P9-CFU-787
2847 147
8520
Book of
Records
$5.00

THE WORLD ALMANAC® BOOK OF RECORDS

FIRSTS, FEATS, **FACTS** & PHENOMENA

THE WORLD ALMANAC® BOOK OF RECORDS

EDITOR Mark Young

PROJECT EDITOR Erik C. Gopel

CONTRIBUTORS Phil Allard, Karen Barrow, Clive Carpenter, Robert Cashill, Mark Coleman, Jennifer Dunham, Jerilyn Famighetti, Shelly Gepfert, Marshall Gerometta, Jacqueline Laks Gorman, Joseph Gustaitis, Lisa Haddock, Richard Hantula, Raymond Hill, Chris Larson, Jean-Claude Lupis, Michelle Dunkley McCarthy, Amanda Moseley, Sean Price, Glenn M. Speer, Christopher J. Steinitz

RESEARCHERS Andrew Steinitz (Chief); Maria Brock Schulman, Kerry Christensen, Emily Keyes, Sara Levin

WORLD ALMANAC BOOKS

EDITORIAL DIRECTOR William A. McGeveran Jr.

EDITORIAL DIRECTOR, CHILDREN'S BOOKS Zoë Kashner

MANAGING EDITOR Elizabeth J. Lazzara

EDITOR Vincent G. Spadafora

ASSOCIATE EDITORS Sarah Janssen; Elizabeth Sheedy

DESKTOP PRODUCTION ASSOCIATE Michael Meyerhofer

DESKTOP PRODUCTION ASSISTANT Sean Westmoreland

DESIGN: BILL SMITH STUDIO

CREATIVE DIRECTOR Brian Kobberger

PROJECT DIRECTOR David Borkman

DESIGN Ron Leighton, Geron Hoy, Mie Tsuchida, Kavita Ramchandran, Eric Hoffsten

PRODUCTION James Liebman, Eric Murray, Steve Scheluchin

WORLD ALMANAC EDUCATION GROUP

CHIEF EXECUTIVE OFFICER, WRC MEDIA INC. Ann Jackson

COO, EVP WRC MEDIA, INC. Rick Nota

PRESIDENT, WORLD ALMANAC EDUCATION GROUP Peter Esposito

GENERAL MANAGER/PUBLISHER Ken Park

ASSOCIATE PUBLISHER Edward A. Thomas

VICE PRESIDENT OF SALES Lola A. Valenciano

MARKETING COORDINATOR Julia Suarez

DIRECTOR OF INDEXING SERVICES Marjorie B. Bank

INDEX EDITOR Walter Kronenberg

The World Almanac Book of Records: Firsts, Feats, Facts & Phenomena

Copyright © 2006 by World Almanac Education Group, Inc.
The World Almanac and The World Almanac Book of Records are registered trademarks of World Almanac Education Group, Inc.

Softcover ISBN-13: 978-0-88687-946-4; ISBN-10: 0-88687-946-9
Hardcover ISBN-13: 978-0-88687-978-5; ISBN-10: 0-88687-978-7
Printed in the United States of America
First Edition 2006

Cover photo credits, see page 486.

WORLD ALMANAC® BOOKS
An Imprint of World Almanac Education Group, Inc.
512 Seventh Avenue
New York, NY 10018
E-Mail: records@waegroup.com

Contents

CONTENTS

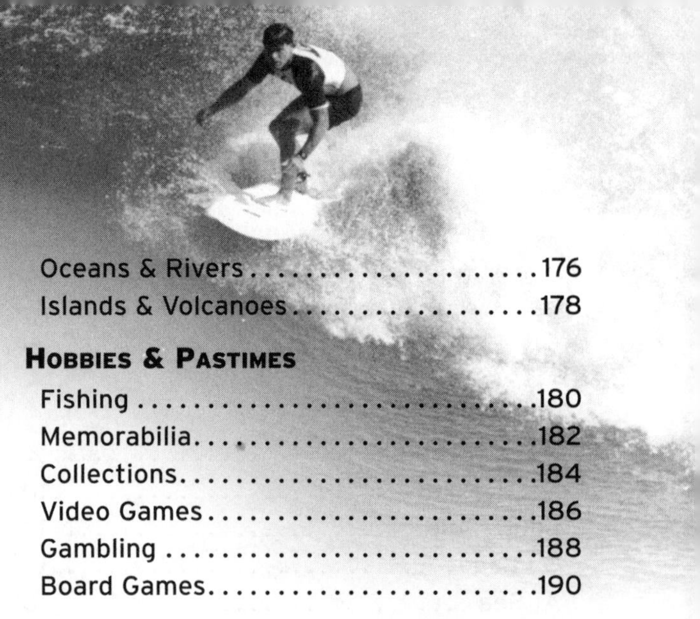

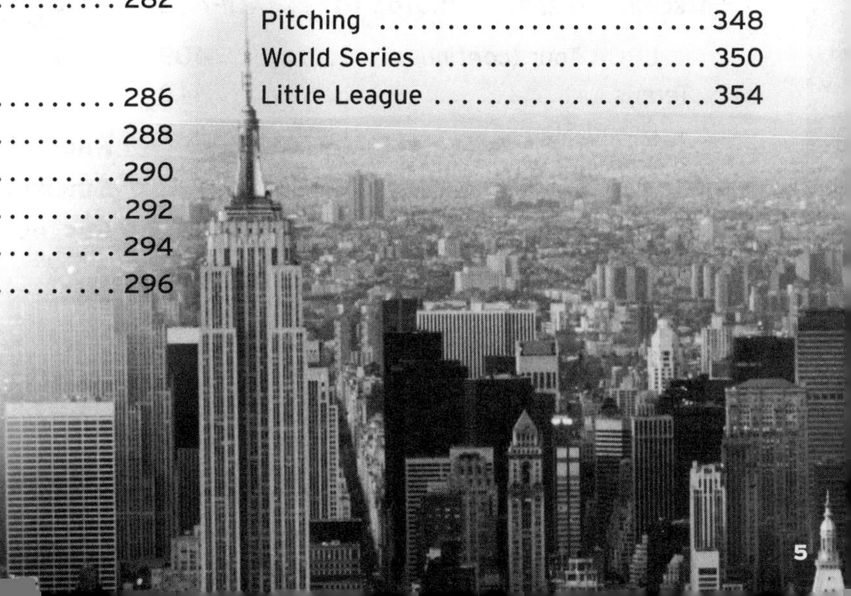

Danny Way at the Great Wall

15-year-old polar explorer Janek Mela

TELL US YOUR STORY

A 15-year-old boy with an artificial leg reached both the North and South Pole in the same year (page 11). An 88-year-old woman sailed across the Atlantic with her son in a small boat (page 17). An American architect conceived low-cost "Earthship" houses constructed out of natural and recycled material (page 123). Skateboarder Danny Way jumped the Great Wall of China (pages 403, 447).

Do you know people like this? Or are you one?

The stories above show everyday folks creating their own special "Firsts, Feats, Facts & Phenomena." *The World Almanac Book of Records: Firsts, Feats, Facts & Phenomena* presents the full spectrum of human record-breaking achievements to amuse, amaze, edify, and inspire.

The famous *World Almanac and Book of Facts*—itself a record-breaker as America's best-selling reference book—has been delivering authoritative and entertaining facts since 1868! We hope this inaugural collector's edition of our new *World Almanac Book of Records* will be the first of another century or so of annual editions. We're counting on your help to help us reach that goal.

We want to hear from you. To make sure we are offering the most fascinating facts possible, we want to hear your stories of record-setting derring-do, offbeat happenings, or serious quests.

THE WORLD ALMANAC BOOK OF RECORDS DOES NOT JUDGE OR CERTIFY RECORDS, but we do want to recognize in our pages as wide a range of achievements as possible. Please send your record-breaking story or curious tale—along with supporting documentation—to:

Tell Us Your Story
World Almanac Book of Records
512 Seventh Ave., 22nd Floor
New York, NY 10018

or

records@waegroup.com

Due to the volume of correspondence, we can only respond to letters (and return materials, such as certificates, photographs, articles, and video) that include a self-addressed stamped envelope with sufficient postage. Because of space limitations, only a limited number of items can be included in *The World Almanac Book of Records*. The editors reserve the right to decide which records make the final selection. We will contact you if your record or story will be used in *The World Almanac Book of Records 2007*.

Thanks for picking up *The World Almanac Book of Records*. We hope you enjoy it and we look forward to hearing from you.

The Editors

Michael Reynolds's "Earthship" house

Mount Everest

MOUNT EVEREST IS THE WORLD'S TALLEST MOUNTAIN, last officially measured in 1999 at 29,035 feet. It straddles the border between Nepal and Tibet. It is known as *Sagarmatha* ("Mighty Brow of the Sky") in Nepal, *Chomolungma* ("Goddess Mother of the World") in Tibet.

In 1802, British administrators in India began the Great Trigonometrical Survey to create an accurate map of the subcontinent. The project took 40 years to reach the Himalayas, in the far north. By the late 1840s, Andrew Waugh was in charge. While measuring Mount Kangchenjunga, then believed to be the world's highest peak, he saw a cluster of new peaks that appeared to be even higher. The highest of these mountains Waugh designated "Peak XV." His team began to take measurements of "Peak XV" in 1847. In 1856, Waugh announced that "Peak XV" was the world's highest mountain, at 29,002 feet. He renamed it in honor of Sir George Everest, his predecessor as surveyor general of India.

MILESTONES

1921: FIRST EXPEDITION In 1921, British mountaineer Lt. Col. Charles Howard Bury led the first official expedition to find a route to the summit. The climbers reached Lhakpa La, a 22,500-foot pass. Guy Bullock and George Mallory, proceeded to the Northern Col (c.23,000 ft) on Sept. 23, 1921. From this point they were able to examine the summit and plot a route, now known as the Northern Route, to reach it.

A second expedition, led by Brig. Gen. Charles G. Bruce, made the first assault to reach the top the following year. In May 1922, Mallory, Teddy Norton, Henry Morshead, Howard Somervell, and five porters set out from Camp IV in a bid to reach the summit. Without supplementary oxygen the attempt was doomed to fail. The porters turned back at 25,000 feet. The British climbers turned back at 26,985 feet. But they had climbed almost 2,400 feet higher than anyone before them.

On the way down Mallory's team met George Finch and Geoffrey Bruce (nephew of the expedition leader) going up. Finch and Bruce carried supplemental oxygen and climbed 27,300 feet before turning back.

1922: DEATHS
On June 7, 1922, during the second Everest expedition, a party led by George Mallory suffered the first fatalities on the mountain. Seven Sherpa climbers were killed in an avalanche below the Northern Col.

Mallory and his companion, Sandy Irvine, died on the mountain in June 1924, the first non-Sherpa climbers to lose their lives while attempting to reach the summit. Mystery still surrounds their deaths, and some historians believe they died descending from the summit.

In 1999, Mallory's body was found at about 27,690 feet. His preserved remains contained no evidence that he had reached the top. Irvine's body has never been found.

1933: FLIGHT
Two British Westland biplanes flew over the peak on April 3, 1933. Powered by turbocharged Pegasus engines adapted for flying in thin air, the planes, conducting the first trigonometrical mapping survey of Everest, were almost downed by violent downdrafts near the summit. The planes were piloted by Flt.-Lt. David McIntyre and Squadron Ldr. Douglas Douglas-Hamilton, the Marquess of Douglas and Clydesdale.

1953: FIRST TO REACH THE SUMMIT Edmund Hillary, a beekeeper from New Zealand, and Tenzing Norgay, a Tibetan-born Sherpa, are the first climbers known to have scaled Mount Everest. Hillary stepped onto the summit at 11:30 AM on May 29, 1953. The two men were part of a British expedition led by Colonel John Hunt.

The team had reached Camp VI, at the foot of the Lhotse Face (23,000 ft), on April 22. On May 26, Charles Evans and Tom Bourdillon reached the South Summit (28,750 ft), but were forced to turn back.

On May 28, Hillary and Tenzing, supported by George Lowe, Alf Gregory, and Ang Nyim, began the team's second assault on the summit. At 27,900 feet, Lowe, Gregory and Ang turned back as planned. Hillary and Tenzing set up camp there and began the final climb the next day. At 9 AM they reached the South Summit. It took them nearly 2 ½ hours to scale the final 300 vertical feet to the top, where the 33-year-old Hillary snapped a picture of Tenzing.

1963: AMERICAN
On May 1, 1963, Jim Whittaker from Seattle, WA, became the first American to scale the world's highest peak, as part of an expedition sponsored by the National Geographic Society.

1975: WOMAN
Junko Tabei, a Japanese climber, became the first woman to reach the summit on May 16, 1975. Twelve days before, she had been buried in an avalanche; a Sherpa spotted her ankle protruding from the snow and rescued her.

1978: ASCENT WITHOUT BOTTLED OXYGEN Reinhold Messner (Italy) and Peter Habeler (Austria) made the first ascent without bottled oxygen, reaching the summit on May 8, 1978.

On August 20, 1980, Messner became the first to get there alone without supplemental oxygen. During his climb he fell into a

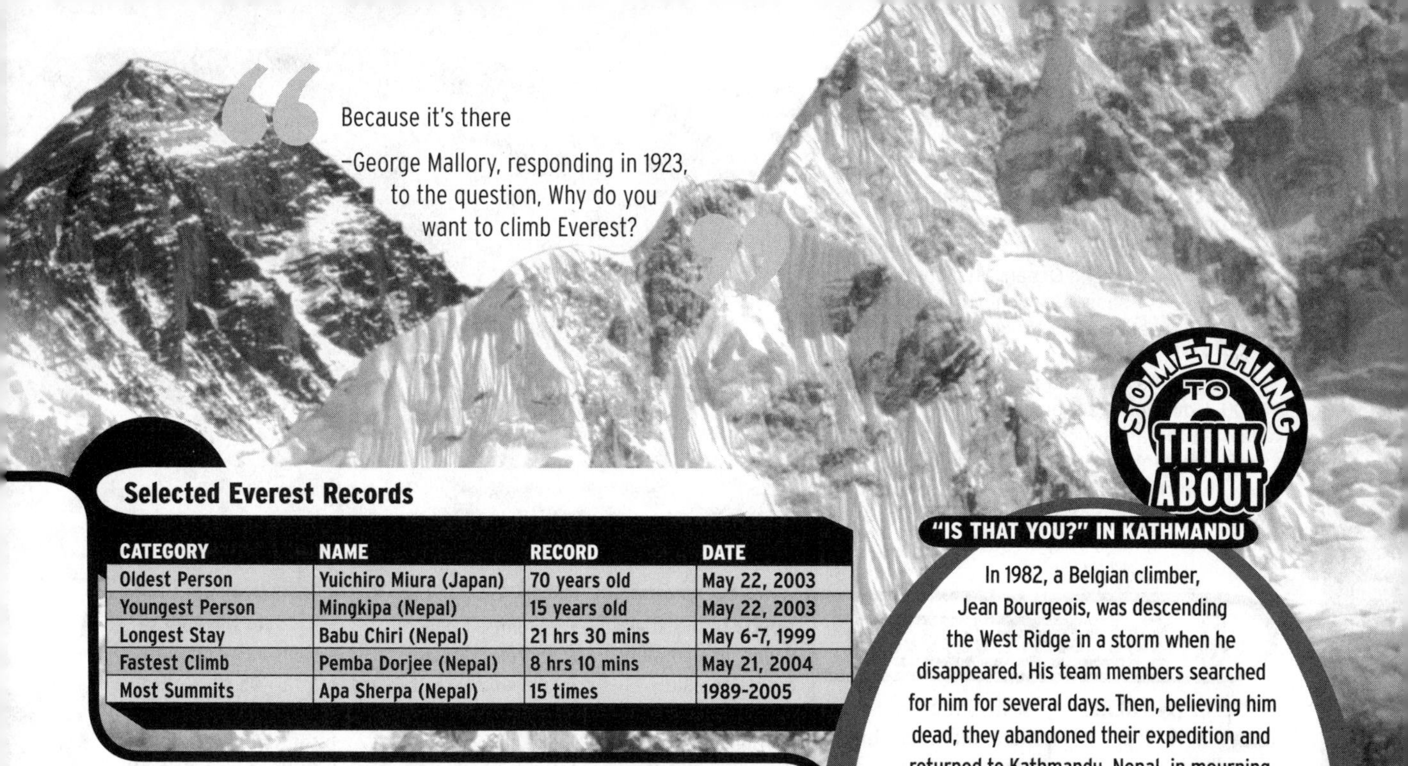

> Because it's there
>
> –George Mallory, responding in 1923, to the question, Why do you want to climb Everest?

Selected Everest Records

CATEGORY	NAME	RECORD	DATE
Oldest Person	Yuichiro Miura (Japan)	70 years old	May 22, 2003
Youngest Person	Mingkipa (Nepal)	15 years old	May 22, 2003
Longest Stay	Babu Chiri (Nepal)	21 hrs 30 mins	May 6-7, 1999
Fastest Climb	Pemba Dorjee (Nepal)	8 hrs 10 mins	May 21, 2004
Most Summits	Apa Sherpa (Nepal)	15 times	1989-2005

crevasse but landed safely on a snow platform.

1988: LIVE TV

The first live TV broadcast from the summit aired on May 5, 1988, on Japan's Nippon Television Network and showed the arrival at the top of two teams of climbers, one from the Tibet side of the mountain and the other from the Nepal side.

A lightweight video camera was carried up the mountain by one of the climbers; special equipment installed at points on the mountainside made the broadcast possible.

1998: AMPUTEE

On May 27, 1998, Tom Whittaker, 49, an outdoor adventure instructor from Prescott, AZ, became the first disabled climber to reach the summit. The British-born climber, who lost his right leg in a 1979 auto accident, used a specially designed lightweight prosthetic leg called a flex foot during his climb. It had built-in crampons to grip the icy surface of the mountain.

2001: BLIND PERSON

Erik Weihenmayer from Golden, CO, became the first blind person to conquer Everest, on May 25, 2001. The 32-year-old who had lost his sight at age 13 due to a rare hereditary disease of the retina, took up rock climbing at 16 and before Everest had climbed Mount McKinley in Alaska, Mount Aconcagua in Argentina, and Mount Kilimanjaro in Tanzania.

All the climbers in his party wore "bear bells" on their jackets, wrists, and ski poles. The sound of the bells kept Weihenmayer in touch with his companions and helped guide him up the mountain.

2005: WEDDING

The first couple to marry on the summit of Everest are Pem Dorjee Sherpa and Moni Mulepati (both Nepalese). On May 30, 2005, the happy pair stood atop the world and exchanged vows. Each put red powder on the other's forehead, a sacred ritual sealing their marriage.

SOMETHING TO THINK ABOUT

"IS THAT YOU?" IN KATHMANDU

In 1982, a Belgian climber, Jean Bourgeois, was descending the West Ridge in a storm when he disappeared. His team members searched for him for several days. Then, believing him dead, they abandoned their expedition and returned to Kathmandu, Nepal, in mourning. But Bourgeois wasn't dead, he was in Tibet. In the storm, Bourgeois had slid off the ridge, but had survived. Finding it impossible to re-climb the slope, he decided to try to make it to the Rongbuk monastery, which he found ruined and empty. After spending several nights in the open he eventually reached a village and was detained by the Chinese authorities. They believed his story, gave him 500 rupees, and packed him off back to Kathmandu, where he was reunited with his astonished colleagues.

LIFTING THE CURSE

Boston Red Sox fan Paul F. Giorgio of Auburn, MA., scaled Everest on May 23, 2001. The Red Sox had not won the World Series since 1918, and many fans believed the team was cursed by the sale of Babe Ruth to the rival New York Yankees in 1919. Many attempts have been made to lift the "Curse of the Bambino," but Giorgio took his efforts to new heights. He carried a Red Sox baseball cap with him to the summit and left it there. In 2004, the Red Sox finally won their first World Series in 86 years.

North Pole

THE RACE TO THE NORTH POLE began in the 19th century as an offshoot to the search for a sea passage connecting the Atlantic Ocean to the Pacific via the Arctic Ocean. That route, the Northwest Passage, was finally navigated in 1905. Credit for reaching the North Pole first is often given to American explorer Robert Peary, who claimed to have gotten there by land in April 1909. However, another American, Frederick Cook, claimed to have reached the Pole earlier, and now many think neither of them made it all the way. If not, then the first successful surface expedition was not made until 1968, by a team headed by American explorer Ralph Plaisted.

The airship Norge *above Spitsbergen, Norway*

MILESTONES

1852: OPEN POLAR SEA In 1845, an expedition led by British naval officer Sir John Franklin foundered trying to find the Northwest Passage. Rescue missions were launched, funded by Franklin's wife, but the men were never found.

In 1852, one of the rescue operations, led by Commander Edward Inglefield, discovered that Smith Sound was navigable. Inglefield proposed that beyond Smith Sound there had to be an open polar sea providing a navigable passage to the Pole. This theory sparked new interest in reaching it.

1876: NEARING THE POLE A two-ship British expedition led by Sir George Nares in 1875 sailed up the Smith Strait (later Nares Strait) located between Ellesmere Island (Canada) and the northwestern coast of Greenland. Using sleds, Nares's team was able to travel over the ice pack, charting the northwest coast of Greenland. One group sledged to within 7 degrees of the North Pole (83° 20'N), before an outbreak of scurvy forced them to give up.

1895: THE *FRAM* In 1893, Fridtjof Nansen launched his epic voyage aboard the *Fram* (a ship specially designed to withstand pressure from the ice) with 12 men, testing his theory of an Arctic Ocean current. The Norwegian explorer believed a ship that sailed into the polar ice pack could drift with the ice from Siberia to the Atlantic Ocean, and possibly the North Pole. When the ship wasn't drifting fast enough, Nansen and Hjalmar Johansen made an attempt to reach the North Pole with dogsleds and kayaks; on Apr. 8 1895, they reached 86° 14'N, the farthest journey north yet achieved, before having to turn back. They traveled to Franz Josef Land, wintered in a homemade hut, and eventually met up with British explorer Frederick Jackson, who rescued them.

The *Fram* reached Norway in Aug. 1896, just one week after Nansen and Johansen had returned.

1897: BALLOON FLIGHT In the mid-1890s Swedish engineer Salomon Andrée developed a plan to fly to the North Pole in a helium-filled silk hot-air balloon. Andrée, with two companions, left Danes Island on July 11, 1897, in a balloon called the *Eagle*. They were never seen alive again. On Aug. 6, 1930, their remains were found on White Island near Franz Josef Land, some 350 miles from their launch spot.

1900: DUKE OF ABRUZZI'S EXPEDITION In 1899, Italian explorer Luigi Amedeo, the Duke of Abruzzi, led a crew of 20 aboard the *Stella Polare* in an attempt to reach the North Pole from Rudolf Island at the northeast point of Franz Josef Land. The boat was cast ashore by ice in Table Bay and stranded for 11 months.

During that time the Duke sent out four expeditions. One of those, a four-man party led by Captain Umberto Cagni, made a bid for the Pole on sleds in spring 1900. After 105 days, their quest failed, but they set a new mark for the farthest journey north at 86° 33'N.

1905: NORTHWEST PASSAGE The legendary Norwegian explorer Roald Amundsen was the first to complete navigation of the Northwest Passage. With his six-man crew aboard the *Gjoa*, Amundsen set sail on June 1, 1903.

The main goal was to measure the position of the north magnetic pole (a point to which compasses are attracted, far short of the geographic pole). For two years, the team was based in a harbor of King William Island, where they pursued scientific study. Amundsen also studied the local Inuit population and their way of life.

Other North Pole Milestones

First Flight[1]	*Norge*	Norway-Italy-United States	May 12, 1926
First Submarine[2]	*U.S.S. Nautilus*	United States	Aug. 3, 1958
First Aircraft Landing	Don Braun[3]	Canada	May 5, 1967
First Sled Dog Across Polar Cap	Wally Herbert[4]	Great Britain	April 5, 1969
First Ship	*Arktika*	Soviet Union	Aug. 16, 1977
First Sled Dog Journey (solo)	Noami Uemura	Japan	April 30, 1978
First Woman (sled dog, supported)	Ann Bancroft	United States	May 2, 1986
First Woman (unsupported)	Helen Thayer	New Zealand	April 27, 1988
First Return Trip (unsupported)	Richard Weber, Mikhail Malakhov[5]	Canada, Russia	June 15, 1995

(1) American aviator Richard Byrd claimed to have flown over the Pole with his pilot Floyd Bennett in a three-engine Fokker monoplane a few days earlier, on May 9, 1926. However, Byrd's claim has been widely disputed. The *Norge*, a blimp designed by Italian engineer Umberto Nobile, flew over the North Pole on its journey from Kings Bay, Spitsbergen, to Teller, Alaska. The crew included Norwegian explorer Roald Amundsen. (2) Under the command of Comdr. William R. Anderson, the sub crossed the North Pole beneath the ice. (3) Braun landed a Bristol freighter 18 miles from the Pole to set down a research group from the Dominion Observatory in Ottawa. (4) Herbert and his three-man team traveled 3,700 miles across the polar ice cap from Point Barrow, Alaska, to near Spitsbergen. The team reached the North Pole on Apr. 5, 1969. Some historians regard Herbert's expedition as the first to reach the North Pole entirely on foot. (5) Weber and Malakhov became the first to reach the Pole and return to starting base without any mechanical assistance. Their 940-mile trip took 121 days, and was made entirely on skis.

In mid-Aug. 1905, the *Gjoa* left its port and headed west. On Aug. 26, the crew saw a schooner, the *Charles Hansen*, in open water approaching them from the west, and knew they had navigated the Northwest Passage. Amundsen wrote: "My boyhood dream—at that moment it was accomplished."

1909: FIRST TO REACH THE POLE–PART ONE There are competing claims as to who reached the North Pole first. On Sept. 2, 1909, the *New York Herald* published a story claiming that Dr. Frederick Cook, a veteran American explorer from Brooklyn, NY, had reached the Pole, along with two Eskimos, on April 21, 1908. Nine days later, the *New York Times* published an account of a second claim; Robert E. Peary, another veteran American polar explorer, claimed to have reached the top of the world, with Matthew Henson and four Eskimos, on April 6, 1909. "He has simply handed the public a gold brick," said Peary of Cook. In fact, there were flaws in both men's accounts.

In 1910, the National Geographic Society certified Peary's claim, and his name went into the history books for generations. But Cook continued to insist he had done it first. The National Geographic Society in 1989 suggested that Peary had fallen short of his goal by 30'-60'. If neither Cook nor Peary got there by land, it is possible no one did for another six decades.

1968: FIRST TO REACH THE POLE–PART TWO The first surface expedition (not in a plane, boat, or sub) to be confirmed as having reached the North Pole was an American group led by Ralph Plaisted. Departing from Canada's Ellesmere Island by snowmobile, the four-man team reached the Pole on April 19, 1968; their position was verified by a U.S. Air Force plane overhead.

SOMETHING TO THINK ABOUT

TEENAGE ADVENTURER

The youngest person to reach the North Pole was Janek Mela, a Polish teenager who had lost an arm and a leg in a 2002 accident. With the aid of an artificial leg, he reached the Pole on April 24, 2004, at the age of 15, in an expedition led by explorer Marek Kaminski. Eight months later on Dec. 31, 2004, Mela, along with Kaminski, reached the South Pole.

Frederick Cook

South Pole

THE SOUTH POLE has been described as "the most remote spot in the world." By the late 19th century, after much attention had been focused on the top of the earth, the South Pole became the final great prize for explorers and adventurers. The result was a "race to the pole," eventually won by Roald Amundsen in 1911.

Today scientists live year-round in the harsh environment of Antarctica and at the Pole itself.

The Southern Party aboard the Nimrod; *(left to right) Wild, Shackleton, Marshall, Adams*

MILESTONES

1895: FIRST LANDING ON ANTARCTICA The first landing party to set foot on Antarctica was a group from an Australian expedition financed and accompanied by Henryk Johan Bull, on Jan. 24, 1895. Bull was a Norwegian based in Melbourne, Australia. With the help of companies eager to find new whaling spots, he funded the voyage of the whaling ship *Antarctic*, which left Australia in 1893. It is disputed which man actually set foot on the continent first, but the crew did land on the coast of Antarctica's Cape Adaire.

1902: SCOTT GETS CLOSE Robert Falcon Scott led his first expedition to the South Pole in 1901. The British-supported expedition was troubled almost from the start. A refitting of Scott's ship, the *Discovery*, in Madeira resulted in a leak that couldn't be fixed until the ship reached New Zealand.

On Jan. 20, 1902, Scott's party landed in Antarctica and began its geographic study. On Nov. 25, 1902, the party became the first to cross the 80th parallel. Using sled dogs, the group pushed farther south and despite the harsh conditions reached 82° 17′ S, the farthest point yet reached by anyone.

Suffering from frostbite, short on supplies, and having lost all of the dog team, Scott decided to turn back on Dec. 31. His expedition was only 480 miles from the Pole, 300 miles closer than anyone before.

1907-1909: SHACKLETON GETS CLOSER The first expedition to find a navigable overland route to the South Pole was Ernest Shackleton's—though the veteran British Antarctic explorer never quite got there.

His team, aboard the *Nimrod*, left England on Aug. 7, 1907. After a period in New Zealand, the expedition reached McMurdo Sound on Jan. 29, 1908. Base camp was set up at Cape Royds, and by Feb. the *Nimrod* withdrew, leaving the men at the Antarctic to prepare for winter and start scientific studies.

In Oct., Shackleton and three others began the trek to the geographic South Pole. On a separate expedition, three members of the party set out to reach the magnetic South Pole, the point to which one end of a compass needle is attracted, about 1,600 miles away from the geographic pole. Led by David, they reached their goal on Jan. 16, 1909.

Shackleton's bid to reach the geographic South Pole fell just short. His party passed Robert Scott's endpoint and, by Jan. 9, got to 88° 23′ S before returning to base. They were just 97 miles from the Pole.

1911: FINAL RACE TO THE POLE British explorer Robert Scott was determined to reach the South Pole first and, with Shackleton's close miss, believed history was his for the making. He did not expect competition from Norwegian explorer Roald Amundsen. Amundsen, a veteran of North Pole exploration, had dreamed of being the first person to reach 90°N; after two American explorers in 1909 claimed to have achieved that goal, he switched his attention south.

Scott's expedition set sail from Great Britain on June 1, 1910. After a stopover in Australia, they arrived at Antarctica's Cape Evans on Jan. 2, 1911.

That same month Amundsen made camp across the Ross Ice Shelf, 400 miles east. Amundsen had told no one of his plans in advance. He only informed his crew on the *Fram* during a stop at the Madeira Islands in the Atlantic Ocean, and from there he sent a telegram to Scott in Australia telling him of his intentions.

Amundsen's party broke camp and set out for the South Pole on Oct. 20, 1911. Alongside Amundsen were four other Norwegians: Oscar Wisting, Olav Bjaaland, Helmer Hanssen, and Sverre Hassel, and a team of 52 dogs. The party used sleds and

Other South Pole Milestones

First Flight Across Antarctica[1]	Lincoln Ellsworth and pilot Herbert Hollick-Kenyon	United States, Great Britain	Nov. 23, 1935–Jan. 16, 1936
First to Fly Over South Pole	Richard Byrd on the *Floyd Bennett* [2]	United States	Nov. 28-29, 1929
First Land Crossing of Antarctica	Commonwealth Trans-Antarctic Expedition [3]	Great Britain, New Zealand, Australia, South Africa	Nov. 24, 1957-Mar. 2, 1958
First Women, South Pole by Land	Victoria Murden, Shirley Metz [4]	United States	Nov. 27, 1988-Jan. 17, 1989
First Antarctic Crossing without Dogs or Machinery[5]	Reinhold Messner, Arved Fuchs	Italy, Germany	Nov. 13, 1989-Feb. 12, 1990
First South Pole (solo)	Erling Kagge	Norway	Nov. 17, 1992-Jan. 7, 1993
First Antarctic Crossing (solo)	Borge Ousland	Norway	Nov. 1996-Jan. 18, 1997

(1) Ellsworth and Hollick-Kenyon did not quite do it; they ran out of fuel 20 miles short of their destination, Little America, and were rescued by a British search team. (2) Byrd, the navigator, was accompanied by Bernt Balchen, pilot, Harold June, wireless operator, and Ashley McKinley, aerial photographer. (3) British explorer and geologist Vivian Fuchs led the multi-national project. It was split into two teams. Fuchs led the team that started from the Weddell Sea and traveled to Scott Station. Edmund Hillary, the New Zealander who was the first to scale Mt. Everest, led a second team that started out from Scott Station on Oct. 14, 1957 and reached the Pole first on Jan. 3, 1958 (Fuchs arrived Jan. 24). Fuchs's team was the first to make the crossing, arriving at Scott Station on Mar. 2, 1958. The party had traveled 2,158 miles in 98 days. The parties traveled by snow tractors. (4) Murden and Metz were part of an 11-person expedition that reached the Pole that day. (5) They used wind-powered sails connected to their sledges, an idea devised by Roald Amundsen.

Roald Amundsen

SOMETHING TO THINK ABOUT

TEST OF ENDURANCE

Ernest Shackleton is probably best known for a heroic expedition that never came close to its goal. In Oct. 1914 he set out from Buenos Aires in his ship *Endurance* hoping to travel by land across Antarctica. But the ship got stuck in an ice pack and eventually became unusable. Shackleton spent many months on the ice with dwindling supplies and months of journeying over a stormy ocean in an open lifeboat. In the end Shackleton and a few men got help for the rest by crossing icy mountains on the island of South Georgia to reach a small whaling settlement there on May 20, 1916. All 28 of Shackleton's crew were eventually saved.

skis to travel across the ice. Meanwhile, Scott's team set out for the Pole on Nov. 1.

The British expedition followed Shackleton's trail, but the Norwegians blazed a new route. That decision paid off. Traveling across the Axel Heiberg Glacier and the Polar Plateau, Amundsen and his companions reached Shackleton's mark on Dec. 7 and got to the South Pole about 3 PM on Dec. 14, 1911. Scott's party finally reached the Pole on Jan. 18, 1912; they found a flag Amundsen had left as a marker of his group's achievement.

The Norwegians had also left a tent with surplus equipment and a message for Scott, asking him to deliver a note to the King of Norway in case they didn't survive the journey home. They did make it back, but Scott and the rest of his party perished, just 11 miles short of one of their supply depots.

SUPERLATIVES

LARGEST ANTARCTIC EXPEDITION

The largest expedition ever mounted to Antartica was Operation High Jump, organized by the U.S. Navy and led by Rear Admiral Richard Byrd. Launched in Dec. 1946, the expedition involved about 4,700 men on a flotilla of 13 ships and 23 aircrafts. The main purpose of the two-year-long mission was a military training exercise for winter warfare with the Soviet Union. The expedition also mapped the Antarctic coastline and polar interior.

On Land

FROM THE SILK ROAD TO THE OREGON TRAIL, PEOPLE HAVE ROAMED THE WORLD on foot, alone or in groups of like-minded travelers, since the beginning of time. The roads are rarely flat or unbroken. Rivers need to be crossed and mountain tops scaled. For some, the challenge was the attraction; others just wanted a new place to settle. Some explored land, others explored trade. They all expanded the horizons of human endeavor. Here are some of their stories and accomplishments.

Lewis and Clark

MILESTONES

1271-95: TRAVELS OF MARCO POLO
The son of a Venetian merchant, Marco Polo first set off to China with his father, Nicolo, and his uncle, Maffeo, in 1271. (The elder Polos had been among the first Europeans to visit the court of Kublai Khan in Beijing, 1266-69.)

Marco Polo's account of his own epic journey, *The Description of the World*, is one of the world's most famous travelogues. The 5,600-mile winding route from Venice to Beijing went through Persia, Afghanistan, the Gobi Desert, and vast sections of the Chinese interior. The party finally arrived at the Great Khan's court in 1275.

A talented linguist, Marco Polo became an emissary to Kublai Khan and traveled on missions to India and Burma, among many other places. His travels were the most extensive of any European for centuries. In his journal he described not just the grand scenery but the lavish lifestyle of the court and the customs of everyday people.

The party returned to Venice in 1295, after a three-year sea voyage. Alas, the public did not believe his stories, and he became known as "the man of a million lies." Even on his deathbed, Marco Polo was still seeking to answer his critics. "I have told only half of what I saw!" he declared.

AROUND 1275-94: JOURNEY OF RABBAN SAUMA
Rabban Sauma, a Christian monk of the Eastern Nestorian sect, from what is now Turkistan in Central Asia, traveled all the way from Beijing, China, to Paris, France. A member of the court of Kublai Khan, Sauma began his journey (more than 7,000 miles) around 1275, keeping a journal along the way.

Sauma traveled with another monk, named Marcus. Their original destination was Jerusalem. After a four-year journey, which included a two-month trek on camel across the Taklimakan Desert in western China, Sauma's party reached Baghdad, but because of the war raging around Jerusalem, they did not try to go there.

In 1287, Sauma set out for Europe as an emissary of Persia's Mongol leaders. He met with Edward I of England in Bordeaux, France, and Philip IV of France in Paris. In 1288, he celebrated mass with the pope in Rome. He eventually returned to Baghdad, where he died in 1294.

1804-06: LEWIS AND CLARK After the Louisiana Purchase of 1803, President Thomas Jefferson commissioned an expedition into the newly acquired American West. Jefferson's secretary, Capt. Meriwether Lewis, led the expedition. He chose William Clark, an expert outdoorsman and army lieutenant, as his co-commander.

Their "Corps of Discovery" of around 40 people included Clark's slave, York; the French trapper and interpreter, Toussaint Charbonneau; and Charbonneau's wife, Sacagawea, a Native American who acted as an interpreter and peacemaker with the tribes they encountered.

The party set off from St. Louis on May 14, 1804. They traveled up the Missouri River through what is now North Dakota and Montana, across the Rocky and Cascade Mountains, and down the Columbia River to the Pacific, which they reached on Nov. 7, 1805.

They climbed mountains and navigated rivers, braving the elements as they pushed through rough, uncharted wilderness. They mapped the area as they went and collected and catalogued specimens of plant and animal life never before seen by European-Americans.

The group set out on their return journey in early 1806 after camping by the Columbia River during the winter, and arrived in St. Louis on Sept. 23, 1806.

1836-69: THE OREGON TRAIL
The Oregon Trail from Independence, MO, to the Columbia River in Oregon, was the main route for America's westward expansion in the mid-19th century. The first couple who traveled the length of the trail in a covered wagon were Marcus and Narcissa Whitman, who arrived in Oregon in 1836.

After a trickle of travelers, the first big wave of emigration west began in 1843. It is estimated that more than 500,000 people made the journey before the trail was superseded by the transcontinental railroad in 1869.

1970-74: FIRST CIRCUMNAVIGATION (ON FOOT)
Dave Kunst of Waseca, MN, is recognized as being the first person to walk around the world. Known as "the Earthwalker," Kunst set out with his brother John on June 20, 1970.

Tragedy struck when John was murdered in Afghanistan in Oct. 1972. Joined by another brother, Pete, Dave continued the quest. Dave's odyssey took him from Waseca to New York City; Lisbon, Portugal to Calcutta, India; Perth to Sydney, Australia; and Los Angeles back to Waseca on Oct. 5, 1974. He walked 14,450 miles across 13 countries on four continents before returning to Waseca on Oct. 5, 1974.

Along the way he met an Australian school teacher named Jenni Samuel. The couple married in 1975.

1981-86: THE SEVEN SUMMITS The first person to climb the seven highest summits of each continent was Richard D. Bass (U.S.). The millionaire oilman and rancher began his quest in 1981. With friend and fellow adventurer Frank Wells, he climbed six of the summits in 1983 (Mt. Aconcagua, Argentina; Mt. McKinley, AK; Mt. Kilimanjaro, Tanzania; Mt. Elbrus, Russia-Georgia; Mt. Vinson Massif, Antarctica; and Mt. Kosciusko, Australia).

Wells, a Hollywood executive, could not join Bass on his subsequent assault on Mt. Everest in 1985. Bass himself reached the summit of the world's tallest peak on April 30, 1985.

Some mountaineering organizations do not recognize Mt. Kosciusko as one of the Seven Summits, since a car can drive to its top. In these cases, Mt. Jaya (the Carstensz Pyramid) in Indonesia, which at 16,500 feet is the tallest peak in Australasia, is used instead. Pat Morrow (Canada) is recognized as the first to have gained this version of the Seven Summits. He started with Mt. Everest in 1982, and finished with Mt. Jaya in 1986.

2001: TRIPLE CROWN The first and so far only person to complete all three National Scenic Trails in one calendar year—the so-called Triple Crown of hiking—is "Flyin" Brian Robinson, of San Jose, CA.

The 40-year-old computer systems engineer, starting out Jan. 1, 2001, completed the Pacific Crest Trail, which runs 2,645 miles from Mexico to Canada, then hiked the 2,588 miles of the Continental Divide Trail in the Rocky Mountains. He topped this off by covering the entire Appalachian Trail (over 2,100 mi) from Georgia to Maine where he finished his record hike on Oct. 27, 2001.

In all, Robinson hiked 7,371 miles in just under 11 months, an average of more than 20 miles per day.

SOMETHING TO THINK ABOUT

ON THE ROAD AGAIN

Country legend Willie Nelson famously sang "On the Road Again," but Rock and Roll Hall of Famer Art Garfunkel actually walked across America. The Queens, NY, native began a 14-year cross-country stroll in spring 1983 from New York City, NY. His journey was broken down into dozens of stages. At the end of each leg of the trip, the singer would mark the spot, and when he returned, sometimes months later, he would begin his walk again from that spot. He reached the Pacific on Sept. 29, 1997.

SUPERLATIVES

SEVEN SUMMITS
YOUNGEST CLIMBER
The youngest person to scale the Seven Summits, as originally understood (see above), was 20-year-old Danielle Fisher of Bow, WA. Her quest began when she climbed Mt. Aconcagua in Argentina on Jan. 5, 2003. She set the new record on June 2, 2005, when she scaled the world's tallest peak, Mt. Everest.

In between she climbed Mt. Kilimanjaro (July 14, 2003), Mt. Elbrus (July 30, 2003), Mt. Kosciusko (Jan. 6, 2004), Mt. McKinley (May 26, 2004), and Mt. Vinson Massif (Jan. 12, 2005).

The youngest man to climb the Seven Summits is Britton Keeshan (U.S.), who was 22 when he completed his final climb in 2004.

SEVEN SUMMITS
OLDEST CLIMBER
The oldest person to climb all seven summits was Ramon Blanco (Spain). The former violin maker was 70 years, 243 days old when he completed his quest atop Mt. Kosciusko, Australia, Dec. 29, 2003.

At Sea

FROM THE PHOENICIAN SAILORS OF ANTIQUITY plying the Mediterranean to modern-day weekend sailors boating off Martha's Vineyard, the sea has attracted humankind for thousands of years. Some have gone in search of adventure; some launched invasions; some went fishing. In the process they discovered new worlds, opened trade routes, and expanded the possibilities of human achievement.

British sailor Ellen MacArthur

MILESTONES

1000: ERIKSSON Leif Eriksson, second son of Erik the Red, the Norse explorer who discovered Greenland, is believed to have been the first European to set foot in North America. According to the *Groenlendinga* Saga (*"The Tale of the Greenlanders"*), around 1000 AD he made landfall in what he called Helluland (perhaps Baffin Island in arctic north eastern Canada). As he sailed along the coast, he visited and named places such as Markland (perhaps Labrador) and Vinland.

The whereabouts of Vinland have been debated, but in 1963 the apparent remains of a Viking settlement were found at L'Anse-aux-Meadows, in northern Newfoundland.

1419: EXPLORER SCHOOL Prince Henry of Aviz (1394-1460), the "Navigator," never actually went to sea. But he pioneered Portugal's exploration of the world's oceans. As governor of the Algarve province in 1419, he created the "Vilo do Infante" near Sagres on Cape Saint Vincent, one of the first centers of study and research for explorers and map makers.

Under Henry's direction, Portugal began to seize overseas territories and build an empire.

1492: COLUMBUS Backed by King Ferdinand and Queen Isabella of Spain, Christopher Columbus assembled a three-ship fleet consisting of the *Santa Maria*, the *Nina*, and the *Pinta* that set sail on Aug. 3, 1492, seeking a westward sea route to the Indies. After a stop in the Canary Islands to take on supplies, the fleet continued west. Landfall was first made at San Salvador Island (also known as Watling Island) in the Bahamas on Oct. 12.

Columbus's voyage established a sea route connecting Europe to the New World.

1498: DA GAMA Although Bartolomeu Dias "discovered" the Cape of Good Hope in 1488, Portuguese explorer Vasco da Gama was the first to complete a sea voyage from Europe to India. Da Gama left Lisbon in July 1497 and sailed around the Cape that November. After skirting Africa's east coast, he sailed across the Indian Ocean, reaching southern India in May 1498.

He was not greeted kindly by the locals and had to fight his way out of the port. But he returned, a hero, to Portugal in 1499.

1519-22: CIRCUMNAVIGATION Ferdinand Magellan had no intention of sailing around the world. His goal was to reach the spice-rich East Indies by sailing west rather than east. With a crew of 270 men and five ships, he set off on Sept. 20, 1519.

His men endured treacherous seas, starvation, and violence. Two ships were lost, and Magellan himself was killed in a skirmish in the Philippines, on April 27, 1521.

The surviving sailors were consolidated into two crews. The *Victoria* continued west while the *Trinidad* turned back. On Sept. 6, 1522, the *Victoria* arrived in Spain. Its 18-member crew was the first to sail around the world.

1773: ANTARCTIC CIRCLE A British expedition led by Capt. James Cook was the first to cross the Antarctic Circle, latitude 66° 33′ S, on Jan. 17, 1773. Cook had been charged by the British admiralty to confirm the existence of a continent in the unexplored section of the Southern Hemisphere.

The expedition left England on July 13, 1772, with two ships—the *Resolution*, which was Cook's flagship, and the *Adventure*. During the three-year expedition, Cook explored the South Pacific and New Zealand. The farthest point south he reached was 71° 10′ S (Jan. 26, 1774), a new record.

1895-98: SOLO CIRCUMNAVIGATION The first person known to complete a circumnavigation of the globe by himself was Joshua Slocum. An experienced sea captain, the Canadian-born sailor left Boston, MA, on April 24, 1895, sailing a 37-foot sloop, *Spray*, which he had refitted himself. He completed his journey on June 27, 1898, in Newport, RI.

1947: KON-TIKI In 1941, Norwegian explorer and archaeologist Thor Heyerdahl published a paper outlining his theory that inhabitants of Peru had sailed across the Pacific on balsa rafts to Polynesia hundreds of years before the arrival of European explorers. In 1947, Heyerdahl and his five-man crew set off from Callio, Peru, to prove that the voyage could be done, on a balsa raft they created using Peruvian raw materials and ancient boat building techniques.

The *Kon-Tiki* completed the 4,300-mile journey in 101 days.

Selected Round-the-World Milestones

CIRCUMNAVIGATION	SAILOR	START/FINISH	DATES
Solo (Non-Stop)	Robin Knox-Johnston (Great Britain)	Falmouth, England	June 14, 1968-April 22, 1969
Solo (Woman)[1]	Krystyna Liskiewicz (Poland)	Las Palmas, Canary Islands	Feb. 28, 1976-Apr. 21, 1978
Solo (Non-Stop, Woman)	Kay Cottee (Australia)	Sydney, Australia	Nov. 29, 1987-June 5, 1988

(1) Naomi James (New Zealand) was the first woman to complete the "classic" solo circumnavigation via Cape Horn. She left Dartmouth, England, on Sept. 9, 1977, and returned to port on June 8, 1978. Liskiewicz sailed through the Panama Canal to reach the Pacific Ocean.

SOMETHING TO THINK ABOUT

OCEAN-GOING OCTOGENARIAN

Helen Tew's lifelong dream was to sail in a small boat across the Atlantic. Her father had taught her how to sail as a little girl but it was her oldest son, Donald, who helped her finally fulfill her dream. The two set sail aboard the *Mary Helen*, a 64-year-old, 26-foot vintage gaff cutter, leaving England on Aug. 1, 2000. Surviving fierce storms and damage to their craft, they arrived in English Harbour, Antigua, after 26 days, 23 hours, 50 minutes. Soon after, Helen Tew celebrated her 89th birthday. Of her journey, she said, "I am tickled pink. To be here, on this boat, has been my ambition for 70 years."

SUPERLATIVES

1960: AROUND THE GLOBE UNDERWATER The first underwater circumnavigation was completed by the *USS Triton* on its maiden voyage, under the command of Capt. Edward Beach. The submarine left New London, CT, on Feb. 15, 1960, but the circumnavigation was officially recognized as beginning on Feb. 24 at St. Peter and St. Paul's Rocks, off the coast of Brazil. The vessel returned to the same spot on April 24, having gone 27,723 miles in 60 days, 21 hours without re-surfacing.

FASTEST CIRCUMNAVIGATION Bruno Peyron of France skippered the 120-foot catamaran *Orange II* in a record circumnavigation of 50 days, 16 hours, 20 minutes, 4 seconds, arriving back at its starting point, Ushant, an island off Brittany, France, on March 16, 2005. In doing so, he captured the Jules Verne Trophy for sailing around the world the fastest.

Peyron and his 13-man crew set the record despite hitting a whale in the South Atlantic.

FASTEST SOLO CIRCUMNAVIGATION At age 28, British sailor Ellen MacArthur completed the fastest solo circumnavigation on Feb. 7, 2005. She sailed her 75-foot trimaran *B&Q* from England on Nov. 28, 2004, and finished her journey in 71 days, 14 hours, 18 minutes, 33 seconds.

MacArthur, who received a congratulatory call from Prince Charles, beat the previous mark, set in 2004 by Francis Joyon (France) at 72 days, 22 hours, 54 minutes, 22 seconds.

OLDEST SOLO CIRCUMNAVIGATOR The oldest person to complete a solo circumnavigation is David Clark. The World War II veteran was 77 when he completed his around-the-world trip on Dec. 7, 2001.

Clark had left Fort Lauderdale, FL, on Dec. 5, 1999, with his only companion, his dog Mickey. Alas, when Clark's ship started taking on water off the coast of South Africa, Mickey went overboard. Clark stayed on in South Africa to raise enough money for a new boat to complete his journey. He christened the new boat *Mickey*.

FASTEST ATLANTIC CROSSING Steve Fossett skippered the 125-foot maxi catamaran *PlayStation* to the fastest crossing of the Atlantic Ocean. He and his crew of nine left Ambrose Point, NY, on Oct. 5, 2001, and arrived at the finish line off Lizard Point, England, in 4 days, 17 hours, 28 minutes, 6 seconds.

In the Air

FROM THE ANCIENT GREEK LEGENDS OF PERSEUS soaring on winged shoes, and Icarus melting his wax wings by flying too close to the sun, to the Wright Brothers, to today's adventurers circumnavigating the globe, the challenges of flight have lifted humankind to new heights.

SR-71

MILESTONES

1783: HOT-AIR BALLOON FLIGHT The hot-air balloon was invented by the Montgolfier brothers, Joseph Michel and Jacques Etienne of France. On June 4, 1783, in Annonay, France, they sent into the air an unmanned globe-shaped balloon made of cloth and paper, and inflated it with heated air produced by a controlled fire in the balloon's basket.

They gave a public demonstration of their flying machine Sept. 19, on the grounds of the Palace of Versailles; Louis XVI and Marie Antoinette witnessed this flight, which carried three passengers: a sheep, a duck, and a rooster.

On Nov. 21, two human passengers, Jean-Francois Pilâtre de Rozier and the Marquis Francois-Laurent d'Arlandes, took off from Versailles in a balloon and soared over Paris. Benjamin Franklin, the U.S. ambassador, was among the witnesses.

1891: GLIDER FLIGHT The first person to fly in a heavier-than-air machine was Otto Lilienthal of Germany, who piloted his own No. 3 Glider monoplane near Potsdam in 1891. The aviation pioneer continued to refine his glider designs until his death on Aug. 10, 1896, from injuries sustained in a crash.

1903: WRIGHT BROTHERS' FIRST FLIGHT That very brief flight took place over a Kitty Hawk, NC, beach on Dec. 17, 1903, and was the culmination of several years of work and experimentation by the two Ohio-based brothers, Orville and Wilbur Wright. Their "Flyer" was not the first flying machine, but it was the first one that could be controlled while in the air.

The 1903 Flyer was a skeletal flying machine built of spruce, ash and muslin, with a wingspan of 40 feet, 4 inches and a weight of just over 605 pounds.

It was ready for flight on Dec. 14, but the first attempt was a failure. Three days later, at about 10:35 AM on Dec. 17, the Flyer finally took off. Orville was able to fly for 12 breathtaking seconds, going a distance of 120 feet, less than the wingspan of a modern Boeing 747.

The Wright brothers flew the plane three more times that morning. On the fourth flight the Flyer was damaged and the most important day in aviation history came to an end.

1909: ACROSS THE CHANNEL A British newspaper offered a £1,000 prize to the first pilot who could fly across the English Channel. The prize was claimed by Louis Blériot of France, who flew a monoplane of his own design, the Blériot XI, from France, on July 25, 1909.

Visibility was poor because of heavy mist, and Blériot navigated by following ships sailing to the English port of Dover. He landed on English soil after only 37 minutes in the air.

1919: NONSTOP ATLANTIC CROSSING In 1913, Britain's *Daily Mail* offered a £10,000 prize for the first nonstop crossing of the Atlantic between the U.S. or Canada and the British Isles. The prize went to British aviators Capt. John Alcock and Lt. Arthur Whitten Brown. They left Newfoundland in a Vickers Vimy bomber on June 14, 1919; after a relatively uneventful 16-hour flight, they crash-landed in a bog in Ireland, then part of Britain.

1927: LUCKY LINDY It was a $25,000 prize offered by philanthropist Raymond Orteig that sparked Charles Lindbergh's solo nonstop flight from New York to Paris. An unknown airmail pilot, he persuaded the Ryan Aeronautical Company to build him a customized aircraft for his attempt. Several World War I aces had already tried for the prize, including Charles Nungesser, who left France May 8, 1927, and was never seen again.

◀ Wilbur Wright (right) and Orville (in plane) during the first flight at Kitty Hawk, NC.

Selected Milestones in Flight

First Helicopter Flight[1]	Breguet-Richet Gyroplanel	Douai, France, Aug. 24, 1907
First Atlantic Crossing[2]	Curtiss Model NC flying boat; Cdr. A.C. Read (U.S. Navy)	May 27, 1919
First Woman to fly across the Atlantic (solo)[3]	Amelia Earhart (U.S.)	May 20-21, 1932
First Woman to fly across the U.S. (solo)	Amelia Earhart (U.S.)	Aug. 24-25, 1932
First Circumnavigation; First Pacific Crossing[4]	Two planes of the U.S. Air Service; 27,553 mi; from Seattle	Apr. 6-Sept. 28, 1924
First Nonstop Circumnavigation[5]	*Lucky Lady II*, Boeing B-50A, James Gallagher, crew of 13	Feb. 26-Mar. 2, 1949
First Mach 2 flight	*Skyrocket*, A. Scott Crossfield (U.S.)	Nov. 20, 1953
First Solo Circumnavigation (no refueling)	Global Flyer, Steve Fossett (U.S.)	67 hours, completed March 3, 2005

(1) Designed by Louis and Jacques Breguet with Charles Richet (all France), the helicopter was steadied by four men holding long poles. The first man to "fly" in a helicopter machine was Paul Cornu (France), who rose briefly in his "flying bicycle" on Nov. 13, 1907. (2) Three flying boats set off from Rockaway, NY. They traveled via Newfoundland, Canada, and the Azores (where two were damaged). The remaining craft flew on to Lisbon, then to Ferrol, Spain. (3) Earhart had been the first woman to cross the Atlantic when she flew as a passenger with pilots Wilmer L. Stultz and Louis E. Gordon in June 1928. (4) The circumnavigation was the brainchild of Col. Billy Mitchell to promote the U.S. Air Service, the forerunner of the U.S. Air Force. He commissioned Donald Douglas to build a fleet of four planes for the attempt. The *Seattle*, the *Chicago*, the *Boston*, and the *New Orleans* left Seattle, WA; only the *Chicago* and *Seattle* completed the journey. Each used nine engines and traveled 27,553 miles. (5) Flight took off from Carswell Air Force Base, near Fort Worth, TX. *Lucky Lady II* was refueled four times in midair.

Undeterred, Lindbergh took off in the *Spirit of St. Louis* at 7:52 AM on May 20 and landed in Paris 33 ½ hours later, at 5:21 PM May 21.

Lindbergh was greeted by a crowd so big he had to shut off his propeller so as not to endanger anyone. An instant hero, he was feted on his return home with a ticker-tape parade June 13 along New York's Fifth Avenue.

1931: AROUND THE WORLD In 1931, former wing walker Wiley Post (U.S.) flew his modified Lockheed Vega, the *Winnie Mae*, around the world. With his navigator, Harold Gatty, Post left New York on June 23. They returned eight days later, after numerous refueling stops.

Two years later Post made the first solo circumnavigation. Using a radio compass and an autopilot, he left Floyd Bennett Field, Long Island, on July 15, 1933, and returned 7 days, 18 hours, 49 minutes later.

1947: BREAKING SOUND BARRIER The first flight to break the sound barrier came on Oct. 14, 1947.

The Bell X-1 test plane, nicknamed *Glamorous Glennis* by the pilot Chuck Yeager after his wife, was carried into the sky in the bomb bay of a B-29. At 21,000 feet, the X-1 was released from the plane and fired its engines. It surpassed Mach 1 (the speed of sound) at 43,000 feet, hitting a speed of Mach 1.06 (about 700 mph).

1986: CIRCUMNAVIGATION NONSTOP *Voyager*, piloted by Jeana Yeager and Dick Rutan, was the first plane to complete a nonstop around-the-world flight without refueling. Designed by Rutan and his brother, Burt, *Voyager* took off from Edwards Air Force Base on Dec. 14, 1986, and returned nine days later. It carried 1,200 gallons of fuel in 17 specially designed tanks.

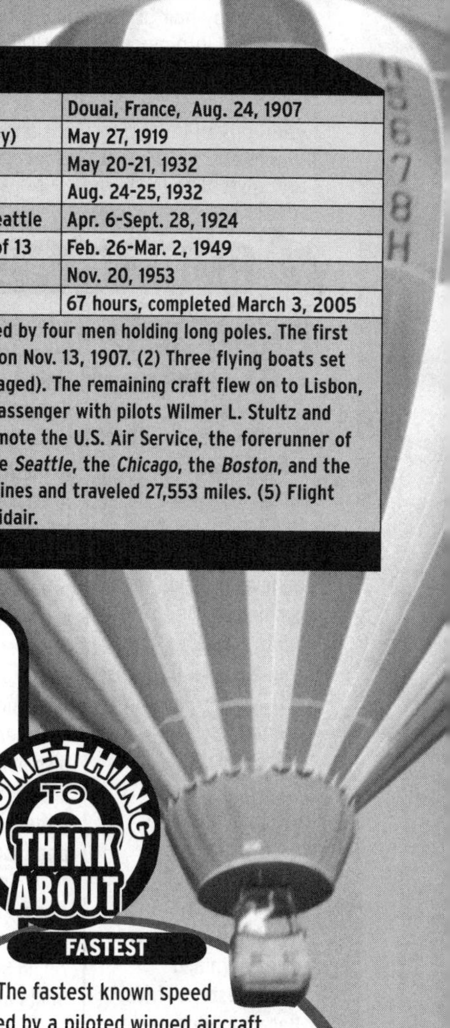

SOMETHING TO THINK ABOUT

FASTEST

The fastest known speed reached by a piloted winged aircraft is 4,520 miles per hour (Mach 6.70) by Air Force Maj. William "Pete" Knight in the X-15A-2 test plane. It rocketed over California on Oct. 3, 1967, at an altitude of 102,100 feet. The fastest speed recognized by the Fédération Aéronautique Internationale (FAI) is Mach 3, set by the U.S military's SR-71 Blackbird on July 28, 1976. Knight's flight was never officially recognized as a record, since the X-15 was launched in midair; according to FAI rules, an aircraft must take off using its own power in order to qualify for the record.

Mammals

THE WORD "MAMMAL" comes from the Latin word for "breast." Mammals are warm-blooded vertebrate animals that nourish their young with mother's milk secreted by mammary glands. They have skin usually covered by hair or fur, and a muscular diaphragm. Mammals have been classified into more than 5,000 species.

There are three types of mammals: Monotremes, such as platypuses, which lay eggs; marsupials, such as kangaroos, that give birth to their young in an immature state and protect them in a pouch; and placental mammals, which nourish their young in the womb through the placenta and give birth to them at a relatively advanced stage of development.

SUPERLATIVES

SPEED

FASTEST LAND MAMMAL
The cheetah, *Acinonyx jubatus*, has been clocked at speeds up to 70 miles per hour over short distances on level ground. When running, it can cover 7.5 to 8.5 yards in a single stride. Its semi-retractable claws give it good traction.

The cheetah was once plentiful across most of Africa and Asia; today the only significant populations left are in the game reserves of eastern and southwestern Africa. Because of poaching, susceptibility to disease, and difficulty breeding in captivity, the cheetah is an endangered species.

FASTEST MARINE MAMMAL The killer whale, *Orchinus orca*, also known as an orca, can swim at speeds up to 35 mph. The largest member of the dolphin family, killer whales live in all oceans of the world, but are most abundant in the Arctic and Antarctic. Although the killer whale can "turn on the jets" when required, it usually cruises at speeds of between 2 and 6 mph.

Over short distances, Dall's porpoise, *Phocoenoides dalli*, has also been measured at speeds of 35 mph. The largest member of the porpoise family, it is found in the northern North Pacific. This porpoise is known for riding bow waves of boats and swimming in zig-zag patterns. It is more social than other porpoises, traveling in schools of 10-20.

FASTEST FLYING MAMMAL
The dwarf bonneted bat, *Eumops bonariensis*, is the smallest of the bonneted bats and can fly 40 mph, reaching 60 mph in groups. These bats are found from southern Mexico to central Argentina and eastern Brazil.

FASTEST PINNIPED
Among pinnipeds, which include seals, sea lions, and walruses, the California sea lion, *Zalophus californianus*, is the fastest swimmer. In short bursts the California sea lion can reach speeds up to 25 mph in the water. This marine mammal can be found off the rocky coast of western North America from Mexico all the way north to British Columbia, Canada.

SLOWEST MAMMAL
The pale-throated three-toed sloth, *Bradypus tridactylus*, travels less than 1 mph at top speed, covering only 6-8 feet per minute.

The sloth is found in the tropical forests of Central and South America, where it spends most of its time hanging upside down from tree branches, lazily sleeping 15-20 hours a day. It travels so slowly that moss grows in its fur.

SIZE

LARGEST MAMMAL
The largest mammal, and the largest animal to ever inhabit the earth, is the blue whale, *Balaenoptera musculus*. Found in all oceans of the world, adult blue whales can grow over 100 feet long, but typically average 70 to 90 feet in length (about as long as three school buses). On average they weigh between 100 and 150 tons; the largest may weigh nearly 200 tons.

An adult can have a heart the size of a Volkswagen Beetle.

Selected Whale Species

WHALE	RECORD LENGTH	RECORD WEIGHT
Blue Whale, *Balaenoptera musculus*	109 ft	140 tons
Fin Whale, *Balaenoptera physalus*	90 ft	97 tons
Sei Whale, *Balaeonoptera borealis*	72 ft	45 tons
Sperm Whale, *Physeter catodon*	67 ft	72 tons
Humpback Whale, *Megaptera novaeangliae*	65 ft	64 tons
Gray Whale, *Eschrichtius robustus*	51 ft	39 tons

Even a newborn blue whale calf is formidable; it measures about 20 feet long and weigh 2 to 3 tons.

LARGEST LAND MAMMAL
The world's largest land mammal is the male African bush elephant, *Loxodonta Africana*. Found in sub-Saharan Africa, it stands up to 12 feet at the shoulder, and on average weighs 4 to 7 tons. An herbivore, the African elephant can consume more than 600 pounds of plant matter a day.

LARGEST FLYING MAMMAL The largest flying mammals are flying foxes, a family of bats. The Malayan flying fox, *Pteropus vampyrus*, is the largest, weighing nearly 2 pounds, with a head and body length of up to 17 inches and a 5-foot wingspan. This nocturnal fruit-eater is found throughout Southeast Asia.

LARGEST RODENT
The world's largest rodent is the capybara, *Hydrochaeris hydrochaeris*. Also known as a carpincho, or water hog, it is found east of the Andes from the Panama Canal to Argentina.

This massive semi-aquatic rodent, which looks like a huge guinea pig, is about 4 feet long, and can weigh over 170 pounds.

The capybara lives in the thick vegetation near lakes, rivers, and swamps, eating mainly grass. Its name means "master of the grasses" in the language of the Guarani Indians.

TALLEST MAMMAL
The giraffe, *Giraffa camelopardalis*, is the tallest mammal in the world. On average, these animals grow to 18 feet, with some reaching almost 20 feet, the height of a typical two-story building. Found mainly in East Africa, some herds still roam as far south as Zambia.

Despite its great length, the giraffe's neck, which typically grows to about 5 feet in length, has the same number of vertebrae (7) as those of most other mammals, including humans.

SMALLEST MAMMAL
The world's smallest mammal is Kitti's hog-nosed bat, *Craseonycteris thonglongyai*, also called the bumblebee bat. An endangered species found only in Thailand, it is about 1.2 inches long and weighs less than an ounce.

There are only an estimated 200 of these bats, living deep in limestone caves along the River Kwai.

SMALLEST NON-FLYING MAMMAL
The world's smallest non-flying mammal is the white-toothed pygmy shrew, *Suncus etruscus*. Found from southern Europe through southern Asia, the pygmy shrew on average measures 1.4 to 2 inches in body length (minus its tail) and weighs 0.05 to 0.09 ounces.

LONGEST HORNS
Excluding pre-historic mammals, the mammal with the world's longest horns is the Indian buffalo, *Bubalus arnee*, also known as the water buffalo. Found mainly in India, the water buffalo has been domesticated in several parts of Asia, from Southeast Asia to India. On average, their horns spread to 3 feet 3 inches from base to tip.

The longest ever measured—13 feet, 11 inches—belonged to a bull that was shot in 1955.

SOMETHING TO THINK ABOUT

RODENT ON FRIDAYS

Meat from the capybara, the world's largest rodent, is a traditional dish in Venezuela. Low in fat and high in protein; it became popular in this largely Roman Catholic country more than a century ago, after the Catholic Church agreed to count capybara meat as fish—so that Catholics could substitute it for meat, which was prohibited on Fridays and at most meals in Lent.

THEY SUCK BLOOD (REALLY)

The common vampire bat, *Desmodus rotundus*, is about the size of a human thumb. Vampire bats are unique among mammals in that they live strictly off the blood of other animals. They feed on cows, pigs, horses, and birds. They are also unique among bats, as they can walk, jump, and even run.

MORE ON

Mammals

SUPERLATIVES

LOUDEST MAMMAL Foghorn blasts of both the male blue whales, *Balaenoptera musculus*, and fin whales, *Balaenoptera physalus*, have been measured at up to 188 decibels, which is louder than the 180-decibel blast of a rocket launch. These whales emit 5-to-25-second, extremely low-frequency sounds—some too low to be detectable by humans.

Both whales need long, deep calls to locate mates among the ambient noises of the sea. Blue whales can communicate over distances of hundreds of miles.

LOUDEST LAND MAMMAL The loudest land mammals are male howler monkeys of the genus *Alouatta*. There are six species, found in the rain forests of Central and South America. Howler monkeys emit loud, guttural howls that can be heard as far as 3 miles away, even through the rainforest's dense vegetation.

Howlers have big necks for their large vocal chords and deep lower jaws for chewing leaves. The loud howls help monkey troops mark territory and avoid conflicts.

MOST ACUTE HEARING Toothed whales (*Odontocetes*), which include dolphins and porpoises, and small bats (*Microchiroptera*) have the most acute hearing among mammals.

Because of poor visibility in their habitats, they use echolocation to bounce sound waves off objects in order to sense their position and find food. Frequencies as high as 250 kHz and as low as 2 kHz can be heard by some bats, with the 30-120 kHz range typical for most. Most whales can hear between 50 Hz to 200 kHz, but typically between 200 Hz to 100 kHz.

The normal hearing range for humans is 20 Hz to 20 kHz.

LONGEST GESTATION The longest gestation period for any mammal is 21-22 months, for both the Asiatic elephant, *Elephas maximus*, and the African elephant, *Loxodonta africana*. Female Asiatic elephants give birth to a calf every 3-4 years, while African elephants give birth every 4-9 years.

SHORTEST GESTATION The shortest gestation period known for a mammal is 12-13 days.

Several mammals complete the conception-to-birth cycle within this short time: the rat-like short-nosed bandicoot, *Isoodon obesulus*, found in Australia and some South Pacific islands; the common North American Virginia opossum, *Didelphis virginiana*; and the rare water opossum, *Chironectes minimus*, of Central America and northern South America.

All these mammals are marsupials; their young are born while still immature and must complete their development in the pouch of their mother.

YOUNGEST BREEDERS The world's youngest breeding mammals are female Norway lemmings, *Lemmus lemmus*; they can become pregnant as young as 14 days old. Found in Scandinavia, these heavily furred rodents range 4-6 inches long and are well-adapted for cold climates.

Females typically give birth to six to eight young at least three or four times a year. They typically do not breed during the long northern winter.

WEIGHT LOSS While nursing her young calves, the female blue whale can lose up to 25% of her body weight. These mothers can produce over 50 gallons of milk per day, with lactation lasting about seven to eight months.

LONGEST-LIVING MAMMAL In April 1999, researchers published a study of bowhead whales, *Balaena mysticetus*, that claimed a male killed by Alaskan Eskimo (Inuit) hunters in 1995 had lived for up to 211 years, radically challenging the notion that no mammal other than humans lives beyond 100 years old.

This research, led by biologist Craig George, was sparked by the discovery of stone arrowheads embedded deep in the blubber of several bowheads. Stone-tipped harpoons fell out of use by the end of the 19th century.

Further examination of 48 frozen bowhead eyeballs by Dr. Jeffrey Bada of the Scripps Institution of Oceanography in La Jolla, CA, placed five males between the ages of 91 and 211 years at death. The 211-year-old whale's life would have spanned the tenure of U.S. presidents from Thomas Jefferson to Bill Clinton.

SOMETHING TO THINK ABOUT

SLEEPING... ONE HALF OF THE BRAIN AT A TIME

Dolphins sleep an average of eight hours a day, but only allow one half of their brain to doze off at a time. These animals must surface in order to breathe and cannot sleep underwater, or they would drown. So sophisticated is the dolphin's sleep system that it naps at the surface of the water, with half of its brain alert and the opposite eye open, while the other half of the brain is asleep with the opposite eye closed. During sleep, the dolphin alternates position to allow each half of the brain to get its turn.

NO NEED TO FLOSS

The only mammals with no teeth are anteaters. What these animals miss in molar power they make up for with the length of their tongues. Typically, an anteater's tongue can extend up to 2 feet. The equipment seems to work pretty well: the giant anteater, *Myrmecophaga tridactyla*, can gulp down over 10 million ants a year.

JANE OF THE CHIMPS

Perhaps the most internationally renowned wildlife researcher is Jane Goodall, the world's foremost authority on wild chimpanzees. Goodall was only 24 years old when she set up camp in 1960 in the Gombe Stream Chimpanzee Reserve in Tanzania. For nearly 10 years she studied chimpanzees, and discovered previously unknown behaviors such as their ability to use straws for extracting termites from nests. (Today, she heads up the Jane Goodall Institute, a global nonprofit organization that educates the public on the environment.)

OLDEST PRIMATE
The world's oldest known primate is Cheeta, the chimpanzee that starred in 12 Tarzan movies in the 1930s and 1940s. While most chimpanzees, *Pan troglodytes*, live about 45 years in the wild and up to 60 years in captivity, Cheeta turned 73 on April 9, 2005.

The movie-making monkey lives in retirement at the Committee to Help the Environments of Endangered and Threatened Apes (CHEETA) Primate Sanctuary in Palm Springs, CA. Cheeta's last screen appearance was in 1967, when he played opposite Rex Harrison in *Doctor Dolittle*.

OLDEST DEER The world's oldest known deer was a red deer, *Cervus elaphus scoticus*, who lived to be 31 years old. Named Bambi by her owners, Johnnie and Nancy Fraser of Kiltarlity, Scotland, the deer was born on June 7, 1963, and died on Jan. 23, 1995. Deer typically only live to half of Bambi's age.

The Frasers decided to have Bambi put to sleep to end her suffering after she had a stroke and was unable to walk anymore.

THICKEST FUR
The mammal with the thickest fur is the sea otter, *Enhydra lutris*. Found in coastal waters from Mexico to Alaska and across the Pacific Ocean in Japan, the sea otter has a super-thick coat with 850,000 to 1 million hairs per square inch.

There are actually two layers of fur, an undercoat and longer guard hairs. This two-layer system serves to protect the sea otter's skin, trapping a layer of air between the coats as insulation from wet and cold.

Birds

BIRDS ARE WARM BLOODED VERTEBRATES that have wings, beaks, and feathers (only birds have feathers). They generally use their wings to fly, but some can't fly; ostriches use their wings for balance, and penguins use them as flippers in the water. Like horses, birds sleep standing up. They can't sweat, but they cool off while flying, and by breathing heavily when on land. Believed to have evolved from dinosaurs long after the mammals and reptiles broke off, birds lay eggs that hatch into their young. There are about 9,000 different species of birds, spread around every part of the globe.

SUPERLATIVES

SPEED AND TRAVEL

FASTEST FLYERS
The peregrine falcon, *Falco peregrinus*, is the world's fastest bird. In a steep dive, called a stoop, it reaches speeds up to 150 mph. A medium-sized raptor, the peregrine falcon can be found on every continent except Antarctica. Smaller and more streamlined than hawks, male peregrine falcons range in size from 15 to 18 inches long and weigh about 1.25 to 3.5 pounds. The female is bigger, at 18 to 21 inches and about 2 pounds in weight.

SLOWEST FLYERS
The world's slowest flying bird is the American woodcock, *Scolopax minor*. It flies, without stalling, at a mere 5 mph, similar to a human's jogging speed. The American woodcock is a shorebird that lives in forests. Its coloring blends in with the forest around it, so that it is difficult to spot.

FASTEST LAND BIRD
The fastest bird on land is the ostrich, *Struthio camelus*. Found in Africa, ostriches can run across level ground at speeds of 45 mph up to 60 mph in short bursts. One of about 40 species of flightless birds, ostriches can weigh as much as 345 pounds and stands an average of 8 feet, 2 inches. Ostriches' strong legs also make them the fastest of all two-legged land animals.

FASTEST SWIMMER
The fastest underwater swimming bird is the gentoo penguin, *Pygoscelis papua*. These birds swim underwater at speeds up to 17 mph. They are found from the Antarctic islands to southern South America; the largest concentrations are on South Georgia, the Falkland Islands, and Iles Kerguelen.

FASTEST WINGBEAT
The bird with the fastest wingbeat in the avian kingdom is the Horned Sungem, *Heliactin bilopha*. Found in Brazil, Bolivia, and Suriname, the Horned Sungem flaps its wings over 90 times per second during normal activity. The hummingbird's wings act like a tiny propeller, allowing the bird to hover for long periods. Hummingbirds can also fly backward and sideways.

SLOWEST WINGBEAT
The birds with the slowest wingbeat are vultures. These are very large birds that eat carrion (animals that have died and started to decay). Vultures have very strong wings and can maintain flight with just one wingbeat per second. There are many species of vultures and they are found around the globe.

LONGEST MIGRATION
The longest migration of any bird is the estimated 22,400 miles traveled each year by the Arctic tern, *Sterna paradisaea*, from above the Arctic Circle down to Antarctica and back. A small bird with a lot of stamina, the Arctic tern weighs less than a quarter pound and is up to 15 inches long.

These birds breed in the Arctic tundra during the northern hemisphere's summer and about 90 days later begin their long journey south. Their path follows the Atlantic coasts of Europe and Africa or the Pacific coast of America. They inhabit Antarctica's pack ice during the southern hemisphere's summer and then journey again back north.

It has been estimated that because it summers twice a year in polar regions, the Arctic tern spends more time in daylight than any other animal.

SIZE

BIGGEST BIRD
Found only in Africa, the ostrich is both the heaviest and the tallest bird. Males are larger than females; some have been measured at more than 9 feet tall, while weighing 345 pounds or more. Unable to fly because it doesn't have a keeled breastbone, the ostrich feeds mainly on seeds and other plant material.

HEAVIEST FLYING BIRD The heaviest bird capable of flying is the great bustard, *Otis tarda*. Over hunted in the past century, it is now found only in patches across Eurasia. Male bustards have been known to reach 44 pounds, grow to 41 inches long, and have wingspans of 7 feet.

SMALLEST BIRD
The world's smallest bird is the bee hummingbird, *Mellisuga* or *Calypte helenae*. These are found in Cuba and on the Isle of Pines (part of New Caledonia in the South Pacific).

The largest bee hummingbirds are just

over 2 inches long. Some adult birds have been estimated at as small as 1 inch long. About the size of a bumblebee, most bee hummingbirds weigh about as much as a U.S. dime ($\frac{1}{20}$ ounce).

LARGEST WINGSPAN The bird with the longest wingspan is the wandering albatross, *Diomedea exulans*. Found in the southern oceans, the wandering albatross has a wingspan of 8-11 feet. Living in one of the world's windiest environments, this bird uses its large wingspan to stay airborne for long periods of time while it searches for food. The wandering albatross can live to be up to 30 years old.

LONGEST LEGS Though the bird with the longest legs is the ostrich, the bird that has the longest legs relative to its body length is the black-winged stilt, *Himantopus himantopus*. The black and white shorebird is found in tropical and subtropical marshes worldwide, including Hawaii. Typically a black-winged stilt's pink legs are 7 to 9 inches long, which is 60% percent of its height, usually about 13.75 to 15.75 inches.

LONGEST BILL The bird with the longest bill is the Australian pelican, *Pelecanus conspicillatus*. Found throughout Australia, Papua New Guinea, and western Indonesia, the Australian pelican has a pouched bill that can reach 18.5 inches in length. The largest of the seven species of pelicans, it has a pouch that can hold up to 14 quarts of water when fully extended.

The bird with the longest bill in proportion to its body size is the sword-billed hummingbird, *Ensifera ensifera*. Found in northern South America, it has a beak over 4 inches long, longer than the rest of its body, excluding the tail. This bird uses its beak to feed from the long, tubular flowers that are plentiful in its environment.

SOMETHING TO THINK ABOUT

PERCHING ON POWER LINES

When you see electrical power lines, you usually see birds perched on top of the wires. How come they don't get electrocuted when wires aren't insulated? It is because electricity flows when there is a difference in voltage. Since they usually are touching only one wire with their two feet, and nothing else, the electricity stays put. However, if a bird stood on two power lines or touched a grounded pole, there would be a potential difference in voltage between the two, and the electricity would travel through the bird from the higher voltage area to the lower. In fact, many large birds are killed each year when their wings touch two power lines at the same time.

POISONOUS BIRDS

There are only six species of poisonous birds and they all live in Papua New Guinea. Five are of the genus *Pitohui* while the sixth is the blue-capped ifrita, *Ifrita kowaldi*. The hooded pitohui, *Pitohui dichrous*; the variable pitohui, *Pitohui kirhocephalus*; and the ifrita are the most poisonous. They all have high concentrations of batrachotoxin (a steroidal alkaloid also found in poison dart frogs) in their belly, breast, and leg feathers, that can numb or paralyze on contact. In local villages the ifrita is called "slek-yakt," which literally means "bitter bird." The poison protects them from wary predators.

Mike, the Wonder Chicken

MIKE, THE WONDER CHICKEN

On Sept. 10, 1945, Lloyd Olsen, from Fruita, CO, lopped off the head of his chicken, Mike, but amazingly, the headless chicken survived "the guillotine." Olsen had connected too far up Mike's head and missed the jugular vein; the brain stem and one ear were still attached. Mike was still alive the next day, and Olsen and his wife Clara didn't have the heart to kill him. Instead they fed the headless chicken directly into his gullet with an eyedropper, and hit the road. "Mike the Wonder Chicken" toured the carnival circuit, where people could get a look at him for 25 cents. Mike died in an Arizona motel in May 1947. "Fowl" play was not suspected. In 2003, his story was the subject of a documentary that aired at the Cannes Film Festival, *Chick Flick: The Miracle Mike Story*. The citizens of Fruita honor his memory with annual Mike the Headless Chicken Days, including the 5-kilometer "Run Like a Headless Chicken" Run.

Reptiles

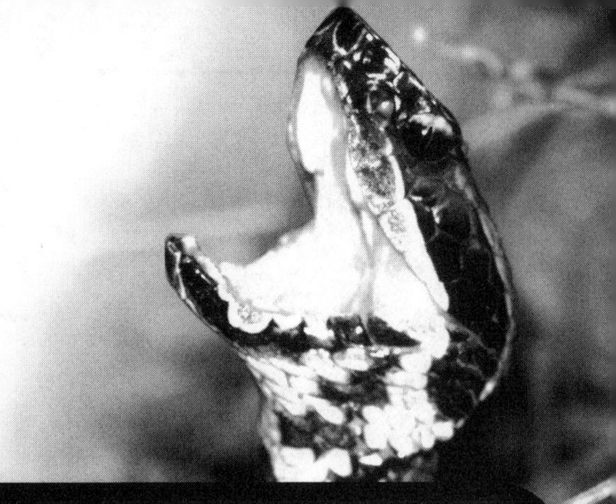

THE WORD "REPTILE" comes from the Latin *repere*, which means "to crawl." There are four orders of reptiles: Squamata (lizards and snakes), Testudines (turtles), Crocodilian (crocodiles and alligators), and Rhynchocephalia (tuataras). Most reptiles do appear to crawl. Aside from that, they are vertebrate animals that typically eat meat, rely on outside heat (such as from the sun) to warm their blood, and reproduce by laying eggs. Reptiles are found on all continents except Antarctica, but usually live in tropical and subtropical climates.

SUPERLATIVES

SNAKES

FASTEST SNAKE
The black mamba, *Dendroaspis polylepis*, has been clocked at speeds of 14 miles per hour for short distances, and is considered the fastest-moving land snake. The name for this aggressive, venomous snake actually comes from the purplish-black color inside its mouth.

MOST TOXIC SNAKE
The western or inland taipan snake, *Oxyuranus microlepidotus*, found in a remote area of Queensland, Australia, produces the most poisonous venom, drop for drop, of any land snake in the world. This snake is not very aggressive. But its venom is 50 times as powerful as the king cobra's, and one big bite could release enough venom to kill more than 100 people or 250,000 mice.

LONGEST FANGS
The venomous gaboon viper, *Bitis gabonica*, has the longest fangs of any snake species. Found in sub-Saharan Africa, it is the largest viper on the continent and has 2-inch-long fangs. The head is typically 5 inches long, and the fangs fold back against the roof of the mouth. The gaboon can swallow animals as big as rabbits. It uses its fangs to grip and poison its prey, then swallows it whole.

LONGEST VENOMOUS SNAKE The king cobra, *Ophiophagus hannah*, is the world's longest venomous snake: it can grow up to 18 feet long. The average length is 13 feet. Found in eastern India, southern China, and throughout Southeast Asia, these snakes carry up to 0.2 ounces of venom, enough to kill an Asian elephant.

SHORTEST VENOMOUS SNAKE
The Namaqua dwarf adder, *Bitis schneideri*, is the world's shortest venomous snake. Found in southern Africa, this sidewinder grows to an average length of 8 inches. Typically, the Namaqua lives in desert habitats. Although its venom is poisonous, the Namaqua rarely bites humans and has never been reported as the cause of a person's death.

HEAVIEST SNAKE
The green anaconda, *Eunectes murinus*, also known as the water boa, is the heaviest species of snakes. Found in the Amazon and Orinoco River basins of South America, the green anaconda is a water snake. It usually weighs over 200 pounds, and some green anacondas have been estimated to weigh up to 500 pounds.

SNAKEBITE DEATHS
The World Health Organization estimates that 125,000 people each year die from snakebites. In Europe and North America more people die from bee and wasp stings. But in Asia, the annual number of snakebite deaths is estimated at 100,000, 80% of the world's total.

It has been estimated that 17 to 20% of snakebites are fatal. But in most cases, deaths could have been prevented if the patient had better access to medical treatment. In India, fewer than 40% of snakebite victims visit a hospital.

LIZARDS

LARGEST LIZARD
The Komodo dragon, *Varanus komodoensis*, is the world's largest lizard. Biologists found the first specimen on the Indonesian island of Komodo in 1911. An adult male komodo can grow to be up to 10 feet long from nose to tail. Komodos usually weigh 200 to 300 pounds and are good eaters; they can consume 80% of their body weight in a single meal.

LONGEST LIZARD
The crocodile monitor, *Varanus salvadori*, is the world's longest lizard. Only found in Papua New Guinea, the crocodile monitor has been measured at 15 feet, 7 inches long. About two-thirds of the lizard's length is in its sturdy, flexible tail, which it uses as a defensive weapon. A climbing reptile, the crocodile monitor flourishes in very hot and humid conditions and spends a lot of time in trees.

SMALLEST LIZARD
The Jaragua sphaero, *Sphaerodactylus ariasae*, and the Virgin Islands dwarf sphaero, *Sphaerodactylus parthenopion*, are the two smallest known lizards (and the smallest reptiles) in

SOMETHING TO THINK ABOUT

LONGEST SNAKE

In Dec. 2003, the Curugsewu Park in Kendal, Java, Indonesia, displayed what it claimed was the world's longest snake, a nearly 49-foot-long reticulated python. The park's snake handler, Imam Darmanto, told reporters that the snake, called Fragrant Flower, had been found on Sumatra in 2002. News of the massive snake was met with skepticism. The previous record-holder was a reticulated python shot in 1912 that measured 32 feet, 9 inches. A British journalist traveled to Java in Jan. 2004 to examine the claim. His measurement came up short of the record: Fragrant Flower was a mere 22 feet long. When questioned about the apparent discrepancy, Darmanto told the reporter, "Look, you must understand that a python's length is not constant."

GATORS OR CROCS?

Should you ever come face-to-face with an alligator or a crocodile and wonder which species confronts you, fear not—look at their noses. An alligator has a rounded snout; a crocodile's is triangular. You can also look at the mouth: the fourth lower tooth can be seen when a crocodile has its mouth closed, but with the alligator the tooth fits into a socket in the upper jaw and can't be seen.

BEWARE: DEAD RATTLESNAKE

A dead rattlesnake can still attack for up to an hour after death. Studies have shown that the muscle reflex to strike an object that touches it is so hard-wired into a snake's body that the signal bypasses processing in the brain.

the world. Both lizards measure a mere 0.63 inches from nose to tail and could curl up inside the face of a dime.

The Jaragua sphaero was discovered in 2001 on the tiny Caribbean island of Beata, near the Dominican Republic, by biologists Blair Hedges, of Penn State University, and Richard Thomas, of the University of Puerto Rico. The dwarf sphaero was found in the British Virgin Islands in 1965.

TURTLES

LARGEST TURTLE
The leatherback sea turtle, *Dermochelys coriacea*, is the largest turtle in the world. These turtles grow up to 9 feet long and 6 feet wide, and can weigh 1,200-1,500 pounds.

Leatherbacks, an endangered species, are so named for the leather-like consistency of their shells. The sea turtles inhabit tropical and sub-tropical oceans and can be found as far north as the British Isles and as far south as Australia. Leatherbacks can dive as deep as whales and feed mostly on jellyfish and squid.

OLDEST SEA TURTLE FOSSIL The discovery of a fossilized sea turtle skeleton, dating to the early Cretaceous period, was reported in April 1998. Japanese paleontologist Ren Hirayama of Teikyo Heisei University found the fossil, *Santanachelys gaffneyi*, at the Santana Formation fossil site in northeastern Brazil, where Hirayama had been working since 1992. Extremely well preserved, the Santana fossil lived about 110 million years ago.

DEEPEST DIVE
In Feb. 2004, Graeme Hays of the University of Wales in Swansea reported that a leatherback turtle tagged with tracking equipment dove to a depth of 2,100 feet in the Atlantic Ocean. This is the deepest known dive for a reptile.

CROCODILES

LARGEST CROCODILE
The "SuperCroc," *Sarcosuchus imperator*, is the largest crocodile ever found. Paleontologist Paul Sereno and herpetologist (snake biologist) Brady Barr estimate the SuperCroc was 37 to 40 feet long and weighed as much as 10 tons. The first of the SuperCroc fossils were discovered in 1960, and Sereno and Barr's fossil excavation in 2000 uncovered dozens of other fossilized remains.

SuperCroc lived about 110 million years ago by the Niger River in what is now African desert. A life-size skeletal cast of the SuperCroc was created as a traveling museum exhibit.

LARGEST LIVING CROCODILIAN The largest crocodile known today is the saltwater crocodile, *Crocodylus porosus*, also known as the estuarine or Indopacific crocodile. Found mainly in India and Bangladesh, these creatures can measure 20 feet or more in length, from nose to tail, with the record so far standing at 23 feet long.

SMALLEST CROCODILIAN
The Cuvier's dwarf caiman, *Paleosuchus palpebrosus*, is the smallest known crocodile. It is found in northern South America. The females of the species rarely grow past 4 feet in length, while full-grown males measure no more than 5 feet long.

Amphibians

AMPHIBIANS are a group of cold-blooded animals that live both in water and on land. The word *amphibian* is a combination of two Greek words, amphi, meaning "both," and *bios*, meaning "life." Amphibians have backbones and generally hatch their young in eggs, which usually need water to grow. Adult amphibians are carnivorous, eating mainly insects, slugs, and worms; tadpoles are mainly vegetarians.

SUPERLATIVES

FROGS AND TOADS

Anura (Salientia), tailless amphibians like frogs and toads, inhabit every continent except Antarctica. They thrive in most environments, but live mainly in wetland areas. The names are often interchanged, but "frog" usually means a smooth-skinned, aquatic species, while "toad" means a rough-skinned, land-based species.

OLDEST FROG-LIKE FOSSIL The earliest frog-like fossil dates to the Early Triassic period, 220-230 million years ago. *Triadobatrachus massinoti* was found in northern Madagascar. Although it looks like a frog, it has a longer body, a tail, and shorter legs. *Prosaliris bitis*, a 190-million-year-old fossil found on a Navajo Indian reservation in Arizona in 1982, has more traits in common with modern frogs, including longer legs for jumping and no tail.

LARGEST FROG

The goliath frog, *Conraua goliath*, is the world's largest frog. Found in the West African rain forests of Cameroon and Equatorial Guinea, this "African giant" has been measured at 12.5 inches long. With back legs extended, some goliaths have been measured at lengths of more than 2.5 feet. First identified in 1906, the goliath can weigh as much as 7.2 pounds, about as much as a domestic cat.

SMALLEST FROG Two frogs vie for the title of world's smallest frog: the Monte Iberia dwarf eleuth, *Eleutherodactylus iberia*, and the gold frogs *Brachycephalus* and *Psyllophryne*. Also known as the Cuban pygmy or litter leaf frog, the eleuth was first found on Cuba's Monte Iberia by Cuban scientist Alberto Estrada in 1996. The gold frog is found in eastern and southern Brazil. Full-grown adults of both species have been measured at 0.4 inches from snout to vent.

FROG JUMPING

Santjie, a sharp-nosed frog (*Ptychadena oxyrhynchus*), leapt a world distance record of 33 feet, 5.5 inches in three leaps at a derby in Kwa-Zulu-Natal, South Africa, in May 1977. Perhaps the most famous frog jumping contest is the Calaveras County Fair & Jumping Frog Jubilee, staged every May in Angels Camp, CA. The fair was inspired by Mark Twain's short story "The Celebrated Jumping Frog of Calaveras County." The longest triple frog jump at the fair was set in 1986 by a bullfrog named Rosie the Ribbiter, who leaped 21 feet, 5.75 inches.

MOST FROG SPECIES

A Wildlife Heritage Trust survey completed in 1999 discovered that Sri Lanka has the world's highest density of amphibian diversity. The Indian Ocean island nation, slightly larger than the state of West Virginia, contains almost 5% of the world's total frog species.

LARGEST FROG GENUS The largest genus of frogs is the *Eleutherodactylus*, with more than 700 species. Known generally as "rain frogs" or "tink frogs," these amphibians are found throughout the tropics of the Western Hemisphere. This genus is also considered to be the largest genus of all vertebrates.

MOST POISONOUS FROG Poison-arrow frogs (*Dendrobatidae*, including *Dendrobates* and *Phyllobates*) are regarded as the most poisonous of the frog species. These brightly colored frogs, found in Central and South America, don't sting or bite but secrete some of the most deadly toxins known to science.

The more than 200 known species of poison-arrow frogs come in most colors of the rainbow, from green to yellow to red. The bright colors fend off potential predators by surprising or confusing them momentarily, giving the frog enough time to escape.

Three of the deadliest dart poison frogs, all *Phyllobates* found in western Colombia, produce batrachotoxin, one of the most potent naturally occurring poisons. These frogs are so poisonous that

SOMETHING TO THINK ABOUT

ADAPTABILITY

Frogs are among the world's most adaptable creatures. There are more than 4,000 species, coming in many shapes and sizes, and many have distinct characteristics. The red-eyed tree frog, found in Central America, has toe pads on its feet; these act like suction cups, enabling the red-eye to cling to branches and leaves. The South American horned frog has powerful jaws and sharp teeth; it gets its nickname, "pac man frog," from using its supersize molars to snap up passing rodents, birds, and other small animals. Wallace's flying frog, found in Malaysia's forest canopies, uses its webbed feet to leap 50 feet between trees. The wood frog can stay partially frozen down to 23°F for several weeks, helping it to survive the harsh winters of its native Canada and northern United States.

BEST EATEN RAW

In May 2003, the *South China Morning Post* (Hong Kong) reported that the Longxi Restaurant in the Baiyun district of Guangzhou, China, had added a new dish to its menu to help lure back diners: giant salamanders. In China a special license is required to serve salamanders, which the restaurant received in April 2003. The chef planned to serve them raw, steeped in a rice wine, or steamed. Initial reports suggested that salamanders, raw or cooked, are not a big attraction to diners.

SALAMANDER QUIRKS

The only amphibian that does not hatch from an egg is the fire salamander; baby fire salamanders develop inside the mother's body. The only amphibian that is a natural cave-dweller is the olm, a pale-skinned creature that lives in total darkness in underground pools of water. Salamanders may be the quietest of amphibians. They cannot hear sounds, and don't emit sounds themselves.

just by rubbing an arrow tip on the skin of an adult frog, hunters can obtain enough poison to kill a large animal. The tiny golden poison frog, *Phyllobates terribilis*, is only 1.5 inches long, but secretes a toxin so powerful that 1 milligram can kill 20,000 mice or 10 humans.

SALAMANDERS

The *caudata*, or "salamander," is the scientific order of amphibians that have tails as adults. This includes animals commonly known as newts and sirens. Salamanders may often be mistaken for lizards, but they have no scales and must stay close to water to survive.

EARLIEST SALAMANDER
Chunerpeton tianyiensis is the oldest-known relative to today's salamanders. The 160-million-year-old fossil was found in northern China by Ke-Qin Gao of the American Museum of Natural History and Neil Shubin of the University of Chicago. It resembles today's largest species: the North American hellbender (*Crytobranchus*) and the Chinese giant salamander (*Andrias*).

LARGEST SALAMANDER
The Chinese giant salamander, *Andrias davidianus*, is the biggest salamander, and biggest amphibian, in the world. It grows to about 70 inches long from tip to tail and weighs more than 25 pounds. A fully aquatic salamander, it has a long body, and two pairs of legs which are usually the same size. Its eyes are tiny and have no eyelids.

SMALLEST SALAMANDER
Thorius arboreus (arboreal minute salamander) is the smallest known salamander. It is found in the state of Oaxaca in Mexico. The largest known female specimen measured 0.866 inches from head-to-tail.

HIGHEST AMPHIBIAN
The *Pseudoeurycea gadovii* is a salamander that lives at an elevation of about 16,400 feet on the Orizaba Volcano in Mexico. It is the world's highest-dwelling amphibian.

CAECILIANS

Caecilians, or *Gymnophia*, are relatively unknown creatures that make up less than 5% of all amphibians and look like large earthworms. These reclusive burrowers are found only in moist tropical soil or water; they eat small fish or invertebrates.

EARLIEST CAECILIAN
Eocaecilia micropodia were found by Farish A. Jenkins Jr. of Harvard University and Denis M. Walsh of the University of London in northeastern Arizona in 1990. They date to the Lower Jurassic period about 175 to 180 million years ago. The fossils had not yet shed their tiny limbs and were about 1.6 inches long.

LARGEST CAECILIAN
Found in the heights of central Colombia, the *Caecilia thompsoni* is the largest caecilian, reaching about 5 feet in length.

LARGEST GENUS OF CAECILIAN The largest genera of caecilian are *Ichtyophis* and *Caecilia* with more than 30 species each. Ichtyophis are found throughout southeastern Asia. *Caecilia* are found in southern Central America south to Bolivia in South America.

Fish

FISH LIVE IN WATER, HAVE BACKBONES, AND BREATHE WITH GILLS rather than lungs. Most fish have scales, but not all do. There are three classes of fish. The Agnatha, the most primitive type of fish, have no jaws. Chondrichthyes, including sharks and rays, are jawed fish with cartilaginous skeletons. Ostheichthyes, such as trout, bass, and salmon, have bony skeletons. Parental care and feeding habits vary between species. Some fish lay eggs and others give birth to live young. Some fish are carnivores while others are vegetarians.

SUPERLATIVES

SLOWEST FISH
The world's slowest known fish is the dwarf sea horse, *Hippocampus zosterae*. Found in the western Atlantic across the Gulf of Mexico and the Caribbean, the dwarf sea horse travels at a speed of about 5 feet per hour.

These tiny creatures, less than 2 inches long, typically live in shallow water, among coral reefs or sea-grass bed. Their rigid body structure is the reason why dwarf sea horses move so slowly in the water. The only parts of their body that can move easily are the small fins on either side of the body and their back.

LARGEST FISH The world's biggest fish is the whale shark, *Rhincodon typus*. Typically, the whale shark grows to a length between 13 and 40 feet but specimens have reached 45 feet, and their weight can exceed 10 tons.

Found in all tropical and warm temperate waters, this gentle ocean giant is harmless to humans. It feeds mainly on plankton.

SMALLEST FISH
The stout infantfish, *Schindleria brevipinguis*, is just over a quarter of an inch long. The species was first recorded in 1979 by Australian Museum's Jeff Leis in the Great Barrier Reef, and only six specimens have ever been found. It is also the smallest and lightest vertebrate.

HEAVIEST BONY FISH The world's heaviest bony fish is the ocean sunfish, *Mola mola*. Found in warm and temperate oceans around the world, it weighs an average of around 2,200 pounds but can reach over 4,000 pounds. The length of the fish is typically between 6 and 10 feet.

There are two claims for the heaviest known specimen: A *Mola mola* hit by an Australian steamship *SS Fiona* about 40 miles off Sydney on Sept. 18, 1908, was towed to port and weighed in at 4,927 pounds. A *Mola mola* caught off the coast of Kamogawa, Japan, in 1996 was weighed at 5,071 pounds. Scientists have expressed doubts as to the accuracy of both measurements, but accept that such sizes are within the realm of possibility. The *mola* diet? Mostly squid and small fish.

LARGEST PREDATORY FISH The world's biggest predatory fish is the great white shark, *Carcharodon carcharias*. Found in temperate waters in most of the world's oceans, it averages between 4.5 and 20 feet long and weighs up to 6,600 pounds.

Scientists know little about the movements of these solitary creatures. Studies have shown that this shark is adapted perfectly to kill its prey: sensory organs in the snout can detect minute movement in the water; the shark's coloring provides excellent camouflage; its large, powerful body allows quick bursts of speed for striking prey; and it has around 3,000 razor sharp teeth in rows that tear into the flesh of its prey.

MOST EGGS The fish that produces the most eggs is the ocean sunfish, *Mola mola*. It has been estimated that a typical female *Mola mola* has as many as 300 million eggs in her single ovary. One beached in the Philippines yielded 17 quarts of eggs. Each of these tiny eggs measures about 0.05 inches in diameter.

MOST POISONOUS FISH The world's most poisonous fish, in terms of being deadly when eaten by humans, are various puffer fish, from the *tetraodontidae* family. Known for their round bodies, which give them common names like blow fish or swell fish, puffers contain the poison tetrodotoxin mostly in their liver, ovaries, intestines, and skin. Females are generally more toxic than males and are the most toxic during mating season.

Eaten as a delicacy in many parts of the world, especially in Japan (where they are called *fugu*), the puffer can kill a human quickly after ingestion if not prepared properly. The fatality rate for poisoned humans is close to 60%, with deaths occurring within 24 hours; there is no known antidote, and treatment is purely symptomatic. However, puffer fish, when prepared properly, are perfectly safe to eat.

MOST VENOMOUS FISH The world's most venomous fish, in terms of injecting a toxin, are three of the five stonefish species: *Synanceia horrida*, *Synanceia trachynis*, and *Synanceia verrucossa*. Found in the shallow waters of the Indo-Pacific region, stonefish have 13 dorsal fin spines that contain highly toxic proteins that inflict intense pain

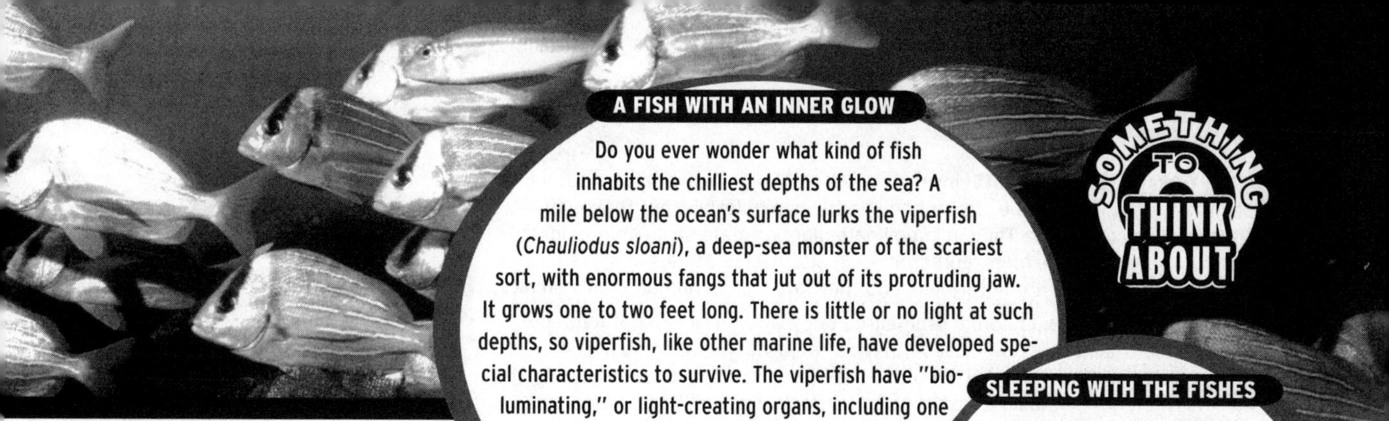

and sometimes death on their prey. They can be deadly to humans, but such deaths aren't common.

Stonefish live on the seabed, usually in tidal inlets, coral islands, sheltered bays, or estuaries, or among weed-covered rocks. They are dangerous only if stepped on or caught. Perfectly camouflaged, stonefish look like encrusted rock or coral, and many unsuspecting swimmers are stung each year.

DEEPEST DWELLING FISH Because of the lack of light and overwhelming pressure, it is difficult for organisms to survive in the extreme deep. Exploring is even more difficult. The greatest depth from which any living species of fish has been recorded is 27,455 feet, more than 5 miles, at the Puerto Rico Trench, where a type of cuskeel, *Abyssobrotula galatheae*, was found by Jørgen G. Nielsen during an expedition in 1977.

Members of the brotulid family of fish are known to survive at such depths. A $6\frac{1}{2}$-inch *Bassaogigas profundissimus* was recovered from the trench in April 1970. More recently another species, *Abyssobrotula galatheae*, also known as "fangtooth," was found in the trench. Scientists know very little about these fish and how they survive in such a harsh environment.

OLDEST GOLDFISH

The oldest known goldfish, named Tish, lived for 43 years in the home of Hilda Hand in Thirsk, England. Won by Hand's son, Peter, at a carnival in Doncaster, England, in 1956, Tish passed away in Aug. 1999. A male goldfish, Tish lived so long that his bright orange scales faded to silver, and he outlived his partner, Tosh, by 24 years. Won by Peter at the carnival too, Tosh died in 1975.

Hilda Hand took over the care of Tish when Peter left home to get married. She told Britain's BBC News that the secret to Tish's long life was "not being overfed, and being put in the sun occasionally."

SOMETHING TO THINK ABOUT

A FISH WITH AN INNER GLOW

Do you ever wonder what kind of fish inhabits the chilliest depths of the sea? A mile below the ocean's surface lurks the viperfish (*Chauliodus sloani*), a deep-sea monster of the scariest sort, with enormous fangs that jut out of its protruding jaw. It grows one to two feet long. There is little or no light at such depths, so viperfish, like other marine life, have developed special characteristics to survive. The viperfish have "bio-luminating," or light-creating organs, including one on a large dorsal fin that helps "call" in fish for mealtime. Some viperfish have large eyes to gather as much light as possible, while others have no eyes at all.

SLEEPING WITH THE FISHES

It's actually pretty difficult to sleep with the fishes, because fish do not "sleep" like most animals. Instead, they enter states of rest. Some fish rest under logs or hide in coral at night. Deep-sea species like sharks and tuna can never stop swimming. Scientists do not know how sharks rest.

SIBLING RIVALRY

Sharks in general aren't friendly toward one another, and baby sand tiger sharks take this to an extreme. Sand tiger sharks can give live birth to two pups per year, meaning they emerge from their mother fully formed and not in eggs. While still inside the womb as embryos, these sharks will eat each other and the other eggs in the ovum, thus enhancing their own chance for survival. Normally, only one emerges from the mother, and it is quite large (some say up to 40 inches) after having feasted on its sibling.

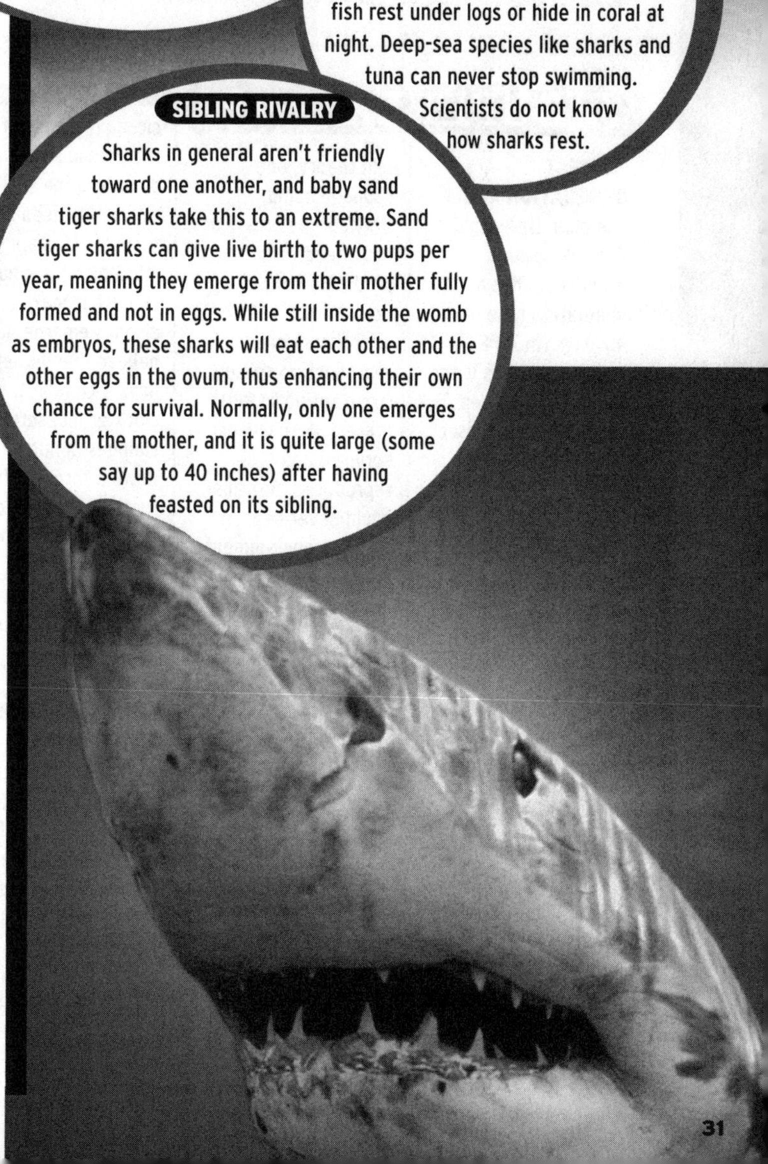

Insects

CREEPY-CRAWLIES, BUGS, PESTS—insects have been called many names, not all of them pleasant. Some people regard insects as a nuisance, but they play a vital part in ecosystems. They help pollinate plants, aerate soil, and provide a source of food for fish, birds, and other animals. Insects can also be destructive (termites and locusts are notorious), and they love to join human family picnics.

An insect has an exoskeleton, a segmented body, and three pairs of jointed legs. All mature insects have a body that can be divided into three parts: head, thorax, and abdomen. Most have compound eyes and a pair of antennae. Adult insects often have wings and can fly. Some insects, such as bees, wasps, ants, and termites, live in amazingly well-organized groups, where members have highly specialized functions and work together with a degree of cooperation that could put human society to shame!

There are more than a million known insect species spread throughout the world, and entomologists estimate that millions more are yet to be discovered.

SUPERLATIVES

FASTEST GENERATION CYCLE

The plum tree aphid, *Rhopalosiphum prunifoliae*, has a generation time of 4.7 days (in 77°F conditions). This is the total time between the birth of one insect to the birth of that insect's offspring.

Female aphids called "stem mothers" reproduce asexually and produce daughters, who in turn rapidly produce more daughters, all summer. A newborn female can carry the embryos of her unborn daughters and even granddaughters developing at the same time within the unborn daughters.

In late summer, some males develop and mate with females; their (female) offspring hatch the next spring.

In theory, one cabbage aphid, *Brevicoryne brassicae*, could lead to the production of 1.6 octillion (1.6 x 10^{27}) offspring in one reproduction season (from spring to fall) if every descendant survived and reproduced. But this could never happen because environmental conditions kill off most young aphids quickly.

LONGEST GENERATION CYCLE

The longest known generation cycle of an insect under normal conditions is 17 years and belongs to the three species of cicada (*Magicicada septendecim*, *M. cassini*, and *M. septendecula*). An adult female cicada lays her eggs in tree branches. When they hatch, the cicada nymphs fall to the ground and tunnel down into the soil, where they feed on roots for 17 years.

Scientists are not sure what makes the cicadas emerge but believe they either have a biological clock or measure the changes in nutrients flowing through the roots. When they do emerge, the nymphs rapidly transform into adults and call loudly to other cicadas to begin the mating process.

Strangely, the life of the adult cicada is very short. The male dies after mating; the female dies after laying all her eggs. A month or two after the female dies, her eggs hatch and the 17-year cycle starts again.

FASTEST WING BEAT

The fastest wing beat of any insect is generated by a midge of genus *Forcipomyia*. These tiny relatives of the mosquito have been found to have a wing beat frequency of 62,760 beats per minute. In comparison, even the fastest hummingbirds only flap their wings about 5,500 times a minute.

LOUDEST INSECT

Cicadas are the loudest insects. Adult male cicadas emit "songs" during the mating season by drumming two membranes against the sides of the abdomen.

There are just under 2,000 species of cicada, and generally the bigger the cicada, the louder its song.

The loudest scientifically measured song belongs to the African cicada, *Brevisana brevis*. A single African cicada is capable of producing a 106.7-decibel sound, which is louder than a subway train.

LONGEST INSECT

The longest insects belong to the order Phasmatodea. Better known as walkingsticks, they uncannily resemble the twigs and branches of their own habitat. Some individual specimens have been measured at up to 22 inches with their legs fully extended.

Even at such lengths, they blend in with their environment, protecting them from predators.

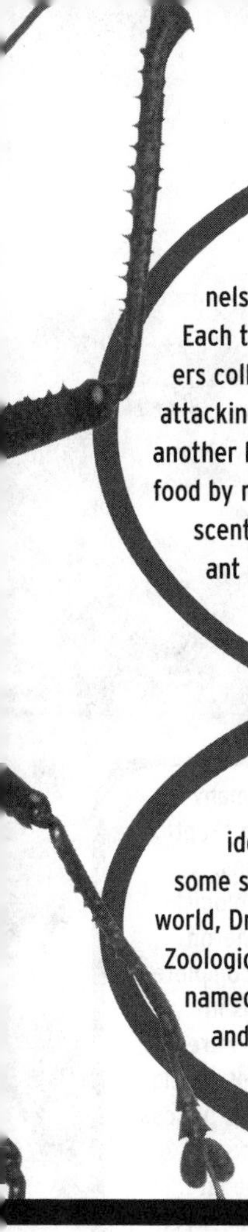

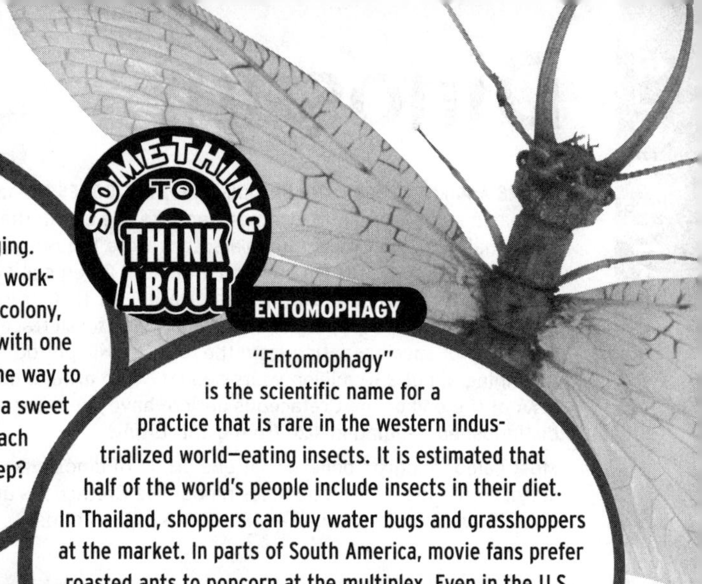

SOMETHING TO THINK ABOUT

AMAZING ANTS

Ants are social insects that live and work cooperatively together in large colonies—usually systems of underground tunnels with mounds formed above by the dirt removed in digging. Each type of ant has a specific function: the queen lays eggs, workers collect food and enlarge the nest, and soldiers defend the colony, attacking ants they recognize as strangers. Ants communicate with one another by touching with their antennas, and can show others the way to food by making a path with a chemical (pheromone) that leaves a sweet scent. Besides being cooperative ants can work very hard; each ant can lift up to 50 times its own weight. Do ants ever sleep? Scientists don't know.

WHEN A NAME BUGS YOU

There are so many animal species waiting to be named that taxonomists can't keep up. Often, the person who identifies the new species gets to name it. This can lead to some strange attempts at humor and unusual tributes. In the insect world, Dr. Neal L. Evenhuis, president of the International Commission on Zoological Nomenclature, has named hundreds of insect species. He has named flies *Pieza pi* and *Pieza rhea*, revealing his love for both puns and pizza. Others look to film actors for inspiration. There is an ant named *Pheidole harrisonfordi*, and a fly named *Campsicnemius charliechaplini*.

ENTOMOPHAGY

"Entomophagy" is the scientific name for a practice that is rare in the western industrialized world—eating insects. It is estimated that half of the world's people include insects in their diet. In Thailand, shoppers can buy water bugs and grasshoppers at the market. In parts of South America, movie fans prefer roasted ants to popcorn at the multiplex. Even in the U.S., each person unintentionally consumes an estimated pound of insects per year: common foods such as tomato sauce, hot dogs, and chocolate all may contain insect parts and eggs. Of course, health codes allow only very low levels of these ingredients.

Walkingsticks can also keep perfectly still for up to six hours at a time.

LONGEST REGULAR MIGRATION Every year as cold weather approaches, the North American monarch butterfly, *Danaus plexippus*, migrates from southern Canada and the northern U.S. to Central Mexico, a trip of about 2,800 miles. From Nov. to March, about 4 million butterflies can be found in an acre, and up to 15,000 on a single branch. Not every monarch gets the chance to migrate. Several generations are born every year, so the migratory butterflies are often the great-grandchildren of the last generation to make the trip.

SHORTEST REPRODUCTIVE LIFE Once mayflies (the Ephemeroptera order) molt into sexual maturity, very few live beyond 48 hours. Many live for such a short time that they don't even develop mouths. Female *Dolania americana* mayflies have been recorded as fully reproductive for less than five minutes. Talk about speed dating: that means five minutes to rise from the water, find a suitable mate, and lay their eggs.

LARGEST ORDER Insects of the order Coleoptera, commonly known as beetles, comprise the largest order in the entire animal kingdom. The number of species in this order has been estimated to be anywhere from 300,000 to 500,000.

It is likely that one out of every four creatures in the world is a beetle (not counting The Beatles, whose spelling emphasizes the famous rock group's "beat").

BIGGEST HOMES The nest of the African termite, *Macratermes michaelseni*, takes decades to build and can range up to 18 feet high, making it the tallest self-constructed home for any animal, relative to size. It can accommodate several million African termites, each about 1 inch long.

The nest is built from sand, soil, and termite saliva. It resembles a huge sandcastle and is air conditioned—by means of air exchange tunnels and a floor layered with wet soil.

Dinosaurs

TO THE ANCIENT GREEKS AND ROMANS, THE HUGE BONES found in the earth came from mythical monsters like the griffin (half-eagle, half-lion). To Chinese scholars, they were the remains of dragons. In 1842, British anatomist Richard Owen coined the term "dinosaur" ("fearfully great lizard") for this strange group of enormous creatures known only from fossil traces. Hundreds of species—dating from the late Triassic period beginning about 230 million years ago (MYA) to around 65 MYA at the end of the Cretaceous period—have since been distingushed, ranging in size from giant to tiny.

Most paleontologists believe that one group of dinosaurs survived the mass extinction closing out the Cretaceous and actually went on to prosper, evolving into today's birds.

MILESTONES

1824: MEGALOSAURUS In 1677, British chemist and naturalist Robert Plot wrote of a massive thighbone that had been unearthed in Oxfordshire. People thought it belonged to a giant. And it did—but not a human one.

In 1824, British geologist William Buckland called the creature *Megalosaurus* ("Great Lizard"). Paleontologists believe that the large meat-eating dinosaurs known as *Megalosaurus* lived in the latter part of the Jurassic period, from 206 to 144 MYA.

1853: LIFE-SIZED REPLICAS British artist Benjamin Waterhouse Hawkins made life-size, concrete-and-brick replicas of extinct animals—among them the dinosaurs *Iguanodon*, *Hylaeosaurus*, and *Megalosaurus*—as the director of the fossil department at the Crystal Palace in London.

A mold of his model *Iguanodon* (a huge duck-billed plant eater that lived in the early Cretaceous, some 144-99 MYA) actually housed a London dinner party for scientists, including Richard Owen, on Dec. 31, 1853. The dinosaur statues still stand in Sydenham Park near London.

1858: DINOSAURS IN NORTH AMERICA While fossil enthusiast William Parker Foulke was vacationing in Haddonfield, NJ, in 1858, he heard about giant bones that had been found in marl pits on a nearby farm 20 years earlier. He organized an excavation that yielded the first significant evidence of dinosaurs in North America and the most complete dinosaur skeleton found up to that point.

The skeleton, from a two-footed *Hadrosaurus*, was revealed to the public on Dec. 16, 1858.

1861: BIRD LINK Two years after Charles Darwin's *Origin of Species* was published, a fossil specimen called *Archaeopteryx lithographica* was found near Solnhofen, Germany.

Archaeopteryx dated from about 150 MYA and came to be considered the earliest known bird. In addition to a birdlike appearance, it had feathers (as well as, scientists established in 2004, a brain big enough for flight).

As early as 1868, British biologist Thomas Huxley described how it also had bones, teeth, and skull like a dinosaur's. Most paleontologists now regard birds ("avian dinosaurs") as belonging to a group of dinosaurs called maniraptors, which also includes dromaeosaurs ("raptors").

1869: DINOSAUR EGGS Geologist Jean-Jacques Pouech discovered what were said to be the first dinosaur egg shells, in southern France in 1864, but many experts were skeptical of their origins.

In 1869, geologist Philippe Matheron found more complete dinosaur eggs in France. They were from the plant-eating *Hypselosaurus priscus* and *Rhabdodon priscus* of the late Cretaceous, between 99 and 65 MYA.

2005: DINOSAUR WITH EGGS In 2005, scientists found in southern China the remains of a dinosaur with two pineapple-sized eggs still inside it. The specimen was an *Oviraptor*, a two-footed theropod, from the late Cretaceous. Analysis showed its reproductive system resembled that of a crocodile while its egg production and laying were similar to a bird's.

SOMETHING TO THINK ABOUT

NAMING DINOSAURS

Dinosaurs may be named after a distinctive feature (such as the three-horned *Triceratops*), their imagined behavior (*Velociraptor*, "speedy thief"), their location upon discovery (*Bavariasaurus*), or the person who found them (*Herrerasaurus*, unearthed by Argentinean Victorino Herrera). The longest genus name is *Micropachycephalosaurus*, for a plant-eating, late Cretaceous "tiny thick-headed lizard" found in China; the shortest, *Minmi*, for an *ankylosaur* discovered near Minmi Crossing in Australia, and *Khaan*, for a birdlike meat eater (the word means "lord" in Mongolian).

SUPERLATIVES

EARLIEST DINOSAUR
Fossils of the 3-foot-long *Eoraptor lunensis* and the 10-13-foot *Herrerasaurus ischigualastensis*, both carnivores found in Argentina, date back to the late Triassic, about 228 MYA. Two jawbones from unnamed plant-eating *prosauropods* found in Madagascar, however, may be slightly older.

LARGEST DINOSAUR
The long-necked *Argentinosaurus huinculensis* is estimated to have been 100-125 feet long and to have weighed about 100 tons. This plant-eating sauropod, which lived during the late Cretaceous, was discovered by a rancher in Argentina in 1987. Its remains, like those of most dinosaurs, are fragmentary.

SMALLEST DINOSAUR
It's sometimes difficult to know how small an extinct species actually was, since juveniles could be mistaken for full-grown adults. A strong contender for the title of smallest nonavian dinosaur is the feathered *Microraptor zhaoianus*. Based on the tail and hind legs dating from the early Cretaceous (125-122 MYA) that were found in northeastern China in 1999, it was estimated to be 16 inches long.

The 2-foot-long *Compsognathus longipes*, a predator during the late Jurassic (145-140 MYA), is sometimes said to be the littlest of the nonavian dinosaurs; it apparently weighed about 6.5 lbs. What these "compys" lacked in size they probably made up for in agility and speed.

SMALLEST AND BIGGEST BRAINS
Large herbivores were most likely the dumbest dinosaurs. The bony-plated *Stegosaurus armatus*, a late Jurassic plant eater the size of a bus that lived 155-144 MYA, had a 2.5-ounce brain the size of a walnut.

Small carnivorous theropods were most likely the smartest nonavian dinosaurs. *Troodon formosus*, a carnivore about 6 feet in length (that, like *Stegosaurus*, roamed western North America, but 80 million years later), had the largest brain capacity of any known nonavian dinosaur in relation to its size.

LONGEST NECK
Euhelopodidae of the *Mamenchisaurus* genus had the longest necks, over half their body length. One *M. hochuanensis* dinosaur had a neck estimated at 36 feet. This four-legged late Jurassic plant eater (130 MYA) was found in China.

LARGEST COLLECTION
The American Museum of Natural History in New York has the world's largest collection of vertebrate fossils, about 1 million specimens in all (with some 600 on display). It also boasts the biggest collection of dinosaur fossils.

Explorers like Roy Chapman Andrews (rumored to have been the inspiration for cinematic adventurer Indiana Jones) risked life and limb in the 1920s to bring in fossil finds from remote and dangerous places, such as the Gobi Desert in Mongolia.

HIGHEST PRICE (AUCTION)
On Oct. 4, 1997, the Field Museum of Chicago paid $8.36 million to acquire "Sue," the largest and most complete *Tyrannosaurus rex* skeleton known. Measuring 42 feet long and weighing in at 12,465 pounds, the specimen is nicknamed for its discoverer, fossil hunter Sue Hendrickson, who found it in South Dakota on Aug. 12, 1990.

One of the largest carnivorous dinosaurs, the T. Rex was built to eat massive herbivores. It had a huge skull with powerful jaws, which held up to 60 double-serrated teeth, some of them larger than a human hand. But paleontologists still debate whether the T. Rex was a predator or a scavenger.

Painting & Sculpture

PEOPLE HAVE EXPRESSED THEMSELVES through painting and sculpture since prehistoric times. Styles, techniques, and tools have evolved over the centuries, but great art retains its appeal, whether preserved in a home, a gallery, or a museum.

MILESTONES

PREHISTORIC PAST: CAVE ART Etching and painting rock surfaces go back tens of thousands of years, and early examples have been found around the world. The art—some more than 30,000 years old—portrayed animals or people hunting. (See "Oldest Paintings" below.)

PREHISTORIC PAST: STONE SCULPTURE The use of stone in sculpture traces back to the late Paleolithic period. The earliest, made 27,000-32,000 years ago, were small and cut from ivory, horn, bone, or stone. One of these, a small ivory horse, was found in a cave in Germany. Animals were common subjects, as were women with emphasized reproductive organs, which are thought to be fertility icons.

The earliest existing stone statues in the Americas are large, lifelike heads built by the Olmecs around 1200 BC in the area that today is Mexico.

3400 BC: CANVAS Fabrics have been used as a surface for paint since ancient times, particularly in China, where silk was commonly used after 1000 BC. But cloth disintegrates over time, so old samples are rare; most experts believe that painted cloth found in a tomb at Gebelein, Egypt, dating back to about 3400 BC, is the oldest remaining example.

Canvas, defined as fabric stretched across a frame for painting, replaced wooden panels as the preferred surface in Western painting by the 15th century.

3000 BC: PAINTBRUSHES Prior to the use of brushes, experts believe artists applied paint by blowing it through hollow tubes.

The use of brushes dates back to ancient Egypt and China. In Egypt around 3000 BC, they consisted of bound softened reed fibers inserted into a handle. In East Asia, where calligraphy and brushwork were greatly prized, brushes were often made of feathers and animal hair.

2200 BC: EASEL Easels became common in the 16th century in Europe, when they were needed to support panels or canvases. But the earliest known depiction of an easel is that in a relief found in the Egyptian tomb of a high-ranking Sixth Dynasty official, Mereruka (c. 2200 BC). Collapsible easels appeared in the 18th century.

George King of Perth Amboy, NJ, patented the first easel in the U.S. in 1863.

12TH CENTURY: OIL PAINT There is no known inventor of oil paint; the earliest reference occurs in the 12th-century manual of techniques, *De Diversis Artibus* (*On Diverse Arts*), by the German Benedictine monk Theophilus. Linseed oil was, and still is, commonly used as a base.

The 15th-century Flemish painter Jan van Eyck popularized the medium, which was considered superior to earlier wax- and water-based paints, such as encaustic and tempera, for its utility and range.

Prepared paints were sold in pig bladders in the 18th century. American artist John Rand invented the collapsible aluminum paint tube in 1841.

15TH CENTURY: FRESCO In frescoes, pigments dissolved in water are applied to wet plaster on a wall. Pigments seep into the wall, forming a colored layer on the surface.

Frescos first appeared in the Mediterranean in the 2nd millennium BC, but were neglected after the fall of Rome. The technique was revived in Renaissance Italy.

15TH CENTURY: PERSPECTIVE The development of linear perspective, which allows objects on two dimensional surfaces to appear smaller as they recede into the distance toward a vanishing point, is credited to Italian Renaissance architect and sculptor Filippo Brunelleschi between 1417 and 1420. Donatello's relief *St. George and the Dragon* (c. 1417) and Masaccio's fresco *Trinity* (c. 1425) are the earliest surviving examples, both in Florence.

The technique was quickly incorporated into painting during the Renaissance.

16TH CENTURY: WATERCOLOR As a medium, watercolors are usually credited to the Renaissance-era German master Albrecht Dürer (1471-1528). They became a tradition in northern Europe in the 16th and 17th centuries.

1943: SYNTHETIC BRUSHES DuPont labs began producing nylon bristles for paintbrushes around 1943, due to shortages of hog bristles from China and Russia during World War II. Today both synthetic and natural-bristle brushes are widely used.

State Hermitage Museum in St. Petersburg, Russia

SOMETHING TO THINK ABOUT

RED ICE IN GREENLAND

In March 2004, Chilean-born Danish artist Marco Evaristti painted an iceberg, floating in the waters off the coast of Greenland, bright red. The artist used 780 gallons of red paint diluted with seawater to create his frozen art. Working in -9 ° F weather, the 40-year-old Evaristti used three fire hoses and the aid of 20 assistants to paint over the 10,000-square-foot tip of the iceberg. The task took two hours.

SUPERLATIVES

OLDEST PAINTINGS The site of Ubirr in Arnhem Land in northern Australia contains the oldest-known paintings and the longest continuously-practiced artistic tradition. The oldest of the site's Aboriginal rock art dates to an estimated 40-60,000 years ago, and the most recent date to the present day. The images range from animals and dynamic stick figures to depictions of encounters with Europeans and present a chronicle of Aboriginal history.

MOST EXPENSIVE PAINTING (AUCTION) The highest price paid for a painting at auction was $104.2 million paid for Pablo Picasso's *Boy With a Pipe* (*The Young Apprentice*) by an unknown bidder at Sotheby's, New York, May 5, 2004.

Painted in 1905, the work is a portrait of a teenage boy known only as "P'tit Louis." Picasso was just 24 years old when he painted it in his Paris studio.

MOST EXPENSIVE SCULPTURE (AUCTION) A Constantin Brancusi sculpture, forgotten for years in an attic, was sold on May 4, 2005, for $27.45 million, the highest price ever paid at auction for a freestanding sculpture. The 4-foot-high marble abstract, *Oiseau dans l'espace* (*Bird in Flight*), was probably carved around 1922.

LARGEST ART MUSEUM The world's biggest art museum is the State Hermitage Museum in St. Petersburg, Russia. Catherine the Great, started it with her private collection in the Winter Palace (built 1754-62). The museum currently includes 322 galleries housing nearly 3 million works of art in four main buildings.

BIGGEST ENDOWMENT The art museum with the world's largest endowment is the J. Paul Getty Museum in Brentwood, Los Angeles, CA. It's the public face of the J. Paul Getty Trust, and in 2004 reportedly had an endowment of $4.4 billion.

The $1 billion museum complex, which opened in Dec. 1997, enabled the Trust to spend a chunk of its endowment, as required by law, without adding pressure on world fine art prices.

BIGGEST ART FAIR European Fine Art Fair is held in Maastricht, Netherlands, every March, covering 290,625 square feet (6.7 acres) of floor space.

In 2005, 200 dealers from 14 countries offered around 30,000 pieces. A portrait by the 17th-century Dutch master Jan Lievens sold for $5.4 million.

BIGGEST PAINTING A finger painting, made by the joint efforts of more than 1,400 Vietnamese children, and displayed in Vietnam's capital city in Sept. 2005, is said to be the biggest painting in the world.

Completed in May 2005 after five hours of work, it covers an area of 8,850 square feet.

BIGGEST RELIEF SCULPTURE The world's largest relief sculpture is of three Confederate Army leaders: President Jefferson Davis, General Robert E. Lee, and General Thomas "Stonewall" Jackson, carved into the north face of Stone Mountain, near Atlanta, GA. The sculpture of the trio, all riding on horseback, covers 1.33 acres. They are 90 feet high, 190 feet wide, and recessed 42 feet into the mountain.

The memorial was conceived by Helen Plane in 1912. Gutzon Borghum, who went on to design Mount Rushmore, was the original sculptor; he quit in 1925 and the project was abandoned until the State of Georgia took over the property in 1958. Walter Hancock completed the project, 1964–69.

Classical Music

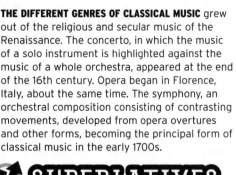

THE DIFFERENT GENRES OF CLASSICAL MUSIC grew out of the religious and secular music of the Renaissance. The concerto, in which the music of a solo instrument is highlighted against the music of a whole orchestra, appeared at the end of the 16th century. Opera began in Florence, Italy, about the same time. The symphony, an orchestral composition consisting of contrasting movements, developed from opera overtures and other forms, becoming the principal form of classical music in the early 1700s.

SUPERLATIVES

MOST PROLIFIC COMPOSER
The most prolific composer, going by total output, was German composer Georg Philipp Telemann (1681–1767), who wrote 125 concerti, 125 orchestral suites, 135 chamber pieces, 87 instrumental solos, 30 or more operas, around 156 passions, oratorios, and masses, some 1,700 cantatas, and 114 songs. His total output was more than 2,500 pieces. Only a small number are well-known today.

The Austrian musical genius Wolfgang Amadeus Mozart (1756–91) was more prolific year by year. Mozart began playing the harp at three and was composing by the age of five. By the time he died at the early age of 35, he had written over 1,000 operas, symphonies, operettas, concerti, masses, serenades, string quartets, sonatas, motets, and other chamber music.

MOST PROLIFIC COMPOSER CONCERTI
The Venetian priest Antonio Vivaldi (1678–1741) may have been one of the most celebrated composers of his age and, with 460 surviving concerti, the most prolific composer of concerti of all time. His *Four Seasons* violin concerti are frequently played today, but a century ago they were unknown.

Soon after his death, Vivaldi's music ceased to be popular and by the end of the 19th century, it was forgotten and much of it lost. The 20th-century revival of baroque music restored his reputation.

MOST PROLIFIC COMPOSER SYMPHONIES
Franz Joseph Haydn (1732–1809) composed a record 106 symphonies, many of them for his wealthy Hungarian patrons, the Esterházy family, in whose household at Eisenstadt he remained for 30 years.

OLDEST ORCHESTRA
The world's oldest existing concert orchestra is the Gewandhaus Orchestra of Leipzig, Germany. Founded by 16 Leipzig merchants in March 1743 as the "Grosse Concert-Gesellschaft," it got its present name from the Gewandhaus (Garment House) Hall, where it performed for a time.

It has been directed by some of the world's best known musicians, including Felix Mendelssohn, Wilhelm Furtwängler, and Kurt Masur.

LONGEST OPERA
The longest opera that is part of the established repertoire is *Die Meistersinger von Nürnberg* ("The Mastersingers of Nuremberg") by Richard Wagner (1813–83). The opera, in three acts, lasts for around five hours, 15 minutes (sometimes longer). It was first performed June 21, 1868.

MOST MUSICIANS REQUIRED SYMPHONY
The *Gothic Symphony* by British composer Havergal Brian (1876–1972) calls for more musicians and singers of any other classical piece. Completed in 1927, it is scored for an orchestra of at least 190 instruments (including such percussion instruments as a "thunder machine," glockenspiel, and birdscare), as well as at least 500 singers in four mixed choirs, a children's choir of 100, and four soloists.

Unsurprisingly, the symphony is seldom performed; the first professional performance didn't come until Brian's 90th birthday in 1966.

Not all of Brian's works are on a massive scale. His 22nd symphony, the *Symphonia Brevis*, lasts a mere nine minutes.

MOST VALUABLE VIOLIN The world's most valuable violin is "The Messiah," believed to have been made in 1716 by Antonio Stradivari, the greatest violin-maker of all time. He made at least 1,116 instruments, of which about 650 still exist.

It is not known for sure whether "The Messiah" is really a Stradivarius or was made by one of Stradivari's sons, but the instrument, whose

Ludwig van Beethoven

tone is considered unsurpassed, is estimated to be worth more than $18 million. It is housed in the Ashmolean Museum in Oxford, England.

The highest price paid for a violin, or any instrument, at auction is $2.03 million, paid by an unidentified bidder for a 1699 Stradivarius known as the "Lady Tennant," at Christie's, New York on April 22, 2005. The "Lady Tennant" got its name when Scottish industrialist Sir Charles Tennant, bought it for his wife in 1900.

QUIETEST WORK

The concert work *4′33″* by U.S. composer John Cage (1912–92) probably deserves the title of quietest piece of music ever composed. The orchestra sits in silence and the "music" is whatever noise, including coughs, comes from the audience during the four minutes, 33 seconds allotted.

Conceived in 1948, the work was first performed in 1952.

BIGGEST PERFORMER

The 1970 orchestral piece *And God Created Great Whales* by U.S. composer Alan Hovhaness (1911–2000) features the largest performer to be heard on the concert platform: the work includes a taped solo by a humpbacked whale.

SOMETHING TO THINK ABOUT

DEAF BUT NOT TONE DEAF

Ludwig van Beethoven (1770-1827), said by many to have been the greatest of all classical composers, noticed he was losing his hearing while still in his 20s, and in the last eight years of his life was totally deaf. In those years he kept a slate for visitors to communicate with him, and composed some of his greatest music, including the *Ninth Symphony* and *Missa Solemnis*, often "singing, howling, and stamping" in a self absorbed fashion that led some to conclude he was crazy.

CONFUSED COMPOSERS

The founder of the famous London Proms concerts, Sir Henry Wood (1869–1944), took a stirring march and transcribed it for the trumpet, organ, and drums, mistakenly attributing it to English composer Henry Purcell (1659–95). The piece, almost universally known as *Purcell's Trumpet Voluntary*, was composed by another Englishman, Jeremiah Clarke (c. 1674–1707), and its real name is *The Prince of Denmark's March*. Clarke became depressed after an unhappy love affair and shot himself to death; he might have become even more depressed if he had known that someone else would get the credit for his best-known tune.

WHICH 1812?

Pyotr Ilyich Tchaikovsky's widely performed *1812 Overture* was not inspired by the *War of 1812*, as many people think. It actually came about when Tchaikovsky (1840-1893), probably Russia's most famous composer, was commissioned to write a piece marking the 70th anniversary of Russia's victory over Napoleon at the outskirts of Moscow in 1812. The *Overture*, first performed in Moscow in 1882, begins softly but becomes louder and louder, ending with the French national anthem *La Marseillaise* and cannon blasts (usually rendered by a bass drum). Tchaikovsky himself was not very enthused about the piece, which he described as "very loud and noisy."

MUSICAL MURDER?

Much has been made of the relationship between Mozart and fellow composer Antonio Salieri (1750-1825), thanks especially to Peter Shaffer's play (1979) and movie (1984) *Amadeus*, which portrayed Salieri as driven by envy to poison the younger and more brilliant Mozart. This legendary scenario was popularized by Nikolay Rimsky-Korsakov (1844-1908), in his 1898 opera *Mozart et Salieri*. In reality, Salieri was in no way a rival to Mozart. They seemed to have gotten along fine, and in some circles, Salieri was the preferred composer. Mozart died from what is largely believed to have been typhoid fever.

Jazz

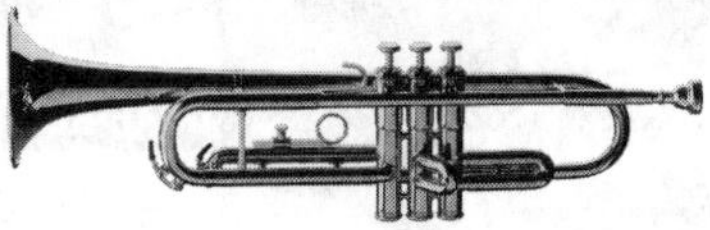

BORN IN THE MISSISSIPPI DELTA CITY of New Orleans during the 19th and 20th centuries, jazz is a musical style blending African and European traditions. It is often called America's only homegrown art form, and has been described as a culture, a subculture, a language, and a way of life. With its elements of the blues, spirituals, ragtime, and other folk music, jazz continues to captivate audiences and aficionados today as it did in its youth in the early 1900s.

1 MILESTONES

19TH - EARLY 20TH CENTURY: NEW ORLEANS The Crescent City's eclectic musical styles (which included European popular and classical traditions, country blues, military music, Creole folk, and black gospel music) merged into a new musical art form at the turn of the 20th century.

Cornetist Buddy Bolden and pianist Tony Jackson dominated the original New Orleans jazz scene. They were followed by cornetist King Oliver and pianist Jelly Roll Morton. The work of these jazz greats is widely credited with establishing the music's characteristics and popularity prior to World War I.

1917-1929: CHICAGO JAZZ In 1917, the notorious red-light district Storyville, where New Orleans' pioneering jazz clubs were located, was closed down. At the same time, with Northern war industries booming and the prospect of less discrimination, many African-Americans left the South for Northern cities, in what is known now as the Great Migration.

New Orleans musicians like King Oliver and trumpeter Louis Armstrong followed their audiences. Chicago became a jazz mecca for all.

1917: FIRST JAZZ RECORDING In Feb. 1917, immediately after their sensational New York debut, the Original Dixieland Jass Band, a quintet from New Orleans via Chicago, recorded "Livery Stable Blues." The record was considered a novelty number, but it introduced audiences to the language of jazz, selling over a million copies in six months.

1923: INTEGRATED JAZZ Recordings brought noted black and white players together first: by July 1923 Jelly Roll Morton had cut sides with the white New Orleans Rhythm Kings. There is some uncertainty about the first interracial live performance, but most authorities credit the Benny Goodman Trio, which performed with their black pianist Teddy Wilson at Chicago's Congress Hotel on April 12, 1936.

1935: "KING OF SWING" Mobbed at Los Angeles' Palomar Ballroom on Aug. 21, 1935, Benny Goodman became known as the "King of Swing." Big bands were bringing jazz to dancers and listeners across America, and swing came as close to being pop music as jazz ever would.

Goodman credited his success to the influence of black musicians on his work, including Fletcher Henderson and other arrangers. Goodman's interracial quartet (Teddy Wilson, drummer Gene Krupa, and black vibraphonist Lionel Hampton) pushed forward the integration of jazz groups.

On Jan. 16, 1938, the swing age reached its peak with Goodman's famous concert at Carnegie Hall in New York. Twelve years later, a recording of the concert became one of the best-selling jazz records of all-time.

1944: BOP Charlie Parker, Dizzy Gillespie, Thelonious Monk, and other radicals developed a new jazz style called rebop, or bebop, or simply bop. Intricate and difficult to play, bop broke out in 1944 on Swing Street—West 52nd Street—in New York.

Influenced by the improvisational work of the legendary Louis Armstrong, a generation of creative jazz musicians took the opportunity to follow their own muses. But the relationship between Gillespie and Parker fractured quickly, and bop began to fade, leaving a legacy of remarkable music.

1949-50: "BIRTH OF THE COOL" Over three sessions in 1949-50, Miles Davis, a young bop trumpeter, assembled a nine-piece band and recorded 12 tracks that became known as the "Birth of the Cool"—something like jazz chamber music.

"Cool" musicians, many from struggling big bands, brought their complex, soft sound to the fore, especially on California's West Coast jazz scene. And a 1950s countermovement centered on the East Coast, "hard bop," soon emerged.

1959: FREE JAZZ When Texas-born saxophonist Ornette Coleman played "free jazz" at New York's Five Spot in 1959, his style raised musical eyebrows. His albums *The Shape of Jazz to Come* and *Free Jazz: A Collective Improvisation* abandoned rigid chord progressions and structure, altering the harmonic/melodic variations that had defined jazz since its infancy.

"The New Thing" was embraced by young revolutionists Cecil Taylor and Archie Shepp and interpreted by veterans like John Coltrane and Sun Ra.

1969: FUSION
Miles Davis released *In a Silent Way* in 1969 and *Bitches Brew* in 1970, launching "fusion" music, a merging of jazz, rock, and funk. As Davis later put it, he switched "because jazz was becoming the music of the museum."

Jazz artists taking to rock and rockers using elements of jazz crisscrossed the music scene.

1997: JAZZ PULITZER
In 1965, three Pulitzer Prize panel members proposed that famed bandleader/composer Duke Ellington receive a special award, but the full Pulitzer committee rejected the idea. Ellington, characteristically, said: "Fate is being kind to me. Fate doesn't want me to be too famous too young." In 1997, a Pulitzer was finally awarded to a jazz composition—Wynton Marsalis's "Blood on the Fields."

Two years later Ellington—who had died in 1974—received a special citation in music from the Pulitzer Prize board.

2004: JAZZ HALL OF FAME On Sept. 30, 2004, the Ertegun Jazz Hall of Fame was dedicated at Lincoln Center in New York City. During the ceremony, the first group of jazz greats were inducted, including Louis Armstrong, Sidney Bechet, Bix Beiderbecke, John Coltrane, Miles Davis, Duke Ellington, Dizzy Gillespie, Coleman Hawkins, Billie Holiday, Thelonious Monk, Jelly Roll Morton, Charlie Parker, Art Tatum, and Lester Young. The Hall of Fame has an interactive design that showcases the lives and accomplishments of these jazz giants.

SOMETHING TO THINK ABOUT

"DJANGOLOGY"

Django Reinhardt (1910–53), born into a Gypsy clan in Belgium, survived a caravan fire that cost him two fingers on his left hand, and somehow developed a nimble, lyrical, harmonically advanced guitar style. By the late 1930s, he was turning the heads of Americans in Paris. Before World War II it was *de rigueur* for visiting jazz greats to join the sessions of his "Hot Club de France."

KING OF JAZZ?

Saxophonist and clarinetist Bhumibol Adulyadej long hosted Friday jam sessions in Bangkok, Thailand. But his day gig has lasted even longer, and is even more unusual. He became king of Thailand in 1946. Benny Goodman, Lionel Hampton, and other American jazz legends have shared the stand with him.

SUPERLATIVES

LARGEST JAZZ FESTIVAL Festival International de Jazz de Montréal has been dubbed the largest in the world. The annual event began in 1980 and now hosts over 500 concerts, 2,000 musicians, and an estimated 2 million jazz pilgrims every summer.

OLDEST CLUB
Famously a music of smoky, crowded, raffish clubs, jazz has many shrines. Since 1935, aficionados have been going downstairs from the sidewalk to Manhattan's Village Vanguard to hear comics, singers, and, by the 1950s, a roster of jazz greats.

Baker's Keyboard Lounge, in Detroit, claims May 1934, an earlier date, as its birthday.

The Green Mill, on Chicago's North Side, although not exclusively a jazz joint, has been featuring jazz even longer. It first opened in 1914 and hosted orchestras led by Isham Jones and Charlie Elgar. The original closed after a shooting in 1930. Both Al Capone and Machine-Gun Jack McGurn hosted there.

MOST JAZZ GRAMMIES Guitarist Pat Metheny has won the most Grammys in jazz categories, with 13. He won his first in 1982 (Best Jazz Fusion Performance for Offramp); his latest came in 2002 for Best Contemporary Jazz Album (*Speaking of Now*).

HIGHEST PRICED INSTRUMENT The highest price paid at auction for a jazz instrument was $148,665 for an alto saxophone owned by Charlie Parker, at Christie's London in Sept. 1994. The American Jazz Museum in Kansas City, MO, Parker's birthplace, purchased the cream-colored Grafton acrylic sax.

Parker had played it in one of the most famous jazz concerts of all-time, the 1953 Massey Hall Concert in Toronto. His quintet on stage that evening included trumpeter Dizzy Gillespie, drummer Max Roach, bassist Charles Mingus, and pianist Bud Powell.

BIGGEST SELLING JAZZ ARTIST The best-selling jazz artist of all-time is saxophonist Kenny G, (real name, Kenneth Gorelick). He has sold over 70 million albums worldwide since releasing his self-titled first album in 1982.

Kenny G also lays claim to the best-selling single jazz album title with 1992's *Breathless*, which has sold 12 million copies.

Theater

Broadway Musicals

MUSICAL THEATER IS ONE OF AMERICA'S MOST POPULAR AND ENDURING ART FORMS. With roots that stretch back to 19th century vaudeville, the musical has expanded beyond the extravagant song-and-dance revues popularized by producer Florenz Ziegfeld in the early 20th century. Musicals came to have story lines, sometimes touching on serious subjects, though comedy and frivolity often reigned. Many musicals have gone from Broadway to stages around the country and world, as well as to the silver screen.

Nathan Lane (left) and Matthew Broderick in The Producers

MILESTONES

1895: FIRST BROADWAY THEATER Developer and producer Oscar Hammerstein I built the huge Olympia Theater—the first on what has become New York City's "Great White Way." He bought an entire block on Broadway, adjoining what later became Times Square, and opened the Olympia on Nov. 25, 1895. Before that, most theaters were located around Herald Square/34th Street.

Today theaters are still clustered between 6th and 9th Avenues and between 41st and 53rd Streets, though the Olympia has been gone since 1935 and only four "Broadway" theaters—the Cadillac Winter Garden, the Marquis, the Palace, and, of course, the Broadway—have actual Broadway addresses.

1907: *ZIEGFELD FOLLIES* Producer Florenz Ziegfeld launched the first of his famous *Follies* musical comedy shows on July 8, 1907, at the rooftop "Jardin de Paris" of the Criterion Theater. Subsequent editions featured famous performers such as Fanny Brice, Eddie Cantor, and W.C. Fields.

Ziegfeld produced 19 Follies through 1931.

1927: *SHOW BOAT* Oscar Hammerstein II, grandson and namesake of Broadway pioneer Oscar Hammerstein I, and composer Jerome Kern broke new ground in musical theater by adapting Edna Ferber's book *Show Boat*. Their show, which opened at the Ziegfeld on Dec. 27, 1927, was the first musical to follow a storyline rather than being a collection of musical numbers and sketches.

Its novelistic plot, mixture of characters, and serious theme made it a hit at the Ziegfeld, where it ran for 575 performances.

1932: PULITZER The political satire *Of Thee I Sing*, which opened at the Music Box Theatre on Dec. 26, 1931, was the first musical to win a Pulitzer Prize for drama.

The show, about a bachelor president who holds a beauty contest for a first lady, was written by George Kaufman and Morrie Ryskind with music by George and Ira Gershwin. It ran for 441 performances.

1929: BROADWAY TO HOLLYWOOD Hollywood found its voice when popular Broadway entertainer Al Jolson starred and sang in the first "talkie," 1927's *The Jazz Singer*. But the first Broadway musical adapted to film was *The Desert Song*.

With the book written by Otto Harbach, Frank Mandel, and Oscar Hammerstein II, and music by Sigmund Romberg, *The Desert Song* opened on Broadway Nov. 30, 1926, and ran for 471 performances. Warner Brothers created the film version, first shown May 1, 1929.

1943: *OKLAHOMA!* The Great Depression wiped out Broadway fortunes, and the increasing popularity of movies over theater discouraged further experiments for some time. Then Rodgers and Hammerstein's *Oklahoma!*, based on the play *Green Grow the Lilacs*, began a five-year run on March 31, 1943. It sparked a new era of narrative storylines in musical theater.

Oklahoma! ran on Broadway for 2,202 performances. It grossed an estimated $7 million and, boosted by the title song (a last-minute addition to the score), spawned the first cast album. Available as a package of six 78 rpm records, the album sold 800,000 copies by the time *Oklahoma!* closed on May 29, 1948.

1949: TONY Cole Porter's musical comedy *Kiss Me, Kate* won five Tonys including the first for Best Musical. (The Tonys, founded two years earlier, didn't originally include a Best Musical category.) The show was inspired by the feuding between theater legends Alfred Lunt and Lynn Fontanne during a Broadway production of Shakespeare's *Taming of the Shrew*. A revival won five awards in 2000.

1961: OSCAR The 1961 film version of *West Side Story* was the first adaptation of a Broadway musical to win the Best Picture

SOMETHING TO THINK ABOUT

GETTING TO KNOW YUL

Yul Brynner famously starred on Broadway as the King of Siam in Rodgers and Hammerstein's *The King and I* (1951-54, 1,246 performances), for which he won a Tony in 1952. He was awarded the Best Actor Oscar in 1956 for the film version. Brynner revived the show on Broadway two more times, in 1977 and 1985, and toured relentlessly, eventually performing the role a kingly 4,625 times. For this achievement he won a special Tony award in June 1985, a few months before his death.

Oscar. (The musical, with music by Leonard Bernstein and lyrics by Stephen Sondheim, had run on Broadway from 1957 to 1959.)

The film won 10 Oscars in all (a then-record) and grossed $44 million at the domestic box office. Films of *My Fair Lady* (1964), *The Sound of Music* (1965), *Oliver!* (1968), and *Chicago* (2002) followed in its golden footsteps.

In 1973, Alan Jay Lerner and Frederick Loewe turned their original film musical, *Gigi*, named best picture of 1958, into a Broadway show, but it flopped.

1964: 3,000-PLUS PERFORMANCES
Fiddler on the Roof opened at the Imperial on Sept. 22, 1964, and ran a then-record 3,242 performances over eight years, winning nine Tonys. It passed the 3,000-mark Dec. 4, 1971; the achievement was marked with a special Tony Award in 1972.

Fed up with the demands of the form, perfectionist director Jerome Robbins never launched another original musical.

1975: 6,000-PLUS PERFORMANCES
With everyday costumes and no sets or stars, Michael Bennett's *A Chorus Line*, a tale of Broadway "gypsies" (dancers) trying out for a new musical, proved itself "One Singular Sensation" after moving uptown from the Off-Broadway Public Theater (originally opened April 16) to the Shubert for its July 25, 1975, Broadway opening.

It ran for an astonishing 15 years, with 6,137 performances.

SUPERLATIVES

LONGEST-RUNNING
With its 7,486th performance on Jan. 9, 2006, Andrew Lloyd Webber's *The Phantom of the Opera* surpassed *Cats*—also by Lloyd Webber—as the longest-running musical on Broadway.

Based on Gaston Leroux's 1910 novel about a disfigured composer haunting the Paris Opera House, the show opened on Broadway on Jan. 26, 1988. Since its premier, the New York production has grossed nearly $600 million in tickets sales, the most for any Broadway show.

BIGGEST SALES ADVANCE *Miss Saigon*, which opened at the Broadway on April 11, 1991, set a record for largest pre-opening advance sales, at $36 million. It was also the first musical to charge $100 for front mezzanine tickets.

With a production cost of $10 million, *Miss Saigon* famously included a near full-size helicopter as a stage prop.

MOST EXPENSIVE
The Walt Disney Company's *The Lion King*, which opened Nov. 13, 1997, cost an estimated $20 million to stage.

Director Julie Taymor's puppet-filled adaptation from the original animated movie won six Tonys, including Best Musical.

BIGGEST FLOP
Broadway's biggest financial flop was *Dance of the Vampires*. The monster musical, based on a Roman Polanski film, starred Michael Crawford. It bled its investors to the tune of $12 million in a 56-performance run that ended Jan. 25, 2003.

A faster flop was the musical *Carrie*, which cost about $7 million and closed after 4 performances.

MOST TONYS
SHOW Adapted from Mel Brooks's 1968 Oscar-winning comedy, *The Producers* took Broadway by storm, when it opened on April 19, 2001. It received a record 15 Tony nominations in 12 categories, then set another record for a show by winning 12, including Best Musical.

MOST TONYS
CAREER Producer-director Harold Prince has been nominated for 36 Tonys and has won a record 20. He won awards for his work with Stephen Sondheim (who holds a record eight wins for a composer) for *Company* (2 in 1971), *Follies* (2 in 1972), *A Little Night Music* (2 in 1973), and *Sweeney Todd* (1 in 1979).

Prince also co-produced the Tony-winning best musicals *The Pajama Game* (1955) and *Damn Yankees* (1956). Both were choreographed by Bob Fosse, who won nine Tonys for his work.

BIGGEST THEATER
The biggest theater on Broadway is the Gershwin on West 51st Street, with 1,933 seats. Originally named the Uris, it opened in Nov. 1972; alas, its first show, the musical *Via Galactica*, was a flop. The theater was renamed for composer George and lyricist Ira Gershwin in 1983.

Drama

IN HIS PLAY *AS YOU LIKE IT* SHAKESPEARE FAMOUSLY WROTE: "ALL THE WORLD'S A STAGE..." Maybe so. Staged storytelling is one of the most ancient and durable forms of artistic expression. Its roots dig deep into all cultures, from classic Greek tragedies to ancient shadow puppet plays from Java, Indonesia, to Shakespeare and Arthur Miller and beyond.

MILESTONES

6TH CENTURY BC: CLASSICAL GREEK DRAMA
Western culture's oldest surviving plays date back to classical Greece (6th century BC). According to legend, Thespis was the first drama director. In the 5th century BC, Sophacles wrote his classics *Antigone* and *Odeipus Rex*.

The plays originated from the practices of the cult of Dionysus, which included performances by men dressed as satyrs—mythological creatures that were half-human and half-goat.

At festivals held in enormous stone amphitheaters for audiences of tens of thousands of people, Greek playwrights produced tragedies and comedies at annual competitions held in Athens. An all-male cast wearing masks spoke in verse.

BEFORE 1 AD: SHADOW PUPPET THEATER The origins of shadow puppet theater (*Wayang Kulit*) are lost in the mists of time, but it is one of the earliest forms of dramatic storytelling. A central part of the artistic culture of Indonesia, *Wayang Kulit* features intricately carved puppets, traditionally fashioned from leather, that are made to perform in front of a simple screen.

14TH CENTURY: NOH Japanese *Noh* drama has its roots in religious theater troupes that formed as early as the 12th century. Zeami, considered the father of *Noh*, was a playwright, actor, director, and philosopher during the 14th and 15th centuries. He wrote the aesthetic manual "The Transmission of the Flower and Style," which became a guide for *Noh* performers.

Traditional *Noh* is performed on a simple, undecorated stage, with three or four musicians, six to eight chanters who tell the story, and two or three actors. A set of simple, stylized gestures communicate the action of the play.

AROUND 1598: GLOBE THEATRE The first permanent British theater for dramatic performances, the Globe Theatre, was built in London around 1598. William Shakespeare staged most of his plays there. The theater has been destroyed and rebuilt many times. The current version stands on the banks of the River Thames in London, England.

1898: MOSCOW ART THEATER
Konstantin Stanislavski founded the Moscow Art Theater in 1898 with dramatist Vladimir Ivanovich Nemirovich-Danchenko. Stanislavski directed, acted, and taught acting—emphasizing the use of authentic emotions.

In the 1930s and 40s, his acting philosophy was widely adopted in the United States, where it became known as "The Method." With Method acting, actors use the mental recall of events in their own lives to recreate the emotions necessary to portray the drama on stage.

SUPERLATIVES

OLDEST SURVIVING GREEK DRAMA The oldest surviving Greek dramas are those of Aeschylus (525-456 BC). He is said to have written about 90 plays in all, but only seven have survived into modern times. These include *Agamemnon*, *The Libation Bearers*, and *The Eumenidies*—which make up a trilogy called *The Oresteia*. The story is about murder and revenge—starting with the death of Agamemnon at the hands of his faithless wife Clytemnestra.

MOST HONORED GREEK PLAYWRIGHT
Sophocles (c. 496-406 BC) wrote more than 100 plays. In the ancient drama festivals, he won 18 first-place honors, more than any other playwright.

Only seven of his tragedies survive intact, but many more exist in fragments. His tragedy *Oedipus Rex*, one of the greatest classics of Western civilization, focuses on the downfall of the mighty King Oedipus who learns that he unwittingly killed his father and married his mother.

LONGEST OPERATING THEATER (WEST END) The Theatre Royal, Drury Lane, opened on May 7, 1663. The doyenne of London's West End, it is the longest operating theater in Great Britain.

LONGEST RUNNING PLAY The world's longest-running play is Agatha Christie's *The Mousetrap*, which opened on Nov. 25, 1952, at the Ambassador Theatre in London.

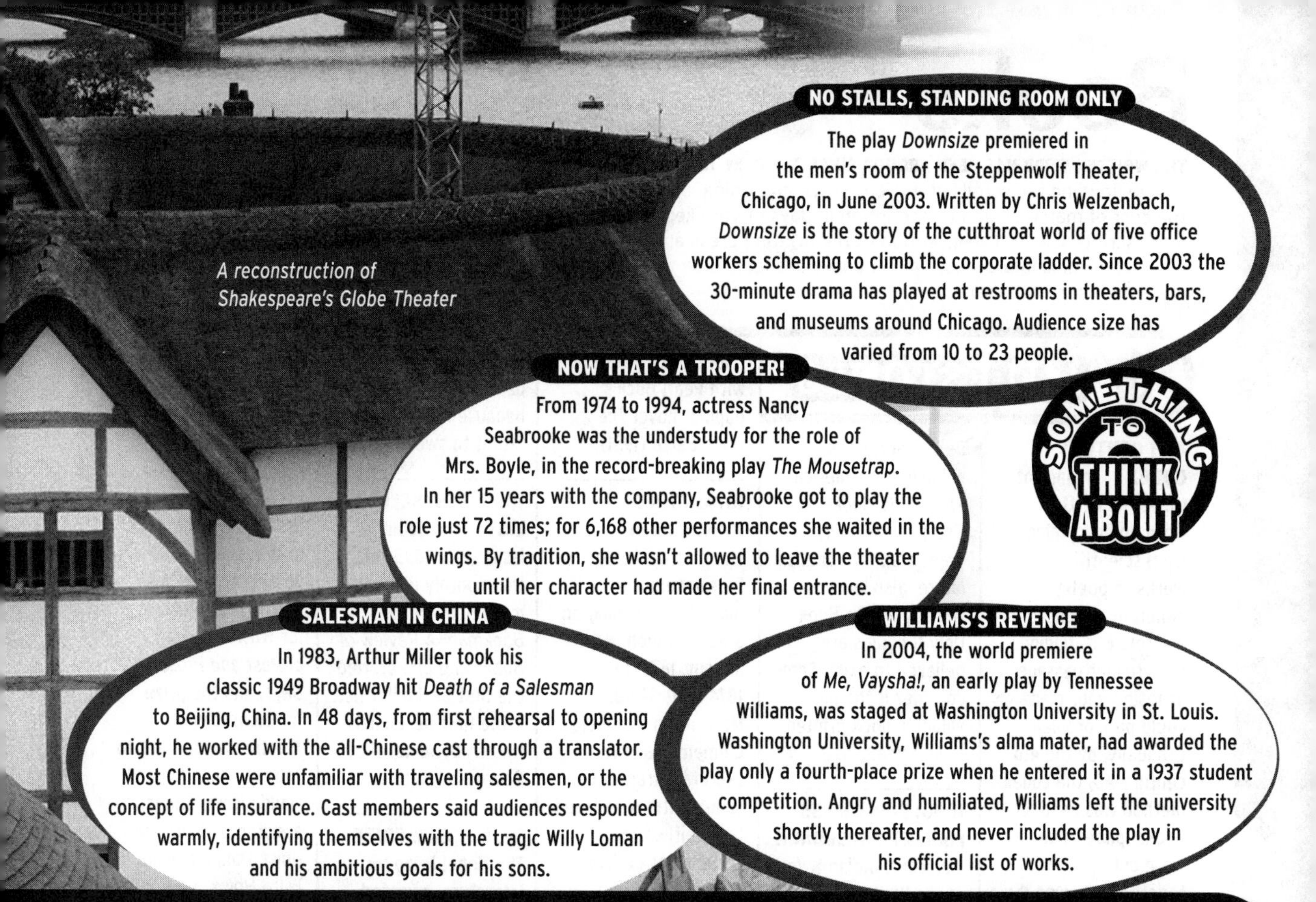

A reconstruction of Shakespeare's Globe Theater

NO STALLS, STANDING ROOM ONLY

The play *Downsize* premiered in the men's room of the Steppenwolf Theater, Chicago, in June 2003. Written by Chris Welzenbach, *Downsize* is the story of the cutthroat world of five office workers scheming to climb the corporate ladder. Since 2003 the 30-minute drama has played at restrooms in theaters, bars, and museums around Chicago. Audience size has varied from 10 to 23 people.

NOW THAT'S A TROOPER!

From 1974 to 1994, actress Nancy Seabrooke was the understudy for the role of Mrs. Boyle, in the record-breaking play *The Mousetrap*. In her 15 years with the company, Seabrooke got to play the role just 72 times; for 6,168 other performances she waited in the wings. By tradition, she wasn't allowed to leave the theater until her character had made her final entrance.

SALESMAN IN CHINA

In 1983, Arthur Miller took his classic 1949 Broadway hit *Death of a Salesman* to Beijing, China. In 48 days, from first rehearsal to opening night, he worked with the all-Chinese cast through a translator. Most Chinese were unfamiliar with traveling salesmen, or the concept of life insurance. Cast members said audiences responded warmly, identifying themselves with the tragic Willy Loman and his ambitious goals for his sons.

WILLIAMS'S REVENGE

In 2004, the world premiere of *Me, Vaysha!*, an early play by Tennessee Williams, was staged at Washington University in St. Louis. Washington University, Williams's alma mater, had awarded the play only a fourth-place prize when he entered it in a 1937 student competition. Angry and humiliated, Williams left the university shortly thereafter, and never included the play in his official list of works.

Christie adapted the whodunit from her radio play "Three Blind Mice." In 1974, the drama moved to the St. Martin's Theatre, without missing a beat.

In 2005, more than 50 years after its opening, *The Mousetrap* was still luring in audiences. Among more than 300 actors who have appeared in the play, David Raven played the role of Major Metcalf 4,575 times, the greatest number of times any actor is known to have played a single part.

LONGEST RUNNING PLAY (BROADWAY) The longest running drama ever on Broadway was Howard Lindsay and Russel Crouse's *Life With Father*. The light-hearted story of a would-be strict father in 1880s New York City wrestling for control of his family, it ran for 3,224 performances from 1939 to 1947.

MOST PULITZER PRIZES FOR DRAMA Eugene O'Neill won a record four Pulitzer Prizes for Drama. He won for *Beyond the Horizon* (1920), *Anna Christie* (1922), *Strange Interlude* (1928), and the autobiographical *Long Day's Journey Into Night* (1957, post-humous production).

MOST TONY AWARDS (BEST PLAY) Three playwrights have won three Best Play Tony Awards. Arthur Miller won for *All My Sons* (1947), *Death of a Salesman* (1949), and *The Crucible* (1953); Neil Simon for *The Odd Couple* (1965), *Biloxi Blues* (1985), and *Lost in Yonkers* (1991); and Tom Stoppard for *Rosencrantz and Guildenstern Are Dead* (1968), *Travesties* (1976), and *The Real Thing* (1984).

MOST TONYS (ACTING) Julie Harris has won a record five Tony Awards for Best Leading Actress in a Play. Her first Tony came for her performance in *I Am a Camera* (1952). Her other awards came for *The Lark* (1956), *Forty Carats* (1969), *The Last of Mrs. Lincoln* (1973), and *The Belle of Amherst* (1977).

MOST OLIVIER AWARDS (ACTING) Dame Judi Dench has won a record seven Olivier Awards (the prestigious British award, named after the famed actor Sir Laurence Olivier). Since 1976, the Olivier Awards have honored the best in British theater. The legendary actress won her first in 1977—when she was named Actress of the Year in a Revival for her role as Lady Macbeth in *Macbeth*.

Books

THE WRITTEN WORD HAS BEEN AROUND SINCE THE CLAY TABLETS of Babylon and the scrolls of ancient Egypt and China, but the cost of materials and transcription in days of yore kept manuscripts scarce. The invention of the printing press and new paper-making processes made books available on a wide scale and promoted literacy.

MILESTONES

4TH CENTURY: CODEX In ancient times the written word on everything from scientific works to poetry was generally produced on a scroll. But, finding a particular passage or losing your place could be a problem. Gradually, by the 4th century AD, the codex method was used for books; paper sheets were cut and sewn together, allowing the reader to turn rather than unscroll.

1456: GUTENBERG Although printing from wooden blocks was used in China as early as the 6th century, Johann Gutenberg invented movable type printing. Working on his press for several years in Mainz, Germany, Gutenberg printed his 42-line Bible (named for the number of lines per column) in 1456.

1640: BAY PSALM BOOK In July 1640, Steven Day printed what is believed to be the first book published in America, *The Whole Booke of Psalmes Faithfully Translated into English Metre*, also known as the *Bay Psalm Book*. Only 11 copies are believed to exist. Some consider it the most valuable book printed in America.

1860: FIRST MASS-MARKET PAPERBACK *Malaeska: Indian Wife of the White Hunter* (1839), by Ann S. Stephens, republished by Beadle & Co. of New York on June 9, 1860, was the first mass market paperback.

Using cheap materials and a standard format for its books, Beadle was able to lower the price of a book from the standard $1 to 10 cents. *Malaeska* sold more than 300,000 copies.

The new trend for cheap books died in the 1890s only to resurge in 1939, when Pocket Books began selling "paperback" versions of popular "hardbacks," starting with Pearl Buck's popular novel *The Good Earth* (1931).

1874: TYPED MANUSCRIPT The first workable typewriters were made by E. Remington & Sons of Ilion, NY, in Sept. 1873. In 1874 in Hartford, CT, Mark Twain (Samuel Clemens) had his secretary transcribe some writings believed to be either *The Adventures of Tom Sawyer* or *Life on the Mississippi on a Remington*—the first typed book manuscript sent to a publisher.

Twain later stopped using the typewriter because it made him "want to swear."

1895: BESTSELLER LIST The debut issue (Feb. 1895) of the monthly literary magazine *The Bookman—A Review of Books and Life* carried the first bestseller list.

The first bestseller was *Trilby*, a novel by George du Maurier.

1901: NOBEL PRIZE The Nobel Prize for Literature, awarded annually since 1901, was awarded for the first time to the French poet René F. A. Sully Prudhomme, best known for *La Justice* and *Le Bonheur*.

1917: PULITZER PRIZES The Pulitzer Prizes, awarded annually for works produced in the previous year, were first given out in 1917. In that year J. J. Jusserand won the first History Pulitzer, for *With Americans of Past and Present Days*, and the prize for Biography or Autobiography went to Laura E. Richards and Maude Howe Elliott, assisted by Florence Howe Hall, for *Julia Ward Howe*.

The first Pulitzer for Fiction was given in 1918 to Ernest Poole for the novel *His Family*, which portrayed a New York family.

Selected Repeat Award Winners

AWARD	MOST WINS
Edgar Award (best mystery novel)	3, Dick Francis (1970, 1981, 1996)
Hugo Award (best science fiction novel)	5, Robert A. Heinlein (1951, 1956, 1960, 1962, 1967)
National Book Award (fiction)	3, Saul Bellow (1954, 1965, 1971)
Nebula Award (science fiction/fantasy)	3, Ursula K. Le Guin (1969, 1974, 1990)
Newbery Medal (best children's book)	2, E. L. Konigsburg (1968, 1997) Joseph Krumgold (1954, 1960) Lois Lowry (1990, 1994) Katherine Paterson (1978, 1981) Elizabeth George Speare (1959, 1962)
Pulitzer Prize (fiction/novel)	2, William Faulkner (1955, 1963) Booth Tarkington (1919, 1922) John Updike (1982, 1991)
Pulitzer Prize (nonfiction)	2, Barbara Tuchman (1963, 1972)

A LOVE OF BOOKS GOING TOO FAR

SOMETHING TO THINK ABOUT

Stephen Blumberg was arrested on March 20, 1990, at his home in Ottumwa, IA, after being found with 23,600 rare books stolen from hundreds of North American libraries. Valued at more than $20 million, his collection of stolen rare books was the largest in U.S. history. Blumberg was tried in 1991 and sentenced to 5 years, 11 months in prison and fined $200,000. He was released on Dec. 29, 1995; included in the terms of his probation was the requirement that he identify himself upon entering any library or bookstore. Blumberg was arrested again two years later for stealing old building fixtures, which had been his obsession before he discovered the wonderful world of books.

The Library of Congress

1926: BOOK-OF-THE-MONTH CLUB *Lolly Willowes, or the Loving Huntsman*, by Sylvia Townsend Warner, the story of a spinster seeking self-determination, was the first book selected by the Book-of-the-Month Club and was sent out to 4,750 members of the club on April 16, 1926. The organization, established in New York City earlier that month, pioneered in providing selected mail-order books to subscribers at a discount.

1942: *TIMES* BESTSELLER LIST The *New York Times* began printing its bestseller list as a regular weekly feature on Aug. 9, 1942 (it had been a monthly feature in somewhat different form since 1935). Rachel Field's *And Now Tomorrow* was the first No. 1 fiction bestseller, while Paul Elliot's *The Last Time I Saw Paris* was the first No. 1 nonfiction bestseller.

1950: NATIONAL BOOK AWARDS The National Book Awards were given out for the first time on March 15, 1950. The Fiction prize went to Nelson Algren for *The Man With the Golden Arm*, the Nonfiction prize to Ralph L. Rusk for *Ralph Waldo Emerson*, and the award for Poetry to William Carlos Williams.

1996: OPRAH'S BOOK CLUB TV personality Oprah Winfrey began Oprah's Book Club in 1996, recommending books on her show and succeeding in getting her many viewers to read quality literature. The first selection, on Sept. 17, 1996, was Jacquelyn Mitchard's *The Deep End of the Ocean*, followed on Oct. 18, 1996, by Toni Morrison's *Song of Solomon* and on Nov. 18, 1996, by Jane Hamilton's *The Book of Ruth*.

SUPERLATIVES

BESTSELLING AUTHOR British mystery writer Agatha Christie is believed to be the world's bestselling author. Her 79 crime novels have sold an estimated 2 billion copies around the world.

BESTSELLING BOOK Most experts agree the world's bestselling book ever is the Bible, which has easily sold billions of copies in more than 2,000 languages and dialects.

MOST ONE-DAY SALES (FICTION) J. K. Rowling's *Harry Potter and the Half-Blood Prince*—the sixth book in the wildly popular children's series—sold an estimated 6.9 million copies in the U.S. alone on July 16, 2005, the day it went on sale (starting just after midnight).

MOST ONE-DAY SALES (NON-FICTION) President Bill Clinton's memoir *My Life* sold an estimated 400,000 copies on June 22, 2004, the day it went on sale. The previous record of 200,000 sold in one day was set by Sen. Hillary Rodham Clinton's memoir *Living History*, on June 9, 2003.

MOST VALUABLE BOOK An original four-volume subscriber set of John James Audubon's *The Birds of America* sold at auction for $8,802,500 on March 10, 2000, setting a world auction record for a printed book.

The previous record had been $7,565,396, paid in 1998 for a 15th-century copy of Geoffrey Chaucer's *Canterbury Tales*.

BIGGEST BOOK *Bhutan: A Visual Odyssey Across The Last Himalayan Kingdom* weighs 133 pounds and measures 5 feet by 7 feet when opened. Copies are sold for $15,000.

BIGGEST LIBRARY With more than 29 million books, the Library of Congress in Washington, DC, is the world's largest library. Founded in 1800 as a reference library for Congress, it was destroyed by the British during the War of 1812. To replace it, Thomas Jefferson sold his personal library containing 6,487 volumes for $23,950 in 1815.

Today, there are nearly 130 million items on about 530 miles of bookshelves. Along with its huge book collection, the library also houses 2.7 million recordings, 12 million photographs, 4.8 million maps, and 58 million manuscripts.

William Shakespeare

THE GREATEST ENGLISH-LANGUAGE DRAMATIST, William Shakespeare (1564-1616), is a somewhat mysterious figure. Records of his baptism, marriage, and death—all in and around Stratford-upon-Avon, England—survive, but not much is known of the details of his life. Some scholars and fans, especially in the late 19th century, have doubted that the Bard wrote any of the plays attributed to him. Some thought he lacked enough education to have written a collection of plays regarded as among the world's greatest literary masterpieces. Claims have been made that Sir Francis Bacon wrote them, or perhaps Edward De Vere, 18th earl of Oxford. Most scholars today consider such claims unlikely.

MILESTONES

1564: BIRTH There is no reliable record of Shakespeare's birth date. Records do show that Shakespeare was baptized at the Church of the Holy Trinity on April 26, 1564, and he was probably born close to that date, in Stratford-upon-Avon, England. His birthday is most often celebrated on April 23, which by coincidence is St. George's Day, the holiday observed to honor the patron saint of England. Shakespeare is known to have died on that date in 1616.

1582: MARRIAGE Shakespeare's exact wedding date is unknown, but a marriage license was issued to him and his bride, Anne Hathaway, on Nov. 27, 1582. She was eight years older than he was.

The couple had three children—Susanna, who was christened on May 26, 1583, and twins Hamnet and Judith, born in 1585. Hamnet died in 1596.

1589: FIRST PLAY There is no consensus among scholars as to which play Shakespeare wrote first. His earliest plays, perhaps going back as far as 1588, include the historical trilogy of *Henry VI* and the comedies *The Two Gentlemen of Verona* and *The Taming of the Shrew.* Of his tragedies, there is a consensus that *Titus Andronicus*, written between 1590 and 1594, was the first.

1594: CHAMBERLAIN'S MEN Little is known about Shakespeare's acting career, but there is evidence that he was a "player" and "actor-manager" before coming to the fore as a dramatist. By 1594 his prominence as a playwright was established. Records show that Shakespeare was then a partner in the Chamberlain's Men, a new company sponsored by Henry Carey, 1st Lord Hunsdon, Lord Chamberlain, who was head of the royal household. Royal accounts show that Shakespeare was paid for the staging of two plays at Queen Elizabeth I's court during Christmas celebrations that year.

The company was renamed the King's Men when they came under the patronage of the new king, James I, in 1603.

1623: COLLECTED PLAYS The first printed collection of Shakespeare's plays, or the First Folio, was published in England around Nov.-Dec. 1623. The 907-page collection contained 36 plays. About 750 copies of the First Folio were printed, and about 230 still exist.

As many as 19 of Shakespeare's plays were printed individually and published in England prior to the release of the First Folio; these appeared in the smaller-sized quarto format.

1879: ROYAL SHAKESPEARE COMPANY The Royal Shakespeare Company (RSC), the most famous Shakespearean company in the world, was formed in 1879, and has performed the Bard's works for millions of theatergoers since. The first play performed by the RSC was *Much Ado About Nothing*, at the original Shakespeare Memorial Theatre at Stratford-upon-Avon, England, on April 23, 1879. The most frequently performed play by the RSC is *A Midsummer Night's Dream*.

In 1961, the Memorial Theatre was renamed the Royal Shakespeare Theatre.

1899: FIRST MOVIE The first known Shakespearean play, or portion of a play, adapted for the screen was the final death scene, Act V, Scene vii, in *King John*. It was performed by the famous English actor-manager Sir Herbert Beerbohm-Tree in 1899.

The first complete Shakespeare play filmed in the U.S. was *Richard III*, released Oct. 15, 1912. In 1996, former projectionist William Buffum of Portland, OR, donated the only known copy of the five-reel film to the American Film Institute Film Festival. It is the oldest complete full-length U.S. feature film.

1948: BEST PICTURE OSCAR The first, and so far only, adaptation of a Shakespeare play to win an Oscar for best picture was *Hamlet* in 1948. The movie starred Laurence Olivier, who won the Best Actor award for his performance in the title role.

Fifty years later, in 1998, *Shakespeare In Love*, a romantic comedy about Shakespeare as a young playwright, took home the Best Picture award.

"THE SCOTTISH PLAY"

It has long been considered unlucky by actors to say the name "Macbeth" in a theater. Thespians usually refer to the work as "the Scottish play." The superstition arises from the play's depiction of witchcraft and the incantations of the three witches, which are claimed by some to be based on genuine chants used by real-life witches. There have been many reports of accidents to actors, equipment and lighting failures, sudden illness, and other problems surrounding performances of *Macbeth*, which also has the distinction of being Shakespeare's shortest tragedy.

UNIVERSAL INFLUENCE

Of the 21 named moons of Uranus, 18 are named for characters from Shakespeare. The tradition began with John Herschel, whose father, British astronomer Sir William Herschel, discovered (but did not name) Uranus in 1781. John Herschel named two moons, Titania and Oberon, after the queen and king of the fairies in *A Midsummer Night's Dream*. When American astronomer Gerald Kuiper discovered a smaller moon in 1948 he named it Miranda, after the heroine in *The Tempest*, thinking the earlier names were from that play.

When *Voyager 2* discovered 10 more moons in 1986, astronomers named nine of them for Shakespearean characters (mostly women): Cordelia, daughter of Lear in *King Lear*; Ophelia, daughter of Polonius in *Hamlet*; Bianca, sister of Kate in *Taming of the Shrew*; Cressida, title character in *Troilus and Cressida*; Desdemona, wife of Othello in *Othello*; Juliet, the heroine of *Romeo and Juliet*; Portia, heroine of *The Merchant of Venice*; Rosalind, daughter of the banished duke in *As You Like It*; and Puck, the mischievous spirit in *A Midsummer Night's Dream*. The six named since have all been from *The Tempest*: Caliban, the slave; Sycorax, Caliban's mother; Prospero, rightful duke of Milan; Setebos, Sycorax's god; Stephano, a drunken butler; and Trinculo, a jester.

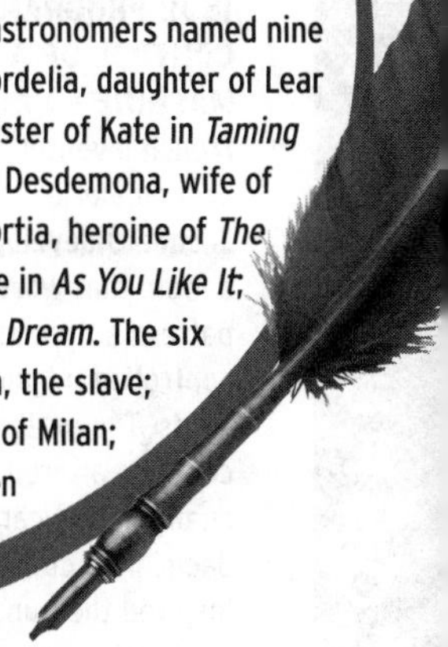

SUPERLATIVES

LARGEST SHAKESPEARE COLLECTION The Folger Shakespeare Library in Washington, DC, houses the largest collection of Shakespeare's work and related materials. It has 79 copies of the First Folio, and more than 200 of the early Shakespeare quartos.

Among other Shakespearean memorabilia, the Folger collection includes playbills, costumes, promptbooks, and much more.

LONGEST, SHORTEST PLAY Shakespeare's longest play (also said to be the most often quoted and possibly the most frequently performed) is *Hamlet*, at 4,042 lines, as counted in one edition by the Folger Shakespeare Library. And the title role in *Hamlet* is by far the longest part in any single Shakespeare play, at 1,507 lines.

The shortest play is *A Comedy of Errors*, at 1,787 lines.

HIGHEST AUCTION SALE On Oct. 9, 2001, an anonymous bidder paid $6,166,000 for an original copy of the First Folio, the most money ever bid at auction for a work by Shakespeare. Sold at Christie's New York, the book was one of only five complete, privately owned copies. It also set an auction record for a 17th-century book.

SOMETHING TO THINK ABOUT

SHAKESPEARE MARATHON

In 1987, Joseph Papp, the founder of New York City's Public Theater and the New York Shakespeare Festival, launched an ambitious project called "The Shakespeare Marathon" to try to perform all of the Bard's plays at either the Public Theater or Central Park's Delacorte Theater in six years. The first production was *A Midsummer Night's Dream*. The great theatrical challenge was completed with the staging of *Henry VIII* in 1997, six years after Papp's death.

MONKEY BUSINESS

There is a saying that a room full of monkeys banging randomly on typewriter keys will eventually write out the works of Shakespeare. One Web site, The Monkey Shakespeare Simulator, has put the saying to the test and simulates a room of monkeys typing at random using a random number generator. So far the closest line generated has been "RUMOUR. Open your ears" from *Henry IV, Part II*.

Software

EARLY COMPUTING MACHINES DID WHAT THEY WERE BUILT TO DO, such as performing simple calculations or running a loom, and no more. Machines that could be instructed, or programmed, to do different things were a step forward. But programming was arduous—operators had to shift wheels, move switches, plug and unplug wires and cables, and so on. The advent of software—sets of instructions stored within the computer—was a major advance. The flexibility and power of today's computers are largely due to software, including complex operating systems and programs that may run millions of lines long.

MILESTONES

1801: PROGRAM CONTROL OF A MACHINE
French inventor Joseph-Marie Jacquard developed a loom that wove a pattern automatically controlled by punch cards. The pattern could be altered by changing the cards. Jacquard's concept inspired the punched cards later used in tabulating machines and computers.

1945: "STORED PROGRAM" COMPUTER
The storage of both instructions and data in a single memory unit—a basic principle underlying modern digital computer design—was described by Hungarian-American mathematician John von Neumann in 1945 in a report on the planned EDVAC (Electronic Discrete Variable Automatic Computer). This approach allowed a computer to manipulate instructions in the same manner as data, which made it easy to reprogram the machine.

The EDVAC was not completed until 1952. The first electronic computer to run stored programs was the Small-Scale Experimental Machine built by British engineers Frederic C. Williams and Tom Kilburn in 1948. Ironically nicknamed the "Baby," it was 16 feet long and weighed half a ton.

1951-52: COMPILER
The first complete compiler—a program that translates programs written in a high-level language readily comprehensible by humans into machine code understandable by computers—was probably the A-0, written by Grace Hopper for the UNIVAC (Universal Automatic Computer) at Remington Rand in 1951-52.

In the course of her long and remarkable career, Hopper helped develop COBOL (COmmon Business Oriented Language), a programming language that enjoyed great popularity in business, and rose to the rank of rear admiral in the U.S. Navy.

1957: EASY-TO-USE LANGUAGE
The first high-level language to be both relatively easy to use and widely used was FORTRAN (FORmula TRANslation), created by John Backus and a team of IBM programmers. Designed for engineers and scientists, it was introduced for the IBM 704 computer in 1957.

Even more popular was a much simpler language, BASIC (Beginners' All-purpose Symbolic Instruction Code), developed in 1963 by Dartmouth College professors John G. Kemeny and Thomas E. Kurtz.

1968: SOFTWARE PATENT When software was first developed, many regarded it as information or formulas and not patentable. Martin A. Goetz, director of the Software Products Division of Applied Data Research, received the first software patent on April 23, 1968, for a "sorting system."

Amid the uproar, a news headline read, "First Patent Is Issued for Software, Full Implications Are Not Yet Known."

1968: GRAPHICAL USER INTERFACE
On Dec. 9, 1968, engineer Douglas Engelbart of Stanford Research Institute demonstrated the first hypertext system, NLS (oN Line System), in San Francisco, CA. Among other features, hypertext allowed the user to move text and data with a mouse (another Engelbart invention).

His philosophy of easy human-computer interaction was the basis of the graphical user interface, or GUI ("gooey").

Xerox PARC's Alto, completed in 1973, was the first to implement icons, menus, and a mouse pointer in GUI. The Alto's commercial version—STAR 8010, released in 1981—was the first retail computer using GUI.

GUI is a key part of such popular operating systems as Apple's Macintosh OS, Microsoft Windows, and Unix/Linux (X Windows).

1969-71: UNIX
The powerful UNIX operating system is a mainstay of larger computers and the basis for the well-known Linux and Macintosh OS X operating systems.

It was first developed by Ken Thompson, Dennis Ritchie, and colleagues at Bell Laboratories in 1969-71. The first edition was released Nov. 3, 1971.

1974: WYSIWYG
"What you see is what you get" (WYSIWYG) is the system in which the on-screen image precisely reflects the final product (printed document or Web page). The Xerox Research Center in Palo Alto, CA, completed the first WYSIWYG word-

◀ *Bill Gates (front, left) and the Albuquerque Group, 1978*

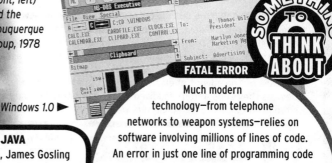

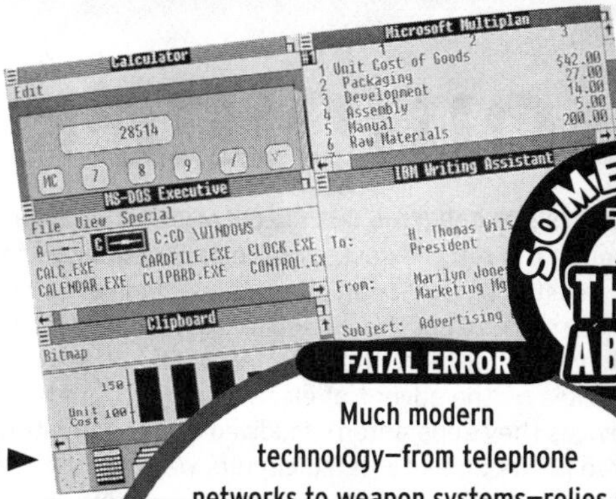

Windows 1.0 ▶

processing program, Bravo, for the Alto computer in 1974.

1974: CP/M
CP/M, the first widely used operating system for microcomputers (computers with a microprocessor), was developed by computer scientist Gary Kildall in 1974. CP/M (Control Program for Microcomputers) was the model for QDOS (Quick and Dirty Operating System), written by programmer Tim Paterson in 1980.

QDOS formed the basis of Microsoft's DOS (or MS-DOS or Microsoft Disk Operating System), which became the primary operating system for IBM and IBM-compatible personal computers.

1975: MICROSOFT
Software goliath Microsoft was founded (as "Micro-soft," dropping the hyphen the next year) by 20-year-old Bill Gates and 22-year-old Paul Allen in Albuquerque, NM, in 1975.

The company began when Gates and Allen wrote a form of BASIC for the new Altair personal computer. They sold their first copy on Feb. 1 and made $16,005 that year with just three employees (including Ric Weiland). They released their first version of Windows (1.0) on Nov. 20, 1985, but it was mostly a "front-end" to MS-DOS.

1991: LINUX
The UNIX-based Linux operating system was introduced by Finnish college student Linus Torvalds as a replacement for Minix, a UNIX variant used for academic purposes.

On Aug. 25, 1991, while still working on his new system, he posted to an Internet newsgroup a charming announcement: "I'm doing a (free) operating system (just a hobby, won't be big and professional...)." He announced his first version Oct. 5.

1995: JAVA
In 1991, James Gosling began work on "Oak" with a team at Sun Microsystems. The end result after four years was the Java programming language. Since it was independent of any platform, it could run on any computer. It also allowed programming code to be embedded in a web page.

It was introduced on May 23, 1995, and bundled with the Netscape Navigator browser the following year. It can be found today in over 1.75 billion devices.

1997: COMPUTER BEATS CHESS CHAMP
In Feb. 1996, world chess champion Garry Kasparov beat IBM computer "Deep Blue" in a 6-game match in the first traditional chess match between a computer and a human champion. In May 1997, "Deep Blue" reversed the result with a 3.5-2.5 victory over Kasparov.

SOMETHING TO THINK ABOUT

FATAL ERROR

Much modern technology—from telephone networks to weapon systems—relies on software involving millions of lines of code. An error in just one line of programming code can be fatal. This point was hammered home back in 1962, when NASA's *Mariner 1* had to be destroyed 293 seconds after takeoff. The omission of a single hyphen in the computer coding had caused *Mariner* to veer off course.

SUPERLATIVES

BIGGEST SOFTWARE COMPANY Microsoft was the world's No. 1 software and services company in 2005, according to a Forbes.com evaluation based on sales ($38.47 billion), profits ($10.00 billion), assets ($64.94 billion), and market value ($273.75 billion). Microsoft's market value was greater than the total for the next nine of the industry's top ten as ranked by Forbes.

MOST WIDELY USED OPEN-SOURCE SOFTWARE Proprietary software written by companies for profit is generally far more widely used than "open-source" programs, whose source code is public, making them freely modifiable. (For example, most personal computers run Microsoft's Windows operating system, and some run Apple's Macintosh OS; relatively few use the open-source Linux.) But there are exceptions. In July 2005, nearly 69.6% of sites on World Wide Web servers used the open-source Apache HTTP program.

HIGHEST PIRACY RATE According to the Business Software Assoc., in 2004, 92% of the software sold in Vietnam was pirated. Ukraine had the second highest piracy rate (91%), followed by China and Zimbabwe (both 90%). The U.S. had the lowest rate (21%), followed by New Zealand (23%) and Austria (25%).

Computer Hardware

DEVICES FOR CARRYING OUT CALCULATIONS ARE NOTHING NEW. Rudimentary abacuses were used in the remote past, as were analog devices for calculating the motions and positions of celestial bodies. Sophisticated mechanical computing machines began to emerge a few centuries ago. But the immediate forerunners of today's fast, powerful digital computers (able to do far more than compute) did not arrive until the 20th century. They were made possible by the advent of electronics (vacuum tubes were faster than the mechanical devices they supplanted), followed by the miniaturizing magic of semiconductor technology (transistors and integrated circuits were far more compact and reliable than vacuum tubes).

MILESTONES

AROUND 80 BC: ANTIKYTHERA MECHANISM The most complicated device known from classical times was found in a shipwreck by divers off the island of Antikythera in 1900-01. This "Antikythera mechanism," a geared device built around 80 BC, was apparently used to help locate stars and planets in the sky.

1623: MECHANICAL CALCULATOR German mathematician Wilhelm Schickard in 1623 built the first machine that could automatically add, subtract, multiply, and divide. He called his machine a "calculating clock."

1833-71: DESIGN FOR PROGRAMMABLE COMPUTER After devising a mechanical calculator ("Difference Engine") in 1822, English mathematician Charles Babbage in 1833 began designing the first programmable computer. He continued working on his "Analytical Engine" until his death in 1871.

The machine, never actually built, was a precursor of today's computers. It was to be programmed with punched cards, a technology successfully demonstrated at the beginning of the 19th century by French engineer Joseph-Marie Jacquard to control the weaving pattern of a loom.

1889: PUNCHED CARD TABULATOR In 1889, American engineer Herman Hollerith received a patent for a punched-card electromechanical tabulating machine that could handle large amounts of statistical data. His equipment quickly proved useful for organizing census data in the U.S. and other countries. His punched cards were a mainstay of data processing into the second half of the 20th century. The tabulator company he founded evolved into IBM.

1937-41: ELECTRONIC COMPUTER American physicist John Atanasoff and graduate student Clifford Berry built the first rudimentary electronic digital computer at Iowa State College (now University). The Atanasoff-Berry Computer (ABC) used vacuum tubes and was not programmable. This device, which could store 3,000 bits (3k) of memory, read punched cards and took about 16 seconds to perform one operation.

1941: PROGRAM-CONTROLLED COMPUTER German engineer Konrad Züse in 1941 built the first fully-functional completely program-controlled computer. The Z3, as it was named, was relay based (nonelectronic)—it used electromechanical switching devices called relays, rather than electronic tubes.

1943: COLOSSUS The first fully electronic programmable computer was the Colossus, built by British electronics engineer Tommy Flowers in 1943. It was designed for a specific task—code breaking—and its development was funded by the British government.

The Colossus was critical in helping British agents decode German documents in the later years of World War II.

1944: HARVARD MARK I The IBM Automatic Sequence Controlled Calculator, a huge relay-based machine better known as the Harvard Mark I, was the world's first large-scale automatic general-purpose digital computer. Built by Howard Aiken at Harvard University, the massive machine was funded by IBM. It contained 500 miles of wiring.

1946: ENIAC American scientists John Mauchly and J. Presper Eckert of the University of Pennsylvania built the first electronic, programmable general-purpose computer. The mammoth 30-ton machine, completed in 1946, used 17,468 vacuum tubes. It was called ENIAC, for "Electronic Numerical Integrator And Computer."

1947: TRANSISTOR American physicists John Bardeen, Walter Brattain, and William Shockley developed the transistor in 1947, launching the semiconductor revolution. Transistors are smaller and use less power than vacuum tubes. The scientists earned the 1956 Physics Nobel Prize for their work.

1954: MASS PRODUCTION The first mass-produced computer was IBM's 650, first sold Dec. 8, 1954. By April 1956, IBM was turning out

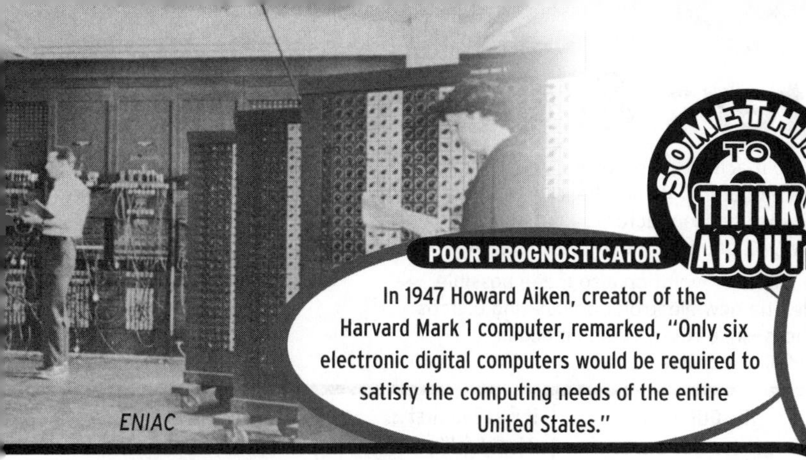
ENIAC

one machine per day. Almost 2,000—mostly used for scientific and engineering research and some business—were sold by the time the model was dropped in 1962.

1958: INTEGRATED CIRCUIT Electrical engineer Jack Kilby of Texas Instruments invented the integrated circuit—a circuit on a semiconductor chip—in late 1958. The achievement earned him a share of the 2000 Nobel Prize in physics.

Soon after Kilby's invention, Fairchild Semiconductor engineer Robert Noyce, working independently, also developed an integrated circuit. Noyce's design was the first to receive a patent, in 1961. He helped found the major chip manufacturer Intel ("INTegrated ELectronics") in 1968.

1971: EASILY PORTABLE STORAGE IBM introduced its first "floppy disk" in 1971. This "floppy," nicknamed for its flexibility, was 8 inches in diameter and held about 80 kilobytes of information. Today's blue-laser DVDs can hold upwards of 27 gigabytes of data, enough to fill about 350,000 of the original floppy disks.

1971: MICROPROCESSOR The first commercial microprocessor (an entire computer processor on a chip) was the four-bit 4004, introduced by Intel in 1971.

1976: APPLE Apple Computer Co. was founded by Steve Wozniak and Steve Jobs on April 1, 1976. Early on, they operated out of Jobs' garage in Los Altos, CA. Their first fully packaged system with a keyboard, the Apple II, was introduced April 15, 1977; it won instant popularity and remained in production, through several upgrades, into 1993.

1982: MACHINE OF THE YEAR For 1982, *Time* magazine instead of naming a "Man of the Year" designated the computer as its "Machine of the Year." *Time* publisher John A. Meyers wrote, "Several human candidates might have represented 1982, but none symbolized the past year more richly, or will be viewed by history as more significant, than a machine: the computer."

1998: QUANTUM COMPUTER A glimpse into what the future of computing technology might hold came in 1998 at UC Berkeley with the demonstration of the first working "computer" based on the principles of quantum mechanics at the University of California, Berkeley.

Current computers are faster and smaller than their ancestors, but still run on simple physics and the binary code of 0s and 1s. The 2-qubit (quantum bit) computer would allow each bit to be 0 and 1 simultaneously—making for faster processing, increased search speed, and better encryption capabilities.

SOMETHING TO THINK ABOUT

POOR PROGNOSTICATOR

In 1947 Howard Aiken, creator of the Harvard Mark 1 computer, remarked, "Only six electronic digital computers would be required to satisfy the computing needs of the entire United States."

BEST PROGNOSTICATOR

In 1952 computers, to the general public, were rare, exotic machines. But on the night of the presidential election that year, CBS-TV used a UNIVAC computer to analyze early returns and predict a winner. Polls had portrayed the race as tight, with Adlai Stevenson the front-runner, but the UNIVAC early on projected a landslide win for Dwight D. Eisenhower. A skeptical CBS news team put off announcing the UNIVAC prediction until late that night. But Eisenhower did win in a landslide, and the computer emerged as a hero.

GOOD PROGNOSTICATOR

In 1965 electronic engineer Gordon Moore, later a cofounder of Intel, predicted that the number of transistors that could be put on a computer chip would double every two years. The time period was later revised to every 18 months, and in this form "Moore's Law" has by and large proved true.

SUPERLATIVES

BIGGEST HARDWARE COMPANY IBM was the world's No. 1 company in "technology hardware and equipment" in 2005, according to a Forbes.com evaluation based on sales ($96.29 billion), profits ($8.43 billion), assets ($109.18 billion), and market value ($152.76 billion).

FASTEST COMPUTER The fastest-working computer, as of early 2006, was the IBM BlueGene/L at the Dept. of Energy's Lawrence Livermore National Laboratory in Livermore, CA. A massively parallel supercomputer with tens of thousands of microprocessors, it was capable of a blazing 280.6 trillion "floating-point" calculations, or flops, per second (280.6 teraflops).

The original Cray-1, produced by supercomputer pioneer Seymour Cray in 1976, had a peak speed considerably below 200 million flops ("megaflops"). Today, leading desktops are capable of a few billion flops ("gigaflops").

Microcomputers & Calculators

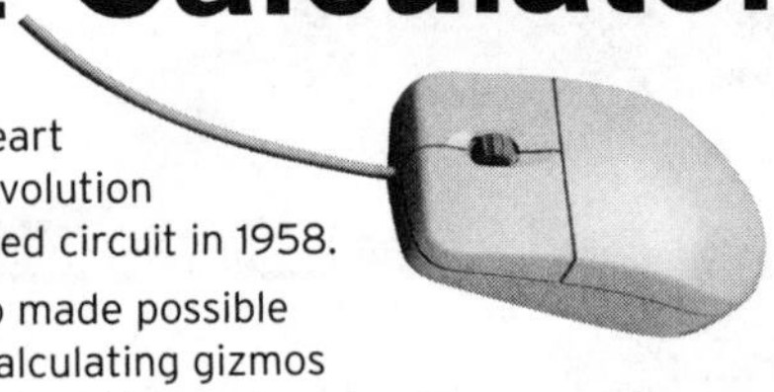

TODAY'S UBIQUITOUS PERSONAL COMPUTERS—desktop machines, laptops, tablets, personal digital assistants—are all microcomputers. At their heart they have a microprocessor, one of the fruits of the semiconductor revolution touched off by the invention of the transistor in 1947 and the integrated circuit in 1958. The miniaturization engendered by the semiconductor revolution also made possible radically smaller calculators. Besides being little, the new electronic calculating gizmos were often far more capable than previous devices—slide rules, adding machines, abacuses, and the like—which for the most part fell out of use.

MILESTONES

1963: MOUSE The pointing device known as a mouse, a basic means of interacting with today's personal computers, was invented by Stanford Research Institute scientist Douglas Engelbart in 1963. A working name used for the device during its development was "bug." Engelbart's patent application called it an "X-Y position indicator for a display system."

According to Engelbart, it got the name "mouse" because the cord originally came out of the back, like a tail. "Very soon we realized that the connecting wire should be brought out the 'front' instead of the back," he said. But it was too late—"mouse" had already scampered into wide use.

1967: POCKET CALCULATOR The electronic handheld calculator was invented by Jack Kilby (one of the inventors of the integrated circuit) and his colleagues at Texas Instruments in 1967. The Texas Instruments project, dubbed "Cal-Tech," produced a battery-powered device that had a thermal printer and could add, subtract, multiply, and divide.

This miniature electronic calculator, as it was called in its patent (granted in 1974), measured $\frac{1}{4}$ x $6\frac{1}{8}$ x $\frac{3}{4}$ inches and weighed a bit under 3 pounds.

1973: XEROX ALTO: PC PRECURSOR The Alto computer, developed at Xerox's Palo Alto Research Center, became operational in 1973. It had a host of features that later became commonplace in personal computers, including a graphical user interface (GUI) and the capability to be networked with other computers.

The GUI used windows, icons, a mouse, and pointers—features that gave rise to the acronym "WIMP" for the interface; its ease of use provoked disdain among some techies.

1974: PROGRAMMABLE POCKET CALCULATOR Hewlett-Packard developed the first programmable handheld calculator, the HP-65, in 1974; it had a built-in magnetic card reader/writer and could run short programs up to 100 lines long. U.S. astronauts used an HP-65 to calculate course-corrections during the 1975 rendezvous of the U.S. *Apollo* and Soviet *Soyuz* spacecraft.

1975: PERSONAL COMPUTER The Altair 8800, created by Micro Instrumentation and Telemetry Systems (MITS) engineers Edward Roberts, William Yates, and Jim Bybee, entered the market in 1975. Available for a few hundred dollars, it was the first widely sold personal microcomputer. The basic model had just 256 bytes of RAM memory (a typical computer today has nearly a million times more RAM).

Users entered data and instructions by means of switches on the front panel; program results were conveyed via lights on the front.

1975: PORTABLE COMPUTER Much more capable, and expensive (a price tag in the $9,000-$20,000 range), than the Altair was the IBM 5100, which was introduced in 1975 as the first "portable" computer. It had a 5-inch screen and weighed about 50 pounds. A carrying case was available as an option.

1976: WORD PROCESSOR In 1976, Altair programmer Michael Shrayer wrote the first word-processing program for personal computers, Electric Pencil.

The first personal computer word processor to achieve smash commercial success was WordStar. Introduced for personal computers in 1979 by MicroPro International, it ranked as an industry standard for several years.

Today's dominant word processor, Microsoft Word, made its debut in 1983 in a version for IBM PCs; in Word's early years the Macintosh version, first shipped in 1984, enjoyed a far better market share than did the one for the IBM PC.

1977: APPLE II The Apple II, introduced in 1977 by Apple Computer, had attractive features such as support for a color display. Although not cheap—the original base model, with 4,000 bytes of RAM, retailed for $1,298—it was not inordinately expensive. By late 1982 more than 750,000 units had been sold.

◀ *Apple Computer*

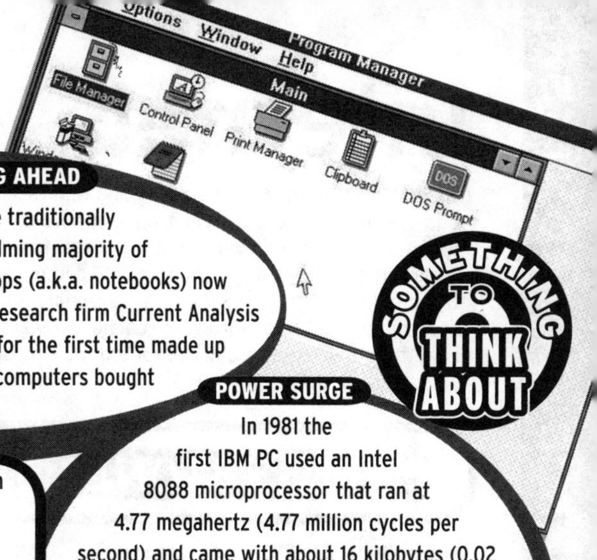

Windows 3.0 ▶

LAPTOPS RACING AHEAD

Desktop machines have traditionally accounted for the overwhelming majority of personal computers in use, but laptops (a.k.a. notebooks) now appear to have caught up. The market research firm Current Analysis reported that in May 2005, laptops for the first time made up more than half of personal computers bought in the U.S.

SOMETHING TO THINK ABOUT

POWER SURGE

In 1981 the first IBM PC used an Intel 8088 microprocessor that ran at 4.77 megahertz (4.77 million cycles per second) and came with about 16 kilobytes (0.02 megabytes) of RAM (upgradable to 256 kilobytes or 0.24 megabytes), but without a hard drive; prices stated at $1,565. Just two decades later, a consumer could get, for a lower price, an IBM desktop machine with an Intel Pentium 4 processor running at more than 1 gigahertz (1 billion cycles per second) and with at least 128 megabytes of RAM.

1981: IBM PC IBM's 5150 Personal Computer, the archetypal IBM PC, was released in 1981.

It was a relatively simple machine, sporting just 16,000 bytes of RAM. But IBM was a prestigious company with a long history in tabulating and computing equipment. Its entry into the personal computer market galvanized the corporate world's acceptance of microcomputers for individuals.

IBM picked a then obscure software company called Microsoft to supply the operating system for its new machine. Most of the explosive growth in personal computer production involved machines from either IBM or manufacturers that imitated IBM's design ("IBM-compatibles").

Meanwhile, Microsoft, which made application programs as well as operating systems for personal computers, came to dominate the software industry.

1984: MACINTOSH
Apple Computer introduced the revolutionary Macintosh in 1984. At a time when people still interacted with personal computers almost exclusively via a text-based "command-line interface," the Macintosh was the first low-cost computer to boast a GUI reminiscent of the innovative Alto.

Its introduction was announced during halftime of Super Bowl XVIII (Jan. 22, 1984) in an iconoclastic TV commercial that was based on George Orwell's novel *1984* about a totalitarian society. *Advertising Age* rated the ad "the greatest commercial ever" in 1995.

1985: WINDOWS
Microsoft released the first version of Windows, a GUI for IBM-compatible machines, in 1985. It was clunky and slow in its initial form, but achieved commercial viability with the introduction of version 3.0 in 1990.

Originally an add-on to Microsoft's DOS operating system, it eventually was developed into a full-fledged operating system.

1996: PALMPILOT
The PalmPilot, introduced in 1996, was not the first handheld computer on the market, but it was the first major commercial success. Its fame was such that as PDAs, or personal digital assistants, became commonplace in the business world, they were sometimes called, regardless of their manufacturer, palm pilots.

2002: 1 BILLION The personal computer industry shipped its 1 billionth machine in April 2002, according to Gartner, a prominent information technology analysis firm.

Gartner predicted that the 2 billion mark would be reached by the year 2008.

SUPERLATIVES

LARGEST PERSONAL COMPUTER COMPANY
Dell has been the world's top source of personal computers. Preliminary figures from industry analyst IDC for third quarter 2005 showed it had 18% share of the world market, topping the 16% share of the No. 2 vendor, Hewlett Packard.

MOST COMMON OPERATING SYSTEM
Market share for personal computer operating systems can be measured in different ways, but the results are usually similar. Looking at desktops, laptops, and the like, as of 2005, Microsoft Windows ran on at least nine-tenths of machines worldwide, with the Macintosh OS and Linux accounting for most of the rest.

The picture was different in the PDA arena, where the players are more numerous and product lifespans shorter, but there too, Microsoft ruled the roost. In first quarter 2005, according to Gartner figures, Microsoft's version of Windows for handhelds claimed a market share of 46%. Research in Motion's operating system, for the Blackberry, held 20.8%; the Palm OS, 20%; Symbian, 9.9%; and Linux, 0.8%.

Internet

THE INTERNET STARTED AS A LINK among U.S. research scientists; today 1 billion or more people around the world connect up to the Internet for a wide variety of purposes, from e-mailing to reading the latest news to shopping. "E-commerce" continues to expand rapidly; the U.S. Commerce Department estimates that online retail sales for 2004 reached $69.2 billion, up 24% from the previous year, and accounted for almost 2% of all consumer purchases in the U.S.

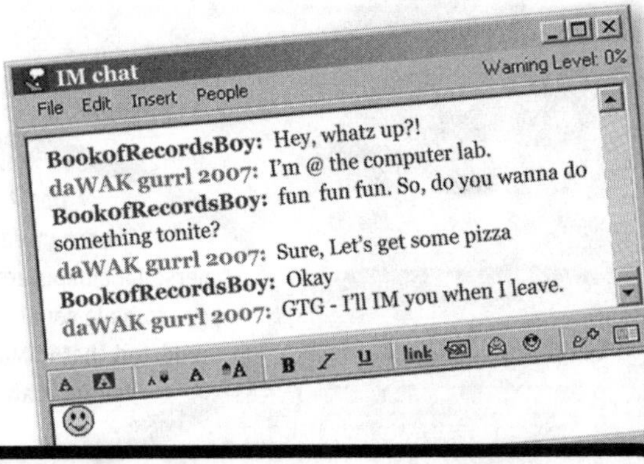

MILESTONES

1960s: BIRTH OF THE IDEA The space race of the 1950s and 1960s led to the creation of the Internet. When the Soviet Union launched *Sputnik I*, on Oct. 4, 1957, the U.S. Defense Department responded by forming the Advanced Research Projects Agency (ARPA), which along with the newly created National Aeronautics and Space Administration (NASA), was given a mandate to regain the country's technological superiority.

In 1967, ARPA allotted $19,800 to study the "design and specification of a computer network." That network became ARPAnet, which evolved into the Internet.

1968: LINKED NETWORKS In 1968, faculty at the Stanford Research Institute and three universities contracted with ARPA to construct four interface message processors (IMPS), as gateways that would let computers enter other systems through telephone lines.

By 1971 ARPAnet had spread to 23 "hosts," computers that provide access to other computers within a network; by 1981, there were over 200, including several overseas.

1971: E-MAIL Ray Tomlinson, an engineer at Bolt, Beranek & Newman (BBN), had a neat idea to create the first electronic mail program by combining a file transfer program, CPYNET, with a system to send and receive messages. One day in 1971 he sent the very first message (between two computers connected by a cable). He thinks it said something along the lines of "TESTING 1, 2, 3, 4."

1978: SPAM Spam, or unsolicited e-mail sent out to large numbers of people at the same time, has cluttered inboxes since 1978, when Digital Equipment Corporation (DEC) advertised a new computer to all ARPAnet addresses on the West Coast. The term was inspired by a sketch from the British TV comedy *Monty Python's Flying Circus*, where the word "spam" is sung repeatedly, drowning out conversation.

The label became widespread in 1994 when two Phoenix attorneys distributed an ad on several thousand USENET newsgroups and got thousands of angry responses. Hormel, maker of the original SPAM® spiced ham, has claimed not to mind the reference so long as it is lowercase and not given as a trademark. It is estimated that spam makes up more than 80% of all e-mail in the U.S. today.

1983: TCP/IP On Jan. 1, 1983, ARPAnet switched its method of transferring information to the two-tiered TCP/IP (Transmission Control Protocol/Internet Protocol). This method involved sending packets of information called "datagrams"—similar to real-life envelopes containing letters—through "gateway" computers, or electronic post offices. Gateway computers read the delivery information and deliver the contents to host computers that "open" the envelope so users can read them. TCP allowed smaller networks to be joined into a greater nexus and has been recognized as giving birth to the modern Internet. The "20th anniversary of the Internet" celebration, in 2003, marked this milestone in technology.

1988: WORM ATTACK On Nov. 2, 1988, Robert T. Morris Jr., a graduate student in computer science at Cornell University, created a self-replicating, self-propagating program now referred to as "the Morris worm."

The experimental program was designed

Other On-line Firsts:

Newspaper	*Toronto Globe and Mail*	1977
Search Engine	Archie; Peter Deutsch, Alan Emtage and Bill Heelan at McGill Univ., Montreal	1990
Banner Ads	On Hotwired.com	Oct. 1994
Audio Streaming	RealAudio	Oct. 1995
Internet-Only Full-Service Bank	First Internet Bank of Indiana	Feb. 22, 1999

SOMETHING TO THINK ABOUT

INTERNET ADDICTION

In China, "Internet Addiction Disorder" (IAD) is said to affect 15% of youths, with withdrawal symptoms including anxiety, depression, irritation, obsessive thinking about the Internet, and even voluntary or involuntary typing movements when Internet use is reduced. Whether afflicted with IAD or not, as of 2005, over 112 million Chinese speakers used the Internet. This makes Chinese the second most widely used language on the Internet, after English.

SEARCH OF SELF DISCOVERY

About one in four Internet users have typed their own names into a search engine to see what information about them is on the Web according to a 2002 survey. While most "vanity searchers" say they found what they expected, 24% were surprised by how much information they found, while 16% were surprised by how little they found.

SUPERLATIVES

BIGGEST USE More people use the Internet for e-mail than any other activity. As of Jan. 2005, about 120 million Americans were e-mail users; over 65 million did so daily. The second most common daily activity was getting news, performed by over 41 million Americans.

Other Internet Superlatives

Most Connected Country (total users)	U.S.	201 million users (July 2004)
Most Connected Country (%)	Sweden	74.6% (July 2004)
Most Connected States (%)	Oregon/ Washington	68% (2002)
Most Used Search Engine	Google	250 million searches/day (Feb. 2003)
Most Visited Site	Yahoo.com	115 million visitors (June 2004)
Largest Internet Service Provider (ISP)	America Online	Approx. 22.7 million subscribers (Sept. 2004)

to connect its host computer to another on the network, use the destination computer's resources to reproduce itself, and then go on to other computers. It was only supposed to infect each computer once, but because of a programming error, it kept repeating itself in an infinite loop on each infected computer. It eventually forced about 10% of all U.S. hosts to shut down. Morris was convicted of violating the Computer Fraud and Abuse Act, sentenced to three years probation and 400 hours of community service, and fined $10,050.

1989-90: WORLD WIDE WEB The World Wide Web is the set of hypertext documents that are found on interlinked HTTP servers all around the world. Tim Berners-Lee, a British physicist at CERN, the European Center for Nuclear Research, in Switzerland, first proposed the idea for an information network in 1989. He launched the first World Wide Web server (nxoc01.cern.ch) on Dec. 25, 1990, and also created Uniform Resource Locators (URLs), the Hypertext Transfer Protocol (HTTP), and Hypertext Markup Language (HTML). The Web evolved into a medium with graphics, audio, animation, and video. CERN declared in 1993 that Web technology could be used by anyone for free, leading to the Web's rapid expansion.

1993: GRAPHICAL BROWSER Berners-Lee's WorldWideWeb and ViolaWWW, programmed by UC-Berkeley student Pei-Yuan Wei, were graphical browsers for Unix. Mosaic, released on Sept. 16, 1993, was the first available for Microsoft Windows, Macintosh, and Unix systems, making Web access practical for the average user. Mosaic was developed at NCSA (National Center for Supercomputing Applications) in Illinois by Marc Andreessen, Jamie Zawinski, and other students who went on to create the Netscape Navigator browser.

1999: WIRELESS PHONE The Nokia 7110, released on Feb. 23, 1999, was the first cellular phone based on the Wireless Application Protocol (WAP) currently used for wireless Internet access. The phone could display Internet text, including a CNN newsfeed.

Robotics

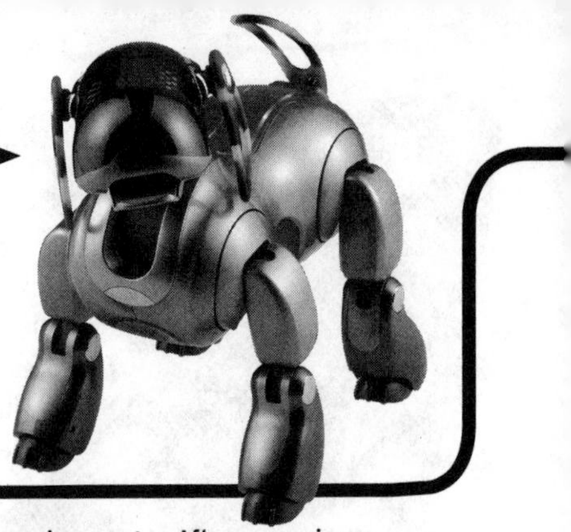

AIBO Entertainment Robot ►

ROBOTS ARE MACHINES THAT CAN INTERACT WITH THEIR ENVIRONMENT automatically, without direct human control. Real-life robots range from simple automatic devices to complex systems whose behavior is governed by computer processors responding to sensory data. Real robots—from assembly-line machines to planetary rovers—operate by and large in accordance with preprogrammed instructions. But robots encountered in science fiction are often endowed with a formidable degree of artificial intelligence, occasionally even a sort of free will.

MILESTONES

3RD CENTURY BC: AUTOMATA Long before people dreamed of robots, they built mechanical figures, or automata, that imitated movements of humans or animals. They were powered in a number of different ways including by falling weights, water, and steam.

Reports of humanlike automata date as far back as third-century-BC China and Greece. An entire orchestra was said to have been crafted for a Han dynasty emperor, and Archytas of Tarentum built a wooden pigeon about 400–350 BC that was probably powered by water.

LATE 15TH-EARLY 16TH CENTURIES: LEONARDO DA VINCI Around 1478 the Florentine artist/scientist Leonardo da Vinci designed a spring-powered three-wheeled cart that, some scholars say, would have been able to move in accordance with programmed instructions. In 1495, he designed an automaton in the form of a knight that could move its legs, hips, arms, and head, sit up, and open and close its jaws.

Later, for French King Louis XII, he made a mechanical lion; it reportedly moved across a long hall and halted in front of Louis, whereupon it opened "its breast which was full of lilies and different flowers."

1730s: VAUCANSON In 18th-century Europe there was a flurry of interest in automata. The most famous were those made by French inventor Jacques de Vaucanson. He produced a weight-powered mechanical flute player in 1738 and a tambourine player and a duck the following year. The duck moved like a real duck and could simulate drinking, eating, and defecating.

In the 1740s Vaucanson developed an automated loom whose operation was guided by perforated cards. It failed to gain acceptance in the weaving industry, but several decades later was improved upon by Joseph-Marie Jacquard, who used punch cards for programming looms.

1788: FEEDBACK CONTROLLER Feedback involves feeding something from the output of a system back to the input.

An early example was the flyball governor introduced by Scottish inventor James Watt in 1788. It automatically regulated the speed of rotating steam engines. As the speed of rotation increased, centrifugal force made the device's two pivoted flyballs swing outward, engaging a throttling valve that slowed the steam flow and the engine, thereby enabling the engine to maintain a more or less constant speed.

1898: REMOTE CONTROL The Croatian-born American electrical engineer Nikola Tesla was the first to implement wireless remote control, applying the then-new technology of radio. He used this technology to steer a boat in a demonstration in May 1898 at New York City's Madison Square Garden.

1920: "ROBOT" Czech writer Karel Capek introduced the word "robot" in his 1920 play *R.U.R.* ("Rossum's Universal Robots"), about an Englishman called Rossum who produces mechanized human-like "robots" (from the Czech *robota*, "compulsory labor") who perform tasks to make life easier for humans.

After an engineer begins to give the robots emotions, they revolt against their human rulers.

1948-49: EMERGENT BEHAVIOR U.S.-born British neurophysiologist W. Grey Walter in 1948-49 built two simple three-wheeled electronic robots, or "turtles," that were not limited to the fixed behavior of previous robots; that is, they could move more independently and respond to the environment in more unpredictable ways.

Named Elmer and Elsie ("ELectro MEchanical Robots," and "Light SEnsitive"), they had light sensors and a contact sensor that allowed them to react with lifelike behavior.

Walter observed "uncertain, randomic, free-will or independent characteristics" in his little robots. They were first displayed at the Festival of Britain in 1951.

1954: INDUSTRIAL ROBOT American engineer George Devol Jr. developed the first robot arm that could be programmed to do different things. He filed for a patent in 1954, and in 1961 sold it to his associate, engineer/entrepreneur Joseph Engelberger, who founded the pioneering industrial robot company Unimation.

Unimation produced the first industrial robot to work on a production line: a 4,000-pound arm called Unimate, which was put into service at the General Motors Ternstedt plant in Trenton, NJ, in 1961. Its job was to remove finished castings from a die-casting machine.

1966-72: A ROBOT WITH "REASON" Called the "first electronic person" by *Life* magazine, the first mobile robot guided by artificial intelligence was developed at the Stanford Research Institute (now SRI International) between 1966 and 1972.

Nicknamed "Shakey" (from the jerkiness of its movements), this wheeled box of electronics boasted simple language, perception, locomotion, and problem-solving capabilities, permitting it to find its way in a structured environment and respond to English commands input into its computer.

1997: EXPLORING PLANETS The National Aeronautics and Space Administration's Pathfinder mission to Mars successfully landed a solar-powered, 25-pound, six-wheeled rover called *Sojourner* on July 4, 1997. It explored the red planet for several weeks, until the connection was lost on Sept. 27.

Sojourner, equipped with a hazard-avoidance system enabling it to make some navigation decisions on its own, was the first such robot system to be deployed on another planet.

1999: AIBO Robotic canines introduced by Sony in 1999 were not only able to walk, respond to surroundings, react to spoken commands, and express "emotions"; they were also capable of learning. Aibo (the name derived from "Artificial Intelligence, roBOt" but also echoed the Japanese *aibo*, "buddy," and *ai*, "love") was the first commercially successful autonomous mobile entertainment robot.

The first run of Aibos, marketed over the Internet, sold out in 20 minutes in Japan (3,000 units) and four days in the U.S. (2,000 units).

SOMETHING TO THINK ABOUT

SAFETY FIRST

A need to prevent robots from appearing to be a menace gave rise to the Three Rules of Robotics formulated by the celebrated science fiction writer Isaac Asimov (1920-92). The laws, in order of priority, required that robots should not harm humans, should (only if consistent with the first law) obey their orders, and (only if not in conflict with the other two laws) protect their own existence. Asimov, who coined the term "robotics," set forth the laws in his 1942 short story "Runaround."

PLAY BALL

On June 7, 2005, a 200-pound, four-wheeled S-3 became the first robot to throw out the first pitch of a Major League Baseball game, at a game between the Pirates and Baltimore Orioles at Pittsburgh's PNC Park. Around the same time, Hiroshima University researcher Idaku Ishii exhibited a robot that could hit fastballs at speeds upwards of 100 mph by analyzing 1,000 images per second to determine the pitch's path.

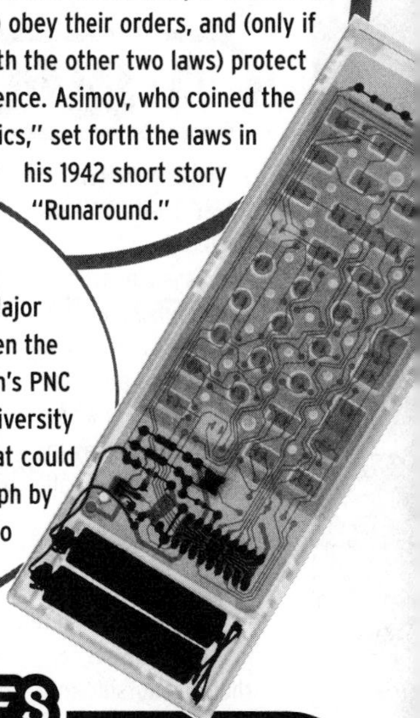

SUPERLATIVES

MOST INDUSTRIAL ROBOTS (COUNTRY) Of an estimated 886,200 functioning industrial robots in the world at the end of 2004, Japan had the most, 352,200, according to the UN Economic Commission for Europe (UNECE).

MOST COMMON HOUSEHOLD ROBOT According to UNECE figures, autonomous vacuum cleaners that clean floors themselves without human guidance made up the vast majority (570,000) of the estimated 607,000 household robots (as of 2003) in the world; robot lawn mowers, with about 37,000 units, held the No. 2 spot.

LARGEST ROBOT COMPETITION The 2005 edition of RoboGames, held in San Francisco, CA, March 25-27, drew 214 teams from 13 countries, with 466 robots taking part; events ranged from sumo wrestling, to maze running, to firefighting, to Aibo soccer and beyond.

TINIEST ROBOT New York University chemists William B. Sherman and Nadrian C. Seeman reported in 2004 the creation of a tiny walker from bits of DNA. Their "precisely controlled DNA biped walking device" could move forward or backward on its two legs, which were only ten nanometers (that is, 10 billionths of a meter) long.

Seeman hopes the machines could make molecular-size assembly lines for nano-manufacturing.

Cameras

Daguerreotype from 1839

"PHOTOGRAPHY," COMES FROM TWO GREEK WORDS MEANING "LIGHT" AND "WRITING," so it is "writing with light." But cameras do much more than just fix an image. As the theater critic Brooks Atkinson once put it, "The virtue of the camera is not the power it has to transform the photographer into an artist, but the impulse it gives him to keep on looking."

MILESTONES

16TH CENTURY: CAMERA OBSCURA During the Renaissance, artists began employing a device known as the *camera obscura* ("dark room") when sketching. It uses the basic principle of all cameras: light that enters a small hole in the wall of a dark room casts an inverted image of the scene that lies outside the wall upon the opposite wall.

The camera obscura effect had been known for centuries when artists and inventors began making adjustments to improve focus. It's mentioned in a 5th century BC Chinese text, and was known to Aristotle. The Muslim scientist Abu Ali al-Hasan Ibn al-Haitham (known in the West as Alhazen) described the camera obscura effect at the beginning of the 11th century.

1727: DISCOVERY OF "SCOTOPHORUS" In 1727, German anatomy professor Johann Heinrich Schulze discovered that chalks dissolved in nitric acid containing silver changed color under light. He called his light-sensitive substance "scotophorus," or "bringer of darkness." The discovery that chemical compounds of silver turn dark on exposure to light became the basis of photography.

1826: FIRST PHOTOGRAPH Using a plate coated with bitumen of Judea and an eight-hour exposure, Joseph Nicéphore Niépce of France, captured a black and white image of the view from an upper window at his estate in 1826. The image, which Niépce called a *heliograph* ("writing with sun"), is as historic as it is murky. Soon after, Niépce captured a much sharper image of a table set for a meal.

1839: DAGUERREOTYPE Louis Jacques Mandé Daguerre, who had worked with Niépce until his death in 1833, perfected the "daguerreotype" in 1839. The daguerreotype method involved a light sensitive silver-plated sheet of copper on which images could be directly reproduced.

He began retailing the camera almost immediately. The daguerreotype exposure times ranged from 3 to 15 minutes, but were soon reduced to about 20 to 40 seconds.

1839: CALOTYPE Just weeks after Daguerre announced his method, English scientist William Henry Fox Talbot introduced the calotype, a technique in which a negative image is developed on paper and could be used to produce endless copies. The British astronomer Sir John Herschel suggested the word "photography" for the process.

1840: CAMERA LENS Hungarian mathematician Josezf Max Petzval of the University of Vienna designed the first lens made specifically for a camera in 1840. The lens gathered almost 15 times more light than other lenses available.

1879: DRY-PLATE PROCESS Charles Harper Bennett invented a gelatin dry-plate process in 1879. Bennett's process eliminated the need for photographers to prepare each plate before taking the picture, and did not require such cumbersome equipment.

1888: KODAK REVOLUTION George Eastman, a dry plate manufacturer in Rochester, NY, introduced the Kodak camera in 1888, with the slogan, "You press the button—we do the rest."

One hitch remained—the camera had to be loaded in a darkroom. The camera came preloaded with enough roll-film to capture 100 pictures; when the film ran out, the camera was mailed to Eastman for processing.

A year later Kodak began selling the Brownie for $1 using 15¢ rolls of film. The affordable "snapshot" was born.

1907: COLOR PHOTOGRAPHY Experiments in color photography began as early as the 1860s, but color processes were not available to the public and usually involved adding color during processing or a special device for viewing images.

Color photography was not commercially available until 1907, when French brothers Auguste and Louis Lumière began marketing their "Autochrome" color process. Autochrome color came from a

layer of red, blue, and green potato starch granules on a glass plate, which selectively exposed the light sensitive layer below.

1924: 35MM CAMERA Ernst Leitz Company, a German optical firm, began marketing the Leica, the first 35mm camera to come into widespread use, in 1924. 35mm cameras used film that was originally intended for motion pictures, and were popular for their compactness. Since then, the 35mm camera has been the camera of choice for both professionals and serious amateurs.

1947: THE FIRST INSTANT PICTURE In 1947 Edwin H. Land invented the Polaroid Land camera, in which the photograph begins to develop right inside the apparatus. The Model 95 went on sale the next year. By 1956, a million Polaroid cameras had been sold.

1986: DISPOSABLE CAMERA Fujifilm began selling the QuickSnap, a single-use camera, in 1986. By 2004, 2 million of the vacation-friendly cameras were sold annually, and disposable camera film made up nearly 20% of developed rolls.

1994: DIGITAL CAMERA Apple introduced its QuickTake 100, the first digital camera meant to be linked to a home computer and used by amateur photographers, in 1994. The camera stored up to 32 images at a resolution of 320 x 240 pixels and cost a little under $1,000. Since then prices have plunged and digital cameras have ballooned in popularity.

POINT, CLICK... DOWNLOAD

In 2003, sales of digital cameras in the United States (12.5 million) surpassed film camera sales (12.1 million) for the first time.

SOMETHING TO THINK ABOUT

SUPERLATIVES

MOST EXPENSIVE CAMERA (AUCTION)
In Jan. 2001, a prototype Phantom camera and its processing accessories sold for $273,065 at Christie's in London, England, shattering the world record for the most expensive camera at auction. The Phantom prototype, which was never commercially manufactured, was designed in 1946 by Noel Pemberton Billing, a former member of the British Parliament.

MOST EXPENSIVE PHOTO In May 2003, Christie's in London auctioned a collection of early daguerreotypes by the pioneer photographer Joseph-Philibert Girault de Prangey. A full plate of the Temple of Jupiter in Athens set a new record auction price for either a daguerreotype or photograph, of $922,488.

LARGEST DIGITAL PHOTOGRAPH
In 2004, the Dutch company TNO Communications produced a photograph with 2.5 billion pixels, 500 times as many as a standard digital image. The picture has not been printed, but if it were, it would measure 22 feet across, and 9 feet tall.

The photo is a composition of 600 overlapping images, all taken automatically with a computer-maneuvered consumer camera. It shows a view of the Dutch town of Delft.

LARGEST PHOTOGRAPHY COLLECTION (U.S.)
The U.S. Library of Congress, which is the largest library in the world, has 12 million photographs in its constantly growing collection. A number of images are available online at www.loc.gov.

The world's biggest museum of photography and film, however, is the George Eastman House in Rochester, NY, with some 400,000 photographs, taken by 14,000 photographers.

Eastman House also has the world's largest collection of American cameras.

Telephones

THE TELEPHONE HAS COME A LONG WAY from the awkward devices of the late 19th century to the small, sleek, cellular models that are an indispensable part of many people's lives today.

◄ *Alexander Graham Bell*

MILESTONES

1876: FIRST TELEPHONE CALL Alexander Graham Bell, a Scottish-born inventor and former teacher of the deaf, said what is widely believed to have been the first sentence over a telephone, on March 10, 1876. According to traditional accounts, Thomas Watson, Bell's assistant, was in the front room of Bell's Boston house awaiting a test of the new invention; as Bell reached for the transmitter, he spilled sulfuric acid on his clothes, so over the phone he cried out, "Mr. Watson, come here, I want to see you."

The details of this story are disputed, but the general idea is not—though there are also other claimants to the invention—see "Something to Think About."

1878: TELEPHONE EXCHANGE The District Telephone Company began operating in New Haven, CT, on Jan. 28, 1878. The switchboard, designed by George W. Coy, served 21 subscribers, and the first operators were teenage boys. Previously, phones had to be directly linked for a call to be made from one to another.

1878: PHONE DIRECTORY The first telephone directory—which listed approximately 50 names on a single page—was issued in New Haven, CT, on Feb. 21, 1878. Most subscribers were businesses.

1879: IN THE WHITE HOUSE Rutherford B. Hayes was the first president to have a phone in the White House; it was installed on May 10, 1879. His first call was to Alexander Graham Bell. After that few calls were actually made from the White House; there weren't many phones to call.

Herbert Hoover was the first president to have a phone on his desk. John F. Kennedy was the first to have a different color than black; he chose turquoise.

1884: LONG DISTANCE The first long-distance call was made on March 27, 1884, between branch managers of the American Bell Telephone Company in Boston and New York. The line worked well for about 90 minutes, then the cable went down somewhere in Connecticut. Public use began Sept. 4.

1886: YELLOW PAGES 21-year-old Reuben H. Donnelley published the first yellow pages business directory on May 15, 1886, for the Chicago Telephone Co.

1889: COIN-OPERATED PHONE William Gray of Hartford, CT, got a patent for a coin-operated telephone on Aug. 13, 1889. The first commercial coin telephone was installed later that year by Southern New England Telephone in the basement of the Hartford National Bank.

1915: TRANS-CONTINENTAL CALL On Jan. 25, 1915, at 4:30 PM EST, Alexander Graham Bell, in New York City, made the first transcontinental call, to San Francisco, CA. After conversing on a modern line, Bell used a model of his first telephone and spoke with his old assistant, Thomas Watson.

When the line opened for public service on March 1, the bill for a three-minute call that distance was $20.70, about $400 in today's dollars.

1956: TRANS-ATLANTIC CABLE After three years of work, a $42 million underwater transatlantic telephone cable, linking the U.S., Canada, and the UK, was activated on Sept. 25, 1956. It ran 2,250 miles from Clarenville, Newfoundland, to Oban, Scotland.

The first conversation took place that day between the chairman of AT&T in New York and the postmaster general in London.

Earlier transatlantic calls had used radio telephony. The new cable could carry 36 calls at a time.

The first fiber optic transatlantic cable, installed in 1988, could handle 40,000 calls at once; later cables handled increasingly more.

1963: PUSH-BUTTON SERVICE The first telephones equipped with "touch tone" push buttons rather than a rotary dial were test-marketed by the Bell System and put into service in Carnegie and Greensburg, PA, on Nov. 18, 1963.

The technology, which enabled calls to be switched digitally, later led to automated menus and functions.

SUPERLATIVES

MOST LAND TELEPHONES As of 2003, China had the most telephone land lines in the world—263 million. Next came the U.S. (181,599,900), Japan (71,149,000), Germany (54,350,000), and India (48,917,000).

MOST CELL PHONES As of 2003, China had the most cell phones of any country in the world—269,000,000. Next came the U.S. (158,722,000), Japan (86,658,600), Germany (64,800,000), and Italy (55,918,000).

HIGHEST RATE OF CELL PHONE SUBSCRIPTIONS At the end of 2003, Taiwan had the highest proportion of cell phone subscriptions, with 110.8 per 100 people, followed by Luxembourg (106.1 per 100 people) and Hong Kong (105.8 per 100). The U.S. ranked 42nd, with 54.3 per 100.

SOMETHING TO THINK ABOUT

YOU MAKE THE CALL

Did Alexander Graham Bell really invent the telephone? Not necessarily. In 1861 the German physicist Johann Philip Reis invented an instrument that could transmit musical tones but not speech. Two other inventors, Oberlin professor Elisha Gray and Italian immigrant Antonio Meucci, were both working on developing a practical telephone at the same time as Bell. Gray filed a caveat, or intention to patent, the same day as Bell, Feb. 14, 1876, but two hours later. When he contested Bell's patent, the U.S. Supreme Court sided with Bell. Meucci had tried to patent his "telectrophone" in 1871 but lacked the funds to complete the process. It is believed that he had set up a working device that allowed him to communicate from room to room with his bedridden wife. Bell's claim was challenged in court but proceedings were delayed and the case was dropped when Meucci died in 1889. In 2002 the U.S. House passed a resolution calling for Meucci's contribution to be recognized.

It also gave rise to *The Pushbutton Telephone Songbook*, which offered directions on how to play 37 tunes on a push-button phone.

Early touch tone phones had only 10 buttons instead of 12; there was no * or #.

1965: SATELLITE Early Bird, the first communications satellite, was launched on April 6, 1956, by Communications Satellite Corp. (COMSAT). It weighed 85 pounds and carried 240 channels for TV, telephone, and data.

On June 28, the first telephone conversation using the satellite took place. The ceremonies involved President Lyndon B. Johnson in Washington, DC, and world leaders in Britain, West Germany, Switzerland, France, and Italy.

Judson LaFlash, an aerospace information specialist in Woodland Hills, CA, made the first commercial satellite call. He spoke with his friend, John Tuttle, in Brussels, Belgium, for 26 minutes, 22 seconds. The call cost $118.80.

1968: 911 In 1967, the Federal Communications Commission had recommended that a single emergency number be adopted by police departments nationwide. AT&T designated 911 as the number; a computer had selected it from numbers not already in use.

The first 911 system went into operation in Haleyville, AL, on Feb. 16, 1968.

1977: CELL PHONE DEMO Early mobile phones were effectively handheld, two-way radios, very limited in range. In Dec. 1977, the first trials of public cell phone service, AT&T's advanced mobile telephone service (AMPS), started in the Chicago area, with 2,000 users. Service was $25 a month for 120 minutes.

Regular service began in Japan in 1979, in Europe in 1981, and in the U.S. in 1982.

Motorola's DynaTAC 8000X was the first handheld cell phone. Available in 1984, it weighed 28 ounces.

1982: AT&T BREAKUP On Jan. 8, 1982, an eight-year-old antitrust suit against AT&T—the world's largest corporation—by the Justice Department was settled, with AT&T agreeing to give up its 22 local Bell System companies, in exchange for being allowed to expand into unregulated areas of business. Seven regional companies took over local phone service from AT&T on Jan. 1, 1984.

1998: INTERNET PHONE SERVICE Internet telephone service—using devices connected to a computer to conduct voice conversations over the Internet to a telephone—was first offered in the U.S. in 1998. The technology utilizes Voice over Internet Protocol (VoIP) software, which was introduced in 1995.

2000: CAMERA PHONE The J-SH04, the first cell phone equipped with a color digital camera, was introduced in Japan in Nov. 2000 by Sharp and J-Phone (now part of Vodafone).

Skyscrapers

WHAT WE CALL SKYSCRAPERS—VERY TALL COMMERCIAL OR RESIDENTIAL BUILDINGS, usually with structural steel frames—began to appear in the late 19th century, as high-strength building materials and safe and efficient modern elevators made it feasible to erect tall buildings in cities, making efficient use of scarce real estate.

This section covers only buildings where at least 50% of the height consists of floors used for residences or businesses. In accordance with standards set by the Council on Tall Buildings and Urban Habitat, height is measured from sidewalk level at the main entrance. Spires, domes, parapets, included; antennas, flagpoles, etc. excluded, unless otherwise noted.

MILESTONES

1885: FIRST STEEL-FRAMED SKYSCRAPER The first skyscraper was the Home Insurance Building in Chicago, IL, built in 1885. Designed by William Le Baron Jenney, it was the first tall building entirely supported by a metal frame.

The building, encased in brownstone, originally had 10 floors, rising 138 feet up. In 1890, two more floors were added, bringing the total height of the building to 180 feet. It was demolished in 1931.

1903: FIRST REINFORCED CONCRETE SKYSCRAPER The first skyscraper built from reinforced concrete was the Ingalls Building in Cincinnati, OH, completed in 1903. Designed by Alfred O. Elzner and George M. Anderson, it had 16 floors and stood 212 feet high. While it was built out of reinforced concrete, the façade was made of marble and glazed brick decorated with terra-cotta.

SUPERLATIVES

WORLD'S TALLEST BUILDING Taipei 101, located in Taipei, Taiwan, is currently the tallest building in the world. Standing 1,666 feet tall with 101 stories, it was completed in 2004, and surpassed the twin Petronas Towers in Kuala Lumpur, Malaysia, which, at 1,483 feet, had held the title since 1996.

Designed by C. Y. Lee & Partners, Taipei 101 would have been 350 feet higher, but was shortened to avoid obstructing airplane paths. It also holds the titles of tallest building measured to the roof, at 1,474 feet, and highest occupied floor, at 1,441 feet.

The Sears Tower in Chicago still holds the record for tallest building as measured to the tip of the antenna—1,729 feet.

TALLEST ALL-RESIDENTIAL BUILDING Q1 in Gold Coast, Australia, is the world's tallest all-residential building. Completed in 2005, it stands 1,058 feet tall (including spire), with 78 stories.

In recent years the title of the world's tallest all-residential building has changed several times. Lake Point Tower in Chicago held the record from 1968 to 1993 at 645 feet. Tregunter 3 in Hong Kong reigned from 1993 to 2001 at 721 feet. The Trump World Tower in New York City took the title in 2001 at 861 feet, until it was topped by the 21st Century Tower in Dubai at 883 feet in 2003.

Currently, there are at least three residential towers in Dubai that have just begun construction and will be taller than Q1. The exact heights of the buildings have not been confirmed.

HIGHEST RESIDENTIAL UNIT The world's highest residential units are located on the 92nd floor of the John Hancock Center in Chicago, at 1,003 feet.

Skyscraper Firsts by Height

MILESTONE	BUILDING	HEIGHT	FLOORS	YEAR COMPLETED
300+ ft	World Building, New York, NY*	309 ft	20	1890 (demolished 1955)
500+ ft	Singer Building, New York, NY	612 ft	47	1908 (demolished 1968)
700+ ft	Metropolitan Life Insurance Tower, New York, NY	700 ft	50	1909
1,000+ ft	Chrysler Building, New York, NY	1,046 ft	77	1930
1,200+ ft	Empire State Building, New York, NY	1,250 ft	102	1931
1,300+ ft	One World Trade Center, New York, NY	1,368 ft	110	1972 (destroyed 2001)
1,400+ ft	Sears Tower, Chicago, IL	1,450 ft	108	1974
1,500+ ft	Taipei 101, Taipei, Taiwan	1,666 ft	101	2004

* *The New York World* was the original publisher of *The World Almanac.*

The lower floors of "Big John" contain stores, offices, garages, a swimming pool, an ice rink, and even a "Cheesecake Factory."

TALLEST HOTEL The world's tallest hotel is the Burj Al Arab Hotel in Dubai, United Arab Emirates. Built in the shape of an Arab sailing vessel known as a *dhow*, the hotel stands 1,053 feet tall (including spire), with 202 two-story suites on 60 stories.

Completed in 1999, the Burj Al Arab is located on a man-made island and is the world's first seven-star hotel.

The Rose Tower in Dubai, which is under construction and scheduled to be completed in 2006, will be 1,093 feet with 72 stories. Rotana will be the hotel tenant.

HIGHEST HOTEL ROOM The world's highest hotel rooms are on the 85th floor of the Jin Mao Tower in Shanghai, at just over 1,069 ft.

The 88-story tower, located in Shanghai's financial district, is also the world's tallest "mixed-use" building. The first 50 floors are used for offices. The next 37 are occupied by the Grand Hyatt Shanghai hotel. The tower's 555 guest rooms are located from the 53rd to the 85th floors.

TALLEST BUILDINGS EVER DESTROYED The tallest and largest buildings ever destroyed were the Twin Towers of the World Trade Center in New York City. Tower One stood 1,368 feet, and Tower Two, 1,362 feet. The towers were felled by a terrorist attack on the morning of Sept. 11, 2001. Each building collapsed when a fire caused by direct hits on each of the skyscrapers by hijacked aircraft melted the steel framework. Approximately 2,800 people were killed, including all passengers and crew aboard the two planes.

The Towers had been a terrorist target in 1993, but the buildings survived the bomb blast in a basement-level garage.

At the time of the Towers' completion in 1972 (Tower One) and 1973 (Tower Two), they were the tallest buildings in the world. Two years later, the Sears Tower in Chicago overtook them.

TALLEST BUILDING EVER DEMOLISHED The tallest building ever demolished under controlled circumstances is the Singer Building in New York City. Completed in 1908, it stood 612 feet tall. In 1967-68 it was dismantled and demolished, along with the 487-foot City Investing Co. Building, to make room for a 54-story office building for U.S. Steel.

TALLEST BUILDING EVER IMPLODED The tallest building ever imploded is the J.L. Hudson Building of Detroit, MI. Standing 397 feet tall, with 26 stories, the Hudson Building was completed in 1928. Once the world's tallest department store, the Hudson was imploded using 2,728 pounds of plastic explosives on Oct. 24, 1998.

SOMETHING TO THINK ABOUT

FASTEST ELEVATORS

The world's fastest elevators are located in Taipei 101, the world's tallest building. Two of the 67 elevators there, the bullet-shaped observation-deck shuttles, travel upward in 43 seconds at a 37 mph (3,314 feet per minute) and downward in 52 seconds at 23 mph. They are 35% faster than the previous record holders in Yokohama's Landmark Tower, which is also Japan's tallest building. Ceramic braking shoes are used, since temperatures would melt traditional bronze brakes. A special system was developed to equalize pressure inside the elevator as it descends, to avoid ruptured eardrums.

TALLEST BUILDING IN AN EARTHQUAKE ZONE

The world's tallest building, Taipei 101, stands 1,666 feet tall, and is located in an earthquake-prone area. During a major earthquake on Mar. 31, 2002, two construction cranes fell from the 56th floor of Taipei 101, killing five people and crushing four cars.

SKYSCRAPER CENTRAL

For most of the 20th century, the center of the skyscraper universe was North America. In 1980, the top ten tallest buildings in the world were all located in North America. In the last quarter-century that situation has changed radically. Today, the center of the skyscraper universe is Asia. Currently, 8 of the 10 tallest buildings in the world are located in Asia. Five of these are in China (including Hong Kong), which also has more buildings 500 feet or higher than any other country (the U.S. is second).

Other Large Structures

FOR OVER 4,000 YEARS—LONG BEFORE THE SKYSCRAPER—the world's tallest and probably most impressive structure was the 480-foot-tall Great Pyramid at Giza. It was surpassed in 1880 when the spire of Cologne Cathedral was built in in Cologne, Germany (513 feet). But big buildings can be impressive whether they are big vertically or horizontally. From traditional structures built in Africa 100 years ago to immense modern-day manufacturing plants, here's a look at some record-holders.

SUPERLATIVES

BIGGEST BUILDING The Boeing Co. airplane assembly plant in Everett, WA, is the biggest building in the world by volume (more than 472 million cubic feet). The plant, which produces 747, 767, and 777 wide-body commercial jets, covers 98.3 acres.

Boeing's massive plant started at 205 million cubic feet in 1968, and was expanded to its current size in 1993.

BIGGEST OFFICE BUILDING U.S. The Pentagon in Arlington, VA, is the largest office building in the U.S., with a volume of 77 million cubic feet covering 29 acres. Construction on the Pentagon, which is the headquarters of the U.S. Dept. of Defense with over 23,000 civilian and military employees, was completed on Jan. 15, 1943, only 16 months after it began.

The Pentagon contains more than 17.5 miles of corridors, but was so efficiently designed that it takes no more than seven minutes to walk between any two points.

LARGEST PARLIAMENT BUILDING The Palace of the Parliament in Bucharest, Romania, is the world's largest Parliament building and one of the world's biggest buildings, with a floor area of nearly 86.5 acres. Opened in 1984, when it was known as the People's Palace, it's 12 stories (282 feet) tall and has additional levels sinking 302 feet into the ground.

The footprint of the building is 787 by 886 feet.

BIGGEST AIRPORT TERMINAL Hong Kong International Airport, which opened in July 1998, is home to the world's largest terminal building. The Y-shaped structure is 0.8 miles (4,167 feet) long from entrance to end and covers 141 acres. It was the eighth busiest passenger airport in 2004 and can process up to 55 flights per hour.

Travelers don't have to hoof it in the vast terminal. An internal shuttle train called the APM (Automated People Mover) departs at least every three minutes and can carry 152 passengers from one end of the terminal to the other, traveling at 38 mph.

BIGGEST DOMED STRUCTURE The Millennium Dome, which is located on the prime meridian line of longitude in London, England, is the largest domed structure in the world. The dome is 1,050 feet in diameter and encloses about 77.7 million cubic feet of space. It's made of translucent Teflon-coated fiberglass, supported by 12,328-foot-long masts and a web of 2,600 cables.

Designed by Richard Rogers, it hosted 10,500 people for London's millennium celebration on Dec. 31, 1999. Officially opening to the general public the next day, the dome housed exhibitions in honor of the new millennium, but closed a year later. It was renamed "The 02" in 2005 and is scheduled to reopen in April 2007 as a sports and entertainment arena.

The 02 may also host events for the 2012 Olympic Games.

The Georgia Dome in Atlanta, completed in 1992, is the largest domed structure in the U.S. Its Teflon-coated fiberglass roof is 840 feet in diameter.

BIGGEST ATRIUM The lobby of the 30-story, pyramid-shaped Luxor resort in Las Vegas, NV, is actually a 29 million-cubic-foot atrium—complete with a 35-foot-tall life-sized replica of the Great Temple of Ramses II. Guests enter the Luxor, which opened in 1993, through a model of the Sphinx, and reach their rooms via "inclinators," or elevators that travel at a 39-degree angle along the inside of the atrium.

The Burj-al Arab hotel in Dubai, United Arab Emirates, claims the tallest atrium at 590 feet.

Rollercoasters

CATEGORY	RIDE (YEAR BUILT)	LOCATION	RECORD
Tallest	Kingda Ka (2005)	Six Flags Great Adventure, Jackson, NJ	456 ft high
Longest (wooden)	The Beast (1979)	Paramount's King Island, Kings Mill, OH	7,400 ft long
Longest (steel)	Steel Dragon (2000)	Nagashima Resort, Japan	8,133 ft long

Kingda Ka ▶

◀ The Pentagon

LARGEST AQUARIUM The Georgia Aquarium, which opened in Nov. 2005 in Atlanta, is the world's largest. More than 8 million gallons of fresh and salt water are contained in its 505,000 square feet of space. The underwater zoo is home to 100,000 creatures representing over 500 species, including two giant whale sharks (the only two in captivity in the U.S.), two beluga whales, and many other sea creatures.

Home Depot co-founder Bernard Marcus donated the $200 million in funds to build the facility, explaining his donation with a simple, "I love big fish, OK?"

LARGEST MUD BUILDING The Grand Mosque in Djenné, Mali, is the largest mud-brick building in the world. The house of worship measures 328 feet long and 131 feet wide, with walls that vary in width between 16 and 24 inches.

Though the building is considered an architectural and historic treasure, it is not the first Grand Mosque built on the site. The original building, completed in the 13th century, was used until 1835, when it was abandoned and fell into disrepair.

The current building, constructed in 1906-07, requires careful maintenance, especially during and after Mali's rainy season.

BIGGEST BASEBALL STADIUM (CAPACITY) The New York Yankees don't just have the most World Series titles (26 through the 2005 season); they also have the biggest stadium capacity in Major League Baseball, with room for 57,545 fans. The Yanks played their inaugural game in "The House That Ruth Built" on April 18, 1923, versus their rivals, the Boston Red Sox.

The Yankee organization built the stadium in the Bronx after being asked to leave the Polo Grounds, where they had split field time with their landlords, the New York Giants baseball team. Yankee Stadium was the first ballpark with three decks, or levels, of seating.

In 2005, the Bronx Bombers announced plans to begin building a new Yankee Stadium with 51,000 seats, set to open not far from its current site in 2009.

LARGEST RETRACTABLE ROOF U.S. Houston's Reliant Stadium, home to the NFL's Houston Texans since 2002, has the largest retractable roof in the U.S. Each half is 240 feet long by 385 feet wide, and the total roof area is 4.25 acres. Two 984-foot rails allow the roof's two halves to open and close, depending on weather conditions. It takes 40 motors about ten minutes to open or close the roof.

The stadium can hold 69,500 football fans. Super Bowl XXXVIII was played (with the roof closed) at Reliant Stadium on Feb. 1, 2004.

LONGEST SKI LIFT Silver Mountain Ski Resort's 3.1-mile-long gondola lift, which opened in Kellogg, ID, in 1990, is the longest uninterrupted single stage ski lift in the world.

Powered by a 1,500-horsepower electric motor, the gondola ascends the mountain at 1,000 feet per minute (about 11 mph). Its 112 cabins can carry 1,600 people per hour up the 4,000-foot ascent. Forty-five towers hold up the 34,450-foot haul rope.

BIGGEST RADIO TELESCOPE The Arecibo radio telescope at the National Astronomy and Ionosphere Center near Arecibo, Puerto Rico, measures 1,000 feet in diameter and 167 feet deep. The bowl-shaped aluminum-paneled dish covers about 20 acres. The panels focus incoming radio waves from outer space onto a detecting platform suspended 450 feet above the dish.

The telescope can also transmit signals, and has been used for radar-reflection studies of the moon and other bodies in the solar system.

LARGEST SPACE ENVIRONMENT SIMULATION CHAMBER The Space Power Facility (SPF), located at NASA's Glenn Research Center in Sandusky, OH, is the world's largest space environment simulation chamber (and largest vacuum chamber). The aluminum chamber is 100 feet wide and 122 feet tall.

SPF recreates the environment hundreds of miles above earth. It can create a high vacuum and temperatures down to -320 °F or simulate solar radiation. The Mars Pathfinder spacecraft and International Space Station hardware are among the many innovations tested there.

Religious Structures

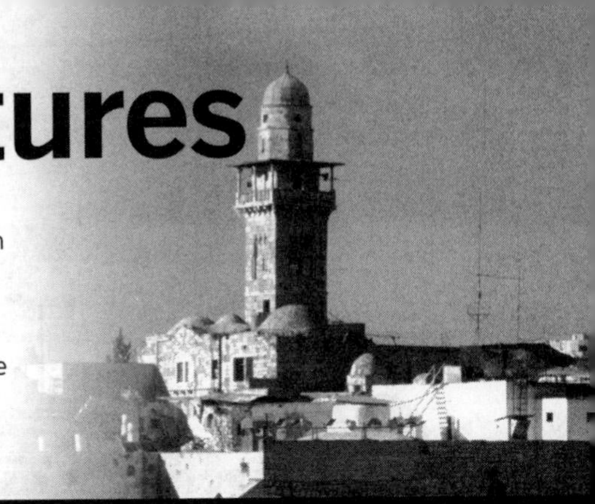

ABOUT TWO-THIRDS OF THE WORLD'S POPULATION BELONGS to one of three religions—Christianity, Islam, or Hinduism—and perhaps five out of six people in the world are affiliated with one religion or another. The churches, mosques, and temples of these faiths are among the world's greatest buildings. Holy places may sometimes be important to more than one religion. Temple Mount in Jerusalem, for example, is important to Jews, Muslims, and Christians, while many sites in India are holy to both Hindus and Muslims.

SUPERLATIVES

OLDEST CHURCH
Several buildings in Syria claim the title of oldest surviving Christian place of worship.

The oldest church in the world still in use is often said to be the church of St. Sergius and Bacchus at Maaloula, Syria. Built on the site of a pagan temple, it has an altar with a rim designed to catch the blood of pre-Christian sacrifices—indicating that the church was built earlier than 325 AD.

There are also several candidates for the oldest known church building. Many archaeologists think that an 85-by-53-foot mud-brick structure excavated at Al Aqabah, Jordan (the Roman port of Aila), may date from about 300 AD, making it the oldest known church.

OLDEST JEWISH TEMPLE The famous Wailing Wall in Jerusalem is the surrounding wall of the Second Temple in Jerusalem (built 515 BC). It is all that remains of that structure, which was destroyed by the Romans in 70 AD, and it is still a holy site for Jews.

The First Temple, known as the Temple of Solomon (built in the 10th century BC), was entirely destroyed by the Babylonians in 586 BC. The Second Temple was built in the same place—in the area known as Temple Mount in Jerusalem—after the Jews returned from exile in Babylon.

OLDEST MOSQUE
The first mosques were built during the life of the Prophet Muhammad (570–632 AD). Muhammad built the first mosque, Masjid al-Nabi (Mosque of the Prophet), in Medina, Saudi Arabia, after fleeing Mecca in 622. Upon his death, Muhammad was buried alongside the mosque.

Over the years, the mosque has been expanded to over 100 times the size of its original fifth-of-an-acre plot, and it is considered the second holiest place in Islam, after Mecca.

OLDEST MINARET
In the earliest mosques, the call to prayer was given directly from the roof of the mosque itself. The use of a minaret, the tower from which the faithful are called to prayer, began with the Mosque of Kairouan in Tunisia. It is thought to have been an adaptation of the square towers of early Christian churches in pre-Islamic Syria.

The lowest section of Kairouan's minaret dates from before 730 AD.

OLDEST BUDDHIST SANCTUARY
The oldest Buddhist sanctuary is believed to be at Sanchi, near Bhopal, India, and dates from about 250 BC.

Located there is the 54-foot Great Stupa, a burial monument begun by the Mauryan king Asoka. It is also the oldest stone structure in India.

LARGEST RELIGIOUS STRUCTURE The world's largest religious structure is Angkor Wat Temple in Cambodia. An immense rectangle covering about 400 acres, Angkor Wat contains concentric walled courtyards surrounding a central structure with five graceful lotus-shaped towers. It was built in the 12th century by King Suryavarman II as a Hindu temple to celebrate the king as the incarnation of the god Vishnu.

In the 12th and 13th centuries, it was used as a Buddhist temple. Around 1431, the city of Angkor was abandoned, and over the following centuries Angkor Wat fell into obscurity.

LARGEST RELIGIOUS STRUCTURE (WOOD)
The world's largest wooden religious structure is the Great Hall of Buddha at Todai-ji Temple at Nara, Japan. Enclosed in the Horyu-ji area along with 40 other buildings, the hall measures 154 feet high, 164 feet long, and 187 feet wide. Rebuilt in 1709 after a fire, it is now only one-third the size of the original structure. It contains the largest metal Buddha statue, which stands about 46 feet high.

The Horyu-ji complex also contains pre-eighth-century Buddhist monuments and, some of the oldest wooden buildings in the Far East.

LARGEST CHURCH
The biggest church in the world is the Basilica of Notre Dame de la Paix (Our Lady of Peace) at Yamoussoukro, the official capital of Côte d'Ivoire in Africa.

SOMETHING TO THINK ABOUT

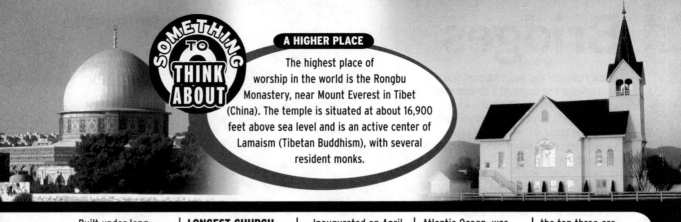

A HIGHER PLACE

The highest place of worship in the world is the Rongbu Monastery, near Mount Everest in Tibet (China). The temple is situated at about 16,900 feet above sea level and is an active center of Lamaism (Tibetan Buddhism), with several resident monks.

Built under long-time president Félix Houphouët-Boigny in his home town, the church was completed in 1989 after just three years. It has the world's highest dome at 489 feet, and seats about 7,000. Pope John Paul II consecrated the Basilica of Notre Dame de la Paix on Sept. 10, 1990.

LARGEST CATHEDRAL

The world's largest cathedral, and the largest U.S. church, is the unfinished Episcopal Cathedral of St. John the Divine in New York City, with a floor area of about 120,000 square feet. The cathedral has the longest nave in the world (601 ft) but lacks its towers and transept. The temporary Gustavino dome, finished in 1911, is 162 feet high.

Construction began in 1892 and has yet to be completed.

LONGEST CHURCH

The longest church in the world is the Spanish Civil War memorial basilica Santa Cruz del Valle de los Caidos (Holy Cross of the Valley of the Fallen) in the Guadarrama Mountains, 25 miles north of Madrid, Spain. A huge crypt tunneled out of solid granite, the church is 853 feet long. It was built by the dictator Francisco Franco, who came to power after his victory in the Spanish Civil War (1936-39). His remains are buried in the basilica.

Valle de Cuelgamuros, on top of the hill from which the church was carved, is the world's tallest free-standing cross, at 500 feet high.

BIGGEST MORMON TEMPLE The largest Latter-day Saints temple is the Tabernacle in Salt Lake City, UT. Construction began in 1853; it was not completed until 1892.

Inaugurated on April 6, 1893, the six-spire temple covers an entire city block and has a total floor area of 253,015 square feet. Its walls are 9 feet thick at the base and its central spire tips off at 233.5 feet.

TALLEST SPIRE

At 528 feet, the tallest church spire is atop the Lutheran Cathedral of Ulm, in southern Germany near Munich. Although the building was begun in 1377, the spire was not completed until 1890.

LARGEST MOSQUE

The Holy Mosque in Mecca (Masjid Al Haram) is the largest mosque in the world, with a total area of about 2 million square feet. It can accomodate more than a million worshippers.

TALLEST MINARET

The world's tallest minaret is that of the Great Mosque Hassan II in Casablanca, Morocco. The mosque, which juts out over the Atlantic Ocean, was completed in 1993. The minaret of the mosque is 656 feet high and houses a green laser beam that points toward Mecca.

BIGGEST SYNAGOGUE

Temple Emanu-El, in New York City, is the biggest synagogue in the world. Built between 1927 and 1929, it has a main sanctuary measuring 147-by-77 feet. Its ceiling rises to 103 feet. There are no interior supporting pillars, which allows for a vast interior space; Temple Emanu-El can seat about 2,500 worshippers.

BIGGEST BUDDHIST TEMPLE The temple of Borobudur, near Jogyakarta, Indonesia, built around 800 AD, with about 2 million cubic feet of gray stone, has more than 3 miles of corridors. These include eight step-like stone terraces; the bottom five are square while the top three are circular and ringed with 72 small stupas—domes built to house a statue of the Buddha. A large 103-foot-tall stupa crowns the top.

The temple was buried under volcanic ash around 1000 but was rediscovered in the early 1800s.

BIGGEST BUDDHA

The world's biggest statue of the Buddha is at Ushiku Arcadia Park, 30 miles north of Tokyo, Japan. The statue, which was completed in 1993, is 328 feet tall (394 ft including its base and platform), twice the height of the Statue of Liberty. It weighs an estimated 4,000 tons.

Bridges

DOWN THROUGH THE AGES BRIDGES HAVE CHALLENGED THE INGENUITY OF BUILDERS and captured the imagination of travelers. Bridges made from twisted vines, bamboo, and other natural materials existed in early antiquity in many parts of the world. Stone bridges were constructed by the Chinese as long ago as 2000 BC, and by Babylonians about 1800 BC. References to a beam bridge, the Ju Bridge, in China date to the Shang dynasty (began 16th century BC).

The Millau Viaduct

SUPERLATIVES

OLDEST BRIDGE
U.S Built in 1697, the stone-arch Frankford Avenue Bridge crosses Pennypack Creek in Philadelphia, PA. A three-span bridge with a length of 75 feet, it was part of the King's Road that connected Philadelphia to New York in colonial times.

The oldest covered bridge, completed in 1827, is the double-span, 278-foot Haverhill Bath Bridge, which spans the Ammonoosuc River in New Hampshire.

OLDEST BRIDGE (IRON) The Iron Bridge spanning 100 feet over the Severn River near Coalbrooke, England, was the first bridge constructed entirely from cast iron. Completed in 1779, it is supported by five arched iron ribs mounted on cast iron bed plates.

LONGEST BRIDGE
The two parallel causeways that run nearly 24 miles across Lake Pontchartrain, a large tidal estuary north of New Orleans, LA, are the world's longest bridges. They connect Metarie on the southern shore to Mandeville on the northern shore. The spans consist of prestressed concrete sections supported by over 9,000 concrete pilings. The first span was completed on Aug. 30, 1956, the second on May 10, 1969. Although they were damaged after Hurricane Katrina hit the area on Aug. 29, 2005, they were able to be reopened a few weeks later.

LONGEST BRIDGE (AUTO-RAIL) During the last Ice Age, Denmark and Sweden were connected by ice. It took until July 1, 2000, for them to be rejoined. The two-level Øresund Bridge between Zealand, Denmark, and Skåne, Sweden, is the world's longest single bridge built for both automobiles and trains. The cable-stayed bridge is 25,738 feet long. Its longest span is 1,614 feet.

LONGEST SUSPENSION BRIDGE
Completed in 1998, the Akashi-Kaikyo Bridge in Kobe-Naruto, Japan, has a main span 6,532 feet long.

This bridge endured a scary moment while under construction. On Jan. 17, 1995, a 6.9-magnitude earthquake struck the area, destroying about 50,000 buildings. The bridge towers moved

Some Other Bridge Records

TYPE	BRIDGE	LENGTH*	COMPLETED
Longest Steel-Arch Bridge	Lupu Bridge, China	1,800 ft	2003
Longest Steel-Arch Bridge (U.S.)	New River Gorge Bridge, Fayetteville, WV	1,700 ft	1977
Longest Concrete-Arch Bridge	Wanxian Bridge, Wanzhou, China	1,378 ft	1997
Longest Continuous-Truss Bridge	Columbia River, OR-WA	1,232 ft	1966
Longest Steel-Plate-and-Box-Girder Bridge	Ponte Costa e Silva Bridge, Rio de Janeiro, Brazil	984 ft	1974

*Length of main span.

SOMETHING TO THINK ABOUT

BRIDGE STEALING

In 2004, a rash of bridge thefts spanned the globe. In February, a 36-foot steel bridge over the river Svalyavka in the Ukraine was stolen, isolating an entire town. In August another bridge, weighing 400 tons, was being stored in a warehouse in Gdansk, Poland, when its owners returned to find it gone. Later in August, thieves dismantled and made off with an entire 40-foot bridge near the Bosnian town of Mostar; the men were sighted loading steel beams into a van and were eventually tracked down.

"GALLOPING GERTIE"

On Nov. 7, 1940, at about 11 AM, the first Tacoma Narrows suspension bridge in Washington State collapsed as a result of strong wind-induced vibrations. An hour before the bridge gave way, state officials had closed it in response to its wave-like movements. "Galloping Gertie" claimed one victim, a dog trapped in a car abandoned on the bridge, and the disaster became especially famous because the structure's twisting and buckling was captured on film. The bridge ruins were placed on the National Register of Historic Places in 1992.

ELEPHANT WALK

The most celebrated engineering feat of its day, the Brooklyn Bridge, with a span of 1,596 feet, was the world's longest suspension bridge when it opened on May 24, 1883. The following year impresario P.T. Barnum marched a herd of 21 elephants, including the colossal "Jumbo," across the span. He said he did it in the public interest to prove that the structure was solid. Maybe, but the publicity certainly didn't hurt.

almost 3 feet apart, but the bridge stood strong and opened with great fanfare three years later.

LONGEST SUSPENSION BRIDGE U.S The Verrazano-Narrows Bridge, which connects the New York City boroughs of Brooklyn and Staten Island, has a main span of 4,260 feet. Because of its length, the towers are 1.5 inches farther apart at their tops than at the base to compensate for the curvature of the earth.

Building the bridge's approaches in a densely populated Brooklyn neighborhood required the demolition of some 800 buildings and the relocation of 7,000 residents. Meanwhile, the population of Staten Island more than doubled after the bridge opened in 1964.

LONGEST CANTILEVER BRIDGE With a central span of 1,800 feet, the Quebec Bridge spanning the Saint Lawrence River in Quebec City, Canada, is the world's longest cantilever bridge (supported in the middle by "cantilever" beams that are anchored by a load on one end).

Unfortunately, it took some time to get it right. Before the bridge was completed on Oct. 17, 1917, sections of it collapsed twice—on Aug. 29, 1907 and on Sept. 11, 1916. The first time, 75 workers died; the second time, 11.

LONGEST CANTILEVER BRIDGE U.S The two Greater New Orleans Bridges, also called the Crescent City Connection, were completed April 1958 and Sept. 1988, and cross the Mississippi River in Louisiana with a span of 1,575 feet.

Before Hurricane Katrina, they were the fifth most traveled toll bridge in the U.S. Although they were undamaged, traffic levels fell considerably.

LONGEST CABLE-STAYED BRIDGE U.S The Arthur Ravenel Jr Bridge spans the Cooper River near Charleston, SC, and opened on July 16, 2005, with a span of 1,546 feet. It replaced the Grace and Pearman bridges—two truss bridges that spanned the river nearby. The demolition of the two older bridges will be completed in 2006.

HIGHEST VEHICULAR BRIDGE The Millau Viaduct, designed by British architect Norman Foster, runs across the river Tarn in the Massif Central mountain range in southwestern France. The bridge opened to traffic Dec. 16, 2004. The deck reaches a maximum height of 885 feet above the water, and the top of its tallest tower is 1,125 feet high—higher than the 984-foot Eiffel Tower.

HIGHEST BRIDGE U.S The Royal Gorge Bridge in Cañon City, CO, is the world's highest suspension bridge. Its deck hangs 1,053 feet over the Arkansas River, but its towers do not extend into the gorge and it does not carry a highway. Now listed on the National Historic Register, the bridge cost $350,000 to build, and opened on Dec. 8, 1929.

MOST BRIDGES (CITY) Hamburg, Germany, located on the Elbe and Alster rivers, near the North Sea, has 2,302 bridges within its confines.

Tunnels & Dams

DAMS AND TUNNELS have been around in some form since ancient times; today these engineering marvels play key roles in the economy, affecting energy, water resources, and transportation.

> "This morning I came, I saw, and I was conquered, as everyone would be who sees for the first time this great feat of mankind."
>
> —President Franklin D. Roosevelt at the opening of the Hoover Dam, Sept. 30, 1935

MILESTONES

2498 BC: OLDEST KNOWN DAM The Sadd el-Kafara dam was built across the Wadi el-Garawi near Helwan, Egypt, by about 2498 BC. It took 10-15 years to construct the 348-foot-long dam, which was 78 feet wide at the base and filled with rubble. It held an estimated 21,188,800-cubic-foot reservoir of water.

The dam was probably breeched before long; it was rediscovered in 1885 by the German archaeologist George Schweinfurth.

1594: TIBI DAM The Tibi dam on the Monegre River near Alicante, Spain, was the world's tallest, at 135 feet, for centuries after its completion in 1594. It is the oldest dam still in use in Europe.

1821: FIRST TRANSPORTATION TUNNEL (U.S.) Completed in 1821, the Orwigsburg Water Tunnel was dug by the Schuylkill Navigation Company along the Schuylkill River at Landingville, PA. It was 450 feet long and 20 feet wide. Later its roof was slowly removed and it eventually became an open-cut canal.

A 729-foot tunnel on the nearby Union Canal at Lebanon, PA, is the oldest tunnel in the U.S. today.

1832: RAILROAD TUNNEL (U.S.) Staple Bend Tunnel on the Allegheny Portage Railroad, near Johnstown, PA, was the first railroad tunnel in the U.S.

The tunnel was later abandoned, but has been restored by the National Park Service.

1841: UNDERWATER TUNNEL French engineer Marc Brunel developed the tunneling shield, which allowed tunnel construction through the soft mud under navigable rivers. Inspired by watching a mollusk tunnel through wood aided by a hard lining around its mouth, Brunel theorized that tunnel diggers could be shielded in an iron box with a removable front.

Brunel began construction on the twin-arch Thames Tunnel in London on March 2, 1825. After floods, fatalities, and delays, the 1,200-foot-long tunnel was finished on Nov. 16, 1841.

1927: HOLLAND TUNNEL The first tunnel built specifically for motor vehicles under a navigable river in the U.S. linked Manhattan and Jersey City, NJ. The twin 8,558-foot and 8,371-foot tubes opened Nov. 12, 1927.

Although the name conjures up visions of tulips and windmills, it was chosen to honor the tunnel's deceased first chief engineer, Clifford Holland.

Vehicle exhaust was the big obstacle to constructing a tunnel for road traffic. To surmount this problem, Holland's 2nd successor, Ole Singstad, developed a two-duct system that used one duct to draw in fresh air and another to suck out exhaust. His innovation became a model for tunnel builders.

1935: HOOVER DAM On Sept. 30, 1935, in the midst of the Great Depression, President Franklin D. Roosevelt dedicated the Hoover Dam, one of history's greatest engineering achievements. Situated on the Colorado River between Nevada and Arizona, the 726.4-foot dam transformed life in the Southwest by supplying electrical power, irrigation, and flood control.

Despite the dangerous working conditions, hot weather, and remote location, the mighty concrete structure was completed two years ahead of schedule.

1968: ASWAN HIGH DAM Egypt's Aswan High Dam was completed in 1968. Its 365-foot high embankment extends across the Nile, and made Lake Nasser one of the world's largest reservoirs.

The expanding lake flooded much of Lower Nubia, which was full of monumental sites. An international effort led by UNESCO saved most of the buildings. For example, two temples carved into a sandstone cliff at Abu Simbel about 1250 BC, during the reign of Ramses II, were cut into 1,036 pieces and reassembled on a cliff 196 feet above its original spot.

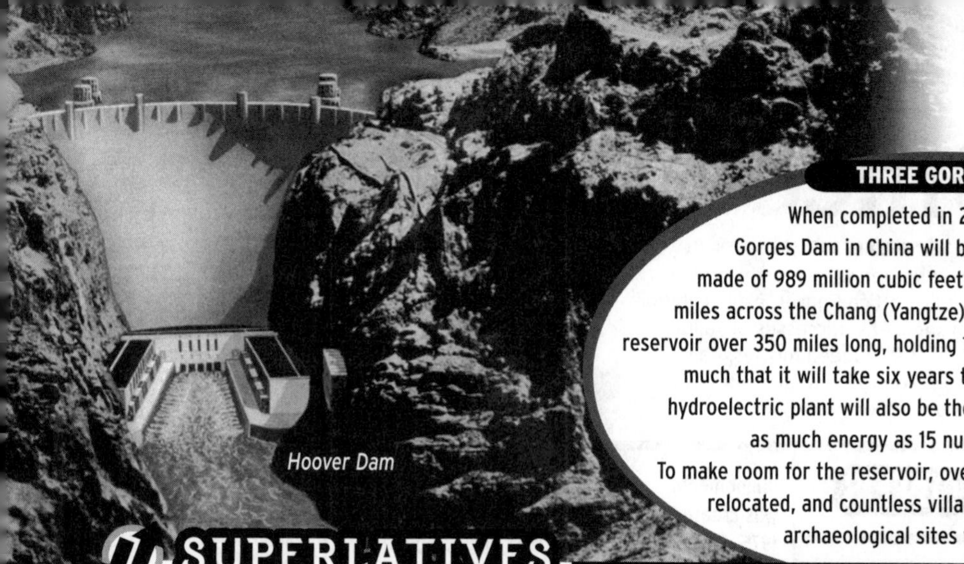

Hoover Dam

SOMETHING TO THINK ABOUT

THREE GORGES DAM

When completed in 2009, the Three Gorges Dam in China will be the world's largest, made of 989 million cubic feet of concrete. Spanning 1.4 miles across the Chang (Yangtze) River, the dam will create a reservoir over 350 miles long, holding 1.39 trillion cubic feet of water, so much that it will take six years to fill. Its 18,200-megawatt hydroelectric plant will also be the world's largest, generating as much energy as 15 nuclear power plants.

To make room for the reservoir, over 1.2 million people are being relocated, and countless villages, burial grounds, and archaeological sites will be flooded.

SUPERLATIVES

LONGEST TUNNEL The Delaware Aqueduct (completed in 1944) that brings water from the Delaware River Basin to New York City contains a tunnel about 85 miles long, from Roundout Reservoir in the Catskill Mountains to Hillview Reservoir in Yonkers, just north of New York City.

LONGEST RAILROAD TUNNEL Japan's Seikan Tunnel, opened in March 1988, connects the islands of Honshu and Hokkaido. For 14.5 of its 33.5 miles it runs 330 feet beneath the seabed. The engineering problems were such that it took 24 years to build.

Three of the four longest railway tunnels are now in Japan. However, when Switzerland's Gotthard AlpTransit tunnel is finished, around 2015, it will be the world's longest, 2 miles longer than Seikan.

LONGEST ROAD TUNNEL The 15.2-mile Laerdal Tunnel in Norway links the cities of Oslo and Bergen. Construction started in March 1995. At its opening on Nov. 27, 2000, a musician blew on a *bukkehorn* (ram's horn) to attract mountain "trolls," played by children dressed in colorful costumes.

LONGEST UNDERWATER TUNNEL The world's longest undersea tunnel is the Channel Tunnel, or "Chunnel," connecting England and France. The Chunnel has two railroad tunnels for freight and passenger trains and a third service tunnel. Passengers may ride the trains or stay in their own vehicles, which can be loaded on specially built rail cars.

The Chunnel opened in May 1994. The span running under the English Channel is 23.6 miles long.

The Brooklyn Battery Tunnel is the longest underwater vehicular tunnel in North America, spanning 9,117 feet underneath New York's East River. It opened May 25, 1950.

TALLEST DAM The Nurek Dam on the Vakhsh River in Tajikistan is 984 feet high above its lowest formation and operates the largest power station in Central Asia. However, the Rogun Dam, also in Tajikistan, will be nearly 1100 feet high when it's completed.

At 770 feet, the tallest in the U.S. is the Oroville Dam, on the Feather River in California.

LARGEST-VOLUME DAM If you go by sheer volume, Syncrude Tailings Dam in Alberta, Canada, is by far the world's biggest dam, at 706,320,000 cubic yards. However, this mammoth dam was not designed for the purpose of holding back water. It's composed of the piled-up material left over from mining operations, and holds back water by its sheer bulk. As mining continues the dam expands.

The New Cornelia Tailings in Ten Mile Wash, AZ, is the largest in the U.S., at 274,026,000 cubic yards.

LARGEST EMBANKMENT DAM Tarbela Dam, completed in 1976 on the Indus River in Pakistan, contains 165 million cubic yards of earth and rock in the main dam, the largest volume for an embankment dam. It is 486 feet high and 9,003 feet long.

LARGEST-CAPACITY HYDROELECTRIC DAM The Itaipu Dam, operated jointly by Brazil and Paraguay, is the world's largest hydroelectric dam, with a capacity of 12,600 megawatts. It is 4.8 miles long wide and 643 feet tall, with a reservoir covering 521 square miles.

After this dam was built the reservoir submerged Paraguay's Guaira Falls, once the largest waterfall in the world.

The Grand Coulee Dam on the Columbia River in Washington is the largest-capacity hydro dam in North America, capable of producing 6,800 megawatts of electricity.

During construction from 1933 to 1942, 11,975,521 cubic yards of concrete was poured. It's 550 feet tall and 5,223 feet wide.

MOVIES

Box Office

UNTIL VARIETY STARTED LISTING THE WEEKLY TALLIES for Hollywood films in the early 1980s, revenue figures were mostly kept quiet by the studios. Nowadays box office figures, especially for each weekend, are widely published. The successes or failures, especially of the most expensive star-studded movies, have become a Monday morning obsession for film fans—who also enjoy delving into Hollywood's box office past.

MILESTONES

1915: MILLION DOLLAR GROSS D.W. Griffith's silent film epic about the Civil War, *The Birth of a Nation,* which premiered in Los Angeles on Feb. 8, 1915 (under the name *The Clansman*), was the first film to gross over $1 million. The movie was an ambitious milestone but deeply flawed in sympathetically portraying the Ku Klux Klan. It was produced for an estimated (then-record) $110,000; it grossed $3 million in the U.S., and $10 million worldwide.

The average cost of a movie ticket in 1915 was 25 cents, but some theaters charged as much as $2 for the Griffith film, while others refused to show it because of its theme.

The first film to run over 100 minutes, *The Birth of a Nation* was also the first to be screened at the White House, on Feb. 18, 1915, for President Woodrow Wilson.

1939: $100 MILLION GROSS Filmed for a lavish $4 million, the Civil War drama *Gone With the Wind* premiered in Atlanta, GA, on Dec. 15, 1939. One of the most beloved movies of all time, it won eight Oscars including Best Picture and Best Actress and grossed $198.7 million in the U.S., partly through various theatrical reissues.

Little-known English actress Vivien Leigh was cast in the plum role of fiery Scarlett O'Hara, beating out over 1,000 contenders for the part, including such Hollywood heavyweights as Joan Crawford and Claudette Colbert.

1975: THE SUMMER BLOCKBUSTER The summer movie blockbuster phenomenon was created in 1975. Backed by an expensive TV marketing campaign and booked into 500 theaters for its June 20 opening, Steven Spielberg's *Jaws* chomped down a $100 million gross in the U.S. in just 59 days, on its way to a total of over $260 million, making it the top box office thriller of all time. When it was released, tickets cost an average of $2.03.

Jaws reached the $100 million mark far faster than any prior $100 million earner. Only three other movies—*The Godfather*, *Gone With the Wind*, and *The Sound of Music*—had previously reached $100 million.

1977: $300 MILLION GROSS George Lucas's *Star Wars* powered past *Jaws* to the top of the U.S. box office charts in 1977. The film opened on May 25 in 34 selected theaters and earned $307 million on its initial release (tickets cost an average of $2.23).

Lucas accepted $175,000 as his writer/director's fee in return for 40% of merchandising rights. Using the billion-dollar profits from those rights, he was able to move his studio out of Hollywood and build a motion picture empire with Lucasfilm Ltd.

1997: $1 BILLION GROSS The first movie to gross more than $1 billion in ticket sales worldwide was James Cameron's *Titanic*, released Dec. 19, 1997. It broke the $300 million mark in 44 days and sailed past $1 billion internationally ($427 million in North America and $575.7 million overseas) by March 1998.

Co-produced by 20th Century Fox and Paramount, the movie cost a record $200 million to make—more than it had cost to build the doomed luxury liner (about $126 million in 1997 dollars).

Titanic also tops the North American box office list, having grossed over $600 million. And at the 1998 Oscar ceremonies, the film won a then-record 11 Academy Awards (tied by *The Lord of the Rings: The Return of the King* in 2004).

2002: $100 MILLION OPENING WEEKEND Released May 3, 2002, on 3,615 screens, *Spider-Man* snared $114,844,116 in its opening weekend, becoming the first film to gross $100 million or more in its first weekend (with a record single-day gross of $43.6 million). It went on to earn another $288.9 million at the domestic box office and $418 million overseas

Spider-Man wore 28 "Spidey suits" in the movie. They cost $22,000 each, and kept getting shredded in battle sequences.

◀ *(left to right) Ian McDiarmid, Ewan McGregor and Hayden Christensen. COURTESY OF LUCASFILM LTD.* Star Wars: Episode III-Revenge of the Sith *© 2005 Lucasfilm Ltd. &™. All rights reserved. Used under authorization. Unauthorized duplication is a violation of applicable law.*

Top Grossing Films by Genre

GENRE	MOVIE	NORTH AMERICAN GROSS
Animation	*Shrek 2* (2004)	$441 million
Comedy	*Home Alone* (1990)	$286 million
Crime	*The Fugitive* (1993)	$184 million
Documentary	*Fahrenheit 9/11* (2004)	$119 million
Fantasy	*Lord of the Rings: The Return of the King* (2003)	$377 million
Gangster	*The Godfather* (1972)	$135 million
Horror	*The Exorcist* (1973)	$233 million
Musical	*Grease* (1978)	$188 million
Religious	*The Passion of the Christ* (2004)	$371 million
Romantic Comedy	*My Big Fat Greek Wedding* (2002)	$241 million
Science Fiction	*Star Wars* (1977)	$461 million
Sports	*Jerry Maguire* (1996)	$154 million
War	*Saving Private Ryan* (1998)	$216 million
Western	*Dances With Wolves* (1990)	$184 million

SOMETHING TO THINK ABOUT

A BIG FAT HIT, BUT NOT NUMBER ONE

The romantic comedy *My Big Fat Greek Wedding* was the sleeper hit of 2002. Released on April 19 in only 8 locations, it went on to gross over $240 million at North American box offices, but it never topped the weekly box office charts. The movie expanded to hit more than 650 theaters by August, but faced competition from *Spider Man, Lord of the Rings: Two Towers, Star Wars Episode II,* and *Harry Potter and the Chamber of Secrets.* During fall 2002, it surpassed *Dances With Wolves* (1990), as the highest-grossing movie never to make the No. 1 slot (since 1982, when such records began to be kept).

THE PRICE OF FAME

One of the most famous lines in movie history, "Frankly my dear, I don't give a damn," Rhett Butler's parting comment to Scarlett O'Hara in the 1939 box-office record-setter *Gone With the Wind* almost didn't make it into the movie. Producer David O. Selznick actually filmed an alternate line of dialogue where Rhett said, "Frankly, my dear, I just don't care," as a reserve in case censors balked at the curse word. However, when the censors did object to the original line, he included it anyway, and paid a $5,000 fine.

SUPERLATIVES

HIGHEST GROSSING MOVIE *Titanic,* starring Leonardo DiCaprio and Kate Winslet, is the highest grossing North American movie of all-time at more than $600 million.

However, if adjustments are made for inflation, then *Titanic* sinks to sixth place on the list. With adjusted figures, *Gone With the Wind* tops the box office, at $1.3 billion in today's money.

HIGHEST-GROSSING MOVIE SERIES The Force has been with them. *Star Wars* (1977), *The Empire Strikes Back* (1980), *Return of the Jedi* (1983), *Star Wars: Episode I–The Phantom Menace* (1999), *Star Wars: Episode II–Attack of the Clones* (2002), and *Star Wars: Episode III–Revenge of the Sith* (2005) have grossed more than $2.1 billion in the U.S. and Canada alone.

The *Star Wars* series is followed by the *James Bond* cycle (1963-), which has shaken and stirred $1.3 billion in 21 movies, *Harry Potter* (2001-), which has grossed $1.1 billion with 4 movies, and the *Lord of the Rings* trilogy (2001-03), which earned just over $1 billion.

HIGHEST GROSSING DIRECTOR The most successful director of all-time in terms of box office gross is Steven Spielberg. A two-time Best Director Academy Award winner, Spielberg has directed more than 20 movies. From his feature debut at the helm of 1974's *The Sugarland Express* to the present, Spielberg's films combined have grossed more than $3.2 billion.

When asked what movies he would most like to be remembered for, Spielberg named *E.T.* and *Schindler's List. E.T.* is his biggest success financially ($435 million), while *Schindler's List* garnered the most Oscars (seven, including Best Director and Best Picture).

MOST WEEKS AT NO. 1 Since records were first kept in 1982, Steven Spielberg's *E.T. The Extraterrestrial* has stayed atop the box office rankings for the most weeks. Released on June 11, 1982, *E.T.* has spent a record 16 weeks in all atop domestic box office charts.

To better connect with a young audience, Spielberg shot the film at eye-level with E.T. and his human friend, Elliot (played by Henry Thomas). The idea clearly paid off.

MOVIES

Academy Awards

THE ACADEMY AWARDS are presented by the Academy of Motion Picture Arts and Sciences and have been staged annually since 1929. The first Oscars were presented in the Blossom Room of the Hollywood Roosevelt Hotel in Los Angeles on May 16, 1929; 15 statuettes were handed out in 14 categories. There were only 250 people in attendance, and a ticket cost $10.

MILESTONES

1929: FIRST OSCARS The winners of the first Oscars were announced in Feb. 1929. Emil Jannings won Best Actor honors for his work in two silent films: *The Last Command* and *The Way of All Flesh*. He had to return to Germany before the ceremony, and requested that he receive his Oscar before leaving Los Angeles so that he could take it home with him. The Academy agreed to his request, and so Jannings became the first person ever presented with the gold statuette.

The other winners included: Outstanding Picture (*Wings*), Best Actress (Janet Gaynor, *7th Heaven, Street Angel*, and *Sunrise*), Best Director, Drama (Frank Borzage, *7th Heaven*), Best Director, Comedy (Lewis Milestone, *Two Arabian Knights*), Writing, Adaptation (Benjamin Glazer, *7th Heaven*), Writing, Original Story (Ben Hecht, *Underworld*), Best Cinematography (Charles Rosher and Karl Struss, *Sunrise*), and Best Art Direction (William Cameron Menzies, *The Dove* and *Tempest*).

There were two special awards, to Warner Bros. (for producing *The Jazz Singer*) and Charlie Chaplin for his work on *The Circus*.

1930: "TALKIE" BEST PICTURE The first ever Best Picture Oscar went to *Wings*, which was a silent film. The first time a Best Picture Oscar went to a "talkie" was at the second ceremonies, in 1930, when The *Broadway Melody*, directed by Harry Beaumont and starring Charles King and Anita Page, won the award.

1932: TIE There have only been five ties in Oscar history. The first came at the 5th Awards in 1932 when Fredric March (*Dr. Jekyll and Mr. Hyde*) and Wallace Beery (*The Champ*) tied for Best Actor. March actually received one more vote than Beery, but Academy rules at the time stated that any nominees within three votes of the winner must be named a winner too. The rules were subsequently changed.

The first true mathematical tie came at the 22nd Awards in 1950 in the Best Documentary (short subject) category. *A Chance to Live and So Much for So Little* were even in the voting and both won the Oscar.

1935: "OSCAR SWEEP" The four major categories at the Academy Awards are: Best Picture, Best Director, Best Actor, and Best Actress. The first time one movie swept all four categories was at the 7th Awards in 1935. That year *It Happened One Night* (1934) was named Best Picture; Frank Capra won Best Director for his work on the film, and its stars, Clark Gable and Claudette Colbert, won the acting awards.

Only two other movies have attained the "Oscar Sweep": *One Flew Over the Cuckoo's Nest* (1975) with Milos Forman (Director), Jack Nicholson (Best Actor), and Louise Fletcher (Best Actress); and *The Silence of the Lambs* (1991) with Jonathan Demme (Director), Anthony Hopkins (Best Actor), and Jodie Foster (Best Actress).

1935: BEST SONG
The Best Song category was introduced at the 7th Awards in 1935. The winner was "The Continental," music by Con Conrad with lyrics by Herb Magidson. It was featured in the movie *The Gay Divorcée*, starring Fred Astaire and Ginger Rogers.

That same year the Academy honored the Best Score for the first time. The Oscar winner was *One Night of Love* (1934).

1937: BEST SUPPORTING ACTOR AND ACTRESS
Oscars for Best Supporting Actor and Best Supporting Actress were first presented at the 9th Awards in 1937. The first recipients were: Walter Brennan (*Come and Get It*) and Gale Sondergaard (*Anthony Adverse*).

1939: DOUBLE ACTING NOMINATIONS
At the 11th Awards in 1939, Fay Bainter became the first person to receive nominations for Best Actress (*White Banners*) and Best Supporting Actress (*Jezebel*) in the same year. She won for *Jezebel*, but the Best Actress award went to her *Jezebel* co-star, Bette Davis.

Receiving nominations in both acting categories in the same year is a rare achievement. It has occurred nine times, most recently at the 75th Awards in 2003, when Julianne Moore received a Best Actress nomination for *Far From Heaven*, and a Best Supporting Actress nod for *The Hours*.

At the 17th Awards in 1945, Barry Fitzgerald received a double nomination for the same performance, as Father Fitzgibbon in

BAD SIGNS?

During the ceremony in 1978, Debby Boone performed Best Song nominee "You Light Up My Life," surrounded by hearing-impaired children apparently signing the lyrics. But viewers who actually knew sign language soon spotted that the kids were not signing at all and flooded the Academy with irate phone calls. The Academy later admitted that the students were recruits from a Los Angeles-area public high school who did not know sign language.

Going My Way. He won the Best Supporting award, with Best Actor honors going to cast-mate Bing Crosby.

Fitzgerald is the only actor to have received two nominations for the same performance. The Academy subsequently changed the rules to prevent such an occurrence from happening again.

1940: AFRICAN-AMERICAN WINNER
Hattie McDaniel was the first African-American to win an Oscar. She won the Best Supporting Actress award at the 12th Awards in 1940 for her performance as "Mammy" in *Gone With the Wind* (1939).

1941: SEALED ENVELOPES The first time the winners were not pre-announced was at the 13th Awards ceremony in 1941. Among the surprised winners that year were: Best Actor, James Stewart (*The Philadelphia Story*), Best Actress, Ginger Rogers (*Kitty Foyle: The Natural History of a Woman*), Best Supporting Actor, Walter Brennan (*The Westerner*), Best Supporting Actress, Jane Darwell (*The Grapes of Wrath*), and Best Director, John Ford (*The Grapes of Wrath*).

1953: TELEVISED CEREMONY
The Academy Awards were first televised on March 19, 1953. The ceremonies, held at the RKO Pantages Theatre in Hollywood and the NBC International Theatre in New York, were broadcast on NBC television. Bob Hope hosted the ceremonies in Los Angeles, and Fredric March made the presentations in New York. *The Greatest Show on Earth* won for Best Picture.

The first color broadcast came in 1966, when *The Sound of Music* won the Best Picture award.

1977: WOMAN BEST DIRECTOR NOMINATION The first woman to get a Best Director nomination was Lina Wertmüller for *Seven Beauties* at the 49th Awards in 1977. The Oscar went to John G. Avildsen for *Rocky*. The Italian director also received a Best Original Screenplay nomination that year, but she lost to Paddy Chayefsky for *Network*.

Only three women have received Best Director nominations: Wertmüller, Jane Campion for *The Piano* (1993), and Sofia Coppola for *Lost In Translation* (2003).

2002: AFRICAN-AMERICAN WINNERS (LEAD ROLE)
Sidney Poitier was the first African-American actor to win the Best Actor award when he won in 1964 at the 36th Awards for his performance as Homer Smith in *Lilies of the Field*.

In 2002 at the 74th Awards, Halle Berry became the first African-American actress to win the Best Actress award. She won for her performance in *Monster's Ball*.

That same evening Denzel Washington became the second African-American actor to win the Best Actor award, for his performance in *Training Day*.

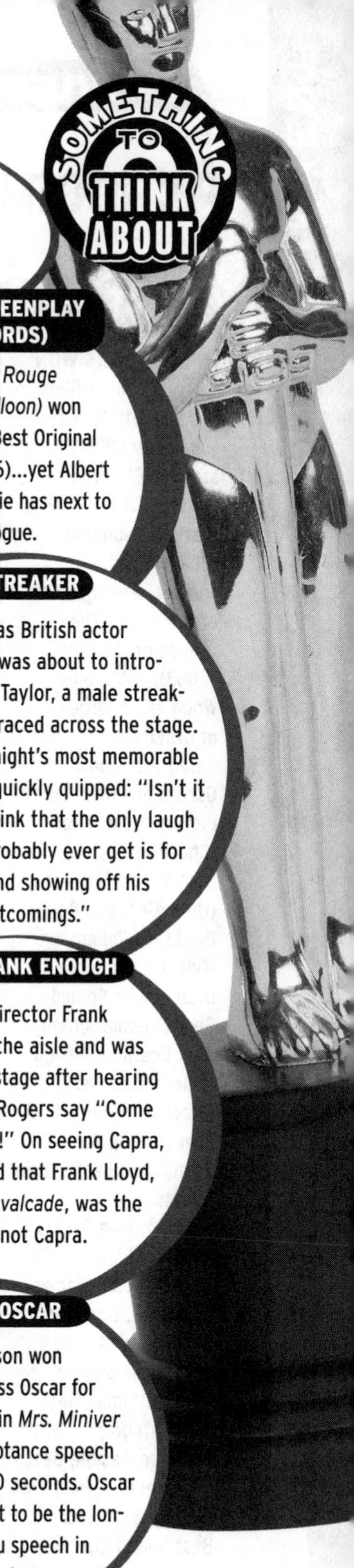

BEST SCREENPLAY (NO WORDS)

Le Ballon Rouge (The Red Balloon) won the Oscar for Best Original Screenplay (1956)...yet Albert Lamorisse's movie has next to no dialogue.

STREAKER

In 1974, as British actor David Niven was about to introduce Elizabeth Taylor, a male streaker, Robert Opal, raced across the stage. In one of Oscar night's most memorable moments, Niven quickly quipped: "Isn't it fascinating to think that the only laugh that man will probably ever get is for stripping and showing off his shortcomings."

NOT FRANK ENOUGH

In 1934, director Frank Capra ran up the aisle and was halfway to the stage after hearing presenter Will Rogers say "Come and get it, Frank!" On seeing Capra, Rogers clarified that Frank Lloyd, director of *Cavalcade*, was the winner, not Capra.

THANKING OSCAR

Greer Garson won the Best Actress Oscar for her performance in *Mrs. Miniver* (1942). Her acceptance speech lasted 5 minutes, 30 seconds. Oscar watchers believe it to be the longest thank-you speech in Awards history.

MOVIES

MORE ON

Academy Awards

SUPERLATIVES

MOST OSCARS WON

MOVIE Three films have won 11 Oscars: *Ben-Hur* (1959), starring Charlton Heston, *Titanic* (1997), starring Leonardo DiCaprio and Kate Winslet, and *The Lord of the Rings: The Return of the King* (2003), with Elijah Wood and a large cast of other stars.

Ben-Hur won Oscars for: Best Picture, Best Actor (Charlton Heston), Best Supporting Actor (Hugh Griffith), Best Director (William Wyler), Best Score, Dramatic or Comedy, Best Cinematography, Best Costume Design (Color), Best Art Direction (Color), Best Film Editing, Best Sound, and Best Special Effects.

Titanic won Oscars for: Best Picture, Best Director (James Cameron), Best Song ("My Heart Will Go On"), Best Original Score (Drama), Best Cinematography, Best Costume Design, Best Art Direction, Best Film Editing, Best Sound, Best Sound Effects (Editing), and Best Visual Effects.

The Lord of the Rings: The Return of the King won Oscars for: Best Picture, Best Director (Peter Jackson), Best Original Song ("Into the West"), Best Original Score, Best Costume Design, Best Adapted Screenplay, Best Art Direction, Best Sound Mixing, Best Film Editing, Best Makeup, and Best Visual Effects.

CLEAN SWEEP

MOVIE *The Lord of the Rings: The Return of the King* (2003) was the biggest Oscar winner to sweep all categories for which it was nominated. Two other films went nine for nine: *Gigi* (1958) and *The Last Emperor* (1987).

MOST OSCARS WON **INDIVIDUAL**

Walt Disney won a record-breaking 26 Oscar awards from 59 nominations, the last awarded posthumously for *Winnie the Pooh and The Blustery Day* at the 41st Awards in 1969. He also holds the record for the most Oscars won in a single year, with four at the 26th Awards in 1954: Best Short Film (Cartoon), *Toot, Whistle, Plunk and Boom*, Best Documentary Short, *The Alaskan Eskimo*, Best Documentary Feature, *The Living Desert*, and Best Short Subject (Two-Reel), *Bear Country*.

MOST OSCARS

DIRECTOR John Ford won four Oscars as Best Director for *The Informer* (1935), *The Grapes of Wrath* (1940), *How Green Was My Valley* (1941), and *The Quiet Man* (1952). The only one of those movies to win the Best Picture award was *How Green Was My Valley*.

MOST OSCARS

ACTOR/ACTRESS

Katharine Hepburn won four Best Actress awards: *Morning Glory* (1933), *Guess Who's Coming to Dinner* (1967), *The Lion in Winter* (1968) (tie with Barbra Streisand for *Funny Girl*), and *On Golden Pond* (1981).

Jack Nicholson and Walter Brennan have won three Oscars, the most for an actor. Nicholson won Best Actor honors for *One Flew Over the Cuckoo's Nest* (1975) and *As Good As It Gets* (1997), and Best Supporting Actor for *Terms of Endearment* (1983). Brennan's were all for Best Supporting Actor (see below).

MOST OSCARS

SUPPORTING ACTOR

Walter Brennan won three Best Supporting Actor Oscars in *Come and Get It* (1936), *Kentucky* (1938), and *The Westerner* (1940).

MOST OSCARS

SUPPORTING ACTRESS

The record for most wins in the Best Supporting Actress category is two, shared by Shelley Winters for *The Diary of Anne Frank* (1959) and *A Patch of Blue* (1965) and Dianne Wiest for *Hannah and Her Sisters* (1986) and *Bullets Over Broadway* (1994).

OLDEST WINNERS

The oldest person to win an Academy Award in an acting category is Jessica Tandy. She won Best Actress for *Driving Miss Daisy* (1989) at age 80 years, 293 days. The oldest actor to win an award is George Burns. The legendary comedian was 80 years, 69 days old when he won a Best Supporting Oscar for his role in *The Sunshine Boys* (1975).

That's not counting actors given honorary Oscars. Groucho Marx was awarded an honorary Oscar in 1974 at age 83 years, 182 days. The silent film star Mary Pickford received an honorary Oscar in 1976 at age 82 years, 356 days.

The oldest actor to win for a lead role is Henry Fonda. He was 76 years, 317 days old when he won Best Actor for *On Golden Pond* (1981).

The oldest actress to win in the Best Supporting Actress category is Dame Peggy Ashcroft. She was 77 years, 93 days old when she won for *A Passage To India* (1984).

YOUNGEST WINNERS

Tatum O'Neal was 10 years, 148 days old when she won the Best Supporting Actress award for *Paper Moon* (1973). Timothy Hutton was 20 years, 227 days old when he won the Best

THE LAST TIME...

The Academy Awards have always been held in California. But in 1953 they started being co-staged in New York City. The last time this happened was in 1957, when Celeste Holm hosted in Hollywood and Jerry Lewis in the Big Apple. The winner for Best Picture ... *Around the World in 80 Days.*

Ian McKellen as Gandalf in The Lord of the Rings: The Return of the King

Supporting Actor award for his performance in *Ordinary People* (1980).

Shirley Temple was awarded an honorary Oscar in 1935 at age 6 years, 310 days.

Marlee Matlin holds the record as the youngest person to win the Best Actress award. She was 21 years, 218 days old when she won for *Children of a Lesser God* (1986). This was her first movie role of any kind.

The youngest actor to win the Best Actor award was Adrien Brody for his performance in *The Pianist* (2002). Brody was 29 years, 343 days old, beating the mark of Richard Dreyfuss, who was 30 years, 156 days when he won for *The Goodbye Girl* (1977).

MOST OSCAR NOMINATIONS

MOVIE *All About Eve* (1950) and *Titanic* (1997) both received a record 14 nominations. *All About Eve* won six awards and *Titanic* won 11.

MOST NOMINATIONS WITHOUT WINNING

MOVIE Two movies, *The Turning Point* (1977) and *The Color Purple* (1985), both received 11 nominations but won no Oscars.

MOST NOMINATIONS WITHOUT WINNING

ACTOR/ACTRESS

The undesirable record for most Oscar nominations without winning the gold statuette is seven, held by two actors: Richard Burton and Peter O'Toole. O'Toole, however, was given an honorary Oscar in 2003. The record for an actress is six, also held by two performers: Deborah Kerr and Thelma Ritter.

MOST NOMINATIONS

INDIVIDUAL

Meryl Streep's Best Supporting Actress nomination for *Adaptation* (2002) was her record 13th nomination in an acting category, breaking her tie with Katharine Hepburn. Streep has won twice: Best Supporting Actress for *Kramer vs. Kramer* (1979) and Best Actress for *Sophie's Choice* (1982).

Jack Nicholson's Best Actor nomination for his performance in *About Schmidt* (2002) was his 12th Oscar nomination, extending his record for an actor. He has won three Oscars in all (see above).

OLDEST NOMINEES

The oldest person to receive an Academy Award nomination in an acting category is Gloria Stuart. She was 87 when she received a Best Supporting Actress nomination for *Titanic* (1997). The oldest actor to receive a nomination is Sir Ralph Richardson. The renowned British stage actor was 82 when he received a Best Supporting Actor nomination for his performance in *Greystoke: The Legend of Tarzan, Lord of the Apes* (1984).

The oldest woman to receive a Best Actress nomination is Jessica Tandy. She was 80 when she received a nomination for *Driving Miss Daisy* (1989). Tandy won the award (see above).

The oldest man to gain a Best Actor nomination is Richard Farnsworth. He was 79 when nominated for *The Straight Story* (1999).

YOUNGEST NOMINEES

The youngest person to receive an Oscar nomination in an acting category is Justin Henry. The child actor was eight when he received a Best Supporting Actor nomination for *Kramer vs. Kramer* (1979). The youngest person to receive a Best Actor nod is Jackie Cooper. He was nine when he received his nomination for *Skippy* (1930-31).

The youngest girl to receive an Oscar nomination is Tatum O'Neal. She was 10 years old when she received a Best Supporting Actress nomination for *Paper Moon* (1973). She won the award (see above).

The youngest actress to receive a Best Actress nomination is Keisha Castle-Hughes. The Australian-born actress was 13 when she received her nomination for *Whale Rider* (2003).

MOVIES

Special Effects

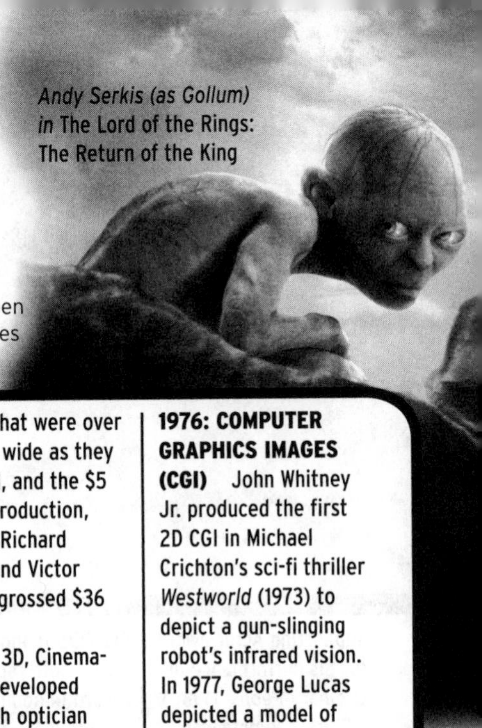

Andy Serkis (as Gollum) in The Lord of the Rings: The Return of the King

ALMOST SINCE THE BEGINNING OF FILM, filmmakers have used technology to wow the crowds. Georges Méliès's *A Trip to the Moon* (1902) (see page 103) and Edwin Porter's *The Great Train Robbery* (1903) dazzled movie-goers with never-before-seen effects. Through advanced technological tricks, make-up, and stunts, the boundaries always advance and "movie magic" continues to thrill, chill, and enthrall.

MILESTONES

ABOUT 1918: BLUE SCREEN Now a standard effect in the making of movie magic, blue-screen technology developed out of "traveling matte" composites developed by cameraman Frank Williams about 1918. In this technology an actor is filmed against a solid blue (or now green) background and isolated as a separate shot. Those shots are later superimposed on other scenes.

1925: ACTORS AND ANIMATION
The Lost World (1925) was the first feature film where live actors shared the frame with models of creatures, painstakingly manipulated frame-to-frame, by hand, by special effects artist Willis O'Brien. At the film's climax, a brontosaurus, terrorizes London.

O'Brien later created the legendary effects for 1933's *King Kong* and in 1949 won an Academy Award for his work with a friendlier big ape in *Mighty Joe Young*.

1939: SPECIAL EFFECTS OSCAR
Special effects were first rewarded at the 1939 Academy Awards, held Feb. 29, 1940. And the Oscar goes to . . . no, not to that year's Best Picture winner, *Gone With the Wind*, for its burning of Atlanta sequence, or to *The Wizard of Oz*, with its flying monkeys. Rather, it was given to honor the work of Fred Sersen and E. H. Hansen in *The Rains Came*. In that 1939 film, an earthquake breaks dams and floods devastate a city in India. The disaster sequence alone was budgeted at $500,000 and used a 50,000-gallon tank for the flood.

1952: 3D FEATURE FILM "A lion in your lap! A lover in your arms!" promised ads for Arch Oboler's African adventure *Bwana Devil* (1952). The movie delivered, with jungle lions seeming to leap out of the screen. 3D works by using color filters on glasses to allow each eye to percieve a different angle, both projected onto the screen.

Bwana Devil was the first feature filmed entirely in 3D. It broke theater attendance records. However, the Production Code Administration denied it a "purity seal" because the 3D love scene was "too torrid."

3D soon faded, though it cropped up in the early 1980s with such films as *Friday the 13th Part 3, 3D* (1982) and later spawned such films as *The Adventures of Shark Girl and Lava Boy* (2005).

1953: CINEMASCOPE
20th Century Fox, hoping to compete with the ever-more-popular TV, released a religious epic, *The Robe*, on Sept. 16, 1953. Its patented widescreen process, called CinemaScope, dazzled audiences with images that were over twice as wide as they were tall, and the $5 million production, starring Richard Burton and Victor Mature, grossed $36 million.

Unlike 3D, CinemaScope, developed by French optician Henri Chrétien, and other widescreen processes became standard in feature-film production. The old ratio of width to height, set in 1932, was 1.33:1 whereas the new ratio was 2.55:1. It was later set at 2.35:1.

1970: IMAX
The widescreen IMAX projection and film system was developed by three Canadians: Graeme Ferguson, Roman Kroitor, and Robert Kerr. They first demonstrated the prototype at EXPO '70 in Osaka, Japan. Ontario Place in Toronto installed the first system in 1971.

IMAX is the largest-sized commercial film produced—ten times larger than normal film with 15-perforation, 70 mm sized frames.

1976: COMPUTER GRAPHICS IMAGES (CGI) John Whitney Jr. produced the first 2D CGI in Michael Crichton's sci-fi thriller *Westworld* (1973) to depict a gun-slinging robot's infrared vision. In 1977, George Lucas depicted a model of the Death Star via computer simulation in *Star Wars, Episode IV: A New Hope*.

These were small steps for the technique, but by the mid-1990s CGI was commonplace in Hollywood feature films, largely replacing stop-motion animation. The first fully CGI film was *Toy Story* (1995).

1981: BEST MAKEUP OSCAR Makeup got its own Oscar for the first time at the 1981 Academy Awards ceremony, held March 29, 1982. Rick Baker's werewolves in *An American Werewolf in London* triumphed over Stan Winston's robots in *Heartbeeps*. Baker, who now runs Cinovation, has won six Oscars for makeup.

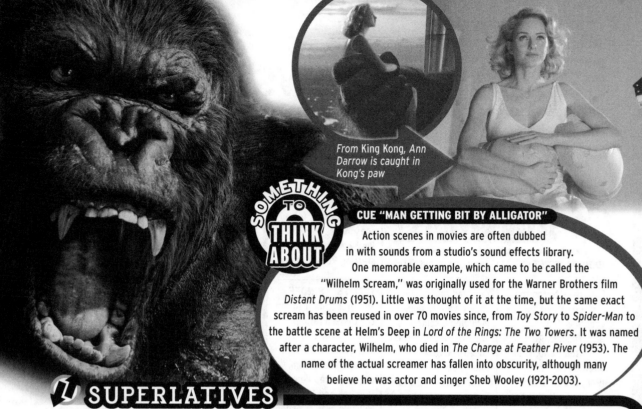

From King Kong, Ann Darrow is caught in Kong's paw

SOMETHING TO THINK ABOUT

CUE "MAN GETTING BIT BY ALLIGATOR"

Action scenes in movies are often dubbed in with sounds from a studio's sound effects library. One memorable example, which came to be called the "Wilhelm Scream," was originally used for the Warner Brothers film *Distant Drums* (1951). Little was thought of it at the time, but the same exact scream has been reused in over 70 movies since, from *Toy Story* to *Spider-Man* to the battle scene at Helm's Deep in *Lord of the Rings: The Two Towers*. It was named after a character, Wilhelm, who died in *The Charge at Feather River* (1953). The name of the actual screamer has fallen into obscurity, although many believe he was actor and singer Sheb Wooley (1921-2003).

SUPERLATIVES

MOST COSTUMES CREATED (FEATURE) Costume designer Herschel McCoy created 10,250 costumes for the epic vision of the Emperor Nero's reign of terror in MGM's *Quo Vadis* (1951), and got an Oscar nomination for his craftwork.

MOST PROSTHETICS AND ARMS CREATED (FEATURE) For *The Lord of the Rings: The Fellowship of the Ring* (2001), New Zealand effects company Weta created more than 48,000 prosthetics and weapons, including 10,000 prosthetic facial appliances and over 3,500 pairs of Hobbit feet.

LARGEST MAKEUP BUDGET (%) John Chambers received an honorary Oscar for his work on *Planet of the Apes* (1968). Eighty artisans labored around the clock to create landmark makeup for 200 actors cast as humanoid apes in the sci-fi classic. Their work "made up" 17% of the total production cost.

MOST OSCARS (SPECIAL EFFECTS) Industrial Light & Magic, the special effects house founded by George Lucas to create the Oscar-winning illusions seen in *Star Wars* (1977), has received a record 14 Academy Awards.

MOST SPECIAL EFFECTS SHOTS Industrial Light & Magic created a record 2,151 visual effects shots—containing 375,040 frames—for *Star Wars: Revenge of the Sith* (2005). Of these shots, 1,269 were animated and featured 185 digital characters. Producing the effects took 6,598,928 hours using a crew of 350 people and multiple computer processing systems.

The first *Star Wars* film in 1977 had only 360 effects shots.

MOST FULLY ANIMATED CGI CREATION The fantasy creature Gollum, as seen in Peter Jackson's *The Lord of the Rings* trilogy, is the most fully animated all-digital character yet produced, with 250 facial expressions and 300 moving muscles. There were 964 control points on the face alone.

Gollum's model was actor Andy Serkis, whose movements were fed into computers via motion capture techniques. Serkis "doubled" again for the giant ape in Jackson's remake of *King Kong* (2005).

HIGHEST STUNT FREE FALL (FROM BUILDING) Legendary stuntman Dar Robinson leapt from the CN Tower in Toronto in 1979 for a scene in the movie *Highpoint* (1984). Robinson plunged 1,136 feet, most of it in free fall. He fell for six seconds, reaching a top speed of 126 mph. He pulled the rip chord on his parachute 300 feet from the ground.

HIGHEST STUNT FALL (AIR MATTRESS) The highest stunt leap into an air mattress for a movie was performed by A.J. Bakunas. He jumped off the roof of a 232-foot-tall building in the movie *Hooper* (1978). The film, which starred Burt Reynolds as stunt man Sonny Hooper, was directed by one of Hollywood's most famous stuntmen, Hal Needham.

TELEVISION

Favorite Shows

NIELSEN MEDIA RESEARCH HAS BEEN KEEPING TABS ON PEOPLE'S TV VIEWING HABITS since 1950. Founded in 1923 by marketer A.C. Nielsen to measure audiences for the radio and advertising industries, the company today places meters in some 5,000 randomly selected TV viewing households that agree to participate. Each household member has a Personal Viewing Button so that the TV audience can also be broken down by age and gender.

Linda Gray & Larry Hagman of Dallas ▲

MILESTONES

1950-51: FIRST NO. 1 SHOW The first show to top the Nielsen ratings for the year was *The Texaco Star Theater*, hosted by Milton Berle. First aired on NBC-TV in 1948, the show was so popular that it has been widely credited with the explosive growth of TV set ownership in the U.S. in the late 1940s and early 1950s.

1952-53: SITCOM The first comedy program to head the season-long rankings table was *I Love Lucy*, for 1952-53. One of the most beloved shows in TV history, it was the top-ranked show for three of the next four seasons.

1955-56: GAME SHOW The top-rated TV show in the 1955-56 season was *The $64,000 Question*, the first No. 1-ranked game show. Hugely popular in the early days of television, game shows fell out of favor after it was revealed that some shows were rigged, including a spinoff to *The $64,000 Question* called *The $64,000 Challenge*.

The most infamous instance involved the show *Twenty One*; repeat-winner Charles Van Doren, whose charismatic performances gave a big boost to ratings, revealed in 1959 to a House committee investigating quiz shows that he was fed the answers prior to the show.

It would be almost 50 years before another quiz show, *Who Wants to Be a Millionaire*, zoomed to the top of the ratings chart, becoming the No. 1 prime-time show for the 1999-2000 season.

1970-71: MEDICAL DRAMA Hospital, or medical, dramas have long been a TV staple. The first to top the Nielsen ratings for a season was *Marcus Welby, M.D.*, in 1970-71, starring Robert Young.

1977-78: SPINOFF The first spinoff to top the Nielsen ratings was *Laverne and Shirley* in the 1977-78 season. The sitcom, which starred Penny Marshall and Cindy Williams, was spawned by *Happy Days*. That classic sitcom, starring Ron Howard as Richie Cunningham and Henry Winkler as "The Fonz," ranked No. 1 in 1976-77.

1980-81: PRIMETIME SOAP The first prime-time soap opera to top the ratings was *Dallas*. This saga of the Ewing oil family topped the charts in the 1980-81 season. The Nov. 21, 1980, broadcast, commonly called "Who Shot J.R.?," but actually titled "Who Done It?," was the second-highest-rated single show of all-time, behind the *M*A*S*H* finale (see page 83).

SUPERLATIVES

LONGEST-RUNNING SHOW Politicians have been interviewed by journalists on NBC's *Meet the Press* for almost 60 years. The radio version, produced by Lawrence Spivak and Martha Roundtree, debuted in 1945. It moved to TV in Nov. 1947, and is still going strong, making it the longest running program in TV history. Tim Russert, its ninth and longest-serving moderator, took the reins in Dec. 1991.

LONGEST-RUNNING PRIME-TIME DRAMA The western series *Gunsmoke* first aired on Sept. 10, 1955, and blows away the competition as the longest-running dramatic series: it ran for 635 episodes over 20 years. James Arness (as Dodge City Marshal Matt Dillon) and Milburn Stone (Doc Adams) were the only original cast members still around for the final episode, aired Sept. 1, 1975.

The show was almost cancelled in 1967 because of poor ratings, but CBS president William S. Paley, a fan, intervened and, in a magic-bullet solution, moved it from Saturday to Monday. The move helped propel the show back into the top ten in ratings.

SOMETHING TO THINK ABOUT

SKATING TO THE TOP

The proliferation of cable TV channels in the past several years has fragmented a viewing audience that once turned in nearly exclusively to the "Big Three" networks (ABC, CBS, and NBC). This made a stellar rating very hard to attain. Only one show in the 1990s or later brought back enough viewers to reach TV's all-time top-10-rated shows. Nearly 46 million homes (48.5%) tuned in to watch the figure-skating showdown between Nancy Kerrigan and her accused "whacker," Tonya Harding, at the XVII Winter Olympics in Lillehammer, Norway, on Feb. 23, 1994. It became the all-time number-six show.

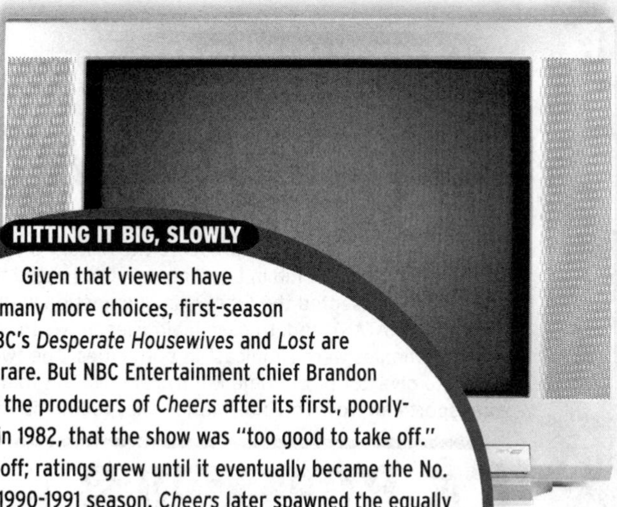

HITTING IT BIG, SLOWLY

Given that viewers have so many more choices, first-season hits like ABC's *Desperate Housewives* and *Lost* are increasingly rare. But NBC Entertainment chief Brandon Tartikoff told the producers of *Cheers* after its first, poorly-rated season in 1982, that the show was "too good to take off." His faith paid off; ratings grew until it eventually became the No. 1 show, in the 1990-1991 season. *Cheers* later spawned the equally successful *Frasier*. Its star, Kelsey Grammer, played the role of Frasier, the slightly neurotic psychiatrist, for 20 straight years between the two programs, tying a record by the *Gunsmoke* actors. NBC's *Seinfeld* also started out in the ratings cellar in 1990, but said farewell on May 14, 1998, with 76.3 million viewers and a stellar 41.3% rating.

LONGEST-RUNNING SOAP A radio serial that debuted in 1937, *Guiding Light* moved to TV on June 30, 1952, where it remains to this day. The ongoing misadventures of the Bauer family in life and love originated on NBC and later moved CBS.

TOP-RATED SOAP Premiering on CBS in 1973, *The Young and the Restless* has been TV's top-rated soap since 1989—a record 16 years.

LONGEST-RUNNING LATE-NIGHT TALK SHOW *The Tonight Show* has been entertaining night owls since Sept. 27, 1954, making it the longest-running show in its after-hours timeslot. The show first aired in New York City with Steve Allen as host. Later, in 1957, the personable Jack Paar took over, turning the show into a lasting success. He was followed by the legendary Johnny Carson (1962-92), and in 1992 by comedian Jay Leno. The show moved to Hollywood, or more accurately, Burbank, CA, in 1972.

LONGEST-RUNNING MORNING SHOW *The Today Show*, broadcast on NBC is TV's longest running morning show. It has aired daily since Jan. 14, 1952. The first host was Dave Garroway; it now features Katie Couric and Matt Lauer.

HIGHEST-RATED EPISODE The highest-rated episode in American TV history was "Goodbye, Farewell, and Amen," the 2 $\frac{1}{2}$-hour finale of *M*A*S*H*, broadcast Feb. 28, 1983. An estimated 106 million viewers, 60.2% of U.S. households with TVs, tuned in to watch the 4077th Mobile Army Surgical Hospital unit in Korea disband after 11 seasons—8 years longer than the Korean fighting itself.

HIGHEST-RATED MINI-SERIES *Roots*, based on the Alex Haley novel that traces his family's history from Africa to slavery to the 20th century, was the highest-rated miniseries of all time. The finale, broadcast Jan. 30, 1977, was the third-highest-rated show in American TV history. Six of the series eight episodes rank in the Top 50 chart for highest-rated TV shows of all time.

HIGHEST-RATED SPORTS EVENT Super Bowl XVI, played on Jan. 24, 1982 between the San Francisco 49ers and Cincinnati Bengals, drew a record 49.1% of American TV households. The 49ers beat the Bengals, 26-21.

NO. 1 SHOW (CONSECUTIVE SEASONS) Bigoted Archie Bunker, played by Carroll O'Connor, may have turned off his son-in-law Mike "Meathead" Stivic, played by Rob Reiner, with his tirades, but droves of viewers tuned in to *All in the Family* (1971-79), making it the No. 1 TV program for its first five seasons, a record. The show set a new standard for realism in sitcoms and produced spin-offs *The Jeffersons*, *Maude*, and *Gloria*.

TOP TEN RANKING (CONSECUTIVE SEASONS) The CBS news magazine show *60 Minutes* ranked in the Nielsen Top 10 for a record 17 straight years, 1979-96. The streak was snapped in 1997, when *60 Minutes* slipped to 11th place.

TELEVISION

Emmy Awards

THE EMMY AWARDS were originally presented by the Academy of Television Arts and Sciences (ATAS), founded in 1946 to preserve the history of TV. The first Emmy ceremony was staged at the Hollywood Athletic Club in Los Angeles, CA, hosted by composer-actor Walter O'Keefe. Starting in 1957, ATAS presented the Emmys in conjunction with the National Academy of Television Arts and Sciences (NATAS), and, to ease jealousies between New York and Hollywood television companies, the ceremonies were simulcast in both cities. The two groups reached an accord in 1977, calling for ATAS to give out prime-time Emmys and NATAS to manage other Emmys, including daytime, news, and sports awards. The information that follows is for prime-time Emmys only.

MILESTONES

1948: EMMY STATUETTE The 15-inch-tall, 5-pound Emmy statuette presented to Emmy winners was designed by Louis McManus in 1948 as a composite of pewter, iron, zinc, and gold. The winged woman holding an atom was created by McManus using his wife, Dorothy, as a model. The wings represent the muse of art, and the atom represents the science behind television.

Originally the award was nicknamed "Immy," for the early "image orthicon" camera tube. It was later changed to Emmy, which academy members thought was more appropriate for a female symbol.

1949: FIRST EMMY WINNER At the first Emmy awards ceremonies, on Jan. 25, 1949, the first of the six Emmys presented was for Most Outstanding Television Personality. It went to 20-year-old ventriloquist Shirley Dinsdale and her puppet Judy Splinters. The award for the Most Popular Television Program went to *Pantomime Quiz*.

The winner for Best Film Made for Television was *Your Show Time*: "The Necklace." The other three awards went to: Paramount Studio's KTLA (best station); Charles Mesak (technical award), and Louis McManus (honorary award).

This ceremony was broadcast only in the Los Angeles area, on KTSL, and since TV did not yet have a coast-to-coast hookup, these Emmys were given only to Los Angeles programs and personalities.

1955: FIRST NATIONAL TV BROADCASTS The Emmy Awards have been televised every year since 1949, except 1954, but the first national broadcast did not come until 1955. The first time the Emmys aired in color was on March 16, 1957.

At the time of the first Emmy ceremony, in 1949, there were 1 million TV sets in the United States; by the time of the first national broadcast in 1955, there were 25 million TVs. In 2004 there were about 247 million TV sets in the U.S.

1960: FIRST AFRICAN-AMERICAN WINNER The first African-American to win an Emmy Award was Harry Belafonte. The singer won Best Variety or Musical Program or Series for his 1959 television musical special, *The Revlon Revue:* "Tonight With Harry Belafonte."

Bill Cosby was the first African-American to win for Best Actor, receiving the award three years in a row, 1966-68, for his role as Alexander "Scotty" Scott in the series *I Spy*.

1960: FIRST SYNDICATED SHOW TO WIN A syndicated program is one that is sold to numerous independent TV stations instead of just one network. The first to win an Emmy was the cartoon series *Huckleberry Hound*, created by Hanna Barbera. Also the first cartoon to win an Emmy, *Huckleberry Hound* was recognized as Best Children's Program.

1969: WITHHELD EMMYS In an experiment, the 1969 winners were chosen by a blue-ribbon panel that was empowered to withhold awards if they didn't think any of the nominees were deserving.

For the first, and so far only time, ever, the panel refused to give an Emmy to any of the nominees in one of the categories, Best Supporting Actor in a Special, passing over Ned Glass, Hal Holbrook, and Billy Schulman.

1973: TRIPLE CROWN The only person to win an Emmy, an Oscar, and a Tony in the same year is director/choreographer Bob Fosse. He won the Emmy for *Singer Presents* "Liza with a Z," an Oscar for *Cabaret*, and two Tony awards for *Pippin*.

1987: CABLE TV ELIGIBILITY Cable television programs first became eligible for Emmy consideration in 1987. The first time a cable network won an Emmy was on Aug. 27, 1988, when two HBO shows won a total of three Emmys: *Dear America: Letters Home From Vietnam* won two Emmys, and *Jackie Mason on Broadway* won one.

The year 2004 marked the first time that cable networks got more total prime time nominations (220) than broadcast networks (206).

(Left to right) *Eva Longoria, Nicollette Sheridan and Felicity Huffman of* Desperate Housewives

SUPERLATIVES

MOST EMMYS

ALL TIME The record for most Emmys won by an individual is 18, by two men: producer-director Dwight Hemion and producer-director-writer James L. Brooks. Hemion, who also holds the record for most individual nominations, with 47, directed the *Tonight Show* with Steve Allen in 1953 and later specialized in celebrity concerts and holiday spectaculars. Brooks won his first Emmy for *The Mary Tyler Moore Show* in 1971, and has been recognized for his work on such classic comedies as *Taxi* and *The Simpsons.*

MOST WINS (SERIES)

ALL TIME The record for most Emmy Awards won by any series is 35, by the sitcom *Frasier* during its 11-year-run (1993-2003). The show won Best Comedy five times, and its star Kelsey Grammer won Best Actor in a Comedy Series five times, 1994-98.

MOST WINS (DRAMA)

ALL TIME Three series have won the Best Drama award four times: *Hill Street Blues,* 1981-84; *L.A. Law,* 1987, 1989-91; and *The West Wing,* 2000-03.

MOST WINS (COMEDY)

ALL TIME The most Best Comedy Emmys won by a series is five by *Frasier*, 1994-98. It was also the first spin-off series of an Emmy-winning comedy (*Cheers*) to win in this category.

MOST WINS (SWEEP)

YEAR The most Emmys won for a show sweeping all the categories it was nominated for was nine, won by "An Evening With Fred Astaire" in 1959. It was the legendary dancer's first television special.

MOST WINS (NETWORK)

YEAR The most Emmys won in a single year by a network was 44, presented to CBS in 1974. The most Emmys won in a single year by a cable channel was 32, by HBO at the 2004 Awards.

MOST WINS (SHOW)

YEAR The most Emmys won in one year by a single production was 11, a feat achieved twice. *Eleanor and Franklin: The White House Years,* a television movie that aired on ABC in 1976, set the record. The mark was tied in 2004 by *Angels In America,* a mini-series first broadcast on HBO in 2003. Besides tying that record, *Angels* also set a new record for most Emmys won by a mini-series, topping the mark of nine set by *Roots* in 1977.

MOST WINS (SERIES)

YEAR The record for most Emmys won by a series in a single season is nine, by *The West Wing* in 2000, its debut season.

MOST NOMINATIONS

ALL TIME The most nominations gained by any television show is 117, by the comedy series *Cheers* from 1983 to 1993. The show won 28 Emmys, including Best Comedy four times, 1983, 1984, 1989, and 1991. The most nominations all-time for a drama is 112, for *ER*. The medical drama has won 21 Emmys, including Best Drama once in 1996.

SOMETHING TO THINK ABOUT

EXCELLENT ANALYSIS

Kelsey Grammer played the character of the pompous psychiatrist Dr. Frasier Crane over a period of 20 years, on two of the four most nominated series in Emmy history: *Cheers* (117 nominations) and *Frasier* (107). Grammer won five Emmys for playing Frasier.

FOOD FOR THOUGHT

At the 1974 Emmys, comedian Lily Tomlin won the Best Variety, Music, or Comedy Special category for *Lily*. Tomlin had no difficulty keeping the momentousness of the award in perspective: "This is not the greatest moment in my life," she said, "because on Friday I had a really great baked potato at Niblick's on Wilshire."

WIRES CROSSED?

At the 1951 Emmys, Groucho Marx was named TV's Most Outstanding Personality. In a typical Groucho gesture, the legendary comedian strode onto the stage, ignored his Emmy statuette, and instead picked up Miss Emmy, the former Miss America Rosemary LaPlanche, and carried her off stage.

TELEVISION

Quiz & Game Shows

QUIZ AND GAME SHOWS HAVE BEEN STAPLES of television since the medium began. A quiz show was aired on the day commercial broadcasting began in the U.S. Today catchphrases like "Come on down!" and "Is that your final answer?" are part of the pop culture lexicon. As for the *Jeopardy!* theme song—well, good luck getting it out of your head.

(left to right) Ken Jennings, Brad Rutter, and the host of Jeopardy!, Alex Trebek ▶

MILESTONES

1941: FIRST TV QUIZ/GAME SHOW
A TV version of *Truth or Consequences*, a popular radio program, was the first game show to appear on American TV, on July 1, 1941. It was a special broadcast and did not become a regular TV show until 1950.

The first regularly scheduled game show, the *CBS Television Quiz*, began airing July 2, 1941.

1951: EMMYS On Jan. 23, 1951, *Truth or Consequences* (CBS) became the first show of the genre to win an Emmy Award, nabbing the prize for Best Game and Audience Participation Show of 1950. The show, airing in prime time, was hosted in its early years by Ralph Edwards, its creator and producer.

1955-56: HIGHEST-RATED TV SHOW
Only two quiz/game shows have been the highest-rated TV show during a season. The first was *The $64,000 Question*, which was the top-rated show for 1955-56.

The second was *Who Wants to Be a Millionaire*, in 1999–2000. *Millionaire*, originally aired in Britain, made its debut on U.S. primetime television in Aug. 1999, with Regis Philbin as host. A syndicated version of the show, hosted by Meredith Vieira, was launched in 2002.

1959: QUIZ SHOW SCANDAL In 1959, a U.S. House of Representatives subcommittee heard testimony from contestants who had appeared on various TV quiz shows—including *21*, *Tic Tac Dough*, *The $64,000 Question*, and *The $64,000 Challenge*—that they had been coached and given questions and answers in advance of their appearances.

The most gripping testimony came from contestant Charles Van Doren, a telegenic Columbia University English instructor from a well-known literary family, who had won $129,000 on *21* in 1956. Van Doren had also been given a lucrative job at NBC; he was fired from NBC and resigned from Columbia after admitting the wrongdoing.

Big-money quiz shows had been extremely popular, but most were canceled in the wake of the scandal.

1975: HOUR-LONG SHOW In 1975, *The Price Is Right* became the first regularly scheduled game show to expand from a half-hour to a full hour run-time.

1999: $1 MILLION WINNER John Carpenter, an IRS collection agent from Hamden, CT, who appeared on *Who Wants to Be a Millionaire* on Nov. 19, 1999, became the first contestant to win $1 million.

In the climactic question, Carpenter identified Richard Nixon as the president who appeared on the TV show *Rowan and Martin's Laugh-In*.

The first person to win the £1 million prize on the British version of *Millionaire* was Judith Keppel, a distant cousin of Camilla Parker-Bowles, who married Prince Charles in 2005. Keppel's big win was broadcast on Nov. 21, 2000.

◀ *Bob Barker at the 34th season premiere of* The Price Is Right

SOMETHING TO THINK ABOUT

THE PASSWORD IS "ARRESTED"

When does winning on a popular game show equal losing? In 1988, a contestant on *Super Password* going by the name of Patrick Quinn was recognized by viewers in Alaska as a fugitive in an insurance fraud case. When he showed up at Mark Goodson Productions offices to pick up the check for $58,600 in prize money, he was arrested.

NAME THAT TOWN!

In 1950, Hot Springs, NM, changed its name to "Truth or Consequences" in honor of the popular game show, accepting a challenge by host Ralph Edwards. In a special election, 1,294 Hot Springs residents voted to rename the town, though 295 locals were against the new name and filed a protest. The issue has gone to the polls several times since then, but each time "Truth or Consequences" won out.

UNKNOWN SUPERSTARS ON QUIZ SHOWS

Hollywood legend Robert Redford and Emmy-winning actress Kirstie Alley both appeared on game shows in their pre-fame days. Redford was given a fishing pole as payment for appearing as a demonstrator on *Play Your Hunch* in 1959. In 1979, the pre-*Cheers* Alley won the $5,000 jackpot on *The Match Game*. She also appeared on *Password Plus* and won $10,000, with the help of partner Lucille Ball.

SUPERLATIVES

LONGEST RUN *The Price Is Right*, which has been on the air continuously since Sept. 4, 1972, is the longest-running quiz or game show broadcast in the United States. An earlier version of the show appeared on TV from 1956 to 1965.

LONGEST TENURE Bob Barker signed a contract in Jan. 2005 to continue hosting *The Price is Right* for an unprecedented 34th season. Barker also hosted the game show *Truth or Consequences* for 18 seasons. In June 2004, the animal-rights activist was inducted into the Academy of Television Arts and Sciences Hall of Fame.

As of 2005, Barker had won 13 Emmys as a host and three as a producer of *The Price is Right*.

MOST CONSECUTIVE APPEARANCES Utah software engineer Ken Jennings made 75 straight appearances on *Jeopardy!*, tying the record set by Ian Lygo (see below).

LONGEST WINNING STREAK (U.S.) Ken Jennings's 74 straight wins on *Jeopardy*! in 2004 is the longest winning streak for an American quiz show contestant. The year before, *Jeopardy!* had eliminated a long-standing rule limiting contestants to five games.

Jennings's loss, aired on Nov. 30, 2004, came in his 75th straight appearance. He was stopped by a "Final Jeopardy" clue to identify the firm whose "70,000 seasonal white collar employees work only four months a year." By then he had given some 2,700 correct answers (in the form of a question, of course), but this time he guessed FedEx Corp., failing to identify tax preparation service H&R Block.

H&R Block softened the blow by offering Jennings free tax preparation and financial services for life, which he accepted.

LONGEST WINNING STREAK (WORLD) Ian Lygo won 75 straight games on the British quiz show *100%* in 1998. He might well have won more, but the show's producers—who feared his winning streak was hurting ratings—decided after his 73rd win that they would change the rules and limit contestants to 25 straight wins. They let him come back for two more games.

MOST PRIZE MONEY WON Brad Rutter, a college dropout and former record-store assistant from Lancaster, PA, has won a record $3,255,102 in his appearances on *Jeopardy!* He first appeared in 2000, and accumulated his record winnings by playing in the show's Tournament of Champions from 2000 to 2005.

$2 million of Rutter's total winnings came from defeating Ken Jennings and Los Angeles writer Jerome Vered in the final round of *Jeopardy!*'s 15-week Ultimate Tournament of Champions in 2005.

Jennings took in $2,520,700 from his record 75 straight appearances on *Jeopardy!*, and won an additional $500,000 for placing second in the Tournament.

Reality TV

REALITY-SHOW PROGRAMMING HAS BEEN PART OF TELEVISION SINCE ITS EARLIEST DAYS, but was a minor part of TV's offerings until the 1990s. Today, reality shows have become a main attraction, filling the airwaves with high-stakes contests, outrageous stunts, and outsized personalities.

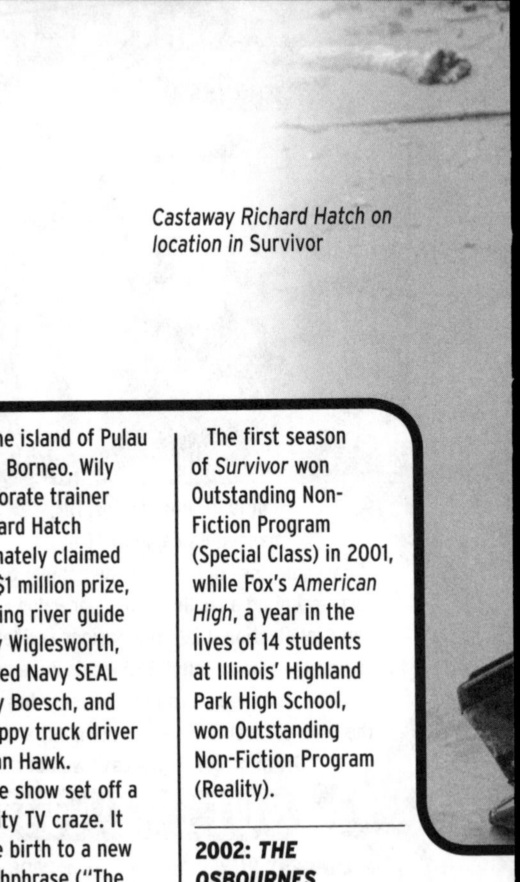

Castaway Richard Hatch on location in Survivor

MILESTONES

1973: *AN AMERICAN FAMILY* Shot over seven months in 1971, *An American Family* (1973) gave PBS viewers a close-up look at the tangled lives of the Loud family of Santa Barbara, CA.

This "fly-on-the-wall" style documentary broke new ground in television. Over 12 one-hour episodes, 10 million viewers (a stunning audience for public television) watched as parents William and Pat Loud endured divorce proceedings, while eldest son Lance, TV's first openly gay "character," unashamedly revealed his homosexuality before the cameras.

PBS revisited the Louds in 1983 and again in 2003, with a chronicle of Lance's final years before his death from hepatitis C and HIV in 2001.

1992: *THE REAL WORLD* The idea of MTV's *The Real World* is to throw together seven different college-age people in an unfamiliar city and record their misadventures and growing pains.

First set in a New York loft (1992), the show attracted its greatest notoriety for the year it took place in San Francisco (1994), as gay AIDS activist Pedro Zamora clashed with irreverent bike messenger David "Puck" Rainey.

In each season, characters face off over issues big and small. The explosive quarrels and occasional sexual intrigue set the tone for reality series to come.

2000: *WHO WANTS TO MARRY A MULTI-MILLIONAIRE* On Feb. 15, 2000, during "sweeps," Fox launched *Who Wants to Marry a Multi-Millionaire*.

Fifty beautiful women competed to win the hand of a wealthy mystery bachelor, a formula that brought in big ratings—and outraged many feminists, conservatives, family groups, and pundits.

The winning bridal contestant, emergency room nurse Darva Conger, wed real estate investor and comedian Rick Rockwell. But the marriage was annulled less than two months later, and Fox cancelled reruns because of allegations of abuse by a former fiancée of Rockwell's.

Multi-Millionaire left heirs, however, spawning a subgenre of courtship-themed reality programs like ABC's *The Bachelor*, NBC's *Average Joe*, and Fox's *Joe Millionaire*.

2000: *SURVIVOR* CBS successfully imported a European reality show to the U.S. in the summer of 2000. *Survivor,* based on Sweden's *Expedition: Robinson* (1997), first featured a series of contests between two "tribes" on the island of Pulau Tiga, Borneo. Wily corporate trainer Richard Hatch ultimately claimed the $1 million prize, besting river guide Kelly Wiglesworth, retired Navy SEAL Rudy Boesch, and scrappy truck driver Susan Hawk.

The show set off a reality TV craze. It gave birth to a new catchphrase ("The tribe has spoken") and made stars of ordinary people, as some contestants went on to publish books and appear in other TV shows or movies.

The show's relatively low production costs (about $1 million per episode), combined with massive ratings averaging 28.3 million viewers, inspired a flood of reality programming.

2001: FIRST EMMYS The Academy of Television Arts and Sciences has dealt with reality (so to speak) in different ways.

The first season of *Survivor* won Outstanding Non-Fiction Program (Special Class) in 2001, while Fox's *American High*, a year in the lives of 14 students at Illinois' Highland Park High School, won Outstanding Non-Fiction Program (Reality).

2002: *THE OSBOURNES* The *bleeping* insanity that was life with rock star Ozzy Osbourne and his unruly family (including dogs) enlivened TV's first "reality sitcom." The Emmy-winning MTV show *The Osbournes*, launched in 2002, was the station's most-viewed show ever. It aired for four seasons (52 episodes), capturing everything from Sharon's meat-tossing rant to Ozzy's ATV accident.

Other celebrity reality stars followed, from pop stars Nick Lachey and Jessica Simpson in *Newlyweds* to "celebutantes"

SOMETHING TO THINK ABOUT

VOTE FOR YOUR FAVORITE . . . GORILLA

Gorillas are the stars of a new *Big Brother*-style reality show. Czech broadcasters launched *Odhaleni* ("Discovery") in Nov. 2005. The show follows one male, two females, and one baby gorilla as they go ape competing for a prize of 12 melons.

GROSS-OUT LAWSUIT

Since 2001, NBC's *Fear Factor* has obliged contestants to devour live cockroaches, have raw sewage dumped on their heads, be locked into bamboo cages and lowered into a swamp full of giant bullfrogs, and drink duck embryo "milkshakes" seconds before being launched off the top of a high-rise building. It's all pretty crazy, but only one "challenge" inspired a dismayed viewer to try to sue the show for emotional distress. In Jan. 2005, Cleveland paralegal Austin Aitken sought legal relief from an episode in which contestants ate dead rats mixed in a blender. He claimed the show made him throw up and run into a doorway. A judge dismissed the $2.5 million suit as frivolous.

SOUR GRIPES

Reality TV made it to China, but government officals there were not enthused by China's *American Idol*-style sensation *The Mongolian Cow Sour Yogurt Super Girl Contest*. As some 400 million viewers watched, 3.27 million voted Li Yuchun as the Super Girl on Aug. 27, 2005. Officials panned the show and its outcome. Li, a frizzy-haired tomboy music student, was deemed a poor role model. China's official paper also asked, "How come an imitation of a democratic system ends up selecting the singer who has the least ability to carry a tune?"

Paris Hilton and Nicole Richie in *The Simple Life*.

2002: *AMERICAN IDOL* Based on the British hit *Pop Idol*, *American Idol* combined the traditional talent-search show à la *Star Search* with events controlled by viewers who voted from home. By 2005, its fourth season, votes totaled 500 million.

In the first season finale, which drew 22.8 million viewers on Sept. 4, 2002, Kelly Clarkson won a major recording contract and guaranteed stardom.

2004: *THE APPRENTICE* "You're fired!" was on everyone's lips as Manhattan real-estate mogul Donald Trump began his search for a new hire through NBC's *The Apprentice* in early 2004. Chicagoan Bill Rancic was the first person hired to a high-paying job through a TV show, leaving the boardroom with a $250,000 post.

Subsequent programs like chef Gordon Ramsay's *Hell's Kitchen*, Virgin Group owner Richard Branson's *The Rebel Billionaire*, and *The Apprentice: Martha Stewart* had other big name employers sizing up prospective employees while viewers watched in suspense.

SUPERLATIVES

BEST RATING
EPISODE The two-hour finale of *Survivor* on Aug. 23, 2000, attracted 51.6 million viewers, making it the highest-rated summer broadcast ever tracked. It generated the best overall ratings for CBS since the 1994 Winter Olympics.

BEST RATING
SEASON The second season of *Survivor*, set in the Australian Outback, emerged as the No. 1-rated program of the 2000-01 TV season, attracting 17.4% of the average audience. The episodes prior to the finale drew an average of 29.2 million viewers.

MOST EXPENSIVE REALITY SHOW
NBC paid $2 million per episode for Mark Burnett's *The Contender* (2005). Burnett, the creator of reality hits *Survivor* and *The Apprentice*, spun *The Contender* around boxing matches in the tradition of *Rocky* (1976). The show was hosted by that film's star, Sylvester Stallone.

LONGEST-RUNNING
The longest-running show in the reality genre is *The Real World*, first broadcast on MTV in 1992. The show's 17th season, based in Key West, FL, premiered in Feb. 2006.

Contestants by then had descended on 14 different U.S. cities (New York twice), plus London and Paris.

MOST COUNTRIES
Currently, there are 40 versions of *Big Brother*, not including knockoffs. The show, where contestants are locked in a house and voted out one by one, premiered in The Netherlands in Sept. 1999, and has been adapted in 35 countries, plus an additional 5 pan-regional networks.

TELEVISION

Technology

CT-100—First RCA all-electric color television

NO SINGLE PERSON INVENTED TELEVISION; it was the product of many inventors working separately and often competitively. And the technology is always advancing. The bulky sets of yesteryear have given way to sleeker units using a variety of technologies to deliver a crisp picture.

MILESTONES

1884: NIPKOW'S SCANNING DISK Paul Gottlieb Nipkow, a German engineering student, patented the first mechanical television system, in 1884.

The key component of his "electric telescope" was a spinning disk in which holes were arrayed in a spiral. As the disk rotated, the image was scanned through the holes and converted into electric signals by a light-sensitive cell. The signals controlled a light source at an identical spinning disk, by means of which the image was re-created.

No one knows if Nipkow ever built a working model of the disk; only his sketches remain. The concept of scanning, however, proved fundamental to TV technology, and Nipkow's disk became the basis of mechanical television systems that enjoyed attention before the rise of electronic TV.

1897: CATHODE-RAY TUBE Karl Ferdinand Braun, a German scientist, invented the cathode-ray tube in 1897. The CRT is a vacuum tube that produces an image when an electron beam hits its phosphorescent surface. First used as a display in 1907, it played a key role in the development of electronic television.

Today, many electronic devices with a display—such as ATMs and video game kiosks—still use a CRT, as do many TV sets.

1923: MECHANICAL TELEVISION Scottish engineer John Logie Baird is widely credited with the development of a practical mechanical television system. In Oct. 1925 he created the first televised image in his laboratory on his "televisor." The image was of a ventriloquist's dummy, named Stooky Bill.

Baird said of the event, "The image of the dummy's head formed itself on the screen with what appeared to me an almost unbelievable clarity."

Baird's TV used a 2-foot revolving disk to scan the image and a similar disk worked in tandem to reproduce it. If the disks went out of sync, the image would blur.

The first public television demonstration occurred in Jan. 1926 at Baird's London lab, with 40 members of the Royal Institution in attendance. Later that year Baird set up the first TV station.

1923: ICONOSCOPE Russian-born American physicist and electronics engineer Vladimir Zworykin developed the first television camera in 1923. Called an iconoscope, it was a tube that converted an optical image into electrical pulses for transmitting television signals.

Zworykin received funding from RCA (Radio Corporation of America) to develop his device in 1930. Finalized in 1933, it proved controversial. He was accused of copying American engineer Philo T. Farnsworth's patented dissector tube (see below) to make improvements to his device.

Farnsworth later won a settlement from RCA, with the company agreeing to pay him royalties.

1927: IMAGE DISSECTOR TUBE Philo T. Farnsworth filed a patent for his "image dissector" tube in Jan. 1927. He held the first public demonstration of an all-electronic television camera in Sept. 1928 at his San Francisco lab.

His tube made much clearer images than the early iconoscope, but it required that the subject be illuminated with a strong, somewhat blinding light.

1929: KINESCOPE Vladimir Zworykin demonstrated a receiver tube called the kinescope in Nov. 1929 at the Institute of Radio Engineers in Rochester, NY. A forerunner of the kinescope was developed by his Russian physics professor, Boris Rosing (St. Petersburg Institute of Technology), in 1907, but it could transmit only still images.

The kinescope had no moving parts and could project a clear image under normal lighting. It is the basis for most CRT displays today.

1940: COLOR TV As early as 1899, Russian researcher A. A. Polumordvinov devised a machine that used a colored Nipkow disk to transmit images.

John Logie Baird demonstrated a mechanical color TV in 1928 using a spinning red-blue-green color wheel but the screen, as was typical of mechanical television systems, was small. (Baird later worked on an electronic TV, the telechrome, which he exhibited in 1944.)

Hungarian-born American engineer Peter Goldmark, led a CBS research team that in 1940 developed a partly mechanical

SUPERLATIVES

WORLD'S LONGEST TV SCREEN A television display installed by Mitshubishi Electric at the Hong Kong Jockey Club in 2003 measures 26 feet by 231 feet, making it as long as a Boeing 747 jetliner. It can show up to three views of a race, along with statistics and odds, at the same time.

TOP CABLE TV NATION Nearly all TV programming is delivered via cable in the Netherlands, which boasts the highest cable penetration in the world—over 96%.

SOMETHING TO THINK ABOUT

LAFF BOX

How did producers ever get studio audiences to laugh so hard at poor sitcom jokes? As you probably know, they don't have to; they can rely on the "Laff Box," which was invented in 1953 by television engineer Charles Douglass. It is used to create canned laugh tracks that can make any joke sound like it was funny.

These days the laugh machine is digital and can offer laughter from around the world. Many sitcoms use the Laff Box, even those with a live studio audience such as *Will & Grace* and *Seinfeld*.

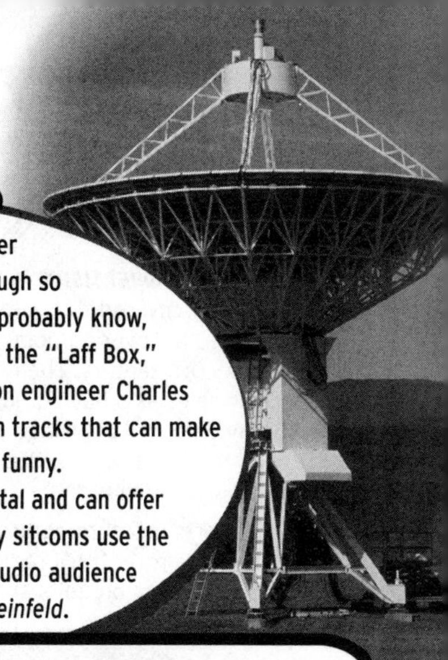

color TV system. It used Baird's disk, a cathode-ray tube, and a kinescope. A competition unfolded with RCA, which favored an all-electronic system, to determine the U.S. industry standard.

Pressed by CBS, the Federal Communications Commission approved the CBS system in Oct. 1950. CBS began regular color broadcasts from New York City in June 1951. But the cost of retrofitting existing black-and-white sets with a pricey adapter, and the technology's small screen size, limited its appeal to consumers. (A 19-inch screen would have required a 5-foot wheel and a 10-horsepower engine.)

The FCC approved a revised electronic system developed by RCA. It is still used today in the U.S. for analog (nondigital) television.

1948: CABLE TV
In the mid-1940s John Walson of Mahanoy City, PA, created the Service Electric Company, which sold, installed, and repaired appliances. His business was in a mountainous area, where TV broadcasts were difficult to receive. To fix this problem, Walson in 1948 placed an antenna on a utility pole atop a nearby mountain and using a cable connected it to the TVs in customers' homes.

This was the first instance of what became known as community antenna television (CATV).

1950: REMOTE CONTROL The first TV remote control was created in 1950 by the Zenith Radio Corp. It was attached to the TV through a wire and could turn the set on and off and change channels. But people complained about tripping over the wire.

1964: PLASMA SCREENS The plasma display, in which each dot on the screen glows like a tiny neon sign, makes possible flat-screen TVs. It became a popular alternative to the traditional CRT TV receiver in the late 1990s.

The technology actually originated much earlier. The plasma screen was invented by Donald Bitzer and H. Gene Slottow of the University of Illinois at Urbana-Champaign, along with graduate student Robert Willson, in 1964. The three were honored with an Emmy for technological achievement in 2002.

1968: LIQUID CRYSTAL DISPLAY
Another common alternative to the cathode-ray tube receiver is the liquid crystal display. In the early 1960s, RCA physical chemist Richard Williams found that the optical properties of liquid crystals could be manipulated by electric impulses.

By 1968, RCA electronics engineer George Heilmeier and his coworkers had developed prototypes for simple LCD screens, which soon came to be used in calculators.

The first color TV using an LCD screen, introduced by Seiko-Epson in 1984, had a 2-inch screen (screen size is measured diagonally across the viewing area). By 2005 Samsung was displaying a screen more than 80 inches in size.

1969: HDTV High-definition television (HDTV) is a group of TV technologies that together yield a much higher-resolution image, and a sharper, more lifelike picture than standard TV.

Early efforts at HDTV relied on analog transmission. NHK (Japan Broadcasting Corp.) experimented with broadcasting quality during the 1964 Tokyo Olympics; the next year, with the support of the Japanese government, it began researching high-definition television. The new technology was first demonstrated in Japan in 1969, and NHK began producing programs in analog HDTV in 1982.

Modern HDTV is digital. In the U.S., Congress mandated in 1997 that all TV signals (including non-HDTV) be digital by Dec. 31, 2006, or when 85% of households are able receive digital transmissions—whichever is later.

MUSIC

Chart Toppers

BILLBOARD ADVERTISING, A TRADE PUBLICATION that originally covered the outdoor advertising industry, switched to covering popular entertainment by the start of the 20th century. The new *Billboard* tracked sheet music sales as a buying guide for jukebox operators. Today *Billboard* publishes a variety of charts, including ones for country, jazz, R&B, classical, electronic, Latin, and Christian music.

The charts measure popularity using Nielsen Broadcast Data Systems to track radio airplay and data from manufacturers on units shipped (minus returns) to follow sales figures.

Alicia Keys and Usher

MILESTONES

1940: FIRST BEST-SELLING RETAIL SINGLE For the week of July 27, 1940, *Billboard*, for the first time, ranked songs by individual recordings (instead of grouping together different recordings of a popular song). "I'll Never Smile Again" (Victor) by Tommy Dorsey and his Orchestra—featuring a young Frank Sinatra—topped the inaugural list.

1944: FEMALE ARTIST AT NO. 1 Dinah Shore's "I'll Walk Alone" (Victor) was the first No. 1 hit for a female artist since the 1940 inception of the singles chart. It topped the chart on Oct. 11, 1944.

1956: ALBUM CHARTS The first weekly album chart was published on March 24, 1956. Just over 11 years later, on May 13, 1967, the chart grew to include 200 albums, leading to what is now known as the Billboard 200. The first album to top the charts was *Belafonte*, by Harry Belafonte.

1958: HOT 100 On Aug. 4, 1958, *Billboard* introduced its "Hot 100," which gave each record a single ranking for combined sales and airplay.

Teen idol Ricky Nelson had the first No. 1 with "Poor Little Fool" (Imperial). Today *Billboard*'s "Hot 100" singles and "Hot 200" albums charts are considered industry standards.

1958: GOLD DISCS On March 14, 1958, the Recording Industry Association of America (RIAA) certified its first gold single (1 million copies sold to U.S. retailers); it was Perry Como's "Catch a Falling Star" (RCA). The same year, the RIAA also certified its first gold album ($1 million in wholesale sales), for the cast recording of the Broadway musical *Oklahoma!* (Capitol).

In 1975, gold album certification rules were revised by the RIAA to require 500,000 copies shipped and $1 million wholesale revenue.

1976: PLATINUM DISCS In 1976, Johnny Taylor's "Disco Lady" (Columbia) became the first single to earn a platinum award for shipping over 2 million copies. The first platinum album, awarded for over 1 million copies shipped and $2 million in sales, was *The Eagles Their Greatest Hits 1971-1975* (Asylum).

The multi-platinum certification was launched in 1984, for the sale of over 2 million albums. Michael Jackson's *Thriller* (Epic) was among the first honored.

1999: DIAMOND DISCS On March 16, 1999, the RIAA pioneered the diamond classification, which celebrates single or album sales that rise over 10 million. The Beatles' *Sgt. Pepper's Lonely Hearts Club Band* (Capitol) was the earliest-released album (1967) to be recognized among the 62 works by 46 inaugural recipients.

The Beatles have a record six diamond awards, including one for their 1968 release *The Beatles* ("The White Album"), their best-selling album in the U.S. (19 million copies sold).

2003: DIGITAL DOWNLOAD CHARTS Reflecting the growing value of online business, *Billboard* introduced its digital downloads chart on July 12, 2003. "Hot Digital Tracks" measures Internet purchases of music files from services such as Apple iTunes and Pressplay.

Beyoncé's "Crazy in Love" featuring Jay-Z was the first No. 1.

SOMETHING TO THINK ABOUT

RINGTONES

When *Billboard* began tracking the sales of ringtone versions of popular songs on Nov. 6, 2004, analysts were surprised that the most popular was "My Boo" by Usher and Alicia Keys, which sold 97,000 units, whereas the most legally downloaded song, U2's "Vertigo," sold only 30,000. By year's end, *Billboard* awarded the first "Ringtone of the Year" award to the bleep-bloop version of rapper 50 Cent's "In Da Club."

MUSIC FOR ALL TASTES

Ever since music charts were first introduced, many hits have topped a variety of them simultaneously. For instance, Elvis Presley's "Hound Dog" topped the pop, black, and country charts in 1956 (three years after Big Mama Thornton's version topped the R&B charts). In one unusual example of boundary-crossing, the million-selling single from Ray Charles's gold album *Modern Sounds in Country and Western Music* (ABC-Paramount) won a 1962 Grammy award for Best R&B Recording for the track "I Can't Stop Loving You."

SUPERLATIVES

MOST WEEKS AT NO. 1 SINGLE "One Sweet Day" (Columbia), performed by Mariah Carey and Boyz II Men, is the longest-running No. 1 single ever; it topped the Billboard 100 for 16 straight weeks before being bumped on March 23, 1996.

The longest streak atop the Billboard 100 for a solo performance is 14 weeks, held by two artists: Whitney Houston and Sir Elton John. Houston's "I Will Always Love You" (Arista) headed the charts for 14 weeks starting Nov. 19, 1992. John's tribute to Princess Diana, "Candle in the Wind 1997" backed with "Something About the Way You Look Tonight" (Rocket), dominated the charts beginning Oct. 2, 1997.

The single with the most total weeks at No. 1 for airplay is "Iris" (Reprise) by the Goo Goo Dolls, which spent 18 weeks as a chart-topper in late 1998.

MOST WEEKS AT NO. 1 ALBUM The *West Side Story* (Sony Classical) soundtrack album, released in 1960, spent a record 54 weeks at the top of the Billboard album chart, beginning May 5, 1962.

MOST CONSECUTIVE NO. 1 SINGLES The record for most consecutive singles hitting No. 1 on the Billboard Hot 100 is held by Whitney Houston, who released seven straight chart toppers from 1985 to 1988. Her streak started with "Saving All My Love for You," and ran to "Where Do Broken Hearts Go."

The pop diva beat the mark of six set by The Beatles and the Bee Gees. Houston's other songs were "How Will I Know," "The Greatest Love of All," "I Wanna Dance with Somebody," "Didn't We Almost Have It All," and "So Emotional."

MOST NO. 1 HITS The Beatles hold the record for most No. 1 pop singles with a whopping 21, from "Can't Buy Me Love" in 1964 to "The Long and Winding Road" in 1970.

As for solo artists, Elvis Presley and Mariah Carey both have had 17 No. 1 pop singles, the most for solo artists. Elvis accrued his hits in the space of $13\frac{1}{2}$ years between April 21, 1956, and Nov. 1, 1969, while Carey racked up her hits in 15 years from Aug. 4, 1990 to Dec. 31, 2005.

Although Elvis is sometimes credited with 18 hits; "Don't Be Cruel" and "Hound Dog" appeared on the same record and are officially considered one single.

YOUNGEST ALBUM CHART TOPPER Stevie Wonder was the youngest performer ever to have a No. 1 album. In 1963, his live album *Little Stevie Wonder–The Twelve Year Old Genius* (Motown) topped the pop charts when he was just 13 years old. The single "Fingertips–Pt 2" also hit No. 1 that same year.

BEST-SELLING ALBUMS The Eagles' compilation *Their Greatest Hits 1971-1975* is the best-selling album of all time, certified at 28 million copies sold since its release in 1976. Michael Jackson's *Thriller*, a 1982 release with Epic, is the best-selling studio album of all time, as well as album by a solo artist, selling an estimated 27 million in the U.S.

Shania Twain set the bar high for female artists. *Come On Over* (Mercury), released in 1997, has sold over 20 million copies and is the best-selling country album of all-time.

GREATEST ADVANCE SALES SINGLE Elton John's tribute to Diana, Princess of Wales, "Candle in the Wind 1997" (Rocket) with lyrics by Bernie Taupin, was performed at her funeral on Sept. 6, 1997. A reworked version, released as a B-side to "Something About the Way You Look Tonight" shipped 8 million copies prior to its release on Sept. 23, fulfilling multi-platinum standards before it could be purchased. It sold another 3 million in two weeks.

BIGGEST ONE-HIT WONDER The biggest-selling one-hit-wonder album in U.S. history is *We Are the World* (Columbia) by USA for Africa. The charity album (with title track written by Lionel Richie and Michael Jackson and featuring an ensemble of 45 artists) sold over 4 million albums, taking the Billboard 200 No. 1 spot for four weeks beginning April 13, 1985.

MUSIC

Grammy Awards

Beyoncé Knowles ▶

THE NATIONAL ACADEMY OF RECORDING ARTS AND SCIENCES (NARAS), an industry group founded in 1957, presents the Grammy (short for Gramophone) Awards annually to recognize achievements the previous year in music recordings. Hosted by comedian Mort Sahl, the first Grammy Awards were presented at the Beverly Hills Hilton Hotel in Los Angeles on May 4, 1959. (When awards are mentioned by year, the date is for the year of the achievement's release.) All records are as of the 47th Grammy Awards, presented Feb. 13, 2005.

MILESTONES

1958: FIRST GRAMMY WINNERS The big winner at the first Grammy Awards was Domenico Modugno. He won the Record of the Year and Song of the Year awards for 1958 for his Italian song *"Nel Blu Dipinto Di Blu"* (also known as "Volare"). The first Album of the Year Grammy went to Henry Mancini for *The Music From Peter Gunn.*

1960: NON-MUSICAL ALBUM OF THE YEAR Comedian Bob Newhart was the first non-musician to win the Album of the Year Grammy, for his album *Button-Down Mind of Bob Newhart*. The only other non-musical winner was Vaughn Meader, who won the 1962 award for *The First Family*, his spoof of President John F. Kennedy and the Kennedy clan.

1961: ROCK AND ROLL The Grammys recognized a Rock and Roll category for the first time at the 1961 Grammys, staged on May 29, 1962. Chubby Checker won for his follow-up hit, "Let's Twist Again."

1970: HAT-TRICK The first performer to sweep the three main Grammy categories in one year was Paul Simon. He won 1970 Grammys for "Bridge Over Troubled Water" as Record, Album, and Song of the Year; Art Garfunkel, the other half of the Simon & Garfunkel duo, shared the Record and Album awards. Three other artists have completed the Grammy hat-trick: Carole King (1971: "It's Too Late," *Tapestry*, and "You've Got a Friend"); Christopher Cross (1980: "Sailing," *Christopher Cross*, and "Sailing"); and Eric Clapton (1992: "Tears in Heaven," *MTV Unplugged*, and "Tears in Heaven").

1972: LIVE BROADCAST The first time the Grammys were broadcast live on national TV was on March 14, 1972. This was also the first time that the awards were staged in New York City (at Madison Square Garden's Felt Forum). The big winner that year was Carole King, who swept the big three awards (see above). She also won Best Female Pop Vocal Performance (for *Tapestry*).

1988: RAP The first time the Grammys designated a category for rap was on Feb. 22, 1989. DJ Jazzy Jeff and the Fresh Prince (Jeff Townes and Will Smith) received the 1988 Best Rap Performance award for "Parents Just Don't Understand." The awards presentation was not televised, and four of the five nominees boycotted the ceremony in response.

1990: REVOKED GRAMMY The only artists to be stripped of their Grammy were the duo Milli Vanilli. They won the 1989 Best New Artist Award in Feb. 1990, but NARAS revoked the honor on Nov. 19, 1990, when Rob Pilatus and Fabrice Morvan admitted that they did not sing on their album *Girl You Know It's True*, and lip-synched when it was performed; the actual singers were Charles Shaw, Brad Howell, and Johnny Davis, who were credited with backup vocals on the album.

1991: GRAMMY SPURNED Irish singer Sinéad O'Connor announced on Feb. 1, 1991, that she would not perform in the Feb. 20 Grammy ceremony or accept any of the four awards for which she was nominated, in protest against "a world that measures artistic ability by material success."

She became the first person to decline a Grammy, which she won as Best Alternative Music Performer for "I Do Not Want What I Haven't Got."

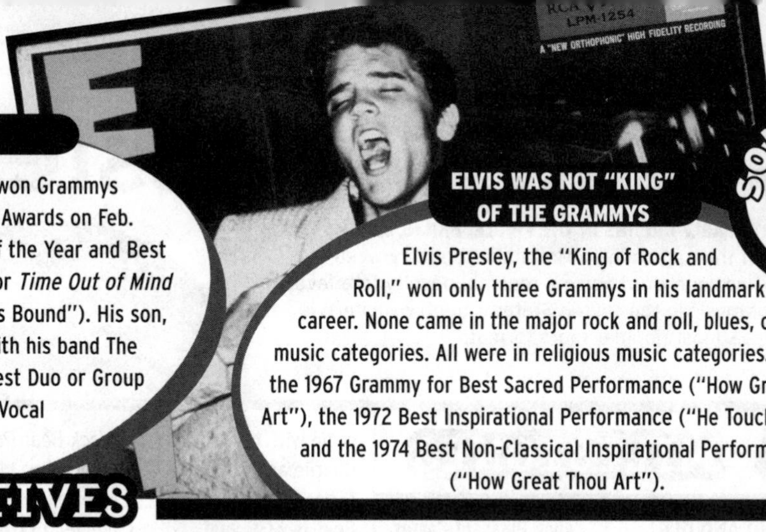

FAMILY AFFAIR

The only time a father and son won Grammys in the same year was at the 40th Awards on Feb. 26, 1998. Bob Dylan won the Album of the Year and Best Contemporary Folk Album Grammys for *Time Out of Mind* and Best Male Rock Vocal ("Cold Irons Bound"). His son, Jakob Dylan, won two Grammys with his band The Wallflowers: Best Rock Song and Best Duo or Group Rock Performance with Vocal ("One Headlight").

SOMETHING TO THINK ABOUT

ELVIS WAS NOT "KING" OF THE GRAMMYS

Elvis Presley, the "King of Rock and Roll," won only three Grammys in his landmark career. None came in the major rock and roll, blues, or pop music categories. All were in religious music categories. He won the 1967 Grammy for Best Sacred Performance ("How Great Thou Art"), the 1972 Best Inspirational Performance ("He Touched Me"), and the 1974 Best Non-Classical Inspirational Performance ("How Great Thou Art").

SUPERLATIVES

MOST GRAMMY WINS **CAREER** Hungarian-born conductor Sir Georg Solti won 38 Grammys, the most by any performer. He won his first Grammy in 1962, for Best Opera Recording (Verdi's *Aida* with the Rome Opera House Orchestra and Chorus). He won his last Grammy posthumously at the 40th annual ceremony on Feb. 26, 1998, six months after his death. It was again for Best Opera Recording (Wagner's *Die Meistersinger von Nurnberg* with the Chicago Symphony Orchestra and Chorus).

MOST WINS (FEMALE ARTIST) **CAREER** At the Grammy ceremonies in 2004, singer and virtuoso fiddler Alison Krauss won three Grammys to reach a record total of 17, more than any other female performer. She was just 19 years old when she claimed the 1990 Best Bluegrass Recording Grammy for her third album (*I've Got That Old Feeling*). She won on Feb. 8, 2004, for Best Country Collaboration with Vocals ("How's the World Treating You") with James Taylor, Best Country Instrumental Performance ("Cluck Old Hen") with Union Station, and Best Bluegrass Album (*Live*) with Union Station.

MOST WINS (PERFORMER) **YEAR** Michael Jackson won eight Grammys in one year, more than any other performer. "The King of Pop" won his record haul at the 26th Grammys on Feb. 28, 1984: Record of the Year ("Beat It"), Album of the Year (*Thriller*), Male Pop Vocal ("Thriller"), Male Rock Vocal ("Beat It"), Best R&B Song ("Billie Jean"), Male R&B Vocal ("Billie Jean"), Producer of the Year (*Thriller*) with Quincy Jones, and Best Record for Children (*E.T. The Extra-Terrestrial*).

MOST WINS (GROUP) **YEAR** Santana, helmed by guitarist Carlos Santana, tied Michael Jackson's eight awards at the 42nd Grammys in 2000.

The legendary group won Record of the Year ("Smooth" featuring Rob Thomas), Album and Rock Album of the Year (*Supernatural*), Duo or Group Pop Performance with Vocal ("Maria, Maria"), Duo or Group Rock Performance with Vocal ("Put Your Lights On" with Everlast), Pop Collaboration with Vocals ("Smooth" featuring Rob Thomas), Pop Instrumental Performance ("El Farol"), and Rock Instrumental Performance ("The Calling" with Eric Clapton).

MOST WINS (FEMALE ARTIST) **YEAR** Four female artists have won five Grammys in a single year. Lauryn Hill set the mark at the 1998 Grammys on Feb. 25, 1999, winning, among other awards, Best New Artist and Album of the Year (*The Miseducation of Lauryn Hill*).

Alicia Keys won her five at the 44th Grammys on Feb. 27, 2002, including Best New Artist and Song of the Year ("Fallin'"). Norah Jones claimed five at the 45th Grammys on Feb. 23, 2003, including Best New Artist, Album of the Year (*Come Away With Me*), and Record of the Year ("Don't Know Why"). Beyoncé Knowles won five at the 46th Grammy Awards on Feb. 8, 2004, including Best Female R&B Vocal Performance ("Dangerously in Love 2"), Best R&B Duo or Group Performance ("The Closer I Get to You" with Luther Vandross), and Best R&B Song ("Crazy in Love" with Jay-Z).

MOST RECORDS OF THE YEAR **CAREER** Paul Simon is the only performer to win the prestigious Record of the Year Grammy three times. His first win came in 1968 for "Mrs. Robinson" (Simon & Garfunkel). He later won for "Bridge Over Troubled Water" (Simon & Garfunkel, 1970), and for "Graceland" (1986).

MOST ALBUMS OF THE YEAR **CAREER** Three performers have won the Album of the Year Grammy three times: Frank Sinatra, Stevie Wonder, and Paul Simon.

"Old Blues Eyes" won for *Come Dance With Me* (1959), *September of My Years* (1965), and *Sinatra: A Man and His Music* (1966). Wonder won for *Innervisions* (1973), *Fulfillingness' First Finale* (1974), and *Songs in the Key of Life* (1976). Simon won for *Bridge Over Troubled Water* (1970, Simon & Garfunkel), *Still Crazy After All These Years* (1975), and *Graceland* (1986).

MUSIC

Country & Western

FROM ITS EARLY ORIGINS IN THE FIDDLE, BANJO, AND MANDOLIN music of the Appalachian Mountains, country-western music has gone from being a regional novelty to a favorite form of music in the United States. Country-western is America's most popular radio format.

1 MILESTONES

1925: GRAND OLE OPRY The heart of country music, *The Grand Ole Opry*, from Nashville, TN, is the oldest continuously broadcast live radio program in the U.S. It debuted on WSM radio Nov. 28, 1925, as the *WSM Barn Dance*. George D. Hay gained national notoriety as the program's emcee and self-proclaimed "Solemn Old Judge." Uncle Dave Macon, a banjo player, is considered the Opry's first bonafide musical star.

Most major country music stars have played at the Opry, and it is largely responsible for Nashville's becoming the country music capital of the U.S.

1927: CARTER FAMILY Known as the "First Family of Country Music," the Carter family changed the sound of country and had an influence on bluegrass, folk, and rock.

Alvin Pleasant Carter, his wife Sara Dougherty, and her cousin Maybelle Addington began playing around southwest Virginia in 1926. Their first recordings in August 1927 for Victor records were an instant hit. They standardized hundreds of Appalachian folk songs and helped bring the music to the more mainstream general public.

In 1970, the Carter family became the first group to enter the Country Music Hall of Fame in Nashville, TN.

EARLY 1930s: BLUEGRASS Bill Monroe fashioned "bluegrass," in homage to his home state of Kentucky. It is typically played with acoustic stringed instruments such as the banjo and guitar, and the songs are usually sung in high-pitched harmonies. In the early 1930s, Monroe performed on radio with his brothers Charlie and Birch. He formed The Bluegrass Boys in 1939, and added legends Lester Flatts and Earl Scruggs in 1944.

Monroe's recording "Blue Moon of Kentucky" is a staple at the Grand Ole Opry. In 1970, Bill Monroe was elected to the Country Music Hall of Fame.

1939: KEEP ON TRUCKIN' Few things say "country music" like a good ol' pick-up truck. Cliff Bruner, bandleader of the Texas Wanderers, is credited with being the first person to record a song about a truck, when he performed Ted Daffan's composition "Truck Driver's Blues" in 1939, with its chorus, "Keep those wheels a-rollin', I ain't got no time to lose."

In 1975 C.W. McCall (aka Bill Fries) helped spread the CB radio craze when he released "Convoy." Co-written with Chip Davis, the single from *Black Bear Road*, went gold in two weeks and inspired a same-titled movie in 1978.

1940S: "HONKY TONK BLUES" Hank Williams Sr., perhaps the most enduring country singer of all time, embodied the "honky tonk" style of country music—which was influenced by blues music and by the yodelling style of Jimmy Rodgers (the "father" of country music).

Williams piled up 27 country top-ten hits in four years, 1949–53, including "Lovesick Blues," "Your Cheatin' Heart," and "I'm So Lonesome I Could Cry."

His 1952 hit "I'll Never Get Out of This World Alive" was released just before he died of a heart attack at age 29 at turn of the new year 1953. Along with Rodgers and Fred Rose (a song writer and impresario), he was a member of the first class of artists elected to the Country Music Hall of Fame, in 1961.

1964: GRAMMYS GO COUNTRY A Country Music category was first included in the Grammy Awards in 1964.

That year, Roger Miller walked away with five Grammies, including Best Country and Western Song and Best Country and Western vocal performance, for "Dang Me." His album *Dang Me/Chug A Lug* also won Album of the Year. Dottie West won Best Female Country Vocalist for "Here Comes My Baby."

1967: COUNTRY MUSIC AWARDS The Country Music Awards (CMAs) began in 1967 as a banquet for the Country Music Association and the press. Eddy Arnold was named the first Entertainer of the Year, and the nontelevised event was hosted by Bobbie Gentry and Sonny James. Dallas Frazier's "There Goes My Everything" was Song of the Year.

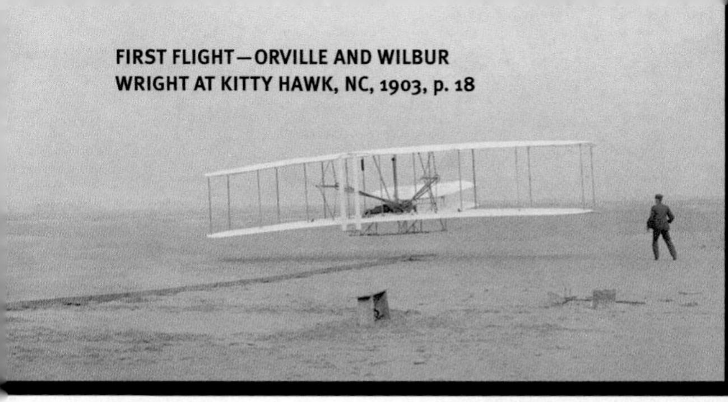

FIRST FLIGHT—ORVILLE AND WILBUR WRIGHT AT KITTY HAWK, NC, 1903, p. 18

ERNEST SHACKLETON'S *NIMROD* IN ANTARCTICA, 1908-09, p. 12

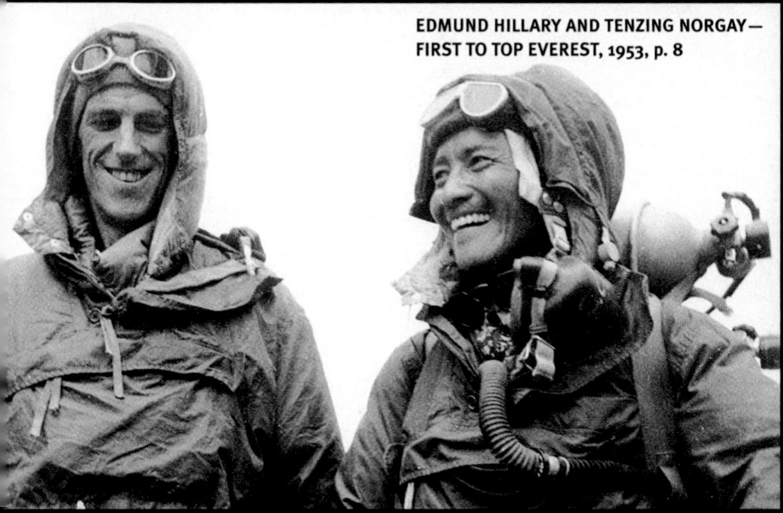

EDMUND HILLARY AND TENZING NORGAY—FIRST TO TOP EVEREST, 1953, p. 8

AMELIA EARHART—FIRST WOMAN TO FLY SOLO ACROSS THE ATLANTIC, 1932, p. 19

TALLEST MOUNTAIN—MT. EVEREST, pp. 8-9

LONGEST INSECT—
WALKINGSTICK, p. 32

VAMPIRE BATS DRINKING BLOOD, p. 21

RATTLESNAKES, DANGEROUS EVEN AFTER DEATH, p. 27

OLDEST PRIMATE—"CHEETA," WITH PHOTO OF CO-STAR "TARZAN," p. 23

MOST POISONOUS FISH—TWO PUFFER FISH, p. 30

FASTEST LAND MAMMAL—CHEETAH, p. 20

FASTEST ON LAND, HEAVIEST, AND TALLEST BIRD—OSTRICH, p. 24

TERMITES: BIGGEST-HOME BUILDERS, p. 33

PABLO PICASSO'S *BOY WITH A PIPE*—HIGHEST PRICE FOR A PAINTING AT AUCTION, 2004, p. 37

ENIAC—FIRST ELECTRONIC, PROGRAMMABLE GENERAL-PURPOSE COMPUTER, 1946, p. 52

CHESS CHAMP KASPAROV PLAYS "DEEP BLUE" COMPUTER, 1996, p. 51

WORKERS AT THE EMPIRE STATE BUILDING, 1931, p. 64

BOB DYLAN GOES ELECTRIC AT THE 1965 NEWPORT FOLK FESTIVAL, pp. 108-109

FIRST AUDIO RECORDING—THOMAS EDISON, 1877, p. 112

TOP-GROSSING MOVIE SERIES—*STAR WARS*, 1977-2005, p. 75

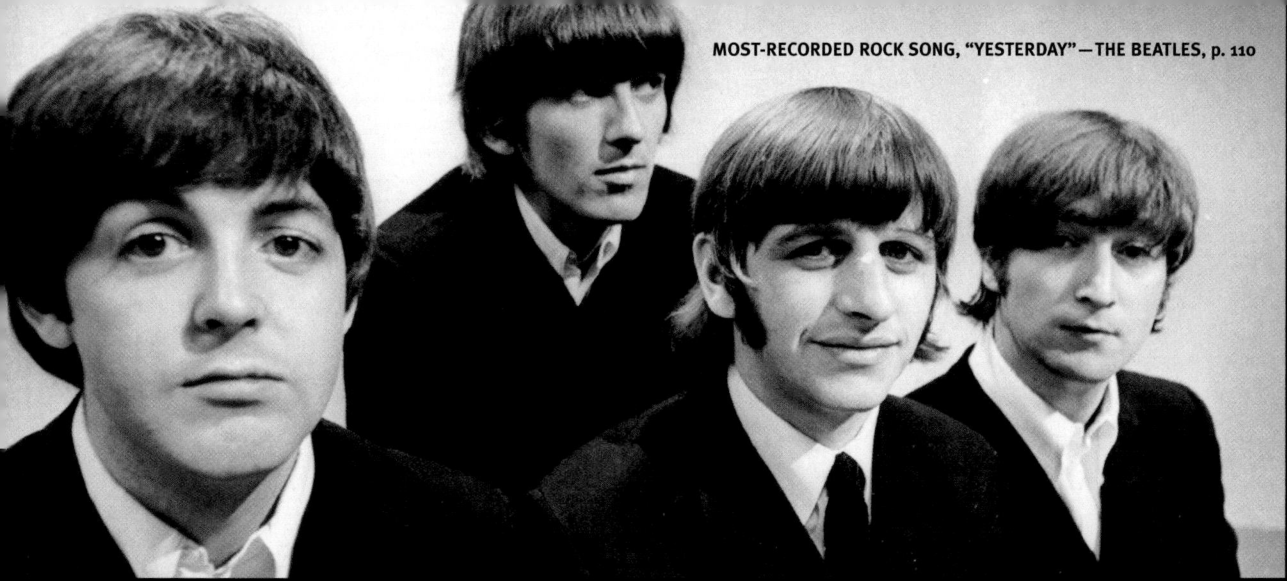

MOST-RECORDED ROCK SONG, "YESTERDAY"—THE BEATLES, p. 110

MOST EXPENSIVE MUSICAL—*THE LION KING*, 1997, p. 43

FIRST SUMMER BLOCKBUSTER MOVIE—*JAWS*, 1975, p. 74

EARLY SPECIAL EFFECTS IN FILM—*A TRIP TO THE MOON*, 1902, p. 80

MOST EMMY NOMINATIONS—*CHEERS*, p. 85

WORST NUCLEAR POWER ACCIDENT—CHERNOBYL, 1986, p. 147

MOST DAMAGING OIL SPILL (U.S.)—*EXXON VALDEZ*, 1989, PRINCE WILLIAM SOUND, AK, p. 147

BIGGEST STONE BUDDHA—LESHAN, CHINA, p. 139

WORST TSUNAMI—INDIAN OCEAN, 2004, p. 147

THE "UNSINKABLE" *TITANIC* HIT AN ICEBERG AND SANK IN 1912; OVER 1,500 DIED, p. 146

TALLEST BUILDINGS EVER DESTROYED—WORLD TRADE CENTER TOWERS, 2001, p. 65

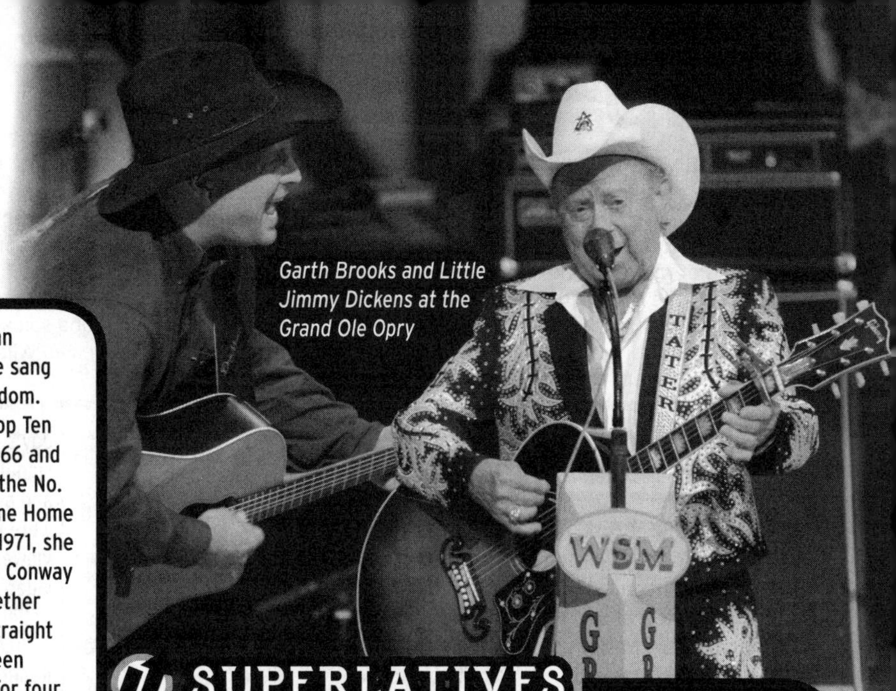

Garth Brooks and Little Jimmy Dickens at the Grand Ole Opry

The first live televised CMA Awards ceremony was in 1969, when Johnny Cash became the first artist to earn five CMA Awards in a single year: Male Vocalist of the Year; Single of the Year for "A Boy Named Sue;" Vocal Group of the Year for work with his wife, June Carter; Entertainer of the Year; Album of the Year for *Johnny Cash at San Quentin Prison*.

1972: FIRST FEMALE ENTERTAINER OF THE YEAR (CMAs)
In 1972, Loretta Lynn became the first woman named Entertainer of the Year by the Country Music Association.

Her life story echoes a myriad of country themes. She was born dirt-poor in the coal mining town of Butcher Hollow, KY, and married at 13. She moved to Custer, WA, in 1951 with her husband, where she began performing. She sang her way to stardom.

Lynn had 13 Top Ten hits between 1966 and 1970, including the No. 1 hit "Don't Come Home a' Drinkin." In 1971, she teamed up with Conway Twitty, and together they had five straight No. 1 hits between 1971 and 1975. For four straight years (1972-75), they were named the Vocal Duo of the Year by the Country Music Association.

1985: FARM AID
Country Legend Willie Nelson helped organize the first Farm Aid concert on Sept. 22, 1985, in Champaign, IL. A crowd of about 80,000 attended and raised more than $7 million for America's financially strapped farmers. The lineup included Nelson, Bob Dylan, Loretta Lynn, Roy Orbison, Tom Petty, and others.

SUPERLATIVES

MOST NO. 1 COUNTRY HITS Conway Twitty holds the record for most No. 1 hit songs on the Billboard Country Music chart, with over 40. His last hit, "Desperado Love," went to No. 1 in 1986. Conway once said that he directed his songs toward women because they "get the message quicker than men do."

MOST CMAs
Vince Gill has won a record 18 CMAs. He won his first in 1990 for Single of the Year ("When I Call Your Name"). To date, his last CMA came in 1999 for Vocal Event of the Year ("My Kind of Woman/My Kind of Man," with Patty Loveless). Gill has also won the award for Entertainer of the Year twice, in 1993 and 1994.

The record for most nominations is Alan Jackson, who was nominated for 72 awards, winning 16.

BEST-SELLING ALBUM The biggest-selling country album of all time is Shania Twain's *Come On Over*. Released Nov. 4, 1997, the Canadian superstar's album has been certified by the Recording Industry Association of America (RIAA) as having sold 20 million copies.

The biggest-selling album by a male country artist is Garth Brooks's *No Fences*. Released Aug. 27, 1990, it was certified as having sold 16 million copies.

Brooks is the only country artist to have four albums certified at 10 million or more copies sold: *The Hits* (10 million), *Ropin' The Wind* (14 million), *Double Live* (15 million), and *No Fences*.

The biggest-selling album by a country group is *Wide Open Spaces* by the Dixie Chicks. Released Jan. 27, 1998, it has sold 12 million copies.

Some Oddball Song Titles

TITLE	WRITTEN BY
May the Bird of Paradise Fly Up Your Nose	Neal Merritt
Jack Daniels If You Please (Knock Me to My Knees)	David Allan Coe
Drop-kick Me Jesus Through the Goalposts of Life	Paul Craft
Get Your Biscuits in the Oven (and Your Buns in the Bed)	Kinky Friedman
All My Ex's Live in Texas	Sanger D. Schafer, Lyndia Shafer
If the Phone Doesn't Ring, It's Me	Jimmy Buffett, Will Jennings, Michael Utley
You Can't Roller Skate in a Buffalo Herd	Roger Miller

Hip-Hop

OutKast

THE SOUND OF HIP-HOP CONSISTS OF TWO BASIC COMPONENTS: RHYMES AND BEATS. It's spoken poetry delivered over pre-recorded samples and/or electronically generated rhythm tracks. Over the years hip-hop has been hailed, and roundly condemned, for its unconventional use of recording technology, and for the frank, provocative lyrics of the most celebrated rappers. The roots of rap reach into the black oral tradition. Participants in the popular competitive game called "the dozens" would engage in an escalating, operatic exchange of rhymed insults. During the late 1940s, jazz singers would accompany complex bebop saxophone solos by "scatting" and improvising lyrics. And in the 1960s comedians like Richard Pryor, Flip Wilson, and Redd Foxx heralded rap's fearless topicality and its raunchy humor.

MILESTONES

1970s: BREAKBEATS DJ Kool Herc (Clive Campbell) invented the DJ breakbeat at South Bronx clubs, house parties, and dances in the mid-1970's.

Herc's style was to play peak after peak of percussive funk momentum, showcasing the rhythmic high points of different songs back-to-back on two turntables. These manual edits were known as breakbeats and Herc's teenage dancing fans were known as the breakers or B Boys.

Two young DJs in the Bronx followed in Herc's footsteps: Grandmaster Flash (Joseph Saddler) and Afrika Bambaataa. By the 1980s, these two had added rappers, drum machines, and synthesizers to the hip-hop mix.

1977: SCRATCHING The wick wikka wikka sound—achieved by a DJ scratching the needle back and forth on a record—became the signature hip-hop hook during the 1980s, thanks to the 1983 hit "Rockit" by Herbie Hancock.

However, scratching was actually invented by Bronx DJ Grand Wizard Theodore (Theodore Livingston) about 1977. A protégé of Grandmaster Flash, Theodore made his discovery by accident when his mother interrupted him while he was practicing at the turntable.

1979: FIRST BILLBOARD TOP 40 HIT Sylvia Robinson, co-founder of Englewood, NJ's Sugar Hill Records, recruited would-be rappers Wonder Mike (Michael Wright), Master Gee (Guy O'Brien), and Big Bank Hank (Henry Jackson) in the local pizzeria and created the Sugarhill Gang.

Assembled in the recording studio with professional musicians covering the disco hit "Good Times" by Chic and borrowed rhymes from Grandmaster Caz (Curtis Fisher), the Sugarhill Gang's debut single "Rapper's Delight" peaked on the Billboard Top 40 at #36 in Jan. 1980. "Rapper's Delight" was the first rap single to "cross over" onto the pop charts.

1980: FIRST GOLD RECORD Kurtis Blow (Kurtis Walker), managed by Russell Simmons, was the first rapper to sign with a major label, Mercury, and his 12-inch single "The Breaks" was the first to sell a million copies, by Aug. 19, 1980.

1984: RAP ON MTV Standing proud in their black leather jackets and Adidas sneakers, the no-nonsense Queens trio Run DMC brought the rap sound to a dynamic new medium.

Rappers Run (Joseph Simmons) and DMC (Darryl McDaniels) and DJ Jam Master Jay's (Jason Mizell) signature rock guitars and dry funky beats were introduced to MTV viewers through their video for "Rock Box" in 1984.

Their producers Rick Rubin and Russell Simmons (Run's older brother) also established the Def Jam record label, building a business empire on hip-hop's newfound visibility.

1986: FEMALE RAP GROUP Cheryl "Salt" James and Sandy "Pepa" Denton were the originators of the first major female rap group, Salt-n-Pepa. Although hip-hop was, and still is, a male-dominated genre, Salt-n-Pepa set the stage for the inclusion of women in rap with their 1986 debut album, *Hot, Cool, and Vicious*.

Two of their biggest hit songs were "Push It" and "The Show Stopper."

1987: NUMBER 1 ALBUM *Licensed To Ill* (Def Jam) by the Beastie Boys became first hip-hop album to top the Billboard Top 200 LP charts on Feb. 28, 1987. Going quadruple platinum by year's end, it was also the fastest-selling debut album in parent-company Columbia Records' 98-year history.

1989: RAP GRAMMY The first time the Grammy Awards recognized a category for rap music was in 1989. DJ Jazzy Jeff & the Fresh Prince won the Best Rap Performance Grammy for "Parents Just Don't Understand."

1991: SAMPLING LAWSUIT On Dec. 16, 1991, Gilbert O'Sullivan successfully sued comedic rapper Biz Markie (Marcel Hall), claiming that his single "Alone Again" had illegally used a sample of the first eight bars from O'Sullivan's 1972 soft-rock hit "Alone Again (Naturally)."

The first complaint judged in court proved to be a creative turning point for hip-

HIP-HOPPING AROUND THE GLOBE

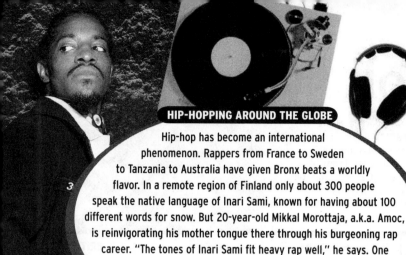

Hip-hop has become an international phenomenon. Rappers from France to Sweden to Tanzania to Australia have given Bronx beats a worldly flavor. In a remote region of Finland only about 300 people speak the native language of Inari Sami, known for having about 100 different words for snow. But 20-year-old Mikkal Morottaja, a.k.a. Amoc, is reinvigorating his mother tongue there through his burgeoning rap career. "The tones of Inari Sami fit heavy rap well," he says. One of his more popular raps begins, *"Kolle Aksu, tääl lii puattam veelkij maksu"*, which can be translated as "Golden Axe, the time for paying the debts has come."

hop as well as a legal precedent, as multi-platinum producers like Dr. Dre responded by employing more keyboards and turning away from outright sampling of old records.

1992: DEATH ROW RECORDS N.W.A. turned heads in interest and outrage with *Straight Outta Compton* in 1988.

It wasn't the first gangsta rap available, but the album, which described the violent and hedonistic world of rappers Ice Cube (O'Shea Jackson), Dr. Dre (Andre Young), and Eazy-E (Eric Wright), hit No. 37 on Billboard and went platinum in 1989 without any major airplay.

Once Ice Cube left for a successful solo career in 1989, the group split but gangsta rap, or G funk, had moved the hip-hop spotlight.

In the hip-hop do-it-yourself spirit, Dr. Dre and Marion "Suge" Knight founded the mega-successful Death Row Records label in 1992. They released a stream of gangsta-style hits with rolling bass grooves and profanity-laced rhymes, including Dre's own *The Chronic* (1992) with Snoop Dogg (Calvin Broadus).

1996-97: THE FEUD As their fame rose in the mid '90s, California-based Tupac Shakur (Lesane Crooks) and Brooklyn rapper Notorious B.I.G. (Chris Wallace) were engaged in an ongoing feud—a verbal turf war pitting east coast hip-hop against the west coast—stemming from a near-fatal mugging Tupac survived in New York in Nov. 1994.

Then, two still-unsolved murders silenced both these talented and troubled voices. Tupac, age 25, was shot in Las Vegas on Sept. 7, 1996, after attending a prizefight.

Within six months, Biggie, age 24, was fatally shot as he left the *Vibe* magazine party after the Soul Train Awards in Los Angeles on Mar. 9, 1997.

2004: RAPPER TURNED EXECUTIVE On Dec. 3, 2004, Brooklyn, NY rapper Jay-Z (Shawn Carter) was named president and CEO of Def Jam record label (now owned by Vivendi/Universal).

Jay-Z had retired from making music in 2003, after releasing a string of 13 successful albums.

SUPERLATIVES

BIGGEST SELLING ALBUM Three rap albums have sold over 10 million copies in the U.S. according to the Recording Industry Assoc. of America: Hammer's *Please Hammer, Don't Hurt 'Em* (1990); Notorious B.I.G.'s *Life After Death* (1997); and OutKast's *Speakerboxxx/The Love Below* (2003).

FASTEST SELLING ALBUM Eminem's *The Marshall Mathers LP* sold 1.76 million copies in its first week in May 2000.

After 50 Cent's *The Massacre* was released five days early in March 2005 to fight piracy, it sold 1.14 million copies in four days, making it the fastest selling album in a shortened release week.

BIGGEST SELLING ARTIST The biggest selling rap artist of all-time is Tupac Shakur, with certified domestic sales in excess of 36.5 million. His debut album *2Pacalypse Now* was released in 1991.

During his lifetime, 2Pac released four albums. More than double that number have been released posthumously.

MOST GRAMMY WINS (YEAR) Stepping out on her own after a successful stint in The Fugees, Lauryn Hill put a progressive spin on the urgent sound of hip-hop with her solo debut album, *The Miseducation of Lauryn Hill*. At the 1998 Grammy Awards, Hill collected five awards for her efforts, including Album of the Year and Best New Artist.

OSCAR RAP Rap star Eminem (along with lyricists Jeff Bass and Luis Resto) won the Best Original Song Oscar at the 2003 Academy Awards for "Lose Yourself." The song was written for the movie *8 Mile* (2002), which was loosely based on the life of Eminem (Marshall Bruce Mathers III).

The rapper refused to sing "Lose Yourself" during the Oscar telecast when the Academy insisted he sing a "sanitized" version of the song, rather than bleep out offensive words. It was the first time in the history of the awards that the winning song was not performed at the ceremony.

MUSIC

Rock & Roll

ROCK AND ROLL MEANS DIFFERENT THINGS to different people. However the music genre is defined, there is no doubt that the emergence of rock and roll music in the mid-20th century sparked a musical, commercial, and cultural revolution that still reverberates. From Chuck Berry to the White Stripes, Robert Johnson to U2, rock and roll features a strong back beat and the electric guitar in all its glory. Rock icons like Elvis Presley and The Beatles transcended their music to become permament fixtures of pop culture.

MILESTONES

1952: MOONDOG CORONATION BALL
Cleveland, OH, disc jockey Alan Freed is widely credited with bringing rhythm and blues to a white audience in the early 1950s with "the Moondog Rock and Roll Party" on the radio station WJW. The phrase "rock and roll" was not new, but Freed popularized it.

Freed, along with promoter Lew Plant, were the driving forces behind the "Moondog Coronation Ball" staged at the Cleveland Arena on March 21, 1952. Promoters underestimated the demand to see such performers as The Dominoes and Tiny Grimes, and over 20,000 fans tried to crowd into the 11,000-seat arena.

Chaos broke out and the event had to be stopped. But this concert is credited with launching the rock and roll frenzy that soon swept pop culture.

1955: "ROCK AROUND THE CLOCK"
Bill Haley and the Comets' "Rock Around the Clock" was the first rock and roll song to go number-one on the pop charts, in June 1955. Written by Jimmy DeKnight and Max Freedman, it was originally recorded by Sonny Dae and His Knights in 1952. Haley and the Comets recorded their rockabilly version on Apr. 12, 1954. That version was originally released as a B-side but became a hit nearly a year later, when it was featured in the movie *Blackboard Jungle*.

1955: "MAYBELLENE"
One of the most influential guitar players in rock history, Chuck Berry hit it big in 1955 with "Maybellene." The song was Berry's version of a novelty country song, "Ida Red."

With his flamboyant guitar licks, and signature "duck walk" the St. Louis native was one of the first African-American artists to reach a large, young, white audience.

1956: ELVIS PRESLEY ON *ED SULLIVAN*
Elvis was paid $50,000 for three performances on *The Ed Sullivan Show*, the most popular program on American television for most of the 1950s and 1960s. His first performance, on Sept. 9, 1956, transformed the rising star into a national phenomenon.

One in three Americans, 52 million people saw Presley's grating, sensually energetic performance of "Don't Be Cruel," "Love Me Tender," "Ready Teddy," and "Hound Dog."

Elvis's rise to becoming the "King of Rock and Roll" was not without controversy. By his third performance on Jan. 6, 1957, the moral clamor over Presley's gyrations had led Ed Sullivan insist that the star's performance be filmed from the waist up.

1957: AMERICAN BANDSTAND
The *American Bandstand* TV show was first broadcast nationally on ABC on Aug. 5, 1957, as an afterschool program, and ran on the network until May 9, 1987 (it continued on cable until Oct. 7, 1989). The program was first broadcast on Philadelphia's WFIL-TV on Oct. 6, 1952, as "Bandstand" with host Bob Horn.

Dick Clark joined the show as a DJ and hosted for 33 years, 1956-1989. The first song played on the national edition was Elvis's "Teddy Bear."

1964: THE BRITISH INVASION When The Beatles appeared on *The Ed Sullivan Show* for three shows beginning on Feb. 9, 1964, "Beatlemania" shook the U.S. An estimated 23 million households, 45.3% of the American audience, tuned in to watch the Beatles play to some 1,500 screaming fans. The rating was a record at the time and still stands as the 24th highest in TV history.

British bands dominated the charts for the next two years, including an unrivaled stint by The Beatles, who managed to take the top five spots on the Billboard Pop Singles chart on April 4, 1964. Other top acts included The Rolling Stones, The Kinks, The Hollies, and Herman's Hermits.

1965: BOB DYLAN GOES ELECTRIC
While some musicians were taking their cue from Chuck Berry

The Beatles invade the U.S., Feb. 1964

SOMETHING TO THINK ABOUT

THE DAY THE MUSIC DIED

Three pioneering rock and roll stars—Buddy Holly, Ritchie Valens, and J.P. Richardson, "The Big Bopper"—died in a plane crash on Feb. 3, 1959. During a three-week, 24-city tour, Holly had decided to charter a plane from Clear Lake, IA, to Fargo, ND, because the tour bus had no heat. The plane crashed shortly after takeoff. This event inspired singer Don McLean's 1972 hit ballad "American Pie," which immortalized it as "the day the music died."

and Elvis, others were building a scene around singers of traditional folk songs like Woody Guthrie and Leadbelly. In the early 1960s, Bob Dylan emerged as the preeminent heir of the growing folk scene which was closely intertwined with the protest movement.

While an album released early in 1965 included electric instruments, Dylan's change of style was brought home during his first set at the Newport, RI, Folk Festival on July 25, 1965. In a seminal moment in rock history, Bob Dylan performed for the first time with an electric guitar in concert.

1966: PSYCHEDELIC

Studio recording advances and a wider array of influences from jazz to Indian sounds took hold of popular rock, and by 1966 musicians stepped out of the typical verse-chorus-verse song structure into longer and less linear sounds. Bands like The Yardbirds began using swirling guitars and novel instruments like harpsichords. Practically everybody followed suit including The Beatles (with recorded sounds played backward) and The Rolling Stones.

Some like Pink Floyd played surreal and dreamy songs that focused on atmosphere and mood. Others like Jimi Hendrix howled onto the scene, using the guitar to make sounds no one thought possible. Hendrix's experiments with distortion, feedback, and sound effects like the wah-wah pedal are legendary and influenced many musicians of the day.

1969: HEAVY METAL

Some bands began pounding out raw recordings focused on louder guitars and heavier drumming. With amps turned to 11, Led Zeppelin's back-to-back albums released in 1969, *Led Zeppelin* (released Jan. 17), and *Led Zeppelin II* (released Oct. 22), both made the Billboard Top 10 and propelled blues-based heavy metal into garages everywhere.

1969: WOODSTOCK

Music festivals at places like Monterey, CA, and the Isle of Wight, England, were becoming popular symbols of the rock and roll cultural revolution in the late 1960s. The Woodstock Festival held on Max Yasgur's farm in Bethel, NY, Aug. 15-17, 1969, made headlines as traffic jams backed up for miles and over 400,000 people stormed the gates. The concert's promoters were unprepared for the enormous response and admission fees had to be abandoned.

Among the many bands and performers on the bill were The Grateful Dead, The Who, Jefferson Airplane, Joan Baez, Joe Cocker, Jimi Hendrix, and The Band.

1975: PUNK

Punk began almost simultaneously as a reaction in both the U.S. and U.K. around 1975, although different punks were reacting to different "establishments" in different scenes. Musically, punk rebuffed the refined and complex rock then popular. It embraced the loud, fast, and sloppy styles emerging over the past five years traced through the Velvet Underground, the Stooges, and the New York Dolls.

Three-chord and two-minute songs dominated most early punk. Some bands like The Ramones echoed 50s rock with songs about teens growing up; others like The Sex Pistols and The Clash made political statements.

LATE 1980s: GRUNGE

Musicians and fans divided punk fused with other influences into hundreds of genres and subgenres. Bands like Mudhoney began playing a combination of punk and early '70s metal called "grunge," in Seattle, WA, in the late 1980s.

Grunge was the first post-punk genre to develop a large commercial following with bands like Soundgarden, Nirvana, and Pearl Jam topping charts in the early 1990s. Nirvana's second album *Nevermind*, released in 1991, is widely credited with sparking the grunge movement around the world.

MORE ON

Rock & Roll

SUPERLATIVES

LARGEST ATTENDANCE (ONE-DAY ROCK CONCERT) "Summer Jam '73" held at Watkins Glen, NY, on July 28, 1973, drew about 600,000 people, although only 150,000 of them actually bought tickets. The show's headliners were the Grateful Dead, the Band, and the Allman Brothers Band.

The "Molson Canadian Rocks for Toronto" ("Toronto Rocks"), a benefit to promote tourism there in the aftermath of the 2003 SARS outbreak, sold more tickets than any other rock show. Held at the city's Downsview Park on July 30, 2003, it drew 489,176 paying customers to see the Rolling Stones, AC/DC, Rush, and 12 other acts.

An estimated 180,000 people saw former Beatle Paul McCartney perform a second show at the Maracaña Stadium in Rio de Janeiro, Brazil, on April 21, 1990—the largest paying audience for a single act. His two shows at the world's largest soccer stadium were his only appearances in South America during an eight-month-long world tour. The first show drew only 60,000 because of heavy rain.

HIGHEST GROSSING TOUR The highest gross for any rock tour is the $320 million generated by the Rolling Stones Voodoo Lounge Tour in 1994-95. Staged in over 60 cities worldwide, the tour easily topped the previous mark (set by the Stones' Steel Wheels Tour, which grossed over $250 million in 1989). Their 2003 "Licks" tour now ranks second, having grossed $299.5 million.

MOST WATCHED CONCERT (LIVE BROADCAST) The Live Aid Concerts, broadcast to 1.5 billion potential worldwide viewers on television July 13, 1985, are considered the most watched concert in history. The 16-hour satellite broadcast reached 150 countries with 80% of the world's TVs.

An estimated 40 million in the U.S. and 30 million in Britain saw an unprecedented collection of rock icons perform for a noble cause.

Organized by Boomtown Rats lead singer Bob Geldof to raise funds for famine relief in Ethiopia, the concerts were held concurrently in Wembley Stadium in London, England, and JFK Stadium in Philadelphia, PA, though some acts performed via satellite.

The lineups included David Bowie, Bob Dylan, Mick Jagger, Elton John, B.B. King, Madonna, Paul McCartney, Queen, Sting, U2, and The Who, among other rock luminaries.

MOST RECORDED SONG The most recorded rock song is "Yesterday," with more than 3,000 cover versions estimated to have been recorded since The Beatles' 1965 recording. Cover artists vary from Ray Charles to the Philadelphia Orchestra.

Although the song is credited to both John Lennon and Paul McCartney, McCartney wrote the song alone (the pair shared credits on their songs regardless of who wrote them).

McCartney said he dreamed the melody of "Yesterday," woke up, and immediately began to work on the music, initially with gag lyrics.

HIGHEST PRICE (ROCK MEMORABILIA) The highest price ever paid at auction for a piece of rock and roll memorabilia was the $2,229,000 paid for a Rolls-Royce that once belonged to The Beatles' John Lennon.

Canadian businessman Jim Pattison placed the winning bid on the 1965 Rolls-Royce Phantom V limousine, complete with psychedelic paintwork, at Sotheby's in New York on June 29, 1985. The luxury automobile was equipped with a TV, telephone, refrigerator, and backseat that converted into a double bed.

In 1987, Pattison donated the car to the province of British Colombia. It is now on public display at Bristol Motors in Victoria, British Columbia.

HIGHEST PRICE (DRUM KIT) The highest price ever paid for a drum kit at auction was $252,487, for the chrome set used by the late Keith Moon. The five-piece Premier-brand kit, auctioned at Christie's in London on Sept. 29, 2004, was used by Moon, the drummer of The Who, from 1968 to 1970.

HIGHEST PRICE (PIANO) A walnut Steinway Model Z upright piano (on which John Lennon composed and recorded "Imagine" in 1971) went for $2.1 million at auction, the highest price tag ever for a rock musician's piano. Pop singer George Michael was

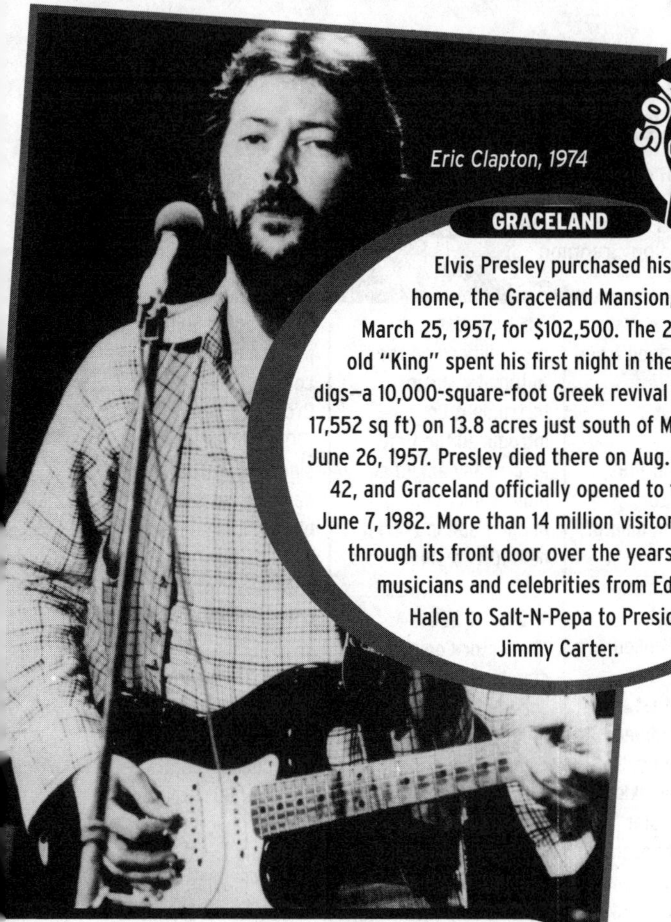

Eric Clapton, 1974

the winning bidder, Oct. 17, 2000, at London's Hard Rock Cafe. He reportedly outbid such music luminaries such as Robbie Williams and Noel and Liam Gallagher.

The previous owner had loaned the piano to The Beatles Story Museum in Liverpool, England, for 10 months before the auction. Michael later returned the piano to the museum.

HIGHEST PRICE (GUITAR)

Eric Clapton's black and white Fender Stratocaster, which the British rock legend played from late 1970 to 1985, is the most expensive guitar ever sold at auction. On June 24, 2004, the guitar, which Clapton dubbed "Blackie," went for $959,500 at Christie's in New York. The Guitar Center instrument chain store, based in Westlake Village, CA, won the bidding.

Auction proceeds were donated to the Crossroads Center in Antigua, a drug treatment center Clapton established in 1998.

SOMETHING TO THINK ABOUT

GRACELAND

Elvis Presley purchased his home, the Graceland Mansion, on March 25, 1957, for $102,500. The 22-year-old "King" spent his first night in the palatial digs—a 10,000-square-foot Greek revival mansion (now 17,552 sq ft) on 13.8 acres just south of Memphis, TN—on June 26, 1957. Presley died there on Aug. 16, 1977, at age 42, and Graceland officially opened to the public on June 7, 1982. More than 14 million visitors have walked through its front door over the years, including musicians and celebrities from Eddie Van Halen to Salt-N-Pepa to President Jimmy Carter.

FIFTY IN FIFTY

In 2003, folk rocker Adam Brodsky from Philadelphia, PA, managed to play all 50 states in 50 days, with a Washington, DC, finale on the 51st. Traveling 23,440 miles, most of it in a white conversion van (he flew only to Alaska and Hawaii), Brodsky played Newark, DE, on Aug. 3 and looped his way through the country, playing bars, cafes, a deli, and a "gumbo shack," before reaching Washington, DC, on Sept. 22.

CAN YOU ROCK IT LIKE THIS?

Not everybody gets to be a rock star, but that hasn't stopped anyone from rocking out behind closed doors before an imaginary crowd, shredding on an imaginary "air guitar." For some, mimicking a guitarist (tongue wagging, kicks, and all) while playing the air has become a thing of pride. The Air Guitar World Championships have been held as part of The Oulu Music Video Festival in Oulu, Finland, since 1996. In 2005, finalists from 13 countries participated. The winner, Michael "Destroyer" Heffels (Netherlands), received his very own guitar and amp.

KNOCKIN' ON HEAVEN'S DOOR

According to a 2005 survey by the British digital cable channel Music Choice, the song its viewers most wanted played at their funeral was "Angels" by British star Robbie Williams. "My Way" by Frank Sinatra held the second spot, followed by Monty Python's "Always Look on the Bright Side of Life."

Selected Auction Records for Celebrities' Guitars

ROCK STAR	ITEM	PRICE	DATE
Kurt Cobain	1960s Mosrite Gospel, Mark IV	$117,500	April 17, 2004
Jerry Garcia	The "Tiger"	$959,000	May 8, 2002
George Harrison[1]	1964 Standard SG Gibson	$567,500	Dec. 17, 2004
Jimi Hendrix	1968 Fender Stratocaster[2]	$295,000	April 25, 1990
Buddy Holly	1945 Gibson Acoustic	$242,000	June 23, 1990,
Pete Townshend	1963 White Gibson SG Special	$181,614	Sept. 29, 2004
Stevie Ray Vaughan	c. 1965 composite Fender Stratocaster ("Lenny")	$623,500	June 24, 2004

(1) Harrison used the guitar on the *Revolver* album. He loaned it to John Lennon, who used it on some songs on the *White Album*. (2) Played by Hendrix at the 1969 Woodstock Festival.

MUSIC

Audio Technology

Edison home phonograph

WHEN A "TALKING MACHINE" WAS DEVELOPED BY THOMAS EDISON IN 1877, IT WAS HAILED AS A MARVEL, clinching his fame as the "inventor of the age." The cylinders he used for recording may seem primitive today. But they marked the beginning of a long series of remarkable innovations in recording technology, ranging from disks, to tapes, to today's various digital formats.

MILESTONES

1877: AUDIO RECORDING Edison made the first audio recording ("Mary had a little lamb") on Dec. 6, 1877. The Wizard of Menlo Park had not planned to spark a new entertainment industry; he was looking for a way to record telephone messages.

The first working model of the "phonograph," as he called it, recorded on tinfoil wrapped around a cylinder; sound caused a needle to vibrate and make indentations in the foil. Because of the fragile nature of tinfoil, none of the original recordings survive.

1888: MUSIC RECORDING The June 29, 1888, cylinder recording of Handel's oratorio "Israel in Egypt" at London's Crystal Palace, made by Edison's foreign sales agent is the oldest known piece of recorded music.

The next year, Edward Easton's District of Columbia Phonograph Co. became the first company to sell cylinders of recorded music. Music by Columbia's U.S. Marine Band and by whistling virtuoso John Yorke Atlee were popular selections.

Early recordings were made using a large conical horn attached to a cutter for wax. (Edison's tinfoil proved a less than satisfactory recording medium.) Impressions in the wax were made by a diaphragm pushed by direct sound pressure, so people would sometimes resort to sticking their heads in the horn and shouting.

1889: MASS PRODUCTION German-born American inventor Emile Berliner developed a practical disc phonograph—dubbed a "gramophone"—in 1887. This provided the answer to a major problem with cylinders: they could only be copied one at a time, while discs could be stamped from a master.

Berliner first licensed his gramophone in 1889, as a novelty, to Kämmerer & Reinhardt, a toy-making firm in Germany. The company mass-produced small hand-cranked gramophones and talking dolls that played hard rubber, celluloid, or zinc discs. Songs like "Twinkle, Twinkle Little Star" (by Berliner himself) and "Jack & Jill" were some selections. To compensate for poor sound quality, lyrics were printed on the disc's other side.

1889: JUKEBOX The coin-operated cylinder phonograph was installed on Nov. 23, 1889, at the Palais Royal Saloon in San Francisco. Louis Glass and William Arnold of the Pacific Phonograph Co. had fitted an Edison phonograph cabinet with a coin mechanism. The nickel machine with four "listening tubes" earned over $1,000 in the first six months of operation.

Bar music without a band became a possibility when the Automatic Music Instrument Co. introduced the first electrically amplified multi-selection phonograph in 1927; it held 10 two-sided discs.

1901: 78 RPM The Victor Company standardized the speed of its records in 1901. It needed a comfortable pace for cranking its spring motor phonograph, and 78 rotations per minute was found to be in keeping with the heart rate. Later, with the advent of electric recording, the speed was adopted as a general standard, and it remained popular until the long-playing record (LP) arrived in 1948.

1901: FLIP SIDE Ademor Petit of Newark, NJ, invented the double-sided disc, with grooves on both sides of the record. He filed a patent application in Jan. 1901 and received the patent in 1904.

1909: ALBUM The Odeon Co. of Germany recorded Tchaikovsky's "Nutcracker Suite," performed by the London Palace Orchestra in April 1909, on four double-sided discs. The package resembled a photo album, and the word "album" was soon used for any collection of records.

1925: 33-$\frac{1}{3}$ RPM J. P. Maxfield of Bell Labs in 1925 introduced a rotation speed of 33-$\frac{1}{3}$ rpm for sound-track records, matching the 11-minute playing time of contemporary film reels (The existing 10-inch, 78-rpm record lasted only a third of that time). In addition to the lower speed, the new records required a 20-inch diameter.

Columbia introduced the first 12-inch long-playing record in 1948. The microgrooved vinyl LP was developed by Peter Goldmark for Columbia Records and could play 23 minutes on each side.

1932: STEREO RECORDINGS Alan Blumlein of Electric & Musical Industries patented the

SOMETHING TO THINK ABOUT

TECHNOLOGY OF CHOICE

CD sales surpassed LP sales in the U.S. for the first time in 1988. During the first six months 70.4 million CDs were sold, while LP sales decreased to 43.5 million units. Only 13% of all U.S. homes had a CD player at that time, while 90% had a turntable or other audio player. Cassettes were still the dominant format though, outselling CDs three to one (208.1 million units).

CAR STEREO

Years before the thud of subwoofers could be heard rolling down streets, some 1956 Plymouth, Dodge, DeSoto, Chrysler, and Imperial cars were the first to incorporate a built-in stereo with their "Highway Hi-Fi." Peter Goldmark and CBS Labs developed this $16\frac{2}{3}$-rpm record player, which held 7-inch ultramicrogroove (one-third the width of a human hair) records mounted in a shockproof case. The unit cost $56.95, and each record played over 45 minutes per side.

"binaural" recording method in London in 1931. The concept, intended for film, came from the simple observation that listeners determine a sound's direction using two ears. Leopold Stokowski, conductor of the Philadelphia Orchestra, made the first "stereophonic" recording, Scriabin's "Poem of Fire," with Bell Labs on March 12, 1932.

1936: REEL-TO-REEL
Magnetic recordings using metallic surfaces existed since 1898 but were very expensive. German engineer Fritz Pfleumer coated strips of paper or film with magnetic powders, a cheaper process that he patented in 1928.

AEG of Berlin made the first public recording on a "Magnetophone," on Nov. 19, 1936. The device remained in Germany until after World War II, when U.S. Signal Corps Captain John Mullin mailed two machines with 50 reels from Frankfurt to California.

1949: 45 RPM
RCA Victor began producing vinyl 7-inch 45s to match a new player in 1949, as a marketing move for cheaper music. The design was completed before a speed was established, and the math determined 45 rpm. Later that year, Capitol became the first record company to support all three existing speeds.

1963: CASSETTE
Royal Philips Electronics launched the compact audio cassette at the Sept. 1963 Berlin Radio Show. It used a new, $\frac{1}{8}$-inch, low-noise polyester tape from BASF and was intended for portable dictation. In 1979, Sony developed the TPS-L2 Walkman as the first portable audio cassette player. The format led U.S. music sales from 1985 until 1991.

1973: COMPACT DISC
Dutch physicists Klaas Compaan and Piet Kramer began to record video images in holographic form on disc for Philips in 1969. The team switched over to an audio format in 1973.

Philips and Sony agreed in 1980 on a standard plastic compact disc that used 16-bit encoding, was 4.7 inches in diameter, and had a maximum playtime of 74 minutes. CDs were first available in the U.S. in 1983; 800,000 were sold there that year. CDs have been the dominant format for U.S. music sales since 1992.

1987: MP3 In 1987, Germany's Fraunhofer Institute, along with Dieter Seitzer of the University of Erlangen, developed a method for compressing audio files that maintained acceptable sound quality while reducing the file size to $\frac{1}{12}$ of the original. It became known as ISO-MPEG Audio Layer-3, or MP3 for short.

MPMan of Korea released the MP-F20, the first portable MP3 player, in 1997; it could hold an hour of audio.

SUPERLATIVES

OLDEST PLAYABLE RECORDING
The oldest existing recording is a talking clock prototype devised by Frank Lambert of the Ansonia Clock Company. After Thomas Edison signed a contract with Ansonia on Jan. 7, 1878, Lambert recorded himself counting off the hours in quick succession on a cylinder made of lead rather than the standard tinfoil.

The scratchy and ghostly recording is now owned by a private collector but can be heard online at tinfoil.com.

OLDEST RECORD LABEL Columbia is the world's oldest continually active record label. The Columbia Phonograph Co. was created by stenographer Edward Easton in the District of Columbia in 1889, as a local selling agency of the North American Phonograph Co. Columbia's music sales made it the most successful subsidiary. When North American went bankrupt in 1894, Columbia became an independent company.

MOST VALUABLE RECORD AT AUCTION A still-sealed, first-pressing stereo copy of the Beatles' "Yesterday . . . and Today" LP (Capitol 1966), with the controversial "Butcher" cover of the Fab Four in white smocks with dismembered dolls, sold for $38,500 at the Good Rockin' Tonight "Ultra Rarities" auction on Aug. 4-5, 1999. It is one of two stereo copies in pristine condition that are known to exist.

Radio

THE BUGGLES SANG THAT "VIDEO KILLED THE RADIO STAR," but radio–technically, the transmission of electromagnetic waves through space, picked up by a receiver and converted to sound–is still very much alive in the 21st century. Radio today offers everything from heavy metal to classical, Rush Limbaugh to Howard Stern, Ryan Seacrest to *All Things Considered*, and traffic and weather every 20 minutes.

MILESTONES

1888: HERTZ WAVES Scottish physicist James Clerk Maxwell theorized in 1864 that invisible electromagnetic waves traveled like light, but it was two decades before German physicist Heinrich Rudolf Hertz detected these electromagnetic waves. In recognition of his discovery, the unit of frequency, measured in cycles per second, is named the hertz.

1890s: WIRELESS RADIO Hertz's discovery prompted a rush of innovation. Leading the way were Croatian-born American Nikola Tesla, Russian physicist Aleksandr Popov, and Italian inventor Guglielmo Marconi.

Tesla presented the first public demonstration of the principles of radio communication, in 1893. Popov made the first radio receiver in 1895, and on June 2, 1896, in Great Britain, Marconi received the first patent for radio.

1900: VOICE OVER RADIO Canadian-American engineer Reginald Fessenden was the first to transmit sound other than Morse code over radio waves. The U.S. Weather Bureau hired him in Jan. 1900 to develop wireless speech so that it could receive weather information from distant points.

Fessenden worked from two stations, one in Washington, DC, and one a mile away on Cobb Island, in the Potomac River. He succeeded on Dec. 23, 1900, when an assistant on Cobb Island heard him ask, "Is it snowing where you are?"

Fessenden is also credited with the first long-distance radio broadcast, on Christmas Eve 1906, airing from Brant Rock, MA, a program of readings and music for boatmen in Boston harbor.

1901: TRANS-ATLANTIC SIGNAL Guglielmo Marconi received the first signal across the Atlantic Ocean. After setting up a receiving station at Newfoundland, Canada, he instructed his assistants at his wireless station at Cornwall, England, to send the Morse code letter *S* on Dec. 11, 1901. In Canada, he and his assistant George Kemp received signals the next day.

Marconi shared the Nobel Prize for Physics in 1909.

1920: COMMERCIAL RADIO Westinghouse received the first commercial broadcasting license, on Oct. 27, 1920, and was assigned the call letters KDKA. The assistant chief engineer, Frank Conrad, had begun airing programs of music and talk from his garage in Wilkinsburg, PA, in late 1919 and had gained a relatively large audience.

In its first official broadcast, on Nov. 2, KDKA covered the Harding-Cox presidential election from a shed atop a building in East Pittsburgh. A daily schedule soon followed, and the first full-time announcer was hired.

1933: FM RADIO Edwin Armstrong single-handedly created wide-band frequency modulation–FM–radio, securing five patents on Dec. 26, 1933. While AM waves drown out interference with stronger signals (amplitude), FM emits a wider span of frequencies at low levels. Sound quality is far superior since it isn't affected by electrical interference, such as storms.

The first public FM broadcast was from Yonkers, NY, on Nov. 5, 1935, for a meeting of the Institute of Radio Engineers in New York City.

1930s-50s: GOLDEN AGE OF RADIO Between 1930 and 1935, radio production and ownership doubled. By 1935, 22,869,000 American homes owned a radio and there were 625 stations.

The airwaves were filled with action-adventure series, including *The Shadow* (1930-54), *Death Valley Days* (1930-51), and *The Green Hornet* (1936-52), and with comedy by entertainers such as Jack Benny (1935-55), Fred Allen (1932-49), George Burns and Gracie Allen (1934-50), and Fibber McGee and Molly (1935-59).

Radio production peaked in 1947, when about 17 million sets were made. Some 37 million homes owned a radio, while 1,100 stations employed over 55,000 full- or part-time entertainers.

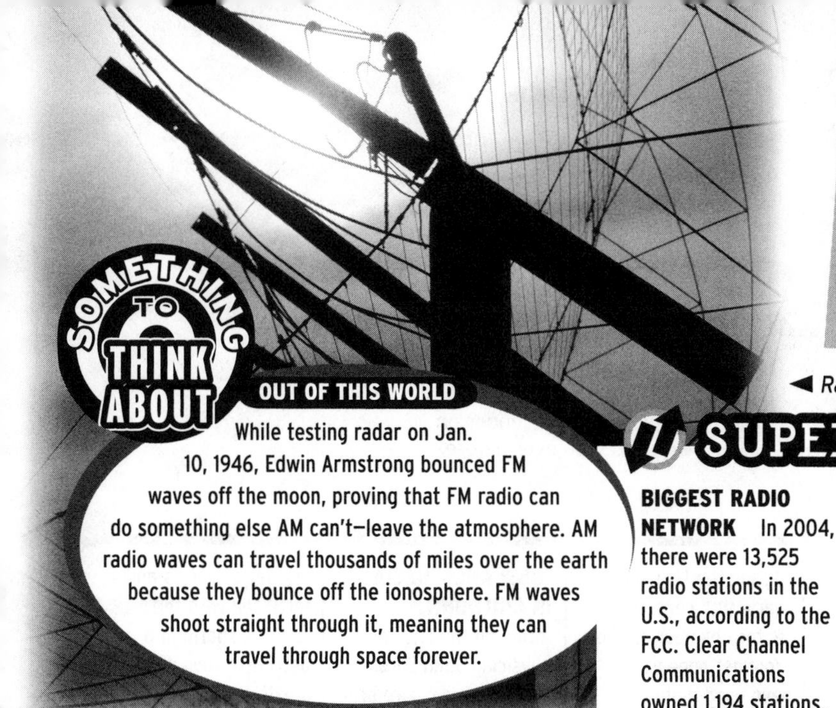

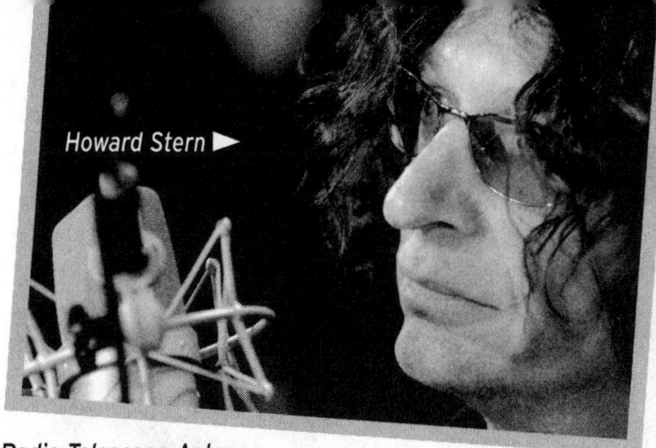

Howard Stern ▶

◀ Radio Telescope Antenna

SOMETHING TO THINK ABOUT

OUT OF THIS WORLD

While testing radar on Jan. 10, 1946, Edwin Armstrong bounced FM waves off the moon, proving that FM radio can do something else AM can't—leave the atmosphere. AM radio waves can travel thousands of miles over the earth because they bounce off the ionosphere. FM waves shoot straight through it, meaning they can travel through space forever.

1947: TRANSISTOR John Bardeen, Walter Brattain, and William Shockley, all scientists at Bell Laboratories in Murray Hill, NJ, invented the transistor on Dec. 23, 1947. It was first publicly demonstrated on June 30, 1948, and went on to replace the vacuum tube and revolutionize electronics. The three won the Nobel Prize for physics in 1956.

The first commercially available transistor radio, announced in Oct. 1954, was the Regency TR-1.

1992: DIGITAL BROADCAST Digital radio, or digital audio broadcasting, was developed in the 1980s. It has CD-quality sound with less interference than FM.

At the World Administrative Radio Conference in March 1992, 127 countries first assigned frequencies for digital audio broadcasting, choosing either low-frequency or satellite bandwidths. In the U.S., the FCC auctioned two eight-year licenses for satellite broadcasting on the S-band in 1997. CD Radio (now Sirius Satellite Radio) paid $83.4 million and American Mobile Radio Corp. (now XM Radio) paid $89.9 million. They launched in 2001.

Since Oct. 10, 2002, AM and FM stations have been permitted to send a digital radio signal alongside their analog signals.

SUPERLATIVES

BIGGEST RADIO NETWORK In 2004, there were 13,525 radio stations in the U.S., according to the FCC. Clear Channel Communications owned 1,194 stations, nearly 900 more than the second-largest network, Cumulus Broadcasting, with 305 stations. Clear Channel stations reached 188 markets, and had revenues of $3.8 billion.

MOST POPULAR FORMAT In 2004, the news and talk format attracted 15.9% of the nation's listener base, according to Arbitron. Country music stations attracted 13.2% of listeners, while the third-most popular format, adult contemporary, drew 12.8% of listeners.

LONGEST WEEKLY CORRESPONDENCE Before retiring at age 95, British-born Alistair Cooke aired "Letter from America" on the BBC for 58 years, from March 24, 1946, to Feb. 20, 2004. He broadcast 2,869 "letters" in all. Aired in Britain and around the world, Cooke's 13-minute essays were hugely popular and made him a cultural icon.

LONGEST-RUNNING RADIO SHOW The Grand Ole Opry, which airs a weekly variety show from its world-famous country and western stage, was first broadcast on WSM in Nashville, TN, on Nov. 28, 1925.

BIGGEST FINE On Nov. 23, 2004, Viacom Inc. agreed to pay a record $3.5 million to the FCC to resolve a number of proposed indecency fines for violations committed by 16 of its Infinity Broadcasting radio stations. The fines covered broadcasts that included the morning *Opie & Anthony Show* and the *Howard Stern Show*.

MOST MARCONI AWARDS Paul Harvey, whose show has aired on more than 1,350 ABC stations across the nation since 1951, has received a National Assoc. of Broadcasters Marconi Award five times for Network/Syndicated Personality of the Year (1989, 1991, 1996, 1998, 2002) since the Marconi awards were established in 1989.

LARGEST RADIO AUDIENCE The largest radio audience for any station is the estimated 149 million listeners worldwide who regularly tune in to the BBC World Service.

Originally known as the "Empire Service," World Service began overseas transmissions on Dec. 19, 1932. Today, the service is broadcast in 43 languages, in 144 capital cities, and from more than 1,200 stations.

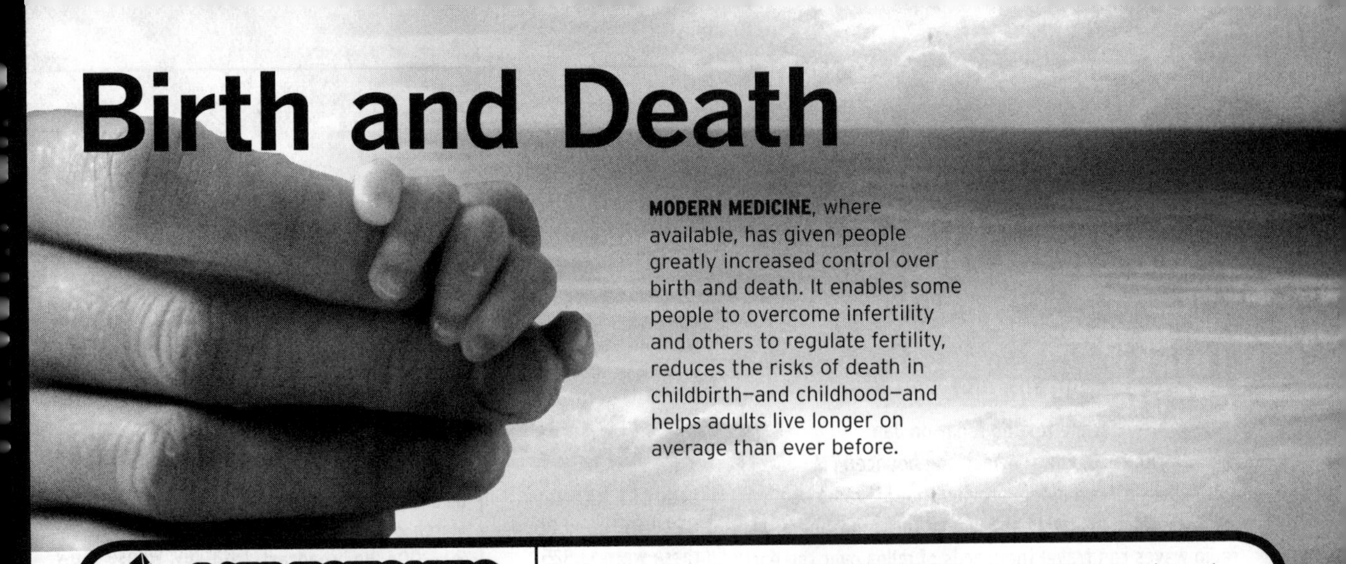

Birth and Death

MODERN MEDICINE, where available, has given people greatly increased control over birth and death. It enables some people to overcome infertility and others to regulate fertility, reduces the risks of death in childbirth—and childhood—and helps adults live longer on average than ever before.

MILESTONES

SECOND MILLENNIUM BC: CESAREAN BIRTH Cesarean birth, or the surgical opening of the walls of a woman's abdomen and uterus in order to deliver a child, gets its name because of the long-held belief that Julius Caesar was born this way. That's not likely since his mother was still alive when he was an adult (women didn't usually survive such operations until many centuries later).

Even if the story is true, Caesar wasn't the first; a cuneiform tablet dating from the second millennium BC in Mesopotamia referred to cesarean-style birth.

However, the first authenticated case of a cesarean birth by a living woman did not occur until 1610. And because of the high risk, this operation—"C section" for short—did not become widespread until the late 19th century, when increased use of antiseptics and advances in surgical techniques made it less dangerous.

AROUND 120 AD: FIRST WRITINGS ON OBSTETRICS The Greek physician Soranus studied at Alexandria and was an expert on obstetrics, gynecology, and pediatrics. His work, *Gynecology*, was an influential medical treatise until the Renaissance. He wrote about midwives, menstruation, breathing techniques, and how to recognize a healthy baby.

AROUND 1600: FORCEPS One of the most significant innovations in improving survivability in birth, forceps were first used by the Chamberlen family of England during the 17th and early 18th centuries. Peter Chamberlen the Younger appears to have used them first but it was kept a family secret until 1673.

The use of forceps in modern times was pioneered by William Smellie, a Scottish physician, who described them in-depth in his 1752 work *A Treatise of the Theory and Practice of Midwifery*. His design remained the most popular in Britain for over two centuries.

1841: BABY BOTTLE Although baby-feeding devices of various kinds have existed since ancient times, in 1841 Charles M. Windship of Roxbury, MA, patented the first glass baby bottle.

Cleverly, he designed it to shape to the mother's breast so that the little one would think the milk was coming straight from Mom.

1853: ANESTHESIA IN CHILDBIRTH Although the English physician John Snow administered chloroform to dozens of women in labor during his career, it was not until he attended the birth of Queen Victoria's eighth child, Leopold, in 1853 that the idea really took hold. If it was good enough for the queen, reasoned British mothers-to-be, it was good enough for them.

1978: TEST-TUBE BABY Dr. Patrick C. Steptoe, a gynecologist, and Dr. Robert G. Edwards, a Cambridge University specialist in reproductive physiology, developed the idea of in-vitro fertilization (IVF). The first birth of a human baby conceived outside a woman's body took place on July 25 in Lancashire, England.

On Nov. 10, 1977, an egg cell had been taken from one of the mother's ovaries and fertilized with the father's sperm in a petri dish. Two and a half days later the embryo was placed in the mother's uterus. The parents were Lesley and John Brown. The 5-pound, 12-ounce baby Louise was delivered by C-section.

1984: FROZEN EMBRYO On March 28, the first baby was born from a frozen embryo at Monash University in Melbourne, Australia. The 5-pound, 13-ounce girl named Zoe was born by C-section.

The first U.S. birth of this kind (a boy) took place two years later in Los Angeles. The mother was 36 years old and had been trying to conceive a child for 15 years.

DEATH DEFYING

Disobeying British authorities, on Nov. 20, 2002, German professor Gunther von Hagens held the first public autopsy in Britain since 1832, in London. Some 500 onlookers paid $19 to view the procedure, while an estimated 1.4 million watched it on TV.

VANQUISHING VAMPIRES

In 1732, German Regimental Field Surgeon Johann Flückinger wrote *Visum et Repertum*, the first official report of the exhumation of a suspected vampire and the driving of a stake through its heart. The suspect was Arnold Paul, who had been buried near the Serbian village of Medvedja. He was dug up because it was believed that he had returned from the dead, killed four people, and harassed many others. Officials continued to excavate the cemetery and found more supposed vampires; these bodies were decapitated and cremated, with the ashes disposed of in the river.

SOMETHING TO THINK ABOUT

SUPERLATIVES

MOST BIRTHS

COUNTRY India had the most births in 2004, with an estimated 24,111,301 babies born. China was second with 16,759,417.

HIGHEST BIRTH RATE

COUNTRY Niger has an estimated rate of 51.3 live births per 1,000 people in 2005, more than double the world rate of 20.2.

LOWEST BIRTH RATE

COUNTRY Germany's birth rate was only 8.3 per 1,000 in 2005, and its neighbor Austria is right behind at 8.8. Nine of the 10 lowest rates are in Europe; the other is Japan at 9.5.

HIGHEST DEATH RATE

COUNTRY Because of a combination of factors, AIDS being chief among them, Botswana in 2005 had the world's highest death rate, estimated at 29.4 deaths per 1,000 people. In comparison, the U.S. had a death rate of 8.25 per 1,000 people.

MULTIPLE BIRTHS

There are many reports of large multiple births, dating back to the 15th century, when a set of septuplets was born in England. But until the 20th century there were no records of groups larger than four surviving.

The first recorded set of surviving quintuplets were the Dionnes of Canada, born May 28, 1934, to Olivia Dionne (all were girls); their birth made medical history, and the children lived in the glare of worldwide publicity.

The first surviving sextuplets were born Jan. 11, 1974, to Susan Rosenkowitz of Capetown, South Africa (3 boys, 3 girls). The first surviving septuplets were born Nov. 19, 1997, to Bobbi McCaughey of Carlisle, IA (4 boys, 3 girls). The latter two mothers were taking fertility drugs.

In 1998 Nkem Chukwu gave birth to octuplets (6 girls and 2 boys). The first was born naturally on Dec. 8, 1998, in Houston, TX. The others were delivered by C-section on Dec. 20. The smallest, 10.3 ounces, died soon after birth.

OLDEST MOM On Jan. 16, 2005, 66-year-old Adriana Iliescu of Romania, who was artificially inseminated using sperm and egg from anonymous donors, gave birth to a daughter after nine years of fertility treatments and two failed pregnancies. The baby, named Eliza Maria, weighed 3.5 pounds.

MOST POPULAR BABY NAMES Based on records kept by the Social Security Administration, the most popular boy's name in the first decade of the 20th century was John and the most popular girl's name was Mary. In the 1990s it was Michael for boys and Ashley for girls. Jacob and Emily went to the top starting in 1999.

HIGHEST LIFE EXPECTANCY AT BIRTH

COUNTRY Andorra (83.5 years) ranked number one in 2005. U.S. life expectancy stood at 77.7 (#46); the worldwide average was 64.11.

LOWEST LIFE EXPECTANCY AT BIRTH

COUNTRY Swaziland, an African nation stricken with poverty, drought, and AIDS, had the lowest life expectancy of any country at a mere 33.22 years at birth in 2005.

DEATH (U.S.)

MOST COMMON CAUSE In 2002, 696,947 people died from heart disease in the U.S. The second most common cause of death was cancer, which killed 557,271.

ACCIDENTAL DEATH (U.S.)

MOST COMMON CAUSE Accidents involving motor vehicles are the biggest cause of accidental death in the U.S.; there were 44,065 in 2002, accounting for 27.3% of all injury deaths. The second leading cause, falls, resulted in 16,257 deaths in 2002.

OLDEST PERSON

The longest verified lifespan in history is that of Jeanne Louise Calment of France, who lived for 122 years, 164 days. She was born Feb. 21, 1875, in Arles and died Aug. 4, 1997, in the same town. She rode her bicycle until she was 100.

LARGEST CEMETERY

Cemetery size is a difficult thing to measure, but the likeliest candidate is the Wadi-e-Salaam (Valley of Peace) cemetery near Najaf, Iraq, which is the most highly prized burial place among Shiite Muslims.

The cemetery, which dates back to the seventh century, holds 2 to 5 million deceased Muslims.

Weddings & Marriage

THE OLDEST RECORD OF A WEDDING DATES TO 2350 BC, in Mesopotamia. Most societies have recognized marriage as a kind of contract, usually formalized in a ceremony, but there is great variety in the customs associated with it. In some cultures even today, marriages are arranged and love is scarcely a consideration.

1 MILESTONES

2800 BC: WEDDING RING The ancient Egyptians gave us the custom of wearing wedding rings and of placing them on the fourth finger of the left hand. The first rings were probably made from the rushes and reeds that grew along the Nile and were worn only by women. The fourth finger of the left hand was chosen because it was believed that a vein in that finger led directly to the heart.

The practice was picked up by the Greeks and Romans. Today, most people wear their wedding rings on that same finger.

AROUND 100 BC: WEDDING CAKE Wedding cakes go back to ancient Rome. By 100 BC it was common for bread-like cake (with no icing) to be broken over the bride's head. Grains symbolized fertility, and Romans believed eating the pieces would ensure a long life of good luck and fertility. Later, wedding cakes were made with meats or fruits, before becoming the sugary confections common today. Cakes with white icing, then meringue, first appeared in the 17th century.

AROUND 7TH CENTURY: RELIGIOUS OBSERVANCE In Christian, Jewish, Hindu, and other traditions, marriage has a religious dimension. It has been considered a sacrament of the Catholic Church since around the 7th century, with the exchange of vows between husband and wife as the vital element. Not until the Council of Trent in 1563 did the Church require that priests preside at the ceremonies.

1812: WHITE HOUSE WEDDING The first White House wedding took place on March 29, 1812, when Dolley Todd Madison's widowed sister, Lucy Washington, married Thomas Todd, a Kentucky justice, in the White House.

The first and only president to marry there was Grover Cleveland. The 49-year-old president wed his former ward, 21-year-old Frances Folsom, on June 2, 1886, in the Blue Room. There have been 17 White House weddings in all.

1840: WHITE WEDDING DRESS Though many women wore white at their weddings before her, the custom was popularized by Queen Victoria. Breaking with a tradition that royal brides should wear silver, she wore a white gown for her wedding to Prince Albert, Feb. 10, 1840, starting a trend that endures to this day.

1980: DIVORCE RATE PEAKS It's commonly thought (and much bemoaned) that the American divorce rate is around 50%. In 2004, there were 7.5 marriages and 3.7 divorces per every 1000 persons. However, when the divorce rate is calculated as the number of people who have ever been married who were subsequently divorced, the rate has not gone up since 1980, when it hit 41%.

2001: SAME-SEX MARRIAGE The Netherlands became the first country in modern times to pass legislation granting marriage status to same-sex couples, on Sept. 12, 2000. The gay marriage law took effect on April 1, 2001. Nearly 2,000 couples were married in the Netherlands in the first six months after the law went into effect.

2003: MARRIAGE IN SPACE The Soviet cosmonaut Yuri Malenchenko married Ekaterina Dmitriev, of Houston, TX, on Aug. 10, 2003, in the first wedding held at least partly in space. At the time of the ceremony, Malenchenko was 240 miles above the earth in the International Space Station, while his bride was in Houston. They had set the date before his arrival home was delayed.

SOMETHING TO THINK ABOUT

MONUMENT TO LOVE

The world's most famous monument to love is the Taj Mahal, a magnificent mausoleum in Agra, India, begun in 1631 by the Mughal Emperor Shah Jahan for his wife, who had died in childbirth. The domed monument, made of white marble inlaid with gemstones, took about 22 years to build and required some 20,000 workers.

OLDER AND WISER?

Since 1890, the U.S. Census has recorded the age people report that they were married for the first time. In 1956, men reported that they were, on average, 22.5 years old upon their first marriage, and women were, on average, 20.1 years old. In 2004, men reported having married at an average age of 27.4 years, women at 25.8 years.

NO CHURCH AISLE REQUIRED

Weddings can take place in caves, underwater, or up in the air, or just about anywhere. On Valentine's Day 2004, 17 couples exchanged vows on the observation deck of the Empire State Building in New York, and in August 2003, 23 couples married at the start-finish line of the Bristol Motor Speedway, hours before that day's NASCAR race.

SUPERLATIVES

OLDEST BRIDE
The oldest known bride was an Australian named Minnie Munro, who was 102 when she married Dudley Reid, only 83, in Point Claire, New South Wales, on May 31, 1991.

LONGEST MARRIAGE
Sir Temulji Nariman and his wife, Lady Nariman, of India were five years old when they wed on Aug. 25, 1852. Sir Temulji died in the summer of 1940, after a marriage of about 88 years.

The longest known marriage in the U.S. was that of Lazarus Rowe and Molly Weber of Greenland, NH. They were married from 1743 until Lazarus's death in 1829, a total of 86 years.

MOST WATCHED WEDDING Charles, the Prince of Wales, married Lady Diana Spencer at St. Paul's Cathedral in London, England, on July 29, 1981, in what was the most watched wedding ever. More than 750 million people around the world saw the nuptials on TV.

Another famous wedding also took place in 1981—on the TV soap opera *General Hospital*—when some 30 million viewers watched the (fictitious) wedding of Luke and Laura. It was the highest rated soap episode in TV history, with 52% of all TV viewers tuned in.

MOST EXPENSIVE WEDDING Probably the most expensive single wedding was the weeklong bash in Dubai, that marked the 1981 marriage of Mohammed, son of Sheikh Rashid Ben Saeed Al Maktoum, to Princess Salama. The bill was estimated at $44 million.

Another expensive ceremony was the dual wedding of brothers, Shushanto and Shimanto Roy, two of India's leading industrialists, in Lucknow, India, in Feb. 2004. The weeklong celebration, which cost an estimated $94 million, included Bollywood stars among the 10,500 guests. Flowers were imported from Thailand, a 110-piece orchestra from Britain, and a troupe of acrobats from China.

The Roy family also paid expenses for more than 100 weddings held in their community at the same time.

MONTH WITH MOST/LEAST MARRIAGES U.S. Summer months are traditionally the favorite time to get married. In 2004, 232,000 marriages took place in July, which beat out August (226,000), September (223,000), and June (215,000, surprisingly back in fourth place).

Despite a smattering of Valentine's Day nuptials, February had the fewest weddings (137,000).

MOST/LEAST MARRIAGES STATES
Among the 50 states, Idaho had the highest percentage of people over age 15 who were part of a married couple, according to the 2000 census—60.0%. New York had the lowest percent, 50.0%, and also the highest percent never married, 31.7%. Arkansas had the lowest percent never married, 21.2%.

Washington, DC, had an even lower percent of married couples—29.9%—with a whopping 48.4% reported as never married.

MOST/LEAST DIVORCES STATE
Nevada had the highest percentage of divorced adults—13.8% of the over-15 population, according to the 2000 U.S. Census. New Jersey had the lowest percentage—7.5%.

Holidays

FESTIVALS occasioned by religious devotion or by planting, harvesting, and the cycle of the seasons have been celebrated around the world for millennia. Ancient Romans celebrated the winter solstice and harvest with Saturnalia—a festival at which sacrifices were offered and gifts were exchanged, as later became a Christmas custom.

MILESTONES

ANTIQUITY: HALLOWEEN The superstitions of Halloween are thought to have originated among the ancient Celts in Ireland and Scotland, who celebrated New Year's Day, Samhain, at that time of year. There are records of children visiting houses the day before to collect money and supplies for their celebrations.

Christians later changed Samhain to All Saints ("All Hallows") Day, celebrated on Nov. 1, and the night before became "All-Hallow-Even" or Hallowe'en. Halloween parties with costumes, apple bobbing, and jack-o-lanterns were common in the U.S. by the 1890s.

ANTIQUITY: FIRST PASSOVER SEDER Passover, described in the Book of Exodus, has been one of the most important Jewish holidays for millennia. *Pesach* (as it is known to Jews) is celebrated around the time of the vernal equinox.

The observance lasts seven days, and begins with a Seder, a ceremonial meal where participants tell the story of Moses and his leading the Hebrew people out of Egypt. The readings, songs, and prayers are contained in a special book, the *Haggada*.

7TH CENTURY AD: RAMADAN This month of fasting and prayer is written into the Koran, the holy book of Islam. For the entire month, Muslims fast from first light to sundown, and are forbidden to drink or smoke. Contributing to charity is considered part of the observance as well. At the end of the month, the fast-breaking is a celebration: Eid Al-Fitr.

14TH CENTURY: VALENTINE'S DAY One tradition holds that this observance developed partly as a Christian alternative to an ancient Roman feast (Feb. 15), dedicated to Lupercus, a fertility god. On that day (Lupercalis), young Roman men and women drew lots to obtain partners for a feast.

Festivities in the Middle Ages became associated with the Christian feast day, Feb. 14, of two Roman martyrs named Valentine who died in the 3rd century. It was also widely believed that birds mated around this time of year.

In the court circles of 14th-century England and France, lovers celebrated the date with gifts and letters. Specialized Valentine cards were being made commercially by the 1840s.

1605: O TANNENBAUM The tradition of decorating a tree for Christmas is said to have begun in Germany in the 16th century. It stems from an older custom. People in the Upper Rhine region adorned their homes with holly or evergreen boughs to ward off evil spirits as the new year approached at the end of the month of Jol (from which "Yule" derives).

The oldest record of a "Christmas tree," decorated with apples, candies, and paper roses, comes from a 1605 diary found in Strasbourg.

1863: THANKSGIVING American colonists celebrated a day of thanksgiving after surviving hardships at Jamestown in 1610 and Plymouth in 1621. George Washington originally set Dec. 18, 1777, as a day of thanks after the Continental Army defeated British troops at the Battle of Saratoga.

It did not become an annual tradition until Oct. 3, 1863, when President Abraham Lincoln heeded a 17-year campaign by magazine editor Sarah Hale and created an annual Thanksgiving holiday in November.

Gimbel's Department Store in Philadelphia held the day's first parade in 1920; Macy's followed in 1924.

The first Thanksgiving NFL game, between the Detroit Lions and Chicago Bears, was broadcast by radio in 1933; TV followed in 1956. President Harry Truman pardoned the first turkey in 1947.

In 1941 Congress followed the initiative of President Franklin D. Roosevelt and moved the day to the fourth Thursday, instead of the last, to avoid having too short a shopping season between Thanksgiving and Christmas.

1894: LABOR DAY In the U.S. and Canada, Labor Day is celebrated on the first Monday in September. The tradition started in the U.S. after the Knights of Labor union held a parade and picnic for about 10,000 workers on Sept. 5, 1882, in New York City. The date was chosen as a halfway point between Independence Day and Thanksgiving.

On June 28, 1894, Congress established it as a federal holiday.

1914: MOTHER'S DAY In 1907 Anna Jarvis of Philadelphia drove the call for a day to celebrate mothers. A successful writing campaign led President Woodrow Wilson to make the second Sunday in May Mother's Day in 1914.

The tradition of wearing or giving carnations on that day may have been inspired by an earlier president, William McKinley, who became known for commonly wearing this flower in his buttonhole.

Father's Day started in Spokane, WA, in 1910 after a city resident called for a day to honor her father, a veteran and widower who raised six children. It did not become official until 1972, when it was proclaimed by President Richard Nixon.

Hallmark estimates that more than 150 million Mother's Day cards were given out in the U.S. in 2005, as well as nearly 95 million Father's Day cards.

1966: KWANZAA African American activist and scholar Maulana (Ron) Karegna created the seven-day festival of Kwanzaa (Dec. 26-Jan. 1) in 1966. The holiday—which draws customs from varied African traditions—celebrates family, community, and culture.

The word "Kwanza" comes from a Swahili phrase meaning "first fruits." An "a" was added to give the word seven letters, matching the seven days. The U.S. Postal Service released its first Kwanzaa stamp in 1997.

1983: MARTIN LUTHER KING DAY Rev. Dr. Martin Luther King Jr., the great civil rights movement leader, was assassinated on April 4, 1968. Soon after, campaigns began to create a federal holiday in his honor, including a 6-million-signature petition.

In 1983, President Ronald Reagan signed a bill making it a federal holiday, beginning in 1986. King's birthday, Jan. 15, was considered too close to the holiday season, so the third Monday was chosen.

The holiday was recognized by all 50 states by 1999.

MATH LOVERS' DELIGHT

In math, the Greek letter π (Pi) stands for the ratio of the circumference of a circle to its diameter. The exact value of Pi cannot be measured, but it has been calculated to more than one trillion decimal places, starting with 3.14159. In honor of this number, math lovers throw parties on March 14 at 1:59 AM or PM (3/14 1:59). Some people eat pie, some watch the movie *Pi*, and some just reflect on how Pi has affected their lives.

SOMETHING TO THINK ABOUT

NO-PANTS DAY

Since its mysterious beginnings around 1986, No-Pants Day (observed on the first Friday in May) has been gaining popularity, especially among college students and other young people. The holiday is simple—men and women shed their trousers and wear only underwear from the waist down. Celebrants from around the world can be viewed on NoPantsDay.com.

SUPERLATIVES

BIGGEST CARNIVAL In some countries with large Catholic populations, the days preceding Ash Wednesday, which opens the penitential season of Lent, are marked by festive celebration, ending on Mardi Gras ("Fat Tuesday").

Salvador, Brazil, throws the world's biggest such event, drawing on average over 2 million revelers. Large groups of marchers (*blocos*) and floats (*trios elétricos*) highlight the five-day celebration. In 2005, about 2.2 million people took to the streets each day, while 470,000 elaborately costumed singers, dancers, and musicians performed. Some 4.25 million gallons of beer and soft drinks were consumed.

In the U.S., New Orleans draws the biggest Mardi Gras crowds, averaging about a million. The New Orleans Mardi Gras is known for its spectacular floats, organized by krewes, or clubs. Since 1870 there has also been a royal court, presided over by Rex, the king. Despite the effects of Hurricane Katrina, City officials hoped to hold the celebration there in 2006.

BEST-SELLING HOLIDAY SINGLE Bing Crosby's rendition of the Irving Berlin tune "White Christmas" has sold over 30 million records since it aired in Oct. 1942. Originally written for a defunct Broadway revue, the song was later used for the movie *Holiday Inn*.

MOST VALUABLE XMAS CARD In 1843, the first known Christmas card was designed by British artist John Calcott Horsley for Sir Henry Cole to send to his friends. It featured a festive family scene and a printed message: "A Merry Christmas and Happy New Year to You."

One of Horsley's cards was sold at auction in the United Kingdom in 2001 for £20,000 (about $28,000), a record. Another pricey Christmas card was hand-drawn by former Beatle John Lennon. The card, sent to the band's manager, Brian Epstein, sold for £5,405 ($8,737) at Christie's in London in 2000.

Housing

The Winchester House

FROM KOROWAI TREEHOUSES IN NEW GUINEA to thatched-roof cottages in Ireland to the cave homes of Andalusia, Spain, humans past and present have lived in a wide variety of dwellings. With housing suited to the particular environment, people have lived comfortably in deserts, high mountains, and polar regions. Today, a few humans are living in the harshest environment of all—space.

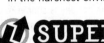

SUPERLATIVES

OLDEST HOUSE

As far back as two million years ago, pre-human primates began taking shelter in caves. The oldest houses for which evidence survives are believed to be about 15,000-20,000 years old. Mammoth bone huts were built as winter homes in Russia and eastern Ukraine near the Dnepr and Desna river valleys and their tributaries.

The large bones were sturdy and didn't rot like wood. In some cases these bone structures were probably covered with mammoth hides. One spectacular camp found in 1965 by a farmer digging in his cellar in Mezhirich, near Kiev, Ukraine, yielded four huts made from the bones of at least 149 animals.

LARGEST PRIVATE HOUSE (U.S.)

The 250-room Biltmore House in Asheville, NC, is said to be the biggest private home in the U.S. It was built by Richard Morris Hunt for the philanthropist George W. Vanderbilt between 1890 and 1895 on a 125,000-acre estate (now reduced to 8,000 acres).

The four-story French Renaissance château has four acres of interior floor space, with a vaulted banquet hall, winter garden, 35 bedrooms, 65 fireplaces, and 43 bathrooms (installed at a time when inside bathrooms were not common). Vanderbilt first received guests at the house on Christmas Eve, 1895. It is still owned by members of the Vanderbilt family, but has been open to the public for tours since March 15, 1930.

MOST EXPENSIVE PRIVATE HOUSE

In 2004, steel magnate Lakshmi N. Mittal paid £70 million (about $125 million) for a 12-bedroom mansion in one of the world's priciest neighborhoods—Kensington Palace Gardens, in London, England. The home has a ballroom, basement pool, and underground parking to accommodate 20 cars.

The mansion's price surpasses the $70 million (HK$540 million) paid in 1997 for Genesis, a 40-room mansion in the exclusive Victoria Peak section of Hong Kong, China.

MOST EXPENSIVE REGION (U.S.)

Real estate agents say that the price of a house depends on three factors: "Location, location, location."

The median U.S. sale price for single-family homes during 2004 was $184,100.

But prices varied by region. The West was most expensive at $265,800, followed by the Northeast at $220,000, the South at $169,000, and the Midwest at $149,000.

Communities varied even more widely. The most expensive zip code in the U.S. as of 2004 was Atherton, CA, just outside of San Francisco, with an average home sale price of $2,496,553.

Only three other places surpassed the $2 million mark, all in California: Santa Barbara, Rancho Santa Fe, and Newport Beach.

California had the highest median home value of any state ($316,600) and the highest percentage of million-dollar homes (4.1%).

OWNERSHIP RATES (U.S.)

In cities, where space is tight and many people struggle to make ends meet, owning a house may be a luxury. In 2004, Aurora, CO, had the highest percentage of ownership (67.2%); it was followed by Wichita, KS (67%), and Virginia Beach, VA (66.9%). At the other end of the spectrum, 79% of the households in Newark, NJ, are renters. The second and third renting capitals are New York, NY (68%), and Miami, FL (62%).

HIGHEST HUMAN DWELLING

Orbiting the Earth every 92 minutes at an average altitude of 220 miles, the International Space Station (ISS) has been continually occupied since Nov. 2, 2000. Construction began on Nov. 20, 1998, and has not been completed (a situation familiar to many home owners).

The craft was designed and assembled in what is said to be the largest cooperative science project in history, involving the U.S., Russia, and 14 other nations.

Top Five Most Expensive Metropolitan Areas*

LOCATION	MEDIAN HOME PRICE
San Francisco-Oakland-Fremont, CA	$686,200
Orange County, CA (Anaheim-Santa Ana)	$656,900
San Diego-Carlsbad-San Marcos, CA	$584,100
Honolulu, HI	$529,100
Los Angeles-Long Beach-Santa Ana, CA	$474,700

© Copyright 2005, National Association of Realtors

*Preliminary figures as of first quarter, 2005; median sales price of existing single-family homes for metropolitan areas

SOMETHING TO THINK ABOUT

SCRAP HOUSE

In the 1970s, architect Michael Reynolds began designing special low-cost, environmentally friendly houses using old tires and aluminum cans as (surprisingly efficient) insulators. He stuffed the tires with dirt, stacked them as walls, and filled them in with aluminum cans, completing 25 solar-powered houses around his home of Taos, NM, by 1979. Once surrounded by soil, the building material is unnoticeable. He began selling the formula as "Earthships" in 1988, and there are now over 2,000 in eight countries; 1,000 in New Mexico alone. He also sells Earthship kits for facilities ranging from a $2,500, 607-square-foot "nest" to a $3,600, 1,450-square-foot two-bedroom, two-bath house with garage.

HOLE N" THE ROCK, MOAB, UT

Beginning in 1940, Albert Christensen blasted and drilled to make a 5,000-square-foot, 14-room home in the side of a sandstone mountain, complete with kitchen, bathroom, fireplace, and an image of Franklin D. Roosevelt's face carved near the entrance. Christensen and his wife, Gladys, moved into the place in 1952 and opened a diner, since turned into a café and gift shop.

After Albert's death in 1957, Gladys continued to live in the cave, promoting her home as a roadside attraction, until 1974. Hole N" the Rock has been preserved as it was when the Christensens lived there. Some 70,000 people tour the home every year.

KEEPING THE GHOSTS ON THEIR TOES

The Winchester House in San Jose, CA, took 38 years to build, from 1834 to 1922, at a cost of $5.5 million. Erected by Sarah Winchester, the widow of millionaire rifle manufacturer Oliver Winchester, the 160-room mansion is an architectural marvel. It includes 13 bathrooms, 52 skylights, 10,000 windows, and 40 bedrooms. It's said that Mrs. Winchester constantly remodeled the house, adding secret passageways and blank walls to fool the resident ghosts. She believed the house was haunted by victims of her husband's guns.

WHERE THE GHOULS ARE AT HOME

Ghost hunter Hans Holzer speculates that a San Diego, CA, landmark could be the most haunted house in America. The Whaley House, built in 1856, was home to the prominent San Diegan Thomas Whaley, his wife, and six children.

Staff and visitors have reported seeing many ghostly guests, including the Whaleys; Yankee Jim, a man who was executed on the property before the Whaleys bought it; a small woman in a gingham dress; a spotted dog; and a red-headed little girl.

The last of the Whaleys died in 1953, leaving the house unoccupied. By 1960, it was a tourist attraction.

The space station currently provides 15,000 cubic feet of living space—with sleeping cabins, kitchen, gym, and bathroom. When completed it will contain six laboratories and provide living space for seven people.

As of June 2005, a total of nearly 30 astronauts have lived aboard the station at one time or another.

LARGEST REFUGEE CAMP

The world's largest-ever haven for refugees was the Hartisheik Camp in Ethiopia. Multitudes of Somalis flocked to the area beginning in 1988 during the collapse of Mohammed Siad Barre's government. The United Nations organized a camp to alleviate the appalling conditions the Somalis were enduring.

Hartisheik was home to more than 600,000 refugees. Services for residents included schools, health centers, and a dam. Beginning in 1997, the UN began sending Somalis back home. After repatriation was completed, the camp closed on June 30, 2004.

Appliances

Ironing, 1908

WHEN YOU RECEIVE AN ELECTRIC NONSTICK EGG POACHER AS A GIFT and it ends up sitting on a shelf, it's tempting to think of household appliances as trivial. But if you reflect upon the hours of backbreaking labor that were required to run a household in the pre-electric era, you realize how useful appliances are.

MILESTONES

1882: ELECTRIC IRON One of the first appliances to be electrified, the iron entered the modern age on June 6, 1882, when Henry W. Seely of New York City patented an electric iron that used a carbon arc to create heat. It also weighed 15 pounds. Safer and lighter irons using electrical resistance were introduced 10 years later by Crompton and Co. and by Edison's General Electric.

1886: DISHWASHER Frustrated by the damage her servants were causing to her fine china, Josephine Cochrane of Shelbyville, IL, designed a hand-spun dishwasher with hot-water jets. Cochrane patented her design on Dec. 28, 1886, and opened a business.

The machine was a success at the World's Fair in Chicago in 1893 but initially appealed mainly to restaurant and hotel owners. It caught on with homemakers in the 1950s, when models became smaller and more affordable. Also, advances in hot water heaters and detergents made it possible to get dishes truly clean, with no soapy residue.

1901: VACUUM CLEANER The vacuum cleaner arrived on the scene in stages, with contributions by several inventors. Two American designs were patented in the 1860s, including a hand-cranked vacuum cleaner devised by a Chicagoan named Ives McGaffey. The first electric vacuum cleaner was patented by British engineer Hubert Cecil Booth in 1901. Booth's contraption worked, but it was a monstrous, unwieldy device, drawn by horses. It was parked outside the site to be cleaned and long hoses attached to the device went in through the windows.

In 1907, a janitor named Murray Spangler from Canton, OH, constructed a portable electric vacuum cleaner out of a fan, a tin soap box, a broom handle, and a pillowcase. He sought to market it and a family friend, William H. Hoover, bought the patent in 1908. Hoover turned Spangler's device into the "Hoover electric suction sweeper," a machine that was soon "sweeping" the country.

1906: AIR CONDITIONER Air conditioning was the brainchild of Willis Haviland Carrier, who hit upon the idea of "dew point control" while standing in a fogbound railroad station. The first unit was commissioned in 1902 by Sackett & Wilhelms Lithographing and Publishing Co. in Brooklyn, NY, because the hot, muggy weather was causing trouble with its ink and printing. Carrier received a patent for his invention on Jan. 2, 1906, the same year the term "air conditioning" was coined, by Stuart Cramer, a textile engineer. The technology was intended for industrial use, but by the 1920s, Carrier was air-conditioning movie theaters, department stores, and even the U.S. House and Senate. Home air conditioning did not become popular until the 1950s.

1908: ELECTRIC WASHING MACHINE Alva Josiah Fisher, an engineer from Evanston, IL, first applied for a patent for his motor-driven washing machine on Sept. 28, 1908. Fisher's washing machine had wringers for squeezing the moisture out of clothes, but the development of two-speed motors eventually made the "spin-dry" cycle possible, and in 1932, John Chamberlin and Rex Basset developed a new prototype.

Bendix Corp. bought their idea and sold the first fully automatic machine in 1937, but modern washing machines did not become popular until after World War II.

1913: MODERN REFRIGERATOR Until mechanical refrigerators were developed, people collected ice over the winter and preserved it for the warmer months in covered pits. In 1803, a Maryland engineer named Thomas Moore patented the "refrigerator," an early version of what came to be known as the icebox, an insulated cabinet that held a block of ice.

Fred Wolf Jr., an engineer from Chicago, filed for the earliest known mechanical refrigerator patent, on Dec. 23, 1913. His "Domelre" ran on electricity and even had ice trays, but he

Something to Think About

NO APPLICATION

For every successful invention, there must be a dozen or so that just don't make it. Patented appliances that you would be hard-pressed to find in a store today include: a motorized ice cream cone that turns ice cream "against a person's outstretched tongue," a "combined earthquake sensor and night light," a "pneumatic shoe lacing apparatus," "a portable hat system that allows you to smoke without damaging the environment" (it includes a fan and a filtration system), "devices for making artificial egg yolks in the form of discs," and "toilet lights" that gently illuminate the bowl for middle-of-the-night bathroom visits.

EXTREME IRONING

If you accept the results of an "Extreme Ironing" competition held in Germany in 2002, the British surpass everyone else in getting wrinkles out of clothes. Two three-person British ironing squads topped nine other countries, winning gold and bronze medals. The teams were challenged with five ironing tasks on different fabrics and in environments ranging from mountainous to forested, to urban and aquatic. Extreme Ironing is a serious sport (well, sort of), whose participants iron on mountain cliffs, on busy city streets, while floating down rivers, and even at the North Pole.

couldn't afford to mass-produce it and sold off the rights in 1916.

1915: ELECTRIC BLENDER Stephen Poplawski of Racine, WI, created the commercial drink mixer associated with milkshakes and soda fountains around 1915. Blenders took off as home appliances with the introduction of the Waring Blender (popularized by bandleader Fred Waring) in 1937 and the Osterizer in 1946.

1919: POP-UP TOASTER Early types of electric toasters were being made by 1900, but they were open-faced contraptions that toasted bread one side at a time.

Charles Strite, of Minneapolis, MN, invented a pop-up toaster with a variable timer in 1919. In 1926 the Waters-Genter Co. used a version of Strite's invention for the "Toastmaster," the first home toaster that toasted both sides simultaneously and ejected the toast at just the right moment. It quickly became the "toast" of the town.

1945: MICROWAVE This popular appliance was accidentally discovered by Percy Spencer, an engineer with the Raytheon Corporation. He was experimenting with a radar device called a magnetron when he realized a candy bar in his pocket was melting. The first food item he tested in the gizmo was popcorn.

He filed for a patent on Oct. 8, 1945, and unveiled the "Radarange," the first oven that used microwaves, in 1947. It was the size of a refrigerator. Countertop microwaves did not go on the market until 1967.

SUPERLATIVES

BIGGEST BLENDER As part of a publicity promotion for Jose Cuervo tequila, actress Jenny McCarthy unveiled the world's largest blender in New York City on April 28, 2005. The machine, which stood 15 feet, 4 inches high, was said to be capable of whipping up some 500 gallons of tequila-laced margarita cocktails. The event launched a one-week countdown to the Mexican holiday of Cinco de Mayo.

LARGEST WASHING MACHINE The world's biggest washing machines for home use are Panasonic's NA-W1350T and NA-W1300T twin-tub washing machines, which can clean nearly 30 pounds of dirty clothes at a time. They were designed for the Middle East, where families tend to be large. According to one Panasonic official, "[They] can easily wash up to 35 *dishdashas* at a single go." (A *dishdasha* is a traditional full-length Arab robe.)

BIGGEST MANUFACTURER Sweden's AB Electrolux is the world's largest home appliance producer, comprising 18 brands including AEG, Electrolux, Eureka, Frigidaire, and Zanussi. It sells over 55 million products in about 150 countries each year ($18.3 billion in sales in 2004). Whirlpool is the largest U.S.-based producer, with net sales of $13.2 billion in 2004.

BIGGEST EXPORTER China is the world's largest exporter of electric appliances for the home. In 2004, China sent $2.35 billion worth of appliances (or 26% of the world's appliance exports) abroad. Germany was the second-largest exporter, shipping out $1.28 billion worth (14%), followed by the U.S. with $743 million (8%). From 2001-04, China was the leading exporter of electric coffee and tea makers (32% of these exports), vacuum cleaners (26%), food processors (24%), microwave ovens (40%), and toasters (68%). About a third of all Chinese appliance exports (32%) go to the U.S.

BIGGEST IMPORTER The U.S. is by far the world's biggest importer of electric appliances for the home. In 2004, $2.85 billion worth of appliances (31% of the world's appliance imports by value) went to the U.S. Germany ranked second, importing $845 million worth, followed by Great Britain with $653 million.

Pets

THE ANCIENT EGYPTIANS SO TREASURED THEIR FURRY COMPANIONS— including cats, dogs, and baboons—that they mummified their pets, some with customized sarcophagi, to preserve their souls for the afterlife. Whether it's cats, dogs, tarantulas, or boa constrictors, pets are treasured by people of all stripes. A survey conducted in 2005 found that 74% of dog owners and 60% of cat owners considered their pet a member of the family.

MILESTONES

1866: ASPCA
The American Society for the Prevention of Cruelty to Animals (ASPCA) was founded by Henry Bergh, who based his work on Britain's Royal Society for the Prevention of Cruelty to Animals (founded 1840). He was given a New York state charter for the ASPCA that went into effect April 10, 1866.

The state legislature passed an animal anti-cruelty law nine days later. By 1867, the ASPCA was operating the first-ever ambulance service for horses. By Bergh's death in 1888, 37 of the 38 states had enacted anti-cruelty laws.

1877: WESTMINSTER DOG SHOW
The prestigious annual Westminster Dog Show was first held May 8-11, 1877, in the Hippodrome at Gilmore's Garden in New York City. Then called the New York Bench Show of Dogs, it was organized by the Westminster Kennel Club and drew 1,201 dogs.

The Best In Show (BIS) award was not instituted until 1907; Warren Remedy, a Fox Terrier, won the top ribbon. He went on to win BIS the next two years, and still holds the record for most wins (3).

1918: CHER AMI
Perhaps the world's most famous carrier pigeon, Cher Ami was awarded the French Croix de Guerre, which honors bravery in combat, in 1918. The U.S. Army Signal Corps used the bird to relay messages across the American sector in Verdun, France.

During his 12th and final mission, Cher Ami was shot by enemy fire, but managed to make it back to his military loft, carrying a message giving the position of the 77th Infantry's "Lost Battalion." Within hours, the 194 soldiers of the Lost Battalion were safely behind U.S. lines.

Cher Ami died from his battle wounds in 1919, but his body was preserved by a taxidermist, and today he is on display at the Smithsonian's National Museum of American History in Washington, DC.

1973: IDITAROD
Staged annually since 1973, the Iditarod Trail Sled Dog Race commemorates a heroic relay to save an Alaskan town from a diphtheria outbreak in 1925. In a race against time, 20 mushers and their teams carried anti-diphtheria serum 674 miles from Nenana, AK, to Nome, AK (where the race ends today), in 127 hours.

The first winner was Dick Wilmarth, who completed the 1,161-mile Southern Route in 20 days, 49 minutes, 41 seconds. The first woman to win was Libby Riddles in 1985.

2004: PET CLONE
Genetics Savings & Clone cloned the first pet for a paying client in 2004. Julie, a flight attendant from Dallas, TX, paid $50,000 on Dec. 10, 2004, for "Little Nicky," an eight-week-old chromatin-transfer clone of her recently deceased Maine Coon cat, Nicky, on Dec. 10, 2004. Julie also adopted Little Nicky's surrogate mother, Maria.

Top Five Registered Cat Breeds (U.S.)*

RANK	BREED	TOTALS
1.	Persian	18,176
2.	Maine Coon	4,162
3.	The Exotic	2,838
4.	Siamese	1,621
5.	Abyssian	1,462

*New registr., Cat Fanciers' Assoc. (2004)

Top Five Registered Dog Breeds (U.S.)*

RANK	BREED	TOTALS
1.	Labrador Retriever	146,692
2.	Golden Retriever	52,550
3.	German Shepherd	46,046
4.	Beagle	44,555
5.	Yorkshire Terrier	43,522

*New registr., The American Kennel Club (2004)

SOMETHING TO THINK ABOUT

EIGHT LIVES LEFT

In March 2005, a wary Torri Hutchinson pulled over to the shoulder on I-15 in Idaho after a fellow motorist persisted in driving alongside her car and pointing at the roof. While Hutchinson sat with the doors locked and the engine running, the Good Samaritan got out of his car and grabbed her cat, Cuddle Bug (also known as C.B.), from the top of the car. Hutchinson had taken her orange tabby out of the car before she left for work, but C.B. (perhaps Clinging Bravely) had secretly jumped up on the roof. The shocked owner estimated she had driven 10 miles with C.B. aboard.

CITY "KITTY"

Claiming he was trying to create a city "Garden of Eden," Antoine Yates of New York, NY, was arrested in Oct. 2003 for keeping Ming, a 425-pound Bengal-Siberian tiger, in his Harlem apartment. Yates had sought treatment at a hospital for a bite he claimed came from a pit bull. Suspicious doctors alerted the police, who had been receiving tips about wild animals in Yates's building. Ming, whom Yates described as "like my brother," was removed from the apartment after a police sharpshooter rappelled down the side of the building and shot the tiger with tranquilizer darts through the window. When police went in to get the tiger, they found another pet no-no: a $5\frac{1}{2}$-foot-long alligator named Al. Ming and Al found more suitable homes at animal sanctuaries in Ohio and Indiana.

SUPERLATIVES

OLDEST DOG BREED
Signs of domesticated Asian wolves date back to about 6750 BC in Mesopotamia. The Saluki, the royal dog of ancient Egypt, is the oldest known present-day domesticated dog breed. Saluki-like remains have been dated as far back as about 4000 BC. Mummified Salukis have been uncovered in tombs of pharaohs that date to 2100 BC.

MOST COMMON PET (U.S.) There were 70.8 million cats living with 33.2 million American families as of 2001, making felines the most abundant U.S. pet.

But dogs are in the most homes; 37.9 million, or 36.1% of American households, have a dog. Pet owners average 1.6 dogs per home as compared to 2.1 cats.

Fish are the most common exotic pet; 49.3 million finned friends live swimmingly in 6.4 million homes.

OLDEST PET CEMETERY (U.S.)
The Hartsdale Pet Cemetery near Yonkers, NY, was started in 1896 after a veterinarian, Samuel Johnson, allowed a client from nearby New York City to bury her dog in his apple orchard. After he related the story to a news reporter, he was bombarded with requests. Over 70,000 pets, including cats, birds, and rabbits, have since found final resting places at the site.

IDITAROD SLED DOG RACE

MOST WINS
Rick Swenson (U.S.) has won a record five Iditarods: 1977, 1979, 1981-82, and 1991. The most wins by a female musher is four by Susan Butcher (U.S.) in 1986-88 and 1990.

FASTEST TIME
Swiss-born Martin Buser holds the record for the fastest Iditarod run. He won the 2002 race, March 12, in a time of 8 days, 22 hours, 46 minutes, 2 seconds.

Prior to the race, Buser received his U.S. citizenship papers, and he carried them with him to the starting line. A day after winning the 2002 race (his fourth victory overall), Buser took the oath of citizenship in Nome.

WESTMINSTER DOG SHOW: BEST IN SHOW

MOST WINS
Out of the 99 BIS awards presented, the Fox Terrier (Wire) breed has won Best In Show at the Westminster Dog Show a record 13 times. The terrier group has won the title 43 times.

OLDEST WINNER
The oldest BIS champion is "Kirby," a papillon officially named Loteki Supernatural Being, from Solon, IA. The first papillon to win Best In Show, he was 8 years, 1 month, 10 days old when he took top dog honors in 1999.

He was also the only dog to win BIS at both Westminster and the World Dog Show in Helsinki, Finland (1998).

YOUNGEST WINNER
The youngest BIS champion was exactly nine months old. Laund Loyalty of Redbank, NJ, a Collie (rough), won the title in 1929.

Shopping

THE PRACTICE OF SHOPPING, SOMETIMES JOKINGLY REFERRED TO AS "RETAIL THERAPY," is ancient. Archaeologists have found the remains of bazaars in Iran that date back as far as 9000 BC. Shopping centers existed in ancient Rome and throughout the Middle East, alongside small shops selling all kinds of items, from food and wine to paper goods. Evidence of credit goes back as much as 3,000 years. Today we have credit cards, debit cards, mass-produced products, brand names, supermarkets, and superstores. And we may order items by mail or over the Internet instead of trudging around. But shopping retains its allure.

The Mall of America ►

MILESTONES

500 BC: FORUM The forum was a large open rectangular space in the center of every Roman town, used for legal, political, and mercantile transactions, as well as public sports, games, and theater. (The word "forum" actually means marketplace.) By 500 BC, the original Roman forum had evolved into a shop-lined marketplace.

Trajan's Market in Rome, named for Emperor Trajan and built by around 112 AD, was the largest of the Roman forums. It had six floors with about 150 shops lining its lower corridors, and large halls above for ceremonies and gatherings.

1838: DEPARTMENT STORE Most early department stores were expansions of existing dry-goods or general stores. Le Bon Marché in Paris was the first, founded by the Videau brothers in 1838. Aristide Boucicaut became a partner in 1852, and the sole owner in 1863. Boucicaut's business method involved buying and selling products at a fixed price on a large scale.

In 1869, construction began on a new building designed by Louis-Charles Boileau. Engineer Gustav Eiffel's elaborate metal frame and latticework gave it a spacious and whimsical interior. The store was expanded twice and, when complete in 1887, covered 568,335 square feet. Boucicaut had died in 1877 but both the business model and architectural design of the store became models for retailers around the world.

1879: FIVE AND TEN Frank Winfield Woolworth opened the world's first "five-and-ten" in Lancaster, PA, on June 21, 1879. Woolworth expanded the idea of selling counter novelty items at a fixed price of a nickel to an entire store of merchandise selling in the range of 5 to 10 cents. The Lancaster store was the first of more than 1,000 opened in Woolworth's lifetime.

1916: PLANNED SHOPPING CENTER Between 1912 and 1916, Arthur Aldis bought and razed a congested commercial strip by the railroad station in the Chicago suburb of Lake Forest. In its place, Howard Van Doren Shaw constructed Market Square, an elm-lined commercial plaza with a pedestrian median strip. All 25 stores, 12 offices, and 28 apartments were collectively owned and centrally heated.

1956: INDOOR MALL The Dayton Co.'s Southdale Shopping Center, in Edina, MN, opened on Oct. 7, 1956, as the first fully enclosed mall in the United States. Victor Gruen designed the 72-store, two-tiered, modernist building. It cost $20 million and offered the new luxury of climate control (set at 75 degrees). It had two department stores as anchors, and a central, sky-lit garden court. It had the largest parking lot of its time, holding 5,200 autos.

Time magazine called it a "pleasure dome with parking."

1995: AMAZON.COM A pioneer in online shopping, Jeff Bezos's Amazon.com opened its electronic doors for business in 1995 as a bookstore with the motto "If it's in print, it's in stock." In Oct. 1997, it became the first online retailer to serve a million unique customers, reaching 10 million in June 1999. Sales expanded to music in June 1998 and other goods in 1999.

Amazon.com posted its first profitable quarter not driven by holiday sales in the fall of 2003.

SOMETHING TO THINK ABOUT

MONEY WELL SPENT?

According to the U.S. Department of Labor, housing accounts for the biggest chunk of the U.S. dollar spent—about 33 cents in 2003. Transportation in 2003 accounted for another 19 cents, and food cost about 14 cents. Insurance, personal care, and health care together accounted for 17 cents. The remaining 17 cents went for entertainment, clothing, alcohol and tobacco, cash contributions, and education. Claiming one of the smallest shares of the average dollar in 2003 was reading materials, at .3 cents.

TOO BUSY TO SHOP

In 2003, the Murcia (Spain) Chamber of Commerce organized a promotion to encourage residents to shop at local merchants. First prize was a 6,000-euro shopping spree (then worth about $6,500). The winner was less than thrilled with the prize. She told organizers that she "couldn't waste the morning" and didn't claim her winnings. The prize was offered to the second-place finisher, Piedad Lopez, who happily had some free time, and went shopping.

TAKING CREDIT

By 1980, 56% of Americans had at least one credit card; by 2000, it was 76%. In 2004, Americans put a total of $1.045 trillion on their Visa cards alone. Total consumer debt is about $40.1 trillion; the average cardholder carries a credit card debt of more than $8,000. Only about 40% of cardholders pay off their balances each month.

SUPERLATIVES

BIGGEST SHOPPING COMPLEX China has been experiencing "mall fever" in recent years, as ever-larger malls are constructed. For less than a year after opening on Oct. 24, 2004, the Golden Resources shopping center, in northwest Beijing, was the biggest shopping complex, with 5.9 million square feet of shopping space and 1,000 stores.

Golden Resources was outdone in early 2005 by the South China Mall in Dongguan. Its 7.1 million square feet contain 1,500 stores, a theme park, pyramid, windmill, and a mile-long river.

BIGGEST MALL (NORTH AMERICA) The West Edmonton Mall, in Alberta, Canada, is the biggest mall in North America. Since its most recent expansion, in 1998, it has 5.3 million square feet of space, with about 800 stores, a hotel, and 110 "eating establishments," as well as an amusement park, aquarium, and miniature golf course.

BIGGEST MALL (U.S.) The Mall of America, opened in 1992 in Bloomington, MN, is the largest mall in the U.S. It is 4.2 million square feet, with about 520 stores, 11,000 employees, an indoor NASCAR speedway, an aquarium, and the largest indoor family theme park in the country.

LARGEST RETAIL CHAIN The world's largest retail company is Wal-Mart, Inc. Founded by Sam Walton, the chain began with a store in Rogers, AK, in 1962, and took the Wal-Mart name in 1969. There are now more than 3,600 Wal-Marts in the U.S. and over 2,300 abroad. The company accounts for 8 percent of U.S. retail shopping (excluding cars).

LARGEST DEPARTMENT STORE Macy's flagship store on Herald Square in New York City opened on Nov. 8, 1902, and expanded in 1924, to claim the distinction of being the world's largest department store. Macy's has more than 1 million square feet of selling space.

Rowland Hussey Macy founded his first store in 1858; first day sales came to $11.06.

OLDEST INDOOR SHOPPING CENTER (U.S.) The Arcade in Providence, RI, is the nation's oldest indoor shopping center. The Greek Revival structure was built in 1828.

BUSIEST SHOPPING DAY The busiest shopping day of the year is usually, but not always, the Saturday before Christmas. In 2004, it was Thursday, Dec. 23. In Jan. 2005, Visa reported that its customers charged a total of $4,837,127,232 on that day.

Chocolate

CHOCOLATE IS PRODUCED FROM ROASTED COCOA BEANS, the seeds of the melon-like fruit of the cacao tree. It started out as a bitter drink, over 2,500 years ago in the tropical lowlands of Central and South America, and was unknown to most of the world until the 16th century. Although solid chocolate didn't appear until the 19th century, it is now popular worldwide, in many different shapes, flavors, and sizes as a holiday treat, an everyday snack, or even an aphrodisiac. According to the International Cocoa Organization, over 3 million tons of cocoa products were consumed worldwide between Oct. 2004 and Sept. 2005.

MILESTONES

600 BC: FOOD OF THE GODS Evidence shows that Maya Indians regularly used cocoa in food and drink as early as 600 BC on Central America's Yucatan peninsula. They mixed cocoa with water and, frequently, with corn and chili peppers to make a frothy, bitter drink called *cacahuatl* or "bitter water." Cocoa beans were held in such high regard that images of them were carved into the walls of Mayan stone temples, and royalty drank chocolate at sacred ceremonies.

The Aztecs, who dominated the area after the 1200s, believed cocoa was a gift from their god Quetzalcoatl, who had stolen it from other gods. The importance of cocoa in Aztec religion and society, along with the limited area in which it could grow, made cocoa beans highly valuable. In fact, the beans were used as currency up until the arrival of the Spanish. According to one Spanish observer at the time, a rabbit could be purchased for ten cocoa beans or a slave for about 100.

16TH CENTURY: CHOCOLATE IN SPAIN In 1519, Spanish conquistador Hernán Cortés sampled the Aztec cocoa drink, but disliked the foam and bitterness. The Spanish added sugar to the drink and served it warm. The Aztecs named the Spanish version *chocolatl* to distinguish it from their own beverage.

Chocolate first appeared in Europe in 1544, when Dominican monks brought a group of Kekchi Mayans to Spain and they gave several jars of their chocolate drink to Prince Philip as a gift. Before the century's end, Spain was processing cocoa beans and sweetening the chocolate drink with vanilla and cane sugar.

1615: CHOCOLATE MIGRATION Chocolate gradually spread across Europe, but it came from the Americas and was too expensive for most people. It was known in Venice, Italy, by 1606. When the Spanish Princess, Anne of Austria, was betrothed to Louis XIII of France in 1615, cocoa was included in her dowry.

Louis' surprise present caught the attention of the French court. Chocolate became a must-have item in Paris, and the joys (and economic potential) of chocolate quickly spread to the rest of Western Europe.

Enamored with the seed, the 18th-century Swedish botanist Linnaeus (Carl von Linné) categorized the plant as *Theobroma* ("food of the gods") *Cacao.*

1657: CHOCOLATE SHOP Chocolate drinking spread across the English Channel from France to Great Britain around 1652. The first known English chocolate house opened in London in June 1657. The shop, owned by a Frenchman, sold both the drink and cocoa powder. But chocolate was taxed so highly that only the rich could afford it.

1765: CHOCOLATE (U.S.) In 1765, John Hanan and Dr. James Baker built the first known chocolate making facility in the U.S at Milton Lower Mills near Dorchester, MA. Hanan imported the cocoa beans from the Caribbean and worked with Baker to create what would later be called Baker's® chocolate, a product still sold today.

1795: MASS PRODUCTION Walter Churchman in 1729 received a patent to manufacture chocolate using a water-powered machine. Joseph Fry of Bristol, England, purchased the company and patent in 1761; by 1764, his chocolate was sold in 53 towns.

In 1795, his son, Joseph Storrs Fry Sr., who had inherited the company, patented a method for using a Watt steam engine to grind cocoa beans; it became a key element in large scale manufacturing.

1828: COCOA PRESS AND "DUTCHING" The invention of the cocoa press in 1828 by Conrad Van Houten of Amsterdam was a major breakthrough in cocoa production. His alkalizing process, where the fat (cocoa butter) was separated from the powder, became known as "Dutching" chocolate. From then on, chocolate drinks had a smoother consistency.

1847: CHOCOLATE BAR "Eating chocolate," the form of chocolate enjoyed most often today, was the brainchild of Joseph Storrs Fry Jr. By combining melted cocoa butter, sugar, and cocoa powder, he created his *chocolat delicieux à manger,* the first chocolate of its kind.

SOMETHING TO THINK ABOUT

SPECIAL EFFECTS

In black and white films (and countless B Movies), plain old chocolate syrup was a useful stand-in for blood. In the infamous shower scene in Alfred Hitchcock's 1960 film *Psycho*, Janet Leigh splattered chocolate syrup down the drain, and in Martin Scorsese's boxing masterpiece *Raging Bull*, a battered Robert DeNiro (as Jake LaMotta) bled chocolate syrup in the ring.

DEEP-FRIED

The Scottish delicacy of deep fried Mars bars supposedly got its start in 1995 at the Haven fish and chip shop in Stonehaven, Scotland. Supposedly, a teen regular, Brian Macdonald, came up with the idea of dipping the bar in batter and flour and frying it at 350 degrees for 30 seconds, crisping the exterior but leaving a greasy, gooey mess inside.

WHY DOES CHOCOLATE TASTE SO GOOD?

Part of the appeal of chocolate is that cocoa butter melts at 97° F—just below normal human body temperature (98.6 °F). It literally melts in your mouth. Chocolate contains phenylethylamine, a mild mood elevator, and is also believed to release endorphins in the brain, which, combined with the serotonin released with sugar, produces feelings of pleasure.

1875: MILK CHOCOLATE
After eight years of research, Daniel Peter of Vevey, Switzerland, devised a way of adding milk to cocoa powder, creating milk chocolate. By removing the water from the milk, the new method ensured the chocolate would not mildew and go bad.

The method was based on the research of a neighboring pharmacist, Henri Nestlé, who had created baby formula and founded the original Nestlé company.

1879: CONCHING
Rodolphe Lindt of Berne, Switzerland, created the conching process—so called for the machine's resemblance to a conch shell—in which heat and metal rollers pulverized cocoa and sugar particles to a smooth consistency. These were the first chocolates that could melt on the tongue or be served as pure gooey goodness.

SUPERLATIVES

BIGGEST PRODUCERS
Côte d'Ivoire (Ivory Coast) produced 1.4 million metric tons of cocoa beans in its 2003-04 season, about 41% of the world's total production. Côte d'Ivoire was followed by Ghana (736,000 metric tons) and Indonesia (415,000 metric tons). The Netherlands processes the most beans. It ground 445,000 tons in 2003-04.

Archer Daniels Midland (ADM) processes the most cocoa of any company, accounting for 15% of the world's cocoa grinding.

BIGGEST CONSUMERS (PER CAPITA) The Swiss consume more chocolate candy per capita than any other people in the world—21.2 pounds per person in 2003. The U.S. was 10th on the list, consuming 11.9 pounds per capita.

BIGGEST SELLING CHOCOLATE (U.S.)
Mars Inc. is the world's largest confectionary company, totaling $9.1 billion in sales in 2004. The chocolate candy sold the most over the counter (not counting vending machines) in the U.S. is M&Ms. In 2004, Mars sold 75.4 million packs ($201.4 million) of the candy that melts in your mouth—not in your hands.

BIGGEST CHOCOLATE CELEBRATION In Perugia, Italy, there is a week-long celebration of chocolate called Eurochocolate. At the 11th annual festival in 2005, more than 900,000 "chocoholics" invaded the town to gobble up 20,000 tons of chocolates from over 130 vendors.

The town even appoints a "chocolate mayor" for the festivities. The largest chocolate bar ever made, weighing 5,026 pounds, was produced by Elah-Dufour United Food Companies and appeared at Eurochocolate in March 2000.

This delicious festival often sets records in chocolate form; its displays have included the largest known chocolate chess board, TV set, Easter egg, and Nativity scene.

Education

IN MODERN SOCIETIES FORMAL EDUCATION takes up a large part of life. Someone who attends preschool and goes on to an advanced degree can spend well over a quarter of a century completing the process.

MILESTONES

AROUND 387 BC: PLATO'S ACADEMY IN ATHENS
This school, named for Akademos, a mythological figure who was associated with its location, is considered the fount of Western education. Classes included such subjects as astronomy, biology, mathematics, political theory, and philosophy. It lasted for some 900 years until the Emperor Justinian closed it in AD 529.

124 BC: EARLY UNIVERSITY, CHINA
After the Han Emperor Wu Ti made Confucianism a state ideology, he established an imperial university in 124 BC to educate bureaucrats for the Chinese imperial system. Within a century it had 3,000 students.

400s AD: EARLY UNIVERSITY, INDIA
Nalanda, the leading center of Buddhist learning in India, was probably founded as a monastery in Bihar during the reign of Kumara Gupta I (AD 414-445). A faculty of around 2,000 professors taught some 10,000 students. Nalanda was destroyed by Muslim invaders in the 12th century.

AROUND 11TH CENTURY: EUROPEAN UNIVERSITIES
There are several claimants to the title of first university in Europe. Salerno (*schola medica salernitana*), a medical school near Naples, was known throughout southern Europe in the 10th and 11th centuries.

The Alma Mater Studiorum for Law at the University of Bologna, founded around 1088, appears to have been the model for the first medieval universities, including Oxford University in England (established by the end of the 12th century).

1551: THE AMERICAS
The oldest university in the Americas is believed to be the Universidad Mayor de San Marcos in Lima, Peru, founded by a royal decree of Spanish King Charles V on May 12, 1551.

Established for the education of the upper crust of society, and modeled after Spain's University of Salamanca, it provided courses in languages, literature, theology, law, and medicine.

1636: HARVARD UNIVERSITY
The first university in the United States was founded in 1636 in Cambridge, MA, with a grant from the General Court of the Massachusetts Bay Colony and was named three years later for John Harvard, an English clergyman who had moved to the colony in 1637.

When he died less than a year later, he left half his estate and about 400 volumes to the school.

1678: WOMAN DOCTORATE
Belonging to an influential Venetian family enabled Elena Lucrezia Cornaro Piscopia to attend the University of Padua in Italy and graduate with a Ph.D. in philosophy on June 25, 1678.

Her pursuit of higher education was encouraged by her father, the procurator of St. Mark's Cathedral in Venice, who had hired several tutors to aid her studies.

1776: PHI BETA KAPPA In the midst of the American Revolutionary War, on Dec. 5, 1776, five students at the College of William and Mary in Williamsburg, VA, established the first college society to have a Greek letter name. Phi Beta Kappa, with its oath of secrecy, initiation rituals, badge, and code of laws, became the model for subsequent U.S. fraternities and sororities.

1837: COEDUCATION
U.S. College education for women and coeducation at the college level began in the U.S. at Oberlin College in Oberlin, OH. Women had taken classes from the Ladies Course at Oberlin since 1834, and in 1837 women participated in the men's degree program for the first time. In another first for Oberlin, Mary Jane Patterson graduated in 1862, becoming the first African-American woman to earn a college degree.

1837: KINDERGARTEN
Friedrich Froebel founded the first kindergarten ("children's garden") in Blankenburg, Germany, in 1837. The renowned German educator believed that play was significant to the development of small children and advocated the use of songs, games, and storytelling in teaching them, a philosophy that revolutionized early childhood education.

SOMETHING TO THINK ABOUT

DREAM COLLEGE

A Princeton Review survey conducted in 2004-05 asked students and parents, "What college would you most like to attend (or see your child attend) were prospects of acceptance or cost not issues?" Students chose New York University in bustling downtown New York City, while parents opted for prestigious Stanford University in Stanford, CA.

A SCHOLARSHIP FOR EVERY SKILL

Many students rely on scholarships to help offset the costs of college. Often these come from government programs or are given through the college to a wide range of students with athletic skills, high academic qualifications, or financial need. But there are quite a few unusual scholarships that target a very narrow field of students. A few examples: Juniata College's scholarship for left-handers; a scholarship for people who are 4'10" or under from the Little People of America Association; the milk industry's Scholar Athlete Milk Mustache of the Year (SAMMY) Award; and a scholarship from the Society of Performers, Artists, Athletes, and Celebrities for Space Exploration for students with "an interest in space music as a means of expressing the beauty and inspiration of our universe."

THE THE MAN WHO KNEW TOO MUCH?

One can make a case that history's smartest person was William James Sidis (1898-1944), the son of Ukrainian-Jewish immigrants to the U.S. He reportedly learned to read at a year and a half and write at three, and finished a seven-year public school course in six months at the age of six. Sidis entered Harvard at 11 and gave a brilliant two-hour lecture to the mathematics club on four-dimensional bodies. In later life, however, Sidis became something of a loner and worked in low-level jobs, leading some critics to offer him as the classic example of a prodigy pushed too hard. He died of a brain hemorrhage at the age of 46.

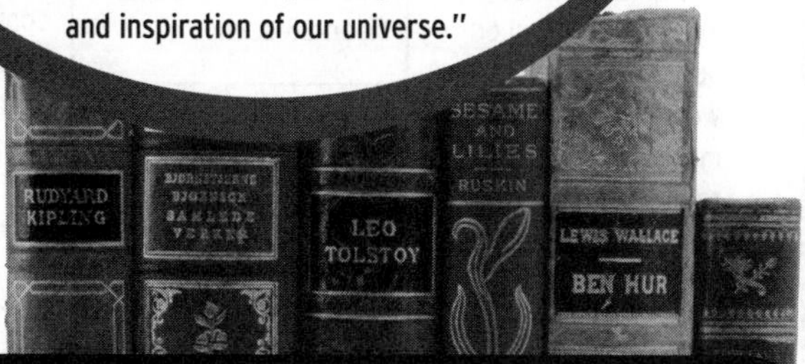

SUPERLATIVES

LARGEST UNIVERSITY

U.S. The University of Texas at Austin and Ohio State University have the largest single-campus enrollments in the U.S. For the fall semester in 2004, Ohio State had the largest enrollment, with 50,995 students at the Columbus campus. In 2004, the University of Texas intentionally lowered the enrollment at its Austin campus to 50,403 students from 51,438 in 2003.

LARGEST HIGH SCHOOL **U.S.**

The nation's three largest high schools are all in the Los Angeles Unified School District. Belmont, Theodore Roosevelt, and John C. Fremont Senior High Schools have over 5,000 students each.

OLDEST DOCTORATE

On June 26, 2004, 93-year-old Rev. Edgar Dowse received his seventh degree from the London School of Theology, in Middlesex, England. Dowse earned his first degree in 1935 when he was 22. He hit the books one last time after his wife, Ivy, died in 1999. All of his degrees are in theology or biblical studies.

HIGHEST TEST SCORES

U.S. In 2003, the most recent year for which there are complete figures, three U.S. states tied for the highest standardized reading test scores (fourth grade) in public schools under the National Assessment of Educational Progress (NAEP) program. Connecticut, Massachusetts, and New Hampshire tied with an average score of 228 (out of 500). New Mexico, at 203, was at the bottom among the 50 states.

HIGHEST PAID TEACHERS

The country that pays the highest average upper-secondary teacher's salary is Switzerland, according to a study conducted in selected nations in 2002. Novice Swiss teachers receive an average salary of $49,484; the average salary with 15 years experience is $63,893; the salary at the top of the scale averages $74,949. The comparative figures for the U.S. (ranked 8th worldwide) are $28,806, $41,708, and $49,862.

HIGHEST MATH & SCIENCE SCORES

EIGHTH GRADE Among 45 countries with eighth-grade students tested in the Third International Math and Science Study (2003), the country with the highest average math and science scores was Singapore, with scores of 605 and 578, respectively. South Korea and Hong Kong ranked second and third, respectively, in math; Taiwan and South Korea ranked second and third in science.

Students in the U.S. scored an average of 504 in math and 527 in science (15th and 9th overall).

HIGHEST ENDOWMENT

COLLEGE Harvard University's endowment assets were valued at $22.1 billion in 2004, the most of any college or university in the U.S. Yale University had the second highest endowment, with $12.7 billion.

At Work

FROM THE PARAMEDIC RACING TO THE SCENE of a crash to the woman hauling water for her family from a distant well, most adults around the world do some sort of work—usually in a job outside the home. Experts number the worldwide labor pool at nearly 3 billion of the world's 6.4 billion people.

Model Ts on the Ford assembly line, 1917

MILESTONES

12TH CENTURY: CRAFT GUILDS Around the beginning of the 12th century, artisans established guilds throughout Western Europe for mutual benefit and regulation of their trades. Guild members were divided into classes: apprentices, journeymen, and masters. Once trained, apprentices became journeymen, but masters made it difficult for journeymen to advance.

In the 14th century, journeymen began forming guilds of their own. These guilds are considered the forerunners of modern labor unions.

1805: LABOR UNION STRIKE U.S. A group of shoemakers and leatherworkers, who in 1794 had formed the Federal Society of Journeymen Cordwainers in Philadelphia, PA, organized the first strike for higher wages in North America, in Nov. 1805. The leaders were convicted in Jan. 1806 of conspiracy to raise their wages and fined $8 each.

1834: FIRST NATIONAL UNION U.S. The National Trades Union was founded on Aug. 28, 1834. By 1836, it had 300,000 members, but the financial panic of 1837 led to a decline in membership and the movement stalled.

The National Cooperative Association of Cordwainers, founded in New York City in 1836, was the first national occupation-specific union.

1894: MINIMUM WAGE The first minimum wage law was enacted by the government of New Zealand in 1894. In the U.S., Massachusetts passed the first minimum wage law, in 1912; eight other states followed suit the next year.

These early U.S. laws were applicable only to women and minors.

1913: ASSEMBLY LINE In 1913, Henry Ford combined conveyors and interchangeable parts at his Highland Park, MI, plant to reduce the time it took to assemble a Model T car from about 12 hours to 93 minutes.

Ford also began paying employees $5 a day, almost double the going rate. (This helped to produce customers who could "af-Ford" his cars.) He reduced the working day to 8 hours, so as to fit in another shift. Eventually, one Model T was being produced every 24 seconds.

1938: FAIR LABOR STANDARDS ACT After decades in which the U.S. Supreme Court struck down laws regulating child labor and minimum wages, and a year of debate in Congress, President Franklin Roosevelt signed into law the landmark Fair Labor Standards Act on June 25, 1938. The law, which is still in effect, required a minimum wage (first set at 25 cents an hour) and at least time-and-a-half pay for working over 40 hours in a week. It also prohibited "oppressive child labor."

1938: XEROX COPIER Chester Carlson, a patent lawyer, made the first successful xerographic reproduction of a glass slide onto wax paper on Oct. 22, 1938, in his New York City apartment. Years of refining and miniaturizing followed, accompanied by rejections from 20 companies, including IBM and General Electric.

The first automatic plain-paper office copier, the Xerox 914, was released on Sept. 16, 1959, by the Haloid Co., later known as the Xerox Corporation.

1970: OCCUPATIONAL SAFETY AND HEALTH ADMINISTRATION The Occupational Safety and Health Administration (OSHA)—an agency of the Department of Labor—was created on Dec. 29, 1970, to prevent work-related illness, injury, and death. Since its creation, workplace deaths have been reduced by over 60%, while injuries and illnesses have decreased by 40%.

1980: POST-IT NOTES Dr. Spence Silver, a researcher at 3M, inadvertently developed a repositionable adhesive in 1968. Its novelty was clear—it would stick quickly but not very well—yet a practical use eluded him.

In 1973 the formula was shown to 3M's commercial tape division, which included a product developer named Art Fry. Fry sang in a church choir and was tired of how bookmarks kept falling out of his hymnal. He began using the adhesive to make them stay put. No further demonstration of practicality was needed, and the Post-it Note was first sold in 1980.

SOMETHING TO THINK ABOUT

FASHION DICTATES

In July 2004, Tom Murry, president of Calvin Klein Inc., sent a memo to his staff reminding them to maintain the "Calvin Klein brand aesthetic." A "visual team" was to ensure that all desks were clear of photos, mementos, toys, or awards, and that all accessories were either black or white. Even desktop patterns for computer monitors had to follow the code and were distributed by the company.

OLDEST WORKER

Ray Crist, a scientist and educator, began working in 1925, at Columbia University in New York, and "retired" three times before finally calling it quits in April 2004 at age 104. In between, he worked at Union Carbide Corp. (1946-63), and taught at Dickinson College (1963-70) and Messiah College (1974-2004). Even in 2004, Crist didn't hang up his lab coat. He kept up his research and writing until he died at age 105 on July 23, 2005. The *Sentinel* of Carlisle, PA, Crist's hometown paper, called him "probably the oldest publishing research scientist in history."

SUPERLATIVES

HIGHEST MINIMUM WAGE U.S. Washington State has the highest minimum wage of any state. As of Aug. 1, 2005, workers there with a 40-hour week earn at least $7.35 an hour, $2.20 more than the federally mandated minimum.

LARGEST UNION NORTH AMERICA The largest union in North America is the Service Employees International Union (SEIU), with 1.8 million active members in the U.S., Canada, and Puerto Rico. SEIU members work primarily in public service, property services, and health care. The union was created by the AFL in 1921, but disaffiliated with the AFL-CIO in 2005 to form the group "Change to Win."

BIGGEST PRIVATE EMPLOYER More than 1.2 million people are employed by Wal-Mart at its 1,353 discount stores, 1,713 super centers, and 551 Sam's Clubs in the U.S. Its workforce in Puerto Rico and 14 other markets around the world numbers more than 400,000. Net sales were $285.2 billion in fiscal year 2005.

HIGHEST-PAID CEO Terry Semel, chief executive officer of Yahoo Inc., topped Forbes' 2005 list of best-paid executives, with a total compensation package of $230.6 million. In 2004, when he earned $26 million, he was 13th on the list. The nine-fold pay hike in a single year was mostly because of stock gains.

HIGHEST OFFICE The highest occupied office space in the world is the 98th floor of the Sears Tower in Chicago, IL, leased by the advertising law firm Gronek & Armstrong. It takes a four-minute elevator ride to reach that floor.

BIGGEST OFFICE BUILDING The Pentagon, in Arlington, VA, covers 29 acres. It has 17.5 miles of corridors and 3,705,793 square feet of office space on its five floors. Construction was completed on Jan. 15, 1943, after just 16 months.

In the terrorist attacks of Sept. 11, 2001, the building's west wing, recently renovated to better protect it from terrorists, was hit by a Boeing 757 jet with 62 people aboard; despite the reinforcements dozens of offices were incinerated and 122 people on the ground were killed.

MOST DANGEROUS JOBS Loggers and aircraft pilots put themselves at greater risk than any other U.S. civilian workers in 2004. Their occupations had the highest fatality rate, with 92.4 fatalities per 100,000 workers. Fishing was the third most dangerous occupation, with a fatality rate of 86.4 per 100,000.

The most deadly job in China, and possibly the world, is coal mining. China is the world's biggest coal producer, and in 2004 alone, 6,027 coal miners died on the job, according to official statistics. Other estimates range even higher. An additional 600,000 are believed to suffer from Black Lung (*pneumoconiosis*).

COMMUTING TIME U.S. Workers in New York State have the longest average commute—30.6 minutes in 2004—followed by those in Maryland (29.7) and New Jersey (29.5).

North Dakota workers can sleep a bit later: they have the shortest average commute of any state at 14.8 minutes.

HIS AND HERS PAYCHECKS U.S. In Alaska, both spouses work in 62.4% of marriages. West Virginia has the fewest two-paycheck households with 41.9%.

OLDEST CONTINUOUSLY OWNED FAMILY BUSINESS The Japanese construction company Kongo Gumi spans 40 generations, back to 578 AD. A Korean carpenter named Shigemitsu Kongo was hired in 593 to build a Buddhist temple in Osaka, by Prince Shotoku, who was one of the first in Japan to embrace what was then a new religion. Kongo stayed in Japan and his descendants have been building Buddhist temples and Shinto shrines ever since.

Money

ALTHOUGH MONEY MAY MAKE THE WORLD GO 'ROUND, coins and paper bills are a relatively recent innovation. At one time or another, people bartered everything from goats to shells, or used precious metals like gold and silver. Metals are long-lasting, beautiful, and have value beyond their use as money. Whether it's gold, a herd of cattle, or beads, economists say that an object must meet three criteria to qualify as legal tender: measure value, store wealth, and work efficiently as a medium of exchange. It also helps if the object is portable, durable, divisible, easy to distinguish, desirable, and scarce.

MILESTONES

1200 BC: CURRENCY Brightly colored seashells were the first known items used specifically as money. They were used as long ago as 1200 BC in China. About 200 years later, China introduced bronze and copper imitations of such shells.

7TH CENTURY BC: COINS The first known true coins were dime-shaped lumps of electrum—a mixture of gold and silver—often stamped with an image of a lion or a bull. They were used in the kingdom of Lydia, in what is now western Turkey.

1023: PAPER MONEY Chinese merchants developed paper money in the ninth century as a type of transferable voucher or IOU good for a set amount of time. In 1023 the Chinese government issued an official paper currency, called *jiaozi*, based on coins. Later dynasties continued using paper money, but inflation rose too quickly and the method faded by 1455.

Printed banknotes for fixed sums were first issued by the Stockholm Bank in Sweden in 1661, but they soon lost value. The first major issue of paper money in Europe was in France in the early 1700s.

1535: WAMPUM Strings of beads, often sewn together into belts, were used by Native Americans in ceremonies and as gifts to seal treaties.

The earliest recorded reference to wampum beads dates from 1535, when they were seen among the St. Lawrence Iroquois. When Europeans began settling eastern North America, coins from their home countries were scarce, and wampum became the primary currency.

1793: FIRST COINS (U.S.) The U.S. Mint was established by Congress on April 2, 1792, in Philadelphia—then the nation's capital. The Mint was the first federal building constructed after the passage of the U.S. Constitution.

The first circulating U.S. coins—11,178 copper cents—were minted in March 1793.

1862: "GREENBACKS" The Civil War forced the U.S. government to issue paper money in order to help pay war expenses. Authorization came from Congress in Feb. 1862, and the government printed more than $400 million worth of these bills in 1862-63.

People called the bills "greenbacks" because of the ink used to print them. Before this, Americans bought things using an odd array of government coins, bonds, foreign money, and banknotes printed by local banks.

1864: "IN GOD WE TRUST" A Baptist minister, Rev. M. R. Watkinson, of Ridleyville, PA, wrote a letter to Secretary of the Treasury Salmon P. Chase, in Nov. 1861, when Union morale was low because of Civil War battlefield defeats, and asked that God be recognized on U.S. money. Chase agreed and decided upon the phrase "In God we trust."

After Congress approved the motto, it appeared for the first time on the new two-cent coin in 1864. Over the next 40 years the motto was used on and off in coinage, and it became mandatory on all coins, except for the penny and nickel, in 1908. It first appeared on paper currency in 1957.

1865: SECRET SERVICE The U.S. Secret Service was created as part of the Treasury Department on July 5, 1865, to stop the age-old problem of counterfeiting. The Secret Service brought the problem under control, and today it still handles counterfeiting cases.

1900: GOLD STANDARD (U.S.) The first country to go on the gold standard was Great Britain, in 1821. The U.S. used gold and silver on and off, and after great debate began backing every paper dollar with pure gold (originally 25.8 grains/dollar) in March 1900. Eventually, the "gold standard" greatly restricted the number of dollars available, stifling economic growth.

Until 1933, people could redeem a bill's value in gold. This was stopped in June 1933 to help end the Great Depression. Today, all U.S. currency is "fiat money." That means it is backed by the people's faith in the economy rather than by precious metals.

1950: CREDIT CARDS Alfred Bloomingdale, Frank McNamara, and Ralph Schneider

BULB BLOOM AND BUST

From 1634 to 1637 the Dutch went crazy over tulips; these bulbs had just been introduced to Europe from Turkey. Prices for just one tulip bulb soared to more than the price of a house. The speculative bubble eventually burst, plunging hapless investors into financial ruin. Before it did, "Tulipomania"—as it's called—introduced the idea of the futures market, a place where contracts for future delivery on goods are bought and sold. Futures markets are used today to buy and sell goods ranging from orange juice to foreign currency.

SOMETHING TO THINK ABOUT

Wampum ▲

MONEY TO BURN

The Chinese traditionally burn fake "hell money," or spirit money, as a way to send cash to dead ancestors. Thanks to advances in technology, they now burn hell checks and hell cash cards as well.

ELECTRONIC MONEY

The U.S. Treasury's Bureau of Engraving and Printing pumps out 37 million paper bills with a face value of about $696 million each day. But more than 90% of the dollar value of transactions exists only as electric impulses in computers and never takes physical form. Electronic money includes purchases using bank cards and Internet transactions.

devised the first credit card that could be used at a variety of businesses. The Diners Club card, released in Feb. 1950, lent customers credit at select restaurants and, eventually, hotels. It was a charge card—all debts had to be paid when the bill was tendered, commonly on a monthly basis.

Bank of America launched the first revolving-credit card, with a credit limit and flexible payment dates, in Sept. 1958. Its BankAmericard evolved into today's Visa.

1967: AUTOMATIC TELLER MACHINE (ATM) De La Rue Automatic Cash System installed the first ATM at Barclays Bank in Enfield, England, in June 1967. The machine accepted carbon paper vouchers set at specific values.

Chemical Bank installed the first machine that read magnetic strips in a Rockville Centre, NY, branch in Sept. 1969.

1988: PLASTIC CURRENCY In Jan. 1988, Australia began printing its $10 note on polymer sheets rather than paper, creating the world's first plastic currency. A complete series, from $5 to $100, was printed in 1992-96.

By 2004, 22 countries were using polymer-based notes.

SUPERLATIVES

LARGEST MONEY
The Pacific Island of Yap in Micronesia still recognizes giant stone disks as legal currency. Some disks are as big as 12 feet in diameter, making them the world's largest known coins.

The stones are rare because they are quarried about 400 miles away on the island of Palau. The big ones are more valuable because they are harder to transport on canoes. They are seldom actually used in trade.

LARGEST DENOMINATION (U.S. DOLLARS) The highest-denominated bill in U.S. history never entered public circulation. A $100,000 note bearing President Woodrow Wilson's portrait was used to shuffle huge sums back and forth between the Federal Reserve System and the Treasury Department.

The biggest denomination ever in circulation was a $10,000 bill with a portrait of former Treasury Secretary and Chief Justice Salmon P. Chase.

Since 1969 the $100 bill, bearing Benjamin Franklin's portrait, has been the largest-denomination bill in circulation.

MOST EXPENSIVE COIN A $20 gold piece, the "1933 Saint-Gaudens double eagle," is the world's priciest coin, fetching about $7.6 million at auction in 2002.

When the U.S. left the gold standard in 1933, its $20 gold coins designed by sculptor Augustus Saint-Gaudens were ordered melted down. One surviving coin was found and acquired by the U.S. in 1996 and became the only such coin ever authorized for sale to a private owner.

RICHEST PEOPLE
William H. Gates III, chairman of Microsoft Corp., has a fortune that *Forbes* magazine estimated at $60 billion in 2005. That makes him the world's richest living person. Alice Walton, daughter of Wal-Mart founder Sam Walton, is the richest living woman, with an estimated net worth of $18 billion. She ranked 13th on the *Forbes* 2005 list of richest people.

MOST PENNIES
Flomaton, AL, gas station operator Edmond Knowles cashed in his loose pennies on June 22, 2005, and set a new record. Knowles, who had been collecting pennies for 38 years, amassed 1,308,459 pennies ($13,084.59). He stored them in four 55-gallon drums and three 20-gallon drums.

Knowles broke the record of 1,048,013 pennies set by Eugene Sukie of Barberton, OH, in Nov. 2004.

Religion

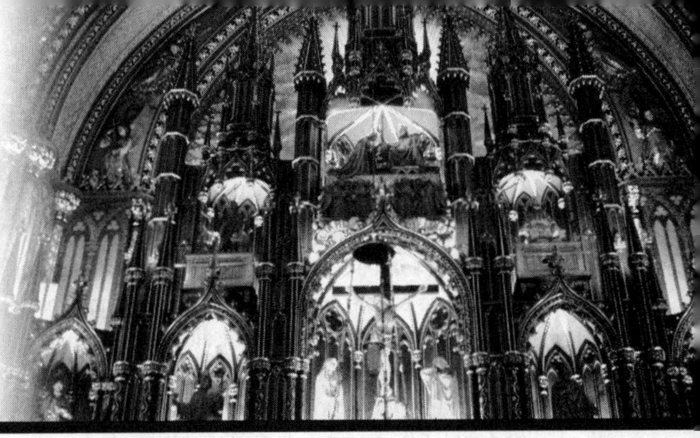

RELIGION HAS EXISTED SINCE PREHISTORIC TIMES, when animism was practiced in hunter-gatherer cultures. Animists believe that both animals and plants have spirits. More than 200,000 people around the world still practice traditional animism, but the most common religions today are Christianity (more than 2 billion followers), Islam (over 1 billion), and Hinduism (almost 1 billion).

MILESTONES

AROUND 2000-1500 BC: ABRAHAM AND JUDAISM According to the Torah, Abraham, the patriarch of Judaism, made a covenant with God in which God promised to protect his "chosen people" if they swore to love and obey him.

Abraham was the first prophet to preach monotheism (the existence of only one God). He and his wife, Sarah, settled in Canaan (present-day Palestine) and had children despite their advanced ages (Sarah was said to be in her 90s). The 12 tribes descended from their grandson, Jacob (also named Israel), are referred to as the Children of Israel, or Israelites.

1300 BC: FIRST RELIGIOUS TEXT The earliest known religious texts are contained in the Hindu *Rig Veda* (meaning "Praise Knowledge"), probably composed around 1300 BC, although some scholars date it much earlier. It contains over 1,000 Sanskrit mantras, most of which are hymns to deities.

AROUND 500 BC: BUDDHISM Buddhism started from the teachings of Siddhartha Gautama (around 563-483 BC), an Indian prince known as the Buddha ("Enlightened One"), who at the age of 29 renounced his life of luxury and began a quest for inner peace.

The Buddha attained enlightenment through realization of the Four Noble Truths: (1) life is suffering; (2) ignorance causes suffering; (3) suffering can be ended by overcoming ignorance and attachment; (4) this involves following the Noble Eightfold Path, eight rules concerning morality, wisdom, and concentration.

AROUND 500 BC: CONFUCIANISM Confucianism started when Confucius (551-479 BC), a government official in China, became discouraged by corruption in the administration and urged reform. He quit his job, traveled widely, and developed a philosophy that became the official state doctrine during China's Han dynasty (202 BC-220 AD).

Confucius's teachings, conserved in the *Analects* and other works, stress upright moral conduct and proper social relations in everyday life.

3RD-4TH CENT. BC: TAOISM Taoism can be traced back to the semi-historical Chinese philosopher Lao Tzu, meaning "Old Master." In the third or fourth century BC, he wrote the *Tao Te Ching* ("The Way and Its Power"), a guide to spiritual life. Taoists believe that practicing *wu-wei* ("doing nothing" strained or unnatural) allows them to achieve unity with the Tao and transcend life and death.

30 AD: CHRISTIANITY The roots of Christianity are based in Jewish tradition and the teachings of Jesus of Nazareth (born about 4-6 BC). A Jewish teacher in Roman-controlled Palestine and Judea, Jesus preached a faith calling for repentance and love of neighbor, and was crucified by the Romans around 29 AD. Christians see him as the Son of God who came on earth to redeem the world.

Accounts of his life and teachings, and writings by Paul and other early Christians, form the New Testament of the Bible.

610: ISLAM In 610 at age 40, Muhammad began spreading the message of Islam (meaning "submission" to God) to the peoples of the Arabian Peninsula. His teachings call for Muslims to practice "the Five Pillars of Islam": profession of faith; prayer five times daily; paying *zakat* ("alms"); dawn-to-dusk fasting during the holy month of Ramadan; and pilgrimage to Mecca at least once a lifetime, if possible.

The faithful regard Muhammad as the last and best of a long line of prophets, including Abraham, Jesus, and other biblical figures.

1053-54: THE GREAT SCHISM The Great Schism between Eastern and Western Christian churches came when Pope Leo IX and Patriarch Michael Cerularius excommunicated each other. The Western churches sided with the Roman Catholic pope, while the Eastern churches followed the Eastern Orthodox Patriarch of Constantinople and others.

Despite attempts at reunification, the churches have remained divided.

1382: FIRST ENGLISH BIBLE In 1382, British scholar and theologian John

Wycliffe (1324-1384) completed the first English translation of the Latin Bible. His translation, the first in more than a millennium, was a handwritten text, distributed by his followers, called Lollards.

Known for his opposition to the organized church, Wycliffe was later called the "Morning Star of the Reformation."

1517: THE REFORMATION
The Protestant Reformation, a protest against the Roman Catholic Church that led to the formation of many separate Christian churches, was sparked by a German monk, Martin Luther (1483-1546).

Luther wrote a list of "95 Theses on Indulgences" in 1517 and posted it on the door of the Wittenberg Cathedral. He started out by opposing the practice of granting "indulgences," reducing punishment after death for sins (especially in return for money), and later rejected other Catholic teachings and practices.

SOMETHING TO THINK ABOUT

BIGGEST BUDDHA

The Great Buddha of Leshan, China, is the world's largest stone sculpture of the Buddha. Carved into a cliff overlooking water, the seated figure is nearly 233 feet high. The head is 32.8 feet wide. The statue was carved over a period of 90 years, from 713 to 803 AD, during the Tang dynasty.

SUPERLATIVES

LONGEST-SERVING POPE The Roman Catholic Church is headed by the pope, the bishop of Rome. St. Peter, the first pope, is said to have served for about 35 years.

The longest documented service of any later pope is the 31 years, 8 months, of Pius IX (elected in June 1846, he died in 1878).

Pope John Paul II, who served from Oct. 17, 1978, until his death on April 2, 2005, was the next longest-serving pontiff, at 26 years, 6 months.

LONGEST-SERVING PATRIARCH
The Ecumenical Patriarch (patriarch of Constantinople) today is considered the leader of Eastern Orthodoxy worldwide. The line of patriarchs dates back to 38 AD, when St. Andrew the Apostle founded the Christian church of Byzantium. The longest reigning patriarch documented was Titus, who served 30 years, from 242 to 272.

LONGEST-SERVING DALAI LAMA
The Dalai Lama (Mongolian for *Ocean of Wisdom*) is the spiritual and temporal leader of Tibetan Buddhists and considered to be a reincarnation of the Buddha. The first Dalai Lama, Gedun Drub, was also the longest serving—for 83 years, from 1391 to 1474.

ALL-TIME BEST SELLER It is impossible to determine exactly how many copies of the Bible have been printed and sold. But the Bible is by far the best-selling book of all-time—estimates range from 2.5 to 6 billion in about 2,000 languages and dialects since the 19th century. Wycliffe International estimates that about 168,000 Bibles are sold or given away every day, and it is estimated that over 90% of homes in the U.S. have at least one Bible.

LONGEST BOOK IN THE BIBLE The longest book in the Bible is the book of Psalms, 150 hymns or poems composed in Hebrew by King David and others over eight centuries beginning around 1300 BC.

The longest psalm by far is Psalm 119 (sometimes numbered 118), which in the New International Version contains more than 2,500 English words. It is an acrostic poem, with each section starting with a different letter of the Hebrew alphabet, from *aleph* (the first letter) to *tav* (the last).

The shortest book in the Bible is 2 John, which contains one chapter in 13 verses (around 300 words).

The shortest verse (John 11:35) is "Jesus wept."

LONGEST *SURA* IN THE KORAN The title of Islam's sacred text, the Koran, means "to read" or "recitation" in Arabic. Each chapter, known as a *sura* ("row" in Arabic), contains revelations said to have been received by the prophet Muhammad.

Every *sura* has a name as well as a number; *Sura* 2 ("The Cow") is the longest, about 12,000 words (in English), with 286 verses.

CRIME

Crimes

SUPERLATIVES

THEFT

BIGGEST ART HEISTS On the morning of Aug. 21, 1911, in the biggest single-painting heist ever, Italian thief Vincenzo Perugia swiped Leonardo da Vinci's *Mona Lisa*, perhaps the most famous painting in the world, from the Louvre Museum in Paris, France.

Perugia, a regular visitor who had worked there briefly, hid overnight in the museum and stole the piece the next day when the museum was closed for maintenance. Dressed like a workman, he walked out with the painting concealed under his smock. The crime still baffled authorities two years later.

Perugia offered the piece to a Florentine art dealer and was immediately arrested. The masterpiece was turned over to the Italian police and put on display in Florence's Uffizi Gallery. Perugia claimed he wanted to return the piece to its home country as compensation for the art stolen by Napoleon I. Viewed as a patriot by many Italians, he served only six months after his guilty verdict.

The biggest multiple-painting art heist occurred on April 14, 1991, when 20 paintings worth an estimated $500 million were stolen from the Van Gogh Museum in Amsterdam, Netherlands. However, the paintings were found in an abandoned car only 35 minutes after they were discovered missing.

BIGGEST MOB HEIST On Dec. 11, 1978, a crew of seven armed robbers stole $5.8 million in jewelry and several currencies from a Lufthansa cargo hangar at John F. Kennedy International Airport in Queens, NY. The thieves, linked to the Lucchese crime family, carted away 72 15-pound cartons of untraceable cash from the hangar, in what was then the largest cash robbery in U.S. history.

"Inside man" Louis Werner, a cargo agent for Lufthansa, was the only suspect convicted. A scant $20,000 of the cash was recovered. Martin Scorsese's 1990 film *GoodFellas* dramatized the crime.

BIGGEST GOLD HEIST On Nov. 26, 1983, six British men stole 3 tons of gold bullion (6,800 bars) worth about $40 million and 1,000 karats of diamonds from the Brinks-Mat Ltd. security depot at Heathrow Airport in London, England. The robbers entered with a key supplied by a Brinks-Mat guard, Anthony Black.

Investigators learned that the thieves had expected cash rather than gold. Two of the thieves were tracked down through their efforts to dispose of the gold, and went to jail.

BIGGEST SAFE DEPOSIT HEIST On July 12, 1987, Valerio Viccei and an accomplice walked into the Knightsbridge Safe Deposit Centre in London, England. The pair inquired about renting a safe deposit box and then overpowered the guards and the manager (later found to be a co-conspirator) to take control of the facility, with a third robber disguised as a guard at the front door.

Five robbers in all entered the vault, looting 113 of 800 occupied boxes for about $50 million worth of cash, jewelry, and valuables. The gang was traced through a bloody fingerprint left behind by Viccei, who had cut himself on the torn metal of a box.

Viccei was sentenced to 22 years in 1989, which he served in Britain until 1992. Suspected of unsolved robberies in his native Italy, he was transferred to a prison there, and in 1996, put under day release with a nightly curfew. He was killed in a shootout with the Italian police in April 2000, following a joyride in a stolen car.

BIGGEST JEWEL HEIST Four thieves stole an estimated $100 million worth of diamonds from safes in the Diamond Center in Antwerp, Belgium, the weekend of Feb. 15-16, 2003. The thieves emptied 123 of the 160 safes in the Center's vault so seamlessly that the crime went undetected until business resumed on Monday.

Despite what investigators called the heist's "artistry," bags containing the heist plans and a name were found discarded on the highway between Antwerp and Brussels, leading police to the suspects. The thieves had been renting office space in the building and their leader, Italian Leonardo Notarbartolo, 51, had been staking out the vault since Nov. 2000, obtaining keys, security passes, and combinations.

Only one diamond—lodged in Notarbartolo's vacuum cleaner—was ever found.

SOMETHING TO THINK ABOUT

ONE IN A MILLION

On March 5, 2004, Alice Pike was arrested for trying to use a $1 million bill to pay for her purchases at a Wal-Mart in Covington, GA. Pike, who told police that her estranged husband had given her the note, tried to buy merchandise worth $1,671.55. She claimed not to know the note wasn't real and had two others in her purse. "You can't keep up with the U.S. Treasury," Pike said.

A BITE OUT OF CRIME

Thieves who stole a pickup truck in White River, IN, on April 8, 2004, might have laughed about their illicit haul, or maybe not. The truck contained some 25,000 pairs of Billy Bob Teeth. The police assumed that the criminals were not aware that the novelty items, which fit over natural teeth to give a goofy grin, were in the truck. When the truck was discovered later in the day, it was stripped of its stereo system and toolboxes. All but 6,000 sets of the teeth were left behind.

MURDER

MOST CONFESSED MOB HITS Convicted of five murders, Richard "The Iceman" Kuklinski is currently serving multiple life sentences and an 85-year stretch without parole at Trenton, NJ, State Prison. Kuklinski claims responsibility for more than 100 murders since he was 14, most of them while living the life of a suburban husband and father of three in Bergen County, NJ.

The freelance hit man for the Gambino crime family favored cyanide but also used knives, lamp cords, crossbows, hand grenades, and firearms to carry out contract hits and settle personal scores.

The Iceman earned his frosty nickname by storing a victim's remains in a Mr. Softee ice cream truck. He has been in prison since his first murder conviction in 1988, and was convicted in 2003 in the 1980 slaying of New York City police officer Peter Calabro, after authorities viewed him mentioning the crime on a TV show.

MOST DEADLY SHOOTING SPREE
On April 28, 1996, armed with several semiautomatic rifles, 28-year-old Martin Bryant fatally shot 35 people and wounded 22 others in Port Arthur, Tasmania, Australia.

He shot two acquaintances in their home before heading to the Broad Arrow Café at the Port Arthur historic site, where he slaughtered 20 and injured 12 others in 90 seconds. Fleeing in his car, he opened fire on people in the parking lot and along the road.

With three hostages in tow, he holed up in a guesthouse and was surrounded by police for an 18-hour standoff. The house burst into flames the next morning and Bryant ran out with his clothes on fire. The hostages were found dead inside.

Bryant was sentenced to 35 life terms without parole.

MOST PROLIFIC SERIAL KILLER
According to investigators, British physician Harold "Fred" Shipman, a general practitioner in Hyde, England, killed at least 215 (and possibly as many as 400) of his patients over several decades (1975-98). All were middle-aged or elderly women killed by lethal injections of morphine.

Shipman's crimes went virtually undetected until 1998, when a victim's daughter noted discrepancies in her mother's will and he was linked to its forgery. Arrested in 1998, he was convicted of killing 15 people and sentenced to 15 life terms. He hanged himself in prison on Jan. 13, 2004.

MOST PROLIFIC SERIAL KILLER (U.S.)
Gary Ridgway, known for years only as the Green River Killer, was sentenced to 48 consecutive life sentences on Dec. 18, 2003, over 20 years after he killed the first of 48 confirmed victims, more than any other U.S. serial killer so far as is known.

Investigators were finally able to identify Ridgway with DNA technology unavailable when he first began killing women, mainly prostitutes and runaways, and disposing of their bodies along the Green River just south of Seattle, WA, in 1982. He avoided the death penalty by confessing his murders and leading investigators to remains.

NARCOTICS

BIGGEST DRUG BUST Thanks to an interagency effort, U.S. Coast Guard personnel captured the sister boats *Lina Maria* and *San Jose*, seizing about 27 tons (55,000 lbs) of pure cocaine in Sept. 2004. The *Lina Maria* was stopped 300 miles southwest of the Galapagos Islands off Ecuador on Sept. 17, and authorities seized 14.5 tons of cocaine. By Sept. 24, the *San Jose* had been overtaken about 500 miles west of the Galapagos with 13 tons of cocaine.

The seized stashes were worth an estimated $1.7 billion.

CRIME

Punishment

IN ANCIENT TIMES, CRIMES WERE AVENGED BY VICTIMS, or their relatives. With the advent of legal systems, the state took over. Evidence of capital punishment is found in some of the earliest historical records; it often involved torture and mutilation–such as drawing and quartering–and was frequently carried out in public. In recent times capital punishment, when used at all, has generally been restricted to crimes such as murder and treason, and attempts have been made to make methods of execution more humane.

Corporal punishment, such as flogging and branding, was used in ancient times to punish non-capital crimes. Jails were originally designed mainly to hold those awaiting trial or sentencing, but in the 1500s, vagrants and petty criminals in England were sent to workhouses and, by the 1600s, many nations were imprisoning debtors and other criminals, often in lurid conditions. Reforms in the 18th and 19th centuries improved prison conditions, and, by the early 20th century, the idea of using prisons to rehabilitate criminals began to take hold.

MILESTONES

1792: GUILLOTINE Beheading has long been used to execute criminals. In medieval Europe, beheadings of common criminals were often botched; the most skilled executioners were reserved for nobility, giving them the privilege of a quicker, less painful death.

In 1789, at the height of the French Revolution, lawmaker and physician Joseph-Ignace Guillotin proposed the use of an efficient decapitation machine for all executions; his name became forever linked with that machine.

The guillotine was first used on Nicholas-Jacques Pelletier, a highway robber, at the Place de Grève, Paris, on April 25, 1792. Its use continued until 1977; the last public execution was in June 1939. Capital punishment was formally abolished in France in Oct. 1981.

1890: ELECTRIC CHAIR Electrocution as a form of capital punishment was first suggested in 1881 by Dr. Alfred P. Southwick, a dentist from Buffalo, NY, who had seen a man die instantly after touching an electric generator.

At the same time, the "war of the currents" was being waged between Thomas Alva Edison, who had begun lighting homes and businesses in New York City with direct current (DC) electricity, and George Westinghouse, who used Nikola Tesla's alternating current (AC). Edison hired Harold P. Brown to design an electric chair, which he hoped would prove that AC electricity was too dangerous for public use.

On June 4, 1888, New York legalized death by electricity and electrocution by alternating current and, in 1889, approved Brown's invention.

At 6:43 AM on Aug. 6, 1890, at New York's Auburn Prison, convicted murderer William Kemmler of Buffalo, NY, became the first person to die in the chair.

Ironically, Edison opposed capital punishment.

1924: GAS CHAMBER Nevada was the first state to use lethal gas as a means of execution. In 1921, it approved this method to execute Gee Jong, a Chinese immigrant convicted of a gang-related murder. Initially, officials planned to pump hydrogen cyanide gas into his cell while he was asleep. As there was no way to contain the gas, they constructed an airtight gas chamber; he was executed in the chamber on Feb. 8, 1924.

1977: LETHAL INJECTION In 1977, Oklahoma became the first U.S. state to approve lethal injection as a means of capital punishment. But Texas was the first state to use it, when convicted murderer Charles Brooks was executed on Dec. 7, 1982, in Huntsville, TX, with an injection of potassium chloride.

1934: FIRST SUPERMAX PRISON In Aug. 1934, Alcatraz Island, a former fort and military prison in San Francisco Bay, CA, became the first supermaximum security facility in the federal prison system, used to incarcerate prisoners deemed too dangerous for other prisons. Known as "The Rock," it operated until 1963, and held a total of 1,545 men throughout its history. Alcatraz is now a national park, and is open to the public.

In all, 34 inmates tried to escape the island prison, though none successfully.

SOMETHING TO THINK ABOUT

SPANDAU PRISON

Built in 1876 in western Berlin, Spandau Prison was used exclusively after the end of World War II to house Nazi war criminals convicted in the Nuremburg trials of 1946. Its seven prisoners were Rudolf Hess, Erich Raeder, Karl Dönitz, Walther Funk, Konstantin von Neurath, Albert Speer, and Baldur von Schirach. Raeder, Dönitz, Funk, and Von Neurath were released in the 1950s. Speer and Von Schirach were released in 1966, leaving Hess as Spandau's lone prisoner for 20 years. In 1987, he committed suicide. The prison was destroyed so that neo-Nazis would not turn it into a shrine. Debris from the demolition was ground up and dumped into the North Sea.

PENAL COLONIES

Since ancient times, exile was used to punish wrongdoers or enemies of those in power, often as an alternative to execution. As early as the 17th century, Russia and later the Soviet Union exiled masses of people to the inhospitable region of Siberia; at their height under Joseph Stalin, the Siberian labor camps, known as the *gulag*, held about 5 million prisoners. Great Britain settled Australia as a means of exile, sending about 160,000 criminals there between 1788 and 1868. France sent thousands of prisoners to Devil's Island (a series of islands off the coast of French Guiana) from 1852 to 1946.

POST-MORTEM EXONERATION

Since 1973, over 120 death-row prisoners in the U.S. have been exonerated. Frank Lee Smith was one such prisoner, but exoneration came too late for him. Smith was convicted of the 1985 rape and murder of an eight-year-old girl in Fort Lauderdale, FL. In the spring of 1999, his lawyers campaigned for DNA testing of evidence in the case, but prosecutors stalled. Meanwhile, Smith died of cancer on Jan. 30, 2000, on Florida's death row. Ten months later, DNA tests cleared Smith. All charges were dropped.

SUPERLATIVES

MOST COMMON METHODS OF EXECUTION **U.S.** As of 2005, the most common method of execution in the U.S. was lethal injection, employed (not always exclusively) in 37 states. From 1977 through the end of 2005, 1,004 people were executed in the U.S, mostly by lethal injection (836) or electrocution (152).

MOST EXECUTIONS **COUNTRY** Capital punishment is legal in 76 countries. According to the human rights group Amnesty International, the People's Republic of China performs over two-thirds of the world's executions; in 2004, at least 3,400 people were executed in China.

MOST EXECUTIONS PER CAPITA **COUNTRY** In 2004, Amnesty International reported that Singapore, a nation of about 4 million, puts more people to death per capita than any other country in the world. Between 1994 and 1999, the country executed 14 people per 1 million residents.

MOST EXECUTIONS **U.S.** After the U.S. Supreme Court overturned death penalty statutes in 37 states in 1972, some states began rewriting them and in 1976 the Court upheld the use of capital punishment under certain conditions.

As of 2005, 38 states, the federal government, and the military had the death penalty. Texas has been the leader in executions, with a total of 355 from 1977 through mid-2005 (Virginia was second with 94). California has the largest death row population—648 prisoners as of early 2005; however, it has executed only 12 prisoners since 1976.

LONGEST SENTENCE **U.S.** Practically speaking, life in prison without parole is the longest term any prisoner can receive. But an Oklahoma County, OK, judge, following recommendations of a jury, sentenced repeat felon Charles Scott Robinson to 30,000 years behind bars, after he was convicted, in Dec. 1994, on six counts involving the repeated sexual assault of a three-year-old girl.

An appellate court upheld the sentence.

CRIME

Investigation

CRIMINAL INVESTIGATION PROCEDURES DATE back to biblical times. Jewish laws given in the Torah set standards for investigating murder, adultery, and other offenses. It is written that a thorough investigation must take place and multiple witnesses must be found if a capital offense is suspected. But from ancient times through the 18th century, most legal cases rested on confessions obtained by torture or on superstitious tests and suspect evidence. Today investigators have an array of techniques at their disposal. Scientific examinations of offender behavior, DNA, shoe and tire prints, bite marks, handwriting, fibers, ballistics, blood splatter patterns, and skeletal remains are a few of the weapons in the arsenal of the modern detective.

MILESTONES

1248: FIRST FORENSICS GUIDE The earliest known written work outlining investigative procedures for forensic science is *Xi Yuan Ji Lu* ("Instructions to Coroners" or "The Washing Away of Wrongs"). The five-volume collection written by Song Ci was in circulation as early as 1247 in China.

Having served as a judge in what is now the province of Fujian, Song Ci wrote his book to help investigators solve crimes fairly. Among the many standards set forth is the requirement that autopsies be performed by trained doctors.

Song Ci discusses how to identify possible causes of violent death. He also suggests that coroners examine the dead body at the scene of the crime. *Xi Yuan Ji Lu* was translated into many languages and is regarded as a foundation stone of forensic science.

1806: "ARSENIC MIRROR" One of the earliest advances in forensic science was the use of the "arsenic mirror" to detect poisoning. The first person to demonstrate traces of arsenic in a human stomach was Valentine Rose in 1806. His work was based on an earlier discovery by Johann Metzger that arsenic, when heated with charcoal, forms an arsenic vapor that collects on a cool surface and forms a black, shiny film.

The next great advance came in 1813, when Spanish chemistry teacher Mathieu Orfila published *Traite des Poisons Tires* ("Treatise of General Toxicology"). This work set the standard for detection of poison in human organs, and not just in the stomach.

Orfila, who became known as "the father of toxicology," became the first to extract arsenic from organs, in 1839.

1829: FIRST POLICE FORCE Sir Robert Peel established the London Metropolitan Police, the world's first modern organized police force. Police officers in London were quickly dubbed "Bobbies" after Sir Robert.

1835: BALLISTICS The science of ballistics began with innovations in gun making. The barrels of firearms were smooth up until the late 18th century, often making it difficult to define a bullet's origins.

In 1835, London policeman Henry Goddard was the first to match a firearm to a crime, when he traced a musket ball to a mould belonging to a suspect.

Albert Llewellyn Hall, a physician from Buffalo, NY, first noted in 1900 that in rifling, every gun maker had a characteristic spiral, and as the gun was used, it left distinct wear patterns on the projectiles it fired. A Massachusetts State Court was the first to accept expert testimony on the issue two years later.

1880: FINGERPRINTS Fingerprinting, originally known as dactyloscopy, was used by ancient Assyrians and Chinese for the signing of legal documents. It is known that in sixth century China fingerprints were used to establish the identity of someone borrowing money.

The use of fingerprints to identify criminals was first outlined by a British missionary-physician working in Japan, Dr. Henry Faulds, in 1880 in an article in the journal *Nature*. He noticed that fingerprints healed to their original form. While working in Tokyo, Faulds appealed to Charles Darwin for help in promoting his work.

To this end, Darwin passed Faulds's findings along to his cousin, British anthropologist Sir Francis Galton. In 1892, Galton published his book *Fingerprints*, which established a system of classification and identification still in use today.

Nowhere in the pages did he credit Faulds with the initial discovery, and Faulds's contribution remained obscure for years.

1891: FINGERPRINT BUREAU The Buenos Aires police department was the first to set up a fingerprint bureau to collect and analyze

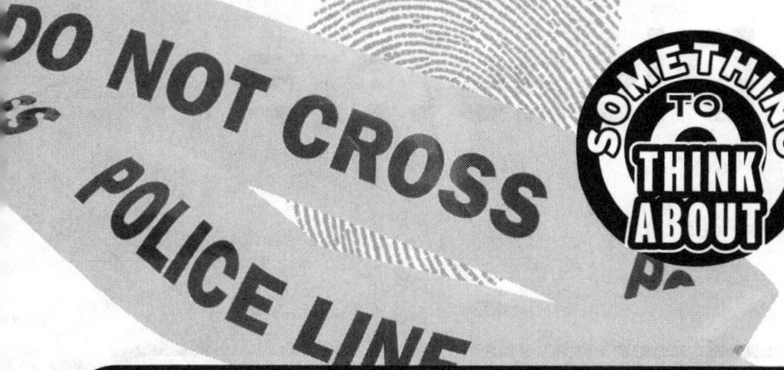

SOMETHING TO THINK ABOUT

THE WHOLE TRUTH AND NOTHING BUT THE TRUTH

William Marston, the creator of an early lie detector, never profited from his machine but gained riches after creating DC Comics' *Wonder Woman* in 1941. One of her special abilities? Anybody ensnared in her golden Lasso of Truth couldn't tell a lie.

fingerprint information during investigations. Created by Croatian-born police officer Ivan Vucetic, head of the Argentine Statistical Bureau, the bureau was set up in 1891. The following year, Vucetic solved his first case using fingerprints, catching 27-year old Francisca Rojas, who had killed her two sons.

1910: FORENSIC LAB

Edmund Locard established the first forensic lab in Lyon, France. Locard first hypothesized the forensics mantra that "every contact leaves a trace" in his book *Exchange Principle*.

The first forensic laboratory in the U.S. was established in 1923 by August Vollmer at the Los Angeles Police Department.

1915: BLOOD TESTING

In Nov. 1901, former University of Vienna professor Dr. Karl Landsteiner discovered that blood cells can be classified by different types, such as O, A, and B, with each group further classified by Rh factor as positive or negative. Landsteiner's work gained him the 1930 Nobel Prize in Physiology or Medicine, and sparked a new method of criminal investigation. Blood typing became another means to identify culprits who leave bodily fluids at crime scenes.

In 1915, Leone Lattes, an Italian professor working in Turin, developed a procedure for blood typing dried blood. This allowed the police to identify stains on clothing and other materials.

1931: LIE DETECTORS

In 1915 William Marston, as a Harvard graduate student, created a device that measured blood pressure, theorizing that blood pressure rises when a person tells a lie. It was highly controversial.

When James Frye of Washington, DC, recanted his confession of second-degree murder in 1923, Marston tested Frye using his device (then known as the "systolic blood pressure deception test"). He concluded that Frye was innocent and offered his findings as evidence. However, the trial judge wouldn't allow the results to be used, and Frye was found guilty. Later, the Court of Appeals also rejected Marston's testimony and set the precedent that any scientific device must have gained general acceptance in its field before being used as evidence.

Leonarde Keeler patented the modern lie-detector test in 1931. The Keeler Polygraph measures blood pressure, pulse rate, breathing, and perspiration. Polygraphs are still controversial and often inadmissible in court since a polished liar can pass the test. CIA agent Aldrich Ames, for example, passed two polygraph tests while spying for the Soviet Union and the Russians in the 1980s and 1990s.

1977: FORENSIC ANTHROPOLOGY

In forensic anthropology, physical anthropologists apply their techniques (identifying skeletal or decomposed remains) to a criminal setting.

The FBI consulted anthropologists for forensics as early as July 1936, when they began contacting Aleš Hrdlika, curator of anthropology at the Smithsonian Museum, to determine whether remains were human. The discipline gained prominence with the founding of the American Board of Forensic Anthropologists in 1977.

Forensic anthropologists seek to determine age, ancestry, gender, and general health of homicide victims.

1988: DNA IN COURT

The first use of DNA evidence in a criminal investigation came in the 1980s in Leicestershire, England.

After a teenage girl was raped and murdered in 1983 near Narborough and another met the same fate in 1986, police turned to DNA pioneer Dr. Alec Jeffreys. A professor at Leicester University, he developed a method to show that each person's DNA "fingerprints" were unique. Jeffreys determined that fluids found on both victims came from the same man. Police requested that all men between the ages of 18 and 30 in three local villages volunteer blood or saliva samples. The Forensic Science Service processed 5,511 samples but didn't find the killer.

Eventually, a woman at a pub overheard a man say he had submitted a sample for his friend Colin Pitchfork. Pitchfork was arrested and tested; his DNA profile matched that of the killer. In 1988 he was convicted on the basis of DNA evidence; he was sentenced to life in prison.

DNA is also used to exonerate wrongly-convicted felons. In 1979, Gary Dotson of Illinois was found guilty of raping Cathleen Crowell and sentenced to 25 years in prison. Several years later, Crowell admitted she had made up the story. But because of a series of legal mishaps, Dotson remained in prison until 1989, when Dotson's attorneys brought in DNA experts who could prove he was innocent.

Accidents & Disasters

"ACCIDENTS WILL HAPPEN," although an individual's lifetime chance of a fatal accident are modest, the National Safety Council estimates that the lifetime odds of death from an accident (estimated specifically for an American born in 2002) are about one in 35.

MILESTONES

79 AD: VESUVIUS After several centuries of lying quiet, Mount Vesuvius—a 4,190-foot volcano overlooking Naples Bay in southern Italy—erupted in 79 AD. On Aug. 24, a heated mud and ash flow swept down the mountain, engulfing the cities of Pompeii, Herculaneum, and Stabiae with debris. When Pompeii was later excavated in 1748, the remains of at least 2,000 people were found.

1871: CHICAGO FIRE Some said it began when a cow kicked over a lantern in a barn, but it was never proven. The fire began around 9 PM on Sunday, Oct. 8, in a barn behind the home of Patrick O'Leary, in Chicago's West Side. Hours later, the entire business district was in flames. The fire burned all day Monday; luckily it rained that night, and the blaze was contained.

An estimated 300 people died and 90,000 were left homeless.

1883: KRAKATAU Most of the volcanic island of Krakatau in Indonesia was destroyed after the volcano that created it erupted on Aug. 26. The 2,667-foot peak collapsed to about 790 feet below sea level, sinking two-thirds of the island and killing more than 3,000 people. A tsunami generated by the collapse killed over 36,000 in Java and Sumatra.

The eruption produced one of the loudest noises in history; it could be heard 3,000 miles away.

1889: JOHNSTOWN FLOOD On June 1, after a night of heavy rains, the South Fork Dam broke on the Little Conemaugh River. A surge of water traveling 40 mph, at a height of sometimes 60 feet, went crashing down on the town of Johnstown, PA, destroying everything in its path. The official death toll reached 2,200, but many victims were never found. It was the deadliest flood in U.S. history.

1896: FIRST FATAL CAR ACCIDENT Bridget Driscoll was crossing the street near the Crystal Palace in London on Aug. 17 when Arthur James Edsall, a cabbie, hit her. Bystanders claimed the car was speeding "as fast as a good horse could gallop," but an expert put the speed at no more than 4.5 mph.

The first U.S. auto fatality came when Henry Bliss was getting off a trolley in New York City on the night of Sept. 13, 1899, and was run over by a passing car.

1906: SAN FRANCISCO QUAKE Around 5 AM on April 18, a magnitude-8.3 earthquake rocked San Francisco and set off massive fires throughout the city. The quake damaged water pipes, hindering efforts to contain the blaze. Fires burned for several days, destroying much of the city. At least 3,000 people were killed, 28,000 buildings were lost, and half the city's population was left homeless.

1912: TITANIC The British luxury liner *Titanic*—on its maiden voyage from Southampton, England, to New York City—struck an iceberg south of Newfoundland just before midnight on April 14. Of more than 2,220 people on board, 1,513 died, including millionaires John Jacob Astor and Benjamin Guggenheim.

The *Titanic* was supposed to be unsinkable because of its 16 watertight compartments, but five were punctured by the iceberg, and the ship sank in under three hours. It was later found that there was only enough lifeboat space for three-fourths of the passengers and crew, and that the ship had been sailing too fast in dangerous waters.

The *Titanic's* wreck was found in 1985 by Robert Ballard and explored the next year.

1952: NUCLEAR REACTOR ACCIDENT The first reactor accident occurred at an experimental facility in Chalk River, Ontario, on Dec. 12, as a result of human error. Because of built up pressure, the reactor's 4-ton lid blew off, and sent radioactive water spurting out. No one was killed, but the reactor core could not be decontaminated and was buried. A trained nuclear engineer, future President Jimmy Carter, was among hundreds who aided in the cleanup.

1953: FIRST FATAL JET CRASH A Canadian Pacific Comet jet crashed on takeoff from the airport at Karachi, Pakistan, on March 3. All 11 on board were killed. The plane, scheduled to begin service on a new route in a few weeks, was on a familiarization flight. It had been diverted from another airport because of fog.

Selected Deadliest Disasters

Deadliest Hurricane[1]	300,000-500,000 deaths	Bangladesh (then East Pakistan)	Nov. 13, 1970
Deadliest Earthquake[2]	830,000 deaths (est.)	Shaanxi, China	Jan. 23, 1556
Deadliest Flood	3.7 million deaths	Huang He (Yellow River), China	July-Nov. 1931
Deadliest Tornado	1,300 deaths	Bangladesh	April 26, 1989
Deadliest Volcano[3]	10,000 deaths	Mount Tambora, Indonesia	April 5, 10-11, 1815

(1) Also referred to as a cyclone. (2) Estimated magnitude, 8.0. (3) Another 82,000 deaths occurred from starvation and disease. Airborne dust from the volcano caused global temperatures to drop, and in 1816, the "year without a summer," there were crop failures and other weather-related disturbances in North America and Europe.

SUPERLATIVES

WORST AIRLINE DISASTER Two Boeing 747s—a KLM Royal Dutch jet and a Pan American World Airways jet—collided on the runway in Tenerife, Canary Islands, on March 27, 1977, killing 582 people.

The weather was foggy, but pilot error was blamed for the crash. The KLM plane had begun accelerating without being cleared by the control tower; it hit the Pan Am jet, causing the two planes to explode. Both had been diverted to Tenerife from the airport at Grand Canary, after separatists seeking independence for the Canary Islands from Spain exploded a bomb there.

WORST SINGLE-PLANE DISASTER A Japan Airlines Boeing 747 crashed into Japan's Mount Ogura northwest of Tokyo on Aug. 12, 1985, killing 520 people. Thirteen minutes after the jet had taken off from Tokyo's Haneda Airport—for a 50-minute fight to Osaka—the crew reported trouble and asked permission to turn back. Minutes later, the plane disappeared from airport radar. Four survivors were rescued the next morning, more than 14 hours after the crash.

Japanese government investigators blamed faulty repairs made to the jet by a Boeing team in 1978.

WORST INDUSTRIAL DISASTER Tons of toxic methyl isocyanate gas leaked from a defective storage tank at a Union Carbide chemical plant in a heavily populated section of Bhopal, India, shortly after midnight on Dec. 3, 1984. The spill killed at least 1,600 people in the hours after. An estimated 16,000 eventually died, and tens of thousands suffered severe damage to eyes, lungs, and kidneys.

A lawsuit settled in 1989 provided $470 million in compensation to victims. Suits by India against Union Carbide and its chairman at the time, Warren Anderson, continue to this day.

WORST NUCLEAR POWER ACCIDENT
The disaster at Chernobyl nuclear power plant near Kiev, USSR (now in Ukraine), on April 26, 1986, was the result of a test in the No. 4 reactor that went horribly wrong, causing explosions and fire. Radioactive fallout spread over much of the Soviet Union, and an estimated 160,000 people had to be evacuated from the region.

Some experts predicted that the accident would lead to tens of thousands of deaths. According to a UN report issued in 2005, most people in the area did not receive a substantial dose of radiation and only 59 people could be determined to have died from the accident so far. However, the report concluded that about 4,000 people could eventually die from disease caused by radiation exposure.

MOST DAMAGING OIL SPILL (U.S.)
On March 24, 1989, the oil tanker *Exxon Valdez* ran aground in Prince William Sound, Alaska, spilling 11 million gallons of oil. The slick covered more than 1,000 miles of coastline, and killed hundreds of thousands of fish and seabirds and thousands of otters.

Joseph Hazelwood, the captain, had reportedly been drinking before the accident; he was tried and acquitted of the most serious criminal charges against him. A court ultimately ordered Exxon to pay those affected by the oil spill $4.5 billion in punitive damages and $2.25 billion in interest. The company also paid about $300 million in compensatory damages to parties affected, $1 billion to settle with the Alaskan and federal governments, and over $2 billion for cleanup.

WORST TSUNAMI
On Dec. 26, 2004, an earthquake measuring 9.0 on the Richter scale triggered a tsunami in the Indian Ocean that slammed into the coastlines of 13 countries, causing widespread destruction.

About 300,000 people were known to have been killed. On the Indonesian island of Sumatra, near the quake's epicenter, at least 235,000 lives were lost; and perhaps 40,000 people were killed in the island nation of Sri Lanka.

The tsunami's waves—which reached heights of over 30 feet by the time they hit shorelines—traveled across the entire Indian Ocean to East Africa.

DEADLIEST RAIL ACCIDENT On Dec. 26, 2004, a passenger train traveling from Colombo to Matara, Sri Lanka, was swamped by a tsunami; 824 bodies were found, but the death toll was estimated at close to 1,200 in all.

Monarchs

THROUGHOUT HISTORY, the most common form of government has been monarchy, where one person—whether called a king, queen, emperor, or another title—has the hereditary right to rule as head of state during his or her lifetime. Monarchs can have absolute power or have primarily ceremonial duties, like today's constitutional monarchs.

Today, 42 of the world's sovereign states are monarchies (including the 15 Commonwealth nations where the British monarch, Queen Elizabeth II, is official head of state). In addition, in Africa and Asia, hundreds of chiefs, sultans, sheikhs, and other hereditary rulers are recognized as traditional leaders of their communities or of states that are not independent tribes.

MILESTONES

3000-2850 BC: FIRST MONARCH The first monarch whose name is known was Menes, who reigned in Egypt sometime between 3000 and 2850 BC. Menes founded the first dynasty of Egyptian kings after he united the separate kingdoms of Upper and Lower Egypt.

1876: TELEPHONE Pedro II, emperor of Brazil from 1831 to 1889, was the first monarch to use a telephone. Alexander Graham Bell demonstrated the telephone to the Brazilian sovereign at the 1876 Philadelphia Exposition.

1932: RADIO BROADCAST Great Britain's George V was the first monarch to address his subjects via radio. The landmark broadcast was a Christmas message written for the king by author and poet Rudyard Kipling, and it was so well received that it became an annual Christmas day tradition for British monarchs to address the country. The king gave the address from the study of Sandringham House in Norfolk, England.

A more famous radio address was that by the British monarch Edward VIII (later the Duke of Windsor) on Dec. 11, 1936, when he announced to a stunned public that he had abdicated the throne in order to be allowed to marry "the woman I love," an American divorcée, Wallis Warfield Simpson.

SUPERLATIVES

YOUNGEST MONARCHS There are several claimants to the title of youngest crowned monarch because some were born as chiefs of state. The best known are King Jean (or John) I of France and King Alfonso XIII of Spain.

When Spain's King Alfonso XII died on Nov. 25, 1885, his wife, Queen Maria Cristina, was pregnant. At the time, the royal couple already had two daughters. If the posthumous baby had been a girl, Alfonso XII's older daughter, the Infanta Maria de las Mercedes, would have become queen. As it turned out, Maria Cristina—who was queen of Spain until her child was born—gave birth to a son, who immediately became king.

A similar situation occurred in 1316, when King Louis X of France died during his wife's pregnancy, on June 5. There was an interregnum until Nov. 15, when the royal widow had a son, who became King Jean I of France at birth. Unfortunately, the infant lived for only five days; he was succeeded by his uncle, Philip V.

SHORTEST REIGN It can be claimed that the shortest known reign was that of King Luis II of Portugal. On Feb. 1, 1908, King Carlos of Portugal, his wife, and their two sons were driving through Terreiro do Paço (now Praça do Comércio), in Lisbon, when operatives associated with *Carbonária*, a suspected republican secret society, opened fire on their carriage, killing the king and mortally wounding the crown prince, Luis Felipe. The crown prince survived for about 15 to 20 minutes, momentarily becoming king.

The shortest reign of an individual who actually served as a monarch was that of Louis XIX of France. In 1830, revolution swept the Bourbon dynasty from the French throne and King Charles X was forced to abdicate on Aug. 2, in favor of his unpopular elder son, Louis, Duke of Angouleme, who legally became Louis XIX.

However, Louis had no doubts that the situation was beyond his control. In line with his father's wishes, he abdicated a few hours after assuming the throne in favor of his nine-year-old nephew, Henri, who for five days was Henri V of France. Parliament then declared a distant

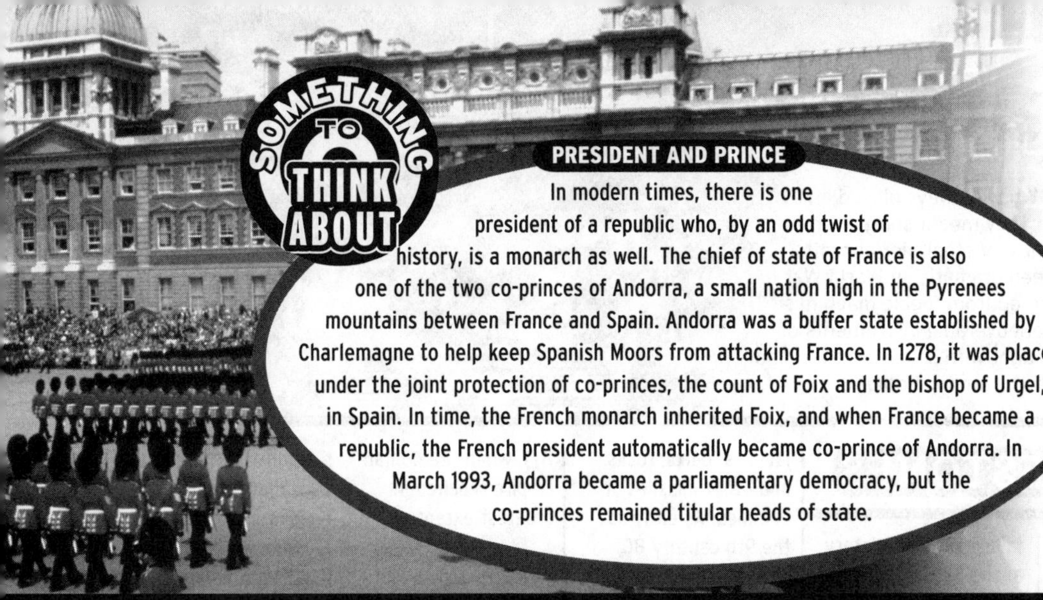

SOMETHING TO THINK ABOUT

PRESIDENT AND PRINCE

In modern times, there is one president of a republic who, by an odd twist of history, is a monarch as well. The chief of state of France is also one of the two co-princes of Andorra, a small nation high in the Pyrenees mountains between France and Spain. Andorra was a buffer state established by Charlemagne to help keep Spanish Moors from attacking France. In 1278, it was placed under the joint protection of co-princes, the count of Foix and the bishop of Urgel, in Spain. In time, the French monarch inherited Foix, and when France became a republic, the French president automatically became co-prince of Andorra. In March 1993, Andorra became a parliamentary democracy, but the co-princes remained titular heads of state.

cousin, Louis Philippe, monarch, with a new title, King of the French.

Henri V ultimately reassumed the throne, in 1848.

LONGEST REIGN
The longest reign for which there is reasonable proof is that of the ancient Egyptian pharaoh (king) Pepi II Neferkare, who came to the throne when he was six years old, around 2325 BC. There is evidence that he reigned for 94 years.

OLDEST RULING HOUSE The oldest ruling family, or house, is the Japanese imperial family. Japan's royalty traces its roots to the nation's first emperor, Jimmu, who began his rule around 660 BC.

The present emperor, Akihito, is the 125th successor to the first emperor. Emperor Akihito ascended to the throne on Jan. 7, 1989. His reign is called *Heisei*, which translates to "the achievement of complete peace on earth and in the heavens."

RICHEST MONARCH
Prior to his death in August 2005, King Fahd Bin Abdulaziz Alsaud of Saudi Arabia's total wealth was estimated at around $30 billion. The richest living female monarch is Queen Beatrix of the Netherlands. Her total wealth is estimated at about $2.5 billion.

SMALLEST MONARCHY
The world's smallest monarchy is the principality of Monaco, which has an area of three-fourths of a square mile, making it smaller than New York's Central Park.

Founded on June 10, 1215, Monaco has been ruled off and on by the House of Grimaldi since Jan. 8, 1297.

The principality's longtime ruler Prince Rainier III, who ascended the throne on May 5, 1949, later married the glamorous American film actress Grace Kelly, who abandoned her career to become Her Serene Highness Princess Grace (she died in 1981 in a car crash).

Rainier died April 6, 2005, to be succeeded by his son, Prince Albert III.

LONGEST CONSECUTIVE FEMALE RULE The longest period in which female monarchs have reigned over a country is the current sequence in the Netherlands, which stands at more than 114 years.

In 1890, King Willem III of the Netherlands was succeeded by his daughter Wilhelmina, who reigned as queen until 1948. Wilhelmina was succeeded by her daughter, Juliana, who in turn was succeeded by her daughter, Beatrix, the present Dutch queen, in 1980.

The line of queens is expected to end with Queen Beatrix, who has no daughters; the heir apparent is a son, the Prince of Orange, Willem-Alexander.

MOST SIBLINGS TO RULE The most brothers and sisters to be reigning monarchs were five of the seven siblings of French emperor Napoléon I (reigned 1804–1814 and 1815).

His brothers Joseph, Louis, and Jerome became (respectively) kings José of Spain, Lodewijk I of Holland, and Hieronymus Napoleon of Westphalia. His sisters Elisa and Pauline became reigning sovereigns of Italian states: Elisa in Tuscany, and Pauline in Guastalla.

MOST MARRIED MONARCH The most married monarch ever is believed to have been Kabaka (king) Suna II of Buganda, which today is part of Uganda. The names of 148 of the principal wives of Suna II, who reigned from 1832 to 1856, are known. The names and number of his junior wives are unknown.

The most married current monarch is King Mswati III of Swaziland, Africa's last absolute monarch. In 2004, the king, who succeeded to the throne in 1986, chose his 13th wife at an annual ceremony at which thousands of maidens danced before him.

Warfare

ADVANCES IN TECHNOLOGY have always played a key role in warfare, whether they meant sharper spears, faster ships, bigger bombs, or stealthier aircraft. Some advances have been dramatic. In World War I, airplanes were transformed from feeble machines to deadly and highly maneuverable instruments of war. World War II was fought with soldiers, tanks, and aircraft, and ended with the atomic bomb.

Omaha Beach, June 6, 1944

MILESTONES

PALEOLITHIC PERIOD: BOW The simple bow is believed to have come into use during the Paleolithic period, which ended about 13,000 BC. The composite bow—made of wood, bone, and sinew—is believed to have been developed by tribes on the central Asian plains around 1500 BC. It was a quick and powerful killer at short range and from horseback.

The Chinese used crossbows during the warring states period (403-221 BC), and around 1000 AD Europeans began using them in battle. Bolts shot from them could pierce heavy armor 1,000 feet away.

The crossbow was later discarded in favor of the longbow—as tall as a man and able to pierce armor more effectively from longer range. Introduced in Europe in the 13th Century, it proved its superiority in the famous English victory at the Battle of Crécy (1346).

ABOUT 2500 BC: CHARIOT Attaching wheeled carts to animals for battle dates back to about 2500 BC in Mesopotamia. The "Standard of Ur," a box-like artifact uncovered in an ancient royal burial site in southern Iraq, depicts four Sumerian chariots, each with a driver and spearman, pulled by donkeys.

Around 2000 BC horses were used to pull chariots, which made them even more effective against enemy foot soldiers. Around 300 BC, cavalry, which were better on difficult terrain, began replacing war chariots.

9TH CENTURY BC: CATAPULT Various machines were used in ancient and medieval times to discharge javelins, darts, rocks, and other missiles at enemies. As early as the 9th century BC, a relief from Nimrud (Iraq) shows a catapult. By 400 BC, catapults were used in Greece.

4TH CENTURY BC: ROMAN LEGIONS While Greek heavily-armed infantry (*hoplites*) fought in close formations and used thrusting spears to assault, Romans began fighting in massive units that were more maneuverable and better able to break enemy formations. The Roman legion consisted of 5,000-6,000 soldiers, mostly infantry. A typical legionnaire wore armor, had a shield (*scutum*); he carried a 5- to 7-foot-long javelin (*pilum*), and a 20-inch sword (*gladius*).

The Roman legions flourished from the time of Julius Caesar (who conquered northern Gaul by 57 BC) to the reign of the Emperor Trajan (AD 98-117), when the Roman Empire reached its greatest extent.

8TH CENTURY: GUNPOWDER The Chinese are generally credited with the discovery of gunpowder—a mixture of saltpeter, charcoal, and sulfur—toward the end of the Tang dynasty (618-907). The earliest written formula dates to 1044 in China, and the earliest known depiction of a cannon is from 1127 in China.

Gunpowder appeared in Europe in the 13th century, when the English philosopher Roger Bacon wrote of the invention. The earliest European depiction of a cannon was in 1327 in England, which oddly shows the cannon firing arrows.

10TH CENTURY: KNIGHTS The first knights were heavily armed peasant horsemen who served feudal lords in return for land or money in the years following the fall of Rome. Later, knights became a privileged warrior class. They fought mainly on horseback and wore heavy chain mail and plate armor. In battle they would typically charge the enemy using lances to break through shield walls and infantry formations.

Over time, knights became associated with a code of chivalry romanticized in popular myths such as *The Song of Roland*.

Knights flourished during the Crusades (1096-1297). But by the 15th century, use of knights began to decline as longbows and other weapons made charging headlong into battle all but suicidal.

15TH CENTURY: RIFLED FIREARMS Around the 15th century, European gun makers began to carve shallow, spiraling grooves on the inside of gun barrels, which caused the bullet to spin when fired, making it fly

USS Ronald Reagan

straighter and farther. However, the round bullets used at the time made loading the guns complicated and time consuming. It wasn't until the 19th century that elongated bullets and better parts made rifles more practical.

1615: FLINTLOCK Early firearms were cumbersome devices, unreliable in wet weather, and slow-loading. The matchlock, developed in 15th-century Germany, used a wick or smoldering cord to ignite the gunpowder inside the barrel. But it was still unreliable and slow.

The flintlock, developed in France in 1615 by the Bourgeoys family, produced a spark from flint striking steel that lit the gunpowder causing the weapon to fire.

Flintlocks were less sensitive to dampness and easier to load. They were adopted by the French army in the mid-17th century, and soon became standard.

1620S: SUBMARINE The first submarine was designed by Dutch engineer Cornelis Drebbel between 1620 and 1624. The vessel, which had a cucumber-shaped hull like some of today's subs, was tested on the Thames River in London. Despite promising trials, the idea didn't catch on.

The first submarine used in warfare was the *Turtle*, an egg-shaped one-man vessel, with a crank that the mariner would use to turn a propeller. Introduced during the American Revolution, it was not a success.

It wasn't until Feb. 17, 1864, that a sub managed to mount a successful attack on a surface craft. The Confederate human-powered submarine *Hunley* blew up the *USS Housatonic* in Charleston, S.C., Harbor, using an explosive device mounted on the end of a long boom protruding from the sub.

German submarines, or U-boats (short for the German word *unterseeboot*), used during World War I, were the first to live up to the sub's potential of being widely deployable, deadly weapons against surface boats.

1849: MINIÉ BULLET Claude-Etienne Minié and Henri-Gustave Delvigne made the rifle more accurate and reliable by inventing the precursor to the modern bullet in 1849. Using the percussion cap invented by Joshua Shaw in 1814, they made a cylindrical, cone-tipped (the classic bullet shape) lead projectile with a hollow base, the Minié ball. It was small enough to muzzle-load easily but would expand to fill the rifle's grooves upon firing, all but eliminating fouling.

1885: AUTOMATIC MACHINE GUN Multiple barrel guns for repeated firing had been around for centuries but they were crude and, in the case of Richard Gatling's famous "Gatling Gun," which could fire up to 3,000 rounds per minute, hand-cranked.

The first machine gun as we know them today was invented by American engineer Hiram Maxim in 1883-85. His single-barreled, belt-fed "Maxim" machine gun was the first to automatically eject spent rounds by using the gun's recoil. The gun could continuously fire 600-700 .45 caliber shells per minute.

1910: AIRCRAFT CARRIER On Nov. 14, 1910, Eugene Ely took off in a Curtiss biplane from a specially built wooden platform on the *USS Birmingham* near Hampton Roads, VA. It was the first time an airplane took off from the deck of a ship.

The first carrier specifically designed to carry airplanes, Britain's *HMS Argus*, commissioned Sept. 16, 1918, was a converted passenger liner fitted with a flight deck. The U.S. Navy's first carrier was the *USS Langley*, a converted coal-carrying ship, commissioned March 20, 1922, at Norfolk, VA.

MORE ON
Warfare

1915: CHEMICAL WEAPONS Chemical weapons were used on a wide scale in World War I. By 1915, first France then Germany had used tear gas in battle, but it was Germany that mounted the first lethal chemical attack. On April 22, 1915, the German army unleashed about 177 tons of wind-borne chlorine gas over 3.7 miles of Allied trenches at Ypres.

The gas, which causes burning in the throat and lungs and suffocates its victims, killed some 5,000 soldiers and injured thousands more. Soon after, the French and British responded in kind. During World War I, it is estimated that more than 90,000 troops were killed by poison gas. A League of Nations ban on chemical weapons went into effect in 1928.

1916: TANK The modern tank was developed during World War I out of a need to break the stalemate caused by trench warfare. Early tanks used the chassis of an American Holt Agricultural Caterpillar Tractor, and were armed with machine guns. Originally called landships, they were later nicknamed "Willie" but given the code name "water tank," which is where we get the term.

On Sept. 15, 1916, the British deployed 49 tanks in the Battle of the Somme near Courcelette, France, with some success. Their usefulness was shown at the Battle of Cambrai in 1917, when British tanks and infantry broke through German lines along a 12-mile front. However, early tanks broke down frequently, and often got bogged down in mud.

1942: FIGHTER JET The first operational fighter jet was Nazi Germany's Messerschmitt Me-262 *Schwalbe* ("Swallow") interceptor, first flown on July 18, 1942. The revolutionary aircraft was a single-seat fighter powered by twin turbojet engines generating 1,986 pounds of thrust. The Me-262 had a maximum speed of 540 mph, a flight ceiling of about 38,000 feet, and an operational range of 650 miles.

The first combat kill by a jet plane came on July 25, 1944, when an Me-262 shot down a British Mosquito photo-reconnaissance plane over Munich.

Selected Modern Warfare Milestones

WEAPON	INVENTOR/CONTRACTOR	YEAR
Breech-loading rifle	Patrick Ferguson (Great Britain)	1776
Shrapnel Shells	Henry Shrapnel (Great Britain)	1784
Colt (revolver)	Samuel Colt (U.S.)	1835
Gatling (machine gun)	Richard J. Gatling (U.S.)	1861
Radar	Sir Robert Watson-Watt	1935
MiG-15 (fighter plane)	Artem I. Mikoyan, Mikhail I. Gurevich (USSR)	1947
AK-47 (assault rifle)	Mikhail Kalashnikov (USSR)	1947
Hydrogen Bomb	U.S. scientists led by Edward Teller	1952
Nuclear Submarine	Electric Boat Corp.	1954
F-117 Stealth Fighter	Lockheed Martin Corp.	1981
B-2 Stealth Bomber	Northrop Grumman Corp.	1989

1944: MISSILES Crude rockets had been used in battle notably by the early Chinese, and in the 19th century by the British army (hence "rockets' red glare"). But it was Nazi Germany that developed and used the first missiles as we know them today.

The German V-1 (*Vergeltungswaffen*-1 or "Vengeance Weapon") was the world's first cruise missile. Armed with a ton of high explosives, each V-1 was 27.1 feet long, and had a wingspan of 17.8 feet and a range of 150 miles. Beginning June 12, 1944, Germany fired 9,521 V-1s from launching points in occupied France at southern England (mainly London), killing 6,184 people and injuring 17,981.

German rocket engineer Wernher von Braun pioneered the V-1's larger, more-sophisticated cousin, the V-2, which was the world's first ballistic missile. Each V-2 had a range of 180-220 miles and carried a 1-ton high-explosive payload. From Sept. 8, 1944, to March 30, 1945, Germany pounded England with 1,115 V-2s, while 1,524 fell on continental Europe, killing about 7,000 people in all (2,754 in London alone).

The first intercontinental ballistic missile (ICBM) was the U.S. Convair B-65 "Atlas." Made operational in 1959, it had a range of 6,300 miles and carried a nuclear warhead.

1945: ATOM BOMB The first atomic bomb was tested on July 16, 1945, at Los Alamos National Laboratory (NM).

Then, at 8:15 AM on Aug. 6, 1945, a B-29 bomber, *Enola Gay*, dropped a uranium (U-235) bomb on Hiroshima, Japan. Code-named "Little Boy," it had an explosive yield of 14 kilotons, enough to destroy an entire city.

The blast, combined with an atom bomb dropped on Nagasaki 3 days later, brought an end to the brutal war, but an estimated 200,000 Japanese died immediately or eventually as a result of the two bombs.

SOMETHING TO THINK ABOUT

SOCCER WAR

In 1969, the national soccer teams of El Salvador and Honduras were paired in a World Cup qualification series that proved to be the last straw in deteriorating relations between the two countries. Over the years, many Salvadorians had drifted over the border into Honduras and squatted; there were about 300,000 by 1960. In 1969, the Honduran government forced the eviction of thousands. As relations deteriorated, the two countries' soccer teams faced each other in a series of games marred by rioting. Border skirmishes escalated, and El Salvador invaded Honduras on July 14, 1969. The so-called "Soccer War" lasted until July 18, when a cease-fire was reached.

SUPERLATIVES

LONGEST WAR
The Hundred Years War between France and England (1337-1453) is the longest war ever fought. On May 24, 1337, the French king Philip VI kicked off the war when he seized the sole French fiefdom held by the English king Edward III. Edward attacked Philip's realms in 1339, and won battles at Crécy (1346) and Poitiers (1356). After a lull in the 1360s, the new French king, Charles V, renewed the campaign in 1369, winning back much of the French land.

Henry V of England invaded in 1415 and defeated the French army at Agincourt, but by the end of the war, the English had lost nearly all of their land in France. No formal treaty was ever signed.

Other leaders who fought in the war included Edward the Black Prince (son of Edward III) and Joan of Arc (France).

BIGGEST WAR
World War II was the biggest war in history in terms of human and material resources expended. In all, 61 countries, representing 1.7 billion people ($\frac{3}{4}$ of the world's population) were sucked into it. A total of 110 million were mobilized for military service including 22-30 million by the USSR, 17 million by German, and 16 million by the U.S. (The USSR had the most on duty at any one time, with a standing army of about 12.5 million.)

Estimates of the financial cost range as high as $1 trillion, which would make World War II more costly than all other wars combined. The human cost, not including more than 5 million Jews and 250,000 Gypsies killed in the Holocaust, is estimated to have been about 53.5 million dead—including 38.6 million civilians.

DEADLIEST WAR (U.S.) The deadliest war fought on U.S. soil was the Civil War (1861-65). It is estimated that 498,333 Americans died on the two sides (364,512 Union, 133,821 Confederate). But only 43% of those deaths came on the battlefield. The rest died of accidents, disease, or privation.

The bloodiest battle of the war was at Gettysburg, PA, July 1-3, 1863. Union forces suffered 23,049 casualties, and Confederate forces 28,063.

The bloodiest one-day battle was at Antietam, MD, on Sept. 17, 1862. That day, there were an estimated 22,720 casualties, including 2,100 Union and 1,550 Confederate deaths.

BIGGEST INVASION
The invasion of France's Normandy coast by Allied Forces seeking to defeat the Germans, known as Operation Overlord, began on June 6, 1944 (D-Day). Under U.S. General Dwight D. Eisenhower, it was the biggest invasion in military history. More than 150,000 troops, including some 73,000 Americans, 62,000 Britons, and 21,000 Canadians, stormed the beaches.

During the landing the Allied forces suffered 10,300 casualties, including 2,500 killed, mostly at Omaha Beach. In the next five days, about 326,500 soldiers, 54,000 vehicles, and over 104,000 tons of supplies went ashore. The operation officially ended on Aug. 19, 1944.

BIGGEST NAVAL BATTLE The Battle of Leyte Gulf took place off the Philippines Oct. 23-25, 1944. It involved 282 ships (218 Allied, 64 Japan), and 1,996 aircraft (1,280 Allied, 716 Japan). Nearly all of Japan's surviving fleet fought—including 7 battleships and 16 cruisers. The first Japanese kamikazes (suicide airplane attacks) were used on Oct. 25.

OLDEST ARMY UNIT
The Pontifical Swiss Guard, which guards the Pope and is based in Vatican City, is the oldest army unit in the world, founded on Jan. 22, 1506. Back then, Swiss mercenaries were coveted for their fighting prowess.

The Swiss Guard saw battle on May 6, 1527, when Rome was sacked by troops of Spanish King and Holy Roman Emperor, Charles V; 147 Swiss Guards were killed defending Pope Clement VII and the Vatican. After that, they never lost another soldier in combat.

Balance

CIRCUS PERFORMERS HAVE AMAZED THE PUBLIC with high-wire feats for hundreds of years. But daring disregard for gravity is not limited to the Big Top or the high-wire. Daredevils, showoffs, and everyday folks looking for a challenge have balanced risk and reward to obtain glory. Here we recognize some of those accomplishments.

Philippe Petit, World Trade Center tightrope walk, 1974

MILESTONES

1859: TIGHTROPE WALK ACROSS NIAGARA FALLS Perhaps the most famous tightrope artist of all time, the Great Charles Blondin was the first person to walk a tightrope strung across the Niagara Falls gorge.

The Frenchman (real name Jean François Gravelet) first crossed the Falls (from the U.S. to Canada) June 30, 1859, on rope 3.75 inches thick. A great showman, Blondin paused during the walk and had a drink of wine from a bottle he hauled up by rope from the tour boat *Maid of the Mist*. After completing the trip in 17 minutes, he had some celebratory champagne and returned to the U.S. side in about six minutes.

It was the first of 21 Niagara crossings by Blondin. Suspended precariously above the Falls, he later rode a bicycle, pushed a wheelbarrow across the span, cooked an omelet, and in perhaps the most dangerous stunt of all (he nearly lost his life when a guy wire broke), carried his 136-pound manager Harry Colcord across on his back.

1919: POGO STICK Ernst Rohmer patented the iron *Sprunggeräth* (literally "Jumping Apparatus") in Germany in 1897, but the basic model for modern pogo sticks came in 1919, when George Hansburg created a device he called the "Pogo Stick."

The Gimbel Brothers Department Store had commissioned the toy maker to produce a new model "jumping stick," after a large order of German-made wood jumping sticks rotted during shipping. Hansburg's all-metal machine featured an enclosed spring, and quickly sparked a craze in the 1920s.

1947: 7-PERSON PYRAMID One of the most famous high-wire circus acts is the "Flying Wallendas," and it was the supreme aerial family's patriarch, Karl Wallenda, who perfected the 7-Person Pyramid (atop a tightrope), in Sarasota, FL, in 1947.

The three-tier pyramid had four men on the bottom, two men on the second level, and a woman sitting, then standing, on a chair at the top of the pyramid. The four-man foundation stood on a tightrope 35 feet above the circus floor; two pairs were yoked together by shoulder bars, as were the two mid-level men standing on the bars.

The Wallendas began performing the spectacular act in 1948. But tragedy struck on Jan. 30, 1962, when the pyramid toppled, killing two Wallendas and paralyzing a third. The Flying Wallendas performed the stunt only seldom thereafter, and no other group has perfected it. But sixth- and seventh-generation performing Wallendas continue to tackle other daring and dangerous stunts.

1974: WORLD TRADE CENTER TIGHTROPE WALK On Aug. 7, 1974, French high-wire artist Philippe Petit and his accomplices secured a tightrope between the 1,360-foot-tall roofs of the nearly completed World Trade Center towers in New York City. In secret, he brought 250 feet of galvanized steel rope, just $\frac{7}{8}$" in diameter, to the top of the South Tower. Assistants on the North Tower used a bow and arrow attached to a fishing line to secure the cable across the span the night before.

The tightrope walk, the culmination of six years of preparations, began at 7:15 AM. Thousands of New Yorkers heading to work stopped and stared.

After eight crossings and 45 minutes spent suspended a quarter of a mile above the Big Apple, Petit finally ended his historic walk. He was arrested and charged with trespassing and disturbing the public order, but public support for Petit was so great that all charges were dropped.

The Port Authority formally thanked him for bringing a bit of majesty to the then-criticized Twin Towers project by having him sign his name on a steel beam near where he performed his feat.

RECORD BREAKER

Philippe Petit

"'It's painful to perform here now with them gone, but I still consider them my towers. If they built them again, I would walk between them again."

–Philippe Petit, in New York City to mark the 31st anniversary of his World Trade Center walk, on Aug. 7, 2005.

SUPERLATIVES

DOMINO TOPPLING (INDIVIDUAL) On Aug. 18, 2003, at the Singapore Expo Hall, Ma Lihua of China pushed one domino and set off a chain reaction that knocked over 303,621 dominoes, the most ever toppled in a chain created by one person.

It took the 24-year-old Beijing resident nearly seven weeks of 13-hour days to align over 9 miles of dominoes, but it took just four minutes for the dominoes to fall.

At one point in the set-up process, cockroaches threatened the entire project when one of the creepy crawlies bumped into a domino. About 8,000 tiles were toppled, which set her back over a day's worth of work. Pandam leaves, thought to repel the insects, were placed around the hall to prevent further "roach rage."

DOMINO TOPPLING (TEAM) The Netherlands' Weijers Domino Productions b.v. is a domino toppling dynasty. The Dutch company has built nine of the ten largest domino chain reactions of all time, dating back to 1986. It holds the current world record, which stands at 4,002,136 dominoes aligned and toppled in Amsterdam, The Netherlands, on Nov. 18, 2005, "World Domino Day."

Celebration of the new record was somewhat tempered by the shooting of a sparrow that had threatened to topple the dominoes ahead of schedule earlier in the week. The bird knocked down 23,000 tiles and was shot by an exterminator with an air gun. More than 5,000 people signed a memorial register on a website in honor of the bird.

POGO STICK, CN TOWER (FASTEST) On July 23, 1999, in Toronto, Canada, Ashrita Furman (U.S.) pogoed up the 1,899 steps of the CN Tower, the world's tallest free-standing structure, in a record time of 57 minutes, 51 seconds.

The New York health food store worker also holds the record for fastest pogo mile (12 minutes, 15 seconds) and longest distance (23.11 miles) on a pogo stick. Other accomplishments include having pogo stick jumped up Mount Fuji in Japan, and aqua-pogoed in the Amazon River.

STILT WALKING, LONGEST JOURNEY Over five months in 1980, Joe Bowen, of Powell, KY, walked 3,008 miles in extra-long stilt strides from Los Angeles, CA, to Bowen, KY. Bowen's epic trek was performed to raise money for muscular dystrophy research. He departed Los Angeles on Feb. 20 and traveled 40 miles per day, completing his journey on July 26 in Bowen, the town founded by his great-great-grandfather.

LONGEST UNICYCLE JOURNEY Rev. Lars Clausen, a Lutheran minister from Holden Village, WA, rode his 36-inch Coker unicycle from Oregon to New York and back across in 2002. During his cross-country journey, he traveled 9,136 miles while visiting all 50 states.

Clausen's trip began on April 22, 2002, in Tillamook, OR. He reached the Statue of Liberty on Aug. 10. The return transcontinental crossing along the Gulf of Mexico was completed on Nov. 12, 2002, at the Santa Monica Pier in CA.

During 205 days in the unicycle saddle, Clausen completed more than 5 million revolutions of the wheel. He beat the previous mark of 3,876.1 miles set by Hans Peter Beck, who rode across Australia from June 30 to Aug. 20, 1985.

TALLEST UNICYCLE On Jan. 29, 2004, Sem Abrahams of Livonia, MI, rode a 114.8-foot-tall unicycle, the tallest ever ridden. A long time unicycle performer, Abrahams recaptured the record he had previously set in 1976 (45 ft), and 1980 (72 ft). The aluminum center post unicycle was custom-built by Kriewall Enterprises, Inc., of Rome, MI.

Abrahams made his record ride at Michigan's Pontiac Silverdome. The unicycle cost $16,000, and Abrahams had to pay an additional $2,500 to rent the stadium.

WHEELIE, LONGEST RIDE On June 25, 1999, Kurt Osburn arrived in Orlando, FL, from Los Angeles, CA, traveling the entire 2,839.6 miles while performing a wheelie on a child's bicycle. The 29-year-old entrepreneur from Fullerton, CA, had started April 13 on his record-setting ride, which took him through eight states in 74 days.

Juggling

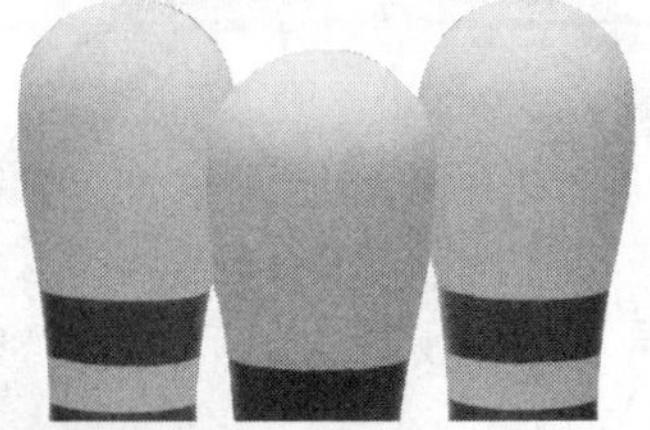

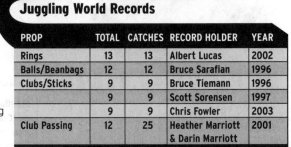

JUGGLING DATES BACK AT LEAST 4,000 YEARS. Paintings of jugglers have been found in tombs in ancient Egypt from as early as 2000 BC and in Greek art by 400 Circus performers, vaudeville acts, and various other entertainers have claimed juggling records over the years, but few of these claims are accepted as fact. The International Jugglers' Association (IJA) was founded in 1947 and recognizes juggling world records achieved in IJA competitions.

Juggling World Records

PROP	TOTAL	CATCHES	RECORD HOLDER	YEAR
Rings	13	13	Albert Lucas	2002
Balls/Beanbags	12	12	Bruce Sarafian	1996
Clubs/Sticks	9	9	Bruce Tiemann	1996
	9	9	Scott Sorensen	1997
	9	9	Chris Fowler	2003
Club Passing	12	25	Heather Marriott & Darin Marriott	2001

SPORT JUGGLING, ALSO KNOWN AS "JOGGLING," combines running with juggling. In most events, competitors juggle three half-pound rubber balls while running standard track and field distances. Joggling competitions range from lengths of 100 meters to the marathon, a distance of 26.2 miles.

The origins of the sport are unknown, but official races have been staged in the United States since 1980. The official governing body for the sport is the International Sport Juggling Federation, founded in 2001.

FOOTBAG WAS INVENTED by John Stalberger and Mike Marshall in Oregon City, OR, in 1972. Stalberger, who was recovering from knee surgery at the time, was looking for exercises that could help him regain his flexibility. One day, he met Marshall, who was kicking around a handmade bean bag. Stalberger joined in and soon a new sport was born.

The pair designed a product, a small leather ball filled with sand or plastic pellets, which they trademarked as "Hacky Sack," and named the sport "footbag." Marshall died in 1975, but Stalberger continued to promote their game. Later Stalberger sold the rights to Hacky Sack to Kransco (operating under the Wham-O label).

The World Footbag Association, founded in 1983, is the official governing body of the sport.

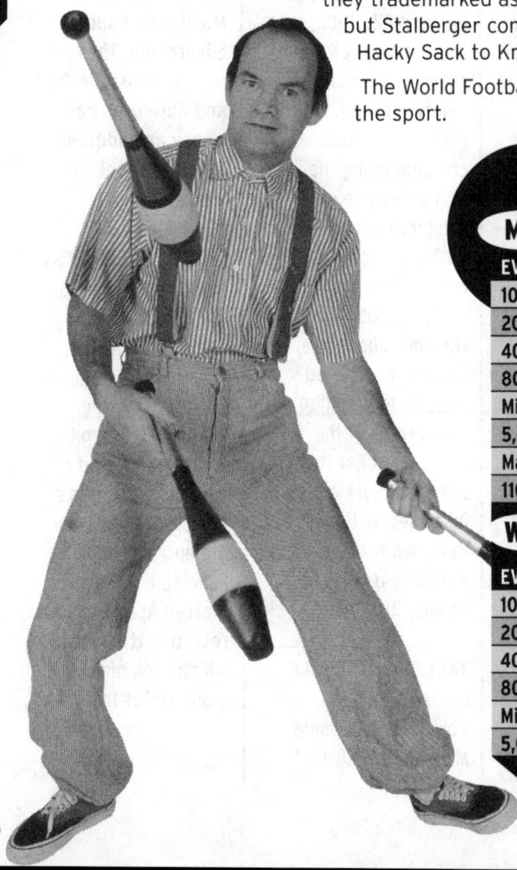

The following world records are recognized by the International Sport Juggling Federation:

Men's Outdoor World Joggling Records (3 balls)

EVENT	TIME	RECORD HOLDER	LOCATION	YEAR
100 meters	00:11.68	Owen Morse	Baltimore, MD	1989
200 meters	00:26.16	Chris Essick	Eugene, OR	2002
400 meters	00:56.90	Chris Essick	Columbia, MO	2000
800 meters	02:28.58	Jamie Whoolery	Reno, NV	2003
Mile	04:42.36	Will Howard	Atlanta, GA	2003
5,000 meters	16:58.80	Kirk Swenson	San Jose, CA	1986
Marathon	3:07:05.00	Zach Warren	Philadelphia, PA	2005
110-m hurdles	00:17.94	Albert Lucas	Branson, MO	1997

Women's Outdoor World Joggling Records (3 balls)

EVENT	TIME	RECORD HOLDER	LOCATION	YEAR
100 meters	00:14.96	Lana Bolin	Montreal, Canada	2000
200 meters	00:34.34	Lana Bolin	Montreal, Canada	2000
400 meters	01:16.00	Christa Rypins	Los Angeles, CA	1990
800 meters	03:19.18	Heather Marriott	Reno, NV	2003
Mile	06:17.00	Kathy Glynn	Baltimore, MD	1989
5,000 meters	25:43.00	Heather Marriott	Reading, PA	2002

HOW DO THEY KEEP IT UP?

Tricia George and Gary Lautt hold the footbag world record in the category "Most Kicks, Open Doubles." It's tough to keep a footbag in the air for five minutes—but to do it all day? Working with a partner adds risk. And how do you practice when you live hundreds of miles apart?

The pair talked to *The World Almanac Book of Records* about how and why they set the footbag record their first time around in 1995. (Three years later they succeeded in breaking their own record!)

To get ready for their first record attempt, Tricia and Gary practiced kicking the footbag separately. Then Tricia traveled from her home in Clackamas, Oregon, to practice with Gary in Chico, California. "We worked out for two hours at a time, doing 15,000 kicks." They planned their record attempt scheduling breaks for rest, food, and the bathroom. "We did 20 kicks each, then passed the footbag," says Tricia.

How many kicks would they be able to do? That number was still up in the air. Once they reached 100,000 kicks, it was hard to stop. "We shot for 111,111. Then we decided we liked the look of 123,456 even better!"

SUPERLATIVES

JUGGLING

SOCCER BALL JUGGLING Milene Domingues, a member of the Brazil squad at the 2003 FIFA Women's World Cup, holds the women's record for continuously juggling a soccer ball, with 55,187 touches in 9 hours, 6 minutes. She performed the feat in 1997 at age 17.

Known in Brazil as *rainha das embaixadinhas*, "the juggler queen," Milene is the former wife of Real Madrid and Brazil soccer superstar Ronaldo.

PING PONG BALLS Tony Ferko of Czechoslovakia juggled seven ping-pong balls with his mouth on Jan. 5, 1987.

BOOMERANG JUGGLING On Sept. 3, 1995, in Strasbourg, France, Yannick Charles of France made 555 consecutive catches with two boomerangs. At least one of the boomerangs was aloft at all times. Charles also holds the single boomerang world record for consecutive catches: 1,215 catches, which he set in Dijon, France, in 1995.

FOOTBAG

OPEN SINGLES The world record for keeping a footbag airborne is 63,326 consecutive kicks (known by players as "hacks"), held by Ted Martin of Des Plaines, IL. Martin set the record on June 14, 1997, at the 1997 Midwest Regionals, held at Lions Park in Chicago. He was "hacking" for 8 hours, 50 minutes, 42 seconds.

Spotters gave Martin drinks and bananas throughout his record-setting run, which topped his previous best set in 1993 by 12,171 kicks. The bag finally dropped when Martin stepped on his foot.

WOMEN'S SINGLES The women's record is held by Constance Constable of Seaside, CA, with 24,713 kicks in 4 hours, 9 minutes, 27 seconds. She set the record on April 18, 1998, at the CA Athletic Club in Monterey, CA.

Constable broke her own record of 18,936 kicks, which she had set on August 1, 1995, in Menlo Park, CA. That record took a mere 3 hours, 14 minutes, 42 seconds.

OPEN DOUBLES Tricia George of Clackamas, OR, and Gary Lautt of Chico, CA, kicked their footbag a record 132,011 times in a row on March 21-22, 1998, at the Lia Way Recreation Center in Chico.

The pair kept the footbag aloft for 20 hours, 34 minutes to beat their own world record, which they had set in Chico on Nov. 12, 1995. That day, George and Lautt stopped at 123,456 kicks, because as they said, "it's a neat number."

The rules for Footbag Doubles state that each person may kick the footbag up to 25 times before passing it.

WOMEN'S DOUBLES The women's doubles world record is 34,543 kicks, by the team of Constance Constable of Seaside, CA, and Tricia George of Clackamas, OR. They set the mark on Feb. 18, 1995, at the Heart of Footbag Freestyle Tournament in Portland, OR. The pair kept the footbag aloft for 5 hours, 38 minutes, 22 seconds.

LARGEST FOOTBAG CIRCLE Andy Linder led a group of 963 people in creating the world's largest footbag circle at the Cornerstone Festival in Bushnell, IL, on July 6, 2001.

Linder's group beat the previous record of 933 people set by St. Patrick High School in Chicago in 1996.

Every member of the circle is required to kick the footbag at least once for the group to qualify.

MOST "HACKS" IN FIVE MINUTES Andy Linder, a psychotherapist from Chicago, IL, set the world record for most consecutive kicks in five minutes on June 7, 1996, with 1,019 hacks. He set the mark at the 1996 Midwest Regional Footbag Championships in Mount Prospect, IL.

The women's record is 804 kicks, set by Ida Fogle at the 1997 World Footbag Championships in Portland, OR, on August 11, 1997.

Food & Drink

EVERYONE EATS TO LIVE. SOME PEOPLE LIVE TO EAT. A few live to do groundbreaking things with food—whether by inventing recipes that become world famous or just by eating ordinary foods in record-breaking amounts. Does that whet your appetite? If so, read on.

Sonya Thomas and Takeru Kobayashi at Nathan's Famous Fourth of July International Hot Dog Eating Contest, July 2005 ▶

MILESTONES

1886: COCA-COLA
The recipe for Coca Cola, made from extracts of coca leaves (containing about 1/400 of a gram of cocaine) and kola nuts, was invented in 1886 by Dr. John S. Pemberton, a pharmacist in Atlanta, GA. At first, the drink also contained wine. When Atlanta briefly enforced Prohibition in 1886-87, Pemberton started making it with carbonated sugar water instead. Pemberton's partner, Frank Robinson, thought up the trademark Coca-Cola, penned in the script still used today.

Pemberton gradually sold off shares in his company, which was ultimately acquired by Atlanta businessman Asa Candler for about $2,300. The rest is history.

In 2004, the company saw over $21.9 billion in sales pour into its coffers—and the drink has been cocaine-free since 1929.

AROUND 1924: CAESAR SALAD
Possibly the world's most widely-served salad, the Caesar Salad was created by Caesar Cardini at his restaurant, Caesar's Place, in Tijuana, Mexico, in 1924.

The origins are not certain, but the most commonly told story is that Cardini's restaurant was overwhelmed one evening by Californians slipping over the border during Prohibition to have a drink with dinner. Fearing he would run out of food, Cardini created a new dish from produce and condiments left in the kitchen—romaine lettuce, lemon juice, olive oil, eggs, Romano cheese, croutons, and condiments. (Anchovies weren't a part of the original recipe.)

Cardini served the dish with great fanfare, and it was an instant hit.

AROUND 1930: TOLL HOUSE COOKIE
The chocolate chip cookie was the creation of Ruth Wakefield of the Toll House Inn near Whitman, MA. Around 1930, she was baking butter drop cookies when she decided to chop up and add a Nestlé's semi-sweet chocolate bar for flavor. Wakefield expected the chunks to melt into the batter. Instead, "Chocolate Crunch Cookies" became a hit with Wakefield's patrons.

Nestlé bars were soon flying off the shelves. Wakefield approached Nestlé and struck a deal—they would print her recipe on their chocolate bar wrapper, and she would receive a lifetime supply of all the chocolate bars she could bake.

2005: SHE ATE THE 6-LB. BURGER
On Jan. 12, 2005, Kate Stelnick, a 19-year-old student at The College of New Jersey, became the first person to down the Ye Old 96er burger at Denny's Beer Barrel Pub in Clearfield, PA. The burger—weighing 6 pounds (96 oz) with 5 pounds of fixins'—was created by the bar's owner, Denny Leigey Jr., in 1998. Leigey's rules require the burger gobbler to eat the 96er within a three-hour time limit. Stelnick, who weighs only 115 lbs, gobbled down the burger in 2 hours, 54 minutes.

Selected Food Feats[1]

FOOD	EATER	AMOUNT	TIME LIMIT	DATE
Chicken Wings	Sonya Thomas	161 (5.09 lbs)	12 min.	Sept. 5, 2004
Corn Dogs	Richard LeFevre	12	10 min.	Sept. 28, 2003
French Fries	Cookie Jarvis	4.46 lbs	6 min.	Mar. 31, 2005
Grilled Cheese Sandwiches	Joey Chestnut	32.5	10 min.	Oct. 22, 2005
Onions (Maui)	Eric Booker	8.5 oz	1 min.	Aug. 8, 2004
Pork Ribs	Joey Chestnut	5.5 lbs	12 min.	July 17, 2005
Sweet Corn	Cookie Jarvis	33 1/2 ears	12 min.	Aug. 24, 2004
Tamales	Levi Oliver	36	12 min. 30 sec.	June 4, 2005
Watermelon	Jim Reeves	13 lbs	15 min.	July 30, 2005

(1) Recognized by the International Federation of Competetive Eating.

SOMETHING TO THINK ABOUT

A WHALE OF A BURGER

Despite protests from anti-whaling activists, the Japanese restaurant chain Lucky Pierrot offers a whale burger on its menu. The deep-fried minke-whale meat burger comes with lettuce and mayonnaise and costs about $3.50 (380 yen).

I'M MELTING

In 2005, Snapple, the soft drink maker, attempted to create the world's largest popsicle. At 35,000 pounds, the icy treat was 25 feet tall, and weighed over 17 tons. It was set to be measured and displayed in Manhattan on June 21, the first day of summer. However, as it was being hauled into an upright position by a crane, officials noticed that pink ice was beginning to turn into mush. Snapple officials decided to halt proceedings, fearing the monster popsicle would break apart and collapse on the crowd. The record attempt was abandoned as kiwi-strawberry goo flooded the street.

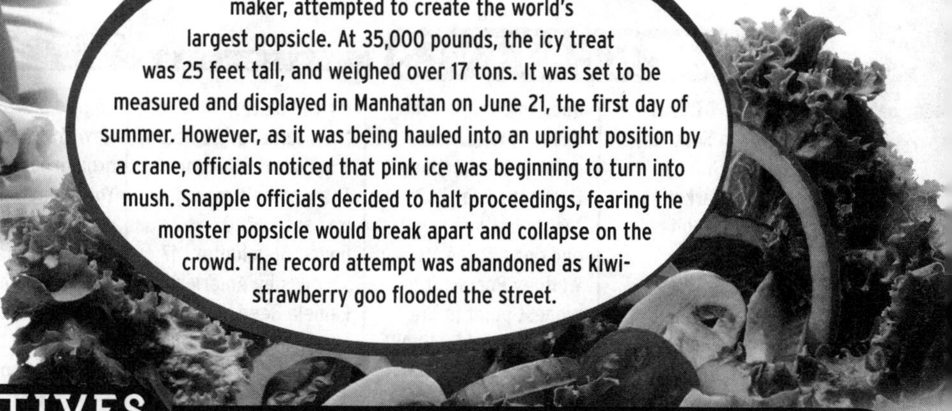

SUPERLATIVES

HIGHEST FORMAL DINNER PARTY

On June 23, 2005, Bear Grylls and Lt. Com. Alan Veal sat down for a three-course meal of asparagus spears followed by poached salmon and a terrine of summer fruits, while suspended from a hot-air balloon at an altitude of 24,262 feet. Both men donned formal naval attire, parachutes, and oxygen masks. After the meal the men toasted Queen Elizabeth II and then sky-dived back to earth.

The balloon, which launched from the grounds of the Ston Easton Park, near Bath, England, was piloted by David Hempleman-Adams. High altitudes were nothing new to Grylls; he climbed Mount Everest in 1998 at age 23.

HOT DOG EATING

The Nathan's Famous Fourth of July International Hot Dog-Eating contest was first staged outside Nathan's original hot dog store at Coney Island in Brooklyn, NY, in 1916. Nathan's record for the most hot dogs consumed within the required 12-minute limit is $53\frac{1}{2}$, by Takeru Kobayashi (Japan) in 2004.

The 132-pound Kobayashi has won five consecutive years. Before he revolutionized hot dog eating in 2001 by eating 50 dogs with his "Solomon method" (breaking each dog in half), the record was $25\frac{1}{8}$.

The women's record is 37 hot dogs by Sonya Thomas, of Alexandria, VA, in 2005. The winner of the annual event receives the coveted Mustard Yellow International Belt.

MOST CHERRY-PIT SPITTING TITLES

The annual International Cherry Spit contest was first staged at Tree-mendous Farm, Eau Claire, MI, in 1974. Rick "Pellet Gun" Krause has won the title a record 12 times: 1980, 1983-1985, 1987-1990, 1995, 1997, 1999, and 2001. The women's title has been won a record five times by his wife, Marlene Tully Krause: 1994, 1996-97, 2000, and 2005.

The longest pit spit gained in the championships is 93 feet, $6\frac{1}{2}$ inches, by Rick's son, Brian "Young Gun" Krause, in 2003. The women's record is 46 feet, 1 inch, by Ann St. Amend in 2004.

MOST COMPETITIVE EATING TITLES

Cookie Jarvis holds 12 official competitive eating titles, including ice cream, 1 gallon, 9 ounces, in 12 minutes; ham and potatoes, 6 pounds in 12 minutes; grapes, 8 pounds, 15 oz. in 10 minutes; and of course, cannoli (cream-filled Italian cookies), 21 in 6 minutes. Cookie appears in contests and for the media in his full-length trench coat, which displays his titles and an air-brushed image of himself (known as "Mini Cookie").

Stamina

Gertrude Ederle ▶

NEW YORK YANKEES FIRST BASEMAN AND BASEBALL LEGEND LOU GEHRIG was called "the Iron Horse" because of his consecutive games streak of 2,130 that ended in 1939. Later, Baltimore Orioles shortstop and third baseman Cal Ripken Jr. surpassed Gehrig's seemingly unbeatable mark in 1996, and became known as "Ironman." These and other feats of stamina require not just physical fitness but mental toughness and the will to keep pushing oneself beyond the normal limits to achieve success.

SUPERLATIVES

ATLANTIC OCEAN SWIM On Sept. 25, 1998, French-born American marketing executive Benoit Lecomte became the first person to complete a swim across the Atlantic (not all in one spurt, of course). Beginning at Cape Cod, MA, on July 16, he covered 3,726 miles in twice-daily stints of two to four hours each, sleeping in between aboard a boat. At one point he took a week-long break in the Azores.

During his marathon swim, Lecomte used a monofin and snorkel as well as a wet suit. At the finish line in Quiberon, France, he proposed to his waiting girlfriend. She accepted.

BADWATER ULTRAMARATHON The Badwater Ultramarathon is 135-mile foot race held each year in July, that starts in Badwater, CA, goes through Death Valley (the lowest point in the Northern Hemisphere at 282 feet below sea level), and ends at the Mt. Whitney Portals (the highest point in the contiguous U.S., 14,491 feet).

During the race, contestants suffer first through intense heat that can reach upwards of 130° F, then through the arduous climb up Whitney, where the thin air takes its toll on their lungs.

The race was the brainchild of American amateur athlete and fitness instructor Al Arnold, who made the run himself for the first time in 1977. In the beginning, competitors raced against the clock along Arnold's route; it wasn't until 1988 that an official race was staged.

In 2000 Anatoli Kruglikov, from Russia, captured the record for the fastest time for the course, at 25 hours, 9 minutes, 5 seconds. The women's record was set in 2003 at 27 hours, 56 minutes, 47 seconds by American Pamela Reed.

BERING STRAITS SWIM On Aug. 7, 1987, 30-year-old Lynne Cox became the first person to swim the 2.7-mile channel dividing Little Diomede Island, AK, from Big Diomede Island (then USSR). It had taken her 11 years to get permission from Soviet authorities to enter into Soviet territory on the swim; she ultimately completed it in 2 hours, 5 minutes, braving water temperatures of about 43° F.

Cox was greeted at the shore by Soviet officials, who toasted her achievement with hot tea.

EMPIRE STATE BUILDING RUN UP The annual race up the Empire State Building in New York City was first organized by the New York Road Runners Club in 1978. Competitors race from the lobby of the building up 1,576 steps to the observation deck on the 86th floor.

The fastest time for the event is 9 minutes, 33 seconds by Australian Paul Crake in 2003. The women's record is 11 minutes, 51 seconds set by Andrea Mayr of Austria in 2005.

The oldest person to complete the race is 93-year-old pianist Chico Scimone of Italy. In 2005, he did it in 49 minutes, 28 seconds, placing him last in the field of 136 runners. It was his 16th time running.

ENGLISH CHANNEL SWIMMING The first person to swim the English Channel without the aid of a life preserver was Capt. Matthew Webb of Dawley, England. Webb set off from the Admiralty Pier at Dover, England, and reached Calais, France, on Aug. 24, 1875. It took 21 hours, 45 minutes. (The distance is about 21 miles in a straight line, but Webb is estimated to have covered about 40 miles in his zig-zag route).

The first woman to swim the Channel was Gertrude Ederle (U.S.). She completed her crossing on Aug. 6, 1926, in a then-record time (men and women) of 14 hours, 31 minutes.

The current speed record belongs to Chad Hundeby (U.S.), who finished in 7 hours, 17 minutes in 1994. The women's record is 7 hours, 40 minutes, set by Penny Lee Dean (U.S.) in 1978.

The oldest person to swim the English Channel is retired airline pilot George Brunstad (U.S.).

GOING THE EXTRA MILE

Runners in the 2005 Lakeshore Marathon in Chicago got a bigger challenge than they bargained for. Organizers inadvertently set the distance at 27.2 miles instead of the regulation 26.2 miles. The mistake was discovered after the race was completed. Race officials issued an apology to the more than 500 runners who completed the race.

SOMETHING TO THINK ABOUT

GOLFING ACROSS MONGOLIA

Andre Tolme, a civil engineer from New Hampshire, took up golf as a 10 year old in 1980. In Sept. 2001, while touring the world, he arrived in Mongolia and decided to golf his way across that remote land. On a map, he divided the country into 18 holes along an east-west route following the Kherlen River. Using only a 3-iron, and accompanied by his caddy, a local named Khatanbaatar, Tolme teed off at the 138,889-yard first hole in Choybalsan on June 4, 2003. Between shots he traveled by jeep and slept in a tent. His 180-day trek finished 1,234 miles later at the 18th hole in Dund-Us. Tolme, who set par at 11,880, shot 12,170 (290 over par). Along the way, he lost 509 balls.

IMPROV MARATHON

Second City, the renowned comedy troupe based in Chicago, stages a 24-hour improv-athon each December. Over the 24-hour period, the group of actors perform a non-stop improv show. Individual actors may leave the stage at times and return later, but there is always somebody on stage improvising. Second City players and alumni, along with guest performers such as Billy Corgan, former lead singer of Smashing Pumpkins, have appeared in "The Second City That Never Sleeps: Letters to Santa" to raise money to buy Christmas presents for needy children.

The uncle of movie star Matt Damon, Brunstad completed his journey three days after his 70th birthday, on Aug. 28, 2004.

The youngest swimmer to do it was 11-year-old Thomas Gregory, in 1988. Soon after Gregory's swim, officials set the minimum age for official attempts on swimming the Channel at 16.

MARATHON WEEK

British adventurers Sir Ranulph Fiennes, 59, and Dr. Michael Stroud, 48, ran 183 miles in what was billed as seven marathons in seven straight days on seven continents.

They started on Monday, Oct. 27, 2003, by running an unofficial marathon in Patagonia, Chile. Fiennes and Stroud then ran in the Falkland Islands (a substitute for Antarctica because of bad weather), Australia, Singapore, London, and Cairo before crossing the finish line in the official New York City Marathon the following Sunday.

The pair crossed the line together in a time of 5 hours, 25 minutes, 46 seconds. They are the only runners known to have run seven marathons in a single week.

SAUNA STAMINA

The annual Sauna World Championships, possibly the world's hottest event, were first held in Heinola, Finland, in 1999. Contestants are supposed to sit still in a sauna for as long as possible.

The temperature is set at 230° F at the beginning of the contest, and water is poured on the coals every 30 seconds. The last person left in the sauna wins the title, provided he or she can walk out without assistance.

The record for the longest time in the sauna came at the 2003 championships, when Finland's Timo Kaukonen lasted 16 minutes, 15 seconds.

NOT A FISH STORY

Former fireman and leukemia survivor Lloyd Scott of England ran a "monstrous" 26.2-mile marathon on the floor of Scotland's famous Loch Ness in 2003.

The first person to complete a marathon run underwater, he got the idea after running several marathons on land wearing a 130-pound 1940s antique Russian deep-sea diving suit. (He had completed the Edinburgh Marathon wearing the suit in a time of 148 hours, 30 minutes, 56 seconds.)

Scott's ground-breaking underwater stint began Sept. 28, 2003, and took him 11 days, 23 hours, 20 days to finish on Oct. 9. He proceeded in spurts of up to five hours each, that being the length of time he could stay under with his equipment.

Really Big

BIGGER MAY NOT ALWAYS BE BETTER. But whether it's the largest pizza or the longest gum-wrapper chain, familiar objects blown up into super-sized creations catch the eye and excite curiosity. Making it the biggest may take expert craftsmanship, organizational skills, or just a lot of patience and persistence.

Whatever it takes, here we review a small sample of some really big deals.

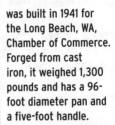

World's biggest chair

SUPERLATIVES

BIGGEST BOOT
As part of its centennial celebrations in 2005, Red Wing Shoes of Red Wing, MN, manufactured the world's largest leather boot. A size $638\frac{1}{2}$ D, the boot is 20 feet long, 7 feet wide, 16 feet high, and weighs 2,300 pounds.

Sixty people, both employees and retirees, volunteered 4,000 hours over 13 months to make the boot. Among its "ingredients": 80 leather hides, 80 pounds of brass for the eyelets, 60 gallons of urethane for the sole, and 1,200 feet of nylon rope for the stitching. Red Wing estimates that it would fit comfortably on a 120-foot-tall person.

TALLEST CHAIR
The world's biggest chair stands in Manzano, Italy, in the heart of the "Chair Triangle," the Friuli-Venezia Giulia region of Italy. To celebrate Friuli craftsmanship, area businesses commissioned the construction of a reproduction of the classic "Marocca" design.

The chair was unveiled on Oct. 7, 1995, in Matteotti Square, Udine. It stands 65.5 feet high, is made from 52.3 cubic yards of laminated red pine, and weighs 50,508 pounds. It took 300 work hours to complete and a further 120 hours to assemble.

On Jan. 6, 1996, the chair was dismantled and reassembled in a square in Manzano, the Chair Triangle's industrial area, where it still sits.

LARGEST FLAG
To mark Bahrain's 33rd National Day, celebrating the country's independence from British rule, the world's largest flag was unfurled on Dec. 13, 2004, outside the national stadium in Manama. The red-and-white Bahraini flag measured 555 feet by 318 feet, and weighed about 7,000 pounds.

Manufactured by the Jiaxing Maosen Flag Company of China, it took 70 people 400 hours to make. Approximately 44,550 yards of fabric were used.

TALLEST FLAGPOLE
The world's tallest freestanding flagpole reaches 416 feet high and stands in Amman, Jordan. Installed on June 10, 2003, the gigantic flagpole weighs 135 tons and is capable of flying a 197-foot by 98-foot flag.

King Abdullah II dedicated the flagstaff, part of a three-phase project that will include the Jordanian Flag Museum and the King Abdullah II Public Gardens.

North Korea boasts that its 525-foot-tall flagpole in Panmunjom is the world's tallest and it is, but it is not freestanding. The flagpole is supported by a radio tower-style structure.

LARGEST FRYING PAN The world's biggest frying pan was built in 1941 for the Long Beach, WA, Chamber of Commerce. Forged from cast iron, it weighed 1,300 pounds and has a 96-foot diameter pan and a five-foot handle.

The skillet was first used at the 1941 Razor Clam Festival (to fry razor clam fritters) and was taken on tours of the Northwest to promote the Long Beach peninsula as a vacation spot.

Although the original pan eventually rusted, a fiberglass replica stands proudly in Long Beach as a permanent reminder of past cookware glory.

LONGEST GUM-WRAPPER CHAIN
On March 11, 1965, a 14-year-old Canadian high school student named Gary Duschl began stringing Wrigley's gum wrappers together. He hasn't stopped.

As of mid-Nov. 2005, his world-record gum-wrapper chain was reported to be 47,514 feet—9 miles—long, made up of 1,111,545 wrappers. That's as long as 132 football fields, or 38 Empire State Buildings.

Now living in Virginia Beach, VA, Duschl keeps the chain at his home in specially made cases. He extends it 3 feet nearly every day, and had no plans to stop working on it.

To mark the milestone of his one-millionth wrapper, Duschl used a Spearmint antique wrapper printed on June 30, 1905, that he bought on eBay.

LARGEST HOCKEY STICK The world's biggest wooden hockey stick stands in Eveleth, MN, the home of the Hockey Hall of Fame (on Hat Trick Avenue). The stick is 110 feet long, weighs 5 tons, and was made by Sentinel Structures, Inc., of Peshtigo, WI. It was put on display on June 18, 2002.

Eveleth natives refer to the record-holder as the "New Big Stick" because it is not the first hockey stick to break records. In 1995, a 107-foot, 3-ton monster was made by Christian Brothers Hockey Sticks of Warroad, MN, from white and yellow aspen. Because of safety concerns, the original Big Stick was removed on July 3, 2001.

There's an even bigger stick in Duncan, BC, Canada, but it's reinforced with steel. Built from Douglas fir beams, it is 205 feet long and weighs 61,000 pounds. The steel adds to the weight and would be an equipment violation in the NHL.

LARGEST MOAI (EASTER ISLAND) The colossal carved statues of Easter Island are among the world's most famous icons, and possibly the most puzzling. Archaeologists have no idea why these stone giants, known as *moai* to islanders, were ever built. There is no written record, but it is estimated that they were carved between 1400 and 1600 AD.

In 1989, archaeologist Jo Anne Van Tilburg published a study of the 887 moai on Easter Island. They average 13 feet high. According to Van Tilburg's calculations, the tallest moai is 71.93 feet high and weighs 145-165 tons. Nicknamed "El Gigante," it stands in the Rano Raraku Quarry, meaning it was never moved to its intended site.

LARGEST PIZZA TO GO The largest pizza that can be ordered from a pizza parlor is the "Ultimate Party Pizza" baked by Paul Revere's Pizza, Mt. Pleasant, IA. For $99.99, pizza-lovers can purchase a prodigious pie that measures 4 feet in diameter and 1,814 square inches. The custom-made pizza contains 170 ounces of dough, 48 ounces of sauce, 6-8 pounds of cheese, and a variety of meats and other toppings.

The owners Joe and Patty Keagle first offered the mega-pizza in Jan. 2001. It can feed 30 to 40 people.

TALLEST TOTEM POLE The tallest totem pole ever erected stood 180 feet, 3 inches, and was designed by Coast Salish Indian carver Richard Krentz. Known as the "Spirit of Lekwammen (Land of the Winds)," it was unveiled Aug. 17, 1994, on Songhees Point in Victoria, Canada. Carved from a 250-year-old red cedar, it took 11 craftsmen (and 250 volunteer helpers) to carve. Because of safety concerns, it was dismantled on Aug. 26, 1997.

There are strict rules governing the authenticity of totem poles. They must be carved from a single piece of wood, reflect Native traditions, and be erected by Native American craftsmen from southeastern Alaska, coastal British Columbia, or northern Washington State. The finished totem must also be raised according to tribal conventions, and secured and blessed by tribal elders.

LARGEST AIRCRAFT CARRIER The world's largest warships are the U.S. Navy's Nimitz class aircraft carriers. These "floating airports" have a full-load displacement of 97,000 tons. The overall length of the Nimitz class vessels is 1,092 feet, with 4½ acres of flight deck.

LONGEST YARD SALE Stretching 450 miles from Gadsden, AL, to Covington, KY, the annual Highway 127 Corridor Sale is said to be the longest yard sale in the world.

Begun in 1987 to encourage tourists to visit the backcountry roads of the region, it is now a 2,000-vendor, four-day event, held in early August, and attracts more than 60,000 bargain hunters (along with expert collectors).

Moai *of Easter Island* ►

Speed

SPEED IS THE TEST OF CHOICE FOR MANY RECORD-BREAKERS– whether it's jumping rope, driving a jet-fuel-propelled car, or figuring out the quickest solution to a Rubik's Cube puzzle. The following individuals and technologies define life in the fast lane.

RECORD BREAKER

Solar Car Racing Champ

"We expected a little more competition. It would be nice to not pass everyone in the first three hours and then just increase the distance between the teams."

–Anne-Marie Rasschaert, team spokesperson, Nuon Solar, 2003-2005 champions of the solar-powered car race

SUPERLATIVES

WORLD LAND-SPEED RECORD One of the most famous world records is the world landspeed record—the fastest average speed attained in a wheeled vehicle driven over a measured mile on land.

The current record of 763.035 mph, or Mach 1.020, was set by British fighter pilot Andy Green on Oct. 15, 1997 at Black Rock Desert, NV.

This record marked the first time that the sound barrier had been broken by a land vehicle—the Thrust SSC, which was powered by two Rolls-Royce Spey 205 turbofans capable of generating 25,000 pounds of thrust.

To break the land speed record, Green was required to drive the Thrust SCC for two 1-mile timed runs within an hour of each other.

Green's official result shattered the 14-year-old record of 633.468 mph set by his boss and Thrust team leader, Richard Noble.

FASTEST SOLAR-POWERED CAR The world's fastest solar-powered car is the Nuna 3, built by the Dutch team Nuon Solar. The yearly World Solar Challenge across Australia is the world's fastest solar-car race.

On Sept. 28, 2005, the Nuna 3, built by 11 students from the Technical University of Delft, won the competition. The vehicle completed the 1,877-mile course from Darwin to Adelaide in a record 29 hours, 11 minutes, at an average speed of 63.85 mph.

The 16-foot-long, 6-foot-wide vehicle looks more like an airplane wing than a car. It has room for a driver, but no steering wheel. Instead, the driver uses two rods that operate the vehicle's three wheels. The surface of the car is covered in solar panels.

BACKWARDS RUNNING The fastest time for the 100 meters while running backwards is 13.6 seconds, set by Ferdie Ato Adobe (Ghana) on July 25, 1991, at Smith College, Northampton, MA. Besides being a speedy retro runner (the official name for backwards running), Adobe was a four-year starter on the University of Massachusetts soccer team and played soccer professionally in Australia and France.

FASTEST HOLE IN ONE/300 GAME DOUBLE
The shortest elapsed time between acing a hole in one at golf and bowling a perfect 300 game is a mere three hours.

Tom Donahue, at the time a 34-year-old head pro at the Grenelefe Golf and Tennis Resort in Haines City, FL, aced the 230-yard fourth hole on Grenelefe's West course on May 10, 1999. Then, after arriving at the Cypress Lanes for that evening's bowling league matches, he capped a perfect day with 22 strikes for a 300 game. It was the third time Donahue had rolled a perfect game.

The oldest person to perform the ace-perfect game double in less than 24 hours is Paul Hughes. The 74-year-old retired plumber from Waunakee, WI, sank a hole in one on Oct. 13, 2003, and posted a 300 game the next day, 22 hours later.

FASTEST GUN SLINGER According to the World Fast Draw Association, Ernie Hill of Litchfield Park, AZ, made the fastest shot in competition. In an elimination contest in 1985, he drew from an open holster of his own design and shot a 4-inch target 8 feet away in 0.208 seconds.

ROPE JUMPING
The most revolutions performed with a jump rope in a minute, according to the International Rope Skipping Federation, is 425. Robert Commers (U.S.) performed the feat on Feb. 23, 1990.

On Oct. 1, 2004, Ranjit Pal (India) completed 136 turns in just 15 seconds.

The record for most rope jumps in 30 seconds while standing on one leg is 94 by Alexandra Toth (Hungary) on July 25, 2004.

FASTEST THREE-LEGGED RACERS
The three-legged race has one of the oldest standing records. The team of Harry Hillman Jr. and Lawson Robertson (U.S.) ran the three-legged 100-yard dash in a time of 11.0 seconds on April 24, 1909.

Hillman was a two-time track Olympian who won three gold medals at the 1904 St. Louis Games. Also an Olympian, Robertson went on to coach the U.S. Track and Field team at the 1936 Berlin Games.

FASTEST PIZZA MAKER U.S. Pizza Team member Brian Edler of Findlay, OH, set a world record

Wife Carrying World Championship

for the fastest time to make five pizza crusts at the 2005 World Pizza Championship in Salsomaggiore, Italy, on Mar. 16.

Edler, who owns four Domino's restaurants in Ohio, won the fastest pizza contest, in a time of 37 seconds, breaking the previous record by five seconds.

Each competitor in the event is given five 7-ounce dough balls, which have to be stretched over 12-inch diameter screens into rounded pizza crusts. The 39-year-old had been making pies since 1981.

FASTEST RUBIK CUBE UNSCRAMBLER

At the start of a speed cubing competition, cubes are scrambled using computer-generated scrambling algorithms. The fastest time for restoring a Rubik's Cube (4x4x4) back to its original state in an official competition is 55.38 seconds, a time set by Chris Hardwick (U.S.) at the 2005 Caltech Dallas Summer Competition.

For speed and consistency, 14-year-old Japanese-born Arcadia, CA, middle-school student Shotaro "Macky" Makisumi is the champ. He set the best average of 5 for the 3x3x3 cube—14.52 seconds, at the Caltech Spring Tournament on April 3, 2004. Macky also holds the record for 2x2x2 average of 5 (6.29 seconds).

FASTEST WIFE CARRIER

The World Wife Carrying Championship was first staged in Sonkajärvi, Finland, in 1992. In the annual contest, contestants carry a woman (who doesn't have to be married to the carrier) of at least 17 years and weighing a minimum of 108 pounds, over an 832-foot obstacle course, including one water "hazard." Along with a trophy and the glory, the winners also receive the equivalent of the wife's weight in beer.

The world record time of 55.5 seconds was set by Margo Uusorg and Birgit Ulricht of Estonia on July 1, 2000.

FASTEST BALL SPORT

The speed of the ball in a typical Jai Alai game is the fastest of any sport. Players launch the ball (pelota) at the court's facing wall using scooped baskets (cestas) that can regularly generate ball speeds over 180 mph. A top speed of 188 mph was clocked at the Newport Jai-Alai, RI, during a game in 1979.

FASTEST ROLLER COASTER

The world's fastest roller coaster is Kingda Ka at Six Flags Great Adventure at Jackson Township, NJ. Unveiled in 2005, Kingda Ka travels from zero to 128 mph in 3.5 seconds, and also reaches a record height of 456 feet. It is the main feature of the theme park's 11-acre Golden Kingdom.

FASTEST CHECKMATE (CHESS) The fastest possible checkmate in chess is four moves. Known as "Fool's Mate," the four-move sequence rarely happens, but is set in motion when white moves the bishop and rook pawns forward one or two squares, exposing the king with the first and third moves. Black's first move (second overall) is to move the queen's pawn one or two squares, allowing the queen to advance on the fourth move to trap the king in checkmate.

The algebraic chess notation is: 1) p-f3; p-e2; 2) p-g4; Q-h4+.

FASTEST CAMERA

Shimadzu's HyperVision HPV-1 camera can capture images up to a rate of one million frames per second in monochrome at a resolution of 312x260-pixels. It can record shock wave propagation in microns.

Countries & Territories

THERE ARE 193 INDEPENDENT COUNTRIES in the world. All are now members of the United Nations except two: Taiwan, which is independently ruled but claimed by the People's Republic of China, and Vatican City. A country is defined in international law as a land possessing a permanent population, a defined area, government, and the capacity to enter relations with other states. (All statistics for 2005 are mid-year estimates.)

United Nations ▶

SUPERLATIVES

LARGEST COUNTRY

AREA The world's largest country in size is Russia, with a total area of 6,592,769 square miles and a land area of 6,562,112 square miles.

LARGEST COUNTRY

POPULATION China is the world's most populated nation. In 2005, it had an estimated population of 1,306,314,000, including the special administrative areas of Hong Kong and Macau, but not including Taiwan.

SMALLEST COUNTRY The world's smallest country in both area and population is Vatican City, which covers only 108.7 acres and had a population of 921 in 2005.

MOST BORDERS Russia and China both border 14 countries. Russia shares its borders with Norway, Finland, Estonia, Latvia, Belarus, Lithuania, Poland, Ukraine, Georgia, Azerbaijan, Kazakhstan, China, Mongolia, and North Korea.

China shares borders with Afghanistan, Bhutan, India, Kazakhstan, North Korea, Kyrgyzstan, Laos, Mongolia, Myanmar (Burma), Nepal, Pakistan, Russia, Tajikistan, and Vietnam.

YOUNGEST COUNTRY Timor-Leste (East Timor) is a former Portuguese colony that first declared its independence on Nov. 28, 1975—and was invaded by Indonesia nine days later.

After a long civil war, the East Timorese were able to decide their own future in a UN-sponsored referendum; 78% opted for independence, which was finally achieved on May 20, 2002.

MOST DEPENDENT TERRITORIES As of 2005 Great Britain claimed the most dependencies (18): Akrotiri, Anguilla, Bermuda, the British Antarctic Territory, British Indian Ocean Territory, British Virgin Islands, Cayman Islands, Dhekelia, Falkland Islands, Gibraltar, Guernsey, Isle of Man, Jersey, Montserrat, Pitcairn Islands, South Georgia and the South Sandwich Islands, St. Helena, and Turks and Caicos Islands. (The Antarctic claims are not recognized by the U.S., which also technically regards Akrotiri and Dhekelia as sovereign military bases rather than dependencies.)

As of 2005 France claimed 16: Bassas da India, Clipperton Island, Europa Island, French Guiana, French Polynesia, French Southern & Antarctic Lands, Glorioso Islands, Guadeloupe, Juan de Nova Island, Martinique, Mayotte, New Caledonia, Reunion, Saint Pierre and Miquelon, Tromelin Island, and the Wallis and Futuna Islands.

LARGEST DEPENDENT TERRITORY

AREA The largest dependent territory, excluding Antarctic dependencies, is Greenland, a dependency of Denmark with an area of 836,330 square miles, but a population of only 56,375 in 2005. In 1979, it was granted self-governing status, but Denmark retains control over foreign affairs.

SMALLEST DEPENDENT TERRITORY

AREA The smallest dependency is the French Indian Ocean atoll of Bassas da India, with an area of about 0.08 square miles. Sitting atop a long-extinct volcano, the volcanic rock and surrounding reef that make up the territory are submerged at high tide.

LARGEST DEPENDENT TERRITORY

POPULATION The dependency with the most people is Puerto Rico, a commonwealth of the U.S. As of mid-2005, it had an estimated population of 3,917,000.

RICHEST PER CAPITA The world's richest country, measured in terms of per capita wealth, is the Grand Duchy of Luxembourg, an important international center of finance and banking. At 998 square miles, it is slightly smaller than Rhode Island, and had an estimated per capita gross domestic product of $58,900 in 2004.

The U.S. ranked 2nd with $40,100.

POOREST PER CAPITA As of 2004, East Timor had the lowest per capita GDP at $400. The country's infrastructure was devastated by pro-Indonesian militias in 1999 prior to independence.

HIGHEST LIFE EXPECTANCY Citizens of Andorra, a tiny principality wedged in the Pyrenees Mountains

between France and Spain, fare well from the standpoint of both death and taxes.

In 2005, they had a life expectancy of 83.5 years at birth, the highest of any country. And while death is still a certainty, Andorrans pay no income tax.

LOWEST LIFE EXPECTANCY The nation whose citizens have the lowest life expectancy is Swaziland, where the average life expectancy had fallen to 33.22 years by 2005 because of HIV-related illnesses.

HIGHEST INFANT MORTALITY The southern African nation of Angola had the world's highest infant mortality rate in 2005, at 187.49 per 1,000 live births.

LOWEST INFANT MORTALITY Singapore had the world's lowest infant mortality rate in 2005 at 2.29 per 1,000 live births.

HIGHEST FERTILITY RATE The country with the highest fertility rate in 2005 was Niger, where women have an average of 7.55 children each over their child-bearing years.

LOWEST FERTILITY RATE Aside from Vatican City, the rich southeast Asian city-state of Singapore has the lowest fertility rate—1.05 children in 2005. Hong Kong and Macau, which are territories of China, have rates of 0.93 and 1.0 respectively.

SOMETHING TO THINK ABOUT

LANDLOCKED²

There are only two double-landlocked nations on Earth—countries that are entirely surrounded by landlocked countries. One is the Central Asian republic of Uzbekistan, whose landlocked neighbors are Afghanistan, Kazakhstan, Kyrgyzstan, Tajikistan, and Turkmenistan. The other is the small Alpine principality of Liechtenstein, which lies between landlocked Switzerland and Austria.

DIVIDED COUNTRIES

Not all countries are in one piece: the territories of 22 different nations are divided by parts of other nations. Some detached pieces are large, such as Alaska, which is separated from the lower 48 U.S. states by Canadian territory, and Kaliningrad, which is separated from Russia by Belarus and Lithuania.

There are, in all, around 260 enclaves—pieces of one country that are completely surrounded by another state. The country with the most separated pieces is India, which has 106 tiny enclaves that are surrounded by Bangladesh. The village of Dahala Khagrabari is an Indian enclave that is surrounded by a Bangladeshi enclave within an Indian enclave in Bangladesh.

Other nations that have many enclaves are Bangladesh (92 enclaves in India) and Belgium (22 in the Netherlands).

MULTI-CONTINENTAL

Eight countries straddle two continents. More than two-thirds of Russia lies in Asia, though about 75% of the population live in the smaller European part. Most of Turkey lies in Europe, but a tiny piece (about 3%) lies in Asia across the Bosporus Strait.

While most of Egypt is in Africa, the Sinai Peninsula is physically part of Asia. Socotra Island, which lies off the Horn of Africa, is part of the west Asian republic of Yemen. Spain's Canary Islands and the Spanish cities of Ceuta and Melilla are physically part of Africa. Similarly, Portugal's Madeira island group is physically part of Africa rather than Europe.

Indonesia consists of 13,700 islands; the eastern islands (including Papua, formerly known as Irian Jaya) are counted as part of Oceania rather than Asia. The U.S. also lies on two continents—the state of Hawaii is part of Oceania.

Cities

Istanbul, Turkey ▶

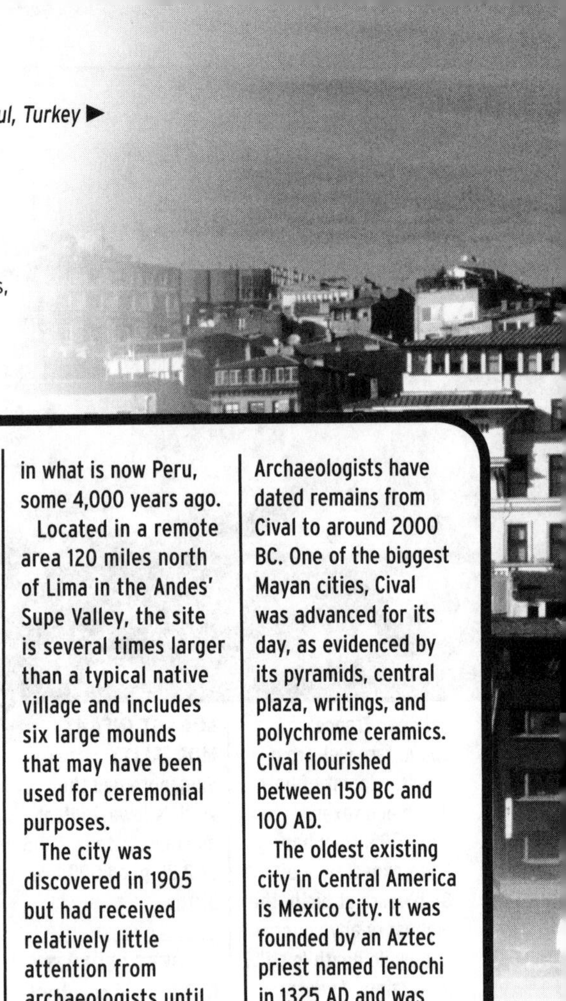

NEARLY 7,000 YEARS AGO IN WESTERN ASIA, farmers began producing crop surpluses that could be used by non-family members, and allowed people to specialize in other work; some became potters, some became weavers, and others became merchants. Towns appeared, and later, larger centers became cities. To be called a city today, in most countries, official recognition is required, but there is no uniform standard. For instance, the U.S. has many cities but Great Britain has only a few.

MILESTONES

4000 BC: FIRST KNOWN CITY
Tell Hamoukar, a settlement between the Tigris and Euphrates rivers (in what is now Syria), is widely regarded as the oldest known city in the world. Founded over 6,000 years ago, the site covers more than 1 square mile and may have been home to 25,000 people.

A joint expedition by the Univ. of Chicago and the Syrian Directorate General of Antiquities began excavations there in the summer of 1999. Archaeologists announced the following spring that many artifacts indicating evidence of a complex society, such as clay seals, porcelain figures, jewelry, and stone carvings, had been unearthed.

3200 BC: FIRST CITY (AFRICA) Memphis, the first capital of unified Egypt, was founded around 3200 BC by Menes. Considered by historians to be the "first imperial city in world history," the ancient city lies within the boundaries of present-day Cairo.

Other settlements thousands of years old are also located in Cairo, which is generally recognized as Africa's oldest city.

3000 BC: FIRST CITY (EUROPE) The settlements of the Minoan civilization on the Greek island of Crete are widely believed to have been Europe's first cities. The ruins of Knossos, on Crete, date back at least 5,000 years. Athens, often said to be Europe's oldest continuously inhabited city, is also more than 5,000 years old.

2600 BC: FIRST CITY (AMERICAS)
The first known city in the Americas was established at Caral, in what is now Peru, some 4,000 years ago.

Located in a remote area 120 miles north of Lima in the Andes' Supe Valley, the site is several times larger than a typical native village and includes six large mounds that may have been used for ceremonial purposes.

The city was discovered in 1905 but had received relatively little attention from archaeologists until recently.

2000 BC: FIRST CITY (CENTRAL AMERICA)
The first known city in Central America was built at Cival, in the Peten region of what is now Guatemala. Archaeologists have dated remains from Cival to around 2000 BC. One of the biggest Mayan cities, Cival was advanced for its day, as evidenced by its pyramids, central plaza, writings, and polychrome ceramics. Cival flourished between 150 BC and 100 AD.

The oldest existing city in Central America is Mexico City. It was founded by an Aztec priest named Tenochi in 1325 AD and was known to the Aztecs as Tenochtitlán.

1565: FIRST CITY (U.S.) Founded by the Spanish explorer Pedro Menendez de Aviles in 1565, St. Augustine, FL, is the oldest U.S. city.

Selected Milestones in the Development of Cities

Schools for Elite	Egypt and Mesopotamia	3000 BC
Sewer Pipe System	Mohenjo-Daro (in what is now Pakistan)	around 2750 BC
Paved Roads	Knossos, Crete	around 1700 BC-1400 BC
Public Libraries	Rome, Italy	around 200 BC
Schools for General Public	Berlin, in Prussia (now Germany)	1717
Gaslight Street Lamps	London, England	1807
Subway Train Line	London, England	1863
Electric Street Lamps	New York City	1882

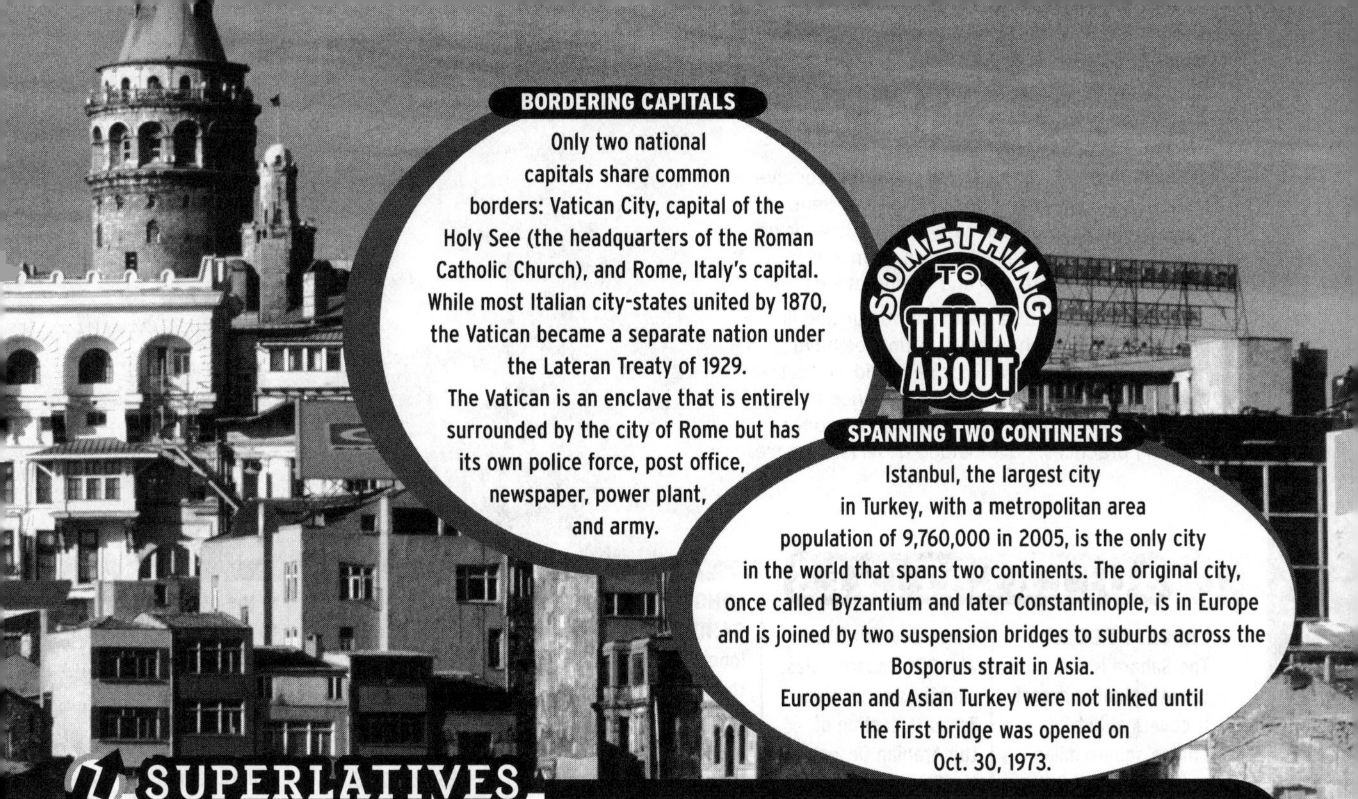

BORDERING CAPITALS

Only two national capitals share common borders: Vatican City, capital of the Holy See (the headquarters of the Roman Catholic Church), and Rome, Italy's capital. While most Italian city-states united by 1870, the Vatican became a separate nation under the Lateran Treaty of 1929. The Vatican is an enclave that is entirely surrounded by the city of Rome but has its own police force, post office, newspaper, power plant, and army.

SOMETHING TO THINK ABOUT

SPANNING TWO CONTINENTS

Istanbul, the largest city in Turkey, with a metropolitan area population of 9,760,000 in 2005, is the only city in the world that spans two continents. The original city, once called Byzantium and later Constantinople, is in Europe and is joined by two suspension bridges to suburbs across the Bosporus strait in Asia. European and Asian Turkey were not linked until the first bridge was opened on Oct. 30, 1973.

SUPERLATIVES

LARGEST CITY (POPULATION) The world's largest urban agglomeration, or metropolitan area, is Tokyo, Japan. As of 2005, it had a population of about 36 million. The city proper population is about 8 million.

In terms of city-proper population, the world's largest city is Mumbai, India, formerly known as Bombay. The population was 11,914,398 as of 2000. Several other big cities had around 10 million people by 2000 and may be in competition to eclipse Mumbai, including Karachi, Pakistan; Shanghai, China; Seoul, South Korea; and São Paulo, Brazil.

LARGEST CITY (AREA) If Chinese municipalities that contain several cities are ignored, the largest city in the world by area is Mount Isa, in Queensland, Australia.

Mount Isa, which is a lead, copper, and zinc mining center, covers 15,900 square miles but had only 21,636 residents according to the latest census (2001).

SMALLEST CITY (POPULATION) The world's smallest city in population is Durbuy, in the Ardennes region of southern Belgium, which has 400 inhabitants. The old buildings of Durbuy line cobbled streets that climb to a castle founded in the 11th century. The area was granted city rights in 1331.

SMALLEST CITY (AREA) The smallest city in area is Vatican City, which covers only 108.7 acres in the heart of Rome—smaller than the 125-acre parking lot for Disney World's Magic Kingdom. It has a population of about 920.

NORTHERNMOST CITY The world's most northerly city is Longyearbyen, capital of the Norwegian Arctic territory of Svalbard. Longyearbyen, at 78°13'N, is a coal-mining center and has only 1,100 residents, but it has the infrastructure of a larger city.

The temperature averages 24°F, and Longyearbyen has as many snowmobiles as people. One out of four Longyearbyen residents say they came for the adventure; about the same number say they have stayed because of low taxes.

SOUTHERNMOST CITY The world's most southerly city is Ushuaia in Argentina, at 54°46'S. The provincial capital of Tierra del Fuego, it sits on the south side of the Andes, 93 miles from Cape Horn. Penguins regularly visit the shores nearby.

There were 29,411 people in Ushuaia in 1991; by 2001 there were 45,598, partly as a result of a government campaign to revitalize the area.

FARTHEST FROM THE OCEAN The most remote city from the sea is Urumqi, capital of the Chinese autonomous region of Xinjiang Uygur. Urumqi, which had a population of 1,359,000 in 2000, is about 1,500 miles from the nearest coast. It was once an important town on the Silk Road.

Deserts

DESERTS ARE DRY REGIONS that generally receive less than 10 inches of precipitation per year, and have a high evaporation rate so that little or no moisture remains. Deserts often form where prevailing winds are dry and temperatures hot.

About one-fifth of the Earth's land surface is desert, and nearly half of all countries have areas that are either arid or semiarid. Desert boundaries are not static—they advance and retreat. Some human activities, such as poor farming practices, have helped deserts advance.

SUPERLATIVES

LARGEST DESERT
The Sahara is the world's biggest desert. It covers about 3.5 million square miles and stretches 3,200 miles across northern Africa from the Atlantic coast to the Red Sea and Egypt, an area about equal to the lower 48 U.S. states combined. The Sahara is so vast, it effectively divides the continent between North Africa and Sub-Saharan Africa.

Despite the common belief that deserts are made of sand, only about 30% of the Sahara is sand. The rest of the surface is covered by gravel and bare rock.

LARGEST EXPANSE OF SAND The largest unbroken expanse of sand in the world is the *Rub al-Khali* or "Empty Quarter," on the Arabian Peninsula, which covers about 250,000 square miles, slightly smaller than Texas. A section of the Arabian Desert, the Empty Quarter occupies around one-fourth of Saudi Arabia, and extends into Oman and the United Arab Emirates.

TALLEST DUNES
The world's tallest sand dunes are located in the Badain Jaran desert of China and the Saharan sand sea of Isaouanne-N-Tifernine in Algeria.

The unique star-shaped dunes of the Badain Jaran rise to approximately 1,640 feet over shallow lakes in northern China. Compound dunes (one on top of another) in the Sahara reach at least 1,300 feet and in some cases have been estimated to be as high as 2,000 feet.

LONGEST LINE OF SAND DUNES The longest sand dunes in the world are found in the Simpson Desert in Queensland, Australia. Occurring nearly every half-mile, these parallel ridges of dunes span about 125 miles and sometimes reach as high as 295 feet.

MOST ARID DESERT
The most arid of the world's deserts is the Atacama Desert in northern Chile. Parts of the desert resemble the dry, cracked surface of Mars.

On average, the Atacama Desert receives less than 0.004 of an inch of rainfall a year, and some areas of the desert have not received rain for 400 years. Some places cannot even host self-sustaining bacteria.

This desert is thought to be between 10 and 15 million years old, making it the oldest desert on Earth.

LARGEST STONE DESERT Not all deserts have substantial areas of sand. Some are seemingly endless plains of pebbles and gravel, dotted with rocks and boulders. The world's largest stone desert is the Gobi, a vast, rocky plateau covering some 500,000 square miles in northern China and much of Mongolia. Only 5% of the Gobi Desert is sand.

LARGEST DESERT CITY The largest city located in a desert is Cairo, Egypt. Although Cairo's downtown area adjoins the Nile River, the city's suburbs extend into the Eastern Desert in one direction and the Western Desert in the other. According to the 1996 Egyptian national census, 6,789,000 people lived within Cairo's city limits in 2005, while the metropolitan area was home to an estimated 11,146,000 people.

LARGEST DESERT
U.S. The largest desert entirely contained within U.S. borders is the Great Basin, which covers about 200,000 square miles in the western U.S. states of Utah, Nevada, Oregon, and Idaho. The Great Basin owes its desert status to the "rain shadow" of the Sierra Nevada Mountains.

The arid expanse contains vast salt flats in many smaller basins, which fill during the infrequent rains. The rainwater evaporates, but leaves behind a layer of salt dissolved from the ground.

Crossing the Sahara, Selected Firsts

MODE OF TRANSPORTATION	ADVENTURER(S)	DATE
Aircraft	Joseph Vuillemin, Julien Chalus (France)	Feb. 18-Apr. 2, 1920
Land Vehicle (with tires)	Georges-Marie Haardt, Louis Audouin-Dubreuil, Paul Castelnau, Rene Estienne, and 6 crew in 5 Citroen caterpillar automobiles (France)	Dec. 15, 1922-Jan. 6, 1923
Hot-Air Balloon	Don Cameron, Julian Nott, Felix Pole (Great Britain), in 2 balloons	1972
Microlight (motorized hang glider)	Richard Meredith-Hardy (Great Britain)	Aug. 25-Oct. 25, 1982

DUNE NOTES

The average diameter of a grain of sand from a dune is between 0.008 and 0.016 of an inch. The grains are so tiny and fluid that even a supercomputer can't track their every move.

Winds can move sand dunes very rapidly across desert regions, sometimes threatening to cover nearby farms and cities. In Egypt's Kharga Depression, the wind can move dunes forward between 66 and 320 feet a year.

In northern China, where the Gobi Desert is expanding by about 950 square miles per year, a "Green Wall" stretching about 2,800 miles from Beijing through Inner Mongolia is being planted to stop the encroaching sands.

Some dunes even make eerie noises. In the deserts of Africa, the Middle East, South Africa, Chile, and Baja California, the combination of spherically smooth sand and extra dry winds causes a low, drawn-out boom that has been mistaken for artillery fire, propeller planes, and even mythical beasts.

Along the coast of Namibia in southwestern Africa, where the Namib Desert meets the ocean, large areas of fog in the early mornings provide enough moisture to sustain a remarkable array of animals. The coastal desert is home to snakes, spiders, beetles, termites, lizards, and moles. Hundreds of thousands of fur seals breed beside the desert, and the coast is home to three-fourths of Africa's flamingos.

SOMETHING TO THINK ABOUT

MARATHON DES SABLES

Founded in 1986, the *Marathon des Sables* ("Marathon of Sands") is one of the most grueling foot races in the world. A six-day, 143-mile trek across part of the Sahara in Morocco, the race is held annually and starts in the town of Ourzazate. The course changes from year to year, and is not revealed until the day before the race begins. While the race takes place in April, competitors may still face temperatures above 100°F, as well as sandstorms, rocky terrain, and sand dunes. To be eligible, runners must submit a certificate from a physician. Any runner requiring more than one IV to replenish fluids during the race is disqualified. The dangers of the race are apparent on the application form, which contains a section called "notification of the corpse repatriation fee." There have been over 6,000 participants since the race's inception. In 2005 Lahcen Ahansal of Morocco won the grueling race for the eighth time.

DESERT SKIING

For skiers who prefer to slalom in the sun, help is at hand. You can find permanent snow in the sun-baked desert at the $277 million, 1.4-million-square-foot Dubai Sunny Mountain Ski Dome in the Gulf emirate of Dubai. Under the dome are ski slopes on an artificial mountain; adjoining the slopes is the gigantic Mall of the Emirates.

Forests

THE FORESTS AND WOODLANDS OF EARTH maintain the balance of Earth's atmosphere through photosynthesis and transpiration. About 20% of the world's oxygen is produced by South America's Amazon rainforest alone. Forest trees account for about two-thirds of the leaf area of all land plants. Tropical rainforests and temperate forests nurture a wide array of living things. Tropical rainforests alone are home to about half of the world's plant and animal species.

MILESTONES

354-280 MILLION YEARS AGO: FIRST FORESTS The first forests to appear on Earth held giant horsetails, club mosses, and ferns that stood up to 40 feet tall. Giant horsetails, with stems as thick as a person's wrist, first appeared around 400 million years ago and thrived after that in the Carboniferous Period. The horsetail forests' compressed remains contributed to the formation of Earth's coal deposits.

1891: FOREST RESERVE ACT The passage of the federal Forest Reserve Act in 1891 permitted the president of the United States to designate Forest Reserves (renamed National Forests in 1907) out of portions of public domain land. The act was intended to remove the threat of logging from tracts of wooded land and to preserve watersheds.

1905: U.S. FOREST SERVICE The United States Forest Service was established on Feb. 1, 1905. Part of the Department of Agriculture, the Forest Service was given a mandate to manage the nation's forests and sustain them for future generations.

Gifford Pinchot, the first chief of the Forest Service, is widely acknowledged as the "father" of the American conservation movement. During his five-year term, Pinchot oversaw the expansion of the national forest system from 60 Forest Reserves covering 56 million acres in 1905 to 150 National Forests covering 172 million acres in 1910.

According to the U.S. Forest Service, the United States in 2005 had 155 National Forests, 20 National Grasslands, and 222 Research and Experimental Forests, as well as other areas of special interest, covering more than 192 million acres of public land, an area about the size of the nation of Turkey.

Most Rapid Deforestation Rates

NATION	% FORESTED LAND AREA (2000)	% FOREST LOST ANNUALLY (1990-2000)
Burundi	3.7	9.0
Haiti	3.2	5.7
Saint Lucia	14.8	4.9
El Salvador	5.8	4.6
Micronesia	21.7	4.5

SUPERLATIVES

LARGEST FORESTED AREA The largest area of forest on Earth is a taiga (coniferous sub-arctic forest) that stretches eastward from Scandinavia through northern Russia to Asia's Pacific coast. Although large areas of trees have been felled, it is estimated that around 4.2 million square miles of virtually continuous coniferous forest still stands.

The West Siberian and other taiga forests cover around 11% (6.4 million square miles) of Earth's land area.

BIGGEST RAINFOREST The Amazon is the world's largest tropical rainforest, with an average temperature around 79°F and average annual rainfall around 80 inches. At 1.6 million square miles in area, it ranges over five countries: Brazil, Colombia, Venezuela, Ecuador, and Peru.

The Amazon rainforest covers half of Brazil, which is the largest country in South America.

This rainforest sustains an overwhelming number of wildlife species, including an estimated 2.5 million insect varieties, tens of thousands of high-order plants, 2,000 fish, and 200 mammal species. One out of every six known bird species makes the Amazon rainforest its home.

Like other rainforests, the Amazon forest is rapidly giving way to chain saws and bulldozers; it is estimated that the world's tropical forest acreage is being lost at a rate equivalent to 120 football fields a minute.

LARGEST TEMPERATE RAINFOREST Temperate rainforests are rare, constituting only 2-3% of the world's forest acreage. They get as much rain as tropical rainforests, but in much cooler temperatures (averaging 40-60°F).

The largest area of temperate rainforest stretches about 1,900 miles north along the Pacific coast from San

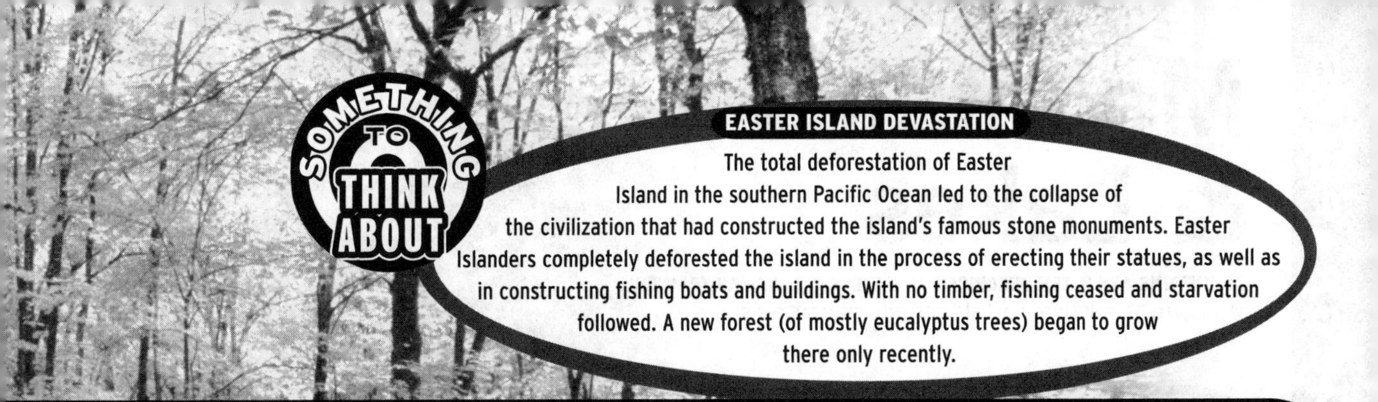

SOMETHING TO THINK ABOUT

EASTER ISLAND DEVASTATION

The total deforestation of Easter Island in the southern Pacific Ocean led to the collapse of the civilization that had constructed the island's famous stone monuments. Easter Islanders completely deforested the island in the process of erecting their statues, as well as in constructing fishing boats and buildings. With no timber, fishing ceased and starvation followed. A new forest (of mostly eucalyptus trees) began to grow there only recently.

Francisco Bay to Kodiak Island in the Gulf of Alaska.

The trees (redwoods, firs, hemlocks, and pines) in this region are some of the tallest in the world. The area receives over 55 inches of rain every year, but its position between the Pacific on the west and mountain chains to the east protects the forests from weather extremes.

LARGEST TROPICAL FOREST RESERVE Tumucumaque National Park in the Amazonian state of Amapa, Brazil, is the world's largest tropical forest reserve. Covering about 15,000 square miles, Tumucumaque is larger than the states of Massachusetts and Connecticut combined.

Created on Aug. 22, 2002, the park is in one of the most inaccessible regions in the Amazon basin. It is 568,000 acres larger than Slonga National Park in the Democratic Republic of Congo, the previous record-holder.

LARGEST AFFORESTATION PROJECT The Chinese government has planted more than 42 billion trees since 1978 across its northern region, creating the world's largest afforestation project. Affectionately known as the "Green Great Wall," this swath of (mostly poplar and jujube) trees already blankets more than 3,000 square miles.

The trees skirt the Gobi and Taklimakan Deserts and were planted to defend against desertification and over-farming, which have ruined vast areas of land in China. Another of the project's goals is preventing desert sandstorms from reaching the national capital in Beijing.

An enormous undertaking, the "Green Great Wall" is expected to take until the year 2050 to complete.

FASTEST DEFORESTATION During the 1990s, an estimated average of 8,915 square miles (roughly the size of New Jersey) was deforested annually in Brazil. The worst period of deforestation came between 1994 and 1995, when estimates rose to 11,200 square miles (an area roughly the size of Maryland) for the year. This is the fastest deforestation ever recorded.

BIGGEST PROPORTIONATE LOSS The nation suffering the most rapid deforestation rate is the small central African nation of Burundi. 9% of its forest land was lost annually between 1990 and 2000.

MOST FOREST Russia has more forested land than any other nation, equal to about half its land area, or about 3.3 million square miles.

The smallest country in South America, Suriname, is largely blanketed by rainforest and can claim the highest proportion of forested land to total area. In 2000, about 90.5% of its total land area was covered by rainforest.

HIGHEST-ALTITUDE FOREST The highest growing trees are of the genus *polylepis* and grow in the Andes Mountains of Ecuador, Peru, Bolivia, and Argentina. Polylepis forests, called *queñua* by locals, have sprung up in the dry volcanic regions around Mt. Sajama in western Bolivia at altitudes over 17,000 feet. Most trees grow 10-30 feet tall, but some have been known to reach as high as 105 feet. The *polylepis* forests are considered the most threatened ecosystems in Bolivia and Peru.

LARGEST NATIONAL FOREST (U.S.) The largest national forest in the U.S. is Tongass National Forest, located on the southeast panhandle of Alaska. At almost 17 million acres, the park abounds in over 400 species of land and marine wildlife, and is especially known for its bald eagles.

Tongass is also home to some of the most spectacular scenery in the country, from glaciers to mountains to thousands of islands separated by the park's many waterways and channels.

DEADLIEST FOREST FIRE (U.S.) On Oct. 8, 1871, while much of the city of Chicago, IL, was destroyed and about 300 people killed in the Great Chicago Fire, a much deadlier forest fire raged to the north. Prolonged drought and heat, "slash and burn" land clearing practices, and high winds had created perfect wildfire conditions in the forests of northeastern Wisconsin and Michigan's Upper Peninsula. About 2,400 square miles of wooded land burned, and the final death toll was estimated at more than 1,180 people.

Mountains & Lakes

MOUNTAINS ARE OFTEN DESCRIBED AS MAJESTIC; LAKES AS TRANQUIL. And both have inspired artists and adventurers alike.

MILESTONES

1615: EUROPEAN DISCOVERY OF THE GREAT LAKES In July 1615, French explorer and founder of Quebec, Samuel de Champlain, first gazed upon Georgian Bay on Lake Huron. Although it is likely that earlier European trappers, hunters, and missionaries had seen some portion of the Great Lakes before, Champlain was the first to record its sighting.

1786: MONT BLANC ASCENT The sport of mountaineering as we know it originated in 18th-century Europe, with attention concentrated mostly on Mont Blanc, the highest peak in western Europe at 15,771 feet.

The first people to climb to the top of Mont Blanc were Jacques Balmat, a crystal hunter, and Michel-Gabriel Paccard, a doctor, both from France. The intrepid pair reached the peak on Aug. 8, 1786, as observers watched their progress from nearby Chamonix, France, through a telescope.

1858: DISCOVERY OF LAKE VICTORIA On Aug. 3, 1858, British explorer John Hanning Speke became the first European to sight Africa's largest lake. He was convinced that Lake Victoria was the source of the Nile, but many in Britain were skeptical and today the source of the Nile is considered to be upstream from Lake Victoria.

1889: KILIMANJARO ASCENT Dr. Hans Meyer, a German geographer from Leipzig, accompanied by Ludwig Purtscheller, an Austrian alpinist, and native guide Mwini Amania, reached the highest peak of the Kilimanjaro massif at 19,340 feet. The team took a difficult route, cutting their way up over a glacier before reaching the peak on Oct. 6, 1889.

1897: ACONCAGUA ASCENT English mountaineer Edward Fitzgerald headed the first successful ascent of the 22,834-foot Mt. Aconcagua in Argentina, the highest peak in the Americas, but he never made it to the peak himself.

The lead Swiss guide, Mathias Zurbriggen, was the first to reach the summit, on Jan. 14, 1897. Fitzgerald had to turn back because of altitude sickness, with about 800 feet to go.

1913: MT. MCKINLEY ASCENT The first documented ascent of Mt. McKinley was made on June 7, 1913, by a party led by Rev. Hudson Stuck, the Episcopal archdeacon of the Yukon Territory, Canada.

1953: MOUNT EVEREST ASCENT The feat was accomplished on May 29, 1953, by New Zealander Edmund Hillary, and Nepalese Sherpa Tenzing Norgay. (See pages 8-9 for more on Everest.)

LARGEST LAKES (by continent)

Africa	Victoria Nyanza, (Kenya, Uganda, Tanzania)	26,828 sq mi
Antarctica[1]	Vostok Subglacial Lake	5,400 sq mi
Asia	Caspian Sea (Russia, Kazakhstan, Turkmenistan, Iran, Azerbaijan)	143,244 sq mi
Europe	Ladoga (Russia)	6,835 sq mi
North/Central America	Lake Superior (U.S., Canada)	31,700 sq mi
Oceania (Australasia)[2]	Lake Eyre (Australia)	3,600 sq mi
South America	Lake Maracaibo (Venezuela)	5,217 sq mi

(1) Vostok is covered by ice over two miles thick. (2) This is the average largest extent of Lake Eyre, which sometimes dries out completely.

HIGHEST MOUNTAINS (by continent)

Africa	Kilimanjaro, Tanzania	19,340 ft
Antarctica	Vinson Massif	16,864 ft
Asia	Everest (Nepal, Tibet)	29,035 ft
Europe[1]	Elbrus (Russia)	18,510 ft
North/Central America	Mt. McKinley (AK, U.S.)	20,320 ft
Oceania (Australasia)	Jaya (New Guinea)	16,500 ft
South America	Aconcagua (Argentina)	22,834 ft

(1) By some definitions, Elbrus is in Asia; the peak in W. Europe is Mt. Blanc (France, Switz.) at 15,771 ft.

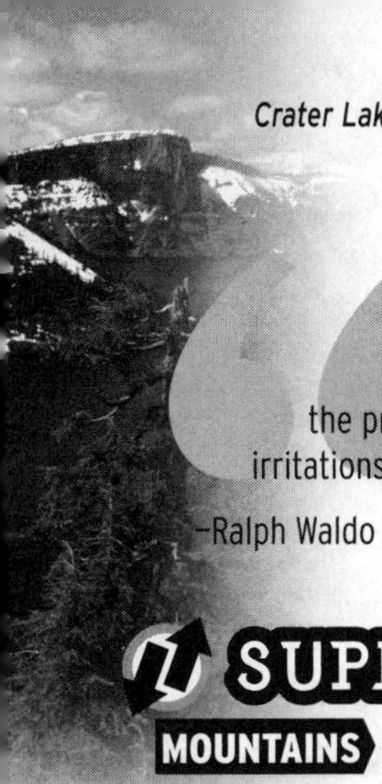
Crater Lake

SOMETHING TO THINK ABOUT

"The influence of fine scenery, the presence of mountains, appeases our irritations and elevates our friendships."

—Ralph Waldo Emerson, 1860

WHOA, NESSIE!

In spring 1933, a new road with splendid views was opened along the west shore of Loch Ness, a narrow 24-mile-long lake near Inverness, Scotland. That April, local hoteliers—John and Aldie Mackay—were driving on the new thoroughfare when Aldie saw "an enormous animal rolling and plunging on the surface." When a reporter for the *Inverness Courier* published their story, he used the word "monster" to describe what they had seen. From that, the legend of the Loch Ness Monster was born, and an otherwise unremarkable body of water speedily became one of the most celebrated lakes in the world.

SUPERLATIVES

MOUNTAINS

HIGHEST MOUNTAIN

WORLD The peak of Mount Everest, the world's highest mountain, is 29,035 feet above sea level. (for more details, see pages 8-9.)

HIGHEST MOUNTAIN

U.S. At 20,320 feet, Mount McKinley in Alaska is the tallest mountain in North America. It was first seen by a European in 1794, when British hydrographer George Vancouver sighted it from Cook Inlet while surveying the region.

Over the years, the majestic peak has gone by several different names. Originally, native Athabascans called it *Denali*, which means "the High One." Russian explorer Andrei Glazunov in 1834 named it "Tenada." In 1889, U.S. prospectors named it after one of their ilk, Frank Densmore. Finally, it was renamed in 1897 for President William McKinley.

The area surrounding the mountain was made into a national park called Denali, in 1912. Since then, over 12,000 climbers have reached the top.

LONGEST MOUNTAIN CHAIN

The mid-ocean ridge is a loose but extensive underwater mountain chain that winds for about 40,000 miles through all the oceans. While not entirely continuous (sometimes gaps take up tens or hundreds of miles), this chain comprises the largest geographical feature in the world.

The ridge begins on the floor of the Arctic Ocean and runs south about 10,000 miles through the Atlantic Ocean, reaching, on average, a width of 1,000 miles and a height of 10,000 feet. It continues from the Atlantic into the southern Indian Ocean, where it splits into two branches, one running toward East Africa, the other up to the west coast of the U.S. and into the Gulf of Alaska. The entire ridge is seismically active.

The ridges play a key role in plate tectonics as molten rock erupts through rifts in their peaks, adding new material to the plates.

LAKES

LARGEST LAKE

A lake is usually defined as a body of water surrounded by land. Some bodies of water that are called seas, such as the salty Caspian and Aral Seas, are really lakes. That being said, the largest lake in the world is the Caspian Sea, which has an area of 143,244 square miles. Five countries touch its shores: Russia, Kazakhstan, Turkmenistan, Iran, and Azerbaijan.

The largest body of fresh water is the Great Lakes of North America. Lakes Superior, Michigan, Huron, Erie, and Ontario altogether cover an area of about 291,080 square miles total including drainage.

DEEPEST LAKE

WORLD Lake Baikal in Russia is the world's deepest lake. Its maximum depth has been measured at 5,712 feet below the surface (over a mile deep).

As might be expected, Lake Baikal has a lot of water in it. It has been estimated that it contains about one-fifth of the world's non-frozen fresh water. In terms of volume, it's the second biggest lake in the world, after the Caspian Sea.

DEEPEST LAKE

U.S. At 1,932 feet, Crater Lake in Oregon is the deepest lake in the U.S. and the seventh deepest in the world. It was formed by the collapse of an ancient volcano, Mt. Mazama, 7,700 years ago.

LOWEST LAKE

The lowest dry point on Earth is the coastal surface of the Dead Sea on the Israel-Jordan border, which lies 1,348 feet below sea level.

HIGHEST LAKE

The highest recorded lake sits at 19,294 feet above sea level inside the crater of Licancabur, a dormant volcano in the Andes on the border between Chile and Bolivia. The extreme environment is believed to resemble that of Mars 3.5 billion years ago.

Because of the thin air and other atmospheric conditions, the area is home to some of earth's most primitive life forms including stromatolites, large humps composed of microorganisms, which date back 3 billion years to the Precambrian Era.

Oceans & Rivers

FOR CENTURIES THE OCEANS on Earth were considered to be four main bodies: the Pacific, the Atlantic, the Arctic, and the Indian oceans. In 2000, the International Hydrographic Organization distinguished a fifth ocean, the 7,848,400-square-mile Southern Ocean, which was defined as including all the Antarctic seas south of 60°S latitude. The oceans contain many smaller bodies of water known as seas or gulfs; in all, about 71% of the planet's surface is covered by saltwater seas and oceans, which are fed by thousands of rivers.

SUPERLATIVES

OCEANS

LARGEST OCEAN

The Earth's largest ocean is the Pacific Ocean, which has an area of about 60,060,000 square miles, including the portion that may be counted as part of the Southern Ocean. The Pacific covers about one-third of the surface of the Earth, and is larger than the world's total combined land area. It contains the Bali, Bering, Coral, East China, Philippine, South China, and Tasman seas, as well as the Sea of Japan, the Sea of Okhotsk, and others.

Excluding the part covered by the Southern Ocean, the Pacific is still about 15 times the size of the U.S. It is also the deepest ocean, with an average depth of 12,925 feet.

SMALLEST OCEAN

The smallest ocean is the Arctic Ocean, which has an area of about 5,427,052 square miles—that is, about 1.5 times the size of the U.S. The Arctic Ocean contains the Barents, Chukchi, Kara, and Laptev seas.

LARGEST SEA

The largest sea is the South China Sea, which is part of the Pacific Ocean. The sea has an area of 1,148,500 square miles. This includes the area formerly known as the Malayan Sea, which is no longer recognized as a separate sea.

SMALLEST SEA

There is disagreement over the extent of many seas, and some "seas," particularly the small ones in Japanese coastal waters, do not always receive recognition. Different geographers recognize between 70 and 90 seas in all. The smallest is often said to be the Sea of Marmara, between the Aegean and Black seas in Turkey. Despite its small area of 4,382 square miles, the Sea of Marmara is relatively deep, reaching down as far as 4,446 feet.

DEEPEST OCEAN TRENCH

The deepest part of the ocean is Challenger Deep in the Mariana Trench, located in the Pacific just east of the Mariana Islands. The spot is named for the British research vessel *Challenger II*, which first located it in 1951.

The first people to reach the bottom, 35,840 feet down, were Swiss scientist Jacques Piccard and U.S. Navy Lt. Don Walsh on Jan. 23, 1960. Their submersible bathyscaphe, *Trieste*, was designed by Jacques and his father Auguste in 1953.

Challenger Deep is actually deeper than Mount Everest, the world's highest mountain (at 29,035 feet), is high. The pressure at the bottom of the Mariana Trench is 16,000 pounds per square inch.

SHALLOWEST SEA

The world's shallowest sea is the Sea of Azov, a "tributary" sea north of the Black Sea. The sea, which lies between Ukraine and Russia, has a maximum depth of only 52 feet.

GREATEST OCEAN CURRENT

The world's greatest ocean current is the Antarctic Circumpolar Current (ACC) or West Wind Drift. The ACC flows across the entire Antarctic continent and eastward through the Atlantic, Indian, and Pacific oceans. It transports more water than any other current, about 100 times the flow of all the world's rivers combined.

The British astronomer Edmund Halley, for whom the comet is named, discovered the ACC while working as a member of a British survey expedition aboard the HMS *Paramore* in 1699-1700.

RIVERS

LONGEST RIVER

At approximately 4,160 miles, including headwaters that flow into Lake Victoria, the Nile is the world's longest river. Starting in Burundi (Central Africa), the Nile river system flows through Tanzania, Uganda, Sudan, and Egypt, and empties into the Mediterranean Sea.

NOT QUITE WHAT YOU SEA

Some so-called seas are, in fact, lakes. Central Asia's Caspian Sea at 143,244 square miles—about the same size as Montana—is not connected to any ocean and is really a lake, the largest in the world. The Aral Sea, shared by Kazakhstan and Uzbekistan, was once the world's fourth-largest lake, but the use of its tributaries for irrigation water has reduced the lake to 6,100 square miles from 24,600 square miles over about 55 years. The Dead Sea and the Sea of Galilee (Lake Tiberias) in the Middle East are also lakes rather than seas.

SOMETHING TO THINK ABOUT

A SOURCE OF MYSTERY

The downstream (northern) portion of the Nile River, with its annual flooding, created the fertile river valley that was the center of ancient Egyptian civilization as long as 7,000 years ago. But the river's source long remained a mystery, because of inhospitable conditions, difficult terrain, and waterfalls that made upper stretches of the river unnavigable. The Spanish missionary Father Pedro Paez discovered the source of one branch, the so-called Blue Nile, at Lake Tana, Ethiopia, around 1618. Several European expeditions searched for the source of the longer branch, the White Nile (the famed Scottish missionary-explorer Dr. David Livingstone died in central Africa while seeking it). Finally, in the early 1860s, two British explorers, John H. Speke and Sir Samuel Baker, identified Lake Victoria, which is fed by the Kagera River, as the probable source; this was confirmed when General Charles Gordon followed the river to the lake in the 1870s.

LONGEST RIVER (ASIA) Chang Jiang (formerly known as the Yangtze River), at approximately 3,964 miles, is the longest river in Asia, and third longest in the world. It flows entirely in China, and empties into the East China Sea.

LONGEST RIVER (EUROPE)
The longest river in Europe is the Volga River. Entirely in Russia, it flows for approximately 2,290 miles and empties into the Caspian Sea.

LONGEST RIVER (NORTH AMERICA)
The longest continuous waterway in North America is the Mississippi-Missouri-Red Rock river system at 3,710 miles. It flows from the Red Rock's source in Beaverhead County, MT, to the Gulf of Mexico.

The longest individual river in North America is the Mississippi. From its source at Lake Itasca, MN, to the Gulf of Mexico, "the Big Muddy" flows 2,340 miles. The Mississippi receives tributaries from 33 states and two Canadian provinces.

LONGEST RIVER (AUSTRALIA)
The longest river in the Australian continent is the Murray-Darling River at approximately 2,310 miles. It flows into the Indian Ocean.

LONGEST RIVER (SOUTH AMERICA)
The Amazon River at 4,087 miles is the longest river in South America, and the second longest in the world.

From its source at Lake Lauricocha in the Peruvian Andes, the Amazon flows through Peru, Colombia, and Brazil before reaching the Atlantic Ocean.

The river was given its name by the Spanish explorer Francisco de Orellana in 1541. He named it Amazon in tribute to what he said were women warriors that he encountered on his journey through the region.

GREATEST RIVER FLOW The Amazon River is the world's greatest river in terms of water carried. It discharges, on average, 6,350,000 cubic feet of water per second. The huge discharge of freshwater from the Amazon River dilutes the saltiness of the Atlantic Ocean for more than 100 miles from the shore.

The Amazon is also the world's largest drainage system. It drains a basin of some 2,300,000 square miles, the majority in Brazil, but also from parts of Peru, Colombia, Ecuador, and Venezuela, an area equivalent to around three-quarters of the U.S.

LARGEST DELTA
The world's largest delta is the combined delta at the Bay of Bengal of the Ganges, Meghna, and Brahmaputra rivers in India and Bangladesh.

The delta covers an area of about 49,420 square miles. This includes the Sundarbans, containing the world's largest area of mangrove forests (about 2,300 sq mi) and an abundance of rare wildlife, including tigers, boars, dolphins, storks, and crocodiles.

Islands & Volcanoes

ISLANDS ARE LAND MASSES SURROUNDED BY WATER, distinguished from continents by their smaller size, but the exact dividing line between an "island" and a "continent" is a matter of convention. The total number of islands on Earth is incalculable; Canada alone has over 50,000. Islands may have distinctive flora and fauna, sometimes even different from those found in islands relatively nearby.

SUPERLATIVES

ISLANDS

LARGEST ISLAND Although Australia might be considered a very big island, it is classified as a small continent. That leaves Greenland (*Kalaallit Nunaat*) as the world's largest island, with an area of 836,330 square miles.

A little over three times the size of Texas, Greenland lies between the Arctic Ocean and North Atlantic Ocean. Ice caps cover about 81% of the surface, but Greenland is still home to about 56,000 people. A territorial possession of Denmark, Greenland began home rule on May 1, 1979.

LARGEST ISLAND NATION Indonesia, with an area of 741,100 square miles, is the biggest independent island nation by several measures. The country comprises over 13,600 islands in the Malay Archipelago, between the Indian Ocean and the Pacific Ocean. It has the largest population of any island nation (241,973,879 in 2005), and Java, one of Indonesia's biggest islands, (48,900 sq mi in area) has the highest population of any island in the world (121,352,608 in 2000).

Madagascar, the world's fourth largest island in area, at 226,658 square miles, is the largest-sized island constituting a single nation.

LARGEST U.S. ISLAND The largest island in the U.S. is Hawaii, one of the eight main islands that make up the state. Also known as "The Big Island," with an area of 4,028 square miles, it was formed by volcanic activity and has mountains that peak above 13,000 feet.

Long Island in New York State is the largest island in the continental U.S., at 1,723 square miles.

LARGEST UNINHABITED ISLAND Devon Island, in the Canadian Arctic, has an area of 21,331 square miles, making it the world's biggest uninhabited island (and 27th largest island in the world). NASA has studied the geology of Devon's Haughton impact crater since 1999; it's believed to be Earth's closest environmental equivalent to Mars.

SMALLEST ISLAND NATION The Pacific nation of Nauru, with an area of 8.2 square miles, is the smallest island nation—about one-tenth the size of Washington, DC. As of mid-2005, an estimated 13,048 people lived on Nauru.

MOST ISOLATED (INHABITED) The most remote inhabited island is Tristan da Cunha, in the South Atlantic, 1,500 miles south of its nearest occupied neighbor—St. Helena, which is itself 1,150 miles off the coast of Namibia, Africa. Tristan da Cunha's north coast is inhabited by about 275 British citizens (the earliest permanent residents arrived in 1816).

LARGEST ARCHIPELAGO The mountainous Malay Archipelago, between the Indian and Pacific Oceans, covers about 1.1 million square miles and stretches from 20° north of the equator to 10° south. The archipelago includes the Philippines, Indonesia, Papua New Guinea, Brunei, and innumerable other islands.

Other Island Records

Largest Lake Island	Manitoulin Island, Lake Huron, Canada	1,068 sq mi
Largest River Island	Bananal Island, Araguaia River, Brazil	7,720 sq mi
Largest Sand Island	Fraser Island, off Queensland, Australia	710 sq mi
Highest Altitude	Three islands in Lake Orba Co, Tibet	17,425 ft
Lowest Altitude	Afrera Ye'ch'ew Hayk, Ethiopia	337 ft below sea level
Most Densely Populated Island	Ap Lei Chau, Hong Kong	186,806 people per sq mi
Most Densely Populated Island Nation	Singapore	16,576 people per sq mi

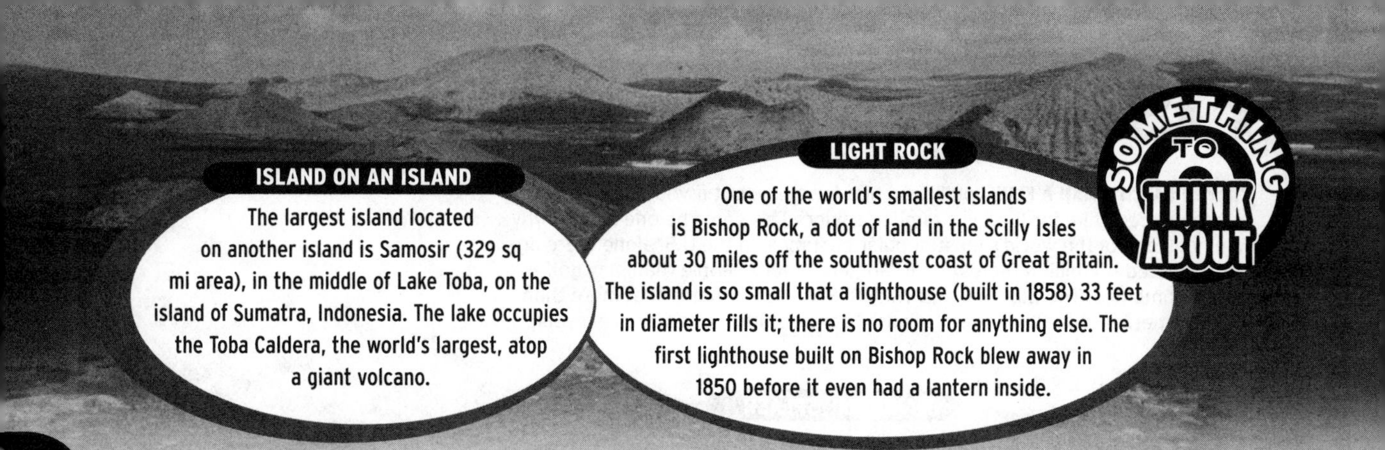

SOMETHING TO THINK ABOUT

ISLAND ON AN ISLAND

The largest island located on another island is Samosir (329 sq mi area), in the middle of Lake Toba, on the island of Sumatra, Indonesia. The lake occupies the Toba Caldera, the world's largest, atop a giant volcano.

LIGHT ROCK

One of the world's smallest islands is Bishop Rock, a dot of land in the Scilly Isles about 30 miles off the southwest coast of Great Britain. The island is so small that a lighthouse (built in 1858) 33 feet in diameter fills it; there is no room for anything else. The first lighthouse built on Bishop Rock blew away in 1850 before it even had a lantern inside.

VOLCANOES HAVE CHANGED THE EARTH'S CLIMATE, created islands, and caused the deaths of millions of people. About 540 volcanoes have erupted on land during recorded history, with an untold number erupting in the sea.

Almost 75% of the world's active volcanoes lie along the so-called "Ring of Fire," which traces the edges of two tectonic plates under the Pacific. It stretches from New Zealand along Asia's eastern coast, to Alaska's Aleutian Islands, and down the western coast of the Americas.

Volcanoes are fissures in the earth's crust above which a cone of material has accumulated, ejected from inside the earth. Many volcanoes were born underwater, and some still form islands today.

VOLCANOES

MOST ACTIVE VOLCANOES (COUNTRY)

Indonesia has 76 historically active volcanoes, 80% of which erupted in the 20th century. Their 1,171 total eruptions in recorded history are surpassed only by Japan's 1,274.

HIGHEST

The world's tallest volcano is Nevados Ojos del Salado in the Andes, along the Argentina-Chile border. The volcano, which is active but has not erupted in at least 1,000 years, is 22,595 feet tall.

HIGHEST (U.S.)

Hawaii's Mauna Kea is the tallest U.S. volcano, at 13,796 feet. The highest active volcano is Mauna Loa (Long Mountain), also in Hawaii; it stands 13,681 feet above sea level.

MOST MASSIVE

Measured from its submarine base in the Hawaiian Trough, Mauna Loa is the world's most massive active volcano. The shield volcano rises 13,681 feet above sea level, and its dome measures 75 miles long by 31 miles wide.

Mauna Loa has a total volume of 10,200 cubic miles, 84% of which is underwater. It last erupted in March 1984.

LARGEST CALDERA

Calderas (large crater-like basins) generally form when an eruption causes the volcano's dome to collapse. A series of four major eruptions, the first 1.2 million years ago, formed the massive Toba Caldera in Sumatra, Indonesia. The world's largest caldera, it covers about 1,400 square miles and contains Sumatra's biggest lake.

The supervolcano's last eruption (74,000 years ago) was the earth's largest in the last 2.5 million years. It spewed 670 cubic miles of magma (2,680 times more than Mount St. Helens did in 1980), and its ash covered the Indian subcontinent.

DEADLIEST ERUPTION

It is estimated that at least 92,000 people died when the Tambora volcano on Sumbawa, Indonesia, erupted in April 1815. About 10,000 people died right away; another 82,000 people died afterward from starvation and disease.

The fallout from the massive eruption is said to have caused a "year without a summer" in 1816. Global average temperatures dropped dramatically, and there were large-scale crop failures and other weather-related disturbances throughout Europe and northeast North America.

DEADLIEST ERUPTION (U.S.)

Mount St. Helens, in Skamania County, WA, blew its top on May 18, 1980, in the deadliest and most destructive eruption ever to occur in the U.S. It killed 57 people and destroyed over 200 homes and 27 bridges.

The explosion reduced the height of the volcano by 1,313 feet and created a crater that measured 1 mile by 2 miles across and 2,100 feet deep. In the first nine hours, 540 million tons of ash fell over more than 22,000 square miles.

LARGEST ERUPTION

About 27.8 million years ago, a volcano erupted with a magnitude of 9.1 in the San Juan Mountains of southwestern Colorado, releasing a dense-rock equivalent (DRE) of 1,080 cubic miles of magma.

It created La Garita caldera and left an ash-flow deposit of about 1,200 cubic miles that now fills the Fish Canyon Tuff.

Fishing

"IF YOU CATCH A MAN A FISH, you'll feed him for a day; but if you teach a man to fish, you'll feed him for life," is a familiar saying. This could be one reason why fishing is one of the world's most popular pastimes. In the U.S. alone there are an estimated 44 million recreational "anglers," more people than play golf and tennis combined. The U.S. Fish and Wildlife Service estimates that more than one in five Americans over the age of six are "gone fishing" at least once a year.

MAKING A "SPLASH"

On Jan. 16, 2004, Cody Mullenix a contractor from Howe, TX, caught a world-record blue catfish in Lake Texoma, TX, using a 14-foot surf rod with 20-pound line. After reeling in the blue monster, Mullenix faced a dilemma. He didn't want to kill it, but he couldn't claim the record if he didn't get it weighed. So he stood in the lake for an hour, holding the fish in the water with his hands, while a friend drove over with a scale. After weighing it, they put it in the back of his pickup and sped it over to a local bait shop where it was stored in a minnow tank; the catfish, dubbed "Splash," weighed in at $121\frac{1}{2}$ pounds, which was ratified by the IGFA as a world record. Mullenix donated Splash to the Texas Parks and Wildlife Department, and it was subsequently put on display in a 26,000-gallon aquarium at the Texas Freshwater Fisheries Center in Athens, TX.

SUPERLATIVES

BIGGEST CATCH

As certified by the International Game Fish Association (IGFA), the largest fish ever caught on a rod was a great white shark (*Carcharodon carcharias*), landed by Alf Dean on a 130-pound test line at Denial Bay, near Ceduna, South Australia, on April 21, 1959. It weighed 2,664 pounds and measured 16 feet, 10 inches long.

Dean, a citrus farmer from Mildura, South Australia, holds two other records for catching great whites (also known as white pointers): 2,536 pounds in 1955 (180-lb line) and 2,344 pounds in 1960 (80-lb line).

MOST WORLD CHAMPIONSHIPS
FRESHWATER

The freshwater world championships have been staged annually since 1957. Two anglers have won four world titles: Bob Nudd and Alan Scotthorne (both from England).

Nudd won his first title in 1990; the Essex-based fishing pro followed with wins in 1991, 1994, and 1999. Scotthorne won three consecutive titles from 1996 to 1998, and tied Nudd's record with his fourth win in 2003.

Scotthorne overcame adversity to win his record-tying fourth title on the River Vah in Slovakia. Two sections of his fishing pole broke during the competition while he was trying to reel in fish—in the first instance a barbell, and in the second a bream. Scotthorne is the only angler to have won three straight world titles.

MOST WORLD CHAMPIONSHIPS
FLY-FISHING

The fly-fishing world championships have been staged annually since 1981. Pascal Cognard (France) has won a record three titles, in 1994, 1997, and 2000.

The 1997 event was staged in Jackson Hole, WY, with the competitors required to fish from drift boats. It is illegal to fish from drift boats in France, so Cognard had rarely participated in this form of fly-fishing. Despite this, he still won the title.

BIGGEST ICE FISHING CONTEST The world's biggest ice fishing competition is the Brainerd Jaycees Ice Fishing Extravaganza staged annually in the "land of 10,000 lakes" on Gull Lake, near Brainerd, MN.

The three-hour fishing festival was first held in 1990, and it regularly attracts more than 10,000 competitors each January. The competition area ($\frac{1}{3}$ square miles on the lake) is predrilled by volunteers with about 24,000 holes.

Along with the freezing conditions, competitors are attracted to Brainerd by the lure of a $150,000 purse and other prizes, including new trucks, ATVs, and fishing gear.

Something to Think About

FAMILY AFFAIR

In 2003, Alan Scotthorne won his record-tying fourth world fishing championship. But he wasn't the only Scotthorne to net a world title that year. Three weeks earlier his wife, Sandra, had won the women's world championship. It was the first time in the history of match fishing that spouses had won world titles in the same year. Historians have speculated that this is the only husband and wife pair to win individual world titles in the same sport in the same year.

THE ONE THAT GOT AWAY

Tall tales of big fish that got away are legendary, but Bob Ploeger's story could top them all. On July 12, 1989, Ploeger, a 63-year retiree from Sandstone, MN, was fishing on Alaska's Kenai River with a guide, Dan Bishop, when he felt the tug of a fish hooked on the line. Neither of them knew they had a king salmon estimated to be close to 100 pounds. Knowing they couldn't maneuver from their drift boat, they boarded a passing powerboat to continue the fight. Sharp, quick struggles would be followed by long lulls. As word spread to the local community, other fishing guides ferried fuel and food to the boat, and onlookers began to line the riverbank. A camera crew from an Anchorage TV station arrived to film the epic struggle In the end the king salmon ruled. After 37 hours he snapped Ploeger's 30-pound test line and swam away. Ploeger went home with the fish story . . .and a videotape that proved it was true.

Saltwater Fish Records (International Game Fish Association)

SPECIES	WEIGHT	CAUGHT BY	LOCATION	DATE
Bass, giant sea	563 lbs 8 oz	James D. McAdam Jr.	Anacapa Island, CA	Aug. 20, 1968
Bluefish	31 lbs 12 oz	James M. Hussey	Hatteras Inlet, NC	Jan. 30, 1972
Cod, Atlantic	98 lbs 12 oz	Alphonse J. Bielevich	Isle of Shoals, NH	June 8, 1969
Flounder, summer	22 lbs 7 oz	Charles Nappi	Montauk, NY	Sept. 15, 1975
Grouper, Goliath	680 lbs	Lynn Joyner	Fernandina Beach, FL	May 20, 1961
Marlin, Atlantic blue	1,402 lbs 2 oz	Paulo Roberto A. Amorim	Vitoria, Brazil	Feb. 29, 1992
Marlin, black	1,560 lbs	Alfred C. Glassell Jr.	Cabo Blanco, Peru	Aug. 4, 1953
Marlin, pacific blue	1,376 lbs	Jay W. deBeaubien	Kaaiwi Pt., Kona, HI	May 31, 1982
Shark, great hammerhead	991 lbs	Allen Ogle	Sarasota, FL	May 30, 1982
Shark, tiger	1,780 lbs	Walter Maxwell	Cherry Grove, SC	June 14, 1964
Shark, white	2,664 lbs	Alfred Dean	Ceduna, Australia	April 21, 1959
Snapper, red	50 lbs 4 oz	Capt. Doc Kennedy	Gulf of Mexico, LA	June 23, 1996
Swordfish	1,182 lbs	L. B. Marron	Iquique, Chile	May 7, 1953
Tuna, Atlantic bigeye	392 lbs 6 oz	Dieter Vogel	Puerto Rico Gran Canaria, Spain	July 25, 1996
Tuna, Pacific bigeye	435 lbs	Dr. Russell V. A. Lee	Cabo Blanco, Peru	April 17, 1957

Freshwater Fish Records (International Game Fish Association)

SPECIES	WEIGHT	CAUGHT BY	LOCATION	DATE
Bass, largemouth	22 lbs 4 oz	George W. Perry	Montgomery Lake, GA	June 2, 1932
Carp, common	75 lbs 11 oz	Leo van der Gugten	Lac de St. Cassien, France	May 21, 1987
Catfish, flathead	646 lbs (pending verification)	Ken Paulie	Chiang Khong, Thailand Mekong River	May 1, 2005
Perch, Nile	230 lbs	William Toth	Lake Nasser, Egypt	Dec. 20, 2000
Pike, northern	55 lbs 1 oz	Lothar Louis	Lake of Grefeern, Germany	Oct. 16, 1986
Salmon, Atlantic	79 lbs 2 oz	Henrik Henriksen	Tana River, Norway	1928
Salmon, chinook	97 lbs 4 oz	Les Anderson	Kenai River, AK	May 17, 1985
Sturgeon, beluga	224 lbs 13 oz	Merete Lehne	Guryev, Kazakhstan	May 3, 1993
Sturgeon, white	468 lbs	Joey Pallotta III	Benicia, CA	July 9, 1983
Trout, lake	72 lbs	Lloyd Bull	Great Bear Lake, NWT, Canada	Aug. 19, 1995
Trout, rainbow	42 lbs 2 oz	David White	Bell Island, AK	June 22, 1970
Walleye	25 lbs	Mabry Harper	Old Hickory Lake, TN	Aug. 2, 1960

Memorabilia

AUCTIONS WERE ONCE THE DOMAIN OF FINE ART AND ANTIQUES, but in the latter part of the 20th century a new market emerged: memorabilia. From baseball cards to movie posters, from presidential manuscripts to lyrics penned by rock stars, items associated with the famous (and infamous) have been up for bid. With the advent of online auction house eBay in 1994, seemingly everything has a price, and usually a buyer. Here we review the eclectic mix of memorabilia that has sparked bidding wars and expanded the auction room.

SUPERLATIVES

ACADEMY AWARD
The highest price ever paid for an Oscar statuette was the $1,542,500 that pop star Michael Jackson shelled out to buy producer David O. Selznick's best-picture award for *Gone With the Wind*, at Sotheby's New York, on June 12, 1999.

Before then, the record price had been $607,500, reaped by Clark Gable's best-actor award for the 1934 comedy *It Happened One Night*. That buyer was two-time Oscar-winning director Steven Spielberg, who later bought two other Oscars (both best-actress Oscars won by Bette Davis, for *Dangerous* in 1936 and *Jezebel* in 1938). Spielberg returned all three trophies to the Academy of Motion Picture Arts and Sciences.

Since 1951, the Academy has required award nominees to agree not to sell their Oscars, making the pre-1951 statuettes even more valuable.

ANIMATION ART The most expensive piece of animation ever is a black-and-white cel from the 1934 Disney cartoon *Orphan's Benefit*. The cel (short for "celluloid"), showing Donald Duck flipping his lid, was purchased for $286,000 at Christie's on May 16, 1989, by an unnamed Canadian collector.

BASEBALL The ball hit by Mark McGwire for his record 70th 1998 home run, on Sept. 27, 1998, set a different kind of record on Jan. 12, 1999, by becoming the most expensive item of sports memorabilia ever sold.

It was acquired by Todd McFarlane, the creator of "Spawn" comics, who paid $3,005,000 ($2,700,000, plus $305,000 commission) at a Guernsey's auction house sale in New York.

BASEBALL BAT
The bat Babe Ruth swung on April 18, 1923, to hit the first home run at Yankee Stadium was sold for $1,265,000, the highest price ever paid for a bat, on Dec. 2, 2004, at Sotheby's New York.

The historic Louisville Slugger, known as "the Holy Grail," was donated by Ruth's agent to the Los Angeles *Evening Herald* as first prize in a high school home-run hitting contest organized by the newspaper in 1923. Ruth signed the bat for the winner, Victor Orsatti, who kept it until he died in 1984. It was sold by Orsatti's nurse, Marcia Tejada, to whom he had left it in his will.

BASEBALL CARD
A mint condition 1909 Honus Wagner became the most valuable baseball card yet when it sold for $1,263,000 on July 15, 2000. Very few cards depicting the Hall of Fame shortstop are known to exist; he is said to have halted their production himself. A nonsmoker, he insisted the American Tobacco Company withdraw his card because he didn't want children buying tobacco.

BASEBALL CONTRACT The contract that sent Babe Ruth from the Boston Red Sox to the New York Yankees on Dec. 26, 1919, for $100,000, sold for nearly 10 times that when it was auctioned by Sotheby's New York on June 10, 2005. Peter Siegel, a New York memorabilia dealer and Yankee fan, was the winning bidder, paying $996,000, the most ever for a sports document.

DRESS The famous—or infamous—beaded Jean Louis dress that Marilyn Monroe wore to serenade President John F. Kennedy at Madison Square Garden on May 19, 1962, sold at Christie's on Oct. 27, 1999, for $1,267,500, making it the most expensive dress ever sold at auction, and the most expensive item of Marilyn Monroe memorabilia.

At that same auction, a platinum eternity band with 35 diamonds (one was missing) that baseball legend Joe DiMaggio gave Monroe after their wedding in 1954 sold for $700,000.

FOOTBALL JERSEY
The highest price ever paid for a football jersey was $284,350,

LIGHTSABER

A pair of lightsabers wielded by Luke Skywalker (Mark Hamill) and Darth Vader (David Prowse) were sold at auction in Beverly Hills, CA, on July 29, 2005. In this instance, the force was with the son, not the father: Luke's lightsaber (used in *Star Wars*, 1977) sold for $206,600, Lord Vader's (used in *The Empire Strikes Back*, 1980) for $118,000.

SOMETHING TO THINK ABOUT

A PARTING OF WAYS

A news story on June 1, 2005, reported that Neil Armstrong, the first man to set foot on the moon, had threatened legal action against a Lebanon, OH, barber for selling clippings of his hair. Marx Sizemore, the owner of Marx' Barber Shop, admitted selling the former astronaut's hair to a Connecticut collector, John Reznikoff, for $3,000. After telling Armstrong of the sale, Sizemore was asked to buy the locks back or donate his profit to charity. The new owner refused to sell the hair back to Sizemore, but said he would make the charitable donation.

"POPEMOBILE"

On May 5, 2005, a 1999 Volkswagen Golf formerly owned by Pope Benedict XVI was sold for $244,600 in an auction on eBay's German website, by a man who bought it from a dealer. The car was once registered to then-Cardinal Joseph Ratzinger, though the cardinal himself apparently never drove it and did not have a drivers' license. The gray hatchback had 46,605 miles on the odometer.

VAMPIRE KIT

An anonymous buyer paid a record $12,000 for a vintage "Vampire Killing Kit" at Sotheby's New York on Oct. 30, 2003. The kit, enclosed in a walnut box, included a wooden stake and mallet, a rosary, crucifix, pistol, and 10 silver bullets. The origins of the kit are unknown. Some experts thought it was an authentic kit sold in Eastern Europe in the 18th and 19th centuries. Others believed it to be a piece of merchandising produced in the early 20th century to take advantage of the popularity of Bram Stoker's book *Dracula*, published in 1897.

The Popemobile ►

for Jim Thorpe's Canton Bulldog uniform. It sold in Dec. 2004 in an internet auction by Leland's, a sports auction house. The sweater dates from about 1916, and features a tan "C" knitted into the fabric.

Thorpe, an Olympic medalist in the pentathlon and decathlon, is also a charter member of the Pro Football Hall of Fame.

LETTER (PRESIDENTIAL ASSASSIN)
The record high price for a letter by a presidential assassin is $79,900. The three-page letter by John Wilkes Booth was dated Feb. 9, 1865, two months before Booth shot President Abraham Lincoln in Ford's Theater, in Washington, DC. In it, Booth asks a friend, Orlando Tompkins, to send him promotional photos of himself; they were later used in the "wanted" posters circulated after the assassination.

The letter was purchased through Skinner auction house by Joe Maddalena, a Los Angeles memorabilia collector, on Nov. 21, 2004.

LYRICS (ROCK SONG)
John Lennon's handwritten lyrics for "All You Need Is Love" used in the Our World satellite broadcast on June 25, 1967, sold for £600,000 (about $1 million) at a Cooper Owen auction in London on July 28, 2005.

MANUSCRIPT
A one-page draft of a pre-Civil War speech in which Abraham Lincoln referred to a nation half free and half slave as a "house divided"—his earliest known use of the phrase—sold for $1.54 million through Sotheby's on Dec. 16, 1992, the most ever paid for a manuscript in the U.S. It was bought by Kaller Historical Documents, Inc. for the New-York Historical Society.

MOVIE PROP Ronald Winston, the president of Harry Winston jewelers, paid $398,500 for the 50-pound Maltese Falcon that was the focus of the 1941 movie of the same name, starring Humphrey Bogart. Winston made his record purchase at Christie's New York on Dec. 7, 1994.

MOVIE SCRIPT
Marlon Brando's annotated script for *The Godfather* knocked Clark Gable's *Gone With the Wind* script out of the top-selling spot by fetching $312,800 at Christie's New York on June 30, 2005. Gable's script had sold for $244,500 in Dec. 1996.

Collections

The "Jenny"

FROM HIGH-PRICED PAINTINGS TO CLASSIC AUTOMOBILES to credit cards, there are ultra-large collections of practically everything and anything. Some are housed in museums and galleries, some in boxes in the basement or the attic. Many have great monetary value, and others . . . well, at least they're worth a look.

SUPERLATIVES

ANTIQUE CARS

The largest known private collection of antique cars was gathered by the late Harold LeMay of Tacoma, WA. The founder of a refuse and recycling company, he collected over 3,000 antique cars. Each year he opened his estate to the public to see the cars.

LeMay died in Nov. 2000, but 400 of his cars are still on display at the annual Car Show and Open House. In 2009, the LeMay Museum will open in a new 750,000-square-foot space next to the Tacoma Dome.

ARMORED VEHICLES

Jacques Littlefield of Portola Valley, CA, had already made a hobby of recreating miniature-scale military vehicles when he purchased a World War II-era American M-3A1 wheeled scout car for $3,500 in 1976. He restored the vehicle himself, and eventually founded the Military Vehicle Technology Foundation, the largest private collection of deactivated armored vehicles, housed in his 12,000-square-foot workshop.

This self-proclaimed "tank nerd" owns 220 military vehicles (including 66 tanks), and even a pair of Soviet-made Scud-missile launchers.

CHINESE FOOD TAKE-OUT MENUS

Harley Spiller, a 46-year-old arts administrator from New York City, has more than 10,000 menus and related objects in his collection of Chinese restaurant memorabilia from over 50 countries.

COCA-COLA ARTIFACTS

The Schmidt Museum of Coca-Cola Memorabilia in Elizabethtown, KY, boasts the largest private collection of items related to the world's top-selling soft drink.

It includes over 80,000 vintage items—such as trays, calendars, jewelry, and signs. Dispensing machines, bottles, and glasses are also on view.

The Schmidt family has operated Coca-Cola bottling plants in the area since 1901. Bill and Jan Schmidt started seriously collecting Coca-Cola artifacts in 1971 to decorate a plant, and they opened their museum in 1976.

CREDIT CARDS

Walter Cavanagh, a retired real estate broker and financial adviser from Shell Beach, CA, owns the world's largest collection of credit cards.

The collection was prompted by a 1969 bet with a friend as to who could obtain the most credit cards in a year—Cavanagh won the bet, 143 to 138.

By 2004, Cavanaugh's collection stood at 1,497 valid credit cards. Added together, his potential credit limit is over $1.7 million.

Cavanaugh stores most of his plastic in safe deposit boxes, but keeps a selection in a specially designed wallet that holds up to 800 cards and extends to 250 feet.

He rarely uses any of the cards and pays any credit card bills in full each month.

GERMS

The American Type Culture Collection stores the world's largest collection of biological cultures in their 106,000-square-foot main facility at George Mason University in Manassas, VA.

Over 153,000 individual strains fill the collection, varying from the most diverse collection of prokaryotes (about 18,000 strains) to 70 lines of stem cells.

MEDICAL ODDITIES

The College of Physicians of Philadelphia houses the Mütter Museum—a two-story gallery of 20,000 medical items.

The founder of the collection, Thomas Mütter, was a pioneer in American medical education. He spent $20,000 building a teaching collection showing many of the illnesses that student would face when they began treating patients.

Among the oddities are the largest colon (27 ft), the skeletons of the first known Siamese twins (Eng and Chang), a tumor removed from Grover Cleveland's hard palate, and the remains of the soap lady—a woman whose body fat turned into adipocere, a fatty wax similar to lye soap, after she died in the mid-19th century.

PREPARED MUSTARD

After Wisconsin assistant attorney general Barry Levenson watched his beloved Boston Red Sox lose the 1986 World Series to the New York Mets, he dejectly wandered until he found himself in the mustard section of a 24-hour supermarket. Levenson decided to buy 12 jars.

His collection grew and in 1991 he left his job to create the Mount Horeb Mustard Museum in Mount Horeb, WI. It now holds over 4,400 jars from over 60 countries.

SOMETHING TO THINK ABOUT

STAR TREKKING

The Las Vegas Hilton is a mecca for Star Trekkers. Fans can browse through the world's largest Star Trek memorabilia store. After loading up on trinkets, they can tour the world's largest permanent collection of Star Trek costumes and props at the History of the Future Museum.

BIG COLLECTION OF TINY THINGS

Erika Nelson, a grassroots artist from Lucas, KS, always loved the large roadside attractions of heartland America. After writing her master's thesis, "Driving Around Looking at Big Things While Thinking About Spam," Nelson began touring these attractions in a wildly decorated bus. Dissatisfied with the miniatures offered at roadside shops, she began crafting her own. Her bus is now a mobile museum for over 55 handcrafted miniature versions of some of the county's "largest" attractions, like a 3-inch version of the 170-foot-tall Brooks Catsup bottle in Collinsville, IL, and a scale model of the "largest river otter," from Fergus Falls, MN. Nelson now tours these roadside attractions in hopes of promoting small-town tourism.

SNOWFLAKE PHOTOS You can find the largest collection of snowflake photographs in the Snowflake Bentley Museum in Jericho, VT.

The collection centers around the work of Wilson "The Snowflake Man" Benson, a Vermont farmer who was a pioneer in photomicrography. He was the first person to photograph a snow crystal (snowflake) in 1885, and the collection contains nearly all of the approximately 5,000 snowflake photographs that Benson took.

SPAM In Sept. 2001, Hormel Foods Corp. opened a 16,500-square-foot museum in Austin, MN, for fans of its canned meat products. Exhibits include thousands of Spam cans, a wall of Spam, a 5-foot replica Spamburger, a Spam exam, and a simulated production line, "Spam, Spam, and more Spam."

STAMP SALE A plate block of four stamps—the inverted "Jenny" (shorthand for a Curtiss JN-4 plane)—was sold Oct. 19, 2005, for a record price of $2.7 million to investment banker Bill Gross.

The stamps were originally purchased in 1918 by William Robey, an avid collector who was on the lookout for inverts the day that the two-color 24-cent stamp for the new airmail system went on sale.

Robey was offered a sheet of inverts at a Washington, DC post office. Only after the sale did the clerk discover the mistake. The clerk admitted to a reporter, "How was I to know the thing was upside down? I never saw a plane before."

After one week, Robey made a return on his investment, receiving $14,976 for a the $24 sheet he had bought. The sheet was broken up and then sold and resold over the decades.

Only two weeks after buying the plate, Gross swapped it with Donald Sundman for his "Z Grill," named for the waffle-like grill on the back that better absorbed postmarks. This rare 1868 stamp, featuring Benjamin Franklin, completed Gross's one-of-a-kind collection of every U.S. stamp from the 19th century.

Video Games

BACK IN THE DAYS OF *PONG*, no one could imagine the high-tech games of today. In just 30 years, video game systems went from devices no more powerful than pocket calculators to systems that, when configured correctly, could guide missiles. In 2004, the video game industry generated about $28 billion in revenue.

MILESTONES

1958: VIDEO U.S. government physicist William Higginbotham unknowingly created what is believed to be the first video game in 1958.

He made *Tennis for Two* out of vacuum-tube transistors and an oscilloscope (for use as a viewing screen) as a display for guests at the Department of Energy's Brookhaven National Laboratories in Upton, NY. The controls consisted of a rotating knob and a serve button, and players had a choice of tennis on the moon (low gravity) or on Jupiter (high gravity).

Believing that he hadn't invented anything significant, Higginbotham didn't patent the device. Even if he had, however, he wouldn't have profited from it—the U.S. owned the rights to all his inventions as a government scientist.

1962: COMPUTER GAME The first computer-driven game was created in April 1962 by a programming team led by Stephen ("Slug") Russell at the Massachusetts Institute of Technology. Called *Spacewar!*, it was a two-player space-battle game designed to demonstrate the capacity of the school's new 17-square-foot mainframe computer.

1966: HOME CONSOLE Ralph Baer came up with the concept of TV games around 1951, while working as a TV engineer at a television-making company called Loral. It wasn't until 1966 that he built a prototype while with RCA-owned Sanders Laboratories. He sold the rights to the system, which came to be known as *The Odyssey*, to Magnavox, which began distribution in May 1972. The $100 system had 22 game cartridges and TV overlays to provide color backgrounds for its ball- and paddle-controlled tennis, hockey, and maze games.

1972: ARCADE GAME The first two coin-operated arcade games were both versions of *Spacewar!*. The first to debut was *Galaxy Game*, a $20,000 contraption built by Bill Pitts and Hugh Tuck that cost 10 cents to play. It sat in a Stanford University coffee house from June 1972 until May 1979, when the display finally burned out.

In 1972, engineers Nolan Bushnell and Al Alcorn founded Atari, the first video game company. Together, they developed its first game, *Pong*.

1976: FIRST "VIOLENT" VIDEO GAME Exidy Games released *Death Race*, a driving game loosely based on a 1975 movie of the same name. Players had to steer a vehicle around a playfield chasing "gremlins" for points. When one was run over, it screamed and turned into a cross that players had to avoid.

Public outcry against the game's violence gained national attention, and it was taken off the market.

1979: THIRD-PARTY DEVELOPER Initially, games were developed in-house by the companies that created the game systems. This changed when the software company Activision was founded; a long-standing dispute over game credits and pay led programmers David Crane, Larry Kaplan, Alan Miller, and Bob Whitehead to leave Atari in 1979 to form the new company.

In 1980, Activision released its first game for the Atari system, *Drag Race*, based on Atari's 1977 arcade game. Activision went on to release other popular games such as *River Raid*, *Kaboom!*, and *Pitfall*, opening the door for other third-party gaming software companies.

1980: 3D GAME While not technically 3D, the 3D-style environment of Atari's *Battlezone* was a first. Its laser-show-like vector graphics and capacity for offscreen actions impressed the U.S. military so much that it commissioned Atari to build modified versions for use in tank training.

1980: ARCADE-TO-CONSOLE Because of the rabid following and popularity of *Space Invaders*, it became the first arcade game licensed for the home console. Atari reached a deal with the Japanese company Taito, the game's creator, in 1980. Over the next few years, the exclusive deal helped to keep Atari at the top of the home-console industry.

Rick Mauer, the Atari programmer who adapted the game for home use, reportedly received only $11,000 for his work. He never designed a game for Atari again.

1980: D-PAD Gumpei Yokoi invented the cross-shaped directional pad used on most game consoles today. In 1980, while developing the Game & Watch, a foldable

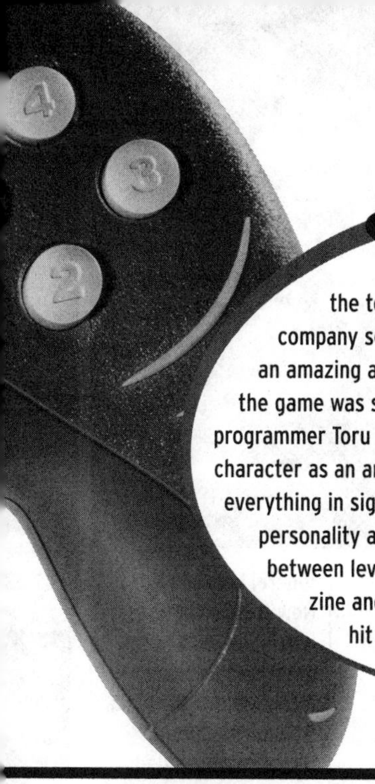

BEST-SELLING ARCADE GAME

Namco's *Pac-Man* is said to be the top-selling arcade title of all time. The company sold about 100,000 units in the U.S. in 1980, an amazing amount by the standards of the day. In Japan, the game was so popular, it caused a coin shortage. Japanese programmer Toru Iwantani designed the game, imagining the main character as an animated pizza racing through a maze and eating everything in sight. It was the first game to feature an animated personality and was also the first to feature cut scenes in between levels. *Pac-Man* made the cover of *Time* magazine and inspired "Pac-Man Fever," a song that hit ninth on the *Billboard* "Top Ten" in March 1984.

TOP SECRET

In April 2000, Sony's PlayStation 2 became the first video game console to face export controls under Japan's Foreign Exchange and Foreign Trade Control Law. The system was so sophisticated that, combined with a video camera, it could be used as a crude missile-guidance system.

SOMETHING TO THINK ABOUT

handheld series for Nintendo, Yokoi found that a joystick was impractical. He came up with a digital control scheme (hence D-pad), which was used on the handheld game. Yokoi later developed Nintendo's Game Boy.

1989: CD-BASED CONSOLE When NEC released the TurboGrafx-16 console, it also sold a $400 portable CD player attachment to run games on compact discs. The 3DO Interactive Multiplayer released four years later was the first console that used exclusively CD technology. Because of its high price, CD-only consoles were not widely accepted until the much cheaper Sony PlayStation was released in Japan in 1994.

1994: RATINGS With increasingly violent games appearing in the early 1990s, such as *Mortal Kombat* (Midway 1992), Senators Joe Lieberman (D, CT) and Herb Kohl (D, WI) urged the game industry to make a rating system to help parents monitor the games their children played.

In Sept. 1994, the Entertainment Software Ratings Board was established as an independent self-regulatory body; since then, ESRB has rated more than 10,000 video games.

More Video Game Firsts

Rom Chip	*Tank*	Kee/Atari	1974
High Scores	*Space Invaders*	Bally/Midway	1978
High Scores w/ Initials	*Asteroids*	Atari	1979
Handheld	*Microvision*	Milton Bradley	1979
Multilevel	*Gorf*	Midway	1981
Polygon Graphics	*I, Robot*	Atari	1983
On CD	*The Manhole*	Cyan Worlds/Activision	1988

SUPERLATIVES

BEST-SELLING PC GAME Electronic Arts' *The Sims* is the biggest-selling computer game. It has been the No. 1 PC series since 2000, with over $500 million in sales. It has been translated into 17 different languages, and more than 13 million copies have been sold worldwide since 2000, along with 23 million expansion packs. *The Sims 2* sold more than 1 million copies at retail stores worldwide within the first 10 days of its Sept. 14, 2004 release.

BIGGEST TOURNAMENT The annual World Cyber Games, begun in Seoul, South Korea, in 2000, has become the world's biggest game event.

The 2005 games, held at the Suntec Singapore International Convention and Exhibition Centre in Singapore, saw over 700 players from 67 countries compete in eight games. Thirty-nine thousand fans were on hand for the World Cyber Games Grand Final, which carried a $435,000 grand prize.

Gambling

GAMBLING USUALLY INVOLVES RISK, chance, and the possibility of a worthwhile reward. For at least as long as human history, people have gambled—on dice, cards, coin flips, dogfights, lotteries, games, elections, wars, or just about any endeavor open to a clear but uncertain outcome. Gambling has always labored under a seedy reputation, but today it thrives as a multi-billion dollar industry where profits are made from losers, not winners. In 2005, gamers in the U.S. lost about $80 billion in legal gambling.

MILESTONES

BRONZE AGE (ABOUT 3000 BC): DICE
The earliest-known dice were made from the anklebones (or knucklebones) of sheep and had four distinct sides. There is evidence that dice games were played across the Mediterranean and Mesopotamia during the Bronze Age.

Cube dice as we know them today go as far back as 2000 BC in ancient Egypt.

800 AD: PLAYING CARDS
Playing cards may have first appeared in China and Korea in ancient times, but cards as we know them date back to India around 800 AD. Crusaders returning from the Middle East likely brought them to Europe by the 1370s.

Decks still vary in number and suits in different countries. The familiar four-suit, 52-card version was first developed in France around 1480.

1500s: LOTTERIES
The first state lottery is believed to have been held in France in 1520, and it became a major source of royal funding. In 17th century America, colonists authorized lotteries to fund public works and private construction. A lottery was held to raise funds for the Jamestown colony in 1612. Later, Yale and Harvard colleges held lotteries for funds, in 1750 and 1772, respectively.

1821: LOTTERY BANS
On Nov. 10, 1821, New York became the first state to ban lotteries because corruption had become rampant. By 1878 every state had barred lotteries, except Louisiana, where a private lottery operated until the 1890s.

1863: MONTE CARLO
In 1861, the tiny country of Monaco gave up 80% of its territory to France in exchange for independence. With few natural resources, Prince Charles III built the country's economy on tourism and gambling and in 1863 hired François Blanc to create Le Casino de Monte Carlo.

1908: PARI-MUTUEL BETTING (U.S.)
The American Jockey Club adopted the pari-mutuel betting system for the 1908 Kentucky Derby on May 5, 1908.

Developed by the Spaniard Joseph Oller in France in 1868, the pari-mutuel (mutual bet) system standardized the distribution of winning bets on a set percentage of the amounts wagered, making winnings clear to spectators.

State taxes on pari-mutuel betting made racing beneficial to local governments.

1941: LAS VEGAS STRIP The first hotel-casino on what was to become the famous Las Vegas Strip was El Rancho Vegas, which opened on April 3, 1941.

El Rancho, owned by Thomas Hull, was so successful that more casinos like it popped up on the Strip, including mobster "Bugsy" Siegel's famous Flamingo in 1946.

1964: NEW HAMPSHIRE SWEEPSTAKES
New Hampshire became the first state in 70 years to hold a legal statewide lottery. At the time, lotteries were technically illegal under federal law. However, New Hampshire took advantage of a legal loophole and tied the lottery to horse racing, which was legal. It was officially called the "New Hampshire Sweepstakes."

Gov. John King bought the first ticket on March 12, 1964, at Rockingham Park.

1988: NATIVE AMERICAN CASINOS
The Indian Gaming Regulatory Act, enacted on Oct. 17, 1988, made it legal for Native Americans to set up gambling operations on tribal lands if gambling wasn't banned throughout the entire state where their lands were located.

The law sparked the rapid rise of casino development on Native American reservations across the country. Today, 28 states have Native American casinos.

SOMETHING TO THINK ABOUT

LUCKY NUMBERS 22, 28, 32, 33, 39

In the March 30, 2005, Powerball drawing, 89 players picked five of the six winning numbers, and 21 got all six. Lottery officials estimated only four or five players would have guessed that many correct numbers, and became suspicious. They found that the players had all picked their numbers from the same source—fortune cookies. Each cookie was baked in a New York City factory and had five of the six "lucky numbers." Those who got those numbers won $100,000, and those who had guessed the sixth won $500,000.

TWICE AS NICE

In June 2005, 55-year-old Donna Goeppert of Bethlehem, PA, won her second $1 million lottery jackpot in six months playing a Pennsylvania Lottery scratch-off ticket. She had previously won $1 million in January.

1,666,667 TO 1

British roofer Mick Gibbs, 59, staked 30 pence (roughly 50 cents) on a complicated accumulator bet in August 2000, which required him to correctly predict the winners of 15 different sporting events for cricket, rugby, and soccer, culminating in the 2001 UEFA Champions League (soccer tournament) winner. The odds for pulling off such a bet were about 1,666,667 to 1. When Bayern Munich beat Valencia in a penalty kick shootout to win the Champions League final, Gibbs defied the odds and won the maximum payout of £500,000 (about $860,000). Gibbs was too nervous to watch the game.

SUPERLATIVES

HEAVIEST BETTING EVENT (U.S.) Gambling on horseraces, dog races, and jai alai are legal in many states, but gambling on other sports is illegal in the U.S. except in Nevada. Despite this, the Super Bowl generates the heaviest betting of the year for any event. For Super Bowl XXXIX in 2005, Nevada's casinos logged legal bets worth a record $90.8 million. Experts estimate that all the office pools and friendly bets add up to at least 50 times that amount.

BIGGEST RESORT CASINO Foxwoods in Ledyard, CT, owned by the Mashantucket Pequot tribal nation, is the biggest casino in the world. Covering a total area of more than 4.7 million square feet, it boasts six casinos of 340,000 square feet in all (almost the size of six football fields) filled with about 7,400 slot machines and 388 tables.

BIGGEST SLOT MACHINE JACKPOT A 25-year-old software engineer from Los Angeles (who chose to remain anonymous), while playing the slots at the Excalibur Hotel-Casino in Las Vegas, NV, made an incredible hit on March 21, 2003. The Megabucks progressive slot machine he was playing announced a jackpot of $39,713,982.25. The lucky guy said he had put about $100 into the machine when he hit.

He beat out the previous record of $34.9 million set in 2000.

BIGGEST POKER PRIZE After 13 hours, 56 minutes of straight no limit Texas Hold'em play, Lebanese-born Australian Joseph Hachem, 39, took home a record $7.5 million from the 2005 World Series of Poker World Championship in Las Vegas at 6:44 AM on July, 16, 2005.

LARGEST LOTTERY PAYOUT On Dec. 26, 2002, 55-year-old Andrew Jackson "Jack" Whittaker Jr. of Scott Depot, WV, won a lump-sum payment of $170.5 million ($111.7 million after taxes) off a Powerball ticket. It was the biggest lottery payout ever won by one person. He took it instead of receiving yearly payments from a $314.9 million jackpot that would have paid out over 30 years.

The largest jackpot ever won was the $363 million Big Game on May 9, 2000, but it was split between two winners: Larry Ross, a 47-year-old swimming pool installer, from Shelby Township, MI, and Joe and Sue Kainz, microbrewers from Tower Lakes, IL. Both chose the lump sum of about $90 million each.

BIGGEST PAYOUT (HORSE RACING) The biggest payout in horse racing history was $2,033,852.40 ($1,627,084.40 after taxes), taken home by Anthony Speelman and Nicholas Cowan (both of Great Britain) on April 19, 1987. The pair parlayed a $64, 9-horse accumulator at Santa Anita Racetrack in Arcadia, CA, into the record winnings. The jackpot had built up over 24 days. The duo picked seven winners in their selections.

Board Games

FROM ANTIQUITY TO THE PRESENT, people have played board games and most likely have argued about the rules. Games like backgammon have been around in some form for thousands of years. In the 20th century, several new board games, like Monopoly®, Scrabble®, and Trivial Pursuit®, quickly became more than holiday gifts. They are part of American popular culture.

MILESTONES

C. 3000 BC: BACKGAMMON
Backgammon is one of the oldest known board games. Games similar to it have been traced back to ancient civilizations in Greece, India, and Mesopotamia; excavators in Iran and Iraq have uncovered boards suitable for playing the game that date back 5,000 years.

Ancient Romans called their version *tabula*, meaning "table" or "board," and this version of the game spread throughout Europe. The name "backgammon" was coined around 1645, most likely a combination of the Middle English words *bac* (back) and *gammen* (game). In 1743, Edmond Hoyle wrote "A Short Treatise on the Game of Backgammon," which established formal rules for the game.

C. 2300 BC: GO
Known as *Go* (Japan), *Baduk* (Korea), or *Weiqi* (China), this game in some form was first played in China about 4,300 years ago, according to one legend. Some believe the game was developed by semi-mythical Chinese Emperor Yao to encourage his son Dan Zhu to think logically; others claim that the game actually appeared much earlier.

Regardless, skill at *Weiqi* ("the surrounding game") was so highly regarded in China by the time of Confucius (c. 600 BC) that it was considered one of the "Four Accomplishments" (brush painting, poetry, and playing the zither were the others).

By the 11th century, the game had spread to Japan and Korea. To this day it remains enormously popular in Japan, South Korea, and China, and its champions are major celebrities.

Despite the game's foundation in logic, no computer program has beaten a pro. The most lucrative competition, the Ing Cup, is held every four years. China's Chang Hao claimed the $400,000 purse over Korea's Choi Cheol Han in 2004.

AD 1550: MODERN CHESS The origins of chess in its earliest versions are lost in antiquity, but most historians consider the Indus Valley of northern India its birthplace. A similar board game called *Chaturanga*, played by four players, appeared in India as early as the sixth century AD.

Versions of the game were also played in Persia and China, and several different versions eventually spread westward.

The modern game was established in Europe around 1550 with the introduction of rules that are standard now: the queen was recognized as the most powerful piece, a pawn could move two squares on its first move, and castling was introduced.

Chess ends with "checkmate," when one player's king is unable to move without being captured; the expression comes from the Persian (and later Arabic) phrase *shah mat* ("the king is dead").

The first truly international chess tournament, held in London in 1851, was won by a German player, Adolf Anderssen.

The International Chess Federation (Fédération Internationale des Échecs; FIDE) was founded in Paris in 1924.

1934: MONOPOLY®
The saga of modern Monopoly begins with Charles B. Darrow, an unemployed heating engineer from Philadelphia, PA, who presented his real estate game to executives at Parker Brothers in 1934.

They unanimously rejected it. Fortunately, he didn't linger on the "free parking" square; with the help of a printer, he produced the game on his own, persuaded a Philadelphia department store to stock it, and promptly sold all 5,000 copies. Darrow then went back to Parker Brothers, who reconsidered and bought the rights.

In 1935, Monopoly sold over 500,000 copies and, the next year, over 3 million. It is now the best-selling board game of all-time, with over 200 million games sold in 80 countries worldwide. Parker Brothers estimates that more than 5 billion little green houses have been distributed for "building" since 1935.

SOMETHING TO THINK ABOUT

BATTLE CHESS

Think board games are all brains and no brawn? The creators of chess boxing might see things differently. The new event, devised by the World Chess Boxing Organization (WCBO), combines "the No. 1 thinking sport and the No. 1 fighting sport" into an 11-round marathon. Players alternate between six four-minute rounds of chess and five two-minute boxing rounds until there's a checkmate or KO. If the 11th round ends in stalemate, the boxer with the most points (as determined by the boxing judges) wins.

MONOPOLY® IS A LONG GAME

The makers of the Monopoly game recognize world records for their game in various categories. For instance, the longest Monopoly game played in a bathtub is four days, three hours. Other unlikely settings for marathon games are: a treehouse (11 days, 22 hours); upside-down (1 day, 12 hours); a moving elevator (16 days); on the back of a fire truck (4 days, 5 hours); and underwater (45 days).

1947: SCRABBLE® Alfred Butts, an unemployed New York City architect, began developing Scrabble in the Depression year of 1931. The original version, called Lexiko, used wooden tiles but no board. Butts added the crossword-grid board and renamed it Criss-Cross Words by 1938.

The points given to each letter were based mostly on Butts's analysis of how often each was used on the front page of *The New York Times*. However, he reduced the number of "S" tiles to four, to limit the use of plurals.

The game was rejected by manufacturers until Butts met entrepreneur James Brunot, who helped him refine the rules. In 1947, they renamed the game Scrabble, which means, "to write in rambling or scrawling characters."

They made Scrabble sets themselves by hand, until the president of Macy's department stores played the game and agreed to carry it in 1952. The next year, Scrabble sold more than one million sets.

1981: TRIVIAL PURSUIT® Canadian journalists Scott Abbott and Chris Haney developed Trivial Pursuit with Haney's brother, John, and Ed Werner. The foursome produced a prototype in 1981 and presented it at the Feb. 1982 Toy Fair in New York City.

As with many other popular board games, the initial reaction to Trivial Pursuit was lukewarm. But players took to the hybrid of general knowledge quiz and board game, and publicity for the game built quickly.

Trivial Pursuit sold 100,000 copies in the U.S. in 1982, 2.4 million in 1983, and in 1984, over 20 million games were sold in six languages.

SUPERLATIVES

MOST EXPENSIVE BOARD GAME (RETAIL)
The world's most expensive retail board game is the deluxe version of Outrage! The purpose of the game is to steal the crown jewels from the Tower of London. In the deluxe edition, the crown jewels are handmade replicas of the real thing. Eighteen karat gold crowns are studded with real rubies, sapphires, emeralds, and diamonds.

First produced in 1992, it currently sells for about $15,000. If that price tag is a little too much for your pocketbook, the regular version sells for $55 and the travel edition for $20.

BIGGEST MONOPOLY® BOARD The biggest permanent Monopoly game is a 930-square-foot playing board made of granite in front of the Children's Discovery Museum in San Jose, CA. Called "Monopoly in the Park," and authorized by Parker Brothers, the game is played using life-sized versions of the Monopoly tokens; there is even prison garb for players who have to "go directly to jail."

Created by Cypress Granite and Memorials of San Jose, the game was dedicated on July 19, 2002.

YOUNGEST GRAND MASTER (CHESS)
Chess players who have attained the title of Grand Master have gotten increasingly younger in the past 10 years. To get the Grand Master title from the International Chess Federation (FIDE), players must have a winning record that adds up to at least 2,500 points. The FIDE system is based on a complicated algorithm that converts percentage scores into rating differences.

Ukrainian Sergei Karjakin, born on Jan. 12, 1990, earned that distinction before he was even a teenager, with a win at a tournament in Sudak, Ukraine, on Aug. 12, 2002. He was 12 years and seven months old.

HIGHEST SCRABBLE® WORD SCORE The most points scored in an official Scrabble competition on one turn is 392, for the word CAZIQUES, the plural for a Caribbean tribal leader. Dr. Karl Khoshnaw came up with the word, and a good placement for it, at a tournament in Manchester, England, in April 1982.

(With luck you could do even better. If you have the right letters to fill in certain blanks across the bottom of the board, with triple word scores and intersecting words, you could get 1,970 points for BENZOXYCAMPHORS.)

The Human Body

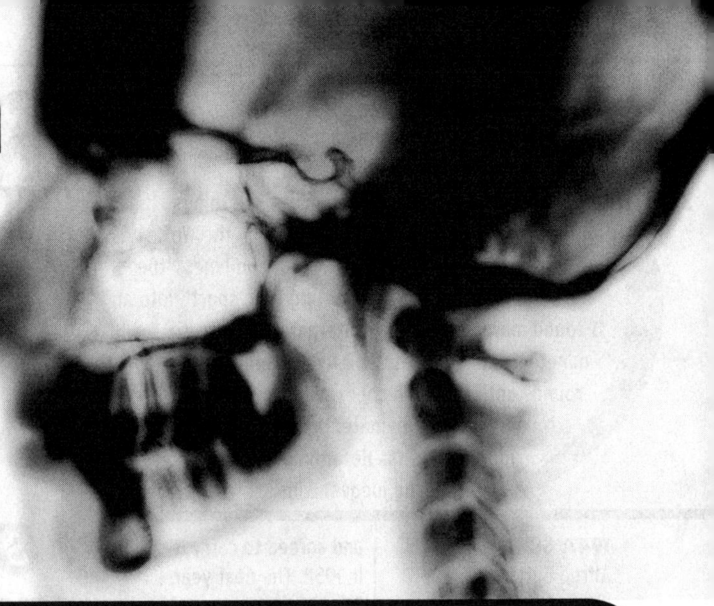

THE ANCIENTS HAD ONLY A RUDIMENTARY KNOWLEDGE of human anatomy, but from the 16th century onward, aided at first by dissections of corpses, physicians began to gain accurate knowledge of the structure, and workings, of the body.

MILESTONES

AROUND 300 BC: FIRST DISSECTIONS Herophilus of Chalcedon (335-280 BC) was the head of a school of medicine in Alexandria, Egypt, and the first person known to have provided instruction in human dissection. In his writings, which are now lost but have been referred to by other ancients, including Galen, he properly identified several organs and established that arteries contain blood rather than air.

100s AD: GALEN Galen, a Greek physician (130-200), wrote over 100 treatises on anatomy. Because laws at the time prohibited dissecting humans, he did his research first by dissecting pigs, dogs, and apes, and later as a doctor for gladiators. His writings and drawings were the basis for most of western medicine for the next 1,000 years.

1491: ANATOMICAL PRINTS The first printed medical text with illustrations was Johannes de Ketham's *Fasciculus Medicinae*. Anatomy diagrams in this text, derived from medieval drawings, allowed for the first widespread sharing of anatomical studies.

1543: MODERN ANATOMY Andreas Vesalius published *De Humani Corporis Fabrica*, a series of books with images and descriptions of the human body based on Vesalius's numerous human dissections. This work was the first with fairly accurate renditions of the human anatomy.

1628: BLOOD CIRCULATION English physician William Harvey correctly asserted in his 1628 treatise "Anatomical Essay on the Motion of the Heart and Blood in Animals" that blood circulates and the heart propels it—a big step toward modern physiology.

It is now known that all blood completes this cycle once every minute through the 93,000 miles of arteries and veins in a human body.

1895: X-RAY On the evening of Nov. 8, 1895, German physicist Wilhelm Conrad Roentgen was experimenting with cathode rays when he realized that paper treated with barium platinocyanide became fluorescent when located nearby. When he placed his wife's hand in front of a photographic plate bombarded by the rays, it captured an image of her bones and wedding ring. Because the nature of the rays was then unknown, he called them X-rays.

1967: CRYONICS The belief that a body preserved at very low temperatures shortly after death can be available for revival by possible future medical techniques gained popularity in the 1960s.

The first person to permanently enter "cryonic suspension" was a 73-year-old retired psychology professor who had succumbed to kidney cancer. Dr. James Bedford had agreed to have his body cooled to -110°F with dry ice and later liquid nitrogen upon his death, which took place on Jan. 12, 1967, near Los Angeles. He is now maintained with about 60 other corpses in "cryocapsules" at the Alcor Life Extension facility in Scottsdale, AZ.

2000: HUMAN GENOME MAP On June 26, the international Human Genome Project and privately held, Maryland-based Celera Genomics both announced that they had completed a "working" draft of the human genetic pattern.

The non-profit Project had been working for ten years, while Celera quickly accomplished the same feat in two. In a completed map released on April 14, 2003, the HGP identified around 30,000 genes and 3 billion base pairs for human DNA. The entire map was made publicly available later that year.

Human Body Superlatives

PART	NAME	LOCATION	AVERAGE MEASUREMENT
Longest Bone	Femur	Thigh	$\frac{1}{4}$ total height
Smallest Bone	Stirrup (Stapes)	Inner ear	length, under 1 in
Largest Organ	Skin		22 sq ft (16% of body weight)
Longest Organ	Small intestine	Abdomen	13 ft
Most Active Organ	Heart	Chest	70 contractions/min
Largest Gland	Liver	Gut	3 lbs
Largest Muscle	Gluteus maximus	Buttocks	2 lbs
Longest Muscle	Sartorius	Thigh: Lower spine to knee	20 in
Smallest Muscle	Stapedius	Middle ear	length, 0.05 in long
Longest Vein	Long saphenous vein	Foot to inner thigh	
Largest Vein	Inferior vena cava	Legs and lower torso to heart	1.2 in diameter
Largest Artery	Aorta	Above heart	diameter, 1 in
Strongest Tendon	Achilles	Back of ankle	supports up to 1,000 lbs
Hardest Substance	Enamel	Teeth	

SOMETHING TO THINK ABOUT

HANDY TO KNOW

The hands and feet account for over half of all the bones in the human body.

SUPERLATIVES

LONGEST APPENDIX
On June 11, 2003, Dr. Riaz Ahmed Khokhar extracted the biggest appendix on record, measuring 9.25 inches long, from a 55-year-old Pakistani man, at the Pakistan Institute of Medical Sciences in Islamabad, Pakistan.

BIGGEST FEET
Matthew McGrory, of Los Angeles, is believed to have had the world's largest feet not caused by a medical condition. His feet were said to be $18\frac{1}{26}$ inches long, and a pair of custom-made shoes, size $28\frac{1}{2}$, cost him more than $22,000.

McGrory weighed 15 pounds when he was born in 1973 and was 5 feet tall by the end of kindergarten; he grew to 7 feet, 6 inches. An actor who appeared in the movie *Big Fish* (2003), he died in Aug. 2005.

MOST VALUABLE HAIR
A baseball-sized clump of Elvis Presley's dyed hair was sold at auction on Nov. 15, 2002, for $115,120, to an anonymous buyer. The jar of jet black hair had been saved by Presley's personal barber, Homer "Gill" Gilleland; he gave it to a friend who put it up for auction in preparation for his retirement.

MOST COMMON BROKEN BONE
The wrist area undergoes frequent use, and abuse, as a favorite way of breaking falls, and the large number of porous bones in the wrist make distal radius fractures the most common kind of fracture—except in the elderly, where hip breaks are the most common. In 2003, 11.7% of all emergency room visits in the U.S. were due to wrist injuries.

MOST COMMON DISLOCATED JOINT
Shoulder dislocations account for almost 50% of all joint dislocations, and an anterior dislocation is the problem in nine out of 10 shoulder patients.

MOST COMMON BLOOD TYPE
O positive is the most common blood type, found in about 37% of the U.S. population. O negative blood, on the other hand, is uncommon (found in under 7%), but is notable in that it can be given to almost any recipient.

LEAST COMMON BLOOD TYPE AB negative is the least common blood type, found in only 1% of the U.S. population.

AB positive found in about 3% of the population is also uncommon, but special, because people with that type can receive transfusions from any other type.

LOWEST SURVIVING BODY TEMPERATURE
On Dec. 13, 1985, when Scott Romfo was 17, he fell asleep in a snowbank, drunk, on a night when temperatures fell below –20°F. When he was found the next morning, he had a body temperature so low (well below 60°F) that the hospital thermometers bottomed out. Romfo survived but had to have all his limbs amputated.

In May 1999, Dr. Anna Elisabeth Baagenholm, 29, went through the ice on a stream in Norway, while skiing off-trail.

She was trapped underwater for about 80 minutes. When she was taken to a hospital her temperature was measured at 56.6°F. Her heart had stopped and she showed no signs of life. She was revived and amazingly kept every limb.

HIGHEST SURVIVING BODY TEMPERATURE
On July 10, 1980, Willie Jones, 52, was taken to Grady Memorial Hospital in Atlanta, GA, suffering from heatstroke.
On admittance, his temperature was measured at 115.7°F. Luckily, doctors were able to bring it back down, and he was released 24 days later.

Organ Transplants

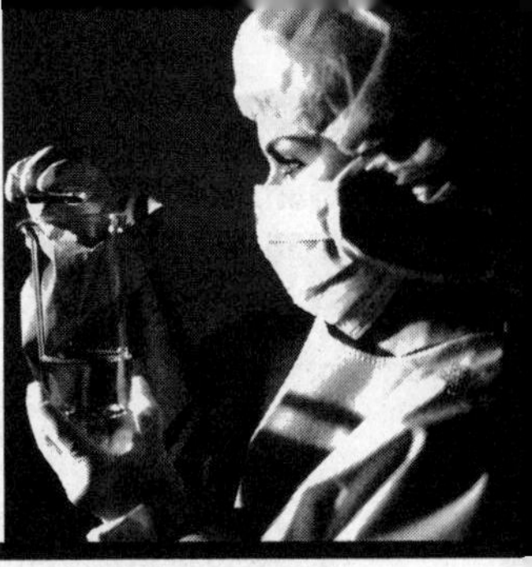

ONCE A MEDICAL DREAM, organ transplants today have become practical; doctors have learned to reduce the heavy risks involved, and are often able to use transplants to improve and prolong the lives of seriously ill patients.

MILESTONES

1905-10: EXPERIMENTAL TRANSPLANTS

French surgeon Alexis Carrel (1873-1944) is known as the founding father of experimental organ transplantation. Carrel was a noted eccentric, who reportedly wore black when performing surgery. But he did pioneering work.

In 1905, he transplanted the kidney of a puppy into the neck of an adult dog and observed the reconnected functioning kidney for several hours. That same year, Carrel and Dr. Charles Claude Guthrie performed a number of surgical grafts with kidneys and thyroids. In 1908, Carrel exhibited a dog that had lived for 17 months with a transplanted kidney. In 1910, he demonstrated that blood vessels could be preserved in cold storage for extended periods of time.

In 1912 he received the Nobel Prize in physiology or medicine.

1935: BLOOD-CIRCULATING PERFUSION PUMP

In collaboration with the aviator Charles Lindbergh, who began experiments in this area of research because of a relative's heart condition, Dr. Carrel designed the first blood-circulating pump that did not cause infection. Using this pump Carrel could perform operations where blood circulation was interrupted for up to two hours without permanent damage. On April 5, 1935, he removed a cat's thyroid gland and was able to keep it alive—perfused with the necessary fluids—for 18 days.

1950: SUCCESSFUL KIDNEY TRANSPLANT

The first human kidney transplant was performed by a team led by Dr. Yu Yu Voronoy in Kiev, Ukraine (then Soviet Union), in the 1930s.

Unfortunately, the patient had the wrong blood type (different from the donor's) and, for this and other reasons, died two days after surgery.

The first successful transplant occurred on June 17, 1950, at the Little Company of Mary Hospital in Chicago, IL. The patient was Ruth Tucker, a 44-year-old woman; the operation was performed by a team led by Dr. Richard H. Lawler. Tucker, who received her new kidney from a cadaver, lived for nearly five years.

The first successful living human-to-human organ transplant occurred on Dec. 23, 1954, when a kidney was transplanted between identical twins in Boston, MA. Dr. Joseph Murray and Hartwell Harrison led the team that transplanted a kidney from Ronald Herrick to his brother Richard. Richard lived eight more years. Ronald suffered no ill effects and returned to college soon after the surgery.

Murray received the Nobel Prize for physiology or medicine in 1990 for his work with kidney transplants.

1967: SUCCESSFUL LIVER TRANSPLANT

A team led by Dr. Thomas Starzl attempted the first human liver transplantation on March 1, 1963, at the University of Colorado in Denver. However, the patient, a three-year-old boy named Bennie Solas, did not survive surgery. After more failures there and in Boston and Paris, France, this procedure was abandoned.

On July 23, 1967, Starzl began again, after successful clinical trials of a new treatment aimed at preventing the body's immune system from rejecting the organ. This time, he operated on an 18-month-old child with a malignant liver tumor. She survived for 400 days before she died of spreading cancer.

1967: HUMAN HEART TRANSPLANT

On Dec. 3, 1967, a human heart transplant was performed by Dr. Christiaan Barnard at Groote Schuur Hospital in Cape Town, South Africa. The donor was Denise Darvall, a 25-year-old auto accident victim. The patient, Louis Washkansky, was a 55-year-old grocer suffering from end-stage heart disease. He lived for 18 days, which was considered a relative success and major step forward.

1981: SUCCESSFUL HEART-LUNG TRANSPLANT

A team led by Dr. Denton Cooley performed the first clinical heart-lung transplantation on Sept. 15, 1968, at the Texas Heart Institute in Houston, TX. But the patient, a two-month-old infant, survived for only 14 hours.

On March 9, 1981, Stanford surgeon Bruce Reitz and his colleagues transplanted the heart and lungs of a 15-year-old traffic accident victim into Mary Gohlke. The 45-year-old Mesa, AZ, newspaper executive was the first successful heart-lung transplant. She survived for five years.

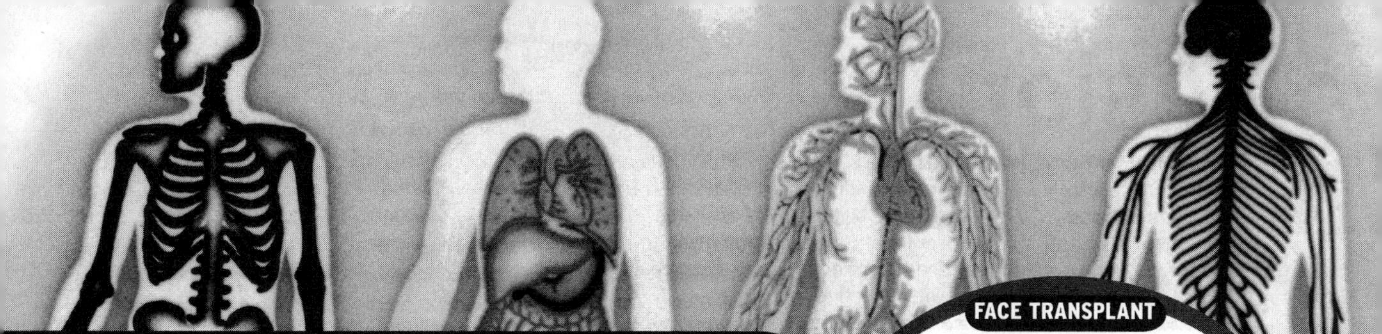

1982: PERMANENT ARTIFICIAL HEART Dr. Denton Cooley implanted the Liotta artificial heart, a $\frac{1}{2}$ pound device connected by tubes to a console, in 47-year-old Haskell Karp of Skokie, IL, on April 4, 1969, as a temporary replacement until a human heart could be found. The patient did survive on the device until April 7, when a human heart transplant operation was performed. But he died the next day of tissue rejection and other complications.

The Jarvik-7 was the first permanent artificial heart. It was implanted on Dec. 2, 1982, into 61-year-old dentist Barney Clark. Powered by air cables running from a 375-pound TV-sized unit into Clark's chest, the pneumatic pump proved that a mechanical heart could save lives. Dr. Clark lived 112 days.

In 1990, the FDA withdrew approval of the Jarvik-7 because of adverse reactions, but a similar device was put into use in 1993.

On July 2, 2001, the first fully contained artificial heart was implanted in a 58-year-old man at Jewish Hospital in Louisville, KY. It sustained Robert Tools of Franklin, KY, for five months before he died from a stroke.

1983: SUCCESSFUL LUNG TRANSPLANT The first single-lung transplantation in a human was performed by a team led by Dr. James Hardy at the University of Mississippi Medical Center, Jackson, MS, on June 11, 1963. However, the patient, John Russell, survived only 18 days before dying of kidney failure. The civil rights activist Medgar Evers, who had been shot to death on his porch earlier that day, was the donor.

The first lung transplant considered successful was performed by a team led by Dr. Joel Cooper on Nov. 7, 1983, at Toronto General Hospital. The patient, Tom Hall, was a 58-year-old hardware executive dying of pulmonary fibrosis. He lived for another six years, three months and 10 days before dying of kidney failure.

1983: CYCLOSPORINE APPROVED In 1971 Dr. Jean F. (Francois) Borel and the Sandoz Laboratories (now Novartis) in Basel, Switzerland, developed cyclosporine, the first drug powerful enough to protect transplant patients from weakened immune systems.

The "miracle drug" was developed from a substance first found in a mushroom that grows on the Hardangervidda, a high plateau in southern Norway. The first tests on humans took place in 1978, and the U.S. Food and Drug Administration approved the drug in 1983.

After the introduction of cyclosporine in 1984, the five-year survival rate for heart transplant recipients has been 60%-65%.

SOMETHING TO THINK ABOUT

FACE TRANSPLANT

The first partial face transplant was performed on Nov. 27, 2005, in Amiens, France, on a 38-year-old woman who had been mauled by a dog. Surgeons used the facial tissue from a brain-dead donor to replace the patient's chin, lips, and part of her nose, including the adjoining muscles, nerves, and blood vessels. The procedure took 15 hours and required the skills of 50 people in two medical teams. While a significant medical advancement, the operation prompted ethical questions about its usefulness and methods, as well as the psychological condition of the patient at the time.

FELINE TRANSPLANT

James Gueth of Melbourne, Australia, paid for his eight-year-old black cat Ninja to receive a kidney transplant in Sept. 2002. Dr. Victor Menrath performed the five-hour surgery at his Brisbane veterinary clinic. The donor was a two-year-old gray tabby named Paddington. The operation and related expenses cost Gueth an estimated $10,000. "Affordability was not an issue," he told the *Herald Sun* (Melbourne).

SUPERLATIVES

MOST TRANSPLANTED ORGANS The most organs received in one transplant procedure is eight. Alessia Di Matteo, a six-month-old Italian baby, received a liver, stomach, pancreas, small and large intestine, spleen, and two kidneys, in surgery performed at the University of Miami on Jan. 31, 2004. She survived for about a year, dying on Jan. 12, 2005. Alessia had a disorder that prevents normal functioning of the stomach, intestines, and kidneys and is generally fatal.

Vision

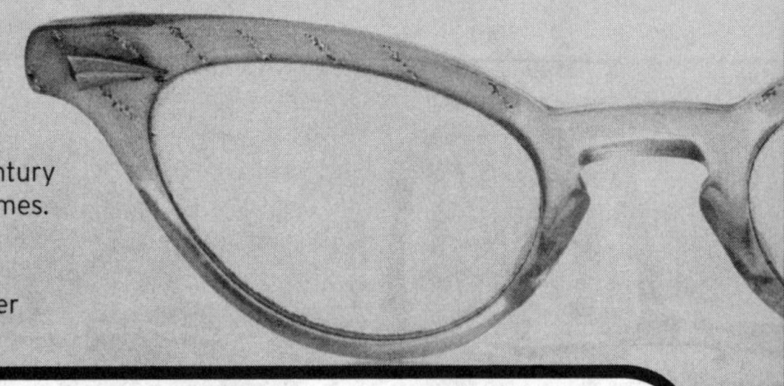

THE CHINESE MAY HAVE HAD A FORM OF EYEGLASSES by the 10th century AD, but these were only simple magnifying glasses placed in frames. In Europe eyeglasses were worn in the Middle Ages, as may be seen in some portraits dating from that time. With the invention of printing, good eyesight assumed more importance, and greater efforts were made to come up with effective eyeglasses.

MILESTONES

AROUND 600 BC: CATARACT SURGERY The earliest known surgery for cataracts (dark spots that block vision) is recorded in Sanskrit manuscripts from around 600 BC. The Hindu surgeon Susruta described pushing aside the clouded eye lens with a needle.

In 1745, the French ophthalmologist Jacques Daviel performed the first modern cataract operation, removing the cataract from the eye.

AROUND 1280: FIRST EYEGLASSES The Roman writer Pliny reported that the emperor Nero (reigned AD 45-68) used a concave emerald set in a ring to help him better see the events staged at the Colosseum. But true eyeglasses came much later. Most likely, the first step in developing true eyeglasses was taken by an Italian lay person in Pisa around 1280, who kept the process a profitable secret.

Alessandro di Spina, a Dominican monk, is credited with sharing the secret with the world. A fellow monk named Giordano da Rivalto first used the word *occhiali* ("eyeglasses") in a 1306 sermon.

Convex lenses for farsightedness became popular in the Middle Ages. Paintings of the late 13th and early 14th centuries depict scholars and religious figures wearing these eyeglasses, which were often associated with wisdom and learning.

Concave lenses were developed in the 15th century to correct problems of nearsightedness. A portrait of Pope Leo X by Raphael, painted in 1517, depicts the pontiff wearing eyeglasses with concave lenses. This portrait is the first evidence of their use.

AROUND 15TH CENTURY: SUNGLASSES It is believed that the first sunglass lenses were created in China during the Ming Dynasty (1368-1644). Made from smoke-colored quartz, the glasses were used more for hiding the wearer's eyes rather than for protecting them from the sun.

Tinted green sunglasses were used in the 17th century. Samuel Pepys, the English diary writer (1633-1703), wrote at one point about his eyes being irritated and bothering him. He thought that if he got some green lenses his eyes would feel better. In a later entry, he had acquired the glasses and his eyes did feel better.

1508: CONTACT LENS IDEA In 1508, Leonardo Da Vinci conceived of a lens that would correct vision defects at the cornea. In his writings, Da Vinci described how one might immerse the eye in a water-filled tube that was sealed with a lens.

In 1827, British astronomer Sir John F. W. Herschel proposed the first practical contact lens design. He suggested applying a layer of gelatin to the eye that would be held in place by a lens. It would be another 60 years before a physical lens would be developed based on the ideas of Herschel.

1727: TEMPLE ARMS Early forms of eyeglasses fitted on the user's nose with a bridge connecting the two lenses. A London optician named Edward Scarlett is believed to have invented spectacles, known as temple eyeglasses, with hinged side-arms that hooked around the ears to hold the glasses in place. Scarlett patented his invention in 1727.

1784: BIFOCALS The first bifocal eyeglasses, employing a divided lens with the top half for clearer distance vision and the bottom half for close-up vision, were devised by Benjamin Franklin in 1784.

One of America's more inventive Founding Fathers, Franklin suffered from poor eyesight in later life. At first he had two sets of glasses, one for seeing close objects, one for distant objects. Tired of having to constantly switch, he cut the lenses of each pair in half and put a piece of each in a frame, creating the bifocal lens.

1887: CONTACT LENSES In 1887, F. E. Muller, a German glass blower, designed the first usable eye-covering lens. He created one for a patient suffering from ulcers on his cornea; the patient wore the lens for 20 years.

In 1888, Adolf Eugene Fick, a Zurich physician, took molds of human cadaver eyes and created a contact lens out of blown glass in order to correct astigmatism. It was Fick who coined the term "contact lens."

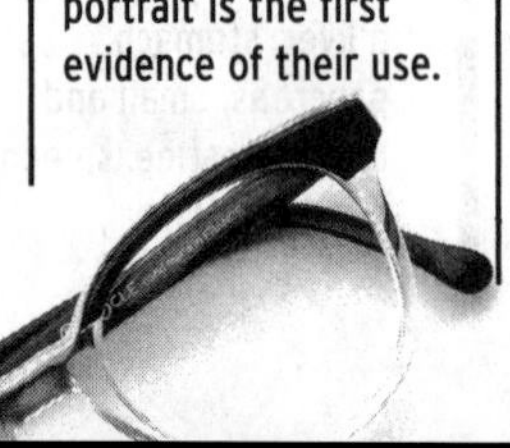

THE SILENT TYPE

Harold Lloyd, the silent film star, set records for popularity at the box office as a prop-oriented comic. Shedding traditional harlequin costumes, Lloyd wore distinguishing tortoise shell spectacles, and popularized the use of glasses, especially horn-rimmed ones, at a time when many people resisted their use.

SOMETHING TO THINK ABOUT

ARTIFICIAL EYE

On Jan. 17, 2000, it was announced a blind man, identified as "Jerry," had regained a form of limited vision with a "bionic eye." The man had been blinded by a blow to his head 26 years earlier. American eye specialist William Dobelle had been working for many years to develop an artificial eye when Jerry became his patient. Jerry had 68 platinum electrodes implanted in his brain 1978 and now wears glasses that are attached to a miniature camera and an infrared rangefinder. The camera sends signals to a small computer carried on the waist, which processes the images and sends signals back to the electrodes. Jerry does not "see" normally, but can visualize a series of dots that outline an object. He can comprehend only images straight ahead and at the equivalent of 20/400 vision.

SUPERLATIVES

OLDEST EYEGLASSES The earliest eyeglasses found so far are an incomplete pair of spectacles dating from the 14th century. The wooden frames were discovered under the floorboards of the Wienhausen monastery in northern Germany during renovations in 1953.

LIGHTEST GLASSES Roberto Carlon and Micromega Corp., based in Venice, Italy, designed the world's lightest eyeglass frames, which weigh about 0.03 ounces. They are hand stitched to the lens with titanium or 14-karat gold thread and are custom designed.

1928: REDUCED-GLARE SUNGLASSES The biggest step in the development of modern sunglasses was the invention of a synthetic polarizing filter by Edwin H. Land in 1928. This was the first modern filter to polarize light so that glare from light reflecting off roadways, water, and other surfaces could be reduced.

In 1932, Land and George Wheelwright III founded their own laboratory outside Boston (Wellesley Hills), and by the mid-1930s, Land had created various types of polarizing material for use in sunglasses, which he patented.

Land received 535 patents in his life—second only to Thomas Edison.

1929: MOLDED CONTACT LENSES Joseph Dallos, a Hungarian physician, perfected a method for taking molds of living eyes in 1929. This breakthrough allowed the development of glass lenses that conformed more closely to individual eyes.

Adolf Mueller-Welt, of Stuttgart, Germany, became the first person to produce large inventories of fluidless lenses that coul be marketed.

1947: CORNEAL LENSES Corneal lenses were a new design for contacts developed by Kevin Tuohy in 1947. From Tuohy's work, Oregon optometrist Dr. George Butterfield developed a new type of corneal lens in 1950. With Butterfield's "microlens," the inner surface follows the eye's shape instead of sitting flat. This better fitting lens was the beginning of the modern design.

1961: SOFT CONTACT LENS The first soft contact lens was developed by Czech chemist Otto Wichterle. He had created a hydrogel, a soft plastic that could absorb water, in the early 1950s. From this he produced the first gel contact lens in his home in Prague in 1961.

Wichterle's lens was easy to manufacture and easy to wear, and sparked a boom in contact lens use around the world.

1995: LASER EYE SURGERY In Oct. 1995 the first laser treatment for eye surgery was approved by the U.S. Food and Drug Administration. The excimer laser produces an ultraviolet beam of light emitted in pulses. It can be used for correcting mild to moderate nearsightedness in a process called photorefractive keratectomy (PRK).

In the PRK procedure, the laser is used to reshape the cornea by removing microscopic amounts of tissue from its outer surface.

A newer procedure, LASIK, approved in 1998, is more complex but can be performed for all degrees of nearsightedness. In LASIK, the surgeon uses a special knife to cut into a flap of corneal tissue, then removes tissue beneath it with the laser.

Drugs

DRUGS ARE POTENT SUBSTANCES used in or on the body for treating, alleviating, or preventing illnesses and disorders. People have used substances derived from plants, animals, and minerals to bring about changes in the body from time immemorial. But a remarkable explosion in the arsenal of therapeutic drugs began in the late 19th century, powered by developments in science and engineering. One wonder drug after another was introduced—ranging from new chemical therapies to antibiotics derived from substances created by living organisms to medicines developed with the help of genetic engineering.

MILESTONES

AROUND 1550 BC: EBERS PAPYRUS The longest (61 ft) and most important extant medical scroll is the ancient Egyptian Ebers papyrus, which dates from around 1550 BC. It describes about 880 prescriptions for everything from toenail pain to eye inflammation to birth control. One remedy for baldness used penis and vulva extracts along with a black lizard. Although not the oldest known health-related papyrus, the Ebers Papyrus is considered to be the most historically important since it is the first one to describe health issues without invoking religion or magic as the means to cure disease.

16TH CENTURY: PARACELSUS The Swiss physician and alchemist Theophrastus Bombastus von Hohenheim (c. 1493-1541), better known under the pseudonym Paracelsus, initiated a revolution in medicine comparable to that wrought in astronomy by his contemporary Copernicus.

Paracelsus (literally, "above or beyond Celsus"—a famous first-century Roman doctor and physician) resisted reliance on the authority of the ancients and sought to base medical practice on chemical and other scientific principles. He rejected the role of astrology in medicine and stressed the healing power of nature.

In 1530 he was credited with the best clinical description of syphilis. He established the role of chemistry in medicine, and today is remembered as a founding father of chemotherapy and also toxicology.

Parcelsus once said, "All substances are poisons: there is none which is not a poison. The right dose differentiates a poison and a remedy."

1897: ASPIRIN The most successful of the drugs resulting from chemists' flurry of activity in the latter part of the 19th century was aspirin. The formula was based on the salicylic acid found in plants that had long been used for easing pain and reducing fever. (Since as far back as 400 BC, Hippocrates had been prescribing willow tree bark and leaves, which contained mildly potent amounts of it.)

On Aug. 10, 1897, Felix Hoffmann, a chemist who worked for the German company Bayer, synthesized a form of salicylic acid called acetylsalicylic acid. Aspirin, as Bayer dubbed Hoffmann's substance, became one of the most widely-used drugs of all time. Today an estimated 80 million tablets are consumed each day in the U.S.

Hoffmann in 1897 also synthesized heroin, and Bayer trademarked the name. At the time it was valued as a cough suppressant, but that drug's future proved less bright.

1928: PENICILLIN Antibiotics are potent microbe-killing or microbe-inhibiting substances that are themselves produced by (or derived from) a micro-organism. Like many discoveries, the dicovery of the first antibiotic, penicillin, came about virtually by accident. In 1928, on returning from vacation, British bacteriologist Alexander Fleming noticed that a type of mold, *Penicillium notatum*, had gotten into one of the unwashed lab dishes containing staphylococci bacteria, and seemed to be destroying the bacteria.

Fleming studied the phenomenon, but the job of purifying the active ingredient (penicillin) and demonstrating its miraculous power against bacterial infection in humans did not get under way until 1939, in an effort led by two Oxford University scientists, Australian-born pathologist Howard Florey and German-born biochemist Ernst Chain.

In 1941 the U.S. began producing penicillin, and in 1945 Fleming, Florey, and Chain won the Nobel Prize in physiology or medicine.

The five top drugs in terms of promotional spending (sales representatives, medical journal ads, and the like) in the U.S. in 2004 are listed below; based on data from the pharmaceutical market researcher IMS Health.

Top Five Drugs (Promotional Spending)

RANK	DRUG	COMPANY	MAJOR USE	SPENDING
1	Lexapro	Forest	Depression, anxiety	$168.5 million
2	Celebrex[1]	Pfizer	Arthritis and other pain relief	$130.2 million
3	Crestor	AstraZeneca	Cholesterol	$125.0 million
4	Bextra[2]	Pfizer	Arthritis and other pain relief	$121.2 million
5	Lipitor	Pfizer	Cholesterol	$114.4 million

(1) Advertising curtailed in December 2004 because drug is associated with increased risk of cardiovascular problems. Carries warning label.
(2) Removed from the market in April 2005 because drug is associated with increased risk of cardiovascular problems and serious skin reactions

SOMETHING TO THINK ABOUT

THALIDOMIDE COMEBACK

It can take years for a drug's risks—and benefits—to come to light. When thalidomide was introduced in the mid-20th century, it was used as a sleeping pill and a treatment for morning sickness during pregnancy. At the time, doctors didn't know of any side effects. Unfortunately, thalidomide turned out to cause birth defects. Thousands of children were born with stunted or missing limbs or other deficiencies. Nearly half failed to live more than a year. Thalidomide was accordingly banned in many countries in the early 1960s. But researchers continued to study it, and in 1998 the U.S. Food and Drug Administration approved its use in treating erythema nodosum leprosum, a complication of leprosy. While thalidomide remains dangerous for pregnant women, it has shown signs of potential effectiveness for such conditions as myeloma and oral ulcers associated with HIV infection.

SUPERLATIVES

MOST COMMON MOOD-ALTERING DRUG Caffeine, a stimulant found in coffee, tea, cola drinks, and chocolate, is generally acknowledged as the world's most commonly used psychoactive drug. Although not an illicit substance, it is sometimes considered a drug of abuse; chronic ingestion can result in dependence, it can cause anxiety and panic attacks and sudden cessation can give rise to possible flu-like withdrawal symptoms. Extremely large doses can cause convulsions, and doses of several grams or more (depending on body weight) could even be fatal.

According to the National Coffee Association, almost 80% of American adults drink coffee at least on occasion, and more than half drink it every day. The Finnish consume the most coffee per capita though, averaging 24.7 pounds a year between 2000 and 2003; almost 95% of Finnish adults drink coffee.

HIGHEST DRUG EXPENDITURE (COUNTRY) The U.S. spends the most per capita on drugs. According to the Organization for Economic Co-operation and Development (OECD), in 2003, U.S. expenditure per person was $728. France, at $606, was No. 2, followed by Canada ($507) and Italy ($498).

HIGHEST DRUG USAGE (STATE) The state with the most retail prescriptions filled per capita in 2003 was Tennessee, with 16.5, compared to a national average of 10.7.

TOP-SELLING DRUG The world's No. 1 drug in terms of sales in 2004 was Pfizer's cholesterol-lowering Lipitor, which boasted global sales of $12 billion and was the first drug in history to surpass $10 billion in sales. In the U.S. 8,500 prescriptions were dispensed per hour.

Lagging behind in second place was another cholesterol drug, Merck's Zocor, which accounted for $5.9 billion in sales.

LARGEST DRUG COMPANY According to *Forbes* magazine's 2005 list of the world's largest companies, U.S.-based Pfizer ranks No. 1 in the Drugs & Biotechnology category, with sales of $52.52 billion, profits of $11.36 billion, and assets of $123.68 billion. Among all companies listed, it ranks 23rd worldwide.

BIGGEST ADVERTISER The drug company that spent the most on advertising in the U.S. in 2004 was Pfizer. According to *Advertising Age*, Pfizer's total U.S. ad spending of $2,957.3 million earned it the No. 4 ranking among all companies.

Other drug-related companies ranking high on the ad-spending list included Johnson & Johnson (No. 10 overall, with $2,175.7 million), GlaxoSmithKline (No. 11, with $1,828.3 million), Novartis (No. 21, with $1,284.6 million), and Merck (No. 24, with $1,250.3 million).

Vaccines

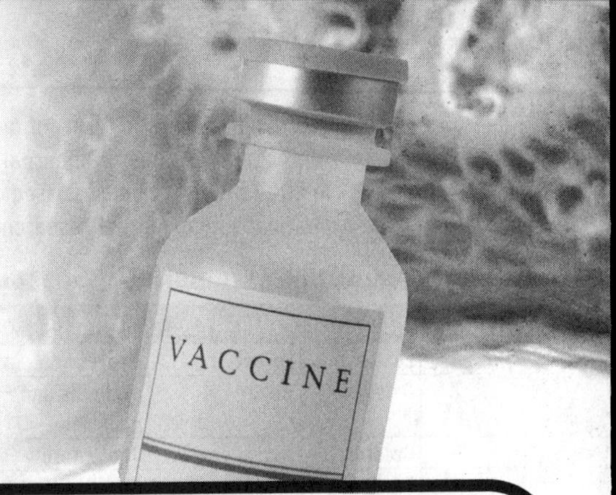

MICROBES, TINY ORGANISMS too small to be seen with the naked eye, have always played a role in people's lives. Most microbes are harmless. Some are even beneficial; without them we would not have leavened bread (made with yeast), yogurt, or alcohol. But others, in the form of fungi, bacteria, or viruses, cause infections and disease. A vaccine works by mildly infecting the body with a small amount of either a weakened or dead virus or bacterium. Because the microbes are weak, the patient isn't likely to get sick, but the body will be immune to future infections of the same type.

MILESTONES

1796: SMALLPOX

Caused by the variola virus, smallpox is believed to have appeared around 10,000 BC in northeastern Africa. It spread along trade routes to Asia Minor, killing up to 60% of those infected and leaving others with disfiguring scars.

Smallpox is the first disease for which an effective vaccine was discovered, before people even knew that viruses existed.

In 1796, an English doctor, Edward Jenner, decided to test the local country lore that people who caught cowpox, a mild viral infection from cows, could not catch smallpox. He took pus from the cowpox-infected hand of a milkmaid named Sarah Nelmes, and inserted it into an incision in the arm of James Phipps, the eight-year-old son of his gardener. Phipps proved immune to cowpox and smallpox. The process became known as vaccination from the Latin word *vacca*, meaning "cow."

No cure for smallpox has ever been found, but the World Health Organization announced in 1980 that the disease had been wiped out. Ali Maow Maalin, a cook in Somalia, was the last person to naturally contract smallpox, in 1977. Today, the virus exists only in laboratories.

1885: RABIES

Rabies is a viral disease most often passed on to people through the bite of an infected animal. It attacks the nervous system, causing brain damage and death. With the help of his associate, Emile Roux, the French scientist Louis Pasteur found that a weakened virus could be used to prevent serious infection.

Through a method called attenuation, a milestone process in modern medicine, Pasteur was able to harvest weaker and weaker strains of the rabies virus. On July 6, 1885, he tested his vaccine on Joseph Meister, a nine-year-old boy bitten 14 times by a rabid dog. Meister never got rabies.

Pasteur's work helped lead to an entirely new field of medical research called bacteriology. Today, rabies is highly curable through a series of shots if administered right away before symptoms appear.

1923: DIPHTHERIA

A bacterial disease that can cause paralysis of the diaphragm and heart failure, this once widespread, deadly disorder was known as "the strangler," and affected mostly children.

Gaston Ramon of the Pasteur Institute in 1923 developed a vaccine against diphtheria, which was not widely used until the early 1930s. In 1949 it was combined with tetanus and pertussis vaccines to form DTP. In the U.S. today there are on average only one to three diphtheria cases a year.

1927: TUBERCULOSIS (TB)

TB is a bacterial lung infection that can be fatal; it causes more deaths worldwide than any other single infectious disease except HIV/AIDS and was declared a "global emergency" by the World Health Organization in 1993.

Beginning in 1908, French bacteriologist Albert Calmette and veterinarian Jean Camille Guerin spent 13 years weakening a strain of cow TB bacteria. They created a living but harmless strain for use as a vaccine, Bacillus Calmette-Guerin, or BCG.

Since its widespread introduction in 1927, BCG has been the most widely used TB vaccine in the world. However in recent years, BCG has been shown to have a low success rate, and it is no longer even recommended for use in the U.S., where the disease is rare (about 5.1 cases per 100,000 people). Instead, those infected are given a cocktail of antibiotics.

1927: TETANUS

Tetanus is the only vaccine-preventable disease that is not communicable. It is acquired through environmental exposure, usually through a wound, and causes severe muscular spasms and contractions, including lockjaw. The bacteria can be found everywhere, but mostly in street dirt.

Gaston Ramon and medical officer Christian Zoeller first demonstrated active immunity to tetanus in human subjects in 1927.

1940s: INFLUENZA

For most people, the flu means a week in

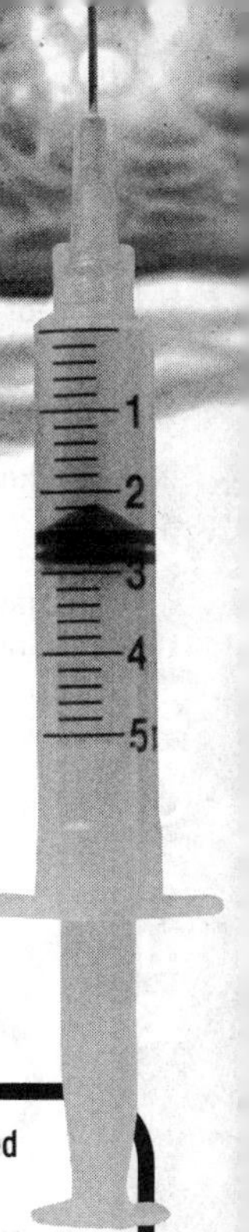

Some Other Vaccines

DISEASE	VACCINE DEVELOPED BY	PLACE	YEAR
Anthrax	George Wright, Thomas Green, & Ralph Kanode Jr.	U.S. Army	1954
Hepatitis A+B	GlaxoSmithKline	U.S.	2001
Leprosy	National Institute of Immunology	India	1998
Lyme disease	SmithKline Beecham	U.S.	1998
Meningitis	Emil C. Gotschlich	U.S. Army	1970
Mumps	Merck & Co	U.S.	1967
Plague	Waldemar M. Haffkine (Russian)	India	1897
Pneumococcal pneumonia	Merck	U.S.	1977
Rubella	Meyer and Parkman, Prinzie and Huygelen, and Plotkin	U.S.	1969
Typhoid	Almroth Wright & Richard Pfeiffer	Britain & Germany	1896
Varicella (Chickenpox)	Michiaki Takahashi	Japan	1974
Yellow Fever	Andrew W. Sellards & Jean Laigret	France	1932

bed with chicken soup, but it is responsible for approximately 36,000, mostly elderly, deaths per year in the U.S.

The word *influenza* originated in 15th-century Italy from the belief that epidemics were due to the "influence" of the stars.

The U.S. Armed Forces Epidemiological Board in the early 1940s commissioned civilian doctors and medical scientists to come up with a vaccine to prevent epidemics among troops during World War II. Since then, the U.S. government has taken an active role in flu immunization.

In 1976, President Gerald Ford authorized $135 million for a national immunization program to fight swine flu, which is closely related to the Spanish flu that killed some 20-50 million people between 1918 and 1919.

Since then, experts have tried to predict each year which strains of flu will be prevalent. They then develop the vaccines needed for the year. These flu shots are effective in most cases, but not foolproof.

1954: MEASLES

At one time, before a vaccine was available, contracting the measles was like a rite of passage. There was an average of more than 500,000 cases annually in the U.S. between 1958 and 1962, mostly among children. The cases were often severe and occasionally fatal.

Researchers John Enders and Tom Peebles isolated the virus in human and monkey kidney tissue culture in 1954, but it took ten years for their strain to be licensed for use in the U.S.

Since 1972, a combination measles, mumps, and rubella (MMR) vaccine has become routine, but measles is still a common and often fatal disease in developing countries today.

1954: POLIO

Poliomyelitis was the scourge of children, paralyzing thousands each year until its peak in the U.S. in 1952. At first, efforts to find a vaccine were stymied because no one realized that polio was caused by several viruses and not just one.

Dr. Jonas Salk, who began researching the disease at the University of Pittsburgh in 1947, developed the inactivated poliovirus vaccine (IPV) in 1952 using three types of killed polio viruses, which stimulated production of antibodies.

On April 26, 1954, the National Foundation for Infantile Paralysis delivered "the shot felt around the world." Over the next year, about 1.8 million schoolchildren in the U.S. and Canada were injected either with a vaccine or with an inactive substance known as a placebo. It was the largest voluntary clinical trial ever, and was immensely successful.

In 1961, Albert Sabin developed the oral polio vaccine using weakened rather than killed strains of the virus. Sabin's vaccine became the preferred method for stopping the virus.

Until 2005, when several cases in the U.S. were reported, there had not been a single locally contracted case in the U.S. since 1979. Worldwide, there were about 1,500 cases reported in 2005.

2005: BIRD FLU

In Aug. 2005, U.S. government researchers reported promising results from clinical tests of a vaccine that could be effective against the avian flu, an often deadly new form of influenza that is transmitted between birds and could begin to spread significantly to humans.

Dentistry

REGULAR BRUSHING AND FLOSSING of teeth is not an invention of modern day parents. Evidence of dental care, and tooth decay, dates back thousands of years. A cuneiform tablet from ancient Sumeria, around 5000 BC suggests that cavities are caused by small worms in the mouth. The first named dentist known to history, Hesy-Re, plied his trade in Egypt around 2600 BC, and the oldest evidence of a surgical operation dates back to 2750 BC in Egypt. The evidence is a human jawbone with two holes just below the root of the first molar, indicating the drainage of an abscessed tooth. Researchers have found a kind of dental floss and toothpick grooves in the teeth of ancient human fossils from Africa to Australia.

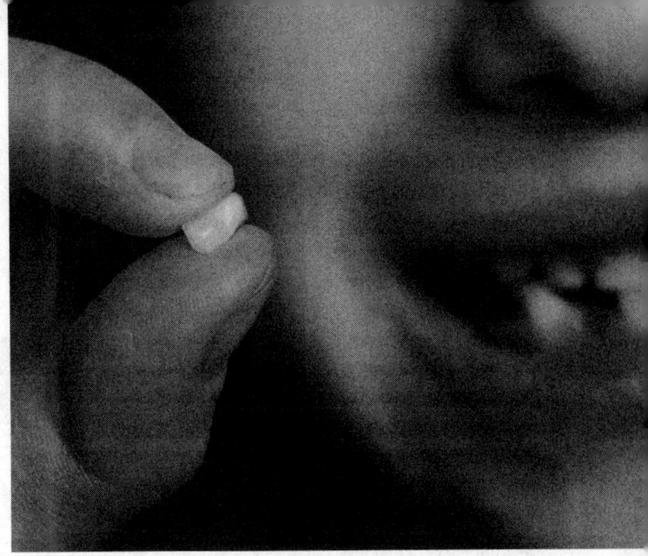

MILESTONES

47 AD: TOOTHPASTE FORMULA The earliest known written toothpaste formula is found in *Compositiones Medicamentorum*, the work of the Roman physician Scribonius Largus from around 47 AD. A doctor at the court of the Roman emperor Claudius, Largus devised three different "toothpaste" mixtures containing such ingredients as vinegar, honey, salt, and very finely ground glass.

1498: TOOTHBRUSH WITH BRISTLES The first toothbrushes made using natural bristles appeared in China in 1498. These brushes used hair from the neck of pigs attached to handles made of bone or bamboo.

Boar's hair was commonly used until 1938, when DuPont Co. introduced nylon bristles.

1790: DENTAL CHAIR Prior to the 18th century the standard dental care position for the patient was to wedge his or her head between the dentist's knees. In the early 1500s, dentists in Milan, Italy, had started the practice of using a chair for dental examinations. But it was Josiah Flagg, an American dentist, who created the first chair actually tailored for dentists, when he attached an adjustable headrest to a wooden chair in 1790.

While James Snell, an English surgeon, is credited with designing the first reclining dental chair in 1832, it was James Beall Morrison, an Ohioan living in London, who designed the first truly adjustable one, in 1867. A heavy base allowed the seat to rotate on a ball and socket joint. It had an adjustable headrest and backrest.

1863: TOOTHPICK MACHINE Benjamin F. Sturtevant patented a toothpick making machine on June 2, 1863, while running his shoe peg factory in Boston. Silas Noble and James P. Cooley of Granville, MA, received a patent for an improved toothpick making machine on Feb. 20, 1872. With their device, 7.5 million toothpicks could be made from one cord of wood.

1874: ELECTRIC DENTAL DRILL In 1864, George F. Harrington of England designed the Erado, the first "motor driven" drill. It used a clockwork mechanism by which a spring could be wound up and then released for two minutes. George F. Green of Kalamazoo, MI, invented a pneumatic drill powered by pedals in 1871.

Green, a mechanic with the S.S. White Company, continued to refine his drill and in 1874 produced the first electric dental drill. Powered by electromagnetic motors, the drill reached a speed of up to 4,000 revolutions per minute. Green received a patent for his device in 1875.

1884: ANESTHETICS The first local anesthetic used in dental care was cocaine, introduced as an anesthetic for eye surgery by Czech-born American ophthalmologist Carl Koller in 1884.

German chemist Alfred Einhorn introduced procaine hydrochloride in 1905 as a replacement for the highly addictive cocaine. The substance was discovered while Einhorn was researching a safe local anesthetic. He named the product Novocaine, from *novus* ("new" in Latin) and *cocaine*. Novocaine quickly became the standard dental anesthetic.

1892: TUBE OF TOOTHPASTE A New London, CT, chemist and dental surgeon named Dr. Washington Wentworth Sheffield

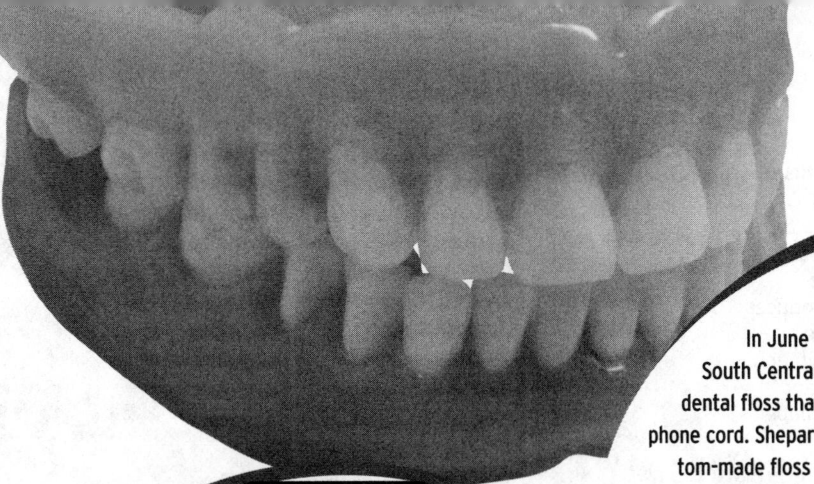

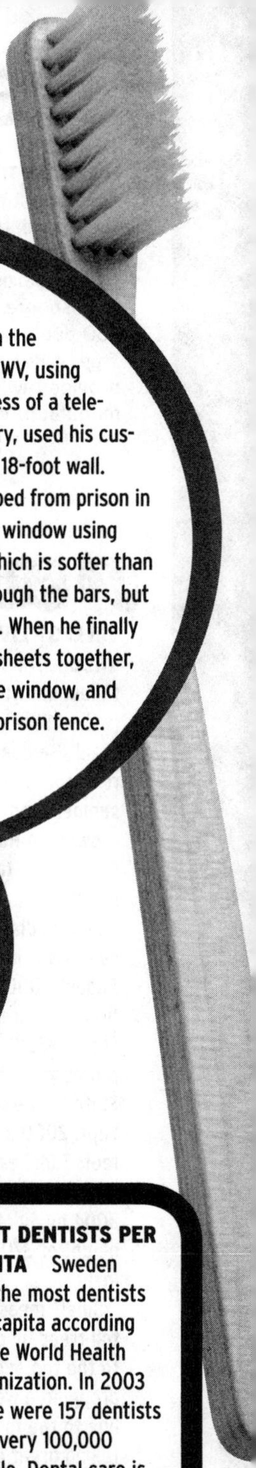

FALSE ARREST

False teeth can be illegal in some states and may even be considered weapons. A Vermont law requires married women to get permission from their husbands in order to buy false teeth. In Louisiana, if you feel the urge to bite someone, then make sure you do it with your natural teeth. Biting another person with natural teeth is legally regarded as simple assault, but if you chomp at someone using false teeth, you can be charged with aggravated assault.

FREE, BUT WERE THEIR TEETH CLEAN?

In June 1994, Robert Shepard escaped from the South Central Regional Jail in South Charleston, WV, using dental floss that he braided into a rope the thickness of a telephone cord. Shepard, who was awaiting trial for robbery, used his custom-made floss rope to scale the recreation yard's 18-foot wall.

In April 2000, convicted murderer Vincenzo Curcio escaped from prison in Turin, Italy, after sawing through the bars on his cell window using dental floss. The prison had bars made of ductile iron, which is softer than steel or normal iron. It took him several days to cut through the bars, but none of the prison's 800 guards noticed his handiwork. When he finally "flossed" through the last of the bars, he tied his bedsheets together, climbed out of the window, and scaled the prison fence.

SOMETHING TO THINK ABOUT

DENTAL CARING

Volunteer dentists, hygienists, and other dental care providers treated 2,200 people at Pittsburg State University in Kansas City, MO, over a three-day weekend at the beginning of May 2004. Dr. Ron Strader, one of the leaders of the Kansas Mission of Mercy clinic, claimed it was "the largest short-term missionary project—anywhere, any time." Eight dental chair and drill units were loaned to the mission team from other dental missions in Virginia. Other equipment belonged to the Kansas Mission of Mercy. After being cleaned and sterilized, all the equipment was taken to Topeka for storage until the group's next free clinic.

first produced toothpaste in a collapsible tube. Sheffield Laboratories, the current name of the company founded by Dr. Sheffield in the 19th century, gives the credit for the idea to his son, Dr. Lucius Tracy Sheffield.

As a young man traveling in Europe, Lucius had seen painters use oil paints stored in metal tubes. His father was already selling his own toothpaste, Dr. Sheffield's Crème Dentrifice, in porcelain jars, but Lucius had a better idea. His father agreed and his company switched to using metal tubes in 1892.

No, no one has yet figured out how to put the paste back in the tube.

SUPERLATIVES

FIRST DENTIST TO WALK TO THE MAGNETIC NORTH POLE Dr. Hannah Shields from Derry, Northern Ireland, became the first Irish woman and the first dentist to walk to the magnetic north pole. Dr. Shields and her teammate, Dr. Christoffer van Tulleken, walked 285 miles from the Polaris Mine in Nunavut, in the Canadian Arctic, as part of the Fujitsu Polar Challenge 2004. The pair finished second in the race, covering the distance in 11 days. In 2003, Dr. Shields came within 318 feet of reaching the top of Mt. Everest before her frostbite had become too severe to continue.

MOST DENTISTS PER CAPITA Sweden has the most dentists per capita according to the World Health Organization. In 2003 there were 157 dentists for every 100,000 people. Dental care is funded partially by the government, and in 2002 the total cost for dental care was approximately $1.56 billion.

Trees

TREES ARE THE WORLD'S LONGEST-LIVING ORGANISMS and largest plants. Excluding Antarctica and Greenland, trees cover nearly a third of the world's land surface. Vital to human existence, they convert carbon dioxide into oxygen, replenishing the atmosphere. It is estimated that one tree produces 260 pounds of oxygen each year, on average. Trees can also prevent soil erosion, bear fruit, and provide raw material for construction, fuel, and manufactured products such as rubber and paper.

SUPERLATIVES

TALLEST LIVING TREE The world's tallest known tree is the "Stratosphere Giant," a coast redwood, *Sequoia sempervirens*, growing in Humboldt Redwoods State Park in California. The tree was discovered by Chris Atkins in August 2000 and first measured by Steve Sillett, a botany professor at Humboldt State University, in Sept. 2000 at 368 feet, 7 inches tall. It was measured in late 2004 by Sillett at a height of 370 feet, 2 inches.

Sillett measures tall trees by climbing to the top and then dropping a weighted line to the forest floor, taking great care not to damage the fragile trees. He uses slack ropes, so as not to damage the bark, and always climbs barefoot.

The Stratosphere Giant bettered the mark of the Federation Giant (now 368 ft, 11 in), which was previously considered the tallest and grows in the same park.

In fact, there is something of a slow horse race at Humboldt for the title of tallest tree. These two trees, plus the National Geographic Society Tree (369 ft, 6 in) and the Paradox Tree (368 ft, 6 in), are all still growing—though tree growth typically slows at great heights—and are measured annually.

ALL-TIME TALLEST TREE A fallen eucalyptus tree measured in the 19th century is considered the tallest tree of all time. Located in Watts River, Victoria, Australia, the dead tree was measured on the ground at 435 feet long in 1872.

LARGEST LIVING TREE The biggest living tree (by trunk volume) is a giant sequoia, *Sequoiadendron giganteum*, located in California's Sequoia National Park. Dubbed "General Sherman" by admirers of the Civil War general in 1879, the colossal tree has a volume of about 52,500 cubic feet and weighs an estimated 6,167 tons—about as much as 41 blue whales or 740 elephants.

In Dec. 2000, the U.S. Geological Survey reported it had used new estimation methods to determine that the tree was probably just over 2,200 years old, a downgrade from previous estimates of 4,000 to 6,000 years old. General Sherman, however, is still growing, adding enough wood each year to make a tree one foot in diameter 100 feet taller.

ALL-TIME LARGEST TREE The most massive tree ever discovered was the "Lindsey Creek Tree," a coast redwood that grew in Northern California. The volume of its trunk was estimated at about 90,000 cubic feet. The tree fell during a storm in 1905.

General Sherman was officially measured in 1975; its volume was then calculated at slightly over 52,500 cubic feet.

More of the General's Vital Statistics

Height above Base	274.9 ft
Circumference at Ground	102.6 ft
Maximum Diameter at Base	36.5 ft
Diameter 60 ft above Base	17.5 ft
Diameter 180 ft above Base	14.0 ft
Diameter of Largest Branch	6.8 ft
Height of First Large Branch above the Base	130.0 ft
Average Crown Spread	106.5 ft
Source: National Park Service	

SOMETHING TO THINK ABOUT

THE SHOE TREE

A 70-foot-tall cottonwood tree, standing just off Highway 50 outside of Middlegate, NV, about 100 miles east of Reno, is one of the must-see roadside attractions in the U.S. Known locally as "The Shoe Tree," the huge tree has hundreds of pairs of footwear of all sizes and styles, from running shoes to roller skates, dangling from its branches. Silhouetted against a surrounding landscape of flat scrubland and a long gray ribbon of highway pavement, "The Shoe Tree" is a dramatic, quirky site. Local lore has it that around 15 years ago, a newlywed couple stopped to camp overnight on the roadside near the tree. When they had a tiff and the new bride said she was going home, the groom tossed her shoes into the tree and told her she would have to walk home barefoot. It's said that the couple quickly made up, and returned to the tree a year later, with their new baby, whose first shoes were thrown into the tree.

PHANTOM PLANTER

Since Jan. 2004, someone has been secretly planting oak trees in the rural Oak Park section of east Ventura County, CA. The "Mystery Tree Planter," as the furtive arborist has been nicknamed, had planted 20 oak trees by July 2005 and has even returned to water them. Officials investigated people living in the adjacent neighborhood, but no one has yet witnessed the covert cultivating. Mike Enge, the district's grounds maintenance supervisor, has suggested forming a watch group, explaining, "We want to talk to him and give him some recognition. We're not looking at punishment."

ANCIENT TREE

The Wollemi Pine, *Wollemia nobilis*, was presumed to have been extinct for 2 million years, until park ranger David Noble found a cluster nestled in a narrow canyon at Australia's Wollemi National Park on Sept. 10, 1994. The oldest fossil of this prehistoric conifer species dates to 90 million years before the present (BP), although scientists believe the Wollemi may have grown up to 200 million years BP. Its leaves are not typical pine needles but are rather fern-like and flat. Samples have shown the Wollemi can grow up to 130 feet tall and 3 feet in diameter and live about 400 years. Yet its ability to develop multiple trunks (coppicing) means the roots could be thousands of years old. It was first planted in the U.S. on Feb. 9, 1998, and has been sold on a limited scale since Oct. 2005.

BIGGEST CHRISTMAS "TREE"

The annual Christmas market in Dortmund, Germany, often claims to be the home of the world's largest Christmas tree. Though Dortmund's Christmas symbol has impressive proportions (145 ft high, 45 ft wide) and is visited by over 2 million people each holiday season, it is not actually a tree. The "World's Largest Christmas Tree" is, in fact, about 1,700 fir trees, stacked closely together in the shape of a giant tree, adorned with over 13,000 twinkling lights.

THE TREE THAT OWNS ITSELF

A large white oak at the top of South Finley Street in Athens, GA, is the descendant of an oak so beloved by its owner, Col. W. H. Jackson, that he deeded the tree to itself upon his death in 1832. A plaque at the oak's base is inscribed with the deed's original words, which gives it "entire possession of itself and all land within 8 feet of the tree on all sides." Although the original tree blew down during a storm in 1942, four years later the citizens of Athens planted a seedling grown from one of the original tree's acorns. The Junior Ladies Garden Club has nurtured it ever since.

OLDEST LIVING TREE SPECIES The Ginkgo, *Ginkgo biloba*, also known as the maidenhair tree, is the world's oldest living tree species. Its origins date back over 250 million years. *Ginkgo biloba* is the only remaining species in the *ginkgoales* order of plants, which thrived during the Jurassic period (195 to 135 million years ago), but declined as the last dinosaurs died off, about 65 million years ago.

Thought to enhance memory and slow the effects of aging, *Gingko biloba* leaves have become one of the most popular herbal supplements in the U.S.

LARGEST TREE SEED The double-coconut palm, *Lodoicea maldivica*, only grows on two small islands of the Seychelles group in the Indian Ocean. The tree, also known as the coco-de-mer, has seeds that weigh up to 40 pounds, and can be a foot long and 3 feet in circumference.

Plants & Gardens

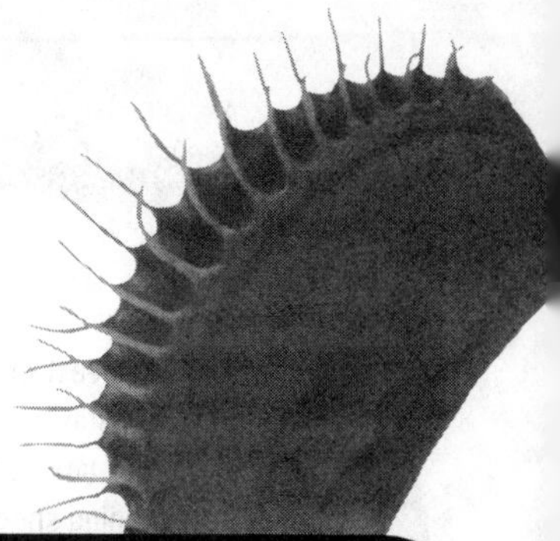

PLANTS HAVE FASCINATED HUMANKIND from the beginning of time. Whether our interest is in their scientific or medicinal properties, or simply to revel in their sheer beauty, the plant kingdom continues to be a source of wonder. And some of that wonder is captured in gardens, from those of the grandest palaces to the very smallest herbaceous borders in a tiny front yard, or an urban roof garden.

MILESTONES

ANTIQUITY: PARADISE The earliest gardens were created by the ancient Persians as walled oases which they called "pairidaeza," a word we know as "paradise."

The earliest surviving Persian garden was built by Cyrus the Great around 550 BC. It followed the traditional garden design, with waterways dividing the lush foliage into four quarters. Today it is a UNESCO World Heritage Site.

Persian garden design remained influential for centuries; one of the best-known Persian gardens is at the Taj Mahal in Agra, India.

AROUND 300 BC: FATHER OF BOTANY Theophrastus of Lesbos, Greece, is considered the father of botany, and his *Enquiry into Plants*, nine volumes of description and classification of the plant kingdom, is considered the most important classical botanical work. It covered more than 300 plants, including some brought back by Alexander the Great from his Asian expedition.

1543: BOTANICAL GARDEN The first modern garden for scientific purposes was founded by Luca Ghini at the University of Pisa in 1543, and contained medicinal herbs, vegetables, and leaves. It moved to its current location in 1591.

The oldest garden still in its original location was founded at the University of Padua on June 29, 1545. Its oldest tree, a palm (*Chamaerops humilis*), dates to 1585.

1593: TULIPS IN HOLLAND Tulips originally grew in Central Asia and Turkey. Their name comes from the vulgar Turkish pronunciation—*tul(i)band*—of the Persian word *dulband*, which means "turban." Ogier Ghiselin de Busbecq, a diplomat for Hapsburg Emperor Ferdinand I, was stationed at the court of Sultan Suleiman the Magnificent from 1555 to 1562. During that time he sent tulip bulbs back to Charles de l'Ecluse, Ferdinand's doctor and prefect of the imperial gardens in Vienna. When de l'Ecluse accepted a professorship at the University of Leiden in 1593, he introduced tulips to the Dutch. The interest in the flower was enormous, and by 1637, "tulipmania" was in full flower.

1648: DISCOVERY OF PHOTOSYNTHESIS Flemish physician and chemist Jan Baptista van Helmont was the first to show that plants obtain nutrients through photosynthesis, the conversion of energy from the sun. To test his hypothesis, he planted a willow tree, weighing both the willow and the soil. Five years later, he weighed the tree and the soil again. Although the willow had gained 169 pounds, the soil had lost practically no weight.

Van Helmont's works were published in 1648, four years after he died, as *The Fount of Medicine*.

1753: PLANT NAMES In the 16th century, naturalists like Valerius Cordus began recording large numbers of new plants, along with their traits. Between 1736 and 1766, Swedish botanist Carolus Linnaeus devised a new taxonomy, sorting plant classes by number of male stamens and orders by female pistils. In *Species Plantarum* (1753), Linnaeus organized about 8,000 plants using binomial nomenclature. His classification system is still used today.

1760: HYBRIDS German botanist Joseph Gottlieb Kölreuter experimented with hybrids between 1760 and 1766, using tobacco plants (*Nicotiana paniculata* and *N. rustica*). While other botanists had grown hybrids earlier in the century, Kölreuter was the first to do so scientifically. He also demonstrated the roles that insects and wind play in pollination.

1830: LAWNMOWER The first mechanical lawnmower was patented in 1830, by Edwin Beard Budding of Gloucestershire, England. His design was based on the rotary blades used in textile mills. The cast-iron mower required two men to operate.

Leonard Goodall, of Warrensburg, MO, patented the first rotary power mower on July 23, 1940. It remains the most popular type in the U.S. today.

SOMETHING TO THINK ABOUT

CAPTURE, KILL, AND DIGEST

Carnivorous plants, of which there are more than 600 species and subspecies, are the stuff of science fiction movies and Broadway plays. There are two types: those with passive traps—pitcher plants, for example, with vaselike leaves—and those with active traps that close up around their prey, like the Venus Fly Trap. In spite of *The Little Shop of Horrors*, carnivorous plants pose no danger to people. Even the largest of carnivorous plants, the nepenthe, captures nothing bigger than the occasional frog.

WHAT'S THAT SMELL?

The world's smelliest flower, *Amorphophallus titanium*, or Titan Arum, also known as corpse flower, looks spectacular but smells horrible. The giant plant emits the smell of rotting flesh so as to attract the insects that pollinate it; it can be detected from half a mile away.

SUPERLATIVES

LARGEST FLOWER The Indonesian flower *Rafflesia arnoldii*, nicknamed the stinking corpse lily, has the biggest bloom of any flower. It grows up to 36 inches wide and weighs as much as 15 pounds, with petals an inch thick. The flower and a related plant, Titan Arum (*Amorphophallus titanium*), both smell like rotting flesh to attract flies and carrion beetles to pollinate them.

SMALLEST FLOWER The *Wolffia angusta* from Australia and the world-spanning tropical *W. globosa* are tiny rootless plants in the duckweed family. Floating on the surface of streams and ponds, the plants, on average are about 0.6 mm long, and weigh about the same as two grains of salt.

LARGEST BULB EXPORTER The Netherlands, which has been one of the leading cultivators of flower bulbs for over 400 years, is the largest exporter of bulbs. It exported $2.2 billion worth of flower bulbs between 2001 and 2004, 62% of the world's total.

The Netherlands is also the lead exporter of cut flowers, selling $7.9 billion worth between 2001 and 2004.

LARGEST SEED COLLECTION The Millennium Seed Bank Project at England's Royal Botanic Gardens has the greatest number of plant seed specimens, with 23,742 samples—from 11,870 identified species—as of July 2005. The Project aims to collect and conserve about 24,000 species, or 10% of the world's seed-bearing flora, by 2010.

LARGEST GREENHOUSE The Eden Project, which opened on March 17, 2001, in Cornwall, Great Britain, houses the largest greenhouse in the world. The Humid Tropics Biome, the larger of its two greenhouses, is a geodesic dome measuring 787 feet long, 361 feet wide, and 164 feet high (11,657,724.6 cubic feet). It replicates four types of tropical rainforest and has an 82-foot high waterfall. The two biomes house over 100,000 plants.

LARGEST HORTICULTURAL SHOW The Hampton Court Palace Flower Show in Surrey, England, is the world's largest horticultural show. In 2005 there were 18 show gardens, 30 small gardens and 6 water gardens, and more than 700 exhibitors. The show takes 2,000 people three weeks to set up.

The gardens are also home to the Great Vine, the oldest and biggest vine in the world, which was planted as a cutting in 1768 by the famous landscape gardener Lancelot "Capability" Brown. Over 120 feet long, it takes up four greenhouses and produces over 500 pounds of grapes annually.

Agriculture

HUMANS WERE HUNTER-GATHERERS until small groups of people began cultivating plants and domesticating animals around 10,000 BC. Early agriculture began near ready water sources, including the Nile River in Egypt, China's Huang He (Yellow) River, and the Indus River on the Indian subcontinent. The earliest evidence of animal domestication comes from the "fertile crescent," which arcs from the eastern Mediterranean coast to the Persian Gulf. With the advent of agriculture, people began living in permanent settlements and building great civilizations.

SUPERLATIVES

LARGEST FARM
The world's largest farms are cattle ranches (known as "stations" in some parts of the world), which require extensive grazing lands to be successful. The world's biggest cattle ranch is said to be Anna Creek Station, in South Australia. It covers over 11,620 square miles, making it bigger than the state of Massachusetts.

MOST FARMS (STATE) The number of farms in the U.S. has dropped by about 66% nationwide since 1940, to 2.11 million in 2004. Meanwhile the size of the average farm has gone up from 174 acres to 443.

Iowa had the greatest number of farms in 2004: 89,700, covering 31.7 million acres. Montana had the most farmland: 60.1 million acres.

CROP PRODUCTION

LARGEST CORN PRODUCERS
The U.S. is by far the world's largest producer of corn, which is grown on about 400,000 U.S. farms. The nation produced 11.8 million bushels of the starchy staple in 2004, or some 42% of the world's crop.

Of all the states, Iowa produced the most corn for grain; its farms yielded 2.24 billion bushels in 2004.

LARGEST WHEAT PRODUCERS China is the world's largest producer of wheat, harvesting 100.6 million tons in 2004, which is 15% of the world's crop.

In the U.S., Kansas grew the most wheat in 2004, producing 314.5 million bushels.

LARGEST BARLEY PRODUCERS Russia produced 19.0 million tons of barley in 2004, which is about 11% of the world total.

North Dakota produced 91.8 million bushels in 2004, more barley than any other state.

LARGEST SOYBEAN PRODUCERS
The U.S. dominates soybean production, harvesting around 94.2 million tons in 2004, which is 42% of world production.

Illinois grew the biggest soybean crop in the U.S., with a harvest of 500 million bushels.

LARGEST RICE PRODUCERS China is the world's largest producer of rice, growing 195.1 million tons in 2004, which is 29% of the world harvest.

Arkansas produced 53.7 million tons of rice in 2004, more than any other state.

LARGEST COTTON PRODUCERS China is the world's largest cotton producer, growing 6.9 million tons (in the 2004-05 growing season), which represented 27% of the world production.

Texas beat all other states, with a crop of 7.5 million bales of cotton (1.8 million tons) in 2004.

LARGEST COFFEE PRODUCERS There is an awful lot of coffee grown in Brazil; the nation produced 2.7 million tons of coffee beans in 2004, representing 32% of the world's crop. That number has more than doubled since 1995.

Hawaii is the only U.S. state that grows coffee, and produced 2,800 tons in 2004.

LARGEST SUGAR PRODUCERS Brazil is the largest sugar producer in the world, growing 453 million tons (from sugarcane) in 2004; this represents 17% of the world's sugar production, both cane and beets.

Florida produced 13.4 million tons of sugarcane for sugar in 2004.

U.S. Per Capita Consumption Of Selected Foods

STATISTICS SHOW THAT AMERICANS ARE EATING A LOT MORE POULTRY

	1940	2003
Red Meat	92.4 pounds	111.9 pounds
Poultry	12.3 pounds	71.2 pounds
Whole Milk	29.2 gallons	7.6 gallons
Low Fat/Skim Milk	4.7 gallons	13.9 gallons
Butter	17.0 pounds	4.2 pounds
Margarine	2.4 pounds	6.2 pounds

SOMETHING TO THINK ABOUT

ANT FARM

Humans weren't the first farmers. Many kinds of bugs were farming 40-60 million years ago. About 210 species of ants, 330 of termites, and 3,400 of beetles today are known to practice some sort of cultivation. Leafcutter ants have developed some of the most advanced techniques. Worker ants of the species collect plant material—leaves, wood, pulp—to fertilize fungus gardens in their hills, which they vigilantly tend, harvesting one type and weeding out foreign spores. When an ant princess colonizes a new nest, she brings along fungus to start a new garden.

SHEER SHREK

In New Zealand, sheep outnumber people by about 10 to 1 (40,049,000 sheep to 4,035,461 people in 2004), so it's hard for one sheep to stand out. But Shrek, a merino ram, can probably lay claim to being the most famous sheep in the country. Shrek was captured in 2004 after six years on the lam, during which he grew a huge fleece. The size drew so much attention that he was sheared on live television by Peter Casserly, a former world champion blade shearer.

It took around 15 minutes for the shears to trim off some 60.6 pounds of fine merino wool, which was auctioned off to raise money for children's charities.

BEEFED UP

Nearly all the beef consumed in the oil-rich Sultanate of Brunei in southeast Asia is produced on the Brunei-owned Wileroo cattle ranch in the Northern Territory of Australia. This 2,262-square-mile ranch by itself is larger than the tiny 2,228-square mile nation on the coast of Borneo.

WHY DID THE CHICKEN CROSS THE ROAD?

In this case, the answer is: to go to traffic court. On March 26, 2005, a chicken owned by Linc and Helena Moore of Johannesburg, CA, wandered into the road by their house. The Moores were issued a $54 citation for violating a state law that forbids livestock on the highway. They appealed the fine, and won the case.

The judge dismissed the ticket after being convinced by the Moore's lawyer that the chicken was a domesticated animal, not livestock.

LARGEST OLIVE PRODUCERS Olive production varies dramatically from one year to the next depending on the climate and other growing conditions. Spain, the leading producer (5.5 million tons in 2004), has nearly 6 million acres of trees, the largest area in the world dedicated to growing olives. The nation grows between 4 and 8 million tons of olives every year, over 30% of the world's supply.

In the U.S., California grows the most olives, usually over 100,000 tons.

LARGEST GRAPE PRODUCERS Italy, the world's biggest grape producer, grew 9.6 million tons of grapes in 2004, 13% of the world's supply.

California was the largest producer in the U.S., growing 5.6 million tons in 2004.

LARGEST COCONUT PRODUCER Indonesia grew 18 million tons worth of coconuts in 2004, about 30% of the world's supply.

LIVESTOCK

MOST CATTLE Brazil had about 192 million cattle in 2004, about 14% of the world's population. India had the second largest supply in 2004 at 185.5 million head, but had led the world until 2002. However, cattle meat is not eaten by adherents of Hinduism, which is India's majority religion.

In the U.S., Texas led the states with 13.9 million head of cattle in 2004. California had the most dairy cows (1.7 million), followed by Wisconsin (1.3 million).

MOST PIGS Almost half of the world's swine live in China, which had about 472.9 million hogs in 2004.

North Carolina had 9.9 million head of hogs in that year, more than any other state.

MOST SHEEP China is home to about 156 million sheep, around 15% of the world's total.

In the U.S., Texas had the most sheep, counting 1.1 million head in 2005.

MOST CHICKENS China has the world's largest poultry population with 4.2 billion chickens, 26% of the world's stocks, in 2004. After at least 30 avian flu outbreaks in China in 2005, Chinese authorities ordered the controlled slaughter of millions of birds; however, this did not substantially affect China's poultry population.

Pennsylvania led the states with 27.9 million chickens in 2004.

The Weather

EVERYBODY COMPLAINS ABOUT THE WEATHER . . . but where is it really the worst? Where is it wettest? hottest? coldest? And where does the sun always shine? Here are the facts about a topic that never gets stale.

New Orleans, LA ►

SUPERLATIVES

HOTTEST The hottest temperature ever recorded on Earth was 136° F, in El Azizia, Libya, on Sept. 13, 1922. The second-hottest, and the highest in the U.S., was 134° F, at Death Valley, CA, on July 10, 1913.

COLDEST The coldest temperature—negative 129° F—was recorded on July 21, 1983, at the Vostok Scientific Station in Antarctica. The U.S. record is negative 80° F, recorded at Prospect Creek Camp, AK, on Jan. 23, 1971. The lowest in the lower 48 was -70° F on Jan. 20, 1954, near Lincoln, MT.

LARGEST TEMPERATURE VARIATION The greatest temperature variation recorded in a single 24-hour period happened in Loma, MT, on Jan. 14 and 15, 1972, when the temperature rose 103 degrees, from -54° F to 49° F.

The steepest spike in temperature was 49 degrees in two minutes, measured at Spearfish, SD, on Jan. 22, 1943. The temperature rose from -4° F at 7:30 AM to 45° F at 7:32, only to drop back to -4° F a few hours later.

The freakish fluctuation was caused by a Föhn wind (known in the region as a Chinook), a strong, warm, dry wind from the south or west. As moist air blowing off the Pacific Ocean travels over the Rocky Mountains, much of the moisture condenses out on the western slopes. This warms the wind, which undergoes further heating and drying as it descends the eastern slopes.

MOST RAIN (AVERAGE) Lloró, Colombia, on the slopes of the Andes Mountains, is probably the world's rainiest place, with an estimated average rainfall of 523.6 inches a year.

In the U.S., trade winds bring short but frequent showers to Mt. Waialeale, HI, almost daily. Its average annual rainfall is about 460 inches (415.08 in 2004).

MOST RAIN (YEAR) The rainiest year ever was at Cherrapunji in northeast India in 1861. From Aug. 1860 to July 1861, monsoons dropped 1,041.78 inches (86.8 ft) on the town. Precipitation there usually averages over 425 inches per year, yet once the monsoons end, droughts are not uncommon.

In the U.S., Pu'u Kukui, HI, received an all-time high of 704.83 inches of rain in 1982.

RAINIEST DAY (24 HOURS) The most rainfall recorded in a 24-hour period is 73.62 inches, at Cilaos on Réunion Island in the Indian Ocean, from March 15 to 16, 1952.

The U.S. record belongs to Alvin, TX, where Tropical Storm Claudette dropped 43 inches over 24 hours on July 25 and 26, 1979.

DRIEST There are many spots in the Atacama Desert of northern Chile where rain has never been recorded. Arica, at the Atacama's northern tip, averaged only 0.03 inches a year for 59 years, and for one 14-year stretch, received no rain at all. Villages in the area receive so little rain that people use nets to capture fog moisture.

In the U.S., the driest place is considered to be Death Valley, CA, which averages 1.96 inches a year. However, Bagdad, CA, in the nearby Mojave desert, received no rain for a record 767 days between Oct. 3, 1912, and Nov. 8, 1914.

MOST SUNSHINE The sunniest place in the world is Yuma, AZ, with an average of 4,055 hours of sunshine each year, out of a possible 4,456. Temperatures in Yuma peak at above 90° F for about 175 days each year.

WINDIEST PLACE The windiest place in the world is around Cape Dennison and Port Martin on Commonwealth Bay, Antarctica, where the wind averages 50 mph annually (winds of more than 200 miles per hour have been recorded there).

In the U.S., wind speed at Mt. Washington, NH, averages 35.3 mph.

Tornadoes produce the strongest winds anywhere. Gusts inside a tornado just outside Oklahoma City on May 3, 1999, were measured with Doppler radar at 318 mph. Apart from tornadoes, the strongest wind gust ever recorded was at Mt. Washington, NH, where a rare southeast gust of 231 mph occurred on April 12, 1934.

MOST SNOW (U.S.) The snowiest place in the U.S. is Valdez, AK, which has averaged 327.2 inches a year for the past 33 years, most of it between October and April. The snowiest large city in the U.S. is Rochester, NY, which has an average of 92.8 inches.

The 24-hour snowfall record was set on April 14 and 15, 1921, at Silver Lake, CO, when 75.8 inches fell. The most snow to fall in

◀ *Gulfport, MS*

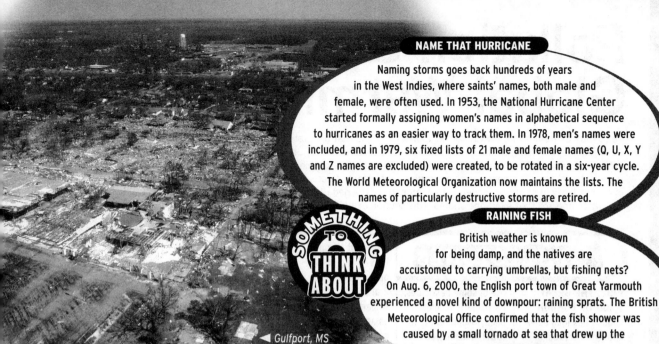

SOMETHING TO THINK ABOUT

NAME THAT HURRICANE

Naming storms goes back hundreds of years in the West Indies, where saints' names, both male and female, were often used. In 1953, the National Hurricane Center started formally assigning women's names in alphabetical sequence to hurricanes as an easier way to track them. In 1978, men's names were included, and in 1979, six fixed lists of 21 male and female names (Q, U, X, Y and Z names are excluded) were created, to be rotated in a six-year cycle. The World Meteorological Organization now maintains the lists. The names of particularly destructive storms are retired.

RAINING FISH

British weather is known for being damp, and the natives are accustomed to carrying umbrellas, but fishing nets? On Aug. 6, 2000, the English port town of Great Yarmouth experienced a novel kind of downpour: raining sprats. The British Meteorological Office confirmed that the fish shower was caused by a small tornado at sea that drew up the fish along with the seawater.

an entire season is the 1,140 inches that fell on Mt. Baker, WA, from July 1998 to June 1999.

BIGGEST HAILSTONE
The heaviest hailstone ever recorded weighed 2.25 pounds and fell in Bangladesh on April 14, 1986. The storm and its heavy hail killed 92 people.

The U.S. has two record hailstones: the biggest and the heaviest. The biggest landed on Aurora, NE, on June 22, 2003, and was 18.75 inches in circumference, weighing 1.3 lbs. A hailstone that fell in Coffeyville, KS, on Sept. 3, 1970 was only 17.5 inches in circumference, but weighed 1.67 lbs.

WINDIEST HURRICANES (U.S.)
Three hurricanes since 1900 have been rated as Category 5—winds in excess of 155 miles per hour—on the Saffir-Simpson scale after landfall in the U.S.: the "Labor Day Hurricane" of 1935, with winds of at least 160 mph, causing over 400 deaths; Camille, which struck the Mississippi coast with winds up to 190 mph on Aug. 17, 1969, causing 256 deaths; and Andrew, which hit South Florida on Aug. 24, 1992, with winds over 160 mph, causing over 50 deaths.

MOST HURRICANES (YEAR) There were a record-setting 27 named storms in the 2005 Atlantic season, including 14 hurricanes (7 major) beginning with Dennis on July 6 and ending with Epsilon, a Category 1, on Nov. 29. (After the 21 scheduled names are used, storms are named for Greek letters).

The season included the most hurricanes that peaked at Category 5, though they made U.S. landfall at lower levels: Katrina, Rita, and Wilma—the last of which reached a record-low pressure for the Atlantic Basin at 882 millibars.

HIGHEST STORM SURGE The highest storm surge ever recorded was at least 42 feet, caused by the Bathurst Bay Hurricane (also known as Cyclone Mahina) which struck Australia on March 5, 1899.

The highest storm surge in the U.S. was caused by Hurricane Katrina, which struck Louisiana, Mississippi, and Alabama on Aug. 29, 2005, making landfall as a Category 4 storm. Its sustained winds of 140 mph produced a storm surge estimated at between 25 and 29 feet, surpassing the 22-foot storm surge that accompanied Camille.

MOST TORNADOES (U.S.) Tornadoes in the U.S.—about 1,000 a year—account for more than half of all tornadoes worldwide. The area from the Rockies to the Appalachians, especially from South Dakota down into Texas, is known as Tornado Alley for good reason: its meteorological conditions make it ripe for the development of twisters.

Oklahoma City, OK, is the most-battered city, struck by 116 tornados between 1893 and 2004. A record 1,819 tornadoes were confirmed nationwide in 2004, including 546 in May alone.

Pollution & Global Warming

THE STUDY OF HUMANITY'S IMPACT ON THE EARTH is a topic that generates much heated debate. Scientists have noted that the global average temperature rose by about one degree Fahrenheit in the 20th century and has been rising more rapidly since the 1970s. While some dispute the causes of global warming, arguing that climate fluctuations occur naturally, there is a large body of scientific evidence to demonstrate the negative impact of pollutants on the air, water, and soil that everyone shares. This section examines some of these issues.

MILESTONES

1952: THE GREAT SMOG OF LONDON
London has long been known for its fog, but it was "London smog," from Dec. 5-9, 1952, that caused one of the most famous air pollution events in history. Industrial and residential emissions like sulfur dioxide, nitrogen oxides, and soot lingered in city's cold and stagnant air. About 4,000 deaths, mostly of people with chronic respiratory or cardiovascular problems, were attributed to the smog during those five days.

1962: SILENT SPRING AND DDT Rachel Carson's groundbreaking book *Silent Spring*, first serialized in *The New Yorker* in 1962, exposed the dangers of unrestrained pesticide use. A marine biologist, Carson presented evidence that the widespread use of some pesticides, particularly dichlorodiphenyltrichloroethane (DDT), endangered humans and wildlife DDT was largely banned in 1972.

1970: EARTH DAY
In 1969, Sen. Gaylord Nelson (D-WI) announced in a speech in Seattle, WA, that there should be a nationwide grassroots demonstration on behalf of the environment on April 22, 1970. About 20 million people participated with "teach-ins" and demonstrations on that day. Earth Day now occurs annually on April 22, and an estimated 500 million people in 174 countries observed Earth Day 2005.

1970: ENVIRONMENTAL PROTECTION AGENCY (EPA) The EPA was created under President Nixon in 1970 and began operating on Dec. 2 of that year, with William Ruckelshaus as administrator. Its creation was ordered with the passage of the National Environmental Policy Act on Jan. 1.

1978: LOVE CANAL
From 1942 to 1953, Hooker Chemicals and Plastics Corp. dumped about 22,000 tons of chemical waste in the Love Canal section of Niagara Falls, NY. The company then donated the land to the local board of education, which built a school there. By 1976, the waste chemicals, including polychlorinated biphenyls, dioxins, and pesticides, began surfacing and the EPA reported a localized increase in cancer and miscarriages. The site was named the first federal environmental disaster area on Aug. 7, 1978, and hundreds of families were evacuated from their homes.

1985: OZONE HOLE
A thin layer of ozone molecules (O_3) in Earth's stratosphere serves as protection from the sun's dangerous ultraviolet rays. Using measurements taken from Oct. 1957 to March 1973 at Halley Bay Observatory in Antarctica, Joseph Farman, Brian Gardiner, and Jonathan Shanklin of the British Antarctic Survey discovered a periodic ozone loss in the atmosphere over Antarctica. The ozone "hole" is not actually a hole but a lower concentration of ozone (below 220 Dobson Units, or about 1 millimeter thick) over Antarctica that forms every August to October.

The main causes of the hole are manmade chlorine and bromine atom compounds like chlorofluorocarbons (CFCs) from aerosol cans, which bond with and break apart the ozone molecules. The size of the ozone hole varies annually. At its peak on Sept. 19, 2005, the hole measured about 10.4 million square miles, which is bigger than North America.

2002: EMISSIONS LAW On July 22, 2002, California became the first state with legal mandatory emissions limits on carbon dioxide and other so-called greenhouse gases for passenger vehicles and light duty trucks. When California passed its first emission mandates for other pollutants in 1990 (now repealed), it became the only state authorized by the EPA to initiate emissions standards tougher than the federal government's. The California Air Resources Board approved regulations Sept. 24, 2004, that aimed to cut emissions

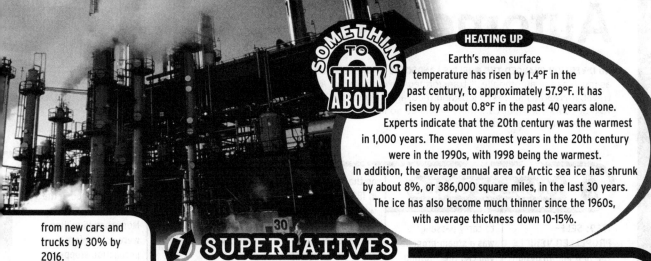

SOMETHING TO THINK ABOUT

HEATING UP

Earth's mean surface temperature has risen by 1.4°F in the past century, to approximately 57.9°F. It has risen by about 0.8°F in the past 40 years alone. Experts indicate that the 20th century was the warmest in 1,000 years. The seven warmest years in the 20th century were in the 1990s, with 1998 being the warmest. In addition, the average annual area of Arctic sea ice has shrunk by about 8%, or 386,000 square miles, in the last 30 years. The ice has also become much thinner since the 1960s, with average thickness down 10-15%.

from new cars and trucks by 30% by 2016.

2005: KYOTO PROTOCOL
The Kyoto Protocol, adopted in its namesake Japanese city on Dec. 11, 1997, took effect Feb. 16, 2005. The agreement requires industrialized nations to collectively reduce greenhouse gas emissions below 1990 emissions levels by 5.2% before 2012, although countries' individual percentage obligations vary. By the terms of the agreement, developing countries, such as China and India, are voluntarily committed to limiting their emissions growth.

The U.S. had a 7% reduction commitment in the agreement, which it signed in 1998 and did not ratify. As of Nov. 2005, 157 nations had ratified the protocol.

SUPERLATIVES

BIGGEST GREENHOUSE GAS PRODUCER
The United States produced 7.6 billion tons of greenhouse gases in 2003, more than any other nation. The U.S. total includes 6.4 billion tons of carbon dioxide—95% of which is from fossil fuel combustion. Total greenhouse gas emissions in the U.S. have increased 13.3% since 1990.

MOST TOXIC RELEASES (U.S.)
Mining debris and rubble spike the toxin numbers by millions of pounds in some states, and the runoff can contaminate drinking water if not properly contained. Alaska reported 540 million pounds of toxic releases in 2003, more than any other state by sheer weight. About 90% of the toxins came from waste rock at one zinc and lead mine facility.

MOST COMMON AIR TOXIN (U.S.)
The most prevalent chemical pouring into the air from stacks, vents, ducts, or pipes nationwide is hydrochloric acid. About 594.5 million pounds, mostly from coal- and oil-burning power plants, were produced in 2003.

Ohio, the largest producer of all air toxins, produced 70,522,155 pounds, or 12%, of all hydrochloric acid.

MOST COMMON SURFACE WATER TOXIN (U.S.)
In 2003, Indiana, the state with the most surface water discharges (23.3 million pounds), released 22.5 million pounds of nitrates into its surface water. The majority (76.6%) of these were a byproduct of treating stainless steel, in a process called "pickling." Nationally, nitrate compounds made up 87.5% of all toxins discharged into water in 2003.

MOST SMOG (U.S.)
Atmospheric ozone serves a purpose, but too much of it at ground level—most of which is produced by auto exhaust and factory emissions—creates unhealthy smog. The greater Los Angeles region consistently reports the worst smog in the nation. The south coast air basin exceeded the EPA's 8-hour smog standard for 84 days in 2005.

MOST HAZARDOUS WASTE SITES (U.S.)
New Jersey was home to 113 of 1,238 "national priority" hazardous waste sites in 2005, more than any other state in the U.S. Pennsylvania and California ranked second and third, with 94 and 93 sites, respectively. Since the Superfund (the federal government program that cleans up hazardous waste sites) began, Pennsylvania has had the most sites cleaned up (85) followed by Michigan (72) and New Jersey (66).

MOST EXPENSIVE SUPERFUND
The cleanup of Bayou Bonfouca in Slidell, LA, from Nov. 1993 to July 1995 cost between $112 and $140 million. A wood treatment plant that discharged creosote had been operating at the site since 1892, and burned down in 1970 (releasing more creosote). The water was so badly polluted that it gave divers second-degree chemical burns.

Automobiles

1997 hybrid Prius

NO INVENTION CHANGED THE WORLD'S LANDSCAPE in the 20th Century as much as the automobile. It transformed how people live and travel. It created millions of jobs and thousands of new businesses. And of course, without cars there would be no interstate traffic jams or back-seat cries of "Are we there yet?"

MILESTONES

1769: SELF-PROPELLED VEHICLE The first known design for a self-propelled vehicle, a spring-driven cart, was drawn up by Florentine artist and scientist Leonardo da Vinci around 1478. Two centuries later, Ferdinand Verbiest, a Flemish Jesuit missionary in China, made a working model of a steam-powered vehicle.

In 1769, French engineer and mechanic Nicolas Joseph Cugnot built the first self-propelled road vehicle, a three-wheel steam-powered military tractor for hauling artillery. It traveled at 2 ½ miles per hour and had to stop about every 15 minutes to build up power.

Cugnot was also the first person involved in a motor vehicle accident, when one of his "cars" ran into a wall.

1801: PASSENGER AUTOMOBILE The first road automobile to carry passengers was a steam-propelled vehicle, the "Puffing Devil," built in 1801 by British inventor Richard Trevithick.

1870: INTERNAL COMBUSTION ENGINE The first vehicle powered by an internal combustion engine was a cart on which Austrian inventor Siegfried Marcus placed a gasoline-powered engine, in 1870.

Practical gasoline-powered vehicles were developed independently by German engineers Karl Benz and Gottlieb Daimler. Benz produced a three-wheel vehicle in 1885 (patented the next year).

In 1886 Daimler created the first four-wheeled auto—a standard horse-drawn stagecoach powered by an engine of about 1.5 horsepower that he designed with engineer Wilhelm Maybach. Daimler improved on the engine and, in 1889, developed a two-cylinder v-shaped version that became the basis for modern automobile engines.

1903: DISC BRAKES British engineer Frederick William Lanchester received a patent on disc brakes in 1903, but more than half a century passed before the disc brake, which uses pads pressing against a disc ("rotor") attached to the wheel hub, began to replace the less powerful and more complicated drum brake. Today, disc brakes can be found on most autos.

1903: WINDSHIELD WIPER Mary Anderson, of Birmingham, AL, was visiting New York City when she noticed drivers continually getting out of their vehicles to wipe snow and ice from their windows. She came up with a device with a swinging arm and rubber blade that the driver could operate from inside—an idea she patented in 1903.

Her windshield wipers were initially criticized as distracting to the driver, but as cars became more popular, the usefulness of windshield wipers became apparent. They were standard equipment on American cars by 1916.

1913: FORD ASSEMBLY LINE The first American automobile maker to use an assembly line was Ransom E. Olds, who probably got the idea from meatpacking plants.

Henry Ford raised the assembly-line manufacture of cars to mass production levels. He introduced his automated assembly line in Dec. 1913 as a cost-cutting measure.

Ford was able to lower the price of the 20-horsepower Model T, "The Tin Lizzie," which had debuted in Oct. 1908, from the original price of $850 to $260 by 1925.

By 1921, 57% of all autos produced in the world were Model Ts. More than 15 million were sold before production stopped in May 1927.

1940: AUTOMATIC TRANSMISSION General Motors introduced the automatic transmission as an option in its 1940 line of Oldsmobiles. GM called the innovation Hydra-Matic drive, and highlighted its ease in an ad campaign that proclaimed, "No gears to shift! No clutch to press!"

In 1941, Chrysler introduced a semi-automatic transmission called Vacamatic. Other manufacturers followed, and automatic transmission was available as an option on most American cars by 1948.

1958: THREE-POINT SEAT BELT Early seat belts, or safety belts, were "lap belts" that went across the thighs and hips. They

SOMETHING TO THINK ABOUT

SELF-PARKING CARS

In late 2003, Toyota unveiled the Intelligent Parking Assist System (IPAS), an option available with its Prius gas-electric hybrid that allows the car to park itself. Only available in Japan, the $2,200 package relies on a built-in computer, steering sensor, rearview camera, and, of course, the driver. Using a dashboard display, the driver defines the parking area for the IPAS and pushes a button to set the car in motion. The computer doesn't recognize objects in its path, so if a person or animal runs out behind the car, the driver has to intervene to avoid a collision.

TOO SECURE

In Oct. 2003, a new bombproof BMW was delivered for Norwegian Prime Minister Kjell Magne Bondevik. The car had one problem: it was too heavy to be registered in Norway. With its armor plating, bulletproof windows, and special equipment, it weighed 4 tons, exceeding Norway's legal limit for a four-person vehicle. The car sat in an Oslo garage for weeks while engineers pondered what to do. Their decision: send it back to the factory to have the motorized, reclining rear seat replaced with a lighter conventional seat.

held people in place but often caused injury during a crash. The modern three-point seat belt, which attaches to the car near a shoulder as well as at the two hips, was invented by Nils Bohlin, an employee of Swedish automaker Volvo.

Bohlin patented the three-point safety belt in 1958 in Sweden. It became standard equipment on all Volvos a year later. Today, it can be found in almost every car and truck in the world—with 80% usage in the U.S.—and has been found by the U.S. National Highway Traffic Safety Administration to reduce fatalities in car accidents by 45%—saving over 15,000 lives in 2004.

1968: AIR BAGS American engineer Allen K. Breed invented the electromechanical automotive air bag in 1968. General Motors offered air bags as an option on some cars in the mid-1970s, but not until 1988 did a carmaker, Chrysler, make air bags standard equipment in its cars.

Though they are not perfect, the National Highway Traffic Safety Administration says air bags reduce the risk of fatalities by 34% in front-end crashes. In the U.S., frontal air bags have been required for the driver and front passenger since the 1998 model year.

1997: HYBRIDS The first mass-produced hybrid car, powered by both a gasoline engine and an electric motor, was the Toyota Prius, which hit the Japanese market in Dec. 1997. The Honda Insight, which went on sale in Dec. 1999, was the first sold in the U.S.

SUPERLATIVES

WORLD'S LARGEST AUTOMAKER General Motors, founded in 1908, has been the world's largest automaker in terms of car sales since 1931. In 2005, the company sold 9.2 million cars worldwide. Japanese car maker Toyota surpassed Ford as the second largest automaker in 2004, and has been predicted to overtake GM by 2007.

LONGEST-PRODUCED CAR The original Volkswagen Beetle was produced for a record 62 years. Austrian automotive engineer Ferdinand Porsche designed the "Bug" under a mandate from the Nazi German government to make a car that was air-cooled, fuel-efficient, and affordable. After several prototypes were made, the first Beetle was manufactured in Wolfsburg, Germany, on July 11, 1941.

The last, number 21,529,464, was made in Puebla, Mexico, on July 30, 2003, and shipped to Volkswagen's Wolfsburg headquarters to be placed in the company museum.

The Beetle supplanted the Ford Model T as the most-produced single-model car. The New Beetle, a sleeker, more modern version of the classic car, was launched by Volkswagen in 1998.

FASTEST (PRODUCTION CAR) The fastest production road car is the Swedish Koenigsegg CCR.

On Feb. 28, 2005, it broke the previous record, set by the McLaren F1, by achieving a top speed of 241 mph on the circular track at the Nardo Prototipo proving ground in Italy.

The CCR has a peak of 806 horsepower at 6,900 rpm.

Driving

Horatio Nelson Jackson, 1903

THERE ARE MORE THAN 230 MILLION REGISTERED VEHICLES in the United States (231 million vehicles for 226 million people of driving age, as of 2003)—good evidence that the automobile is an integral part of the fabric of American culture. Along with cars, trucks, and SUVs come traffic jams, parking meters, and long, long highways. And the joys of the open road.

MILESTONES

1868: TRAFFIC LIGHT The first known traffic light actually preceded the automobile. Railroad engineers Saxby & Farmer installed a 20-foot-high gas-lit signal at the junction of Bridge and Great George Streets in London to control the bustling crowds around the nearby House of Commons. Even then a green light for either street meant "go"; a red light, along with two semaphore-like arms, meant "stop."

The light was rotated manually by a policeman and was first used on Dec. 17, 1868.

1893: LICENSE PLATES The first numbered license plates were introduced in Paris in 1893.

The first U.S. state requiring drivers to register (or "license") their cars was New York. As of April 25, 1901, New York drivers (starting with George Chamberlain of Harrison) had to pay a $1 fee and file their names, addresses, and vehicle descriptions with the state. That year, 954 cars were registered.

The first state to issue permanent metal license plates—as opposed to ones made from paper and displayed in the car window—was Connecticut, in 1937.

1902: TRIPLE A In the early 1900s roads were primarily for horses and were muddy and unmarked. In 1902, a group of auto enthusiasts in Chicago formed the American Automobile Association (AAA). They set up contract agreements with service stations to help stranded members.

Today, AAA has about 45 million members in North America.

1903: DRIVE ACROSS U.S. The first person to drive his own vehicle coast-to-coast across the U.S. was Dr. Horatio Nelson Jackson of Burlington, VT. Accompanied by his mechanic, Sewall K. Crocker, and his dog "Bud," he set out from San Francisco to New York in his 20-horsepower Winton on May 23, 1903, reportedly to win a $50 bet. Driving at a top speed of 30 mph, he took 63 days, 12 hours, 30 minutes to get there.

Jackson donated his car, and Bud's goggles, to the Smithsonian Institution.

1935: PARKING METER The parking meter was the brainchild of Carl Magee, director of the Oklahoma City, OK, Chamber of Commerce. He completed a working prototype in late 1933, and the first group of 175 meters was installed on 14 blocks in that city on July 16, 1935. It cost five cents to park for one hour.

1956: INTERSTATE HIGHWAYS The Federal-Aid Highway Act, signed by President Dwight D. Eisenhower in June 1956, authorized the building of an interstate highway system across the U.S.

The idea of a national highway system to connect states and major cities and accommodate the nation's growing vehicle traffic was first proposed in the 1930s. Work aiming in that direction was halted during World War II, but Eisenhower revived the program in the early 1950s.

By 1996, when work was nearly complete, the system included almost 43,000 miles of roads.

Five Longest Interstate Highways

HIGHWAY	CITIES LINKED	DISTANCE
I-90	Seattle, WA and Boston, MA	3,085.27 miles
I-80	San Francisco, CA and Teaneck, NJ	2,906.77 miles
I-40	Barstow, CA and Wilmington, NC	2,554.29 miles
I-10	Los Angeles, CA and Jacksonville, FL	2,459.96 miles
I-70	Cove Fort, UT and Baltimore, MD	2,175.46 miles

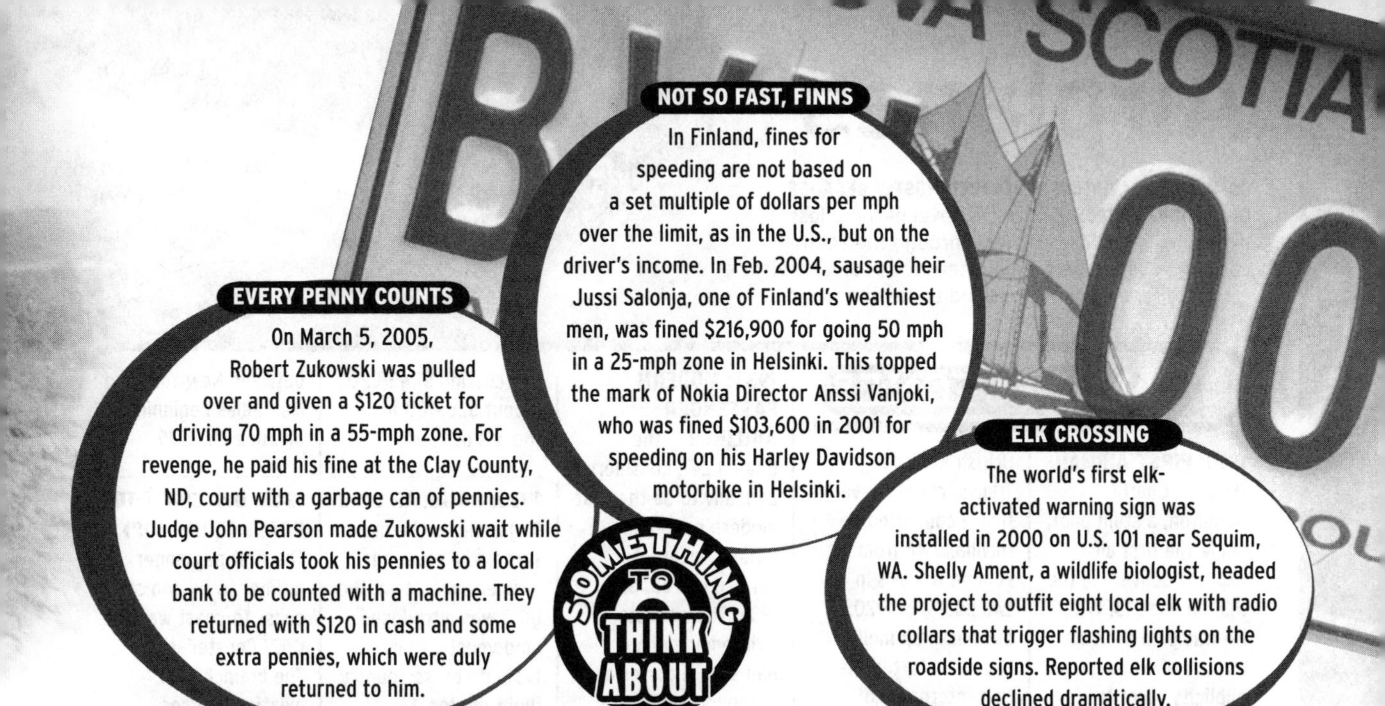

SOMETHING TO THINK ABOUT

EVERY PENNY COUNTS

On March 5, 2005, Robert Zukowski was pulled over and given a $120 ticket for driving 70 mph in a 55-mph zone. For revenge, he paid his fine at the Clay County, ND, court with a garbage can of pennies. Judge John Pearson made Zukowski wait while court officials took his pennies to a local bank to be counted with a machine. They returned with $120 in cash and some extra pennies, which were duly returned to him.

NOT SO FAST, FINNS

In Finland, fines for speeding are not based on a set multiple of dollars per mph over the limit, as in the U.S., but on the driver's income. In Feb. 2004, sausage heir Jussi Salonja, one of Finland's wealthiest men, was fined $216,900 for going 50 mph in a 25-mph zone in Helsinki. This topped the mark of Nokia Director Anssi Vanjoki, who was fined $103,600 in 2001 for speeding on his Harley Davidson motorbike in Helsinki.

ELK CROSSING

The world's first elk-activated warning sign was installed in 2000 on U.S. 101 near Sequim, WA. Shelly Ament, a wildlife biologist, headed the project to outfit eight local elk with radio collars that trigger flashing lights on the roadside signs. Reported elk collisions declined dramatically.

SUPERLATIVES

WORST TRAFFIC The worst area for traffic congestion in the U.S. is Los Angeles/Orange County, according to the Texas Transportation Institute's latest annual study, based on 2003 federal data. In 2003, each driver there wasted 93 hours in rush-hour traffic on average. One consolation—this was five hours less than in 2002, and 10 less than in 2000.

The report found that, nationally, American drivers lost over 3.7 billion hours sitting in traffic in 2003, and wasted nearly 2.3 billion gallons of fuel from idling engines.

LONGEST ROAD TRIP
In 1984, a Swiss couple, Emil and Liliana Schmid, decided to fulfill a dream and spend a year driving through North and Central America. They set off Oct. 16 in their 1982 Toyota Land Cruiser FJ60, and the adventure lived up to their hopes.

The Schmids continue to drive everywhere in the very same Land Cruiser. As of Nov. 2005 they had covered 364,704 miles: 52,088 in Europe, 107,725 in North America, 47,310 in South America, 60,639 in Africa, 24,209 in Australia, and 72,733 in Asia.

So far, the Schmids have spent 7,429 days on their tour, traveled in 150 countries, and consumed 38,067 gallons of gas. At the end of 2005, they were touring through Southeast Asia. Their ongoing drive can be followed on the Schmids' Web site at: www.weltrekordreise.ch

FASTEST SPEED DRIVEN (BLIND)
Mike Newman, a 41-year-old bank manager from Sale, England, who has been legally blind since age 11, set the world land speed record for a blind (or blindfolded sighted driver) on Aug. 13, 2003. He drove a specially adapted Jaguar XRJ 4.2 sports car at an average of 144.75 mph on the runway at Elvington airfield, North Yorkshire, England.

As the only person allowed in the car, Newman received radio instructions from his coach and stepfather (also named Mike Newman), who followed at four car lengths behind him. The Newmans broke the record of 141 mph set by Alistair Weaver (a sighted driver who wore a blindfold) in 2002.

LONGEST SKID MARKS The world's longest skid marks, covering nearly 6 miles across the Bonneville Salt Flats, UT, were made by Craig Breedlove, during an attempt to set a 1-mile land speed record on Oct. 15, 1964. Breedlove, driving a *Spirit of America* jet-powered car, lost control almost immediately; the parachute snapped off the back of the car and the vehicle hurtled across the flats, smashing through trees and finally plunging into a pond.

Breedlove climbed out shaken but unharmed. Having broken the 400-mph barrier in 1963, he went on to become the first to pass the 500- and 600-mph marks, in 1964 and 1965.

SHORTEST INTERSTATE
The shortest two-digit interstate highway is I-73. It runs from Emery to Greensboro, NC, for 12.27 miles.

Airplanes

COMMERCIAL AVIATION DEVELOPED MOSTLY BECAUSE OF BUSINESS NEEDS, but as air travel became less expensive and more efficient through the 20th century, aviation became a means for people to visit far-flung family and friends and to see the world.

MILESTONES

1910: FIRST AIRMAIL (U.S.) Charlie Hamilton, a stunt pilot, made the first air express delivery in the U.S. on June 13, 1910. He was paid $10,000 as part of a newspaper publicity stunt to deliver letters between New York City, NY, and Philadelphia, PA. The round-trip normally took nearly 11 hours (only 3:34 in the air). He averaged 49 mph and cruised at 500–600 ft.

1914: COMMERCIAL FLIGHT (U.S.) The first regularly scheduled passenger air service was inaugurated Jan. 1, 1914, on a 21-mile route running across Tampa Bay from St. Petersburg to Tampa, FL. The plane was a Benoist Type XIV seaplane, and the first passenger was a former St. Petersburg mayor, Abe C. Phiel, who had won the trip in an auction.

1919: COMMERCIAL FLIGHT (WORLD) On Aug. 25, 1919, British Aircraft Transport and Travel flew a converted de Havilland 4A from London to Paris in two hours. In 1920, businessman Inglis Uppercu started the first international flights from the U.S. They initially ran between Key West, FL, and Havana, Cuba.

1926: FLIGHT ATTENDANT Men were the first flight attendants (then known as stewards) for commercial flights starting in 1926. They carried bags and served beverages.

A nurse named Ellen Church became the first female flight attendant, May 15, 1930, on a flight from Oakland, CA, to Chicago.

Boeing's early qualifications for female flight attendants were very specific: they had to be nurses, unmarried, under 25 years old, less than 115 lbs, and no taller than 5 feet 4 inches.

1933: MODERN PASSENGER AIRLINER The Boeing 247, considered by many to be the first modern passenger airliner, went into service on Feb. 8, 1933. The all-metal twin-engine plane had such features as autopilot, wing flaps, de-icing equipment, and retractable landing gear.

The plane accommodated 10 passengers (and 3 crew), flew at about 160 mph, and took some 20 hours to fly between New York and Los Angeles.

1935: PACIFIC ROUTE Pan American, the company that pioneered service to South America, flew its first planes across the Pacific Ocean (delivering air mail) in 1935. The route, from San Francisco to Manila, (in the Philippines), via Hawaii, Midway Is., Wake Is., and Guam, was completed by the *China Clipper* Nov. 22-29, 1935.

Regular passenger service began Oct. 21, 1936, with a round-trip costing $1,438.20 (about $20,000 in today's dollars).

1936: DOUGLAS DC-3 Regarded as the most successful passenger airliner ever flown, the DC-3 was introduced on domestic routes in 1936. Its cross-country flight on Dec. 17, 1935, with American Airlines, took 13 hours, 4 minutes—a record at the time.

Production of the DC-3 ended in 1944 after 10,000 planes, representing 90% of the world's commercial aircraft, had been produced. About 2,000 of these planes are still flying today.

1939: TRANS-ATLANTIC FLIGHTS On March 26, 1939, the Pan American B-314 mail service plane called the *Yankee Clipper* left Baltimore, MD, on a trial run and arrived at Foynes, Ireland, on April 11 after a few stops. Regular mail service began May 20, 1939.

Pan Am took the first step in passenger service with flights between New York and Marseilles beginning on June 28, 1939.

1945: U.S. COAST-TO-COAST (NON-STOP) The first passenger airliner to fly non-stop coast-to-coast was the C-121 Constellation. The brainchild of aviation pioneer Howard Hughes, it was built in near secrecy by Lockheed Aircraft in the early 1940s.

During its first demonstration flight, on April 17, 1944, Hughes and Jack Frye flew from Burbank, CA, to Washington, DC, in a record 6 hours 58 minutes, averaging 355 mph.

The C-121 could carry between 57 and 100 passengers over a distance of 3,000 mi. It had a pressurized cabin so that it could fly above 20,000 ft without requiring oxygen masks.

TWA introduced regularly scheduled non-stop New York-to-Los Angeles passenger service on Oct. 19, 1953.

SOMETHING TO THINK ABOUT

SKY HIGH BID

On Dec. 1, 2003, Hungarian-born U.S. engineer Ferenc Gaspar won a highly competitive bidding war for a Concorde nose-cone at an auction held in London, England. The self-described "Concorde fanatic" bid $551,600 for the distinctive droop snout protuberance that was one of the trademarks of the supersonic airliner. His bid was almost 10 times the expected price.

1952: JETLINER
On May 2, 1952, the first commercial jetliner, a British Overseas Aircraft Corporation (BOAC) de Havilland Comet, flew from London to Johannesburg, South Africa. It could fly at 35,000 ft, where there is much less turbulence, and cut London-New York travel time from 18 to 12 hours.

In 1953 and 1954, however, three Comets crashed, apparently because of metal tears due to the stress of depressurization. A redesigned model was inaugurated in 1958, but the plane never regained its initial success.

1958: THE BOEING 707
The Boeing 707 began commercial flight on Oct. 26, 1958, from New York to Paris; the trip took 8 hours, 41 minutes, flying at a then-incredible speed of 575 mph. The first completely standardized airplane, it carried over 150 passengers.

1961: IN-FLIGHT MOVIE
TWA showed its first in-flight movies, to first-class passengers only, on July 19, 1961, when New York-to-California travelers saw *By Love Possessed* with Lana Turner. *Come September,* with Rock Hudson, was the first film shown on international flights, a month later.

1969: "JUMBO JET"
The maiden flight of the Boeing 747, the "Jumbo Jet," took place Feb. 9, 1969, and the 747 was put into regular service by Pan Am on Jan. 22, 1970. The plane, which can seat 524 passengers and stay in flight 17 hours at a time, remains the most popular wide-bodied plane today.

1976: SUPERSONIC AIRLINER The first supersonic passenger airliner was the Anglo-French Concorde. Its maiden test flight took place in Toulouse, France, on March 2, 1969, but the first supersonic flight wasn't until Oct. 1. Because the Concorde could reach a speed of Mach 2, its frame had to deal with extremely high temperatures due to friction, so a special aluminum alloy was used to prevent it from melting. The first commercial flights took place on Jan. 21, 1976.

A British Airways Concorde flew from London to Bahrain, and an Air France one flew from Paris to Rio de Janiero.

Although it flew from New York to London or Paris in about 3.5 hours, the plane was never a commercial success. Only 16 models were ever made, and the service ended with the last passenger flight on Oct. 23, 2003.

SUPERLATIVES

LARGEST AIRCRAFT
The world's largest passenger aircraft, the Airbus A380, was introduced in Toulouse, France, on Jan. 18, 2005, and had its first test flight April 27. The Airbus has a near 262-foot wingspan and double-decker seating for 555 people. On the ground, its huge weight is supported by 20 landing-gear wheels. The A380 can fly about 9,300 miles without refueling.

LONGEST NON-STOP ROUTE Singapore Airlines flies the longest non-stop commercial route, from Singapore to New York City (Newark Airport). The flight is about 10,335 miles and takes over 18 hours. The route, in both directions, was added to the schedule on June 28, 2004.

BUSIEST AIRPORT
The world's busiest airport in terms of passenger totals is Hartsfield-Jackson Atlanta International Airport. In 2004, Hartsfield processed 83,606,583 arrivals and departures, compared to Chicago O'Hare's 75,533,822.

The busiest non-American airport is London's Heathrow, which processed 67,344,054 passengers in 2004.

LARGEST AIRLINE
The world's largest airline is American Airlines, a subsidiary of AMR Corporation. Its more than 1,000 aircraft serve over 240 cities in 40 countries with more than 3,800 flights daily.

LONGEST NON-STOP COMMERCIAL FLIGHT
A Boeing 777-200LR Worldliner flew 13,420 miles, setting the record for the longest non-stop commercial flight on Nov. 10, 2005. The jet had traveled from Hong Kong the day before and flew over the Pacific Ocean, North America, and the Atlantic Ocean without stopping or refueling. It landed in London's Heathrow Airport after 22 hours, 42 minutes. Those aboard (including 8 pilots and 27 passengers) saw two separate sunrises during the marathon flight.

Ships & Shipping

Panama Canal

SHIPS ARE AN EFFICIENT AND COST-EFFECTIVE MEANS TO CARRY PRODUCTS to the marketplace. Even after the advent of trains, planes, and trucks, shipping lanes are still humming with commerce. But life on the water is not all work and no play. Grand liners and giant cruise ships have taken passengers to ports of call worldwide in luxury and comfort for over a century.

MILESTONES

ABOUT 3000 BC: PLANK BOATS The oldest-known constructed boats, rather than those carved from logs, are Egyptian plank boats, which date to about 3000 BC. These 60 to 80-foot vessels were made up of wooden planks lashed together over a wood framework. They were powered by at least 20 oarsmen; sails were also used.

ABOUT 900 BC: PHOENICIAN SHIPS Phoenicians were known throughout the Mediterranean world for their well-crafted boats. From their homeland in what is now Lebanon, Phoenician mariners used their single-mast, broad-beamed "round ships" to set up colonies across the Mediterranean all the way to Spain. They even sailed onto the Atlantic Ocean north to Britain and south to Cape Verde.

800-1100 AD: VIKING LONGSHIPS The people of Scandinavia, the Norse or Vikings, were great mariners who created strong, single-mast, ocean-faring vessels.

The "longships" were made by overlapping split wood planks (known as the "clinker" or "lapstrake" technique) fastened together with lashings or, later, iron nails. The Norse sailed in longships westward to Iceland, Greenland, and North America; east down the Volga to the Caspian Sea; and south to Africa and the Middle East. Longships also carried Viking warriors on raids.

1787: STEAMBOAT Although Robert Fulton is most associated with steamboats, the first successful steamboat in the U.S. was built by John Fitch, who launched a 45-foot steamboat on the Delaware River on Aug. 22, 1787.

Fitch, however, was not able to turn his invention into financial success. That achievement was Fulton's, whose 146-foot *Clermont* first steamed from New York City to Albany, NY, in Aug. 1807.

1843: LARGE IRON SHIP Isambard Brunel launched the *SS Great Britain* on July 19, 1843. It was the first iron-hulled ocean-going ship, and the first to be driven with a screw propeller instead of paddles. At the time, the 322-foot *Great Britain* was the biggest ship in the world.

Despite its innovative design, the *Great Britain* was too expensive to operate, and changed hands and roles several times. Finally, it was beached in the Falkland Islands in 1937, and left to wither away.

In 1970, the ship was salvaged and towed back to Bristol, England, where it was originally built. The *Great Britain* was restored and today rests in a drydock where it is open to visitors.

1869: SUEZ CANAL Ancient Egyptians had sailed between the Mediterranean and Red Seas through a system of canals. But by the 8th century AD, the waterways had become unnavigable.

After gaining approval from the Egyptian viceroy, French engineer Ferdinand de Lesseps, in April 1859, began building a canal from Port Said on the Mediterranean coast to the Red Sea. The 120-mile Suez Canal opened on Nov. 17, 1869. It is the longest canal in the world without locks.

1886: FIRST OIL TANKER The world's first true oil tanker, that is, a vessel with oil storage tanks built into the hull as opposed to a cargo vessel that carried oil in barrels, was the British-built, German-owned *Glückauf* ("Lucky"). Launched on Aug. 7, 1886, the 299-foot *Glückauf* could carry 2,600 tons of oil, that could be pumped directly into its 16 tanks.

However, the boat did not last long. The *Glückauf* accidentally ran aground off Fire Island, NY, in March 1893. Luckily, it wasn't carrying oil. Its remains are still visible today.

1914: PANAMA CANAL In 1880, Suez Canal builder Ferdinand de Lesseps led a French effort to dig a sea-level canal across Panama to connect the Atlantic and Pacific Oceans. But the project was plagued by yellow fever, difficult weather, and budget problems. Also the terrain was too rugged. In 1889, the project was ended.

Then in 1904, the U.S. took up the task. The American canal used a series of locks and an artificial lake, which made construction easier. But workers faced many of the same troubles as the French, until John Stevens, a

well-known railroad builder, took over as chief engineer. Unlike his predecessors, Stevens took care of living conditions first by building sanitation systems and eradicating yellow fever. Conditions improved and the project took off.

Despite his success, Stevens resigned from the project in 1907. In his place, President Theodore Roosevelt assigned Lt. Col. Thomas Goethals, who saw the project to its end. The canal was officially opened on Aug. 15, 1914.

1956: FIRST CONTAINER SHIP Malcolm McLean, a trucking entrepreneur from North Carolina, came up with the idea for standardized cargo containers while in New Jersey, waiting for dockworkers to unload cargo from his delivery truck onto a ship. McLean thought that it would be faster if they could just take the entire trailer off and load it onto the boat. A few years later, he purchased some ships and founded SeaLand, which began operating in 1956 using his new standardized containers. His idea and business flourished.

As the years went by, more ports were outfitted to deal with the new containers. Today, about 90% of cargo is now shipped in containers.

SOMETHING TO THINK ABOUT

ON THE ROCKS

Can you imagine an aircraft carrier almost a mile long, two football fields wide, and made entirely of ice? During WWII, the British government looked into building aircraft carriers made of a material called pykrete, which was a mixture of ice and sawdust. Unlike regular ice, pykrete was as strong as steel, and could withstand bomb blasts better than any material around. Aircraft carriers made from this would've been virtually unsinkable. An experimental model was made on a lake in Canada. But the high cost of the boats along with the end of the war kept the idea literally "on ice."

Queen Mary 2

SUPERLATIVES

BIGGEST SHIP
The oil tanker *Knock Nevis* (formerly the *Seawise Giant*, the *Happy Giant*, and the *Jahre Viking*) is the world's biggest ship. It is 1,504 feet long, 226 feet wide, and has a deadweight of 564,763 tons. It was built for C.Y. Tung between 1979 and Dec. 1980 by the Sumitomo Corporation at its Oppama, Japan, shipyard and is now owned by Fred Olsen Production.

Capable of carrying 4.4 million barrels of crude, the *Knock Nevis* has too deep a draft to enter most ports. It is currently used as a storage and offloading facility in the oil fields off the coast of Qatar.

LARGEST CONTAINER SHIP Samsung Heavy Industries of South Korea launched the world's two largest container vessels on July 11, 2005—the *MSC Pamela* and *Susanna.*

Owned by Offen Shipping of Germany, the twin 1,106-foot long, 151-feet wide vessels weigh 109,600 tons each and have the capacity to carry 9,200 20-foot-equivalent-unit (TEU) containers at a top speed of 29 mph (25.2 kn).

BIGGEST PASSENGER SHIP The *Queen Mary 2*, launched on Jan. 12, 2004, weighs 151,400 tons, is 1,132 feet long, and 147.5 feet high at the beam of the bridge wings. It's over twice as long as the Washington Monument.

The luxury liner carries 2,620 passengers and 1,253 crew and has 10 restaurants, five swimming pools, a casino, a ballroom, and a planetarium.

LARGEST SAILBOAT
The 5,000-ton *Royal Clipper* is 439 feet long and has five masts, each 197 feet tall, that hold a total of 42 sails. The ship was built for Star Clippers cruises and carries 227 guests and 106 crew.

BUSIEST PORT
The world's busiest port in terms of volume of TEUs per year is Hong Kong, China. In 2004, the Asian port handled 22 million TEUs. It was the 12th time in the last 13 years that Hong Kong had topped the busiest port rankings.

Singapore was a close second with 21.3 million TEUs. In terms of shipping tonnage, Singapore handles the most, over 1.04 billion tons of goods in 2004.

BUSIEST PORT (U.S.)
North America's busiest port in terms of volume of TEUs is the Port of Los Angeles, CA. In 2004, the port handled over 7.3 million TEUs. However, the Port of South Louisiana handled the most volume of tonnage with over 248 million.

Railways

WITH THE EXPLOSION OF MANUFACTURING IN THE INDUSTRIAL REVOLUTION, railways became the dominant form of transportation in 19th-century Europe, replacing horse-drawn carts.

Despite heavy competition from motor vehicles and aircraft, railways are still important today for transporting both passengers and freight.

Transcontinental Railroad, 1869

MILESTONES

1804: FIRST STEAM LOCOMOTIVE British engineer/inventor Richard Trevithick made the world's first steam railway locomotive at Penydaren Ironworks in South Wales. On Feb. 21, 1804, the engine traveled 9.5 miles to what is now Abercynon.

It reached a top speed of 5 miles per hour while towing 10 tons of iron and 70 men in five wagons.

1825: PASSENGER TRAIN On Sept. 27, 1825, the first public passenger train, pulled by George Stephenson's locomotive Active (later renamed Locomotion), ran 25 miles from Darlington to Stockton, in England, carrying 450 people at 15 miles per hour.

On Sept. 15, 1830, the English industrial cities of Liverpool and Manchester (40 mi apart) became the first cities in the world to be linked by rail.

1832: STREETCAR Philadelphian John Stephenson built the first urban light rail system, in New York City on Nov. 26, 1832, for the New York and Harlem Railroad. For 12.5 cents each, up to 60 people could ride in the horse-drawn, open-top, double-decker John Mason.

Since rails eliminated most of the friction, the horses could pull the large load with less effort.

1863: SUBWAY The first underground railway opened in London on Jan. 10, 1863. It ran 3.75 miles between Paddington (Bishop's Road) and Farringdon St.

The route was made using a "cut and cover" method, where tracks were laid in a trench, covered with a brick-lined tunnel, and paved over. The tunnels had ventilation shafts so steam from the locomotives could escape.

The City and South London Railway, which opened in Dec. 1890, was the first subway powered by electricity. Each train on the "Tube" could carry only 96 passengers.

The system experienced frequent blackouts, despite being powered by the country's largest power plant.

The first U.S. subway line opened Sept. 1, 1897, in Boston. It was a light rail system in which electrified streetcars went underground downtown to reduce congestion.

1869: TRANS-CONTINENTAL RAILROAD (U.S.) The first railway system crossing the U.S. was completed on May 10, 1869, when the golden spike was nailed at Promontory Summit, 85 miles northwest of Salt Lake City, UT.

Between 1865 and 1869, the Union Pacific Railroad had worked westward from Omaha, NE, laying 1,086 miles of iron rails, spikes, and ties. The Central Pacific Railroad had laid 689 miles moving eastward from Sacramento, CA.

1879: ELECTRIC RAILWAY The first electric railway to supply power through the rails was a miniature locomotive demonstrated by German electrical engineer Ernst Werner von Siemens at the Berlin Trade Fair in 1879. The engine pulled three carriages along a 985-foot circular track at a speed of 4.5 miles per hour.

Siemens also put the first electric streetcar into operation, on May 16, 1881, in Germany. The tiny cart traveled up to 25 miles per hour between Lichterfelde's Anhaltischen station, near Berlin, and the nearby Prussian Cadet School.

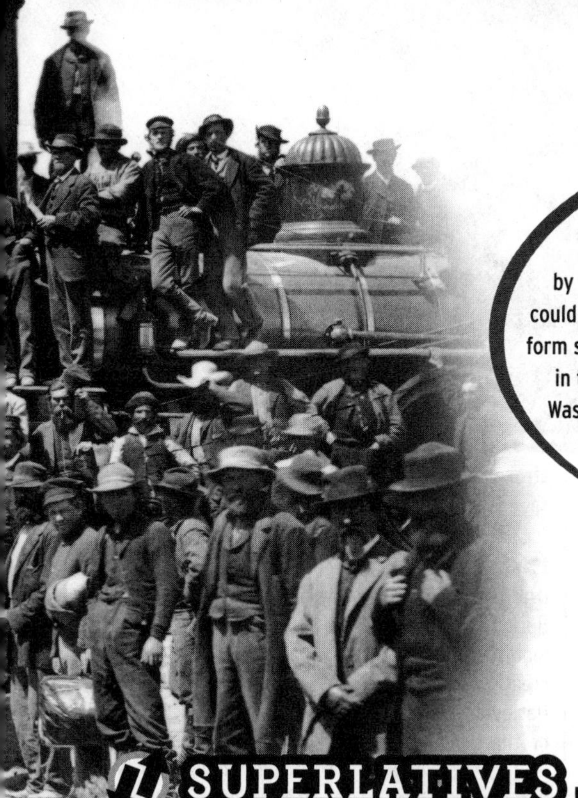

SOMETHING TO THINK ABOUT

MAKING THE CLOCKS RUN ON TIME

Before the transcontinental railroad was completed, travel was slow enough that people traveling east or west adjusted their watches by "sun time," or one minute for every 12 miles. Once trains could travel from New York to San Francisco in under a week, a uniform system was needed to organize the 300 or so "local sun times" in the U.S. At the request of railways, the Naval Observatory in Washington, DC, set four time zones, Eastern, Central, Mountain, and Pacific, at noon (Eastern Time) on Nov. 18, 1883.

LARGEST MODEL RAILROAD SET

Bruce Zaccagnino has constructed a floor-to-ceiling world of HO-, O-, and G-gauge trains in "Northlandz," a warehouse in Flemington, NJ. The exhibit, open to the public, features 8 miles of track winding through a landscape of 8-foot skyscrapers and mountains up to 30 feet high. All the while, Zaccagnino sits dead center, performing on his pipe organ. Ironically, the model-train-loving organist says he has never ridden in a real train.

SUPERLATIVES

LONGEST LINE The Trans-Siberian Railroad is the world's longest single rail system, stretching 5,778 miles from Moscow's Yaroslavl Station to the city of Vladivostok.

In 1891, Tsar Alexander III had decided to connect his Pacific port, Vladivostok, with European Russia, a feat completed in 1904. The line passes through 295 stations and seven time zones.

MOST EXPANSIVE SYSTEM North American railroads run along more than 173,000 miles of track in Canada, Mexico, and the U.S.

In 2003, the seven U.S. Class I freight railroad companies (Burlington Northern and Santa Fe Railway, CSX Transportation, Grand Trunk Corp., Kansas City Southern Railway, Norfolk Southern Combined Railroad Subsidiaries, Soo Line Railroad, and Union Pacific Railroad) operated 98,944 miles of the 141,509-mile U.S. network.

DEEPEST RAILWAY The 33.5-mile Seikan tunnel crosses under the Tsugaru Strait 14.5 miles from Japan's main island of Honshu to the northern island of Hokkaido, reaching a record 787 feet below sea level halfway across.

Digging began in 1964 and was not completed until 1988. Some 2,900 tons of explosives and 168,000 tons of steel were used in the construction.

BIGGEST SUBWAY SYSTEM The New York City subway system has 277 underground stations, 468 in all, on 660 miles of track. Running 24 hours a day, the fleet of subway trains traveled 352 million miles in 2004 and carried 1.4 billion fares.

Times Square is the busiest station. The 191st Street station in Manhattan, at 180 feet below street level, is the deepest.

FASTEST PASSENGER TRAIN The three-car MLX01 maglev (MAGnetic LEVitation) train reached a top speed of 361 mph with passengers, while racing over 11.4 miles of track at the Yamanashi Maglev Test Center in central Japan, Dec. 2, 2003.

That's about twice as fast as Japan's current "bullet" trains and almost three times faster than the fastest roller coaster (Kingda Ka at Six Flags Great Adventure, in Jackson, NJ, which reaches 128 mph).

MOST EXPENSIVE RAIL LINE "The Chunnel," between Folkestone, England, and Sangatte, France, cost $21 billion to complete. It runs under the English Channel for 23.6 miles.

Digging began on both sides of the Strait of Dover in 1987–88 and was completed in 1991; the tunnel officially opened May 6, 1994.

HIGHEST RAILWAY More than four-fifths of the 695-mile Qinghai-Tibet railway, running from Golmud in northwest China's Qinghai province to Lhasa in Tibet, is being built at elevations above 13,000 feet.

Construction began June 29, 2001; the line was expected to open in 2007.

Bicycles & Motorbikes

ABOUT 100 MILLION BICYCLES ARE MANUFACTURED WORLDWIDE each year. That makes bikes the world's most popular vehicle, topping cars by about 35 million.

A "Penny-Farthing" ▶

MILESTONES

1839: FIRST BICYCLE Two-wheeled vehicles propelled by the feet were works in progress in the late 17th century; they were typically called "hobby-horses." Scottish blacksmith Kirkpatrick Macmillan first added pedals and cranks to a frame with handlebars in 1839.

Macmillan never patented or tried to market his device. It weighed 57 pounds and could reach speeds of 14 mph. In 1846, Gavin Dalzell began marketing a model based on Macmillan's design that became widely used in England.

1872: PENNY-FARTHING More properly called the Ariel Highwheeler, the Penny-Farthing was invented by British engineers James Starley and William Hillman. Instantly recognizable by its small rear wheel and enormous front wheel (over 4 feet tall), the "Penny-Farthing" (nicknamed for two British coins, one large, one small) was inspired by the French *velocipedes*, which were nicknamed "bone shakers."

In the U.S., the Penny-Farthing was known as the "ordinary" because it became so common.

1884-87: CIRCUMNAVIGATION (BIKE) Thomas Stevens started out from San Francisco April 22, 1884, on a 50-inch standard Columbia bicycle. He reached Boston Aug. 4, 1884, completing the first transnational bike ride.

Stevens then sailed to Liverpool, England, cycled through Europe to Turkey (arriving July 2, 1885), and took a boat and train to the northwest Indian border. After pedaling across India, he took a boat from Calcutta to Hong Kong, then biked through Japan. He returned to San Francisco via steamship, arriving Jan. 7, 1887.

1885: MOTORCYCLE Sylvester Roper of Roxbury, MA, invented a steam-powered cycle propelled by a charcoal-fired engine, which he first exhibited at New England fairs and circuses in 1869.

But credit usually goes to German engineer Gottlieb Daimler. On Aug. 29, 1885, Daimler patented a one horse power (hp) engine, which he tested on a wooden bicycle with two small, spring-loaded outrigger wheels (similar to training wheels).

Large-scale production didn't begin until 1894, when Hildebrand & Wolfmüller, based in Munich, Germany, made about 200 2.5-hp, two-cylinder, four-stroke bikes capable of speeds up to 25 mph.

1903: HARLEY-DAVIDSON® The Harley-Davidson motorcycle was the creation of William Harley and three brothers—Arthur, Walter, and William Davidson. Their first motorcycle, constructed in a 10 x 15-foot wooden shed in Milwaukee, WI, was a racing machine with a $3\frac{1}{8}$-inch bore and $3\frac{1}{2}$-inch stroke.

In 1908, Walter Davidson scored a perfect 1,000 points at the Federation of American Motorcyclists Endurance and Reliability Contest, and a motorcycle legend was born.

1912-13: CIRCUMNAVIGATION (MOTORCYCLE) Journalist Carl Clancy from South Egremont, MA, was the first person to travel around the world on a motorbike. Riding a four-cylinder Henderson, Clancy circled the world in 1912-13 to study new automobile routes.

After reaching Europe, Clancy followed an 18,000-mile route through the Sahara, Egypt, Sri Lanka, India, Japan, and the U.S., completing his journey in New York City. His journey was featured in the Oct. 1, 1913, edition of *World Motorcycle Review*.

1924: MOTOCROSS On March 29, 1924, British motorcycle enthusiasts held the "Southern Scott Scramble" in Surrey, England, in which 80 riders raced 50 miles over rugged hills and rough terrain. Only 40 participants finished the race.

The winner, Arthur Sparks, completed the "Scramble" in 2 hours, 1 minute, 51 seconds. The event is generally considered the birth of "motocross," that is, cross-country motorcycle racing.

A restored 1903 "Serial No. 1" Harley-Davidson motorcycle. (Harley-Davidson Archives—Copyright Harley-Davidson) ▶

1970s: MOUNTAIN BIKE It probably didn't take long for a rider to take a bike off-road, but mountain biking as a sport didn't begin until the 1970s. Thrill seekers in California's San Francisco Bay Area began pairing "fat" tires (over 2 in. wide) with heavyweight bikes, usually Schwinns from the 1930s. These "clunkers" often weighed over 40 pounds and had motocross handlebars and drum brakes that let riders maneuver treacherous slopes.

Russ Mahon of Cupertino, CA, rode with the Morrow Dirt Club and is credited with first adding the 10-speed *derailleur*, a device for shifting gears.

In Sept. 1979, Gary Fisher and Charlie Kelly, like-minded pioneers from nearby San Anselmo, CA, formed the Mountain Bikes company, which sold the first line of off-road, heavy-duty bikes (built by Tom Ritchey), and provided a name for the new biking phenomenon.

1976: MOUNTAIN BIKE RACE Charlie Kelly and Fred Wolf organized the first official downhill mountain bike race, held near Fairfax, CA, on Oct. 21, 1976. The *Repack* course dropped 1,300 feet over 2 miles. In that first race, only one of seven riders, Alan Bond, finished (5 min, 12 sec).

Mountain biking made its Olympic debut at the Atlanta Summer Games on July 30, 1996. Bart Brentjens (Netherlands) and Paola Pezza (Italy) took the first gold medals in their respective events.

1982: RACE ACROSS AMERICA The first official Race Across America (then called the Great American Bike Race) was staged in 1982. Lon Haldeman, 24, from Harvard, IL, set out from California's Santa Monica Pier on Aug. 4 and arrived at New York's Empire State Building on Aug. 14, after pedaling 2,968 miles in 9 days, 20 hours, and 2 minutes. Only three other cyclists managed to complete the race.

SOMETHING TO THINK ABOUT

PEDAL PROTEST

On June 11, 2005, cyclists in several countries, including the United States, Spain, Israel, and France, took part in World Naked Bike Ride 2005. The event was staged to protest so-called gas-guzzling cars, as well as traffic congestion, and to encourage bike riding. In London, about 100 naked riders, risking saddle sore, pedaled 6 miles bearing a banner that said, "Oil is not a bare necessity but a crude obsession."

SUPERLATIVES

ONE-HOUR CYCLING Timed cycling records are subject to interpretation depending on the type of equipment used. The most frequently cited record, monitored by the Union Cycliste Internationale (UCI), allows cyclists to use only bikes with innovations developed before 1972, to prevent technology from overpowering skill. Under these guidelines, Czech record holder Ondrej Sosenka pedaled a record 30.9 miles in 1 hour at the Krylatskoje Olympic Velodrome in Moscow, Russia, on July 18, 2005.

Speed records made outside this standard are considered "best hour performance." Chris Boardman (Great Britain) holds that record after completing 35.0 miles in an hour at England's Manchester Velodrome on Sept. 6, 1996.

FASTEST RACE ACROSS AMERICA The official Race Across America solo record is held by Pete Penseyres, who in July 1986 covered 3,107 miles in 8 days, 9 hours, and 47 minutes—an average speed of 15.40 mph.

Seana Hogan holds the women's record with a 2,912-mile journey in 1995 covered in 9 days, 4 hours, and 2 minutes (13.23 mph).

BICYCLE SPEED RECORD On Oct. 3, 1995, Dutch pro cyclist Fred Rompelberg reached a speed of 167 mph at Bonneville Salt Flats, UT. He achieved this by riding behind a speeding dragster fitted with an air dam, which reduced air resistance.

Rompelberg was also the first man to break 100 mph on a bicycle, on Oct. 22, 1988.

MOTORCYCLE SPEED RECORD On July 14, 1990, Dave Campos of Albuquerque, NM, set the motorcycle land speed record at 322.150 mph at the Bonneville Salt Flats, UT. Campos drove a 23-foot-long rocket-shaped Harley streamliner called "Easyrider," powered by a pair of Ruxton-Harley-Davidson engines.

MOST EXPENSIVE MOTORCYCLE (AUCTION) On Nov. 13, 2004, Bonhams & Butterfields auctioned a 1936 Brough Superior SS-100 for $145,000 ($164,500 with premium and taxes) at the Petersen Automotive Museum in Los Angeles.

The British-manufactured bike, once used by George Brough himself, was one of only 75 now known to exist. It has an overhead valve engine and can reach 100 mph.

MOST CYCLISTS PER CAPITA (COUNTRY) In 2003, the Netherlands reported 13.4 million licensed bike riders, or about 83% of the total population. Seven out of eight Dutch people over age 15 have a bike; about 25% cycle to work.

Advertising

ARCHAEOLOGISTS HAVE FOUND EVIDENCE OF ADS DATING BACK TO THE BABYLONIANS in 3000 BC. Notices painted on buildings were among the first forms of advertising; signs have been unearthed from ancient Rome offering property for rent and from Pompeii calling attention to a nearby tavern. Today, advertising besieges us from all types of media, including print, broadcast, and now the Internet.

MILESTONES

1704: FIRST NEWSPAPER AD (U.S.) *The Boston News-Letter*, the first continuously published newspaper in America, carried the first known American newspaper ad, on May 1, 1704. It was placed by William Bradford for a mill and plantation in Oyster Bay, Long Island.

1800: AD AGENCY The first known advertising agency was established in Warwick Square, London, by James White in 1800.

1880: COPYWRITER John Wanamaker, founder of the famous Philadelphia department store, hired John E. Powers in 1880 as the world's first full-time advertising copywriter. While Wanamaker had been running ads since 1974, Powers ushered in a fresh, direct, appealing style. He became known as the "father of honest advertising," reputedly once even telling consumers, "We have a lot of rotten gossamers and things we want to get rid of."

Wanamaker was also the first merchant to place a half-page newspaper ad (in 1874) and a full-page ad (in 1879).

1882: FIVE-FIGURE AD BUDGET Procter & Gamble, at Harley Procter's behest, began promoting Ivory soap nationally in 1882 in newspapers, magazines, and outdoor advertisements, with an ad budget of $11,000. The ads emphasized Ivory's purity and the fact that it floated. They often used color and included poems, humor, and fantastical drawings.

One critic wrote in 1884 that Ivory soap's ads in *Harper's Monthly* were almost worth the magazine's price.

1911: SEX APPEAL In May 1911, Woodbury Soap, a product that had been around for decades, began using the slogan "The Skin You Love to Touch" in its advertising, along with paintings of comely young couples embracing. It's considered the first use of sex appeal in advertising.

1914: FEDERAL TRADE COMMISSION (FTC) Government supervision of the advertising industry began after the Federal Trade Commission Act was passed on Sept. 26, 1914. It included a provision allowing the new FTC to issue cease-and-desist orders against false advertising.

EARLY 1920s: MADISON AVE. New York City's Madison Avenue began attracting advertising agents as early as Sept. 1915, when the Advertising Men's League (soon to be the Advertising Club) of New York leased a club in the Madison Square hotel. Enough agencies had moved to Madison Ave. by April 1923 that one reporter called it the "advertising centre of New York."

1922: RADIO ADS The Queensboro Corp., a real estate firm, bought the first radio commercial, called "toll broadcasting," on AT&T's station WEAF in New York, NY, for $100. For 10 minutes on Aug. 28, 1922, H.M. Blackwell promoted a new tenant-owned apartment complex in Jackson Heights, Queens, called Hawthorne Court.

1941: TV COMMERCIALS The FCC allowed commercial TV broadcasting to begin on July 1, 1941. NBC's WNBT in New York City was the first station to show ads.

The first TV commercials, for Bulova watches, Ivory soap, Spry shortening, and Sun Oil Co. (now Sunoco), were shown to an audience of about 2,000 families.

1970: CIGARETTE ADS CURBED Congress passed the Public Health Cigarette Smoking Act in 1970, banning cigarette ads on TV and radio.

In 1998, under an agreement reached between 46 state governments and the tobacco industry, five of the biggest U.S. tobacco manufacturers agreed to additional ad restrictions to protect youth. These included bans on most outdoor advertising, on cartoon mascots—like Joe Camel—and on paying for product placement in movies and TV.

USING YOUR HEAD

Andrew Fisher, a 20-year-old Omaha, NE, Web-page designer, was really using his head when he auctioned off his forehead on eBay as advertising space in Jan. 2005. Fisher got $37,375 to wear a temporary tattoo of the logo of SnoreStop, a snoring remedy, on his forehead for 30 days. It wasn't the first time the gimmick had been used. On March 21, 2003, people attending first-round games at the NCAA basketball tournament in Boston's FleetCenter were asked to wear Dunkin' Donuts logos on their foreheads for three hours; some received minimum wage and some did it for the fun. And in April 2004, about 40 people paraded around New York's Times Square for $11 per hour wearing logos to promote Toyota's Scion tC Coupe.

"1984"

Perhaps the most famous Super Bowl commercial of all time was the Apple Corp. "1984" spot announcing the upcoming launch of the Macintosh computer, which aired during Super Bowl XVIII. Directed by Ridley Scott (*Alien*, *Gladiator*), the ad cost $700,000 to produce. Such was the buzz generated by the commercial that "1984" is widely credited with sparking the trend of introducing new ads during the Super Bowl. Almost incredibly, the spot aired nationally just once. It cost $1.5 million to air, but the money spent was made back in the first day of sales.

SOMETHING TO THINK ABOUT

SPARE THE CHILDREN

The Children's Television Act of 1990 limited commercials aired during children's TV programs to 10.5 minutes per hour on weekends and 12 minutes per hour on weekdays.

SUPERLATIVES

HIGHEST AD RATES Commercials run during the annual Super Bowl telecast have by far the highest ad rates in broadcasting. A 30-second spot during Super Bowl XXXIX on Feb. 6, 2005, went for $2.4 million. In contrast, the most expensive commercials on regular prime-time shows cost about $400,000.

The Super Bowl is the most widely watched sports event in the U.S., attracting some 90 million viewers, and ads shown during the game are often talked about for years. During Super Bowl I in 1967, a 60-second ad cost less than $10,000.

The finale of the NBC sitcom *Friends* in May 2004 charged an average of $2 million per spot, a record for any non-sporting program.

MOST EXPENSIVE AD A Chanel No. 5 commercial shot by Baz Luhrmann, who directed *Moulin Rouge* (2001), and starring Nicole Kidman cost about $33 million to make. A Chanel publicist opined that the three-minute spot was "a film, not an advert."

LARGEST AD BUDGET (U.S.) Of all U.S. companies, Procter & Gamble spent the most on measured advertising in 2004, with expenditures of $3.0 billion, followed by General Motors with $2.8 billion.

In unmeasured advertising, including promotions and direct marketing, the ranks were reversed, with GM spending $4.0 billion and P&G spending $3.9 billion.

The two companies have held top spots for 30 of the past 50 years. Time Warner placed third in both categories ($1.9 billion measured expenditures and $3.3 billion unmeasured).

MOST ADVERTISING The auto industry spends more on advertising than any other industry ($20.5 billion in 2004). Of this amount, $8.9 billion was spent on television ads, the most for any advertising medium. Retail companies came in second, spending $17.3 billion in 2004, followed by telecom and Internet companies, at $9.1 billion.

BIGGEST VENUE Companies spend the most national advertising dollars on direct mail. An estimated $52.2 billion was spent in the U.S. on mailing 39.6 billion pieces of mail in 2004.

LONGEST CLIENT RELATIONSHIP Unilever hired the J. Walter Thompson Co. in Nov. 1902 to advertise Lifebuoy soap. Unilever is still with the agency—the longest known client relationship in advertising history.

LARGEST BILLBOARD The world's biggest billboard—443 feet long and 79 feet high, and weighing 2 tons—was built on the side of the Fort Dunlop tire factory in Birmingham, England, in 2002.

A nearby highway is one of England's most congested, as 800,000 drivers crawl by each week.

OLDEST AD AGENCY (U.S.) William James Carlton began selling ad space in newspapers and founded Carlton & Smith in 1864. Four years later, he hired a 24-year-old bookkeeper, James Walter Thompson, who soon began selling ads too.

In 1877, Thompson bought the agency (paying $500 for the business and $800 for the furniture); he renamed it the J. Walter Thompson Co.

The name was changed again, to JWT, in 2005.

Magazines & Newspapers

WHEN ALEXIS DE TOCQUEVILLE VISITED THE UNITED STATES in 1831-32, he was struck by the number and power of newspapers. "The power of the periodical press," he wrote in his classic *Democracy in America*, "is only second to that of the people." But he complained that "three-quarters of the enormous sheet . . . are filled with advertisements, and the remainder is frequently occupied by political intelligence or trivial anecdotes." De Tocqueville's observations characterize how many modern readers view newspapers and magazines today.

MILESTONES

59 BC: *ACTA DIURNA* Julius Caesar decreed that the *Acta Diurna* ("Daily Acts"), a daily authorized record of political, military, and social events in Rome, be posted throughout the city for public reading in 59 BC. Many consider it the first forerunner of today's newspapers.

1556, 1605: NEWSPAPERS The first monthly newspaper (of a sort) that we know of, *Notizie scritte* ("Written Information"), was published by the Venetian government in 1556. In 1605, Johann Carolus of Strasbourg began printing *Relations: Aller Furnemmen*, generally considered to be the first weekly newspaper.

1609: COLONIAL NEWSPAPERS The three-page *Publick Occurrences, Both Forreign and Domestick*, considered the first newspaper in the 13 Colonies, was suppressed by the governor of the Massachusetts Bay Colony, in 1609, having lasted only one issue.

The weekly *Boston News-Letter*, first issued by postmaster John Campbell for the week of April 17, 1704, lasted 72 years.

1650, 1783: DAILY PAPERS In July 1650, German printer Thimotheus Ritzsch began putting out his Leipzig newspaper six days a week, making it in effect the world's first daily newspaper.

The *Pennsylvania Evening Post and Daily Advertiser*, published in Philadelphia by Benjamin Towne, was the first daily in America (1783).

1731: MODERN MAGAZINE Britain's *Gentleman's Magazine* (or *Trader's Monthly Intelligencer*), which survived until 1907, is considered the first magazine of the modern kind, offering essays, stories, reports of political debates, and other material designed to entertain readers and inform them on issues of the day. Founded by Edward Cave under the pseudonym Sylvanus Urban in Jan. 1731, it was the first periodical to call itself a "magazine," and sold for six pence.

1735: ZENGER ACQUITTED When the printer John Peter Zenger, founder of the *New York Weekly Journal*, printed articles criticizing the colonial governor of New York, he was charged with seditious libel in Nov. 1734. His lawyer Andrew Hamilton argued that the allegations were true and therefore not libelous. A jury found him not guilty, Aug. 5, 1735; the verdict marked a victory for American freedom of the press.

1741: MAGAZINES (U.S.) In Jan. 1741, the printer Andrew Bradford published the first American colonial magazine, *American Magazine*, in Philadelphia as a monthly on regional politics. He had asked Benjamin Franklin to edit the magazine, but the two were unable to agree on content. They separated and Franklin promptly created the second magazine in the colonies, *General Magazine, and Historical Chronicle, for all the British Plantations in America*.

Published within days of each other, the two publications were soon battling for circulation; both folded by midyear.

1835: *HERALD* FIRSTS The first issue of the *New York Herald*, on May 6, 1835, was produced in a Wall Street cellar, ran four pages long, and sold for a penny. Publisher James Gordon Bennett's emphasis on "human interest," lurid crime, and scandalous news set a style that still sells papers today.

The paper was also the first in the U.S. to illustrate news articles, employ foreign correspondents, and print financial news from Wall Street.

1886: LINOTYPE Installed at the *New York Tribune*, Ottmar Mergenthaler's linotype machine may have been the greatest advance in printing since Gutenberg. It could cast full lines of type in a molten metal mold for printing, then be melted and reused. A single operator could set, justify, and distribute type, quickly making mass printing and rapid circulation feasible.

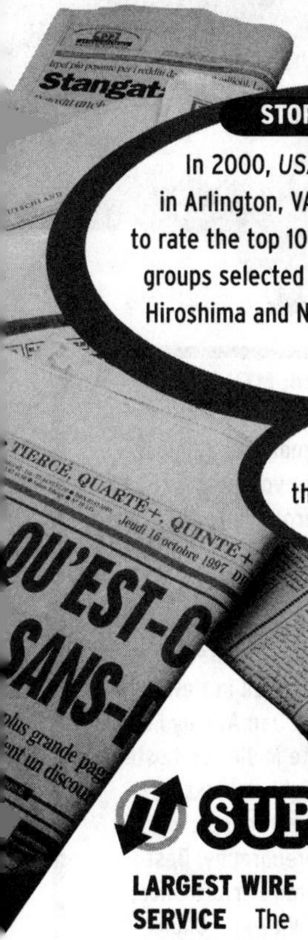

SOMETHING TO THINK ABOUT

STORY OF THE CENTURY

In 2000, *USA Weekend* and the Newseum in Arlington, VA, polled journalists and readers to rate the top 100 stories of the 20th century. Both groups selected the dropping of atomic bombs on Hiroshima and Nagasaki in 1945 as the top story.

WILL CIRCULATION PLUNGE TOO?

The Feb. 2004 issue of *Trail*, a British magazine devoted to hiking, included directions for hiking down *Ben Nevis*, Britain's tallest mountain. Unfortunately, the route excluded a crucial turn, meaning that anyone who followed the guide as printed would plunge off the mountainside. Editors quickly realized their error, and apologized. Scotland's Mountaineering Council posted a caution on its Web site: "The descent bearing which was provided on Page 105 of *Trail* Feb. 2004 is WRONG—it would take you over the north face."

DECLINING COMPETITION

In 1900 there were 2,326 daily newspapers in the United States. In 2000 there were 1,480, and in 2003 only 1,456.

BELATED APOLOGY

On April 13, 1993, the *Hartford Courant* apologized to President Thomas Jefferson. The newspaper had vehemently opposed Jefferson's election 193 years earlier, in 1800, editorializing that the country would be irrevocably damaged by his victory. In honor of Jefferson's 250th birthday, the newspaper printed a formal apology, commenting that "It's never too late to admit a mistake."

SUPERLATIVES

LARGEST WIRE SERVICE The Associated Press (AP) was formed in 1848 by six New York dailies to cooperatively finance the cost of gathering national news. It is the oldest newswire service in the U.S. and the largest worldwide, with 3,700 employees working in 242 international bureaus.

HIGHEST CIRCULATION

NEWSPAPER The newspaper with the highest circulation in the world is Japan's *Yomiuri Shimbun*. Its morning edition had a circulation of 14,246,000 copies in early 2005. The highest-circulation English-language daily is the British tabloid *The Sun*, which sold 3,461,000 copies daily in late 2005. In the U.S., *USA Today* has the greatest daily circulation, at an average of 2,603,000 copies in late 2005. *The Wall Street Journal* ranks second (1,821,000) followed by *The New York Times* (1,673,000).

HIGHEST AD REVENUE

MAGAZINE The magazine with the highest advertising revenue in the U.S. is *People* as of late 2005 according to the Publisher's Information Bureau. Rounding out the top four were *Better Homes and Gardens*, *Time* and *Sports Illustrated*. General Motors was the most prolific advertiser, placing 4,870 ad pages in 2004.

WEIGHTIEST AMERICAN MAGAZINE The heaviest street-stand magazine ever published was the Feb.-March 1999 issue of *Brides* magazine. The nuptial monster weighed 4 pounds, 9 ounces and had 1,242 pages (1,065 of which were advertisements).

MOST PULITZERS The Pulitzer Prize was created by American newspaper pioneer and media baron Joseph Pulitzer, and first presented in 1917. Most, though not all, of the prize categories are for journalism and the judging is administered by the Columbia University School of Journalism. *The New York Times* has won the most journalism Pulitzers of any newspaper. Since the paper won its first award in 1918, the *Times* and its journalists have won 91 Pulitzer Prizes.

MOST ELLIES The American Society of Magazine Editors (ASME) created the "Ellie" award in 1966 to honor the best in magazine journalism each year. By 2005 *The New Yorker* had received a record 44 Ellie awards.

OLDEST EXISTING NEWSPAPER (U.S.) The *Hartford Courant*, first published on Oct. 29, 1764, as the *Connecticut Courant*, is the oldest continuously published newspaper in the U.S.

The *New York Post* is the oldest continuously published daily, operating since its foundation on Nov. 16, 1801 by Alexander Hamilton.

OLDEST EXISTING MAGAZINE (U.S.) The oldest magazine still printed in the U.S. is *Scientific American*, created by Rufus Porter on Aug. 28, 1845. The magazine was originally a weekly broadsheet. Porter sold it within 10 months for $800.

Music Videos

THANKS TO MTV, which celebrated its 25th anniversary in 2006, music videos are part of the cultural landscape. But the form that "killed the radio star" is older than the MTV "Moonman." Indeed, production of short-form music videos began in the 1940s, decades before anyone said "I want my MTV."

MILESTONES

1940: PANORAM JUKEBOX
Short-form music videos were first made available for public viewing on the Panoram Jukebox, a product of Mills Novelty Co. of Chicago.

Customers at bars, hotels, and restaurants could pay a dime to watch a three-minute montage of assorted "soundies"—eight clips of various styles of music, with musicians lip-synching and miming playing their instruments.

1972: "JOHN, I'M ONLY DANCING" To publicize his first U.S. tour, David Bowie hired Mick Rock to record four "video clips," to be shown as filler on late-night TV. For the first video, Bowie lip-synched to a record of his song "John, I'm Only Dancing" during a pre-concert rehearsal at London's Rainbow Theatre on Aug. 19, 1972. The video cost under $200 to produce and was broadcast in several U.S. cities later that year.

Rock critic Lester Bangs said the clip represented "the very moment the modern idea of a video was born." Over a decade later, Bowie, along with The Beatles and director Richard Lester (for *A Hard Day's Night*), received the first Video Vanguard Award, at the 1984 MTV Video Music Awards.

1974: MUSIC VIDEO TV SHOW
Graham Webb, an Australian radio and TV personality, created the first show based entirely on promotional music video clips, in Feb. 1974. What began in Sydney as the *Saturday Today Show* was renamed *Sound Unlimited* when it went national.

When Webb wanted to air a song that didn't have a video, he sent staff out to film one. Russell Mulcahy, one of his staffers, directed the first video shown on MTV (see below).

1981: VIDEO GRAMMY AWARD
At the 23rd Annual Grammy Awards, on Feb. 25, 1981, former Monkees member Michael Nesmith was awarded the first Video of the Year Grammy. He won for his hour-long home video program *Michael Nesmith in Elephant Parts*, reflecting the freestyle antics of The Monkees.

The Beatles and The Monkees (whose 1966-68 TV show mixed comedy with music-video-style performances) helped lay the foundation for music videos as they moved away from performance shots to short narrative films.

1981: MTV LAUNCHED
The music video revolution officially began on Aug. 1, 1981, with the launch of MTV: Music Television in just 2.1 million cable-subscribing households. The programming kicked off at midnight, with The Buggles' "Video Killed the Radio Star" (directed by Russell Mulcahy)—though, in fact, exposure on the channel did make radio stars of many acts.

The second video aired was Pat Benatar's "You Better Run"—followed by dead air, to the consternation of the channel's first "VJs" (video jockeys).

In March 1982, the station launched its "I Want My MTV" marketing campaign. Soon it seemed like just about everyone had MTV, as the station went on to launch spin-off channels like VH1 and CMT, and international versions in over 100 nations and 17 languages worldwide.

1984: GRAMMY AWARD (SHORT FORM) The Grammys introduced a category for short-form, MTV-style videos at its 26th annual event, held Feb. 28, 1984. The winner was Duran Duran, for its stylish and sexy "Girls on Film/Hungry Like the Wolf." Their album *Duran Duran* also won Best Video Album.

1984: MTV VIDEO MUSIC AWARDS
Intended as a hipper, more youthful alternative to the Grammys, the first "Moonman" statuettes were awarded Sept. 14, 1984, at Radio City Music Hall in New York City. Dan Aykroyd and Bette Midler co-hosted.

Michael Jackson swept the Best Choreography, Best Overall Performance, and Viewer's Choice categories with "Thriller."

Other winners included the breakdancing robots from jazz pianist Herbie Hancock's video "Rockit," which took home five Moonmen.

1992: DIRECTOR CREDIT While directors play a crucial part in how a music video looks, it wasn't until Dec. 1, 1992, that MTV began including the director in video credits. Only Country Music Television (which is owned and operated by MTV) had done so earlier.

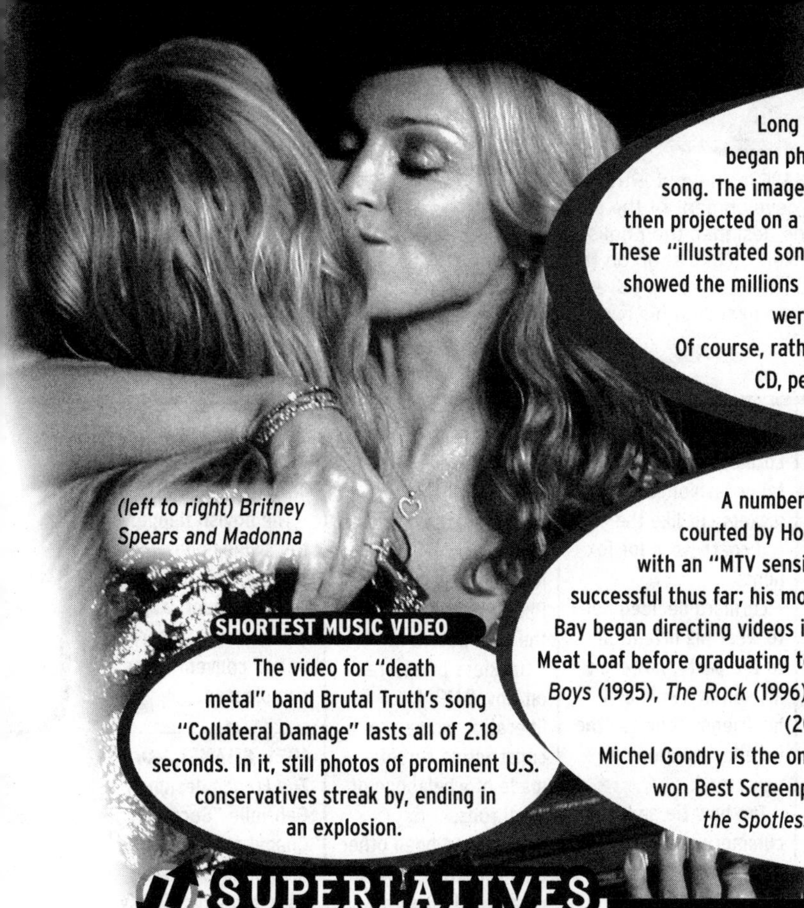

(left to right) Britney Spears and Madonna

FACE THE MUSIC

Long before MTV, in the 1890s, George Thomas began photographing people acting out the lyrics of a song. The images were printed on glass and brilliantly hand-colored, then projected on a theater screen while musicians performed the song live. These "illustrated songs" were wildly popular—over 10,000 theaters nationwide showed the millions produced from 1890 to 1914—and, like music videos, they were used to help sell copies of new songs.

Of course, rather than being able to download an MP3 or buy the CD, people had to settle for buying a copy of the sheet music.

SOMETHING TO THINK ABOUT

DIRECTOR'S CHAIR

A number of music video directors have been courted by Hollywood to direct feature films enlivened with an "MTV sensibility." Michael Bay is the most commercially successful thus far; his movies have grossed more than $770 million in the U.S. Bay began directing videos in 1988 for the likes of Donny Osmond, Tina Turner, and Meat Loaf before graduating to the big screen with a string of turbo-charged hits: *Bad Boys* (1995), *The Rock* (1996), *Armageddon* (1998), *Pearl Harbor* (2001), *Bad Boys II* (2003), and *The Island* (2005).

Michel Gondry is the only video director to go on to receive an Oscar. He won Best Screenplay in 2004 for writing *Eternal Sunshine of the Spotless Mind* alongside Charlie Kaufman and Pierre Bismuth.

SHORTEST MUSIC VIDEO

The video for "death metal" band Brutal Truth's song "Collateral Damage" lasts all of 2.18 seconds. In it, still photos of prominent U.S. conservatives streak by, ending in an explosion.

SUPERLATIVES

MOST GRAMMYS
ARTIST Three performers have won two Grammy Awards for Best Short-Form Video: Peter Gabriel (the only back-to-back winner, in 1992 for "Digging in the Dirt" and 1993 for "Steam"), Michael Jackson (1989's "Leave Me Alone" and 1995's "Scream"), and Janet Jackson, a co-winner for "Scream" and 1997's "Got 'Til It's Gone."

Michael Jackson was also featured in the 1985 winner, the famine relief video "We Are the World—The Video Event."

MOST GRAMMYS
DIRECTOR
Director Mark Romanek has won three Best Short-Form Video Grammys, more than any other director. He was honored as the director of Janet and Michael Jackson's "Scream" (1995), Janet Jackson's "Got 'Till It's Gone" (1997), and Johnny Cash's cover of Nine Inch Nails' "Hurt" (2003).

MOST VMAs
ARTIST Madonna, whose image has morphed again and again on MTV since her first videos ("Everybody" and "Burning Up") started airing in 1983, has been nominated for a record 67 Video Music Awards and has won 19, more than any other artist.

MOST VMAs (VIDEO OF THE YEAR)
After debuting as the Best New Artist at the 1999 VMAs, Eminem has won Video of the Year twice, for "The Real Slim Shady" (2000) and "Without Me" (2002).

Missy Elliott has also won Video of the Year twice, once as a performer (2003's "Work It") and once as a producer, on "Lady Marmalade" featuring Christina Aguilera, Lil' Kim, Mya, and Pink (2001).

MOST VMAs
DIRECTOR
Spike Jonze's humorous videos for Weezer (1995's "Buddy Holly") and Fatboy Slim (1999's "Praise You" and 2001's "Weapon of Choice," with a dance routine by actor Christopher Walken) have brought him a record three VMA Best Direction awards.

Jonze's offbeat style transcends genre; he earned a Best Director Oscar nomination for 1999's *Being John Malkovich*, a first for a director primarily associated with music videos.

MOST EXPENSIVE MUSIC VIDEO
Michael Jackson and Janet Jackson's collaboration "Scream" (1995), with director Mark Romanek, cost $7 million to produce. In 2001 it ranked 9th on VH1's "100 Greatest Videos of All-Time" list.

Michael Jackson's groundbreaking 13-minute video "Thriller," which was made for about $1 million in 1983, earned the top spot on VH1's list.

Fashion

THE MODERN FASHION INDUSTRY BEGAN TO TAKE SHAPE in the mid-19th century, thanks to the commercially successful development of the sewing machine in the mid-1850s, and the first bona fide designer, the Englishman Charles Frederick Worth. In 1858, Worth set himself up in a shop on the then unfashionable rue de la Paix in Paris and, instead of sewing dresses according to the instructions of his customers, began selling his own designs.

Gibson Girl

1 MILESTONES

17TH CENTURY: PERIWIG
Large curled wigs, some powdered, came into fashion across Europe during the 17th and 18th centuries. The trend was started in the French royal court in 1624, when, supposedly, Louis XIII wore a wig to hide his balding head.

Styles represented specific ranks, certain positions of dignity, and even political beliefs. They were also used to protect the head from lice. Wigs are still worn today by British judges and barristers.

1873: LEVIS
Levi Strauss was a German immigrant who worked with his siblings in the dry goods business. In 1853, he traveled from Louisville, KY, to San Francisco, CA, to join a brother-in-law with a supply of goods.

Strauss sold most of his goods en route, but his stock of canvas, which was intended for tents, was the wrong type. So, he used the fabric for overalls.

When Strauss's first batch of overalls sold out, he switched to twill-weaved heavy cotton. While popular, the overalls were no different from other brands until Jacob Davis, a Nevada tailor, suggested that copper rivets be added at stress points to increase durability.

The date of that patent, May 20, 1873, is considered the birthday of denim jeans.

1886: TUXEDO JACKET The tuxedo jacket was created by Pierre Lorillard IV, a tobacco heir and owner of the Tuxedo Club and much of Tuxedo Park, NY, in 1886.

Tired of the long-tailed jacket worn at formal gatherings, Lorillard wanted a tail-less jacket to wear at his country club's Autumn Ball. At Lorillard's request, his tailor fashioned black jackets cut like the red coats worn for fox hunts.

Lorillard decided not to wear his invention to the party; however, his son Griswold and his friends took to "the tuxedo," sparking a new trend.

The bow tie and cummerbund were added to the tuxedo ensemble later.

1890-1900s: "GIBSON GIRL"
At the turn of the century, American style was dominated by the "Gibson Girl," created by the illustrator Charles Dana Gibson for fashion magazines. First seen in *Life*, she also graced the pages of *Collier's Weekly*, *Harper's New Monthly*, and *Scribner's*.

The Gibson Girl was athletic, cosmopolitan, and born into a self-made family. She wore high-necked dresses, demure shirtwaists, and long, flowing skirts cinched at her tiny waist. Her hair was styled in a wild chignon—a roll of hair fastened at the neck.

1914: BRASSIÈRE
New York socialite Mary Phelps Jacob obtained the first patent for a backless brassière on Nov. 3, 1914, liberating women from constricting corsets made of whalebone or steel rods.

There had been other undergarments that resembled Jacob's bra, but hers was the first to be patented as a "brassière." This bra was no Victoria's Secret push-up; it merely flattened the breasts, and provided no support. Cup sizes weren't developed until later.

The sports bra was created by Hinda Miller and Lisa Lindahl by sewing two jockstraps together; they patented the "jogbra" in 1977.

1920s: "THE FLAPPER"
After World War I, women bobbed their hair, donned close-fitting cloche hats, and wore shift dresses that bared legs and arms.

The boyish flapper of the swinging jazz age danced, smoked, drank bootleg liquor, wore makeup, and generally defied convention as she pleased.

1921: CHANEL NO. 5
The French designer Gabrielle "Coco" Chanel revolutionized fashion in the 1920s with her simple, easy-to-wear but elegant knit clothes, a reversal from the heavy garments women had been wearing.

Chanel was the first fashion designer to launch her own line of perfume. In May 1921 she chose the fifth fragrance perfumer Ernest Beaux presented to her, dubbing it Chanel N°5. That's why you've never heard of "Chanel N°4."

In 1926, Chanel introduced "the little black dress," the simple but stunning number that goes everywhere and always looks smashing.

◀ *Bob Hope and Raquel Welch, 1967*

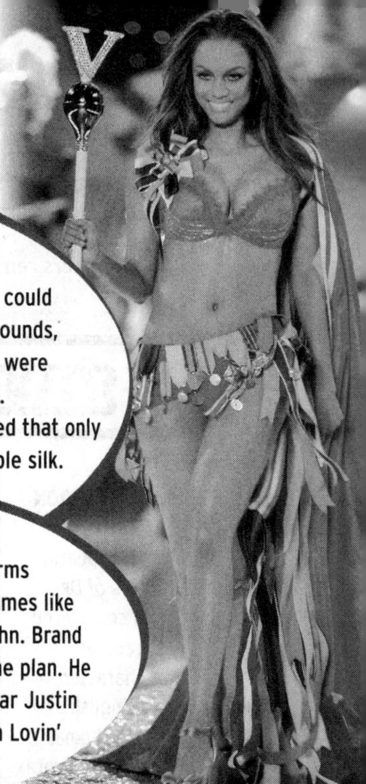

Tyra Banks models at Victoria's Secret Fashion Show, 2005 ▶

SOMETHING TO THINK ABOUT

THE REAL FASHION POLICE

During the Middle Ages, sumptuary laws enacted throughout Europe regulated the extravagance of the clothing that certain classes could wear. Some rules were based on economic or moral grounds, some were meant to assimilate foreigners, and some were meant simply to help preserve class distinctions. One such law, issued in 1574 by Elizabeth I in England, stated that only members of the royal family were allowed to wear purple silk.

McBLING

When McDonald's planned to update their employees' uniforms in 2005, they turned to big fashion names like Rocawear, Tommy Hilfiger, and Sean John. Brand consultant Steve Stoute came up with the plan. He also inked McDonald's deal with pop star Justin Timberlake in 2003 to sing their "I'm Lovin' It" slogan.

1946: BIKINI In May 1946, French swimsuit designer Jacques Heim came out with a two-piece bathing suit named "Atome" in tribute to its skimpy size. The idea failed to catch on.

A few months later, French automotive engineer Louis Réard copied the style and named it after an atoll in the Pacific Ocean where atomic bombs were being tested—Bikini.

1947: "NEW LOOK" On Feb. 14, 1947, French designer Christian Dior introduced Paris to his extravagant style, using yards of fabric in voluminous skirts paired with narrow shoulders and a cinched waist.

This style was dubbed the "New Look." Its success helped restore Paris to a dominant position in fashion.

1960: MR. BLACKWELL'S WORST DRESSED Former fashion designer and socialite Richard Blackwell thought up his infamous "Worst Dressed Women List" in 1960, along with his "Best Dressed List."

Italian actress Anna Magnani topped the first worst-dressed list, published in the Sunday newspaper supplement *American Weekly* on Oct. 30, 1960.

Four divas have topped Mr. Blackwell's Worst Dressed Women List twice: Zsa Zsa Gabor in 1962 and 1963 (the only back-to-back worst-dressed "winner"), Barbra Streisand in 1964 and 1967, Cher in 1984 and 1999, and Britney Spears in 2000 and 2005.

Blackwell has included men on the list nine times, starting with Milton Berle in 1966. The first man to top the list was shock jock Howard Stern in 1995.

1965: MINISKIRT The British designer Mary Quant opened her first boutique, Bazaar, in London in 1955. Quant is credited with introducing miniskirts in 1965.

The short skirts, often worn with bright tights, were a huge success.

SUPERLATIVES

MOST EXPENSIVE JEWELRY (AUCTION) Saudi sheik and jeweler Ahmed Fitaihi paid $16,548,750 on May 17, 1995, for an internally flawless, pear-shaped, grade D 100.10-carat white diamond at a Sotheby's auction in Geneva, Switzerland, a world record price for any piece of jewelry. He named the stone "Star of the Season."

MOST VALUABLE SHOES Stuart Weitzman designed a pair of the diamond-studded stiletto "Cinderella" sandals with a 4 ½-inch heel and 565 diamonds (including one 5-carat amaretto stone) set in platinum.

The shoes, estimated to be worth $2 million, were worn by singer Alison Krauss at the 2004 Academy Awards ceremony.

MOST FASHION AWARDS Marc Jacobs, who has worked for Perry Ellis and Louis Vuitton, has received seven awards from the Council of Fashion Designs of America (CFDA), including the Perry Ellis Award for new talent in 1987 for his first collection, three for Accessory Designer of the Year (1998/99, 2003, 2005), two for womenswear (1992, 1997), and one for menswear (2002).

Comics & Animation

FROM MICKEY MOUSE TO SHREK, Superman to the X-Men, Fred Flintstone to Homer Simpson—cartoon characters are among the most beloved figures in American pop culture. Be it movies, comic books, television shows, or comic strips, the demand for cartoon characters remains insatiable.

MILESTONES

1809: FIRST REGULAR CARTOON CHARACTER Dr. Syntax, appearing in *The Tours of Dr. Syntax*, is considered the first regular cartoon character. Drawn by English caricaturist Thomas Rowlandson, Dr. Syntax was a dull, blundering schoolmaster who often found himself in disastrous situations. Rowlandson illustrated the lyric storylines, by William Combe, with comic pictures. They began appearing in *The Poetical Magazine* in 1809 and were published in separate volumes starting in 1812.

In an early example of merchandising, Dr. Syntax's image soon appeared on mugs, puppets, dinnerware, toys, and other products snapped up by an eager public.

1842: COMIC BOOK (U.S.) *The Adventures of Mr. Obadiah Oldbuck*, a translation of a pirated copy of Rodolphe Töpffer's 1837 Swiss comic *Les Amours de M. Vieux Bois*, was the first comic book published in the U.S., on Sept. 14, 1842. The 40-page book, a supplement to the magazine *Brother Jonathan*, told its story in successive panels incorporating words and pictures.

1896: SUCCESSFUL COMIC STRIP (U.S.) The Yellow Kid—a bald, barefoot child with flapping ears and a quizzical buck-toothed smile—made his first appearance in Richard Felton Outcault's comic strip *At the Circus in Hogan's Alley* on May 5, 1895, in the Sunday *New York World*. Mickey Dugan, a.k.a. The Yellow Kid (so-nicknamed for the color of his long, dirty nightshirt), soon became the strip's star.

The strip's popularity boosted newspaper sales and inspired an outpouring of merchandise. In an 1896 bidding war, the *New York Journal* outbid the *World* for Outcault's comic strip, which he renamed *The Yellow Kid.*

1928: TALKING CARTOON The first released talking cartoon, Walt Disney's *Steamboat Willie*, premiered Nov. 18, 1928, at the Colony Theater in New York City. First made as a silent film to which sounds and the song "Turkey in the Straw" were added, the cartoon starred Mickey Mouse as a playful deckhand on a river liner.

1929: ADVENTURE STRIP Two epic strips—*Tarzan of the Apes*, based on the novels by Edgar Rice Burroughs and drawn by Harold (Hal) Foster, and *Buck Rogers in the 25th Century*, created by Philip Nowlan and drawn by Richard (Dick) Calkins—were introduced on the same day, Jan. 7, 1929.

1929: INDEPENDENTLY PUBLISHED COMIC BOOK The four-color, tabloid-sized *The Funnies* was the first U.S. comic book published independently of a newspaper or magazine. It ran for 13 issues in 1929.

In 1934, *Famous Funnies: A Carnival of Comics* became the first comic book sold at newsstands, for a price of 10 cents.

1937: FEATURE-LENGTH ANIMATED MOVIE Walt Disney's *Snow White and the Seven Dwarfs*, which premiered at Carthay Circle Theatre in Los Angeles on Dec. 21, 1937, was the first feature-length animated film. It was a huge undertaking that took almost four years to complete. About 500 artists created some 250,000 drawings, seven reels, and 81,200 cels (the transparent plastic sheets on which characters were painted) for the 83-minute final cut; the budget was an unprecedented $1.4 million. Snow White was also Disney's first attempt at animating a human character.

A multi-plane camera was invented specifically for the movie. It photographed the animation cels in distanced layers—much like characters on a stage—to allow for more realistic shadows and depth.

1938: SUPERHERO The age of superheroes began with the first appearance of Superman over 13 pages in *Action Comics No. 1*, dated June 1938.

As teenagers back in 1933, writer Jerry Siegel and illustrator Joe Shuster originally conceived of Superman as an extraterrestrial villain out to conquer the world. The pair reconsidered and made him a hero instead. The noble visitor from a distant planet (Krypton), who was imbued with awesome powers, made his way into radio, animation, TV, and film—and he still appears in comic books.

Comic book legend holds that Siegel and Shuster sold the rights to Superman to

The Simpsons

National Periodicals (now DC Comics) for only $130.

1950: *PEANUTS* APPEARS The first *Peanuts* strip appeared on Oct. 2, 1950. Its creator, Charles Schulz, introduced Charlie Brown in the first panel; Snoopy (based on Schulz's childhood dog, Spike) was brought in two days later.

The last daily installment of the beloved strip appeared on Jan. 3, 2000, a month before Schulz's death. But Charlie Brown, Snoopy, Linus, Lucy, and their friends live on in old strips that continue to run in newspapers.

1963: ANIMÉ Japanese animation styles, which were heavily influenced by American animation and comic book art, developed after World War II. On Jan. 1, 1963, Osamu Tezuka's *Astro Boy* became the first animated color cartoon series to air in Japan.

Tezuka was already famous for leading the Manga (comics) industry's 1947 revival. He first drew Tetsuwan Atom (Astro Boy) in 1951 as a comic book side character. The show focused on the adventures of a futuristic robot boy with 100,000-horsepower strength and large, glassy eyes, and set the standard for Animé style. *Astro Boy* ran for 193 episodes, through 1966.

2002: OSCAR *Shrek* (2001), an unconventional fairy tale about an endearing ogre who goes on a quest with a talkative donkey to rescue a princess, won the first Academy Award for Best Animated Feature, on March 24, 2002.

Before the category was created, Disney's *Snow White* and Pixar's *Toy Story*, the first entirely computer animated feature film, had both won special achievement awards, in 1938 and 1995.

When Walt Disney won his 1938 Oscar, he received one standard-sized statuette and seven miniature ones.

SOMETHING TO THINK ABOUT

EAT YOUR GREENS

Popeye, the salty spinach-eating sailor, was the first cartoon character to have a monument dedicated to him. On March 26, 1937, at the second annual Spinach Festival in Crystal City, TX (the "Spinach Capital of the World"), a 6-foot painted concrete statue of Popeye made by San Antonio architect Max M. Sandfield was unveiled in front of a city building. The spinach industry wanted to thank E.C. Segar, who had created *Popeye* in 1929 and whom they credited with a 33% increase in spinach consumption.

SUPERLATIVES

MOST SYNDICATED COMIC STRIP
Garfield, drawn by Jim Davis and starring a fat, lazy cat who loves lasagna, had its premiere on June 19, 1978, in 41 newspapers. From those humble beginnings, the strip has become the most widely syndicated in the world, appearing in 2,570 newspapers and read by 263 million people around the world each day.

LONGEST RUNNING COMIC BOOK
The Dandy Comic, published in Great Britain by D.C. Thomson, debuted on Dec. 4, 1937, and has been published continuously ever since, making it the world's longest running comic book. Many different characters have been shown in its pages over the years. The Dandy Bellboy—who gave the comic its name—used to appear on the front cover and at the end of each story, but was never in the comic itself.

An original first issue (one of 10 known), including its "free" metal whistle bonus, fetched $36,394 from an anonymous bidder at Hamer Auctions in England on Sept. 7, 2004, a record price for a British comic.

LONGEST RUNNING PRIME-TIME ANIMATED SERIES
From 1987 to 1989, the Simpson family—drawn somewhat differently—appeared in animated shorts on *The Tracey Ullman Show*. Matt Groening, the creator, was offered his own half-hour show, and on Dec. 17, 1989, *The Simpsons* aired as a holiday special with an episode titled "Simpsons Roasting on an Open Fire." The first regular episode, "Bart the Genius," appeared on Jan. 14, 1990.

The irreverent series—following the exploits of Homer, Marge, Bart, Lisa, and Maggie Simpson and their friends and neighbors in Springfield—is now TV's longest running prime-time animated show, as well as its longest running situation comedy series. *The Simpsons* has won 15 Emmys, including eight Outstanding Animated Program awards, and it was contracted to air through at least 2008.

TOP-GROSSING ANIMATED FILM
Shrek 2, the sequel to the award-winning *Shrek*, became the top-grossing animated movie of all-time by the end of 2004. Its total North American gross was $441,226,247, and its worldwide gross was $918,506,048.

Toys

Gold engine made for Lionel Trains' 100th anniversary

WHAT WOULD CHILDHOOD BE WITHOUT TOYS? There were stone marbles in Egypt in 3000 BC, and crude wooden dolls have been found in ancient graves. Some more recent toys have shown amazing longevity, and learning their origins can be almost as fun as it is to play with them.

MILESTONES

1880: STEIFF ANIMALS German seamstress Margarete Steiff grew up confined to a wheelchair. For Christmas 1880, she made some elephant-shaped pin cushions which quickly became popular as children's toys.

In 1886 Steiff sold 5,170 stuffed elephants and began expanding to other animals. The animals were displayed to great acclaim at the 1893 Leipzig trade fair. The button in the ear to show authenticity was added in Nov. 1904.

Steiff's stuffed animals are highly prized collectors' items today.

1900: ELECTRIC TRAINS In 1900, when Americans were entranced by the sleek passenger trains that were crossing the country, 22-year-old Joshua Lionel Cowen of New York City attached a small, battery-run electric fan motor he had invented to the bottom of a model railroad flatcar. He sold the toy train to a store owner as a window advertising display.

Electricity was new and most toy trains were spring-loaded or ran on burning alcohol. Although Cowen's was not the first model electric train displayed, it was the first one to become popular on a national level. Cowen began a sales catalog in 1902 for engines and model accessories.

1903: TEDDY BEARS In Nov. 1902, President Theodore (Teddy) Roosevelt went bear hunting near Smedes, MS. But when the guide clubbed a bear and tied it to a tree for Roosevelt to shoot, he rejected the idea as unsportmanlike. *Washington Post* illustrator Clifford Berryman created a cartoon of the event that became famous.

A Brooklyn, NY, store owner, Morris Michtom, had his wife stitch up some plush bears, which they called teddy bears—supposedly with Roosevelt's permission. Within a few years, Michtom's firm, the Ideal Novelty and Toy Co., was mass-producing teddy bears.

Steiff also added a bear to their line of stuffed animals in 1903.

1913: ERECTOR SET Inspired by watching workers construct an electrical system with riveted steel girders, A. C. Gilbert—the 1908 Olympic pole vaulting champ—created a construction set for kids with steel beams, wheels, motors, pulleys, and gears.

Gilbert began selling the Mysto Erector Structural Steel Builder in 1913, with the first major ad campaign launched for a toy. The tag line was "Hello Boys! Make Lots of Toys."

Gilbert went on to amass some 150 patents.

1918: LINCOLN LOGS The inventor of Lincoln Logs, John Lloyd Wright, was the son of famed architect Frank Lloyd Wright. John joined his father for a trip to Tokyo in 1916 to oversee construction of the Imperial Hotel, built with interlocking cantilevered beams to withstand earthquakes.

When they returned to America, John designed sturdy interlocking wooden log-shaped blocks for use as toys, and began selling Lincoln Logs in 1918.

1918: RAGGEDY ANN When newspaper cartoonist Johnny Gruelle's daughter Marcella found an old rag doll in her grandmother's attic, he painted a new face on it with a red nose, and gave the doll oven-mitt hands.

Father and daughter named it Raggedy Ann after James Whitcomb Riley's poems, "The Raggedy Man" and "Orphan Annie".

Tragically, Marcella became deathly ill with smallpox. Gruelle distracted her with stories about Raggedy Ann, and also began incorporating the doll into his cartoons. Marcella soon passed away. Gruelle eventually patented the doll and began to sell them in 1918.

1952: MR. POTATO HEAD About 1950, model maker George Lerner created plastic pieces shaped like eyes, ears, noses, and mouths, equipped with prongs so they could be pushed into fruits or vegetables to make funny faces. Sales were low until 1952, when Hasbro began marketing the pieces as Mr. "Potato Head." It was the first toy ever advertised on TV.

A spouse, Mrs. Potato Head, arrived in 1953, and the pair finally got plastic bodies in 1964.

When Mr. Potato Head celebrated his 50th birthday on Feb. 5, 2002, he was given his own American Association of Retired People (AARP) membership card.

1955: LEGO Danish carpenter Ole Kirk Christiansen founded his toy company in

Some Record-Setting Toy Sales

Teddy Bear	Steiff bear (Teddy Girl)	$171,000 (London)	Dec. 5, 1994
Action Figure	1963 G. I. Joe Prototype	$200,001.10 (San Diego, CA)	July 17, 2003
American Tin Toy	"Charles" Hose Reel c. 1875 (fire wagon)	$231,000 (New York)	Dec. 16, 1991
Model Train	1906 Märklin spirit-fired gauge V steam train	$165,783.74 (London)	Dec. 17, 2001

Some Classic Toys

TOY	INVENTOR	DATE
Crayola Crayons	Binney & Smith	1903
View-Master	Harold Graves & William Gruber	1939
Slinky	Richard James	1943
Wiffle Ball	David Mullany	1953
Matchbox Toys	Leslie Smith and Rodney Smith	1954
Trolls	Thomas Dam	1956
Etch A Sketch	Arthur Granjean (France)	1959
G.I. Joe	Hasbro	1964
SuperBall	Norman Stingley	1965
Big Wheels	Ray Lohr	1969
Nerf Ball	Reyn Guyer	1969
Rubik's Cube	Erno Rubik (Hungary)	1974
Dungeons & Dragons	Gary Gygax	1974
Cabbage Patch Kids	Xavier Roberts	1978
Super Soaker	Lonnie Johnson	1982
Furby	Dave Hampton	1998

1934, naming it LEGO, for *leg godt* ("play well").

In 1949, the company began making interlocking plastic blocks that were hollow underneath, sold only in Denmark.

The LEGO System of Play, 28 sets of bricks and 8 vehicles, was first sold in 1955 and introduced in the U.S. in 1961. LEGO people were added in 1978.

One reason why these simple bricks are so popular is the impressive variety—there are 915,103,765 ways to connect six two-by-four bricks.

1956: PLAY-DOH In 1954, Joseph McVicker was running his family's failing cleaning products business in Cincinnati, OH, when he saw his daughter playing with a soft wallpaper cleaning product. He gave some to his sister-in-law, a nursery school teacher in Mountain Lakes, NJ, and her students loved it. McVicker made a non-toxic version and added color variety.

After selling some to the Cincinnati school system, McVicker and his brother Noah formed a company to make and sell the compound as Play-Doh in 1956. They sold $1.34 million worth of Play-Doh in 1957 alone. That's a lot of dough.

SUPERLATIVES

BEST-SELLING FASHION DOLL Ruth Handler, who founded Mattel toys with her husband, realized that her daughter, Barbara, wanted to play with a teenage doll—not the traditional baby doll.

In 1956, on vacation in Europe, Handler saw a "Lilli" doll—based on a racy German comic—and brought some to the designers at Mattel. They unveiled a shapely 11 1/2-inch doll with vinyl skin and rooted hair, named Barbara Millicent Roberts, or "Barbie," at the Toy Fair in New York on March 9, 1959.

Dolls and accessories were added—including boyfriend Ken in 1961 (named after Handler's son)—and are updated every year.

Dolls are the second most profitable toy category after infant toys, and Barbie is queen, with more than 1 billion sold since 1959. At Mattel, the world's largest toy maker, Barbie accounts for a third of all sales. The company estimates that American girls age 2-11 own an average of 10 Barbies each.

Barbie—who has had more than 80 careers, including astronaut, athlete, doctor, and bride (the best-selling outfit)—has her own fan club and conventions. If she were life-size, should would be 5'9", measuring 36-18-33.

Museums

THE WORD "MUSEUM" is derived from the Greek *mouseion*, meaning a temple or other building dedicated to the nine Muses. The artifacts kept in ancient Greek temples were sometimes exhibited to the public, and European churches and monasteries in the Middle Ages sometimes displayed jewels, statues, manuscripts, and saints' relics.

By the 16th century, the palaces of the wealthy contained prized collections of art and natural curiosities; gradually, many such collections were opened to the public, and by the 18th century, museums as we know them were established in Europe.

MILESTONES

ABOUT 290 BC: FIRST *MOUSEION* The Alexandrian Library and Museum was founded in Alexandria, Egypt, by Ptolemy I about 290 BC. Objects such as surgical and astronomical instruments, animal hides, elephant tusks, statues, and portrait busts were housed there and used for teaching. The library and museum were sacked and burned several times; the worst destruction came in 47 BC when the Romans set fire to the facility.

1683: FIRST PUBLIC MUSEUM The first public museum in the modern sense probably was the Ashmolean Museum, opened to the public by Oxford University in 1683. It housed a collection of rare objects, including gems, minerals, and botanical specimens, donated to the university by the antiquarian Elias Ashmole. This was also the first institution to be called by the English name "museum."

1753: BRITISH MUSEUM The British Museum in London was founded by an act of Parliament on June 7, 1753, based primarily on some 70,000 artifacts donated by the British physician and naturalist Sir Hans Sloane, who died that year. It opened on Jan. 15, 1759.

Among the museum's highlights are extensive collections of Egyptian antiquities, including the Rosetta Stone, and Greek and Roman antiquities. The museum houses the celebrated Elgin Marbles from the ancient Greek Parthenon, which were brought to England in 1806 by the British diplomat Lord Elgin to prevent either the Turks or French from getting them. Today, Greece wants them back as part of their heritage.

1769: UFFIZI The Uffizi Gallery in Florence, Italy, was built as government offices for Cosimo I of the ruling Medici family between 1560 and 1580. Designed by Giorgio Vasari, it connects Palazzo della Signoria, Florence's city hall, with another Medici facility, the Palazzo Pitti. When the Medici line ended in 1737, the city inherited the building and art. The Uffizi opened to the public in 1769. It contains works by most major Renaissance artists, including paintings, sculptures, drawings, and prints.

1773: FIRST MUSEUM (U.S.) The Charleston Museum in Charleston, SC, dedicated to the natural history of the region, was founded on Jan. 12, 1773. It was the first museum in the American colonies, and is the oldest U.S. museum in continuous existence.

1793: LOUVRE Construction of the Louvre began in Paris in 1546 during the reign of Francis I, who decided to transform a medieval fortress into a luxurious residence that would also hold his art collection. It was a royal residence until 1682. In 1793, during the French Revolution, it was opened to the public.

The museum today is one of the largest in the world. Among its treasures are the *Venus de Milo* and Leonardo da Vinci's *Mona Lisa*.

1805: ART MUSEUM (U.S.) The Pennsylvania Academy of the Fine Arts was established in Philadelphia on Dec. 26, 1805, by artist Charles Willson Peale and 70 other Philadelphians, and opened in 1807. It was the first successful U.S. art museum.

Visitors today can view Peale's self-portrait *The Artist in His Museum*, as well as works by Mary Cassatt, Thomas Eakins, and Alexander Calder.

1824: SCIENCE MUSEUM (U.S.) The Franklin Institute Science Museum in Philadelphia, founded by Samuel Vaughan Merrick and William H. Keating on Feb. 5, 1824, became the first U.S. science museum. Originally located in Independence Hall, it opened in its current location in 1934. It houses a planetarium, an IMAX theatre, and science exhibits.

1846: SMITHSONIAN The Smithsonian Institution was founded by an act of Congress on Aug. 10, 1846, under the terms of a bequest from British scientist James Smithson to create "an establishment for the increase and diffusion of knowledge among men."

Smithson died in 1829 and the legacy was accepted by Congress in 1836, but it was not until May 1, 1847, that the cornerstone of the first building, known as the Castle, was laid.

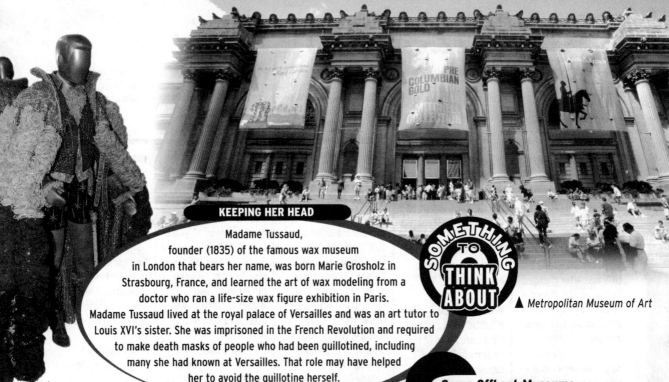

▲ *Outfit from the Liberace Museum*

▲ *Metropolitan Museum of Art*

SOMETHING TO THINK ABOUT

KEEPING HER HEAD

Madame Tussaud, founder (1835) of the famous wax museum in London that bears her name, was born Marie Grosholz in Strasbourg, France, and learned the art of wax modeling from a doctor who ran a life-size wax figure exhibition in Paris. Madame Tussaud lived at the royal palace of Versailles and was an art tutor to Louis XVI's sister. She was imprisoned in the French Revolution and required to make death masks of people who had been guillotined, including many she had known at Versailles. That role may have helped her to avoid the guillotine herself.

SUPERLATIVES

1976: BLOCKBUSTER EXHIBIT
"The Treasures of Tutankhamen," 55 artifacts from the tomb of Egypt's "King Tut", began a tour of U.S. museums on Nov. 17, 1976, at the National Gallery in Washington, DC. By the time the tour ended at San Francisco's M.H. de Young Memorial Museum on Sept. 30, 1979, the exhibit had drawn an estimated 8 million people, making it the world's first traveling museum "mega-event."

King Tut and his riches returned to the U.S. in a bigger exhibit of more than 130 artifacts in 2005-07.

BIGGEST MUSEUM COMPLEX (WORLD)
The Smithsonian Institution, based in Washington, DC, is the world's biggest museum complex, with about 144 million items housed in 18 museums. More than 20 million people visited Smithsonian museums in 2004.

Units based in Washington include the Hirshhorn Museum and Sculpture Garden, National Air and Space Museum, American Art Museum, National Museum of American History, National Portrait Gallery, and National Museum of the American Indian, along with the National Zoo.

BIGGEST MUSEUM (U.S.) The Metropolitan Museum of Art, founded in 1870, is the largest individual U.S. museum. The 2-million-square-foot building spans four city blocks along New York's Central Park. Its holdings of over two million objects range from superb collections of ancient, Egyptian, Middle Eastern, and Asian art to contemporary European and American works. It includes an Egyptian temple that was moved from its original site and reassembled in the museum.

Some Offbeat Museums

MUSEUM	LOCATION
America Sanitary Plumbing Museum	Worcester, MA
Britt Hobo Museum	Britt, IA
Burlingame Museum of Pez Memorabilia	Burlingame, CA
Cockroach Hall of Fame Museum	Plano, TX
Daredevil Museum	Niagara Falls, NY
Dog Mushing Museum	Fairbanks, AK
Dr. Pepper Museum	Waco, TX
Flashlight Museum	Fridley, MN
Haverstraw Brick Museum	Haverstraw, NY
International UFO Museum and Research Center	Roswell, NM
Johnny Gruelle Raggedy Ann & Andy Museum	Arcola, IL
Liberace Museum	Las Vegas, NV
Lunchbox Museum	Salem, AL
Mount Horeb Mustard Museum	Mount Horeb, WI
Museum of Bad Art	Dedham, MA
Museum of Dirt	Boston, MA
National Buffalo Museum	Jamestown, ND
Spam Museum	Austin, MN
Toilet Seat Art Museum	Alamo Heights, TX
Vent Haven (Ventriloquist Museum)	Fort Mitchell, KY
World Famous Asphalt Museum	Sacramento, CA
World Kite Museum	Long Beach, WA

The Wizard of Oz

***THE WIZARD OF OZ* HAS BEEN PART OF AMERICAN POP CULTURE** for over a century. L. Frank Baum's novel is a classic of children's literature, while the 1939 movie is one of the most beloved films of all time. Somewhere over the rainbow, perhaps there is a person who doesn't know the phrase "Follow the yellow brick road," but in Kansas (and the other 49 states) there is hardly a man, woman, or munchkin who doesn't recognize its origin.

MILESTONES

1900: FIRST OZ BOOK The first Oz book, *The Wonderful Wizard of Oz*, was published on May 15, 1900. (The title was later changed to simply *The Wizard of Oz.*) The author, L. Frank Baum, had been a newspaper editor and then a traveling salesman for a china company.

He started making up stories on his travels, to tell to his children when he returned home.

Baum was already a successful author by 1899, when his book *Father Goose* became the best-selling children's book of that year. He achieved the same distinction in 1900 with the first Oz book.

1902: FIRST STAGE PRODUCTION The first of a number of *Wizard of Oz* stage musicals opened in Chicago on June 16, 1902, and then went on tour, reaching Broadway on Jan. 20, 1903. After a $9\frac{1}{2}$-month run, it toured again for several years.

Baum had written a fairly straightforward adaptation of his book, but the producer and director turned it into a comic opera and vaudeville extravaganza.

1908: SCREEN PRODUCTION Many films were made of the Oz story before the famous 1939 version. The first, *The Fairylogue and Radio Plays*, a combination of film and live action on stage, appeared in 1908. Baum created and narrated the production, which flopped.

1939: MOVIE PREMIERE The MGM classic *The Wizard of Oz*, produced by Mervyn LeRoy, had its official premiere in Hollywood on Aug. 15, 1939. Thousands of fans lined the streets and filled the bleachers erected outside of Grauman's Chinese Theatre, where a temporary yellow brick road led to the entrance.

1940: OSCAR NIGHT When the 12th Annual Academy Awards were announced on Feb. 29, 1940, *The Wizard of Oz* won two Oscars, Herbert Stothart's for Original Score, and Harold Arlen and E. Y. Harburg's for Best Song ("Over the Rainbow," which had almost been cut from the film). It was also nominated for Best Picture, Art Direction, Cinematography, and Special Effects.

Judy Garland got a special miniature Juvenile Award, which she later called the "Munchkin Award."

Gone with the Wind won nine of its 15 nominations that evening, including Best Picture, in what many consider the strongest year in film history. Victor Fleming, the credited director of both films, won Best Director for *Gone with the Wind.*

1949: RE-RELEASE MGM first re-released *The Wizard of Oz* in April 1949. Other re-releases followed.

1956: TV *The Wizard of Oz* was shown on TV for the first time on Nov. 3, 1956.

The CBS program was introduced by Bert Lahr (who had played the Cowardly Lion), Liza Minnelli (Garland's daughter, then 10 years old), and 13-year-old fan Justin Schiller, who two months later founded the International Wizard of Oz Club. An estimated 45 million people tuned in.

The film was broadcast next on Dec. 13, 1959, and hosted by comedian Red Skelton and his 12-year-old daughter. It attracted a huge audience again and the broadcast became an annual tradition.

On March 15, 1970—the first airing since Garland's accidental overdose death on June 22, 1969—Gregory Peck introduced the film with a tribute to its legendary star.

1977: COMMEMORATIVE PLATES Eight limited-edition plates painted with scenes from *The Wizard of Oz* were issued by the Edwin M. Knowles China Company in 1977, making it the first film honored with a commemorative plate collection.

1990: OZ STAMP In 1990 the U.S. Postal Service included *The Wizard of Oz* in a set of commemorative stamps honoring the 50th anniversaries of four classic motion pictures from 1939. (The others were *Gone With the Wind*, *Stagecoach*, and *Beau Geste.*)

Resembling a miniature movie poster, the stamp depicted Judy Garland in her role as Dorothy.

1998: AFI BEST FILMS *The Wizard of Oz* was named No. 6 on the list of 100 Best American Movies of All Time by the American Film Institute (AFI) in 1998.

(Film buffs know that the top five movies on the list were *Citizen Kane, Casablanca, The Godfather, Gone with the Wind*, and *Lawrence of Arabia.*)

2004: AFI BEST SONGS "Over the Rainbow" was named No. 1 on the AFI's list of 100 top movie songs of all time in 2004.

SOMETHING TO THINK ABOUT

LOTS OF DIRECTION

Five directors were involved in making *The Wizard of Oz*. The original director, Richard Thorpe, filmed for 10 days, until producer Mervyn LeRoy replaced him with George Cukor (LeRoy did not use any of Thorpe's footage). Cukor did not shoot any actual scenes, but he changed the look of the film by redesigning sets, costumes, and makeup (Dorothy's and the Scarecrow's, in particular); he then left to begin work on *Gone with the Wind*. Victor Fleming took over and did most of the actual directing, but he too eventually left for *Gone with the Wind*. King Vidor finished the film, largely directing the sepia-toned "Kansas scenes." Producer Mervyn LeRoy directed some transitional scenes himself. Fleming is the credited director of two of the most beloved movies in Hollywood history, but none of the other contributing directors appears on the credits of either film.

OZ FESTS

Many towns around the U.S. stage annual Oz festivals. Among them are the Wizard of Oz Festival in Chesterton, IN (site of the Wizard of Oz Museum); Oz Fest in Chinnenango, NY (Baum's hometown); Ozfest (formerly Oztober) in Liberal, KS (site of a tourist attraction called Dorothy's House); and the Judy Garland Festival in her hometown of Grand Rapids, MI.

PROJECT OZMA

Project Ozma, one of the first projects of SETI (Search for Extraterrestrial Intelligence), began in April 1960. Named after the Queen of Oz, which according to the books was a land "very far away, difficult to reach, and populated by strange and exotic beings," the project lasted until July 1960. Project Ozma was an attempt to detect interstellar radio transmissions; it didn't find any.

MUNCHKIN LAND

132 Munchkins appeared in the film; 124 were played by adults and eight by children. Most of the voices, however, were dubbed by professional singers. There is a widely circulated urban myth that one of the Munchkin actors committed suicide during filming, and that his body can be seen in the background of the Tin Man's forest scene. It is actually a bird.

SUPERLATIVES

AUTHOR OF THE MOST OZ BOOKS L. Frank Baum wrote the first 14 books in the Oz series, but another author wrote more. After Baum's death in 1919, Ruth Plumly Thompson took over the series, and wrote 19 Oz books, published between 1921 and 1939.

Another seven were written by others.

MOST ACTORS FOR A SINGLE OZ ROLE Three actors were cast as the Tin Man at one time or another.

Ray Bolger was originally cast in that role, but asked to play the Scarecrow instead. Buddy Ebsen, originally cast as the Scarecrow, became the Tin Man and began filming, but was hospitalized two weeks later when he developed a severe allergic reaction to aluminum dust in his makeup. Jack Haley finally performed the role in the film.

ACTOR PLAYING THE MOST OZ ROLES Frank Morgan played five roles in the film—the Wizard, Professor Marvel (in Kansas), the Emerald City gatekeeper, the cabbie driving the Horse of a Different Color, and the Wizard's guard.

HIGHEST PRICE FOR OZ MEMORABILIA
A whopping $666,000 was paid on May 24, 2000, by collector David Elkouby for a pair of ruby slippers worn by Garland in the film. Anthony Landini had originally bought that pair at auction for $165,000 in June 1988; another pair was sold a week later at the same price.

Seven pairs are believed to have been made for the film, but the whereabouts of only five are known; one is in the Smithsonian; another is owned by actress Debbie Reynolds.

Archaeology

ARCHAEOLOGY IS THE SCIENTIFIC STUDY OF THE MATERIAL REMAINS—tools, artwork, weapons, household items, and so on—of past human life. The archaeologist both recovers the past (through excavations and other activities) and tries to understand it. An archaeological find can be quite modest—a couple of ancient coins, a broken vase—or it can be spectacular, such as a complete ancient city forgotten for centuries.

MILESTONES

1738: HERCULANEUM AND POMPEII One of the earliest and most spectacular archaeological finds came about when the French Bourbon King Charles III, who ruled over Naples, heard stories of unearthed artifacts in an area near Naples and funded a project to excavate the site, with architect Joaquin de Alcubierre in charge.

In 1738 the Theater of Hercules was uncovered with an inscription that identified it as part of the city of Herculaneum. Alcubierre then dug a series of large holes and tunnels searching for more treasures, often with little regard for fragile items.

In 1748 he found another, more accessible Roman metropolis, which he called Civita. Its true name, found 15 years later, was Pompeii. Swiss engineer Karl Weber, who joined the project in 1750, was very methodical, digging carefully and recording all his findings.

Both cities had been buried by the eruption of Mount Vesuvius on August 24, 79 AD.

1782: EARLY AMERICAN EXCAVATION When he was temporarily out of politics and living on his estate, Thomas Jefferson noted Indians passing by and stopping mournfully at a site along the Rivanna River. He had the site carefully excavated in layers, anticipating modern archaeological methods, and found skeletons there in what proved to be a large Indian burial mound.

1799: ROSETTA STONE In 1799, troops of Napoleon Bonaparte, who had invaded Egypt the year before, came across a tablet near the town of Rosetta (Rashid) containing parallel texts in two Egyptian scripts and Greek writing. Scholars, using their knowledge of Greek, started deciphering the Egyptian scripts.

On Sept. 27, 1822, the French scholar Jean-François Champollion announced that the translation was done, the first breakthrough in understanding the long-lost language of the pharaohs.

1870: TROY For centuries, Europeans had read tales of the ancient city of Troy, whose destruction was recounted in Homer's epic poems, but there was doubt that it ever really existed.

In 1870, Heinrich Schliemann, a German businessman and amateur archaeologist, who had financed his own expedition to western Turkey, excavated a mound called *Hissarlik* ("Place of Fortresses"). There he found gold and silver treasure and other signs of past civilization and concluded that the area was indeed the site of ancient Troy.

Over the next 65 years, excavations carried out by others confirmed his conclusion.

1879: CAVE PAINTINGS The Spanish nobleman Marcelino Sanz de Sautuola had been visiting a cave near Altamira in northern Spain for a few years and found interesting bones and tools there. On one summer visit in 1879 he brought along his little daughter Maria. While he was digging for artifacts, Maria noticed paintings of bison on the ceiling. Marcelino was reminded of prehistoric art he had seen at an exhibit in Paris.

The paintings were found to be authentic and dated to about 16,000–14,000 BC. Altamira cave has since been called the "Sistine Chapel of Rock Art."

1900: MINOAN PALACE British archaeologist Arthur Evans had good reason to believe there were valuable remains on Crete; he had previously found a number of fascinating carved sealstones there. He began a series of excavations, culminating in the discovery (1900) of a great royal palace from the 2nd millennium BC. His findings confirmed that that the ancient civilization on Crete referred to by the Greeks was real.

The term "Minoan" was coined by Evans, who named the civilization after Minos, the name of several possibly legendary Cretan kings.

1922: KING TUT'S TOMB There is probably no archaeological find more famous than the tomb of the Egyptian boy pharaoh Tutankhamen, who reigned in the 14th century BC. By the time it was found, most other Egyptian tombs had long been plundered by grave robbers.

For years British archaeologist Howard Carter and his patron, Lord Carnarvon

(George Herbert), had searched the area known as the Valley of the Kings for an intact tomb. Carter was about ready to quit when he decided to try once more.

On Nov. 4, 1922, his expedition unearthed a stairway that led to a door. The seal on the door had not been broken, meaning that the tomb was untouched.

Carter waited for Lord Carnarvon to arrive from England, and they opened the tomb on Feb. 17, 1923. The golden treasures they found astounded the world and gave archaeologists new insights into ancient Egyptian culture.

1947: DEAD SEA SCROLLS One of the greatest finds in biblical archaeology was made by Arab shepherd boys of the Taamireh Bedouin tribe, who spotted a curious hole in a large rock on the western shore of the Dead Sea in the area of Khirbet Qumran. Below the rock was a cave holding large clay jars containing manuscripts or scrolls, preserved in large degree because of the dry air. Apparently written at various times between around 200 BC and AD 68, they were attributed to a previously unknown Jewish sect and shed new light on Jewish history and culture.

Among the documents discovered were two of the oldest known copies of the Book of Isaiah and fragments of every book in the Old Testament except Esther, as well as hymn books, commentaries, and other works.

1947: CARBON-14 DATING Until Willard Libby came along, archaeological dating had a large element of guesswork. Libby, a professor of chemistry at the University of Chicago, realized that by measuring the proportion of radioactive carbon-14 (C14) in objects, he could determine their age.

In 1947, Libby and his colleagues found that after 5,568 years, half the C14 in an original sample will have decayed into nitrogen, and after another 5,568 years, half of that remaining material will have decayed, and so on.

The half-life of radiocarbon was recalculated to 5,730 plus or minus 40 years in 1962. Today, there are over 130 radiocarbon dating laboratories around the world.

Libby's discovery is considered one of the greatest archaeological breakthroughs of the 20th century.

Machu Picchu

SOMETHING TO THINK ABOUT

CITY IN THE SKY

High in the Andes Mountains, 7,972 feet above sea level, and about 50 miles northwest of Cuzco, Peru, lies the site of the ancient Incan city Machu Picchu. The city covered about 5 square miles and contained terraces built around a central plaza and linked by numerous stairways. The American explorer Hiram Bingham discovered Machu Picchu in 1911. He thought it might have been one of the last Inca strongholds before they were conquered by the Spanish. However, the Spanish made no record of Machu Picchu, leading researchers to believe that the city had been long abandoned. Its history remains a mystery.

SUPERLATIVES

LARGEST ANCIENT SCULPTURE COLLECTION

In 1974, workers digging a well near Xi'an, China, came upon fragments of a life-sized warrior figure. Archaeologists were called to the site, and after further investigation discovered vaults containing thousands of life-sized terracotta soldiers and their horses and chariots. They had come upon the tomb of the Chinese emperor Qin Shi Huangdi, who ruled between 221 and 210 BC.

The Chinese government built the Terracotta Army Museum in 1975. It houses the original pit, which holds the 6,000 soldiers and horses found there, and two other pits containing figures of cavalrymen, horses, infantrymen, and wooden chariots.

OLDEST COIN

Although there are several candidates for the claim, what may be the oldest coin yet discovered is known as the "Lydian Lion" third stater. (A "stater" is a coin used by ancient Greek city-states, and was also a fixed unit of weight; a third stater is a coin with $\frac{1}{3}$ of that value.)

The coin, which bears the head of a lion, is made of electrum, an alloy of gold and silver that occurred naturally in rivers, and is believed to have been minted by King Alyattes in Sardis, Lydia, Asia Minor (what is now Turkey), around 600-575 BC.

BIOTECHNOLOGY

Agriculture & Food

BIOTECHNOLOGY INVOLVES THE APPLICATION OF SCIENCE AND TECHNOLOGY TO LIVING ORGANISMS. Before the 20th Century it involved applications such as brewing and food production. Since the mid-20th Century its development has been closely linked to advances in genetic engineering. The application of biotechnology to agriculture has led to new forms of crops and increased farm production. But modern genetic modification techniques have caused controversy. Although many experts claim that there is no difference in principle between manipulating molecules through biotechnology and traditional breeding techniques, others worry that genetic modification could end up causing unexpected harm.

MILESTONES

C. 7000 BC: FERMENTED BEVERAGES
The earliest evidence of fermented beverages dates back 9,000 years to the Neolithic village of Jiahu in Henan Province of eastern China. Potsherds dated between 7000 BC and 6600 BC were analyzed by a team of researchers led by Patrick McGovern of the University of Pennsylvania. The pottery revealed traces of hawthorn fruit or grapes mixed with honey and rice; the researchers determined that the sugar and yeast needed for fermentation had been present.

1780: ARTIFICIAL INSEMINATION
Artificial insemination is a key technique on the modern farm; it allows top-quality animals to be bred quickly.

Although there are claims that artificial insemination was performed on horses in the Middle East almost 2,000 years ago, the roots of the modern-day practice are much more recent. Italian scientist and priest Lazzaro Spallanzani conducted the first successful experiment in this field in 1780, when he artificially inseminated a poodle that later gave birth to three pups. A few years later, Scottish surgeon John Hunter performed the first successful artificial insemination of a human.

Supported by the government, Russian scientist Ilya Ivanovich founded a center for artificial insemination in 1901. He developed a program for impregnating horses. Over the next three decades he extended his method for collecting semen to such farm animals as cattle, sheep, and pigs.

1809: FOOD STORAGE
In 1795, the Society for the Encouragement of Industry, a French organization created by Napoleon Bonaparte, offered a 12,000-franc cash prize to the scientist who could develop a method for food preservation. The purpose of the contest was to aid the military. Napoleon knew that an army marches on its stomach and that, if good food could be preserved, his troops would be healthier in both mind and body.

The prize was awarded in 1809 to Nicolas Appert for inventing what is known as food canning. Under Appert's new method, food was cooked in open kettles and placed in glass jars, which were sealed by corks wired in place. The jars were then heated by submersion in boiling water.

In 1810 an English inventor, Peter Durand, patented the idea of using tin-plated cans. Commercial canning was introduced into the U.S. in 1821 by the William Underwood Company of Boston.

1860s: PASTEURIZATION
French chemist and microbiologist Louis Pasteur revolutionized the farm and food industries when he developed a method of heating wine and milk in order to kill, or make inactive, the microbes that can spoil or ferment these products. His process, called "pasteurization," is widely used today to make food and drink safe for public consumption.

1879: GENETICS IN FOOD PRODUCTION
Inspired by Charles Darwin's book on hybrid vigor, William James Beal, a professor of botany and horticulture at Michigan Agricultural College (now Michigan State University), performed the first controlled cross-fertilization, combining two varieties of corn to make a unique third.

Beal's work had a major impact on the use of genetic science to increase production yields of crops. Crops that he grew increased their yields by as much as 53%.

1939: FREEZING SPERM The biggest step toward improving artificial insemination was learning how to freeze sperm to extend its life, thus allowing for a more extensive and efficient use of livestock. In 1939, University of Wisconsin biochemist

SOMETHING TO THINK ABOUT

CLONE AUCTION

The rights to the first calf clone sold at auction fetched $82,000 on Oct. 6, 2000, at the 34th World Dairy Expo in Madison, WI. Billed as the "auction of the millennium," the event featured indoor fireworks, a light show, and a musical performance before the bidding started. Spencer Landswerk of Minneapolis, MN, acting on behalf of the Landox Syndicate, placed the high bid on the as yet unborn animal, an exact copy of a champion Holstein named Lauduc Broker Mandy from Carrousel Farms of Orangeville, IL. Mandy II was cloned by Infigen, Inc., of DeForest, WI, and was born on Sept. 2, 2001.

Paul Phillips and his graduate assistant Henry Lardy discovered that the phospholipids and lipoproteins in egg yolk could protect sperm from shock during cooling. By 1950, with the development of chemicals that extend the life of the sperm, antibiotics to prevent bacterial contamination, and a switch to using liquid nitrogen instead of dry ice and alcohol, artificial insemination with frozen sperm had become common practice on farms.

1946: "GREEN REVOLUTION"
While assessing Japan's postwar agricultural problems, American agronomist S. Cecil Salmon unknowingly began what was later called the "Green Revolution," a scientific effort to alleviate world hunger. He acquired seeds from 16 different strains of wheat plants from Norin, Japan. One of them was the dwarf Norin No. 10 strain, a type with little foliage and a heavy grain head. Salmon distributed these seeds to wheat breeders in the U.S., including Orville Vogel of Washington State University.

Over the next 13 years, Vogel used the seeds to make various hybrid crosses of the wheat varieties. Finally, in 1959, he produced the Gaines strain, the first semidwarf strain of wheat suitable for commercial use. It was rugged and allowed for greater production.

Norman Borlaug of the International Center for Maize and Wheat Improvement in Mexico, crossed the Gaines strain with Mexico's best wheat varieties. He introduced these new dwarf grains to India in 1966 to help with its wheat crisis. Native Indian wheat grew too high when fertilized with nitrogen, and it collapsed under its own weight; this had caused widespread famine in India during the 1950s.

Borlaug's new dwarf wheat variety was an immediate success. It allowed Indian wheat production to surge from 12 million metric tons in 1965 to over 20 million metric tons in 1970. Borlaug's work in India became a model for other countries. He was awarded the 1970 Nobel Peace Prize and is known as "father of the Green Revolution."

1986: GENETICALLY ENGINEERED CROP
On May 30, 1986, the first genetically engineered crop, of tobacco, was planted on a Wisconsin farm. This field test was conducted by Agracetus (now Monsanto), a biotechnology company in Middleton, WI, and required approval from the U.S. Environmental Protection Agency and the U.S. Department of Agriculture. The tobacco plants were modified to resist a bacterial disease called crown gall that causes tumors on plant roots; the disease disrupts water and nutrient flow within an infected plant and can inhibit its growth and reproduction.

This was only the second time that living genetically engineered organisms were deliberately released into the environment. The first was when a gene-altered virus in a swine vaccine underwent field tests in 1985.

1994: GENETICALLY ENGINEERED FOOD The Flavr Savr tomato was the first genetically engineered food approved by the U.S. Food and Drug Administration. Developed by Calgene of Davis, CA (now owned by Monsanto), it was first sold in American supermarkets in May 1994. The genetic modification produced a tomato that could ripen longer on the vine and still be firm enough for shipping.

1996: DOLLY THE SHEEP The first mammal to be cloned from an adult cell was a sheep called Dolly. Born on July 5, 1996, she was created by scientists at Scotland's Roslin Institute using a cell from a mammary gland. The announcement of her existence touched off a storm of controversy over the ethics of cloning.

Dolly was put to sleep on Feb. 14, 2003, at the age of six, after having been diagnosed with a progressive lung disease that normally affects older sheep. She had previously suffered from a form of arthritis.

Dolly was mounted and is now displayed at the Royal Museum of Edinburgh, Scotland. During her brief life, she gave birth to Bonnie in 1998 and then to three more lambs in 1999, all of them conceived by natural means.

BIOTECHNOLOGY

Health

BIOTECHNOLOGY HAS MADE POSSIBLE THE CREATION OF NEW DRUGS and synthetic hormones, plus lots of improvements in treatment. But some of its applications, often involving genetic engineering, have sparked ethical and legal controversy.

MILESTONES

1860s-1870s: BACTERIOLOGY

The field of bacteriology came about largely through the work of French scientist Louis Pasteur. Beginning in the 1860s, Pasteur studied specific bacteria to understand how microorganisms develop, spread, and can be stopped. His work helped lay the foundation for the germ theory of disease, pointing to microorganisms as the cause of contagious illness. The fact that Pasteur was already a renowned scientist helped this revolutionary theory gain acceptance.

The German biologist Ferdinand J. Cohn wrote the first systematic classification of bacteria into genus and species. His three-volume treatise was published in 1872. Cohn placed them in the plant kingdom. They were later included in the kingdom *Monera* (prokaryotes) and more recently have tended to be classified by many scientists as one of three "domains" into which living things are grouped, the other two being the *Archaea* and *Eukarya* (eukaryotes).

1909-10: CHEMOTHERAPY

Salvarsan, the first "chemotherapeutic" agent for humans, was discovered by German scientist Paul Ehrlich in 1909. Ehrlich introduced the term "chemotherapy" to refer to the use of synthetic chemicals to treat disease. He envisioned drugs that would attack the organism but not the person—like a precision bomb. (Ehrlich used the phrase "magic bullet.")

The idea came to him in 1891 while researching tuberculosis and cholera at the Moabit Hospital in Berlin. He noticed that methylene blue dye would selectively stain malaria. This meant that chemicals could be targeted toward organisms of a specific chemical makeup.

Looking for a treatment for syphilis, Ehrlich began testing arsenic compounds that had been proven effective against a variety of diseases. After testing almost 1,000 compounds, his Japanese assistant Sachahiro Hata found that a previously discarded preparation, known as #606 (now called arsphenamine), worked in killing the infection. This discovery led to the production of the arsenic drug called salvarsan at the Hoechst labs in Germany on July 10, 1910.

1912: VITAMINS

While Pasteur had proven that germs could cause diseases, others began to suspect that the absence of certain substances could also be at fault. For example, British physician James Lind had recommended in 1747 that sailors eat citrus fruits (containing vitamin C) to prevent scurvy. In 1896, Dutch physician Christiaan Eijkman linked beriberi breakouts to diets where rice had been mechanically stripped of its nutritious husks, which contain vitamin B1. (It was actually his apprentice, Gerrit Grijns, who first proposed that the cause was vitamin deficiency rather than an added toxin.)

The concept that vitamins were needed for proper growth wasn't accepted until the British biochemist Sir Frederick Gowland Hopkins in 1912 published the results of a study where he concluded that people need vitamins in their diet. Eijkman and Hopkins shared the 1929 Nobel Prize in physiology or medicine.

The Polish-born biochemist Casimir Funk coined the term "vitamines" ("vital amines") while working in London in 1912. At the time Funk incorrectly thought that vitamin B was chemically an "amine" (any of certain compounds derived from ammonia). The *e* was eventually dropped from the word.

1970: ONCOGENES

Oncogenes (from the Greek *onkos* meaning "tumor") are genes that under certain conditions can cause normal cells to become cancerous, that is, subject to uncontrolled growth. This may occur if the oncogene is damaged or altered through exposure to a carcinogen—a cancer-causing substance or biological agent—or through inheritance of a defect.

A breakthrough in scientists' understanding of oncogenes came when research into the Rous sarcoma virus (RSV), a virus known to cause cancer in chickens, yielded a key finding. In 1970, various scientists, including Steve Martin, Peter Duesberg, and Peter Vogt, identified the *src* gene as a specific gene in RSV that can change healthy cells to cancerous ones.

Later, in a paper published in 1976, researchers Michael Bishop and Harold Varmus showed that certain genes already present in

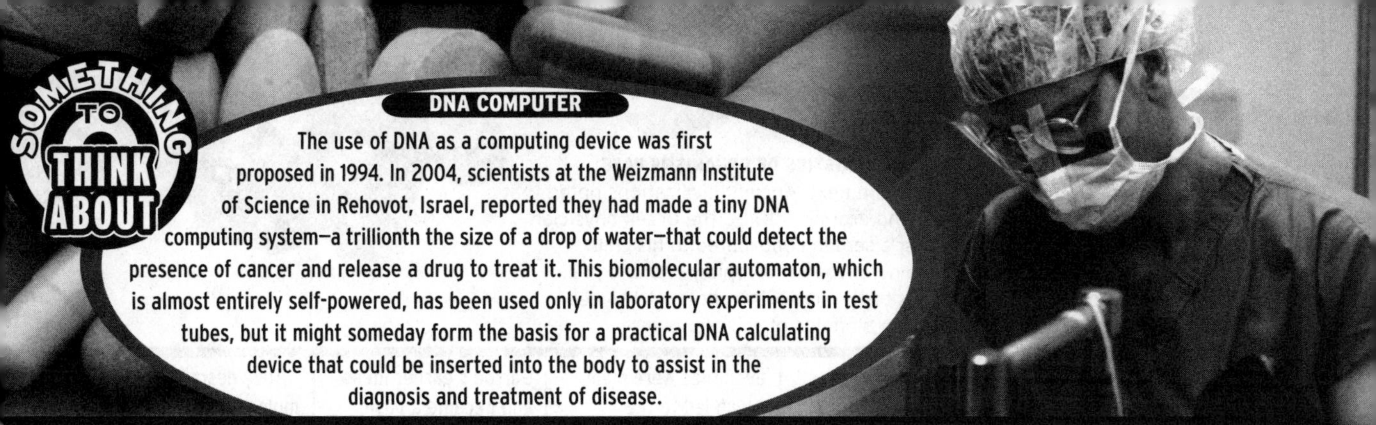

SOMETHING TO THINK ABOUT

DNA COMPUTER

The use of DNA as a computing device was first proposed in 1994. In 2004, scientists at the Weizmann Institute of Science in Rehovot, Israel, reported they had made a tiny DNA computing system—a trillionth the size of a drop of water—that could detect the presence of cancer and release a drug to treat it. This biomolecular automaton, which is almost entirely self-powered, has been used only in laboratory experiments in test tubes, but it might someday form the basis for a practical DNA calculating device that could be inserted into the body to assist in the diagnosis and treatment of disease.

normal cells, called proto-oncogenes, could mutate to become oncogenes. This discovery put the spotlight on the activity of oncogenes in normal cells and their part in causing cancer. For their work in this field, Bishop and Varmus won the 1989 Nobel Prize in physiology or medicine.

The first known tumor-suppressor gene (anti-oncogene) was isolated in 1986, when it was discovered that the retinal tumor retinoblastoma developed when the tumor-suppressor gene *Rb* was lost or became inactive.

1975: AMES TEST

In 1975 biochemist Bruce Ames of the University of California at Berkeley developed the Ames Test to screen for potential cancer-causing elements in the environment or in foods. Using chopped rats' liver as a medium, he tested whether chemicals damaged DNA cells of modified *Salmonella typhimurium* bacteria. Since most cancer-causing agents also cause mutations, the ability to detect mutagenic properties of various substances more quickly and cheaply revolutionized the study of cancer-causing agents.

1975: MONOCLONAL ANTIBODIES

Antibodies are great. They fight diseases without hurting the body cells, at least ordinarily. They can stay in your system to prevent further infection by the specific disease they fight (that's how vaccines work). And they can help doctors detect the presence of diseases or drugs. Monoclonal antibodies can also be mass-produced for use in diagnosis and treatment.

In 1975, German immunologist Georges J. F. Köhler and British immunologist César Milstein developed monoclonal antibodies by fusing clones of a single B lymphocyte (a type of white blood cell that produces antibodies) with myeloma tumor cells. These hybrids, known as hybridomas, multiply at the abnormally fast speed of a tumor and produce a continuous supply of monoclonal antibodies.

For their work the two men—along with Danish immunologist Niels K. Jerne, who made theoretical contributions to the understanding of the immune system and monoclonal antibodies—shared the 1984 Nobel Prize in physiology or medicine.

1977: HUMAN PROTEIN MADE IN A BACTERIUM

In 1977, the American biotechnology company Genentech used bacteria to make the human hormone somatostatin. Founded in 1976 by financier Robert Swanson and biochemist Herbert Boyer, Genentech was created to develop commercial applications for recombinant DNA technology.

In 1973, Boyer, who worked at the University of California at San Francisco, and Stanley Cohen of Stanford University developed one of the key techniques permitting the transfer of genes from one organism to another. In 1977, with the help of this technique, somatostatin was produced by modified *E. coli* bacteria. This commercial development was a landmark in the creation of the biotechnology industry.

In 1978, Genentech created the first synthetic human insulin, which in 1982 became the first drug produced by genetic engineering to be approved by the U.S. Food and Drug Administration.

1980: PATENTS FOR LIVING THINGS

On June 16, 1980, the U.S. Supreme Court, voting 5-4 in the case *Diamond v. Chakrabarty*, ruled that genetically altered life forms can be patented. This controversial decision resulted from a patent application filed by Indian microbiologist Ananda Chakrabarty in 1972 while working for General Electric. Chakrabarty had created via genetic engineering a microorganism that could break down crude oil. It was used to help clean up oil spills in the ocean.

Chakrabarty's initial application for a U.S. patent was denied on the grounds that living things are not patentable. After a successful appeal to the Court of Customs and Patent Appeals, the case made its way to the U.S. Supreme Court.

The first patent for a genetically engineered plant was issued in 1985 to Molecular Genetics, Inc. for a type of corn. Philip Leder and Timothy Stewart of Harvard College received the first animal patent on April 12, 1988, for an "oncomouse," genetically modified to be extra-susceptible to cancer.

Genetics

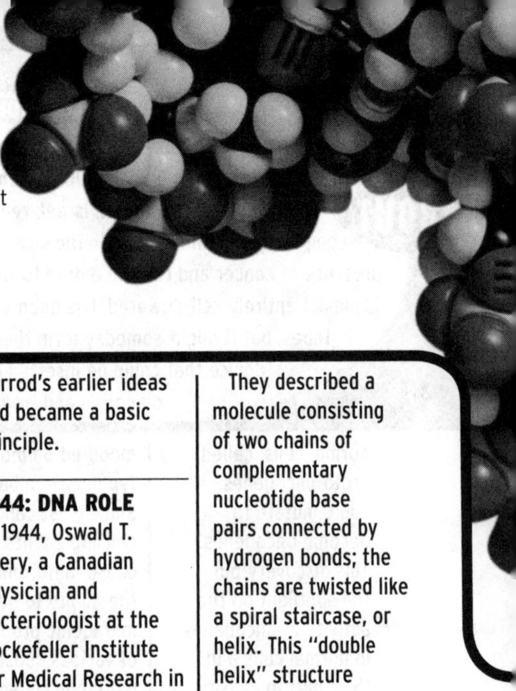

GENETICS IS THE STUDY OF HOW CHARACTERISTICS OF ORGANISMS PASS and change from one generation to the next. Ancient civilizations noted that children resembled their parents, and around 400 BC the Greek physician Hippocrates theorized that a father's semen contributed to his child's characteristics. Modern genetics, one of the most rapidly changing fields of scientific inquiry, traces its roots to the mid-19th century. Advances in genetics have had a major impact on all fields of science.

MILESTONES

1866: MENDEL'S LAWS The work of an Austrian monk named Gregor Mendel was the most significant early breakthrough in the study of genetics. In 1866, he published a paper outlining the general laws governing heredity. Mendel demonstrated that characteristics are passed from one generation to the next as discrete units of inheritance—what we now call genes. His conclusions were the culmination of years of painstaking research breeding thousands of pea plants.

The significance of Mendel's work was not recognized until 1900, 16 years after his death, when three scientists rediscovered his paper and independently verified his laws with further research.

1908: GENES AND DISEASE In 1908, Sir Archibald Garrod, an English physician working at a London hospital, became the first person to connect Mendel's "laws of inheritance" to the inheritance of disease. He studied patients with alkaptonuria, a rare disorder that causes urine to darken when exposed to air. After analyzing distribution patterns of this disease in families, he found they conformed to Mendel's laws.

Fifty years passed before biochemists were able to prove Garrod's hypothesis.

1910: GENES AND CHROMOSOMES
The work of Thomas Hunt Morgan, a Columbia Univ. embryologist, established the field of classical experimental genetics. In 1910, Morgan concluded that male traits of fruit flies, *Drosophila melanogaster*, obeyed the laws of Mendelian inheritance. More important, while observing a mating experiment, he noted that all the white-eyed flies were male, which led to the realization that some traits are sex-linked. This suggested the existence of sex (X and Y) chromosomes, and prompted the landmark hypothesis that genes are located on chromosomes.

In 1915, Morgan published *The Mechanism of Mendelian Heredity*, in which he first described sex-linked traits and other genetic patterns.

1941: GENE-PROTEIN CONNECTION
In the 1930s and early 1940s at Stanford Univ., George Beadle, a geneticist, and Edward Tatum, a biochemist, investigated the "one gene, one enzyme" hypothesis. They reported in 1941 that experiments with *Neurospora crassa* bread mold suggested that each protein or enzyme is the result of the expression of one gene.

The realization that genes produce proteins substantiated Garrod's earlier ideas and became a basic principle.

1944: DNA ROLE
In 1944, Oswald T. Avery, a Canadian physician and bacteriologist at the Rockefeller Institute for Medical Research in New York City, showed that deoxyribonucleic acid (DNA) was the material of heredity.

Avery had tried for more than a decade to determine how "rough" bacteria could acquire the "smooth" traits from strains of the same bacteria. With his colleagues Colin MacLeod and Maclyn McCarty, Avery purified the "transforming factor," showed it to be DNA, and determined that it is central to heredity.

1953: DNA STRUCTURE
In 1953, British biophysicist Francis Crick and American biochemist James Watson determined the molecular structure of DNA at the Cavendish Laboratory in Cambridge, England. They described a molecule consisting of two chains of complementary nucleotide base pairs connected by hydrogen bonds; the chains are twisted like a spiral staircase, or helix. This "double helix" structure was fundamental to a coherent understanding of how inherited characteristics are passed on from one generation to the next.

Crick and Watson's conception showed how DNA could carry genes and self-replicate and recombine during reproduction. With British biophysicist Maurice Wilkins they ultimately, in 1962, received the Nobel Prize in physiology or medicine.

1957: GENETIC PRINCIPLES
Francis Crick, speaking at University College London in Sept. 1957, outlined his theory that the function of genes was to produce proteins. This radical theory, although still

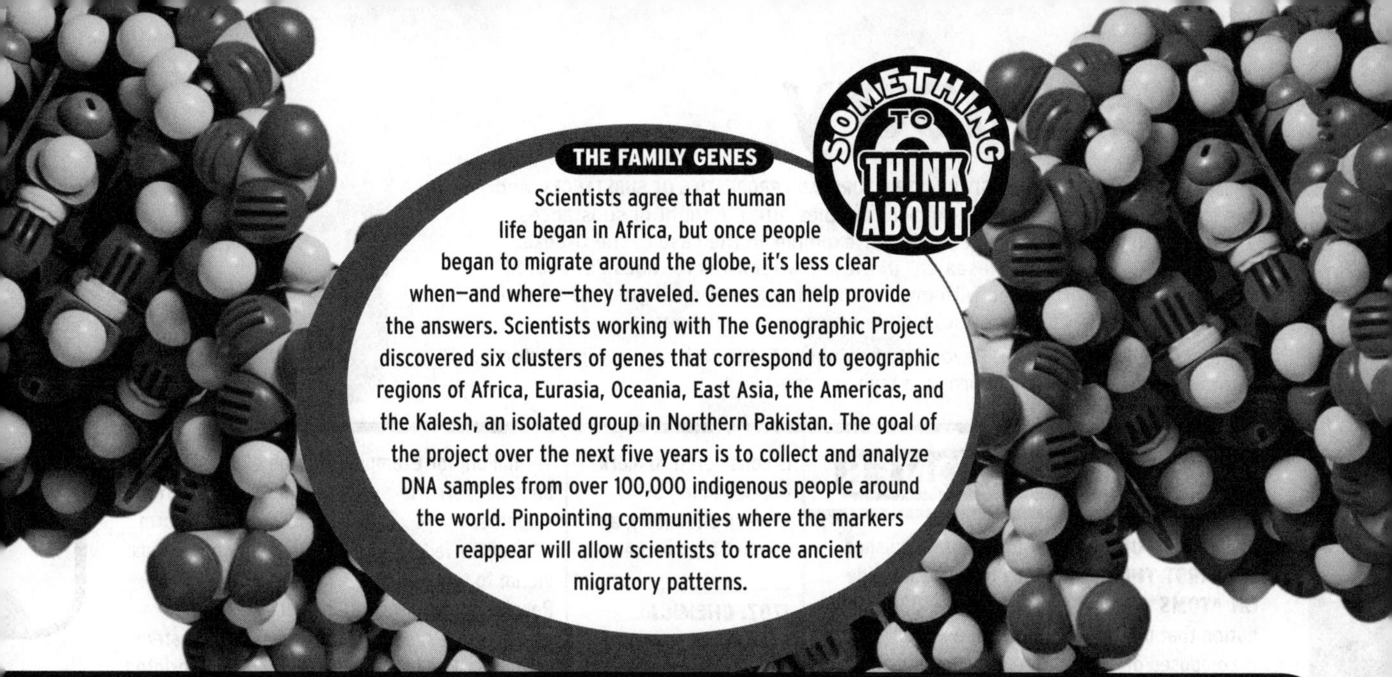

SOMETHING TO THINK ABOUT

THE FAMILY GENES

Scientists agree that human life began in Africa, but once people began to migrate around the globe, it's less clear when—and where—they traveled. Genes can help provide the answers. Scientists working with The Genographic Project discovered six clusters of genes that correspond to geographic regions of Africa, Eurasia, Oceania, East Asia, the Americas, and the Kalesh, an isolated group in Northern Pakistan. The goal of the project over the next five years is to collect and analyze DNA samples from over 100,000 indigenous people around the world. Pinpointing communities where the markers reappear will allow scientists to trace ancient migratory patterns.

unproven, changed the face of genetic research.

Crick identified two key principles of genetics. The "sequence hypothesis" holds that the order of the bases in a molecule of DNA forms a code determining the sequences in which amino acids combine to form various proteins. The "central dogma" holds that while information from DNA is transmitted from DNA and RNA (ribonucleic acid, a molecule similar to DNA and crucial in protein formation) to proteins, information cannot be transmitted from a protein back to DNA.

1961: CRACKING THE CODE In 1961 Marshall Nirenberg of the U.S. National Institutes of Health took a giant step toward deciphering the genetic code. In experiments involving the RNA required for protein synthesis, carried out with German researcher Heinrich Matthaei, he identified the first codon. (A codon is a sequence of three bases of DNA, known as a "triplet," that codes for an amino acid, and amino acids are the building blocks of protein.)

By 1966, Nirenberg and associates had deciphered the code of all 64 RNA codons for 20 amino acids. Two years later, he split the Nobel Prize in physiology or medicine with geneticists Har Gobind Khorana and Robert W. Holley.

1972: RECOMBINANT DNA Paul Berg of Stanford Univ. announced in 1972 the creation of the first recombinant, or hybrid, DNA molecules. Using restriction enzymes, which cut DNA molecules at specific points, and ligases, enzymes that join pieces of DNA together, he combined DNA elements from two organisms.

Berg opened the way to the development of recombinant genetic engineering. He was awarded the 1980 Nobel Prize in chemistry, along with Walter Gilbert and Frederick Sanger (see below).

1977: SEQUENCING DNA In 1977, Harvard's Walter Gilbert and Cambridge's Frederick Sanger developed separate techniques allowing scientists to rapidly determine the sequence of nucleotides in DNA. Both men used recently discovered enzymes and electrophoresis on a polyacrylamide gel, a process that makes nucleotide order visible.

The techniques allow scientists to quickly learn the entire sequence of a gene, which can be up to 30,000 bases long. For their work, Gilbert and Sanger, along with Paul Berg, received the 1980 Nobel Prize in chemistry.

2000: HUMAN GENOME PROJECT A massive project to map all human genes—collectively known as the human genome—was launched by the U.S. government in the late 1980s under sponsorship of the Department of Energy and the National Institutes of Health. Other countries, including France, Germany, Italy, Japan, the United Kingdom, and Canada, joined in.

The private company Celera Genomics began its own genome sequencing project in the late 1990s, using a faster technique. Celera and the public Human Genome Project in 2000 jointly announced achievement of a rough working draft of the genome, published the following year. Final completion of the project was announced in 2003.

Chemistry

CHEMISTRY STUDIES THE COMPOSITION, STRUCTURE, AND PROPERTIES OF SUBSTANCES, and the interactions between them. Ancient peoples often thought of substances as composed of a few basic elements—for example, in the case of the Greeks, fire, water, earth, and air. "Research" in these matters was for ages dominated by alchemy, an effort tinged with mysticism and aimed at such goals as turning base metals into gold and developing life-preserving medicines.

It wasn't until the Scientific Revolution beginning in the 17th century in Western Europe that chemistry was born as a true science.

MILESTONES

FIFTH CENTURY BC: FIRST THEORY ON ATOMS The notion that matter is composed of tiny particles was introduced by the ancient Greek philosopher Democritus (around 460-370 BC) and, presumably, his teacher Leucippus, whose views are known via Democritus.

Democritus called these tiny particles *atomos*, Greek for "not divisible." He held that they were indestructible, had different sizes and shapes but the same content, and existed apart from each other. He thought their collisions and combinations into groups were responsible for all change in the universe.

FOURTH CENTURY BC: ARISTOTLE'S ELEMENTS The atomic theory of Democritus and his followers languished by history's wayside for some 2,000 years, eclipsed by the enormous influence of the Greek philosopher Aristotle (384-322 BC). Aristotle adhered to the traditional theory of the four elements—fire, water, earth, and air—which were said to be composed of varying proportions of the qualities heat, cold, moisture, and dryness.

1661: BOYLE AND SCIENTIFIC CHEMISTRY Anglo-Irish chemist Robert Boyle is credited with being the first scientist to define elements as small, distinct "corpuscles," or particles, that mix to form substances—an approach he set forth in his landmark work *Sceptical Chymist*, published in 1661.

Boyle's work, marked by a focus on experimentation and the scientific method, is considered to mark the beginning of modern chemistry, as distinct from alchemy.

1787: CHEMICAL LANGUAGE Another founder of modern chemistry was the French scientist Antoine-Laurent Lavoisier, who helped pioneer quantitative experimentation. In a 1787 work he and three other French scientists laid the foundation for the chemical classification system used today, replacing the traditional confusing nomenclature, including alchemic designations, with a system based on chemical composition.

Lavoisier identified 33 simple substances, or elements, classified into four groups (gases, nonmetals, metals, and earths) according to their properties. Under the new system, the name of a chemical compound reflected the two elements supposed to compose it. Vermillion, for example, became mercuric sulphide.

Lavoisier fell victim to the French Revolution. Sentenced to death in a show trial, he asked to be given 15 days to finish his work. The judge famously rejected the request, proclaiming, "The Republic has no need for scientists." Lavoisier was quickly executed, on May 8, 1794.

1803: ATOMIC THEORY In 1803, British chemist and physicist John Dalton proposed an atomic theory that elaborated on the ancient idea of indivisible building blocks called atoms.

Dalton concluded that matter was composed of atoms and that the atoms of one element differed in weight from the atoms of other elements. He calculated the atomic weights of different elements based on their proportion to the weight of hydrogen. He also proposed that the same elements may combine in different proportions to form different compounds.

Dalton's atomic theory was first published in *System of Chemistry*, printed by his friend Thomas Thomson in 1807.

1811: AVOGADRO'S LAW In 1811, Italian chemist Amedeo Avogadro introduced a clear distinction between an atom and a molecule—the basic particle of a substance that still held the properties of that substance.

Dalton thought the smallest unit of, for example, ordinary nitrogen gas was a nitrogen atom, but this conflicted with experimental results. Avogadro noted that the problem was resolved if each nitrogen molecule consisted of two atoms. He also put forth the principle now known as Avogadro's law: equal volumes of different gases, under the same temperature

SOMETHING TO THINK ABOUT

LONGEST WORD

Most dictionary compilers decline to regard chemical names as words, since they are merely a string of chemical designations and symbols. Still, there are many chemical names lacking such symbols, which might reasonably count as words. The chemical names of proteins traditionally listed the constituent amino acids, but these can be numerous and unwieldy. A few decades ago the authoritative *Chemical Abstracts* began using shorter names for proteins. But the longest known name published before the switch, for a protein familiarly known as tryptophan synthetase, maintains its claim to the longest-word crown.

It totals 1,913 letters

methionylglutaminylarginyltyrosylglutamylserylleucylphenylalanylalanylglutaminylleucyllysylglutamylarginyllysylglutamylglycylalanylphenylalanylvalylprolylphenylalanylvalylthreonylleucylglycylaspartylprolylglycylisoleucylglutamylglutaminylserylleucyllysylisoleucylaspartylthreonylleucylisoleucylglutamylalanylglycyla ...

and pressure conditions, contain the same number of molecules.

Avogadro's analysis was not accepted until almost 50 years later, when another Italian chemist, Stanislao Cannizzaro, calculated atomic weights based on Avogadro's hypothesis.

1814: CHEMICAL SYMBOLS Swedish chemist Jöns Jakob Berzelius, tired of using confusing and cumbersome chemical symbols, many of them stemming from alchemy, introduced in 1814 a streamlined system for abbreviating the names of elements. He proposed using one or two letters derived from the elements' Latin names—for example, He for helium and Fe for iron (*ferrum*). Many of these symbols are still used today.

1869: PERIODIC TABLE Russian chemist Dmitry Mendeleyev in 1869 classified chemical elements into families taking into account both atomic weight and common properties. He used a tabular arrangement, in rows and columns, that, somewhat revised, is still used today.

As he grouped the elements, Mendeleyev left gaps in the table, correctly predicting the existence of elements not yet discovered.

1901: FIRST NOBEL PRIZE IN CHEMISTRY The first Nobel laureate in chemistry was Dutch physical chemist Jacobus Henricus van't Hoff of Berlin University. He won in 1901 for his work relating thermodynamics to chemical reactions and his studies of the properties of solutions.

SUPERLATIVES

MOST TOXIC COMPOUND (MAN-MADE) Comparing toxicity can be difficult, but some experts believe the most toxic compounds made by humans belong to a group of cholorinated hydrocarbons called dioxins. The most toxic dioxin known is 2, 3, 7, 8-tetrachlorodibenzo-p-dioxin (TCDD).

Dioxins are formed as a by-product when chlorine-containing chemicals, such as plastics, are burned, and in such processes as pesticide manufacturing and paper bleaching. Depending on their toxicity and the amount of exposure, dioxins may cause scarring, cancer, heart disease, diabetes, nerve damage, and reproductive problems.

The defoliant Agent Orange contains dioxin. Ukrainian President Viktor Yushchenko was poisoned with dioxin in Sept. 2004 while running for office.

MOST COMMON ELEMENT (UNIVERSE) Hydrogen accounts for about 75% of all known normal matter in the universe by mass. (But scientists believe that mysterious "dark matter" makes up most of the actual matter in the universe.)

MOST COMMON ELEMENT (ATMOSPHERE) The most common element in the Earth's atmosphere is nitrogen. It accounts for about 78% of the atmosphere by volume.

MOST ABUNDANT ELEMENT (CRUST) Oxygen is the most abundant element in the Earth's crust. The element and its compounds make up 49% of the Earth's crust by weight.

HIGHEST DENSITY (SOLID) The densest known solids at room temperature are osmium and iridium. The measured density of osmium is greater, while the density as calculated from the crystal structure is greater for iridium.

HIGHEST DENSITY (GAS) The densest gas at normal temperature and pressure (0° Celsius, or 32° Fahrenheit, and 1 atmosphere) is radon, at 0.6074 pound per cubic foot (9.729 kg per cubic meter).

HIGHEST BOILING POINT Rhenium has the highest known boiling point, 10,104.8°F (5,596°C). Carbon has the highest melting point, 6,422°F (3,550°C).

LOWEST BOILING POINT Helium has the lowest melting and boiling points, −457.96°F (−272.2°C) and −452.074°F (−268.93°C), which are close to absolute zero (−459.67°F, −273.95°C) the coldest that temperatures can get.

Mathematics

MATHEMATICS EVOLVED OUT OF OUR NEED TO COUNT, MEASURE, AND COMPARE. We still use it for these purposes, but now people think of math more broadly as the study of patterns and structures, sometimes extremely abstract. Mathematics has proved extraordinarily useful. It gives science a language for describing the world quantitatively, so that predictions can be tested.

MILESTONES

AROUND 3,000 BC: FIRST WRITTEN NUMBERS The oldest physical evidence of written numbers comes from about 5,000 years ago, in the form of clay tablets from Sumer (in Mesopotamia) and Egyptian hieroglyphics.

Like Roman numerals later, these earliest systems did not use positional notation. In other words, different symbols were used for 10, 100, 1,000, and so on instead of using just "1" and "0" and letting the position of the decimal point indicate magnitude.

AROUND 300 BC: PRIME NUMBERS The Greeks launched math in something like its modern form: as a search for general truths to be proved by deductive methods.

Much of Greek mathematics dealt with geometry, but the Greeks made discoveries in other areas too. Probably the best-known proof that there are an infinite number of prime numbers—integers (whole numbers) greater than 1 that are divisible only by themselves and 1—dates back to Euclid about 300 BC.

9TH CENTURY: ALGEBRA With the fall of the Roman Empire, mathematical knowledge largely disappeared in Western Europe, but it survived in the Muslim world, as Islamic scholars embraced and extended Greek learning, adding to it the convenience of Arabic numbers (which came from India originally).

Algebra—which uses symbols such as letters to represent numbers in arithmetic expressions—gets its name from *al-jabr*, an Arabic word for "restoring"; more specifically, the name comes from *The Book of Restoring and Balancing*, a text on algebra by the 9th-century mathematician Muhammad ibn Musa al-Khwarizmi.

1614: LOGARITHMS In the late Middle Ages, Greek and Islamic knowledge began to filter into Europe. Before long there was a rising tide of mathematical discoveries.

In 1614, John Napier, a Scotsman, published tables of logarithms. Logarithms—the powers, or exponents, to which a certain base number must be raised to produce specific numbers—made it much easier to perform multiplication and division, raise numbers to powers, and extract roots.

Tables of logarithms, along with slide rules based on logarithms, were, in their day, as great an aid to calculation as computers and calculators in ours.

1637: ANALYTIC GEOMETRY The 17th-century French philosopher René Descartes helped introduce key concepts of analytic geometry, a fusion of algebra and geometry. The idea of using numbers to find a point on the surface was known to the ancient Greeks, but Descartes in 1637 was the first to systematize the use of coordinates.

1637: FERMAT'S LAST THEOREM The French mathematician Pierre de Fermat made a variety of important discoveries, but he is best known for "Fermat's last theorem." This is the statement that the equation $x^n + y^n = z^n$ has no solutions when x, y, and z are all positive integers and n is an integer greater than 2. (For n = 2, there are infinitely many solutions in integers.)

In 1637, Fermat wrote in the margin of a book that he had found a "marvelous" proof of the proposition, but the margin was too small for him to write it out! It was some 350 years later, in 1994, when a valid proof was actually published, by Princeton professor Andrew Wiles. It took seven years for Wiles, at age 40, to solve the problem. He had been intrigued by it since he was 10 years old.

Most mathematicians think Fermat was probably mistaken in believing he had a proof himself.

LATE 1600s: CALCULUS The English scientist Isaac Newton and German philosopher Gottfried Wilhelm Leibniz both invented differential and integral calculus, which deal with the changes in a function as the independent variable approaches zero.

Newton made his key discoveries in 1665-66, and Leibniz only about a decade later. But Leibniz was the first to publish, in 1684-86. Although Leibniz got a few hints from Newton, the two men by and large worked independently.

Today's standard notations of $\int$ (for integration) and *d* (differentiation) were introduced by Leibniz.

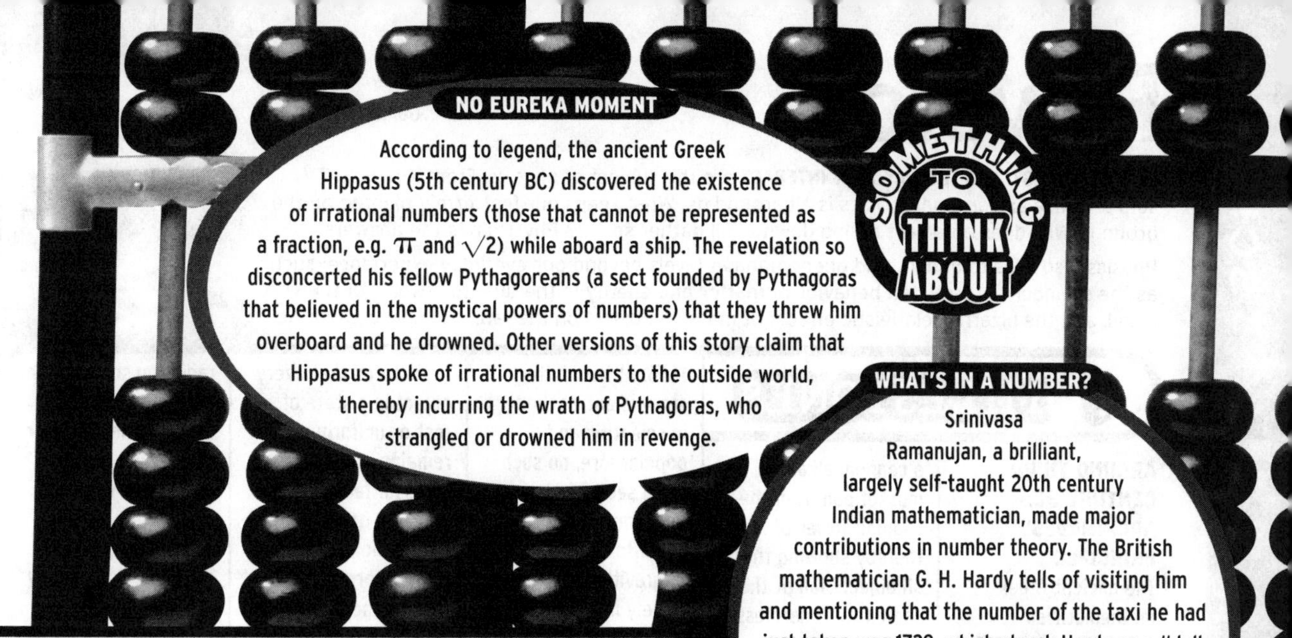

SOMETHING TO THINK ABOUT

NO EUREKA MOMENT

According to legend, the ancient Greek Hippasus (5th century BC) discovered the existence of irrational numbers (those that cannot be represented as a fraction, e.g. π and $\sqrt{2}$) while aboard a ship. The revelation so disconcerted his fellow Pythagoreans (a sect founded by Pythagoras that believed in the mystical powers of numbers) that they threw him overboard and he drowned. Other versions of this story claim that Hippasus spoke of irrational numbers to the outside world, thereby incurring the wrath of Pythagoras, who strangled or drowned him in revenge.

WHAT'S IN A NUMBER?

Srinivasa Ramanujan, a brilliant, largely self-taught 20th century Indian mathematician, made major contributions in number theory. The British mathematician G. H. Hardy tells of visiting him and mentioning that the number of the taxi he had just taken was 1729, which struck Hardy as a "dull number." Ramanujan immediately replied that, on the contrary, 1729 was a very interesting number, being the smallest number that could be written in two different ways as the sum of two cubes: $1^3 + 12^3$ or $9^3 + 10^3$.

18TH CENTURY: EULER The prolific Leonhard Euler, of Switzerland, is estimated to have written a third of all mathematics-related publications in the last three-quarters of the 18th century. He produced almost half his work after he became fully blind around the age of 50.

Euler made major advances in number theory, calculus, and many other areas, including topology—the study of the properties of geometric figures that do not change under actions such as bending or stretching.

In 1736, for example, he solved the now famous Königsberg bridge problem, proving it was impossible to cross all seven bridges in the Prussian city of Königsberg without crossing at least one more than once.

19TH CENTURY: NON-EUCLIDEAN GEOMETRY In the 19th century mathematicians began exploring systems of geometry that do not satisfy all the basic axioms of Euclid's traditional geometry—in particular, the axiom that one, and only one, line parallel to a given line can be drawn through a point that does not lie on that given line.

The German mathematician and scientist Johann Carl Friedrich Gauss was a pioneer in this area, and a child prodigy. Once, when his class was told to add all the integers from 1 to 100, he gave the correct answer—5,050—almost instantly; he had noticed that there were 50 pairs of numbers (1 + 100, 2+ 99, and so on) that each summed to 101, so the total had to be 50 x 101.

19TH CENTURY: GROUPS Groups—sets of things with a binary operation (such as multiplication) and certain other characteristics (such as the existence of an identity, or unit element)—have many applications in math and physics. The brilliant French mathematician Evariste Galois studied permutations of roots of algebraic equations, and his work led him to an early formulation of the algebraic notion of group.

Galois died in 1832, at the age of only 21, from wounds suffered in a duel apparently fought over a woman. He had spent much of the night before writing about his mathematical theories.

SUPERLATIVES

MOST ACCURATE PI Pi (π) is the ratio of a circle's circumference to its diameter. It's an irrational number (that is, like the square root of 2, it can't be expressed exactly as the ratio of two integers). Thus, any decimal value given for pi is only approximate—but you can get more and more accurate by adding more and more decimal places.

The current record—achieved in 2003 by Yasumasa Kanada of the University of Tokyo—is 1.2411 *trillion* digits after the decimal point.

LARGEST PRIME In Jan. 2006, American chemistry professor Steven Boone and math professor Curtis Cooper found the biggest prime number yet discovered: it's 9,152,052 digits long. The number is a "Mersenne prime," meaning that it can be expressed as 2 raised to some power, then minus 1. In this case, the number is $2^{30,402,457}$ minus 1.

They were taking part in the Great Internet Mersenne Prime Search (GIMPS) project, which gives individuals software to help search for Mersenne primes.

Physics

Galileo ►

MATTER, ENERGY, AND THE WAY THEY INTERACT are the subject of physics. From X-rays to TV sets to space exploration, physics is all around us. What keeps our feet firmly planted on the ground? Why does an object rolling down a hill gather speed? Physics has the answers.

Physics also tries to understand phenomena at levels beyond our everyday experience—such as the strangely interrelated behavior of matter and energy in the quantum world of the very small, and the bizarre, relativistic effects of massive objects on the fabric of space and time.

MILESTONES

AROUND THIRD CENTURY BC: ARCHIMEDES' PRINCIPLE
The ancient Greek mathematician Archimedes (287-212 BC) formulated many of the basic ideas used in the study of physics. He is perhaps best known for "Archimedes' principle," which holds that all bodies immersed in fluid are buoyed by a force with a magnitude equal to the weight of the fluid they displace.

According to legend, he discovered this principle while taking a bath, and, after excitedly crying out "*Eureka*!" ("I've found it!"), leaped from his tub to run naked through the streets in celebration.

1589-92: UNIFORMLY ACCELERATED MOTION Tradition holds that the great Italian scientist Galileo Galilei, while teaching mathematics at the University of Pisa in 1589-92, dropped a cannonball and a musket ball from the Leaning Tower of Pisa, thereby showing that all objects fall at the same rate regardless of their mass. This principle, known today as the law of uniformly accelerated motion of falling bodies, was surprising at the time since it contradicted the traditional view (advanced by Aristotle) that an object's speed of fall depends on its weight.

While some historians claim that Galileo didn't actually perform the experiment atop the leaning tower, the discovery itself is not in question. Galileo himself proved the law theoretically in his work *De Motu* ("On Motion").

1687: NEWTON AND GRAVITY British mathematician and physicist Isaac Newton is said to have been inspired to study gravity when he saw an apple fall from a tree sometime around 1666. Although the story is entrenched in scientific and popular lore, no such thing seems to have happened.

Newton's study of gravity was largely inspired by the findings of the French thinker René Descartes and German astronomer Johannes Kepler. It culminated in 1687 with the publication of *Philosophiae Naturalis Principia Mathematica* ("*The Mathematical Principles of Natural Philosophy*").

The *Principia* set forth innovative theories of physics and celestial mechanics, including Newton's law of universal gravitation, which states that any two objects attract each other with a force directly proportional to the product of their masses and inversely proportional to the square of the distance between them.

1687: NEWTON'S LAWS OF MOTION
The *Principia* also laid out Newton's three laws of motion. The first states that every object in a state of rest or uniform motion remains in that state unless affected by an external force. The second holds that when a force acts on a body, the body's acceleration is equal to the force divided by the object's mass. The third says that "for every action, there is an equal and opposite reaction."

Newton's first law can be demonstrated by yanking a tablecloth out from under place settings on a table covered with plates. If you can do it without letting the tablecloth's motion exert force on the dishes (not easy or recommended), they won't crash to the floor. The objects at rest remain at rest.

1900: QUANTUM THEORY In 1900, German physicist Max Planck analyzed the difference in color in light radiated by hot, glowing matter at different temperatures. He theorized that emission (and absorption) of electromagnetic radiation such as light occurs in discrete units of energy (later called quanta) and postulated that the energy of a unit of radiation equals the radiation's frequency multiplied by a universal constant of nature, now known as Planck's constant (6.626×10^{-34} joule-second).

His work, for which he won the 1918 Nobel Prize in physics, laid the foundation for the quantum theory of matter and energy.

1905: EINSTEIN'S WONDROUS YEAR
In 1905 the German-born American scientist Albert Einstein, then working in Bern, Switzerland, revolutionized physics with a series of epochal papers.

Building on Planck's work, he explained the photoelectric effect (the emission of electrons from a metal when struck by light) by regarding light as discrete particles of energy (photons), with energy proportional to the frequency. His work on

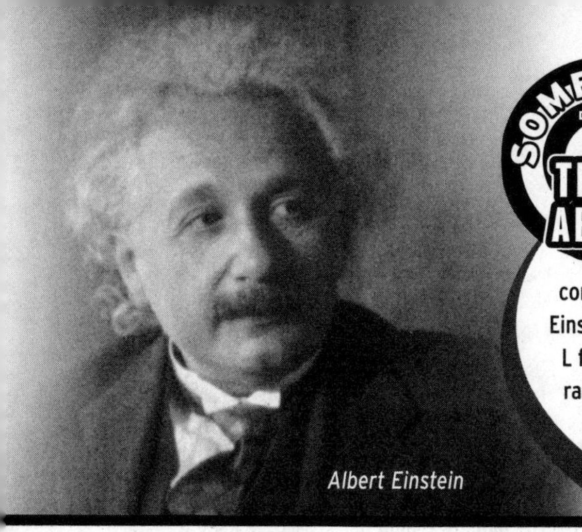
Albert Einstein

SOMETHING TO THINK ABOUT

$L = MV^2$

One of the most famous products of Einstein's wondrous year of 1905 was his statement of the equivalence of mass and energy. This is commonly written $e = mc^2$, where c is the speed of light. But Einstein said it differently. He used V for the speed of light and L for energy: "If a body releases the energy L in the form of radiation, its mass is decreased by L/V^2." It wasn't until the 1920s that the formulation was modified, in accordance with then-common usage, and took on the form familiar today.

the photoelectric effect earned him the Nobel Prize in physics in 1921.

Another 1905 paper by Einstein made a major contribution to statistical mechanics and helped convince many scientists that atoms were actual entities; it showed that Brownian motion—the constant movement of particles suspended in a fluid—could be attributed to the random bombardment of the particles by tiny atoms or molecules.

Yet another 1905 paper set forth Einstein's "special" theory of relativity, which presented a new linkage of space and time, based on the assumption that the laws of physics and the speed of light (in a vacuum) remain the same in all frames of reference, whether moving or at rest.

A little over a decade later Einstein introduced a more comprehensive "general" theory of relativity. It supplanted Newton's theory of gravity with the concept of the curvature of the space-time continuum near massive objects.

1911-13: ATOMIC MODEL British physicist Ernest Rutherford, the 1908 Nobel chemistry laureate, proposed in 1911 that an atom consists of a positively charged nucleus surrounded by negatively charged electrons.

Two years later, Danish physicist Niels Bohr refined Rutherford's model with the help of quantum principles. Bohr theorized that electrons orbited the nucleus at uniformly different levels, and that when an electron moved between levels, electromagnetic radiation could be emitted, at a frequency determined by the difference in energy between the two levels.

Bohr received the 1922 Nobel Prize in physics for his work.

1926: MATTER WAVES
In 1926, Erwin Schrödinger, an Austrian physicist, developed a formula explaining the wavelike nature of matter. Known as the Schrödinger equation, it is a foundation for wave mechanics.

Schrödinger shared the 1933 Nobel Prize in physics with British physicist Paul Dirac (who had been led by his quantum studies to predict the existence of the positron, a positively charged counterpart to the electron).

1927: UNCERTAINTY PRINCIPLE In 1927, German physicist Werner Heisenberg published the uncertainty principle, which states that it is impossible to determine the exact position and momentum of a particle simultaneously, because neither can be measured without affecting the other. In 1932, Heisenberg won the Nobel Prize in physics.

SUPERLATIVES

HIGHEST TEMPERATURE SUPERCONDUCTOR
Superconducting substances have the extraordinarily useful property of offering zero resistance to the flow of electric current.

For most of the period since superconductivity was discovered in 1911 by Dutch physicist Heike Kamerlingh Onnes, the only substances known to exhibit it did so at extremely low temperatures, not far from absolute zero (−459.67°F). But recent decades have seen a surge of new discoveries, and the current record holder for highest-temperature superconductor is a compound composed of mercury, thallium, barium, calcium, copper, and oxygen, at −211°F.

COLDEST TEMPERATURE RECORDED In 2003, a team of researchers at MIT cooled sodium atoms to half-a-billionth of a degree above absolute zero (-459.67°F, -273.15°C), the coldest temperature ever recorded. At such drastically low temperatures, atoms cannot be kept in containers, since they would stick to the surface. To confine the atoms, the researchers used magnetic fields.

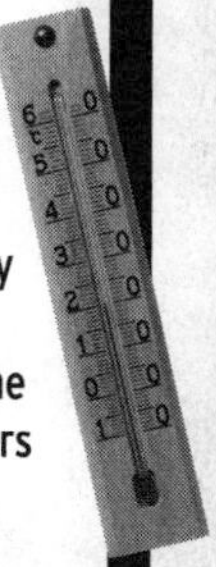

MOST NOBEL PRIZES IN PHYSICS U.S. physicist John Bardeen shared the physics Nobel in 1956, for helping develop the transistor, and received another in 1972, for his contributions to the theory of superconductivity.

Polish-born French chemist Marie Curie earned two Nobels for her work relating to radioactivity, including a share of the 1903 physics prize, but her second Nobel, in 1911, was in chemistry.

ENERGY

Electricity

THE HARNESSING OF ELECTRICITY AS AN ENERGY SOURCE radically altered human existence. Electrical energy can be transformed into heat, light, and mechanical energy, and so serve a myriad of purposes, from lighting up the biggest cities to charging the smallest mupic players.

Grand Coulee Dam ►

MILESTONES

600 BC: ELEKTRON The term "electricity" comes from the Greek word for amber, *elektron*. The Greek philosopher Thales of Miletus (c. 625-546 BC) is said to have observed that when a piece of amber is rubbed with fur or wool it attracts lightweight objects. If rubbed long enough, a spark is generated. This phenomenon later became known as static electricity.

1663: ELECTROSTATIC GENERATOR German physicist Otto von Guericke invented the electrostatic generator. His device consisted of a solid sulfur ball, attached to a spindle (axis) and a wooden cradle. Holding a hand or a cloth pad against the ball as it was spun on its axis produced static electricity.

1733: POSITIVE/NEGATIVE In a 1733 paper, French scientist Charles François de Cisternay du Fay identified two forms of electricity: vitreous, made by glass, and resinous, made by a resin such as amber.

Fourteen years later one of America's founding fathers, Benjamin Franklin, said that the two types of "electrical fire" were actually two different aspects—positive (plus) and negative (minus)—of the same thing.

1745: LEYDEN JAR Today's capacitors—devices for storing electrical energy—descend from a simple apparatus invented in 1745 by German physicist Ewald Georg von Kleist and independently, a little later, by Dutch physicist Pieter van Musschenbroek, a professor at the University of Leiden. Van Musschenbroek's work was better known, and the device came to be called a Leyden jar.

1800: VOLTAIC CELL Italian physicist Alessandro Volta invented Voltaic cells and piles (stacks of cells), the first modern batteries. Volta's piles used alternating zinc and silver or copper disks separated by cloth and immersed in weak acid to generate a steady current.

The volt, a unit that measures electric potential difference or electromotive force, was named for Volta.

1820: ELECTROMAGNETIC REACTION French physicist André Marie Ampère in 1820 discovered the principle of electromagnetic reaction: if a current is passed through a conductor located in a magnetic field, the field exerts a mechanical force on it.

The ampere ("amp"), the basic unit of electric current, was named for him.

1831: ELECTROMAGNETIC INDUCTION In 1831, British physicist and chemist Michael Faraday discovered electromagnetic induction, in which a changing magnetic field can induce an electric current. American scientist Joseph Henry came upon this principle a year earlier, but Faraday was the first to publish his findings.

The discovery led directly to the development of the electric generator.

1837: TELEGRAPH The first commercially practical systems of electric telegraphy were developed in the U.S. by inventor Samuel F. B. Morse in 1837 and in Great Britain the same year by physicist Charles Wheatstone and engineer William F. Cooke.

Morse used a simple code in which messages were transmitted by electric pulses passing over a single wire.

1879: INCANDESCENT LIGHT BULB Thomas Edison did not invent the light bulb, but he did patent the first commercially successful incandescent light bulb. He demonstrated his first working model, which used a carbon filament, on Oct. 21, 1879.

British chemist Joseph Swan created a commercial bulb at about the same time as Edison, and Edison paid for his and Swan's companies to merge in England. Modern incandescent lamps generally use tungsten filaments.

1883: AC INDUCTION MOTOR The invention of the alternating-current (AC) induction motor is usually attributed to Croatian-born American

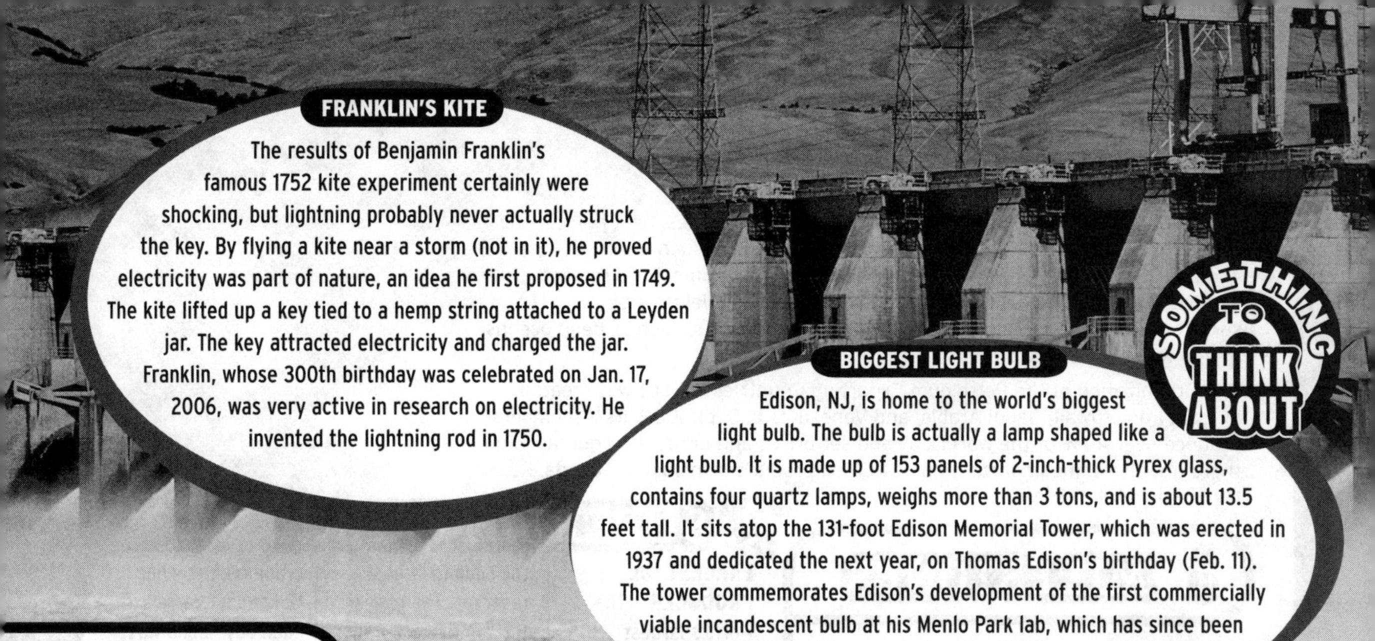

FRANKLIN'S KITE

The results of Benjamin Franklin's famous 1752 kite experiment certainly were shocking, but lightning probably never actually struck the key. By flying a kite near a storm (not in it), he proved electricity was part of nature, an idea he first proposed in 1749. The kite lifted up a key tied to a hemp string attached to a Leyden jar. The key attracted electricity and charged the jar. Franklin, whose 300th birthday was celebrated on Jan. 17, 2006, was very active in research on electricity. He invented the lightning rod in 1750.

SOMETHING TO THINK ABOUT

BIGGEST LIGHT BULB

Edison, NJ, is home to the world's biggest light bulb. The bulb is actually a lamp shaped like a light bulb. It is made up of 153 panels of 2-inch-thick Pyrex glass, contains four quartz lamps, weighs more than 3 tons, and is about 13.5 feet tall. It sits atop the 131-foot Edison Memorial Tower, which was erected in 1937 and dedicated the next year, on Thomas Edison's birthday (Feb. 11). The tower commemorates Edison's development of the first commercially viable incandescent bulb at his Menlo Park lab, which has since been destroyed but was located in the town that now bears his name. The tower stands on the lab's former site.

physicist and engineer Nikola Tesla, who built his first working model in 1883 and filed patent applications four years later. He was hired by Thomas Edison in 1884 but quit Edison's lab the following year after a dispute over payment.

A "war of the currents" soon broke out between Tesla's AC and Edison's direct-current (DC) system. AC was superior due to its long-distance power transmission, and Tesla and his sponsor, entrepreneur/engineer George Westinghouse, ultimately won out.

The first large-scale electric generators in North America used Tesla's AC generators. They were installed at Niagara Falls and began operation on Aug. 26, 1895, sending electricity via power lines to Buffalo, NY, 20 miles away, on Nov. 16, 1896.

SUPERLATIVES

LARGEST POWER PLANT (U.S.)

The biggest U.S. power plant, calculated by net generation, is the Palo Verde Nuclear Generating Station located 50 miles west of Phoenix, AZ. It generates more than 28 million megawatt-hours per year.

LARGEST CAPACITY (U.S.)

The U.S. power plant with the greatest generating capacity is located at the Grand Coulee Dam on the Columbia River, 85 miles west of Spokane, WA. Its summer capability exceeds 7,000 megawatts.

LARGEST ELECTRICITY PRODUCER

The U.S. is the world's largest net producer of electricity. In 2004 its combined utilities generated 3.97 trillion kilowatt-hours. Nearly half was made using coal.

The U.S. is also the world's biggest consumer of electricity, using 3.717 trillion kilowatt-hours in 2004.

WORST BLACKOUT (U.S.)

The worst blackout in U.S. history occurred on Aug. 14, 2003. It was triggered by a power failure in Ohio that affected large areas of the northeastern U.S., from Michigan to New York City, and parts of Ontario, Canada.

More than 60 million people were without power at the height of the blackout. Some 50 million were without power for as long as two days.

MOST-CONCENTRATED GENERATION OF ELECTRICITY

In Sept. 2001 the U.S. Department of Energy's Atlas pulsed-power facility successfully discharged for the first time some 20 million amps of electricity through an aluminum cylinder the size of a tuna can.

The facility, now located at the department's Nevada Test Site, creates such extreme conditions to help understand processes occurring in the explosion of nuclear weapons (whose testing is banned).

MOST POWERFUL BATTERY SYSTEM

Fairbanks, AK, is home to the world's most powerful battery system, designed by the French battery maker Saft. BESS—the Battery Energy Storage System—uses 13,760 rechargeable nickel-cadmium cells to supply emergency power during the area's frequent outages. Temperatures in Fairbanks can reach -60°F in winter, so it is vital to keep electricity flowing.

BESS provides 27 megawatts for 15 minutes, which gives the utility company time to get backup systems working.

Oil

THE MODERN WORLD RELIES HEAVILY ON OIL to power industries, heat homes, and fuel transportation and also as raw material in products such as plastics, paints, and fertilizers. A finite resource, oil is one of the world's most desired and lucrative commodities. It is often difficult to find and extract—oil fields lie beneath the surface of some of the world's most hostile environments, such as deep oceans, frozen wastelands, and deserts.

The Organization of the Petroleum Exporting Countries (OPEC) was created by Iran, Iraq, Kuwait, Saudi Arabia, and Venezuela in Sept. 1960. Its 11 members produce over 40% of the world's oil and set prices and production quotas. But there are also some important non-OPEC oil producers, including Canada, Russia, Mexico, and the U.S.

MILESTONES

1846: KEROSENE Canadian physician and geologist Abraham Gesner distilled a form of fuel oil from coal in 1846. He named the "coal oil" *kerosene*, from the Greek words for wax and oil. His Kerosene Gaslight Company first lit Halifax, Nova Scotia, in 1850.

Polish pharmacist Ignacy Lukasiewicz first extracted kerosene from liquid oil seeping from the ground in 1853. Kerosene replaced expensive and increasingly rare whale oil, and its production gave rise to the petroleum industry. It is now used mainly in aviation fuel.

1848: FIRST WELLS Russians drilled the first oil well at Bibi-Heybat, Azerbaijan, in 1848. It was about 70 feet deep.

"Rock oil," as it was known, was first drilled in North America by Canadian carriage maker James Williams at Oil Springs, Ontario, in 1858. The next year, on Aug. 27, Edwin Drake struck oil near Titusville, PA. The reservoir he tapped was shallow—only 69.5 feet deep—and the oil flowed readily and was easily distilled.

An oil craze swept America soon after his discovery.

1947: OFFSHORE DRILLING Oil was first drilled offshore as early as 1896 near a wharf in the Summerland Oil Field of California. The first true offshore oil well was built by Kerr-McGee Corp. about 40 miles from Morgan City, LA, in 1947, beginning a new phase in the petroleum industry.

SUPERLATIVES

LARGEST OIL PRODUCER The world's largest producer of crude oil is Saudi Arabia, which produced 8.9 million barrels a day of crude oil in 2004, representing 12.6% of the world's supply. Most of its exports go to Asia and the Pacific. Oil accounts for 90-95% of Saudi Arabia's total exports (about $115.6 billion in net oil export revenues in 2004) and almost 40% of its gross domestic product.

The U.S. state that produces the most oil is Texas, which pumped out 1,073,000 barrels a day in 2004.

LARGEST OIL RESERVES Saudi Arabia has oil reserves estimated at 264.3 billion barrels (2005), representing 23% of the world's reserves. Iran (132.5 billion barrels) has the second largest reserves. The rest of the top five are Iraq (115 billion barrels), Kuwait (101.5 billion barrels), and United Arab Emirates (97.8).

It is estimated that Canada has about 170 billion barrels of oil contained in the "oil sands" of northern Alberta. Until recently, extracting the oil from the tar, clay, and sand mixture, was not possible technologically or economically. Taking the oil sand reserves into account would give Canada the world's second largest reserves after Saudi Arabia.

LARGEST OIL CONSUMER The United States was the world's largest refined petroleum consumer in 2004, using 20.7 million barrels a day—27% of the world's total. It was also the largest importer of crude oil, receiving 12.1 million barrels each day. China was the second largest consumer (6.5 million barrels a day) followed by Japan (5.4 million barrels a day).

LONGEST PIPELINE The *Druzhba* ("Friendship") pipeline runs over 2,500 miles from Samara, Russia, to Mozyr, Belarus, where it splits into two separate lines. One pipe goes to Schwedt, Germany, while the southern pipe goes to Százhalombatta, Hungary.

LARGEST OIL FIELD **WORLD** The largest oil field in the world is the Ghawar field in Saudi Arabia. The 174-mile-long, 16-mile wide oil field is located near the Persian Gulf. Its discovery in 1948 made Saudi Arabia a major oil-producing country. Ghawar

SOMETHING TO THINK ABOUT

"OIL" DRINK TO THAT

In 1972, a huge spherical oil storage tank along Detroit's I-75 highway at the Marathon oil refinery was painted to look like a baseball, to honor the Detroit Tigers. In 2003, the tank was repainted as a basketball to honor the Detroit Shock's 2003 WNBA championship win. The following year, the tank was given yet another coat of paint to celebrate the Detroit Pistons' 2004 NBA championship.

"OIL" EAT THAT

Many marine microorganisms naturally "eat" petroleum. This is done by oxidizing hydrocarbons into carbon dioxide and water over a period of several years. Recently, oil spill cleanup crews have been using these microbes for bioremediation—the use of living organisms to remove contaminants from an environment. Crews either spray cultivated bacteria or grow native bacteria with fertilizer to speed up the process. The method was first used to help clean up the *Exxon Valdez* spill that dumped about 11 million gallons of oil into Prince William Sound, AK, on March 24, 1989.

produces 55–60% of Saudi Arabia's crude oil each year. In 1948, it contained about 125 billion barrels; its current reserves are around 70 billion barrels—about 6% of the world's proven total. That's greater than the known combined reserves of the United States and all of Asia and the Pacific.

LARGEST OIL FIELD

U.S. The reserves around Prudhoe Bay, AK, are the largest in the U.S. This field contained 13 billion barrels of crude oil when discovered in 1968. Today, under 4 billion barrels remain.

LARGEST FLOATING OIL PLATFORM

Located about 150 miles southeast of New Orleans, LA, BP's Thunder Horse platform was dedicated Feb. 26, 2005. With quarters for 229 people, it lies above the largest known reserves in the Gulf of Mexico. The semi-submersible platform hull was built in South Korea and has a displacement of 130,000 metric tons. It's capable of extracting 250,000 barrels of oil per day. Its opening was delayed after it tilted during Hurricane Dennis in July 2005; it is expected to begin production in the summer of 2006.

TALLEST OIL PLATFORM The Petronius oil platform located about 130 miles southeast of New Orleans, LA, in the Gulf of Mexico is the world's tallest oil platform. It is partly supported by buoyancy, and stands 2,001 feet above the seabed, in 1,754 feet of water.

Co-owned by ChevronTexaco and Marathon Oil, the platform went into operation on July 9, 2000. At peak operational capacity it can pump out 60,000 barrels per day from the reserves buried 10,000 feet below sea level.

ACTIVE OIL RIGS

According to oil field services company Baker Hughes Inc., there were 3,021 active oil rigs worldwide in Nov. 2005. The U.S. ran 1,486 rigs including 667 in Texas alone.

Although the number has been increasing in recent years, it's still down from a record 5,624 active rigs worldwide in 1981, of which 3,969 were in the U.S.

LARGEST OIL REFINERY The central refinery of Petróleos de Venezuela, S.A. at Paraguaná near Punta Fijo has a refining capacity of up to 940,000 barrels of crude oil each day. It refines 71% of the nation's total oil output.

The U.S. has the largest capacity to refine oil of any country, capable of turning out 16.8 billion barrels each day. The largest refinery in the U.S. is ExxonMobil's refinery at its Baytown, TX, complex. The plant had the capacity to refine 557,000 barrels of crude oil per day in 2004.

MOST EXPENSIVE GAS

Consumers in Iceland paid the equivalent of $6.21 per gallon for gasoline at the pump in Nov. 2004, followed by the Netherlands ($6.13), Norway ($6.09), and Great Britain ($5.91). The United Kingdom paid the most for diesel ($6.06) followed by Norway ($5.45), Liechtenstein, Sweden, and Switzerland (all $5.19). All of these countries have high gas taxes.

At that time, U.S. consumers paid $2.02 per gallon for gas and $2.15 for diesel.

MOST PROFITABLE OIL CORPORATION

According to the Fortune Global 500, the most profitable oil corporation in 2004 was Exxon Mobil, with a net income of $25,330 million. The company sold 8.2 million barrels of refined products each day in 2004. Royal Dutch/Shell had the largest revenues, at $337.5 billion.

Nuclear Energy

THE IDEA THAT MATTER IS MADE UP OF TINY PARTICLES—atoms—is an ancient one, but the existence of atoms was not proven until around the turn of the 20th century. Scientists discovered that an atom consists of still smaller entities; it has a nucleus of protons and (usually) neutrons and is surrounded by tiny electrons. Scientists also found that an abundance of energy could be produced through fission (splitting a nucleus) or fusion (combining two nuclei).

Nuclear reactors that generate electricity rely on fission, as did the first "atomic" bombs. Fusion, capable of generating far more energy, is the process that powers stars. It has not yet been harnessed as a practical source of energy on earth, except in "thermonuclear" weapons.

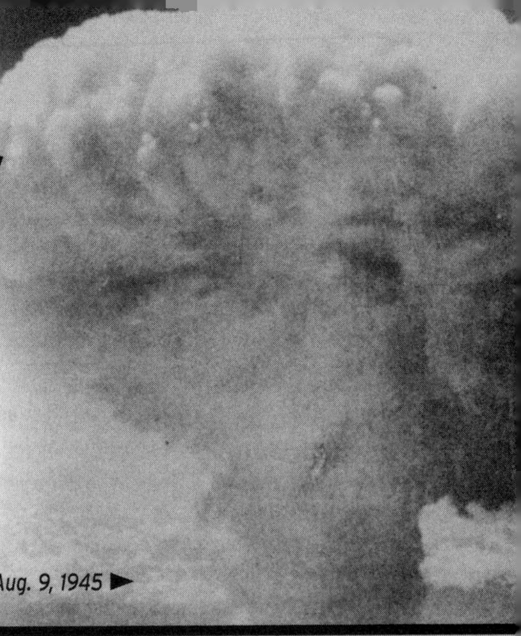

Atomic bombing of Nagasaki, Aug. 9, 1945 ▶

MILESTONES

1896: RADIOACTIVITY
In the old days, atoms were thought to be indivisible solid particles. In 1896, French physicist Antoine Henri Becquerel changed all that when he placed a photographic plate near uranium. The plate turned black, even when an object like a piece of glass or paper was between the two. The mysterious emanations from the uranium, furthermore, seemed to have an electric charge.

Becquerel had discovered radioactivity, which would later be found to consist of subatomic particles and high-energy electromagnetic radiation.

1898: THE CURIES
French husband-and-wife chemists Marie and Pierre Curie began studying radioactivity following Becquerel's discovery. They found that the amount of radiation given off by uranium (or thorium, which Marie found was also radioactive) depended solely on the amount of the substance and was closely linked to the substance's atoms.

1932: NEUTRON
British physicist James Chadwick discovered the neutron in 1932. He showed that neutrons had about the same mass as protons, another subatomic particle with a positive charge, but had no electric charge. Since the neutron had no charge, it would not be repelled if directed at an atomic nucleus.

The Hungarian-born physicist Leó Szilárd soon conceived of releasing energy from atoms through a series of atom-neutron collisions. He thought certain atoms might split when hit by a neutron, releasing energy along with more neutrons, which could cause other atoms to release energy and neutrons, thereby creating a "chain reaction."

1938-39: FISSION
Fission of uranium through bombardment with neutrons was achieved in experiments by German physical chemist Otto Hahn and chemist Fritz Strassmann in 1938, as shown in a theoretical analysis published the following year by Austrian-Swedish physicist Lise Meitner and British physicist Otto Robert Frisch, who coined the term "nuclear fission."

1942: CHAIN REACTION
A controlled chain reaction was first achieved Dec. 2, 1942, in an atomic "pile"—a fission reactor—erected on a squash court below the stands of the University of Chicago's Stagg Field under the leadership of Italian-born American physicist Enrico Fermi. The reactor was part of the U.S. government's secret Manhattan Project during World War II.

1945: ATOMIC BOMB
The Manhattan Project culminated on July 16, 1945, in the explosion of the world's first atomic bomb, code named "The Gadget," at the Trinity test site at Alamogordo, NM.

Scientists were not sure what to expect from the device. Some even believed that the chain reaction could ignite the Earth's atmosphere. Less than a month after the Trinity test, the U.S. used two atomic bombs against Japan.

The first bomb, dropped on Hiroshima, was equal to 15,000 tons of TNT; the second bomb, used on Nagasaki, was equal to 21,000 tons. See "Warfare," page 151.

1952: FUSION BOMB
The U.S. dropped the first "hydrogen" bomb—a 10.4 megaton fusion, or thermonuclear, device called Mike—at Eniwetok Atoll in

Nuclear Power Plant ▶

SOMETHING TO THINK ABOUT

FUTURE SHOCK

The practical exploitation of atomic energy was envisioned as early as 1914 by British writer H. G. Wells in his science fiction novel *The World Set Free*. The book described enormously destructive "atomic bombs" that lay waste to major cities in a 1956 war. Wells's imaginative picture of the future, which reportedly influenced Szilárd (see Milestones), was inspired by the research of British chemist Frederick Soddy, who went on to win the 1921 Nobel Prize in chemistry for his work on radioactivity and isotopes.

LOTSA HALF-LIVES

Much of the "high-level" radioactive waste produced by nuclear power stations and weapons plants will be dangerous for a very long time. Plutonium-239, for example, has a half-life of 24,100 years—that is, it takes 24,100 years for the substance's radioactivity to be reduced by half. Finding secure places to store such materials for thousands of years is a worldwide problem. The U.S. alone has accumulated roughly 160,000 spent fuel assemblies from power plants—representing about 45,000 tons of spent fuel. If the assemblies were all kept in one place, they would cover an area the size of a football field to a depth of $5\frac{1}{2}$ yards.

the Pacific Ocean during Operation Ivy on Oct. 31, 1952. The experiment produced a flash brighter than 1,000 suns, and obliterated the island.

1957: NUCLEAR POWER PLANT
Between 1947 and 1955, various prototypes of nuclear reactors were built in Great Britain, Canada, the U.S., France, and Russia. The first nuclear power plant used for commercial electricity generation was a 1500-megawatt facility located on the Ohio River in Shippingport, PA, near Pittsburgh. It began operations in 1957 and closed in 1982. It became the first reactor to be decontaminated.

Due to cost and safety concerns, no new power plants have been ordered in the U.S. since 1977.

SUPERLATIVES

MOST NUCLEAR POWER GENERATED
The country with the highest proportion of its electricity generated by nuclear energy is France, at 78% in 2004. The proportion in the U.S. was only 20%, but the U.S. had the world's highest total output of nuclear electricity, 788.6 billion kilowatt-hours; France was second in output, at 426.8 billion.

MOST NUCLEAR POWER REACTORS
The U.S. has the most electricity-generating nuclear reactors in the world, with 103. (France, with 59, ranks No. 2.) Illinois has the most power reactors among the U.S. states: 11, at six installations.

MOST POWERFUL NUCLEAR EXPLOSION
The "Tsar Bomba" detonated by the Soviet Union on Oct. 30, 1961, produced a record energy yield equivalent to at least 50 megatons of TNT.

The device, which weighed about 27 metric tons, was dropped by a bomber over the Arctic Ocean island of Novaya Zemlya. The blast produced a mushroom cloud 40 miles high, and its atmospheric shockwave traveled around the Earth three times.

BIGGEST NUCLEAR ARSENAL Natural Resources Defense Council experts estimated in early 2005 that Russia had about 7,200 operational nuclear warheads in its active arsenal—some 3,800 strategic warheads and 3,400 non-strategic (for use by tactical aircraft, naval forces, and ballistic missile and air defense systems). The number of Russian warheads in reserve or retired status was thought to be in the neighborhood of 10,000-12,000.

The U.S. was believed to have over 5,300 operational nuclear warheads—4,530 strategic and 780 non-strategic (gravity bombs and nuclear Tomahawk land-attack cruise missiles)—with an additional 5,000 or so warheads in reserve or inactive status.

The stockpiles of other nuclear powers include about 400 weapons in France and China, 200 in Britain, 50-150 in India and Pakistan, and a few suspected to be in the possession of North Korea. Israel is also believed to have 75-200 nuclear weapons.

LARGEST SCIENTIFIC INSTRUMENT The Large Hadron Collider, slated to go into operation in 2007 at the European Organization for Nuclear Research (CERN), will be used to observe what happens when high-energy beams of protons and heavier particles slam into each other. It uses a ring-shaped tunnel that measures nearly 17 miles in circumference and lies beneath the French-Swiss border.

Time

EARLY HUMANS MEASURED TIME BY OBSERVING the daily and annual motion of the Earth and Moon. Scientists, engineers, and astronomers have narrowed the divisions of time over the centuries from day and night to hours and minutes to nanoseconds and even smaller units. And devices for calculating time have evolved from sundials to digital wristwatches and atomic clocks.

MILESTONES

3500 BC: FIRST SUNDIAL The first sundials date back to about 3500 BC in ancient Egypt. The Egyptians used the length and location of shadows cast on the ground to define rudimentary time elements like morning and afternoon and the longest and shortest days of the year. Early gnomons—the gnomon is the shadow-making object in a sundial—ranged from small sticks to huge obelisks.

Around 1500 BC, the Egyptians progressed to smaller, more accurate sundials that divided the daylight time into 10 periods plus dawn and dusk.

ABOUT 1500 BC: WATER CLOCK Ancient Egyptians developed the first water clocks as early as 1500 BC. A water clock uses a controlled, constant flow of water into or out of a vessel, similar to sand in an hourglass, to mark the passage of time. The Greeks are widely credited with making the instruments, which they called *clepsydras* (water thieves), more accurate and useful. Water clocks were an advance over sundials because they worked 24 hours a day.

1300s: MECHANICAL CLOCKS It is not known when engineers developed the first mechanical clocks, but large mechanical clock towers were standing in several Italian cities by the early 14th century.

The biggest advance in developing these clocks was the invention of the escapement, a weight-driven mechanism that moves gears forward in equal rhythm, allowing the teeth of the gears to "escape" one at a time in a regulated fashion.

The earliest known description of an escapement was in the works of French architect Villard de Honnecourt in 1250.

AROUND 1500: SPRING-POWERED CLOCKS German locksmith Peter Henlein invented the spring-powered clock between 1500 and 1510. Henlein replaced the heavy weights powering earlier mechanical clocks with springs, which drastically reduced clock size.

He also created the first portable timepiece, a spring-driven device known as the Nüremberg "egg" because of its shape.

Some sailors used the eggs—about the size of softballs—to tell time while standing at their watches at sea, eventually lending the word *watch* to all portable timepieces.

1582: GREGORIAN CALENDAR In AD 730, St. Bede announced that the original Julian calendar, in use since 46 BC, was 11 minutes, 14 seconds too long annually. The problem gradually worsened, but nothing was done to remedy it until 1582, when Pope Gregory XIII announced that the day following Oct. 4 would be Oct. 15, compensating for the accumulated extra time, and introduced the Gregorian calendar, which is still in use today.

AROUND 1656: PENDULUM CLOCKS In about 1583, the great Italian scientist Galileo Galilei first stated that the frequency of a pendulum's swing remains almost constant, a property known as isochronism. This principle was the basis for the idea of using pendulums to make more accurate clocks.

The Dutch scientist Christiaan Huygens built the first clock based on a pendulum around 1656. His clock, which had an error of less than one minute per day, was by far the most accurate clock of its time. Later refinements by Huygens made it accurate within 10 seconds per day.

1784: DAYLIGHT SAVING TIME While serving as an envoy to France, Benjamin Franklin proposed a method of adjusting time schedules to conserve fuel, in a lighthearted essay published in *The Journal of Paris* (1784).

British builder William Willett was the first person to seriously promote the practice, in a pamphlet, "The Waste of Daylight" (1907). He proposed reducing the four Sundays in April by 20 minutes each—then adding back the time over four Sundays in September.

Daylight saving time was implemented in World War I, in an effort to conserve fuel; Germany and Austria were the first to adopt it, moving clocks an hour forward on April 30, 1916, with the lost hour to be restored in October. Other countries followed suit. The system proved unpopular and fell out of use, but was revived during World War II.

In 1966, Congress passed a law requiring that all states using daylight saving time follow the same rules. Today the system is used in almost all of the U.S., and by about 1 billion people around the world.

1884: PRIME MERIDIAN The International Meridian Conference in Oct. 1884 in Washington, DC, officially adopted the longitude of Greenwich, England, as the prime meridian. Greenwich was chosen in part because Greenwich Observatory's sea charts were practically standard among sailors.

The conference also determined that all countries would adopt a universal 24-hour day based on the prime meridian's location.

1927: FIRST QUARTZ CLOCK Canadian engineer Warren A. Marrison at Bell Telephone Laboratories in New York City built the first quartz crystal-regulated clock in 1927. Marrison used the regular vibrations of a quartz crystal in a circuit to control the timepiece, removing the need for gears.

The Seiko Quartz-Astron 35SQ was the first quartz wristwatch available for retail; it debuted on Dec. 25, 1969, in Tokyo, Japan, with a $1,250 sticker price.

1949: ATOMIC CLOCK In 1949, American physicist Harold Lyons led a program at the U.S. National Bureau of Standards (now the National Institute of Standards and Technology) to use the vibration of ammonia molecules to measure time. Later atomic clocks used the superior standard vibrations of cesium atoms.

The first commercial cesium atomic clocks became available for $20,000 in 1958.

1967: PRECISE SECOND In 1967 the official definition of a second was calculated to the vibrations of the cesium-133 atom rather than being based on astronomical bodies. A second was formally defined as 9,192,631,770 vibrations of the cesium atom, at the 13th General Conference on Weights and Measures.

SOMETHING TO THINK ABOUT

TIMELESS MUSEUM

The first permanent exhibition dedicated to the history and innovation of Swatch watches was opened in the Arese Jacini Palace of Cesano Maderno, Italy (near Milan), on March 16, 2003. Avid Swatch watch collector Fiorenzo Barindelli donated his record-holding 4,000-plus-piece Swatch collection to the town of Cesano Maderno, on the condition that the watches be displayed in a museum setting.

SUPERLATIVES

MOST PRECISE CLOCK In July 2001, the National Institute of Standards and Technology announced that a team of physicists led by Scott Diddams had developed the most precise clock ever created. This timepiece improved on the basic atomic clock design by using the higher-frequency vibrations of visible light to give more accurate time, and few could find fault with the result. The clock loses only one second in 100 million years.

SMALLEST ATOMIC CLOCK The National Institute of Standards and Technology built the smallest atomic clock in the world in Aug. 2004. This tiny ticker is about the size of a rice grain, and does not gain or lose more than a second in 300 years.

HIGHEST PRICE PAID AT AUCTION **CLOCK** A Louis XVI clock made for the Duc de Choiseul sold for $3,001,294 at auction on July 8, 1999, to an unidentified telephone bidder at Christie's in London, England. The golden clock portrays seconds, minutes, hours, sunrise, sunset, phase of the moon, date, day of the week, and position of the sun in the zodiac.

HIGHEST PRICE PAID AT AUCTION **WATCH** The highest price paid for a watch sold at auction was $11,002,500, for a Patek Philippe watch belonging to New York financier Henry Graves Jr., at a Sotheby's auction on Dec. 2, 1999. The "Supercomplication" took four years (1928-32) to create. Delivered to Graves in Jan. 1933, it weighed 1.2 pounds, had two faces, and displayed 24 pieces of information, including a rotating celestial chart of the New York City sky.

MOST COMPLEX TIMEPIECE The Calibre 89, made in 1989 to commemorate watchmaker Patek Philippe's 150th anniversary, is the most complex timepiece yet created.

The 18-carat gold pocket watch weighs 2.44 pounds, has 33 functions and 1,728 unique parts, and took nine years to complete. Among the watch's features is a celestial chart with 2,800 stars.

TALLEST CLOCK TOWER The NTT DoCoMo Yoyogi Building in Tokyo, Japan, has a clock 50 feet in diameter near the top of its 787-foot tower. The clock was installed in 2002 as part of the Japanese mobile phone giant NTT DoCoMo's 10th anniversary.

ASTRONOMY

Planets

Saturn ▶

THE NINE PLANETS IN OUR SOLAR SYSTEM are usually broken into two groups called the inner planets and outer planets. The four inner ones are (in order from the Sun) Mercury, Venus, Earth, and Mars. The five outer planets are Jupiter, Saturn, Uranus, Neptune, and Pluto (though Pluto is closer to the Sun than Neptune for about 20 years of its 248-year orbit). Between Mars and Jupiter is a belt of about 30,000 asteroids, or mini-planets.

MILESTONES

4.5 BILLION YEARS AGO: PLANETS BORN
According to the prevailing theory, our solar system formed about 4.5 billion years ago from a giant rotating cloud of loosely packed gas and dust. As the cloud contracted, it rotated faster and heated up. Most of the mass became the Sun, which contains over 99% of all the solar system's matter. Much of the rest became the planets.

430 BC: MOVING SPHERES
People used to think that Earth was stationary. The first known theories about Earth's movements come from the Greek thinker Philolaus, who claimed in 430 BC that the Sun and planets, in separate spheres or circular shells, all circled around a central fire.

In 350 BC, another Greek thinker, Heracleides, refined the notion of the spheres, but placed the Earth at the center of the universe and suggested that all the other bodies moved around it. Aristotle further refined these notions almost 60 years later.

141 AD: EARTH FIRST
The Greek thinker Ptolemy worked out a complex system that seemed to prove that Earth is at the center of the universe. His view of the heavens remained widely accepted for the next 14 centuries. But to keep Earth at center stage, many corrections to Ptolemy's calculations had to be made over time, until the system became a wild mess of orbits and revolutions.

1543: COPERNICAN REVOLUTION
Polish astronomer Nicolaus Copernicus (1473-1543) laid the groundwork for overturning Ptolemy's theory of an Earth-centered, or geocentric, universe in his 1543 treatise *De Revolutionibus Orbium Coelestium* ("On the Revolutions of the Heavenly Spheres"). He argued that planetary motions could be better explained in a Sun-centered, or heliocentric, universe. Even to many readers who could understand Copernicus, this theory seemed too jarring to be believed.

1609: ELLIPTICAL ORBITS
In 1609 German mathematician Johannes Kepler showed that planets did not move in perfect circles around the Earth, as in Ptolemy's system, but in more oval or elliptical paths around the Sun.

1609: GALILEO AND HIS TELESCOPE
Legend has it that a Dutch boy found that putting two lenses together made faraway objects seem to jump toward him. He told this to lens maker Hans Lippershey, who put the two lenses in a metal tube to create the first telescope, in 1608.

Italian scientist Galileo Galilei, in 1609, built his own telescope, which magnified objects to look 20 times bigger. He discovered four moons orbiting Jupiter—something that Ptolemy said was impossible.

Other evidence gathered by Galileo convinced him that Copernicus was right in his view of a Sun-centered heavens. However, this did not go over well with the Catholic Church. A devout Christian, Galileo argued that the intention of the the Bible is to teach "how to go to heaven, not how the heavens go." (The quote was actually borrowed from Cardinal Baronius, an early contemporary of Galileo's.)

In the end, Galileo was still condemned by the Vatican for heresy and placed under house arrest.

1631: PLANETARY TRANSIT OBSERVED
On Nov. 7, 1631, French mathematician Pierre Gassendi first observed a planetary transit—where one heavenly object moves across the visible face of a larger one. Gassendi observed Mercury moving across the face of the Sun.

In 1639, English astronomer Jeremiah Horrocks observed a transit of Venus across the face of the Sun. This led him to suggest that observations of a transit taken from different spots on Earth could be used to calculate the planet's distance from Earth, and that a series of such calculations could yield the size of the entire solar system.

1781: URANUS
Before telescopes, people could see only the five planets closest to Earth. In 1781, German-born British astronomer

SEVEN-PERSON PYRAMID—THE WALLENDAS, p. 154

TALLEST CHAIR—65.5 FEET HIGH, MANZANO, ITALY, p. 162

MARATHON OF THE SANDS—ANNUAL SIX-DAY RACE ACROSS 143 MILES OF THE SAHARA, p. 171

HIGHEST FORMAL DINNER PARTY—BEAR GRYLLS & ALAN VEAL, 2005, p. 159

FASTEST SOLO SAILING TRIP AROUND THE WORLD—ELLEN MACARTHUR, 2005, p. 17

FASTEST AND TALLEST ROLLER COASTER—KINGDA KA, NEW JERSEY, p. 66 and p. 165

WORLD TRADE CENTER TIGHTROPE WALK—PHILIPPE PETIT, AUG. 7, 1974, p. 154

LARGEST CATFISH—CAUGHT IN THAILAND'S MEKONG RIVER, 2005, p. 181

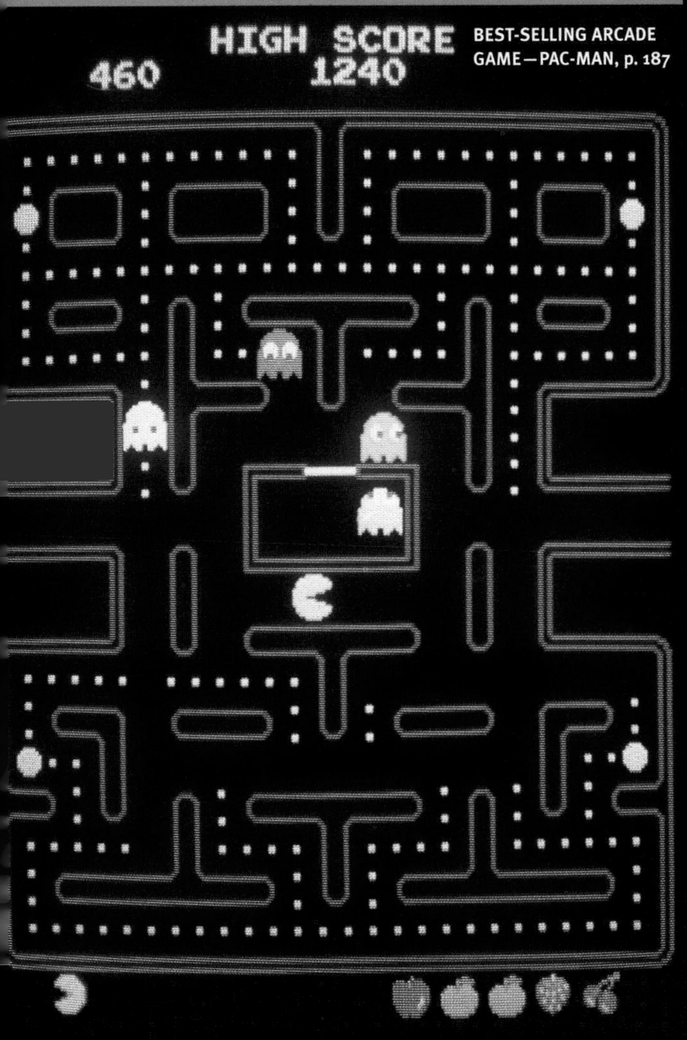

BEST-SELLING ARCADE GAME—PAC-MAN, p. 187

BIGGEST AND BEST-SELLING BOARD GAME—MONOPOLY, pp. 190-191

HIGHEST PRICE FOR STAMP—INVERTED "JENNY" WITH UPSIDE-DOWN AIRPLANES, p. 185

LARGEST LIVING TREE—"GENERAL SHERMAN," A GIANT SEQUOIA, SEQUOIA NATIONAL PARK, CA, p. 204

WORST-SMELLING FLOWER—TITAN ARUM, A.K.A. CORPSE FLOWER, p. 207

HURRICANE KATRINA—HIGHEST U.S. STORM SURGE, 2005 p. 211

ICEBERG IN KULUSUK GREENLAND—POLLUTION AND GLOBAL WARMING, p. 212-213

TORNADOES, p. 211

MICHAEL JACKSON—MOST EXPENSIVE MUSIC VIDEO, PICTURED IN 1975 AND 2005, p. 231

FIRST RINGTONE CHART-TOPPER—USHER, p. 93

THE FIRST EVER "BIKINI"—DESIGNED BY LOUIS RÉARD IN 1946, p. 232-233

THE SIMPSONS—LONGEST-RUNNING PRIME-TIME ANIMATED SERIES, p. 235

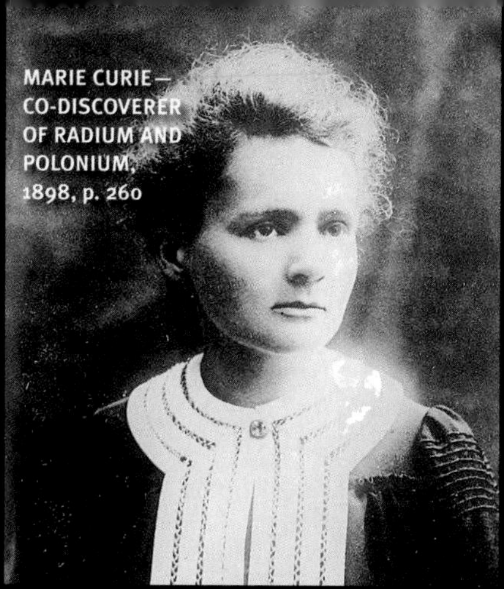

MARIE CURIE—CO-DISCOVERER OF RADIUM AND POLONIUM, 1898, p. 260

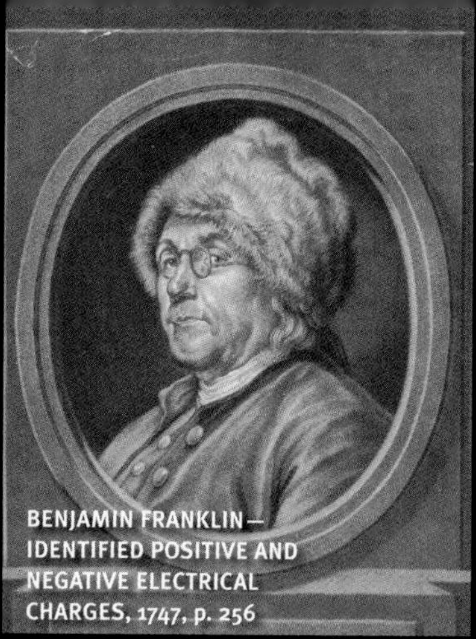

BENJAMIN FRANKLIN—IDENTIFIED POSITIVE AND NEGATIVE ELECTRICAL CHARGES, 1747, p. 256

SIR ISAAC NEWTON—DEVELOPED THE LAW OF GRAVITATION AND THREE LAWS OF MOTION, 1687, p. 254

WORST ELECTRICAL BLACKOUT (U.S.), AFFECTED 60 MILLION PEOPLE IN U.S. AND CANADA, AUG. 14, 2003, p. 257

LARGEST ANCIENT SCULPTURE COLLECTION—TERRACOTTA WARRIORS, EXCAVATED IN XI'AN, CHINA, P.243

FIRST PRIVATE SPACEFLIGHT—*SPACESHIPONE* WITH TEST PILOT BRIAN BINNIE, 2004, p. 279

SECOND MAN ON THE MOON—EDWIN "BUZZ" ALDRIN, PHOTOGRAPHED BY FIRST MAN ON THE MOON, NEIL ARMSTRONG, 1969, p. 278

FIRST U.S. SPACE WALK—ED WHITE, 1965, p. 279

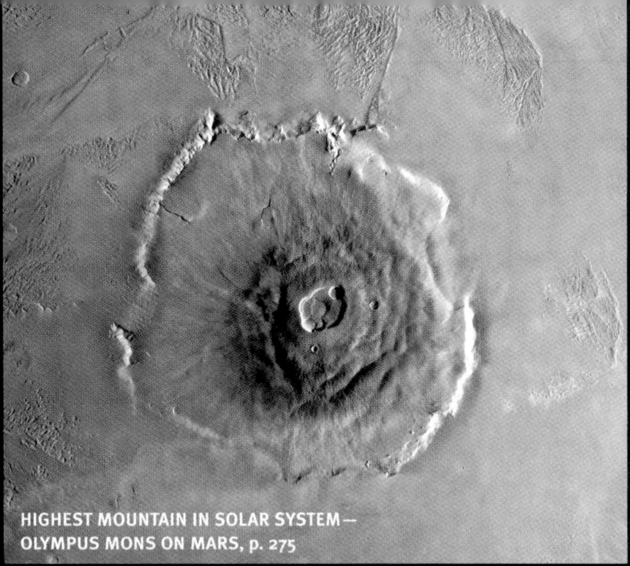
HIGHEST MOUNTAIN IN SOLAR SYSTEM—OLYMPUS MONS ON MARS, p. 275

LARGEST RINGS—SATURN, p. 273

"PILLARS OF STAR CREATION" IN THE EAGLE NEBULA, PHOTOGRAPHED BY THE MOST POWERFUL SPACE TELESCOPE—HUBBLE, 1995, p. 284

The Moon ►

Selected Planetary Records

Largest Planet	Jupiter	88,846 mi wide at equator
Smallest Planet	Pluto	1,485 mi average diameter
Fastest Orbit around Sun	Mercury	29.75 mi per second
Slowest Orbit around Sun	Pluto	2.93 mi per second
Gets Closest to Sun	Mercury	28.6 million mi
Gets Farthest from Sun	Pluto	4.5 billion mi
Longest Day	Mercury	175.94 Earth days
Shortest Day	Jupiter	about 10 Earth hours
Most Moons	Jupiter	63 known
Largest Moon	Ganymede (Jupiter)	3,270 mi wide at equator
Hottest Planet	Venus	867°F average surface temperature
Coldest Planet	Pluto	-369°F average surface temperature

Sir William Herschel discovered a sixth planet, Uranus, using a 7-foot reflecting telescope.

1846: NEPTUNE
Uranus's orbit suggested to some scientists that there had to be a body beyond that planet exerting a gravitational pull. In 1845, two astronomers—Englishman John Couch Adams and Frenchman Urbain J.J. Le Verrier—independently predicted the location of the planet that came to be called Neptune.

In 1846, Johann Galle, using a telescope, observed Neptune for the first time.

1930: PLUTO Pluto's discovery was also spurred by a theory. Unexplained problems with the orbits of Uranus and Neptune led astronomers to believe that another large planet existed beyond their orbits. Their calculations later proved inaccurate, but not before American astronomer Clyde Tombaugh at the Lowell Observatory discovered Pluto.

It wasn't the massive body astronomers had predicted; it's so small—smaller than Earth's moon—and its orbit is so strange that some astronomers hesitate to call it a planet. The International Astronomical Union is officially counting it as a planet, at least for the time being.

SOMETHING TO THINK ABOUT

STILL MORE PLANETS?

In July 2005, astronomers at the California Institute of Technology's Palomar Observatory reported that an object they had discovered in 2003, orbiting the Sun but three times as far away as Pluto, should be classified as the 10th planet, based on their estimates of its size and motion. The exact size of the object could not be determined, but they say it is bigger than Pluto.

SUPERLATIVES

BIGGEST STORM
Jupiter's Great Red Spot is a giant storm of swirling gases so big that three Earths could fit inside. Winds there blow more than 25,000 miles per hour. The Great Red Spot has been raging for at least 300 years. Scientists think this is because unlike Earth, Jupiter has no surface features to slow down the ferocious winds.

BIGGEST EXPLOSION
In 1994, 21 giant fragments of the comet Shoemaker-Levy 9 slammed into Jupiter. One of the biggest fragments hit with a force 100,000 times as great as that of the largest nuclear device ever set off. The impacts left dark bruises the size of Earth on Jupiter's surface. If even smaller fragments of a comet were to hit Earth, the resulting dust and smoke could change the climate drastically and destroy many forms of life. The odds of this happening in the next few centuries or so are very small, perhaps one in several thousand.

BIGGEST RINGS
All four of the solar system's gas giants—Jupiter, Saturn, Uranus, and Neptune—have rings around them. From a distance, these rings look solid. But they are really orbiting fields of ice and rocks.

Saturn has the largest and most dramatic rings. They begin about 4,000 miles above the clouds and extend about 260,000 miles into space. On average the rings of Saturn are only about 700 feet thick.

Mars

MARS, WITH ITS DISTINCTIVE BLOOD-RED COLOR, is easily distinguishable by the naked eye. The ancient Babylonians called it the "Star of Death." In China and Japan it was known as the "Fire Star." The ancient Romans named it Mars after their god of war.

There is no basis for thinking that there is intelligent life on Mars, but the idea has long appealed to people's imaginations. Martians are (often unfriendly) characters in countless science fiction stories, and the red planet figures in over 100 films including such gems as *Invaders from Mars, Horses on Mars, Biker Mice from Mars,* and even *Abbott and Costello Go to Mars.*

MILESTONES

300s-200s BC: MARS'S MOTION Eudoxus of Cnidus, a contemporary of Plato, offered an early, but incorrect, explanation for the bewildering movement of Mars in the sky. Observed from the Earth at the same time every night, Mars appears to move from west to east, but about every two years, it seems to reverse direction for a couple of months. Around 340 BC, Eudoxus theorized that the observed "retrograde" motion of Mars was created by the independent movements of several nested spheres centered on the Earth.

About 100 years later, Aristarchus of Samos argued that Mars's retrograde movement is an illusion created by the Earth's revolution around the Sun. His theory did not catch on; instead until the Renaissance, Western astronomy was dominated by the theory presented in Ptolemy's *Almagest* (c. 137 AD), which placed the Earth at the center of the universe.

1543: COPERNICAN THEORY Astronomer Nicolaus Copernicus, in his major work, published in 1543, placed the Sun at the center of the solar system—which explained the observed retrograde motions of Mars, Jupiter, and Saturn.

1659: FIRST ACCURATE DRAWING Christiaan Huygens of Holland, using a telescope with a 2-inch lens, made the first drawing of Mars that accurately depicts some of its key features. He also observed that the features appeared in the same place on the Martian surface at about the same time each night, leading him to correctly deduce that a Martian day was about 24 hours long.

1666: CALCULATION OF ROTATION By following the location of features on Mars's visible surface at the new Paris Observatory, Giovanni Domenico Cassini in 1666 calculated its rotation to take 24 hours, 40 minutes, close to the 24 hours, 39 minutes, 35 seconds calculated by astronomers today.

1830: MARS MAP Johann Mädler and Wilhelm Beer, amateur astronomers in Berlin, in 1830 issued the first map of the surface of Mars. A special compound lens telescope, built by Bavarian optician Joseph von Fraunhofer, gave Mädler and Beer extremely clear images on which to base their map. Craters on Mars now bear their names.

1877: OBSERVATION OF MOONS Using a telescope at the U.S. Naval Observatory, Asaph Hall in 1877 first discovered the two moons of Mars. Their names, Phobos and Deimos, mean "Fear" and "Terror" in Greek, and are the sons of Ares, the war God in ancient Greek mythology.

1895: MARTIAN "CANALS" In his book *Mars* (1895), Percival Lowell argued that straight lines visible on Mars's surface were canals built by an advanced civilization. This popularized the idea that intelligent life once existed on Mars.

Lowell's book was based in part on the work of Italian astronomer Giovanni Schiaparelli, who had reported seeing *canali* (which actually means "channels") on Mars in 1877. In 1909, astronomer Eugene M. Antoniadi concluded that the geometric network of lines was an optical illusion, an opinion since confirmed.

1898: *WAR OF THE WORLDS* H.G. Wells's 1898 classic science-fiction story made popular the frightening notion that Mars might be inhabited by intelligent beings looking to invade their planetary neighbor Earth.

1938: MARS INVADES EARTH Orson Welles's Oct. 30, 1938, broadcast of a radio play based on H.G. Wells's *War of the Worlds* terrified millions of Americans, who were convinced by its news-bulletin style that an actual invasion was occurring.

Welles had inserted names of actual New Jersey towns and streets into the classic science fiction story, and though the program was identified as fiction four times during the hour-long broadcast, hysteria ensued.

1964: SUCCESSFUL PROBE The NASA probe *Mariner 4* soared past Mars on July 14, 1964, and took a series of close-up photos. The pictures indicated little chance of existing life.

SOMETHING TO THINK ABOUT

LIFE ON MARS?

Although *Viking 1*'s touchdown on Mars in 1976 was a proud technological achievement, many scientists were gravely disappointed by what it found—or rather, didn't find. Images that came back across the cosmos were of a lifeless planet. But in 1996, NASA released a report on an ancient meteorite from Mars called Allan Hills 84001, found in Antarctica 12 years earlier. The report stated that the rock contained chemical, mineral, and structural evidence that microscopic life might have existed on Mars more than three billion years ago. Most scientists believe conditions on the red planet were warmer and wetter long ago—much more earthlike than Mars is today. Scientists received the report with both enthusiasm and skepticism and, though the evidence is still inconclusive, the rock remains one of the most intriguing of all Martian discoveries.

1976: MARS LANDING At 7:53 AM EDT on July 20, 1976, the unmanned U.S. spacecraft *Viking 1* landed on the Martian surface. Within hours, detailed photographs of the desolate Martian landscape were relayed to Earth.

1997: SOJOURNER Launched in 1996, the Mars *Pathfinder* probe landed on Mars on July 4, 1997. Soon after it deployed *Sojourner*, a small, six-wheeled, 25-pound rover, the first ever sent to the red planet. *Sojourner* spent months investigating rock features and sending back pictures of the surface. Two larger rovers, *Spirit* and *Opportunity*, landed on two seperate locations of the planet in January 2004. As of early 2006, they were still operating.

2002: WATER ON MARS Using data collected by *2001 Mars Odyssey*, which began its Mars mapping mission in Feb. 2002, scientists reported evidence of huge amounts of ice just below the Martian surface.

Scientists say that where there is water there may once have been some form of life.

SUPERLATIVES

NEAREST TO EARTH Because the orbital paths of the Earth and of Mars have different shapes, and because Mars takes nearly twice as long to complete its orbit, the distance between the two planets varies considerably.

E. Myles Standish of the Jet Propulsion Laboratory calculated the distance between Mars and the Earth from 3000 BC to 3000 AD. The closest Mars gets to the Earth during that whole time is 34,579,948 miles, on Sept. 8, 2729.

On Aug. 27, 2003, astronomers worldwide rushed to their telescopes to view Mars from only 34,646,418 miles away, the closest it has been in thousands of years.

The farthest distance Mars ever gets from the Earth is 249.4 million miles.

LARGEST CRATER The biggest crater on Mars, Hellas Planitia, an impact crater in the southern hemisphere, is 1,300 miles wide and over 3.7 miles deep.

BIGGEST CANYON The Valles Marineris canyon system on Mars is about 2,500 miles long and reaches a depth of 4.35 miles. Its widest point, in Melas Canyon, is an astounding 120 miles across.

HIGHEST MOUNTAIN (SOLAR SYSTEM) Mars is home to the massive Olympus Mons, the largest mountain in the solar system.

Olympus Mons rises 15.5 miles above the Martian surface, making Mount Everest, at 5.5 miles high, look fairly modest. It measures more than 311 miles across its base.

Olympus Mons and three other enormous shield volcanoes were discovered by *Mariner 9*, which mapped the red planet in 1971.

Stars

TO AN ASTROPHYSICIST A STAR IS AN INCANDESCENT SPHERE of gas that emits electromagnetic radiation and may be classified by mass, size, temperature, and luminosity. For the rest of us, stars in the sky are sources of wonder and delight. And to this day, some people scrutinize horoscopes because they believe, or like to imagine, that the far-flung stars can affect their destinies.

MILESTONES

ABOUT 270 BC: CONSTELLATIONS The poem *Phaenomena,* composed by the Greek poet Aratus around 270 BC, contains the oldest-known written description of the constellations (groups of stars), although it is a versification of an earlier astronomical work by the mathematician Eudoxus of Cnidos. Aratus identified 44 constellations.

About 150 AD, Ptolemy, a Greek astronomer and mathematician who worked in Alexandria, Egypt, wrote the *Almagest*, which set forth a geometric theory to account for the apparent motions and positions of the planets, Sun, and Moon against the background of fixed stars. The *Almagest* listed 48 constellations, 47 of which have the same names today.

134 BC: STAR CATALOG Inspired by a nova, or "new star," he observed in 134 BC while at Rhodes, the Greek astronomer Hipparchus developed a catalog of about 850 stars. He was the first observer to fashion a scale of magnitude to indicate a star's apparent brightness as seen from Earth (visual magnitude). His incremental scale, originally numbering from 1 to 6 (brightest to faintest), is still in use although it has been refined and extended in range.

A star's absolute magnitude is based on how bright it would look if it were 10 parsecs (32.6 light-years) from Earth.

1718: MOVEMENT OF FIXED STARS Edmund Halley (of comet fame) published a paper in 1718 comparing current star locations with those recorded by the ancient Greeks. After studying the star catalogs he concluded that Aldebaran, Sirius, and Arcturus had moved half a degree over nearly 2,000 years—which indicated that stars are not fixed in the sky, as had been believed, but change their position relative to one another.

1838: MEASURING DISTANCE German astronomer and mathematician Friedrich Wilhelm Bessel calculated the first relatively accurate determination of the distance of a star in 1838. He detected a parallax, or shift in position, of the star 61 Cygni when viewed from opposite sides of the Earth's orbit, and used this shift, with the help of trigonometry, to calculate the star's distance: some 3 parsecs, or 10 light-years, away.

British astronomer Thomas Henderson had made parallax measurements for the star Alpha Centauri in 1832, but rigorous rechecking delayed his distance announcement until after Bessel's.

1859: COMPOSITION In 1859, German chemist Robert Bunsen and physicist Gustav Kirchhoff developed spectroscopy, a method of analyzing the makeup of substances through the spectrum of light they give off. Kirchhoff compared spectral patterns from elements on Earth to the Sun's spectrum and identified several shared elements, including iron, calcium, magnesium, sodium, nickel, and chromium.

The method is now used by astronomers to ascertain not only the chemical composition of stars but also their temperature, pressure, density, magnetic fields, and velocity.

1916: BLACK HOLES Basing his conclusions on Albert Einstein's general theory of relativity, German physicist Karl Schwarzschild postulated, in 1916, the existence of an extremely dense body whose gravitational force is so strong that nothing, including light, can escape from it. The term "black hole," however, was not used until American physicist John Wheeler coined it more than 50 years later.

One of the problems with studying black holes is that, since they don't emit light, they can't be seen. But astronomers have found strong evidence for their existence by observing their effects.

1922: CONSTELLATIONS (OFFICIAL) The International Astronomical Union (IAU) in 1922 officially adopted the list of 88 constellations that is currently used. Eight years later the Belgian astronomer Eugène Delporte, working on behalf of the IAU, fixed the boundaries between constellations, so that today every star, nebula, or galaxy can be located within the borders of a constellation.

1924: OTHER GALAXIES Edwin Hubble used the largest telescope of his day (the 100-inch Hooker), at Mount Wilson Observatory, near Pasadena, CA, to observe and photograph distant spiral nebulae.

He noticed the existence of Cepheid variable stars in the Andromeda nebula. These stars—used by astronomers to help determine distances—indicated that the Andromeda spiral nebula was located too far away to be within our Milky Way galaxy and was actually a massive star system in its own right. Hubble reported these findings in 1924. Further observation showed that Andromeda was moving away from the Milky Way.

Although previous astronomers had speculated that our galaxy was not the only one, Hubble was the first to prove it was one of many in an expanding universe.

1963: QUASARS Dutch-born U.S. astronomer Maarten Schmidt in 1963 performed a spectroscopic study of the light from a distant starlike object called 3C 273, which was located in the same place as one of a number of mysterious radio-wave sources that astronomers had detected.

His analysis indicated that 3C 273 was receding from Earth at a phenomenal rate of nearly 30,000 miles per second and was about 2 billion light-years away. To be visible at such a distance, the object had to have an extraordinarily high energy output.

Astronomers later discovered thousands of such remote objects, and called them quasars (for "*quasi*-stell*ar* radio source," although not all emit radio waves).

Today, quasars are generally thought to be associated with the centers of certain types of galaxies and may be powered by supermassive black holes.

1967: PULSARS Graduate student Jocelyn Bell was helping Cambridge University radio astronomer Antony Hewish search the sky for radio-wave sources that might be quasars in Oct. 1967 when she noticed a bit of "scruff" on one of her recording rolls. It turned out she had discovered the first pulsar—a rapidly rotating neutron star (that is, a star made up mostly of neutrons) that emits brief sharp pulses of energy.

SOMETHING TO THINK ABOUT

STAR POWER

Human civilization could be wiped out in a flash if a nearby star were to explode. A reminder of the destructive power lurking in the heavens came on Dec. 27, 2004, when Earth satellites and telescopes detected a super-explosion on the surface of SGR 1806-20, a type of neutron star called a magnetar because of its extraordinarily powerful magnetic field. In the first 200 milliseconds the star released as much energy as the Sun generates in 250,000 years. If such a blast occurred 10 light-years from us, it would destroy the protective ozone layer in the Earth's atmosphere, potentially leading to the extinction of species. Luckily, SGR 1806-20 is about 50,000 light-years away.

SUPERLATIVES

BRIGHTEST STAR The brightest star in the night sky, in visual apparent magnitude, is Alpha Canis Majoris, better known as Sirius or the Dog Star. A mere 8.6 light-years away, it's located in the constellation Canis Major (the Large Dog).

The most luminous known star, that is, the brightest in terms of absolute magnitude, may be LBV 1806-20, located about 45,000 light-years from Earth. Astronomers estimated in early 2004 that it was 5 million to 40 million times brighter than the Sun. Surprisingly, it cannot be seen by normal light-detecting telescopes, since its light is blocked by dust in the Milky Way.

NEAREST STAR The star nearest to Earth is the Sun. The next closest star is Proxima Centauri, which is 4.22 light-years away.

This small red star is the nearest member of the Alpha Centauri triple star system. It is so faint that its existence was unknown until 1915, and it can be seen only through a telescope.

NEAREST GALAXY The Canis Major dwarf galaxy, discovered in 2003, lies about 25,000 light-years away from our solar system. It is a satellite of our Milky Way galaxy.

The nearest major galaxy is the Andromeda galaxy, which is nearly 3 million light-years away and compares in size to our Milky Way Galaxy.

FARTHEST GALAXY Astronomers using the Hubble Space Telescope collected photos of what is called the Hubble Ultra Deep Field (HUDF) from Sept. 24, 2003, to Jan. 16, 2004. The photos detected light from galaxies that existed as early as 700 million years after the Big Bang (95% of the way back to the estimated time of the Big Bang, 14 billion years ago).

The HUDF contains roughly 10,000 galaxies in the constellation Fornax, located below Orion. If observed by ground-based instruments, this area of the sky appears largely empty. The ability to see the galaxies in such a young state is due to their distance from Earth—up to 13 billion light-years.

Human Spaceflight

WITH THE LAUNCH OF *SPUTNIK I*, the first artificial earth-orbiting satellite, by the Soviet Union in Oct. 1957, the U.S. and Soviet Union entered into an out-of-this-world competition to conquer space. Embarrassed by early Soviet successes, the U.S. government accelerated its space efforts, and in 1958, the National Aeronautics and Space Administration (NASA) was created. The focus of the "space race" rapidly switched from putting machines into orbit to sending humans into space, and in 1961, President John F. Kennedy called for "landing a man on the moon and returning him safely to earth" by the end of the decade.

MILESTONES

1961: FIRST MANNED FLIGHT AND EARTH ORBIT On April 12, 1961, Soviet cosmonaut Yuri A. Gagarin became the first human in space, and the first launched into orbit. His *Vostok 1* spacecraft took off from the Baikonur Cosmodrome in Kazakhstan. He circled the Earth once at a maximum altitude of 203 miles; the flight lasted 108 minutes.

1961: AMERICAN IN SPACE On May 5, 1961, the first American astronaut, Alan B. Shepard Jr., was launched into space for a suborbital flight lasting 15 minutes, 28 seconds, aboard the Mercury spacecraft *Freedom 7*. It lifted off from Cape Canaveral, FL, at 9:34 AM and reached an altitude of 116.5 miles before falling back to Earth and splashing down in the Atlantic.

1962: EARTH ORBIT (U.S.) On Feb. 20, 1962, John H. Glenn Jr. became the first U.S. astronaut to orbit Earth. On his 4-hour, 55-minute flight aboard the Mercury vessel *Friendship 7*, he orbited Earth three times.

1965: SPACE WALK On March 18, 1965, Soviet cosmonaut Aleksei Leonov performed the first space walk. Leonov left the *Voskhod 2* spacecraft, piloted by Pavel I. Belyayev, for 10 minutes. During that time his spacesuit expanded, making it difficult for him to reenter the vessel.

1965: ORBIT CHANGE On March 23, 1965, Virgil I. "Gus" Grissom and John W. Young became the first astronauts to perform an orbital path change other than the de-orbit maneuver. The pair, piloting the *Gemini 3*, fired thrusters to change the direction of their orbit and drop to a lower altitude.

1966: ORBITAL DOCKING The first orbital docking of two spacecrafts in Earth's orbit occurred on March 16, 1966, between *Gemini 8* and an *Agena* target vehicle. They had been launched about 100 minutes apart that morning. The *Gemini 8* crew, Neil A. Armstrong and David R. Scott, rendezvoused with *Agena* six hours later, with Armstrong successfully completing the docking maneuver.

Success almost turned to tragedy as the docked spacecraft suddenly tumbled out of control. Armstrong undocked *Gemini 8* but nearly passed out before gaining control. Eleven hours after takeoff, *Gemini 8* made an emergency splash-down in the Pacific Ocean. Armstrong and Scott survived unharmed.

1968: MANNED MOON ORBIT The first humans to complete a lunar orbit, and see the far side of the Moon, were the crew of *Apollo 8*—Frank Borman, James A. Lovell, and William A. Anders. The mission was launched on Dec. 21, 1968. They reached the Moon Dec. 24 and completed ten orbits before heading home. Splash-down was on Dec. 27.

1969: MOON LANDING On July 20, 1969, humans first landed on the Moon. Neil Armstrong was the first human to walk on the Moon, joined by Edwin E. "Buzz" Aldrin Jr. The first human footprint on the lunar surface was Armstrong's left foot.

The *Apollo 11* mission, crewed by Armstrong, Aldrin, and Michael Collins, had been launched July 16. Armstrong and Aldrin, in the lunar module *Eagle*, landed at the Sea of Tranquility. About six hours later, at 10:56 P.M. Eastern Standard Time, Armstrong stepped out onto the surface. The two stayed on the Moon for 21 hours, 36 minutes, 21 seconds.

Apollo 11 splashed-down in the Pacific July 24, ending and climaxing a history-making project launched by President Kennedy eight years earlier.

1971: LUNAR ROVER The *Apollo 15* mission, launched July 26, 1971, crewed by David Scott, James B. Irwin, and Alfred M. Worden, was the first to carry the lunar rover, a four-wheeled vehicle designed specifically for driving on the Moon. It had a top speed of 11 miles an hour. Using the rover, Scott and Irwin explored more of the surface than the three previous lunar missions combined.

1971: SPACE STATION The former Soviet Union launched the first orbital space station, *Salyut 13*, on April 19, 1971. It was first occupied by the crew of *Soyuz 11*, which docked with the station on June 6, 1971.

Tragedy struck this historic mission when the three cosmonauts aboard *Soyuz 11*, Georgi T. Dobrovolskiy, Vladislav N. Volkov, and Viktor I. Patsayev, died during reentry from loss of pressurization in the cabin.

1973: AMERICAN SPACE STATION On May 14, 1973, NASA launched *Skylab*, the first U.S. orbital station. Eleven days later, three astronauts, Pete Conrad Jr., Joseph P. Kerwin, and Paul J. Weitz, took up positions aboard the station. Three crews worked on *Skylab* during extended visits through Feb. 1974.

The unmanned craft disintegrated during Earth reentry over a

Other Spaceflight Milestones

MILESTONE	NAME	SPACECRAFT	DATE
First African American	Guion S. Bluford Jr.	*Challenger*	Aug. 30, 1983
First Native American	John B. Herrington	*Atlantis*	Nov. 23, 2002
First Hispanic American	Franklin R. Chang-Diaz	*Columbia*	Jan. 12, 1986
First Woman	Valentina V. Tereshkova (U.S.S.R.)	*Vostok 6*	June 16, 1963
First American Woman	Sally K. Ride	*Challenger*	June 18, 1983
First Woman Commander (U.S.)	Eileen M. Collins	*Columbia*	July 23, 1999
First Married Couple	Mark C. Lee, N. Jan Davis	*Endeavour*	Sept. 12, 1992
First American Space Walk	Edward H. White 2nd	*Gemini 4*	June 3, 1965

"That's one small step for man, one giant leap for mankind."

–Neil Armstrong, July 20, 1969

sparsely populated region of Western Australia on July 11, 1979.

1975: JOINT VENTURE The first joint Soviet-U.S. space venture was the Apollo-Soyuz Test Project of July 1975.

Three U.S. astronauts, Vance Brand, Thomas P. Stafford, and Donald "Deke" K. Slayton, docked their *Apollo* spacecraft with the Soviet *Soyuz 19* vessel on July 17. Soon after, Stafford and Slayton entered the *Soyuz* through the docking module to be greeted by the two cosmonauts, Aleksei Leonov and Valery Kubasov.

The docking and historic meeting were broadcast on TV in both countries. During the mission the crews shared meals, conducted experiments together, and held a joint press conference.

1981: SPACE SHUTTLE The first space shuttle, *Columbia*, had its maiden flight on April 12, 1981, with John W. Young and Robert L. Crippen at the controls. *Columbia* lifted off from Cape Canaveral and landed 54 hours, 21 minutes later at Edwards Air Force Base in California.

1984: UNTETHERED SPACE WALK American astronauts Bruce McCandless II and Robert L. Stewart performed the first untethered space walks on Feb. 7, 1984. Wearing backpacks called Manned Maneuvering Units (MMU) that cost $60 million each to develop, they took turns soaring around the shuttle. McCandless flew as far as 320 feet away.

1984: SATELLITE CAPTURE AND REPAIR The first in-flight capture, repair, and redeployment of an orbiting satellite came during the *Challenger* mission launched on April 6, 1984. The five-man crew captured the crippled research satellite *Solar Max* on April 10, repaired it, and released it back into space April 12.

1986: *MIR* SPACE STATION The core unit of the *Mir*, the world's first permanently manned space station, was launched Feb. 20, 1986.

Equipped with docking stations to accommodate six visiting spacecraft at once, *Mir*, which means "peace" in Russian, was planned as a three-year project. The station stayed aloft for 15 years, finally crashing to the Pacific Ocean in a controlled ending on March 23, 2001.

1998: INTERNATIONAL SPACE STATION The first assembly stage of the International Space Station occurred during the *Endeavour* shuttle mission launched Dec. 4, 1998. The shuttle carried the U.S.-built *Unity* connecting module to Russian-built *Zarya* control module. The *Zarya* module was launched into orbit Nov. 20, 1998. The *Unity* module was joined to *Zarya* on Dec. 6, the first step in the construction of the ISS.

2000: INTERNATIONAL SPACE STATION RESIDENTS The first permanent residents of the ISS were U.S. astronaut William A. Shepherd and Russian cosmonauts Yuri Gidzenko and Sergei Krikalev. The three-man *Soyuz* crew was launched from the Baikonour Cosmodrome on Oct. 31, 2000, and docked with the space station Nov. 2. This crew stayed on board four months, before being relieved.

2004: PRIVATELY-FUNDED LAUNCH On June 21, 2004, *SpaceShipOne*, piloted by Mike Melvill, became the first privately-sponsored craft to carry a human into space. The craft, designed by Dick Rutan and funded by Microsoft pioneer Paul Allen, made the required two flights within two weeks, Sept. 29 and Oct. 4, to win the $10 million Ansari X Prize for its creators.

On the third flight, piloted by veteran test pilot Brian Binnie (Melvill piloted the second flight), it was lifted to 50,000 feet by an airplane, the *White Knight*, then ascended by rocket power to 367,442 feet, breaking the 1963 record height for a winged aircraft set in 1963.

THE LAST TIME...

The last time humans walked on the Moon was Dec. 14, 1972. Astronauts Eugene Cernan and Harrison "Jack" Schmitt landed on the lunar surface Dec. 11. They left a plaque that said:

"Here Man completed his first exploration of the Moon, Dec. 1972 A.D. May the spirit of peace in which we came be reflected in the lives of all mankind."

MORE ON Human Spaceflight

SUPERLATIVES

YOUNGEST HUMAN IN SPACE The youngest person to travel in space is Soviet cosmonaut Gherman S. Titov. He was 25 years, 329 days old when his *Vostok 2* spacecraft was launched on Aug. 6, 1961. The fourth person to fly in space, Titov was the first to spend more than 24 hours. His mission lasted 25 hours, 18 minutes, and completed 17 orbits of Earth.

YOUNGEST WOMAN IN SPACE The youngest woman to travel in space is Valentina V. Tereshkova. The Soviet cosmonaut was 26 years old when she embarked aboard *Vostok 6* on June 16, 1963.

OLDEST ASTRONAUT The oldest person to travel in space is John H. Glenn (D, OH), who was 77 years old, and a U.S. senator, when he flew aboard the space shuttle *Discovery* mission launched Oct. 29, 1998. His flight came 36 years after he became the first American to orbit Earth. President Bill Clinton attended the launch at the Kennedy Space Center, the first president to witness a shuttle takeoff.

HIGHEST ALTITUDE The three-man crew of *Apollo 13*, James Lovell, Fred Haise, and Jack Swigert, were a record 249,200 miles from Earth on April 14, 1970. The mission's scheduled lunar landing had to be abandoned when an explosion damaged the spacecraft; the crew had to move into the lunar module as a lifeboat to bring them back to Earth. The crippled craft had to fly around the Moon in order to use its gravitational pull to slingshot them on a trajectory back to Earth.

LARGEST CREW The biggest crew on a single mission was the eight-person crew of the space shuttle *Challenger* launched Oct. 30, 1985. There were five Americans, two West Germans, and a Dutch astronaut. This international mission was designated D-1, for Deutschland.

LONGEST SHUTTLE FLIGHT The longest space shuttle mission, on *Columbia*, lasted 17 days, 15 hours, 53 minutes, 26 seconds, from Nov. 19 to Dec. 6, 1996. *Columbia* broke its own record, set just four months earlier. A five-person crew was aboard the record-breaking mission, Kenneth D. Cockrell, Kent V. Rominger, Tamara E. Jernigan, Thomas D. Jones, and Story Musgrave.

Originally planned to last 15 days, the mission was extended due to bad weather near the landing area at the Kennedy Space Center in Florida.

SHORTEST FLIGHT The shortest completed manned spaceflight was Alan B. Shepard Jr.'s 15 minute, 28 second, suborbital flight in *Mercury 3*, on May 5, 1961.

LONGEST IN SPACE **MISSION** The longest time spent in space in a single mission was 437 days, 18 hours, by Russian cosmonaut Dr. Valery Polyakov. He was launched to the Mir space station on Jan. 8, 1994, aboard Soyuz TM-18 and returned in Soyuz TM-20 on March 22, 1995.

LONGEST IN SPACE (U.S.) **MISSION** The longest time spent in space in a single mission, by a U.S. astronaut, is 196 days. Two astronauts, Carl Walz and Daniel Bursch, hold this record. They were members of the *Expedition 4* crew, with Soviet cosmonaut Yury Onufrienko, that flew to the International Space Station aboard the space shuttle *Endeavour* on Dec. 5, 2001. Bursch and Walz returned aboard *Endeavour* on June 19, 2002.

LONGEST TIME IN SPACE (WOMAN) **MISSION** The longest time spent in space during a single mission by a woman is 188 days by American astronaut Shannon Lucid from March 22 to Sept. 26, 1996. She lived aboard the *Mir* space station with two male cosmonauts and orbited Earth 3,008 times during her marathon journey.

LONGEST TIME IN SPACE **CUMULATIVE** Russia cosmonaut Sergei Krikalev has logged the most cumulative time in space. On Aug. 14, 2005, while aboard the International Space Station, he broke the previous record of 747 days held by fellow cosmonaut Sergei Avdeyev. By the time Kirkalev returned to Earth on Oct. 10, 2005, he had accumulated a total of 803 days, 9 hours and 39 minutes in space. Kirkalev first flew aboard the Soviet space station *Mir* in 1988 and was the first Russian to fly a space shuttle mission in Feb. 1994.

LONGEST IN SPACE (U.S.) **TOTAL** When he returned to Earth on April 29, 2004, astrophysicist Michael Foale had traveled 374 days, 11 hours, 19 minutes in space, a record for an American astronaut. He beat the record of Carl Walz, set in 2002. Foale set the record during his sixth mission in space. He first flew into space on March 24, 1992, aboard Atlantis on an eight-day mission.

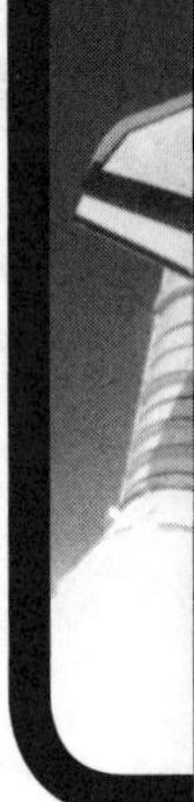

FASTEST SPEED The fastest any human has ever traveled is 24,792 mph, by the three-man crew of *Apollo 10*, Thomas Stafford, Eugene Cernan, and John Young. Their spacecraft attained this speed returning from the Moon on May 26, 1969. The craft was traveling at 6.88 miles per second.

LONGEST ON THE MOON The longest time spent on the Moon was 74 hours, 59 minutes, 40 seconds, by American astronauts Eugene Cernan and Harrison Schmitt. Members of the *Apollo 17* mission, they landed there Dec. 11, 1972, and departed Dec. 14.

The third member of the crew, Ronald Evans, orbited the Moon for a record 147 hours, 48 minutes. He stayed on board the command module while Cernan and Schmitt were on the lunar surface.

MOST SPACE JOURNEYS The most missions flown in space is seven,

LUNAR MENU

The first meal eaten on the Moon by Neil Armstrong and Buzz Aldrin consisted of four bacon squares, three sugar cookies, peaches, pineapple-grapefruit drink, and coffee.

GOLF ON THE MOON

The first, and so far only, lunar golf shots were made by Alan B. Shepard on Feb. 6, 1971. Shepard had stashed a makeshift six-iron on board *Apollo 14*. Like a typical duffer on the first tee with the world watching, he whiffed on his first swing, but he made contact after that. Despite the fun-loving astronaut's later claims, he didn't hit a ball into orbit, just into the history books.

SOLAR ECLIPSE

The first, and so far only, humans to see the Sun eclipsed by Earth were the crew of *Apollo 12*, Pete Conrad, Dick Gordon, and Alan Bean, on Nov. 14, 1969.

SOMETHING TO THINK ABOUT

HAIRCUT

The first haircut in space occurred aboard *Skylab 2*. The barber was Charles Conrad Jr., who cut the hair of Paul Weitz. Perhaps only by coincidence, the first medical doctor to fly in space, Dr. Joseph P. Kerwin, was on the same flight.

Most Days in Space (U.S. Astronauts)

	ASTRONAUT	TOTAL
1.	Michael Foale	374 days
2.	Carl Walz	231 days
3.	Daniel Bursch	227 days
4.	Shannon Lucid	223 days
5.	Ken Bowesox Susan Helms	211 days 211 days

by two astronauts: Jerry L. Ross and Franklin Chang-Diaz. Ross completed his seventh mission on April 19, 2002. He had first traveled into space aboard the space shuttle *Atlantis* on Nov. 26, 1985. Chang-Diaz completed his seventh mission on June 19, 2002. He had first flown aboard the shuttle *Columbia* on Jan. 12, 1986.

LONGEST SPACE WALK The longest space walk was 8 hours, 56 minutes, set by Jim Voss and Susan Helms on an International Space Station/Discovery mission March 11, 2001. The pair installed new hardware on the ISS and relocated a docking port.

MOST SPACE WALKS Russian cosmonaut Anatoliy Y. Solovyov completed 16 space walks during three missions from 1990 to 1998. Soloyov first flew into space aboard *Soyuz TM-5* on June 7, 1988. He didn't make his first space walk until his second mission on July 17, 1990. It was one of two space walks he made in 10 days from the *Mir* space station, the last one coming on July 26. He performed four space walks during 12 days in Sept. 1992, and three space walks in July 1995.

He made his final six space walks during his seven-month stay aboard *Mir*, from Aug. 5, 1997 to Feb. 19, 1998.

MOST SPACE WALKS AMERICAN The record for most space walks by an American astronaut is nine, by Jerry L. Ross. He performed two space walks during his first mission in space from *Atlantis* in 1985. On his last mission in April 2002, he also performed two walks, bringing his total space-walking time to 58 hours, 18 minutes.

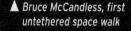

▲ *Bruce McCandless, first untethered space walk*

Unmanned Flight

UNMANNED SPACE FLIGHT has an exciting and varied history. From the shocking Soviet launch of *Sputnik* during the height of the Cold War to telecommunications satellites orbiting high above Earth to the *Voyager* spacecraft now speeding away from the solar system, unmanned spacecraft have looked back at Earth and explored distant worlds far beyond the reach of human travel.

Martian landscape ▶

MILESTONES

1957: *SPUTNIK* The so-called Space Age began on Oct. 4, 1957, when the Soviet Union launched *Sputnik 1*—the world's first artificial satellite—from the Baikonur Cosmodrome in the Soviet Republic of Kazakhstan.

The mission of the 183-pound, volleyball-sized satellite was to take readings of the upper atmosphere and to prove that spacecraft could achieve orbit.

Sputnik 1 circled the Earth once every 98 minutes. It fell out of orbit in Jan. 1958.

1957: DOG IN SPACE Just a few months after the launch of *Sputnik 1*, the Soviet Union on Nov. 3 launched *Sputnik 2*, which carried the first living animal into space—a stray dog originally named Kudryavka ("Little Curly") but later renamed Laika ("Barker"). The Soviets at first reported that Laika died without pain 10 days after blastoff, but later admitted that she succumbed to heat prostration within two days because thermal insulation ripped off and temperatures reached 104° F.

Sputnik 2 completed 2,570 orbits in 162 days before burning up in Earth's atmosphere on April 14, 1958.

1958: *EXPLORER 1* On Jan. 31, 1958, the U.S. launched *Explorer 1*, its first satellite, into orbit from Cape Canaveral, FL. The project was headed by Wernher von Braun (a German scientist who designed the V-2 rocket for the Nazi regime during World War II) at the U.S. Army Ballistic Missile Agency headquarters at Huntsville, AL.

Explorer 1 was a 30.8-pound cylindrical craft that contained scientific instruments. During its flight, *Explorer 1* sent back data proving the existence of the Van Allen belts—doughnut-shaped radiation belts that surround Earth.

1958: NASA FOUNDED The success of the *Sputnik* program brought about the "space race" between the U.S. and Soviet Union. As a result, on July 29, 1958, President Dwight Eisenhower signed the Space Act, which created the National Aeronautics and Space Administration (NASA).

1959: FIRST LUNAR LANDING The Soviet probe *Luna 2* was the first spacecraft to land on the moon. As planned, it crash-landed on the lunar surface on Sept. 14, 1959, and was destroyed on impact.

On Oct. 7, 1959, *Luna 3* became the first spacecraft to photograph the far side of the Moon.

Luna 9 was the first to make a soft landing on the Moon, Feb. 3, 1966. *Surveyor* was the first American craft to make a soft landing on the Moon on June 3, 1966.

1960: WEATHER SATELLITE NASA's first weather satellite was *TIROS 1* (Television InfraRed Observation Satellite) built by the Army Signal Corps. The 270-pound *TIROS 1* was launched from Cape Canaveral on April 1, 1960. During its 78-day operation period, *TIROS 1* provided the first images of weather patterns from space. Later in 1962, TIROS satellites began continuous monitoring of Earth's weather.

The first GOES (Geostationary Operational Environmental Satellite), which provides continuous weather imaging from a fixed point, was launched on Oct. 16, 1975.

1960: COMMUNICATIONS SATELLITE NASA successfully launched a communications satellite, *Echo 1*, from Cape Canaveral on Aug. 12. The paper-thin (0.005 inches) mylar polyester balloon was 100 feet wide and weighed 397 pounds.

While *Echo 1* was in orbit, microwave signals for radio, TV, and telephone were bounced off the satellite's shiny surface across the nation and to Europe. The shiny surface also made it visible to the unaided eye; it was probably seen by more people than any other artificial object in space.

1962: COMMERCIAL SATELLITE AT&T launched the first privately-owned satellite, *Telstar 1*, in conjunction with NASA from Cape Canaveral on July 10, 1962. The 34 $\frac{1}{2}$-inch ball was designed at Bell Labs. It could relay signals, images, and video across the Atlantic for up to 102 minutes every day.

Regular broadcasting and commercial telephone use via satellite did not occur until after COMSAT's (COMmunications SATellite Corp.) *Early Bird* satellite was launched on April 6, 1965.

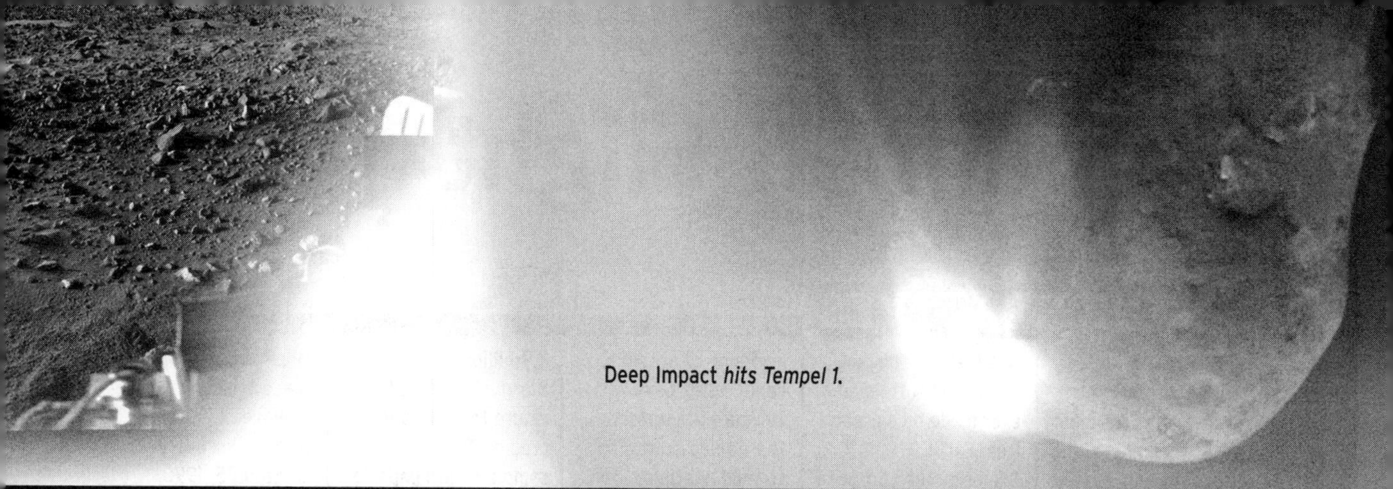

Deep Impact *hits Tempel 1.*

1966: FIRST PLANETARY LANDING On March 1, 1966, the Soviet craft *Venera 3* crashed on the surface of Venus, and thus became the first probe to impact another planet.

Launched from the Baikonur Cosmodrome on Nov. 16, 1965, the craft successfully reached its destination. However, *Venera 3*'s communications systems failed before any information could be transmitted.

The Soviets were able to receive data about the surface only after *Venera 7* entered Venus's atmosphere and landed on the surface on Dec. 15, 1970.

Venera 7's landing capsule took temperature readings for 23 minutes before the intense heat and atmospheric pressure of Venus destroyed it. *Venera 9* was the first to send back a surface image of Venus on Oct. 22, 1975.

1972: LAND-SURVEYING SATELLITE The first U.S. Earth Resources Technology Satellite (ERTS), which today are called Landsats, was launched on July 23, 1972, from Vandenberg Air Force Base, CA. These satellites used multispectral optical filters to make observations of Earth's terrain and natural events in great detail.

1973: GRAVITATIONAL PULL In 1961, Michael Minovitch, a 24-year-old UCLA graduate student, developed a "gravity-assist" theory (often compared to an inter-planetary billiards bank shot) according to which a spacecraft would use a planet's gravity to alter the craft's direction and sling it onward with renewed speed. *Mariner 10*, launched on Nov. 3, 1973, was the first to apply this concept.

The mission required the calculation of thousands of timed trajectories from Earth to Venus and Venus to Mercury. Like clockwork, *Mariner 10* passed within 3,585 miles of Venus on Feb. 5, 1974, and, using a gravity boost from Venus, was slung toward Mercury. It passed within 440 miles of Mercury on March 29, 1974.

During that and two later flybys, *Mariner 10* mapped about half of the planet's Moon-like craggy surface.

1973: FIRST JUPITER PROBE Launched March 2, 1972, NASA's *Pioneer 10* traveled over 365 million miles, reaching speeds up to 82,000 mph, to be the first craft to visit Jupiter.

During its 641-day trip, the craft also became the first to pass through the asteroid belt.

On Dec. 3, 1973, it arrived within 81,000 miles of the planet. After taking photos, it recorded Jupiter's radiation and magnetic properties and showed that the planet is not solid like Earth, but liquid and gaseous.

Pioneer 10 was the first craft to travel beyond the orbit of Pluto, where it took readings of the extra-solar environment. Its last, weak signal was heard on Jan. 23, 2003.

In early 2006, it was estimated to be over 8.3 billion miles from the Sun, and about 3.9 billion miles past the most distant point in Pluto's orbit.

1976: *VIKING 1* AND *2* The Viking probes were the first to land on Mars. Launched on April 5 and Sept. 7, 1975, the identical probes were each composed of an orbiter and a lander, which carried an array of instruments and cameras designed to take readings of the Martian atmosphere and search for possible life on the red planet. *Viking 1* and *Viking 2* landed on Mars on July 20 and Sept. 3, 1976.

2005: *DEEP IMPACT* Comets are big balls of ice and dust that have remained mostly frozen since the early days of the solar system, 4.5 billion years ago. Scientists theorized that if a probe were to hit a comet at extraordinary speeds, the amount of dust kicked up from impact could reveal clues to the solar system's early history.

Launched on Jan 12, 2005, *Deep Impact* sped toward comet Tempel 1. On July 4, the flyby craft launched a refrigerator-sized impact probe that sped toward the comet at 22,680 mph. The impact probe hit the comet and sent up a huge plume of debris. The flyby craft filmed the explosion and aftermath. Data from the impact were under analysis.

MORE ON

Unmanned Flight

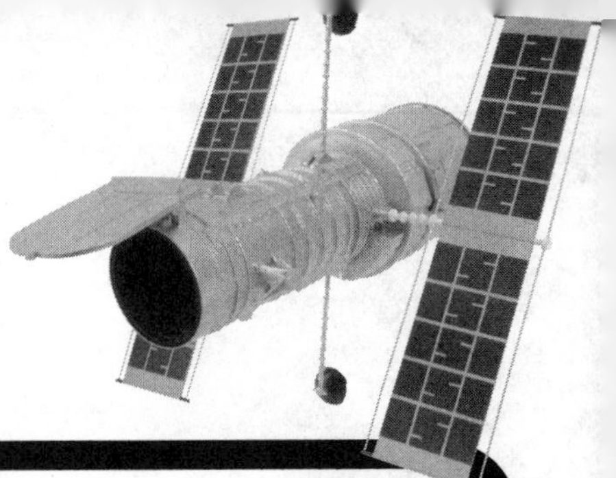

SUPERLATIVES

MOST DISTANT SPACECRAFT *Voyager 1* has traveled farther than any other craft, since its launch on Sept. 5, 1977. Along with its twin craft, *Voyager 2*, its initial goal was to visit and study Jupiter and Saturn, but its accomplishments went far beyond that.

Voyager 1 returned the first photo of the entire solar system on Feb. 14, 1990, and has since become the premier space-pioneer. It surpassed the distance traveled by *Pioneer 10* on Feb. 17, 1998, and by Jan. 1, 2006, *Voyager 1* was over 9 billion miles from the Sun or about 98 times the distance from the Earth to the Sun.

NASA estimates that *Voyager 1* may stay operational until 2020 and become the first spacecraft to leave our solar system.

MOST DISTANT LANDING When the *Huygens* probe landed on Titan, one of Saturn's many moons and the second largest in the solar system, on Jan. 14, 2005, it was the most distant successful soft landing ever made by a probe from Earth.

Built by the European Space Agency (ESA), the *Huygens* probe was launched with the U.S.-built *Cassini* spacecraft on Oct. 15, 1997. When *Huygens* landed on Titan, it was over 750 million miles from home. *Huygens* also transmitted the first close-up surface photos of another planet's moon.

LONGEST ORBITAL SURVEY (PLANET) The *Galileo* spacecraft surveyed Jupiter and its moons for over 2,845 days, from Dec. 7, 1995, until Sept. 21, 2003, when it was intentionally incinerated in the planet's atmosphere.

After its launch on Oct. 18, 1989, *Galileo* made the first flyby of an asteroid (Gaspra, on Oct. 29, 1991) and later found an asteroid (Ida) with its own moon (Dactyl), in Feb. 1994.

Galileo gathered information on many of Jupiter's moons, including Europa, where it found evidence of possible liquid water beneath Europa's icy surface. The *Galileo* craft also studied another moon, the volcanic Io, and showed that Io was more geologically active than previously believed. Three times during its period of operation, Galileo's mission was extended.

MOST DISTANT SOLAR-POWERED SPACECRAFT Solar arrays, the iconic "wings" seen on many space stations and satellites, are a useful source of energy when near the Sun, but this rapidly diminishes the farther out a craft travels. The *Stardust* spacecraft, which was powered by solar energy, got 253 million miles from the Sun by April 18, 2002. At that point, the 71 square feet of panels on its two solar arrays generated only 13% of the power they produced near Earth.

The craft then arced back on its mission toward comet Wild 2, where it took detailed photos and collected comet particle samples. After the 2.9-billion-mile trip, *Stardust* was set to return to Earth and drop a 101-pound sample return capsule on Jan. 15, 2006.

LONGEST TRAVELING SPACECRAFT Launched on Dec. 16, 1965, and originally designed to last only six months, *Pioneer 6* is the oldest intact artificial satellite still in space. Its mission was to enter solar orbit and to take readings of the solar wind, and cosmic and solar rays. Solar cells have kept it powered all these years.

NASA has only periodically tracked the craft since it was decommissioned in 1997. On Dec. 8, 2000, NASA scientists successfully contacted *Pioneer*, to commemorate its 35th year of operation. The craft was still operational at the time. It is believed to still be in solar orbit.

MOST POWERFUL SPACE TELESCOPE The Hubble Space Telescope, which is in orbit 350-375 miles above Earth, is the most powerful optical space telescope. Deployed by the space shuttle *Discovery* on April 25, 1990, *Hubble* is equipped with various high-tech instruments for observing space, including a 94-inch reflecting telescope.

Hubble can also record cosmic infrared and ultraviolet emissions, which cannot be recorded as precisely on Earth because of atmospheric distortion. *Hubble* allows scientists to look deep into space (over 12 billion light years) and explore many phenomena including black holes, other galaxies, and the birth and death of stars.

Currently, scientists say that *Hubble's* batteries and gyroscopes will only last a few more years. If they aren't replaced, *Hubble* will stop functioning and fall out of orbit as early as 2013.

Because of safety concerns within the shuttle program, NASA is looking into

a possible robotic mission to service the telescope.

OLDEST SPACE JUNK The oldest known artificial object in space that is still being continuously monitored is *Vanguard 1*. Part of an Air Force test launch on March 17, 1958, the 3-pound, 6.5-inch aluminum sphere surveyed Earth and its atmosphere until it stopped operating in May 1964. Today, it's tracked by the 1st Space Control Squadron (see "Something To Think About").

MOST PLANETS ENCOUNTERED *Voyager 2*, launched on Aug. 20, 1977, has flown by four planets, not including Earth, in the solar system: Jupiter, Saturn, Uranus, and Neptune.

It made its closest approach to Jupiter on July 9, 1979. Later it visited Saturn on Aug. 5, 1981. *Voyager 2* went on to become the only spacecraft to fly by Uranus, on Jan. 24, 1986, and later Neptune on Aug. 25, 1989.

MOST COMETS DISCOVERED Almost half of the officially recognized comets in the solar system have been discovered by images transmitted from the *Solar and Heliospheric Observatory* (SOHO). A joint NASA-ESA project, the SOHO satellite was launched on Dec. 2, 1995, to study the Sun's characteristics. Images taken by SOHO are public domain and amateur "comet hunters" are encouraged to report comets they see in the photos that may have been overlooked by astronomers.

The 1,000th comet detected using images from SOHO was found by Toni Scarmato, a high school teacher and amateur astronomer from Italy, on Aug. 5, 2005.

SOMETHING TO THINK ABOUT

SOLAR WINDS

The *Genesis* spacecraft, launched on Aug. 8, 2001, was designed to collect solar wind (charged particles that stream out from the Sun) and return specimens to Earth using a return capsule. Upon re-entry, the capsule was designed to deploy parachutes to slow its descent. Hollywood stunt pilots in helicopters would then swoop in for a mid-air catch. After 29 months collecting samples, the capsule was deployed on Sept. 8, 2004. However, the parachutes did not open and *Genesis* crashed into the Utah desert at 193 mph. Luckily, the most important specimens survived intact.

MESSAGE IN A BOTTLE

When *Voyagers 1* and *2* were launched in 1977, they carried information about Earth for any intelligent life forms they might encounter. Each craft carries a gold-plated copper disk designed by astronomer Carl Sagan and other scientists. The discs are records containing sounds of Earth, including 90 minutes of music and 55 spoken greetings. They also contain 115 analog-encoded images. Along with a cartridge and needle, each record is stored in an aluminum case. On the case is a diagram of how to play the record.

SPACE JUNKIES

Since 1981, the 1st Space Control Squadron (SPCS) has been responsible for tracking all "space junk" bigger than 4 inches as part of the Air Force's Space Control Center at Cheyenne Mountain, CO. This includes defunct satellites, pieces of rockets, and items that have fallen off spacecraft. The SPCS uses data from 30 sensors positioned around the globe.

As of Aug. 2005, the SPCS was tracking an estimated 13,400 objects, of which about 20% were active satellites. One of the main jobs of the SPCS is "collision avoidance analysis" for space shuttle and space station missions. NASA has changed shuttle flight paths 12 times and the ISS's path six times because of SPCS data.

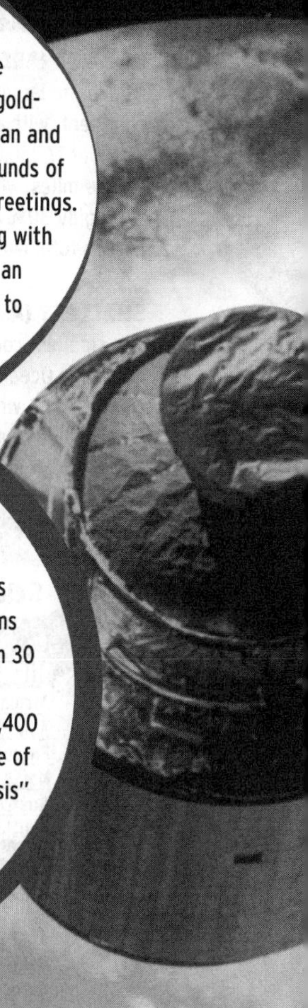

Continents

THERE IS SOME DISAGREEMENT CONCERNING THE NUMBER OF CONTINENTS and their respective extents. But most geographers recognize seven: Africa, Antarctica, Asia, Australia (also known as Oceania or Australasia to include distantly-scattered islands), Europe, North America, and South America.

The boundaries of some continents, particularly Europe, Asia, and the Americas are disputed, but generally Europe and Asia are separated by the physical boundary of the Ural Mountains, and Central America is considered a part of North America. So-called attendant islands–islands near continents, such as the Caribbean islands near North America–are commonly considered part of the nearest landmass.

SUPERLATIVES

LARGEST (AREA)
Asia is the largest continent, with an area of about 17,350,000 square miles, which is roughly 30% of Earth's total land area.

SMALLEST (AREA)
The smallest continent in area is Oceania (Australasia) which has an area of about 3,254,339 square miles.

LARGEST (POPULATION)
The largest continent in population is Asia, which in 2005 was home to about 3.9 billion people. However, this figure does not include Russians, of whom about 25% live in Asia.

SMALLEST (POPULATION)
Antarctica, which has no permanent residents, is the smallest continent by population. Antarctica hosts scientific and meteorological research stations staffed by scientists from around two dozen different nations.

MOST COUNTRIES
The continent containing the most sovereign nations is Africa, which is home to 53 sovereign nations on the mainland, plus seven European territorial possessions, and the disputed Western Sahara territory in Africa claimed by Morocco.

FEWEST COUNTRIES
With no permanent residents, Antarctica has no sovereign nations. Only 12 sovereign nations can be found on the mainland of South America, not including French Guiana, an overseas department of France.

Selected Continent-by-Continent Records

HIGHEST LIFE EXPECTANCY (2005)		
Africa	Libya	76.50 years
Asia	Singapore	81.62 years
Europe	Andorra	83.51 years
North America	Canada	80.10 years
Australia/Oceania	Australia	80.39 years
South America	Chile	76.58 years

HIGHEST BIRTH RATE (2005)		
Africa	Niger	51.33 per 1,000
Asia	Afghanistan	47.02 per 1,000
Europe	Moldova	15.77 per 1,000
North America	Haiti	36.59 per 1,000
Australia/Oceania	Marshall Islands	33.52 per 1,000
South America	Paraguay	29.43 per 1,000

LOWEST LIFE EXPECTANCY (2005)		
Africa	Swaziland	33.22 years
Asia	Afghanistan	42.90 years
Europe	Moldova	65.18 years
North America	Haiti	52.92 years
Australia/Oceania	Kiribati	61.71 years
South America	Guyana & Bolivia	65.50 years

LOWEST BIRTH RATE (2005)		
Africa	Tunisia	15.50 per 1,000
Asia	Japan	9.47 per 1,000
Europe	Germany	8.33 per 1,000
North America	Canada	10.84 per 1,000
Australia/Oceania	Australia	12.26 per 1,000
South America	Uruguay	14.09 per 1,000

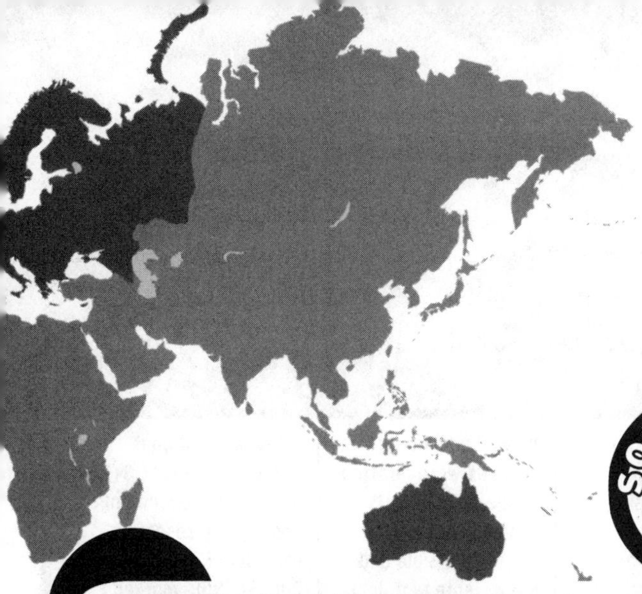

OCEANIA OR AUSTRALASIA?

The geographic label Oceania describes islands between Asia and the Americas. It is used because the Pacific Ocean (rather than a landmass) unites far-flung islands into a continent. On the other hand, Australasia generally groups together only Australia, New Guinea, New Zealand and nearby larger islands; it thus describes a smaller area than Oceania. However, both words are in common use.

SOMETHING TO THINK ABOUT

PANGAEA, LAURASIA, AND GONDWANALAND

German geologist and meteorologist Alfred Wegener proposed in 1912 that all of the continents were once joined as a single landmass, which he called Pangaea (meaning "all earth"). As part of his continental drift theory, Wegener argued that Pangaea was whole until the late-Triassic Period (208-245 million years ago), when it separated into "Laurasia" (the present-day Northern continents) and "Gondwanaland" (the present-day Southern continents). The two pieces gradually receded, creating the Atlantic Ocean. Geological evidence found in the jigsaw puzzle-like coastlines of distant continents, supports the theory. For instance, ancient rock formations on the Brazilian coast match those found in West Africa.

Selected Continent-by-Continent Records

LARGEST COUNTRY (AREA)

Africa	Sudan	967,498 sq mi
Asia*	China	3,705,405 sq mi
Europe*	Ukraine	33,090 sq mi
North America	Canada	3,855,101 sq m
Australia/Oceania	Australia	2,967,908 sq mi
South America	Brazil	3,286,487 sq mi

*With an area of 6,592,769 square miles, Russia would be the biggest country if it were counted wholly on either Asia or Europe.

SMALLEST COUNTRY (AREA)

Africa	Seychelles	176 sq mi
Asia	Maldives	116 sq mi
Europe	Vatican City (Holy See)	0.17 sq mi
North America	Saint Kitts and Nevis	101 sq mi
Australia/Oceania	Nauru	8 sq mi
South America	Suriname	63,039 sq mi

LARGEST CITY (METRO, 2005)

Africa	Cairo, Egypt	11,146,000
Asia	Tokyo, Japan	35,327,000
Europe	Moscow, Russia	10,672,000
North America	Mexico City, Mexico	19,013,000
Australia/Oceania	Sydney, Australia	4,388,000
South America	São Paulo, Brazil	18,333,000

RICHEST NATION*–PER CAPITA GDP (2004)

Africa	South Africa	$11,100
Asia	Japan	$29,400
Europe	Luxembourg	$58,900
North America	United States	$40,100
Australia/Oceania	Australia	$30,700
South America	Uruguay	$14,500

* By per capita Gross Domestic Product adjusted to purchasing power parity

POOREST NATION*–PER CAPITA GDP (2004)

Africa	Burundi	$532
Asia	Timor Leste	$363
Europe	Ukraine	$6,300
North America	Haiti	$1,500
Australia/Oceania	Tuvalu	$1,100
South America	Bolivia	$2,600

* By per capita Gross Domestic Product adjusted to purchasing power parity

Antarctica

WITH AN AREA OF ABOUT 5.5 MILLION square miles in summer, and double that in winter, Antarctica is the fifth-largest continent (larger than only Australia and Europe). About 98% of the landmass is covered by ice. While the continent has no permanent population, Antarctica is home to research bases from 27 nations; the temporary population is about 4,000 in the summer and 1,000 in the winter. For detailed information on the South Pole, see pages 12-13.

MILESTONES

1820s: FIRST SIGHTING For centuries, people speculated about the existence of an "unknown southern land" (*Terra Australis Incognita*). One map dated 1513 shows a large southern continent.

In 1820, three expeditions—one American, one British, and one Russian—neared Antarctica around the same time. The Russian team, led by Fabian Gottlieb von Bellingshausen, was probably the first to see Antarctica; they spotted an ice shelf on Jan. 20, 1820, but didn't realize its significance.

Antarctica's continental status was not established until the 1840s, when three separate expeditions—led by Jules Dumont d'Urville (France), Charles Wilkes (U.S.), and Sir James Ross (Britain)—sailed along much of the ice-covered coastline.

Antarctica was extensively mapped by the Norwegian-born American explorer Finn Ronne in the 1940s.

1898: FIRST WINTER SURVIVAL (60° SOUTH) In March 1898, *Belgica*, a Belgian ship with a multinational crew that included future polar explorer Roald Amundsen, was trapped in pack ice in the Bellingshausen Sea as winter approached. The crew was forced to stay for the next winter. They finally managed to wedge the ship free from the ice after 12 months.

1903: RESEARCH STATION The Scottish National Antarctic Expedition of 1902-04, led by William Bruce, established the first permanent Antarctic research station in the South Orkney Islands on Nov. 1, 1903.

By 2004, Antarctica was home to 82 stations, maintained by 27 countries. Only about half are occupied year-round. Researchers there study everything including astronomy, botany, atmospheric conditions, and meteorology.

1911: SOUTH POLE REACHED A five-man party led by Norwegian explorer Roald Amundsen became the first to reach the South Pole, on Dec. 14, 1911. See pages 12-13.

1935: FIRST WOMAN Caroline Mikkelsen, wife of Norwegian whaling captain Klarius Mikkelsen, became the first woman to set foot on Antarctica, at the newly discovered Vestfold Hills on Feb. 20, 1935.

1956-57: SOUTH POLE STATION The U.S. Navy's Operation Deep Freeze II began construction of the Amundsen-Scott South Pole Station in late 1956. Construction supplies were airlifted to the pole. A party of 18 scientists, led by Dr. Paul Siple and Navy Lieutenant John Tuck, became the first people to winter there, at Earth's southernmost point.

A new station was completed nearby in 1975 as a geodesic dome. The newest station, elevated above ground, will be completed in 2006 and is about 330 feet from the geographic South Pole. This station and the ceremonial South Pole marker are both on top of a glacier, which moves toward the geographic Pole at a rate of about 30 feet per year.

1959: ANTARCTIC TREATY Beginning in the 1920s, Great Britain, Australia, New Zealand, Argentina, Norway, France, and Chile claimed parts of the Antarctic mainland and established administrative bodies for their respective territories.

The International Geophysical Year (IGY), a worldwide agenda of geophysical research from July 1, 1957, to Dec. 31, 1958, marked the beginning of long-term systematic investigation of the continent.

The Antarctic Treaty, which aimed to maintain the IGY's peaceful, scientific exploration of Antarctica, was signed by 12 nations on Dec. 1, 1959, and went into effect on June 23, 1961. Under the treaty, Antarctica is demilitarized. Treaty nations agreed to put sovereignty claims on hold and set aside the continent for research.

The United States, which became the sixth nation to ratify the treaty, on Aug. 10, 1960, does not recognize territorial claims, and reserves the right to make claims of its own.

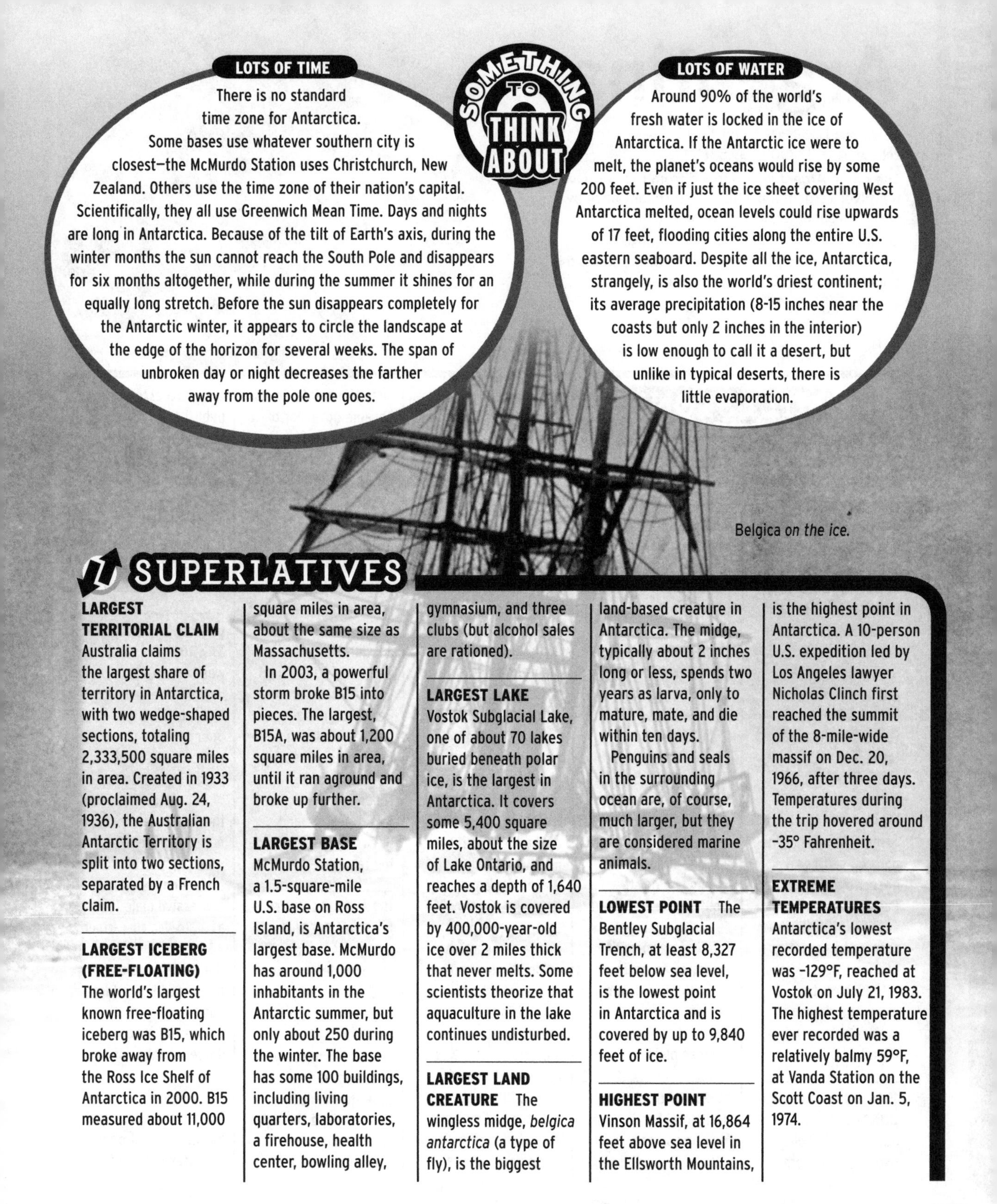

Belgica *on the ice.*

SOMETHING TO THINK ABOUT

LOTS OF TIME

There is no standard time zone for Antarctica. Some bases use whatever southern city is closest—the McMurdo Station uses Christchurch, New Zealand. Others use the time zone of their nation's capital. Scientifically, they all use Greenwich Mean Time. Days and nights are long in Antarctica. Because of the tilt of Earth's axis, during the winter months the sun cannot reach the South Pole and disappears for six months altogether, while during the summer it shines for an equally long stretch. Before the sun disappears completely for the Antarctic winter, it appears to circle the landscape at the edge of the horizon for several weeks. The span of unbroken day or night decreases the farther away from the pole one goes.

LOTS OF WATER

Around 90% of the world's fresh water is locked in the ice of Antarctica. If the Antarctic ice were to melt, the planet's oceans would rise by some 200 feet. Even if just the ice sheet covering West Antarctica melted, ocean levels could rise upwards of 17 feet, flooding cities along the entire U.S. eastern seaboard. Despite all the ice, Antarctica, strangely, is also the world's driest continent; its average precipitation (8-15 inches near the coasts but only 2 inches in the interior) is low enough to call it a desert, but unlike in typical deserts, there is little evaporation.

SUPERLATIVES

LARGEST TERRITORIAL CLAIM Australia claims the largest share of territory in Antarctica, with two wedge-shaped sections, totaling 2,333,500 square miles in area. Created in 1933 (proclaimed Aug. 24, 1936), the Australian Antarctic Territory is split into two sections, separated by a French claim.

LARGEST ICEBERG (FREE-FLOATING) The world's largest known free-floating iceberg was B15, which broke away from the Ross Ice Shelf of Antarctica in 2000. B15 measured about 11,000 square miles in area, about the same size as Massachusetts.

In 2003, a powerful storm broke B15 into pieces. The largest, B15A, was about 1,200 square miles in area, until it ran aground and broke up further.

LARGEST BASE McMurdo Station, a 1.5-square-mile U.S. base on Ross Island, is Antarctica's largest base. McMurdo has around 1,000 inhabitants in the Antarctic summer, but only about 250 during the winter. The base has some 100 buildings, including living quarters, laboratories, a firehouse, health center, bowling alley, gymnasium, and three clubs (but alcohol sales are rationed).

LARGEST LAKE Vostok Subglacial Lake, one of about 70 lakes buried beneath polar ice, is the largest in Antarctica. It covers some 5,400 square miles, about the size of Lake Ontario, and reaches a depth of 1,640 feet. Vostok is covered by 400,000-year-old ice over 2 miles thick that never melts. Some scientists theorize that aquaculture in the lake continues undisturbed.

LARGEST LAND CREATURE The wingless midge, *belgica antarctica* (a type of fly), is the biggest land-based creature in Antarctica. The midge, typically about 2 inches long or less, spends two years as larva, only to mature, mate, and die within ten days.

Penguins and seals in the surrounding ocean are, of course, much larger, but they are considered marine animals.

LOWEST POINT The Bentley Subglacial Trench, at least 8,327 feet below sea level, is the lowest point in Antarctica and is covered by up to 9,840 feet of ice.

HIGHEST POINT Vinson Massif, at 16,864 feet above sea level in the Ellsworth Mountains, is the highest point in Antarctica. A 10-person U.S. expedition led by Los Angeles lawyer Nicholas Clinch first reached the summit of the 8-mile-wide massif on Dec. 20, 1966, after three days. Temperatures during the trip hovered around -35° Fahrenheit.

EXTREME TEMPERATURES Antarctica's lowest recorded temperature was -129°F, reached at Vostok on July 21, 1983. The highest temperature ever recorded was a relatively balmy 59°F, at Vanda Station on the Scott Coast on Jan. 5, 1974.

Argentina

Total Area: 1,068,302 sq mi
Population (est. 2005): 39,537,943

The name *Argentina* is derived from the Latin word for silver (*argentum*) which was brought back by early European explorers to the region.

Modern Argentina is the second biggest South American country in area (after Brazil) and third in population (after Brazil and Colombia).

MILESTONES

PRE-1516: AMERINDIANS Before the Spanish arrived, the area that is now Argentina was sparsely populated by native tribes. Art found in the *Cueva de las Manos* ("Cave of the Hands"), depicting animals and hands, dates back 9,500-13,000 years. Northern tribes farmed in settlements, while hunters and gatherers migrated through the treeless central Pampas plains and the southern desert plateaus of Patagonia. The Incan Empire (1438-1533) controlled Argentina's far northwest. By the late 19th century, most Amerindian settlements were wiped out.

1516-80: EUROPEAN CONTACT In 1516 Juan Díaz de Solís explored southern South America seeking a southwest passage to the East Indies. He claimed the area for Spain and headed up Argentina's Río de la Plata, where Charrua tribe members killed him and most of his small party.

In 1536, Pedro de Mendoza founded Buenos Aires (meaning "Fair Winds"), but hostile locals forced the Spanish out in 1541. The city, now Argentina's largest, was not reoccupied until 1590. In 1553, Spanish colonists from Peru established Santiago del Estero, the first permanent colony in Argentina, and colonists began raising imported livestock on the Pampas plains.

1812: FLAG Three horizontal bands—light blue on top and bottom, with white in the middle—have made up the Argentine flag since Feb. 18, 1812, when it was first raised by revolutionary leader General Manuel Belgrano. Later, in 1818, a sun with a human face, the Incan "Sun of May," was added to the center. Argentina's flag day is June 20, the date of Belgrano's death.

1816: INDEPENDENCE Spain ruled Argentina for centuries, first as a part of the Viceroyalty of Peru (1620) and, from 1776, as part of the Viceroyalty of La Plata (with Bolivia, Paraguay, and Uruguay). On May 25, 1810, Buenos Aires residents overthrew colonial rule there and established a provisional government.

Independence was officially declared July 9, 1816, but anarchy and civil war persisted until military strongman General Juan Manuel de Rosas became governor of Buenos Aires Province in 1829. He crushed his opposition and created an Argentine Confederation.

1853: REPUBLIC OF ARGENTINA The Rosas regime was toppled in 1852, and a federal constitution was adopted the next year. Buenos Aires Province proclaimed its independence from the new republic in 1854. But the secession movement was defeated, and Buenos Aires rejoined the republic in 1859.

1872: *EL GAUCHO MARTÍN FIERRO* Like the American cowboy, the gaucho of the pampas ("grasslands") is a mythic figure celebrated in story and song. Author José Hernández immortalized the Latin American cowboy in the epic poem *El Gaucho Martín Fierro*, published in 1872. Seven years later a second installment was published.

Hernández's work is considered to be among the greatest achievements of Latin American literature.

LATE 19TH CENTURY: TANGO The tango was born in the downtrodden working-class districts of Buenos Aires sometime after 1870. Based on a wide mix of influences, including the Cuban dance *habañera*, tango is an expression of attraction, as an aggressive male leads a passive female partner.

Many believe the dancers' roles originated in the large number of men competing for a limited number of women.

The tango spread to Paris around 1910, and has been a ballroom mainstay ever since.

SOMETHING TO THINK ABOUT

WHERE'S THE PARTY?

Prior to the 2004 Olympic Games, no Argentine athlete or team had received a gold medal since the 1952 Helsinki Games, when Tranquilo Cappozzo and Eduardo Guerrero won the double sculls in rowing. But in just one day, the half-century drought turned into a flood. On the morning of Aug. 28, 2004, the men's soccer team beat Paraguay, 1-0, to win the gold medal. That evening, the men's basketball team defeated Italy, 84-69, to win Argentina's second gold of the day. No nation had ever won both of these golds in the same Olympics.

LEAVE IT TO BEAVERS

In the 1940s, around 50 beavers were introduced to Tierra del Fuego, an island across the Strait of Magellan, in hopes that they would reproduce and boost the Argentine fur industry. Now, with no native predators and beaver fur out of fashion, over 250,000 of the voracious, rapidly reproducing rodents wreak ecological havoc, damming streams, creating lakes, and destroying roads. Argentine authorities, fearing the beavers will swim across the Strait and colonize the mainland, are exploring population management options.

1946-55: PERÓN ERA

Colonel Juan Domingo Perón was elected president in Feb. 1946. His victory was credited to the *descamisados* ("shirtless ones") of the working class, and to his wife, Eva Duarte Perón, the much-adored "Evita." A former actress who served as Perón's labor and social services liaison, Evita was instrumental in creating new social policies that extended the Peronista party's support before her death in 1952. She remains a cult celebrity to this day.

The Perón administration, marked by controversial constitutional overhauls and suppression of dissent, was overthrown by the military in 1955 and Perón went into exile. He returned in 1973, and was again elected president. His third wife, Isabel Perón, succeeded him, as the first female president of a Latin American nation, after his death in 1974.

1976-83: DIRTY WAR

For seven years after a military coup toppled the presidency of Isabel Perón, the government waged the "Dirty War," intended to wipe out leftist and anti-government dissent. After elections in 1983, a "truth commission" uncovered evidence of government-sanctioned human rights violations, but there were few prosecutions.

It is estimated that the government kidnapped, tortured, and killed 10,000 to 30,000 people, known as los desaparecidos ("the disappeared").

SUPERLATIVES

BIGGEST DEFAULT

Between Dec. 2001 and Jan. 2002, Argentina defaulted on its estimated $132 billion foreign debt, the biggest default in world history by a sovereign nation. During the financial turmoil, President Fernando de la Rua and three successive presidents resigned in two weeks before Eduardo Duhalde took office on Jan. 2, 2002.

HIGHEST BEEF CONSUMPTION

Brazil, Argentina's northern neighbor, may produce the most beef, but Argentines eat the most per capita.

The U.S. Department of Agriculture estimates that each person in Argentina will consume 121.5 pounds of beef in 2005.

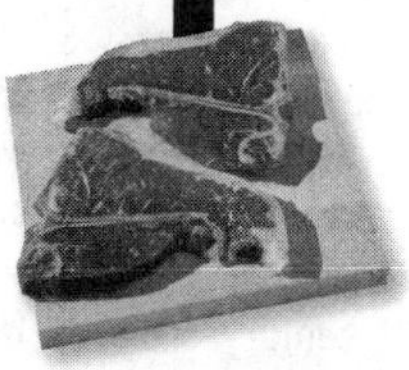

Selected Argentine National Records

Highest Point	Cerro Aconcagua	22,834 ft
Longest River	Paraná	2,485 mi
Largest City	Buenos Aires (metro, 2005)	pop. 13,349.000
Tallest Buildings	El Faro I & II (Buenos Aires)	558 feet
Southernmost City (world)	Ushuaia	55° S lat., in Tierra del Fuego islands
First Nobel Laureate	Carlos Saavedra Lamas	1936, Peace Prize
First Oscar Winner	*The Official Story/La Historia Oficial*	1985, Best Foreign Language Film
First Grammy Winner	Lalo Schifrin, *The Cat*	Best Original Jazz Composition, 1964

Australia

Sydney Opera House ►

Total Area: 2,966,136 sq mi
Population (est. 2005): 19,485,000

Australia is both a continent and a nation. The nation, about the same size as the lower 48 U.S. states, also includes the island state of Tasmania and several hundred smaller islands. As long ago as the second century AD, European legends told of a lost southern continent, and the name Australia comes from the Latin word *australis* ("southern"). Modern-day Australia grew out of British colonial rule and is still heavily influenced by British culture, from its love of cricket to driving on the left-hand side of the road.

MILESTONES

60,000 YEARS AGO: ABORIGINES The Australian continent was populated at least 60,000 years ago by Aborigines and Torres Strait Islanders. Recent scholarship suggests that Aboriginal tribes may have first settled in Australia as long as 100,000 years ago. They lived in small nomadic communities.

1522: EUROPEAN CONTACT The first European to sight Australia was the Portuguese navigator Cristóvão de Mendonça in 1522. The Dutch explored much of the Australian coast in the 17th century, and named the territory New Holland. In 1770, the English explorer James Cook claimed the eastern part of the continent for the English crown.

1788: PENAL SETTLEMENTS After the American Revolution ended the export of British convicts to the Americas, Britain sought other means of alleviating its overcrowded prisons. On Jan. 26, 1788, ships carrying 759 convicts arrived in the colony of New South Wales and founded Sydney Cove (later Sydney), the first permanent European settlement in Australia.

Convict labor, guaranteed to most free settlers, was crucial in building the colonies. By the time Britain stopped sending convicts in 1852, over 150,000 men and women, mostly petty criminals, had been sent to New South Wales and Tasmania.

1858: AUSTRALIAN RULES FOOTBALL A hybrid of rugby, soccer, and American football, "Aussie Rules" was devised in 1858 by Tom Wills and three others. The first club was founded that year in Melbourne. Today, Australian Football League (AFL) teams play in every major Australian city. The most successful club is the Melbourne-based Carlton, which has won 16 grand finals since 1896.

1861: MELBOURNE CUP The most famous horse race in Australia is the Melbourne Cup, begun in 1861, 14 years before the Kentucky Derby. Most of the country stops for a moment to watch, or listen to, the broadcast of the race, run annually on the first Tuesday in November at Flemington racetrack.

1901: COMMONWEALTH By 1830, Britain had laid claim to all of Australia. The various territories began discussing unification in the 1880s, and a constitutional convention was held in 1897-98. In 1900, the British Parliament approved the constitution and it went into effect Jan. 1, 1901, establishing the Commonwealth of Australia. With the 1931 Statute of Westminster the British Parliament recognized Australia's autonomy.

1901: FLAG The national flag of Australia was first raised on Sept. 3, 1901, but not officially approved until Feb. 1903. This flag, designed by the winner of a public competition, is a dark blue field with Great Britain's Union Jack in the top left-hand corner and seven stars representing the Southern Cross constellation.

1908: CAPITAL Australia, like the U.S., built a national capital rather than designating an existing city. After a six-year-long search, Canberra, a rural settlement on the Molongo river was chosen as the site in 1908.

Although Parliament was transferred there from Melbourne in 1927, early development was slowed by the 1930s depression and World War II. The city grew quickly after the 1950s into a major city.

1956: MELBOURNE OLYMPICS The 1956 Summer Olympics in Melbourne were the first to be held in the Southern Hemisphere. Due to Australia's strict quarantine rules, the equestrian events were held in Stockholm, Sweden.

Forty-four years later, the Olympics came to Australia again, when Sydney hosted the 2000 Summer Games. Australia, the U.S., and Germany are the only three countries that have hosted the Summer Games in more than one city.

1984: ANTHEM The national anthem of Australia, "Advance Australia Fair," was officially adopted on April 19, 1984, replacing the British national anthem. The words and music had been composed years earlier by Peter Dodds McCormick, and the anthem was first performed in Sydney in 1878.

Selected Australian National Records

Highest Point	Mount Kosciuszko	7,310 ft
Longest River	Murray-Darling	2,310 mi
Largest Lake	Lake Eyre (South Australia)	3,700 sq mi
Tallest Building	Q1 (Gold Coast)	1,058 ft
Largest City	Sydney (metro, 2005)	pop: 4,388,000
Longest-Serving Prime Minister	Robert Menzies	18 years, 5 months (1939-41, 1949-66)
First Olympic Champion	Edwin Flack (track, 1,500m, 800m)	1896 Athens Games
First Nobel Prize	Howard Florey	1945, Medicine
Highest Grossing Movie (Australian)	*Crocodile Dundee* (1986)	$328 million

SUPERLATIVES

LARGEST MONOLITH The world's largest monolith, now called Uluru (formerly known as Ayers Rock), is in central Australia. The huge, bright red sandstone rock, which is sacred to Australia's Aboriginal people and a major tourist attraction, is 2.2 miles long and 1.5 miles wide.

LARGEST REEF The Great Barrier Reef is the largest system of coral reefs on earth, extending more than 1,200 miles along Australia's northeastern coast. One of the most complex ecosystems in the world, the reef is home to more than 4,000 species of molluscs, sponges, and crustaceans, as well as 400 types of coral, 1,500 species of fish, and dozens of species of birds.

HIGHEST BATTING AVERAGE (CRICKET) Although England is the home of cricket, many of the game's most revered records are held by Australians. The record for highest batting average in test cricket (games between national all-star teams) is held by Don Bradman. Widely regarded as the greatest batsman of all time, he played in 52 matches for Australia (1928-48) and had a test batting average of 99.94 runs (6,996 runs in 80 innings).

LARGEST KOALA RESERVE The world's biggest koala reserve is the Lone Pine Koala Sanctuary in Queensland. More than 130 koalas live on the 50-acre reserve, located near Brisbane. The reserve is also home to one of the world's largest kangaroo populations.

"STOLEN GENERATIONS"

From 1905 until 1971, the Australian government forcibly took Aborigine children from their parents and placed them in institutions. The policy sought to integrate Aborigines into what was considered mainstream society, at the expense of involuntarily separating families. These children became known as the "stolen generations."

SOMETHING TO THINK ABOUT

HOP TO IT

In 2004, Lulu, an eastern grey kangaroo became the first marsupial to receive the Australian Animal Valour Award. The kangaroo raised an alarm when owner Len Richards was knocked unconscious by a falling tree limb at his cattle ranch in Victoria. Lulu stayed with him and made such a commotion that farm hands went over to investigate the problem. Lulu's actions are credited with saving Richards's life.

SOAP STARS

Australia's most successful television program is the soap opera *Neighbours*, first broadcast in March 1985 and now seen in 57 countries worldwide. Past cast members include pop stars Kylie Minogue and Natalie Imbruglia; the Academy Award-winning actor Russell Crowe had a recurring guest role.

Notable Dates of Colonization

New South Wales	Named 1770; first European settlement 1788
Tasmania	1825
Western Australia	1829
South Australia	1834
Victoria	Separated from NSW in 1851
Queensland	Separated from NSW in 1859

Brazil

Total Area: 3,286,487 sq mi
Population (est. 2005): 186,112,794

A former Portuguese colony, Brazil is the biggest country in South America (and fifth in the world) in size, covering nearly half (47%) of the continental land mass and bordering every other South American country except Chile and Ecuador. Brazil is also the world's fifth largest country in population. About 150 million Brazilians (nearly four out of five) are Roman Catholic, the largest number for any country in the world.

MILESTONES

8000 BC: FIRST ROCK PAINTING
The earliest known rock paintings in the Western Hemisphere are in the Caverna da Pedra Pintada (Cave of Painted Stone) located along the lower Amazon River near present-day Monte Alegre. More than 10,000 years old, the colorful iron oxide-based paintings depict human figures and animals. They were first reported by British naturalist Alfred Russel Wallace in 1849.

1500: FIRST EUROPEAN EXPLORERS
Vicente Yáñez Pinzón, a Spanish navigator who commanded the *Niña* for Christopher Columbus in 1492, was the first European known to make land in Brazil. He landed near what is now Recife on Jan. 26, 1500, but did not stay long because the 1494 Treaty of Tordesillas divided South America between Spain and Portugal, and he was on Portuguese territory. After a brief exploration of the Amazon River, Pinzón and his party continued north to Guiana.

Soon afterward, on Apr. 22, 1500, Portuguese explorer Pedro Alvares Cabral staked claim to Brazil for the King of Portugal, declaring it the "Island of the True Cross." The land soon became known as *terra do Brasil* ("land of Brazil"), named after the tropical red brazilwood sent back to Portugal by traders and explorers.

1541: AMAZON EXPLORATION
Francisco de Orellana was the first European to navigate the Amazon River, in 1541, while on orders to find supplies for the Spanish explorer Gonzalo Pizarro. During the journey down the river from Ecuador, Orellana's crew clashed with a group of long-haired natives that they believed to be women, and whom they named after the Amazons in Greek mythology. Orellana also named the river the Amazon, after these female warriors.

The first person to accurately estimate that the Amazon originated in the Peruvian Andes was a Jesuit missionary, Cristoval de Acuna, who wrote down his theory in 1641. Its exact source, the farthest point of origin from the river's basin, was pinpointed by a National Geographic expedition led by Andrew Pietowski in July 2000. A 46-year-old Polish-born math teacher from Carmel, NY, Pietowski used a global positioning system, accurate within 3-6 feet, to locate the source on a slope of Nevado Mismi.

1822: FIRST EMPEROR
Dom Pedro of Portugal declared himself Emperor Pedro I, on Dec. 1. His father, Prince John, a Portuguese royal, had fled to Brazil in 1807 to escape the occupation of his country by French forces. When he went back, he left Dom Pedro as his regent. But driven by Brazil's demand for autonomy from Portugal, Dom Pedro rejected his father's orders and crowned himself emperor.

1889: FIRST REPUBLIC Brazil was first declared a republic on Nov. 15, 1889, when Emperor Dom Pedro II was deposed. While he was away in Europe, his regent, Princess Isabel, had abolished slavery; on his return angry slave owners organized a militia against him. The coup occurred without bloodshed and the emperor and his family went into exile in France.

1889: NATIONAL FLAG The instantly recognizable national flag of Brazil was adopted by decree. There have been minor changes to the flag since, but Raimundo Teixeira's basic concept of a celestial sphere set against the national colors of green and yellow is still the predominant design. The sphere portrays the sky of Rio de Janeiro on the night of the revolution of Nov. 15. The 27 stars represent the 26 states and the federal district of Brazil.

1960: CAPITAL CITIES
The port city of Rio de Janeiro was Brazil's capital from 1763 to April 21, 1960, when the new city of Brasília was dedicated as the capital. The 1891 constitution called for a future Federal District in the heart of the country. Not until 1956 did the actual design and construction begin, under President Juscelino Kubitschek.

The new capital was designed by Brazilian architect and urban planner Lúcio Costa. Its layout resembles an airplane, symbolizing progress, and a crucifix, honoring Brazil's Catholic heritage.

Selected Brazilian National Records

Highest Point	Pico de Neblina (in Amazonas)	9,889 ft
Longest River	Amazon	4,087 mi
Largest City	Sao Paulo (metro, 2005)	pop. 18,333,000
Largest Snake	Anaconda	19 ft, 235 lbs
Longest Private Beach	Comandatuba Island	10 mi
Greatest Tree Diversity	Atlantic Rainforest (in Southern Bahia)	more than 450 species in a single hectare
Longest-Serving Head of State	Emperor Pedro II	58 years (1831-89)
First Grammy Award Winner	Gilberto/Getz by Brazilian João Gilberto and Stan Getz	1965, Album of the Year
Oldest Soccer Franchise	Ponte Preta	founded in 1900
Most Career International Goals	Pelé	97
Most Career International Games	Cafu (active)	133 (Sept. 1990-Aug. 2005)
First Olympic Champion	Guilherme Paraense (rapid-fire pistol)	1920 Antwerp Games

SUPERLATIVES

LARGEST FLAG

The largest flag to fly from a flagpole is a Brazilian flag that stands in the federal capital, Brasília. It measures 229 feet, 8 inches by 328 feet, 1 inch, and is replaced monthly. The flagpole stands 361 feet.

Each flag flown at the Três Poderes Square in Brasília is funded alternately by a different state. The flags are raised in special ceremonies conducted in turn by different branches of the Brazilian armed services.

LARGEST RAINFOREST

The Amazon is the world's largest tropical rain forest. Spanning 1.6 million square miles, it ranges over nine states and covers half of Brazil's territory. There are over 200 known ethnic groups surviving in the area, with close to 170 indigenous languages still spoken.

The rain forest sustains an estimated 2.5 million insect species and tens of thousands of high-order plant species, plus 2,000 fish, 950 bird, and 200 mammal species.

LARGEST COFFEE PRODUCER

Brazil is the world's leading producer of coffee. The official estimate for Brazil's coffee production in 2004-05 is 36.1 million to 40.5 million bags, or about 423 billion cups of coffee per year. Brazil by itself accounts for about a third of world coffee production.

Brazil is also the world's largest producer of sugar cane, frozen concentrated orange juice (though Brazilians do not generally drink OJ), and tropical fruits, and has the world's largest commercial cattle inventory, with about 190 billion head.

LARGEST HYDROELECTRIC POWER PLANT

The world's most powerful power station is the Itaipu hydroelectric plant on the Paraná River, along the border between Brazil and Paraguay. Opened in 1984, the station has a rated capacity of 14,000 megawatts, and provides 25% of Brazil's total electricity, and 95% of Paraguay's. The plant is operated jointly by the two countries.

In 1994, the American Society of Civil Engineers deemed it one of the seven wonders of the modern world.

SOMETHING TO THINK ABOUT

UNIVERSAL GARBAGE

Brazil has the longest coastline in South America, spanning 4,654 miles. In 2002, a cleanup of a 42-mile stretch of the Costa dos Coqueiros (the Coconut Coast) in the state of Bahia produced litter from 730 different brands of consumer items.

SURFING THE AMAZON

The *pororoca*, "the mighty noise," is a giant swell that crashes some 400 miles up the Amazon and during a full moon from late February through March. The wave can be heard from miles away and can reach a height of 16 feet and speeds of 20 miles per hour, making it an irresistible challenge for extreme surfers. In March 2003, 43-year-old Brazilian surfer Picuruta Salazar rode the *pororoca* for 37 minutes, traveling 7.6 miles down the Amazon in the Amapa section in northeast Brazil.

Salvador, Brazil

Canada

Total Area: 3,855,101 sq mi
Population (est. 2005): 32,805,041

Canada is the world's second largest country (after Russia) in total area (including inland water), but ranks only 33rd in population. Over 60% of Canadians live in the eastern provinces of Ontario and Quebec, and 90% live within 100 miles of the U.S. border. Canada has two official languages, English and French, with most French-speaking Canadians living in Quebec, Ontario, and New Brunswick.

Mario Lemieux

MILESTONES

1000: FIRST EUROPEAN EXPLORERS
Around 1000 AD, well before Christopher Columbus came to the Americas, Leif Ericson, the son of Eric the Red, is believed to have landed at L'Anse aux Meadows, Newfoundland.

The remains of a Viking village there were discovered in 1961 by the Norwegian explorer Dr. Helge Ingstad and his archaeologist wife, Anne Stine Ingstad. It is the only authenticated site with traces of European settlement in North America prior to the 17th century.

1759: CURLING
The sport of curling (in which two teams of four slide curling stones over ice toward a target) came to Canada in 1759 with Scottish settlers and was played informally before 1800. It was so popular that British troops during the French and Indian War melted cannonballs to make playing stones. The largest bonspiel, or grand curling match, in the world is the 12-event Manitoba Curling Association Bonspiel, held annually in Winnipeg.

1867: BIRTH OF A NATION In 1867, The United Provinces of Canada (Ontario and Quebec), Nova Scotia, and New Brunswick agreed to the British North America Act (renamed the Constitution Act in 1982), which formed the new Dominion of Canada. After the British Parliament approved, Canadians celebrated their autonomy on July 1, 1867.

John Alexander MacDonald, the driving force behind the confederation, was Canada's first prime minister.

1873: MOUNTIES
The Royal Canadian Mounted Police (RCMP) is the only police force that serves on national, federal, provincial, and municipal levels. The RCMP was created in 1873 as the North-West Mounted Police to avoid a Canadian "wild west" in the newly settled western and northern parts of the country. In 1920 the name was changed to the present one.

The Mounties' scarlet jacket, breeches, and riding boots were designed to replicate the British military uniform. Even the Stetson hat became an official part of the uniform, in 1904.

1875: FIRST HOCKEY GAME Forms of hockey had been played around Canada since the mid-1800s, but the first modern games were played in Montreal in 1875. The earliest written rules of hockey were published on Feb. 27, 1877, in the *Montreal Gazette* newspaper.

The roots of today's National Hockey League go back to 1885, when the Amateur Hockey Association of Canada was formed in Montreal. In 1890, the Ontario Hockey Association became the world's first formally organized hockey league.

1886: TRANSCONTINENTAL RAILWAY The first transcontinental railway in Canada, the Canadian Pacific Railway (CPR), was built to persuade British Columbia to join the Dominion of Canada by linking it with the eastern provinces. Construction started in 1882 and ended in 1885.

The first passenger train left Montreal on June 28, 1886, and arrived six days later at the Pacific gold rush town of Port Moody, British Columbia.

1922: FIRST SNOWMOBILE
While most people on a cold winter's day may be happy to be snowed-in with a mug of hot chocolate, one teenager's love of travel and the outdoors drove him to create the snowmobile for the long Canadian winters. Joseph-Armand Bombardier, from Quebec, invented the first motorized snow vehicle in 1922, when he attached a Ford Model-T engine and wooden propeller to the family sleigh. He was 15 years old.

Bombardier was granted his first patent in 1937, and in 1959 he sold the first of over 2 million Ski-Doo® snowmobiles.

1965: NATIONAL FLAG The Maple Leaf was not used on Canada's flag until 1965, following many spirited debates in Parliament and across Canada. Before 1965, Canada used the British Red Ensign as a symbol of its link with Britain.

In 1964, with Canada's 100th birthday only three years away, Prime

Selected Canadian National Records

Highest Point	Mt. Logan, Yukon Territories	19,550 ft
Longest River	Mackenzie	1,200 mi [1]
Highest Waterfall	Della Falls, British Columbia	1,443 ft
Largest Bay (world)	Hudson Bay	7,623 mi (coastline)
Largest Coastline (world)	51,485 mi (includes 52,455 islands)	
Coldest Temperature	Snag, Yukon Territories	-81.4° F on Feb. 3, 1947
Snowiest City	Gander, Newfoundland	174.5 in. total annual snowfall
Largest City	Toronto, Ontario (metro, 2005)	pop., 5,060,000
Longest-Serving Prime Minister	William Lyon Mackenzie King (1874-1950)	22 years (1921-26; 1926-30; 1935-48).
Shortest-Serving Prime Minister	Charles Tupper	May-July 1896
First Female Prime Minister	Kim Avril Campbell (b. 1947)	June-Dec. 1993
First Female Governor General	Right Hon. Jeanne Mathilde Sauvé (1922-93)	1984-90

[1] Including its tributaries, the Slave, Peace and Findlay Rivers, it flows for 2,635 miles.

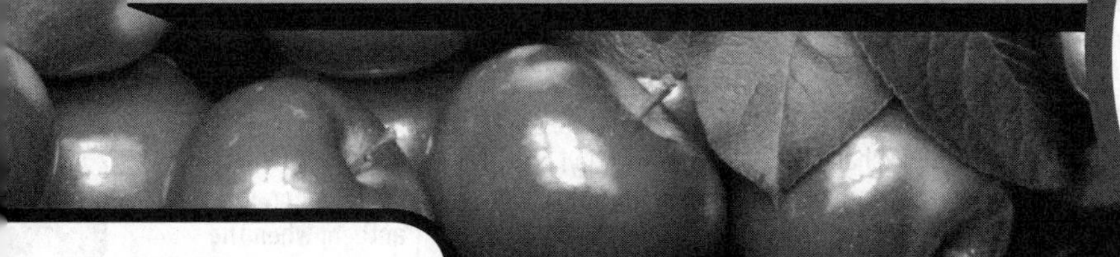

SOMETHING TO THINK ABOUT

THE BIG APPLE

Each of the more than 3 million McIntosh apple trees in North America shares a "family tree" that goes back to the very first McIntosh. Scottish immigrant John McIntosh found an abandoned apple grove in 1811 near Dundela, Ontario. After he transplanted some of the trees, one in particular produced superior fruit. McIntosh's son, Allen, proceeded to graft branches from that tree to the others so they all produced good fruit. McIntosh apples now make up 40% of Canada's apple crop.

Minister Lester B. Pearson organized a committee to create a truly Canadian flag. The new national flag was raised for the first time on Feb. 15, 1965, at noon on Parliament Hill in Ottawa.

1980: NATIONAL ANTHEM "O Canada" was proclaimed Canada's national anthem on July 1, 1980, 100 years after it was first sung. The music was composed by Calixa Lavallée. The French words were written by Sir Adolphe-Basile Routhier, while the English words are from a poem written in 1908 by Mr. Justice Robert Stanley Weir.

SUPERLATIVES

LONGEST HIGHWAY The Trans-Canada Highway between Victoria, British Columbia, and St. John's, Newfoundland, is the world's longest national highway at 4,860 miles. The first post was planted in Victoria in 1912. While some sections were completed early on, the more difficult terrain had to wait until federal funding arrived in 1950. The Trans-Canada Highway was officially completed on Sept. 3, 1962.

MOST MAPLE SYRUP Canada produces about 85% of the world's supply of maple syrup, with more than 10,000 maple syrup producers. In 2004, Canada produced 5.9 million gallons of maple syrup, valued at nearly Can$149 million.

OLDEST ORGANIZED SPORT Lacrosse is the oldest organized sport in North America. Native tribes played "baggataway" to settle disputes and train young warriors for battle. The earliest European record of lacrosse dates back to 1863, when lacrosse was Canada's most popular sport.

In 1910, the Montreal Shamrocks played the New Westminster Salmonbellies in British Columbia for the Minto Cup Senior Championships. The game was attended by over 15,000 fans, 3,000 more than the total population of New Westminster at the time.

TALLEST STRUCTURE The CN Tower in Toronto is the world's tallest self-supporting structure at 1,815 feet, 5 inches. Completed in 1976 after 40 months of construction, it has been cited by the American Society of Civil Engineers as one of the seven wonders of the modern world, and every year almost 2 million visitors ascend the tower.

Thanks to six high-speed elevators, it takes under a minute to travel the 1,136 feet up the concrete shaft to the lookout. The more adventurous can take the stairs—all 1,769 open to the public.

MOST DONUTS Canada has more donut shops per capita than any other country. The nation's most popular donut chain is Tim Horton's, with over 2,300 shops selling over 3 million donuts a day. The business is named after its founder Miles Gilbert "Tim" Horton, who played on the Toronto Maple Leafs hockey team for 18 years (1952-70), through four Stanley Cup championships.

China

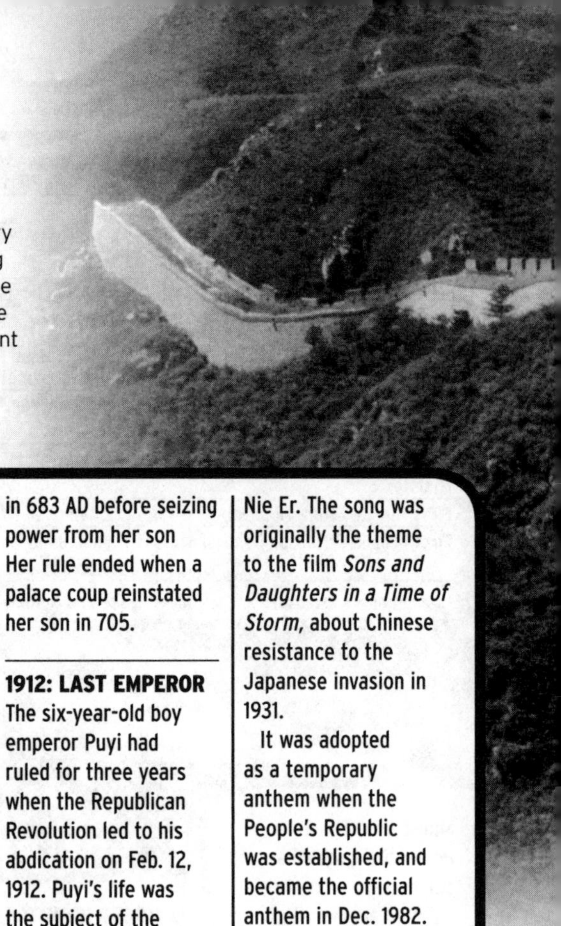

Total Area (People's Republic): 3,600,946 sq mi
Population (People's Republic, est. 2005): 1,306,313,812

China, one of the world's oldest civilizations, is the most populous country in the world today, as well as the fourth largest in total area. Mao Zedong defeated the Nationalist forces under Chiang Kai-shek and established the (Communist) People's Republic of China on the mainland, Oct. 1, 1949. The Nationalists fled to the island of Taiwan, and set up a separate government there. Mainland China considers Taiwan its 23rd province.

MILESTONES

2737 BC: TEA
A Chinese legend credits Emperor Shen Nong with the discovery of tea in 2737 BC, after leaves from a nearby plant fell into his boiling water. The earliest surviving written reference to tea dates back to around 350 BC. Tea was first used as a medicine; it gained popularity as a daily beverage by the 3rd century AD.

1500s BC: CHINESE SCRIPT More than 100,000 fragments of engraved cattle shoulder blades and turtle shells are the earliest records of the Chinese language.

During the Shang dynasty (about 1550-1040 BC), emperors would brand these "oracle bones" with a hot poker and predict future events, such as harvests, from the heat cracks. Afterward, an engraver would etch the prediction into the bone or shell, creating a vast library of writing.

221 BC: UNIFICATION
Ying Zheng, king of the Qin (Ch'in) state, unified the last Chinese feudal states in 221 BC to become the first emperor of all China. His "Dragon Empire" lasted only 15 years, but its many accomplishments included joining the earliest parts of the Great Wall and standardizing the Chinese language.

When he died in 210 BC he was buried in Xi'an in an elaborate underground mausoleum, the largest preserved in China. Discovered in 1974, it contained an army of 6,000 life-size terra-cotta figures in battle formation.

138 BC: SILK ROAD The 4,000-mile route to the Mediterranean dates back to the expeditions of Zhang Qian, an emissary of Emperor Wudi. He first set off to central Asia along the Great Wall in 138 BC, from what is now Xi'an. Soon after, traders followed, exchanging Chinese silk for western wool, spices, and horses.

The demand for silk was so high in Europe that around 550 AD Byzantine Emperor Justinian ordered two Persian monks who had once lived in China to secretly bring silkworms to Constantinople. The vast trade network was named the "Silk Road" in the 1870s by German geologist Baron Ferdinand von Richthofen.

683 AD: FIRST (AND ONLY) EMPRESS
Wu Zetian used her role as a concubine in the imperial court to gain access to the emperor's study, and eventually became the wife of Emperor Gao Zong. She waited seven years after Gao Zong's death in 683 AD before seizing power from her son Her rule ended when a palace coup reinstated her son in 705.

1912: LAST EMPEROR
The six-year-old boy emperor Puyi had ruled for three years when the Republican Revolution led to his abdication on Feb. 12, 1912. Puyi's life was the subject of the 1987 movie, *The Last Emperor*, directed by Bernardo Bertolucci.

1949: FLAG The red and yellow flag of China was adopted as the national flag when the People's Republic was founded. The red symbolizes revolution, the large yellow star represents the Communist Party, and the four smaller stars, arranged in a vertical arc, symbolize the Chinese people.

1982: NATIONAL ANTHEM "March of the Volunteers" was written in 1935 by Tian Han with music by Nie Er. The song was originally the theme to the film *Sons and Daughters in a Time of Storm*, about Chinese resistance to the Japanese invasion in 1931.

It was adopted as a temporary anthem when the People's Republic was established, and became the official anthem in Dec. 1982.

2003: FIRST TAIKONAUT Yang Liwei, an ex-fighter pilot, was the first Chinese launched into space. He spent 21.5 hours on Oct. 15-16, 2003, orbiting the earth 14 times in the *Shenzhou 5*. China is only the third country to launch a human to space.

"Taikonaut" was coined by western media, from *Taikong*, meaning "space." Chinese officials prefer the term *yuhangyuan* ("space navigator").

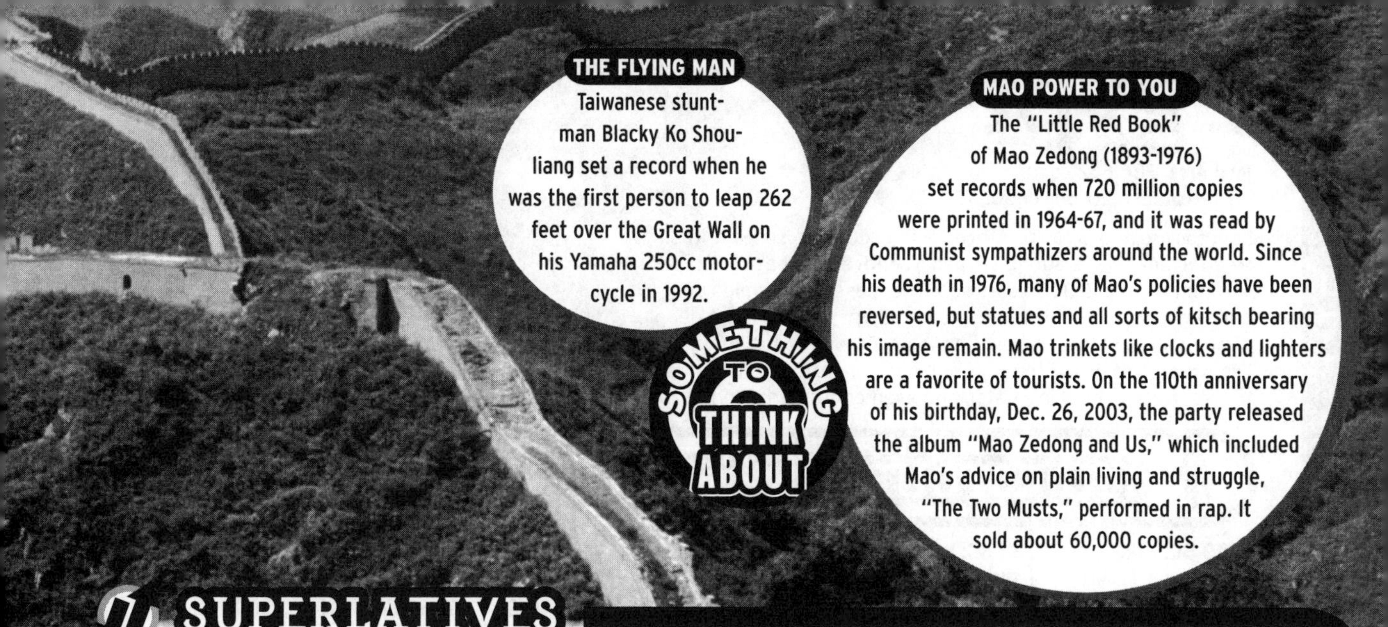

THE FLYING MAN

Taiwanese stuntman Blacky Ko Shouliang set a record when he was the first person to leap 262 feet over the Great Wall on his Yamaha 250cc motorcycle in 1992.

SOMETHING TO THINK ABOUT

MAO POWER TO YOU

The "Little Red Book" of Mao Zedong (1893-1976) set records when 720 million copies were printed in 1964-67, and it was read by Communist sympathizers around the world. Since his death in 1976, many of Mao's policies have been reversed, but statues and all sorts of kitsch bearing his image remain. Mao trinkets like clocks and lighters are a favorite of tourists. On the 110th anniversary of his birthday, Dec. 26, 2003, the party released the album "Mao Zedong and Us," which included Mao's advice on plain living and struggle, "The Two Musts," performed in rap. It sold about 60,000 copies.

SUPERLATIVES

GREAT WALL
The world's longest fortification wall ever built, the Great Wall of China was originally a system of separate walls protecting individual feudal states. Around 220 BC, Emperor Shi Huangdi ordered that the various walls be joined to defend against attacks from the north.

Eventually, the wall extended more than 4,000 miles, from the Yellow Sea in the east to Gansu province in the west.

OLDEST TEAHOUSE
The two-story Huxinting (Heart of Lake Pavilion) Teahouse in the Old Town of Shanghai was originally constructed by Pan Yunduan around 1559-77 as part of his Yuyuan Garden. It became a teahouse in 1855. Today, it is visited by tourists and dignitaries, who can sip tea while enjoying views of the garden and lake.

HIGHEST REGION
Tibet, an isolated area in southwest China, with huge mountain ranges along its borders and in the south, is the highest region on earth, with an average elevation of over 16,000 feet. Five of the world's ten highest mountains—including the highest, Everest—are partly in Tibet.

Although independent for much of its history, Tibet has remained under tight Chinese control since the early 1950s.

MOST TABLE TENNIS CHAMPS Table tennis (Ping-Pong) is immensely popular in China, where it is known as "National Ball." In 1971 a U.S. table tennis team became the first official American delegation to enter Communist China. Since 1971, Chinese women's singles players have won 13 of the 17 World Championships, all seven World Cups, and all five Olympic gold medals. The men's singles players have won 8 of 17 World Championships, 11 of 24 World Cups, and 2 of 5 Olympic golds.

MING PORCELAINS
On Nov. 17, 2004, a rare porcelain bowl from the classic Ming Dynasty (1368-1644) sold at auction at Bonhams & Butterfields in San Francisco for $5,726,250, an American record price for Chinese porcelain.

"MADE IN CHINA"
China has been the world's fastest growing economy in recent years, and now ranks second in GDP, after the U.S. It is also the second largest exporter to the U.S., behind Canada, supplying 12% of America's imported goods. Chief exports include electronics, clothes, toys, and over 90% of America's fireworks.

Two out of three imported U.S. flags come from the Communist nation, which, despite its official atheism, is also the leading exporter of artificial Christmas trees and ornaments.

Selected Chinese National Records

Highest Point (world)	Mount Everest (Tibet, Nepal)	29,035 ft
Lowest Point	Turpan Pendi	505 ft below sea level
Longest River	Yangtze (Chang)	3,915 mi
Largest City	Shanghai (metro, 2005)	pop. 12,665,000
Tallest Building	Jin Mao Tower (Shanghai)	1,380 ft
Busiest Seaport (world)	Hong Kong	264,441,000 metric tons in 2004
Largest Palace Complex (world)	Forbidden City (Gu Gong), now the Palace Museum	178 acres; palace covers 37 acres and over 9,000 rooms
Largest Square (world)	Tiananmen Square	122 acres

Egypt

Total Area: 386,662 sq mi
Population (est. 2005): 77,505,756

Egypt is located in North Africa on the southern shore of the Mediterranean Sea. Along Egypt's Nile River a great civilization sprung up some 5,000 years ago. The massive pyramids built to bury Egypt's pharaohs survive today. Egypt has the most people of any nation in the Arab world. About 94% are Muslims, and 95% live within 12 miles of the Nile, still a major resource for irrigation, transportation, drinking water, and even energy production.

MILESTONES

3000 BC: FIRST DYNASTY Around 3000 BC, Menes founded the first dynasty of Egyptian rulers (pharaohs), uniting a kingdom that extended from Upper Egypt around the Nile delta to Aswan in Lower Egypt.

200s BC: LIBRARY OF ALEXANDRIA The Library of Alexandria is believed to have been built in the 3rd century BC by Ptolemy I of Egypt. At its height it held 500,000 or more scrolls; ships wishing to dock in Alexandria had to hand over any writings they had to be copied and added to the library. The library was eventually destroyed and its manuscripts lost. Much damage came in a 47 BC fire set by the Romans.

In 2002, work was completed on a massive modern library complex, the Bibliotheca Alexandrina, near the old one.

51 BC: LAST PHARAOH Egypt's last pharaoh was the legendary Cleopatra VII, who took the throne in 51 BC at the age of 17. She ruled jointly with her younger brother, Ptolemy XII, until he exiled her; Julius Caesar fell in love with her and restored her as pharaoh in 47 BC after he conquered Egypt.

After Caesar's assassination, she fell in love with the Roman general Mark Antony. In 31 BC, Mark Antony's rival Octavian (later the Emperor Augustus) invaded Egypt. On hearing a false report of Cleopatra's death, Mark Antony committed suicide, leaving Cleopatra alone to face the Romans.

She killed herself—according to legend, by allowing an asp to bite her—and Octavian made Egypt into a Roman province.

969 AD: CAPITAL The city of Cairo was founded by the Fatimids, a Shi'a Muslim dynasty originating in North Africa, in 969 AD, north of the ancient capital of Memphis. After the sack of Baghdad by the Mongols in 1258 AD, it became the most important city in the Muslim world for philosophy, science, and trade.

Today, the Cairo metropolitan area is the largest urban center in Africa.

1799: ROSETTA STONE In 1799 soldiers in Napoleon's army unearthed a 45" x 28" stone near the Egyptian town of Rosetta (Rashid); on it was a pharaoh's decree dating from 196 BC.

The words were written in three scripts: hieroglyphs (the most ancient, used for priestly decrees), ancient Greek, and demotic (the everyday language of ancient Egypt).

Scholars, who understood the Greek, spent the next two decades de-coding the heroglyphic language. On Sept. 27, 1822, the French scholar Jean-François Champollion announced that the translation was done.

1952: MONARCHY OVERTHROWN On July 23, 1952, a group of military officers overthrew Egypt's last monarch, the unpopular King Farouk, and in 1954 Gamal Abdel Nasser took control of the government. Although he ruled in an authoritarian manner and faced serious opposition from within his country, he was one of the most popular modern leaders in the Arab world.

1958: NATIONAL FLAG The flag of Egypt consists of horizontal red, white, and black stripes with a golden eagle in the middle. The red symbolizes struggle for independence against the British, the white, the bloodless 1952 revolution, and the black the end of British colonial rule. The flag was established in 1958.

In 1984 the eagle was added to replace a hawk; it was the symbol used by the famous Muslim general Saladin, who ruled Egypt in the 12th century and fought off the Crusaders.

1979: PEACE WITH ISRAEL On Mar. 26, 1979, Egypt became the first Arab country to make peace with Israel. President Anwar Sadat, Israeli Prime Minister Menachem Begin, and U.S. President Jimmy Carter established the framework for the treaty in Sept. 1978 at Camp David, the U.S. presidential retreat.

Israel agreed to withdraw its forces from the Sinai Peninsula and dismantle its settlements there, while Egypt officially recognized Israel.

Selected Egyptian National Records

Highest Point	Mount Catherine (Jabal Katrina)	8,668 ft
Lowest Point	Qattara Depression	436 ft below sea level
Largest Lake	Lake Nasser	1,550 sq mi
Largest City	Cairo (metro, 2005)	pop. 11,146,000
Tallest Building	Cairo Tower (Cairo)	614 ft

THE ORIGINAL DELTA

The fertile Nile delta, one of the world's largest, is 120 miles wide at the Mediterranean coast. Its triangular shape led the ancient Greeks to compare it to the triangular Greek letter delta, and the word delta is used today for the mouth of any river, where deposits of sediment build up as the current slows before entering a larger body of water.

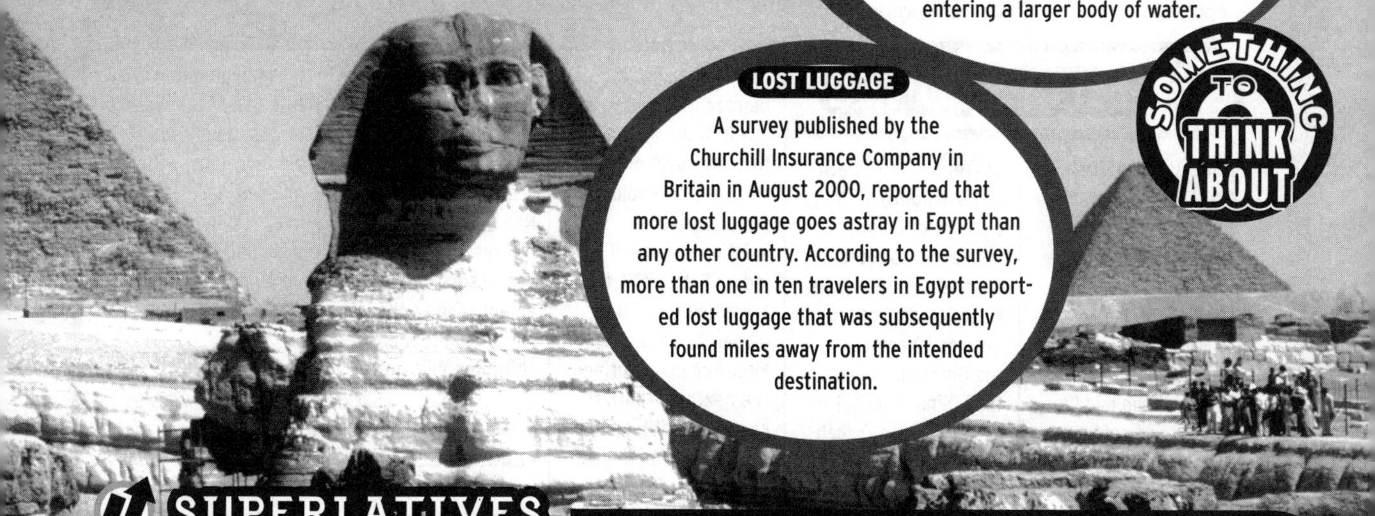

SOMETHING TO THINK ABOUT

LOST LUGGAGE

A survey published by the Churchill Insurance Company in Britain in August 2000, reported that more lost luggage goes astray in Egypt than any other country. According to the survey, more than one in ten travelers in Egypt reported lost luggage that was subsequently found miles away from the intended destination.

SUPERLATIVES

LONGEST RIVER
At approximately 4,160 miles, the Nile is the world's longest river. Starting in Burundi (Central Africa), it empties into the Mediterranean Sea. About 550 miles upstream is the Aswan High Dam, and behind it lies Lake Nasser, the world's second-largest artificial lake (1,550 sq mi in area).

LARGEST PYRAMID
Among the ancient Egyptians' greatest achievements are the massive granite and limestone structures built as tombs and monuments to pharaohs.

Of the 97 known pyramids, the most notable is the Great Pyramid of Giza, erected around 2250 BC for the pharaoh Khufu. It consists of over 2 million limestone and granite blocks, each weighing about 2.5 tons, which had to be dragged from quarries and put into place. The base takes up an area equal to about 10 football fields, and at 480 feet, the pyramid was the tallest structure on Earth until the 19th century. Historians aren't sure how workers were able to build it, but a series of ramps and pulleys may have been used.

Of the Seven Ancient Wonders of the World, this is the only one still surviving today.

GREAT SPHINX
A sphinx is a mythological creature with the head of a man and the body of a lion. The Great Sphinx at Giza is both the largest statue of a sphinx in the world and the largest ancient Mediterranean statue. Its origins and purpose are unknown. The Great Sphinx is 240 feet long and 66 feet tall with its head 20 feet wide.

OLDEST STONE STRUCTURE The step pyramid of Djoser at Saqqara is the oldest large stone structure in the world. It was built for the pharaoh Djoser by his minister, Imhotep, around 2630 BC. Before then, Egyptians used mud bricks as their main building material, which limited the possible size of buildings. By using large limestone blocks as Imhotep did, they were able to construct a building that reached 197 feet.

Originally built as four steps, then expanded to six, the pyramid at Saqqara is earlier than the Great Pyramids at Giza by about 100 years and lacks the smooth sides or polished surface that those later structures had.

OLDEST UNIVERSITY
Al-Azhar University in Cairo, which dates back almost to the founding of the city in 969 AD, is said to be the oldest university in existence today. It was originally a mosque, but by 975 lectures and other scholarly activities focusing on religious and political issues became regular occurrences.

Today, al-Azhar continues its focus on religious studies, but also offers other programs.

France

Total Area: 211,209 sq mi
Population (est. 2005): 60,656,178

France is the third-largest European nation in area, after Russia and Ukraine, and has about as many people as the United Kingdom (fewer than Russia or Germany). It is renowned for its wines and fashions, castles and cathedrals, rich culture, languages, and history; and the capital city of Paris is the most popular tourist destination in the world.

MILESTONES

200s BC: NATIONAL CAPITAL Paris, the capital and largest city of France, is more than 2,000 years old. The Gallic tribe known as Parisii settled on what is now the Île de la Cité at the middle of the third century BC. The area was a regional capital for the Romans, who ruled there for some 500 years following the conquests of Julius Caesar.

During the city's redesign (1852-70) under Napoleon III, urban planner Georges Haussmann replaced the winding medieval neighborhoods with the famous six-story buildings and tree-lined boulevards of today, like the Champs-Élysées. The modern city covers 41 square miles and has about 2 million residents.

842 AD: FRANÇAIS The oldest known document in a form of French is the *Oath of Strasbourg* of 842, a treaty of loyalty between two brothers, Charles the Bald (later Holy Roman Emperor Charles II) and Louis the German. In Aug. 1539, King Francis I made Parisian French the official language, and the *Académie Française* was formed in Feb. 1635, by the chief minister to Louis XIII, Cardinal Richelieu, to watch over the language and develop a dictionary with precise definitions.

French replaced Latin as a common language for international communication, and it is still a working language of the European Union, the Olympics, and the United Nations. It is spoken as a first or second language by 125 million people around the world.

1789: REPUBLIC On July 14, 1789, a group of Parisians rose up against the monarchy and stormed the Bastille, an old fort and royal prison. The French Revolution swept away the existing order and led, in Sept. 1793, to the abolition of the monarchy under the First Republic; during the next year both the king, Louis XVI, and his wife, Marie Antoinette, were beheaded by guillotine. The Republic lasted until Napoleon Bonaparte's Nov. 9-10, 1799, coup d'état.

Bastille Day was declared a national holiday in 1880 and has been celebrated ever since.

1792: "LA MARSEILLAISE" The French national anthem was composed by Officer Claude Joseph Rouget de Lisle on the night of April 25, 1792, in Strasbourg. Originally titled "Chant de guerre pour l'armée du Rhin," it was renamed for the volunteer troops from Marseilles, who sang it as they entered Paris in Aug. 1792. It was declared the national song on July 14, 1795.

"La Marseillaise" was banned under Napoleon I (1799-1814) and his immediate successors, but was established as the national anthem by the Third Republic in 1879.

1794: NATIONAL FLAG The colors of Paris, blue and red, were included in flags of the French Revolution with the white of French royalty, in three vertical bands. In 1794 the French tricolor was made official. It went out of favor after Napoleon's defeat at Waterloo in 1815, but was brought back in July 1830 when the "citizen king" Louis Philippe was enthroned.

1796: THE LOUVRE Once a sumptuous royal palace, the Louvre, on the north bank of the River Seine in Paris, was opened to the public as a museum in Aug. 1793. It is one of the world's largest and greatest art museums, with 8 miles of galleries and over a million works, including the *Venus de Milo* and the *Mona Lisa*.

1858: HAUTE COUTURE Charles Frederick Worth was an English linen drapery apprentice in Paris when he got the idea to create his own high-quality, made-to-measure dresses, instead of simply following customers' specifications. He opened Worth & Bobergh in 1858 with his business partner Otto Bobergh and 20 staffers at 7 rue de la Paix, and won the influential patronage of the fashion-conscious Empress Eugenie, wife of Napoleon III.

Worth used models to showcase his designs and became the first "status" designer, attracting European nobles and royalty as clients.

SOMETHING TO THINK ABOUT

DON'T DIE IN LE LAVANDOU... IT'S ILLEGAL

In Sept. 2000, the mayor of Le Lavandou, Gil Bernardi, enacted a law that banned dying in his French Riviera town. With the only cemetery packed, and plans to build a new one rejected by a court in Nice on environmental grounds, Mayor Bernardi issued the decree to draw attention to the impasse. He admitted that, as for its enforceability, "there is no punishment for dying."

WHAT'S IN A NAME?

In Oct. 2003 a group of French villages held the first meeting of "Villages of Lyric or Burlesque Names" in a hamlet outside of Toulouse called Mingocebos, which means "Eat Onions" in the old regional language. Those attending came from such villages as Beaufou ("Beautiful Insane"), Cocumont ("Cuckold Hill"), and Saligos ("Filthy Pig").

PARLEZ-VOUS GERMAN?

In modern French, only about 400 words are of Germanic origin, but both *franc* ("free") and *français* ("French") are among them, derived from the Germanic word *Franko* ("freeman").

SUPERLATIVES

OLDEST PAINTINGS Europe's oldest paintings were famously found on the walls of a cave at the foot of a cliff in the Ardèche Gorges, in southern France. The paintings, which feature animals such as horses, owls, rhinoceroses, and mammoths, range from 23,000 to 32,000 years old. The Chauvet Cave was named after Jean-Marie Chauvet, who, along with two friends, discovered it on Dec. 18, 1994.

LONGEST REIGNING MONARCH The longest reigning monarch in all of European history was Louis XIV, who ascended the French throne at the age of five and reigned for 72 years (1643-1715), for most of the time as sole absolute ruler.

At his famous palace in Versailles, the Sun King arose each day at 8:30 AM and dressed in an elaborate ritual observed by about 100 male courtiers. At 11:30 PM each day he performed a similar ritual in reverse form.

MOST POPULAR TOURIST DESTINATION In 2003, 75 million people visited France, accounting for 10.9% of the world's total tourism. Paris is the world's most visited city, with some 36 million tourists a year, making it the world's most popular tourist destination, according to the World Tourism Organization.

BIGGEST TOURIST ATTRACTION The biggest single tourist attraction in France is the Eiffel Tower, drawing in about 6 million visitors per year. Built by structural engineer Alexandre-Gustave Eiffel to commemorate the 100th anniversary of the French Revolution, the Eiffel Tower was the tallest structure in the world when it was unveiled for the Paris World's Fair on Mar. 31, 1889.

The 984-foot (1,063 ft with flagpole and antenna), $1.5 million open-lattice wrought-iron tower was considered an eyesore during its two-year construction and was supposed to have been torn down after 20 years, but it became hugely popular once built.

FROMAGE The French eat more cheese than any other people in the world. In 2003 they ate about 1.5 million tons of it—nearly 42 pounds per person.

ROUGE OU BLANC France produces 17.5% of the world's wines, and the French are among the world's biggest wine consumers, drinking an average of almost 15 gallons per person each year.

The most expensive wine ever sold is a 1787 Chateau Lafite from Bordeaux that once belonged to Thomas Jefferson; it was auctioned off at Christie's in Dec. 1985 for $155,242 to the late American publisher Malcolm Forbes.

Selected French National Records

Highest Point	Mt. Blanc	15,771 ft
Longest River	Loire	634 mi
Highest Waterfall	Gavarnie, Hautes-Pyrénées	1,385 ft
Largest City	Paris (metro, 2005)	pop. 9,854,000
Tallest Bridge (world)	Millau Bridge	1,115 ft
Longest-Serving President	Charles De Gaulle	12 years (1944-46, 1959-69)
Most Expensive Champagne	Heidsieck Monopole Goût Américain 1907	$4,068, at Christie's, Oct. 22, 1998
First Cannes Film Festival	Palme d'Or awarded to 11 films	Sept. 20-Oct. 5, 1946
First Tour de France Winner	Maurice Garin (France)	1,509 mi in 94h 33' 14" July 1-19, 1903
Most Caps (Rugby Union)	111, Philippe Sella	1982-95

Germany

Total Area: 137,847 sq mi
Population (est. 2005): 82,431,390

Located in central Europe, Germany, which is about the size of the state of Montana, has land borders with nine countries and is the most populous European country other than Russia. After the defeat of the Nazi regime in World War II, it was divided into sectors, with Communist East Germany separated from the free western sectors. On Oct. 3, 1990, a day now recognized as Germany's national holiday, East and West Germany reunited.

Neuschwanstein Castle

MILESTONES

1871: DEUTSCHES REICH Germany was unified after Prussia's victory in the Franco-Prussian War, when the kingdoms of Bavaria, Württemberg, Baden, and Hesse-Darmstadt joined the North German Confederation, a union of Prussia and 22 states created in 1867 by Prussian Prime Minister Otto von Bismarck. King William I of Prussia was proclaimed German Emperor, or Kaiser, at Versailles on Jan. 18, 1871, and Bismarck became Germany's first chancellor.

1871: NATIONAL CAPITAL King Frederick I made Berlin the Prussian royal residence in 1701, and the city became Germany's first capital in 1871. From 1949 to 1990, East Berlin was the capital of East Germany, while Bonn served as the West German capital. Berlin became the capital again in 1999 after the reunification of Germany.

1919: NATIONAL FLAG The German flag consists of three equal horizontal bands of black, red, and gold, and was adopted as the national flag under the Weimar Republic in 1919. When the Nazis came to power in 1933, the flag was replaced with the infamous swastika. The original flag was re-adopted by West Germany after the war.

1933-45: THIRD REICH Under Aldolf Hitler, Germany launched persecutions of Jews that led to the murder of millions of Jews and others in the Holocaust. Hitler invaded Poland in 1939, precipitating World War II.

1945: V-E DAY On May 7, 1945, Nazi Germany surrendered. Allied commanders designated the following day, May 8, as Victory in Europe, or V-E, Day. Germans often refer to this time as the *Stunde Null*, or "Zero Hour," when the country literally started over.

1950s: "ECONOMIC MIRACLE" After four years of occupation, France, Great Britain, and the U.S. created the Federal Republic of Germany, or West Germany, in 1949. The country rebuilt its devastated cities and industries, and formed a new government. In what is known as the "Economic Miracle," West Germany became one of the world's most prosperous countries.

1961-90: BERLIN WALL Between 1949 and 1961, some 2.5 million people emigrated from East to West Germany via Berlin. On Aug. 12, 1961, the Soviet Union approved the construction of a wall closing off East Berlin. Originally built with barbed wire and cinder blocks, it was later replaced with concrete, and armed watchtowers and minefields were added. The wall ran 27 miles through the city itself and approximately 96 miles around West Berlin, which was entirely within East German territory.

During the Wall's existence there were about 5,000 successful escapes; some 200 others were killed trying to cross, and an estimated 75,000 people were imprisoned for trying to escape.

Mass demonstrations forced authorities to open the Wall on Nov. 9, 1989, marking the beginning of the end of the East German state. Destruction of the wall officially began June 9, 1990, and took five months. Several slabs were left as monuments.

Selected German National Records

Highest Point	Zugspitze (Bavarian Alps)	9,721 ft
Lowest Point	Freepsum Lake	6.5 ft below sea level
Longest River	Rhine	537 mi in Germany; total length, 820 mi
Largest City	Rhem-Ruhr North (metro, 2005)	pop. 6,566,000
First Kindergarten (world)	Founded by Friedrich Froebel	Bad Blankenburg in 1837
Longest-Serving Chancellor	Helmut Kohl	16 years (1982-98)
First Female Chancellor[1]	Angela Merkel	Nov. 22, 2005-present
Most Nobel Prizes for Literature (world)	9	1902, 1908, 1910, 1912, 1929, 1946, 1966, 1972, 1999
Most National Team Games (soccer)	150, Lothar Matthäus	1980-2000
Most Goals (National Team)	68, Gerd Müller	1967-74
First Volkswagen Beetle	Designed by Ferdinand Porsche	prototype built in 1932, first production in April 1939

(1) First chancellor to have grown up in former East Germany

SUPERLATIVES

OKTOBERFEST

On Oct. 12, 1810, Prince Ludwig of Bavaria married Princess Therese of Sachsen-Hildburghausen in Munich. As part of their celebrations, a horse race was held five days later on the fields in front of the city gates. Known by local Bavarians as Wiesen, or "fields," the celebration evolved into an annual 16-day festival ending on the first Sunday in October.

The festival includes a parade through Munich featuring beer wagons, floats, riflemen, and revelers in traditional costumes. By tradition, Munich's mayor taps the first beer keg to open the event, now the biggest beer festival in the world.

FASTEST HIGHWAY

The world's fastest highway system is Germany's Autobahn, which for the most part has no speed limit, only a recommended top speed of 130 kilometers per hour (80 mph).

The Autobahn now stretches 7,444 miles across most parts of Germany, making it the world's second-largest superhighway system, after that of the U.S. (much bigger, at 46,667 miles).

LARGEST AIRLIFT

On June 23, 1948, the Soviet Union laid claim to Berlin, and blocked all rail, road, and water access to the Western-held half. On June 26, the U.S. and Great Britain began a massive airlift to fly supplies into West Berlin.

At the height of the operation an Allied aircraft landed in Berlin every minute. Ultimately, 278,228 flights would be made and 2,326,406 tons of food and supplies would be delivered to Berlin.

On May 12, 1949, the Soviet Union lifted the blockade, and the airlift ended Sept. 30.

GERMAN AMERICANS

Since 1820, when U.S. immigration records were first officially kept, Germany has been the biggest source of immigrants to the U.S. Between 1820 and 2003, about 7 million Germans settled in America and today, nearly 48 million Americans claim some German descent.

During the Third Reich, hundreds of thousands of Germans fled to the U.S. These immigrants, many of them Jewish, included such prominent figures as physicist Albert Einstein, film director Billy Wilder, and musician Bruno Walter.

SOMETHING TO THINK ABOUT

BEST GERMAN WORDS

The Goethe Institute and the German Language Council pored over 22,838 entries from 111 countries between May and Aug. 2004 to declare *Habseligkeiten* ("belongings") the most beautiful sounding word in the German language. *Rhabarbermarmelade* ("rhubarb jam") was dubbed the coolest.

LEANING TOWER OF COLOGNE

Germany got its own leaning tower after work on a new underground transit line in Cologne tipped the red-brick tower of the Church of St. John the Baptist by several feet in 2004. The city's transit authority was still trying to figure out whether to right the 130-foot-high tower, or keep the steel beams currently stabilizing it. Hundreds of tourists have ventured off the beaten track to have their picture taken in front of the tower.

Greece

The Parthenon ►

Total Area: 50,942 sq mi
Population (est. 2005): 10,668,354

Greece, a country in southeastern Europe at the lower end of the Balkan peninsula, has a culture stretching back thousands of years. Its influence on art, architecture, religion, philosophy, and politics permeates Western countries today. Modern Greece replaced its monarchy with a parliamentary republic in 1974.

The beautiful Greek islands, in the Aegean and Ionian seas, make up one-fifth of the country's total area.

MILESTONES

AROUND 3000 BC: TWO CULTURES
Stone Age civilizations appeared on the Balkan peninsula as early as 7000 BC. By 3000 BC, as the Bronze Age began, two major cultures developed. One (later called Mycenaean) centered on the mainland; the other, now called Minoan, on the nearby island of Crete. The Minoans dominated culture and trade until around 1500 BC, when the Mycenaeans gained prominence.

AROUND 1400 BC-500 BC: GREECE EMERGES In the 13th and 12th centuries BC, the Dorians, armed with iron weapons, pushed southward into the region, driving many inhabitants of Greece out into Asia Minor. After these and other invasions and migrations, the Greeks gradually settled into a single identity as Hellenes, and established colonies from the western Mediterranean to the Black Sea. But Greece was not one unified nation; it was a group of city-states, most notably Athens and Sparta, ruled (800 BC-500 BC) first by aristocrats and later by tyrants.

AROUND 776 BC: OLYMPIC GAMES
The ancient Olympic Games were first staged in Olympia in 776 BC. Only one event was staged at the original Games, a 200-meter sprint won by Koroibos, a cook from Elis.

Part religious holiday, part sports and arts festival, the ancient Games began with the lighting of a flame at the altar of Zeus. The ending of the celebration was marked by the dousing of the flame.

As the Games grew in popularity more events were added, including wrestling (708 BC), boxing (688 BC) and chariot racing (408 BC). The Olympics ran for more than a thousand years before Emperor Theodosius I of Rome abolished the Games in 393 AD. He regarded them as an inappropriate pagan festival.

AROUND 9TH CENTURY BC: ILIAD AND ODYSSEY
The two great ancient Greek epic poems, the *Iliad* and the *Odyssey*, were probably composed in the 9th century BC, whether by one person (traditionally the blind poet Homer) or many, and were sung by Greek bards.

The *Iliad* recalls the last year of the Trojan War, when Greek armies invaded the ancient city of Troy (Ilium) in modern-day Turkey, an event historians believe did take place, around the 12th century BC. The story revolves around the "wrath of Achilles," the Greek warrior who eventually slays Hector, son of the Trojan king, in single-handed combat. The *Odyssey* relates the adventures of the Greek hero Odysseus during his eventful journey home after the war.

508 BC: DEMOCRACY
In 508 BC, the Athenian statesman Cleisthenes led an uprising against despotic rule and established one of the world's first, and most extensive, democracies. At the age of 18, all Athenian men had the right to meet in an Assembly and vote on measures, which were passed by a show of hands or by secret ballots using pebbles.

5TH-4TH CENTURY BC: GOLDEN AGE OF ATHENS
After wars with Persia that ended in 479 BC, Athens emerged as the most powerful of the Greek states. Its leader Pericles (ruled c. 460-429 BC) built the great Parthenon and promoted arts and culture.

The Golden Age of Athens produced such figures as the philosophers Socrates and Plato, the playwrights Aristophanes and Sophocles, and historians Thucydides and Herodotus. It faded when rivalries between Athens and Sparta led in 431 BC to the Peloponnesian War.

336 BC: ALEXANDER THE GREAT
As Greek states fought one another, their northern neighbors, the Macedonians, took over; eventually, Alexander the Great (ruled 336-323 BC) made Greece part of a vast empire stretching from Egypt to northern India. Greek culture would influence the entire area for hundreds of years, in what is known as the Hellenistic period.

AROUND 146 BC: ROMAN RULE AND BYZANTIUM After winning independence from the Macedonians, Greece was conquered by Rome and incorporated into its empire in 146 BC. When Rome fell in the 5th century AD, power shifted to the Eastern Empire centered around Constantinople, (modern-day Istanbul, Turkey), also called Byzantium.

Until the 11th century AD, Greece was part of the Byzantine Empire. During this time Greek language and Orthodox Christianity unified the people of Greece.

1460, 1830: OTTOMAN RULE AND INDEPENDENCE In 1460, the bulk of Greek lands fell under the Ottoman Empire. After nearly four centuries, the Greeks successfully fought Turkish rule, winning independence (over a complete area) in 1830. Continuing to fight for their ancestral lands, the Greeks recaptured Thessaly in 1881, Epirus and Macedonia in 1913, and all of Thrace in 1918.

1864: NATIONAL ANTHEM Inspired by the Greek war of independence, Dionysios Solomos wrote the poem *Hymn to Freedom* in 1823-1824. In 1828, Nicolaos Mantzaros set the hymn to music. Running 158 stanzas, the song is often limited to the first two. It was made the national anthem in 1864.

1896: MODERN OLYMPIC GAMES In 1896, 1,503 years after they were last held, the Olympic Games were revived by Frenchman Baron Pierre de Coubertin. He wanted to stage the first modern Games in Paris, but after Greek officials backed de Coubertin's plan, the first Games were moved to Athens.

At the first modern Olympics, 241 athletes (all male) from 14 nations competed in 43 events.

1978: NATIONAL FLAG The current Greek flag was adopted by law on Dec. 22, 1978. The white cross in the left hand corner, representing Christianity, dates to the first blue and white Greek flag in 1822. The blue and white colors are those of the Greek Orthodox Church; legend has it that the blue also represents the sea, while the white stripes suggest the crests of waves.

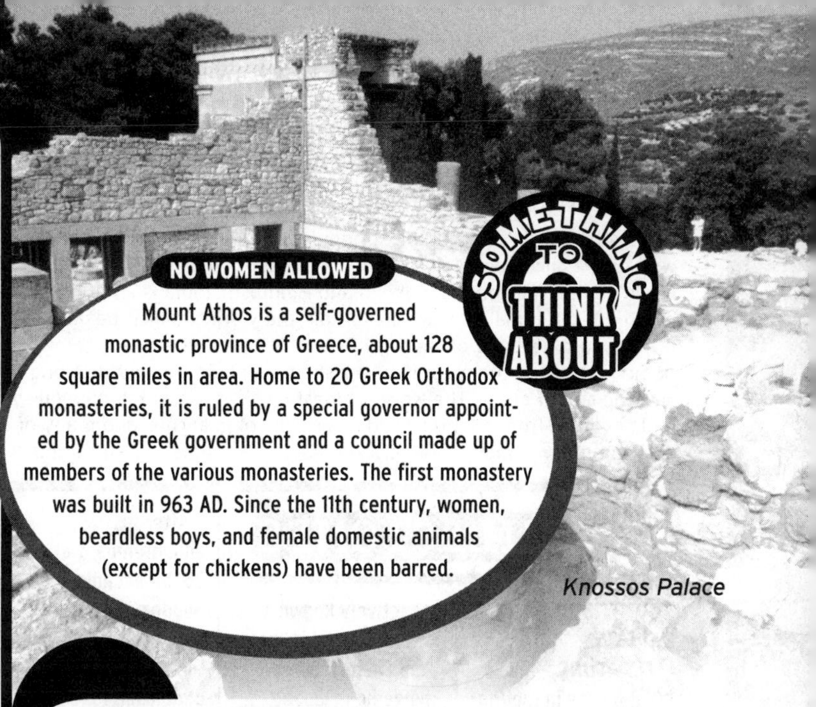

Knossos Palace

SOMETHING TO THINK ABOUT

NO WOMEN ALLOWED

Mount Athos is a self-governed monastic province of Greece, about 128 square miles in area. Home to 20 Greek Orthodox monasteries, it is ruled by a special governor appointed by the Greek government and a council made up of members of the various monasteries. The first monastery was built in 963 AD. Since the 11th century, women, beardless boys, and female domestic animals (except for chickens) have been barred.

Selected Greek National Records

Highest Point	Mount Olympus	9,570 ft
Longest River	Aliakmnon	185 mi
Largest City	Athens (metro, 2005)	pop., 3,238,000
Tallest Building	Athens Tower 1	338 ft
First Nobel Laureate	Giorgios Seferis	1963, Literature
First Oscar Winner	Katina Paxinou	1943 Best Supporting Actress, *For Whom The Bell Tolls*

SUPERLATIVES

OLDEST MARATHON FINISHER The oldest person to complete a full marathon race is Dimitrion Yordanidis of Greece. He ran the Athens Marathon on Oct. 10, 1976, his 98th birthday. The nonagenarian completed the course in 7 hours, 33 minutes.

LONGEST HUMAN-POWERED FLIGHT On April 23, 1988, Greek cyclist Kanellos Kanellopoulos flew the human-powered aircraft *Daedalus 88* for a record 72 miles across the Aegean Sea, from Crete to Santorini on the island of Thira.

The journey, which took 3 hours, 53 minutes, 30 seconds, attempted to recreate the mythical flight of Daedalus, who according to legend escaped Crete with his son, both on wings constructed with feathers and wax. (While Daedalus made it safely, his son Icarus's wings melted after he flew too close to the sun.)

Kanellopoulos safely maintained an altitude of about 15 feet above the ocean. However, *Daedalus 88* didn't quite reach Santorini. Its tail craft broke just 10 yards short of the beach, and *Daedalus 88* ditched into the surf.

India

Total Area: 1,269,345 sq mi
Population (est. 2005): 1,080,264,388

India is the world's second most populous country and is the only nation besides China with over 1 billion people. The world's largest democracy is also the birthplace of two of the world's great religions: Buddhism and Hinduism. India is a nation of vast diversity. In the north are the Himalayas, which contain the world's tallest peaks. In the subtropical plains of the south lie some of the world's largest cities where technology flourishes; yet it is also home to some of the most impoverished people in the world. Along with Pakistan, India was the site of one of the world's oldest civilizations, the Indus Valley civilization. Modern India evolved from a long period of British colonial rule, and many of its institutions, from parliamentary democracy to cricket, have their roots in that period.

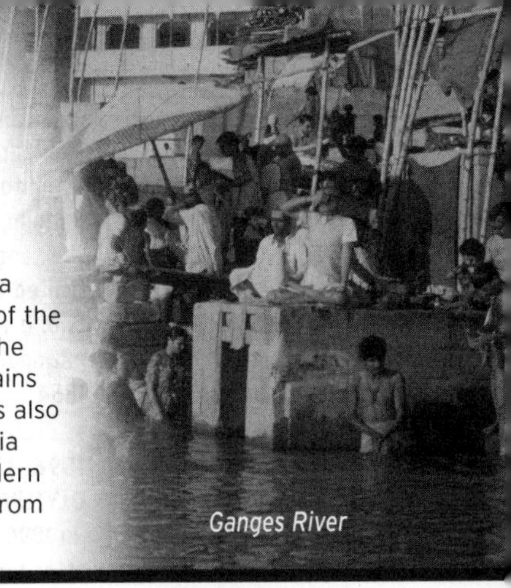

Ganges River

MILESTONES

ABOUT 1500 BC: EARLIEST LITERATURE The 1,028 hymns in the *Rig-Veda* are considered the oldest of the four Vedas, which are the basis of Hinduism. The Vedic mantras are ceremonial hymns to deities and include instructions for various rituals. They were first spoken as early as 1500 BC, after tribes collectively known as Aryans arrived in India from Eastern Europe. The Vedic language later became Sanskrit.

ABOUT 500 BC: BUDDHISM Siddhartha Gautama, a prince in the Himalayan foothills of present-day Nepal, left his royal life and traveled as a beggar throughout northeast India in search of enlightenment.

After his enlightenment at age 35, he became the Buddha. He outlined the Four Nobel Truths, the foundation of Buddhism. (See page 138.)

1588: GOLDEN TEMPLE AT AMRITSAR The Sikh faith was founded by the Guru Nanak in the 15th century. Its most sacred site, the Harimandir (or "Golden Temple") at Amritsar, was built between 1588 and 1601. It houses the original *Adi Granth*, or "First Book," the sacred scripture of the Sikhs.

The Temple was built in the center of a lake, now called *Amrit Sarovar* ("Pool of Nectar"), dug by order of the fourth Guru, Ram Das Sahib, from 1577 to 1581. The city was built around (and named after) this body of water.

1500s-1600s: EAST INDIA COMPANIES Portuguese explorer Vasco da Gama rounded the southern tip of Africa and reached Calicut, India (now Kozhikode), on May 20, 1498. Traders eager to capitalize on the faster, sea-based route raced to create trading posts throughout the 1500s. Several nations consolidated their traders into companies, beginning with England on Dec. 31, 1600.

The English East India Co. created its first permanent trading post at Surat in 1619, and in effect ruled most of India by 1761.

1648: TAJ MAHAL The Islamic Mughals invaded India from Afghanistan in 1526 and brought the tradition of Persian *charbagh* gardens—terraced parks full of lush foliage and reflecting pools. After Emperor Shah Jahan's second wife died giving birth to their 14th child on June 17, 1631, he

Selected Indian National Records

Highest Point[1]	Mt. Kanchenjunga	28,209 ft
Longest River[2]	Ganges	1,560 mi
Largest City[3]	Mumbai (metro, 2005)	pop. 18,336,000
Longest-Serving Prime Minister	Jawaharlal Nehru	15 years, 9 months (Aug. 15, 1947-May 27, 1964)
Tallest Building	SD Towers (Mumbai)	689 ft
First Woman Prime Minister[4]	Indira Gandhi	Jan. 19, 1966
First Nobel Laureate[5]	Rabindranath Tagore	1913, Literature
First Astronaut	Rakesh Sharma	April 2, 1984 (aboard *Soyuz T-11*)

(1) K2 or Mt. Godwin Austen, the world's second highest mountain, at 28,250 feet, lies in the disputed territories in Kashmir, controlled by Pakistan but claimed by India. (2) Only 800 miles of its course flows through India. (3) Previously known as Bombay. (4) The daughter of Jawaharlal Nehru, Mrs. Gandhi served two terms: (1966-1977, 1980-1984). She was assassinated by her bodyguards on Oct. 31, 1984. (5) Two British nationals born in India won the Nobel Prize prior to 1913: Sir Ronald Ross in 1902 for physiology/medicine, and Rudyard Kipling in 1907 for literature.

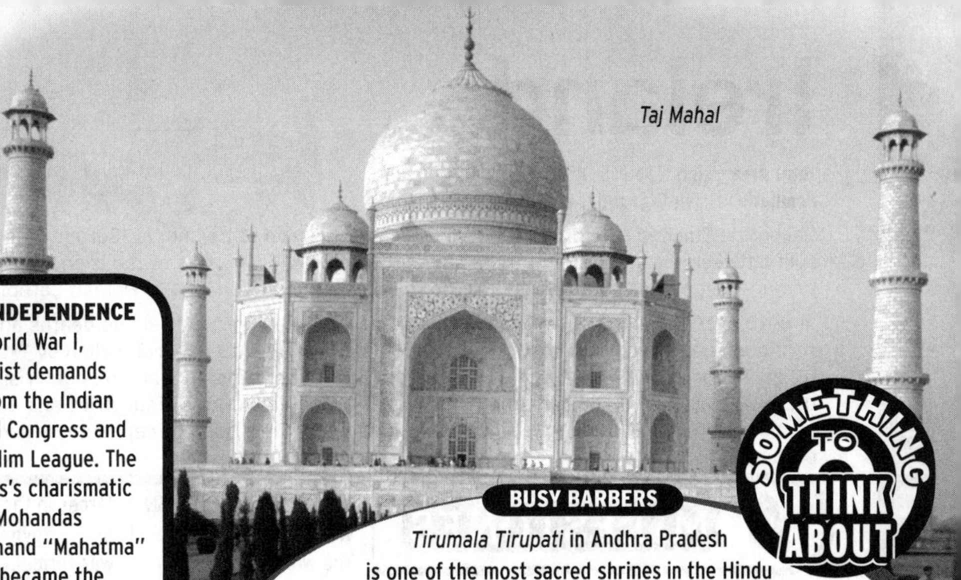
Taj Mahal

created a *charbagh* for her on the banks of the River Yamuna at Agra. At the south end, Ustad Ahmad designed the opulent Taj Mahal, a 243-foot-tall white marble tomb with a tapered dome, completed in 1648.

1858: EMPIRE OF INDIA The East India Company's rule was often crude and cruel. On May 10, 1857, native ("sepoy") troops rebelled and tried to reinstate the Mughal Emperor Bahadur Shah II. The uprising was put down by British troops in June 1858, after which the British government took control of India. On Jan. 1, 1877, Britain's Queen Victoria was declared Empress of India.

1947: FLAG The national flag of India, adopted July 22, 1947, comprises a tricolor of saffron, white, and green. Saffron represents Hinduism, green Islam, and white the peace it was hoped would exist between them. At the center of the white band is a blue *Chakra*, a symbolic wheel of law, a symbol that dates from the second century BC.

1947: INDEPENDENCE After World War I, nationalist demands grew from the Indian National Congress and the Muslim League. The Congress's charismatic leader, Mohandas Karamchand "Mahatma" Gandhi, became the national leader of the resistance movment.

Gandhi's use of non-violent protest gained large support. After years of passive resistance and boycotts, India became an independent nation on Aug. 15, 1947. On the same day, the subcontinent was partitioned, creating the nation of Pakistan for Muslims.

Gandhi was assassinated on Jan. 13, 1948. India officially became a republic on Jan. 26, 1950.

1974: NUCLEAR TEST On May 18, 1974, India conducted its first nuclear test, an underground explosion at Pokhran, officially labeled a "peaceful nuclear explosion" and nicknamed "Smiling Buddha."

SOMETHING TO THINK ABOUT

BUSY BARBERS

Tirumala Tirupati in Andhra Pradesh is one of the most sacred shrines in the Hindu religion. At least 5,000 pilgrims visit the temple and complex each day. Hindus consider it a privilege to shave their heads at the shrine in a vow called tonsuring. Over 500 barbers are in constant demand and work in a five-story building around the clock in three shifts. The shorn locks are gathered and auctioned off. They brought in $6.9 million in the 2004-05 season.

SUPERLATIVES

MOST MOVIES India's film industry is the world's largest. Known as "Bollywood," it is centered in Mumbai (formerly Bombay) and features films with a mix of singing, dancing, fight scenes, and drama. In 2004, there were 934 authorized film releases and over 3 billion admission tickets sold. By comparison, there were 483 films released by Hollywood in 2004, with 1.54 billion tickets sold.

Dadabhai Phalke, the father of Indian cinema, made the country's first movie in 1913. It was based on a story from the ancient epic known as the *Mahabharata*.

The first Bollywood movie nominated for an Oscar was *Mother India*, made by Mehboob Khan in 1957.

MOST FIELD HOCKEY GOLD MEDALS India has won the Olympic men's field hockey tournament a record eight times: 1928, 1932, 1936, 1948, 1952, 1956, 1964, and 1980. The team dominated Olympic play for 32 years from when it first entered the Games from 1928 to 1956, winning every single match (25-0), and six straight golds.

LARGEST TEA PRODUCER India is the world's largest tea producer and consumer. India produced 820,216 metric tons of tea in 2004, slightly ahead of China. Because Indians consume most of their tea, India is not the largest exporter; that distinction goes to Kenya.

LARGEST CRICKET STADIUM The world's largest cricket stadium in terms of seating capacity is Eden Gardens in Calcutta. Built in 1871, it's also India's oldest. It currently has a capacity of 100,000 spectators.

Ireland

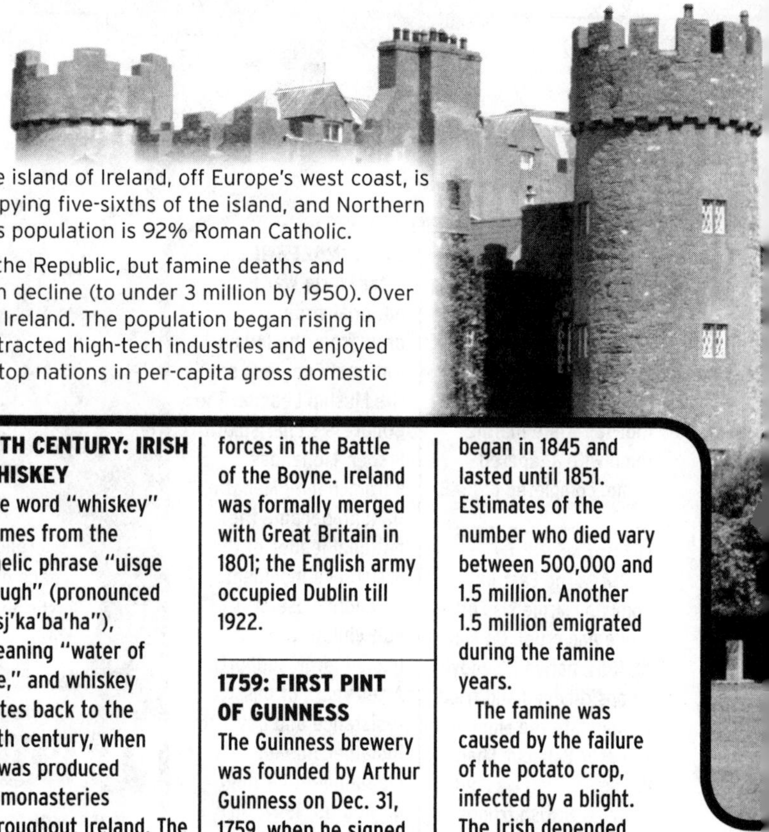

Total Area (Irish Republic): 27,135 sq mi
Population (Irish Republic; est. 2005): 4,015,676

Called the Emerald Isle for its lush green fields, the island of Ireland, off Europe's west coast, is split between the independent Irish Republic, occupying five-sixths of the island, and Northern Ireland, part of the United Kingdom. The Republic's population is 92% Roman Catholic.

In 1840 over 6 million people lived in what is now the Republic, but famine deaths and continued poverty caused a long-lasting population decline (to under 3 million by 1950). Over 50 million people of Irish descent now live outside Ireland. The population began rising in the 1990s, as Ireland, dubbed "the Celtic Tiger," attracted high-tech industries and enjoyed economic growth. It now ranks among the world's top nations in per-capita gross domestic product.

MILESTONES

ABOUT 5725 BC: EARLIEST ARTIFACTS The oldest artifacts found in Ireland were unearthed below Toome Bay, north Lough Neagh, Northern Ireland. A carbon date to about 5725 BC was obtained for woodworking and flint at the site.

4TH CENTURY BC: CELTS Celtic tribes arrived in Ireland around the 4th century BC; their culture flourished and eventually spread to Scotland and elsewhere.

430s AD: ST. PATRICK Born probably in southwest England, Patrick was carried off as a youth by Irish marauders who kept him as a herdsman in Ireland; he escaped but returned around 431 as a priest and later bishop, seeking to convert the Irish to Christianity. According to tradition he used a shamrock to illustrate the mystery of the Trinity; it came to be a symbol of Ireland, and Patrick became Ireland's patron saint.

1014: BRIAN BORU Around 795, the Vikings began a series of invasions along Ireland's east coast, where they founded several settlements, including Dublin, and eventually took the cities of Waterford and Limerick.

In 1014, after nearly 200 years, the Irish king Brian Boru overthrew the Vikings in the Battle of Clontarf. Although he was murdered in his tent at the end of the battle, his name was carried on by his descendants, the O'Brien clan.

12TH CENTURY: IRISH WHISKEY The word "whiskey" comes from the Gaelic phrase "uisge baugh" (pronounced "isj'ka'ba'ha"), meaning "water of life," and whiskey dates back to the 12th century, when it was produced in monasteries throughout Ireland. The monks obtained it by distilling malted barley and other cereals, which had been fermented with yeast.

1169: ENGLISH RULE The Norman rulers of Britain first invaded Ireland in May 1169, when they helped Dermot MacMurrough, deposed king of Leinster, capture Dublin and other towns. Bitter Anglo-Irish conflicts continued over the centuries.

Henry VIII was declared King of Ireland in 1541. The English scored a major victory in July 1690 when William of Orange defeated Irish forces in the Battle of the Boyne. Ireland was formally merged with Great Britain in 1801; the English army occupied Dublin till 1922.

1759: FIRST PINT OF GUINNESS The Guinness brewery was founded by Arthur Guinness on Dec. 31, 1759, when he signed a 9,000-year lease on a building in St. James's Gate, Dublin. About 20 years later he developed a new porter stout that he named after himself; it made his fortune.

By 1883 Guinness was the world's biggest brewery. Nowadays about 10 million glasses of Guinness are downed worldwide each day. In Ireland, most patrons don't request Guinness by name; they just ask the barkeep for a pint of "black."

1845-51: POTATO FAMINE The Irish Potato Famine (often called The Hunger) began in 1845 and lasted until 1851. Estimates of the number who died vary between 500,000 and 1.5 million. Another 1.5 million emigrated during the famine years.

The famine was caused by the failure of the potato crop, infected by a blight. The Irish depended upon the potato as the main item in their diet; a single acre of potatoes could support a family for a year.

1916-22: NATIONALIST REVOLT On April 24, 1916, Easter Monday, Irish nationalists seized several public buildings in Dublin. Outside the main post office, Padraic Pearse declared the formation of an independent Irish Republic. British soldiers swiftly crushed the "Easter Rebellion" and executed the ringleaders.

SUPERLATIVES

LARGEST ISLAND
The largest island off the coast of Ireland is mountainous Achill Island, Co. Mayo. Famous for its dramatic cliffs and sandy beaches, it is only 56 square miles in area, and is connected to the mainland by a bridge.

TALLEST OBELISK
The tallest obelisk in Ireland is the Spire; this thin, stainless steel monument built to mark the new millennium rises 394 feet above O'Connell Street in Dublin. Finally completed in 2003, it was not warmly received by the locals, some of whom dubbed it "The Stiletto in the Ghetto."

LARGEST CRYSTAL BALL The crystal ball that descends at midnight in New York's Times Square on New Year's Eve to signal the start of a New Year was built by the Waterford Crystal Company of Ireland. In use for that event since the year 2000, it weighs 1,070 pounds and is 6 feet in diameter. It contains 504 Waterford crystal triangles, along with 696 multicolored light bulbs, 96 strobe lights, and 90 rotating mirrors.

SOMETHING TO THINK ABOUT

TRULY SQUARE

There are several public "squares" in Dublin, but only one of them is a true square: Mountjoy Square measures 600 feet in length and width.

MIDDLE GROUND

The geographical center of Ireland lies in County Roscommon, 2 miles south of the town of Athlone. Set along both banks of the Shannon River, Athlone was chosen as the site of the principal transmitters of RTE (Ireland's radio and television network) in 1933 because of its central position.

Selected Irish National Records

Highest Point	Carrantouhill, County Kerry	3,415 ft
Longest River	Shannon	224 mi
Largest City	Dublin (metro, 2005)	pop. 1,033,000
Tallest Building	Cork County Hall (Cork)	211 ft
Largest Church	St. Patrick's Cathedral (Dublin)	
Most Famous Artwork	Book of Kells, illuminated Scripture manuscript	created around 700 AD
First Nobel Prize Winner	William Butler Yeats	1932, Literature
First Olympic Champion	Patrick O'Callaghan, hammer throw	1928 Amsterdam Games

The harsh response fueled sympathy for the Republican cause, strengthening *Sinn Fein* ("Ourselves Alone"), a nationalist political movement founded by Arthur Griffith in 1905.

Sinn Fein gained seats in the British parliament, and on Jan. 21, 1919, 28 Irish members met in Dublin and adopted a Declaration of Independence. This led to guerrilla warfare and harsh reprisals by British troops called "Black and Tans."

A compromise measure enacted in Dec. 1920 created two Irish parliaments, one for the 6 northeastern counties, another for the remaining 26. The Dail Eireann (Assembly of Ireland) approved an "Irish Free State" with allegiance to the British crown on Jan. 7, 1922, but treaty opponents of ties with Britain waged guerrilla war against the Free State.

1926: "THE SOLDIER'S SONG" (AMHRÁN NA BHFIANN)
"The Soldier's Song," or *Amhrán Na bhFiann* as it is known in Gaelic, was officially adopted as Ireland's national anthem in 1926. Written by Peadar Kearney and Patrick Heeney in 1907, it gained widespread popularity as the anthem of Irish independence.

1937: NATIONAL FLAG
The Irish flag, a tricolor of green, white, and orange, was first flown in public on March 7, 1848, in Waterford, when Thomas Francis Meagher, leader of the nationalist Young Ireland Movement, addressed a crowd assembled in the street. It was officially adopted as the Irish national flag in 1937. The green represents the older Gaelic and Anglo-Norman element in the population, and the orange the Protestant supporters of William of Orange, while the white symbolizes the ideal of peace between the traditions.

1937: REPUBLIC OF EIRE In 1937, Eamonn de Valera, president of the Executive Council, introduced a new constitution to the Dail Eireann. After much debate, it was adopted, coming into effect Dec. 29. The Irish Free State turned into a "sovereign, independent, democratic state" with a president as head of state and *taoiseach* as prime minister, or head of government.

1938: FIRST PRESIDENT
The first president of Ireland was Dr. Douglas Hyde, who took office June 25, 1938. A leading figure in the preservation of the Irish language, he was nonpolitical, and, though Protestant, was the unanimous choice of the Irish parliament.

1990: FEMALE PRESIDENT
The first woman to become president of the Republic was Mary Robinson, on Dec. 3, 1990. A lawyer, she left the post in 1997 to become UN High Commissioner for Human Rights.

Israel

Total Area: 8,019 sq mi
Population (est. 2005): 6,276,883

The state of Israel is located on the east coast of the Mediterranean Sea. The region was the site of some of the world's oldest civilizations, and of the Promised Land where the Jewish people first settled during the second millennium BC. The ancient kingdom, founded shortly after 1000 BC, fell to a succession of conquerors, and the Jewish population declined over time; Jews eventually were dispersed to many parts of the world. The modern state of Israel was established in 1948 after many decades of Jewish immigration back to Palestine and fighting between Jews, Arabs, and British and French colonial powers. While about 20% of Israel's population is non-Jewish, Israel is the world's only officially Jewish state.

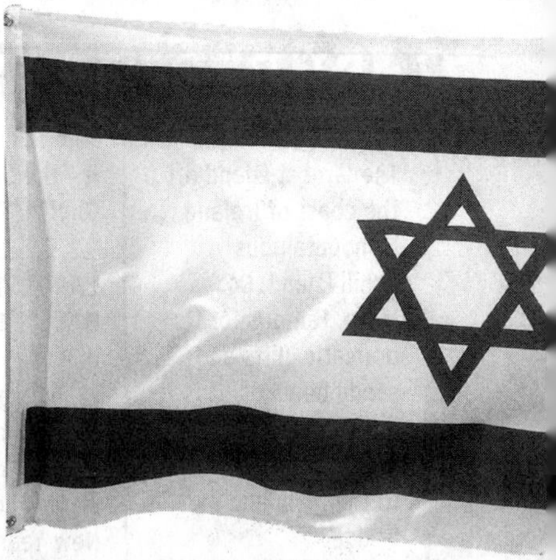

MILESTONES

1882: FIRST ALIYAH Modern Jewish immigration to Palestine occurred in several waves, known as Aliyahs. During the first Aliyah (1882-1903) about 25,000 Jewish immigrants from Europe arrived. By the end of the 1930s, there were about 475,000 Jews in British-mandated Palestine, an estimated 40% of the population.

These were all part of the so-called Zionist movement, aimed at unifying the Jewish people and returning them to their homeland. "Zion" is the name of the hill on which the ancient Temple of Jerusalem stood.

1897: ZIONIST CONGRESS The first Zionist Congress was convened in Basel, Switzerland, Aug. 29-31, 1897. The Hungarian Theodor Herzl and other activists, greatly disturbed by the prevalence of anti-Semitism in Europe, worked to organize Jews across Europe. The Congress laid out a program for the establishment of a Jewish homeland in Palestine.

1909: KIBBUTZ The first kibbutz was founded around 1909 by Jewish settlers in Deganya at the edge of the Sea of Galilee.

Like others that followed, this kibbutz ("community") was a collective village where all property was held in common and each member worked in a designated role according to capacity in return for food, housing, medical care, and so forth in accordance with his or her need. The hot climate and barren land was unfamiliar to many of the first pioneers; it was thought the settlers had a better chance of success if they pooled resources.

1948: INDEPENDENCE DAY On May 14, 1948, amid civil war in British-mandated Palestine, Polish-born David Ben-Gurion (born David Gryn), the first prime minister of Israel, declared Israel's independence. This event marked the first time since ancient times that a Jewish state existed in the world.

1948: HEBREW LANGUAGE Modern Hebrew, *Ivrit*, was declared the official language of Israel in 1948 and is the only language spoken in the world today that is based on an ancient written form. Hebrew gradually ceased to be a spoken language in Roman times, but Hebrew literature has been produced continuously.

Modern Hebrew was developed in the 19th and 20th centuries, largely by the Lithuanian-born scholar Eliezer Ben-Yehuda. He created over 4,000 new words from biblical Hebrew roots.

1948: FLAG The flag of Israel was legally adopted on Oct. 28, 1948, and is based on the flag of the Zionist movement. In the middle is the Star of David, which appeared on King David's shield, according to tradition. The blue stripes at the top and bottom of the flag are based on the blue fringes of Jewish prayer shawls.

1950: JERUSALEM AS CAPITAL On Jan. 23, 1950, the Israeli Knesset (parliament) declared Jerusalem to be the capital of Israel. However, because of Arab claims to East Jerusalem, most countries today have their embassies in Tel Aviv.

1979: CAMP DAVID ACCORDS The first Israeli prime minister to secure peace with one of Israel's neighbors was Menachem Begin. U.S. President Jimmy Carter hosted negotiations with Egyptian President Anwar al-Sadat at Camp David, the presidential retreat in Maryland, and the historic peace accord between Egypt and Israel was signed in Washington, DC, on March 26, 1979.

2003: ASTRONAUT The first Israeli astronaut was Ilan Ramon, a colonel in the Israeli air force who served as a mission specialist on the ill-fated *Columbia* space shuttle flight that blasted off on Jan. 16, 2003. An electrical engineer, the 48-year-old Ramon died with six others when *Columbia* broke apart during reentry into the Earth's atmosphere on Feb. 1, 2003.

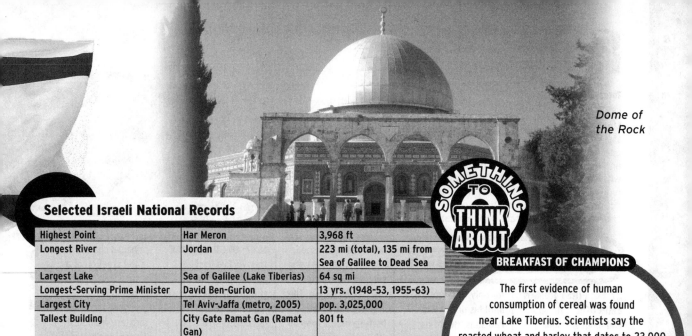

Dome of the Rock

Selected Israeli National Records

Highest Point	Har Meron	3,968 ft
Longest River	Jordan	223 mi (total), 135 mi from Sea of Galilee to Dead Sea
Largest Lake	Sea of Galilee (Lake Tiberias)	64 sq mi
Longest-Serving Prime Minister	David Ben-Gurion	13 yrs. (1948-53, 1955-63)
Largest City	Tel Aviv-Jaffa (metro, 2005)	pop. 3,025,000
Tallest Building	City Gate Ramat Gan (Ramat Gan)	801 ft
First Woman Prime Minister	Golda Meir	1969-74
First Olympic Gold	Gal Fridman, Windsurfing	2004, Athens Games
First Nobel Prize	Samuel Joseph Agnon	1966, Literature

SOMETHING TO THINK ABOUT

BREAKFAST OF CHAMPIONS

The first evidence of human consumption of cereal was found near Lake Tiberius. Scientists say the roasted wheat and barley that dates to 23,000 years ago resembles modern-day breakfast cereals. Interestingly, a nearby site claims to have the earliest evidence of bedding, dating to roughly the same era.

SUPERLATIVES

LOWEST POINT ON EARTH Israel borders the Dead Sea, which, at 1,348 feet below sea level, is the lowest point on Earth. The Dead Sea waters also have the highest salt and mineral content in the world averaging 30% salinity near the surface, making it one of the world's most popular natural spas. Locals like to say that anybody can float on its waters.

LARGEST DIAMOND MARKET The Israel Diamond Exchange is the world's biggest diamond market, where about 20,000 people buy, sell, and appraise diamonds every day. The exchange sees about 50% of the world's rough cut diamonds, and two thirds of those are then sold in the U.S.

In response to concerns over the use of diamond revenues to fund African rebel groups' military activities, Israel was also the first country to adopt the Kimberley Process, which certifies diamonds as "conflict free."

OLDEST HEBREW SCRIPTURES
The Dead Sea Scrolls are one of the most important archeological finds in Israel. These scrolls were discovered by Bedouin shepherds at Qumran in 1947 and contain the earliest manuscripts of Hebrew Scriptures, some dating to the third century BC. Other scrolls in the Qumran collection date to the first century AD and illustrate common teachings between Judaism and early Christianity.

WESTERN WALL
The most visited site in Israel is the most holy site in Judaism, the Western Wall in Jerusalem. Often called "The Wailing Wall" by non-Jews because of the heartfelt prayers performed by visitors, it is all that remains of the Second Temple destroyed by the Romans in 70 AD.

Since then, Jews from around the world have made pilgrimages to the site. Many visitors, including Pope John Paul II in 2000, write a prayer on a slip of paper that is inserted into a crack in the wall. There are organizations that will deliver prayers to the Wall on behalf of those who cannot visit.

THE MACCABIAH
In 1932, the first international Jewish Olympics, known as The Maccabiah, were held in Tel Aviv. The games were created to foster unity among Jews worldwide, and the first event involved 390 athletes from 14 countries.

The games were suspended from 1935 to 1950. Since 1953, the Maccabiah has been held every four years in Israel and is both the world's largest Jewish event and the third largest sporting event in the world. The 17th Maccabiah games were held July 10-21, 2005.

Italy

The Coliseum

Total Area: 116,306 sq mi
Population (est. 2005): 58,103,033

Modern Italy was formed in the mid-19th century from city-states formed in the Middle Ages. The boot-shaped Italian peninsula jutting into the Mediterranean Sea was the seat of the ancient Roman Empire, and much of its history is intertwined with that of the Roman Catholic Church. Italy today has the highest proportion of (at least nominal) Catholics—97%—of any country in the world, and Vatican City, headquarters of the church, is a tiny separate nation located inside Rome.

MILESTONES

27 BC: FIRST ROMAN EMPEROR The first and longest reigning Roman emperor was Augustus, who ruled from 27 BC to 14 AD. Born Gaius Octavius (Octavian) in 63 BC, he was the great nephew and adopted son of Julius Caesar. He slowly gained influence after Caesar's assassination (44 BC), and especially after defeating Marc Antony and Cleopatra (31 BC).

In 27 BC he was given the title Augustus.

394 AD: LAST ROMAN EMPEROR The last person to rule over an undivided Roman empire was Theodosius the Great.

Theodosius at first ruled only in the eastern part; he took over the west as well in Sept. 394, two years after the western emperor was killed in a revolt. But he ruled the united empire for only four months, until his death. His two sons, Honorius and Arcadius, split the empire between them, and it was never united again.

EARLY 1300s: *DIVINE COMEDY* The Florentine poet Dante Alighieri composed one of the first, and greatest, pieces of literature written in Italian, as opposed to Latin. Dante began writing his *Divine Comedy* around 1307 and finished it shortly before his death in 1321.

Hundreds of editions have been published, and it inspired artists such as Boccaccio and Michelangelo. The country's first long feature film, *L'Inferno* (1911), was based on the epic poem.

1400s: RENAISSANCE In prosperous Florence, figures such as the architect Filippo Brunelleschi (1377-1446; built the dome of the Cathedral of Santa Maria dei Fiore), the sculptor Donatello (1386?-1466), and the painter Masaccio (1401-27?) applied lessons learned from classical manuscripts and ruins to develop new forms of art that started off the Italian Renaissance, with its many works of genius.

1637: OPERA HOUSE The world's first public opera house still in operation today is the Tron family's Teatro San Cassiano. It opened in Venice in 1637, with a performance of Francesco Manelli's *L'Andromeda*.

1830: PIZZERIA Naples is the home of pizza. The first pizzeria is believed to be the Antica Pizzeria Port'Alba, which opened there in 1830 and is still in business today.

1830-61: RISORGIMENTO Giuseppe Mazzini, Count Camillo Cavour, and Giuseppe Garibaldi were the three principal characters in the creation of a unified Italy. Starting in the 1830s, they gradually reclaimed territory from Austria, France, Spain, and the Papal States through military campaigns and political alliances, uniting most of Italy into one kingdom under King Victor Emmanuel II by 1861.

1870: NATIONAL CAPITAL By March 17, 1861, Italy—excluding Rome and Venice—was a unified kingdom with Turin as its capital. The seat of government was moved to Florence in 1865. Italian troops eventually entered Rome on Sept. 20, 1870, and the capital was moved there.

Selected Italian National Records

Highest Point	Monte Bianco de Courmayeur	15,577 ft
Longest River	Po	405 mi
Tallest Volcano in Europe	Mount Etna	10,900 ft
Largest City	Milan (metro, 2005)	pop. 4,007,000
Tallest Building	Telecom Italia (Naples)	423 ft
Most Expensive Italian Old Master Painting at Auction	Jacopo da Pontormo, *Portrait of a Halberdier* (1537)	$35,200,000 in May 1989 to the J. Paul Getty Museum
First Gladiatorial Match	The sons of Junius Brutus Pera ordered slaves to fight to the death to honor their father at his funeral	264 BC
Oldest Soccer Franchise	Genoa	Sept. 7, 1893

Leaning Tower Of Pisa

SOMETHING TO THINK ABOUT

THE JULIET CLUB

Though it has been four centuries since Shakespeare's heroine Juliet first died for her love on stage, thousands of letters are still sent to Romeo's darling in her hometown of Verona. The letters, from Italy and all over the world, sometimes are addressed simply to "Juliet, Verona, Italy," and most are from women. The first of these modern letters arrived at Juliet's tomb in 1937, a year after the release of George Cukor's movie *Romeo and Juliet*. Since 1990, seven "Juliet secretaries" have responded to every letter. The club also awards the "Dear Juliet Prize" on St. Valentine's Day to the authors of the most beautiful letters received that year.

CAPPUCCINO GOUGING

When Italy switched over to the euro in 2002, inflation was felt everywhere, as stores rounded up prices on practically everything. But when a retired man from Ladispoli near Rome was charged one euro on Jan. 1, 2002, for the morning cappuccino that cost 1,500 lire (0.77 euro) the day before, he sued the Quelli Della Notte coffee bar for price-gouging. On Jan. 15, 2004, a judge ruled in the man's favor and ordered the bar to refund the 23 euro cents and cover legal fees.

1943-45: LIBERATION Allied forces invaded Sicily in July 1943 and liberated the entire country from Nazi control by April 1945. This ended nearly 20 years of rule under the fascist dictator Benito Mussolini, as well as German domination during World War II.

1946: THE REPUBLIC After the war, calls for a republican form of government forced King Victor Emmanuel to give up the throne. Italy then declared itself a republic, adopted a new constitution, and set about rebuilding.

1946: VESPA Corradino D'Ascanio designed the popular Italian scooter, the Vespa, in 1946. Modeled in part on aircraft landing gears, the Vespa 98 was first produced in April 1946 in Pontedera, Tuscany. It had three gears and a top speed of 45 miles per hour.

1947: FERRARI On May 11, 1947, Enzo Ferrari debuted his first car with the "Prancing Horse" on the hood, the legendary Ferrari automobile. The first Ferrari was a 12-cylinder Spider Tipo 125 with a top speed of 114 mph. Two weeks later in Rome, the Ferrari won its first automobile race.

1947: NATIONAL FLAG The Tricolore became Italy's official flag on March 24, 1947, but it had been used by smaller Italian republics as early as 1797. It became the national standard with the unification of Italy in 1861. The use of vertical green, white, and red bands was influenced by France, which controlled much of northern Italy in the 1790s.

SUPERLATIVES

OLDEST ROMAN ROAD The first Roman road, Via Appia, still handles pedestrian and vehicular traffic today. In 312 BC, as Rome was gaining power, a prominent early Roman politician, Appius Claudius, ordered the road's construction.

About 20 feet wide, the Appian Way was intended to speed military travel and trade. Beginning at Rome's Porta San Sebastiano, the oldest segment stretched 132 miles south to Capua.

In 71 BC, Marcus Licinius Crassus had 6,000 captives from Spartacus's failed slave rebellion crucified along the road.

OLDEST UNIVERSITY (EUROPE) The University of Bologna is considered the oldest in Europe. It separated from the nearby ecclesiastical school around 1088, and received its charter from Holy Roman Emperor Frederick in 1158. Original studies included civil and canon law. Schools of medicine and philosophy were founded around 1200.

OLDEST FILM FESTIVAL (WORLD) The first Venice International Film Festival was staged in 1932 as part of the 18th Venice Biennale. It opened with a screening of Rouben Mamoulian's *Dr. Jekyll and Mr. Hyde*. Although there were no official awards, an audience referendum voted René Clair's *A nous la liberté* (France) best film and Nikolaj Ekk best director for *Putjovka v zizn* (USSR).

Japan

Total Area: 145,883 sq mi
Population (est. 2005): 127,417,244

Japan (official name *Dai Nippon*–"Great Origin of the Sun") consists mostly of a crescent-shaped archipelago stretching 1,500 miles from Hokkaido near Russia's Siberian Sakhalin Island in the north to semitropical Ryukyu Islands off the coast of Taiwan in the southwest. The four main islands (out of 6,852 in all) are, from north to south, Hokkaido, Honshu (considered the mainland), Shikoku, and Kyushu.

MILESTONES

AROUND 10,000 BC: ISLANDS SETTLED It is believed that humans first arrived in Japan about 500,000 BC when it was still connected to the mainland. Around 10,000 BC, melting ice caused sea levels to rise, forming islands, and Japan's earliest civilizations flourished in isolation. The people subsisted by hunting, gathering, and fishing. Their pottery, from about 10,000 to 8,000 BC, is among the world's oldest.

40 BC: CHRYSANTHEMUM THRONE Japan's monarchy, named after the flower in its coat of arms, is the world's oldest. According to tradition, Emperor Jimmu founded the monarchy in 40 BC and the current emperor, Akihito, is the 125th *tenno* (heavenly ruler or god-king). Japanese tradition held that the emperors were deities descended from the sun goddess Amaterasu Omikami, Japan's founder. This belief was renounced after Japan's defeat in World War II.

6TH CENTURY: SUMO WRESTLING Sumo began around 500 AD as part of Japanese harvest rituals and was refined during the Edo period (1603-1867) as entertainment for the merchant class. Two opponents (*rikishi*) wearing loincloths (*mawashi*) try to drive each other out of a circular ring or force some part of the other's body to the ground. *Yokozuna*, the highest rank, has been achieved by fewer than 70 wrestlers in the past 300 years.

The most successful sumo wrestler is Mitsugu Akimoto, known as Chiyonofuji, who won 1,045 career bouts from 1970 to 1991.

681: SHINTO Shinto, the ancient religion of Japan, holds that sacred spirits can be found in both living and non-living things. Shinto was not even named or organized until Buddhism arrived and began to overshadow it. In 681, Emperor Temmu called for the compilation of Japanese myths and cultural practices to lay a foundation for Shinto and distinguish it from Buddhism.

Presently, over one-half of all Japanese people practice both Shinto and Buddhism.

1192: FIRST SHOGUN By the 12th century, the emperor's power had weakened. In 1185, after a five-year war, Minamoto Yoritomo, head of the Minamoto clan, set up a military capital at Kamakura, near Tokyo. The emperor was given a reduced role in government. After seven years, Yoritomo took the title of *shogun* ("generalissimo") and formed a military dictatorship. In the shogunate, the samurai became a warrior upper class and followed a rigid code of ethics.

1854: OPENING TO THE WEST After almost 200 years of isolation, Japan was induced to open its ports to trade with the U.S. and sign a treaty, following the arrival in Feb. 1854 of a naval fleet commanded by Com. Matthew Perry. Many Japanese were angered, and began to favor a stronger government that could better fight off foreign domination. This led to the restoration of the emperor in 1867, when Prince Mutsuhito became Emperor Meiji.

In 1868, the shogunate was toppled. In 1889, Japan adopted a constitution.

1904-05: RUSSO-JAPANESE WAR Japan and Russia went to war over each country's expansion into Korea and China. Japan defeated Russia and in the process decimated the Russian fleet. It was the first time in modern history that an eastern nation defeated a European one. The war also established Japan as a world power.

1941-45: WORLD WAR II Shortly before 8 AM on Sunday, Dec. 7, 1941, Japanese carrier-based airplanes attacked the U.S. Pacific Fleet at Pearl Harbor, HI, destroying the fleet there and bringing the U.S. into World War II. By early 1945, with the fall of Okinawa, Japan was clearly losing in the Pacific, but the Japanese did not surrender until Aug. 14, after the U.S. dropped atomic bombs on Hiroshima (Aug. 6) and Nagasaki (Aug. 9).

1945-52: REBUILDING Japan surrendered to the Allies on Sept. 2, 1945. Then came a period

Selected Japanese National Records

Highest Point	Mount Fuji	12,389 ft
Longest River	Shinano	228 mi
Largest City	Tokyo (metro, 2005)	pop. 35,327,000
Tallest Building	Yokohama Landmark Tower (Yokohama)	972 ft
Longest-Ruling Monarch	Emperor Showa (Hirohito)[1]	62 years (Dec. 25, 1926 to Jan. 7, 1989)
First Olympic Gold Medalist	Mikio Oda, men's triple jump	1928 Amsterdam Games
First Japanese-born Major League Baseball Player	Masanori Murakami, pitcher (San Francisco Giants)	Sept. 1, 1964 to Oct. 1, 1965
First Nobel Laureate	Hideki Yukawa	1949, Physics
First Oscar Winner	*Rashomon*	1951, Honorary Award for Best Foreign Film
First Japanese-born Grammy winner	Seiji Ozawa, conductor; with Itzhak Perlman, soloist, and Boston Symphony Orchestra (1980)	Best Classical Performance, Instrumental Soloist (Or Soloists) with Orchestra; *Berg Violin Concerto/* Stravinksy: *Violin Concerto in D*
Biggest Bank (world)	Mizuho Holdings	$1.136 trillion

(1) Longest-reigning since reliable historical information has been available.

SUPERLATIVES

MOST MOVIES IN SAME ROLE Kiyoshi Atsumi appeared 48 times as the character "Tora-san" in the beloved Japanese comedy movie series *Otoko wa Tsurai yo* ("It's Tough Being a Man"). One of Japan's most popular stars, Atsumi was awarded the prestigious People's Honor award shortly after his death in 1996.

MOST VENDING MACHINES While the U.S. has the most vending machines in all, Japan has the most per capita. There were about 5.6 million vending machines (called *jido-hanbaiki*) in 2001—about one for every 23 people. They sell everything, from eggs to toys to underwear to pet beetles.

SOMETHING TO THINK ABOUT

EMPEROR OF SWAT

Sadaharu Oh is professional baseball's all-time leading home-run hitter. In his long career for the Yomiuri Giants (1959-1980), Oh hit 868 dingers, which is 113 more than Hank Aaron's Major League record of 755. Oh honed his unique style of batting through the martial art of Aikido training and practice with the Japanese longsword.

KARAOKE

From *karappo* (empty) and *okesutura* (orchestra), the term *karaoke* once referred to bar bands who would accompany singing customers. When Inoue Daisuke, a musician from Nishinomiya, couldn't travel to a gig in 1970, he sent a tape instead. It went so well that he leased 11 homemade coin-operated boxes to bars in nearby Kobe. The idea quickly became a hit in Japan; by the 1990s it had spread to the U.S. Americans spend over $200 million a year on Karaoke equipment and music. Daisuke himself never made any money on his idea. He never tried karaoke singing himself until his 59th birthday in 1999.

of U.S. occupation. Japan was stripped of its mainland claims in Asia, and reforms were enacted. A democratic constitution took effect in 1947, and on April 28, 1952, Japan's full sovereignty was restored. Japan grew to become a major world economic power.

1999: FLAG At the heart of the *Hinoma*, Japan's national flag, is the sun, a red circle that is surrounded by white. A state symbol for centuries, the flag was not officially recognized by Japan's Parliament (the Diet) until 1999.

Mexico

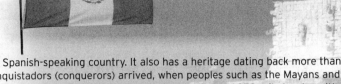

Total Area: 761,606 sq mi
Population (est. 2005): 106,202,903

Mexico is the world's most populous Spanish-speaking country. It also has a heritage dating back more than a millennium before the Spanish conquistadors (conquerors) arrived, when peoples such as the Mayans and Aztecs developed advanced civilizations in the region. To the north, Mexico shares a 1,958-mile border with the U.S., and its culture and history are widely intermingled with those of its northern neighbor. About 25 million people, more than half of the Latino population in the U.S., are of Mexican descent.

MILESTONES

1ST OR 2ND CENTURY BC: CITY OF THE GODS The remains of the ancient "City of the Gods," 30 miles northeast of present-day Mexico City, suggest that it was a major urban center, the first in the Americas. Settlement began there in the 1st or 2nd century BC, and by 200 AD, the city commanded enough labor to construct its famed stepped pyramids, or ziggurats.

At its peak the city sprawled over 8 square miles and housed up to 200,000 people, but around 700-800 it was destroyed by fire. Its language—and even name—at the time are unknown; it is now called by the name the Aztecs gave it centuries later, Teotihuacán ("City of the Gods").

6TH CENTURY AD: CHICHÉN ITZÁ
Mayan culture was peaking when its Itza tribe settled Mexico's Yucatán Peninsula around 515. The tribe named the settlement Chichén Itzá ("Mouth of the Wells of Itza") to honor two sacred wells there. Though the settlement was abandoned for several centuries, upon return the Mayans constructed an elaborate city with temples, pyramids, a ball court, and an astronomical observatory.

As Mayan civilization began to decline around 900, and the Itzá left, the militaristic Toltec tribe of central Mexico took over the city until its decline around 1200.

1325: AZTECS AND TENOCHTITLÁN
Around the 1200s a group of tribes from the north arrived in Mexico, and by 1325 the leading Mexica, or Aztec, tribe had started a settlement in a marshy area that later became the site of Mexico City. Mexica legend had foretold the founding of a great civilization in a marshy area where a cactus grew out of a rock and, perched on the cactus, an eagle ate a snake. According to legend, Mexica priests saw the omen on arriving there.

Mexica built an elaborate city with dams, canals, pyramids, temples, and palaces; early Spanish explorers called it "the Venice of the New World." Over two centuries the Aztec empire expanded to stretch from central Mexico to what is now the Guatemalan border.

1519-21: CONQUISTADORS
The Spanish invasion of the Aztec Empire, led by Hernán Cortés, was sparked by rumors of vast reserves of gold and silver. Cortés landed near modern-day Veracruz on April 21, 1519, and conquered the Aztecs within two years.

Initially, Aztec Emperor Montezuma II believed Cortés was the god Quetzalcoatl ("the Plumed Serpent") and had welcomed him with gold and silver. But tensions escalated and, with the population weakened by new European diseases, the Spanish captured the city on Aug. 13, 1521. Cortés had Tenochtitlán razed and built Mexico City on the ruins.

1810-21: INDEPENDENCE
Mexico's independence was sparked on Sept. 16, 1810, by Miguel Hidalgo y Costilla, a Catholic priest. Angered by the treatment of native peoples by the Spanish, he called on the Amerindians and mestizos of his parish to rise up. The Spanish were vanquished in a long, bloody conflict that lasted over 10 years.

Captured and executed in 1811, Hidalgo became known as "the father of the Revolution." Every year at midnight on Sept. 16, Mexicans celebrate independence by shouting his rallying cry, "Viva Mexico."

1823: FLAG
The nation's tricolor flag of red, white, and green was first proposed by Emperor Agustín de Iturbide in 1821. The green represents the independence movement; the white, Catholic purity; and the red, unity. The emblem of the eagle, snake, and cactus represents Aztec lore from the founding of Tenochtitlán. The flag was officially adopted April 14, 1823.

1846-48: MEXICAN-AMERICAN WAR
The U.S. drive for expansion led to land disputes with Mexico. War was officially declared May 13, 1846. It ended with the signing of the Treaty of Guadalupe Hidalgo on Feb. 2, 1848. The victorious U.S. gained more than 525,000 square miles of territory, stretching from California to Texas. The Gadsden Purchase of 1853 gave an additional strip of territory to the U.S.

Selected Mexican National Records

Highest Point	Pico de Orizaba o Citlaltépetl Volcano	18,855 ft
Longest River	Rio Grande (portion)	1,248 mi
Largest Lake	Chapala	314 sq mi
Largest City	Mexico City (metro, 2005)	pop. 19,013,000
Tallest Building	Torre Mayor (Mexico City)	738 ft
Longest-Serving Head of State (since 1821).	Porfirio Díaz	30 years (1876-1880; 1884-1911)
First Nobel Laureate	Alfonso García Robles	1982, Peace Prize
First Oscar Winner	Anthony Quinn[1]	1952, Best Supporting Actor, *Viva Zapata!*
First Mexican-born Grammy winners	Los Tigres del Norte	1987 Best Mexican-American Performance for *"Gracias! America Sin Fronteras"*

(1) Born Antonio Rudolfo Oaxaca Quinn in Chihuahua, Mexico, Anthony Quinn also won another Best Supporting Actor Oscar for *Lust for Life* (1956).

SOMETHING TO THINK ABOUT

OUR LADY OF GUADALUPE

According to Catholic legend, in Dec. 1531 the Virgin Mary appeared to St. Juan Diego, a Catholic Nahua Indian, on Tepeyac Hill in Guadalupe. Afterward, Juan Diego asked the bishop of Mexico to build a church on the site as the apparition had requested. For proof of what he'd seen, he offered Castilian roses wrapped in his cape, which bore an image of the Virgin. The bishop built the chapel, and millions converted to Christianity. Every year, millions of travelers visit the Basilica of Our Lady of Guadalupe (constructed 1974-76) in Mexico City, where the cape bearing the Virgin's image is displayed.

DAY OF THE DEAD (EL DÍA DE LOS MUERTOS)

On el Día de los Muertos (the Day of the Dead), Mexico celebrates the Catholic holy-day of All Souls (Nov. 2). Families remember deceased loved ones and welcome their spirits home. Time is spent preparing their favorite meals. Balloons or toys are placed on the graves of children, and flowers, bread, and votive candles on those of adults. The day isn't supposed to be sad, but rather a chance to celebrate and remember. Skull-shaped candy made of amaranth seeds, sugar, and chocolate is a favorite treat, while decorative skulls, coffins, and skeletons line homes.

1854: ANTHEM On Nov. 12, 1853, President General Mariano Arista invited poets to compete to write the words for a national anthem. The winning entry was Francisco González Bocanegra's *Mexicanos al Grito de Guerra* ("Mexicans to the Cry of Battle"). Spaniard Jaime Nunó's tune "God and Freedom" won the music competition. The anthem was first performed on Sept. 16, 1854, Mexican Independence Day.

1933: MEXICAN-BORN MAJOR LEAGUER Mel Almada (Baldomero Melo Almada Quiros) was the first Mexican to play major league baseball in the U.S. Almada played for four teams and batted .284 during his seven-season career, starting in 1933.

On July 25, 1937, he scored nine runs in a double-header for the Washington Senators, tying the record for runs scored over 18 innings.

1968: OLYMPICS The 1968 Olympic torch followed Christopher Columbus's route from Palos, Spain, to San Salvador before heading to Mexico City for the first, and so far only, Olympic Games staged in a Latin American country. The city's altitude, 7,710 feet, was the highest on record for the Summer Games and hindered endurance event competitors while helping sprinters break records.

Mexico won a record nine medals (3 each of gold, silver, and bronze), including two golds in boxing.

SUPERLATIVES

LARGEST CRATER (WORLD) 65 million years ago, an asteroid 7.5-9 miles wide crashed into the earth with a blast equaling that of 100 million megatons of TNT. The collision kicked up enough dust to darken the world for years. Most scientists believe it partly or wholly caused the extinction of 75% of the earth's species, including the dinosaurs. The Chicxulub crater, on the northern tip of the Yucatán Peninsula, is about 112 miles in diameter and is now buried under a half mile of sediment.

New Zealand

Total Area: 103,738 sq mi
Population (est. 2005): 4,035,461

Located in the South Pacific Ocean, New Zealand is geographically remote from other nations. Australia, its nearest neighbor, is more than 1,000 miles away. Composed of two major islands (North and South Islands) and a number of smaller islands, New Zealand has a coastline of 9,404 miles, more than half the coastal length of the U.S. The country's rugged grandeur was the backdrop to one of the most successful movie trilogies of all-time, *The Lord of the Rings*, directed by native Kiwi Peter Jackson.

MILESTONES

C. 950 AD: FIRST MAORI SETTLEMENT New Zealand was mostly unpopulated until the first Maori settlers arrived from Polynesia about 1,000 years ago. They sailed to New Zealand in *waka hourua* (double-hulled sailing canoes). At the time, the eastern coast of the North Island was inhabited by the Moriori people; some were absorbed into the Maori settlers and others went to the Chatham Islands.

The islands that would become New Zealand remained unknown to the rest of the world until 1642, when they were sighted by the Dutch explorer Abel Janszoon Tasman. Though Tasman named the islands "Staten Landt," Dutch mapmakers labeled the land "Nieuw Zeeland."

1840: TREATY OF WAITANGI In the 1840s, New Zealand was still populated mainly by Maori, but British missionaries and other settlers were active on the islands. An unsuccessful French attempt at colonization led the British to conclude the Treaty of Waitangi with the Maoris on Feb. 6, 1840. Signed by Maori chieftains, it ceded New Zealand to the British for guarantees that Maori landownership rights would be protected.

However, as European settlement increased, many Maoris lost their land, leading to a series of violent uprisings. A permanent peace was established in 1871, when the Maori gained representation in New Zealand's Parliament.

1893: WOMEN'S SUFFRAGE On Sept. 19, 1893, New Zealand became the first nation in the world to give all women the right to vote in national elections. The parliamentary passage of the Electoral Bill was the culmination of years of women's suffrage campaigns dating back to 1870, when the writings of Mary Muller first sparked political debate on the topic.

1898: OLD AGE PENSIONS New Zealand was the first nation to introduce a pension for senior citizens. The 1898 Pensions Act established a state-funded pension for people aged 65 and over.

1902: FLAG New Zealand briefly had a flag chosen by British colonials and a Maori council, in the 1830s, but it was replaced by the British Union Jack in 1840. The islands didn't have their own flag again until March 24, 1902, when the British Parliament approved the New Zealand Ensign Act. The design, adopted on June 12, 1902, consists of a dark blue field with the British flag in the top left-hand corner and the constellation of the Southern Cross represented by four five-pointed red stars.

1907: DOMINION OF NEW ZEALAND New Zealand gained self-government in 1907, when it became a dominion of Great Britain, and the nation's sovereignty was recognized by the Statute of Westminster in 1931, although New Zealand's Parliament did not formally adopt the statute until 1947.

1988: BUNGEE JUMP FACILITY New Zealander A.J. Hackett, who had bungee-jumped off the Eiffel Tower in June 1987, opened the first commercial bungee jump facility at the Kawaru Bridge, Queenstown, on Nov. 12, 1988. That day 28 people paid about $75 each to leap off the 141-foot-high bridge with a bungee cord attached to their ankles.

1997: WOMAN PRIME MINISTER Jenny Shipley became the first woman to serve as New Zealand's prime minister on Dec. 8, 1997.

She was appointed to succeed Jim Bolger as leader of the National Party, and so became prime minister of the coalition government.

The original coalition collapsed on Aug. 18, 1998, but with the support of a new coalition Shipley continued to serve, until her party lost the national election held Nov. 27, 1999.

Selected New Zealand National Records

Tallest Building[1]	Sky Tower, Auckland	1,076 ft
Highest Point	Mount Cook, or Aoraki	12,349 ft
Largest Island	South Island	58,384 sq mi
Largest City	Auckland (metro, 2005)	pop. 1,152,000
Largest Lake	Lake Taupo	237 sq mi
Longest-Serving Prime Minister	Richard John Seddon	13 years, 41 days, 1893-1906
First Nobel Laureate	Ernest Rutherford	1908, Chemistry
First Olympic Champion[2]	Malcolm Champion	4 x 200M freestyle relay (1912 Stockholm Games)

(1) Includes antenna. (2) Born in New Zealand, Champion was a part of the Australia-New Zealand Olympic team that competed in 1908 and 1912.

SUPERLATIVES

MOST NATIONAL ANTHEMS New Zealand is one of only two countries in the world (the other is Denmark) to have two official national anthems. One is the British "God Save the Queen," played in New Zealand only when a British royal is present. At other times, "God Defend New Zealand" is played.

The words of the latter were written by Irish-born Thomas Bracken in 1879, to music composed by John Joseph Woods in 1875. In 1977 this anthem was elevated to equal status with "God Save the Queen."

SOUTHERNMOST CAPITAL Wellington, which became the capital in 1865, is the southernmost capital city in the world. It was originally known as *Te Upoko o te Ika a Maui* ("the head of Maui's fish" in Maori). According to Maori legend, a fish pulled to the surface by Polynesian navigator Maui became the North Island, on which Wellington is situated.

LONGEST PLACE NAME New Zealand's longest place name, and one of the longest place names in the world, is *Taumatawhakatangihangakoauauotamateaturipukakapikimaungahoronukupokaiwhenuakitanatahu*, which means "the place where Tamatea, the man with the big knees, who slid, climbed, and swallowed mountains, known as 'landeater,' played his flute to his loved one." Locals call it "Taumata."

OLDEST WOODEN SHIP The world's oldest wooden merchant ship still afloat is the *Edwin Fox*, which is kept at Picton in Marlborough, South Island. Built in 1853 out of Burmese teak, the *Edwin Fox* is also the last surviving ship that had been chartered to take convicts from Britain to Australia.

All that remains of the ship today is an open hulk, but it still floats.

NO PENNIES FROM NEW ZEALAND

In 1989 New Zealand withdrew all one-cent and two-cent coins from circulation. If an item costs $1.01 or $1.02, and the customer is paying cash, then the price is rounded down to $1. If the product costs $1.03 or $1.04, the price is rounded up to $1.05. The government announced in 2005 that it also intends to do away with the five-cent coin, believing it will make transactions simpler and save taxpayers another $2.8 million in minting costs.

SOMETHING TO THINK ABOUT

DON'T MESS WITH THE CHEERLEADERS

New Zealand's national rugby team traditionally performs the *Haka*, a Maori war dance, before each game. The fierce chant, accompanied by foot-stamping, chest-beating, and tongue-baring, is intended to fill opponents with unease. In translation, the song goes "It is death! It is death!/It is life! It is life!/ This is the hairy person/who caused the sun to shine/Keep abreast! Keep abreast!/ The rank! Hold fast!/Into the sun that shines!"

WHAT'S IN A NAME?

Not only does New Zealand have two national anthems, it has two official names: New Zealand and *Aotearoa*. The latter is the nation's Maori name and means "land of the long white cloud."

KAKAPO AND SHEEP

New Zealand is home to one of the world's rarest and most unusual birds: the flightless kakapo, a ground-living parrot. The kakapo, once widespread, at first had no mammalian predators; when settlers introduced new animals the kakapo was nearly wiped out, because it could not fly to escape. Only about 60 of the protected parrots now survive. Sheep in New Zealand are far more plentiful. There are 40 million of them, or about 10 times as many sheep as people.

Nigeria

Total Area: 356,669 sq mi
Population (est. 2005): 128,765,768

Nigeria is Africa's most populous country. Located on the western coast of Africa, it is home to people from nearly every native African ethnic group—some 250 cultures in all. The four biggest ethnic groups, making up 60% of the population, are Hausa, Fulani, Yoruba, and Igbo. Nigeria was ruled by Britain during the first half of the 20th century; in the post-colonial era the nation has struggled with civil war and dictatorship. In 1999, Nigeria held its first democratic election in decades. Its official language is English, but many indigenous languages are spoken.

MILESTONES

500 BC: NOK The Nok tribe is one of the earliest known to have settled in large areas of what is Nigeria today. Remnants of the Nok culture indicate that the tribe was thriving as early as 500 BC. Its best-known art works are terracotta sculptures of human figures, which are the earliest known in sub-Saharan Africa. Skilled artists and craftsmanship were respected in Nok culture, a tradition that spread to other West African societies.

16TH CENTURY: SLAVE TRADE North Africans sold slaves to Europeans for centuries before the discovery of the New World. When Europeans began arriving in America, the demand for African slaves increased, driven by a need for cheap labor to harvest the new land's riches.

For 400 years (from the 16th to the 19th centuries), Portuguese, Spanish, and British traders took large numbers of slaves (10 to 30 million) from Africa, mostly with the cooperation of local rulers. The majority of the slaves were from the area now occupied by Benin, Togo, and Nigeria.

1861–1960: COLONIAL PERIOD As part of its territorial expansion in the 19th century, Britain colonized the port of Lagos in 1861. With a West African base for its trade routes, Britain quickly moved to expand its sphere of influence in the region. By 1901, the British had declared Nigeria a protectorate, and in 1914 they established complete control, declaring it a colony.

Over time, the British territory split into regions dominated by different ethnic groups—the Hausa-Fulani in the North, the Yoruba in the southwest, and the Igbo in the southeast. Rivalries exploded into civil war following independence in 1960.

1956: FIRST OIL FIND After nearly 50 years of exploration, the Royal Dutch Shell Company in 1956 became the first to discover oil deposits in Nigeria large enough for commercial development. The first offshore oil finds were made by three American companies, Gulf, Mobil, and Texaco, in 1963.

Nigeria is Africa's largest oil producer and currently the 11th largest in the world.

1958: NATIONAL FLAG Nigeria's national flag, designed in 1958 by Taiwo Akinkunmi, is three vertical stripes, green, white, and green. The green represents agriculture, and the white represents peace and unity.

1967-70: BIAFRA WAR An Igbo-led military junta ruled Nigeria in the mid-1960s, sparking tensions with other ethnic groups. After a 1966 massacre of up to 10,000 Igbos in the North, the eastern-based Igbo military rulers declared eastern Nigeria the Republic of Biafra in May 1967. A three-year civil war ensued, with Biafra surrendering in Jan. 1970.

Despite intense ethnic polarization and at least 1 million dead, the resulting government followed a policy of non-retribution. Subsequent division of Nigeria into smaller states produced better representation for individual ethnic groups.

1976: ABUJA: A PLANNED CAPITAL In 1976, the Nigerian government decided to move its capital from the coastal city of Lagos to a more central location, developing the nation's first planned city.

Designed by the Department of Architecture at Ahmadu University in Zaria, Abuja was built in the 1980s and officially became the nation's capital in 1991. It is located amid rolling grasslands in an area not closely identified with any one ethnic group and has a relatively pleasant climate and environment.

Towering over the nearby government offices is Aso Rock, a granite outcrop 1,300 feet high. The name "Aso Rock" for Nigerians represents the seat of government.

Selected Nigerian National Records

Highest Point	Mt. Dimlang	6,700 ft
Longest River	Niger	2,600 mi (total); about 690 mi in Nigeria
Largest City	Lagos (metro, 2005)	pop., 11,135,000
Tallest Building	National Oil Headquarters (Lagos)	272 ft
Longest-Serving Head of State (post-1960)	Olusegun Obasanjo, former military ruler, current president	3 years, 7.5 months as military ruler (1976-79); elected president 1999; reelected 2003
First Olympic Medalist	Nojim Maiyegun, Light Middleweight Boxing, bronze medal	1964 Tokyo Games

SUPERLATIVES

LARGEST OIL AND GAS RESERVES (AFRICA) · Nigeria and Libya have the biggest crude oil reserves in Africa. Depending on who's doing the measuring, each country has reserves ranging somewhere between 20 billion and 40 billion barrels. Similarly, Nigeria and Algeria have the biggest natural gas reserves in the continent. Estimates for each country range between 120 trillion and 180 trillion cubic feet of gas.

1986: NOBEL LAUREATE
Wole Soyinka, a playwright, poet, novelist, and critic, was the first black African to win the Nobel Prize for literature, in 1986. Soyinka was born in Nigeria in 1934 as a member of the Yoruba tribe. Although his works are in English, he drew heavily upon Yoruba myth and culture, and is known for combining satire with perceptive views of Nigeria's post-colonial troubles.

2002: MUSLIMS AND CHRISTIANS About 50% of Nigerians are Muslim, 40% percent are Christian, and 10% practice indigenous spiritual beliefs. About a third of Nigeria's 36 states, mainly in the heavily Muslim north, follow *sharia* (Islamic law). Religious and ethnic differences between the Muslim north and the Christian/animist south continue to produce tension, riots, and bloodshed.

SOMETHING TO THINK ABOUT

CHILL OUT

In 2000, Mohammed Bah Abba, a schoolteacher from northern Nigeria, developed a simple refrigeration system that uses no electricity and costs about 30 cents to make. The Pot-in-Pot refrigeration device consists of two porous ceramic pots. One is slightly smaller and placed inside the other. The area in between is packed with wet sand, and the whole system is covered with a damp cloth and put in a dry, well-ventilated place. Water evaporating from the wet sand trapped between the two pots cools the inner pot that holds the perishable food. Abba developed the Pot-in-Pot as a practical way for desert cultures to preserve food safely.

FROM AFRICA TO "I LOVE LUCY"

Though they may have been unaware, generations of *I Love Lucy* fans got a small snapshot of Nigerian influence in the New World. In several episodes of the hit 1950s TV series, Cuban-born bandleader Desi Arnaz (as Ricky Ricardo) performs "Babalu," a Spanish song about an African deity. Yoruba slaves from Nigeria and Benin spread worship of the god Babalu and other nature spirits (*orishas*) throughout the Caribbean and the Americas. Over the years, African influence in religion and other aspects of life became part of mainstream Caribbean and Latin American cultures. Today, Yoruba spiritual practices can be found around the world under many names, including Santería and Voodoo.

419 FRAUD

Nigeria has the dubious distinction of being the birthplace of the 419 Fraud, a new variant of an old confidence game. More than 2,000 versions of the con, which violates section 419 of Nigeria's criminal law, have been reported. The scheme is carried out by phone, fax, letter, or e-mail. Typically, the con artist requests help transferring a huge sum of money out of Nigeria, promising the targets a windfall in return. They are later asked to send money—for bogus taxes, attorney's fees, or some other purpose—and in the end, the swindlers vanish with the money. Concerned about its international reputation, the government is working to root out "unscrupulous Nigerians" and their foreign collaborators.

North Africa

ALGERIA

Total Area: 919,595 sq mi
Population (est. 2005): 32,531,853

Though many ancient civilizations left traces in Algeria, the Arab and Islamic legacy dating to the 8th century AD left the strongest impact. In the 19th century the French took control of Algeria from the Ottoman Empire. In the 1950s, the National Liberation Front (FLN) began its fight to end French colonialism and achieved Algerian independence in 1962. The FLN has since dominated the political scene, going so far as to use the military to overturn the 1991 elections that would have brought the fundamentalist Islamic Salvation Front (FIS) to power.

ALGERIA		
Highest Point	Tahat	9,852 ft
Lowest Point	Chott Melrhir	131 ft below sea level
Longest River	Chéliff	420 mi
Largest City	Algiers (metro, 2005)	pop. 3,260,000
Tallest Building	Martyr's Tower (Algiers)	328 ft
Longest-Serving President	Chadli Benjedid	13 years (Feb. 7, 1979-Jan. 11, 1992)
First Olympic Medalist	Mohamed Zaoui, Bronze, Boxing	1984 Los Angeles Games
First Olympic Gold	Hassiba Boulmerka, Women's 1500m run	1992 Barcelona Games
First Oscar-winning film	*Z*	Best Picture, Directing, Editing, Writing, & Foreign Language Film (1969)

LIBYA

Total Area: 679,362 sq mi
Population (est. 2005): 5,765,563

The state of Libya came into existence in 1951 after the unification of three former colonial territories: Tripolitania, Cyrenaica, and Fezzan. After 18 years, King Idris I, the first and only king of Libya, was overthrown by a military coup led by Colonel Muammar al-Qaddafi. Qaddafi, who in still in power, sees himself as a revolutionary leader who has established a new system of governance known as *jamahiriya* or "state of the masses."

LIBYA		
Highest Point	Bikku Bitti	7,438 ft
Lowest Point	Sabkhat Ghuzayyil	154 ft below sea level
Largest City	Tripoli (metro, 2005)	pop. 2,093,000
Longest-Serving Leader	Muammar al-Qaddafi	36 years (Sept. 1969-present)
Biggest Export	Crude oil	1.34 mil barrels per day (2004)

MOROCCO

Total Area: 172,414 sq mi
Population (est. 2005): 32,725,847

Prior to the expansion of Islam to the region in the 7th century AD, North Africa was dominated by the Berbers. Several dynasties of Arab and Berber rulers extended their influence through Algeria, Tunisia, Libya, and large areas of Spain and Portugal before losing their empire. Until the 20th century, Morocco withstood the Ottomans but would struggle for independence from the Spanish and French. In 1956, the exiled ruling family was officially reinstated and Mohammad V took the title of King of independent Morocco. Today, Morocco is a constitutional monarchy that held its first parliamentary elections in 1997.

SOMETHING TO THINK ABOUT

PASS THE PARSLEY!

On July 11, 2002, a dozen Moroccan soldiers seized a tiny uninhabited island about 200 yards off Morocco's coast, near Gibraltar, named Perejil ("Parsley") by the Spanish for its indigenous flora. Spain, which had laid claim to the bare rock since withdrawing from mainland Morocco in 1956, immediately deployed warships. Spanish Special Forces conducted a bloodless raid on July 17, capturing the remaining Moroccan soldiers there. The dispute ended July 22 when Spain and Morocco formally agreed to return the islet to its demilitarized status.

MOROCCO		
Highest Point	Jebel Toubkal	13,665 ft
Lowest Point	Sebkha Tah	180 ft below sea level
Longest River	Draa	700 mi
Largest City	Casablanca (metro, 2005)	pop. 3,743,000
Tallest Building	Casablanca Twin Center Towers (Casablanca)	377 ft
Longest-Serving Leader	Hassan II	38 years (Feb. 26, 1961- July 23, 1999)
First Olympic Medalist	Rhadi ben Abdesselem, Silver, marathon Men	1960 Rome Games
First Olympic Gold	Nawal El Moutawakel[1], Women's 400m hurdles	1984 Los Angeles Games
World's tallest minaret	The Great Hassan II Mosque, Casablanca	689 ft

(1) Nawal El Moutawakel was the first woman from an Islamic country to win an Olympic medal.

TUNISIA

Total Area: 63,170 sq mi
Population (est. 2005): 10,074,951

Although it did not become an independent country until 1956, Tunisia has been a center of civilization since it was the seat of the Carthaginian Empire. Over the centuries various empires—from the Fatimids and Almohads to the Ottomans and the French—have ruled the land. Since independence, the Tunisian Republic has been dominated by a single party.

TUNISIA		
Highest Point	Jebel ech Chambi	5,066 ft
Lowest Point	Shatt al Gharsah	56 ft below sea level
Longest River	Majardah	290 mi
Largest City	Tunis (metro, 2005)	pop. 2,063,000
Tallest Building	Palais de Congress, Tunis	262 ft
Longest-Serving Leader	Habib Ali Bourguiba	30 years (July 25, 1957-Nov. 7, 1987)
First Olympic Medalist	Mohamed Gammoudi, Silver, Men's 10,000m run	1964 Tokyo Games
First Olympic Gold	Mohamed Gammoudi, Men's 5,000m run	1968 Mexico City Games
Oldest Mosque (N. Africa)	Great Mosque, Kairouan	AD 774 (original 670)

SUPERLATIVES

"GREAT MANMADE RIVER" Desert covers about 95% of Libya. Yet beneath its arid surface are aquifers containing over 2,400 cubic miles of water. Construction on what's known as "The Great Manmade River" began on Aug. 28, 1984 and is ongoing although sections are activated. Many consider it the world's largest engineering project. Over $19.58 billion has been spent so far, largely supported by Libya's other great underground resource—oil.

The aqueducts (13 ft in diameter) wind downhill through five systems to coastal cities and farms. The wells (up to 1,800 ft deep) currently yield about 62 billion gallons per year, mostly for irrigation. When finished, about 1,300 wells will produce 8.5 million cubic yards (1.7 billion gallons) of water per day.

LARGEST COLISEUM (N. AFRICA) The Amphitheater of El Jem, built in Tunisia about AD 200, measures 532 by 387 feet, with a circumference of 1,461 feet. It is believed to have seated 30,000 people on three or four stories. It's the largest Roman-built coliseum in North Africa and the third largest in the world after Rome's and Capua's.

Pakistan

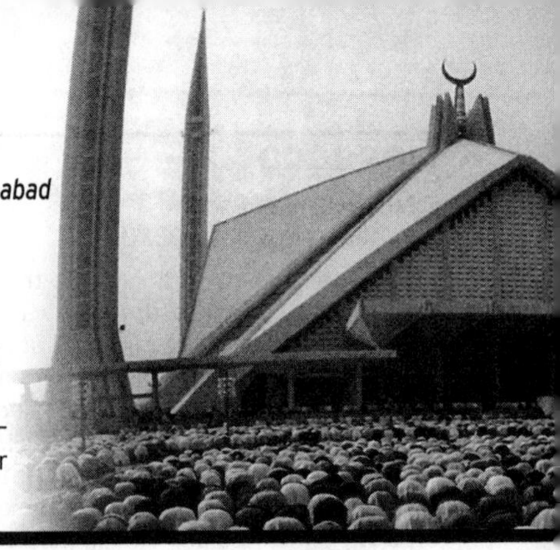
Faisal Mosque in Islamabad

Total Area: 310,403 sq. mi.
Population (est. 2005): 162,419,946

Pakistan is a relatively young nation with a long, rich past; the area was part of the ancient Indus Valley or Harappan civilization. When British India gained independence in 1947, the Muslim-majority regions were partitioned into East and West Pakistan, with India in between. East Pakistan later became Bangladesh.

West Pakistan, which is Pakistan today, is home to more than 150 million Muslims—according to many reckonings, the world's second-largest Muslim population, after Indonesia.

MILESTONES

2500-1700 BC: INDUS CIVILIZATION One of the world's major ancient civilizations sprang up on the Indus River in northern Pakistan over 4,000 years ago. Its name is unknown, but scientists and historians refer to it as the Indus or Harappan civilization. The mud-brick cities of Harappa, Ganweriwala, and Mohenjo-daro ("Mound of the Dead") were highly advanced, with many large public buildings. Mohenjo-daro, abandoned about 1950 BC, had streets laid out on a grid plan and the world's first known sewage system.

1175-1206: ISLAM The first permanent Islamic presence in the region was established between 1175 and 1206, when Muhammad of Ghur began a series of invasions from Persia into the northern Indian subcontinent, eventually conquering the area from Lahore to Bengal. In 1206, his successor, Qutb-ud-Din, established the Dehli Sultanate. After a series of different dynasties, this area, with much of India, in 1526 fell under the rule of the Islamic Mughal dynasty, which lasted until the growth of British rule in the 19th century.

1930s: ROOTS OF INDEPENDENCE The idea of a homeland for British India's Muslims emerged in the 1930s as nationalist feelings grew. In 1906, under the leadership of Pakistan's Quaid-i-Azam, or "Great Leader," Muhammad Ali Jinnah, they formed the Muslim League, the Muslim answer to the mostly Hindu Indian National Congress, which also sought an end to British rule.

In 1930, the poet Muhammad Iqbal proposed the formation of an independent Muslim state. In 1933, in the pamphlet *Now or Never*, British Muslim students suggested the name *Pakistan* for such a state. In Urdu, one of Pakistan's major languages, it means "land of the pure."

1947: PARTITION Two days after the British withdrew from India, on Aug. 15, 1947, they partitioned the subcontinent between India, with a majority Hindu population, and Pakistan, with a majority Muslim population. Between the announcement on June 3, 1947, and the actual withdrawal, communal violence erupted throughout the subcontinent, and hundreds of thousands died. Millions of Muslims fled from India to live in the new Pakistan, while Hindus and Sikhs fled back to India.

The new nation of Pakistan included Muslim areas in the northwest (West Pakistan) and the Muslim Bengali region (East Pakistan). The two regions were about 1,000 miles apart, on opposite sides of India.

1947: FLAG The national flag of Pakistan was designed by Muhammad Ali Jinnah, and adopted in Aug. 1947.

It has a dark green background with a white bar along the side. At the center is a white crescent and white five-pointed star. The green represents Islam, while the white bar represents non-Muslim minorities. The crescent and star—traditional Muslim symbols—represent progress and knowledge respectively.

1948: KASHMIR DISPUTE At the time of partition, the prince of Kashmir ruled the territory independently. Pakistan and India clashed over which of them should control the province.

Although Kashmir had a majority Muslim population, its Hindu leader decided to join India on Oct. 26, 1947. Frustrated, Pakistan began raiding Kashmir, and a war erupted. The UN negotiated a peace agreement and a partition of Kashmir, effective Jan. 1, 1949, but sporadic fighting has continued.

1952: INDIA CRICKET TOUR Cricket is the national sport of both India and Pakistan. The rivalry between their teams is considered by many the most intense in all of sports.

The teams first played each other in an official Test Match (national all-star squads playing over a scheduled five-day match) in Oct. 1952 in Delhi, India. India won convincingly by an innings and 70 runs.

Ongoing political disputes have disrupted the cricket rivalry, with both governments barring games between the teams during the

SOMETHING TO THINK ABOUT

KHYBER PASS

For centuries the mountain pass winding about 35 miles between Kabul, Afghanistan, and Peshawar, Pakistan, has been used as a passage to India. Steep mountain precipices wall in the road, which varies in width from 15 to 450 feet. The road was completed in 1879 and a railway was completed in 1920.

1960s and 1970s. In recent years, the teams have played more frequently.

1956: REPUBLIC OF PAKISTAN The country's first decade was marked by unrest and political turmoil. The first prime minister, Liaquat Ali Khan, was assassinated in Oct. 1951, and disputes between East and West Pakistan made it difficult to build institutions necessary to establish the new nation. But on Sept. 30, 1955, the four provinces of West Pakistan were legally integrated, and on March 2, 1956, a new constitution was adopted, which declared Pakistan an Islamic republic.

1971: BANGLADESH On March 26, 1971, East Pakistan voted to create an independent state and, with Indian assistance, formed the nation of Bangladesh. Since then, the former West Pakistan has been known as Pakistan.

1988: FEMALE PRIME MINISTER Benazir Bhutto became the first woman to head the government of an Islamic state when she became prime minister of Pakistan on Dec. 1, 1988. The daughter of Zulfikar Ali Bhutto, who had served as both president and prime minister, Bhutto served two terms: 1988-1990 and 1993-1996.

1998: NUCLEAR TEST On May 28, 1998, Pakistan tested five underground nuclear devices at the Chagai Hills test site, which lies in a desert area in the southwest, near the border with Iran and Afghanistan. The tests were in response to a series of underground nuclear weapons tests conducted by India two weeks earlier.

Although India had tested its first nuclear device in 1974, it claimed at the time it was for non-military purposes. Now both countries are acknowledged nuclear powers.

Selected Pakistani National Records

Highest Point[1]	Tirich Mir	25,263 ft
Longest River[2]	Indus	1,800 mi
Largest City	Karachi (metro, 2005)	pop. 11,819,000
Tallest Building	MCB Towers (Karachi)	351 ft
Longest-Serving Head of State	Pres. Muhammed Ayub Khan	10 years, 5 months (Oct. 28, 1958-Mar. 25, 1969)
First Olympic Medalists	Men's Field Hockey Team (silver)	1956 Melbourne Games
First Female Olympian	Shabana Akhtar (100 and 200-m sprints)	1996 Atlanta Games
First Nobel Laureate	Abdus Salam	1979, Physics

(1) The highest mountain in Pakistani-controlled territory is K2, or Mount Godwin-Austen, the world's second highest mountain, at 28,251 feet. It lies in the disputed territories in Kashmir, controlled by Pakistan but claimed by India. (2) Most of the river's 1,800-mile course flows through Pakistani territory, although its source and headwaters are in Tibet.

SUPERLATIVES

YOUNGEST CRICKET PLAYER The youngest person to play in an international Test Match is Hasan Raza. He was 14 years, 227 days old when he played for Pakistan against Zimbabwe at Faisalabad on Oct. 24, 1996.

LONGEST WINNING STREAK (SQUASH) Between April 9, 1981, and Nov. 12, 1986, legendary squash player Jahangir Khan put together the longest winning streak in squash, and possibly the longest in any sport. Between his loss to Geoff Hunt (Australia) in the 1981 British Open final, and defeat by Ross Norman (New Zealand) in the 1986 World Open final, Khan won 555 straight matches.

LARGEST MOSQUE The Faisal Mosque in Islamabad, Pakistan's capital, is the second largest in the world, with an area of about 2,041,968 square feet. Built in 1980, it can accommodate 10,000 worshippers in the main prayer hall and up to 700,000 in courtyards and surrounding areas.

YOUNGEST COMPUTER PROFESSIONAL In 2004, Arfa Karim Randhawa became the youngest known Microsoft certified computer professional at 9 years, 9 months, 11 days old. She first became interested in computers at age five.

Poland

Total Area: 120,728 sq mi
Population (est. 2005): 38,557,984

Poland's borders have shifted over time and long periods of foreign rule. At various points, Poland was ruled or controlled by Lithuania, Russia, Prussia, Austria, Nazi Germany, and the Soviet Union. In 1989, the Communist government yielded to pressure and allowed free elections. The new Polish Republic entered NATO on March 12, 1999, and the European Union on May 1, 2004.

Ogrodzieniec Castle

MILESTONES

966: UNIFIED POLAND The nation of Poland has existed in several forms during its history. Mieszko I (c. 922–992), the prince of Poland, was baptized in 966, and viewed conversion to Christianity as a way to unite the various tribes and raise their status in relation to the powerful Catholic-ruled Holy Roman Empire. The first unified Polish state stretched north to the Baltic Sea and south to the Carpathian Mountains.

1025: FIRST KING
The first king of Poland was Boleslav I. The son of Mieszko I, he succeeded his father as prince of Poland in 992. Also known as "Boleslav the Brave" and "Boleslav the Mighty," he petitioned the pope for recognition as king. In 1025, the pope finally gave his blessing and Boleslav was crowned, though his reign was brief; he died the same year.

1384: FIRST QUEEN
The first and only woman to rule as queen of Poland was Queen Jadwiga, who reigned from 1384 until her death from childbirth complications in 1399. She was just 10 years old at the time of her coronation.

Two years after ascending the throne, Jadwiga married the grand duke of Lithuania, Wladyslaw, who was 23 years older. Their union united Poland and Lithuania to create a vast realm that stretched from the Baltic Sea to the steppes of Ukraine. She was named a saint by Pope John Paul II in 1997.

1919: FLAG The present red and white flag of Poland was officially adopted on Aug. 1, 1919, during the reconstruction of Poland toward the end of World War I. The colors had first appeared together on a Polish national emblem in the 16th century. Red and white were first adopted as national colors in Feb. 1831, during an uprising against Russian rule.

1927: NATIONAL ANTHEM The national anthem of Poland is "*Jezscze Polska nie zginela*" ("Poland is not yet lost"), also called "Dabrowski's Mazurka."

The tune, a lively *mazurka* (folk dancing tune), was written by Józef Wybicki in 1797, while serving in Italy with the Polish Legion—an expatriate army led by Jan Henryk Dabrowski that fought for Napoleon. The patriotic chorus urges Dabrowski to lead his army back to Poland and free the nation from foreign rule. "Dabrowski's Mazurka" became Poland's national anthem on Feb. 26, 1927.

1978: ASTRONAUT
Miroslaw Hermaszewski became the first Pole in space on June 27, 1978. The former fighter pilot was launched aboard the Soviet spacecraft *Soyuz 30*, which docked with the Soviet space station *Salyut 6*. The mission lasted 7 days, 22 hours, 2 minutes; Hermaszewski returned to earth on July 5, 1978.

1978: POLISH POPE
John Paul II (born Karol Wojtyla in Wadowice, Poland, on May 18, 1920) was elected Oct. 16, 1978, as the first non-Italian pontiff in 456 years and first Polish pope ever. The "pilgrim pope" traveled a total of about 725,000 miles, more than all his predecessors combined. By the time of his death on April 2, 2005, he had made 104 pastoral trips outside of Italy, visiting 129 countries.

On his visits to Poland, the first in 1979, John Paul drew huge throngs and promoted ideals of democracy and freedom that weakened the hold of the Communist government.

It is estimated that over 2 million pilgrims filed past his bier in St. Peter's Basilica prior to his funeral at the Vatican; it was the largest funeral on record for a pontiff, with more than 70 heads of state in attendance.

1980: SOLIDARITY
After World War II, Poland was ruled by a repressive Communist government tied to the Soviet Union. But on Aug. 14, 1980, striking workers at the Gdansk shipyard—led by Lech Walesa, an electrical engineer turned dissident—joined with workers at other factories, and formed a threat that

Selected Polish National Records

Highest Point	Mt. Rysy; Tatra Mountains	8,199 ft
Longest Cavern	Wielka Sniezna system	11 mi
Longest River	Wisla (or Vistula)	651 mi
Largest Lake	Lake Sniardwy	44 sq mi
Largest City	Katowice (metro, 2005)	pop. 2,914,000
Tallest Building	Palace of Culture and Science (Warsaw)	757 ft
Longest Bridge	Wyszogród Bridge	4,101 ft
Longest Reign	Kazimierz IV	45 years (1447-92)
Longest-Serving President	Ignacy Moscicki	13 years (1926-39)
Longest-Serving Prime Minister	Józef Cyrankiewicz	22 years (1947-52, 1954-70)
First Olympic Champion	Halina Konopacka, women's discus	1928 Amsterdam Games
First Oscar	*Tango*	1982 animated short film

THE BIGGER THEY ARE...

The Warszawa Radio mast was once the world's tallest structure. Built in 1974 in Konstantynów, the mast stood 2,120.6 feet tall and was supported by guy wires. It was used to transmit programs from Warsaw Radio and Television Center until it collapsed on Aug. 8, 1991, during renovation work.

(Right to left) Former Pres. George H.W. Bush, Lech Walesa, and Pres. George W. Bush ▼

SOMETHING TO THINK ABOUT

KING-SIZE KIELBASA

Kielbasa, a sausage that is a staple of the Polish diet, comes in many shapes, sizes, and compositions. One of the more unusual tributes to Kielbasa is a giant two-link sausage sculpture unveiled in Mundare, Alberta, Canada, on June 8, 2001. Built to honor the town's tradition of producing the Polish delicacy, it stands 42 feet high and weighs 6 tons. The culinary giant is unfit for human consumption, however; its ingredients are mainly plastic and fiberglass.

could not be ignored. The Solidarity labor union was officially formed in Sept. 1980, though a year later it was outlawed and Walesa was arrested.

In 1983, Walesa received the Nobel Peace Prize, and pressure mounted on the regime. In early 1989, the government held "roundtable talks" with Solidarity leaders that led to free elections in June—the first in postwar Eastern Europe. Later that year, Walesa was elected president, a position he held until 1995.

1992: WOMAN PRIME MINISTER Poland's first and so far only female prime minister was Hanna Suchocka, who held office from July 10, 1992, to Oct. 18, 1993.

1995: POLE AT BOTH POLES To the delight of pun lovers everywhere, the first person to travel on foot to both the North and South Poles in the same year was Marek Kaminski, a Pole from Gdansk. Bipolar Kaminski reached 90° N on May 23, 1995, and reached its polar opposite on Dec. 26, 1995, after walking 870 miles over 53 days, pulling a 265-pound supply sled.

SUPERLATIVES

MOST OLYMPIC TITLES, WALKING Polish legend Robert Korzeniowski has won a record four Olympic gold medals in race walking. He won his first gold in the 50-kilometer event at the 1996 Atlanta Games. Four years later he swept both men's races, the 20-K and 50-K walks, at the 2000 Games in Sydney. In 2004 he won his third straight 50-K gold medal at the Athens Games.

NOBEL LAUREATE IN TWO DISCIPLINES The only scientist to win a Nobel Prize in two different science disciplines was Marie Curie.

Born in Poland in 1867 as Marie Sklodowska, the famed scientist spent most of her life in France and was the first female professor at the Sorbonne. She won the 1903 Nobel Prize for physics (jointly with her husband, Pierre Curie) for their discovery of the elements radium and polonium. Curie also won the 1911 Prize in chemistry for her work in extracting pure radium.

LONGEST POLKA STREAK Both Poland and the Czech Republic claim to be the originators of the polka. While that debate continues, the American Polka King is unquestionably Jimmy Sturr, who has won 14 Grammy Awards and a record 18 straight Grammy nominations in the polka category.

His streak ended in 2004, when his album, *Rock 'N Polka*, did not receive a Best Polka Album nomination. The gracious Sturr sent congratulatory messages to all the polka nominees.

Russia

Total Area: 6,592,769 sq mi
Population (est. 2005): 143,420,39

Russia has produced some of the world's greatest authors, composers, and dancers, along with some of the world's most notorious despots. Once the dominant republic of the Soviet Union, Russia by itself today is still the world's largest country in area, straddling the continents of Europe and Asia and stretching from the Pacific Ocean to the Black Sea.

The Cathedral of the Assumption, left, at the Kremlin

MILESTONES

AROUND 1000 AD: THE RUS
The birthplace of Russia is modern Ukraine, where the Rus people, of Scandinavian origin, established a series of principalities along the Dnieper valley toward the end of the first millennium. Kiev, now the capital of Ukraine, emerged first as the leading state, then Novgorod to the north. The grand principality of Moscow became the dominant Russian state under Ivan I (reigned 1328-41).

1547: FIRST TSAR
The first tsar of Russia was Prince Ivan IV, later known as "Ivan the Terrible." He became grand prince of Moscow at age three. On Jan. 16, 1547, at age 16, he became the first Russian ruler crowned as emperor or tsar ("Caesar").

He started out as a reformer but turned into a despot. In 1570 he killed thousands of people in Novgorod, believing they were plotting against him. In 1581, in a fit of rage, he killed his oldest and favorite son.

1613: ROMANOVS
The Romanov dynasty, which ruled Russia for over 300 years, began when Mikhail Romanov was elected by an assembly as tsar, on Feb. 21, 1613. He is credited with unifying Russia and reforming the army.

The dynasty, which ended with the 1917 Russian Revolution, included such major figures as Peter the Great (ruled 1682-1725) and Catherine the Great (ruled 1762-96).

1773: BOLSHOI BALLET One of the oldest ballet troupes in the world, the Bolshoi Ballet started out in 1773 with classes given at an orphanage in Moscow.

1865-69: *WAR AND PEACE* One of the world's most famous novels, *War and Peace* written by Leo Tolstoy, was published between 1865 and 1869. The epic work tells the story of five Russian families during the Napoleonic wars.

1885: FABERGÉ EGGS
The world-famous, jewel-encrusted Fabergé Eggs were created by Peter Carl Fabergé, a Russian-born French Huguenot, in 1885. The first egg was an Easter morning present from Tsar Alexander III to his wife, Tsarina Maria.

1917: RUSSIAN REVOLUTION
The Russian Revolution was actually two revolutions that took place in March and November 1917 (Gregorian calendar). The first led to the collapse of tsarist rule. Then, after a brief attempt at democratic rule under Aleksandr Kerensky, the Bolsheviks under Vladimir Lenin seized power in the so-called Bolshevik Revolution.

Tsar Nicholas II and his family, along with a doctor and three servants, were executed on the night of July 16-17, 1918, by a firing squad in a basement in Ekaterinburg. They were reburied in a St. Petersburg cathedral 80 years later.

1920s-50s: STALIN'S PURGES Under the totalitarian rule (1924-53) of Joseph Stalin, more than 10 million people were killed. A notable example of Stalin's terror was a forced famine in the Ukraine in the 1920s and 30s, which led to some 7 million deaths.

"Uncle Joe" also established iron control within his Communist Party. Real or imagined opponents were executed or sent to labor camps (*gulags*) in Siberia, where millions worked in barely habitable conditions, often dying from exhaustion or disease.

1941-44: SIEGE OF LENINGRAD One of the most remarkable episodes of World War II was the refusal of the citizens of Leningrad (now St. Petersburg) to surrender to the German forces that surrounded their city on Sept. 8, 1941. Despite almost constant bombardment and inhuman conditions, Leningrad held out for nearly 900 days.

The city was finally relieved by the Red Army on Jan. 27, 1944. It is estimated that more than a million residents died during the siege.

1957 & 1961: SPACE FIRSTS On Oct. 1, 1957, the Soviet Union launched the world's first artificial satellite, *Sputnik I*, into orbit. *Sputnik I* was only about the size of a basketball and could do little else besides transmit a "beeping" signal.

SUPERLATIVES

BIGGEST EXPLOSION
The greatest recorded explosion on Earth happened on June 30, 1908, in the Tunguska River valley. The explosion, the equivalent of 1,000 Hiroshima-type atom bombs, is believed to have been caused by a stony asteroid exploding just before striking the Earth. The resulting dust was seen to brighten the sky as far away as London.

LONGEST ESTUARY
The Ob River has the world's longest estuary at 550 miles long. Some 50 miles wide, the Ob River is also the widest river in the world that freezes. The longest Russian waterway with a single name, the Ob River is 2,286 miles long.

DEEPEST LAKE
Russia's Lake Baikal is the deepest lake in the world. It is 5,315 feet deep, extending 3,822 feet below sea level.

GREATEST TEMPERATURE RANGE Verkhoyansk in Siberia has the world's greatest temperature range. It has recorded a low of -90°F and a high of 98°F.

LONGEST RAILROAD
The Trans-Siberian Railroad is the longest continuous railroad on Earth. The 5,778-mile journey on the main line, from Moscow to the Pacific port of Vladivostok, crosses eight time zones and takes seven days to complete.

Selected Russian National Records

Highest Point	Mount Elbrus	18,510 ft
Longest River[1]	Lena	2,734 mi
Largest Lake (world)[2]	Caspian Sea	143,244 sq mi
Largest City	Moscow (metro, 2005)	pop. 10,672,000
Longest-Reigning Tsar	Ivan IV	51 years (1533-84)
Tallest Building	Moscow State University (Moscow)	787 ft
First Olympic Champion	Nikolai Panin-Kolomensky, figure skating	1908 London Games
First Nobel Prize	Ivan Pavlov	1904, Medicine

(1) The Yenisey and Angara rivers when combined run a total length of 3,694 mi. (2) The Caspian Sea is shared between Russia, Kazakhstan, Turkmenistan, Iran, and Azerbaijan.

SOMETHING TO THINK ABOUT

FOR WHOM THE BELL DIDN'T TOLL
The Tsar-Kolokol III bell, which is 21 feet high, 20.3 feet in diameter, and weighs about 400,000 pounds, is the largest bell in the world, but it has never rung. Before it could be raised into a bell tower and put into service it was cracked in the Moscow fire of 1737, and it now resides silently on a pedestal next to the tower. The bell is so big that its interior was once used as a small chapel.

GIRL FROM OUTER SPACE
Valentina Tereshkova, the first woman in space, married another cosmonaut, Andrian Nikolayev. Their daughter, Elena, born in 1964, was the first person born to parents that have both been in space.

SEAMSTRESS EXPRESS
Perhaps the most frivolous ruler in Russia's long history was the Tsarina Elizabeth (ruled 1741-62), who reportedly never wore a dress twice and often changed her clothes several times during a ball or dinner. After her death, her wardrobe was found to contain 15,000 dresses.

But it represented a major boost for Soviet prestige.

On April 12, 1961, the Soviet Union achieved new glory when Soviet cosmonaut Yuri Gagarin became the first person in space. He orbited Earth for 108 minutes aboard his craft, *Vostok 1*.

LATE 1980s-1991: END OF SOVIET ERA
As Communist leader Mikhail Gorbachev attempted reforms in the 1980s, under the slogans *glasnost* ("openness") and *perestroika* ("restructuring"), the government came under increasing pressure from nationalist and independence movements that led to the splintering of the Soviet Union into 15 separate countries.

In June 1991, Boris Yeltsin became the first popularly elected Russian president in history. On Dec. 26, 1991, Russia emerged an independent state with roughly half the population and $\frac{3}{4}$ of the area of the old Soviet Union.

1991: FLAG
The present red, white, and blue national flag of Russia was first used on Jan. 20, 1705. The tricolor design was abandoned after the Russian Revolution in favor of the red and gold hammer-and-sickle flag of the Soviet Union. But it returned when the Soviet Union collapsed in Dec. 1991; President Boris Yeltsin made the flag official on Dec. 11, 1993.

Saudi Arabia

Total Area: 756,985 sq mi
Population (est. 2005): 26,417,599

Saudi Arabia, which occupies about four-fifths of the Arabian Peninsula, is the only country in the world named after its ruling family—the al-Saud. The country is home to the Islamic holy cities of Mecca and Medina and is an Islamic state adhering to religious principles taught by the puritanical 18th-century reformer Muhammad bin Abdul Wahhab. About 92% of the population is Muslim. The modern-day kingdom was established in 1932 by King Abdul Aziz al-Saud.

MILESTONES

622: ISLAM The prophet Muhammad was born in the city of Mecca in 570 AD. According to Muslim tradition, in 610 AD he began to be visited by the Angel Gabriel who delivered to him the Word of God, known as the *Koran*. Muhammad began to teach that only one God should be worshiped, criticizing the worship of idols at the Kaaba in Mecca; as a result, he and his followers were forced out of the city and fled to Medina, where Muhammad established the first Muslim community. This migration, in 622 AD, is known as the Hijra. It marks the beginning of the Islamic calendar.

The direction Muslims face when conducting prayers is known as Qiblah. For the first two years after the Hijra, the early Muslims faced Jerusalem when conducting their prayers. Since 624 AD the custom has been to face the holy city of Mecca.

AROUND 1750: ROOTS OF AL-SAUD DYNASTY Around 1750 a local ruler of the town of Diriyah named Muhammad bin Saud joined forces with a Muslim reformer named Muhammad bin Abdul Wahhab, whose teachings became known as Wahhabism. With the help of Abdul Wahhab's religious credibility, the Saud family was able to use its wealth and military power to extend its influence across many cities of Arabia.

The Saudi expansion was viewed hostilely by the Ottoman Empire. The early Saudi conquest came to an end in 1818, when the Ottoman army, led by Ibrahim Pasha of Egypt, destroyed Diriyah.

1932: FIRST KING In 1901, 21-year-old Abdul Aziz al-Saud (also known as Ibn Saud) succeeded his father to become the leader of the al-Saud family. He set out to reclaim lands that his family had once controlled and extend his family's power as far as he could. In Jan. 1902, Abdul Aziz took the city of Riyadh, launching a 30-year conquest of the Arabian Peninsula.

On Sept. 23, 1932, with much of the peninsula firmly under Saudi control, he proclaimed the area the kingdom of Saudi Arabia and named himself as king. He ruled the country until his death on Nov. 9, 1953, at the age of 73. His family rules Saudi Arabia to this day.

1932: CAPITAL The capital city of Riyadh is located near the site of Diriyah, the original native walled settlement of the Saud family. When Abdul Aziz ibn Saud renewed the movement of Saudi conquest, Riyadh was captured in 1902 and became the base of operations for his unification of the Arabian Peninsula.

The city was named "Riyadh," meaning "gardens," because of the greenery that grew in the area when the local wadi, or seasonal river, flooded.

It was declared the capital in 1932, and eventually all ministries and government offices moved there.

1938: DISCOVERY OF OIL Oil was first discovered in Saudi Arabia at Dhahran on March 3, 1938, by Standard Oil of California (Socal, today known as Chevron). The Saudi oil industry was boosted by the great need for petroleum during World War II. In 1944, Socal's Arabian affiliate changed its name to Arabian American Oil Co. (Aramco). Although Saudi Arabia's oil industry began small, it grew substantially, as shown in the following table of average petroleum production, in million barrels of oil per day:

1960	1.31
1970	3.80
1980	9.90
1990	6.41
2000	8.40
2003	8.85

Following the fall of the Soviet Union in 1992, Saudi Arabia became the world's largest oil producer, and it still is the largest producer and exporter.

1950: NATIONAL ANTHEM *"Sarei Lil Majd Walaya"* ("Hasten to Glory and Greatness") was adopted as the national anthem of Saudi Arabia in 1950. The lyrics were written by Ibrahim Khafaji and were set to music by Abd al-Rahman al-Khateeb.

Selected Saudi National Records

Highest Point	Jabal Sawda'	10,280 ft
Longest Wadi (seasonal river)	Wadi Al-Rummah	370 mi
Largest City	Riyadh (metro, 2005)	pop. 5,514,000
Tallest Building	Kingdom Center (Riyadh)	992 ft
Largest Dairy Farm (world)	Al Safia	160,000 gallons milk/day
Longest Pipeline (nation)	East-West crude oil pipeline	740 mi
Largest Mosque (world)	The Holy Mosque in Mecca	about 2 million sq ft
Longest-Reigning King	King Fahd bin Abdul Aziz al-Saud	23 years (1982-2005)
Richest Citizen	Prince Alwaleed bin Talal Alsaud	net worth, $21.5 billion
First Muslim in Space	Prince Sultan Ibn Salman	1985, aboard the space shuttle Discovery.

SOMETHING TO THINK ABOUT

THANK ALLAH IT'S WEDNESDAY

Because Friday is the Muslim day of prayer, the weekend in Saudi Arabia is on Thursday and Friday, with the working week running from Saturday to Wednesday.

1973: NATIONAL FLAG
Saudi Arabia's national flag is based on the flag flown by the Prophet Muhammad in the earliest days of Islam. Green is the symbolic color of Islam, which is why many Muslim countries, including Saudi Arabia, use it in their flags. The Arabic writing on the flag means "There is no god except God; Muhammad is the Messenger of God." This phrase is the creed of all Muslims. The one element not related to Islam is the sword, added during King Abdul Aziz ibn Saud's conquest of the areas of Najd and Hijaz.

On March 15, 1973, a modified flag design was adopted by royal decree, with a smaller inscription and a straight-bladed saber. The Saudi flag is the only national flag today that features writing alone as the central part of its design.

SUPERLATIVES

MOST OIL With an estimated 262 billion barrels of recoverable oil, Saudi Arabia has the largest oil reserves in the world, amounting to about 25% of the world's total proven reserves. Saudi Arabia can produce more oil per day than any other country in the world—at maximum capacity, about 10.5 million barrels of oil per day.

The world's largest oilfield, Ghawar, at 70 billion barrels, and offshore oilfield, Safaniya, at 35 billion barrels, are within Saudi Arabian borders.

The largest offshore oil-loading facility in the world is Ras Tanura in the Persian Gulf. Here ships line up to receive up to 6 million barrels of oil per day for distribution around the world.

ISLAM'S HOLIEST CITY Mecca, in Saudi Arabia, is considered to be the most holy city for Muslims, being Muhammad's birthplace and the location of the Kaaba, or House of God—a small building that Muslims believe was built by the Prophet Abraham and his son, Ishmael. Muslims are required to make a pilgrimage (called the Hajj) to Mecca once in their lives if they are physically and financially able. The Hajj is meant to be a return to a state of spiritual purity. Every year some 2 million Muslims make the Hajj during the holiday of Eid al-Adha.

DESALINATION Saudi Arabia has no lakes or permanent rivers. Most of the kingdom's water comes from desalination plants that draw water from the sea and remove the salt, making it drinkable. Saudi Arabia desalinates more water from its 30 plants than any other country in the world.

The Jubail desalination plant is also the world's largest. Every day about 714 million gallons of drinkable water are generated and pumped to the kingdom's cities and towns.

THE EMPTY QUARTER The Empty Quarter (*Rub al-khali*), found (in part) in south and southeastern Saudi Arabia, is the largest stretch of sand in the world. As the name implies, practically nobody lives in this desolate area, which covers about 250,000 square miles in all, making it slightly smaller than the state of Texas.

In 1930-31, Bertram Thomas, a British civil servant, became the first European to travel through this desert.

Scandinavia

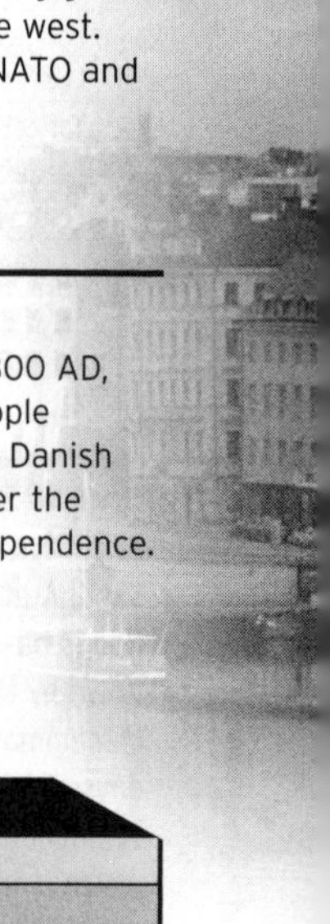
Stockholm, Sweden ▶

THE SCANDINAVIAN PENINSULA OF NORTHERN EUROPE contains the kingdoms of Norway and Sweden, but the term Scandinavia also includes Denmark to the south. Finland and Iceland are also often considered part of Scandinavia and are included here.

DENMARK

Denmark united as single kingdom around 700 AD. For most of the Middle Ages, it was the dominant Scandinavian state, and in 1397 it achieved a temporary union of all Scandinavia. Denmark gained overseas possessions in the 15th century, but lost them in the 19th and early 20th centuries. It became a constitutional monarchy in 1849.

Total Area: 16,639 sq mi
Population (est. 2005): 5,432,335

FINLAND

For much of its history, Finland was dominated by Sweden (13th century to 1809), Russia (from 1809 to 1919), or the Soviet Union (1939-91). During the Cold War, Finland played a balancing game between appeasing the Soviets and reaching out to the west. After the collapse of the Soviet Union, Finland joined NATO and the European Union and adopted the euro.

Total Area: 130,128 sq mi
Population (2005 est.): 5,223,442

ICELAND

Iceland may have been settled by Irish monks before 800 AD, but it remained largely unoccupied until 870 when people from Norway (Vikings) came. In 1381, Iceland became a Danish possession. In 1918 it became a separate kingdom under the Danish monarch and on June 17, 1944, it achieved independence.

Total Area: 39,769 sq mi
Population (est. 2005): 296,737

Selected Scandinavian National Records

DENMARK		
Highest Point	Yding Skovhøj	568 ft
Largest City	Copenhagen (metro 2005)	pop. 1,091,000
Longest Reigning Monarch	Christian IV	59 years, 10 months (1588-1648)
First Prime Minister	Adam Wilhelm (Count Moltke)	March 22, 1848
First Olympic Medalist	Viggo Jensen, Silver, weightlifting, one hand lift	1896 Athens Games
World's Oldest National Flag	The Dannebrog	c. 1478[1]

(1) According to tradition, the Dannebrog fell from heaven during a battle at Lyndanisse, Estonia on June 15, 1219. Its first known mention was in 1478.

FINLAND		
Highest Point	Haltiatunturi	4,357 ft
Largest City	Helsinki (metro, 2005)	pop. 1,103,000
Tallest Building	Fortum (in Espoo)	285 ft
Longest-Serving President	Urho Kekkonen	25 years, 8 months, 12 days (Feb. 16, 1956-Oct. 28, 1981)
First Female President	Tarja Halonen	March 1, 2000-present
First Olympic Medalist	Werner Weckman, Gold, wrestling	1908 London Games
Most Successful Olympian (Scandinavia)	Paavo Nurmi	12 medals (9 gold, 3 silver), track and field (1920, 1924, 1928)

ICELAND		
Highest Point	Hvannadalshnjúkur	6,952 ft
Largest City	Reykjavik (metro, 2005)	pop. 190,000
Largest Glacier	Vatnajökull	3,205 sq mi
World's Largest Lava Flow	Mt. Laki eruption, 1783	218 sq mi[1]
Tallest Building	Gullsmári 7 (Kópavogur)	140 ft
Longest-Serving and First Female President	Vigdis Finnbogadóttir	16 years (Aug. 1, 1980-July 31, 1996)
First Nobel Laureate	Halldór K. Laxness	1955, Literature
First Olympic Medalist	Vilhjálmur Einarsson, silver, triple jump	1956 Melbourne Games

(1) Iceland is one of the most volcanically active regions on Earth; around one-third of the Earth's total lava flow in the last 500 years has been on Iceland.

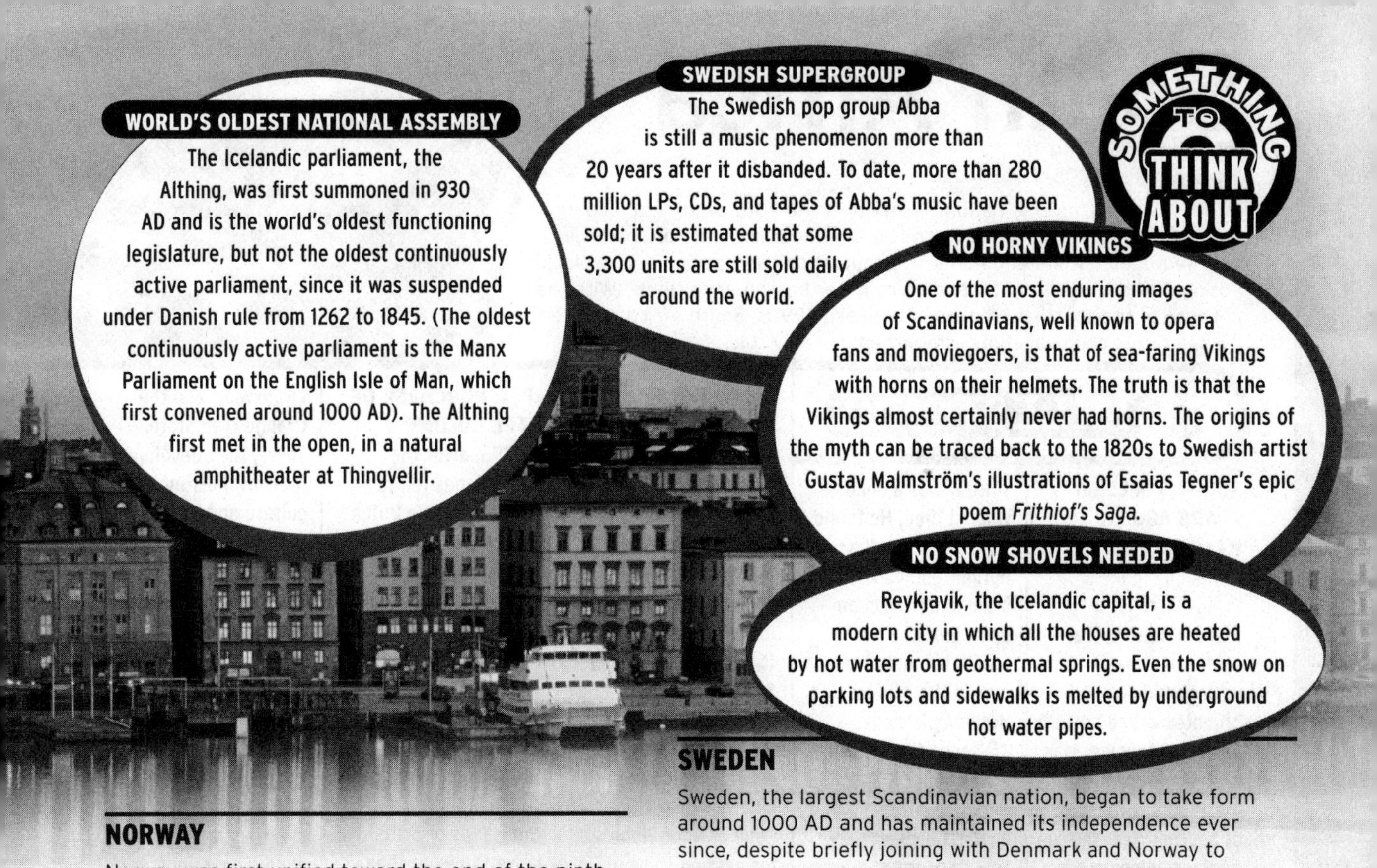

SOMETHING TO THINK ABOUT

WORLD'S OLDEST NATIONAL ASSEMBLY

The Icelandic parliament, the Althing, was first summoned in 930 AD and is the world's oldest functioning legislature, but not the oldest continuously active parliament, since it was suspended under Danish rule from 1262 to 1845. (The oldest continuously active parliament is the Manx Parliament on the English Isle of Man, which first convened around 1000 AD). The Althing first met in the open, in a natural amphitheater at Thingvellir.

SWEDISH SUPERGROUP

The Swedish pop group Abba is still a music phenomenon more than 20 years after it disbanded. To date, more than 280 million LPs, CDs, and tapes of Abba's music have been sold; it is estimated that some 3,300 units are still sold daily around the world.

NO HORNY VIKINGS

One of the most enduring images of Scandinavians, well known to opera fans and moviegoers, is that of sea-faring Vikings with horns on their helmets. The truth is that the Vikings almost certainly never had horns. The origins of the myth can be traced back to the 1820s to Swedish artist Gustav Malmström's illustrations of Esaias Tegner's epic poem *Frithiof's Saga*.

NO SNOW SHOVELS NEEDED

Reykjavik, the Icelandic capital, is a modern city in which all the houses are heated by hot water from geothermal springs. Even the snow on parking lots and sidewalks is melted by underground hot water pipes.

NORWAY

Norway was first unified toward the end of the ninth century, but periods of civil war and division followed. It was united under Denmark (1381-1814), then Sweden (until 1905, when it became an independent kingdom).

Total Area: 125,182 sq mi
Population (est. 2005): 4,593,041

SWEDEN

Sweden, the largest Scandinavian nation, began to take form around 1000 AD and has maintained its independence ever since, despite briefly joining with Denmark and Norway to form the Kalmar Union under one monarch in 1397. It became powerful under the Vasa dynasty in the 16th and 17th centuries. Since 1818, Sweden has been a constitutional monarchy with the prime minister position becoming head of government in 1876.

Total Area: 173,732 sq mi
Population (est. 2005): 9,001,774

NORWAY		
Highest Point[1]	Galdhøpiggen	8,100 ft
Longest Fjord (Scandinavia)	Sogn Fjord	127 mi[2]
Largest City	Oslo (metro, 2005)	pop. 808,000
Tallest Building	Radisson SAS Plaza Hotel (Oslo)	384 ft
Longest-Reigning Monarch	Christian IV	60 years (c. 1588-1648)
First Prime Minister	Peder Anker	1814-22
First Female Prime Minister	Gro Harlem Brundtland	Feb. 4 - Oct. 13, 1981 (1986-89)
Longest-Serving Prime Minister	Frederik Due	17 years (1841-58)
First Nobel Laureate	Björnstjerne Björnson	1903, Literature

(1) Glittertinden used to be the highest, but its ice cap has largely melted, lowering its height. (2) The Sogn Fjord is more than 3 miles wide at its widest point and has a maximum depth of water of 4,291 feet.

SWEDEN		
Highest Point	Kebnekaise	6,926 ft
Largest City	Stockholm (metro, 2005)	pop. 765,582
Tallest Building	Turning Torso (Malmö)	623 ft
Longest-Reigning Monarch	Magnus Eriksson	45 years (1319-64)
First Prime Minister	Louis de Geer	1876-80
First Olympic Medalists	August Nilsson, Karl Gustav Staaf, Gustaf Söderström, gold, tug of war[1]	1900 Paris Games

(1) A combined Sweden-Denmark team won the gold. The six-man team comprised the Swedish trio and three Danish athletes.

South Africa

Total Area: 471,010 sq. mi
Population (est. 2005): 44,344,136

South Africa is a diverse nation. For most of the 20th century, the country was ruled by the white-minority population under a system of apartheid that segregated white and non-white populations and denied native blacks voting rights, access to jobs, and many other basic human rights. With the collapse of the apartheid regime in the early 1990s, South Africa restored human rights and peacefully established majority rule.

MILESTONES

ABOUT 3 MILLION YEARS AGO: WALKING PRIMATES Although older fossils were later found in East Africa, evidence of early upright-walking primates called australopithecines was first discovered in the Sterkfontein Valley of South Africa. The findings helped prove that Africa, rather than Asia, was the cradle of humankind.

In 1924, Dr. Raymond Dart discovered fragments of an australopith's skull in a cave at Taung. Dart studied the specimen, called the "Taung Baby" since it was a child when it died. He found that it likely walked upright and had a brain larger than an ape's but smaller than a human's. He named the species *Australopithecus africanus* ("southern African ape").

4TH-5TH CENTURY AD: EARLIEST KNOWN TRIBES The pastoral Khoikhoi and hunter-gatherer San (Bushmen) were South Africa's earliest modern human inhabitants and lived in the west and southwest areas of today's South Africa.

Iron-using Bantu-speaking peoples moved into the region by about the 8th century AD. Their descendants became the Zulu, Xhosa, Swazi, and Sotho.

1652: FIRST DUTCH SETTLEMENT In April 1652, Jan van Riebeeck established a supply camp in a harbor near the Cape of Good Hope for passing ships of the Dutch East India Company on their way to India and other eastern trade routes. The port spurred Dutch settlement in South Africa and would eventually expand to become present-day Cape Town.

1814: PURCHASE OF CAPE COLONY In 1795, after the Netherlands fell to the French, the Dutch East India Company was ailing. Fearing growing French power, the British sent troops to occupy the Cape. The Dutch ceded the territory to the British for £6 million in an 1814 Treaty.

After 1820, thousands of British moved to what they dubbed the Cape Colony. English became the official language in 1822.

1835: VOORTREKKERS After Britain assumed control of the Cape Colony in 1814, many Dutch colonists became discouraged with the new laws and customs. The "Great Trek" of 1835-43 was a mass migration of primarily Dutch settlers, known first as Boers and today as Afrikaners, into the eastern lands set aside by the British for native tribes. They formed two land-locked Republics, the South African Republic (Transvaal) and the Orange Free State. There, they developed their own distinctive culture and language, Afrikaans.

1899-1902: BOER WAR When vast gold deposits were discovered in the primarily Dutch Witwatersrand region in 1886, British miners flooded the area, creating Johannesburg almost overnight. The Afrikaaners heavily taxed these *Uitlanders*, or "foreigners," and tensions escalated.

Threatened by a growing British army, Transvaal and Orange Free State declared war on Oct. 12, 1899. The British won a bloody 3-year war, known as the Boer War, and the Treaty of Vereeniging, signed on May 31, 1902, unified all the territories as a dominion of the British Empire.

1910: UNION OF SOUTH AFRICA The Union of South Africa was officially ratified on May 31, 1910. Of the four

Selected South African National Records

Highest Point	Njesuthi Mountain	11,181 ft
Longest River	Orange	1,429 mi
Largest City	Johannesburg (metro, 2005)	pop. 3,288,000
Tallest Building	Carlton Centre Office Tower (Johannesburg)[1]	730 ft
Longest-Serving Prime Minister	JBM Hertzog	15 years, 2 months (1924-39)
First Olympic Medalist	Reginal Walker, gold, 100-meter, track; Charles A. Hefferon, silver, marathon	1908 London Games
First Nobel Laureate	Max Theiler	1951, Physiology/Medicine

(1) Tallest building in Africa

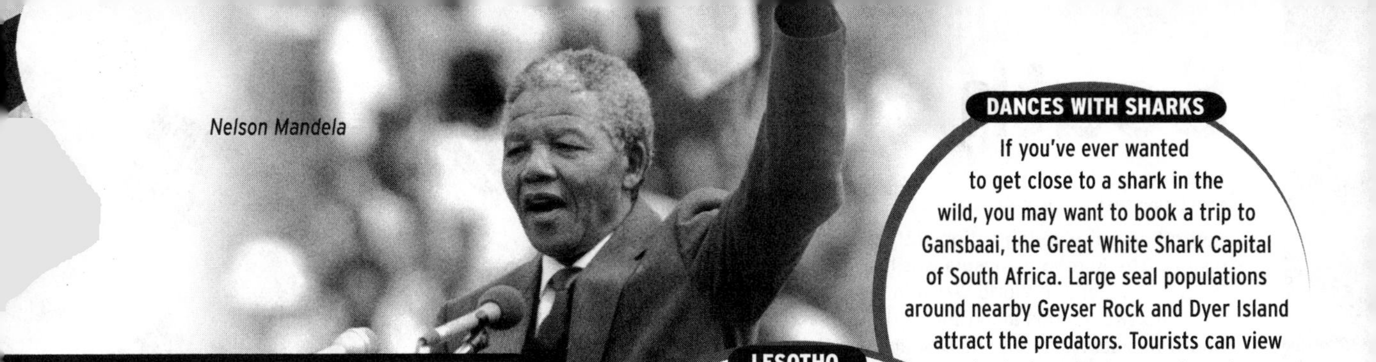

Nelson Mandela

colonies comprising the union, Cape Colony, Natal, Orange Free State, and Transvaal, only Cape Colony allowed blacks to vote in elections—and only the property holders among them.

1948: APARTHEID In 1948, the ruling National Party, consisting mostly of Afrikaners, officially instituted the policy of *apartheid*, an Afrikaans word meaning "apartness." The apartheid laws created a segregated society, in four classes: whites, blacks, coloreds (those of mixed white and black descent), and Asians.

The system forced nonwhites to carry passes, created separate "homelands," for blacks, barred interracial marriage, and imposed other restrictions.

After decades of struggle by groups such as the African National Congress (ANC), along with strong international pressure, the apartheid system ended; it was fully revoked in 1994.

1990: RELEASE OF MANDELA A leading ANC member and co-founder of *Umkonto we Sizwe* ("Spear of the Nation"), Nelson Mandela was arrested on terrorism charges on Aug. 5, 1962, and was later sentenced to life in prison. He continued his anti-apartheid campaign behind bars and became the focal point of resistance.

In 1989, President F.W. de Klerk legalized the ANC, and Mandela was freed on Feb. 11, 1990, after 27 years in prision. In democratic elections on April 27, 1994, Mandela was elected South Africa's first black president.

1994: FLAG South Africa's multi-color flag, formally adopted in 1994, has no official meaning, although the range of color and converging "Y" design are apparently meant to suggest diversity unifying. The colors are based on past flags, including the old South African flag and the ANC flag.

SOMETHING TO THINK ABOUT

DANCES WITH SHARKS

If you've ever wanted to get close to a shark in the wild, you may want to book a trip to Gansbaai, the Great White Shark Capital of South Africa. Large seal populations around nearby Geyser Rock and Dyer Island attract the predators. Tourists can view sharks from boats or underwater cages. April to December is peak viewing time.

LESOTHO

The Kingdom of Lesotho is a constitutional monarchy in the Drakensberg mountains, surrounded entirely by South Africa. The "Kingdom in the Sky" was formed about 1818 under King Moshoeshoe , who successfully fended off invading Zulus and Boers. It became a British protectorate (Basutoland) in 1868, but the people refused to join the South African nation. After apartheid was installed in South Africa, unification became impossible and Lesotho gained independence on Oct. 4, 1966.

SUPERLATIVES

LEADING GOLD PRODUCER South Africa has been the world's leading gold producer since the early 20th century. At the high point in 1970, the nation supplied 77.8% of the world's annual gold production. Its share had dropped to 14.5% by 2003. Although gold was not discovered in South Africa until the 1880s, South African mines have produced 39% of all the gold mined in the world since 1840. South Africa still has the largest reserves.

BIGGEST DIAMONDS The biggest and best diamonds in the world got their start at DeBeer's Cullinan mine (previously known as Premier Mine) in Cullinan, Gauteng.

Found in 1986, the 545.67-carat Golden Jubilee is the world's biggest cut diamond. The 138-facet topaz-colored gem was purchased in 1996 by a Thai businessman for King Bhumibol Adulyadej of Thailand in celebration of his 50th year as sovereign.

The world's biggest uncut diamond —weighing 3,106 carats (roughly 23 ounces)—was discovered in 1905, also at the Premier Mine. Purchased for King Edward VII of Great Britain, the stone was split into 11 stones, including the 530.2-carat Cullinan I (The Great Star of Africa), second in size only to the Golden Jubilee, and the 317.4-carat Cullinan II (The Lesser Star of Africa). Cullinan I was set in St. Edward's Scepter while Cullinan II adorned his Imperial State Crown; both are in the Tower of London.

The gems were named for mine owner Sir Thomas Cullinan.

AIDS CRISIS South Africa has the highest number of people living with HIV/AIDS in a single nation. As of the end of 2004, about 6.3 million people were living with the virus, 14% of South Africa's population.

South Korea

Total Area: 32,023 sq mi
Population (est. 2005): 48,640,671

South Korea is a young nation with an ancient history. The Korean peninsula was liberated from Japan at the end of World War II in 1945, and then split into two nations along the 38th parallel. The South was controlled by the U.S. and the North by the Soviet Union. In 1948, South Korea held its first elections; it was established as the Republic of Korea later that same year.

MILESTONES

2333 BC: KOREAN BEGINNINGS The Korean nation, according to its mythology, began with a visit by a god named Hwanung. Hwanung transformed a bear into a woman and married her.

Their offspring, Tangun, established a capital city at the site of present-day Pyongyang, founding the Choson ("Land of the Morning Dawn") Kingdom in northwestern Korea. This was said to have happened in 2333 BC, the starting point of the Korean calendar.

AROUND 1ST CENTURY BC: TAE KWON DO Tae Kwon Do, roughly meaning "the way of feet and fists," is a traditional martial art developed in South Korea and practiced all over the world. It began as several different tribal rituals and was developed by the militaries of the Three Kingdoms (Silla, Koguryo, and Paekche), as a hybrid of these different martial art styles.

South Korea introduced the sport in exhibition at the 1988 Olympic Games in Seoul, and it is now part of official competition.

1145, 1285: *SAMGUK SAGI* AND *SAMGUK YUSA* Two defining pieces of Korean literature were written to celebrate the famed "Three Kingdoms" period that brought arts, literature, and Buddhism to the cultural life of the peninsula. Under orders from King Injong, the Confucian scholar Kim Busik compiled a history book called *Samguk Sagi* ("History of the Three Kingdoms") in 1145. In 1285, a monk, Iryeon, wrote *Samguk Yusa* ("Memorabilia of the Three Kingdoms"), which added legends and memorabilia.

1446: *HANGUL* ALPHABET As a result of China's cultural influence, written Korean used Chinese characters until 1446, but the difficulty of memorizing the many characters meant that few outside the upper class learned to write. The situation led King Sejong (1397-1450) to ask that linguists develop an alphabet based on how Koreans talked.

The resulting alphabet, *hangul*, has undergone minimal changes since then.

1882: U.S.-KOREA TREATY On June 6, 1882, growing fears of Japanese imperialism led to a historic treaty between the U.S. and Korea. This agreement ended a long-standing policy that had closed off the peninsula to Western merchants and had resulted in Korea's international nickname, "The Hermit Kingdom."

1948: NATIONAL ANTHEM The lyrics for South Korea's national anthem, "Aegukga" ("Love the Country"), have gone through several changes, and they were often sung to Western tunes, most commonly "Auld Lang Syne." Ahn Eak-tay, a Korean who actually spent most of his life abroad in Spain, felt his country deserved an original composition, which he produced in 1935. It gained popularity after Korea's liberation in 1945 and was officially recognized in 1948.

A copyright dispute was resolved in March 2005, when Ahn's Spanish widow agreed to sign over the rights to the South Korean government.

1950: NATIONAL FLAG The basic pattern of the flag—a white field with a red and blue disk surrounded by four groups of black bars—was officially

Selected South Korean National Records

Highest Point	Halla-san Mt. (Cheju Island)	6,398 ft
Longest River	Naktong	325 miles
Largest City	Seoul (metro, 2005)	pop. 9,592,000
Tallest Building	Tower Palace Three-Tower G (Seoul)	865 ft
Longest-Serving President	Park Chung-Hee	16 years (1963-79)

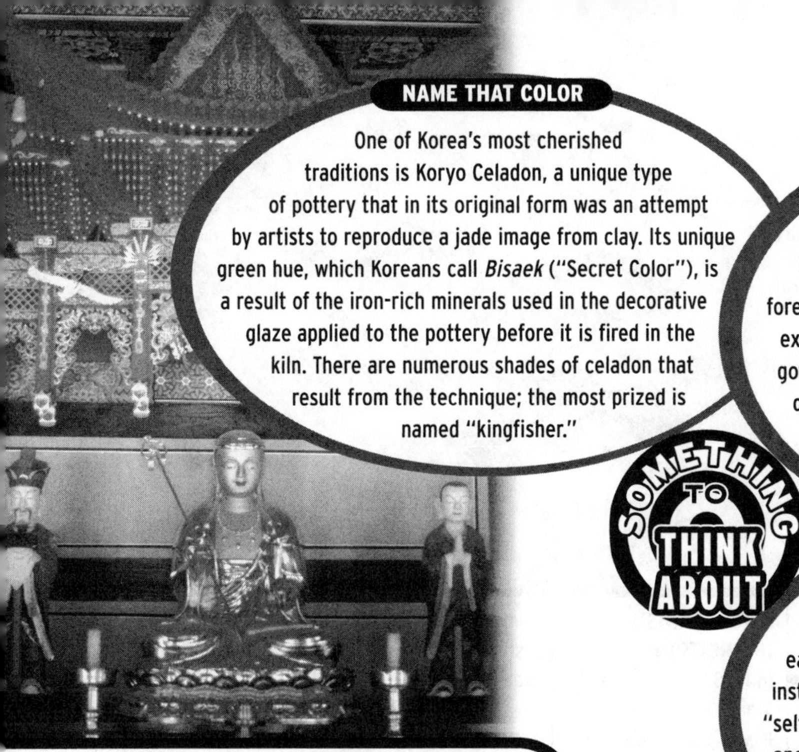

NAME THAT COLOR

One of Korea's most cherished traditions is Koryo Celadon, a unique type of pottery that in its original form was an attempt by artists to reproduce a jade image from clay. Its unique green hue, which Koreans call *Bisaek* ("Secret Color"), is a result of the iron-rich minerals used in the decorative glaze applied to the pottery before it is fired in the kiln. There are numerous shades of celadon that result from the technique; the most prized is named "kingfisher."

GINSENG JINGLE

South Korea produces Panax ginseng, which many consider the finest quality ginseng in the world. The ginseng herb is native to Korean forests and is perhaps Korea's oldest and most famous export. The Korean Ginseng Corp., organized by the government in 1899, is charged with maintaining the quality of its red ginseng. The U.S. and China are South Korea's largest global competitors in ginseng production.

SOMETHING TO THINK ABOUT

DATING BY BLOOD

A dating trend has spread like wildfire through South Korea, in which young people are increasingly defining each other's personality traits by their blood types. For instance, type-B men are considered out of favor for being "selfish and hot-headed" (in the words of one unlucky dater) and are unlikely to have much success on the dating scene if they reveal their secret. Pop culture has adopted this stereotype—in 2004, a song called "Type-B Men" topped the Korean charts.

adopted in 1950. The pattern of red yang and blue yin portrays a balanced universe of opposite forces, while the groups of black lines (called trigrams) symbolize heaven, earth, water, and fire and are arranged in a manner that reflects harmony.

1950-53: KOREAN CONFLICT On June 25, 1950, North Korea's military invaded South Korea in an attempt to unify the peninsula by force. The United States led a United Nations coalition in South Korea's defense, while the Soviet and Chinese militaries supported North Korean troops. Casualties numbered over one million in the resulting three-year war. A 1953 armistice provided for a Demilitarized Zone (DMZ), which still divides the peninsula between North Korea and South Korea.

2000: NORTH-SOUTH SUMMIT In 2000, the leaders of North and South Korea met for the first time in over a half-century, to consider plans for reunification. Although the ensuing agreement was brief and vague, it was hailed as a breakthrough.

Later in 2000, South Korean President Kim Dae Jung became the first Korean to be awarded the Nobel Peace Prize.

SUPERLATIVES

MOST BROADBAND-WIRED COUNTRY As of Dec. 2004, South Korea was home to 25 broadband subscribers per 100 inhabitants, making it the most broadband-wired country in the world. Its nearest rival is Hong Kong, with 21 subscribers per 100 inhabitants. Typical access fees are between $30 and $50 per month.

MOST ARMED BORDER Running 151 miles along the border between North and South Korea, the Demilitarized Zone (DMZ) is the most heavily fortified border in the world—and only 25 miles from Seoul.

The border was established on July 27, 1953, with the armistice ending the Korean War, and the DMZ became more militarized in 1974 after four tunnels were found under it.

Several other tunnels have been found since, and in 2004, three holes were found in the fence.

KIMCHI—MOST POPULAR FOOD Kimchi is considered the national dish of South Korea. It is made by fermenting cabbage leaves with red peppers, radishes, and lots of garlic and ginger.

One national survey found that kimchi constitutes 12.5% of the average total daily food intake. Most cities and villages will have a "Gimjang" festival in the late fall, devoted to preparing Kimchi, which is considered a winter staple.

Spain

Total Area: 194,897 sq mi
Population (est. 2005): 40,341,462

The Kingdom of Spain occupies almost the entire Iberian peninsula in western Europe, uniting the historical kingdoms of Castile, León, Aragón, and Navarre. Other Spanish provinces include the Balearic Islands (in the western Mediterranean Sea) and the Canary Islands (west of Morocco in the Atlantic). Spain dominated early European exploration of the Western Hemisphere and established Darien, the first permanent European settlement in the continental Americas, in present-day Colombia. In 2004, 94% of the population was Roman Catholic.

MILESTONES

1140: SPANISH LITERATURE The earliest known significant work in Spanish is *El cantar de mío Cid* ("The Song of the Cid"), an epic poem composed around 1140. The verses chronicle the heroic deeds of a Castilian warrior, Rodrigo Díaz de Vivar—by an unknown author (about 1040–99), known by the Arabic title *al-sidi* (lord) or *El Cid Campeador* (the Lord Champion).

The epic was composed in Castilian Spanish, the national language of Spain today and the first language of 74% of the people.

1300s: FLAMENCO Roma, or gypsies, are often credited with developing flamenco in Spain beginning in the 14th century. The exact origins of the word "flamenco" are unknown, but some believe it comes from the Arabic *felah-mengus*, meaning "wandering country person." Flamenco blossomed in various forms: *el cante* (the song), *el baile* (the dance), and, after the mid-19th century, *la guitarra* (flamenco guitar). Traditional songs and dances of Andalusia were also a major early influence.

In the second half of the 19th century, *cafés cantante* (singing cafes) sprung up in Seville and launched flamenco's Golden Age. Only four people have won the prestigious "llave de oro del cante" (Golden Key of Song Award): Tomás "el Nitri," Manual Vallejo, Antonio Mairena, and Camarón de la Isla.

1478: SPANISH INQUISITION In 1478 King Ferdinand V and Queen Isabella I, with the pope's approval, started a campaign to root out heresy, at first among Jews. This Spanish Inquisition tortured or executed thousands of Jews in its first few years, then focused on Muslims and on Protestants. Then, in 1492, all the Jews in Spain were ordered to leave the country, or else convert to Christianity. The Inquisition, which did not officially end until 1834, became a symbol of tyrannical cruelty.

Although Spain and Roman Catholics were not alone in persecuting alleged dissidents, and inquisitions were common throughout Europe, the Spanish Inquisition was thorough and effective, and flourished under a string of Spanish monarchs.

1479: BIRTH OF SPAIN By 1479, Ferdinand and Isabella separately ruled their kingdoms of Aragón and Castile, which together made up much of what is now Spain. In 1492 they conquered Granada, the last Muslim stronghold on the Iberian peninsula. That same year Queen Isabella sponsored the first voyage of Christopher Columbus, which gave Spain its initial claims in the Americas.

1720s: BULLFIGHTING The traditional Spanish bullfight is called *la fiesta brava* ("the brave festival"), or more popularly *la corrida*, meaning "the bullfight." Contests involving bulls were first documented in wall frescos in Knossos, Crete (around 1500 BC); in Spain, bullfighting became a customary part of medieval feast day celebrations. The tradition has changed little since the 1720s, when matador Francisco Romero (1698-1763) introduced *el estoque* (the sword) and *la muleta* (the cloth). Madrid erected the first permanent bullring in 1749.

In 2004, Spain hosted 1,912 bullfights involving 11,054 bulls. Madrid hosted 313 events, the most of any city. Madrid also houses the largest bullring in the country, Las Ventas, with a capacity of 23,669.

1770: "MARCHA REAL" (NATIONAL ANTHEM) The origins of the tune are disputed; some claim it was composed by a German, while others say it was originally French. Manuel

Selected Spanish National Records

Highest Point (mainland)	Mulhacén	11,411 ft above sea level
Highest Point (Canary Islands)	Pico de Teide	12,198 ft
Longest River	Tagus	626 mi
Largest City	Madrid (metro, 2005)	pop. 5,145,000
Tallest Building	Gran Hotel Bali (Benidorm)	Benidorm; 610 ft
Longest-Serving Prime Minister	Felipe González Márquez	Dec. 2, 1982–May 5, 1996
Longest-Serving Monarch	King Philip IV	44.5 years (March 31, 1621–Sept. 17, 1665)
Most Int'l Goals (soccer)	Raúl (Gonzáles)	39, 1996-present
Most Int'l Games (soccer)	Andoni Zubizarreta	126 caps, 1985-1998

SOMETHING TO THINK ABOUT

MOST BARREN LANDSCAPE

Timanfaya National Park is a barren volcanic field on Lanzarote, the easternmost island in the Canary Islands off the coast of Morocco. Volcanic eruptions from 1730 to 1736 and during the 19th century (mainly in 1824) made it so much like the surface of the moon that NASA studied its terrain in preparation for lunar missions. The park's restaurant, El Diablo, offers steaks cooked on a sizzling crater.

Espinosa first printed the score in 1761 as "Marcha Granadera" in a Spanish infantry bugle book. King Charles III decreed it to be his "March of Honor" on Sept. 3, 1770. There are no official lyrics, though many playwrights and poets have written verses at different times.

1785: NATIONAL FLAG The Spanish flag, first hoisted in 1785, consists of three horizontal bands of red (top), yellow (double width), and red (bottom), with the royal seal on the yellow band. The shield includes the coats-of-arms for Castile, León, Aragón, and Navarre, and is flanked by two crowned pillars (the Pillars of Hercules, which represent the two sides of the Gibraltar Strait) bearing the motto *Plus Ultra* ("further beyond"). Elements of the flag have been changed many times since 1785, but the colors have stayed the same.

1947: NO MONARCH MONARCHY General Francisco Franco (1892-1975), who became Spain's dictator after leading right-wing forces to victory in the bloody Spanish civil war (1936-39), declared the Spanish government a monarchy in 1947. This idea may have helped gain him some popularity, but Spain remained a monarchy in name only, since Franco decreed that no king could assume the throne until he died, was incapacitated, or freely stepped aside.

At Franco's death on Nov. 25, 1975, Juan Carlos I, the grandson of a former monarch, became Spain's king.

SUPERLATIVES

LARGEST OLIVE PRODUCER Spain is the top producer and exporter of olives and olive oil in the world. In 2004, the nation produced 4.6 million metric tons of olives. Olive groves cover about 6 million acres across Spain.

LARGEST ANNUAL FOOD FIGHT The festival of *La Tomatina,* celebrated the last Wednesday in August in the town of Buñol, is world-famous for its hour-long tomato fight in the town square at high noon. According to the most reliable accounts, the first tomato fight started in 1945 as a mishap at a parade honoring the town's patron saint. It has evolved into an organized event, with trucks dumping crushed red tomatoes on the streets an hour before bombardment commences.

In 2004, five trucks dumped 143 tons of tomatoes onto the square and a record 40,000 people participated in the food fight.

Participants must follow festival guidelines: crush all tomatoes before tossing them, refrain from throwing outside of the designated hour, and do not tear anyone's clothes. By the time the fight is over, the streets run red with rivers of tomato juice up to 10 inches deep.

MOST UEFA CHAMPIONS LEAGUE TITLES Real Madrid has won the Union of European Football Associations Champions League, the most prestigious competition in European club soccer, a record nine times. Originally contested as the European Cup from 1956 to 1998, the competition was dominated by Real Madrid from the beginning. Led by soccer legends Alfredo di Stéfano and Ferenc Puskas, Madrid won the first five cups, (1956-1960).

United Kingdom

Total Area: 94,525 sq mi
Population (est. 2005): 60,441,457

The United Kingdom, consisting of Great Britain (England, Scotland, and Wales) and Northern Ireland, is slightly smaller than the state of Oregon. This not-so-big island nation, with its historically powerful navy, built a vast overseas empire through trade and military conquest. The empire is gone, but the influence of Britain in its former colonies and in the world at large remains significant.

MILESTONES

C. 3100 BC: STONEHENGE Located north of Salisbury, England, Stonehenge is one of England's most famous artifacts. Consisting of huge bluestone structures arranged in concentric circles, it was built in three major stages between about 3100 and 2400 BC. Archaeologists still can only speculate as to its intended purpose; most theorize it served an astronomical or ceremonial function.

5TH CENTURY: ENGLISH The word "English" is derived from the name of the Angles who, along with the Saxons and Jutes, migrated from Germany to England in the fifth century.

The oldest written Old English document in existence is the 42-word *Caedmon's Hymn* (or Hymn of Creation), written around 670 AD.

802: FIRST KING The British monarchy began with Egbert, King of Wessex. Exiled to the continent in his youth, he returned in 802 and conquered the neighboring kingdoms of Kent, Cornwall, and Mercia. By 830 he was sovereign of East Anglia, Sussex, Surrey, and Northumbria, using the title of Bretwalda (ruler of the British).

1215: MAGNA CARTA The Magna Carta (Great Charter), often described as the basis of liberty in England, was accepted by King John on June 15, 1215. It established a legal relationship between the king and barons.

AROUND 1550: CRICKET The earliest record of cricket in some form, from 1598, notes a game of "crecket" played by kids in Guildford, Surrey, around 1550. Today's rules, though revised, are still based on those made by the Marylebone Cricket Club (MCC) of London in 1788. A game, called a test, can last five days.

1745: NATIONAL ANTHEM "God Save The King" was first performed in London in 1745 as a show of support to King George II in the wake of his army's defeat by the Scottish Highland army led by Prince Charles Edward Stuart. It quickly became common practice to play the tune whenever the King made a public appearance. It is not known who wrote the words or tune; the earliest copy of the words appeared in *Gentleman's Magazine* in 1745.

1762: SANDWICH While the concept of a sandwich is probably as old as sliced bread, the word can be traced to John Montagu, fourth Earl of Sandwich and Lord of the Admiralty (1718-92), who, according to one tradition, liked to gamble at cards so much that he made a meal out of cold beef between slices of bread so he could continue playing while he ate.

The earliest written record of the term comes from a Londoner's 1762 journal entry.

1801: UNION JACK When the Kingdoms of England and Wales, Scotland, and Ireland united in 1801, the current Union Flag, or Union Jack, was designed by combining three emblems: the red cross of St. George for England, the diagonal white cross of St. Andrew for Scotland, and the diagonal red cross of St. Patrick for Ireland.

Selected UK National Records

Highest Point	Ben Nevis, Scotland	4,406 ft
Lowest Point	The Fens, East England	13 ft below sea level
Longest River	Severn	200 mi
Largest Lake	Lough Neagh, Northern Ireland	153 sq mi
Largest City	London (metro, 2005)	pop. 7,615,000
Longest-Reigning Monarch	Queen Victoria	63 years, 7 months (1837-1901)
First Prime Minister	Sir Robert Walpole	1721-42
First Female Prime Minister	Margaret Thatcher	1979-90
Longest-Serving Prime Minister	Sir Robert Walpole	20 years, 314 days

The term "Union Jack" has uncertain origins, but many scholars believe it came from sailor slang for the small national flag flown from the jack-staff of a ship.

1860s: FISH AND CHIPS In London in the 1850s, fried fish and potatoes were sold as street food wrapped in newspaper bundles. Joseph Malin supposedly opened the first "chippy" in London's East End in 1860 and called it Malin's of Bowin.

1872: INTERNATIONAL SOCCER The first international soccer match was played at Hamilton Crescent in Glasgow, Scotland, on Nov. 30, 1872, when an English all-star team met its Scottish counterpart. The match ended in a scoreless tie.

1928: OXFORD ENGLISH DICTIONARY The Philological Society of London reached a deal with Oxford University Press in 1879 to create an English dictionary that would examine the language from Anglo-Saxon times onward. The editors planned to finish in 10 years, but it took five just to get to "ant." The whole first edition was finally completed in 1928.

The 20-volume second edition, published in 1989, has 231,000 main entries, backed by over 2.4 million quotations, and weighs 138 pounds. A third edition was begun online in 2000.

1940: WW II—BATTLE OF BRITAIN By June 1940, the Nazis controlled most of Europe and focused on capturing Great Britain. Adolf Hitler ordered a massive air campaign against the British Isles to pave the way for a later amphibious troop landing.

Britain's new prime minister, Winston Churchill, vowed to fight, and with superior radar technology and aircraft, England won superiority in the skies.

Germany, which lost some 1,700 planes, was forced to back off from the plan in September. However, England's cities, especially London, continued to suffer nighttime bombing raids into early 1941.

SOMETHING TO THINK ABOUT

RULE BRITANNIA

In 1914, on the eve of World War I, the British Empire took up about one-fifth of the world's land surface. Whether they knew it or not, one out of every four people in the world owed their allegiance to the British crown. The empire included the Dominion of Canada, the Commonwealth of Australia, a large chunk of Africa, and the lands that became India, Pakistan, and Burma (Myanmar). With such far-flung possessions, it was literally true that "the sun never set on the British Empire."

WHAT'S IN A NAME?

On July 17, 1917, in the midst of World War II, King George V by proclamation changed the name of the British Royal Family from Saxe-Coburg-Gotha to the name currently used, the English-sounding "Windsor," taken from the name of the royal castle. He made the change to avoid attaching a Germanic name to the royal family during the war with Germany.

SUPERLATIVES

LARGEST FERRIS WHEEL The 443-foot high British Airways London Eye, which sits along the river Thames, is the biggest Ferris wheel ever made. Over 1,700 people in five countries built its components. The wheel's 32 carriages can carry over 15,000 people each day and give them a view in every direction of over 25 miles.

The London Eye opened Feb. 1, 2000, and is due to be dismantled in 2008.

BIGGEST LEEK The leek has long been an emblem of Wales, but the world's largest leek was grown in England. Fred Charlton, a 65-year-old retired miner from Easington, England, nurtured the plant, which weighed in at a record 17 lbs, 13 oz at the 2002 UK National Giant Vegetable Championship. It was over 4 feet tall.

The secret? Plenty of water, horse manure, and dried animal blood every 10 days.

LARGEST RADIO AUDIENCE The largest radio audience for any program is the estimated 146 million listeners worldwide who regularly tune in to the BBC World Service, originally known as the "Empire Service."

The first overseas transmissions were sent on Dec. 19, 1932. Today, the service is broadcast in 43 languages, in 139 capital cities, and from over 1,200 stations.

BASEBALL

Team by Team

MAJOR LEAGUE BASEBALL HAS TWO LEAGUES: the National League (NL), founded in 1876, and American League (AL), founded in 1901. The Atlanta Braves (then Boston Red Caps) and Chicago Cubs (then White Stockings) are the only current franchises that go back to the first NL season.

The tables below cover records and milestones for each team through the 2005 season.

SUPERLATIVES

MOST NL PENNANTS
The Los Angeles Dodgers franchise won a record 21 NL titles, the last nine after the team moved from Brooklyn to Los Angeles in 1958.

MOST AL PENNANTS
The New York Yankees, hold a record 39 AL titles, which is also the record for the major leagues.

Team by Team First season for each team is in parentheses.

ARIZONA DIAMONDBACKS (1998, NL)			
World Series Title	2001		
Most Home Runs	209	Luis Gonzalez	1999-2005
Most RBIs	701	Luis Gonzalez	1999-2005
Most Wins	103	Randy Johnson	1999-2004

ATLANTA BRAVES (1876, as Boston Red Caps, NL)			
World Series Titles	1914[1], 1957[2], 1995		
Most Home Runs	733	Hank Aaron	1954-74[3]
Most RBIs	2,202	Hank Aaron	1954-74[2]
Most Wins	356	Warren Spahn	1942-64[4]
(1) as Boston Braves; (2) as Milwaukee Braves; (3) Milwaukee Braves, 1954-65; (4) Boston Braves, 1942-52, Milwaukee Braves, 1953-64.			

BALTIMORE ORIOLES (1901, as Milwaukee Brewers, AL)			
World Series Titles	1966, 1970, 1983		
Most Home Runs	431	Cal Ripken Jr.	1981-2001
Most RBIs	1,695	Cal Ripken Jr.	1981-2001
Most Wins	268	Jim Palmer	1965-84

BOSTON RED SOX (1901, as Boston Americans, NL)			
World Series Titles	1903[1], 1912, 1915, 1916, 1918, 2004		
Most Home Runs	521	Ted Williams	1939-42, 1946-60
Most RBIs	1,844	Carl Yastrzemski	1961-83
Most Wins	192	Cy Young	1901-08
	192	Roger Clemens	1984-96
(1) as Boston Pilgrims			

CHICAGO CUBS (1876, as Chicago White Stockings, NL)			
World Series Titles	1907-08		
Most Home Runs	545	Sammy Sosa	1992-2004
Most RBIs	1,879	Cap Anson	1876-97
Most Wins	201	Charley Root	1926-41

CHICAGO WHITE SOX (1901, AL)			
World Series Titles	1906, 1917, 2005		
Most Home Runs	448	Frank Thomas	1990-2005
Most RBIs	1,465	Frank Thomas	1990-2005
Most Wins	260	Ted Lyons	1923-46

CINCINNATI REDS (1882, as Cincinnati Red Stockings, NL)			
World Series Titles	1919, 1940, 1975-76, 1990		
Most Home Runs	389	Johnny Bench	1967-83
Most RBIs	1,376	Johnny Bench	1967-83
Most Wins	179	Eppa Rixey	1921-33

CLEVELAND INDIANS (1901, as Cleveland Blues, AL)			
World Series Titles	1920, 1948		
Most Home Runs	334	Jim Thome	1991-2002
Most RBIs	1,084	Earl Averill	1929-39
Most Wins	266	Bob Feller	1936-41, 1945-56

COLORADO ROCKIES (1993, NL)			
Most Home Runs	271	Todd Helton	1997-2005
Most RBIs	915	Todd Helton	1997-2005
Most Wins	53	Pedro Astacio	1997-2001

DETROIT TIGERS (1901, AL)			
World Series Titles	1935, 1945, 1968, 1984		
Most Home Runs	399	Al Kaline	1953-74
Most RBIs	1,804	Ty Cobb	1905-26
Most Wins	222	Hooks Dauss	1912-26

FLORIDA MARLINS (1993, NL)			
World Series Titles	1997, 2003		
Most Home Runs	143	Mike Lowell	1999-2005
Most RBIs	578	Mike Lowell	1999-2005
Most Wins	49	A.J. Burnett	1999-2005

HOUSTON ASTROS (1962, as Houston Colt .45s, NL)			
Most Home Runs	449	Jeff Bagwell	1991-2005
Most RBIs	1,529	Jeff Bagwell	1991-2005
Most Wins	144	Joe Niekro	1975-85

KANSAS CITY ROYALS (1969, AL)			
World Series Title	1985		
Most Home Runs	317	George Brett	1973-93
Most RBIs	1,595	George Brett	1973-93
Most Wins	166	Paul Splittorff	1970-84

LOS ANGELES ANGELS OF ANAHEIM, 1961 (as Los Angeles Angels, AL)			
World Series title	2002		
Most Home Runs	290	Tim Salmon	1992-2004[1]
Most RBIs	1,043	Garret Anderson	1994-2005[2]
Most Wins	165	Chuck Finley	1986-99[3]
(1) California Angels, 1992-96, Anaheim Angels, 1997-2004; (2) California Angels, 1994-96, Anaheim Angels, 1997-2004; (3) California Angels, 1986-96, Anaheim Angels, 1997-99.			

LOS ANGELES DODGERS (1890, as Brooklyn Bridegrooms, NL)			
World Series titles	1955[1], 1959, 1963, 1965, 1981, 1988		
Most Home Runs	389	Duke Snider	1947-62[2]
Most RBIs	1,271	Duke Snider	1947-62[2]
Most Wins	233	Don Sutton	1966-80, 1988
(1) as Brooklyn Dodgers; (2) Brooklyn Dodgers, 1947-57.			

MILWAUKEE BREWERS (1969, as Seattle Pilots, NL[1])			
Most Home Runs	251	Robin Yount	1974-93
Most RBIs	1,406	Robin Yount	1974-93
Most Wins	117	Jim Slaton	1971-77, 1979-83
(1) Team was in AL from 1969-97.			

MINNESOTA TWINS (1901, as Washington Senators, AL)			
World Series titles	1924[1], 1987, 1991		
Most Home Runs	559	Harmon Killebrew	1954-74[2]
Most RBIs	1,540	Harmon Killebrew	1954-74[2]
Most Wins	417	Walter Johnson	1907-27[3]
(1) as Washington Senators; (2) Washington Senators, 1954-60; (3) Washington Senators, 1907-27.			

NEW YORK METS (1962, NL)			
World Series titles	1969, 1986		
Most Home Runs	252	Darryl Strawberry	1983-90
Most RBIs	733	Darryl Strawberry	1983-90
Most Wins	198	Tom Seaver	1967-77, 1983

NEW YORK YANKEES (1901, as Baltimore Orioles, AL)			
World Series titles	1923, 1927-28, 1932, 1936-39, 1941, 1943, 1947, 1949-53, 1956, 1958, 1961-62, 1977-78, 1996, 1998-2000		
Most Home Runs	659	Babe Ruth	1920-34
Most RBIs	1,995	Lou Gehrig	1923-39
Most Wins	236	Whitey Ford	1950-67

OAKLAND ATHLETICS (1901, as Philadelphia Athletics, AL)			
World Series titles	1910-11[1], 1913[1], 1929-30[1], 1972-74, 1989		
Most Home Runs	363	Mark McGwire	1986-97
Most RBIs	1,178	Al Simmons	1924-32, 1940-41, 1944[2]
Most Wins	284	Eddie Plank	1901-14[2]
(1) As Philadelphia Athletics; (2) Philadelphia Athletics.			

PHILADELPHIA PHILLIES (1883 as Philadelphia Quakers, NL)			
World Series title	1980		
Most Home Runs	548	Mike Schmidt	1972-89
Most RBIs	1,595	Mike Schmidt	1972-89
Most Wins	241	Steve Carlton	1972-86

PITTSBURGH PIRATES (1887, as Pittsburgh Alleghenys, NL)			
World Series titles	1909, 1925, 1960, 1971, 1979		
Most Home Runs	475	Willie Stargell	1962-82
Most RBIs	1,540	Willie Stargell	1962-82
Most Wins	202	Wilbur Cooper	1912-24

ST. LOUIS CARDINALS (1892, as St. Louis Browns, NL)			
World Series titles	1926, 1931, 1934, 1942, 1944, 1946, 1964, 1967, 1982		
Most Home Runs	475	Stan Musial	1941-63
Most RBIs	1,951	Stan Musial	1941-63
Most Wins	251	Bob Gibson	1959-75

SAN DIEGO PADRES (1969, NL)			
Most Home Runs	163	Nate Colbert	1969-74
Most RBIs	1,138	Tony Gwynn	1982-2001
Most Wins	100	Eric Show	1981-90

SAN FRANCISCO GIANTS (1883, as New York Gothams, NL)			
World Series titles	1905, 1921-22, 1933, 1954[1]		
Most Home Runs	646	Willie Mays	1951-72[2]
Most RBIs	1,860	Mel Ott	1926-47[1]
Most Wins	372	Christy Mathewson	1900-16[1]
(1) as New York Giants; (2) New York Giants, 1951-57.			

SEATTLE MARINERS (1977, AL)			
Most Home Runs	398	Ken Griffey Jr.	1989-99
Most RBIs	1,261	Edgar Martinez	1987-2004
Most Wins	130	Randy Johnson	1989-98

TAMPA BAY DEVIL RAYS (1998, AL)			
Most Home Runs	120	Aubrey Huff	2000-2005
Most RBIs	421	Aubrey Huff	2000-2005
Most Wins	35	Victor Zambrano	2001-2004

TEXAS RANGERS (1961, as Washington Senators, AL)			
Most Home Runs	372	Juan Gonzalez	1989-99, 2002-03
Most RBIs	1,180	Juan Gonzalez	1989-99, 2002-03
Most Wins	139	Charlie Hough	1980-90

TORONTO BLUE JAYS (1977, AL)			
World Series titles	1992-93		
Most Home Runs	336	Carlos Delgado	1993-2004
Most RBIs	1,058	Carlos Delgado	1993-2004
Most Wins	175	Dave Stieb	1979-92, 1998

WASHINGTON NATIONALS (1969, as Montreal Expos, NL)			
Most Home Runs	234	Vladimir Guerrero	1996-2003[1]
Most RBIs	905	Tim Wallach	1980-92[1]
Most Wins	158	Steve Rogers	1973-85[1]
(1) as Montreal Expos.			

BASEBALL

Hitting

MILESTONES

1882: HITTING FOR THE CYCLE The first player to hit for the cycle (single, double, triple, and home run in a game) was Charles "Curry" Foley for the Buffalo Bisons (NL) on May 25, 1882. The first player to hit for the cycle in the American League (AL) was Harry Davis of the Philadelphia A's on July 10, 1901.

1916: SWITCH-HIT HOME RUNS The first player to hit home runs from both sides of the plate in a single game was Wally Schang for the Philadelphia A's on Sept. 8, 1916, against the New York Yankees.

1973: DESIGNATED HITTER The first player to step into the batter's box as a designated hitter was Ron Blomberg of the New York Yankees on April 6, 1973. He walked in his first plate appearance and went 1-for-3 in the game against the Boston Red Sox in the season opener at Fenway Park.

APRIL 8, 1974: AARON PASSES RUTH Atlanta Braves outfielder Hank Aaron hit his 715th career home run to break Babe Ruth's all-time home run record that had stood since 1935. Aaron had tied Ruth's record on opening day of the 1974 season in Cincinnati. In the Braves' home opener, Aaron hit number 715 over the wall in left-center off Los Angeles Dodgers pitcher Al Downing in the fourth inning.

SUPERLATIVES

HITS (GAME)
The most hits ever accrued by one player in a single game is nine (7 singles, 2 doubles). Johnny Burnett of the Cleveland Indians accomplished the feat during a grueling 18-inning game on July 10, 1932.

Two players are tied for the record for a nine-inning game with seven hits: Wilbert Robinson of the Baltimore Orioles, on June 10, 1892; Rennie Stennett of the Pittsburgh Pirates, on Sept. 16, 1975.

HOME RUNS (GAME)
The most home runs in a game is four, a feat achieved by 15 players: Bobby Lowe, Boston Beaneaters (NL) on May 30, 1894; Ed Delahanty, Philadelphia Phillies, on July 13, 1896; Lou Gehrig, New York Yankees, on June 3, 1932; Chuck Klein, Philadelphia Phillies, on July 10, 1936; Pat Seerey, Chicago White Sox, on July 18, 1948; Gil Hodges, Brooklyn Dodgers, on Aug. 31, 1950; Joe Adcock, Milwaukee Braves, on July 31, 1954; Rocky Colavito, Cleveland Indians, on June 10, 1959; Willie Mays, San Francisco Giants, on April 30, 1961; Mike Schmidt, Philadelphia Phillies, on April 17, 1976; Bob Horner, Atlanta Braves, on July 6, 1986; Mark Whiten, St. Louis Cardinals, on Sept. 7, 1993; Mike Cameron, Seattle Mariners, on May 2, 2002; Shawn Green, Los Angeles Dodgers, on May 23, 2002; and Carlos Delgado, Toronto Blue Jays, on Sept. 25, 2003.

Klein, Seerey, and Schmidt were playing in extra-inning games.

RBI (GAME)
The most RBIs in a game by a single player is 12. Two players have done this: Jim Bottomley of the St. Louis Cardinals, on Sept. 16, 1924; and Mark Whiten, also of the Cardinals, on Sept. 7, 1993.

HITTING STREAKS
Joe DiMaggio, the "Yankee Clipper," hit safely in a record 56 consecutive games in 1941. His streak began at Yankee Stadium with a base hit off Eddie Smith of the Chicago White Sox, on May 15. It ended when DiMaggio went 0-for-3 with a walk against the Cleveland Indians at Municipal Stadium on July 17. During the streak, DiMaggio batted .408 with 56 singles, 16 doubles, 4 triples, and 15 home runs through 223 at-bats.

Two players are tied for having the most hits in a row, at 12. Pinky Higgins of the Boston Red Sox did it over four games, June 19-21, 1938. And Walt "Moose" Dropo of the Detroit Tigers tied the record over three games on July 14-15, 1952.

"You can't think and hit at the same time."

–Yogi Berra, 1946

WELL-TRAVELED SLUGGER

SOMETHING TO THINK ABOUT

Todd Zeile is the only player in major league history to have hit a home run for 11 different teams. Zeile set his obscure record when he hit two home runs for the Montreal Expos on Sept. 5, 2003, against the Florida Marlins in Puerto Rico. He had previously blasted round-trippers for the St. Louis Cardinals, Chicago Cubs, Philadelphia Phillies, Baltimore Orioles, Los Angeles Dodgers, Florida Marlins, Texas Rangers, New York Mets, Colorado Rockies, and the New York Yankees. Zeile retired at the end of the 2004 season having played his final season with the New York Mets. In his career Zeile hit 253 home runs over 16 seasons.

Triple Crown Winners[1]

YEAR	PLAYER, TEAM	AVG.	HR	RBI
1901	Nap Lajoie, Philadelphia A's (AL)	.422	14	125[2]
1909	Ty Cobb, Detroit Tigers (AL)	.377	9	115[2]
1912	Heinie Zimmerman, Chicago Cubs (NL)	.372	14	99[2]
1922	Rogers Hornsby, St. Louis Cardinals (NL)	.401	42	152
1925	Rogers Hornsby, St. Louis Cardinals (NL)	.403	39	143
1933	Jimmie Foxx, Philadelphia A's (AL)	.356	48	163
1933	Chuck Klein, Philadelphia Phillies (NL)	.368	28	120
1934	Lou Gehrig, New York Yankees (AL)	.363	49	165
1937	Joe Medwick, St. Louis Cardinals (NL)	.374	31	154
1942	Ted Williams, Boston Red Sox (AL)	.356	36	137
1942	Ted Williams, Boston Red Sox (AL)	.343	32	114
1947	Ted Williams, Boston Red Sox (AL)	.343	32	114
1956	Mickey Mantle, New York Yankees (AL)	.353	52	130
1966	Frank Robinson, Baltimore Orioles (AL)	.316	49	122
1967	Carl Yastrzemski, Boston Red Sox (AL)	.326	44	121

(1) Led the AL or NL in batting average, home runs, and RBIs in the same season. (2) RBIs not officially adopted until 1920.

Selected Major League Hitting Records

Season

RECORD	TOTAL	PLAYER	TEAM	YEAR
Batting Average (Min. 100 games)	.440	Hugh Duffy	Boston Beaneaters	1894
At Bats	705	Willie Wilson	Kansas City Royals	1980
Runs	192	Billy Hamilton	Philadelphia Phillies	1894
Hits	262	Ichiro Suzuki	Seattle Mariners	2004
Home Runs	73	Barry Bonds	S.F. Giants	2001
RBI	191	Hack Wilson	Chicago Cubs	1930
Total Bases	457	Babe Ruth	N.Y. Yankees	1921
Slugging Avg.	.863	Barry Bonds	S.F. Giants	2001
Grand Slams	6	Don Mattingly	N.Y. Yankees	1987
Walks	232	Barry Bonds	S.F. Giants	2004
Stolen Bases	130	Rickey Henderson	Oakland A's	1982

Career

RECORD	TOTAL	PLAYER	TEAM	YEAR
At Bats	14,053	Pete Rose	Cincinnati Reds, Philadelphia Phillies, Montreal Expos	1963-86
Batting Average (Min. 10,000 AB)	.367	Ty Cobb	Detroit Tigers, Philadelphia A's	1905-28
Hits	4,256	Pete Rose	Cincinnati Reds, Philadelphia Phillies, Montreal Expos	1963-86
Runs	2,295	Rickey Henderson	Oakland A's, N.Y. Yankees, Toronto Blue Jays, San Diego Padres, Anaheim Angels, N.Y. Mets, Seattle Mariners, Boston Red Sox, L.A. Dodgers	1979-2003
Home Runs	755	Hank Aaron	Milwaukee-Atlanta Braves, Milwaukee Brewers	1954-76
RBI	2,297	Hank Aaron	Milwaukee-Atlanta Braves, Milwaukee Brewers	1954-76
Stolen Bases	1,406	Rickey Henderson	Oakland A's, N.Y. Yankees, Toronto Blue Jays, San Diego Padres, Anaheim Angels, N.Y. Mets, Seattle Mariners, Boston Red Sox, L.A. Dodgers	1979-2003
Total Bases	6,856	Hank Aaron	Milwaukee-Atlanta Braves, Milwaukee Brewers	1954-76
Slugging Avg. (Min. 4,000 total bases)	.690	Babe Ruth	Boston Red Sox, N.Y. Yankees, Boston Braves	1914-35
Grand Slams	23	Lou Gehrig	N.Y. Yankees	1923-39
Walks	2,190	Rickey Henderson	Oakland A's, N.Y. Yankees, Toronto Blue Jays San Diego Padres, Anaheim Angels, N.Y. Mets, Seattle Mariners, Boston Red Sox, L.A. Dodgers	1979-2003

BASEBALL

Pitching

◀ *Walter Johnson*

MILESTONES

1876: FIRST NO-HITTER The first officially recognized no-hitter was pitched by George Bradley of the St. Louis Brown Stockings in a 2-0 win against the Hartford Dark Blues on July 15, 1876. Since then, 234 no-hitters have been pitched in the majors.

1880: PERFECT GAME In a perfect game, no batter reaches any base during a full game of at least nine innings. The first officially recognized perfect game was thrown by Lee Richmond of the Worcester Ruby Legs in a 1-0 win over the Cleveland Blues on June 12, 1880.

Through the 2005 season, there have been 17 perfect games pitched in the majors. Randy Johnson of the Arizona Diamondbacks pitched the most recent perfect game vs. the Atlanta Braves on May 18, 2004.

1893: 60 FEET, 6 INCHES The standard pitching distance was set at 60 feet, 6 inches in 1893. At the same time, it was ruled that the pitcher's rear foot must maintain contact with the pitching rubber.

1947: FIRST AFRICAN-AMERICAN PITCHER Brooklyn Dodger Dan Bankhead became the first African-American pitcher in the majors when he pitched in relief against the Pittsburgh Pirates on Aug. 26, 1947. He hit a home run in his first plate appearance, but in $3\frac{1}{3}$ innings on the mound, he gave up 10 hits and eight earned runs to the Pirates. Pittsburgh won, 16-3.

1956: CY YOUNG AWARD Inaugurated in 1956, the Cy Young Award is given to the best pitcher in baseball as judged by the Baseball Writers' Association of America. Don Newcombe of the Brooklyn Dodgers won the first award. Since 1967, separate awards have been given to the best pitchers in each league.

1969: LOWERING THE PITCHING MOUND The pitcher's mound was limited to 15 inches in height in 1904. It remained at that height until 1969, when it was lowered to 10 inches.

Selected Major League Pitching Records

Season

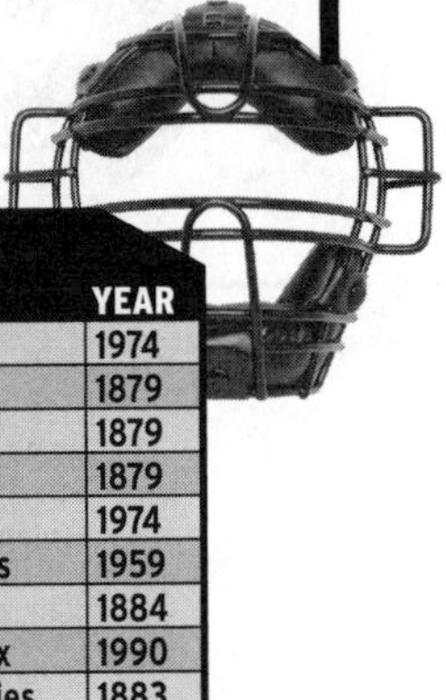

RECORD	TOTAL	PLAYER	TEAM	YEAR
Games	106	Mike Marshall	LA Dodgers	1974
Starts	75	Will White	Cincinnati Reds	1879
Complete Games	75	Will White	Cincinnati Reds	1879
Innings Pitched	680	Will White	Cincinnati Reds	1879
Innings (Relief)	208.1	Mike Marshall	LA Dodgers	1974
Highest Win Pct. (16 or more decisions)	.947 (18-1)	Roy Face	Pittsburgh Pirates	1959
Games Won	59	Charley "Old Hoss" Radbourn	Providence Grays	1884
Saves	57	Bobby Thigpen	Chicago White Sox	1990
Games Lost	48	John F. Coleman	Philadelphia Phillies	1883
Lowest ERA (300 or more innings)	1.12	Bob Gibson	St. Louis Cardinals	1968
Home Runs Allowed	50	Bert Blyleven	Minnesota Twins	1986
Walks	289	Amos Rusie	NY Giants	1890
Strikeouts	441	Charley "Old Hoss" Radbourn	Providence Grays	1884

SUPERLATIVES

MOST NO-HITTERS
Hall of Famer Nolan Ryan pitched a record seven career no-hitters. He threw his first "no-no" for the California Angels in a game against the Kansas City Royals (a 3-0 win), on May 15, 1973, and the last for the Texas Rangers vs. Toronto Blue Jays (3-0), on May 1, 1991.

CONSECUTIVE NO-HITTERS The only player to pitch a no-hitter in back-to-back starts is Johnny Vander Meer of the Cincinnati Reds. He did it on June 11, 1938, against the Boston Bees, a 3-0 win, and on June 15, 1938, vs. the Brooklyn Dodgers, a 6-0 win.

MOST STRIKEOUTS (GAME) The most strikeouts in nine innings is 20, a record reached four times by three pitchers: Roger Clemens, first for the Boston Red Sox vs. Seattle Mariners on April 29, 1986, and again for the Red Sox at the Detroit Tigers on Sept. 18, 1996; Kerry Wood, Chicago Cubs vs. Houston Astros, May 6, 1998; and Randy Johnson, Arizona Diamondbacks vs. Cincinnati Reds, May 8, 2001.

Johnson pitched the first nine innings of an 11-inning game. In a 16-inning game, Tom Cheney of the Washington Senators threw 21 strikeouts vs. Baltimore Orioles on Sept. 12, 1962.

MOST CONSECUTIVE STRIKEOUTS
The most consecutive strikeouts is 10, by Tom Seaver of the New York Mets. He sent down 10 straight San Diego Padres on April 22, 1970.

OLDEST PITCHER (START) The oldest pitcher (and oldest major league player) was Satchel Paige of the Kansas City A's. He was 59 years, 80 days old when he last pitched, on Sept. 25, 1965.

YOUNGEST PITCHER
The youngest pitcher (and youngest major league player) was Joe Nuxhall of the Cincinnati Reds. He made his Reds debut on June 10, 1944, at age 15 years, 314 days. It was his only appearance of the season. He didn't pitch again in the majors until 1952.

MOST CY YOUNG AWARDS
Roger Clemens has won a record seven Cy Young Awards. He won three times with the Boston Red Sox, 1986-87 and 1991; twice with the Toronto Blue Jays, 1997-98; once with the New York Yankees, in 2001; and most recently with the Houston Astros in 2004.

Selected Major League Pitching Records

Career

RECORD	TOTAL	PLAYER	TEAM	YEARS
Games	1,252	Jesse Orosco	NY Mets, LA Dodgers, Cleveland Indians, Milwaukee Brewers, Baltimore Orioles, St. Louis Cardinals, San Diego Padres, NY Yankees, Minnesota Twins	1979, 1981-2003
Starts	815	Cy Young	Cleveland Spiders, St. Louis Cardinals, Boston Red Sox, Cleveland Indians, Boston Braves	1890-1911
Complete Games	749	Cy Young	Cleveland Spiders, St. Louis Cardinals, Boston Red Sox, Cleveland Indians, Boston Braves	1890-1911
Innings Pitched	7,356	Cy Young	Cleveland Spiders, St. Louis Cardinals, Boston Red Sox, Cleveland Indians, Boston Braves	1890-1911
Innings Pitched (Relief)	1,870	Hoyt Wilhelm	NY Giants, St. Louis Cardinals, Cleveland Indians, Baltimore Orioles, Chicago White Sox, California Angels, Atlanta Braves, Chicago Cubs, LA Dodgers	1952-72
Highest Win Pct. (200 or more decisions)	.795	Al Spalding	Boston Braves, Chicago Cubs	1871-77
Games Won	511	Cy Young	Cleveland Spiders, St. Louis Cardinals, Boston Red Sox, Cleveland Indians, Boston Braves	1890-1911
Saves (since 1969)	478	Lee Smith	Chicago Cubs, Boston Red Sox, St. Louis Cardinals, NY Yankees, Baltimore Orioles, California Angels, Cincinnati Reds, Montreal Expos	1980-97
Games Lost	316	Cy Young	Cleveland Spiders, St. Louis Cardinals, Boston Red Sox, Cleveland Indians, Boston Braves	1890-1911
Lowest ERA (2,000 or more innings pitched)	1.82	Ed Walsh	Chicago White Sox, Boston Braves	1904-17
Shutouts	110	Walter Johnson	Washington Senators	1907-27
Home Runs Allowed	505	Robin Roberts	Philadelphia Phillies, Baltimore Orioles, Houston Astros, Chicago Cubs	1948-66
Walks	2,795	Nolan Ryan	NY Mets, California Angels, Houston Astros, Texas Rangers	1966, 1968-93
Strikeouts	5,714	Nolan Ryan	NY Mets, California Angels, Houston Astros, Texas Rangers	1966, 1968-93

The World Series

Yankee Stadium ►

ALTHOUGH VARIOUS CHAMPIONSHIP GAMES WERE PLAYED BETWEEN DIFFERENT BASEBALL LEAGUES IN THE 1880S, the first official World Series was played in 1903. Barney Dreyfuss, owner of the National League (NL) champion Pittsburgh Pirates, invited the winners of the American League (AL) pennant, the Boston Pilgrims, to play his team in a best-of-nine championship series to decide the best team in baseball. The two rival leagues had feuded since the founding of the AL in 1901, and Dreyfuss saw the playoff series as a means to building better relations.

In an upset, the Pilgrims won the series, 5-3. The following year, the National League's New York Giants refused to play Boston in a second World Series, but in 1905 the Giants agreed to play the Philadelphia A's, and the World Series became a permanent baseball fixture. It has been a best-of-seven series since 1905, except for three best-of-nine series, 1919-1921.

Apart from 1904, the only time the Series wasn't played was in 1994, when a players' strike forced the cancellation of the baseball season.

MILESTONES

1903: FIRST GAME The first World Series game was played on Oct. 1, 1903, at Boston's Huntington Avenue Base Ball Grounds. Cy Young started for the Pilgrims, Deacon Phillipe for the Pirates. Pittsburgh won the game, 7-3. The Pirates' right fielder Jimmy Sebring hit the first home run in Series history.

1905: COMBINED 0.00 ERA At the second World Series in 1905, the New York Giants beat the Philadelphia A's, 4-1. The Giants pitchers combined for an ERA of 0.00. Christy Mathewson threw shutouts in Games One, Three, and Five, and Joe McGinnity pitched a 1-0 shutout in Game Four. The A's won Game Two, 3-0, but as all the runs resulted from Giants' errors, the Giants pitcher, McGinnity, was not charged with any runs. This series was also first in which all games were shutouts.

1906: "SAME CITY" SERIES The first time the World Series was played between teams from the same city was in 1906, when the Chicago Cubs played the Chicago White Sox. The Cubs, winners of a then record 116 games during the regular season, were expected to beat the White Sox, a team known as the "Hitless Wonders," but the White Sox never trailed in the Series, which they won 4-2.

1909: DECIDING GAME SEVEN The first time the World Series went to a deciding Game Seven was in 1909. The Pittsburgh Pirates and the Detroit Tigers split the first six, and the climactic seventh game was played at Detroit's Bennett Park on Oct. 16. The Pirates jumped to an early 2-0 lead and went on to win 8-0 behind a complete game shutout from rookie Babe Adams. It was Adams's third complete-game win in the Series.

1920: UNASSISTED TRIPLE PLAY The first, and so far only, unassisted triple play in a World Series game came in Game Five of the 1920 Series between the Cleveland Indians and Brooklyn Dodgers. Indians shortstop Bill Wambsganss caught a line drive from Dodgers pitcher Clarence Mitchell. Wambsganss stepped on second to erase Pete Kilduff, and tagged out Otto Miller, who had been running from first base.

1920: GRAND SLAM The first grand slam hit in World Series history came in Game Five of the 1920 Series between the Indians and the Dodgers (the same game as the only unassisted triple play). Indians outfielder Elmer Smith hit the historic homer off Burleigh Grimes in the first inning.

Cleveland pitcher Jim Bagby hit a home run in the fourth inning, becoming the first pitcher to hit a World Series dinger. The Indians won the game, 8-1, and went on to take the Series, 5-2.

1927-28: CONSECUTIVE SWEEPS The first team to sweep consecutive World Series was the 1927-28 New York Yankees. The Bronx Bombers swept the Pittsburgh Pirates, 4-0, in 1927, and the St. Louis Cardinals, 4-0, in 1928.

1947: PINCH HIT HOME RUN Yogi Berra of the New York Yankees hit the first pinch hit home run in a World Series in Game Three of the 1947 Series at Ebbets Field on Oct. 2, 1947. Berra's bomb was in vain, as the Dodgers won the game, 9-8.

1947: AFRICAN-AMERICAN The first African-American player in a World Series game was Jackie Robinson of the Brooklyn Dodgers. The All-Star second baseman started in Game One of the 1947 Series at Yankee Stadium on Sept. 30.

The first African-American player to hit a home run in the Fall Classic was Larry Doby. His historic home run came in Game Four of the 1948 Series for the Cleveland Indians against the Boston Braves.

In 1952, Joe Black of the Brooklyn Dodgers became the first African-American pitcher to win a Series game when he beat the New York Yankees in Game One, 4-2.

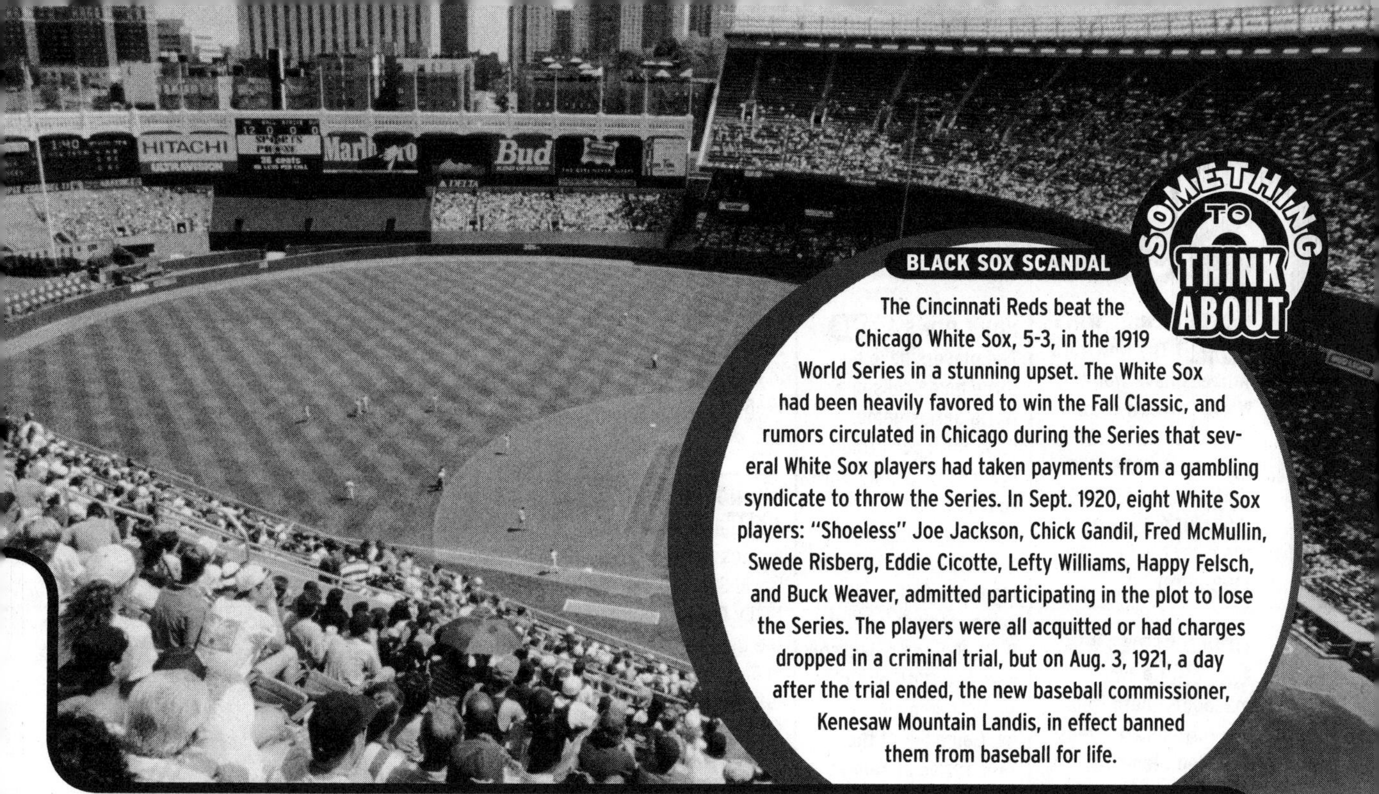

SOMETHING TO THINK ABOUT

BLACK SOX SCANDAL

The Cincinnati Reds beat the Chicago White Sox, 5-3, in the 1919 World Series in a stunning upset. The White Sox had been heavily favored to win the Fall Classic, and rumors circulated in Chicago during the Series that several White Sox players had taken payments from a gambling syndicate to throw the Series. In Sept. 1920, eight White Sox players: "Shoeless" Joe Jackson, Chick Gandil, Fred McMullin, Swede Risberg, Eddie Cicotte, Lefty Williams, Happy Felsch, and Buck Weaver, admitted participating in the plot to lose the Series. The players were all acquitted or had charges dropped in a criminal trial, but on Aug. 3, 1921, a day after the trial ended, the new baseball commissioner, Kenesaw Mountain Landis, in effect banned them from baseball for life.

1955: MVP The first Series MVP was Brooklyn Dodgers pitcher Johnny Podres in 1955. He pitched two complete games in the Series with a 1.00 ERA, as the Dodgers finally beat the New York Yankees, 4-3.

1956: PERFECT GAME The first, and so far only, perfect game pitched in a World Series was hurled by Don Larsen for the New York Yankees in Game Five of the 1956 Series. Larsen faced Brooklyn Dodgers pitcher Sal Maglie, the winning pitcher in Game One. Larsen had given up a 6-0 Yankee lead by the second inning of Game Two and the Yankees lost it 13-8.

It was a different story in Game Five. Larsen needed only 97 pitches to shut down the Dodgers. The final out was a strikeout of Dale Mitchell. The Yankees won Game Five, 2-0, and went on to win the Series, 4-3.

1960: SERIES-WINNING HOME RUN The only player to hit a home run in the bottom of the ninth of Game Seven to win the World Series was Bill Mazeroski for the Pittsburgh Pirates in 1960, against the New York Yankees.

In the ninth inning of Game Seven the score was tied at 9-9, when Mazeroski stepped to the plate. Maz was the first batter in the inning for the Pirates, and the normally light-hitting second baseman slammed Ralph Terry's second pitch over the left field wall to win the game and the Series.

The only other Series-ending home run came in 1993, when Toronto Blue Jays player Joe Carter hit a long ball to end Game Six. The Blue Jays had taken a 3-1 lead in the Series versus the Philadelphia Phillies and seemed determined to defend the World Series crown they had won the year before. But the Phillies won Game Five and the series returned to Toronto.

In Game Six, the Phillies held a 6-5 lead with star relief pitcher Mitch Williams on the mound for the bottom of the ninth. With two runners on and one out, Carter came to the plate. With the count 2-2, the outfielder hit a low fastball over the left field fence to win the Series for the Blue Jays.

1971: NIGHT GAME The first World Series game played at night was Game Four of the 1971 Series at Three Rivers Stadium in Pittsburgh on Oct. 13. The Pittsburgh Pirates beat the Baltimore Orioles, 4-3.

1984: MANAGER WINNING IN BOTH LEAGUES Sparky Anderson led the Detroit Tigers to the 1984 World Series championship. With the win, Anderson became the first, and so far only, manager to lead a team from the National League and the American League to a World Series title. Anderson had managed the Cincinnati Reds to titles in 1975 and 1976.

1987: INDOORS The first World Series game played indoors was Game One of the 1987 Series played at the Hubert H. Humphrey Metrodome in Minneapolis. The Twins beat the St. Louis Cardinals, 10-1. This was the first seven-game series in which each home team won every home game. The Twins won the Series, 4-3.

More on

The World Series

SUPERLATIVES

WORLD SERIES WINS TEAM The New York Yankees have won the World Series a record 26 times: 1923, 1927-1928, 1932, 1936-1939, 1941, 1943, 1947, 1949-1953, 1956, 1958, 1961-1962, 1977-1978, 1996, 1998-2000.

WORLD SERIES WINS MANAGER Two managers—both from the New York Yankees—have led teams to seven World Series titles. Joe McCarthy led the New York Yankees to the titles in 1932, 1936-1939, 1941, and 1943. Casey Stengel, led the Bombers to Series wins in 1949-1953, 1956, and 1958.

SERIES BATTING .300 OR OVER Babe Ruth batted .300 or above in a record six World Series, 1921, 1923, 1926-1928, 1932. His highest Series batting average was .625 (10-16) in 1928.

HITS GAME Paul Molitor of the Milwaukee Brewers had a record five hits in Game One of the 1982 World Series on Oct. 12, at Busch Stadium in St. Louis.

HOME RUNS GAME Two players have hit three home runs in a World Series game. Babe Ruth performed the feat twice, in Game Four at Sportsman's Park, St. Louis, on Oct. 6, 1926, and in a clinching Game Four at the same stadium, on Oct. 9, 1928. Reggie Jackson matched Ruth on Oct. 18, 1977, in a clinching Game Six of the 1977 Series at Yankee Stadium. He hit each home run on the first pitch of his at-bat.

RBI GAME Bobby Richardson of the New York Yankees drove in a record six runs in Game Three of the 1960 World Series at Yankee Stadium on Oct. 8, versus the Pittsburgh Pirates.

STRIKEOUTS GAME George Pipgras holds the undesirable record for most strikeouts by a batter in a World Series. The New York Yankees pitcher struck out five consecutive times in Game Three of the 1932 World Series at Wrigley Field, Chicago, on Oct. 1.

On the other hand, pitcher Bob Gibson of the St. Louis Cardinals struck out a record 17 Detroit Tigers batters in Game One of the 1968 World Series, in a 4-0 win.

INNINGS PITCHED GAME The most innings pitched in a World Series game is 14, by Babe Ruth for the Boston Red Sox in Game Two of the 1916 Series at Braves Field on Oct. 9. Ruth pitched a complete game to beat the Brooklyn Robins, 2-1.

OLDEST PITCHER GAME The oldest pitcher to start a World Series game is Jack Quinn of the Philadelphia Athletics. He was 45 years, 3 months, 7 days old when he started Game Four of the 1929 Series. He pitched five innings versus the Chicago Cubs. The A's won the game, 10-8.

SAVES SERIES The only pitcher to save four games in the World Series is John Wetteland of the New York Yankees, in the 1996 Series. Wetteland won the Series MVP award.

OLDEST MANAGER The oldest manager to lead a team to a World Series title was Jack McKeon, who was the skipper of the Florida Marlins when they won the 2003 World Series. McKeon, at 72 years, 11 months, and 2 days old, beat the record of Casey Stengel, who was 70 years old when he managed the New York Yankees to the 1960 World Series title.

LONGEST WORLD SERIES The 1989 World Series between the San Francisco Giants and the Oakland Athletics finished in a four-game sweep for the A's. But this was no ordinary Series. Minutes before the start of Game Three in San Francisco's Candlestick Park, a devastating earthquake struck Northern California. Measuring 6.9 on the Richter Scale, the earthquake killed 63 people.

Fay Vincent, the commissioner of baseball, postponed the Series for 10 days, until Oct. 27. The A's won the next two games, to win a Series that took a record 15 days to play.

Both teams donated portions of their World Series shares to families affected by the tragedy.

World Series Records (Single Series)

RECORD	TOTAL	PLAYER	TEAM	YEAR
Batting Average	.750	Billy Hatcher	Cincinnati Reds (vs. Oakland A's)	1990
At Bats	36	Jimmy Collins	Boston Red Sox (vs. Pittsburgh Pirates)	1903
Runs	10	Reggie Jackson	NY Yankees (vs. LA Dodgers)	1977
	10	Paul Molitor	Toronto Blue Jays (vs. Philadelphia Phillies)	1993
Hits	13	Bobby Richardson	NY Yankees (vs. St. Louis Cardinals)	1964
	13	Lou Brock	St. Louis Cardinals (vs. Detroit Tigers)	1968
	13	Marty Barrett	Boston Red Sox (vs. New York Mets)	1986
Home Runs	5	Reggie Jackson	NY Yankees (vs. LA Dodgers)	1977
RBI	12	Bobby Richardson	NY Yankees (vs. Pittsburgh Pirates)	1960
Total Bases	25	Reggie Jackson	NY Yankees (vs. LA Dodgers)	1977
	25	Willie Stargell	Pittsburgh Pirates (vs. Baltimore Orioles)	1979
Slugging Pct.	1.727	Lou Gehrig	NY Yankees (vs. St. Louis Cardinals)	1928
Walks	13	Barry Bonds	SF Giants (vs. Anaheim Angels)	2002
Stolen Bases	7	Lou Brock	St. Louis Cardinals (vs. Boston Red Sox)	1967
	7	Lou Brock	St. Louis Cardinals (vs. Detroit Tigers)	1968

World Series Records (Career)

RECORD	TOTAL	PLAYER	TEAM	YEARS
Games Played	75	Yogi Berra	New York Yankees	1947, 1949-1953, 1955-1958, 1960-1963
Games Pitched	22	Whitey Ford	New York Yankees	1950, 1953, 1955-1958, 1960-1964
At Bats	259	Yogi Berra	New York Yankees	1947, 1949-1953, 1955-1958, 1960-1963
Batting Average (Min. 50 AB)	.418	Pepper Martin	St. Louis Cardinals	1928, 1931, 1934
	.418	Paul Molitor	Milwaukee Brewers, Toronto Blue Jays	1982, 1993
Hits	71	Yogi Berra	New York Yankees	1947, 1949-1953, 1955-1958, 1960-1963
Runs	42	Mickey Mantle	New York Yankees	1951-1953, 1955-1958, 1960-1964
Home Runs	18	Mickey Mantle	New York Yankees	1951-1953, 1955-1958, 1960-1964
RBI	40	Mickey Mantle	New York Yankees	1951-1953, 1955-1958, 1960-1964
Stolen Bases	14	Eddie Collins	Philadelphia A's, Chicago White Sox	1910-1911, 1913-1914, 1917, 1919
	14	Lou Brock	St. Louis Cardinals	1964, 1967-1968
Total Bases	123	Mickey Mantle	New York Yankees	1951-1953, 1955-1958, 1960-1964
Slugging Pct.	.755	Reggie Jackson	Oakland Athletics, New York Yankees	1973-1974, 1977-1978, 1981
MVP Awards	2	Bob Gibson	St. Louis Cardinals	1964, 1967
	2	Sandy Koufax	Los Angeles Dodgers	1963, 1965
	2	Reggie Jackson	New York Yankees	1973, 1977
Wins	10	Whitey Ford	New York Yankees	1950, 1953, 1955-1958, 1960-1964
ERA (Min. 25 IP)	0.36	Jack Billingham	Cincinnati Reds	1972, 1975-1976
Saves	9	Mariano Rivera	New York Yankees	1996, 1998-2001, 2003
Shutouts	4	Christy Mathewson	New York Giants	1905, 1911-1913
Innings Pitched	146.0	Whitey Ford	New York Yankees	1950, 1953, 1955-1958, 1960-1964
Complete Games	10	Christy Mathewson	New York Giants	1905, 1911-1913
Strikeouts	94	Whitey Ford	New York Yankees	1950, 1953, 1955-1958, 1960-1964
Losses	8	Whitey Ford	New York Yankees	1950, 1953, 1955-1958, 1960-1964

Little League

Dan Quayle, former Little League player ►

LITTLE LEAGUE BASEBALL IS THE WORLD'S LARGEST ORGANIZED YOUTH SPORTS PROGRAM, and a genuine piece of Americana. A lumberyard clerk named Carl Stotz came up with the Little League concept in 1938. With his wife, Grayce, and enthusiasts George and Bert Beeble, who were brothers, he started the first league in 1939 in their hometown of Williamsport, PA.

There were only three teams that first season. As time went on, the "little league" concept spread to other towns. An article in *The Saturday Evening Post* in 1949 served as a catalyst for even greater expansion. As of 2005, there were nearly 200,000 teams across the U.S., plus organizations in more than 100 other countries. The Little League World Series is played in Williamsport every year in late August. Players must be 11 or 12 years old as of Aug 1.

MILESTONES

1939: FIRST LITTLE LEAGUE GAME
The first organized Little League game was played on June 6, 1939, in Williamsport, PA; Lundy Lumber defeated Lycoming Dairy, 23-8. Lycoming Dairy came back to win the season's first-half title, and faced second-half champ Lundy Lumber in a best-of-three series. Lycoming Dairy won the final game of the series, 3-2.

1947: LITTLE LEAGUE WORLD SERIES
The inaugural Little League World Series (LLWS) was staged in Williamsport in August 1947, and was called the National Little League Tournament. A dozen teams competed for the championship, 11 from Pennsylvania and one from New Jersey (Hammonton).

In the championship game, Maynard-Williamsport, PA, defeated Lock Haven, PA, 16-7. The winner's 16 runs is still the most ever in a championship game.

1950: INTERNATIONAL EXPANSION
Little League expanded outside the U.S. in 1950, when leagues were formed in Panama. The popularity of baseball in Central America, combined with the large number of American workers living in the region, fueled its expansion.

By the following year international Little Leagues had expanded into Canada, Cuba, Hawaii, and Puerto Rico.

1953: LITTLE LEAGUER TO THE MAJORS On July 21, 1953, pitcher Joey Jay became the first graduate of Little League (Middletown, CT) to reach the Major Leagues, when the 17-year-old made his debut with the Milwaukee Braves.

A 1961 All-Star, Jay played for two teams in the majors from 1953 to 1966. He won 99 games, 75 of them with the Cincinnati Reds, for whom he played in the 1961 World Series.

1953: TELEVISION BROADCAST
The Little League World Series was televised for the first time in 1953, broadcast by CBS. Then-rookie announcer Jim McKay called the play-by-play. Birmingham, AL, defeated Schenectady, NY, 1-0, in one of only two 1-0 finals in World Series history.

1957: INTERNATIONAL CHAMPION
In 1957 Monterrey, Mexico, became the first non-U.S. team to win the Little League World Series, as Angel Macias pitched the first perfect game in a championship final. Monterrey defeated La Mesa, CA, 4-0.

1966: PLAYER IN BOTH SERIES
Boog Powell, who played for Lakeland, FL, in the 1954 Little League World Series, became the first player to appear in both the LLWS tournament and the Major League World Series when he played first base for the Baltimore Orioles in the 1966 Series. In 1954, Powell's Little League team lost to Schenectady, NY, 16-0, in their first-round game, but in 1966 his Baltimore Orioles defeated the L.A. Dodgers in four straight games.

1987: LITTLE LEAGUE HALL OF FAMER The first former Little Leaguer to gain induction to the Baseball Hall of Fame was Jim "Catfish" Hunter. A 1974 AL Cy Young Award winner and eight-time all-star, Hunter was elected to the Hall in 1987.

2004: LLWS VETERANS WORLD SERIES DUEL
The first time a former Little League World Series player pitched to another LLWS alumnus in the Major League World Series was during Game Two of the 2004 Series. Boston Red Sox catcher Jason Varitek faced St. Louis Cardinals pitcher Jason Marquis in the seventh inning. Varitek played for Altamonte Springs, FL, in the 1984 LLWS, and Marquis for South Shore, Staten Island, NY, in the 1991 LLWS.

Varitek flied out to center field.

Home Runs

Game	3	Roger Miller, Tuckahoe, VA	1968
	3	Chih Hsiang Lin, Chinese Taipei (Taiwan)	1995
	3	Tetsuya Furukawa, Japan	1998
3-Game Series	5	Lloyd McClendon, Gary, IN	1971
5-Game Series	7	Chin-Hsiung Hsieh, Chinese Taipei (Taiwan)	1996

Strikeouts

6-inning Game	18	Kalen Pimentel (Rancho Vista, CA)	2005
	18	Chen Chao-An, Chinese Taipei (Taiwan)	1979
9-inning Game	22	Chin-Mu Hsu, Chinese Taipei (Taiwan)	1971

Little Leaguers in the Hall of Fame

PLAYER	INDUCTION
Jim "Catfish" Hunter (P)	1987
Carl Yastrzemski (LF)	1989
Jim Palmer (P)	1990
Tom Seaver (P)	1992
Rollie Fingers (P)	1992
Steve Carlton (P)	1994
Mike Schmidt (3B)	1995
Don Sutton (P)	1998
George Brett (3B)	1999
Nolan Ryan (P)	1999
Robin Yount (SS)	1999
Gary Carter (C)	2003
Wade Boggs (3B)	2005

SUPERLATIVES

MOST CHAMPIONSHIPS Teams representing Chinese Taipei (Taiwan) have won a record 17 Little League World Series titles. The first championship won by the Asian island Little Leaguers came in 1969. Other titles came in the years 1971-74, 1977-81, 1986-88, 1990-91, and 1995-96.

MOST CHAMPIONSHIPS **STATE** Teams from California have won the LLWS five times. The first team from the Golden State to win was El Cajon in 1961. The other teams to win were San Jose in 1962, Granada Hills in 1963, and Long Beach in both 1992 and 1993. In 1992, Long Beach lost the championship game to Zamboanga City, Philippines, 15-4, but was awarded the title when the Philippine team was disqualified a month later after it was discovered that they had fielded ineligible players.

LONGEST LLWS GAME The longest LLWS game in terms of innings was played on Aug. 23, 1998, between Toms River, NJ, and Jenison, MI. Toms River won, 13-9, after 11 innings; the game lasted three hours, 11 minutes.

The longest game time-wise, however, was an international semi-final played between Nuevo Leon, Mexico, and Corundu, Panama, on Aug. 26, 2004. That 10-inning game lasted three hours, 50 minutes; Nuevo Leon won, 6-2.

SOMETHING TO THINK ABOUT

WHITE HOUSE LITTLE LEAGUER

George W. Bush is the first former Little League player to reach the White House. The 43rd president played catcher as a Little Leaguer in Midland, TX, from 1955 to 1958. In 2001, he became the first president to attend the Little League World Series, in Williamsport. Former Vice President Dan Quayle also played Little League.

TRIPLE CROWNERS

Two players have played in the Little League World Series, the College World Series, and the World Series. They are Ed Vosberg and Jason Varitek. Vosberg played in the 1974 LLWS (Tuscon, AZ, runner-up), the 1980 College World Series (Arizona, champions), and the 1997 World Series (Florida Marlins, champions). Varitek played in the 1984 LLWS (Altamonte Springs, FL, runner-up), the 1994 College World Series (Georgia Tech, runner-up), and the 2004 World Series (Boston Red Sox, champions).

LITTLE LEAGUE FIELD DIMENSIONS

Regulation distance between bases on fields for 12-year-olds and below is 60 feet (Major League base paths are 90 ft). The distance from the rubber on the pitcher's mound to home plate for 12-year-olds and below is 46 feet (Major League dimensions are 60 ft, 6 in). The distance from the back of home plate to the outfield fence is a local league option, but the Little League organization recommends 200 feet.

FOOTBALL

NFL Team by Team

THE FIRST PRO FOOTBALL PLAYER ever was William ("Pudge") Heffelfinger. A former Yale All-America guard, he was paid $500 to play for the Allegheny Athletic Association against the Pittsburgh Athletic Club on Nov. 12, 1892. Heffelfinger scored the only touchdown of the game, giving Allegheny the victory.

The National Football League (NFL) traces its roots to the American Professional Football Association (AFPA), formed in Canton, OH (under a slightly different name), on Aug. 20, 1920. It began with 10 teams. Four others joined in the league's first year. The Akron Pros won the first APFA title. On June 24, 1922, the APFA changed its name to the National Football League.

In 1946 the All-America Football Conference (AAFC) began play; it merged with the NFL for the 1950 season. The American Football League (AFL) played its first season in 1960 and merged with the NFL ten years later. The tables below cover records and milestones for each team through the 2005 season.

Team by Team

First season for each team is in parentheses. Years given for NFL champions are regular-season

ARIZONA CARDINALS (1920, as Chicago Cardinals)

NFL Champion	1925[1], 1947[1]	
Most Points	1,380	Jim Bakken, 1962-78[2]
Rushing Yards	7,999	Ottis Anderson, 1979-86[2]
Passing Yards	34,639	Jim Hart, 1966-83[2]
Receiving Yards	8,497	Roy Green, 1979-90[3]

(1) Chicago Cardinals; (2) St. Louis Cardinals; (3) with St. Louis Cardinals, 1979-87, Phoenix Cardinals, 1988-90.

ATLANTA FALCONS (1966)

Most Points	620	Morten Andersen, 1995-2000
Rushing Yards	6,631	Gerald Riggs, 1982-88
Passing Yards	23,468	Steve Bartkowski, 1975-85
Receiving Yards	7,349	Terance Mathis, 1994-2001

BALTIMORE RAVENS (1996)

NFL Champion	2000	
Most Points	1,114	Matt Stover, 1996-2005
Rushing Yards	6,669	Jamal Lewis, 2000-05
Passing Yards	7,148	Vinny Testaverde, 1996-97
Receiving Yards	2,893	Todd Heap, 2001-05

BUFFALO BILLS (1960, AFL; 1970 NFL)

AFL Champion	1964, 1965	
Most Points	1,011	Steve Christie, 1992-2000
Rushing Yards	11,938	Thurman Thomas, 1988-99
Passing Yards	35,467	Jim Kelly, 1986-96
Receiving Yards	13,095	Andre Reed, 1985-99

CAROLINA PANTHERS (1995)

Most Points	964	John Kasay, 1995-2005
Rushing Yards	2,530	Tshimanga Biakabutuka, 1996-2001
Passing Yards	12,690	Steve Beuerlein, 1996-2000
Receiving Yards	7,751	Muhsin Muhammad, 1996-2004

CHICAGO BEARS (1920, as Decatur Staleys)

NFL Champion	1921[1], 1932-33, 1940, 1941, 1943, 1946, 1963, 1985	
Most Points	1,116	Kevin Butler, 1985-95
Rushing Yards	16,726	Walter Payton, 1975-87
Passing Yards	14,686	Sid Luckman, 1939-50
Receiving Yards	5,059	Johnny Morris, 1958-67

(1) as Chicago Staleys

CINCINNATI BENGALS (1968, AFL; 1970, NFL)

Most Points	1,151	Jim Breech, 1980-92
Rushing Yards	8,061	Corey Dillon, 1997-2003
Passing Yards	32,838	Ken Anderson, 1971-86
Receiving Yards	7,101	Isaac Curtis, 1973-84

CLEVELAND BROWNS[1] (1946, AAFC; 1950, NFL)

AAFC Champion	1946-1949	
NFL Champion	1950, 1954-55, 1964	
Most Points	1,349	Lou Groza, 1950-59, 1961-67
Rushing Yards	12,312	Jim Brown, 1957-65
Passing Yards	23,713	Brian Sipe, 1974-83
Receiving Yards	7,980	Ozzie Newsome, 1978-90

(1) The Browns moved from Cleveland to Baltimore for the 1996 season, and a new NFL franchise was started in Baltimore, the Ravens. Cleveland received an expansion franchise that began play in the 1999 season; the records of the original Browns were transferred to the new team.

DALLAS COWBOYS (1960)

NFL Champion	1971, 1977, 1992-93, 1995	
Most Points	986	Emmitt Smith, 1990-2002
Rushing Yards	17,162	Emmitt Smith, 1990-2002
Passing Yards	32,942	Troy Aikman, 1989-2000
Receiving Yards	11,904	Michael Irvin, 1988-99

DENVER BRONCOS (1960, AFL; 1970, NFL)

NFL Champion	1997-98	
Most Points	1,556	Jason Elam, 1993-2005
Rushing Yards	7,607	Terrell Davis, 1995-2001
Passing Yards	51,475	John Elway, 1983-98
Receiving Yards	10,877	Rod Smith, 1995-2005

DETROIT LIONS (1930, as Portsmouth Spartans)

NFL Champion	1935, 1952-53, 1957	
Most Points	1,420	Jason Hanson, 1992-2005
Rushing Yards	15,269	Barry Sanders, 1989-98
Passing Yards	15,710	Bobby Layne, 1950-58
Receiving Yards	9,174	Herman Moore, 1991-2001

GREEN BAY PACKERS (1921)

NFL Champion	1929-31, 1936, 1939, 1944, 1961-62, 1965-67, 1996	
Most Points	1,054	Ryan Longwell, 1997-2005
Rushing Yards	8,207	Jim Taylor, 1958-66
Passing Yards	53,615	Brett Favre, 1992-2005
Receiving Yards	9,656	James Lofton, 1978-86

HOUSTON TEXANS (2002)

Most Points	339	Kris Brown, 2002-05
Rushing Yards	3,195	Domanick Davis, 2003-05
Passing Yards	10,624	David Carr, 2002-05
Receiving Yards	2,806	Andre Johnson, 2003-05

INDIANAPOLIS COLTS (1953, as Baltimore Colts)		
NFL Champion	1958-59[1], 1970[1]	
Most Points	995	Mike Vanderjagt, 1998-2005
Rushing Yards	9,226	Edgerrin James, 1999-2005
Passing Yards	39,768	Johnny Unitas, 1956-72[1]
Receiving Yards	12,331	Marvin Harrison, 1996-2005
(1) Baltimore Colts		

JACKSONVILLE JAGUARS (1995)		
Most Points	764	Mike Hollis, 1995-2001
Rushing Yards	8,367	Fred Taylor, 1998-2005
Passing Yards	25,698	Mark Brunell, 1995-2003
Receiving Yards	12,287	Jimmy Smith, 1995-2005

KANSAS CITY CHIEFS (1960, AFL, as Dallas Texans; 1970, NFL)		
AFL Champion	1962, 1969	
NFL Champion	1969	
Most Points	1,466	Nick Lowery, 1980-93
Rushing Yards	5,933	Priest Holmes, 2001-05
Passing Yards	28,507	Len Dawson, 1962-75[1]
Receiving Yards	7,810	Tony Gonzalez, 1997-2005
(1) with Dallas Texans, 1962, Kansas City Chiefs, 1963-75.		

MIAMI DOLPHINS (1966, AFL; 1970, NFL)		
NFL Champion	1972[1]-73	
Most Points	830	Garo Yepremian, 1970-78
Rushing Yards	6,737	Larry Csonka, 1968-74, 1979
Passing Yards	61,361	Dan Marino, 1983-99
Receiving Yards	8,869	Mark Duper, 1982-92
(1) The only team to win every game in a season was the Miami Dolphins in 1972. Coached by Don Shula, the Dolphins went 14-0 in the regular season, and won two playoff games, then defeated the Washington Redskins, 14-7, in Super Bowl VII to complete a 17-0 season.		

MINNESOTA VIKINGS (1961)		
Most Points	1,365	Fred Cox, 1963-77
Rushing Yards	6,818	Robert Smith, 1993-2000
Passing Yards	33,098	Fran Tarkenton, 1961-66, 1972-78
Receiving Yards	12,383	Cris Carter, 1990-2001

NEW ENGLAND PATRIOTS (1960, AFL as Boston Patriots; 1970, NFL)		
NFL Champion	2001, 2003-04	
Most Points	1,156	Adam Vinatieri, 1996-2005
Rushing Yards	5,453	Sam Cunningham, 1973-79, 1981-82
Passing Yards	29,657	Drew Bledsoe, 1993-2001
Receiving Yards	10,352	Stanley Morgan, 1977-89

NEW ORLEANS SAINTS (1967)		
Most Points	1,318	Morten Andersen, 1982-94
Rushing Yards	4,529	Deuce McAllister, 2001-2005
Passing Yards	21,734	Archie Manning, 1971-82
Receiving Yards	7,854	Eric Martin, 1985-93

NEW YORK GIANTS (1925)		
NFL Champion	1934, 1938, 1956, 1986, 1990	
Most Points	646	Pete Gogolak, 1966-74
Rushing Yards	8,787	Tiki Barber, 1997-2005
Passing Yards	33,462	Phil Simms, 1979-93
Receiving Yards	7,797	Amani Toomer, 1996-2005

NEW YORK JETS (1960, AFL, as New York Titans; 1970, NFL)		
AFL Champion	1968	
NFL Champion	1968	
Most Points	1,470	Pat Leahy, 1974-91
Rushing Yards	10,302	Curtis Martin, 1998-2005
Passing Yards	27,057	Joe Namath, 1965-76
Receiving Yards	11,732	Don Maynard, 1960-72

OAKLAND RAIDERS (1960, AFL; 1970, NFL)		
AFL Champion	1967	
NFL Champion	1976, 1980, 1983[1]	
Most Points	863	George Blanda, 1967-75
Rushing Yards	8,545	Marcus Allen, 1982-92[1]
Passing Yards	19,078	Ken Stabler, 1970-79
Receiving Yards	14,734	Tim Brown, 1988-2003[1]
(1) Los Angeles Raiders, 1982-94.		

PHILADELPHIA EAGLES (1933)		
NFL Champion	1948-49, 1960	
Most Points	881	Bobby Walston, 1951-62
Rushing Yards	6,538	Wilbert Montgomery, 1977-84
Passing Yards	26,963	Ron Jaworski, 1977-86
Receiving Yards	8,978	Harold Carmichael, 1971-83

PITTSBURGH STEELERS (1933)		
NFL Champion	1974-75, 1978-79, 2005	
Most Points	1,343	Gary Anderson, 1982-94
Rushing Yards	11,950	Franco Harris, 1972-83
Passing Yards	27,989	Terry Bradshaw, 1970-83
Receiving Yards	8,723	John Stallworth, 1974-87

ST. LOUIS RAMS (1937, as Cleveland Rams)		
NFL Champion	1945, 1951[1], 1999	
Most Points	993	Jeff Wilkins, 1997-2005
Rushing Yards	7,245	Eric Dickerson, 1983-87[1]
Passing Yards	23,758	Jim Everett, 1986-93[1]
Receiving Yards	12,278	Isaac Bruce, 1994-2005[1]
(1) Los Angeles Rams, 1946-94		

SAN DIEGO CHARGERS (1960, AFL as L.A. Chargers; 1970, NFL)		
AFL Champion	1963	
Most Points	1,076	John Carney, 1990-2000
Rushing Yards	7,361	LaDainian Tomlinson, 2001-05
Passing Yards	43,040	Dan Fouts, 1973-87
Receiving Yards	9,585	Lance Alworth, 1962-70

SAN FRANCISCO 49ERS (1946, AAFC; 1950, NFL)		
NFL Champion	1981, 1984, 1988-89, 1994	
Most Points	1,130	Jerry Rice, 1985-2000
Rushing Yards	7,344	Joe Perry, 1950-60, 63
Passing Yards	35,124	Joe Montana, 1979-92
Receiving Yards	19,247	Jerry Rice, 1985-2000

SEATTLE SEAHAWKS (1976)		
Most Points	810	Norm Johnson, 1982-90
Rushing Yards	7,817	Shaun Alexander, 2000-05
Passing Yards	26,132	Dave Krieg, 1980-91
Receiving Yards	13,089	Steve Largent, 1976-89

TAMPA BAY BUCCANEERS (1976)		
NFL Champion	2002	
Most Points	538	Martin Gramatica, 1999-2003
Rushing Yards	5,957	James Wilder, 1981-89
Passing Yards	14,820	Vinny Testaverde, 1987-92
Receiving Yards	5,018	Mark Carrier, 1987-92

TENNESSEE TITANS (1960, AFL, as Houston Oilers; 1970, NFL)		
NFL Champion	1960-61[1]	
Most Points	1,060	Al Del Greco, 1991-2000[1]
Rushing Yards	10,009	Eddie George, 1996-2003[1]
Passing Yards	33,685	Warren Moon, 1984-93[1]
Receiving Yards	7,935	Ernest Givins, 1986-94[1]
(1) Houston Oilers, 1960-96; Tennessee Oilers, 1997-98; Tennessee Titans, 1999-present.		

WASHINGTON REDSKINS (1932, as Boston Braves)		
NFL Champion	1937, 1942, 1982, 1987, 1991	
Most Points	1,206	Mark Moseley, 1974-86
Rushing Yards	7,472	John Riggins, 1976-79, 1981-85
Passing Yards	25,206	Joe Theismann, 1974-85
Receiving Yards	12,026	Art Monk, 1980-93

FOOTBALL

NFL Offense

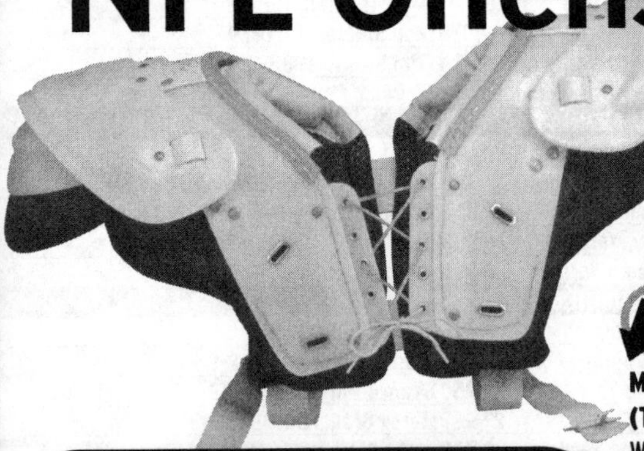

Emmitt Smith (22) and John Keith (28) ▶

SUPERLATIVES

MOST POINTS (TEAM) The Washington Redskins beat the New York Giants, 72-41, on Nov. 27, 1966, setting the record for most points scored by a team in a regular-season NFL game. This game also set the record for most points in any NFL game, 113.

On the other side of the ledger, the Redskins hold the dubious distinction of allowing the most points in a game. In the 1940 NFL championship game, the Chicago Bears beat them, 73-0.

PERFECT KICKING SEASON Only four kickers in NFL history have completed a season without missing a field goal (with minimum of 15 attempts): Tony Zendejas, Los Angeles Rams, 17 in 1991; Gary Anderson, Minnesota Vikings, 35 in 1998; Jeff Wilkins, St. Louis Rams, 17 in 2000; Mike Vanderjagt, Indianapolis Colts, 37 in 2003.

LONGEST PLAYS

RUN FROM SCRIMMAGE During a Monday night game on Jan. 3, 1983, Dallas Cowboy running back Tony Dorsett ran 99 yards for a touchdown against the Minnesota Vikings, setting the NFL record for longest run from the line of scrimmage.

PASS COMPLETION The record for longest pass completion is 99 yards—done 10 times, all for touchdowns: Frank Filchock of the Washington Redskins (to Andy Farkas) vs. Pittsburgh Steelers, Oct. 15, 1939; George Izo of the Redskins (to Bobby Mitchell) vs. Cleveland Browns, Sept. 15, 1963; Karl Sweetan of the Detroit Lions (to Pat Studstill) vs. Baltimore Colts, Oct. 16, 1966; Sonny Jurgensen of the Redskins (to Gerry Allen) vs. Chicago Bears, Sept. 15, 1968; Jim Plunkett of the Los Angeles Raiders (to Cliff Branch) vs. Redskins, Oct. 2, 1983; Ron Jaworski of the Philadelphia Eagles (to Mike Quick) vs. Atlanta Falcons, Nov. 10, 1985; Stan Humphries of the San Diego Chargers (to Tony Martin) vs. Seattle Seahawks, Sept. 18, 1994; Brett Favre of the Green Bay Packers (to Robert Brooks) vs. Bears, Sept. 11, 1995; Trent Green of the Kansas City Chiefs (to Marc Boerigter) vs. San Diego Chargers, Dec. 22, 2002; and Jeff Garcia of the Browns (to Andre Davis) vs. Cincinnati Bengals, Oct. 17, 2004.

FIELD GOAL Two players are tied for the longest field goal at 63 yards: Tom Dempsey for the New Orleans Saints vs. Detroit Lions (Nov. 8, 1970) and Jason Elam for the Denver Broncos vs. Jacksonville Jaguars (Oct. 25, 1998).

MILESTONES

1906: FORWARD PASS The first recorded forward pass in a pro football game was thrown by Massillon quarterback George Parratt to Dan Riley against Benwood-Moundsville on Oct. 27, 1906.

1912: SIX POINTS FOR TOUCHDOWN Pro football rules were changed to increase the point total for a touchdown from five to six in 1912.

1933: PASSING FROM LINE OF SCRIMMAGE On Feb. 25, 1933, the NFL legalized the forward pass from anywhere behind the line of scrimmage. Before then, a forward pass could not be attempted from within 5 yards of the line of scrimmage.

1934: 1,000-YARD RUSHER Chicago Bears halfback Beattie Feathers became the first player to gain 1,000 yards rushing in a single season in 1934. He amassed 1,004 yards on 101 carries. It was his rookie year.

1964: SOCCER-STYLE KICKER The Buffalo Bills signed Cornell's Pete Gogolak, making him the first soccer-style kicker in pro football. Gogolak played 11 NFL seasons for two teams, the Bills and the New York Giants. He kicked 173 career field goals and 344 points after touchdown (PATs).

1973: 2,000-YARD RUSHER The first player to run for over 2,000 yards in a season was O.J. Simpson of the Buffalo Bills. He gained 2,003 yards on 332 carries.

Selected NFL Offense Records

MOST POINTS				
Game	40	Ernie Nevers	Chicago Cardinals vs. Chicago Bears	Nov. 28, 1929
Season	176	Paul Hornung	Green Bay Packers	1960
Career	2,434	Gary Anderson	Pittsburgh Steelers, Philadelphia Eagles, San Francisco 49ers, Minnesota Vikings, Tennessee Titans	1982-2004
TOUCHDOWNS SCORED				
Game	6	Ernie Nevers	Chicago Cardinals vs. Chicago Bears	Nov. 28, 1929
	6	Dub Jones	Cleveland Browns vs. Chicago Bears	Nov. 25, 1951
	6	Gale Sayers	Chicago Bears vs. San Francisco 49ers	Dec. 12, 1965
Season	28	Shaun Alexander	Seattle Seahawks	2005
Career	208	Jerry Rice	San Francisco 49ers, Oakland Raiders, Seattle Seahawks	1985-2004
RUSHING YARDAGE				
Game	295 yards	Jamal Lewis	Baltimore Ravens vs. Cleveland Browns	Sept. 14, 2003
Season	2,105 yards	Eric Dickerson	Los Angeles Rams	1984
Career	18,355 yards	Emmitt Smith	Dallas Cowboys, Arizona Cardinals	1990-2004
RUSHING TOUCHDOWNS				
Game	6	Ernie Nevers	Chicago Cardinals vs. Chicago Bears	Nov. 28, 1929
Season	27	Priest Holmes	Kansas City Chiefs	2003
		Shaun Alexander	Seattle Seahawks	2005
Career	164	Emmitt Smith	Dallas Cowboys, Arizona Cardinals	1990-2004
PASSING YARDAGE				
Game	554 yards	Norm Van Brocklin	Los Angeles Rams vs. New York Yanks	Sept. 28, 1951
Season	5,084 yards	Dan Marino	Miami Dolphins	1984
Career	61,361 yards	Dan Marino	Miami Dolphins	1983-1999
PASSING COMPLETIONS				
Game	45	Drew Bledsoe	New England Patriots vs. Minnesota Vikings (OT)	Nov. 13, 1994
Season	418	Rich Gannon	Oakland Raiders	2002
Career	4,967	Dan Marino	Miami Dolphins	1983-1999
TOUCHDOWN PASSES THROWN				
Game	7	Shared by 5 players		
Season	49	Peyton Manning	Indianapolis Colts	2004
Career	420	Dan Marino	Miami Dolphins	1983-1999
RECEIVING YARDS				
Game	336	Willie Anderson	Los Angeles Rams vs. New Orleans Saints (OT)	Nov. 26, 1989
Season	1,848	Jerry Rice	San Francisco 49ers	1995
Career	22,895	Jerry Rice	San Francisco 49ers, Oakland Raiders, Seattle Seahawks	1985-2004
RECEPTIONS				
Game	20	Terrell Owens	San Francisco 49ers vs. Chicago Bears	Dec. 17, 2000
Season	143	Marvin Harrison	Indianapolis Colts	2002
Career	1,549	Jerry Rice	San Francisco 49ers, Oakland Raiders, Seattle Seahawks	1985-2004
TOUCHDOWN RECEPTIONS				
Game	5	Bob Shaw	Chicago Cardinals vs. Baltimore Colts	Oct. 2, 1950
	5	Kellen Winslow	San Diego Chargers vs. Oakland Raiders	Nov. 22, 1981
	5	Jerry Rice	San Francisco 49ers vs. Atlanta Falcons	Oct. 14, 1990
Season	22	Jerry Rice	San Francisco 49ers	2002
Career	197	Jerry Rice	San Francisco 49ers, Oakland Raiders, Seattle Seahawks	1985-2004

FOOTBALL

NFL Defense

SUPERLATIVES

FEWEST POINTS ALLOWED In 1932, the opponents of the Chicago Bears scored just 44 points in 14 games, the NFL record for the fewest points allowed by a team in a season. The Bears were 7-1-6 that season after beating the Portsmouth Spartans in a playoff game, 9-0, for the NFL title. The teams tied at the end of the regular season.

MOST SHUTOUTS Two teams have posted 10 shutouts in a season. In 1926, the Pottsville Maroons became the first team to shut out 10 opponents (they won 9 games and tied one). The following year, the 1927 New York Giants also posted 10 shutouts, and also won nine of those games and tied one.

The Maroons finished third in 1926, while the Giants won the NFL title in 1927.

MOST SACKS The 1984 Chicago Bears recorded an NFL season-record 72 sacks.

On Dec. 16, 1984, the Bears tied the NFL record for the most sacks in a game with 12 against the Detroit Lions. Three other teams tied this record: the Dallas Cowboys, against the Pittsburgh Steelers on Nov. 20, 1966, the St. Louis Cardinals, against the Baltimore Colts on Oct. 26, 1980, and the Dallas Cowboys against the Houston Oilers on Sept. 29, 1985.

MOST FUMBLES FORCED The record for the most forced fumbles in a season is 50, by two teams—the 1963 Minnesota Vikings and the 1978 San Francisco 49ers.

FEWEST YARDS ALLOWED (RUSHING) The 1942 Chicago Bears gave up only 519 rushing yards, the fewest rushing yards allowed in a single NFL season. That season, the Bears won the Western Division, posting an 11-0 record, but lost to the Washington Redskins in the NFL title game, 14-6.

FEWEST YARDS ALLOWED (PASSING) The fewest passing yards allowed in a season is 545 yards by the 1934 Philadelphia Eagles. The Eagles' tough pass defense didn't help them much, though. The Eagles finished fourth (out of 5 teams) in the Eastern Division, posting a 4-7 record.

FEWEST TOUCHDOWNS ALLOWED Two teams have played an entire NFL season allowing just six touchdowns—the 1932 Chicago Bears and the 1933 Brooklyn Dodgers. The Bears went on to win the 1932 NFL Championship under head coach Ralph Jones. The Dodgers' defense did not lead them to a title.

FEWEST TOUCHDOWNS ALLOWED (RUSHING) Three teams have played an entire season allowing just two touchdowns: the 1934 Detroit Lions, the 1968 Dallas Cowboys, and the 1971 Minnesota Vikings.

Despite their stingy defense, none of the teams won the NFL Championship in those years. The Lions finished second to the Chicago Bears in the Western Division, posting a 10-3 record. The Cowboys lost in the playoffs to the Cleveland Browns, 31-20. The Vikings lost in the playoffs to the Cowboys, 20-12.

MOST POINTS ALLOWED In 1981, the Baltimore Colts gave up 533 points, the most points allowed in a season by any NFL team. They gave up 68 touchdowns that year, also an NFL record. The Colts were 2-14 that season, tied for the worst record in the league with the New England Patriots.

FEWEST INTERCEPTIONS The NFL team record for the fewest interceptions made in a season is three, held by the 1982 Houston Oilers. As a result of a 57-day players' strike, the NFL season was only nine games that season. The Oilers finished with a 1-8 record, which was not the worst in the NFL. The Baltimore Colts went 0-8-1 that year.

MOST FIRST DOWNS ALLOWED The 1981 Baltimore Colts' defense holds the dubious honor of allowing the most first downs in a season: 406.

In stark contrast, the record for fewest first downs allowed in a season is 77, set by the Detroit Lions in 1935.

FEWEST SACKS The NFL single-season record for fewest sacks is 11, held by the 1982 Baltimore Colts. That season the Colts' defense also set the NFL record for fewest opponent turnovers, 11. The Colts played only nine games in 1982 because of the NFL players' strike.

FEWEST FORCED FUMBLES Three teams share the record for fewest forced fumbles in a season with 11: the 1956 Cleveland Browns, the 1982 Baltimore Colts, and the 1998 Tennessee Titans.

LONGEST PLAYS

INTERCEPTION RETURN The record for the longest interception return by an individual is 103 yards, held by two players: Vencie Glenn of the San Diego

Selected NFL Defensive Records

MOST SACKS (SINCE 1982)				
Game	7	Derrick Thomas	Kansas City Chiefs vs. Seattle Seahawks	Nov. 11, 1990
Season	22.5	Michael Strahan	New York Giants	2001
Career	200	Bruce Smith	Buffalo Bills, Washington Redskins	1985-2003
INTERCEPTIONS*				
Season	14	Dick ("Night Train") Lane	Los Angeles Rams	1952
Career	81	Paul Krause	Washington Redskins, Minnesota Vikings	1964-79
* The record for most interceptions in a game is four, held by many players.				
INTERCEPTIONS YARDS				
Game	177 yards	Charlie McNeil	San Diego Chargers vs. Houston Oilers	Sept. 24, 1961
Season	349 yards	Charlie McNeil	San Diego Chargers	1961
Career	1,483 yards	Rod Woodson	Pittsburgh Steelers, San Francisco 49ers, Baltimore Ravens, Oakland Raiders	1987-2003
INTERCEPTIONS FOR TOUCHDOWNS*				
Season	4	Ken Houston	Houston Oilers	1971
	4	Jim Kearney	Kansas City Chiefs	1972
	4	Eric Allen	Philadelphia Eagles	1993
Career	12	Rod Woodson	Pittsburgh Steelers, San Francisco 49ers, Baltimore Ravens, Oakland Raiders	1987-2003
*The record for most interceptions returned for touchdowns in a game is two, held by many players.				
FUMBLES RECOVERED*				
Season	9	Don Hultz	Minnesota Vikings	1963
Career	29	Jim Marshall	Cleveland Browns, Minnesota Vikings	1960-79
*The record for the most opponents' fumbles recovered in a game is three, held by many players.				
FUMBLES RECOVERED FOR TOUCHDOWN*				
Career	5	Jessie Tuggle	Atlanta Falcons	1987-2000
* The record for the most fumbles recovered and returned for touchdowns in a season is two, held by many players.				

Chargers against the Denver Broncos on Nov. 29, 1987; and Louis Oliver of the Miami Dolphins against the Buffalo Bills on Oct. 4, 1992. Both Glenn and Oliver ran for touchdowns.

On Nov. 3, 1996, two players, James Willis and Troy Vincent, combined for a 104-yard touchdown return for the Philadelphia Eagles against the Dallas Cowboys. Willis intercepted the ball and ran 14 yards before pitching to Vincent, who ran 90 yards for the score.

FUMBLE RETURN Two players hold the record for the longest fumble return, both for touchdowns, at 104 yards: Jack Tatum of the Oakland Raiders against the Green Bay Packers on Sept. 24, 1972; and Aeneas Williams of the Arizona Cardinals against the Washington Redskins on Nov. 5, 2000.

MISSED FIELD GOAL RETURN Chicago Bears cornerback Nathan Vasher captured the record for the longest play in NFL history when he returned a missed field goal 108 yards for a touchdown. The feat took place during a game in Chicago against the San Francisco 49ers on Nov. 13, 2005. San Francisco kicker Joe Nedney lined up for a 52-yard field goal attempt and missed wide to his left. Vasher fielded the ball deep in his own end zone and bolted up the sideline for the score.

THE LAST TIME...

The last time a defensive player won the Super Bowl Most Valuable Player award was in Super Bowl XXXVII, played on Jan. 26, 2003. The Tampa Bay Buccaneers' free safety Dexter Jackson was named MVP. He intercepted two Rich Gannon passes in the first half to spark the Bucs' 48-21 rout of the Oakland Raiders.

FOOTBALL

The Super Bowl

THE GREEN BAY PACKERS BEAT THE KANSAS CITY CHIEFS, 35-10, at the Los Angeles Memorial Coliseum, on Jan. 15, 1967, in what became known as Super Bowl I. At that time, it was called the AFL-NFL World Championship Game.

The game pitted the champions of the National Football League (NFL) against the American Football League (AFL) champs. The two leagues had been fierce rivals since the AFL began play in 1960. In June 1966, the two leagues agreed to merge, but they would not officially unite until the 1970 season. They also agreed to stage a title game between their respective champions at the end of their 1966 seasons.

The NFL first used the name Super Bowl in 1969 (for the third match-up) and added the Roman numeral designation starting with Super Bowl V. Lamar Hunt, owner of the Kansas City Chiefs, is credited with having coined the name Super Bowl, after watching his daughter play with a toy ball called a Super Ball.

MILESTONES

1967: FIRST TOUCHDOWN The Green Bay Packers' Max McGee scored the first Super Bowl touchdown. The wide receiver made a spectacular one-handed catch of a Bart Starr pass for a 37-yard TD in the first quarter of Super Bowl I. These were the first points of any kind in Super Bowl play, and gave the Packers a 7-0 lead (with the extra point).

McGee caught 7 passes for 138 yards, and scored two touchdowns in the game. He had only caught four passes all season. The night before the game, McGee had left the Packers' hotel after curfew and returned at 7:30 AM. He figured he had no chance of playing in the game anyway, and that a little fun wouldn't do any harm. But when Boyd Dowler was injured on the fourth play, Packers coach Vince Lombardi called on McGee. The receiver thought at first that Lombardi was calling him over to fine him for breaking curfew, not to send him into the game. "I almost fainted," McGee said later.

1967: RUSHING TOUCHDOWN Jim Taylor, of the Packers, scored on a 14-yard run in the second quarter of Super Bowl I to give Green Bay a 14-7 lead (with the extra point).

1967: FIELD GOAL Mike Mercer, the Kansas City Chiefs kicker, booted the first field goal in Super Bowl history. It was a 31-yarder in the second quarter of Super Bowl I that reduced the Green Bay lead to 14-10.

1967: SUPER BOWL MOST VALUABLE PLAYER Bart Starr, quarterback for the Green Bay Packers, was the first Super Bowl MVP. The future Hall of Famer was 16 of 23 for 250 yards passing, with 2 TDs, and 1 interception.

Starr led the Packers to victory again in Super Bowl II (33-14, against the Oakland Raiders) and won the MVP award again, thus becoming the first two-time Super Bowl MVP.

1969: AFL WIN The first AFL victory in the Super Bowl came in Super Bowl III, when the New York Jets beat the Baltimore Colts, 16-7. This game is regarded by football historians as the most significant in Super Bowl history, as the Jets victory gave the upstart AFL credibility in the eyes of the media, the fans, and the NFL.

The Colts had been heavy favorites to beat the Jets, but in the week leading up to the game, Jets quarterback Joe Namath "guaranteed" that his team would win. Namath won the MVP award even though he didn't throw a single touchdown pass. He is still the only quarterback to win the Super Bowl MVP award without having thrown a TD pass in the game.

1971: ROOKIE HEAD COACH The first rookie head coach to win the Super Bowl was Don McCafferty, who led the Baltimore Colts to a 16-13 victory over the Dallas Cowboys in Super Bowl V.

Only one other person won it in his first season as an NFL head coach—George Seifert, who won Super Bowl XXIV with the San Francisco 49ers

1971: MVP FROM DEFENSE The first defensive player to win the Super Bowl MVP award was Dallas Cowboys linebacker Chuck Howley in Super Bowl V. During the game, he had two interceptions and a fumble recovery, but the Cowboys still lost to the Colts, 16-13.

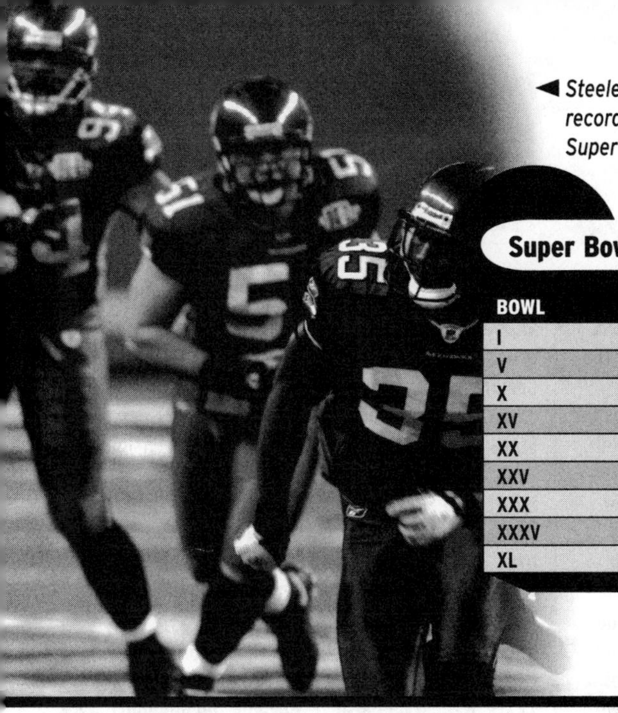

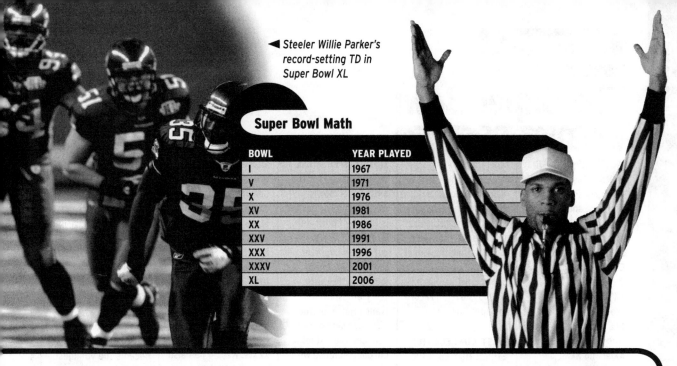

◀ *Steeler Willie Parker's record-setting TD in Super Bowl XL*

Super Bowl Math

BOWL	YEAR PLAYED
I	1967
V	1971
X	1976
XV	1981
XX	1986
XXV	1991
XXX	1996
XXXV	2001
XL	2006

Howley was the first, and so far only, player from a losing team to be named Super Bowl MVP.

1971: FOURTH-QUARTER COMEBACK The Baltimore Colts staged the first successful fourth-quarter comeback during Super Bowl V. Trailing the Dallas Cowboys, 13-6, at the end of the third quarter, the Colts rallied and scored 10 points in the final quarter. The game-winning score came on a 32-yard field goal by rookie kicker Jim O'Brien with five seconds remaining.

1978: INDOOR GAME Super Bowl XII was the first to be held indoors, at the Louisiana Superdome in New Orleans, where the Dallas Cowboys beat the Denver Broncos, 27-10 on Jan. 15, 1978. It is also the only one to date where two players were named Co-Super Bowl MVPs. Defensive end Harvey Martin and defensive tackle Randy White, of the Cowboys, shared the award.

1979: REMATCH The first time two teams met for a repeat Super Bowl matchup came during Super Bowl XIII, when the Pittsburgh Steelers faced the Dallas Cowboys for the second time in four years.

The Steelers had beaten the Cowboys, 21-17, in Super Bowl X. But in the second meeeting, the stakes were even higher, since the victor would be the first three-time winner. The Steelers won, 35-31, in an all-time classic.

1981: WILD-CARD WINNER The Oakland Raiders beat the Philadelphia Eagles, 27-10, in Super Bowl XV to become the first wild-card team to win the Super Bowl. Raiders' owner Al Davis described the win as his team's "finest hour."

1986: $1 MILLION ADVERTISING RATE Television advertising rates hit $1 million per minute for Super Bowl XX. The game, broadcast by NBC, was one of the biggest blowouts in Super Bowl history; the Chicago Bears crushed the New England Patriots, 46-10.

1988: AFRICAN-AMERICAN QUARTERBACK The first, and so far only, African-American starting quarterback to lead his team to a Super Bowl championship was Doug Williams of the Washington Redskins, in Super Bowl XXII.

In the second quarter, with the Denver Broncos leading 10-0, Williams orchestrated a scoring outburst unseen in Super Bowl history. He led scoring drives of 80, 64, 74, 60, and 79 yards to give the Redskins a 35-10 halftime lead. The Redskins won, 42-10, and Williams was named MVP.

1996: NATIONAL ANTHEM–HALFTIME SHOW PERFORMER The first artist to sing the National Anthem before the Super Bowl and be the lead performer during the halftime show was Diana Ross. The Motown diva sang "The Star Spangled Banner" before Super Bowl XVI in Detroit, and was the halftime show star at Super Bowl XXX in Tempe, AZ, which included a memorable exit on a helicopter.

1997: SPECIAL TEAMS MVP Desmond Howard of the Green Bay Packers was named Super Bowl MVP for Super Bowl XXXI, a first time for a special teams player. The kick return specialist rewrote the Super Bowl record book in leading the Packers to a 35-21 win over the New England Patriots. He set a Super Bowl record for longest kickoff return, 99-yards for a TD, and tied the mark for all-purpose yards, with 244.

MORE ON

The Super Bowl

SUPERLATIVES

MOST SUPER BOWL WINS The Dallas Cowboys, Pittsburgh Steelers, and San Francisco 49ers each won a record five Super Bowls. The Cowboys took Super Bowls VI, XII, XXVII, XXVIII, and XXX; the Steelers won IX, X, XIII, XIV, and XL; the 49ers won XVI, XIX, XXIII, XXIV, and XXIX.

MOST CONSECUTIVE WINS Seven teams have won back-to-back Super Bowls. The first was the Green Bay Packers, who won Super Bowls I and II. The other six are: Miami Dolphins, VII and VIII; Pittsburgh Steelers, who did it twice, IX and X; and XIII and XIV; San Francisco 49ers, XXIII and XXIV; Dallas Cowboys, XXVII and XXVIII; Denver Broncos, XXXII and XXXIII; and New England Patriots, XXXVIII and XXXIX.

MOST SUPER BOWL APPEARANCES The Dallas Cowboys have played in a record eight Super Bowls. Their first trip to the NFL's biggest game was Super Bowl V, where they were beaten by the Baltimore Colts, 16-13. The following season, the Cowboys returned to the Super Bowl and won, beating the Miami Dolphins, 24-3, in Super Bowl VI. The Cowboys overall record in Super Bowls is 5-3.

MOST CONSECUTIVE SUPER BOWLS The Buffalo Bills are the only team to play in four straight Super Bowls. The Bills were the AFC representative in Super Bowls XXV, XXVI, XXVII, and XXVIII, and on each occasion the star-crossed Bills came up short, losing every game.

In Super Bowl XXV, the Bills suffered the narrowest loss in Super Bowl history when the New York Giants beat them by one point, 20-19. In the end it all came down to Buffalo kicker Scott Norwood. He could have won the game in the final seconds on a 47-yard field goal, but he missed. It was one of the most heartbreaking losses in sports history.

MOST SUPER BOWL WINS (COACH) The most Super Bowls won by a head coach is four, by Chuck Noll. During the 1970s, Noll put together one of the greatest teams in NFL history with Terry Bradshaw and Franco Harris on the offensive side of the ball, and the "Steel Curtain" defense with players such as Jack Lambert and "Mean" Joe Greene. Noll led his gritty Steelers to victory in Super Bowls IX, X, XIII, and XIV.

MOST SUPER BOWL APPEARANCES (COACH) Don Shula was the head coach in a record six Super Bowls. He led the Baltimore Colts to Super Bowl III, and the Miami Dolphins to Super Bowls VI, VII, VIII, XVII, and XIX. His record was two wins and four losses. His victories came with the Dolphins in Super Bowls VII and VIII.

MOST NATIONAL ANTHEM PERFORMANCES When Aaron Neville joined Aretha Franklin to sing the national anthem at Super Bowl XL, he joined two other groups who had performed the honor twice. The Grambling State University Tiger Marching Band strutted in Super Bowls II and IX. Singers from the Air Force Academy Chorale were featured at Super Bowl VI and joined a larger chorus at Super Bowl XXXIX. Neville had also sung the anthem at Super Bowl XXIV.

MOST SUPER BOWLS (CITY) New Orleans, LA has hosted a record nine Super Bowls. "The Big Easy" first staged the game on Jan. 11, 1970, Super Bowl IV, at Tulane Stadium. Since then New Orleans has hosted Super Bowls, VI, IX, XII, XV, XX, XXIV, XXXI, and XXXVI. Since Super Bowl XII, all Super Bowls played in New Orleans have been played at the Louisiana Superdome.

HIGHEST TELEVISION RATING Super Bowl XVI, San Francisco 49ers vs. Cincinnati Bengals, drew the highest television rating ever for a Super Bowl, and was 4th highest rated show in American television history. Super Bowl XVI had a 49.1 rating, which meant that 73 percent of American homes with television sets had the game on.

YOUNGEST QUARTERBACK TO WIN At the age of 23 years, 340 days, Ben Roethlisberger of the Pittsburgh Steelers became the youngest quarterback to lead a team to a Super Bowl win. In only his second NFL season, "Big Ben" led the AFC 6th-seeded Steelers to a victory in Super Bowl XL, breaking the record formerly held by New England Patriots quarterback Tom Brady, who was 24 years, 184 days old when he won Super Bowl XXXVI.

MOST SUPER BOWL LOSSES (TEAM) There is a three-way tie for the record for most Super Bowl losses for a team: The Minnesota Vikings lost in Super Bowls IV, VIII, IX, and XI; the Denver Broncos lost in Super Bowls XII, XXI, XXII and XXIV; the Buffalo Bills lost in Super Bowls XXV, XXVI, XXVII and XXVIII.

Single Game

Yards Passing	414	Kurt Warner, Rams (vs. Titans)	XXXIV
TD Passes	6	Steve Young, 49ers (vs. Chargers)	XXIX
Points Scored	18	Roger Craig, 49ers (vs. Dolphins)	XIX
	18	Jerry Rice, 49ers (vs. Broncos)	XXIV
	18	Jerry Rice, 49ers (vs. Chargers)	XXIX
	18	Ricky Watters, 49ers (vs. Chargers)	XXIX
	18	Terrell Davis, Broncos (vs. Packers)	XXXII
Receptions	11	Dan Ross, Bengals (vs. 49ers)	XVI
	11	Jerry Rice, 49ers (vs. Bengals)	XXIII
Receiving Yards	215	Jerry Rice, 49ers (vs. Bengals)	XXIII
Rushing Yards	204	Timmy Smith, Redskins (vs. Broncos)	XXII
All-Purpose Yards	244	Andre Coleman, Chargers (vs. 49ers)	XXIX
	244	Desmond Howard, Packers (vs. Patriots)	XXXI
Interceptions	3	Rod Martin, Raiders (vs. Eagles)	XV

Big Plays

Longest TD Pass	85 yards	Jake Delhomme, Panthers (to Muhsin Muhammad vs. Patriots)	XXXVIII
Longest Run From Scrimmage	75 yards	Willie Parker, Steelers (vs. Seahawks)	XL
Longest Field Goal	54 yards	Steve Christie, Bills (vs. Cowboys)	XXVIII
Longest Punt	63 yards	Lee Johnson, Bengals (vs.49ers)	XXIII
Longest Kick Return	99 yards	Desmond Howard, Packers (vs. Patriots)	XXXI
Longest Punt Return	45 yards	John Taylor, 49ers (vs. Bengals)	XXIII

Career

Yards Passing	1,142	Joe Montana, 49ers	XVI, XIX, XXIII, XXIV
TD Passes	11	Joe Montana, 49ers	XVI, XIX, XXIII, XXIV
Points Scored	48	Jerry Rice, 49ers, Raiders	XXIII, XXIV, XXIX, XXXVII
TDs Scored	8	Jerry Rice, 49ers, Raiders	XXIII, XXIV, XXIX, XXXVII
Receptions	33	Jerry Rice, 49ers, Raiders	XXIII, XXIV, XXIX, XXXVII
Receiving Yards	589	Jerry Rice, 49ers, Raiders	XXIII, XXIV, XXIX, XXXVII
Rushing Yards	354	Franco Harris, Steelers	IX, X, XIII, XIV
Interceptions	3	Chuck Howley, Cowboys	V, VI
	3	Rod Martin, Raiders	XV, XVIII
	3	Larry Brown, Cowboys	XXVII, XXVIII, XXX
Most Games	6	Mike Lodish, Bills, Broncos	XXV, XXVI, XXVII, XXVIII, XXXII, XXXIII
Most Wins	5	Charles Haley, 49ers, Cowboys	XXIII, XXIV, XXVII, XXVIII, XXX
MVP Awards	3	Joe Montana, 49ers	XVI, XIX, XXIV

SOMETHING TO THINK ABOUT

FAN-ATIC

Les Boatwright, a longtime San Francisco 49ers fan, died just before Super Bowl XXIII in 1989. But he had already purchased two tickets for the game in Miami. After Boatwright's body was cremated, his two sons decided to take the urn with his ashes to the game with them. The 49ers beat the Cincinnati Bengals, 20-16.

BETTER LATE THAN NEVER

John Madden, head coach of the Oakland Raiders, was so nervous before Super Bowl XI that on the morning of the game he told the driver of the team bus to leave for the stadium from the hotel without realizing that five players were not aboard. The players, who had to get to the stadium on their own, thought they had been late for the bus and tried to hide from Madden in the locker room. Madden, realizing his mistake, was avoiding them. But all was well in the end, as the Raiders beat the Vikings, 32-14.

FOOTBALL

NCAA Division I-A

THE NATIONAL COLLEGIATE ATHLETIC ASSOCIATION (NCAA) was originally known as the Intercollegiate Athletic Association of the United States (IAAUS), launched in New York City in Dec. 1905, and officially constituted on March 31, 1906, with 62 charter members. Its purpose was to organize collegiate football and standardize rules. Renamed in 1910, the NCAA has kept official football statistics since 1937. In 1973, the NCAA reclassified its football competition into three levels of play: Divisions I, II, and III. Five years later, in 1978, Division I football was further subdivided into Division I-A and I-AA.

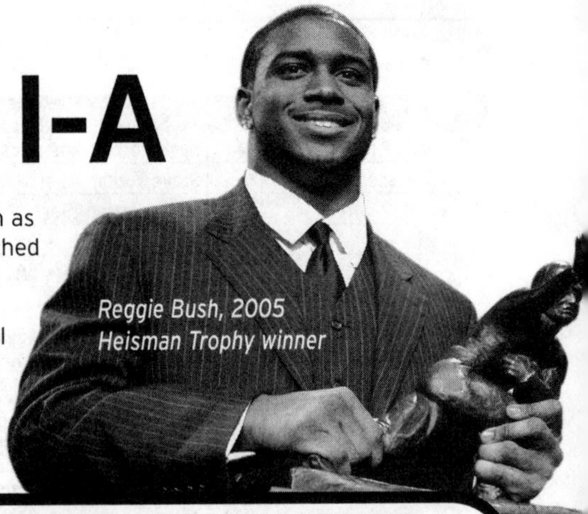

Reggie Bush, 2005 Heisman Trophy winner

MILESTONES

1869: FIRST INTERCOLLEGIATE GAME Historians recognize the first college football game as having been played at College Field, New Brunswick, NJ, on Nov. 6, 1869, between Rutgers and Princeton (Rutgers beat Princeton, 6-4).

The game at that time looked more like rugby than modern-day football and was played with 25 men on the field for each team. Under the rules of the contest, a "score" (the equivalent of a modern field goal) was worth one point and was called a "game." The first team to score six games out of 10 won the contest.

1880: ELEVEN MEN Football innovator Walter Camp's plan to standardize the size of teams to 11 men per side was officially adopted in 1880. While a junior at Yale, Camp had attended the 1878 football convention in Springfield, MA, and promoted the idea. It was rejected at first, but Camp tried again and finally got his way. This was a radical rule change that opened up the game considerably.

1882: FIRST AND TEN The concept of "downs" and "yards to gain" was introduced by Walter Camp. It was sparked by the infamous "block game," played between Princeton and Yale in 1881.

In order to preserve their unbeaten records, both teams played conservatively and did not try to advance the ball when they had possession, angering the crowd. In order to force teams to move the ball forward or lose possession, Camp proposed: "If on three consecutive fairs and downs a team shall not have advanced the ball five yards, nor lost ten, they must give up the ball to opponents at the spot of the fourth down." This "yards to go" rule formed the basis for modern football. It was adopted on Oct. 12, 1882.

1889: ALL-AMERICA TEAM The All-America team is believed to have been the brainchild of Caspar Whitney, who was part owner of the magazine *This Week's Sport*. Whitney's idea was to honor the best college player annually at each of the 11 positions on the field.

It is widely reported that he enlisted the help of his close friend and Yale coach Walter Camp to select the first All-America team that appeared in 1889.

1890: ARMY-NAVY GAME The first Army-Navy Game was played at West Point on Nov. 29, 1890. The Navy's Midshipmen shut out the Cadets of Army, 24-0. Cadet Denis Michie is widely credited with being the driving force behind the first game. In fact, Army's home stadium at West Point is named for him.

In 105 contests through 2004, each service academy won 49 games; 7 games were tied.

1902: BOWL GAME The first College Bowl game was the Rose Bowl played at Tournament Park, Pasadena, CA, on Jan. 1, 1902. The inaugural bowl game pitted Stanford against Michigan. Undefeated Michigan, coached by Fielding "Hurry Up" Yost, had won all 12 games that season, and crushed Stanford, 49-0.

1906: FORWARD PASS The forward pass was legalized by the Intercollegiate Athletic Association of the United States in 1906. John Heisman, a well-known college coach, was the main proponent of this innovation, as a way to change the static nature of the game that led to so much violent play.

The Football Rules Committee, headed by Walter Camp, had opposed the idea for several years. But they relented after the 1905 season, which was plagued by injuries (149 serious injuries and 18 deaths). President Theodore Roosevelt had added his voice to the debate on violence in football, calling for rough play to be outlawed.

Besides defusing the "rough play crisis," the rule change served as a major catalyst for the sport's ensuing surge in popularity.

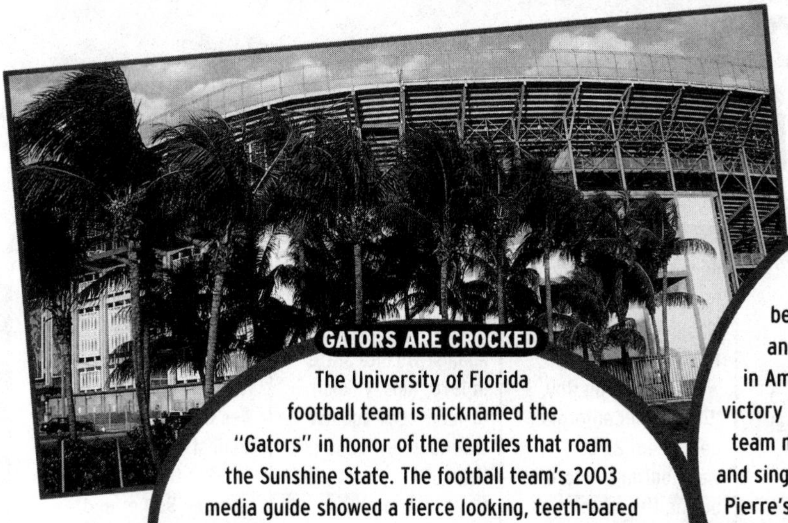

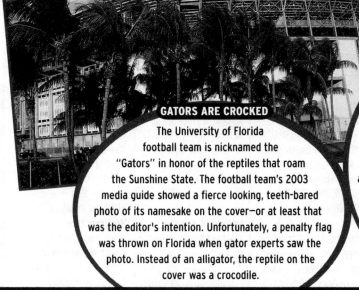

◀ *Orange Bowl Stadium*

SOMETHING TO THINK ABOUT

GATORS ARE CROCKED

The University of Florida football team is nicknamed the "Gators" in honor of the reptiles that roam the Sunshine State. The football team's 2003 media guide showed a fierce looking, teeth-bared photo of its namesake on the cover—or at least that was the editor's intention. Unfortunately, a penalty flag was thrown on Florida when gator experts saw the photo. Instead of an alligator, the reptile on the cover was a crocodile.

BIGGEST LITTLE GAME

Massachusetts rivals the Williams College Ephs and the Amherst College Lord Jeffs have been facing off on the gridiron since 1884. Their annual game, known as the "Biggest Little Game in America," features one of the more unusual college victory traditions. Whenever Williams beats Amherst, every team member marches from the stadium—still in uniform and singing the college fight song—a quarter of a mile to St. Pierre's Barber Shop on Spring Street in Williamstown. The entire squad crams into the place, the blinds are drawn, and the team then celebrates. Besides smoking the traditional winners' cigars and singing anti-Amherst chants, the upperclassmen shave the heads of the freshmen.

1932: HEISMAN TROPHY The Heisman Trophy, given annually to college football's best player, was first awarded in 1935. Originally called the DAC Trophy, the award is presented by the Downtown Athletic Club of New York City.

In the first year, it was limited to players east of the Mississippi. The following year, the pool of eligible players was expanded to the entire country. The first winner was Jay Berwanger, a halfback from the University of Chicago.

The award was renamed the Heisman Trophy in 1936 in honor of the Downtown Athletic Club's athletic director and renowned coach John Heisman, who died earlier that year.

1939: TELEVISED GAME The first televised college game was between Fordham University and Waynesburg College. It was broadcast on Sept. 30, 1939, on what is now WNBC in New York, a local station.

Thought to be a major coup at the time, the telecast had little lasting effect. Since the broadcast signal was weak and TV sets were scarce, the TV audience was minuscule.

Beginning with the 1951 season, the NCAA approved the broadcast of football on Saturday afternoons. At that time, networks were limited to transmitting just one game per region.

The first televised prime-time game was between the Rebels of Ole Miss and the Crimson Tide of Alabama. The game, broadcast by the ABC network on Oct. 4, 1969, was a classic. The Crimson Tide held off the Rebels, 33-32, despite Ole Miss's quarterback Archie Manning's throwing for 436 yards and three touchdowns.

1940: RESULT REVERSAL In 1940, Cornell apparently beat Dartmouth, 7-3, on a last-second touchdown score. But a review of the game film showed that Cornell's winning touchdown pass came on an illegal fifth down play. Two days later, Cornell coaches reviewed the game film and discovered the mistake. In an act of outstanding sportsmanship, Cornell officials notified Dartmouth of the referee's error and forfeited the game.

1958: TWO-POINT CONVERSION The option for a two-point conversion attempt after a touchdown is scored, as an alternative to kicking a point after attempt (PAT), was approved by the NCAA for the 1958 season.

1961: AFRICAN-AMERICAN HEISMAN WINNER Syracuse halfback Ernie Davis became the first African-American Heisman Trophy winner, in 1961. In the balloting he received 53 points more than the runner-up, Ohio State's Bob Ferguson, also an African-American.

2002: FEMALE PLAYER The first female player to participate in a Division I-A football game was New Mexico place-kicker Katie Hnida, in the Las Vegas Bowl against UCLA, played on Dec. 25, 2002. Hnida attempted an extra point, but it was blocked in New Mexico's 27-13 loss.

Hnida became the first female player to score in a Division I-A game, on Aug. 30, 2003. She kicked two extra points in New Mexico's 72-8 victory over Texas State-San Marcos.

NCAA Division I-A

SUPERLATIVES

MOST NATIONAL CHAMPIONSHIPS The national college football champion has been chosen by various ranking, poll, and voting systems since 1869. Yale is recognized as having won the most national titles with 17 (1874, 1876-77, 1880-84, 1886-88, 1891-92, 1894, 1900, 1907, and 1909).

In the modern era, since the introduction of the Associated Press poll in 1936, Notre Dame has won the most. The Fighting Irish have won eight titles: 1943, 1946-47, 1949, 1966, 1973, 1977, and 1988.

MOST BOWL WINS The Crimson Tide of Alabama have won a record 30 bowl games. Their first Bowl victory was the 1926 Rose Bowl.

Overall Alabama has played in a record 51 bowls, and won the Sugar Bowl, eight times, 1962, 1964, 1967, 1975, 1978-80, 1993; Rose Bowl, four times, 1926, 1931, 1935, 1946; Orange Bowl, four times, 1943, 1953, 1963, 1966; Sun Bowl (now John Hancock Bowl), three times, 1983, 1986, 1988; Cotton Bowl, three times, 1942, 1981, 2006; Liberty Bowl, twice, 1976, 1982; and (once each) the Aloha Bowl (1985); Blockbuster Bowl (1991); Gator Bowl (1993); Florida Citrus Bowl (1995); Outback Bowl (1997); and Independence Bowl (2001).

MOST WINS Michigan has won the most games of any college team. Including bowl games, the Wolverines have won 849 games out of 1,165 played, from 1879 to 2005.

LONGEST WINNING STREAK The longest winning streak (no losses, no ties) in Division 1-A football, including bowl games, is 47 games by Coach Bud Wilkinson's Oklahoma Sooners, 1953-57. Their streak was ended on Nov. 16, 1957, when Notre Dame beat them 7-0.

LONGEST UNDEFEATED STREAK The longest undefeated streak (no losses, but ties are allowed) in Division 1-A football, including bowl games, is 63 games by the Washington Huskies, 1907-17. The streak was stopped on Nov. 3, 1917, when California beat them 27-0. Washington's record during the streak was 59 wins, 4 ties.

LONGEST LOSING STREAK The record for consecutive losses in Division I-A football is 34 games, by the Northwestern Wildcats. This most undesirable of streaks started on Sept. 22, 1979, and was finally snapped three years later on Sept. 25, 1982, when Northern Illinois succumbed to the Wildcats, 31-6.

LONGEST RUN FROM SCRIMMAGE The NCAA Division I-A record for the longest rushing yardage gained on a single play is 99 yards. This was achieved by five players. The first to perform the feat was Kansas Jayhawks back Gale Sayers during a game against Nebraska in 1963.

His mark was matched by: Max Anderson of Arizona State against Wyoming in 1967; Ralph Thompson of West Texas A&M against Wichita State in 1970; Kelsey Finch of Tennessee against Florida in 1977; and Eric Vann of Kansas against Oklahoma in 1997.

LONGEST PASS COMPLETION The NCAA Division I-A record for longest pass completion is 99 yards, a distance achieved 15 times. The first 99-yard play came on a Fred Owens pass to Jack Ford for Portland against St. Mary's (CA) in 1947.

It was later matched by: Bo Burris to Warren McVea of Houston against Washington State in 1966; Colin Clapton to Eddie Jenkins of Holy Cross against Boston University in 1970; Terry Peel to Robert Ford of Houston against Syracuse in 1970; Peel and Ford combined again vs. San Diego State in 1972; Cris Collinsworth to Derrick Gaffney of Florida against Rice in 1977; Scott Ankrom to James Maness of TCU against Rice in 1984; Gino Torretta to Horace Copeland of Miami (FL) against Arkansas in 1991; John Paci to Thomas Lewis of Indiana against Penn State in 1993; Troy De Gar to Wes Caswell of Tulsa against Oklahoma in 1996; Drew Brees to Vinny Sutherland of Purdue against Northwestern in 1999; Dan Urban to Justin McCariens of Northern Ill. against Ball State in 2000; Jason Johnson to Brandon Marshall of Arizona against Idaho in 2001; Jim Sorgi to Lee Evans of Wisconsin against Akron in 2003; and Dondrial Pinkins to Troy Williamson of South Carolina against Virginia in 2003.

LONGEST FIELD GOAL The longest field goal made in NCAA Division I-A history is 67 yards. The first player to kick from such a long distance was Texas kicker Russell Erxleben during a game against Rice in 1977.

Fourteen days later, Steve Little, who played for Arkansas, tied the record while playing Erxleben's team.

The following season Joe Williams joined the exclusive club. He

Selected NCAA Division I-A Records

MOST POINTS (NON KICKERS)

Game	48	Howard Griffith	Illinois vs. Southern Illinois	Sept. 22, 1990
Season	234	Barry Sanders	Oklahoma State	1988
Career	468	Travis Prentice	Miami (Ohio)	1996-99

TOUCHDOWNS SCORED

Game	8	Howard Griffith	Illinois vs. Southern Illinois	Sept. 22, 1990
Season	39	Barry Sanders	Oklahoma State	1988
Career	78	Travis Prentice	Miami (Ohio)	1996-99

RUSHING YARDAGE

Game	406	LaDainian Tomlinson	TCU vs. UTEP	Nov. 20, 1999
Season	2,628	Barry Sanders	Oklahoma State	1988
Career	6,397	Ron Dayne	Wisconsin	1996-99

PASSING YARDAGE

Game	716	David Klingler	Houston vs. Arizona St.	Dec. 2, 1990
Season	5,833	B.J. Symons	Texas Tech	2003
Career	17,072	Timmy Chang	Hawaii	2000-2004

PASSING COMPLETIONS

Game	55	Rusty LaRue	Wake Forest vs. Duke	Oct. 28, 1995
	55	Drew Brees	Purdue vs. Wisconsin	Oct. 10, 1998
Season	479	Kliff Kingsbury	Texas Tech	2002
Career	1,231	Kliff Kingsbury	Texas Tech	1999-2002

TOUCHDOWN PASSES THROWN

Game	11	David Klingler	Houston vs. Eastern Wash.	Nov. 17, 1990
Season	54	David Klingler	Houston	1990
Career	388	Timmy Chang	Hawaii	2000-04

RECEIVING YARDAGE

Game	405	Troy Edwards	Louisiana Tech vs. Nebraska	Aug. 29, 1998
Season	2,060	Trevor Insley	Nevada	1999
Career	5,005	Trevor Insley	Nevada	1996-99

RECEPTIONS

Game	23	Randy Gatewood	UNLV vs. Idaho	Sept. 17, 1994
Season	142	Manny Hazard	Houston	1989
Career	300	Arnold Jackson	Louisville	1997-2000

FIELD GOALS MADE

Game	7	Mike Prindle	Western Mich. vs. Marshall	Sept. 29, 1984
	7	Dale Klein	Nebraska vs. Missouri	Oct. 19, 1985
Season	31	Billy Bennett	Georgia	2003
Career	87	Billy Bennett	Georgia	2000-03

TOP FIVE NCAA DIVISION I-A COACHES (WINS)

WINS	COACH	TEAMS
359	Bobby Bowden	Stamford, 1959-62; West Virginia, 1970-75; Florida State, 1976-2005
354	Joe Paterno	Penn State, 1966-2005
323	Paul "Bear" Bryant	Maryland, 1945; Kentucky, 1946-53; Texas A&M, 1954-57; Alabama, 1958-82
319	Glenn "Pop" Warner	Georgia, 1895-96; Cornell, 1897-98, 1904-06; Carlisle, 1899-1903, 1907-14; Pittsburgh, 1915-23; Stanford, 1924-32; Temple, 1933-38
314	Amos Alonzo Stagg	Springfield, 1890-91; Chicago, 1892-1932; Pacific, 1933-46

SUPERMAN FREE SAFETY

Former Princeton free safety Dean Cain holds the Division I-AA record for most interceptions per game in a season with 1.2 (12 in 10 games in 1987). A knee injury prevented him from going pro, so instead, he turned to acting. In what turned out to be a fitting role, Cain played Superman in the TV series *Lois & Clark* from 1993 to 1997.

FOOTBALL UNIVERSITY

Some schools are better than others at producing NFL-quality players. Out of 1,692 players on NFL rosters at the start of the 2005 season, Florida State contributed the most with 42. Tennessee and Florida both had 37 players, and Ohio State and Georgia came next with 35 each. Other schools who were well-represented in the NFL in 2005 included: Michigan (34); Univ. of Miami (33); Auburn (31); Notre Dame (30); and Louisiana State (30).

SOMETHING TO THINK ABOUT

made his record kick for Wichita State during a game against Southern Illinois in 1978.

MOST INTERCEPTIONS BY A PLAYER (SEASON) Washington Huskies DB Al Worley set the Division I-A single-season record in 1968 when he picked off 14 passes over 10 games.

Worley also holds the record for most interceptions per game, with 1.4.

MOST SACKS BY A PLAYER (SEASON) DE Terrell Suggs was a monster for the Arizona State Sun Devils. He recorded a whopping 24 sacks during the 2002 season over a total of 14 games.

Suggs also holds the per game record, with 1.75 sacks.

MOST HEISMAN TROPHY WINS Only one player has won the Heisman Trophy Award more than once—Ohio State running back Archie Griffin.

The Buckeye back first won the Heisman Trophy in 1974. He won the award again the following season in 1975.

BASKETBALL

NBA Team by Team

THE FIRST PRO BASKETBALL LEAGUE in the U.S. was the National Basketball League (NBL), founded in 1898—but it lasted just two seasons.

Today's National Basketball Association (NBA) was created from the merger of two leagues following the 1948-49 season: the Basketball Association of America (BAA) and the NBL, a new version of which had started play in 1938. The NBA recognizes the 1947 championship, won by the Philadelphia Warriors in the BAA, as its first title.

The first NBA season consisted of 17 teams, 10 originally from the NBL and 7 from the BAA. Eight franchises from the original NBA are still in action: the Boston Celtics, New York Knicks, Golden State Warriors (originally Philadelphia Warriors), Philadelphia 76ers (Syracuse Nationals), Atlanta Hawks (Tri-Cities Blackhawks), Detroit Pistons (Fort Wayne Zollner Pistons), Los Angeles Lakers (Minneapolis Lakers), and Sacramento Kings (Rochester Royals).

The American Basketball Association (ABA) began play in 1967. After nine seasons, it merged with the NBA. Four ABA teams joined the NBA for the start of the 1976-77 season: the Denver Nuggets, Indiana Pacers, New York Nets, and San Antonio Spurs. The Spurs are the only former ABA team to win the NBA championship, taking the title in 1999, 2003, and 2005.

The tables below cover records and milestones for each team through the 2004-05 season.

SUPERLATIVES

MOST NBA CHAMPIONSHIPS The Boston Celtics have won a record 16 NBA titles: 1957, 1959-66, 1968-69, 1974, 1976, 1981, 1984, and 1986.

MOST WINS (SEASON) The most wins in the NBA regular season is 72, by the Chicago Bulls. Led by Michael Jordan, the Bulls had a 72-10 record for a .878 winning percentage in their 1995-96 season. The Bulls went on to win the NBA title, beating the Seattle Supersonics, 4-2, in the Finals.

MOST CONSECUTIVE WINS The longest winning streak in the NBA is 33 wins by the Los Angeles Lakers. The Lakers' streak began with a 110-106 win over the Baltimore Bullets on Nov. 5, 1971, at home, and was ended on Jan. 9, 1972, by a 120-104 loss to the Milwaukee Bucks on the road.

Team by Team

First season for each team is in parentheses.

ATLANTA HAWKS (1949 as Tri-Cities Blackhawks)		
NBA Champions	1958 (as St. Louis Hawks)	
Most Points	23,292	Dominique Wilkins, 1982-94
Most Assists	3,866	Doc Rivers, 1983-91
Most Rebounds	12,851	Bob Pettit, 1954-65[1]
(1) Milwaukee Hawks, 1954; St. Louis Hawks, 1955-65		
BOSTON CELTICS (1946)		
NBA Champions	1957, 1959-66, 1968-69, 1974, 1976, 1981, 1984, 1986	
Most Points	26,395	John Havlicek, 1962-78
Most Assists	6,945	Bob Cousy, 1950-63
Most Rebounds	21,620;	Bill Russell, 1956-69
CHARLOTTE BOBCATS (2004)		
Most Points	1,105	Emeka Okafor, 2004-05
Most Assists	591	Brevin Knight, 2004-05
Most Rebounds	795	Emeka Okafor, 2004-05
CHICAGO BULLS (1966)		
NBA Champions	1991-93, 1996-98	
Most Points	795	Michael Jordan, 1984-93, 1994-98
Most Assists	5,012	Michael Jordan, 1984-93, 1994-98
Most Rebounds	5,836	Michael Jordan, 1984-93, 1994-98
CLEVELAND CAVALIERS (1970)		
Most Points	10,389	Brad Daugherty, 1986-94
Most Assists	4,206	Mark Price, 1986-95
Most Rebounds	5,227	Brad Daugherty, 1986-94
DALLAS MAVERICKS (1980)		
Most Points	16,643	Rolando Blackman, 1981-92
Most Assists	511	Derek Harper, 1983-94, 1996-97
Most Rebounds	4,589	James Donaldson, 1985-92

DENVER NUGGETS (ABA: 1967 as Denver Rockets; NBA: 1976)		
Most Points	21,645	Alex English, 1979-90
Most Assists	3,679	Alex English, 1979-90
Most Rebounds	6,630	Dan Issel, 1975-85
DETROIT PISTONS (1948 as Fort Wayne Zollner Pistons)		
NBA Champions	1989-90	
Most Points	18,822	Isiah Thomas, 1981-94
Most Assists	9,061	Isiah Thomas, 1981-94
Most Rebounds	9,430	Bill Laimbeer, 1981-94
GOLDEN STATE WARRIORS (1946 as Philadelphia Warriors)		
NBA Champions	1947 (BAA)[1], 1956[1], 1975	
Most Points	17,783	Wilt Chamberlain, 1959-65[2]
Most Assists	4,855	Guy Rodgers, 1958-66[3]
Most Rebounds	12,771	Nate Thurmond, 1963-74[4]
(1) Philadelphia Warriors (2) Philadelphia Warriors, 1959-62, San Francisco Warriors, 1963-65 (3) Phil. Warriors, 1958-62, S.F. Warriors, 1963-65 (4) SF Warriors, 1963-71		
HOUSTON ROCKETS (1967 as San Diego Rockets)		
NBA Champions	1994-1995	
Most Points	26,511	Hakeem Olajuwon, 1984-2001
Most Assists	4,402	Calvin Murphy, 1970-83[1]
Most Rebounds	13,382	Hakeem Olajuwon, 1984-2001
(1) San Diego Rockets, 1970-71		
INDIANA PACERS (ABA: 1967; NBA: 1976)		
ABA Champions	1970, 1972-73	
Most Points	25,279	Reggie Miller, 1987-2005
Most Assists	4,141	Reggie Miller, 1987-2005
Most Rebounds	7,643	Mel Daniels, 1968-74

LOS ANGELES CLIPPERS (1970 as Buffalo Braves)

Most Points	12,735	Randy Smith, 1971-79[1]
Most Assists	3,498	Randy Smith, 1971-79[1]
Most Rebounds	4,471	Loy Vaught, 1990-98

(1) Buffalo Braves, 1971-78, San Diego Clippers, 1978-82

LOS ANGELES LAKERS (1948 as Minneapolis Lakers)

NBA Champions	1949-50[1], 1952-54[1], 1972, 1980, 1982, 1985, 1987-88, 2000-02	
Most Points	25,192	Jerry West, 1960-74
Most Assists	10,141	Magic Johnson, 1979-91, 1995-96
Most Rebounds	11,463	Elgin Baylor, 1958-72[1]

(1) Minneapolis Lakers, 1958-60

MEMPHIS GRIZZLIES (1995 as Vancouver Grizzlies)

Most Points	7,801	Shareef Abdur-Rahim, 1996-2001[1]
Most Assists	1,675	Mike Bibby, 1998-2001*
Most Rebounds	3,070	Shareef Abdur-Rahim, 1996-2001[1]

(1) Vancouver Grizzlies

MIAMI HEAT (1988)

Most Points	9,248	Glen Rice, 1989-95
Most Assists	3,507	Tim Hardaway, 1995-2001
Most Rebounds	4,544	Rony Seikaly, 1988-94

MILWAUKEE BUCKS (1968)

NBA Champions	1971	
Most Points	14,211	Kareem Abdul-Jabbar, 1969-75
Most Assists	3,272	Paul Pressey, 1982-90
Most Rebounds	7,161	Kareem Abdul-Jabbar, 1969-75

MINNESOTA TIMBERWOLVES (1989)

Most Points	15,681	Kevin Garnett, 1995-2005
Most Assists	3,525	Kevin Garnett, 1995-2005
Most Rebounds	8,601	Kevin Garnett, 1995-2005

NEW JERSEY NETS (ABA: 1967 as Jersey Americans; NBA: 1974 as New York Nets)

ABA Champions	1974[1], 1976[1]	
Most Points	10,440	Buck Williams, 1981-89
Most Assists	2,363	Kenny Anderson, 1991-96
Most Rebounds	7,576	Buck Williams, 1981-89

(1) New York Nets

NEW ORLEANS HORNETS[1] (1988 as Charlotte Hornets)

Most Points	9,839	Dell Curry, 1988-98[2]
Most Assists	5,557	Muggsy Bogues, 1988-98[2]
Most Rebounds	3,479	Larry Johnson, 1991-96[2]

(1) For the 2005-06 season, the Hornets were officially called the New Orleans/Oklahoma City Hornets. The franchise was forced to relocate from its home city in the wake of Hurricane Katrina (2) Charlotte Hornets 1988-2002

NEW YORK KNICKS (1946)

NBA Champions	1970, 1973	
Most Points	23,665	Patrick Ewing, 1985-2000
Most Assists	4,791	Walt Frazier, 1967-77
Most Rebounds	10,759	Patrick Ewing, 1985-2000

ORLANDO MAGIC (1989)

Most Points	10,650	Nick Anderson, 1989-99
Most Assists	2,776	Scott Skiles, 1989-94
Most Rebounds	3,691	Shaquille O'Neal, 1992-96

PHILADELPHIA 76ERS (1949 as Syracuse Nationals)

NBA Champions	1955[1], 1967, 1983	
Most Points	21,586	Hal Greer, 1958-73[2]
Most Assists	6,212	Maurice Cheeks, 1978-89
Most Rebounds	11,256	Dolph Schayes, 1949-64

(1) Syracuse Nationals (2) Syracuse Nationals, 1958-63; Philadelphia 76ers, 1963-73

PHEONIX SUNS (1968)

Most Points	15,666	Walter Davis, 1977-88
Most Assists	6,518	Kevin Johnson, 1988-2000
Most Rebounds	6,937	Alvan Adams, 1975-88

PORTLAND TRAIL BLAZERS (1970)

NBA Champions	1977	
Most Points	18,040	Clyde Drexler, 1983-94
Most Assists	5,319	Terry Porter, 1985-95
Most Rebounds	5,339	Clyde Drexler, 1983-94

SACRAMENTO KINGS (1948 as Rochester Royals)

NBA Champions	1951 (as Rochester Royals)	
Most Points	22,009	Oscar Robertson, 1960-70[1]
Most Assists	7,731	Oscar Robertson, 1960-70[1]
Most Rebounds	9,353	Sam Lacey, 1970-82[2]

(1) Cincinnati Royals (2) Cincinnati Royals 1970-72, Kansas City Royals 1972-81

SAN ANTONIO SPURS (ABA: 1967 as Dallas Chaparrals; NBA: 1976)

NBA Champions	1999, 2003, 2005	
Most Points	20,790	David Robinson, 1989-2003
Most Assists	4,474	Avery Johnson, 1992-93, 1994-2001
Most Rebounds	10,497	David Robinson, 1989-2003

SEATTLE SUPERSONICS (1967)

NBA Champions	1979	
Most Points	16,573	Gary Payton, 1990-2003
Most Assists	6,721	Gary Payton, 1990-2003
Most Rebounds	7,729	Jack Sikma, 1977-86

TORONTO RAPTORS (1995)

Most Points	9,103	Vince Carter, 1998-2004
Most Assists	1,791	Alvin Williams, 1997-2004
Most Rebounds	2,025	Vince Carter, 1998-2004

UTAH JAZZ (1974 as New Orleans Jazz)

Most Points	36,374	Karl Malone, 1985-2003
Most Assists	15,806	John Stockton, 1984-2003
Most Rebounds	14,601	Karl Malone, 1985-2003

WASHINGTON WIZARDS (1961 as Chicago Packers)

NBA Champions	1978 (as Washington Bullets)	
Most Points	15,551	Elvin Hayes, 1972-81[1]
Most Assists	3,822	Wes Unseld, 1968-81[2]
Most Rebounds	13,769	Wes Unseld, 1968-81[2]

(1) Baltimore Bullets, 1972-73, Capitol Bullets, 1973-74, Washington Bullets, 1974-81 (2) Balt. Bullets 1968-73, Capitol Bullets, 1973-74, Wash' Bullets, 1974-81

NBA Regular Season

MILESTONES

1891: BASKETBALL'S ORIGINS Basketball was invented by Dr. James Naismith, a 30-year-old Canadian-born physical education instructor teaching at the YMCA Training School (now Springfield College), in Springfield, MA. In the fall of 1891, Naismith was asked to devise a game that could be played indoors in winter, to give students a more interesting activity than calisthenics.

In mid-December. Naismith set down the rules for his new game. He nailed two peach baskets to the opposite walls of a gym at a height of 10 feet (the height of the balcony), and began to teach his students basketball.

In the first game, played Dec. 21, 1891, the teams were made up of nine men. The game lasted 30 minutes and was played with a soccer ball. A basket was worth just one point; one William R. Chase scored the only basket; for a 1-0 win. There was no hole in the bottom of the basket, the ball had to be retrieved using a ladder.

Naismith published the original 13 rules for his game in the school newspaper, the *Triangle*, on Jan. 15, 1892.

1896: FIRST PRO GAME The first documented professional basketball game was played in Trenton, NJ, on Nov. 7, 1896. The court was surrounded by a 12-foot-high wire-mesh fence. Two teams of YMCA players, from Trenton, NJ, and Brooklyn, NY, were paid $15 each to play; Trenton won, 16-1. Fred Cooper, of Trenton, scored a game-high six points and also received an extra dollar for being team captain.

1895: FREE-THROWS The free-throw line was moved 5 feet closer to the basketball from its original distance of 20 feet to 15 feet. The following year, the points for a free throw were reduced from three to one. Also in 1896, points given for a field goal were changed from three to two.

It wasn't until 1924, that the player who was fouled was required to take the free-throw. Prior to that, teams usually had a specialist that took all the shots from the free-throw line.

1954: 24-SECOND CLOCK The 24-second clock, which requires that teams shoot the ball within that amount of time after gaining possession, was the brainchild of Danny Biasone, owner of the NBA's Syracuse Nationals.

The NBA had been losing fans because of the boring pace of play; Biasone proposed that a shot clock would speed up play and make the game more attractive to watch.

The NBA adopted the 24-second clock for the 1954-55 season and it had an immediate impact. During its first season, NBA teams averaged 93.1 points, an increase of 13.6 points over the previous one. Fans enjoyed the faster pace and higher scores.

1961: THREE-POINT FIELD GOAL The three-point field goal was introduced by the American Basketball League. The ABL set the three-point line at 22 feet, 8 inches. The American Basketball Association (ABA) used the three-point line in 1967 at its inception. It would be 13 years (June 3, 1980) before the NBA voted to adopt the three-point goal permanently.

The NBA set its three-point line at 23 feet, 9 inches, measured from the middle of the basket (on the ground) to the top of its arc (it is only 23 feet on its extreme left and right sides).

1966: FIRST AFRICAN-AMERICAN HEAD COACH Bill Russell was named player-coach of the Boston Celtics, following the retirement of the legendary Arnold "Red" Auerbach at the end of the 1965-66 season. Russell led the Celtics to back-to-back NBA titles in 1968 and 1969.

1997: FIRST WOMAN REFEREE The first woman to referee an NBA game was Violet Palmer. Her first NBA regular season game was the Dallas Mavericks' 90-88 win over the Vancouver Grizzlies on Oct. 31, 1997. Palmer, a veteran college and women's pro leagues referee, was hired for the 1997-98 season at the age of 33 by the NBA along with one other female official, Denise "Dee" Kantner.

Reggie Miller

Selected NBA Records

MOST POINTS				
Game	100	Wilt Chamberlain	Philadelphia Warriors vs. NY Knicks	March 2, 1962
Season	4,029	Wilt Chamberlain	Philadelphia Warriors	1961-62
Career	38,387	Kareem Abdul-Jabbar	Milwaukee Bucks, LA Lakers	1969-89
MOST ASSISTS				
Game	30	Scott Skiles	Orlando Magic vs. Denver Nuggets	Dec. 30, 1990
Season	1,164	John Stockton	Utah Jazz	1990-91
Career	15,806	John Stockton	Utah Jazz	1984-2003
MOST REBOUNDS				
Game	55	Wilt Chamberlain	Philadelphia Warriors vs. Boston Celtics	Nov. 24, 1960
Season	2,149	Wilt Chamberlain	Philadelphia Warriors	1960-61
Career	23,924	Wilt Chamberlain	Philadelphia-SF Warriors, Philadelphia 76ers, LA Lakers	1959-73
MOST FIELD GOALS MADE				
Game	36	Wilt Chamberlain	Philadelphia Warriors vs. NY Knicks	March 2, 1962
Season	1,597	Wilt Chamberlain	Philadelphia Warriors	1961-62
Career	15,837	Kareem Abdul-Jabbar	Milwaukee Bucks, LA Lakers	1969-89
MOST THREE-POINT FIELD GOALS MADE				
Game	12	Donyell Marshall	Toronto Raptors vs. Philadelphia 76ers	March 13, 2005 (ties Kobe Bryant)
Season	267	Dennis Scott	Orlando Magic	1995-96
Career	2,560	Reggie Miller	Indiana Pacers	1987-2005
MOST FREE THROWS MADE				
Game	28	Wilt Chamberlain	Philadelphia Warriors vs. NY Knicks	March 2, 1962
	28	Adrian Dantley	Utah Jazz vs. Houston Rockets	Jan. 4, 1984
Season	840	Jerry West	LA Lakers	1965-66
Career	9,787	Karl Malone	Utah Jazz, LA Lakers	1988-2004

SUPERLATIVES

MOST GAMES PLAYED Robert Parish played in a record 1,611 NBA regular season games for four teams (primarily the Boston Celtics) over 21 seasons.

LONGEST SCORING STREAK (10 OR MORE POINTS) The most consecutive NBA games where a player scored at least 10 points each game is 866, done by Michael Jordan (Chicago Bulls and Washington Wizards), between March 25, 1986, and Dec. 26, 2001.

YOUNGEST TRIPLE-DOUBLE On Jan. 19, 2005, LeBron James became the youngest player on NBA history to record a triple-double in a single game—a feat accomplished when a player reaches double digits in point, rebounds, and assists. The 20-year-old Cleveland Cavaliers forward scored 27 points, 11 rebounds, and 10 assists during Cleveland's 107-101 win over Portland. James recorded another triple double three nights later in a 105-87 win over Golden State.

MOST CONSECUTIVE FREE THROWS Micheal Williams of the Minnesota Timberwolves sank 97 consecutive free throws from March 24 to Nov. 9, 1993. His streak was snapped when he missed a foul shot in the second quarter of a game lost to the San Antonio Spurs.

TALLEST PLAYER Two players are tied for the tallest ever in NBA history. Manute Bol and Gheorghe Muresan, both centers, stood 7 feet, 7 inches. Bol, a Dinka tribesman from Sudan, played from 1985 to 1995, for four different teams, and ranks second in the NBA for career blocks per game, with 3.34. Muresan, from Romania, played six seasons, 1993-2000, for two teams. During the 1995-96 and 1996-97 seasons, Muresan led the NBA in field-goal percentage, with a .584 and .604 respectively.

MOST POINTS BY PLAYER (SINGLE GAME) On March 2, 1962, Wilt Chamberlain of the Philadelphia Warriors scored 100 points in a single game against the New York Knicks in Hershey, PA. His final basket came after he had missed twice; his teammates grabbed the rebounds after each miss and got the ball back to him. On the third try, he dunked for the final two points to reach 100.

The final score was Philadelphia 169, New York 147.

MOST MVP AWARDS Kareem Abdul-Jabbar won a record six NBA MVP awards. He won three with the Milwaukee Bucks in 1971, 1972, and 1974; and three with the Los Angeles Lakers in 1976, 1977, and 1980.

BASKETBALL

NBA Playoffs

Bill Russell (6), Wilt Chamberlain (13), John Havlicek (17) and Keith Erickson (24) ►

MILESTONES

1947: FIRST PLAYOFFS
Although not officially in existence until 1949, the NBA recognizes 1947 as its first playoff year. In that year, six Basketball Association of America (BAA) teams competed in the playoffs: the St. Louis Bombers, Philadelphia Warriors, Chicago Stags, New York Knicks, Cleveland Rebels, and Washington Capitols. The Warriors beat the Stags, 4-1, in the Finals.

1949: OVERTIME GAME
PLAYOFFS The first NBA playoff game that extended into overtime was the New York Knicks' 103-99 win over the Baltimore Bullets on Mar. 26, 1949, in New York. The Knicks also won the first double-overtime playoff game, beating the Boston Celtics in the Boston Garden on Mar. 26, 1952.

1951: GAME SEVEN
FINALS
The first Game Seven in the NBA Finals was played between the Rochester Royals and the New York Knicks on Apr. 21, 1951. The Royals beat the Knicks in Rochester, 79-75, to win the NBA title.

1952: OVERTIME GAME **FINALS**
The first overtime game in the NBA Finals came in 1952. The Minneapolis Lakers beat the New York Knicks, 83-79, in Game 1 on Apr. 12, 1952. This was the first of two games that went into overtime in the '52 Finals; the Knicks won Game 4 in overtime, 90-89. (Eventually, the Lakers won the series in seven games.)

1959: SWEEP
FINALS The Boston Celtics were the first team to sweep the NBA Finals when they defeated the Minneapolis Lakers, 4-0, in the 1959 Finals. The Celtics won the first two games in Boston, and clinched the franchise's second NBA crown with two wins in St. Paul, MN. Both teams scored at least 100 points in each game.

In all, seven teams have won the NBA Finals in a sweep. The last sweep came in 2002 when the Los Angeles Lakers beat the New Jersey Nets.

SUPERLATIVES

MOST GAMES PLAYED
PLAYOFFS Kareem Abdul-Jabbar played in a record 237 NBA playoff games for two teams: the Milwaukee Bucks, 1970-74, and Los Angeles Lakers, 1977-89. The Hall of Famer also holds the record for most playoff minutes accumulated, at 8,851. He played on six championship teams, with the Bucks in 1971, and with the Lakers in 1980, 1982, 1985, and 1987-88. He won the NBA Finals MVP award twice, in 1971 and 1985.

MOST CHAMPIONSHIPS
PLAYER Bill Russell played in a record 72 NBA Finals games for the Boston Celtics, 1957-66 and 1968-69. The Hall of Famer also holds the record for most Finals minutes accumulated, at 3,185.

Russell played on a record 11 NBA championship teams with the Celtics, in 1957, 1959-66, and 1968-69. For the last two title victories, Russell also served as the team's head coach. He is the only player-coach to win an NBA title.

MOST CHAMPIONSHIPS WON **COACH**
The record for most NBA titles won by a coach is nine, held by two coaches: Red Auerbach and Phil Jackson. Auerbach led the Boston Celtics to their first NBA title in

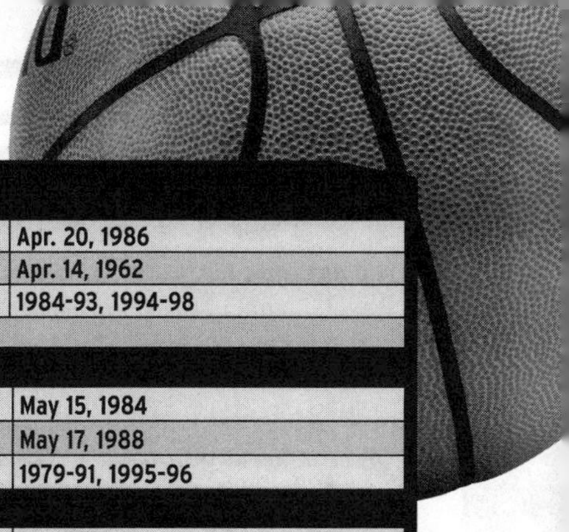

Selected NBA Playoff Records

MOST POINTS				
Game	63*	Michael Jordan	Chicago Bulls vs. Boston Celtics	Apr. 20, 1986
	61	Elgin Baylor	LA Lakers vs. Boston Celtics	Apr. 14, 1962
Career	5,987	Michael Jordan	Chicago Bulls	1984-93, 1994-98
* Double OT				
MOST ASSISTS				
Game	24	Magic Johnson	LA Lakers vs. Phoenix Suns	May 15, 1984
	24	John Stockton	Utah Jazz vs. LA Lakers	May 17, 1988
Career	2,346	Magic Johnson	LA Lakers	1979-91, 1995-96
MOST REBOUNDS				
Game	41	Wilt Chamberlain	Philadelphia Warriors vs. Boston Celtics	Apr. 5, 1967
Career	4,104	Bill Russell	Boston Celtics	1956-69
MOST STEALS				
Game	10	Allen Iverson	Philadelphia 76ers vs. Orlando Magic	May 13, 1999
Career	395	Scottie Pippen	Chicago Bulls, Houston Rockets, Portland Trail Blazers	1987-2003
MOST BLOCKED SHOTS				
Game	10	Mark Eaton	Utah Jazz vs. Houston Rockets	Apr. 26, 1985
	10	Hakeem Olajuwon	Houston Rockets vs. LA Lakers	Apr. 29, 1990
Career	476	Kareem Abdul-Jabbar	Milwaukee Bucks, LA Lakers	1969-75, 1976-89
MOST FIELD GOALS MADE				
Game	22	Elgin Baylor	LA Lakers vs. Boston Celtics	Apr. 14, 1962
	22	Rick Barry	San Francisco Warriors vs. Philadelphia 76ers	Apr. 18, 1967
Career	612	Jerry West	LA Lakers	1962-63, 1965-66, 1968-70, 1972-73
MOST FREETHROWS MADE				
Game	19	Bob Pettit	St. Louis Hawks vs. Boston Celtics	Apr. 9, 1958
Career	455	Jerry West	LA Lakers	1962-63, 1965-66, 1968-70, 1972-73

1957, then won eight straight titles from 1959 to 1966. Jackson led the Chicago Bulls to six titles, 1991-93 and 1996-1998, and coached the Los Angeles Lakers to three championships, 2000-2002.

MOST PLAYOFF WINS COACH

Phil Jackson has the most victories by a coach in the playoffs. Through the 2004-05 season, he has won 175 postseason games over 15 seasons with two teams: the Chicago Bulls, 1989-97, and the Los Angeles Lakers, 1999-2004.

Jackson also holds the NBA career playoff record for highest winning percentage, at .717 (175 wins, 69 losses). He is second on the all-time playoff games coached list, with 244 games. The record is held by Pat Riley, who coached 255 games with three teams: the Los Angeles Lakers, 1981-89, New York Knicks, 1991-94, and Miami Heat, 1995-2000.

HIGHEST CAREER SCORING AVERAGE PLAYOFFS

Michael Jordan has the highest NBA playoff career scoring average, at 33.4 points per game. The Chicago Bulls guard scored 5,987 points in 179 playoff games over 13 seasons.

HIGHEST FREE-THROW PERCENTAGE CAREER

The highest career free-throw percentage in NBA playoff history (minimum 10 made) is .944, shot by Mark Price of the Cleveland Cavaliers. In 47 career playoff games, 1987-90, 1991-95, he made 202 of 214 free throws. In the 1990 playoffs, he was a perfect 30 for 30 from the free-throw line in five games.

HIGHEST FIELD-GOAL PERCENTAGE CAREER

The highest career field-goal percentage in NBA playoff history (minimum 150 made) is .627, shot by James Donaldson. In 51 career playoff games for four teams—the Seattle Supersonics, the Dallas Mavericks, the New York Knicks, and the Utah Jazz—Donaldson made 153 of 244 field goals over nine seasons, 1981-95.

MOST MVP AWARDS

Los Angeles Lakers guard Jerry West won the first NBA Finals MVP award in 1969. Michael Jordan of the Chicago Bulls won a record six NBA MVP awards in 1991-1993 and 1996-1998.

Men's NCAA Tournament

THE NATIONAL COLLEGIATE ATHLETIC ASSOCIATION (NCAA) first staged its men's Division I basketball tournament in 1939. Eight teams played in the first event, with the championship game played on the campus of Northwestern University in Evanston, IL. Oregon beat Ohio State, 46-33, to win the first NCAA title.

MILESTONES

1944: FIRST CHAMPIONSHIP GAME OVERTIME Dick McGuire of Dartmouth sank a basket from half-court at the buzzer to send the 1944 NCAA Championship Game into overtime.

This was the first time that the title game required an extra period of play. But McGuire's buzzer-beater was in vain. Utah defeated Dartmouth, 42-40, in overtime to win the title.

1950: NCAA, NIT DOUBLE City College of New York (CCNY) won both the NCAA and the NIT tournaments in the same year, in 1950, the first and only time this feat was achieved.

Coached by Nat Holman, CCNY beat top-ranked Bradley in both title games, winning the NCAA championship game, 71-68, and the NIT championship, 69-61.

1951: EXPANDED FIELD The tournament field was expanded for the first time in 1951, from eight teams to 16. Kentucky, coached by Adolph Rupp, won the 1951 championship, 68-58, over Kansas. Further expansion came in 1953 (to 22 teams). Over the next two decades, the number fluctuated between 22 and 25 teams until 1975, when the field increased to 32 teams, and 1985, when the number was set at 64.

1954: TELEVISED FINAL The first time the NCAA championship game was televised nationally was in 1954, when La Salle, led by MVP Tom Gola, beat Bradley, 92-76.

1966: AFRICAN-AMERICAN STARTING FIVE The first team to win the NCAA Tournament with a starting five of all African-American players was Texas Western (now UTEP) in 1966. The unheralded non-conference school, coached by Don Haskins, beat Adolph Rupp's national powerhouse Kentucky, 72-65. Bobby Joe Hill led Western with 20 points. They are still the only Texas team to win the title.

1984: AFRICAN-AMERICAN COACH John Thompson was the first black coach to win the NCAA championship. His Georgetown squad, led by center Patrick Ewing, beat Houston, 84-75, to win the 1984 title.

THE LAST TIME...

The last time two teams from the same state played each other in the NCAA title game was in 1962. Cincinnati beat Ohio State, 71-59, in Louisville, KY. It was the second straight year the teams had faced each other in the championship game. The Bearcats beat the Buckeyes the previous year too, winning 70-65 in overtime.

SUPERLATIVES

MOST TITLES UCLA has won a record 11 NCAA titles, 1964-65, 1967-73, 1975, and 1995. The first 10 were under coach John Wooden, who led the Bruins to a record 10 consecutive Final Fours between 1967 and 1976. Jim Harrick coached UCLA to its 1995 championship.

MOST FINAL FOUR APPEARANCES The North Carolina Tar Heels have made the Final Four a record 16 times, between 1946 and 2005. They won the NCAA title four times—in 1957, 1982, 1993, and 2005.

MOST GAMES PLAYED Christian Laettner of Duke played in a record 23 NCAA tournament games, 1989-92. In his four years at Duke, the Blue Devils advanced to the Final Four each year. He led Duke to back-to-back NCAA championships in 1991 and 1992.

MOST MVP AWARDS The only player to win three NCAA tournament MVP awards is Lew Alcindor (now Kareem Abdul-Jabbar). He led UCLA to three straight NCAA titles, 1967-69.

Perhaps the most dominant college basketball player in history, Alcindor scored 39 points in two games at the 1967 Final Four, 53 points in 1968, and 62 in 1969.

HIGHEST-RATED GAME The 1979 title game, when Michigan State beat Indiana State, 75-64, featured a showdown between Earvin "Magic" Johnson (Michigan St.) and Larry Bird (Indiana St.). It was the highest-rated NCAA championship game of all time. Broadcast by NBC, the game gained a 24.1 rating and a 38 share.

BIGGEST VICTORY MARGIN The biggest blowout in an NCAA

Selected NCAA Tournament Records

MOST POINTS				
Game	61	Austin Carr	Notre Dame vs. Ohio	1st round, 1970
Final Four Game	58	Bill Bradley	Princeton vs. Wichita St.	3rd place game, 1965
Championship Game	44	Bill Walton	UCLA vs. Memphis	1973
Final Four	87	Bill Bradley	Princeton	1965
Career	407	Christian Laettner	Duke	1989-92 (23 games)
MOST ASSISTS				
Game	18	Mark Wade	UNLV vs. Indiana	semifinal, 1987
Final Four Game	18	Mark Wade	UNLV vs. Indiana	semifinal, 1987
Championship Game	11	Rumeal Robinson	Michigan vs. Seton Hall	1989 (OT)
Final Four	23	Rumeal Robinson	Michigan	1989
Career	145	Bobby Hurley	Duke	1990-93 (20 games)
MOST REBOUNDS				
Game	34	Fred Cohen	Temple vs. Connecticut	regional semifinal, 1956
Final Four Game	27	Bill Russell	San Francisco vs. Iowa	final, 1956
Championship Game	27	Bill Russell	San Francisco vs. Iowa	1956
Final Four	50	Bill Russell	San Francisco	1956
Career	222	Elvin Hayes	Houston	1966-68 (13 games)

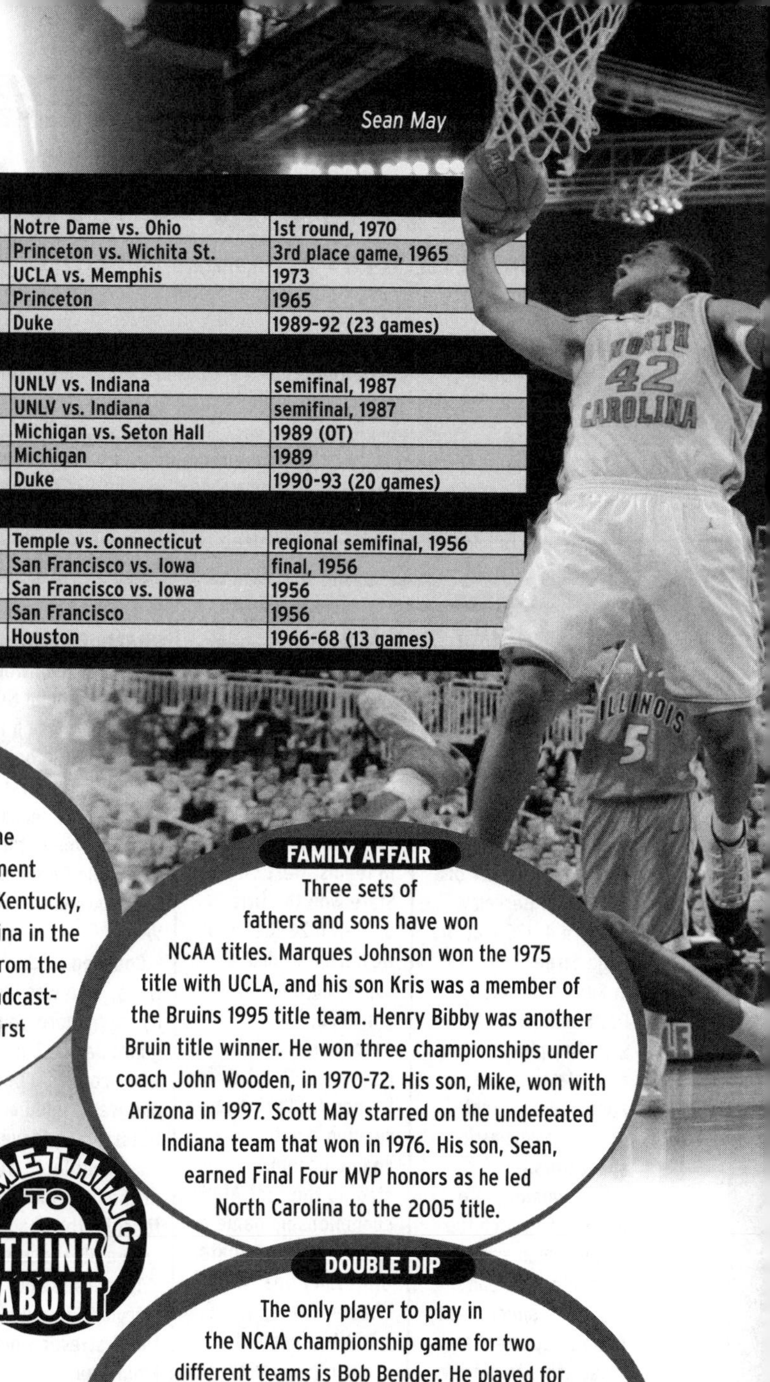

Sean May

WIN AND GO HOME

Three coaches ended their collegiate coaching careers by winning the NCAA title game. John Wooden, the "Wizard of Westwood," announced his retirement before the 1975 NCAA title game. His Bruins beat Kentucky, 92-85. After Marquette's victory over North Carolina in the 1977 title game, coach Al McGuire walked away from the coaching ranks, and went on to a career in broadcasting. In 1988, Larry Brown led Kansas to its first NCAA title since 1952; he then left the Jayhawks for the NBA.

FAMILY AFFAIR

Three sets of fathers and sons have won NCAA titles. Marques Johnson won the 1975 title with UCLA, and his son Kris was a member of the Bruins 1995 title team. Henry Bibby was another Bruin title winner. He won three championships under coach John Wooden, in 1970-72. His son, Mike, won with Arizona in 1997. Scott May starred on the undefeated Indiana team that won in 1976. His son, Sean, earned Final Four MVP honors as he led North Carolina to the 2005 title.

DOUBLE DIP

The only player to play in the NCAA championship game for two different teams is Bob Bender. He played for Indiana in 1976, helping the Hoosiers win the title and complete an undefeated season. Two years later he played for Duke in the Blue Devils' loss to Kentucky. Steve Krafcisin played in the Final Four for two schools: North Carolina in 1977 and Iowa in 1980. The Tar Heels advanced to the title game, but lost to Marquette, 67-59. Iowa was eliminated in the semifinal by Louisville, 80-72.

championship game was UNLV's 30-point victory over Duke in 1990, 103-73, surpassing the previous record set by UCLA in 1968 when they beat North Carolina, 78-55.

LONGEST GAME

North Carolina beat Kansas, 54-53, in the 1957 championship game in three overtimes, making this the longest NCAA final yet. Lennie Rosenbluth led the Tar Heels in scoring, with 20 points, but fouled out of the game in the final quarter of regulation time. The game was won by Joe Quigg, who sank two free throws with six seconds left.

It was the Tar Heels' second triple overtime game of the Final Four. They had beaten Michigan State in the semifinal game, 74-70.

SOMETHING TO THINK ABOUT

Women's NCAA Division I

SENDA BERENSON AND CLARA BAER ARE CONSIDERED THE PIONEERS of women's college basketball. Berenson, director of physical education at Smith College in Northampton, MA, created a "divided-court" version of basketball in 1892 with seven players per team. Berenson's version, based on James Naismith's original rules, also required players to remain in their assigned zone, which reduced the physical demands of the game. A year later, Baer introduced "Basquette," her adaptation of Naismith's game, at Sophie Newcomb Memorial College in New Orleans, LA.

Acceptance of women's basketball was slow, in the face of prejudices and unfounded fears about the safety and propriety of girls playing sports. It wasn't until 1969 that the first national invitational women's basketball tournament was held. In 1972 the passing of Title IX brought increased funding and acceptance to women's college athletics. Since 1982 the NCAA women's basketball tournament has been recognized as the official national championship.

MILESTONES

1896: FIRST COLLEGE GAME The first intercollegiate women's basketball game was played between Stanford and the University of California, Berkeley, on April 4, 1896, at the Page Street Armory in San Francisco, CA. Stanford won, 2-1. They played a nine-player, three-zone game in front of 700 enthusiastic spectators.

Only women were allowed to watch the game, which was such a novelty that San Francisco papers sent female reporters and illustrators to get the story.

1969: NATIONAL COLLEGE INVITATIONAL The first national collegiate basketball tournament was staged at Pennsylvania's West Chester State College in 1969. Organized by host coach Carol Eckman, the single-elimination tournament included 16 teams. West Chester State won the title on March 22, beating Western Carolina, 65-39, in the final.

In 1972, the Association of Intercollegiate Athletics for Women (AIAW) began running a national championship, staging the first AIAW championship game on March 19. Immaculata University beat West Chester State, 52-48.

The tournament grew in popularity and the NCAA took notice. In 1982, 32 teams played in the first women's NCAA basketball tournament; that same year, the AIAW disbanded.

1982: NCAA CHAMPIONSHIP Louisiana Tech won the first official NCAA Women's Division I championship on March 28, 1982. The first-ranked Lady Techsters beat Cheyney State, 76-62, at Old Dominion's Scope Arena in Norfolk, VA.

Coached by Sonja Hogg, Tech was led by sophomore point guard Janice Lawrence, who scored 20 points and was named Most Outstanding Player. Louisiana Tech, winner of the last AIAW title, finished the season with a 35-1 record.

Tennessee and Maryland rounded out the first-ever women's Final Four.

1984: FIRST DUNK The first dunk in women's college basketball was slammed down by West Virginia center Georgeann Wells at a Dec. 21, 1984, game against Charleston.

The 6 foot, 7 inch junior from Columbus, OH, scored the basket with 11:58 remaining in the game to give the Lady Mountaineers an 85-80 lead. As it happened, Wells, sick with a stomach ailment, had almost missed the game! West Virginia won the matchup, 110-82.

The next dunk did not come until Dec. 4, 1994, when Charlotte Smith of North Carolina dunked on North Carolina A&T.

1984: REPEATS USC, with forward Cheryl Miller, was the first team to win back-to-back NCAA titles. The Lady Trojans beat Louisiana Tech, 69-67, in 1983, and retained their title with a 72-61 victory over Tennessee in 1984.

1988: MALE CHAMPIONSHIP COACH The first time a team coached by a man won the NCAA title was in 1988, when Leon Barmore led Louisiana Tech to its second championship with a 56-54 win over Auburn. Barmore had been an assistant coach to Sonja Hogg when Tech won the first NCAA title in 1982.

Only one other man has coached a championship women's team; Geno Auriemma has led Connecticut to five NCAA titles (1995, 2000, 2002-04).

1998: "THREE-PEAT" Tennessee became the first team to win three consecutive national titles. Coach Pat Summitt led the Lady Volunteers to titles in 1996, 1997, and 1998.

Connecticut was the only other team to go back-to-back-to-back; Geno Auriemma's Lady Huskies won titles from 2002 to 2004.

Selected NCAA Division I Records

MOST POINTS				
Game	60	Cindy Brown	Long Beach State (vs. San Jose State)	Feb. 16, 1987
Season	1,062	Jackie Stiles	Southwest Missouri State	2001
Career	3,393	Jackie Stiles	Southwest Missouri State	1997-2001
MOST ASSISTS				
Game	23	Michelle Burden	Kent State (vs. Ball State)	Feb. 6, 1991
Season	355	Suzie McConnell	Penn State	1987
Career	1,307	Suzie McConnell	Penn State	1984-88
MOST REBOUNDS				
Game	40	Deborah Temple	Delta State (vs. Alabama-Birmingham)	Feb. 14, 1983
Season	534	Wanda Ford	Drake	1985
Career	1,887	Wanda Ford	Drake	1983-86
MOST FIELD GOALS MADE				
Game	27	Lorri Bauman	Drake (vs. Southwest Missouri State)	Jan. 6, 1984
Season	392	Barbara Kennedy	Clemson	1982
Career	1,259	Joyce Walker	Louisiana State	1981-84
MOST THREE-POINT FIELD GOALS MADE				
Game	12	Cornelia Gayden	Louisiana State (vs. Jackson State)	Feb. 9, 1995
Season	126	Lisa McMullen	Alabama State	1991
Career	391	Erin Thorn	Brigham Young	1999-2003
MOST FREE THROWS MADE				
Game	23	Shaunda Greene	Washington (vs. Northern Illinois)	Nov. 30, 1991
Season	275	Lorri Bauman	Drake	1982
Career	907	Lorri Bauman	Drake	1981-84
MOST STEALS				
Game	14	6 tied for 14		
Season	191	Natalie White	Florida A&M	1995
Career	624	Natalie White	Florida A&M	1991-95
MOST BLOCKED SHOTS				
Game	15	Amy Lundquist	Loyola (CA) (vs. Western Illinois)	Dec. 20, 1992
Season	152	Amie Williams	Jackson State	2003
Career	428	Genia Miller	Cal. State Fullerton	1987-91

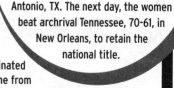

Sophia Young

SOMETHING TO THINK ABOUT

"HUSKY" FROM CHEERING In 2004, the University of Connecticut became the only school ever to win both the men's and women's NCAA Division I championships in the same season. The men cut down the nets first, beating Georgia Tech, 82-73, on April 5 in San Antonio, TX. The next day, the women beat archrival Tennessee, 70-61, in New Orleans, to retain the national title.

SUPERLATIVES

MOST NCAA TITLES Tennessee's Lady Volunteers have won a record six NCAA titles: in 1987, 1989, 1991, and 1996-98, all of them under Coach Pat Summitt.

MOST FINAL FOUR APPEARANCES Tennessee has made the Final Four in the NCAA tournament a record 16 times, between 1982 and 2005.

MOST OUTSTANDING PLAYER AWARDS Three players have won two NCAA tournament Most Outstanding Player awards. Cheryl Miller was the first to win two, while leading USC to back-to-back titles in 1983-84. Chamique Holdsclaw of Tennessee was named at the 1997 and 1998 tourneys, and in 2004, Connecticut's Diana Taurasi won her second consecutive award.

LONGEST CHAMPIONSHIP GAME The only championship game to go into overtime was the 1991 title showdown between Tennessee and Virginia at the Lakefront Arena in New Orleans, LA. The Lady Cavaliers led, 60-55, with 1:25 left in the game. With seven seconds remaining, Dena Head tied the score with two free throws. The Lady Vols took the game, 70-67, over Virginia, which had eliminated them in overtime from the tournament the previous year.

THE LAST TIME...

The last "Most Outstanding Player" of the NCAA Tournament who did not play for the winning team was Dawn Staley of Virginia in 1991. The future Olympic guard led the Lady Cavaliers to the title game, where they lost in overtime to Tennessee. Thirteen years later, Staley carried the American flag at the Opening Ceremony of the 2004 Athens Olympics.

BASKETBALL

WNBA

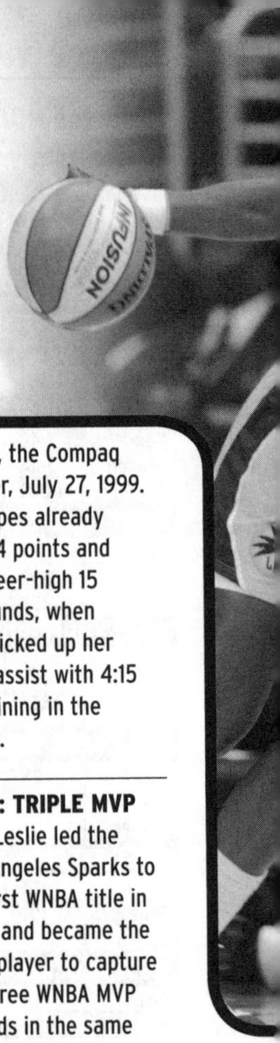

THE LAUNCH OF THE WOMEN'S NATIONAL BASKETBALL ASSOCIATION (WNBA) was approved by the Board of Governors of the National Basketball Association (NBA) on April 24, 1996. Brandishing the slogan, "We Got Next," the WNBA started in June 1997, with eight teams (Charlotte Sting, Cleveland Rockers, Houston Comets, New York Liberty, Los Angeles Sparks, Phoenix Mercury, Sacramento Monarchs, and Utah Starzz) divided into two conferences (East and West). Since then, the WNBA has undergone expansion, contraction, and relocation. There were 13 franchises for the 2005 season.

MILESTONES

1996: FIRST PLAYERS Sheryl Swoopes and Rebecca Lobo were the first players to sign contracts with the WNBA. The pair, teammates on the 1996 U.S. Olympic gold-medal-winning team and former NCAA players of the year, both turned down offers from the rival American Basketball League (ABL) to join the WNBA. In the inaugural season, Lobo played for the New York Liberty, and Swoopes for the Houston Comets.

The league held its first draft on April 28, 1997. The Comets had the first pick and selected Tina Thompson.

1997: FIRST OFFICAL GAME The Los Angeles Sparks hosted the first WNBA game, at the Great Western Forum, on June 21, 1997. Sparks guard Penny Toler scored the league's first basket, but LA's home debut was a disappointment since the visiting New York Liberty won, 67-57.

1997: WNBA CHAMPIONS The Houston Comets, led by Cynthia Cooper (the league's first MVP), became the first WNBA champions with a 65-51 victory over the New York Liberty.

The WNBA's first playoff format was single elimination, including the final. The championship game was played on the Comets' home court at The Summit. Houston won the first four WNBA titles, 1997-2000.

1999: FIRST TRIPLE-DOUBLE Houston Comets forward Sheryl Swoopes recorded the WNBA's first triple-double. The All-Star scored 14 points, 15 rebounds and 10 assists in an 85-46 win over Detroit on her home court, the Compaq Center, July 27, 1999. Swoopes already had 14 points and a career-high 15 rebounds, when she picked up her 10th assist with 4:15 remaining in the game.

2001: TRIPLE MVP Lisa Leslie led the Los Angeles Sparks to its first WNBA title in 2001 and became the first player to capture all three WNBA MVP awards in the same year: All-Star Game MVP, League MVP, and Finals MVP.

Selected WNBA Regular Season Records

SCORING				
Game	46	Katie Smith	Minnesota Lynx vs. LA Sparks (OT)	July 7, 2001
Season	739	Katie Smith	Minnesota Lynx	2001
Career	4,732	Lisa Leslie	LA Sparks	1997-2005
Avg. Points per game (Career)	21.0	Cynthia Cooper	Houston Comets	1997-2003
Field Goal Percentage (Career)	.581	Tamika Williams	Minnesota Lynx	2002-05
MOST ASSISTS				
Game	16	Ticha Penicheiro	Sacramento Monarchs vs. Cleveland Rockers	July 29, 1998
	16	Ticha Penicheiro	Sacramento Monarchs vs. Los Angeles Sparks	Aug. 16, 2002
Season	236	Ticha Penicheiro	Sacramento Monarchs	2000
Career	1,591	Ticha Penicheiro	Sacramento Monarchs	1998-2005
MOST REBOUNDS				
Game	24	Chamique Holdsclaw	Washington Mystics vs. Charlotte Sting	May 23, 2003
Season	357	Yolanda Griffith	Sacramento Monarchs	2001
Career	2,540	Lisa Leslie	LA Sparks	1997-2005
DEFENSIVE STATISTICS				
Most Steals (Career)	520	Sheryl Swoopes	Houston Comets	1997-2005
Most Blocks (Career)	726	Margo Dydek	Utah Starzz; San Antonio Silver Stars; Connecticut Sun	1998-2005

◄ *Los Angeles Sparks' Lisa Leslie (left) and New York Liberty's Vickie Johnson.*

SOMETHING TO THINK ABOUT

NO LOSS LOBO

Baseball has Cal Ripken Jr.'s "ironman streak" (2,632 games), and Joe DiMaggio's hitting streak (56 games), but women's basketball has the Rebecca Lobo streak. During her senior season at the University of Connecticut (1994-95), Lobo led the Huskies to a 35-0 record and a national title. She then joined the U.S. Olympic basketball team, which posted a 60-0 record on its way to the 1996 gold medal at the Atlanta Games. At the start of her WNBA career, Lobo led the New York Liberty to seven straight wins. Finally, after 102 straight wins on three teams over more than three years, Lobo finally played on a losing team, on July 7, 1997. The Phoenix Mercury beat Lobo's Liberty, 69-50. It was Lobo's first loss since North Carolina upset Connecticut in the regional finals of the 1994 NCAA tournament.

2002: SLAM DUNK
The league's first dunk was thrown down by Los Angeles Sparks center Lisa Leslie. The 6'5" All-Star scored the historic basket, a one-handed breakaway, with 4:44 remaining in the first half during the Sparks' 82-73 loss to the Miami Sol at the Staples Center in Los Angeles, July 30, 2002.

2003: INTERNATIONAL MVP In 2003, Australian forward Lauren Jackson (Seattle Storm) became the first international player to win the WNBA MVP. The 6'5" Aussie led the league in scoring, averaging 21.2 points per game. At 22 years of age, she was also the league's youngest MVP.

2004: CHAMPIONSHIP WOMAN COACH
Anne Donovan led the Seattle Storm to its first championship in 2004, with a 2-1 win over the Connecticut Sun. The other women to lead teams to the WNBA Finals were Nancy Darsch (New York Liberty) in 1997 and Cheryl Miller (Phoenix Mercury) in 1998.

SUPERLATIVES

MOST WNBA TITLES
The Houston Comets have won a record four WNBA championships between 1997 and 2000. All four were won under coach Van Chancellor. Cynthia Cooper won WNBA Finals MVP honors all four times.

MOST MVP AWARDS
Sheryl Swoopes (Houston Comets) is the only three-time WNBA League MVP. She won the award in 2000, 2002, and 2003. In the closest vote in the award's history, Swoopes won the 2005 award over Lauren Jackson (Seattle Storm) by two points, 327 to 325.

LONGEST GAME (ELAPSED TIME)
The longest WNBA game yet was played between the Orlando Miracle and the Cleveland Rockers on June 8, 2002. The game turned out to be a triple-overtime contest that lasted a total of 2 hours, 57 minutes.

Orlando managed to pull away with a 103-99 victory. Orlando's Shannon Johnson scored 11 of her 35 points in the third overtime period to lead the hometown Miracle to the win.

MOST OVERTIMES
The only WNBA game to go to quadruple overtime was played in Seattle, WA, on July 3, 2001, when the Washington Mystics beat the Seattle Storm, 72-69. The Storm's Semeka Randall had sent the game into OT when she tied the game at 50-50 with 31 seconds remaining.

Mystic guard Helen Luz settled the game when she hit back-to-back three-pointers in the fourth overtime to give Washington a six point lead they didn't relinquish.

MOST CONSECUTIVE FREE THROWS
The record for the most consecutive free throws made in WNBA history is 66, held by Cleveland Rockers forward Eva Nemcova.

From June 14, 1999, to June 5, 2000, she did not miss from the foul line. Her streak came to an end with a miss against Orlando on June 7.

BIGGEST TURNAROUND
In 2002, the Detroit Shock went a shocking 9-23 for the season, the worst record in the league. Midway through the 2002 season former Detroit Pistons "enforcer" Bill Laimbeer took over as head coach of the Shock. He inherited a team with no wins and 10 losses, and he put a jolt into the team, which went 9-13 the rest of the way.

In 2003, the Shock went from last place to first place, posting a league-leading 25-9 season, 16 more wins than the previous season, the biggest season-to-season turnaround in WNBA history. The Shock maintained its electric play in the playoffs. In the Finals, the Shock doused the Los Angeles Sparks, 2-1, to win the franchise's first WNBA championship.

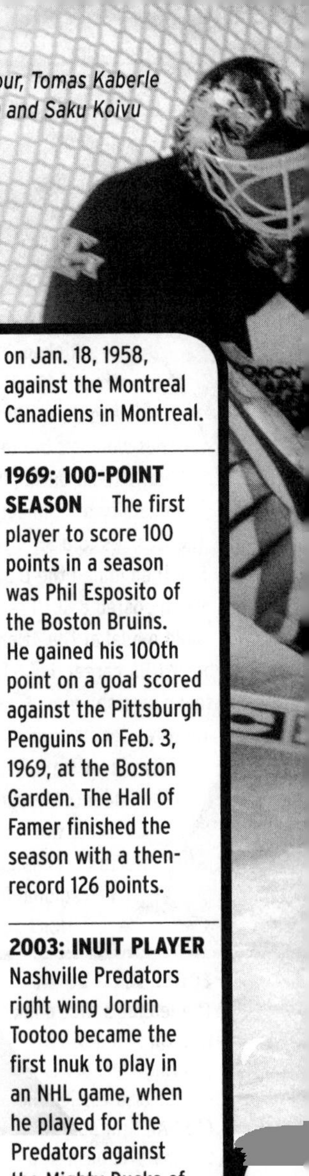

(left to right) Ed Belfour, Tomas Kaberle (Toronto Maple Leafs) and Saku Koivu (Montreal Canadiens)

NHL Regular Season

MILESTONES

1917: DIVING GOALTENDERS For its first season in 1917-18, the National Hockey League (NHL) passed a new rule allowing goaltenders to fall to the ice to make a save. Prior to this, goalies were penalized for this technique.

1924: FIRST U.S. FRANCHISE The first U.S. franchise in the NHL was the Boston Bruins. Owner Charles Adams paid a $15,000 expansion fee to gain admission to the league.

The Bruins' first NHL game was a 2-1 win over the Montreal Maroons at the Boston Arena on Dec. 1, 1924.

1927: THREE PERIODS For the 1927-28 season, the NHL reorganized the game time from two 30-minute periods to three 20-minute periods separated by 10-minute intermissions.

1930: FACE MASK Clint Benedict of the Montreal Maroons was the first NHL goalie to wear a face mask. After his nose was broken by a shot from Howie Morenz in a game on Jan. 7, 1930, Benedict returned to action on Feb. 20 wearing a homemade face mask.

It was uncomfortable so Benedict didn't wear it for long. The goalie face mask wasn't used for another 30 years, until Jacques Plante brought it back. After being hit in the face on Nov. 1, 1959, by a shot from Andy Bathgate, Plante went to the dressing room, got stitched, and came back wearing a cream-colored mask. Soon, most goalies sported face masks.

1942: "ORIGINAL SIX" The Brooklyn Americans withdrew from the NHL before the start of the 1942-43 season, leaving just six NHL franchises: the Boston Bruins, Chicago Blackhawks, Detroit Red Wings, Montreal Canadiens, New York Rangers, and Toronto Maple Leafs. They are now referred to as "the original six." The NHL did not expand again until 1967.

1944-45: FIRST 50-GOAL SEASON Maurice Richard of the Montreal Canadiens had the first 50-goal season. "The Rocket" scored his 50th and final goal of the season on March 18, 1945, against the Boston Bruins in Boston. Bruins goaltender Harvey Bennett gave up the historic goal.

1958: BLACK PLAYER The first player of African descent to skate in an NHL game was Willie O'Ree. The Fredericton, New Brunswick, native played his first game for the Boston Bruins on Jan. 18, 1958, against the Montreal Canadiens in Montreal.

1969: 100-POINT SEASON The first player to score 100 points in a season was Phil Esposito of the Boston Bruins. He gained his 100th point on a goal scored against the Pittsburgh Penguins on Feb. 3, 1969, at the Boston Garden. The Hall of Famer finished the season with a then-record 126 points.

2003: INUIT PLAYER Nashville Predators right wing Jordin Tootoo became the first Inuk to play in an NHL game, when he played for the Predators against the Mighty Ducks of Anaheim on Oct. 9, 2003.

SUPERLATIVES

MOST GOALS SCORED BY A TEAM The most single-game goals scored by a team was 16, by the Montreal Canadiens. On March 3, 1920, the Canadiens pounded the Quebec Bulldogs, 16-3, in Quebec City.

LONGEST WINNING STREAK The most consecutive games won by an NHL team is 17, by the Pittsburgh Penguins. The Penguins, then the two-time defending champs, started their streak on March 9, 1993. Their final win came on April 10, in a 10-4 victory over the New York Rangers.

LONGEST WINLESS STREAK The dubious distinction of having the longest winless streak belongs to the Winnipeg Jets, at 30 games. From Oct. 9 to Dec. 20, 1980, they lost 23 games and tied seven. The Jets snapped the streak with a 5-4 win over the Colorado Rockies on Dec. 23, 1980.

LONGEST GOAL-SCORING STREAK (PLAYER) The most consecutive NHL games with at least one goal scored in a game is 16, by Harry "Punch" Broadbent of the Ottawa Senators, during the 1921-22

SOMETHING TO THINK ABOUT

ONLY ONE GOALIE ALLOWED

Although there is no evidence that any NHL team ever attempted to play two goaltenders on the ice at one time, the league passed a rule for the 1931-32 season stating that each team was allowed only one goaltender on the ice at one time. The rule is still on the books.

Other Selected NHL Records

MOST GOALS				
Game	7	Joe Malone	Quebec Bulldogs vs. Toronto St. Pats	Jan. 31, 1920
Season	92	Wayne Gretzky	Edmonton Oilers	1981-82
Career	894	Wayne Gretzky	Edmonton Oilers, LA Kings, St. Louis Blues, NY Rangers	1979-99
MOST ASSISTS				
Game	7	Billy Taylor	Detroit Red Wings vs. Chicago Blackhawks	Mar. 16, 1947
	7	Wayne Gretzky	Edmonton Oilers vs. Washington Redskins	Feb. 15, 1980
	7	Wayne Gretzky	Edmonton Oilers vs. Chicago Blackhawks	Dec. 11, 1985
	7	Wayne Gretzky	Edmonton Oilers vs. Quebec Nordiques	Feb. 14, 1986
Season	163	Wayne Gretzky	Edmonton Oilers	1985-86
Career	1,963	Wayne Gretzky	Edmonton Oilers, LA Kings, St. Louis Blues, NY Rangers	1979-99

MOST POINTS				
Game	10	Darryl Sittler	Toronto Maple Leafs vs. Boston Bruins	Feb. 7, 1976
Season	215	Wayne Gretzky	Edmonton Oilers	1985-86
Career	2,857	Wayne Gretzky	Edmonton Oilers, LA Kings, St. Louis Blues, NY Rangers	1979-99
MOST POWER-PLAY GOALS				
Season	34	Tim Kerr	Philadelphia Flyers	1985-86
Career	270	Dave Andreychuk	Buffalo Sabres, Toronto Maple Leafs, NJ Devils, Colorado Avalanche, Tampa Bay Lightning	1982-2004
MOST SHUTOUTS				
Season	22	George Hainsworth	Montreal Canadiens	1928-29
Career	103	Terry Sawchuk	Detroit Red Wings, Boston Bruins, Toronto Maple Leafs, LA Kings, NY Rangers	1949-70

season. Broadbent scored 25 goals during the streak.

LONGEST ASSIST STREAK (PLAYER) Wayne Gretzky of the Los Angeles Kings, had an assist in a record 23 straight games, during the 1990-91 season. "The Great One" had 48 assists during the streak.

LONGEST POINTS STREAK (PLAYER) During the 1983-84 season, Wayne Gretzky of the Edmonton Oilers, scored in a record 51 consecutive games. He amassed 153 points (61 goals, 92 assists).

FASTEST GOAL The fastest goal made from the start of a game is five seconds—a feat performed by three players: Doug Smail of the Winnipeg Jets vs. the St. Louis Blues in Winnipeg on Dec. 20, 1981; Bryan Trottier of the New York Islanders vs. the Boston Bruins in Boston on March 22, 1984; and Alexander Mogilny of the Buffalo Sabres vs. the Toronto Maple Leafs in Toronto on Dec. 21, 1991.

MOST PENALTY MINUTES (GAME) In a game against the Philadelphia Flyers on March 11, 1979, L.A. Kings defenseman Randy Hold racked up a record 67 penalty minutes from nine penalties, all of which came in the first period. His first penalty, a minor, came at 10:25 into the game. Then Holt took a double major and a misconduct for fighting with Flyers defenseman Frank Bathe at 14:58.

The big one came soon after when Holt instigated a bench-clearing brawl and ended up getting a major and a misconduct. Holt sat out the rest of the game and was suspended for 3 more. He is also the only player to be given more penalty minutes than the actual length of the game.

NHL Stanley Cup

THE STANLEY CUP IS NAMED FOR LORD SIR FREDERICK ARTHUR, Lord Stanley of Preston, 16th earl of Derby, a hockey lover and onetime governor-general of Canada (1888-93). He donated a trophy to be played for annually; the Cup was first presented in 1893 to the Amateur Hockey Association champions, the Montreal Amateur Athletic Association (AAA). After that, teams competed annually in a challenge (playoff) contest for Lord Stanley's Cup.

The National Hockey Association (NHA), forerunner of the National Hockey League (NHL), took possession of the Cup in 1910. In later years the format for the championship series changed several times, as did the various hockey federations. However, the NHL, formed in 1917 after the NHA folded, was the only league to consistently compete for the Cup. Its champion would play against the champion of one of the other leagues. Finally, in 1927 after the Western Hockey League folded, the NHL playoffs became the Stanley Cup playoffs.

MILESTONES

1894: FIRST FINALS In the first Stanley Cup finals the Montreal AAA beat the Montreal Victorias, 3-2, on March 17, 1894, to advance to a championship game against the Ottawa Capitals. On March 22, the AAA defeated the Capitals, 3-1, to win the Cup.

1917: AMERICAN CHAMPION The Stanley Cup was won by a U.S.-based franchise for the first time in 1917, when the Seattle Metropolitans beat the Montreal Canadiens, 3-1. The first American NHL franchise to win the Cup was the New York Rangers; they defeated the Montreal Maroons, 3-2, in 1928. The Rangers wouldn't win again until 1994.

1919: CANCELED FINALS The Stanley Cup finals have been canceled in midstream only once, in 1919. The Montreal Canadiens and Seattle Metropolitans were in the midst of the series when an epidemic of Spanish influenza struck. Five games had been played, with the series tied at 2-2-1. Several players caught the flu, including Canadien Joe Hall, who died from it.

1919: GAME SEVEN The first time the Stanley Cup finals were scheduled as a seven-game series was in 1919. That series wasn't completed (see above), and the seven-game format was dropped until 1938-39. The first Game Seven was played in 1942 between the Toronto Maple Leafs and Detroit Red Wings on April 18, at Maple Leaf Gardens. The Maple Leafs won, 3-1, clinching both the series and the Cup.

1937: PENALTY SHOT Alex Shibicky of the New York Rangers was awarded the first penalty shot in a Stanley Cup finals game on April 15, 1937. Detroit goalie Earl Robertson faced Shibicky and was able to save the shot.

There never was a successful penalty shot in a Stanley Cup playoff game until Wayne Connelly of the Minnesota North Stars came around. He beat Terry Sawchuk of the Los Angeles Kings on April 9, 1968, during a quarterfinals game.

1950: GAME SEVEN SUDDEN DEATH The Detroit Red Wings sealed a come-from-behind victory in the seventh game of the 1950 Stanley Cup against the New York Rangers on April 23 to become the first overtime champs. With the game tied at 3, the teams went 8:31 into a second overtime before a low backhand shot by utility forward Pete Babando was deflected off a defenseman's shin pad and past goalie Chuck Rayner.

There has only been one other Game Seven overtime goal, also by a Red Wing. In 1954, a shot by Tony Leswick was disastrously redirected by Montreal Canadien Doug Harvey four minutes into overtime.

1996: PENALTY SHOT (OVERTIME) The first penalty shot awarded in the overtime of a Cup game was taken by Joe Juneau of the Washington Capitals on April 24, 1996. He faced Ken Wregget of the Pittsburgh Penguins but failed to convert.

To date, the only other penalty shot awarded in overtime was taken by Aleksey Morozov of the Pittsburgh Penguins. He faced Montreal Canadien goalie Andy Moog, on April 23, 1998. He too failed to convert the penalty shot.

2005: CANCELED SEASON On Feb. 16, 2005, the National Hockey League canceled its 2004-2005 season. It was the first time a major North American sport had canceled its season because of a labor dispute. The Stanley Cup playoffs were also tabled.

The only other time the Cup was not awarded was in 1919 (see above).

THE LAST TIME...

The last team to win the Stanley Cup with a roster made up of only players from Canada was the Philadelphia Flyers in 1975.

Patrick Roy

Selected Playoff Records

MOST GOALS				
Game	5	Newsy Lalonde	Montreal Canadiens vs. Ottawa Senators	March 1, 1919
	5	Maurice Richard	Montreal Canadiens vs. Toronto Maple Leafs	March 23, 1944
	5	Darryl Sittler	Toronto Maple Leafs vs. Philadelphia Flyers	April 22, 1976
	5	Reggie Leach	Philadelphia Flyers vs. Boston Bruins	May 6, 1976
	5	Mario Lemieux	Pittsburgh Penguins vs. Philadelphia Flyers	April 25, 1989
Season	19	Reggie Leach	Philadelphia Flyers	1976
	19	Jari Kurri	Edmonton Oilers	1985
Career	122	Wayne Gretzky	Edmonton Oilers, LA Kings,St. Louis Blues, NY Rangers	1979-97
MOST ASSISTS				
Game	6	Mikko Leinonen	NY Rangers vs. Philadelphia Flyers	April 8, 1982
	6	Wayne Gretzky	Edmonton Oilers vs. LA Kings	April 9, 1987
Season	31	Wayne Gretzky	Edmonton Oilers	1988
Career	260	Wayne Gretzky	Edmonton Oilers, LA Kings, St. Louis Blues, NY Rangers	1979-97
MOST POINTS				
Game	8	Patrik Sundstrom	NJ Devils vs. Washington Capitals	April 22, 1988
	8	Mario Lemieux	Pittsburgh Penguins vs. Philadelphia Flyers	April 25, 1989
Season	47	Wayne Gretzky	Edmonton Oilers	1985
Career	382	Wayne Gretzky	Edmonton Oilers, LA Kings, St. Louis Blues, NY Rangers	1979-97
MOST SHUTOUTS				
Season	7	Martin Brodeur	New Jersey Devils	2003
Career	23	Patrick Roy	Montreal Canadiens, Colorado Rockies	1986-2003
MOST WINS				
Career	151	Patrick Roy	Montreal Canadiens, Colorado Rockies	1986-2003

SUPERLATIVES

MOST CUP WINS
The Montreal Canadiens have won the Stanley Cup a record 24 times. The franchise won its first Cup as a member of the NHA in 1916, and the other 23, from 1924 to the last one in 1993, as a member of the NHL. Official NHL stats count only 23, because they do not recognize NHA Cup victories.

MOST CONSECUTIVE CUPS The Montreal Canadiens won the Cup for five straight years, 1956-1960. In the finals they beat the Detroit Red Wings (4-1, 1956), Boston Bruins (4-1, 1957; 4-2, 1958), and Toronto Maple Leafs (4-1, 1959; 4-0, 1960).

MOST CONSECUTIVE FINALS The Montreal Canadiens reached the finals for 10 straight years, 1951-60. They ended up with six wins, four losses.

MOST CONSECUTIVE PLAYOFFS
The record for most consecutive years for a team to qualify for the playoffs is 29, accomplished by the Boston Bruins (1968-96). During this streak the Bruins won two Stanley Cups, in 1970 and 1972.

LONGEST PLAYOFF STREAK
The Pittsburgh Penguins won 14 straight playoff games over two seasons. The streak began on May 9, 1992, with the first of three wins over the New York Rangers. The Penguins then swept the Boston Bruins in four games in the conference finals and downed the Chicago Blackhawks in four straight in the finals to win the Cup for the second straight year.

The following season the New Jersey Devils lost three straight to Pittsburgh in the first round of playoffs but stopped the streak April 25, 1993, with a 4-1 win at home.

LONGEST OVERTIME GAME The longest overtime game in the playoffs, on March 24, 1936, lasted 176 minutes, 30 seconds. The Detroit Red Wings beat the Montreal Maroons, 1-0, after the long defensive struggle ended on Mud Bruneteau's goal at 16:30 of the sixth overtime period.

MOST WINS COACH
Scotty Bowman won a record nine Stanley Cups with three different teams during his Hall of Fame career. He led the Montreal Canadiens to five Cups (1973, 1976-79), the Pittsburgh Penguins to one (1992), and Detroit Red Wings to three (1997-98, 2002).

MOST MVP AWARDS
The Conn Smythe Trophy has gone to the playoffs MVP since 1965. Patrick Roy won it a record three times, in 1986 and 1993 with the Montreal Canadians and in 2001 with the Colorado Avalanche.

AUTO RACING

NASCAR

THE NATIONAL ASSOCIATION FOR STOCK CAR AUTO RACING (NASCAR) was founded in Daytona Beach, FL, on Dec. 14, 1947, by "Big" Bill France, a race promoter. The first NASCAR championship, known as Strictly Stock, was staged in 1949. Known later as the Grand National, the Winston Cup, and (since 2004) the Nextel Cup, it is the premier stock car race series in the world, attracting millions of fans to what is now a 36-race schedule.

MILESTONES

1948: FIRST RACE WINNER Red Byron, one of the legends of the pioneer days of stock car racing, won the first officially sanctioned NASCAR race at Daytona Beach, FL, on Feb. 15, 1948, driving a Ford Modified.

The following year, Byron took the first championship, winning two races in six starts and $5,800 in prizes.

1949: WOMAN DRIVER NASCAR's first woman driver, Sara Christian, competed for the first time at the Charlotte (NC) Fairgrounds Speedway on June 19, 1949. She finished in 14th position.

1950: PAVED SUPERSPEEDWAY
In the early days, the tracks were either dirt or beach courses. The first Cup race on a paved track was run at the new Darlington (SC) Raceway, on Sept. 4, 1950. That race, the Southern 500, was also the first one run over 500 miles. The race, featuring only two caution flags and lasting over six hours, was won by Johnny Mantz in a 1950 Plymouth.

1951: WEST OF THE MISSISSIPPI
NASCAR's roots are in the Southeast, but the first race west of the Mississippi was staged early in the sport's development, on Apr. 8, 1951, at the half-mile Carrell Speedway in Gardena, CA. Marshall Teague won the 100-mile race in a '51 Hudson Hornet, averaging 61.047 mph.

1954: ROAD RACE Although predominantly an oval track circuit, NASCAR does race on road courses too. The first road race was the International 100, staged at Linden (NJ) Airport, June 13, 1954. Al Keller won in a Jaguar XK140, the only non-American-made car to win a NASCAR race to date.

1959: DAYTONA 500
The inaugural Daytona 500, NASCAR's most prestigious event, was raced at the high-banked 2.5-mile Daytona International Speedway on Feb. 22, 1959. The first race was won in a photo finish by Lee Petty over Johnny Beauchamp.

The drivers were so close at the finish line that Petty's victory was not made official for 61 hours. He was declared the winner by 2 feet after officials reviewed newsreel footage.

1960: TWO-WAY RADIO Team owner and crew chief Bud Moore introduced the use of two-way radio to communicate between driver and pit crew in the World 600 at Charlotte Motor Speedway, June 19, 1960.

1963: AFRICAN-AMERICAN WINNER
The first and thus far only African-American driver to win a NASCAR race was Wendell Scott. He won the Jake 200 at Speedway Park in Jacksonville, FL, on Dec. 1, 1963.

At first the race promoter, fearing a riot, declared Buck Baker the winner instead, giving him the trophy and the $1,000 first-place prize. Hours later, following an official protest, Scott was named the winner and awarded the $1,000. He never did get the trophy.

1970: 200 MPH
Buddy Baker became the first driver to top the 200-mph mark in a stock car, during a test-run at the Alabama International Speedway on March 24, 1970. Now called the Talladega Superspeedway, the 2.66-mile tri-oval is the longest track on the circuit.

The first driver to post an official qualifying lap over 200 mph was Benny Parsons. He clocked 200.176 mph in gaining the pole for the 1982 Winston 500 at Talladega on May 2, 1982.

1977: WOMAN AT DAYTONA 500 Janet Guthrie became the first woman driver to qualify for the Daytona 500 on Feb. 20, 1977. She qualified in 24th place on the grid and finished 12th.

1992: NIGHT RACE
The first Cup race under lights was run at the Charlotte Motor Speedway on May 16, 1992. Davey Allison edged Kyle Petty by a half-car length in a dramatic finish.

Allison lost control of his car after crossing the finish line, and hit the wall at about 160 mph. He ended up with a bruised lung, bruised legs, and a concussion—and a victory worth $300,000.

Jeff Gordon car #24

Jeff Gordon

RECORD BREAKER

"I got into him a little bit, he got loose, and I hope he'll understand tomorrow."

–Jeff Gordon, after bumping Rusty Wallace on the last lap of the 2002 Sharpie 500 to win his first race in 31 starts.

SUPERLATIVES

MOST NASCAR CHAMPIONSHIPS Two drivers have won a record seven NASCAR titles: Richard Petty (the King), 1964, 1967, 1971-72, 1974-75, and 1979; and Dale Earnhardt in 1980, 1986-87, 1990-91, and 1993-94.

MOST CONSECUTIVE TITLES The only driver to win three Cup titles in a row is Cale Yarborough. His "three-peat" came in 1976-1978.

MOST WINS CAREER The record for the most wins in NASCAR's premier series is 200, by Richard Petty. His first victory was on Feb. 28, 1960, at the Southern States Fairgrounds in Charlotte, NC.

His last trip to Victory Lane came in the Pepsi Firecracker 400 at the Daytona International Speedway on July 4, 1984.

Since 1972 (modern era), the most career wins is 84, by Darrell Waltrip. DW's first win came at the 1975 Music City 420. His last was the 1992 Mountain Dew Southern 5000.

MOST WINS SEASON In 1967, Richard Petty won a record 27 races, including a record 10 straight.

MOST WINS DAYTONA 500 Richard Petty won a record seven Daytona 500 races. The first came in 1964, five years after his father, Lee, had won the inaugural event. The others came in 1966, 1971, 1973-74, 1979, and 1981.

FASTEST The fastest average speed attained in a NASCAR series race is 186.288 mph, set by Bill Elliott at Talladega Superspeedway, AL, on May 5, 1985, in winning the Winston 500. He "smoked" the previous record of 177.602 mph set by Buddy Baker at the 1980 Daytona 500.

OLDEST WINNER Harry Gant won the Champion 400 at the Michigan International Speedway on Aug. 16, 1992, at a record age of 52 years, 219 days.

YOUNGEST WINNER Donald Thomas was only 20 years, 129 days old, a record, when he won a 1952 race at Lakewood Speedway in Atlanta.

MOST LEAD CHANGES Since 1976, when records began being officially monitored, the most lead changes in a single race was 75, in the 1984 Winston 500, at the Talladega Superspeedway.

Cale Yarborough was the last man up front when the checkered flag was waved. He was one of 13 different drivers to head the field, and overtook Harry Gant on the backstretch of the track on the last lap for his 80th career win.

NASCAR Track Records

	WINS	DRIVER	YEARS
Superspeedway (career)	55	Richard Petty	1958-92
Superspeedway (season)	11	Bill Elliott	1985
Superspeedway (consecutive)	5	Jeff Gordon	1998
Short Track (career)	139	Richard Petty	1958-92
Short Track (season)	23	Richard Petty	1967
Short Track (consecutive)	10	Richard Petty	1967
Road Courses (career)	7	Jeff Gordon	1992-2004
Road Courses (consecutive)	6	Jeff Gordon	1997-2000

AUTO RACING

Indianapolis 500

THE INDIANAPOLIS 500 WAS FIRST RUN MAY 30, 1911, at the Indianapolis Motor Speedway, a test track built in 1909 by a local car dealer named Carl Fisher. The 2.5-mile track was originally made of crushed stone and tar, but in the first race on it, on Aug. 19, 1909, the surface broke up, causing the deaths of two drivers, two mechanics, and two spectators. The owners immediately paved it over with 3.2 million bricks, and "the Brickyard" was born.

Two years later, the first Indy 500 was a great success, and the next year the total purse was nearly doubled from $27,550 to $52,225. Held annually on Memorial Day weekend, the 33-car, 200-lap Indy 500 offers auto racing's highest purse and has the largest crowd attendance for a one-day sports event in the world. The grandstands hold permanent seating for about 250,000 people, and thousands more can watch from the 224-acre infield.

Danica Patrick ▶

MILESTONES

1911: FIRST WINNER
Ray Harroun won the inaugural race in 1911. Driving a Marmon Wasp, he completed the race in 6 hours, 42 minutes, 8 seconds, at an average speed of 74.602 miles per hour. Harroun, who was relieved by Cyrus Patschke for about 35 laps at the midpoint of the race, won a first-place prize of $14,250.

1911: FIRST FATALITY Prior to 1924, the race always included some two-seater cars, which carried a mechanic along with the driver. On lap 13 of the 1911 race, driver Arthur Greiner hit the southeast wall. He broke his shoulder; his mechanic, Sam Dickson, was killed.

1916: HELMETS
The first drivers to wear steel helmets in American automobile racing were Eddie Rickenbacker and Pete Henderson in the 1916 Indy 500. Rickenbacker, the World War I flying ace who bought the track in 1927, dropped out on the ninth lap with a steering problem. Henderson finished sixth behind the winner, Dario Resta of Italy.

Crash helmets were not mandatory until the 1935 race. Roll bars and fireproof overalls were made compulsory in 1959.

1925: 100 MPH
The first driver to run the 500 at an average speed over 100 mph was Pete DePaolo. He won the 1925 race in a Duesenberg averaging 101.127 mph. He also set a one-lap record at the time of 114.285 mph.

1936: DRINKING MILK IN VICTORY LANE In 1936 Louis Meyer toasted his third Indy 500 win by chugging a bottle of buttermilk in his garage. As he drank, a photographer snapped his picture. When the photo appeared in the newspaper, Indiana's dairy farmers loved it so much that they asked the Speedway to give the winner milk the next year, and a tradition was born.

1936: ASPHALT The track was first partially paved with asphalt in 1936 to cover the rough portions of bricks in the turns. Paving continued over the years, and was completed in 1961. All that remains of the original brick track is a 36-inch strip at the start/finish line known as the "Yard of Bricks."

1939-40: BACK-TO-BACK WINS
The first driver to win consecutive Indy 500s was Wilbur Shaw. He took the checkered flag in 1939 and 1940. Only four other drivers have defended their titles: Mauri Rose (1947-48), Bill Vukovich (1953-54), Al Unser (1970-71), and Helio Castroneves of Brazil (2001-02).

1946: "GENTLEMEN, START YOUR ENGINES" This famous command was first ordered at the 1946 Indy 500. The track had been closed for four years during World War II and now had new ownership: Anton "Tony" Hulman Jr. and former Indy 500 champion Wilbur Shaw. At the finale of the pre-race ceremonies, Hulman uttered the now-traditional order. (But the wording is changed when women participate.)

1952: NO RELIEF
The first time the Indy 500 was completed without the use of relief drivers was in 1952. Troy Ruttman won with an average speed of 128.922 mph, a record at the time.

1967: TURBINE-POWERED CAR
The first turbine-powered car raced at the Brickyard was Parnelli Jones' STP turbocar in 1967. Jones led for 171 laps in his "whoosh mobile" before a bearing burned out on Lap 196, ending his run. He placed sixth behind winner A.J. Foyt Jr.

Indianapolis 500 Career Leaders

Most Starts	35	A.J. Foyt Jr.	1958-92
Most Poles	6	Rick Mears	1979, 1982, 1986, 1988-89, 1991
Most Laps (leading)	664	Al Unser Sr.	1965-93
Most Miles	12,272.5	A.J. Foyt Jr.	1958-92

SOMETHING TO THINK ABOUT

FIRST IN LINE

For 37 straight years between 1948 and 1985, Larry Bisceglia was first in line on opening day at the Indianapolis Motor Speedway. A lifelong fan, Bisceglia first came to the Indy 500 in 1925. At the 1948 race, he heard that the first person in line on opening day always gets a free ticket. The next year he was at the front of the line, and a new tradition began. In 1959, track owner Tony Hulman presented him with an engraved silver cup. In 1967, the Ford Dealers of Indiana gave him a camper van for his annual trip from Long Beach, CA. The next year, he arrived at the track 60 days before opening day, a personal record. Poor health prevented Indy's No. 1 fan from waiting in line in 1986, and he was too ill to make the Memorial Day Classic after that. He died in Dec. 1988, having set a record that is unlikely to be broken.

1977: 200 MPH
The first official 200-mph laps turned at the Speedway were driven by Tom Sneva during the qualifying session for the 1977 race.

The next year, Sneva became the first driver to gain the pole with a four-lap average speed above 200 mph, at 202.156 mph.

1977: WOMAN DRIVER
On May 22, 1977, Janet Guthrie became the first woman to qualify for the Indianapolis 500. Her historic first race ended early, when the timing gear broke on lap 27; she placed 29th out of 33. Earlier in 1977, Guthrie had become the first woman to run in the Daytona 500.

Guthrie raced in the Indy 500 three times, from 1977 to 1979. Her best finish was ninth, in 1978.

1991: AFRICAN-AMERICAN DRIVER
The first African-American to qualify for the race was Willy T. Ribbs on May 12, 1991. He qualified in 29th place with a qualifying speed of 217.358 mph. He dropped out of the race on the fifth lap with engine trouble and placed 32nd in the race.

2005: WOMAN LAP LEADER On May 29, 2005, Danica Patrick became the first woman to lead the Indy 500 when she went to the front on the 56th lap. She led three times for a total of 19 laps.

The 23-year-old rookie driver retook the lead for the third time with 28 laps left. Dan Wheldon of England, the eventual winner, passed her with six laps remaining. Patrick finished fourth, the highest finish by a woman driver.

SUPERLATIVES

MOST INDY 500 WINS
Three drivers have won a record four Indy 500s: A.J. Foyt Jr., in 1961, 1964, 1967, and 1977; Al Unser in 1970-71, 1978, and 1987; and Rick Mears in 1979, 1984, 1988, and 1991.

LOWEST POSITION ON GRID (WINNER)
Two drivers have won the Indy 500 from 28th position on the starting grid. The first was Ray Harroun in the inaugural race in 1911. His feat was matched by Louis Meyer in 1936.

FASTEST WINNER
The record time for winning the Indy 500 is 2 hours, 41 minutes, 18.404 seconds, by the Dutch driver Arie Luyendyk in 1990. His average speed in that race was 185.981 mph.

In a race that saw seven lead changes among three drivers, Luyendyk took the lead for good on Lap 168. There were only four cautions in the race.

SLOWEST WINNER
Ray Harroun won the first Indy 500 in 1911, with the slowest time in the race's history—6 hours, 42 minutes, 8 seconds, with an average speed of 74.602 mph.

OLDEST WINNER
The oldest Indy 500 winner was Al Unser. He won his record-tying fourth Indy 500 in 1987 at age 47 years, 360 days.

YOUNGEST WINNER
Troy Ruttman was 22 years, 80 days old when he won the 1952 race, the youngest driver to win the Indy 500.

CLOSEST FINISH
The closest margin of victory came in 1992 when Al Unser Jr. barely edged out Scott Goodyear by 0.043 seconds.

Unser took the lead with 10 laps to go when Michael Andretti dropped out with a fuel pump problem. Goodyear closed on the leader and an exciting last-lap chase ensued. Unser was loose coming off Turn 3, but just managed to edge the hard-charging Goodyear at the finish line. Unser's father, Al Sr., finished third, the only other driver on the lead lap.

FASTEST QUALIFIER
The record average speed for four laps qualifying is 236.986 mph, set by Dutch Driver Arie Luyendyk in a Reynard-Ford-Cosworth in 1996. In that year, he also set the one-lap qualifying record of 237.498 mph.

SOCCER

FIFA World Cup

THE FIFA (FÉDÉRATION INTERNATIONALE DE FOOTBALL ASSOCIATION) World Cup final, staged every four years, is the most widely watched sporting event in the world; an estimated 1.5 billion viewers watched the championship game between Brazil and Germany in Yokohama, Japan, on June 30, 2002. The first World Cup was staged in Uruguay in 1930. The first tournament included 13 teams; the format today allows for 32 teams to qualify for the finals.

Brazil's Ronaldo (left) and Ronaldinho celebrate at the 2002 World Cup final match ▶

MILESTONES

JULY 13, 1930: FIRST GOAL The first goal in the history of the World Cup finals was scored by Lucien Laurent of France. It came on July 13, 1930, during the opening match of the finals, a 1-0 win over Mexico in Montevideo, Uruguay.

JULY 19, 1930: HAT-TRICK The first hat-trick in the finals was scored by Guillermo Stabile of Argentina. He scored three goals in Argentina's 6-3 win over Mexico on July 19. Stabile only played in the game because team captain Manuel Ferreira had to return to Buenos Aires to take a law school exam. He ended up as the leading scorer in the 1930 finals, with eight goals.

1934: OVERTIME The first game extended to overtime in World Cup finals was at the 1934 championship played in Rome, Italy, on June 10, 1934. Italy was tied, 1-1, with Czechoslovakia at the end of regulation but won the game, 2-1, in the extra period on a goal by Angelo Schiavo.

1938: NON-HOST WINNER The first two World Cups went to the host nation: Uruguay in 1930 and Italy in 1934. The first time a host country lost was in 1938, when Italy won the championship that was held in France. The defending champs knocked out the hosts in the second round, 3-1, and went on to beat Hungary, 4-2, in the final. Host nations have won 6 of the 17 World Cups so far played.

1958: SCORELESS TIE The first 0-0 tie wasn't played until the sixth finals in 1958. England and Brazil played the no-goals draw in pool play.

1982: PENALTY KICK SHOOTOUT FIFA introduced the penalty kick shootout to decide tied elimination games in 1982.

The first game to be decided in this manner was the 1982 semifinal between West Germany and France in Seville, Spain, on July 8. The game was tied 3-3 at the end of the overtime period. West Germany won the penalty-kick shootout, 5-4. Didier Six and Maxime Bossis missed penalty kicks for France, while Uli Stielike missed for West Germany.

The game-winning spot kick was converted by Horst Hrubesch.

SUPERLATIVES

MOST CHAMPIONSHIPS
TEAM Brazil has won a record five World Cups. The South American giants first won the title in Sweden in 1958, the first time a country won the trophy at finals staged outside its own continent. It was also the first World Cup tournament for the legendary Pelé, who scored six goals in the tournament, including two against Sweden in the finals.

Four years later, Brazil sucessfuly defended its title in Chile. In 1970, Brazil became the first team to win the trophy for a third time.

It would be 24 years before Brazil claimed its fourth title, in the U.S. in 1994. In 2002, Brazil beat Germany, 2-0, to win the World Cup for the fifth time, with both goals scored by the sensational Brazilian forward, Ronaldo. No other country has won more than three World Cups.

MOST CHAMPIONSHIPS
PLAYER Brazilian legend Pelé holds the record for championships, with three. He played on Brazil teams that won the title in 1958, 1962, and 1970.

MOST CHAMPIONSHIPS
COACH Italy's Vittorio Pozzo is the only coach to have won two championships. He led Italy to the title in 1934 and 1938.

MOST APPEARANCES
TEAM The only country to qualify for all World Cup finals is Brazil. The five-time champions have played in all 18 finals held from 1930 to 2006.

MOST GOALS (GAME)
TEAM The most goals scored by one team in a World Cup finals game is 10, by Hungary. The "Magyars" beat El Salvador, 10-1, in Elche, Spain, on June 15, 1982.

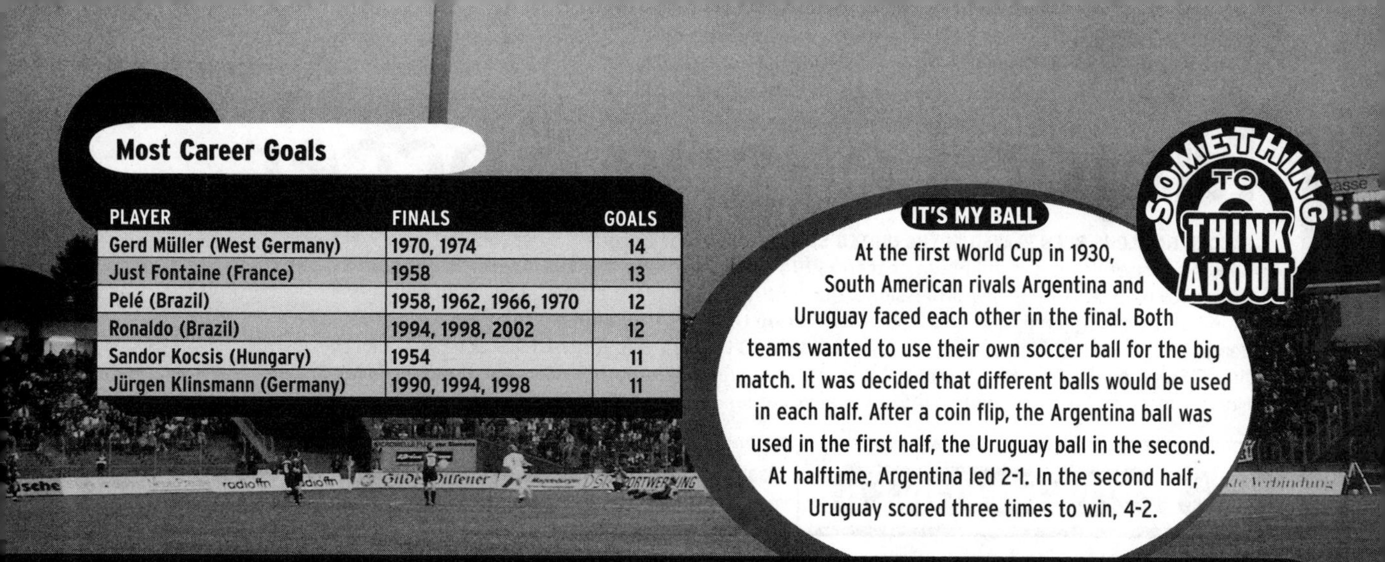

Most Career Goals

PLAYER	FINALS	GOALS
Gerd Müller (West Germany)	1970, 1974	14
Just Fontaine (France)	1958	13
Pelé (Brazil)	1958, 1962, 1966, 1970	12
Ronaldo (Brazil)	1994, 1998, 2002	12
Sandor Kocsis (Hungary)	1954	11
Jürgen Klinsmann (Germany)	1990, 1994, 1998	11

SOMETHING TO THINK ABOUT

IT'S MY BALL

At the first World Cup in 1930, South American rivals Argentina and Uruguay faced each other in the final. Both teams wanted to use their own soccer ball for the big match. It was decided that different balls would be used in each half. After a coin flip, the Argentina ball was used in the first half, the Uruguay ball in the second. At halftime, Argentina led 2-1. In the second half, Uruguay scored three times to win, 4-2.

Second-half substitute Laszlo Kiss led Hungary with three goals, all scored within six minutes, and Tibor Nyilasi and Laszlo Fazekas each had two goals. Jozsef Toth, Gabor Poeloeskei, and Lazar Szentes also scored.

One consolation for El Salvador was that Luis Ramirez scored his country's first-ever goal in the finals.

Hungary's 1982 achievement bested a record previously set by the 1954 Hungary team. That team, known as the Magical Magyars, beat South Korea, 9-0. That record was tied by Yugoslavia at the 1974 World Cup, when that team beat Zaire, 9-0.

MOST GOALS (CHAMPIONSHIP GAME) **TEAM** The most goals scored by one team in a World Cup championship game is five, by Brazil in 1958. Coached by Vicente Feola, the Brazilians beat host nation Sweden, 5-2, for the nation's first world championship. Brazil's goals came from Vava (2), Pelé (2), and Mario Zagallo. This match also set the record for most total goals in a final, with seven.

MOST FINAL TOURNAMENTS **PLAYER** Two players have played in five World Cup finals: Antonio Carbajal (Mexico) and Lothar Matthäus (West Germany/Germany).

The goalkeeper Carbajal played in the 1950, 1954, 1958, 1962, and 1966 finals. Midfield star Matthäus played in the 1982, 1986, 1990, 1994, and 1998 finals.

MOST GAMES **PLAYER** Lothar Matthäus played in a record 25 World Cup finals games for West Germany/Germany in five finals, 1982-1998. He captained West Germany to victory in 1990. He also played in the 1986 final against Argentina.

MOST GOALS (GAME) **PLAYER** The most goals scored by one player in a World Cup game is five, by Oleg Salenko (Russia) vs. Cameroon at Stanford Stadium, Palo Alto, CA, on June 28, 1994. Salenko scored in the 16th, 41st, 45th, 73rd, and 75th minutes, with one goal coming on a penalty kick.

Nine players had shared the previous record of four goals in a game.

MOST GOALS (FINALS) **PLAYER** The most goals scored in one finals tournament is 13, by Just Fontaine (France) in 1958. In six games, Fontaine scored three vs. Paraguay, two vs. Yugoslavia, one vs. Scotland, two vs. Northern Ireland, one vs. Brazil, and four vs. West Germany. France finished third in the tournament, losing to Brazil in the semifinals, 5-2. Fontaine's four-goal haul against West Germany came in the third-place playoff game.

MOST GOALS (FINALS) **CAREER** The most goals scored in a career at the World Cup finals is 14, by Gerd Müller (West Germany). The stocky sharpshooter was the leading scorer at the 1970 finals in Mexico, with 10 goals. He scored four goals in the 1974 finals staged in West Germany. These included the two most important goals of the tournament, the winning goals in the semifinal vs. Poland (1-0) and in the final vs. Holland (2-1).

Only one player has scored a hat-trick in the World Cup final. England striker Geoff Hurst scored three goals vs. West Germany in the 1966 final. Two of Hurst's goals came in overtime of England's 4-2 triumph.

THE LAST TIME...

The last time a penalty kick was awarded in the World Cup final was in 1990. Referee Edgardo Codesal Mendez of Mexico called a foul on Argentina defender Roberto Sensini for his tackle on Germany forward Rudi Voeller. With the game tied at 0-0, Andreas Brehme stepped up to take the kick in the 85th minute. The fullback scored the only goal in the 1-0 match, giving West Germany the Cup.

Major League Soccer

SOCCER HAS LONG BEEN PLAYED IN THE UNITED STATES, but Major League Soccer (MLS) is relatively new. As part of its successful bid to host the 1994 FIFA World Cup, the U.S. Soccer Federation agreed to help start up a new professional outdoor league in the United States. On Dec. 17, 1993, Alan I. Rothenberg, chairman and CEO of World Cup USA 1994, announced the formation of Major League Soccer. Its inaugural season was 1996, with 10 teams vying for the MLS Cup. MLS was the first FIFA-recognized Division 1 professional league launched in the U.S. since the demise of the North American Soccer League (NASL) 12 years earlier.

MILESTONES

APRIL 6, 1996: FIRST GOAL The first goal in MLS play was scored by forward Eric Wynalda of the San Jose Clash in the league's inaugural game. Wynalda scored two minutes from the end of the game, off a Ben Iroha pass, to secure a 1-0 win for the Clash over visiting D.C. United.

MAY 15, 1996: HAT-TRICK D.C. United forward Steve Rammel scored the first hat-trick in MLS history. His historic three-goal haul came during a 5-2 win over the visiting Columbus Crew.

OCT. 20, 1996: MLS CUP CHAMPIONS D.C. United captured the first MLS Cup after a 3-2 sudden death overtime victory over the Los Angeles Galaxy at Foxboro Stadium in Foxboro, MA.

In a game played in a driving rainstorm, the Galaxy held a 2-0 lead with 17 minutes remaining, but United scored two goals to send the game into overtime. Defender Eddie Pope scored the Cup-winning goal on a header off a Marco Etcheverry corner kick. Etcheverry was named the first MLS Cup MVP.

1999: FIRST SOCCER STADIUM The first major league stadium built specifically for soccer in the U.S. was for the Columbus Crew in Columbus, OH. The venue was named Crew Stadium after the team.

The first MLS game played there was on May 15, 1999. The home team Crew beat the New England Revolution, 2-0, on goals by Jeff Cunningham and Stern John.

2000: FIRST TIE ALLOWED For the first four seasons all MLS games had to secure a result; any game ending in a tie would be decided in a shootout. For the league's fifth season, in 2000, MLS fell into line with the rest of the world's soccer leagues and began allowing ties. Following a tie in regulation play, teams would play two sudden death overtime periods of five minutes. If the teams were still tied, then a tie would be declared, and each team awarded a point for the season standings. As in the rest of the soccer world, a tie is worth one point, a win is worth three, and a loss is worth zero. Playoff games go on to penalty kicks if no result is reached in overtime.

The New England Revolution and Miami Fusion were the first teams to tie when they finished a game 1-1.

2004: FIRST PLAYOFF GAME DECIDED BY PENALTIES The first MLS playoff game to be decided on penalties was the 2004 Eastern Conference Championship game on Nov. 6, 2004. D.C. United beat the New England Revolution on penalty kicks, after the teams had played to a 3-3 tie through regulation and overtime.

The tie was decided when United goalkeeper Nick Rimando saved Clint Dempsey's penalty attempt, giving them the advantage. D.C. United advanced to the MLS Cup final, where they beat the Kansas City Wizards, 3-2.

Landon Donovan

MOST MLS TITLES
The most MLS Cup titles won by a team is four, by D.C. United. They took the first two MLS Cup titles in 1996 and 1997. They faltered against the Chicago Fire in the 1998 title game, but came back in 1999 and won a third championship. After a five-year drought, United topped the MLS world again when it won the Cup in 2004.

MOST GOALS (MLS CUP FINAL)
Landon Donovan of the San Jose Earthquakes is credited with having scored the most goals by an individual in an MLS Cup final, with two. His pair of goals came during the 2003 Cup in the Earthquakes' 4-2 win over the Chicago Fire.

Donovan holds the record for career goals in championship games, having scored three overall. His other goal came in the 2-1 win over the Los Angeles Galaxy in the 2001 MLS Cup.

MOST GOALS (TEAM)
The most goals scored by a team in any MLS game is 8, by the Los Angeles Galaxy. The record was reached in an 8-1 victory over the Dallas Burn in Dallas on June 4, 1998.

The most lopsided win in MLS history (later tied by the Chicago Fire's 7-0 win over the Kansas City Wizards on July 4, 2001), the game also featured the fastest hat-trick in league history. Harut Karapetyan, who came on as a substitute in the second-half, scored three goals in five minutes (82nd, 85th, and 87th). He had not scored all season prior to the game.

The other goals for the Galaxy were scored by Ezra Hendrickson (2 goals), Clint Mathis, Greg Vanney, and Brazilian striker Welton. Dallas had been down a player since the 18th minute when Leonel Alvarez was ejected from the game.

YOUNGEST PLAYER
Freddy Adu is the youngest person ever to play soccer in MLS history. The soccer phenom was 14 years old when he played his first game for D.C. United on Apr. 3, 2004. He went in as a second-half substitute in the opening game of the season in a 2-1 win over defending MLS champion San Jose Earthquakes.

The Ghanian-born Adu made more league history when he became the youngest player to score a goal. It came two weeks later on Apr. 17, 2004, in D.C. United's 3-2 loss to the MetroStars at Giants Stadium.

SOMETHING TO THINK ABOUT

"MAMA" MIA

On May 9, 2001, Tampa Bay Mutiny striker Mamadou Diallo became the fourth MLS player to score four or more goals in a game. He scored all his team's goals, yet still didn't play on the winning team. The game with the Los Angeles Galaxy ended in a 4-4 tie. While Diallo's effort didn't spark a victory, Abdul Thompson Conteh's four-goal haul led D.C. United to a 5-0 victory over the New England Revolution. The following season, Diallo scored four goals against the Galaxy again, this time playing for the MetroStars. And this time, his double brace propelled his team to a 5-0 win.

MLS RECORDS

MOST GOALS				
Game	5	Clint Mathis	MetroStars at Dallas Burn	Aug. 26, 2000
Season	27	Roy Lassiter	Tampa Bay Mutiny	1996
Career	100	Jason Kreis	Dallas Burn, Real Salt Lake	1996-2005
MOST ASSISTS				
Game	4	Carlos Valderrama	Tampa Bay Mutiny vs. New England Revolution	Aug. 30, 1997
	4	Chris Henderson	Kansas City Wizards vs. MetroStars	June 20, 1999
Season	26	Carlos Valderrama	Tampa Bay Mutiny	2000
Career	114	Carlos Valderrama	Tampa Bay Mutiny, Miami Fusion, Colorado Rapids	1996-2002
MOST POINTS†				
Game	10	Clint Mathis	MetroStars at Dallas Burn	Aug. 26, 2000
Season	58	Roy Lassiter	Tampa Bay Mutiny	1996
Career	270	Preki	Kansas City Wizards, Miami Fusion	1996-2005

†(2 points for a goal, 1 for an assist)

SOCCER

FIFA Women's World Cup

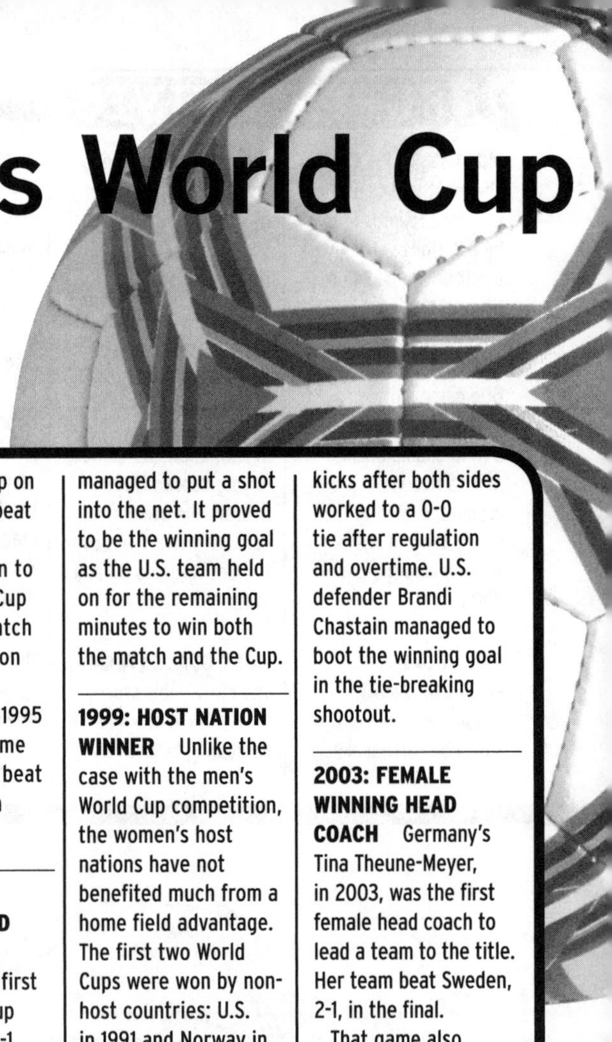

THE FIRST FEDERATION INTERNATIONALE DE FOOTBALL (FIFA) WOMEN'S WORLD CUP was held in China in 1991, with 12 teams competing. Since then, the tournament has been held every four years, and the number of teams has grown to 16. The last Women's World Cup was held in the U.S. in 2003. The competition was moved there from China because of the SARS outbreak in that country. The next Women's World Cup will be held in China in 2007.

MILESTONES

NOV. 16, 1991: FIRST WOMEN'S WORLD CUP GOAL The first goal ever scored in a Women's World Cup finals was by Li Ma of China. Her historic strike came on Nov. 16, 1991, during the opening match of the finals, in a 4-0 win over Norway in Guangzhou, China.

NOV. 16, 1991: SHUTOUT The first shutout at the finals was posted by China goalkeeper Zhong Honglian. She stoned Norway, and even managed to block a penalty kick, as the Chinese won the first-ever finals game, 4-0.

NOV, 17, 1991: HAT-TRICK Carolina Morace of Italy scored the first hat-trick in the World Cup finals. She put away Italy's last three goals in a 5-0 rout of Chinese Taipei (Taiwan) on Nov. 17, 1991.

NOV, 24, 1991: OVERTIME Germany and Denmark played the first game that extended to overtime, in a 1991 quarterfinal played in Zhongshan, China, on Nov. 24. The teams were deadlocked at 1-1 by the end of regulation. But Germany was able to pull out a 2-1 win in the extra period on a goal by Heidi Mohr.

Later that same day in Jiangmen, the Norway-Italy quarterfinal game also went into overtime. With the game tied at 2-2 after 90 minutes, Norway took the match, 3-2, on a Tina Svensson penalty kick in the 96th minute.

NOV. 29, 1991: FEMALE REFEREE The first woman to referee a Women's World Cup Finals game was the Brazilian official Claudia de Vasconcelos. She took charge of the Sweden vs. Germany game at the 1991 World Cup on Nov. 29. Sweden beat Germany, 4-0.

The first woman to referee a World Cup championship match was Ingrid Jonsson of Sweden. She officiated at the 1995 championship game in which Norway beat Germany, 2-0, on June 18.

NOV. 30, 1991: WOMEN'S WORLD CUP CHAMPION The U.S. took the first Women's World Cup after a gripping 2-1 win over Norway in Guangzhou, China, on Nov. 30, 1991. The two teams fought to a 1-1 tie going into the final minutes of the game before U.S. striker Michelle Akers managed to put a shot into the net. It proved to be the winning goal as the U.S. team held on for the remaining minutes to win both the match and the Cup.

1999: HOST NATION WINNER Unlike the case with the men's World Cup competition, the women's host nations have not benefited much from a home field advantage. The first two World Cups were won by non-host countries: U.S. in 1991 and Norway in 1995. The first, and so far only, time a host country won was when the U.S. did so in 1999. The championship game between the U.S. and China was settled by penalty kicks after both sides worked to a 0-0 tie after regulation and overtime. U.S. defender Brandi Chastain managed to boot the winning goal in the tie-breaking shootout.

2003: FEMALE WINNING HEAD COACH Germany's Tina Theune-Meyer, in 2003, was the first female head coach to lead a team to the title. Her team beat Sweden, 2-1, in the final.

That game also marked the first time when both head coaches contesting the championship game were women. Marika Domanski Lyfors was the head coach for Sweden.

All-Time Goals (Top Five)

PLAYER/TEAM	FINALS	GOALS
Michelle Akers (USA)	1991, 1995, 1999	12
Sun Wen (China)	1991, 1995, 1999, 2003	11
Bettina Wiegman (Germany)	1991, 1995, 1999, 2003	11
Ann Kristin Aarones (Norway)	1995, 1999	10
Heidi Mohr (Germany)	1991, 1995	10

SOMETHING TO THINK ABOUT

NOT A HARD TICKET

The smallest crowd for a Women's World Cup game was 250, for the Nigeria vs. Canada game played in Helsingborg, Sweden, on June 8, 1995. The hardy few were rewarded with a six-goal thriller. Canada jumped out to a 2-0 lead early in the game. In the second half, Canada led 3-1. But the Nigerians rallied to tie the game 3-3 on goals by Patience Avre and Adaku Okoroafor.

Mia Hamm

FASTEST RED CARD

The fastest red card in Women's World Cup history was issued to Alicia Ferguson of Australia in the second minute of a game against China, on June 26, 1999, at Giants' Stadium in East Rutherford, NJ. Making her World Cup debut, the 17-year-old Ferguson hadn't even touched the ball when she made a clumsy challenge on China's Jie Bai, which provoked American referee Sandra Hunt to produce a red card, ejecting her from the game. China went on to beat the shorthanded Aussies, 3-1.

SUPERLATIVES

MOST CHAMPIONSHIPS

TEAM The U.S. has won the most championships, with two World Cups. The first came in China in 1991, and the second came eight years later in the U.S. Coincidentally, the U.S. earned that second World Cup after a victory over China in the final.

MOST CHAMPIONSHIPS

PLAYER Seven players have played on two World Cup-winning teams: Michelle Akers, Brandi Chastain, Kristine Lilly, Joy Fawcett (née Biefield), Julie Foudy, Carla Overbeck, and Mia Hamm. All seven players were members of the U.S. squad that won Cups in 1991 and 1999.

MOST GOALS SCORED IN ONE GAME

TEAM The most goals scored by one team in a World Cup Finals game is eight. Two teams have done this, Sweden and Norway.

Sweden beat Japan, 8-0, in Foshan, China, on Nov. 19, 1991. Lena Videkull and Anneli Andelen each had two goals; Malin Lundgren, Helen Nilsson, and Pia Sundhage also scored. Japan's miserable day was compounded when Sweden's eighth goal came on an own goal by Sayuri Yamaguchi.

As for the other record-holder, Norway beat Nigeria, 8-0, in Karlstad, Sweden, on June 6, 1995. Kristin Sandberg scored a hat-trick and Ann Kristin Aarones had two goals. Hege Riise, Linda Medalen, and Tina Svensson scored the other three.

MOST GOALS SCORED IN A TOURNAMENT

TEAM Two teams are tied at 25 for most goals scored in a World Cup Finals tournament: the U.S. in 1991, and Germany in 2003. In pool play, the U.S. beat Sweden, 3-2, Brazil, 5-0, and Japan, 3-0. The U.S. went on to beat Taiwan, 7-0, in the quarterfinals, and Germany, 5-2, in the semifinals. In the championship game, the U.S. beat Norway, 2-1.

Germany also won the World Cup during their record-setting goal spree. In pool play, Germany beat Canada, 4-1; Japan, 3-0; and Argentina, 6-1. Later they beat Russia, 7-1, in the quarterfinals, and the U.S., 3-0, in the semifinals. In the championship game, Germany beat out Sweden, 2-1, in sudden death, or "Golden Goal," overtime.

MOST GOALS SCORED IN FINALS

TEAM The U.S. holds the record for most goals in Finals history. In 24 games over four tournaments, the two-time champions have scored 73 goals.

MOST GOALS SCORED

PLAYER U.S. forward Michelle Akers once scored five goals in a match against Chinese Taipei (Taiwan), contributing to a 7-0 win at New Plaza Stadium, Foshan, China, on Nov. 24, 1991. Akers scored in the 8th, 29th, 33rd, 44th, and 48th minutes, with one goal coming on a penalty kick.

MOST FINALS TOURNAMENT GOALS SCORED

PLAYER Michelle Akers, with 10 goals in the 1991 competition, holds the record for most scored by a single player in one tournament. In six appearances, she scored in four matches. Akers scored in order of play: one goal vs. Brazil, two goals vs. Japan, five goals vs. Taiwan (Chinese Taipei), and two goals vs. Norway.

The U.S. won the tournament, with Akers's two goals in the Final versus Norway clinching the title.

MOST CAREER GOALS SCORED IN FINALS

PLAYER In her World Cup tournament career, Michelle Akers has managed to put 12 in the back of the net. The powerful sharpshooter was the leading scorer at the 1991 Finals in China with 10 goals (see above). In two games during the 1995 campaign in Sweden, she failed to score. But at the 1999 Finals, she scored two goals.

GOLF

The Majors

IN 1930, BOBBY JONES (U.S.) ACHIEVED A GRAND SLAM, BY WINNING the U.S. Open, British Open, U.S. Amateur, and British Amateur championships in one calendar year. When Arnold Palmer (U.S.) won the Masters and U.S. Open in 1960, the men's Grand Slam was redefined as winning the Masters, U.S. Open, British Open, and PGA Championship in a calendar year. He failed to win the British Open, so his Slam bid was derailed, but it captured the public's imagination. Jones is still the only golfer to complete a Grand Slam. Tiger Woods (U.S.) won all four majors consecutively from the 2000 U.S. Open to the 2001 Masters; this feat was called the "Tiger Slam."

Tiger Woods ▶

SUPERLATIVES

MOST MAJORS Jack Nicklaus (U.S.) won a record 18 major championships: 6 Masters (1963, 1965-66, 1972, 1975, 1986); 4 U.S. Open (1962, 1967, 1972, 1980); 3 British Open (1966, 1970, 1978); and 5 PGA (1963, 1971, 1973, 1975, 1980).

CAREER GRAND SLAM Five players have won all four majors: Gene Sarazen (U.S.), 1 Masters, 2 U.S. Open, 1 British Open, 3 PGA; Ben Hogan (U.S.), 2 Masters, 4 U.S. Open, 1 British Open, 2 PGA; Jack Nicklaus (see above); Gary Player (S. Africa), 3 Masters, 1 U.S. Open, 3 British Open, 2 PGA; and Tiger Woods, 4 Masters, 2 U.S. Open, 2 British Open, 2 PGA.

THE MASTERS

Bobby Jones and Clifford Roberts started the Masters tournament in 1934 at the Augusta National Golf Club in Augusta, GA. It has been staged there ever since.

Horton Smith (U.S.) won the first Masters by one shot over Craig Wood (U.S.).

MOST WINS Jack Nicklaus has won the coveted Masters green jacket a record six times: 1963, 1965-66, 1972, 1975, and 1986.

CONSECUTIVE WINS Three golfers have repeated as champs: Jack Nicklaus, 1965-66; Nick Faldo (England), 1989-90; and Tiger Woods, 2001-02.

BIGGEST VICTORY, YOUNGEST Tiger Woods won the 1997 Masters by a record 12 shots over Tom Kite (U.S.). That year Woods also became the youngest Masters' champion ever, at 21 years, 104 days old.

LOWEST 72-HOLE SCORE The Masters record for lowest 72-hole score is 270, set by Tiger Woods in 1997.

LOWEST 18-HOLE SCORE The lowest Masters score for 18 holes is 63, achieved by Nick Price (Zimbabwe) in 1986 and Greg Norman (Australia) in 1996.

OLDEST CHAMPION Jack Nicklaus, "The Golden Bear," was 46 years, 2 months, 23 days old when he won the 1986 Masters.

U.S. OPEN

The Newport Golf Club (RI) was the site of the first U.S. Open in 1895; Horace Rawlins (England) won it by two shots over Willie Dunn (U.S.). The tournament is held on a different course each year.

The format changed from 36 to 72 holes in 1898. By 1965 play was spread over four days.

MOST WINS Four players have won four times: Willie Anderson (Scotland), 1901, 1903-05; Bobby Jones, 1923, 1926, 1929-30; Ben Hogan, 1948, 1950-51, 1953; and Jack Nicklaus, 1962, 1967 1972, 1980.

MOST CONSECUTIVE WINS The only player to win three straight U.S. Open titles was Willie Anderson, in 1903-1905.

BIGGEST VICTORY MARGIN Tiger Woods won the 2000 U.S. Open by a record 15 shots over Ernie Els (S. Africa) and Miguel Jimenez (Spain).

LOWEST 72-HOLE SCORE The U.S. Open record for lowest 72-hole score is 272, by four players: Jack Nicklaus in 1980; Lee Janzen in 1993; Tiger Woods in 2000; and Jim Furyk in 2003.

LOWEST 18-HOLE SCORE The lowest score shot for 18 holes is 63, by Johnny Miller in 1973, Tom Weiskopf in 1980, and Jack Nicklaus in 1980.

OLDEST CHAMPION Hale Irwin was 45 years, 15 days old when he won at Medinah Country Club in a 1990 playoff over Mike Donald.

YOUNGEST CHAMPION John J. McDermott won the first of his back-to-back U.S. Open titles in 1911, at age 19 years, 10 months, 14 days.

THE LAST TIME...

The last time a golfer won the first three legs of the Grand Slam was in 1953, when Ben Hogan won the Masters, U.S. Open, and British Open titles. He could not get back from the British Open in time to play in the PGA Championship.

SOMETHING TO THINK ABOUT

WINNING DEBUT

With his victory in the 2003 British Open, Ben Curtis (U.S.) became the first golfer to win a title in his first major championship appearance since Francis Ouimet (U.S.) won the 1913 U.S. Open. Curtis also was the first player since Tom Watson (U.S.) in 1975 to win the British Open in his first try, and the first to earn his initial PGA Tour victory at a major since John Daly (U.S.) won the 1991 PGA Championship. Before the British Open, Curtis ranked 396th in the official World Golf Ranking; he jumped to 35th.

BRITISH OPEN

The first British Open Championship was played in Prestwick, Scotland, in 1860. Willie Park won the inaugural event by two shots over Tom Morris Sr.

Competition was expanded from 36 to 72 holes over two days in 1892. Locations vary for the Open, but all venues must be coastal links courses.

MOST WINS Harry Vardon (Scotland) won the Claret Jug a record six times: 1896, 1898-99, 1903, 1911, and 1914.

MOST CONSECUTIVE WINS The only player to win four straight British Open titles is Tom Morris Jr. (Scotland). Young Tom won from 1868 through 1870 and in 1872 (event not held in 1871). Morris's father Tom (Old Tom) had won back-to-back titles in 1861-62.

BIGGEST VICTORY MARGIN Tom Morris Sr. won the 1862 British Open by a record 13 shots over Willie Park Sr. (Scotland) in a 36-hole event.

Over 72 holes the biggest margin is eight shots, achieved four times by three players: John H. Taylor (England) in 1900 and 1913; James Braid (Scotland) in 1908; and Tiger Woods in 2000.

LOWEST 72-HOLE SCORE The British Open record for lowest 72-hole score is 267, shot by Greg Norman in winning the 1993 championship at Royal St. George's GC, England.

LOWEST 18-HOLE SCORE The lowest score shot for 18 holes in any British Open is 63, achieved by seven players: Mark Hayes (U.S.) in 1977; Isao Aoki (Japan) in 1980; Greg Norman in 1986; Paul Broadhurst (England) in 1990; Jodie Mudd (U.S.) in 1991; Nick Faldo in 1993; and Payne Stewart (U.S.) in 1993.

OLDEST CHAMPION Tom Morris Sr. was 46 years, 99 days old when he won the 1867 title.

YOUNGEST CHAMPION Tom Morris Jr. was 17 years, 5 months, 8 days old when he won the 1868 title.

PGA CHAMPIONSHIP

The first PGA Championship was played at the Siwanoy Country Club in Bronxville, NY, in 1916. From 1916 to 1957, the tournament was a match-play event. Jim Barnes (England) won the first title, 1-up over Jock Hutchinson (U.S.) in the final.

The format was switched to 72-hole medal play for the 1958 event, won by Dow Finsterwald (U.S.).

MOST WINS Two players have won a record five PGA Championships: Walter Hagen (U.S.), 1921, 1924-1927; and Jack Nicklaus, 1963, 1971, 1973, 1975, and 1980. Hagen's four straight wins from 1924 to 1927 is the record for the most consecutive victories.

BIGGEST VICTORY MARGIN In the match-play format, the biggest victory was Paul Runyan's (U.S.) 8-and-7 win over Sam Snead (U.S.) in 1938. The largest margin of victory in medal play is seven shots, by Jack Nicklaus in 1980.

LOWEST 72-HOLE SCORE The PGA Championship record lowest 72-hole score is 265, shot by David Toms (U.S.) in winning the 2001 title at the Atlanta Athletic Club in Duluth, GA.

LOWEST 18-HOLE SCORE The lowest 18-hole score in any PGA Championship is 63, a feat achieved by nine players: Bruce Crampton (Australia) in 1975; Raymond Floyd (U.S.) in 1982; Gary Player in 1984; Vijay Singh (Fiji) in 1993; Brad Faxon (U.S.) in 1995; Michael Bradley (U.S.) in 1995; Jose Maria Olazabal (Spain) in 2000; Mark O'Meara (U.S.) in 2001; and Thomas Björn (Denmark) in 2005.

OLDEST CHAMPION Julius Boros (U.S.) was 48 years, 4 months, 18 days old when he won the 1968 title by one shot over Arnold Palmer and Bob Charles.

YOUNGEST CHAMPION Gene Sarazen, "The Squire," was 20 years, 5 months, 22 days old when he won the 1922 title. He beat Emmet French (U.S.), 4-and-3, in the final.

GOLF

PGA Tour

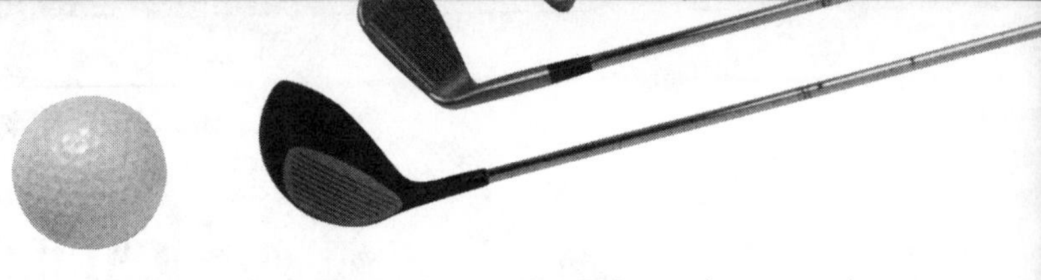

ORGANIZED PROFESSIONAL GOLF IN THE UNITED STATES dates back to the late 19th century. In the 1920s, pro tournaments were regularly staged around the country, and the first "playing pros" group was formed in 1932. The 1950s saw an explosion in golf's popularity, and in the late 1960s the touring professionals split from the existing Professional Golf Association of America (PGA) to form a separate group. The split was healed in 1968 with the creation of the Tournament Players Division of the PGA, This group was renamed the PGA Tour in 1975.

MILESTONES

1926: FIRST $10,000 PURSE The inaugural Los Angeles Open in 1926 offered the first five-figure purse in golf history. Harry Cooper won by three shots over George Von Elm. Nicknamed "Lighthorse," by Damon Runyon for his fast pace of play, Cooper pocketed a check for $3,500.

1933: CORPORATE SPONSOR The Hershey Chocolate Company was the first corporation to sponsor a professional golf tournament—the 1933 Hershey Open.

1938: WOMEN AND MEN Babe Didrikson Zaharias was the first woman to play in a men's professional golf tournament. She received a sponsor invitation to play in the 1938 Los Angeles Open, and shot 84-81, missing the cut. She played in three other men's events, the 1945 Los Angeles Open (missed final round cut), 1945 Phoenix Open (shot 67, finished 33rd), and 1945 Tucson Open (42nd).

It was 58 years before another woman pro entered a PGA Tour event. Annika Sorenstam played in the 2003 Bank of America Colonial, on a sponsor exemption. She missed the cut.

1948: AFRICAN-AMERICAN PLAYERS The first African-American golfers to play in a professional event were Ted Rhodes and Bill Spiller, who competed in the 1948 Los Angeles Open. Spiller finished 33rd and Rhodes came in 35th. At the time, PGA policy left the decision to allow non-white players to the tournament's sponsors.

In 1961 the PGA Tour was officially integrated.

The first African-American to win an official PGA Tour title was Pete Brown at the 1964 Waco Turner Open.

1954: $100,000 PURSE The Tam O'Shanter World Championship of Golf was the first tournament to offer a $100,000 purse, in 1954. Bob Toski won the $50,000 first-place prize.

1983: ALL-EXEMPT TOUR Under a system introduced in 1983, touring pros received a qualifying exemption for an entire season or more by meeting stated criteria, such as finishing in the top 125 of the money list or winning designated tournaments. This virtually eliminated Monday qualifying from the pro tour.

1986: MILLION-DOLLAR PURSE The 1986 Panasonic Las Vegas Invitational offered the first $1 million purse in PGA Tour history. Greg Norman won the 90-hole event by seven shots over Dan Pohl for a prize of $207,000.

Selected PGA Tour Scoring Records

RECORD	SCORE	PLAYER	EVENT
Lowest Score (18 holes)	59	Al Geiberger	1977 Memphis Classic (2nd round)
	59	Chip Beck	1991 Las Vegas Invitational (3rd round)
	59	David Duval	1999 Bob Hope Chrysler Classic (5th round)
Lowest Score (72 holes)	254	Tommy Armour III	2003 Valero Texas Open
Lowest Score (90 holes)	324	Joe Durant	2001 Bob Hope Chrysler Classic
Most Strokes Under Par (72 holes)	31	Ernie Els	2003 Mercedes Championship
Most Strokes Under Par (90 holes)	36	Joe Durant	2001 Bob Hope Chrysler Classic
Fewest Putts (18 holes)	18	Sam Trahan	1979 IV Philadelphia Golf Classic (4th round)
	18	Mike McGee	1987 FedEx St. Jude Classic (1st round)
	18	Kenny Knox	1989 MCI Heritage Classic (1st round)
	18	Andy North	1990 Anheuser-Busch Golf Classic (2nd round)
	18	Jim McGovern	1992 FedEx St. Jude Classic (2nd round)
	18	Corey Pavin	2000 Bell Canadian Open (2nd round)
Fewest Putts (72 holes)	93	Kenny Knox	1989 MCI Heritage Classic
	93	Mark Calcavecchia	2002 Greater Greensboro Chrysler Classic
Most Consecutive Cuts	142	Tiger Woods	ended May 2005 at Byron Nelson Championship

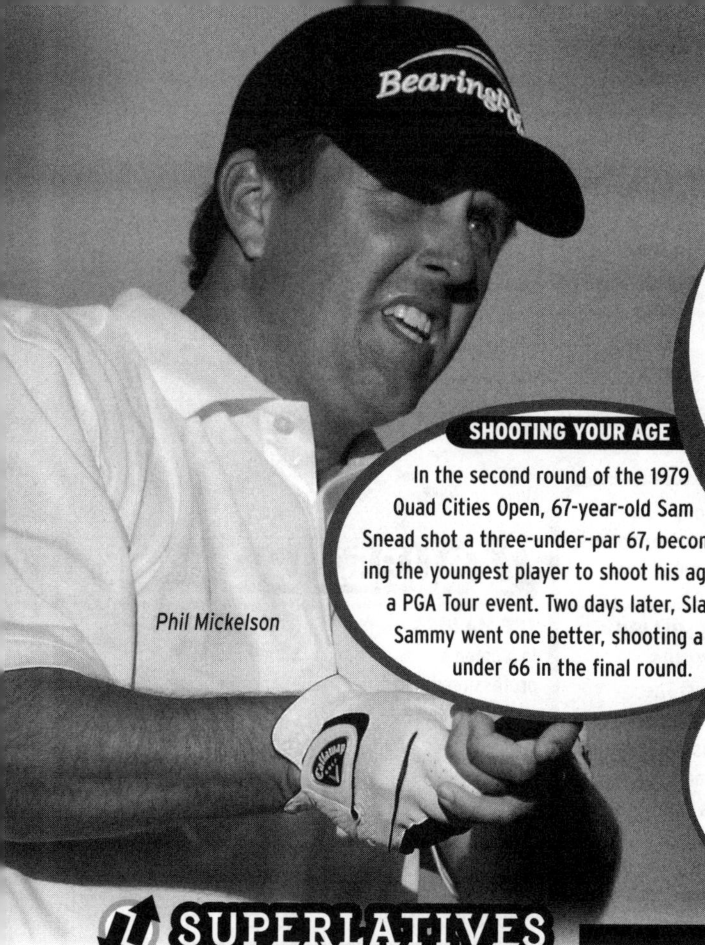

Phil Mickelson

SOMETHING TO THINK ABOUT

SHOOTING YOUR AGE

In the second round of the 1979 Quad Cities Open, 67-year-old Sam Snead shot a three-under-par 67, becoming the youngest player to shoot his age in a PGA Tour event. Two days later, Slammin' Sammy went one better, shooting a four-under 66 in the final round.

THE WHEELS CAME OFF

Four players have experienced the sinking feeling of teeing off in a final round with a six-shot lead only to let it slip away and lose the tournament. The first was Bobby Cruickshank at the 1928 Florida Open. He wasn't joined in the record books until 41 years later, when Gay Brewer blew his big lead at the 1969 Danny Thomas-Diplomat Classic. Hal Sutton lost his lead at the 1983 Anheuser-Busch Golf Classic, before a huge television audience. And in the final round of the 1996 Masters, Greg Norman saw his lead wilt by the 11th hole. When playing partner and winner Nick Faldo was asked what he said to Norman at the end, he replied, "I just hugged him."

ACE ASSIST

The first player to make a hole-in-one on a par-4 in a PGA Tour event is Andrew Magee. In the first round of the 2001 Phoenix Open, his tee shot at the 332-yard 17th hole found the bottom of the cup—with an assist from Tom Byrum's putter. Playing in the group ahead, Byrum was lining up a putt when Magee's tee ball bounced up onto the green, hit Byrum's putter, and was redirected into the hole. Quipped caddy Rusty Uresti, "It was the first putt Tom made all day."

SUPERLATIVES

MOST WINS

CAREER The record for the most wins in official PGA Tour events is 82 by Sam Snead. His first victory came in 1936; his last in 1965. Snead's best year on tour was 1950, when he won 11 titles.

He led the Tour in most season wins four times: 1938, 1941, 1950, and 1952 (tied with Jack Burke Jr.).

MOST WINS

SEASON Byron Nelson won 18 tournaments in 1945, including a record 11 consecutive wins (see below).

MOST CONSECUTIVE WINS In 1945, Byron Nelson won 11 straight PGA-sanctioned tournaments: the Miami International Four Ball, Charlotte Open, Greater Greensboro Open, Durham Open, Atlanta Open, Montreal Open, Philadelphia Inquirer Invitational, Chicago Victory National Open, PGA Championship, Tam O'Shanter Open, and Canadian Open.

Nelson earned $30,250 during the winning streak. He also won a 12th tournament in Spring Lake, NJ, but it is not counted as an official event since the purse was below the PGA minimum.

MOST WINS

SINGLE EVENT Sam Snead won the Greater Greensboro Open eight times, in 1938, 1946, 1949-50, 1955-56, 1960, and 1965.

MOST CONSECUTIVE WINS

SINGLE EVENT The record for same event consecutive wins is four, held by four golfers: Tom Morris Jr. in the British Open (not a PGA event), 1868-70 and 1872 (no event in 1871); Walter Hagen in the PGA Championship, 1924 to 1927; Gene Sarazen in the Miami Open, 1926, 1928-30 (no event in 1927); and Tiger Woods in the Bay Hill Invitational, 2000-2003.

MOST CONSECUTIVE YEARS Longtime rivals Jack Nicklaus and Arnold Palmer each won at least one tournament in 17 straight years. Palmer's streak ran from 1955 (Canadian Open) to 1971 when he won the PGA Team Championship, with Nicklaus as his partner.

Nicklaus won two tournaments a year from 1962 (including his first profesional win, at the U.S. Open in a classic duel with Palmer) to 1978 when he won four PGA events plus the British and Australian Opens.

THE LAST TIME...

The last time an amateur golfer won a PGA Tour event was in 1991, when Phil Mickelson won the Northern Telecom Open in Phoenix, AZ.

GOLF

LPGA Tour

THE FIRST WOMEN'S PROFESSIONAL GOLF ASSOCIATION was founded in 1944 by three players: Hope Seignious, Betty Hicks, and Ellen Griffin. They called their group the Women's Professional Golf Association (WPGA). After three years of financial struggle, the WPGA seemed on the verge of folding when the Wilson Sporting Goods company stepped in to underwrite the Tour in 1947. The name was changed to the Ladies Professional Golf Association (LPGA) and three years later, the LPGA received its official charter.

Michelle Wie ▶

MILESTONES

1950: FOUNDING MEMBERS When the LPGA was officially founded in 1950, the original 13 founding members were Alice Bauer, Patty Berg, Bettye Danoff, Helen Dettweiler, Marlene Hagge, Helen Hicks, Opal Hill, Betty Jameson, Sally Sessions, Marilynn Smith, Shirley Spork, Louise Suggs, and Babe Zaharias.

1962: ROOKIE OF THE YEAR The LPGA created a Rookie of the Year award in 1962. The first winner was Mary Mills. She earned more than $8,000 in her first year on Tour.

1963: TELEVISED EVENT The first nationally televised LPGA event was the final round of the 1963 U.S. Women's Open, held at the Kenwood CC in Cincinnati, OH. The tournament was won by Mary Mills, who beat Sandra Haynie and Louise Suggs by two shots.

The first event televised nationally for all four rounds was the 1982 Nabisco Dinah Shore tournament, which was won by Sally Little.

1976: $100,000 SEASON The first player to win more than $100,000 in a season on the LPGA Tour was Judy Rankin in 1976. That season she won six tour events and $150,734 in prize money.

1978: TRIPLE CROWN WINNER In 1978, rookie sensation Nancy Lopez burst onto the LPGA Tour and gave unprecedented media exposure to the Tour. Lopez won nine tournaments that year and became the first, and so far only, player to win Rookie of the Year, LPGA Player of the Year, and Vare Trophy (lowest average score) honors in the same season.

1981: $1 MILLION IN EARNINGS

CAREER The first female golfer to surpass the $1 million mark in career earnings was Kathy Whitworth. The LPGA Tour's all-time career-wins leader passed the seven-figure milestone when she finished third at the 1981 U.S. Women's Open.

1996: $1 MILLION IN EARNINGS

ROOKIE In 1996, Karrie Webb, a 21-year-old phenomenon from Australia, became the first rookie in golf history (man or woman) to surpass $1 million in season earnings. She won four events that season and earned $1,002,000. Needless to say, she was the runaway winner of the 1996 Rookie of the Year award.

SUPERLATIVES

THE MAJORS
In women's professional golf three events—the U.S. Women's Open, the Titleholders Championships, and the Western Open—were the major championships from 1946 to 1954. In 1955, the Women's LPGA Championship was added to the major's roster.

The U.S. Open and the LPGA Championship have remained majors since, but the roster of majors has changed several times over the years. Currently, the Nabisco Championship and the British Women's Open are the other two majors.

CAREER GRAND SLAM Seven players have completed the career Grand Slam, winning all the major tournaments at least once during their career: Babe Zaharias (completed her Grand Slam in 1948 - three events), Louise Suggs (1957), Mickey Wright (1962), Pat Bradley (1986), Juli Inkster (1999), Karrie Webb (2001), and Annika Sorenstam (2003).

SUPER CAREER GRAND SLAM
Karrie Webb is the only golfer to win five designated Grand Slam events during her career. The Australian player won the 1999 du Maurier Classic, the 2000 Nabisco Championship, the 2000 and 2001 U.S. Open, the 2001 LPGA Championship, and the 2002 British Open.

The Du Maurier Classic ended in 2000 and was replaced as a major by the British Open in 2001. With her victory in the 2002 British Open, Webb's feat was dubbed the "Super Career Grand Slam."

LARGEST FREE-FLOATING ICEBERG—B15A, ANTARCTICA, p. 289

MT. KILIMANJARO—TALLEST MOUNTAIN IN AFRICA, p. 174

BIGGEST CUT DIAMOND—545.67-CARAT "GOLDEN JUBILEE" FROM SOUTH AFRICA, ABOUT THE SIZE OF A DOUGHNUT HOLE, p. 337

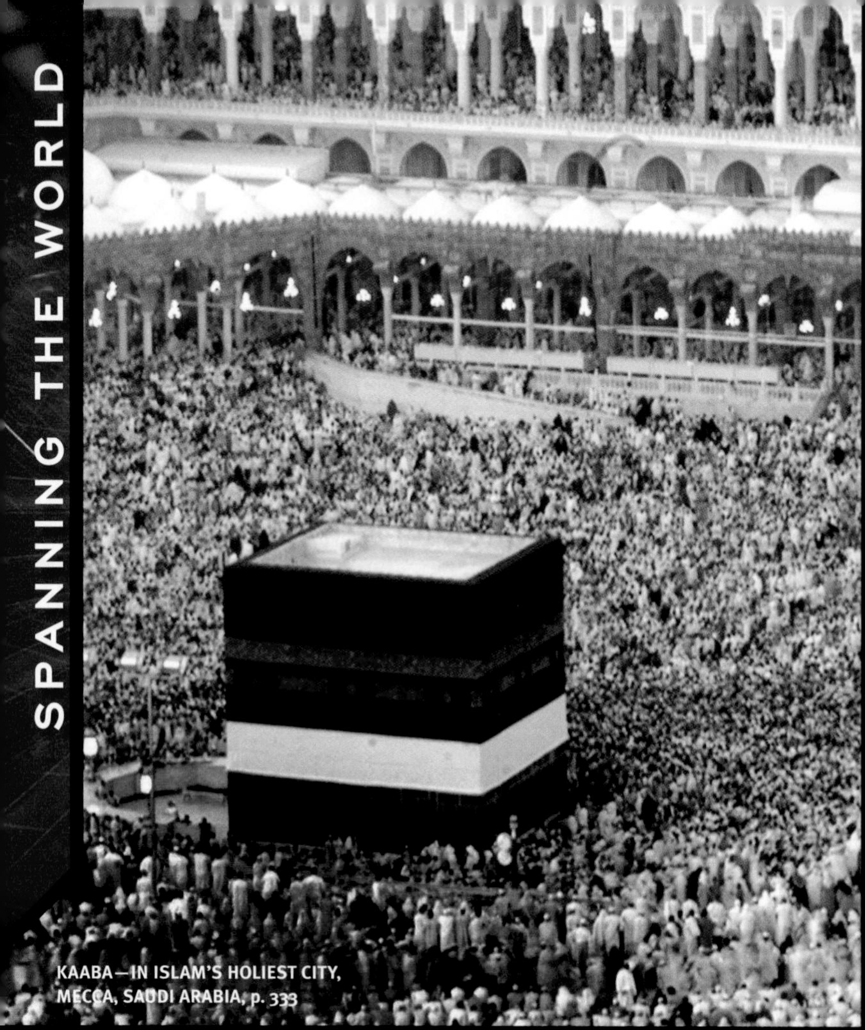

KAABA—IN ISLAM'S HOLIEST CITY, MECCA, SAUDI ARABIA, p. 333

CHICHÉN ITZÁ RUINS—ANCIENT MAYAN SETTLEMENT, MEXICO, p. 318

PARTHENON—CONSTRUCTED IN THE GOLDEN AGE OF ATHENS, p. 306

MOST MOVIES—INDIA'S "BOLLYWOOD" FILM STUDIOS (SHOWN: *DEVDAS* FROM 2002), p. 309

MOST MEDALS, ONE OLYMPIAD—
MICHAEL PHELPS (SHARED), 2004, p. 445

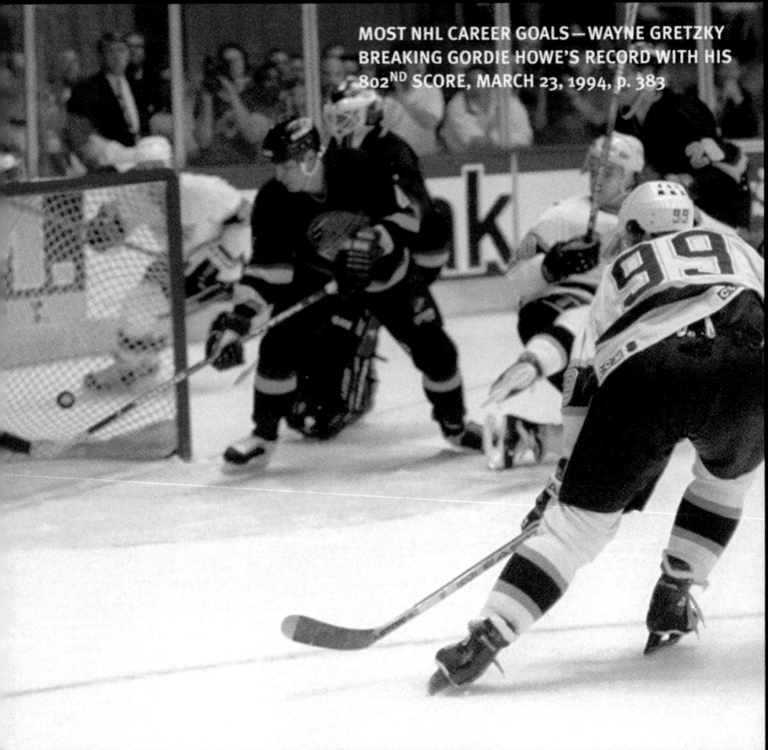

MOST NHL CAREER GOALS—WAYNE GRETZKY
BREAKING GORDIE HOWE'S RECORD WITH HIS
802ND SCORE, MARCH 23, 1994, p. 383

DANNY WAY JUMPS THE GREAT WALL
OF CHINA, JULY 9, 2005, p. 447

INDY 500 FIRST FEMALE LEADER—DANICA PATRICK, p. 389

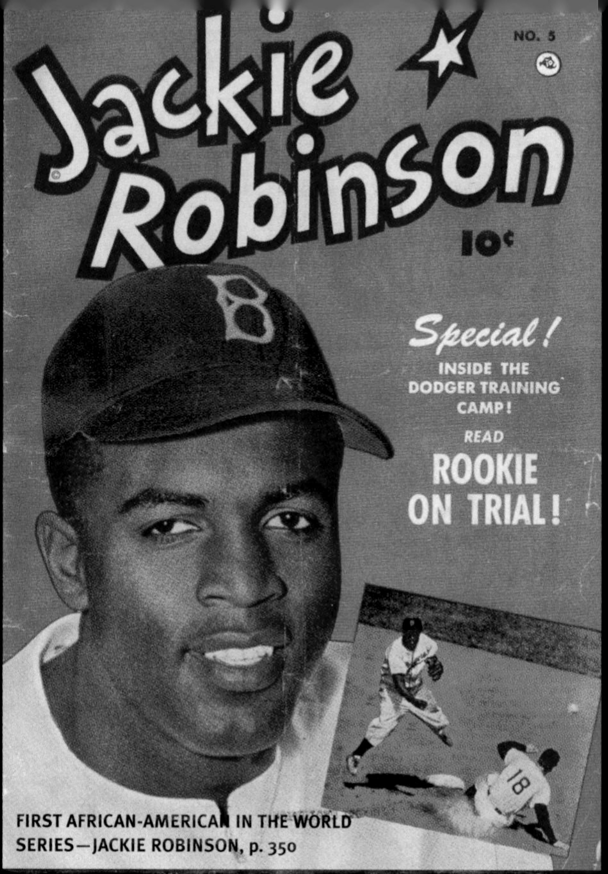

FIRST AFRICAN-AMERICAN IN THE WORLD SERIES—JACKIE ROBINSON, p. 350

GOLF'S MAJOR TOURNAMENT STARS—JACK NICKLAUS (LEFT), TIGER WOODS (RIGHT), pp. 396, 397

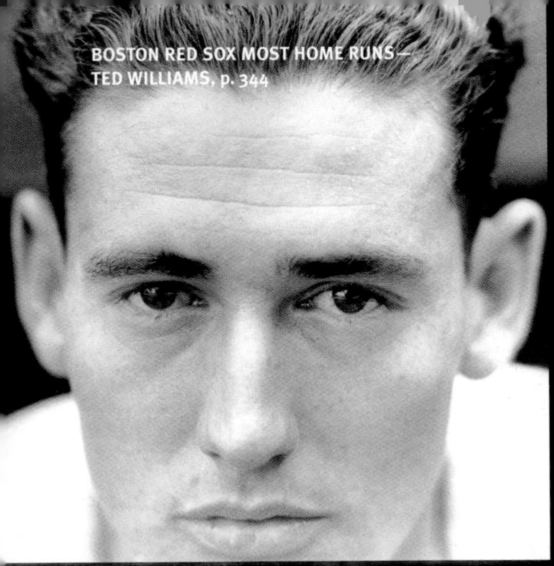

BOSTON RED SOX MOST HOME RUNS—TED WILLIAMS, p. 344

MOST NASCAR SEASON TITLES—DALE EARNHARDT (SHARED); PICTURED WITH SON DALE JR. (LEFT), p. 387

MOST MLS CUP FINAL GOALS—LANDON DONOVAN, p. 393

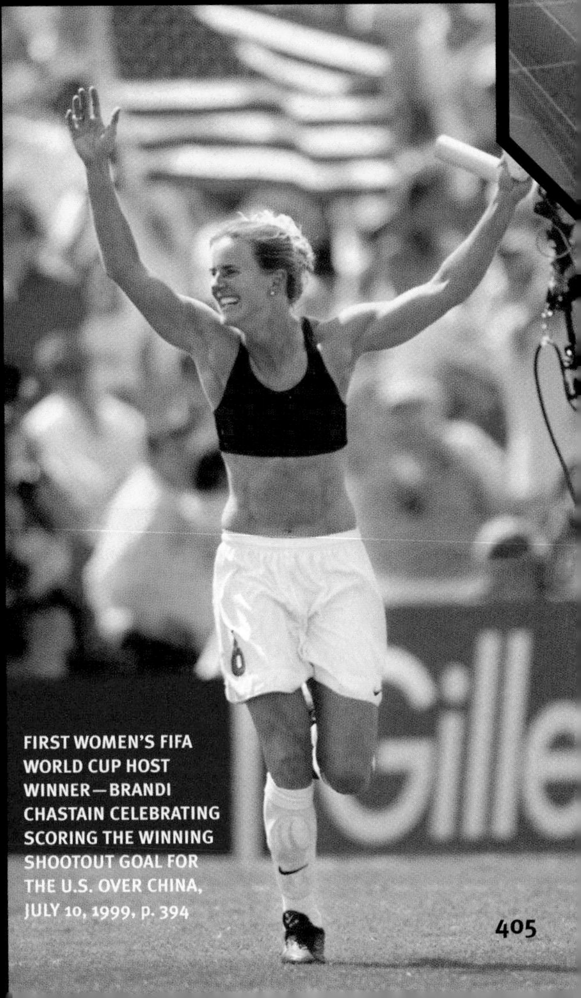

FIRST WOMEN'S FIFA WORLD CUP HOST WINNER—BRANDI CHASTAIN CELEBRATING SCORING THE WINNING SHOOTOUT GOAL FOR THE U.S. OVER CHINA, JULY 10, 1999, p. 394

MOST NBA FINALS MVP AWARDS—MICHAEL JORDAN SINKS THE WINNING HOOP TO WIN HIS 6TH NBA TITLE AND MVP AWARD WITH THE CHICAGO BULLS, JUNE 14, 1998, p. 375

MICHAEL JORDAN, p. 375

MOST NFL TOUCHDOWNS (SEASON)—SHAUN ALEXANDER, 2005, p. 359

YOUNGEST NBA PLAYER WITH TRIPLE DOUBLE—LEBRON JAMES, 2005, p. 373

CLEVELAND BROWNS MOST CAREER RUSHING YARDAGE—JIM BROWN, PICTURED IN 1960, p. 356

MOST NFL TOUCHDOWN PASSES (SEASON)—PEYTON MANNING THROWING HIS 49TH TD PASS, DEC. 26, 2004, p. 359

NBA GREATS BILL RUSSELL (LEFT) AND WILT CHAMBERLAIN, 1967, pp. 370–375

WNBA HIGHEST CAREER SCORING AVERAGE—CYNTHIA COOPER, p. 380

IVORY-BILLED WOODPECKER—THOUGHT EXTINCT FOR 40 YEARS, REDISCOVERED IN ARKANSAS IN 2005, p. 467

LARGEST PRESIDENTIAL PORTRAITS, MT. RUSHMORE (SD), pp. 456-457, 489

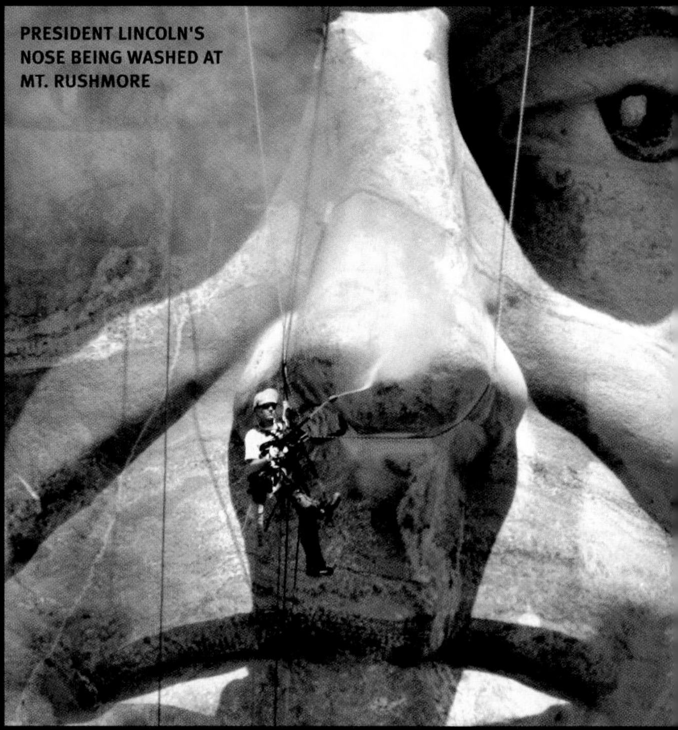

PRESIDENT LINCOLN'S NOSE BEING WASHED AT MT. RUSHMORE

LAS VEGAS-PARADISE—FASTEST-GROWING METROPOLITAN AREA, p. 476

LONGEST RIVER IN NORTH AMERICA—THE MISSISSIPPI, PICTURED FROM SPACE (ABOUT 10 MILES ALONG AR, LA, MS SHOWN), p. 454

LPGA Tour Scoring Records

RECORD		PLAYER	EVENT
Lowest Score (18 holes)	59	Annika Sorenstam	2001 Standard Register PING (2nd Round)
Lowest Score (72 holes)	259	Wendy Doolan	2003 Welch's/Fry's Championship
Most Strokes Under Par (18 holes)	13	Annika Sorenstam	2001 Standard Register PING (2nd Round)
Most Strokes Under Par (72 holes)	27	Annika Sorenstam	2001 Standard Register PING
Largest Margin of Victory (72 holes)	14 strokes	Cindy Mackey	1986 MasterCard International Pro-Am
Largest Come-from-Behind Win	10 strokes	Mickey Wright	1964 Tall City Open
		Annika Sorenstam	2001 The Office Depot hosted by Amy Alcott
Most Holes in One	11 times	Kathy Whitworth	Career record

MOST MAJORS WON

CAREER The most majors won in a career is 15 by Patty Berg. She won one U.S. Open (1946), seven Titleholders (1937, 1938, 1939, 1948, 1953, 1955, 1957), and seven Western Opens (1941, 1943, 1948, 1951, 1955, 1957, 1958).

OLDEST WINNER

MAJOR Fay Crocker is the oldest player to win a major Championship. She won the 1960 Titleholders Championship at the age of 45 years, 7 months, 1 day.

YOUNGEST WINNER

CAREER Sandra Post is the youngest player to win a major championship. She won the 1968 LPGA Championship at the age of 20 years, 19 days.

LPGA TOUR

MOST WINS

CAREER The record for the most official LPGA Tour event wins is 88, held by Kathy Whitworth. Her first victory came in 1962 at the Kelly Girl Open, and her last in 1985 at the United Virginia Bank Classic. Whitworth's best year on Tour was 1968, when she won 10 titles.

She led the Tour in season wins seven times: 1965 through 1967, 1968 (tied with Carol Mann), 1971, 1972 (tied with Jane Blalock), 1973.

MOST WINS

SEASON Mickey Wright won 13 tournaments in 1963. That season, Wright won 40% of the LPGA events (13 of 32), and recorded 27 top-10 finishes in 28 starts.

MOST WINS

CONSECUTIVE In 1978, Nancy Lopez was the first to win five LPGA tournaments in a row: Greater Baltimore Classic, Coca-Cola Classic, Golden Lights Championship, LPGA Championship, and the Bankers Trust Classic. These were not consecutive Tour events, but were events she consecutively entered.

Annika Sorenstam matched Lopez with five consecutive wins in 2004-2005, concluding her streak with a win at the Kraft Nabisco Championship in March 2005.

The record for winning consecutively scheduled LPGA Tour events is held by three players at four wins: Mickey Wright (1962 and 1963), Kathy Whitworth (1969), and Sorenstam (2001).

OLDEST WINNER

The oldest player to win an official LPGA Tour event is Beth Daniel. The Hall of Fame player was 46 years, 8 months, 29 days old when she won the 2003 BMO Financial Group Canadian Women's Open.

YOUNGEST WINNER

Marlene Hagge was 18 years, 14 days old when she won the 1952 Sarasota Open, the youngest player to win an LPGA Tour event. Hagge, who turned professional two weeks before her 16th birthday, won 26 events during her Hall of Fame career.

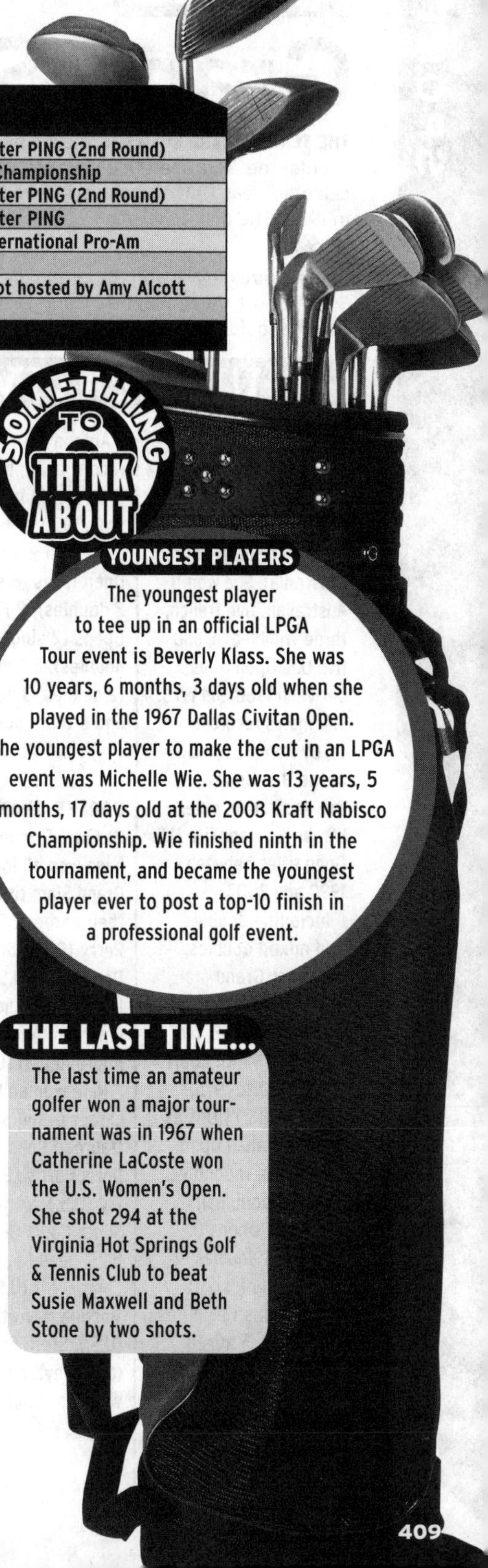

SOMETHING TO THINK ABOUT

YOUNGEST PLAYERS

The youngest player to tee up in an official LPGA Tour event is Beverly Klass. She was 10 years, 6 months, 3 days old when she played in the 1967 Dallas Civitan Open. The youngest player to make the cut in an LPGA event was Michelle Wie. She was 13 years, 5 months, 17 days old at the 2003 Kraft Nabisco Championship. Wie finished ninth in the tournament, and became the youngest player ever to post a top-10 finish in a professional golf event.

THE LAST TIME...

The last time an amateur golfer won a major tournament was in 1967 when Catherine LaCoste won the U.S. Women's Open. She shot 294 at the Virginia Hot Springs Golf & Tennis Club to beat Susie Maxwell and Beth Stone by two shots.

Venus Williams

Grand Slams

THE TENNIS GRAND SLAM is achieved by winning all four designated Grand Slam events—the Australian Open, French Open, Wimbledon, and U.S. Open—in one calendar year. Only five players have done this. The first was Donald Budge (U.S.) in 1938. The only other man was Rod Laver (Australia), who did it twice (1962 and 1969).

Three women have won the Grand Slam: Maureen Connolly (U.S., 1953), Margaret Smith Court (Australia, 1970), and Steffi Graf (Germany, 1988). Graf also won an Olympic gold medal in 1988, becoming the only player to win the "Golden Slam."

SUPERLATIVES

MOST GRAND SLAM TITLES The most singles titles won in the Slams is 24, by Margaret Smith Court (Australia). She won 11 Australian, five French, three Wimbledon, and five U.S. Open titles between 1960 and 1973. The men's record is 14, by Pete Sampras of the U.S. He won two Australian, seven Wimbledon, and five U.S. Open titles between 1990 and 2002.

Including doubles and mixed doubles, the most Grand Slam events won by any player is 62, by Margaret Smith Court. From 1960 to 1975, Court won 21 titles at the Australian Open (11 singles, 8 doubles, 2 mixed doubles), 13 French Opens (5 singles, 4 doubles, 4 mixed doubles), 10 Wimbledons (3 singles, 2 doubles, 5 mixed doubles), and 18 U.S. Opens (5 singles, 5 doubles, 8 mixed doubles).

Among men the record is 28, by Roy Emerson (Australia). From 1959 to 1971, he picked up 9 Australian Open titles (6 singles, 3 doubles), 8 French Opens (2 singles, 6 doubles), 5 Wimbledons (2 singles, 3 doubles), and 6 U.S. Opens (2 singles, 4 doubles).

CAREER GRAND SLAM Five men have won all four Grand Slam titles in their careers: Fred Perry (Great Britain), Don Budge (U.S.), Rod Laver (Australia), Roy Emerson (Australia), and Andre Agassi (U.S.).

Nine women have career Grand Slams: Maureen Connolly (U.S.), Doris Hart (U.S.), Shirley Fry (U.S.), Margaret Smith Court (Australia), Billie Jean King (U.S.), Chris Evert (U.S.), Martina Navratilova (U.S.), Steffi Graf (Germany), and Serena Williams (U.S.).

AUSTRALIAN OPEN

The Australian Open began as the 1905 Australasian Championships, and the venue varied. In fact, the event was staged in New Zealand in 1906 and 1912. But in 1972, it was decided that Melbourne, Australia, would be the permanent host city. Women first played in the tournament in 1922.

It was named the Australian Championships in 1927 and the Australian Open in 1969. It has been considered a Grand Slam event since 1927.

MOST WINS **SINGLES** Margaret Smith Court earned 11 Australian Open singles titles, the most ever by a player. She won every Open between 1960 and 1966, again in 1969-71 and 1973.

The most wins by a man is six by Roy Emerson. He won in 1961 and 1963-67.

MOST WINS **DOUBLES** The most titles won by a doubles team is 10, by Nancye Wynne Bolton and Thelma Coyne Long (both Australian). The pair combined to win the doubles from 1936 to 1940, 1947 to 1949, and 1951 to 1952. Long won two other titles with Mary Hawton, for a record 12 doubles titles.

YOUNGEST CHAMPIONS **SINGLES** The youngest winner of the Australian Open is Martina Hingis (Switzerland). She won the 1997 Open at age 16 years, 117 days. The youngest men's champion is Ken Rosewall (Australia). He won the 1953 Open at age 18 years, 2 months.

FRENCH OPEN

The first French championships were first held in 1891 but were restricted to members of French tennis clubs until 1925. For that reason Grand Slam records only include the French Open from 1925 onwards. The tournament has been played at the Stade Roland Garros in Paris since 1928.

MOST WINS **SINGLES** The most singles titles won at the French Open is seven by Chris Evert (U.S.). She won in

THE LAST TIME...

The last time a player won the men's singles at Wimbledon using a wooden racket was John McEnroe (U.S.) in 1981. He beat Bjorn Borg in four sets, 4-6, 7-6, 7-6, 6-4. It was McEnroe's first Wimbledon win, and snapped Borg's record-breaking, five-year winning streak.

SOMETHING TO THINK ABOUT

HOME SWEET HOME

The American men enjoy playing in the U.S. Open. In the "Open era" (since 1968), the singles championship has been won 19 times by seven American players. Other hosts of Grand Slam events during the same period have been less successful. At the Australian Open, five Australian players in all won a total of seven titles since 1968; the last Aussie to win was Mark Edmondson in 1976. Only one French player won the French Open in the same span, Yannick Noah (1983). And no British player has won the men's title at Wimbledon since Fred Perry won his third straight in 1936.

MOST WIMBLEDON TITLES

Billie Jean King and Martina Navratilova have both won a record 20 tennis titles at Wimbledon (singles and doubles combined). But the record for most Wimbledon titles of any kind goes to Bernard Neal, a retired engineering professor—who has won 37 croquet titles at the All England Lawn Tennis and Croquet Club.

1974-75, 1979-80, 1983, and 1985-86. The most wins in the men's event is six by Bjorn Borg (Sweden). He won in 1974-75 and from 1978 to 1981.

MOST WINS
DOUBLES
Gigi Fernandez (U.S.) and Natasha Zvereva (Belarus) won five times—each year from 1992 to 1995, and again in 1997. Martina Navratilova won a record total of seven doubles titles while playing with four different partners.

YOUNGEST CHAMPIONS
The youngest winner of the French Open is Monica Seles (then Yugoslavia). She won the 1990 Open at the age of 16 years, 169 days. The youngest men's champion is Michael Chang (U.S.). He won the 1989 Open at the age of 17 years, 109 days.

WIMBLEDON

Held at the All England Lawn Tennis and Croquet Club, in Wimbledon, England, the world's most prestigious tennis tournament is officially called the "Lawn Tennis Championships."

First held in 1877, Wimbledon started out as a challenge event, meaning the defending champion automatically qualified for the following year's final and played only one match, which was against the winner of the challenger event.

Beginning in 1922, the "challenge round" was done away with, along with automatic qualification for the previous year's winner. In 1884 a competition for women was added, as well as men's doubles.

MOST WINS
SINGLES Martina Navratilova won a record nine singles titles at Wimbledon. She held the Venus Rosewater Dish (the prize for the event) aloft at Center Court in 1978, 1979, 1982-87, and 1990.

Two men have won seven titles in their careers: William Renshaw (Great Britain) in 1881-86 and again in 1889; and Pete Sampras, 1993-95, 1997-2000. All of Renshaw's victories came during the "challenge round" era.

MOST WINS
DOUBLES The most doubles titles won at Wimbledon by one team is eight by Lawrence and Reginald Doherty (Great Britain). They won the title in 1897-1901 and 1903-05.

YOUNGEST CHAMPIONS
The youngest Wimbledon singles champion is Charlotte "Lottie" Dod (Great Britain). She won the 1887 title at the age of 15 years, 285 days. The youngest men's winner is Boris Becker (Germany), who was 17 years, 227 days old when he won the 1985 championship.

UNITED STATES OPEN

The first official U.S. championship was held in 1881. The U.S. Open was played under a challenger format, much like that of Wimbledon, from 1884 to 1911. In 1968 and 1969, separate amateur and professional championships were held.

MOST WINS
SINGLES
Molla Bjurstedt Mallory (U.S.) won the U.S. Open eight times, the most by anyone. She won the women's singles title in 1915-18 and 1920-22, and in 1926. Three players have won the men's singles title seven times: Richard Sears (U.S.), 1881-87; William Larned (U.S.), 1901-02 and 1907-11; Bill Tilden (U.S.), from 1920-25, and in 1929.

MOST WINS
DOUBLES The team of Althea Louise Brough and Margaret Osborne duPont won a record 12 doubles titles. They won in 1942-50 and 1955-57. DuPont had previously won the doubles with Sarah Fabyan in 1941, which gives her a record total of 13.

YOUNGEST CHAMPIONS
The youngest singles champion at the U.S. Open was Tracy Austin (U.S.), who won the 1979 Open at the age of 16 years, 271 days. The youngest men's champion is Pete Sampras. He was 19 years, 28 days old when he won in 1990.

TENNIS

ATP and WTA Tours

UNTIL 1968, ONLY AMATEURS were allowed to play in Grand Slam events, the sport's prestigious tournaments, and they had little influence over how things were done. This changed as more and more top players turned pro to play in rival tournaments. The French Open and Wimbledon allowed professionals to play in 1968, the start of the "Open era," and in effect the start of modern-day professional tennis. In 1972, the men formed their own group, the Association of Tennis Professionals (ATP). The Women's Tennis Association (WTA) followed the next year. Since then pro tennis has evolved from a series of mini-tours, independent tournaments, and Grand Slam events into two unified series of events known as the ATP Tour and the WTA Tour.

Jimmy Connors ►

MILESTONES

1968: FIRST "OPEN ERA" EVENT The first tennis tournament of the "Open era" was the 1968 British Hard Court Championships, won by Ken Rosewall (Australia). The next month, Rosewall won the first Grand Slam title of the era, the 1968 French Open.

1970: WOMEN'S PRO CIRCUIT In 1970, Billie Jean King led eight other women players to form their own Virginia Slims professional circuit. The spark for the breakaway was the purse for the 1970 Pacific South West Open in Los Angeles, which provided over eight times more prize money for men than for women ($12,500 compared to $1,500).

Supported by *World Tennis Magazine* editor Gladys Heldman and Joe Cullman of Philip Morris, the first Virginia Slims event was played in Houston on Sept. 23, 1970, with a purse of $7,500. The following year, the Virginia Slims Circuit was increased to 19 tournaments. In 1971, King became the first female athlete to win more than $100,000 in a season, raking in $117,000.

1973: BOYCOTT In 1973, the men's pro group, Association of Tennis Professionals (ATP), called for a boycott of the Wimbledon Championships, the sport's most prestigious event, to protest the suspension of ATP member Nikki Pilic by the Yugoslavia Federation for missing a Davis Cup match. The boycott was honored by the majority of ATP members.

1973: ATP RANKINGS The first official ATP ranking of players was introduced on Aug. 23, 1973. Ilie Nastase (Romania) was the first player to lead the rankings, a position he held for the rest of the year to become the first end-of-the-season No. 1 ranked player. Nastase held the top spot for 40 weeks before John Newcombe (Australia) took it on June 3, 1974.

1975: WTA RANKINGS The women's computer ranking was introduced on Nov. 3, 1975. Chris Evert (U.S.) was the first player to lead the rankings, a position she held for 140 weeks before Martina Navratilova (U.S.) took the No. 1 spot on July 10, 1978.

1971: A MILLION IN EARNINGS **CAREER** The Australian Rod Laver was the first player to pass $1 million in career earnings. "Rocket" shot past the mark in Dallas, TX, in 1971 on the last stop of the 20-city, million-dollar "World Championship of Tennis" tour. As runner-up, his $20,000 purse gave him a year's total of $292,717 in prize money and a nine-year career total of $1,006,947. He retired as the all-time money leader in 1978 with $1,564,213.

1976: A MILLION IN EARNINGS (WOMEN) **CAREER** Chris Evert was the first female athlete to earn more than $1 million in career earnings. She passed the million-dollar mark when she won the 1976 Colgate Series Championships in Palm Springs, CA. Evert had turned professional in 1971.

1979: A MILLION IN EARNINGS **SEASON** The first player to top the season money list with over $1 million in prize money was Bjorn Borg (Sweden) in 1979. That year he won $1,008,742, just edging out John McEnroe (U.S.), who also topped the million mark. McEnroe earned $1,001,745 in prize money that season.

1982: A MILLION IN EARNINGS (WOMEN) **SEASON** The first female tennis player to earn more than $1 million in a season was Martina Navratilova in 1982. That year Navratilova won 15 Tour events, including the French Open and Wimbledon, and $1,475,055 in prize money. Her match record that year was 90 wins, 3 losses, and she posted a then-record .968 winning percentage.

The following year, Navratilova posted an 86-1 record, with a .989 winning percentage, which still stands as the all-time Tour record.

SUPERLATIVES

MOST SINGLES TITLES **CAREER** The record for most singles tournaments won is 167 by Martina Navratilova. She won her first title in 1974 and her last in 1994.

The record for most men's singles titles is 109, held by Jimmy Connors (U.S.). He won his first title in 1972 and his last in 1989.

SINGLES TITLES **SEASON** The record for most singles titles won in a season is 21, held by Margaret Court (Australia) in 1970. The men's record is 16, set by Guillermo Vilas (Argentina) in 1977.

WEEKS AT NO. 1 The record for most total weeks ranked as No. 1 by the WTA is 377, held by Steffi Graf (Germany). The 1988 "Golden Grand Slam" winner (she won all four Grand Slam tournaments and that year's Olympic gold medal) first topped the rankings on Aug. 17, 1987. Between 1987 and 1997, Graf held the No. 1 rank seven different times.

The record for the most total weeks ranked as No. 1 by the ATP (men) is 286, held by Pete Sampras (U.S.). The seven-time Wimbledon champion was first ranked No. 1 on Apr. 12, 1993. Between 1993 and 2000, Sampras held the No. 1 ranking on 11 separate occasions. His longest streak at the top was 102 weeks from April 15, 1996, to March 30, 1998.

STRAIGHT WEEKS AT NO. 1 The record for most consecutive weeks ranked No. 1 by the WTA is 186, held by Steffi Graf. She rose to the top on Aug. 17, 1987, and held on until she was overtaken by Monica Seles (Yugoslavia) on March 11, 1991.

The ATP record is 160 weeks, held by Jimmy Connors. He rose to the top on July 29, 1974, and held the top spot until overtaken by Bjorn Borg (Sweden) on Aug. 23, 1977.

YOUNGEST NO. 1 The youngest player to top the WTA rankings was Martina Hingis (Switzerland). She officially became the world's No. 1 female player on March 31, 1997, at the age of 16 years, 6 months, 1 day, and held the spot for 80 weeks. She lost the ranking to Lindsay Davenport (U.S.) on Oct. 12, 1998.

The youngest player to top the ATP rankings is Lleyton Hewitt (Australia). He became the world's No. 1 ranked male player on Nov. 19, 2001, at the age of 20 years, 8 months. He lost the spot to Andre Agassi (U.S.) on Apr. 28, 2003.

LONGEST WINNING STREAK The longest winning streak in the "Open era" is 74 matches by Martina Navratilova in 1984. Her streak was snapped by Helena Sukova (Czechoslovakia) on Dec. 6, 1984, in the semifinal of the Australian Open.

The men's record is 49, by Bjorn Borg in 1978.

SOMETHING TO THINK ABOUT

NO SURFACE TENSION

Seven-time French Open champion Chris Evert is known for her modesty, but she could claim to be the greatest clay court player of all time. She holds the record for the most wins at the French Open, the premier clay court event, and from Aug. 12, 1973, to May 12, 1979, she won 125 consecutive matches on clay. Her streak was finally snapped by Tracy Austin in the semi-finals of the 1979 Italian Open in Rome.

ENDLESS POINT

In a second-set tie-breaker between Vicki Nelson-Dunbar and Jean Hepner at the 1984 Ginny of Richmond, the two volleyed back and forth 29 minutes for one point. During the point the ball crossed the net 643 times before Hepner hit an overhead into the net. Nelson-Dunbar won the tie-breaker.

CAREER WINS - MEN (TOP FIVE)

1. Jimmy Connors	109
2. Ivan Lendl	94
3. John McEnroe	77
4. Pete Sampras	64
5. Bjorn Borg	62
Guillermo Vilas	62

CAREER WINS - WOMEN (TOP FIVE)

1. Martina Navratilova	167
2. Chris Evert	154
3. Steffi Graf	107
4. Margaret Court	92
5. Evonne Goolagong-Cawley	68

THE LAST TIME...

The last time four players from one country all played in the semifinal of an ATP event was at the 2003 Hamburg Open, when the Final Four were all from Argentina: Agustin Calleri, Guillermo Coria, Gaston Gaudio, and David Nalbandian.

Track & Field

HUMANS HAVE PROBABLY COMPETED IN RACING, JUMPING, AND THROWING since the dawn of history. There are wall paintings of running, high-jump, and javelin-style events on the tombs of Egyptian pharaohs dating back to 3800 BC. The ancient Olympics in Greece featured organized running, jumping, and throwing; and there is evidence of professional running and walking competitions in Europe from the 12th century onward. But sports historians mark the 19th century as the beginning of modern-day track and field. Standards for competition were set during this time, and official meets held. Track and field has become the centerpiece of modern-day Olympics.

MILESTONES

1876, 1956, 1989: FIRST HIGH JUMP OVER 6, 7, 8 FEET The first person to jump over a bar set at 6 feet was British high jumper Marshall Brooks in 1876 at Oxford, England. About 80 years later, Charles Dumas became the first to leap over the 7-foot mark on June 29, 1956 at the U.S. Olympic Trials in Los Angeles. Later that year he went on to win the gold medal at the Melbourne Olympics.

The 8-foot barrier was broken by Javier Sotomayor of Cuba on July 29, 1989, in San Juan, Puerto Rico. To date, he is the only person to leap over 8 feet, which is the equivalent of jumping over the crossbar of a soccer goal.

1887: CROUCH START (100 YARDS) In the old days, all sprinters began the 100-yard dash from a standing position. This changed in 1887 when U.S. sprinter Charles H. Sherrill became the first athlete to use the technique of starting from a crouch position. Before a race, Sherrill dug small foot holes in the track.

In 1928, George Breshnahan and William Tuttle invented the starting block to help produce a more reliable start, but the IAAF did not allow the blocks until 1937.

1892: SUB-11 SECONDS 100 METERS British sprinter Cecil Lee became the first to run the 100 meter in less than 11 seconds. His time was 10.8 seconds. The first woman to run the 100m in less than 11 seconds was Renate Stecher of East Germany in 1973. Her time was 10.9 seconds.

1895: WOMEN'S TRACK MEET The first women's track and field meet was staged at Vassar College in Poughkeepsie, NY, on a rainy Nov. 9, 1895. As part of their "field day," the college women "stripped down to their bloomers" and competed in the 50-yard, 100-yard, and 220-yard dashes, a running broad jump, and a running high jump. The class of 1897 won the most points.

1912: INTERNATIONAL AMATEUR ATHLETIC FEDERATION (IAAF) The world governing body for track and field, the IAAF, was founded July 17, 1912, in Stockholm, Sweden, two days after the end of the Olympics staged there. The initial meeting was attended by 17 national associations and it was agreed that the IAAF would be inaugurated in Berlin in 1913.

One of its first tasks was to produce an official listing for world records in the sport, which it did in 1914. There were 53 men's records for running, hurdling, and relay racing. There were also 30 for race walking, and 12 for field events, including the decathlon.

In 2001, the IAAF changed its name to the International Association of Athletics Federations.

1928: WOMEN'S OLYMPIC TRACK EVENTS The International Olympic Committee (IOC) voted 12-5 in favor of allowing women to compete in women-only track and field events at the 1928 Amsterdam Olympics. Only five events were scheduled: 100m, 800m, 4 x 100m relay, high jump, and discus. The first Olympic track and field gold medal for women went to Halina Konopacka of Poland. She won the discus with a world record throw of 129 feet, 11 $\frac{1}{2}$ inches.

Elizabeth Robinson, a 16-year-old high school student from Riverdale, IL, won the gold medal in the 100m with a time of 12.2 seconds. The 800m was won by Karoline Radke of Germany in a world record time of 2 minutes, 16.8 seconds.

(Despite this, the IOC banned all women's events longer than 200m for 32 years, believing that "feats of endurance" were dangerous to women's health.)

Liu Xiang (center), Charles Allen (left), and Yoel Hernandez at the 2004 Olympic Games

THE LAST TIME...
The last American to win the 1500-meter Olympic gold was Mel Sheppard, at the 1908 Summer Olympics in London. "Peerless Mel" also was the first man to win gold medals in both the 800-meter and 1500-meter runs, setting world records at the time for both. Sheppard was elected to the U.S. Olympic Hall of Fame in 1989.

The 4 x 100m relay was won by Canada in a world record time of 48.4 seconds. In addition, Canadian Ethel Catherwood, known as "the Saskatoon Lily," won the high jump with a leap of 5 feet, 2 ½ inches.

1954: FOUR-MINUTE MILE The legendary Roger Bannister of Britain was the first to break the four-minute barrier, on May 6, 1954. The British medical student completed his historic run in a time of 3:59.4 at Oxford University's Iffley Road Track.

Paced by Chris Brasher and Chris Chataway, Bannister completed his "miracle mile," representing the Amateur Athletics Association in a meet versus Oxford University.

However, his world record lasted less than six weeks before Australian runner John Landy ran 3:58.0 on June 21, 1954.

1968: FOSBURY FLOP In 1936, the IAAF changed the rules of the high jump to permit the jumper to leap over the bar without having to cross it feet first. With the introduction of the cushioned landing mat, high jump technique changed dramatically. The most radical style, and now by far the most popular, was the Fosbury Flop, a leap that requires the jumper to go backwards over the bar.

Dick Fosbury popularized the jump after developing it almost by accident in the mid-1960s. Frustrated by his inability to execute a western roll, he switched to the sideways scissors kick style; from this position he gradually developed his backwards style. Fosbury gained worldwide attention when he won the gold medal at the 1968 Olympic Games in Mexico City.

Unknown to most, including Fosbury, the backwards flop had actually been done before, in 1963, by jumper Bruce Quande, but his flop didn't catch on.

OCT. 14, 1968: SUB-10-SECOND 100 METERS American sprinter Jim Hines was the first sprinter to be electronically timed at under 10 seconds for the 100m when he won the gold medal at the Mexico City Olympics on Oct. 14, 1968. His time of 9.95 seconds stood as a world record for 15 years.

He had run 100m in 9.9 seconds at the U.S. Olympic Trials in Sacramento, CA., on June 20, 1968, but that was manually timed. Beginning in 1977, the IAAF recognized only electronically-timed world records.

OCT. 18, 1968: OVER 29 FEET The first person to record a long jump farther than 29 feet was Bob Beamon on Oct. 18, 1968, at the Mexico City Olympics. Prior to Beamon's leap, no one had ever jumped farther than 27 feet, 4 ¾ inches (8.35m).

Beamon's jump of 29 feet, 2 ½ inches surpassed the previous world record by 21 ¾ inches, and even went beyond the length of the rail used for the optical measuring device. A steel tape had to be used to measure the jump. His record stood for 23 years.

1976: METRIC RECORDS
From its formation in 1912, the IAAF had agreed to authorize and recognize world records for both imperial and metric distances. But in 1976, the IAAF scrapped recognition of most records for imperial measurements, such as the 100-yard and 440-yard races. The only nonmetric world record race still ratified by the IAAF is the mile.

1983: WORLD CHAMPIONSHIPS
The first official world track and field championships were staged in Helsinki, Finland, in Aug. 1983. The championships were originally held every four years, in the year preceding the Summer Olympics. Since 1991, they've been held every two years.

MORE ON:

Track & Field

SUPERLATIVES

MOST OLYMPIC MEDALS The most track and field medals won during a person's Olympic career is 12, held by Paavo Nurmi of Finland. The legendary "Flying Finn" won nine gold medals and three silver medals at the 1920, 1924, and 1928 Games.

Merlene Ottey of Jamaica has the record for the most career Olympic track medals won by a woman, with eight.

The sprinter won three silver medals and five bronze medals at the 1980, 1984, 1992, 1996, and 2000 Games.

MOST GOLD MEDALS (ONE OLYMPICS) Paavo Nurmi won a record five gold medals at the 1924 Paris Olympics. He stood atop the podium after the 1,500m, 5,000m, 10,000m, 3,000m (team), and cross-country (team) events.

MOST CONSECUTIVE OLYMPIC GOLD MEDALS (ONE EVENT) Two athletes have won four consecutive Olympic gold medals in individual track events. Al Oerter of the U.S. won the discus in 1956, 1960, 1964, and 1968. Carl Lewis of the U.S. won the long jump in 1984, 1988, 1992, and 1996.

World records are ratified by the IAAF.

Men

EVENT	RECORD	ATHLETE, COUNTRY	LOCATION	DATE
100m	00:09.77	Asafa Powell, Jamaica	Athens, Greece	June 14, 2005
200m	00:19.32	Michael Johnson, U.S.	Atlanta, GA	Aug. 1, 1996
400m	00:43.18	Michael Johnson, U.S.	Sevilla, Spain	Aug. 26, 1999
800m	01:41.11	Wilson Kipketer, Denmark	Cologne, Germany	Aug. 24, 1997
1,500m	03:26.00	Hicham El Guerrouj, Morocco	Rome, Italy	July 14, 1998
1 Mile	03:43.13	Hicham El Guerrouj, Morocco	Rome, Italy	July 7, 1999
2,000m	04:44.79	Hicham El Guerrouj, Morocco	Berlin, Germany	Sept. 7, 1999
3,000m	07:20.67	Daniel Komen, Kenya	Rieti, Italy	Sept. 1, 1996
5,000m	12:37.35	Kenenisa Bekele, Ethiopia	Hengelo, Netherlands	May 31, 2004
10,000m	26:17.53	Kenenisa Bekele, Ethiopia	Brussels, Belgium	Aug. 26, 2005
3,000m Steeplechase	07:53.63	Saif Saaeed Shaheen, Qatar	Brussels, Belgium	Sept. 3, 2004
110m Hurdles	00:12.91	Colin Jackson, Great Britain	Stuttgart, Germany	Aug. 20, 1993
	00:12.91	Xiang Liu, China	Athens, Greece	Aug. 27, 2004
400m Hurdles	00:46.78	Kevin Young, U.S.	Barcelona, Spain	Aug. 6, 1992
High Jump	2.45 m	Javier Sotomayor, Cuba	Salamanca, Spain	July 27, 1993
Pole Vault	6.14 m	Sergey Bubka, Ukraine	Sestriere, Italy	July 31, 1994
Long Jump	8.95 m	Mike Powell, U.S.	Tokyo, Japan	Aug. 30, 1991
Triple Jump	18.29 m	Jonathan Edwards, Great Britain	Gothenberg, Sweden	Aug. 7, 1995
Shot Put	23.12 m	Randy Barnes, U.S.	Westwood, CA	May 20, 1990
Discus	74.08 m	Jurgen Schult, East Germany	Neubrandenburg, Germany	June 6, 1986
Hammer	86.74 m	Yuriy Sedykh, USSR	Stuttgart, Germany	Aug. 30, 1986
Javelin	98.48 m	Jan Zelezny, Czechoslovakia	Jena, Germany	May 25, 1996
Decathlon	9,026 pts	Roman Sebrle, Czech Republic	Gotzis, Austria	May 27, 2001
4 x 100m Relay	00:37.40	U.S. (Mike Marsh, Leroy Burrell, Dennis Mitchell, Carl Lewis)	Barcelona, Spain	Aug. 8, 1992
	00:37.40	U.S. (Jon Drummond, Andre Cason, Dennis Mitchell, Leroy Burrell)	Stuttgart, Germany	Aug. 21, 1993
4 x 400m Relay	02:54.20	U.S. (Jerome Young, Antonio Pettigrew, Tyree Washington, Michael Johnson)	Uniondale, U.S.	July 22, 1998
20km Walk	1:17:21.0	Jefferson Pérez, Ecuador	Paris Saint-Denis, France	Aug. 23, 2003
50km Walk	3:36:03	Robert Korzeniowski, Poland	Paris Saint-Denis, France	Aug. 27, 2003

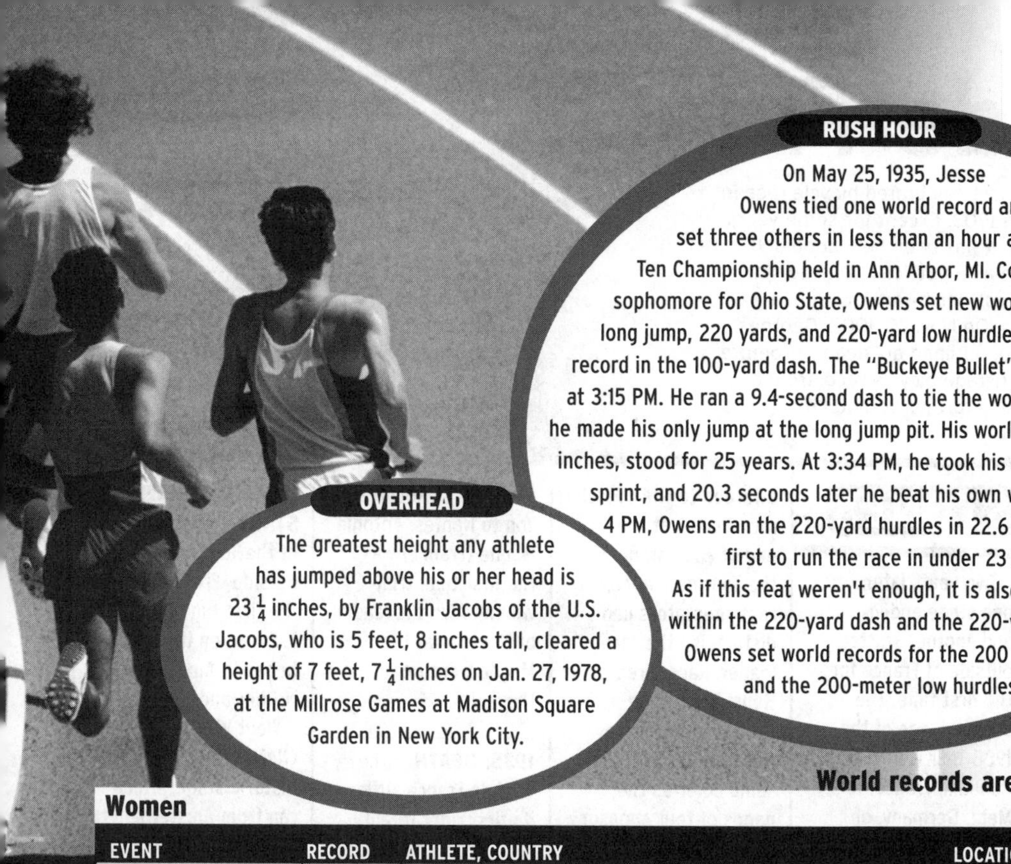

SOMETHING TO THINK ABOUT

RUSH HOUR

On May 25, 1935, Jesse Owens tied one world record and set three others in less than an hour at the Big Ten Championship held in Ann Arbor, MI. Competing as a sophomore for Ohio State, Owens set new world marks in the long jump, 220 yards, and 220-yard low hurdles, and he tied the record in the 100-yard dash. The "Buckeye Bullet" lined up for the 100 at 3:15 PM. He ran a 9.4-second dash to tie the world mark. At 3:25 PM, he made his only jump at the long jump pit. His world record of 26 feet, $8\frac{1}{4}$ inches, stood for 25 years. At 3:34 PM, he took his mark for the 220-yard sprint, and 20.3 seconds later he beat his own world record. Finally at 4 PM, Owens ran the 220-yard hurdles in 22.6 seconds. He was the first to run the race in under 23 seconds.

As if this feat weren't enough, it is also believed that within the 220-yard dash and the 220-yard hurdles, Owens set world records for the 200 meters, and the 200-meter low hurdles.

OVERHEAD

The greatest height any athlete has jumped above his or her head is $23\frac{1}{4}$ inches, by Franklin Jacobs of the U.S. Jacobs, who is 5 feet, 8 inches tall, cleared a height of 7 feet, $7\frac{1}{4}$ inches on Jan. 27, 1978, at the Millrose Games at Madison Square Garden in New York City.

World records are ratified by the IAAF.

Women

EVENT	RECORD	ATHLETE, COUNTRY	LOCATION	DATE
100m	00:10.49	Florence Griffith-Joyner, U.S.	Indianapolis, IN	July 16, 1988
200m	00:21.34	Florence Griffith-Joyner, U.S.	Seoul, South Korea	Sept. 29, 1988
400m	00:47.60	Marita Koch, East Germany	Canberra, Australia	Oct. 6, 1985
800m	01:53.28	Jarmila Kratochvilova, Czechoslovakia	Munich, Germany	July 26, 1983
1,500m	03:50.46	Junxia Qu, China	Beijing, China	Sept. 11, 1993
1 Mile	04:12.56	Svetlana Masterkova, Russia	Zurich, Switzerland	Aug. 14, 1996
2,000m	05:25.36	Sonia O'Sullivan, Ireland	Edinburgh, Scotland	July 8, 1994
3,000m	08:06.11	Junxia Wang, China	Beijing, China	Sept. 13, 1993
5,000m	14:24.68	Elvan Abeylegesse, Turkey	Bergen, Norway	June 11, 2004
10,000m	29:31.78	Junxia Wang, China	Beijing, China	Sept. 8, 1993
3,000m Steeplechase	09:01.59	Gulnara Samitova, Russia	Iraklion, Greece	July 4, 2004
100m Hurdles	00:12.21	Yordanka Donkova, Bulgaria	Stara Zagora, Bulgaria	Aug. 20, 1988
400m Hurdles	00:52.34	Yuliya Pechenkina, Russia	Tula, Russia	Aug. 8, 2003
High Jump	2.09 m	Stefka Kostadinova, Bulgaria	Rome, Italy	Aug. 30, 1987
Pole Vault	5.01 m	Yelena Isinbayeva, Russia	Helsinki, Finland	Aug. 12, 2005
Long Jump	7.52 m	Galina Chistyakova, USSR	Leningrad, USSR	June 11, 1988
Triple Jump	15.50 m	Inessa Kravets, Ukraine	Gothenberg, Sweden	Aug. 10, 1995
Shot Put	22.63 m	Natalya Lisovskaya, USSR	Moscow, USSR	June 7, 1987
Discus	76.80 m	Gabriele Reinsch, East Germany	Neubrandenburg, Germany	July 9, 1988
Hammer	77.06 m	Tatyana Lysenko, Russia	Moscow, Russia	July 15, 2005
Javelin	71.70 m	Osleidys Menendez, Cuba	Helsinki, Finland	Aug. 14, 2005
Heptathlon	7291 pts	Jackie Joyner-Kersee, U.S.	Seoul, South Korea	Sept. 24, 1988
4 x 100m Relay	00:41.37	East Germany (Silke Gladisch, Sabine Rieger, Ingrid Auerswald, Marlies Gohr)	Canberra, Australia	Oct. 6, 1985
4 x 400m Relay	03:15.17	USSR (Tatyana Ledovskaya, Olga Nazarova, Maria Pinigina, Olga Bryzgina)	Seoul, South Korea	Oct. 1, 1988
10km Walk	41:56.23	Nadezhda Ryashkina, USSR	Seattle, WA	July 24, 1990
20km alk	1:25:41	Olimiada Ivanova, Russia	Helsinki, Finland	Aug. 7, 2005

Tour de France

THE TOUR DE FRANCE, the most celebrated bicycle race in the world, was first held in 1903. Except for some years during World Wars I and II, it has been held annually ever since. The race began as a publicity stunt to sell the sports newspaper *L'Auto,* which was facing heavy competition for circulation. On Nov. 20, 1902, Géorges Lefèvre, a writer for *L'Auto*, outlined an idea to promote the newspaper with a multistage bicycle race around France to Henri Desgrange, a former cycling champ and Lefèvre's boss at *L'Auto*.

MILESTONES

1903: FIRST STAGE WINNER The first Tour de France stage, from Paris to Lyon, began on July 1, 1903. A former chimney sweep, Maurice Garin (France) won the 290-mile stage from Paris to Lyon by 55 seconds.

1903: TOUR DE FRANCE WINNER Maurice Garin won the inaugural Tour de France in 1903. He was first in a field of 60 riders. Garin won three of the six stages and completed the 1,509-mile Tour in 94 hours, 33 minutes, 14 seconds, at an average speed of 15.96 mph.

1906: BEYOND FRANCE The race expanded beyond France for the first time during the 1906 Tour. Although all stages started and ended in French territory, some crossed into Germany, Spain, and Italy.

Two years later, one stage ended and another started outside of France for the first time. The second stage of the 1908 Tour wound from Roubaix, France, to Metz, Germany, on July 15. The third stage started in Metz on July 17 and ran to Belfort, France.

1909: NON-FRENCH WINNER The first non-French national to win the Tour de France was François Faber (Luxembourg) in 1909. Known as "The Giant from Colombes," Faber overcame not just the competition and the terrain, but cold, freezing rain, mud, and high winds.

The 1909 race is widely regarded by Tour historians as having suffered the worst weather in race history.

1919: YELLOW JERSEY The yellow jersey (*le maillot jaune*) is awarded to the overall race leader at the end of each stage of the Tour de France, so that spectators can distinguish the race leader. Race director Henri Desgrange used a yellow jersey because it was the same color as the pages of tour sponsor *L'Auto.*

It was first worn on July 18, 1919, when Tour leader Eugène Christophe (France) swapped his gray team jersey for the yellow one before Stage 11.

Though Christophe had led the race from Stage 4, he did not sport *le maillot jaune* all the way to Paris: he lost the lead on Stage 14 when the frame of his bike broke. Firmin Lambot (Belgium) went on to win the race, and Christophe finished third.

1934: INDIVIDUAL TIME TRIAL The first individual time trial was staged during the 1934 Tour de France. Held on July 27, the 51.5-mile time trial was run from La Roche-sur-Yon to Nantes. Antonin Magne (France) was the first time trial winner. Also the leader of the race at the time, Magne went on to win the Tour.

1935: DEATH The Tour de France suffered its first rider fatality in 1935. As Francesco Cepeda (Spain) was descending the Col du Galibier in the Alps during Stage 7 of the race on July 11, 1935, a tire loosened from Cepeda's bike and he fell into a ravine and fractured his skull. He died three days later.

1952: L'ALPE D'HUEZ One of the signature stages of the Tour is the climb of L'Alpe d'Huez. The climb up to the mountain's summit is so steep that it is rated "beyond category" by Tour officials.

In 1952, Fausto Coppi (Italy) won Stage 10, the first stage to end at L'Alpe d'Huez, and went on to win the 1952 Tour.

1954: INTERNATIONAL START The beginning of the Tour was staged outside France for the first time in 1954, when the race began in Amsterdam, Netherlands.

Wout Wagtmans (Netherlands) won the historic stage, which ran from Amsterdam to Brasschaat, Belgium.

1975: CHAMPS-ELYSÉES FINISH The finish line for the Tour de France was set on the Champs-Elysées, Paris's most famous thoroughfare, for the first time in 1975. To the delight of the thousands of Parisians lining the capital's streets, Bernard Thévenet (France) won the Tour.

1986: AMERICAN WINNER Greg Lemond became the first American rider to win the Tour de France, in 1986. It was the first of three Tour wins for Lemond. He also won in 1989 and 1990.

THE LAST TIME...

The last Frenchman to win the Tour de France was Bernard Hinault in 1985. A five-time winner, Hinault finished second to Greg Lemond (U.S.) in his last Tour in 1986.

Lance Armstrong

SUPERLATIVES

MOST WINS Lance Armstrong (U.S.) has won a record seven Tours de France. The Texan won seven years in a row, with victories from 1999 to 2005, after which he announced he would retire from the competition.

OLDEST WINNER
The oldest winner of the Tour was Firmin Lambot (Belgium). He was 36 years old when he won the race in 1922.

YOUNGEST WINNER
Henri Cornet (France) was the youngest Tour winner ever. He was 20 years old when he won in 1904.

Cornet's win was one of the most controversial in Tour history. The race finished on July 23, but the official results were not posted until Dec. 2. The first four finishers were all disqualified, giving the victory to Cornet.

NARROWEST WINNING MARGIN Greg Lemond's (U.S.) 1989 victory over Laurent Fignon (France) was the closest finish in Tour de France history. Lemond beat Fignon by a mere eight seconds.

The pair had raced for 23 days, covering 2,030 miles. Fignon held a 50-second lead heading into the final stage, which was a time trial from Versailles to Paris, but Lemond won the stage and took the Tour.

BIGGEST WINNING MARGIN The biggest margin of victory in Tour de France history was 2 hours, 49 minutes. Maurice Garin set the record at the inaugural Tour de France in 1903.

LONGEST TOUR
The 1926 Tour de France was the longest Tour ever. The 3,567-mile route ran over 17 stages from June 20 to July 18. Lucien Buysse (Belgium) won the race in 238 hours, 44 minutes, 25 seconds.

LONGEST STAGE
The longest stage in the history of the Tour was a 302-mile "spin" from Les Sables d'Olonne to Bayonne in 1919. Jean Alavoine (France) won this endurance challenge, the fifth stage of the 1919 Tour.

MOST TOURS
Joop Zoetemelk (Netherlands) competed in a record 16 Tours de France. The Dutch rider first raced in the Tour in 1970, and he rode his last Tour in 1986. One of the legends of the sport, Zoetemelk won the 1980 Tour, finished second a record six times, and completed all 16 Tours he raced.

MOST STAGE WINS **TOUR** Three riders have won eight stages in one Tour.

Charles Pelissier (France) was the first cyclist to perform this feat in 1930. Tour legend Eddy Merckx (Belgium) matched Pelissier's record twice, in 1970 and 1974. The only other rider to win eight stages was Freddy Maertens (Belgium) in 1976.

Neither Pelissier or Maertens won the Tour in their record-setting years, but Merckx won in both 1970 and 1974.

MOST STAGE WINS **CAREER** Eddy Merckx won a record 34 individual stages during his Tour de France career. The five-time winner (1969-72, 1974) raced in only seven Tours, in 1969-1972, 1974-1975, 1977. He won six stages in the 1969 race, eight stages in 1970, four stages in 1971, six stages in 1972, eight stages in 1974, and two stages in 1975.

Swimming

SWIMMING DATES BACK TO the earliest time of human development. Drawings in the so-called "Cave of Swimmers" in southwest Egypt are thousands of years old. The literature and art of ancient Greece and Rome are sprinkled with references to recreational swimming. During the Middle Ages, however, swimming for recreation was discouraged, partly because of fears that it might spread disease.

Modern swimming competition started in England in the early 19th century when swimming clubs were formed. Though not included in the ancient Olympics, swimming was a big part of the first modern Olympics in 1896, and all later summer Olympics. Those early races took place outdoors in open water. Today, the sport is a highly calibrated event, with races decided by small fractions of a second.

Olympic Swimmers

MILESTONES

1538: SWIMMING LESSONS The first swimming instruction manual known to us today was *Colymbetes*, written by a German named Nicolaum Wynman in Augsburg, Germany, in 1538. Wynman had a practical purpose in producing the work; he wanted people to learn how to swim so that they would not drown—and not that many people did know. The manual included diagrams and descriptions of various strokes.

In 1696, French author Melchisedech Thevenot wrote what later became a standard reference for swimming, *The Art of Swimming*. A significant feature of the book was its description of the breaststroke, in terms similar to the way it is done today.

1798: LITTLE STUDY BOOK OF SWIMMING One of the most influential swimming instruction books ever published was *Kleines Lehrbuch der Schwimmkunst zum Selbstunterricht*, written in 1798, by German physical education instructor Johann Guts Muths.

The book's title roughly translated is *Little Study Book of the Art of Swimming for Self Study*. It established a three-step approach to swimming instruction that, you could say, still holds water today. Guts Muths proposed that beginners first get used to the water using floatation aids. The second step was to practice swimming strokes on land before trying them in the water. Finally, the student would dive into the real thing.

1873: ARMSTROKE ("THE TRUDGEN") At an international swim meet staged by the Swimming Society in London, England, in 1844, European swimmers saw the front crawl for the first time. Two Native American swimmers named Flying Gull and Tobacco represented the U.S. at the meet. Up until then, European swimmers primarily used the breaststroke. Native Americans, on the other hand, used a front crawl style that had been part of their culture and was actually faster. Because of it, they were able to beat the Europeans.

For some time, the British resisted the "totally un-European" style, and stuck to the breaststroke. It wasn't until 1873 that the front crawl was reintroduced to Britain. John Trudgen, who had learned the front crawl while in South America, returned to Britain and taught his variation of the front crawl. "The Trudgen," a hand-over-hand stroke propelled by a scissors kick, became increasingly popular as swimming times dropped steeply. In 1901, F.V.C. Lane swam 100 yards in one minute, which was 10 seconds faster than the breaststroke record over the same distance.

AROUND 1902: AUSTRALIAN CRAWL Perhaps the biggest advance in competitive swimming was the widespread use of the Australian crawl, starting around the beginning of the 20th century. Developed by the sons of British-born Australian swimming teacher Frederick Cavill, the Australian crawl was a variation of the Trudgen stroke where, instead of a scissor kick, a flutter kick was used. At an international meet in England in 1902, an Australian swimmer easily beat the rest of the field using Cavill's technique, which was quickly adopted by the rest of the swimming community. Now it is the stroke almost always used in a free-style event.

1908: FÉDERATION INTERNATIONALE DE NATATION (FINA) FINA, the world governing body for swimming, was founded in 1908 with an initial membership of eight countries.

1912: WOMEN SWIMMERS IN THE OLYMPICS The first Olympics to allow female swimmers were

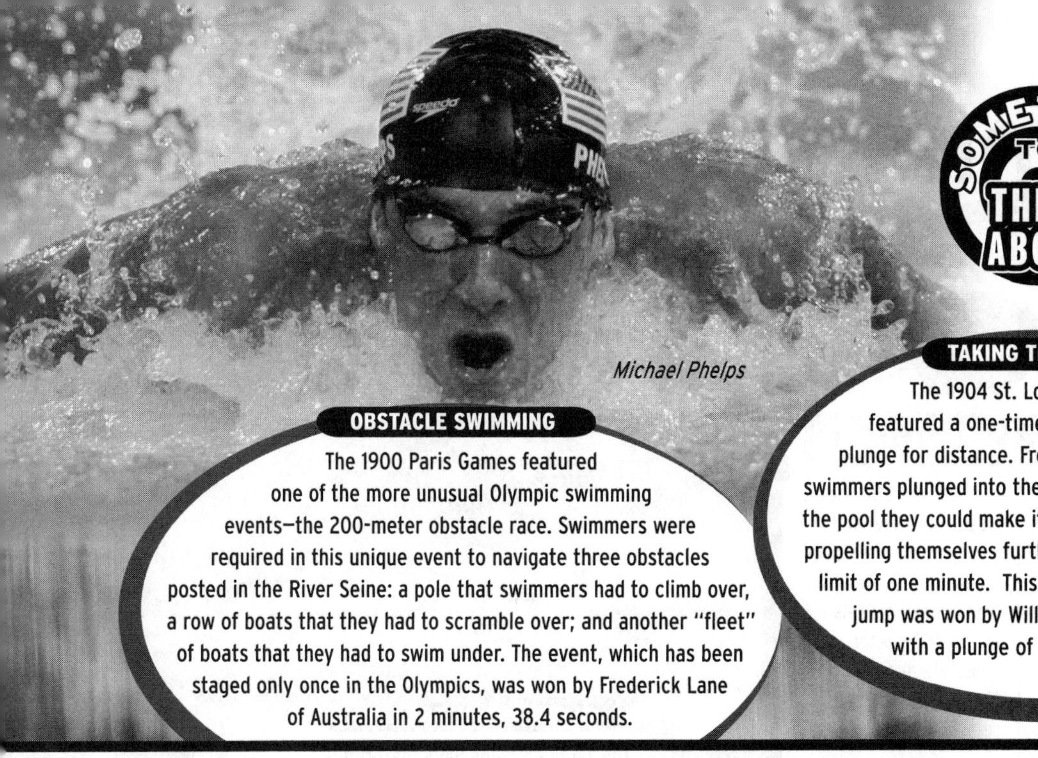

Michael Phelps

SOMETHING TO THINK ABOUT

OBSTACLE SWIMMING

The 1900 Paris Games featured one of the more unusual Olympic swimming events—the 200-meter obstacle race. Swimmers were required in this unique event to navigate three obstacles posted in the River Seine: a pole that swimmers had to climb over, a row of boats that they had to scramble over; and another "fleet" of boats that they had to swim under. The event, which has been staged only once in the Olympics, was won by Frederick Lane of Australia in 2 minutes, 38.4 seconds.

TAKING THE PLUNGE

The 1904 St. Louis Games also featured a one-time Olympic event, the plunge for distance. From a standing start, the swimmers plunged into the pool to see how far across the pool they could make it without taking a breath or propelling themselves further. They were given a time limit of one minute. This water version of the long jump was won by William Dickey of the U.S. with a plunge of 62 feet, 6 inches.

the 1912 Stockholm Games. Female swimmers competed in two events—the 100-meter freestyle and the 4 x 100 meter freestyle relay.

Fanny Durack of Australia won the first women's swimming gold medal, which came in the 100-meter freestyle.

Durack was almost a no-show. Australian Olympic officials thought it was a waste of money to send a woman swimmer to the games. She and fellow Australian swimmer Wilhelmina Wylie were forced to pay their own way. In the end, Durack and Wylie finished first and second, respectively, in the Olympic final.

1922: FIRST SUB-ONE-MINUTE 100 METERS American swimmer Johnny Weissmuller was the first person to swim 100 meters in under a minute. One of the greatest swimmers of all-time, Weissmuller performed the feat on July 9, 1922, in 58.6 seconds. He won three gold medals at the 1924 Paris Olympics, and two more at the 1928 Amsterdam Olympics.

A versatile swimmer, Weissmuller was also a member of the U.S. water polo team that won a bronze medal in 1924. He gained even greater fame in Hollywood, where he starred as Tarzan in a series of jungle adventure films in the 1930s and 1940s.

1924: LANE DIVIDERS
The first time floating lane dividers were used in competition was at the 1924 Paris Olympics. That Olympiad also saw the introduction of lines on the bottom of the pool to help guide swimmers.

1943: BUTTERFLY
Dave Armbruster and Jack Sieg are credited with having developed the butterfly stroke. Armbruster, a coach at the University of Iowa, wanted to find a way to lower the resistance of swimmers performing the breaststroke. In 1934, he combined the more efficient over-arm stroke of the crawl with the old breaststroke kick.

A year later, Jack Sieg, a member of the Iowa swim team, added a dolphin kick technique to the stroke. Working together, Armbruster and Seig refined the new technique to create the butterfly style.

Breaststroke swimmers, impressed by the increase in speed, adopted the new style quickly but were barred from using it in competition. It wasn't until 1953 that the butterfly stroke was accepted as an independent style for competition by FINA.

Jiro Nagasawa became the first world record holder in the butterfly style on Sept. 17, 1954. The first time butterfly races were included in the Olympic Games was 1956.

1973: WORLD SWIMMING CHAMPIONSHIPS
The first official world swimming championships were staged in Belgrade, Yugoslavia, in 1973. They were held sporadically following the inaugural event, with gaps ranging from two to five years in between.

The Worlds are now part of the FINA World Championships, which include the four aquatic sports: swimming, diving, water polo, and synchronized swimming, and are held in odd numbered years.

MORE ABOUT

Swimming

SUPERLATIVES

MOST OLYMPIC GOLD MEDALS CAREER
U.S. swimmer Mark Spitz holds the record for the most career Olympic gold medals for swimming, with a total of nine. The legendary athlete won two gold medals (in the 4 x 100-meter and 4 x 200-meter relays) at the 1968 Mexico City Games, and seven gold medals at the 1972 Munich Games.

His haul in Munich is the record for most gold medals won at one Olympiad. He won the 100-meter and 200-meter freestyle, 100-meter and 200-meter butterfly, 4 x 100-meter and 4 x 200-meter freestyle, and 4 x 100-meter medley.

MOST MEDALS ONE OLYMPICS
Michael Phelps won a record eight medals at the 2004 Athens Olympics. The American swimmer won six golds in: the 100-meter and 200-meter butterfly; 200-meter and 400-meter individual medley; 4 x 200-meter freestyle relay; and 4 x 100-meter individual medley relay. He also won bronze medals in the 200-meter freestyle and the 4 x 100-meter freestyle relay.

MOST MEDALS CAREER
The record for most Olympic swimming medals won in a career is 12, by American swimmer Jenny Thompson. She competed in four Olympic Games from 1992 to 2004, and won eight gold medals, three silver medals, and one bronze medal. All of her gold medals came as a member of relay teams.

SOMETHING TO THINK ABOUT

OLYMPIANS OF THE APES

The Tarzan movies have featured two Olympic swimming champions in the title role. Johnny Weissmuller, who won five career gold medals at the 1924 and 1928 Games, starred in a total of 12 Tarzan films between 1932 and 1948. Clarence "Buster" Crabbe, who won the 400-meter freestyle gold medal at the 1932 Games, starred in 1933's *Tarzan the Fearless*. Crabbe holds the distinction of being the only actor to have played Tarzan, Buck Rogers, and Flash Gordon—in the movies. Adolph Kiefer (U.S.), who won the gold in the 100-meter men's backstroke in the 1936 Berlin Games, turned down an offer to play Tarzan in the movies after learning the pay—$17 per month.

PHOTO FINISH

At the 1960 Olympic Games in Rome, the men's 100-meter freestyle had one of the closest and most controversial finishes in Olympic history. Australia's John Devitt and Lance Larson of the U.S. seemed to touch the wall simultaneously. Three of the judges thought Larson had won and three thought Devitt had won. Although the electronic time registered that Larson was first by 4/100 of a second, the chief judge, Hans Runströmer, awarded the gold medal to Devitt. U.S. officials challenged the decision for several years, but the result was never changed. In response to the dispute that erupted, Swiss Timing developed electronic touch plates.

CHILLY DIP

The swimming competition at the first Olympic Games of the modern era—in Athens, Greece, in 1896—was held in the Bay of Zea near Piraeus. On April 11, when the 100-meter freestyle was raced, the water temperature was a mere 55 degrees Fahrenheit. Alfred Hajos of Hungary, who won the gold medal, later said of the experience, "The icy water almost cut into our stomachs." Hajos also won the 1,200-meter freestyle that same day.

World Records

Swimming world records are ratified by the Fédération Internationale de Natation (FINA). The following are for records set in 50-meter pools.

Women

EVENT	RECORD	ATHLETE, COUNTRY	LOCATION	DATE
50m Freestyle	00:24.13	Inge de Bruijn, Netherlands	Sydney, Australia	Sept. 22, 2000
100m Freestyle	00:53.52	Jodie Henry, Australia	Athens, Greece	Aug. 18, 2004
200m Freestyle	01:56.64	Franziska Van Almsick, Germany	Berlin, Germany	Aug. 3, 2002
400m Freestyle	04:03.85	Janet Evans, U.S.	Seoul, South Korea	Sept. 22, 1988
800m Freestyle	08:16.22	Janet Evans, U.S.	Tokyo, Japan	Aug. 20, 1989
1,500m Freestyle	15:52.10	Janet Evans, U.S.	Orlando, FL	March 26, 1988
50m Backstroke	00:28.25	Sandra Voelker, Germany	Berlin, Germany	June 17, 2000
100m Backstroke	00:59.58	Natalie Coughlin, U.S.	Fort Lauderdale, FL	Aug. 13, 2002
200m Backstroke	02:06.62	Kristina Egerszegi, Hungary	Athens, Greece	Aug. 25, 1991
50m Breaststroke	00:30.45	Jade Edmiston, Australia	Montreal, Canada	July 31, 2005
100m Breaststroke	01:06.20	Jessica Hardy, U.S.	Montreal, Canada	July 25, 2005
200m Breaststroke	02:21.72	Leisel Jones, Australia	Montreal, Canada	July 29, 2005
50m Butterfly	00:25.57	Anna-Karin Kammerling, Sweden	Berlin, Germany	July 30, 2000
100m Butterfly	00:56.61	Inge de Bruijn, Netherlands	Sydney, Australia	Sept. 17, 2000
200m Butterfly	02:05.61	Otylia Jedrzejczak, Poland	Montreal, Canada	July 28, 2005
200m Ind. Medley	02:09.72	Yanyan Wu, China	Shanghai, China	Oct. 17, 1997
400m Ind. Medley	04:33.59	Yana Klochkova, Ukraine	Sydney, Australia	Sept. 16, 2000
4 x 100m Freestyle Relay	03:35.94	Australia (Alice Mills, Lisbeth Lenton, Petria Thomas, Jodie Henry)	Athens, Greece	Aug. 14, 2004
4 x 200m Freestyle Relay	07:53.42	U.S. (Natalie Coughlin, Carly Piper, Dana Vollmer, Kaitlin Sandeno)	Athens, Greece	Aug. 18, 2004
4 x 100m Medley Relay	03:57.32	Australia (Giaan Rooney, Leisel Jones, Petria Thomas, Jodie Henry)	Athens, Greece	Aug. 21, 2004

Men

EVENT	RECORD	ATHLETE, COUNTRY	LOCATION	DATE
50m Freestyle	00:21.64	Alexander Popov, Russia	Moscow, Russia	June 16, 2000
100m Freestyle	00:47.84	Pieter van den Hoogenband, Netherlands	Sydney, Australia	Sept. 19, 2000
200m Freestyle	01:44.06	Ian Thorpe, Australia	Fukuoka, Japan	July 25, 2001
400m Freestyle	03:40.08	Ian Thorpe, Australia	Manchester, England	July 30, 2002
800m Freestyle	07:38.65	Grant Hackett, Australia	Montreal, Canada	July 27, 2005
1,500m Freestyle	14:34.56	Grant Hackett, Australia	Fukuoka, Japan	July 29, 2001
50m Backstroke	00:24.80	Thomas Rupprath, Germany	Barcelona, Spain	July 27, 2003
100m Backstroke	00:53.17	Aaron Peirsol, U.S.	Indianapolis, IN	April 2, 2005
200m Backstroke	01:54.66	Aaron Peirsol, U.S.	Montreal, Canada	July 29, 2005
50m Breaststroke	00:27.18	Oleg Lisogor, Ukraine	Berlin, Germany	Aug. 2, 2002
100m Breaststroke	00:59.30	Brendan Hansen, U.S.	Long Beach, CA	July 8, 2004
200m Breaststroke	02:09.04	Brendan Hansen, U.S.	Long Beach, CA	July 11, 2004
50m Butterfly	00:22.96	Roland Schoeman, South Africa	Montreal, Canada	July 25, 2005
100m Butterfly	00:50.40	Ian Crocker, U.S.	Montreal, Canada	July 30, 2005
200m Butterfly	01:53.93	Michael Phelps, U.S.	Barcelona, Spain	July 22, 2003
200m Ind. Medley	01:55.94	Michael Phelps, U.S.	College Park, MD	Aug. 9, 2003
400m Ind. Medley	04:08.26	Michael Phelps, U.S.	Athens, Greece	Aug. 14, 2004
4 x 100m Freestyle Relay	03:13.17	South Africa (Roland Schoeman, Lyndon Ferns, Darian Townsend, Ryk Neethling)	Athens, Greece	Aug. 15, 2004
4 x 200m Freestyle Relay	07:04.66	Australia (Grant Hackett, Michael Klim, William Kirby, Ian Thorpe)	Fukuoka, Japan	July 27, 2001
4 x 100m Ind. Medley	03:30.68	U.S. (Aaron Peirsol, Brendan Hansen, Ian Crocker, Jason Lezak)	Athens, Greece	Aug. 21, 2004

Diving

MODERN-DAY DIVING traces its roots to the gymnastics movement that developed in Germany and Sweden in the late 19th century. As a safety measure, gymnasts would commonly practice over water to learn new acrobatic moves.

Men's diving events were added to the Olympics at the 1904 Games in St. Louis, MO. Women's diving was not officially recognized on the Olympic program until the 1912 Stockholm Games. Synchronized diving was added to the Olympic program at the 2000 Sydney Games.

Greg Louganis at the 1988 Summer Olympic Games

MILESTONES

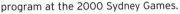

1883: "PLUNGING" COMPETITIONS The earliest diving competitions were "plunging" events. In the manner of a modern swim-racing dive off the blocks, the diver "plunged" into the pool with the aim of making as much distance as possible.

The first known official plunging competition was the British National Plunging Championships, staged in 1883.

1904: FIRST OLYMPIC GOLD The first Olympic gold medal won by a diver was the platform gold medal won by George Sheldon of the U.S. at the 1904 St. Louis Games. Georg Hoffman of Germany took the silver; Frank Kehoe of the U.S. won the bronze.

The first Olympic gold medal won by a female diver, in 1912, went to Greta Johansson of Sweden. The 17-year-old easily beat her countrywoman Lisa Regnell, who took the silver medal. Isabella White of Great Britain won the bronze.

1918: ERNST BRANSTEN "The Father of American Diving," Ernst Bransten was a Swedish diving coach who immigrated to the U.S. in 1918, following World War I, and transformed the sport of diving.

Among Bransten's innovations was dry-land training. He installed a diving board over a sand pit, allowing divers to practice approach and takeoff techniques. Bransten sparked a boom in American diving that resulted in American divers sweeping the two gold medals in the men's 3-meter springboard and 10-meter platform at every Olympics from 1920 to 1952.

SUPERLATIVES

MOST OLYMPIC GOLD MEDALS (CAREER) The most career diving gold medals won in Olympic competition is four. Three divers have done this: Pat McCormick of the U.S., Greg Louganis of the U.S., and Fu Mingxia of China.

McCormick won the women's springboard and platform events at the 1952 Helsinki Games and the 1956 Melbourne Games. Louganis won the men's springboard and platform events at the 1984 Los Angeles Games and the 1988 Seoul Games. Fu Mingxia won the women's platform at the 1992 Barcelona Games and the 1996 Atlanta Games, and the women's springboard in 1996 and at the 2000 Sydney Games.

MOST CONSECUTIVE OLYMPIC GOLD MEDALS The only diver to win the same event at three straight Olympiads is Klaus Dibiasi of Italy. Coached by his father Carlo, who competed in the 1936 Berlin Games, Dibiasi won the platform event at the 1968 Mexico City Games, the 1972 Munich Games, and the 1976 Montreal Games. The Austrian-born Dibiasi had won a silver medal in the platform competition at the 1964 Tokyo Games.

MOST OLYMPIC MEDALS (CAREER) The most diving medals won in Olympic competition is seven, by Dmitri Sautin of Russia. He won two gold medals on the platform in 1996 and synchronized platform in 2000; one silver in the synchronized springboard in 2000; and four bronze on the springboard in

Most Olympic Gold Medals Per Event

EVENT	GOLD	DIVER	COUNTRY	YEARS
Springboard (Men)	2	Greg Louganis	USA	1984, 1988
	2	Ni Xiong	China	1996, 2000
Platform (Men)	3	Klaus Dibiasi	Italy	1968, 1972, 1976
Springboard (Women)	2	Pat McCormick	USA	1952, 1956
	2	Ingrid Kraemer	Germany	1960, 1964
	2	Min Gao	China	1988, 1992
	2	Fu Mingxia	China	1996, 2000
Platform (Women)	2	Dorothy Poynton-Hill	USA	1932, 1936
	2	Pat McCormick	USA	1952, 1956
	2	Fu Mingxia	China	1992, 1996

Acapulco cliff diver

THE LAST TIME...

The last time a non-Chinese diver won either of the men's two individual diving competitions at an Olympic Games was 1996, when Dmitri Sautin of Russia won the platform event. Since the 1992 Barcelona Olympics, Chinese divers have won six of the eight golds in the men's springboard and platform events. Mark Lenzi of the U.S. won the other gold on springboard in 1992.

1992, 2000, and 2004, and on the platform in 2000.

OLDEST GOLD MEDALIST The oldest diver to win an Olympic gold medal is Hjalmar Johansson of Sweden. He won the men's platform at the 1908 London Games at the age of 34 years, 186 days.

But Johansson was a hero at the Games for another reason. During the competition, British diver George Cane crashed into the water and knocked himself out; Johansson promptly jumped into the water and pulled him out.

YOUNGEST OLYMPIC GOLD MEDALIST The youngest diver, and youngest in any sport ever to win an Olympic gold medal, is Marjorie Gestring of the U.S. The Los Angeles native was 13 years, 268 days old when she won the springboard gold medal at the 1936 Berlin Games.

SOMETHING TO THINK ABOUT

DARE DIVERS

The cliff divers (*clavadistas*) of Acapulco, Mexico, leap off of a 130-foot-high cliff into a 12-foot-wide inlet of rough surf. They have to leap almost horizontally to avoid the jagged ledges of rock below, and carefully time their leaps with the ocean waves to avoid injury. The practice became a tourist attraction in the 1930s, and was later popularized on ABC's *Wide World of Sports*. Cliff diving became an international competitive sport in 1996, when the World High Diving Federation held its first Cliff Diving World Championships and set the regulation jumping height at 75-92 feet. By the time those divers break the surface of the water, they are nearing speeds of 55-60 mph.

DIVING-SWIMMING

Although diving as a sport developed as an offshoot of gymnastics, it is most closely associated with swimming. In the history of the Olympic Games four athletes have won medals in both sports at the same Games. The first was by Georg Hoffman of Germany at the 1904 St. Louis Games, he won the silver medal both in platform diving and in the 100-meter backstroke. Eighteen-year-old Aileen Riggin of the U.S. and Hjordis Torpel of Sweden became the first women to win medals in both sports at the 1924 Paris Olympics. Riggin won the silver medal in springboard diving, and a bronze in the 100-meter backstroke. Torpel won a bronze in the women's platform and in the 4 x 100 meter freestyle relay. The other athlete to complete this unusual double is Katherine Rawls of the U.S. She won a silver medal in the springboard event at the 1936 Berlin Games and two days later won a bronze in the 4 x 100m freestyle relay.

GYMNASTICS

Women

WOMEN'S GYMNASTICS was not officially recognized on the Olympic program until 1928, when a team competition was included in the Amsterdam Games. Female gymnasts did not participate in the Olympics again until 1936 in Berlin. Individual apparatus events were not recognized at the Olympics until 1952, when the balance beam, the floor exercise, the uneven bars, and the vault were added to the program. An all-around competition was also included at the 1952 Helsinki Games for the first time.

MILESTONES

1928: FIRST OLYMPIC GOLD MEDAL The first women's gymnastics Olympic gold medal was a team medal awarded to the Netherlands squad at the 1928 Amsterdam Games. The 12-woman team easily won the gold by 27.75 points over second-place Italy (316.75 points to 289.00 points). Great Britain took the bronze.

Women gymnasts of 1928 competed for only one event—the team competition. This remained unchanged until the 1952 Olympics, when individual medals were awarded for uneven bars, balance beam, floor exercise, and the all-around vault.

1952: INDIVIDUAL GOLD MEDAL Mariya Gorokhovskaya of the Soviet Union won the first individual Olympic gold medal in women's gymnastics during the 1952 Helsinki Games for the first Olympic women's all-around competition.

1972: BACK SALTO (BALANCE BEAM) The first female gymnast to perform an aerial back somersault on a balance beam was Olga Korbut of the Soviet Union during the 1972 Munich Games. The 4 foot 11 inch, 85-pound Soviet gymnast stole the show with her innovative moves and marked a watershed in women's gymnastics.

Prior to Korbut's acrobatic routines in Munich, gymnasts had performed routines that concentrated on grace and line, rather than technical difficulty. Following her success in Munich, the sport moved to a more and more technically demanding approach.

1976: PERFECT 10 Nadia Comaneci of Romania was the first gymnast, woman or man, to score a perfect 10 mark in Olympic competition. The 14-year-old gymnast first got a perfect score in her uneven bars routine at the 1976 Montreal Games.

In all, the 4 foot, 11 inch Comaneci was awarded seven perfect scores of 10 at the Montreal Games! She won three gold medals at the Games (all-around, balance beam and uneven bars), one silver in the team event, and a bronze in the floor exercise.

1976: PERFECT EVENT In addition to her perfect 10, Nadia Comaneci of Romania became the first gymnast to win an apparatus event with a combined perfect possible score of 20.00 points. In both of her performances on the uneven bars she gained perfect 10 scores.

Her feat was matched at the 1988 Seoul Games by Daniela Silivas, also of Romania. She too scored a perfect combined 20.00 points in the uneven bars.

1982: THE YURCHENKO VAULT Widely regarded as one of the most daring (and dangerous) moves in gymnastics, "the Yurchenko" was first performed in 1982 by Soviet gymnast Natalia Yurchenko, a former women's all-around world champ.

Yurchenko's self-titled move was radical in that it involved a flip on the runway causing the gymnast to leap backwards onto the vault. Yurchenko ran down the runway, executed a flip with a half-turn from the approach, and landed on the takeoff board facing the runway, rather than the horse. On hitting the horse, Yurchenko performed a one-and-a-half backward somersault and then stuck a two-footed landing.

Most Olympic Gold Medals Per Event

EVENT	GOLD	GYMNAST	COUNTRY	YEARS
Team	3	Larisa Latynina	USSR	1956, 1960, 1964
	3	Polina Astakhova	USSR	1956, 1960, 1964
	3	Lyudmila Turischeva	USSR	1968, 1972, 1976
All-Around	2	Larisa Latynina	USSR	1956, 1960
	2	Vera Caslavska	Czechoslovakia	1964, 1968
Balance Beam	2	Nadia Comaneci	Romania	1976, 1980
Floor Exercise	3	Larisa Latynina	USSR	1956*, 1960, 1964
Uneven Bars	2	Polina Astakhova	USSR	1960, 1964
	2	Svetlana Khorkina	Russia	1996, 2000
Vault	2	Vera Caslavska	Czechoslovakia	1964, 1968

*Tied with Agnes Keleti of Hungary

Carly Patterson

PODIUM PENALTY

At the 1988 Seoul Games, the U.S. missed the bronze medal in the women's team event by three-tenths of a point to East Germany because of a technicality. During the performance of Kelly Garrison-Steves, the team alternate Rhonda Faehn removed the springboard from under the bars that Garrison-Steves used to mount the apparatus. Faehn then stood to one side away from the bars and watched the routine. Her assistance in moving the springboard was perfectly legal, but Faehn had broken a rule by staying on the stage to watch the performance instead of returning to the team area. This little infraction cost the U.S. a half-point penalty and turned out to be the crucial difference.

SOMETHING TO THINK ABOUT

CLOSEST FINISH

At the 1992 Barcelona Games, Tatyana Gutsu of the Unified Team beat Shannon Miller of the U.S. in the all-around by .012 points (39.737 to 39.725), the closest-ever finish in the event. The competition came down to the vault. Miller went first and gained a 9.975 score. Gutsu needed to gain a 9.939 to win. On her first vault of two, with the best score counting, the Ukrainian gymnast bobbled her landing and only posted a 9.925. With one chance left, she stuck her landing and scored 9.950 points to capture the gold.

SUPERLATIVES

MOST OLYMPIC GOLD MEDALS CAREER

The most gold medals won in Olympic competition, by either a woman or man, is nine by Larisa Latynina of the Soviet Union, over three Olympiads.

Latynina won the all-around competition, the floor exercise, the vault, and team competition at the 1956 Melbourne Games. In Rome in 1960, she won the all-around, the floor exercise, and the team competition. Finally, at the 1964 Tokyo Games, she won gold in the floor exercise and the team competition.

MOST OLYMPIC GOLD MEDALS SINGLE OLYMPICS

The most gold medals won at a single Olympics by a female gymnast is four. This feat has been accomplished by four gymnasts: Agnes Keleti of Hungary (1956), Larisa Latynina of the Soviet Union (1956), Vera Caslavska of Czechoslovakia (1964), and Ecaterina Szabo of Romania (1984). Keleti and Latynina both won four golds at the 1956 Melbourne Games.

MOST OLYMPIC GOLD MEDALS INDIVIDUAL EVENTS

Vera Caslavska of Czechoslovakia won seven gold medals in individual events, the most by a female gymnast. In 1964, she won the all-around competition, the vault, and the balance beam. In 1968, she won the vault, the floor exercise, and the uneven bars.

MOST OLYMPIC GOLD MEDALS TEAM

The Soviet Union holds the record for the most team competition golds won by any nation, with nine Olympic golds. It held the streak from 1952 to 1988, with the exception of the boycotted 1984 games. Additionally, the Commonwealth of Independent States, which included most of the former Soviet republics, won the gold in 1992.

The Soviet Union far outpaced their nearest competitor, Romania, which holds only three team golds. No other team has won the gold more than once.

MOST OLYMPIC MEDALS CAREER

The most medals won in Olympic competition, by either a man or woman, is 18 by Larisa Latynina of the Soviet Union. She won a total of nine gold medals, five silver, and four bronze between 1956 and 1964.

MOST MEDALS SINGLE OLYMPICS

The record for the most medals won at a single Olympic Games by a female gymnast is seven, held by Mariya Gorokhovskaya of the Soviet Union. At the 1952 Helsinki Games, she won two gold and five silver medals. Her golds came in the all-around and team competitions. She won her silvers in the team exercise with portable apparatus, the vault, the uneven bars, the beam, and the floor exercise.

Men

GYMNASTICS COMPETITIONS date back to ancient times and were part of the earliest Olympic Games. The ancient Greeks saw gymnastics as an outlet for achieving symmetry between body and mind, and practiced the exercises in "gymnasiums," which also were places for discussion of the arts and philosophy.

Modern-day gymnastics came together in the late 18th century through the efforts of pioneering teachers, whose work led to the growth of the sport in Europe and later the rest of the world.

MILESTONES

1774: GYMNASTICS AND EDUCATION
The first teacher known to incorporate gymnastics into the physical education curriculum was Johann Bernhard Basedow of Germany. When he founded his own private school, the Philanthropinum, in Dessau, Germany, in 1774, he introduced a curriculum of structured physical activity for his students.

Basedow believed that education in the classroom was improved by linking lessons to the outside world.

1793: "GYMNASTICS FOR YOUTH"
The most influential book in the creation of modern gymnastics is Johann Christoph Friedrich Guts-Muth's *Gymnastics for Youth*, written in 1793.

Known as "the Grandfather of Gymnastics," Guts-Muth taught at Germany's Schnepfenthal Institute for 50 years. He emphasized the use of apparatus such as the balance beam, climbing poles, and ropes as part of the gymnastics program.

1813: NEW TECHNIQUES
In 1813, Swedish physical education instructor Pehr Henrik Ling, persuaded King Charles XIII of Sweden to fund the Royal Gymnastics Central Institute, where a new system of gymnastics that emphasized posture and movement, rather than skill on apparatus, was introduced.

Ling's methods were quickly adopted throughout Europe and expanded the sport beyond its emphasis on balance beams and other equipment. Most of Ling's exercises could be performed in big classes in open areas.

1881: EUROPEAN GYMNASTICS FEDERATION
The world's first international sports organization, the European Gymnastics Federation (EGF), was created on July 23, 1881, by three founding nations: Belgium, France, and the Netherlands.

Because of the EGF's work in promoting the sport, gymnastics was accepted into the Olympic program at the first modern Olympic Games in 1896. Gymnastics, along with track and field, swimming, and fencing, is one of only four sports to have been on the program at all Games of the modern era.

The EGF later changed its name in 1921 to the International Gymnastics Federation with the inclusion of the U.S., and continues to be the governing body of the sport.

1980: PERFECT 10
Aleksandr Dityatin of the Soviet Union was the first male gymnast awarded a perfect 10 in Olympic competition. He received the 10 for his vault performance during the all-around competition at the 1980 Moscow Games.

Four other gymnasts also scored 10s at the 1980 Games (which were boycotted by the U.S., China, and about 60 other nations).

They were Stoyan Deltchev (Bulgaria, in the horizontal bars), Alexander Tkachyov (Soviet Union, in the parallel bars), Zoltan Magyar (Hungary, in the pommel horse), and Michael Nikolay (East Germany, in the pommel horse).

SUPERLATIVES

MOST OLYMPIC GOLD MEDALS — CAREER

The most gold medals won in Olympic competition for gymnastics is eight, by Sawao Kato of Japan, over three Olympiads.

Kato won the all-around competition, floor exercise, and team competition at the 1968 Mexico City Games. At the 1972 Munich Games, he won the all-around, the team competition, and the individual parallel bars.

He also landed gold on the individual parallel bars and team competition at the 1976 Montreal Games.

MOST OLYMPIC GOLD MEDALS — SINGLE OLYMPICS

The most gold medals ever awarded to a male gymnast during a single Olympic Games is six, by Vitaly Scherbo. At the 1992 Barcelona Games, he represented the Unified Team, the official name of the former Soviet republics that competed together in Spain.

The 20-year-old Minsk-born Scherbo won gold in the team competition, the all-around, the parallel bars, the vault, the rings, and pommel horse, and tied for first place in the pommel horse with Pae Gil-su of North Korea.

MOST OLYMPIC GOLD MEDALS — INDIVIDUAL EVENTS

Boris Shakhlin and Nikolay Andrianov, both of the Soviet Union, have each won a record six individual Olympic gold medals.

Shakhlin won the pommel horse in 1956 and 1960, the all-around competition, parallel bars, and vault in 1960, and horizontal bars in 1964. Andrianov won the floor exercise in 1972 and 1976, the all-around and rings in 1976, and the vault in 1976 and again in 1980.

MOST OLYMPIC GOLD MEDALS — TEAM

Japan holds the most gold medals won for team competition in men's gymnastics. They won every team medal awarded from 1960 to 1972 (5), and came back to take the gold in 2004.

MOST OLYMPIC MEDALS — CAREER

Nikolay Andrianov of the Soviet Union won the most gymnastics gold medals in Olympic competition with 15.

He won seven gold medals, six in individual events (see above) and one in the team event in 1980. As for silver, he won five, two in the team event in 1972 and 1976, the parallel bars in 1976, the all-around competition in 1980, and the floor exercise in 1980.

Lastly, Adrianov took home three bronze medals, one in vault in 1972, the pommel horse in 1976, and the horizontal bar in 1980.

MOST MEDALS — SINGLE OLYMPICS

Aleksandr Dityatin of the Soviet Union won eight medals during the 1980 Moscow Games, the most by a man at a single Olympics.

Dityatin won three gold, four silver, and one bronze. His gold medals came in the team event, the all-around, and the rings. He won silver in the horizontal bars, parallel bars, pommel horse, and vault. Dityatin won bronze in the floor exercise.

"LEG-ENDARY" FEAT

At the 1904 St. Louis Games, George Eyser of the U.S. won six medals, including gold in the vault and parallel bars. Eyser's accomplishment was all the more remarkable because his left leg had been amputated years earlier, after he was hit by a train. The American gymnast is the only athlete with a wooden prosthesis to win an Olympic medal.

SOMETHING TO THINK ABOUT

MORE "LEG-ENDARY" FEATS

At the 1976 Montreal Games, Japanese gymnast Shun Fujimoto broke his left leg during his floor exercise routine in the team competition but didn't tell anyone. Despite the pain, he performed his whole pommel horse routine, gaining a mark of 9.5. Later, on the rings, Fujimoto performed flawlessly and was able to complete a solid dismount on his broken leg and received a 9.7 mark, while further injuring himself by dislocating his knee. At this point he submitted to medical treatment and withdrew from the Games. In no small part because of Fujimoto's heroic efforts, Japan won the team gold medal.

Boxing

BOXING IS ONE OF THE WORLD'S OLDEST SPORTS—it was part of the ancient Greek Olympics. In the 18th century, prizefighting, as it was called, gained widespread popularity in Britain, and boxing became part of the modern Olympics in 1904.

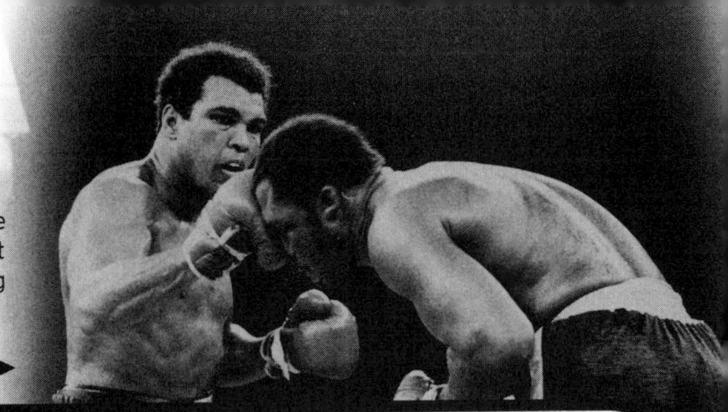

"Thrilla in Manila:" Muhammad Ali (left) and Joe Frazier ▶

MILESTONES

1719: FIRST HEAVYWEIGHT CHAMP The first acknowledged heavyweight champion was James Figg, a 6-foot, 185-pound Londoner who fought bare-knuckle "trials of manhood." He held his ground as "champion of England" from 1719 to about 1730, taking on all challengers.

Figg supposedly lost only one of his more than 270 matches, and that happened when he was sick.

1865: QUEENSBERRY RULES The basic rules of modern boxing were first drafted in 1865, when John G. Chambers, under the patronage of John Sholto Douglas, Britain's eighth Marquess of Queensberry, developed regulations to replace the London Prize Ring Rules. Rounds were now set at three minutes, and padded gloves were required. If one man went down, the other had to go to his corner, and if a downed man failed to get up in 10 seconds, his opponent was ruled the winner.

Bare-knuckle bouts did not cease immediately but rapidly declined in number. John L. Sullivan (U.S.) was the last bare-knuckle champion.

After winning the title in 1882 he continued to fight mostly bare-knuckle. He claimed the Marquess of Queensberry title in an 1885 win, but lost to "Gentleman Jim" Corbett (U.S.) in an 1892 world heavyweight title match fought under the Queensberry Rules.

1908: FIRST BLACK HEAVYWEIGHT CHAMP Owner of a lifetime record of 77-13-14, Jack Johnson was the sport's first African American heavyweight champion, wearing the crown from 1908 to 1915. The 6'1", 200-pound Johnson developed his skills fighting in "battle royals"—brutal spectacles that pitted several black men against each other until the last man standing won. Johnson was continually denied the opportunity to fight for the boxing title despite having an undefeated record since 1905.

Finally, World Heavyweight Champion Tommy Burns of Canada agreed to a fight. On Dec. 26, 1908, in Sydney, Australia, Johnson knocked him out in the 14th round. He became undisputed champ on July 4, 1910, in Reno, NV, when he knocked out Jim Jeffries (U.S.).

Johnson endured racism in the U.S. and lived abroad from 1914 to 1920. He lost the title to the Jess Willard (U.S.) in Havana, Cuba, April 5, 1915, when he was knocked out in the 26th round.

1937: LOUIS ERA BEGINS On June 22, 1937, Joe Louis defeated James ("Cinderella Man") Braddock in the eighth round in Chicago to win the heavyweight belt, beginning the longest championship reign (all divisions) in modern boxing history (nearly 12 years). He won 68 of his 71 matches in his career, and was only the second black man to hold the heavyweight title.

His bouts with Max Schmeling of Germany, darling of the Nazi regime (although not a Nazi himself), were legendary. "The Brown Bomber" lost to Schmeling in a non-title bout on June 19, 1936, before a crowd of more than 60,000 at Yankee Stadium in New York City. But on June 22, 1938, Louis won a New York rematch with the German, knocking him out in the first round.

1955: UNDEFEATED CHAMP Rocky Marciano was the only heavyweight champion to retire undefeated. Although he had an extremely short reach of only 68 inches, he is considered by many boxing historians to be the hardest raw puncher ever. On Sept. 23, 1952, he won the crown by defeating Jersey Joe Walcott in the 13th round in front of over 40,000 fans in Philadelphia's Municipal Stadium.

In his last fight he defeated Archie Moore, Sept. 21, 1955, in Yankee Stadium. His lifetime record was 49-0 with 43 KOs.

1960: FIRST CHAMP TO REGAIN TITLE Floyd Patterson was the first man to regain a heavyweight title. He won the title left vacant by Marciano's retirement with a five-round knockout of Archie Moore on Nov. 30, 1956, in Chicago.

Just under 21 years, 11 months old, Patterson was the youngest world heavyweight champ ever. He defended his title four times before being knocked out by Ingemar Johansson of Sweden on June 26, 1959; then regained the belt in a June 20, 1960, rematch.

On Sept. 25, 1962, Sonny Liston (U.S.) took the title with a first-round knockout.

Jack Johnson

SOMETHING TO THINK ABOUT

LAST BARE-KNUCKLE TITLE

The last bare-knuckle heavyweight title bout in the U.S. was fought on July 8, 1889. John L. Sullivan, the first American professional boxer, and Jake Kilrain went 75 rounds (2 hours, 16 minutes, 25 seconds) before Kilrain's corner finally threw in the sponge. The match was staged in the sweltering heat of a pine forest in Richburg, MS.

1967: ALI STRIPPED OF TITLE On April 28, 1967, Muhammad Ali officially refused induction into the U.S. military in Houston, TX, as a conscientious objector, and his boxing license was suspended by the New York State Athletic Commission. Other state commissions quickly followed suit, and he was stripped of his world title.

Born Cassius Clay in Louisville, KY, he adopted the name Muhammad Ali after becoming a Muslim in March 1964. The name change came shortly after he won the heavyweight belt from Sonny Liston on Feb. 25.

Ali returned to the sport on Oct. 26, 1970, earning a three-round technical knockout against Jerry Quarry in Atlanta, GA, the only state where he could fight. The following year Ali challenged the titleholder, Joe Frazier, in a March 8 match. He won a unanimous decision after a grueling 15 rounds in what was called the "Fight of the Century."

A few months later the U.S. Supreme Court reversed Ali's conviction for draft evasion. He regained the heavyweight title from George Foreman in the famous "Rumble in the Jungle" (Oct. 30, 1974), fought in Kinshasa, Zaire. Then Ali recorded two wins over Frazier, the last being the brutal "Thrilla in Manila" (Oct. 1, 1975), which Ali won by technical knockout.

SUPERLATIVES

LONGEST REIGN

Joe Louis was world heavyweight champion for 11 years and 252 days, from June 22, 1937, to his retirement on March 1, 1949. The Brown Bomber defended his title a record 25 times.

OLDEST CHAMP

With his 10th round knockout of titleholder Michael Moorer on Nov. 5, 1994, George Foreman became the oldest heavyweight champion, at 45 years, 299 days old. He defended the International Boxing Federation (IBF) version of the title on April 22, 1995, against Axel Schulz (Germany), at 46 years, 132 days, eking out a 12th-round decision.

Foreman gave up the IBF belt on July 3 after refusing a rematch with Alex Schulz. Previously, the World Boxing Association (WBA) had stripped Foreman of its title after he refused to fight the WBA's top-rated challenger, Tony Tucker.

YOUNGEST CHAMP

At 20 years, 145 days, Mike Tyson became the youngest heavyweight titleholder in boxing history when he knocked out World Boxing Council (WBC) Champion Trevor Berbick on Nov. 22, 1986.

Tyson went on to capture the WBA and IBF versions of the heavyweight belt from James ("Bonecrusher") Smith (March 7, 1987) and Tony Tucker (Aug. 1, 1987), respectively. The Tucker bout made Tyson the youngest ever undisputed heavyweight champ, at 21 years, 32 days.

TALLEST CHAMP

Standing 7 feet tall, Nikolay Valuev of Russia became the tallest world heavyweight champion ever when he won a points decision over WBA champion John Ruiz (U.S.) on Dec. 17, 2005, in Berlin, Germany.

HEAVIEST BOUT

Nikolay Valvev of Russia became the heaviest heavyweight champion. For his Dec. 17, 2005, title fight with John Ruiz, Valvev weighed in at exactly 300 pounds.

For a match on Dec. 11, 2004, Vitali Klitschko weighed in at 250 pounds and Britain's Danny Williams at 270 pounds, making their combined weight the greatest ever for a world heavyweight title bout. Klitschko won.

LIGHTEST CHAMP

The lightest heavyweight champion was Britain's Bob Fitzsimmons. A former middleweight titleholder, he weighed 167 pounds and stood 5 ft, 11.75 inches tall when he knocked out "Gentlemen Jim" Corbett to win the title in Carson City, NV, on March 17, 1897.

WORST PRO RECORD

The heavyweight champ with the worst career record was James Braddock, who held the title belt in 1935-36. His winning percentage of 60.7% is the lowest of any titleholder. His final pro record was 51-26-7.

Wrestling

WRESTLING IS ONE OF THE WORLD'S OLDEST SPORTS. It is depicted in Egyptian wall paintings from 5,000 years ago and was featured in the ancient Olympic Games. The two most widely performed styles of wrestling are Greco-Roman and freestyle, both of which are featured in modern-day Olympics. But there are many other styles of wrestling.

GRECO-ROMAN AND FREESTYLE

Contestants in Greco-Roman wrestling must apply all holds above the waist, using only their hands and arms. Wrestlers are not allowed to employ tripping or tackling, or use their legs to secure a hold. Greco-Roman wrestlers engage their opponents from a standing position and attempt to bring them to the ground so that the shoulders strike the mat simultaneously. In freestyle wrestling, which evolved from a style called "catch as catch can," almost any fair hold is allowed. The only ones not permitted are those that could injure an opponent, such as strangleholds. A fall is achieved when one wrestler pins both of his opponent's shoulders to the mat for one second.

NCAA WRESTLING

The current weight classes in the adapted-freestyle NCAA competition are (in pounds): 125, 133, 141, 149, 157, 165, 174, 184, 197, and heavyweight (197-plus).

SUMO WRESTLING

Sumo wrestling is one of Japan's national sports and places great emphasis on ritual and tradition. Weight, size, strength, and agility are extremely important. Wrestlers, or *rikishi,* often weigh more than 300 pounds and wear only loincloths, which opponents usually grab. Kicking, gouging, and hair pulling are prohibited, but pushing, pulling, slapping, throwing, and grappling are permitted.

A wrestler wins a match by driving his adversary out of a 15-foot ring or by forcing his opponent to touch the ground with any part of his body other than the soles of his feet. Matches often last no more than a few seconds. The Makuuchi Division is the top league.

MILESTONES

GRECO-ROMAN AND FREESTYLE

1896: MODERN OLYMPICS Greco-Roman wrestling was included in the first modern Olympic Games in April 1896. Germany's Karl Schumann won the gold medal in the heavyweight class, defeating Georgios Tsitas of Greece in a match that was fought over two days. The pair wrestled for 40 minutes without a decision before the referee called the match because of darkness. The bout continued the next morning, with Schumann finally throwing Tsitas by the hip to win the tournament.

Freestyle wrestling was added to the Olympics in 1904.

1912: FILA The International Wrestling Federation of Associated Wrestling Styles (FILA) was created in 1912 to organize the rules of the game. It now has 146 affiliated national federations.

2004: WOMEN COMPETE IN OLYMPICS Olympic Womens' Wrestling (freestyle) made its debut at the 2004 Athens Games. The first women to win medals were: Irini Merleni, Ukraine (48 kg); Saori Yoshida, Japan (55 kg); Kaori Icho, Japan (63 kg); and Xu Wang, China (72 kg).

NCAA WRESTLING

1928: FIRST NCAA CHAMPIONSHIPS Organized by the then chairman of the NCAA rules committee, Dr. Raymond Clapp, the first NCAA wrestling championships were held at Iowa State Univ. in 1928. Oklahoma A&M (today Oklahoma State) won four of the seven individual titles and the team title over Iowa State. Under coach Ed Gallagher, Oklahoma A&M had been undefeated since 1922.

SUMO WRESTLING

1632: *YOKOZUNA* The highest rank in sumo wrestling is *yokozuna*. A complicated ranking system determines *yokozuna* status in modern-day sumo, but the practice dates back to the 17th century when Akashi Shiganosuke became the first *yokozuna* in 1632. Formal record keeping began in 1789 when Tanikaze Kajinosuke was made the fourth *yokozuna*. In all, 68 *rikishi* (wrestlers) have achieved the rank.

1993: *YOKOZUNA* (NON-JAPANESE) Hawaii native Akebono Taro (born Chad Rowan) became the 64th *yokozuna* on Jan. 27, 1993; the first non-Japanese *rikishi* to do so. The 23-year-old Akebono reached the pinnacle in five years, the shortest time ever.

When he retired on Jan. 22, 2001, Akebono had been ranked as grand champion through 48 tournaments (he won 11), the fourth-longest for a *yokozuna*. His career record was 654-232-181.

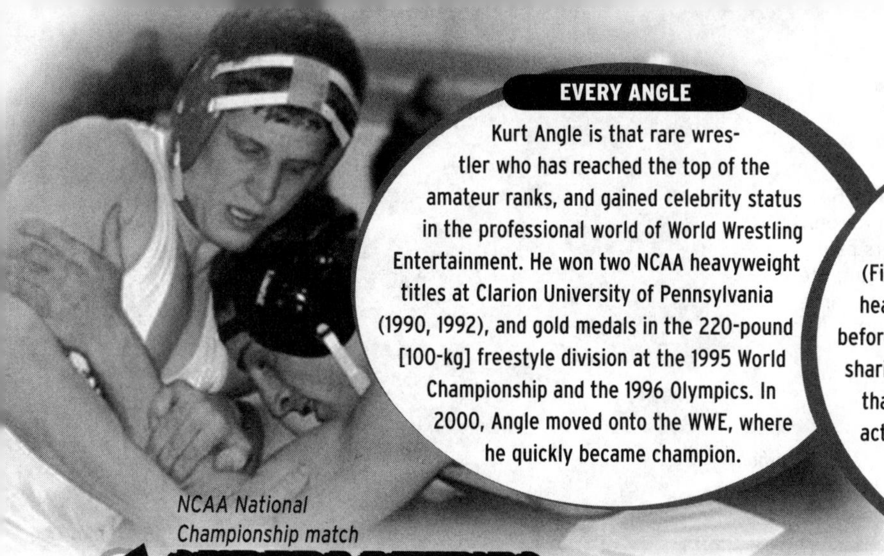

NCAA National Championship match

EVERY ANGLE

Kurt Angle is that rare wrestler who has reached the top of the amateur ranks, and gained celebrity status in the professional world of World Wrestling Entertainment. He won two NCAA heavyweight titles at Clarion University of Pennsylvania (1990, 1992), and gold medals in the 220-pound [100-kg] freestyle division at the 1995 World Championship and the 1996 Olympics. In 2000, Angle moved onto the WWE, where he quickly became champion.

SOMETHING TO THINK ABOUT

NO WIN SITUATION

At the 1912 Stockholm Games, Anders Ahlgren (Sweden) faced Ivar Böhling (Finland) for the Greco-Roman light-heavyweight gold. The match lasted nine hours before officials declared the bout a draw. Instead of sharing the top spot on the podium, officials ruled that a gold medal could only be awarded to an actual winner. So the pair stood on the second step of the podium and received silver medals, while the gold medal space was left empty.

SUPERLATIVES

GRECO-ROMAN AND FREE-STYLE

MOST OLYMPIC GOLDS Four wrestlers have won three Olympic wrestling golds: Carl Westergren (Sweden) won the Greco-Roman middleweight class (1920), light-heavyweight (1924), and heavyweight (1932); Ivar Johansson (Sweden) won the Greco-Roman welterweight and the freestyle middleweight classes (1932) and the Greco-Roman middleweight class (1936); Aleksandr Medved (USSR) won the freestyle light-heavyweight class (1964), and heavyweight (1968, 1972); and Aleksandr Karelin (USSR, CIS, Russia) won the Greco-Roman super-heavyweight class (1988, 1992, 1996).

MOST OLYMPIC MEDALS The most medals won in Olympic wrestling is five by Wilfried Dietrich (Germany). He won one gold (freestyle heavyweight, 1960), two silver (Greco-Roman super heavyweight, 1956 and 1960), and two bronze (Greco-Roman super heavyweight, 1964, freestyle heavyweight, 1968).

LONGEST BOUT (OLYMPICS) Martin Klein (Russia) and Alfred Asikainen (Finland) grappled under the beating sun for over 11 hours in an outdoor arena during a semifinal showdown in the Greco-Roman middleweight class at the 1912 Stockholm Games.

Although short breaks were taken every half-hour, when Klein finally pinned Asikainen for the victory he was so exhausted from his marathon effort that he was unable to participate in the gold medal match. Sweden's Claes Johanson won the gold on Klein's default.

NCAA WRESTLING

LONGEST WINNING STREAK Iowa State senior Cael Sanderson won his 159th straight match on March 23, 2002, and in addition to achieving the longest winning streak, he became the first wrestler to go undefeated in his college career.

With the win, which came in the 197-pound (89-kg) weight class, Sanderson captured his fourth consecutive NCAA title. He continued on to an Olympic gold in 2004 for the 163-185 pound (74-84 kg) freestyle.

MOST TEAM TITLES Oklahoma State has won the most NCAA team titles, with 33 (as Oklahoma A&M, 1928-31, 1933-35, 1937-42, 1946, 1948-49, 1954-56; as Oklahoma State, 1958-59, 1961-62, 1964, 1966, 1968, 1971, 1989-90, 1994, 2003-05. They are followed by Iowa (20), Iowa State (8), and Oklahoma (7).

MOST CONSECUTIVE TEAM TITLES Iowa won a record nine straight NCAA titles from 1978 to 1986.

MOST TITLES (COACH) Iowa coach Dan Gable guided his team to 15 Division I wrestling championships between 1978 to 1997. Gable also led Iowa to the longest winning streak in history, garnering nine straight titles from 1978 to 1986 (see above). His team's career record was 355-21-2 (a .932 win percentage).

SUMO WRESTLING

MOST WINS (CAREER) In terms of total matches, Chiyonofuji Mitsugu, 58th *Yokozuna*, won 807 matches while in the Makunouchi Division. Percentage-wise, Taiho Koki, 48th *Yokozuna* and youngest ever at 21 years, 3 months, won 83.8% of his Makunouchi matches over nine years. Taiho also won a record 32 tournaments, one more than Chiyonofuji.

HEAVIEST SUMO WRESTLER Samoan-born Salevaa Atisanoe, known in Sumo circles as Konishiki, "The Dump Truck," was the heaviest known sumo wrestler. He regularly tipped the scales at over 580 pounds before retiring in Nov. 1997, after 16 big years.

Bowling

THE PROFESSIONAL BOWLING ASSOCIATION (PBA) was founded in 1958 by Eddie Elias, an Akron, OH, attorney. The 33 founding members paid $50 each to help fund the fledgling circuit; the PBA Tour started the following year with three events and a combined prize of $49,500.

Earl Anthony

MILESTONES

1959: FIRST MULTIPLE TOURNAMENT WINNER Hall of Fame bowler Dick Weber won two of the first three PBA Tour events in its inaugural season of 1959. He won both the Dayton Open and the Paramus-Eastern. The other tournament that first year, the Empire State, was won by Lou Campi.

1961: TELEVISED PBA FINALS The 1961 PBA Invitational staged in Paramus, NJ, was the first PBA Tour finals event aired on TV. Roy Lown of Baltimore, MD, won the tournament and received a prize of $15,000, by far the largest payday of the season. Of the 11 tournaments staged on the tour that year, only one other event offered a first-place prize of more than $4,000, the PBA National Championship. Dave Soutar won and took home a $6,000 first place check.

1965: CORPORATE SPONSOR In 1965, Eddie Elias persuaded the Firestone Tire Company to sponsor the tour's most prestigious annual event, the Tournament of Champions. Staged in Akron, OH, at that time home to both the PBA Tour and Firestone, it marked the first time corporate sponsorship was ever paired with a nationally televised sporting event. Billy Hardwick of San Mateo, CA, won the then-unprecedented first prize of $25,000.

1967: TELEVISED PERFECT GAME Jack Biondolillo rolled the first perfect game on live national TV at the 1967 Firestone Tournament of Champions on April 1, 1967. Biondolillo beat Les Schissler, 300-216. To date, 16 bowlers have rolled a 300 game during a televised national PBA tournament.

1969: TRIPLE CROWN In professional bowling three events make up the Triple Crown: the Bowling Proprietors' Association of America (BPAA) U.S. Open (first contested in 1942), the Tournament of Champions (1965), and the PBA World Championship (1959). No bowler has won all three events in one season.

The first player to complete the career Triple Crown was Billy Hardwick. He won the PBA World Championship, then called the PBA Nationals, in 1963, the Tournament of Champions in 1965, and finally the U.S. Open in 1969. Three other players have completed the career Triple Crown: Johnny Petraglia, Mike Aulby, and Pete Weber.

1975: $100,000 SEASON In 1975, Earl Anthony won seven titles and became the first bowler to win more than $100,000 in earnings for the season. That year he won $107,585.

1982: $1 MILLION CAREER EARNINGS Earl Anthony, the all-time career wins leader in PBA Tour history, became the first bowler to top $1 million in career earnings in 1982 when he won the Toledo Trust PBA National Championship.

1986: $100,000 PERFECT GAME In 1986, True Value Hardware Stores offered a $100,000 bonus to any player who could bowl a perfect game during a televised finals. The following year, on Jan. 31, 1987, Pete McCordic won the prize when he rolled a perfect game in his opening game of the Greater Los Angeles Open finals. It was the first 300 game bowled on a nationally-televised event in 13 years. Mats Karlsson of Sweden won the tournament, for a first place prize of $18,000.

1980: 7-10 SPLIT The first bowler to convert the almost impossible 7-10 split in a televised PBA Tour event was Mark Roth at the 1980 ARC Alameda Open. Only two other bowlers, John Mazza and Jess Stayrook, have made the shot in televised tournaments. Both converted the 7-10 split in 1991—Mazza in the Bud Light Classic and Stayrook in the Tucson Open.

PBA Tour Scoring Records

RECORD	TOTAL PINS	PLAYER	EVENT
6 Games	1,635	Norm Duke	1994 True Value Open
	1,635	Dave Wodka	1998 Brunswick Circuit Pro Bowling Classic
8 Games	2,165	Billy Hardwick	1968 Japan Gold Cup
9 Games	2,357	Dave D'Entremont	2002 PBA Flagship Open
12 Games	3,083	Mike Aulby	1996 Greater Baltimore Open
16 Games	4,095	John Mazza	1996 Merit Mixed Doubles Championship
18 Games	4,696	Norm Duke	1994 True Value Open
24 Games	6,109	Pete Webber	1996 Merit Mixed Doubles Championship
26 Games	6,783	Mike Aulby	1995 Peoria Open
32 Games	7,940	Parker Bohn III	1999 Oronamin C Japan Cup
34 Games	8,740	Mike Aulby	1995 Peoria Open
42 Games	10,544	Mike Aulby	1995 Peoria Open

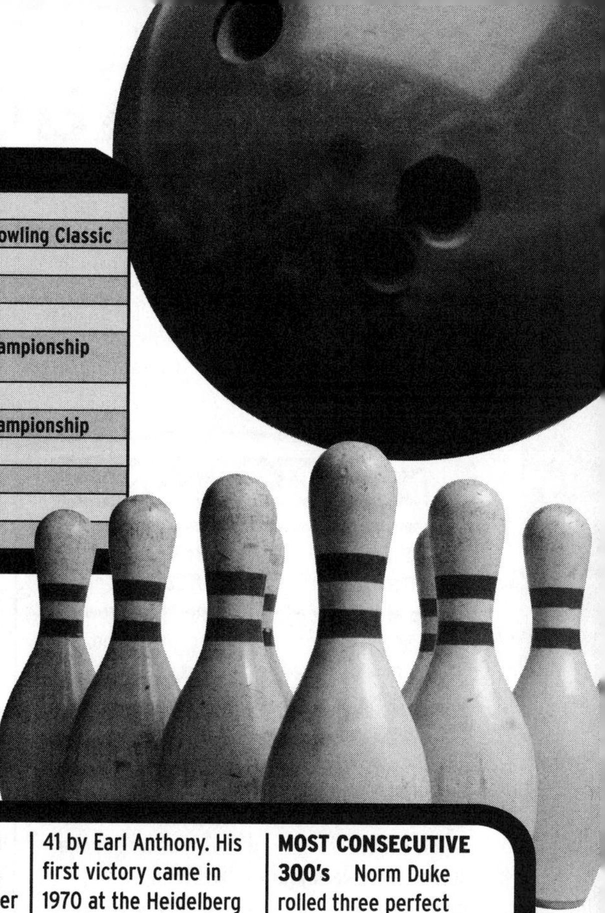

SUPERLATIVES

MOST TRIPLE CROWN TITLES The most Triple Crown titles won in a career is eight by Earl Anthony. He won six PBA World Championships (1973-75, 1981-83), and two Tournament of Champions (1974, 1978).

MOST U.S. OPEN TITLES Two bowlers have won the U.S. Open four times: Don Carter (1953, 1954, 1957, 1958), and Dick Weber (1962, 1963, 1965, 1966).

MOST PBA WORLD CHAMPIONSHIP TITLES Earl Anthony's six PBA titles is the all-time record (see above).

MOST TOURNAMENT OF CHAMPIONS TITLES Two bowlers have won the Tournament of Champions three times: Mike Durbin (1972, 1982, 1984), and Jason Couch (1999, 2000, 2002). Couch is the only bowler to win the event consecutively. The event was not held in 2001.

MOST MAJORS In bowling, four tournaments are considered the majors: the three PBA Triple Crown events and the American Bowling Congress (ABC) Masters Tournament (1901); the ABC Masters is open to qualified professionals and amateurs. The most major titles won is 10, by Earl Anthony. The Hall of Fame bowler won eight Triple Crown events (see above), and two ABC Masters titles (1977, 1984).

MOST ABC MASTERS TITLES Mike Aulby has won the ABC Masters a record three times. He won his first title in 1989. His other victories came in 1995 and 1998. Only two bowlers have won back-to-back ABC Masters titles: Dick Hoover, 1956 and 1957; Billy Welu, 1964 and 1965.

PBA TOUR

MOST WINS (CAREER) The record for the most official PBA Tour event wins is 41 by Earl Anthony. His first victory came in 1970 at the Heidelberg Open in Seattle, and his last was in 1983 at the Toledo Trust PBA National Championship. Anthony's best year on tour was 1975 when he won seven tournaments.

MOST WINS (SEASON) Mark Roth won eight tournaments in 1978.

MOST CONSECUTIVE 200's During the 1993 season, Walter Ray Williams Jr. shot a score of at least 200 in 61 consecutive rounds. That year, Williams won a Tour-leading seven tournaments and $296,370 in earnings.

MOST CONSECUTIVE 300's Norm Duke rolled three perfect games in a row over two rounds at the 1996 Brunswick Johnny Petraglia Open on Apr. 10. The tournament was won by Walter Ray Williams Jr.

OLDEST WINNER The oldest player to win an official PBA Tour event is John Handegard. He was 57 years, 139 days old when he won the 1995 Northwest Classic.

YOUNGEST WINNER Norm Duke was 18 years, 345 days old when he won the 1983 Cleveland Open, the youngest player to win a PBA Tour event.

Horse Racing

HORSE RACING IS ONE OF THE WORLD'S OLDEST SPORTS. Organized races were held at the Olympics in ancient Greece as early as 700 BC. Racing was highly popular in the Roman Empire. It spread in Europe when knights returned from the Crusades with Arabian, Barb, and Turk horses. These were bred with English horses to create the Thoroughbred breed still used in racing today. The sport was introduced in America during colonial times when the first Thoroughbreds were brought over from Europe. Today, there are racetracks all around the U.S., with the center of the industry in Kentucky.

MILESTONES

1665: FIRST U.S. RACETRACK Built in 1665 at Hempstead Plains in Long Island, NY, the Newmarket racetrack was the first track in the U.S. and was named for the famous track in England. During colonial times, two meets were staged there each year, one in the spring and one in the fall.

1730: FIRST THOROUGHBRED The first Thoroughbred imported from Britain to America was Bulle Rock in 1730. The 21-year-old stallion was a son of the Darley Arabian, one of the three "foundation stallions" of the modern Thoroughbred horse, originally brought to England from the Mediterranean.

It is estimated that by the turn of the 19th century more than 300 Thoroughbreds had been imported to the U.S.

1867: BELMONT STAKES The oldest of the Triple Crown races, the Belmont Stakes, was first run on June 19, 1867, at Jerome Park, NY. Named for jockey club president August Belmont, the inaugural race was won by the filly Ruthless, who beat DeCourcey by a neck. Ridden by Gilbert Watson Patrick ("Gilpatrick"), Ruthless covered the $1\frac{5}{8}$-mile course in 3:05.

1873: PREAKNESS STAKES The second of the Triple Crown races was first run on May 27, 1873, at Pimlico Race Course in Baltimore, MD.

The inaugural race was won by Survivor, with George Barbee holding the reins. Survivor covered the $1\frac{1}{2}$ miles in 2:43, beating six other horses by 10 lengths, the largest Preakness margin of victory to this day.

1875: KENTUCKY DERBY The first leg of the Triple Crown and the most famous horse race in America, the Kentucky Derby, was first run on May 17, 1875, at Churchill Downs in Louisville, KY.

The inaugural race was won by Aristides. Ridden by Oliver Lewis, Aristides covered the $1\frac{1}{2}$ miles in $2{:}37\frac{3}{4}$. Lewis was also the first African-American jockey to win a Triple Crown race.

1930: TRIPLE CROWN The phrase "Triple Crown" was first used to describe the Kentucky Derby, Preakness, and Belmont by *Daily Racing Form* sportswriter Charles Hatton in 1930. Hatton used the term to describe the wins of Gallant Fox. Only one horse, Sir Barton in 1919, had won all three races prior to 1930.

Since Gallant Fox's sweep, only nine other horses have won the Triple Crown: Omaha in 1935, War Admiral in 1937, Whirlaway in 1941, Count Fleet in 1943, Assault in 1946, Citation in 1948, Secretariat in 1973, Seattle Slew in 1977, and Affirmed in 1978.

1968: FEMALE JOCKEY Following a hard-fought legal battle, Kathy Kusner became the first woman to obtain a jockey license in 1968. The first woman to actually ride in a pari-mutuel (betting) race in North America was 20-year-old Diane Crump. She rode Bridle 'n Bit, in a $1\frac{1}{8}$-mile seventh race at Hialeah Park, FL, on Feb. 7, 1969, finishing 10th in a field of 12 horses.

Fifteen days later, 19-year-old Barbara Jo Rubin became the first woman to ride a winner when she finished first while riding Cohesian in Charles Town, WV.

1993: FEMALE WINNER OF A TRIPLE CROWN RACE Julie Krone in 1993 became the first female jockey to win a Triple Crown race. She won the Belmont Stakes aboard Colonial Affair on June 5.

Krone's historic victory is the first, and so far only, Triple Crown race won by a female jockey. It was her fourth attempt at a Triple Crown race, and the eighth attempt for any female rider.

1984: BREEDERS' CUP The Breeders' Cup (officially since 2001 the Breeders' Cup World Thoroughbred Championships) is the season-ending championship of American Thoroughbred racing. First held Nov. 10, 1984, at Hollywood Park, CA, it is the richest day in racing, with each of the eight races offering purses of at least $1 million.

The climax of the day is the Breeders' Cup Classic, which has a purse of about $4 million—the biggest single prize in American horse racing.

Selected Records from Triple Crown Races:

Preakness Stakes ($1\frac{3}{16}$ miles)

Most Wins (jockey)	6	Eddie Arcaro	1941, 1948, 1950-51, 1955, 1957
Most Wins (trainer)	7	Robert W. Walden	1875, 1878-82, 1888
Fastest Time	1:53 $\frac{2}{5}$	Tank's Prospect	1985
	1:53 $\frac{2}{5}$	Louis Quatorze	1996
Biggest Margin	11 $\frac{1}{2}$ lengths	Smarty Jones	2004

The Belmont Stakes ($1\frac{1}{2}$ miles)

Most Wins (jockey)	6	Jim McLaughlin	1882-84, 1886-88
	6	Eddie Arcaro	1941-42, 1945, 1948, 1952, 1955
Most Wins (trainer)	8	James Rowe Sr.	1883-84, 1901, 1904, 1907-08, 1910, 1913
Fastest Time	2:24	Secretariat	1973
Biggest Margin	31 lengths	Secretariat	1973

Kentucky Derby ($1\frac{1}{4}$ miles)

Most Wins (jockey)	5	Eddie Arcaro	1938, 1941, 1945, 1948, 1952
	5	Bill Hartack	1957, 1960, 1962, 1964, 1969
Most Wins (trainer)	6	Ben Jones	1938, 1941, 1944, 1948-49, 1952
Fastest Time	1:59 $\frac{2}{5}$	Secretariat	1973
Biggest Margin	8 lengths	Old Rosebud	1914
	8 lengths	Johnstown	1939
	8 lengths	Whirlaway	1941
	8 lengths	Assault	1946

SUPERLATIVES

MOST WINS

JOCKEY Laffit Pincay Jr. rode a career record 9,530 winners from 48,487 mounts, with earnings of $237,417,045. He broke Bill Shoemaker's previous career wins mark of 8,833 on Dec. 10, 1999, when he rode Irish Nip to victory at Hollywood Park, CA.

Pincay's first victory came aboard Huelen on May 19, 1964, at Presidente Remon in his native Panama. His first win on a U.S. track came later on July 1, 1966, aboard Teacher's Art at Arlington Park, IL.

Pincay broke two bones in his neck from a fall on March 1, 2003, and shortly after that announced his retirement.

MOST WINS

SEASON 19-year-old Kent Desormeaux rode a season-record 598 winners from 2,312 mounts in 1989, breaking Chris McCarron's 15-year-old record of 546 winners.

HIGHEST EARNINGS

HORSE The highest career earnings in purse-money by any horse on North American tracks is $9,999,815 by Cigar. The 1995 Breeders' Cup Classic winner posted a career record of 19 wins, four seconds, and five thirds in 33 races. Among those 19 victories was a 16-race winning streak from Oct. 28, 1994, to July 13, 1996.

Cigar also holds the record for the most money won by a North American-based horse in a single year—$4,910,000 in 1996.

OLDEST RACE

The oldest continuously staged race in North America is the Phoenix Breeders' Cup, run yearly since 1831. Originally called the Phoenix Stakes, the Phoenix Breeders' Cup is raced in October at the Keeneland racetrack in Kentucky.

MOST TRIPLE CROWNS

JOCKEY The only jockey to ride horses to two Triple Crowns is Eddie Arcaro. He rode Whirlaway to the Triple Crown in 1941, and repeated the feat with Citation in 1948. In 18 years, "The Master" rode a record 17 winners in Triple Crown races (5 Kentucky, 6 Preakness, and 6 Belmont).

MOST TRIPLE CROWNS

TRAINER Two trainers have each led two horses to winning the Triple Crown: Sunny Jim Fitzsimmons trained Gallant Fox in 1930 and Omaha in 1935 (the first Triple Crown Winners); Ben Jones trained Whirlaway in 1941 and Citation in 1948.

THE LAST TIME...

The last filly to win a Triple Crown race was Winning Colors. She won the Kentucky Derby in 1988. The last filly to win the Preakness was Nellie Morse in 1924. The last filly to win the Belmont was Tanya in 1905. Winning Colors in 1988 and Genuine Risk in 1980 are the only two fillies to race in all three Triple Crown races.

Tests of Strength

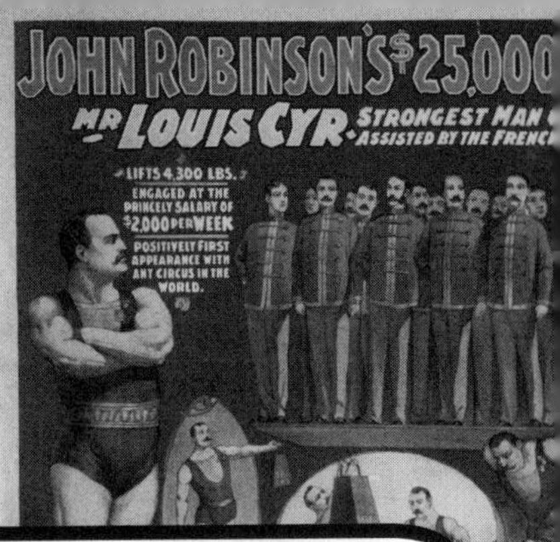

FEATS OF STRENGTH AND COURAGE HAVE BEEN PROMINENT IN LITERATURE AND MYTHOLOGY since the earliest times. In Greek mythology, for example, Atlas held the earth and heavens on his back, and Hercules, even as an infant, managed to strangle two serpents placed in his cradle. Organized individual and team tests of strength have been part of the real world for centuries. From tug-of-war contests to Olympic women's weightlifting competitions, lifters have strained sinews and awed spectators across the generations.

MILESTONES

AROUND 2000 BC: TUG-OF-WAR A contest of strength between two teams stationed at each end of a long rope, tug-of-war is one of the oldest known sporting contests. There is a depiction of a tug-of-war style contest on an Egyptian tomb dating back to 2000 BC. Ancient paintings and other works of art show that similar types of contests were staged in China, Korea, and India as well.

AROUND 11TH CENTURY: HIGHLAND GAMES Hundreds of years ago, Scottish clans first gathered in the Highlands for a festival of music, dancing and sports, but the exact date and year are unknown.

The current Highland Games can be traced to the reign of King Malcolm (1058-93). During the fall hunt, members of the different clans competed to be the strongest man in Scotland. The Games included traditional Scottish feats of strength such as tossing the caber (tree trunk), stone throwing, and even twisting the legs off a cow.

The Games were banned by English authorities after their victory over the Scots at the Battle of Culloden in 1746. They were revived at Braemar by 1800 and, in 1832, regulations were put in place and prize money was awarded.

1890s: LOUIS CYR Towards the end of the 19th century strongmen became popular vaudeville acts. Many were mere tricksters but Quebec strongman Louis Cyr was widely regarded (and always billed) as "the world's strongest man." He toured Canada, the U.S., and various countries in Western Europe performing feats of strength.

While many of his feats may have been exaggerated, they were not illusions. In one trademark stunt, first performed on Dec. 10, 1891, Cyr held back four horses or resisted their pull in front of 10,000 people at Montreal's Sohmer Park.

Another feat which he officially debuted on May 27, 1895, in Boston, involved lifting the 18 heaviest men in the audience on a platform for a total weight of over 4,000 pounds.

1896: OLYMPIC LIFTING The first Olympic Games of the modern era, staged in Athens, Greece, in 1896, featured two lifting events: the two-handed lift and the one-handed lift.

Launceston Elliott (Great Britain) won the one-handed lift (and Britain's first ever Olympic gold medal) when he lifted 71 kg (about 156 lbs).

Viggo Jensen (Denmark) won the silver. Later in the two-handed lift, the pair reversed positions. Jensen and Elliott both raised 111.5 kg (about 245 lbs), but the judges awarded Jensen the gold because of his better technique.

1952: WORLD WRISTWRESTLING CHAMPIONSHIPS Wristwrestling (armwrestling) has been around since ancient times. The World Wristwrestling Championships humbly began in a barroom at Gilardi's saloon in Petaluma, CA, in Oct. 1952 with local contestants.

Over the next 10 years, its organizer, Bill Soberanes, transformed the local event into the World Wristwrestling Championship. The contest got some of its earliest publicity from an unlikely source, a *Peanuts* comic strip series in 1968. The Championship moved to Reno, NV, in 2003 but is still held every October.

1972: FAILED DRUG TEST (OLYMPICS GAMES) The first time the Summer Olympics required comprehensive drug testing of athletes was at the 1972 Munich Games. Of the seven athletes who tested

Weightlifting Records (Heaviest Weight Category)

MEN'S +105 KG			
Snatch	Rezazadeh Hossein (Iran)	213 kg (469.6 lbs)	Sept. 14, 2003, Qinhuangdao, China
Clean and Jerk	Rezazadeh Hossein (Iran)	263 kg (579.8 lbs)	Aug. 25, 2004, Athens, Greece
Total	Rezazadeh Hossein (Iran)	472 kg (1,040.6 lbs)	Sept. 26, 2000, Sydney, Australia
WOMEN'S +75 KG			
Snatch	Ding Meiyuan (China)	137 kg (302 lbs)	Nov. 21, 2003, Vancouver, Canada
Clean and Jerk	Tang Gonghong (China)	182 kg (401.2 lbs)	Aug. 21, 2004, Athens, Greece
Total	Tang Gonghong (China)	305 kg (672.4 lbs)	Aug. 21, 2004, Athens, Greece

positive, two were weightlifters: Walter Legel (Austria) and Arjomand Mohamad Nasehi (Iran), both for ephedrine.

Perhaps, the sport's biggest black eye came at the 1988 Seoul Games. The Bulgarian weightlifters won four of the first five gold medals. Then, two of the team's gold medalists, Miktko Grablev and Anguelov Guenchev, tested positive for steroids. Soon after, the Bulgarian delegation withdrew the entire team from the Games.

1977: WORLD'S STRONGEST MAN COMPETITION Now known as the MET-Rx World's Strongest Man Contest, this made-for-TV competition was first staged in 1977 at Universal Studios in Los Angeles. The winner was former Olympian Bruce Wilhelm of Sunnyvale, CA, who, along with the other competitors, had to deal with temperatures of 108°F during the event.

1983: TRIPLE STRENGTH On Oct. 25, 1983, Bulgaria's 19-year-old Stefan Topurov became the first person to lift three times his own bodyweight overhead in competition. He accomplished the feat at the World Championships in Moscow, USSR. Lifting in the featherweight class (132 pounds), Topurov raised 396 pounds in the jerk section of the competition.

2000: WOMEN'S WEIGHTLIFTING Women's weightlifting was officially added to the Olympics at the 2000 Sydney Games, and included seven weight categories.

The first gold medal was won by Izabela Dragneva (Bulgaria) in the flyweight division. However, just days later, Dragneva was stripped of her medal after having failed a drug test. The gold medal was awarded to American Tara Nott of Stilwell, KS.

SOMETHING TO THINK ABOUT

MORE THAN PULLING HIS WEIGHT

At the 1936 Berlin Olympics, Egyptian weightlifter Khadr Sayed El Touni won gold in the middleweight class with a total lift of 387.5 kg (852 pounds). The breakdown was: press-117.5 kg; snatch-120.0 kg; jerk-150 kg. Not only did he set world records in each lift, but El Touni also lifted 15 kg, or 33 pounds, more than the total of the light-heavyweight gold medalist. In the light-heavyweight division (one above middleweight), Louis Hostin (France) won gold with a total of 372.5 kg (820 pounds).

MORE THAN PULLING HER WEIGHT

At the 2002 Nevada Powerlifting Championships, 90-year-old Effie Nielson of Salt Lake City, UT, set three world records in her age category. The great-grandmother, weighing in at 105 pounds, set records for the squat (80 lbs), bench press (50 lbs), and dead-lift (135 lbs).

SUPERLATIVES

YOUNGEST WORLD RECORD-HOLDER Naim Süleymanoðlu, also known as Naim Suleimanov (Turkish, born in Bulgaria), was the youngest lifter to set a weightlifting world record for any weight class. "The Pocket Hercules" set world records in the clean and jerk (160 kg, 352.5 lbs) and total (285 kg, 628.25 lbs) at the Record Makers Meet in Allentown, PA, on March 26, 1983, at age 16 years, 62 days.

OLDEST WORLD RECORD-HOLDER The oldest person to set a weightlifting world record is Norbert Schemansky (U.S.). He snatched 164.2 kg (362 lbs) in the then-unlimited heavyweight class in Detroit, MI, on April 28, 1962, at the Michigan State championships, at age 37 years, 333 days.

MOST OLYMPIC GOLD MEDALS Four weightlifters have won three gold medals in Olympic competition: Naim Süleymanoðlu (Turkey), in 1988 (60 kg), 1992 (60 kg), and 1996 (64 kg); Pyrros Dimas (Greece), 1992 (82.5 kg), 1996 (83 kg), 2000 (85 kg); Kakhi Kakhishvili (Greece, born in Georgia), 1992 (90 kg for the Unified Team), 1996 (99 kg), 2000 (94 kg); and Halil Mutlu (Turkey), 1996 (54 kg), 2000 (56 kg), 2004 (56 kg).

MOST WORLD'S STRONGEST MAN TITLES Two men have won four World's Strongest Man titles: Jon Pall Sigmarsson (Iceland) in 1984, 1986, 1988, and 1990; Magnus Ver Magnusson (Iceland) in 1991, and 1994-1996.

MOST TUG-OF-WAR CHAMPIONSHIPS Since eight-person team tug-of-war was added to the World Games in 1981, Switzerland has won a record five gold medals in the two weight classes (1989, 1993, 2005 for 640 kg and 1981, 1993 for 720 kg). When tug of war was an Olympic sport from 1900 to 1920, two gold medals each were won by Great Britain (1908, 1920) and Sweden (1900, 1912).

On Ice

Apolo Anton Ohno ►

ICE SPORTS GO BACK HUNDREDS OF YEARS. In northern Europe, blades made of animal ribs or antlers were attached to boots for travel across the ice. Today's ice sports include figure and speed skating, as well as bobsled, luge, and skeleton, in which the blades, or runners, are on sleds, not feet. Curling is played on ice, but not on skates.

FIGURE SKATING

Figure skating evolved from a sport based on strict technical requirements—"school figures"—into one known for artistry and acrobatic jumps. The first world championships were held in 1896. A category for women was established 20 years later. Figure skating was part of the Summer Olympics in 1908 and 1920, and has been a staple of the Winter Olympics since they began in 1924.

SPEED SKATING

There are two forms of speed skating: long track, in which skaters race against the clock on a 400-meter track; and short track, in which skaters race against one another on a 111-meter track. Men's long-track world championships were first held in 1869 and the sport was part of the first Winter Olympics in 1924. Women's long track became an Olympic sport in 1960. Men's and women's short track debuted at the 1992 Games.

CURLING

Curling is played on ice by two teams attempting to score points by sliding granite stones toward a target. The stones generally weigh about 42 pounds and have handles bolted to them by which the players "shoot" them. Curling became an Olympic sport in 1998.

BOBSLED, LUGE, SKELETON

Three ways of sliding down a twisting, steeply banked track of ice are the bobsled, luge, and skeleton. In bobsledding, two- or four-member teams, led by a driver, compete in a streamlined, four-runner sled made of fiberglass and steel. In luge, racers plunge down the track in small sleds, feet first and face up. In skeleton, single riders go head first, face down. Bobsleds can top 100 mph; luge and skeleton can reach 80 mph.

MILESTONES

1860s: INTERNATIONAL STYLE An American named Jackson Haines originated the modern style of figure skating in the 1860s, bringing elements of dance to the rigid, formal manner that was prevalent at the time. His style came to be known as "International Style."

1882: "AXEL" At the first official figure skating competition, in Vienna, Austria, Axel Paulsen (Norway) performed a jump that would become known as the axel: he jumped off from the forward inside edge of one foot, and landed on the back outside edge of the opposite foot. Then the sport's most difficult jump, Paulsen's axel wowed, but he still only finished third in the event.

1909: SALCHOW A year after winning the first Olympic skating gold medal, Sweden's Ulrich Salchow performed his "salchow" jump for the first time. In a salchow, now considered a basic jump, the skater pushes off from the back inside edge of one skate, and lands on the back outside edge of the other.

1913: LUTZ The lutz jump was invented by Austrian skater Alois Lutz and first performed in competition in 1913. While moving in a backward curve, he used the toe pick to rotate in the opposite direction, and took off from the back outside edge of his skate—a very difficult maneuver—and landed on the other back outside edge.

1952: TRIPLE JUMP Two-time Olympic champion Dick Button (U.S.) was the first skater to perform a triple jump in competition—a triple loop—on his way to winning the gold at the 1952 Olympics.

The first woman was Petra Burka of Canada, at the 1962 Canadian Championships.

1988: QUADRUPLE JUMP Kurt Browning of Canada performed the first quadruple jump in competition, completing a quad toe loop at the 1988 World Championships.

Miki Ando, 14, of Japan, was the first female, performing a quadruple salchow at the Junior Grand Prix Final in The Hague, Netherlands, Dec. 14, 2002. Ando still finished only third.

SUPERLATIVES

FIGURE SKATING

MOST OLYMPIC GOLDS Three figure skaters have won three gold medals: Gillis Grafstrom (Sweden), for men's title in 1920, 1924, and 1928; Sonja Henie (Norway), women's title in 1928, 1932, and 1936; and Irina Rodnina (USSR), pairs title, in 1972 (with Aleksei Ulanov), and 1976 and 1980 (with Aleksandr Zaitsev).

MOST WORLD TITLES Three skaters have achieved 10 world championships: Ulrich Salchow (Sweden) won the men's title, 1901-05 and 1907-11; Sonja Henie (Norway), the women's title, 1927-36; and Irina Rodnina (USSR) the pairs title, with Aleksei Ulanov (1969-72), and Aleksandr Zaitsev (1973-78).

HIGHEST-RATED WOMEN'S SPORTS EVENT (TV) The women's short program at the 1994 Olympics in Lillehammer, Norway, in which American skaters Nancy Kerrigan and Tonya Harding competed, produced the highest TV ratings ever for a women's sports event. A month before, Kerrigan's knee was injured in an assault at the U.S. championships, and close associates of Harding's were implicated. But Harding was allowed to compete in the Olympics. Kerrigan went on to win the silver medal, behind Ukraine's Oksana Baiul; Harding placed eighth.

SPEED SKATING

MOST OLYMPIC GOLDS (LONG TRACK) Lidiya Skoblikova (USSR) has won a record six Olympic golds: two at the 1960 Games, 1,500-m, 3,000-m; and four at the 1964 Games, 500-m, 1,000-m, 1,500-m, 3,000-m.

Two men tie for most golds, with five: Clas Thunberg (Finland) won three in 1924 (1,500-m, 5,000-m, all-around) and two in 1928 (500-m, 1,500-m). Eric Heiden, the legendary American skater, won five golds, all in one year, 1980.

MOST OLYMPIC GOLDS (SHORT TRACK) The most gold medals won in short track competition is four. Chun Lee-Kyung (South Korea) won the women's 1,000-m and 1,000-m relay in 1994 and 1998. Two men have won three golds: Kim Ki-Hoon (South Korea), 1,000-m in 1992 and 1994, and 1,000-m relay in 1992; and Marc Gagnon (Canada), 500-m in 2002, 5000-m relay in 1998 and 2002.

Selected Long Track-World Records

DISTANCE	SKATER	TIME	PLACE, DATE
MEN			
500 m	Hiroyasu Shimizu (Japan)	34.32	Salt Lake City, UT, March 10, 2001
1,000 m	Gerard van Velde (Netherlands)	1:07.18	Salt Lake City, UT, Feb. 16, 2002
1,500 m	Shani Davis (U.S.)	1:43.33	Salt Lake City, UT, Jan. 9, 2005
5,000 m	Jochem Uytdehaage (Netherlands)	6:14.66	Salt Lake City, UT, Feb. 9, 2002
10,000 m	Jochem Uytdehaage (Netherlands)	12:58.92	Salt Lake City, UT, Feb. 22, 2002
WOMEN			
500 m	Catriona LeMay Doan (Canada)	37.22	Calgary, Canada, Dec. 9, 2001
1,000 m	Christine Witty (U.S.)	1:13.83	Salt Lake City, UT, Feb. 17, 2002
1,500 m	Cindy Klassen (Canada)	1:53.87	Salt Lake City, UT, Jan. 9, 2005
3,000 m	Claudia Pechstein (Germany)	3:57.70	Salt Lake City, UT, Feb. 10, 2002
5,000 m	Claudia Pechstein (Germany)	6:46.91	Salt Lake City, UT, Feb. 23, 2002

BOBSLED, LUGE, SKELETON

MOST OLYMPIC GOLDS (BOBSLED) Two East German riders, Meinhard Nehmer and Bernard Germeshausen, won three gold medals each. They teamed to win the two-man bob in 1976 and were members of the winning four-man sled in 1976 and 1980.

MOST OLYMPIC GOLDS (LUGE) Georg Hackl (Germany) won a record three Olympic titles, 1992, 1994, and 1998. In women's singles East Germany's Steffi Martin Walter is the only two-time champion, winning in 1984 and 1988.

CURLING

MOST WORLD TITLES Canada has won the most gold medals in the men's and women's World Curling Championships. The men's team won 29 times between 1959 and 2005. The women's 13 victories came between 1980 and 2004.

SOMETHING TO THINK ABOUT

BARREL JUMPING

The spectacular sport of barrel jumping on ice took off in the early 20th century. Speed skating tracks in those days were marked by barrels of various sizes, an irresistible challenge to skaters, who started lining them up and making jumps. In 1925, speed skater Edmund Lamy jumped 27 feet, 8 inches over barrels on Saranac Lake, NY. The current world record is 29 feet, 5 inches, set by Canada's Yvon Jolin Jr. on Jan. 25, 1981, in Terrebonne, Quebec.

SECOND TO NONE

Although the first women's world figure skating championships weren't held until 1906, Britain's Madge Syers competed in the 1902 Worlds with the men, coming in second to the legendary Ulrich Salchow (Sweden). He was so impressed that he offered Syers his gold medal, saying she deserved to win.

Skiing

SKIING AS A COMPETITIVE SPORT dates back to Norway in the mid-1800s, and quickly spread throughout Scandinavia. The first international ski tournament was held in 1892 near Christiana (now Oslo), Norway. The exploration of the Swiss Alps at the turn of the 20th century popularized skiing as both a sport and a recreational activity in the rest of Europe. This section looks at traditional snow sports such as alpine and cross-country skiing, ski jumping, and biathlon; the more modern snow sports of freestyle skiing and snowboarding are reviewed in Extreme Sports, pages 448-449.

MILESTONES

1931: WORLD CHAMPIONSHIPS The first alpine world championships were held in Mürren, Switzerland, in Feb. 1931.

Swiss skiers Walter Prager and David Zogg won the downhill and slalom events, respectively; Esme Mackinnon of Britain won both events in the women's competition.

1936: OLYMPIC DEBUT Alpine skiing was added to the Winter Olympics at the 1936 Garmish-Partenkirchen Games in Germany. Men and women competed in the Alpine Combined event (one downhill run, two slalom runs).

Franze Pfnür (Germany) claimed the men's gold medal, and Christl Cranz (Germany) won gold in the women's competition.

1967: FIS WORLD CUP The FIS World Cup, the season-long multi-race competition to determine the best overall male and female skiers and the best in each event, debuted in 1967. The brainchild of French journalist Serge Lang, the World Cup was recognized by the International Ski Federation (FIS), and has grown into one of the world's most popular sports competitions.

The first overall men's champion was Jean-Claude Killy (France), and the women's cup was claimed by Nancy Greene (Canada).

ALPINE SKIING Alpine skiing gets its name from the Swiss Alps, where the downhill discipline first evolved in the late 1800s and early 1900s. It consists of four races: two "speed" races—downhill and super-giant slalom (super-G)—and two "technical" events—slalom and giant slalom. The International Ski Federation recognized the downhill and slalom as events in Feb. 1930.

CROSS-COUNTRY (NORDIC) SKIING Cross-country skiing, also known as Nordic skiing, originated in Scandinavia thousands of years ago as a means of transportation. It evolved into a popular Scandinavian recreational activity and sport in the late 19th century. Men's cross-country skiing was included in the first Winter Olympics at Chamonix, France in 1924. Women's events debuted as an Olympic medal sport in 1952. A season-long World Cup competition, based on the Alpine skiing format, was introduced in 1982.

SKI JUMPING Ski jumping traces its roots to ski carnivals in Norway in the mid-1800s, and the first officially measured jump took place in 1860. In 1892, the Norwegian royal family donated the King's Cup, which was to be given to the winner of the annual Holmenkollen competition, held in Oslo, Norway, sparking growth of the sport. Ski jumping has been included in every Winter Olympic Games.

BIATHLON The biathlon combines cross-country skiing and rifle marksmanship. Its origins can be traced back hundreds of years, to when early inhabitants of Scandinavia hunted on skis. In Europe's Great Northern War (1700-21), the Norwegian and Swedish armies used ski units. In 1767, ski units guarding the Norwegian-Swedish border organized the first recorded biathlon competition. Men's biathlon was added to the Winter Games in 1960, women's in 1992.

NORDIC COMBINED Nordic combined features ski jumping (two jumps) followed by a cross-country race. It combines the technical prowess needed in ski jumping with the strength and endurance required in cross-country. Only men compete in the sport at the Olympics.

Most World Cups (by Event)

	MEN			WOMEN		
EVENT	SKIER	TITLES	YEARS	SKIER	TITLES	YEARS
Downhill	Franz Klammer (Austria)	5	1975-78, 1983	Annemarie Moser-Pröll (Austria)	7	1971-75, 1978-79
Super G	Hermann Maier (Austria)	5	1998-2001, 2004	Katja Seizinger (Germany)	5	1993-96, 1998
Giant Slalom	Ingemar Stenmark (Sweden)	9	1975-82, 1984	Vreni Schneider (Switzerland)	4	1987, 1989, 1991, 1995
Slalom	Ingemar Stenmark (Sweden)	8	1975-81, 1983	Vreni Schneider (Switzerland)	7	1989-95

Bode Miller

SOMETHING TO THINK ABOUT

SKIING DOWN MT. EVEREST

The first person to complete an uninterrupted ski descent of Mount Everest, from the summit to Base Camp, was Davo Karnicar of Slovenia. He reached the summit in the early hours of Oct. 7, 2000, with his climbing partner, Slovenian Franc Oderlap. Karnicar, who made the final ascent in ski boots, descended more than 2 vertical miles on his skis in less than five hours. In 1996, he had abandoned an attempt to ski Everest due to bad weather, and lost two fingers to frostbite.

"THE BIRKIE"

The largest cross-country skiing race in North America is the American Birkebeiner, better known as "The Birkie." In Feb. 2005, 3,945 skiers completed the 32-mile course from Cable to Hayward, WI. Based on Norway's Birkebeiner Rennet, which commemorates the escape to safety of Norway's heir to the throne during a civil war in 1206, the American Birkie has been held annually since 1973.

150 MPH ON SKIS!!!

Speed skiing is billed as the "fastest non-motorized sport on Earth." Skiers compete on a specially prepared track, wearing clothing and equipment designed to maximize aerodynamics. Philippe Goitschel of France set the men's world record in 2002 in Les Arcs, France, clocking a speed of 155.8 mph. In Les Arcs that same year, Karine Dubouchet of France set the women's world record, 150.53 mph.

SUPERLATIVES

MOST OLYMPIC GOLD MEDALS — ALPINE
Four men and four women have won three Alpine Olympic golds: The first was Austria's Anton "Toni" Sailer, who swept the men's events at the 1956 Cortina d'Ampezzo Games (downhill, slalom, giant slalom). His record was matched by France's Jean-Claude Killy at the 1968 Grenoble Games. The other men were Italy's Alberto Tomba (slalom, 1988; giant slalom, 1988, 1992) and Norway's Kjetil André Aamodt (super-G, 1992, 2002; Alpine combined, 2002).

The triple-gold women are: Switzerland's Vreni Schneider (slalom, 1988, 1994; giant slalom, 1988); Italy's Deborah Compagnoni (super-G, 1992; giant slalom, 1994, 1998); Germany's Katja Seizinger (downhill, 1994, 1998; Alpine combined, 1998); and Croatia's Janica Kostelic (slalom, giant slalom, Alpine combined, 2002).

MOST OLYMPIC MEDALS — ALPINE
Norway's Kjetil André Aamodt claims the men's Alpine record with seven Olympic medals: three gold, two silver, two bronze (1992-2002).

Two women have won five career medals: Vreni Schneider (Switzerland), three gold, one silver, one bronze (1988-94), and Katja Seizinger (Germany), three gold, two bronze (1992-98).

MOST WORLD CUP WINS Sweden's Ingemar Stenmark won a record 86 World Cup races (46 giant slalom, 40 slalom), 1974-89. The women's record is 62 by Austria's Annemarie Moser-Pröll, 1970-79.

MOST OLYMPIC GOLD MEDALS — CROSS-COUNTRY
Norway's Björn Dæhlie has won a record eight golds: 10 km (1994, 1998), 15 km freestyle pursuit (1992, 1994), 50 km (1992, 1998), and 4 x 10-km mixed relay (1992, 1998).

Among women, Lyubov Egorova, who represented the Unified Team in 1992 and Russia in 1994, has won a record six gold: 5 km (1994), 10 km freestyle pursuit (1992, 1994), 15 km (1992), and 4 x 5-km relay (1992, 1994).

MOST OLYMPIC MEDALS — CROSS-COUNTRY
Norway's Björn Dæhlie has won a record 12 Olympic medals: eight gold and four silver, (1992-98). Raisa Smetanina (Soviet Union, 1976-88, Unified Team in 1992), won 10 medals: four gold, five silver, one bronze (1976-92).

MOST OLYMPIC GOLD MEDALS — SKI JUMPING
Finland's Matti Nykänen has won four gold medals: large hill (1984), normal hill, large hill, and team (1988). In 1984, two nearly flawless jumps helped him win the large hill by the largest margin in Olympic history (17.5 points).

MOST OLYMPIC GOLD MEDALS — BIATHLON
Norway's Ole Einar Bjoerndalen has won a record five gold medals: 10 km (1998, 2002); 12.5 km (2002); 20 km (2002); and 4 x 7.5-km relay (2002).

MOST OLYMPIC GOLD MEDALS — NORDIC COMBINED
Two skiers have won three gold medals: Ulrich Wehling of East Germany (individual, 1972, 1976, 1980) and Samppa Lajunen of Finland (individual, sprint, team, 2002).

Olympic Games

THE EXACT ORIGINS OF THE ANCIENT OLYMPICS are unknown, but the first written evidence of the Games dates to about 776 BC. Staged to honor the Greek god Zeus, the Games were held in Olympia, Greece, every four years for nearly 1,200 years, until the Roman Emperor Theodosius abolished them in AD 393.

Over 1,500 years later, owing largely to the efforts of Frenchman Baron Pierre de Coubertin, the Olympics were revived in Athens, Greece, in 1896, and subsequently were held every four years. Since 1994 the Winter and Summer Games have alternated even-numbered years. The 2006 Winter Games were to be held in Turin (Torino), Italy; future Olympic sites include Beijing (Summer 2008), Vancouver, Canada (Winter 2010), and London (Summer 2012).

MILESTONES

776 BC: FIRST OLYMPIC CHAMPION Only one event was staged at the earliest-known Games, a sprint over a distance of 1 *stadion* (about 200 yards). It was won by Koroibos, a cook from Elis.

As the Games grew in popularity, more events were added, including wrestling (708 BC), boxing (688 BC), and chariot racing (408 BC). The standard attire was simple; most ancient Olympians competed naked.

1896: MODERN ERA The first Olympic Games of the modern era opened in Athens on April 6, 1896; 241 male athletes from 14 countries took part. The first modern Olympic champion was American James Connolly. He won the hop, step, and jump (triple jump) with a leap of 44 feet, 11.75 inches.

1900: WOMEN Female athletes were allowed to compete for the first time at the 1900 Games in Paris. The first woman to earn a gold medal was Britain's Charlotte Cooper, who won the women's singles in tennis.

1920: OLYMPIC FLAG AND OATH The Olympic flag was flown for the first time at the opening ceremony of the 1920 Games in Antwerp, Belgium. The Olympic oath, sworn by an athlete from the host nation on behalf of all competing athletes, also made its debut at the Antwerp Games. It was sworn by Victor Boin, a water polo medalist in 1908 and 1912.

1924: WINTER GAMES The first Winter Olympics were staged in Chamonix, France, Jan. 25-Feb. 4, 1924. According to the Olympic Charter, only events on snow or ice can be part of the Winter Games program.

1936: TORCH RELAY At the ancient Olympics a flame burned for the duration of the festival. The first modern Olympics to feature a flame were the 1928 Games in Amsterdam. The torch relay tradition began in 1936 when a torch was lit at the ancient site of Olympia and carried in relay to Berlin; there the Olympic flame was lit at opening ceremonies by Germany's Fritz Schilgen. At the 1968 Summer Olympics in Mexico City, Enriqueta Basilio (Mexico) became the first woman to light it.

1936: JESSE OWENS German Nazi leader Adolf Hitler expected the 1936 Berlin Games to demonstrate the superiority of the "Aryan" race. Germany did lead the medal count, but the top individual performer was African-American track star Jesse Owens. He racked up four golds, in the 100 meters, long jump, 200 meters, and 4 x 100-m relay.

1972: OLYMPIC TERRORISM At the 1972 Games in Munich, Germany, Palestinian terrorists broke into the Olympic Village, killed an Israeli coach and athlete, and took nine other Israelis as hostages.

After a tense standoff, the terrorists and captives were taken to a nearby airport, where a gun battle ensued. All the hostages were killed, as were five terrorists and a German policeman. The Games were suspended for another 34 hours to honor the victims, then resumed following an Olympic Stadium memorial service.

SOMETHING TO THINK ABOUT

GOLD MEDALIST

Only one person has won gold medals at both the Summer and Winter Olympics: Edward Eagen (U.S.), a Rhodes Scholar who captured the light-heavyweight boxing title at the 1920 Antwerp Games and was on the victorious four-man bobsled team at the 1932 Lake Placid Games.

KIDDIE COXSWAIN

The youngest Olympic gold medalist is believed to be a French boy who coxed for Roelof Klein and Francoise Brandt (Netherlands) when the Dutch pair won the coxed pairs rowing title in 1900. He joined the crew at the last minute, posed for a photograph after the event, and then disappeared. No one knows his name or age; Olympic historians tried to track him down for decades.

SUMMER ON ICE

Figure skating as an Olympic sport dates to 1908, when it was included in the London Summer Games. Ice hockey made its debut in the summer too, at the 1920 Antwerp program.

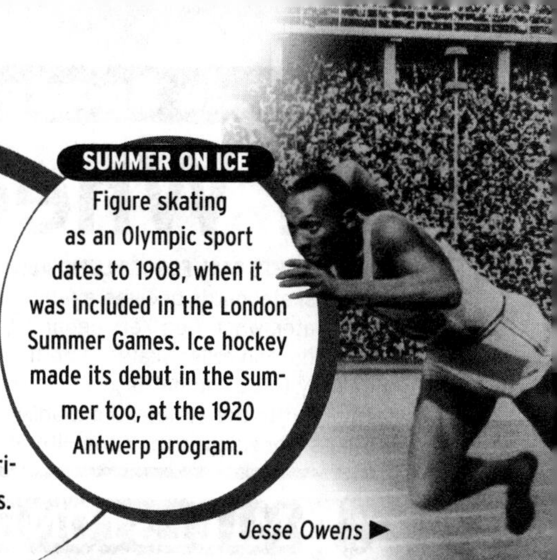

Jesse Owens ▶

SUPERLATIVES

MOST GOLD MEDALS

CAREER The most gold medals won in Olympic competition by a single individual is nine, a mark shared by four Olympians: distance runner Paavo Nurmi (Finland), gymnast Larisa Latynina (Soviet Union), swimmer Mark Spitz (U.S.), and sprinter Carl Lewis (U.S.).

Nurmi won gold in the 10,000 m and the individual and team cross-country races at the 1920 Antwerp Games; the 1,500 m, 5,000 m, 3,000-m team, and individual and team cross-country races at the 1924 Games in Paris; and the 10,000 m at the 1928 Amsterdam Games.

Latynina won the all-around competition, floor exercise, vault, and team competition at the 1956 Games in Melbourne, Australia; the all-around, floor exercise, and team competition at the 1960 Games in Rome; and the floor exercise and team competition at the 1964 Games in Tokyo.

Spitz needed just two Olympiads to tie the record. He swam to gold in the 4 x 100-m and 4 x 200-m relays at the 1968 Mexico City Games, then won a record seven gold medals at the 1972 Munich Games (see below).

Lewis earned gold at the 1984 Los Angeles Games in the 100 m, 200 m, 4 x 100-m relay, and long jump; at the 1988 Games in Seoul, South Korea, in the 100 m and the long jump; at the 1992 Games in Barcelona, Spain, in the long jump and 4 x 100-m relay; and at the 1996 Games in Atlanta, GA, in the long jump.

MOST GOLD MEDALS

ONE OLYMPIAD

Spitz's record seven gold medals at the 1972 Games came in the 100-m and 200-m freestyle, 100-m and 200-m butterfly, 4 x 100-m and 4 x 200-m freestyle, and 4 x 100-m medley. He set new world records in every event.

The most gold medals won by a woman in a single Olympiad is six, by East German swimmer Kristin Otto at the 1988 Seoul Games.

MOST MEDALS

CAREER Soviet gymnast Larisa Latynina picked up a record 18 Olympic medals between 1956 and 1964 (9 gold, 5 silver, 4 bronze). The male athlete with the most medals is Soviet gymnast Nikolai Andrianov, who picked up 15 between 1972 and 1980 (7 gold, 5 silver, 3 bronze).

MOST MEDALS (U.S.)

Swimmer Jenny Thompson holds the record for most medals won by an American. She totaled 12 in four Olympiads from 1992 to 2004 (8 gold, all in relay events; 3 silver; 1 bronze).

The most medals won by an American man is 11, a mark shared by three athletes: shooter Carl Osburn (1912, 1920, 1924), swimmer Mark Spitz (1968, 1972), and swimmer Matt Biondi (1984, 1988, 1992).

MOST MEDALS

ONE OLYMPIAD

The most medals won at one Olympiad is eight, by two athletes: gymnast Aleksandr Dityatin (Soviet Union) and swimmer Michael Phelps (U.S.).

Dityatin amassed three gold, four silver, and one bronze at the 1980 Moscow Games. Phelps picked up six gold and two bronze at the 2004 Games in Athens.

"The Baltimore Splash" did not swim in the final of the 4 x 100-meter medley relay, but per Olympic rules he received a gold medal for the event because he swam in heats for the victorious team.

Gymnast Maria Gorokhovskaya (Soviet Union) holds the record for most medals won at a single Olympiad by a female. She totaled seven at the 1952 Games in Helsinki, Finland (2 gold, 5 silver).

The record for an individual winning the same event the most times in a row is four, by three Olympians. Sailor Paul Elvstrøm (Denmark) took gold in the Finn class, 1948-1960; Al Oerter (U.S.) in the discus, 1956-68; and Carl Lewis (U.S.) in the long jump, 1984-96.

OLDEST MEDALIST

At the 1920 Antwerp Games 72-year-old shooter Oscar Swahn (Sweden) became the oldest person to win a medal in the modern Olympics, taking the silver in the running deer double-shot team event.

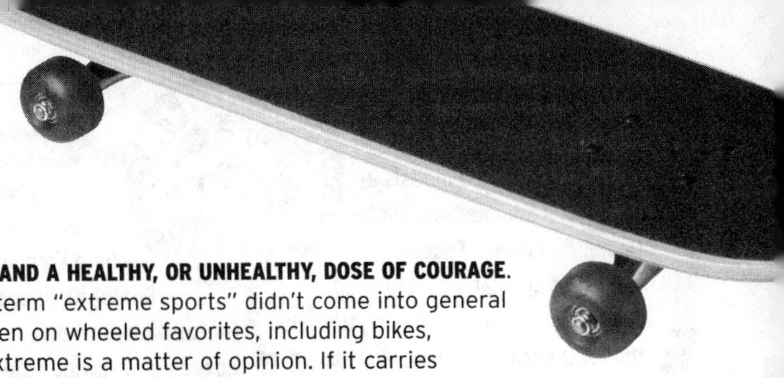

On Wheels

EXTREME SPORTS CALL FOR ATHLETIC ABILITY, PERSEVERANCE, AND A HEALTHY, OR UNHEALTHY, DOSE OF COURAGE. Although skateboards became a fad in the late 1950s, the term "extreme sports" didn't come into general use until later, when Gen Xers began trying new stunts, often on wheeled favorites, including bikes, skateboards, and roller skates. Whether or not a sport is extreme is a matter of opinion. If it carries a "don't try this at home" disclaimer and if fear is an integral part of the activity, then it may just be extreme. But to the athlete, the moniker becomes less important than the adrenaline rush that carries the rider's wheels over the edge—literally.

1 MILESTONES

1863: "QUAD" SKATE
Businessman James Plimpton, of Medford, MA, re-designed roller skates, which back then were called "parlor skates," for increased balance and safety. He placed four wheels—two pairs—in a rectangular or box formation separate from the bottom of the skate, which in his words were "like the wheels of a wagon."

Before the new alignment, most skates were in-line like ice skates. Pimpton patented the new wheel alignment in 1863. Skating rinks soon sprung up.

In-line skates were still produced by some manufacturers. But they did not come back into fashion until the 1980s when rollerblades came along.

1959: SKATEBOARD
Kids had been riding scooters without handles for decades. But by 1959, skateboards were starting to come into their own in southern California.

The first skateboards were crudely made by enthusiasts who simply nailed steel wheels to a wooden two-by-four. After it became apparent that broken bones were a common hazard of skateboarding, many safety experts and community groups sought unsuccessfully to ban skateboarding, and the hobby was here to stay.

The popularity of the skateboard's aquatic brother, the surfboard, helped popularize "sidewalk surfing" throughout the U.S.

1965: PROFESSIONAL SKATEBOARDS (CLAY WHEELS, KICKTAIL)
Larry Stevenson of Santa Monica, CA, made the first professional skateboards with clay wheels in 1962, under the Makaha brand. Clay wheels were an improvement over the steel wheels because they had better traction and made controlling the board easier.

Stevenson in 1971 patented the kicktail (for the LX10), which was an upward curve on the board that also improved control. By 1965, over 30 million pro boards were sold, and regular tournaments started to spring up.

1972: URETHANE WHEELS
Before 1972, skateboard wheels were made of clay or steel. Then in 1972, Frank Nasworthy of Encinitas, CA, started using (poly)urethane wheels with ball bearings that were originally designed for use with roller skates. Unable to sell the idea to companies, he handed them out to friends and called them "Cadillac Wheels."

The urethane wheels were more flexible, provided better grip, and kept more constant speeds for performing tricks and riding on ramps.

1976: SKATEPARKS
The first skateboard parks in the U.S. opened almost simultaneously in early 1976. SkatBoard City, later renamed Skateboard City, was opened in Port Orange, FL. Around the same time, Carlsbad Skatepark in North San Diego County, CA opened.

Carlsbad, covered with dirt in the 1980s, was demolished by developers in May 2005. Skateboard City also closed in the 1980s; today it is a go-cart track.

1978: "OLLIE"
The no-handed jump, where the board appears to "stick" to the rider's feet, got its name from its inventor's nickname, Alan "Ollie" Gelfand.

The Florida-based Bones Brigade skater propelled himself and his board into the air by leaning on the back tailboard and quickly shifting forward.

Today, most tricks are based on the ollie. In 2004, "ollie" was recognized as a word by the Oxford English Dictionary.

1980: ROLLERBLADES
Modern rollerblades were created in 1980 by brothers Scott and Brennan Olson of Minneapolis, MN. After seeing a pair of in-line skates at a local sporting goods store, the brothers decided to make their own using their hockey boots to do some off-ice hockey training. They attached urethane wheels and rubber brakes to the boot shaft.

The Olsons began to sell reproductions to friends and later formed their own company, Rollerblade, Inc. They sold the business to investors in 1984.

1995: X GAMES
The first X Games took place June 24-July 1, 1995, in Middletown, Newport, and Providence, RI, and Mt. Snow, VT. Originally called "The

◀ *Danny Way jumping over the Great Wall of China*

RECORD BREAKER

Tony Hawk

"The impact of the spin and the force that you hit with when you fall is like getting in a car wreck every time you fall."

–Tony Hawk on attempting the "9."

Most X Games Gold Medals (per event)

Vert (BMX)	Dave Mirra	6	1997-99, 2001-02, 2004
Dirt (BMX)	T. J. Lavin	2	1997, 1999
	Ryan Nyquist	2	2000, 2003
	Corey Bohan	2	2004-05
Freestyle Park (BMX)	Dave Mirra	7	1996-2000, 2004-05
Vert Singles (skateboarding)	Bucky Lasek	4	1999-2000, 2003-04
Moto X Freestyle	Travis Pastrana	5	1999-2001, 2003, 2005
Moto X Step Up	Tommy Clowers	4	2000-02, 2005

ESPN Extreme Games," the name was changed to the "X Games" the following year. Extreme athletes competed in 27 events across nine "alternative" sports: Bungy Jumping, Eco-Challenge, In-line Skating, Skateboarding, Skysurfing, Sport Climbing, Street Luge, Biking, and Water Sports.

A distinct Winter X Games was staged for the first time Jan. 30-Feb. 2, 1997, at Big Bear Lake, CA.

1999: "9" Legendary skateboarder Tony Hawk landed the first 900, an aerial trick where the athlete rides up into the air from a halfpipe, makes $2\frac{1}{2}$ rotations, and lands back on the halfpipe. Hawk made his jump on June 27, 1999, at the Summer X Games in San Francisco. However, the history-making 900 did not count because time had run out. Hawk made it count for the first time on Aug. 17, 2003, at the X Games Final.

2001: IN-LINE DOUBLE BACK FLIP Taig Khris performed the first double backflip on in-line skates on Aug. 18 at the 2001 Summer X Games.

2002: MOTO X BACK FLIP In May 2002, a then-little known rider named Caleb Wyatt recorded the first successful Moto X stunt biking back flip in competition. Others soon followed.

Mike "The Godfather" Metzger performed two of these flips back-to-back at the 2002 Gravity Games in Cleveland, OH.

SUPERLATIVES

MOST X GAMES MEDALS As of 2005, Dave "The Miracle Boy" Mirra has won 20 X Games medals, the most for any athlete.

Mirra also holds the record for most X Games gold medals won by an individual, with 14. All Mirra's gold medals came in BMX competitions.

MOST WINS Tony Hawk has won the most professional skateboarding contests with 73. During his legendary career, Hawk also placed second in 19 competitions. A pro by 14, he has competed in more than 100 professional competitions.

BIGGEST SKATEBOARD RAMP Skateboarder Danny Way achieved a famous first when he jumped over the Great Wall of China. Way, who had already held the record for distance jumped at 75 feet, needed a big ramp to perform the unprecedented stunt. So he and his team built the MegaRamp. At nine stories, it was the biggest skateboarding structure ever made. It required over 60,000 screws and 410 sheets of plywood.

Using his giant ramp, on July 9, 2005, Way, in front of thousands, became the first person to jump the Great Wall without a motor vehicle and land successfully. For his accomplishment, Way received a piece of the wall.

On Snow

EXTREME SPORTS ARE BUILT FOR THE COLD. Once the domain of skiers and snowshoers, winter has been invaded more recently by extreme athletes looking to take their summer obsessions into the snow, trading in skateboards for snowboards. TV coverage and Olympic recognition have made extreme winter sports as mainstream as any other winter pastime.

MILESTONES

1922: SNOWMOBILE In 1922, Canadian Joseph-Armand Bombardier, at the age of 15, attached a Ford Model-T engine and a propeller to the family sleigh.

This first snowmobile was meant as a practical means of transportation in snowy Quebec.

He went on to develop a recreational ski mobile named Ski-Doo®. Over 2 million Ski-Doo® snowmobiles have been sold.

1965: "SNURFER" Chemical engineer Sherman Poppen invented the "Snurfer," a precursor to the modern snowboard, in 1965 in Muskegon, MI. Looking to increase the stability of skis for his daughter, Poppen bound two 36-inch downhill skis together and attached a rope to the tip for steering. The device was a success around his neighborhood. Sensing its potential, he licensed the "Snurfer" to Brunswick Corp., which went on to produce it. The name came from Poppen's wife as a combination of the words "snow" and "surfer."

1972: SWALLOWTAIL Dimitrije Milovich in 1972 patented a design for the "Swallowtail," the first modern snowboard. The model combined elements of surfboard and ski design to create the first modern snowboard. Milovich began making and selling the boards in 1974 and developed the popular swallowtail-style board, which was characterized by a split and tapered back. In 1975, he established the Winterstick brand.

1977: BURTON SNOWBOARDS Jake Burton Carpenter, who owned a Snurfer as a child, moved to Stratton Mountain, VT, in 1977 and founded his snowboard company, Burton. Carpenter, working out of a barn, experimented with various prototypes, and ended up attaching the first non-releasable bindings to snowboards.

Burton is now the world's largest board maker and distributes products to more than 30 countries.

1982: NATIONAL SNOWBOARDING CHAMPIONSHIP The first National Snowboarding Championships were held at Suicide Six in Woodstock, VT, in March 1982. The event—the last time that Snurfers and snowboards raced against each other in official competition—included a steep downhill run, nicknamed "The Face," that was won by Tom Sims.

Despite the perilous icy conditions, boarders were clocked at speeds of more than 60 mph.

1987: TWIN TIPS Canadians Neil Daffern and Dave and Ken Achenbach, of Barefoot Snowboards, designed the first snowboard that was curved identically at both ends. This gave the rider more maneuverability in freestyle boarding, and allowed riders to face the slope or halfpipe either regular or fakie (backward), unlike before, when they would actually have to turn the whole board.

1993: SNOWBOARDING GOVERNING BODY The Fédération Internationale de Ski (FIS), the international governing body for skiing, officially put snowboarding under its jurisdiction in June 1994 and began planning future competitions, including a nine-stop 1994-95 World Cup Tour.

The International Snowboard Federation (ISF) had already been around since 1989 and, in response, asked the International Olympic Committee (IOC) for recognition and control over an international snowboarding league. In a controversial decision, the IOC chose the FIS as the governing body instead.

Since then the FIS has helped the sport to become more mainstream. As for the ISF, it folded in 2002.

1997: WINTER X GAMES The first Winter X Games were staged Jan. 30 to Feb. 2, 1997, at Big Bear Lake, CA. Events at the inaugural games included ice climbing, super-modified shovel racing, snow mountain bike racing, snowboarding, and a crossover combination event.

1998: SNOWMOBILE RACING SnoCross (snowmobile racing) was the first motorized sport in X Games history. It debuted at the 1998 Games, with Toni

Multiple exposure of Shaun White winning the men's slopestyle event at the 2005 Winter X Games.

SOMETHING TO THINK ABOUT

REALLY EXTREME SNOWBOARDING

When the sport of snowboarding was invented in the 1970s many resorts refused to let snowboarders on their slopes. This gave rise to "backcountry" snowboarding—that is, snowboarding on unmarked slopes or non-resort areas. Even now that most resorts allow snowboarding, backcountry boarding is still popular despite its added risks. Over the last 20 years, U.S. backcountry skiers and snowboarders have been about 24 times more likely to die in avalanches than in-bounds skiers and riders.

Haikonen (Finland) the first winner of a SnoCross event.

1998: OLYMPIC RECOGNITION
Snowboarding debuted at the 1998 Winter Olympics in Nagano, Japan. Events included giant slalom and halfpipe competitions for men and women. In 2002, giant slalom was replaced by parallel giant slalom where two snowboarders race against each other through gates.

2000: SUPERPIPE
Mark Anolik is credited as the first to snowboard a halfpipe; he did it in 1979 when he happened upon an area behind a dump in Tahoe City, CA, with natural curves that had the overall shape of a half-pipe.

The snowboard half-pipe was first used for official competition at the World Snowboarding Championships at Soda Springs Ski Bowl in California in 1983.

Finally, at the 2000 X Games, the 400-ft long SuperPipe was added to the snowboarding competition. Because of the SuperPipe's 14-foot walls that allowed athletes to get even higher in the air, tricks became more spectacular.

2003: WINTER AND SUMMER X GAMES ATHLETE In 2003 at age 16, Shaun White, of Carlsbad, CA, became the first athlete to compete in both the Summer and Winter X Games in two different sports in the same year. At the 2003 Winter X Games, White won the slopestyle and SuperPipe competitions in snowboarding, and also took home the title of the best athlete of that year's X Games.

During the 2003 Summer X Games, White competed in skateboarding and finished sixth in the men's vert.

SUPERLATIVES

MOST OLYMPIC MEDALS (SNOWBOARDING)
In the short history of Olympic snowboarding, only two boarders have won two medals: Karine Ruby (France) and Ross Powers (U.S.). Ruby won a gold medal in the giant slalom at the 1998 Nagano Games, and a silver medal in the parallel giant slalom at the 2002 Salt Lake City Games. Powers won a bronze in 1998, and a gold in 2002 in the men's halfpipe.

MOST WORLD TITLES (SNOWBOARDING)
Karine Ruby of France has won a record six FIS World Championship titles, including two in the giant slalom (1996, 2001), three in the snowboard cross (1997, 2001, 2003), and one in the parallel slalom (2001). Among the men, Canadian Jasey-Jay Anderson has won a record three World Championships: the giant slalom (2001), parallel slalom, and the parallel giant slalom (2005).

MOST CONSECUTIVE X GAMES MEDALS Blair Morgan has won seven consecutive SnoCross X Games medals. At the 2005 Winter X Games, Morgan won his fourth gold medal, and became the second athlete to win four X Games golds in the same event (Aleisha Cline has four gold medals in women's Skier X). In 2004, "Air Blair" earned a bronze even though he was still recovering from injuries suffered during a 2003 Moto X incident.

YOUNGEST X GAMES CHAMPION Tucker Hibbert was 15 years old when he won the SnoCross gold medal in 2000, becoming the youngest person to win an X Games title. The Minnesota native later finished second in the event in 2002, 2004, and 2005. Now a professional motocross racer, Hibbert only races snowmobiles in official competition once a year during the Winter X Games.

Hibbert's father, Kirk, became the oldest X Games athlete when he competed in his son's event at age 43 in the 2000 games.

FASTEST SPEED (SNOWBOARD)
The fastest speed ever recorded on a snowboard was 125.459 mph by Australian boarder Darren Powell. He set the mark at Les Arcs, France, on May 2, 1999.

FASTEST SPEED (BICYCLE) The fastest anybody has ever ridden a non-motorized bicycle on snow was 138 mph. Eric Barone of France reached the speed on the Aiguille Rouge in Les Arcs, France, on April 21, 2000.

U.S. History

Total Area: 3,718,712 sq mi
Population (est. 2005): 295,734,134

"America is so vast that almost anything said about it is likely to be true, and the opposite is probably equally true," wrote novelist James T. Farrell, a native of Chicago.

MILESTONES

1500s: FIRST EUROPEAN SETTLERS St. Augustine, FL, was founded by Spain on Sept. 8, 1565. It is the oldest European settlement in the U.S.

The English soon followed and in July 1585 founded a colony on Roanoke Island, North Carolina. But the settlement was poorly planned and disbanded within a year.

A second English attempt to colonize the area was led by John White who landed on Roanoke in July 1587. A month later, White went back to England for supplies. He was going to return immediately, but was delayed when war broke out with Spain. Supply ships finally returned to Roanoke in 1590, but, mysteriously, the colony was abandoned.

The only clue as to what may have happened to them was the word "Croatoan," which was carved into a tree nearby and may have referred to a local Native American tribe.

Historians are still trying to figure out what happened. Some think that the natives massacred the colonists. Others believe that the colonists went to live with the natives and assimilated.

1607: JAMESTOWN The Virginia Company founded Jamestown, the first permanent English colony in what is now the U.S., on May 14, 1607.

Life was not easy. The colony endured famine and conflict with Indians. After the first eight months, only 38 of the original 120 settlers were still alive. But the colony survived and grew.

Years later the people of Jamestown created the first general assembly in the U.S., the House of Burgesses. It first convened in Jamestown on July 30, 1619.

1620: MAYFLOWER COMPACT English Puritans first landed near present-day Provincetown, MA, in Nov. 1620. Before establishing a new colony, the colonists created what can be considered America's first written constitution, the *Mayflower Compact* (named for their ship, the *Mayflower*). The short document was basically a pledge by the signers to form a body politic.

After exploring the coast, the Pilgrims found a spot, which they named Plymouth Colony after the port in England from which they had set out.

1775-83: INDEPENDENCE Longstanding tensions between the American colonies and Great Britain came to a head on April 19, 1775, when British soldiers met a group of armed local militia at Lexington, MA. When ordered to disperse, the colonists refused. What happened next is unclear, but according to legend, somebody discharged his weapon in the "shot heard around the world." There the revolution began.

A further engagement that day in nearby Concord forced the British to withdraw to Boston.

A year of fighting later, it was clear that the colonies had to make a clean break from the Brits. In Philadelphia, PA, on July 2, 1776, the Continental Congress met to ratify a "Declaration of Independence." It set out democratic principles and a list of grievances against England's King George III. On July 4, 1776, the declaration was adopted by Congress.

Combat came largely to an end on Oct. 19, 1781, after the battle of Yorktown in Virginia, when British Gen. Charles Cornwallis surrendered to an American and French force under George Washington.

The Treaty of Paris, which officially ended the war, was signed on Sept. 3, 1783.

1787: CONSTITUTION In order to unite and govern the colonies following independence, the Continental Congress drew up the Articles of Confederation, which went into effect on March 1, 1781.

SOMETHING TO THINK ABOUT

GREEN MOUNTAIN BOYS

Vermont's Green Mountain Boys helped expel the British from Ft. Ticonderoga during the American Revolution in 1775. But they were originally formed to fight New Yorkers. New Hampshire and New York in the mid-1700s both claimed Vermont. Ethan Allen was one of many Vermonters who didn't want to be part of New York, so in 1770 he formed the Green Mountain Boys—a gang of thugs who intimidated settlers from New York. When the Revolution broke out, differences were set aside to beat the British. After the war, Vermont became an independent republic. It joined the U.S in 1791 after New York gave up its claims to the region.

LAND OF THE FREE

"The Star-Spangled Banner" was written by Francis Scott Key as he watched the British assault on Ft. McHenry in Baltimore Harbor on Sept. 13-14, 1814, during the War of 1812. Originally titled "Defence of Fort McHenry," it was put to music at the suggestion of Key's wife's brother-in-law. The tune it came to be associated with was a British drinking song written by John Stafford Smith called "To Anacreon in Heaven." The "Star Spangled Banner" became popular with Union soldiers during the Civil War. But it did not become the U.S. National Anthem until Congress declared it in 1931.

Under the Articles, each state had one vote in the Congress, but the body had no power to tax the states, which in effect made it powerless. By 1786, it was clear that the Confederation was not an effective government framework.

Over 16 weeks (May 25-Sept. 17) in 1787, 55 delegates from 12 states (Rhode Island abstained) met in Philadelphia to create a new constitution.

Small states wanted congressional representation by state, while larger ones wanted representation by population. What came about was known as the "Great Compromise." Two legislative bodies were created: the Senate, where each state was given two votes; and the House of Representatives, where representation was proportionate to population. In another "compromise" of sorts, for the purpose of deciding representation, a slave was counted as $\frac{3}{5}$ of a free man.

Delaware was the first state to ratify the new Constitution, on Dec. 7, 1787. Other states followed, and the new government went into effect on June 21, 1788.

Rhode Island was the only state to hold out, but its citizens quickly changed their minds after Congress threatened to treat them as a foreign country. The state ratified the Constitution on May 29, 1790.

The first 10 amendments, now known as the Bill of Rights, were added on Dec. 15, 1791.

1803: LOUISIANA PURCHASE French Emperor Napoleon Bonaparte needed cash for a looming war with Britain. So he offered to sell French lands on the western side of the Mississippi River to the U.S.

President Thomas Jefferson's ministers, initially expecting to buy only the city of New Orleans, were offered the 827,192-square-mile Louisiana Territory for just $15 million. The U.S. accepted on April 30, 1803.

1838-39: "TRAIL OF TEARS" On May 28, 1830, President Andrew Jackson passed the Indian Removal Act, which forced about 100,000 Indians to exchange their territory east of the Mississippi for lands in present-day Oklahoma. Many tribes resisted, most notably the Cherokee Nation. But anti-Indian feeling was prevalent, and the Cherokee did not have many friends in the U.S. government.

After the act was passed, some of the Cherokee moved but most remained in their homes. They were driven off their land in May 1838 by troops under Gen. Winfield Scott, and forced to march to their new lands. This march was known as the Trail of Tears because over $\frac{1}{4}$ of the 16,000 exiles died from famine, disease, and exhaustion.

More on

U.S. History

1849: GOLD! James W. Marshall found gold on Jan. 24, 1848, while constructing John Sutter's sawmill in present-day Coloma, CA. Word spread, and by May 1849, thousands of would-be gold miners flooded California to stake their claims.

Most of these "forty-niners" didn't find any gold, but the ensuing population explosion led to California's statehood in 1850.

1861-65: CIVIL WAR Slavery was a heated issue for the young nation, and with the creation of each new state, the debate over slavery re-emerged. Congressional acts, including the Missouri Compromise (1820) and the Kansas-Nebraska Act (1854) were temporary fixes, but in the end, there was no compromise.

In 1860 Republican Abraham Lincoln was elected president. Fearing the Republicans would act in the interest of northern industry and the abolitionists, South Carolina seceded on Dec. 20, 1860, and soon ten other southern states followed suit. Over the next four years, the U.S. endured the bloodiest war in its history.

1862: HOMESTEAD ACT Passed by Congress in 1862, the revolutionary Homestead Act allowed settlers to claim up to 160 acres of federal land (as long as nobody else had claimed it first) if they promised to live on their plot for five years. About 10% of the U.S., over 270 million acres, was granted to 1.6 million homesteaders.

The law was repealed in 1972; however, some lands in Alaska were still open to homesteading as late as 1986.

1863: EMANCIPATION On Jan. 1, 1863, President Lincoln issued the Emancipation Proclamation, which freed all slaves in states that were "in rebellion." The proclamation applied to slaves and laid a firm legal foundation for slavery's total abolition, which came in 1865 with ratification of the 13th amendment. The subsequent 14th (1868) and 15th (1870) amendments gave African Americans citizenship and, for men, the right to vote.

1917-18: WORLD WAR I The U.S. did not want to enter World War I; the country was neither economically nor militarily prepared. But a series of incidents culminating in the interception of the infamous "Zimmerman Telegram" prompted Congress to declare war on the Central Powers on April 6, 1917.

About 1.66 million American troops were deployed in France before the war ended on Nov. 11, 1918. Though little was gained by the U.S. (except for U.S. industry, which made a fortune on the war), the U.S. established itself as a world power.

1920: WOMEN'S SUFFRAGE The territory of Wyoming on Dec. 10, 1869, became first in the nation to give women the right to vote. A constitutional amendment giving all women the right to vote was introduced in Congress on Jan. 10, 1878, but it sat there for decades. In that time, 11 states passed laws allowing women to vote.

Finally, on Aug. 18, 1920, Tennessee ratified the 19th amendment, which allowed the measure to go into effect.

1929: STOCKS CRASH The post-war economic boom came to a screeching halt when the New York Stock Exchange—the world's largest—began a series of crashes on Oct. 24, 1929, losing a record 22.6% on "Black Monday," Oct. 28, and another 12.8% on "Black Tuesday," Oct. 29. Over the next few weeks, the market dropped even further; many fortunes, big and small, were lost, and the world headed into a deep depression.

1933: NEW DEAL When Franklin D. Roosevelt was inaugurated on March 4, 1933, unemployment was at a record high 24.9%. To restore the economy, he proposed the most sweeping economic legislation in U.S. history over a period from March 9-June 16. It was called the "New Deal."

Many of Roosevelt's initiatives were branded as Communistic by detractors, and some were struck down by the courts. But others, such as the Securities and Exchange Commission, the Works Progress Administration, and Social Security, survived and changed the face of the U.S. government.

The Liberty Bell

1941-45: WORLD WAR II Just before 8 AM on Dec. 7, 1941, a surprise attack by Japanese submarines and carrier-based planes devastated the U.S. fleet at Pearl Harbor naval base in Hawaii. During the attack, 2,403 Americans were killed and 1,178 wounded. Congress declared war on Japan by 4 PM Dec. 8, and on Germany and Italy Dec. 11.

The U.S. was not prepared to fight a major war. But in a short time, U.S. industry began churning out vehicles and munitions on an unprecedented scale. Women took over many of the jobs left by men, and were able to keep the Allied war machine running.

After years of war, Germany surrendered on May 7, 1945. President Harry Truman dropped two atomic bombs, first on Hiroshima Aug. 6, then Nagasaki Aug. 9. Japan sued for peace, and formally surrendered on Sept. 2 aboard the USS *Missouri* in Tokyo Bay.

1962: CUBAN MISSILE CRISIS On Oct. 22, 1962, President John F. Kennedy announced that the Soviets were deploying nuclear missiles in Cuba capable of hitting most of the U.S.

To prevent a possible nuclear armageddon, secret talks opened up with Soviet Premier Nikita Khrushchev, who backed down on Oct. 28. In return, President Kennedy promised not to invade Cuba, and to remove U.S. nuclear missiles from Turkey.

1964: CIVIL RIGHTS ACT On Aug. 28, 1963, Martin Luther King Jr. led over 200,000 people in a march on Washington, D.C., calling for the passage of federal civil rights legislation.

Initially sponsored by President John Kennedy, the Civil Rights Act was signed into law by President Lyndon Johnson on July 2, 1964. It banned discrimination in public businesses and facilities, and in employment and unions.

Congress passed the Voting Rights Act of 1965 on Aug. 6; it suspended (and amendments later banned) use of literacy or other voter-qualification tests that had been used to keep black people from voting.

1964-73: VIETNAM The Vietnam conflict was the longest in U.S. history, and one of the most divisive. The U.S. had been trying to curb Communist expansion in Vietnam since 1955. An alleged attack by three N. Vietnamese gunboats on the USS *Maddox* destroyer in the Tonkin Gulf on Aug. 2, 1964, prompted Congress to pass a resolution for increased involvement.

The first U.S. combat ground-forces arrived in S. Vietnam on March 6, 1965. In the following years, the war expanded into Cambodia and Laos.

In April 1969, U.S. forces peaked at 543,400, while a massive anti-war movement was going on at home. A ceasefire was signed Jan. 27, 1973. Without U.S. support, South Vietnam fell to the Communists by 1975.

In all, 58,000 U.S. troops died in the conflict.

2001: SEPTEMBER 11TH ATTACKS The deadliest terrorist attack in U.S. history came on Sept. 11, 2001. Members of Osama bin Laden's al-Qaeda terrorist network hijacked four U.S. passenger airliners and flew two into the World Trade Center twin towers in New York City (which had withstood a previous bombing on Feb. 26, 1993), bringing both towers crashing down within 100 minutes of the first impact.

A third hijacked jetliner crashed into the Pentagon outside Washington, DC, and a fourth crashed hear near Shanksville, PA, after passengers apparently tried to subdue their captors. About 3,000 people died in the attacks, including over 2,700 in New York.

In the wake of the attack, the U.S. launched a "War on Terrorism" and in 2003 began a controversial war to depose the regime of Saddam Hussein in Iraq.

U.S. Facts

SUPERLATIVES

LARGEST STATE

AREA The largest U.S. state is Alaska, which has a total area of 663,267 square miles, about 429 times the size of Rhode Island (the smallest state at 1,545 square miles).

LARGEST COUNTY

AREA The vast expanses of Alaska are divided into several large, sparsely populated "geographical census areas," counting these as equivalent to counties. Yukon-Koyukuk, at 145,900 square miles, is the largest county in the U.S. (almost as big as Montana).

The largest county in the contiguous U.S. is San Bernardino County, CA, at 20,105 square miles total area. The smallest is Arlington County, VA, at 26 square miles.

LARGEST STATE

POPULATION According to U.S. Census Bureau figures for 2004, California is the most populous state, with 35.9 million residents, followed by Texas (22.5 million) and New York (19.2 million).

LARGEST COUNTY

POPULATION Los Angeles county in California is the most populous county in the U.S., with 9,937,739 people in 2004. The second largest is Cook County, IL, which contains the city of Chicago. It had a population of 5,327,777 in 2004.

LARGEST CITY

POPULATION New York City is the nation's largest city, with about 8,104,079 people in 2004.

MOST CROWDED STATE New Jersey is the most densely populated state, with 1,173 people per square mile of land in 2004. That number has grown from 250.7 in 1900 and 642.8 in 1950. It might surprise visitors that 37% of New Jersey is still forested land.

Alaska is the least densely populated state (1.2 people per sq mi) followed by Wyoming (5.2 people per sq mi).

NORTHERNMOST POINT
The northernmost point in the U.S. is Point Barrow, AK, which sits at 71° 23′ N. The northernmost city is Barrow, AK, which sits at 71° 17′ N.

The northernmost point in the 48 contiguous states is the Northwest Angle, MN, at 49° 23′ N.

Vacationers visiting the Minnesota resort towns on the Lake of the Woods must pass through Canada to reach the Angle by land.

SOUTHERNMOST POINT
The southernmost point in the U.S. is Ka Lae (South Cape) Island in Hawaii, at 18° 55′ N. The southernmost city is Hilo, HI, at 19° 44′ N.

In the 48 contiguous states, the southernmost point is Key West, FL, at 24° 33′ N (although the privately-owned Ballast Key is farther south). The so-called Conch Republic is less than 100 miles from Cuba. Its surrounding reefs are treacherous and natives made lucrative careers of salvaging wrecks for most of the 19th century.

EASTERNMOST POINT Because Alaska's Aleutian Islands extend into the eastern hemisphere, they technically contain the easternmost point in the U.S., which is Pochnoi Point, on Semisopochnoi Island, at 179° 46′ E. This is 70 miles away from the westernmost point.

The easternmost point on the lower 48 is West Quoddy Head, ME, marked by a lighthouse, at 66° 57′ W. The easternmost city is Eastport, ME, at 66° 59′ W.

WESTERNMOST POINT
The westernmost point in the U.S. is Amatignak Island, AK, at 179° 06′ W; however, the Aleutian Islands continue another 300 miles west to Cape Wrangell on Attu Island. The westernmost city is Atka, AK, at 174° 12′ W.

In the 48 contiguous states, the westernmost point is Cape Alava, WA, at 124° 44′ W, in Olympic National Park.

HIGHEST MOUNTAIN
The highest mountain in North America is Mount McKinley (Denali), towering 20,320 feet over Alaska. The 14,494-foot-high Mount Whitney in California is the highest point in the lower 48, and about 80 miles from the lowest point.

LOWEST POINT
The Badwater Basin in Death Valley, CA, plunges 282 feet below sea level. What used to be a lake over 2000 years ago has now dried to a crunchy salt bed.

LONGEST RIVER (NORTH AMERICA)
The longest continuous waterway in North America is the Mississippi-Missouri-Red Rock river system at 3,710 miles. It flows from the Red Rock's source in Beaverhead County, MT, to the Gulf of Mexico, mouth of the Mississippi.

The longest individual river in North America is the Mississippi. From its source at Lake Itasca, MN, to the Gulf of Mexico, "the Big Muddy" flows 2,340 miles. The Mississippi receives tributaries from 33 states and two Canadian provinces.

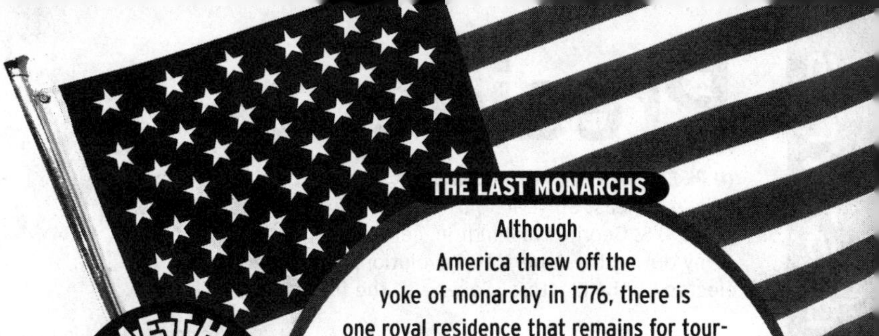

SOMETHING TO THINK ABOUT

LADY LIBERTY

Standing an inch over 151 feet and weighing some 312,000 pounds, the Statue of Liberty is the largest gift given by one country to another. Designed by Frédéric Bartholdi and Alexandre Gustave Eiffel as "Liberty Enlightening the World," it took nine years to construct in France. It was shipped in 350 pieces (in 214 crates) from France to New York Harbor in June 1885, and dedicated on Oct. 28, 1886, on Liberty Island.

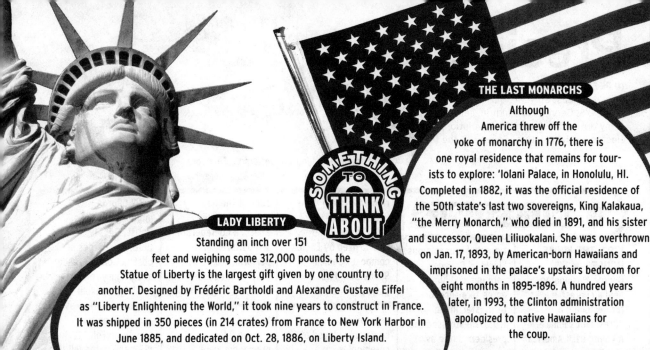

THE LAST MONARCHS

Although America threw off the yoke of monarchy in 1776, there is one royal residence that remains for tourists to explore: 'Iolani Palace, in Honolulu, HI. Completed in 1882, it was the official residence of the 50th state's last two sovereigns, King Kalakaua, "the Merry Monarch," who died in 1891, and his sister and successor, Queen Liliuokalani. She was overthrown on Jan. 17, 1893, by American-born Hawaiians and imprisoned in the palace's upstairs bedroom for eight months in 1895-1896. A hundred years later, in 1993, the Clinton administration apologized to native Hawaiians for the coup.

LARGEST GORGE
It is not called the Grand Canyon for nothing—the Arizona landmark is 277 miles long, 600 feet to 18 miles wide, and one mile deep. The deepest gorge, however, is Hells Canyon on the Snake River crossing the Oregon/Idaho border. At its deepest, it is 7,900 feet down.

DEEPEST WELL
The Bertha Rogers 1 gas well in the Anadarko Basin of Washita County, OK, plunges to a depth of 31,441 feet—about 6 miles. Lonestar Petroleum Company completed the well in 1974 after a year and a half of drilling.

TALLEST STRUCTURES
America's wonders are more than just natural. Chicago's Sears Tower, opened in 1974, stands 1,450 feet tall and remains the tallest building in North America.

It is, however, dwarfed by the nation's tallest free-standing structure, the considerably less urban KVLY-TV tower. Completed Aug. 13, 1963, in Blanchard, ND, over 33 working days, it rises 2,063 feet.

TALLEST MONUMENT
The tallest constructed monument in the world is the Gateway Arch in St. Louis, MO, commemorating the Louisiana Purchase. The stainless steel arch designed by architect Eero Saarinen and completed on Oct. 28, 1965, soars to a height of 630 feet.

LARGEST GOLD REPOSITORY
The world's largest gold repository is the U.S. Bullion Depository at Fort Knox, KY. Its glittering assets amount to $6.2 billion. During its history, the fort has also guarded the original Declaration of Independence, the manuscript of Lincoln's Gettysburg address, and the British and Hungarian crown jewels.

WORST NATURAL DISASTER The worst U.S. natural disaster in terms of loss of life, is the hurricane that roared through the island of Galveston, TX, on Sept. 8, 1900. Bearing 130 mph winds and 15.5-foot storm surges, the hurricane completely flooded the island, killed over 6,000 and destroyed nearly three-fourths of the city.

LARGEST PRE-COLUMBIAN SETTLEMENT
The Cahokia Mounds, made between 700 and 1400 AD in southwest Illinois, cover a 2,200-acre area, with 68 remaining earthen mounds. At the city's peak between 1050 and 1200, it grew to cover 6 square miles with as many as 20,000 people living among more than 100 mounds.

The largest surviving mound, Monks Mound, is about 100 feet tall and covers 16 acres.

THE LAST TIME...

Thomas Jefferson hoped America would become an agrarian nation and for much of its history, it was. During Jefferson's lifetime, the rural population was always over 90% of the total. However, the 1910 U.S. census was the last to record a greater percentage of rural folks to urbanites—54.4% of U.S. residents were listed as rural. The percentage continues to drop, still; in the 2000 census, only 21% of the population was reported as rural.

Presidents

TO BE ELIGIBLE FOR THE PRESIDENCY, one must be a native-born citizen, at least 35 years old, and have lived at least 14 years in the U.S. George Washington, commander of the Continental Army during the American Revolution, was unanimously elected by the Electoral College as the first president in 1789.

Presidents Washington, Jefferson, Theodore Roosevelt, and Lincoln on Mt. Rushmore

MILESTONES

1792: THE WHITE HOUSE In 1792, George Washington held a contest for designing a "President's Palace." A young Irish-American architect named James Hoban won. The cornerstone was laid on Oct. 13, 1792; the building was completed in 1801 at a total cost of $232,372. John Adams and his wife, Abigail, became the first residents in Nov. 1800 as the building was being finished.

The white façade comes from a lime-based whitewash used in 1798 to protect the sandstone from the elements. The earliest written mention of "White House" is in a letter dated Mar. 18, 1812, by Representative Abijah Bigelow (MA). In Sept. 1901, Theodore Roosevelt made the name official.

1792: TWO TERMS Washington wanted to retire to his home, Mt. Vernon, after one term, but a unanimous Electoral College vote induced him to agree to a second term (starting in 1793). He stressed the president's role as temporary, declining a third term.

The tradition limiting a president to two terms continued until it was broken by Franklin D. Roosevelt. The 22nd Amendment to the Constitution made the limit official in 1951.

1825: FATHER AND SON John Quincy Adams was the first son of a president to also become president. He served for one term, from 1825 to 1829; his father, John Adams, also served one term, from 1797 to 1801. In the only other case, George H. W. Bush became president in 1989, and his son George W. Bush followed suit in 2001.

1828: "HAIL TO THE CHIEF" Created for a stage adaptation of Sir Walter Scott's romantic poem "The Lady of the Lake," "Hail to the Chief" was written by English composer James Sanderson. First played in the U.S. in 1812, it quickly became popular and was commonly played at ceremonies.

John Quincy Adams was the first president to be honored by "Hail to the Chief," on July 4, 1828, but it was John Tyler's wife, Julia, who first thought to have the Marine Band announce the president's arrival with the song. The Department of Defense officially made it a musical tribute to the president in 1954.

1857: BACHELOR James Buchanan was a lifelong bachelor. While president (1857-61), he made his orphaned niece, Harriet Lane, White House hostess.

Grover Cleveland was a bachelor when he took office in 1885, but married Frances Folsom the next year.

1865: ASSASSINATED Abraham Lincoln was fatally shot in the back of the head by actor John Wilkes Booth, a Confederate sympathizer, at a performance of *Our American Cousin* at Ford's Theatre in Washington, DC, April 14, 1865.

Three later presidents were assassinated: James Garfield (July 2, 1881, by Charles J. Guiteau in Washington, DC), William McKinley (Sept. 6, 1901, by Leon Czolgosz in Buffalo, NY), and John F. Kennedy (Nov. 22, 1963, by Lee Harvey Oswald in Dallas, TX).

1868: IMPEACHED No president has been removed from office by the process outlined in the Constitution. However, two were impeached.

In a battle for political power following the Civil War, Andrew Johnson was impeached by the House on Feb. 24, 1868. The Senate fell one vote short of the two-thirds majority needed to convict him.

Bill Clinton was impeached by the House, Dec. 19, 1998, on charges of obstruction of justice and perjury related to alleged sexual misconduct. He was acquitted by the Senate on Feb. 12, 1999; the votes fell 17 short of the needed majority.

(A House committee recommended President Richard Nixon's impeachment in 1974, but he resigned before the full House could vote.)

1893: BACK IN OFFICE Grover Cleveland is the only president who served two nonconsecutive terms, in 1885-89 and 1893-97; he is officially counted as both the 22nd and 24th president.

1910: FIRST PITCH William Howard Taft started the tradition of the presidential "first pitch" of baseball season, on April 14, 1910, in Washington DC. Since then every president but Jimmy Carter has opened at

Selected Birth Firsts of the Presidents

Log Cabin	Andrew Jackson	March 15, 1767	Waxhaw settlement, SC
Immigrants' Son	Andrew Jackson	March 15, 1767	Parents came from Ireland, 1765
Born Citizen	Martin Van Buren	Dec. 5, 1782	Kinderhook, NY
Outside the 13 Colonies	Abraham Lincoln	Feb. 12, 1809	near Hodgenville, KY
West of the Mississippi	Herbert Hoover	Aug. 10, 1874	West Branch, IA
Big City	Theodore Roosevelt	Oct. 27, 1858	New York, NY
West of Rockies	Richard Nixon	Jan. 9, 1913	Yorba Linda, CA
In Hospital	Jimmy Carter	Oct. 1, 1924	Plains, GA
Baby Boomer	Bill Clinton	Aug. 19, 1946	Hope, AR

Other Selected Firsts

Rode on a Train	Andrew Jackson	Baltimore and Ohio RR	June 6, 1833
Had Telephone Installed	Rutherford B. Hayes	White House	May 10, 1879
Rode in an Automobile	William McKinley	Stanley Steamer	Oct. 14, 1899
Gave Radio Broadcast	Warren G. Harding	Long Island, NY	Nov. 5, 1921
Gave TV Broadcast	Franklin D. Roosevelt	New York World's Fair	April 30, 1939
Gave Live TV Press Conference	John F. Kennedy	White House	Jan. 25, 1961
Held Internet Chat	Bill Clinton	Virtual town hall meeting	Nov. 8, 1999

SOMETHING TO THINK ABOUT

AFTER THE WHITE HOUSE

Only two presidents have held federal office after leaving the White House. John Quincy Adams served nine terms in the House of Representatives (1830-48). William Howard Taft was appointed Chief Justice of the Supreme Court by President Warren Harding in 1921.

William Howard Taft

John Quincy Adams

least one season during his tenure. A true fan, Woodrow Wilson was the first to attend a World Series; he threw out the first pitch of Game Two during the 1915 Phillies vs. Red Sox series on Oct. 9.

1942: STATE OF THE UNION The phrase "State of the Union" was informally used in 1942 under Franklin D. Roosevelt. Before that the speech was known as the Annual Message.

George Washington delivered the first Annual Message to Congress in person on April 30, 1789, as part of his inaugural address. He gave the first regular Annual Message on Jan. 8, 1790. Beginning with Thomas Jefferson on Dec. 8, 1801, the Annual Message was a letter submitted to Congress, until Woodrow Wilson revived delivering it in person in 1913.

Warren Harding was the first to have his speech broadcast over radio, Dec. 8, 1922. Harry Truman was the first to deliver a televised annual address, Jan. 6, 1947.

1942: CAMP DAVID In 1942, Franklin D. Roosevelt established a presidential retreat at Camp Shangri-La, 70 miles away from the capital, in the Catoctin Mountains of Maryland. Named after the remote mountain monastery in James Hilton's novel *Lost Horizon*, it was renamed Camp David by President Dwight Eisenhower in 1953 for his grandson.

1960: CATHOLIC John F. Kennedy was the first and only Roman Catholic to be elected president. (The first Catholic to run for president, New York Governor Al Smith, had been defeated by Herbert Hoover in 1928.) The most common religious affiliations among the presidents have been Episcopalian (11) and Presbyterian (7).

1962: NUCLEAR FOOTBALL After the 1962 Cuban Missile Crisis, President John Kennedy approved "the football," a briefcase containing the authorization codes for a nuclear strike. Since then, a high-ranking military aide with the briefcase chained to his wrist has followed the president on every trip.

1974: RESIGNATION The only president to resign was Richard Nixon. When an attempted burglary and wiretapping of the Democratic National Committee headquarters at the Watergate complex in Washington, DC, on June 17, 1972, was linked to Nixon, public trust began to plummet. After the House Judiciary Committee recommended impeachment in July 1974, Nixon officially resigned on Aug. 9.

2000: ELECTION SETTLED BY SUPREME COURT In the 2000 presidential election, Al Gore narrowly defeated George W. Bush in the popular vote, but the outcome in the Electoral College hinged on Florida's 25 electoral votes. A series of legal challenges and recounts followed. On Dec. 12, the U.S. Supreme Court in effect voted to block manual recounting and leave standing a popular vote total in Florida that gave Bush the state's electoral votes, and the White House.

MORE ON

Presidents

Presidents Ford, Nixon, George H.W. Bush, Reagan, and Carter

SUPERLATIVES

LEAST ELECTORAL COLLEGE VOTES (INCUMBENT PRESIDENT) The lowest Electoral College tally for an incumbent president running for reelection was the eight received by William Howard Taft in 1912.

Taft, who had won the 1908 election and served one term, was defeated in the 1912 election after his mentor, former President Theodore Roosevelt, joined the race as a third-party candidate. That year Woodrow Wilson won with 435 Electoral College votes; Roosevelt got 88.

MOST ELECTORAL COLLEGE VOTES The most Electoral College votes received by any presidential candidate was 525 by President Ronald Reagan in 1984, securing his second term as president.

The only president to be elected unanimously by the Electoral College was George Washington. In 1789, at the first presidential election, he received all 69 electoral votes, and in 1792 he won all 132 votes. In 1820, James Monroe received every Electoral College vote except one, from a New Hampshire delegate who voted for John Quincy Adams.

CLOSEST ELECTION (ELECTORAL COLLEGE) In the controversial 1876 election between Rutherford B. Hayes and Samuel Tilden, Tilden won the popular vote but eventually lost the election by one electoral vote.

While Tilden was originally on top, 184 votes to 165, the 20 votes of Florida, Louisiana, South Carolina, and Oregon were in dispute. After several months, an Electoral Commission created by Congress awarded all 20 votes to Hayes on March 2, 1877.

LARGEST POPULAR VOTE MAJORITY The greatest majority won in the popular vote was by Richard Nixon in 1972. He defeated George McGovern by a record 17,994,460 votes (47,165,234 to 29,170,774) to win reelection.

LARGEST ELECTORAL COLLEGE MAJORITY The greatest Electoral College majority was won by President Franklin D. Roosevelt in 1936. He defeated Alfred Landon by a record 515 Electoral College votes (523 to 8).

SHORTEST INAUGURAL SPEECH The shortest inaugural speech was delivered by George Washington at his second inauguration, on March 4, 1793. His speech lasted just 90 seconds, delivered in the Senate Chamber of Congress Hall in Philadelphia. It contained just 136 words.

LONGEST INAUGURAL SPEECH William Henry Harrison spoke for two hours at his inauguration on March 4, 1841.

After his inauguration, which was held outdoors on a cold, wet day, Harrison caught a cold that developed into pneumonia. Unable to recover, he died on April 4.

SHORTEST TERM At 32 days, William Henry Harrison served the shortest term as president. The aristocratic Harrison had defeated Martin Van Buren in the 1840 election, running as a humble farmer who put down an Indian uprising at Tippecanoe.

LONGEST-SERVING PRESIDENT Franklin D. Roosevelt was the longest-serving president. He was elected a record four times, in 1932, 1936, 1940, and 1944, and served for 12 years, 39 days. He died in office on April 12, 1945. In 1951, the 22nd Amendment was passed, limiting presidents to two terms.

MOST VETOES The most vetoes issued by any president is 635, by Franklin D. Roosevelt (1933-45). The most vetoes in one term was 414, by Grover Cleveland in his first term (1885-89).

BEST ATHLETE Gerald Ford (served 1974-77) was probably the best athlete among the presidents, despite an image he acquired as president for being clumsy.

In college he started on the University of Michigan Wolverines' national championship football teams of 1932 and 1933 and was MVP of the 1933 team. He received offers to play pro football which he turned down. Later in life, Ford was an avid skier and golf and tennis player.

PRESIDENTIAL RELATIVES In 1905, when Franklin D. Roosevelt married his distant cousin, Eleanor (niece of then-President Theodore Roosevelt), he became related by blood (5) or marriage (6) to 11 former presidents: Theodore Roosevelt, John Adams, John Quincy Adams, Ulysses S. Grant, William Henry Harrison, Benjamin Harrison, James

Other Presidential Superlatives

Oldest to Take Office	Ronald Reagan	69 years, 349 days
Youngest to Take Office	Theodore Roosevelt, took office after McKinley's assassination	42 years, 322 days
Youngest Elected	John F. Kennedy	43 years, 236 days
Longest-living	Ronald Reagan	died at age 93 (in 2004)
Tallest	Abraham Lincoln	6 feet, 4 inches
Shortest	James Madison	5 feet, 4 inches
Biggest Feet	Warren G. Harding	size 14 shoes
Heaviest	William Howard Taft	332 pounds in 1911
Most Children	John Tyler	14, by two wives
Most Common Religion	Episcopalian	11 presidents
Most Common Home State	Virginia	8 presidents
Most Common Alma Mater (undergraduate)	Harvard	5 presidents
Most Common Political Party	Republican	18 presidents

TIME "MAN OF THE YEAR"

Since Franklin D. Roosevelt was chosen as *Time* magazine's sixth "Man of the Year" in 1932, every president except for Gerald Ford has been selected at least once. Roosevelt was selected three times: 1932, 1934, and 1941. The other presidents to be selected multiple times were Dwight D. Eisenhower (1944 and 1959), Harry S. Truman (1944 and 1945), Lyndon B. Johnson (1964 and 1967), Richard Nixon (1971 and 1972), Ronald Reagan (1980 and 1983), Bill Clinton (1992 and 1998), and George W. Bush (2000 and 2004). In 1998, President Clinton was named "Co-Man of the Year" along with independent prosecutor Kenneth Starr.

SOMETHING TO THINK ABOUT

ELECTED WITHOUT POPULAR VOTE

In 1824, the first year the popular vote was recorded, the vote was split four ways, with Andrew Jackson having the highest total. None of the four candidates went on to win a majority in the Electoral College. John Quincy Adams, with 84 votes (all from New England), ran behind Jackson (99) but ahead of William H. Crawford (41) and Henry Clay (37). Adams was elected by the House when Clay put his support (and votes) behind him. Several other presidents since then have been elected despite losing in the popular vote: Rutherford B. Hayes in 1876, Benjamin Harrison in 1888, and George W. Bush in 2000. The 1800 presidential election finished in a 73-73 Electoral College tie between Thomas Jefferson and Aaron Burr; Jefferson won the presidency through a vote in the House of Representatives.

PRESIDENT HANSON?

While George Washington is recognized as the first U.S. president, eight men served as president of the Congress between the adoption of the Articles of Confederation in 1781 and the ratification of the U.S. Constitution in 1789. John Hanson, a Maryland congressman, was the first, chosen unanimously by Congress after the Articles were adopted; he served one year, from Nov. 5, 1781, to Nov. 3, 1782.

MAYFLOWER DESCENDANTS

John Adams, John Quincy Adams, Zachary Taylor, Ulysses S. Grant, James Garfield, Franklin D. Roosevelt, George H. W. Bush, and George W. Bush can all trace their American heritage to the first permanent settlement in New England—the Colony of New Plymouth, established by 101 Pilgrims in Dec. 1620.

FOURTH OF JULY

By a strange quirk of fate, the fourth of July, Independence Day, is also the date on which most presidents have died. Three presidents have passed away on that date. Rivals John Adams and Thomas Jefferson died within hours of each other on July 4, 1826, and James Monroe died on July 4, 1831.

Madison, William Howard Taft, Zachary Taylor, Martin Van Buren, and George Washington.

HAND-SHAKING

William McKinley (1897-1901) is believed to hold the record for presidential hand-shaking, having been informally timed at a rate of 1,800 people per hour. The "McKinley grip" consisted of squeezing with his right hand and holding the elbow with his left.

Shortly after his election in Nov. 1897, a reporter watched McKinley shake hands with 504 people in 17 minutes, or about one handshake every two seconds.

CONGRESS

U.S. Senate

Rebecca Felton, seated, 1st female U.S. senator. ▶

THE U.S. CONGRESS HAS TWO CHAMBERS, THE SENATE AND THE HOUSE OF REPRESENTATIVES. Senators are elected for six years, and there are two from each state, regardless of population. Since 1929 the membership of the House has been fixed at 435; the number from each state depends on its population at the latest census. All House members serve two-year terms.

MILESTONES

1788: FIRST SENATORS ELECTED The distinction of being the first persons elected to the U.S. Senate fell to two men: Robert Morris and William Maclay. They were elected to office from Pennsylvania on Sept. 30, 1788. The Pennsylvania legislature voted Maclay the first-ever senator by a vote of 66 to 1. Morris won the second seat by the closer margin of 37 to 31.

1789: FIRST SESSION The U.S. Senate convened for the first time on March 4, 1789, in New York City. Of the 22 eligible members (only 11 states had ratified the Constitution at the time of the first meeting), only eight attended the first session. They met in a second-floor chamber of Federal Hall.

1789: QUORUM With 12 members present in the Senate, a quorum for business was established for the first time on April 6, 1789. As its first item of business, the Senate elected John Langdon of New Hampshire as president pro tempore and invited the House of Representatives to its chamber to count the electoral ballots for president and vice president. George Washington was elected president, and John Adams vice president.

1790: MEETING IN PHILADELPHIA During the second session of the first Congress, convened in Jan. 1790, a measure was passed that provided for a permanent seat of government along the Potomac River, including a house for the president and a legislative hall, to be ready by Dec. 1800.

While that site was being prepared, Congress agreed to move the government to Philadelphia. The final session of the first Congress met in Philadelphia on Dec. 6, 1790. Congress would meet in Philadelphia for nearly 10 years before moving to Washington, DC.

1800: MEETING IN WASHINGTON, DC On Nov. 17, 1800, the Senate took up residence in the "crowded, leaky, and unheated" ground-floor chamber of the unfinished Capitol in Washington, DC (now the old Supreme Court chamber). A decade later (Feb. 10, 1810), the Senate moved to a larger chamber on the Capitol's second floor, now known as the "old Senate chamber."

With the territorial expansion of the U.S. in the 1800s, the Senate became too crowded and needed larger quarters again. On Jan. 4, 1859, the Senate's 64 members moved to a larger chamber in the Capitol's new north wing.

The Senate continues to meet in this chamber today.

1816: FORMER SENATOR ELECTED PRESIDENT The first person to serve as a senator and then be elected president of the U.S. was James Monroe. The Virginian was elected to the Senate in 1790, and served there until 1794, when President George Washington appointed him minister to France. He was elected president in 1816, and won a second term in 1820.

1870: AFRICAN-AMERICAN SENATOR The first African-American to serve in the U.S. Senate was Hiram R. Revels (R, MS). Elected during Reconstruction by the Mississippi state legislature to fill a vacancy as the state prepared to rejoin the Union, Revels took the oath of office on Feb. 25, 1870. His brief term ended on Mar. 3, 1871.

1913: POPULAR ELECTION OF SENATORS Prior to the ratification of the 17th Amendment to the Constitution in 1913, senators had been selected by state legislatures. With the passage of the 17th Amendment, the election of senators was by popular vote. The amendment was proposed by Congress on May 13, 1912, and ratified on April 8, 1913.

1920: INCUMBENT SENATOR ELECTED PRESIDENT The first incumbent senator to be elected president was Warren G. Harding. An Ohio Republican, he won his Senate seat in 1914 and defeated James M. Cox in the 1920 presidential election. Taken ill while returning from a trip to Alaska, Harding died in office in San Francisco, CA, on Aug. 2, 1923.

1922: WOMAN SENATOR The first woman to serve as a U.S. senator was Rebecca Felton (D, GA). Appointed on Oct. 3, 1922, by Governor Thomas Hardwick to fill a Senate vacancy, Felton was 87 years

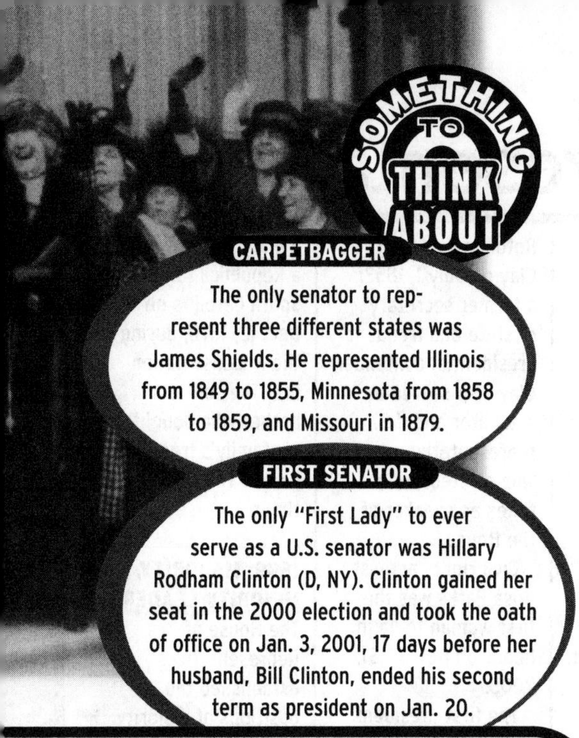

SOMETHING TO THINK ABOUT

CARPETBAGGER

The only senator to represent three different states was James Shields. He represented Illinois from 1849 to 1855, Minnesota from 1858 to 1859, and Missouri in 1879.

FIRST SENATOR

The only "First Lady" to ever serve as a U.S. senator was Hillary Rodham Clinton (D, NY). Clinton gained her seat in the 2000 election and took the oath of office on Jan. 3, 2001, 17 days before her husband, Bill Clinton, ended his second term as president on Jan. 20.

old when she took the oath of office on Nov. 21, 1922.

Historians claim Hardwick had appointed her so that he would not be creating a strong rival when he ran for the Senate seat himself in Nov. 1922. She never did run against Hardwick, but the governor lost after all, to fellow Democrat Walter George. When the Senate convened on Nov. 21, George stepped aside for one day so that Felton could be officially sworn in and claim the distinction of being the first female senator.

The first woman elected to the Senate was Hattie Caraway (D, AR). Appointed to fill the vacancy created by her husband's death, she took the oath of office on Nov. 13, 1931.

On Jan. 12, 1932, she won a special election to become the first woman elected to the Senate. She served until Jan. 2, 1945, setting many landmarks along the way, including becoming the first woman to preside over the Senate, on May 9, 1932.

2005: NON-ENGLISH SPEECH FROM SENATE FLOOR When Sen. Mel Martinez (R, FL) addressed the Senate in his debut speech on Feb. 2, 2005, his first three sentences were in Spanish. Both Univision, the Spanish-language cable network, and CNN En Español broadcast the speech live. The unprepared stenographer simply wrote "Speaking Spanish."

SUPERLATIVES

LONGEST-SERVING SENATOR
The longest-serving member of the Senate was Strom Thurmond (SC), who served 48 years from the end of the 83rd Congress on Dec. 24, 1954, to the start of the 107th on Jan. 3, 2003. He changed parties from Democrat to Republican in 1964.

OLDEST The greatest age at which anyone has served in the Senate is 100 years, 1 month, by Strom Thurmond, who retired soon after his 100th birthday.

YOUNGEST The Constitution sets the minimum age for senators at 30 years old. Contrary to the rules, the youngest-ever senator, John H. Eaton (R, TN), appointed on Sept. 5, 1918, was 28 years, 4 months, 29 days old when he was sworn in on Nov. 16, 1818.

The youngest person elected to the Senate was Armistead Thomson Mason (R, VA). He was sworn in on Jan. 22, 1816, at age 28 years, 5 months, 18 days.

LONGEST TIME FOR SAME TWO SENATORS Senators Strom Thurmond and Ernest Hollings (D) both represented South Carolina, from Nov. 9, 1966, to Jan. 3, 2003 (36 years).

MOST CONSECUTIVE ROLL CALL VOTES
The record for most consecutive roll call votes cast in the Senate was 10,252 by William Proxmire (D, WI). From April 20, 1966, to Oct. 18, 1988, Proxmire didn't miss a single vote.

LONGEST SPEECHES
The longest continuous speech in Senate history was given by Wayne Morse (Ind., OR), who spoke for 22 hours, 26 minutes without interruption on April 24-25, 1953. "The Tiger of the Senate" was speaking on the Tidelands Oil Bill.

The longest filibuster ever—but with one bathroom break—was given by Strom Thurmond (D, SC), when he spoke for 24 hours, 18 minutes against the 1957 Civil Rights Act on Aug. 28-29.

MOST LOPSIDED SENATE During the 75th Congress (1937-39), Democrats outnumbered Republicans 76 to 16, the biggest margin since Reconstruction, when Republicans held the majority. (The other 4 seats were held by minor parties or independents.)

CLOSEST RACE
In Nov. 1974, John Durkin (D) and Louis Wyman (R) faced off in New Hampshire in the closest election in Senate history. After two recounts, Wyman was declared the winner by two votes.

Ultimately the two agreed to a new election, held Sept. 16, 1975. This time Durkin won by a resounding 27,000 votes.

MOST COSTLY RACE
In 2000, Jon Corzine (D, NJ) spent more of his own money—an estimated $60 million—than any other Senate candidate in history, in his bid for an open seat. He won with 50% of the vote.

CONGRESS

U.S. House of Representatives

MILESTONES

1776: GOLD MEDAL The first Congressional Gold Medal awarded by the Continental Congress was to General George Washington on March 25, 1776. Since the American Revolution, Congress has awarded gold medals as its highest expression of appreciation for distinguished achievements and contributions.

The first women to receive the Gold Medal were Margaret Aldrich and Anna Bouligny, in 1938, for setting up hospitals in Puerto Rico to treat soldiers in the Spanish-American War.

1789: SPEAKER In the first Congress, convened in New York in April 1789, the House chose Frederick A.C. Muhlenberg (PA) as its chief officer, or speaker.

1808: FROM CONGRESS TO WHITE HOUSE The first person to serve as a House member and later be elected president was James Madison. The Virginian served three House terms, ending in 1797. He was elected president for two terms, beginning in 1809.

James Polk (D, TN) was the first House speaker to later be elected president, in 1845. The first incumbent representative to go on to the White House was James Garfield (R), who represented Ohio for 17 years before becoming the 20th president in 1881.

John Quincy Adams (Whig, MA) was the only president to be elected to Congress after leaving the White House, serving from 1831 until his death in 1848.

1812: FIRST GERRYMANDER The term Gerrymandering—redrawing congressional electoral district boundaries in a particular, often bizarre, way so as to give one party an advantage over its rivals—was first used in 1812 when Jeffersonians led by Massachusetts Governor Elbridge Gerry redistricted in favor of their party. When a critic noted that one of the new districts was shaped like a salamander, someone replied that it must be a "Gerrymander." Soon after, *Boston Gazette* cartoonist Elkanah Tisdale satirically depicted the oddly shaped district as the mythical "Gerry-mander" beast.

1824: ADDRESS BY A FOREIGN DIGNITARY The Marquis de Lafayette, a French general and Revolutionary War hero, gave a speech before a joint session of Congress on Dec. 10, 1824. He was one of just three world figures who were not current heads of state to address such a session. The others were Polish Solidarity leader Lech Walesa in 1989 and Nelson Mandela, then deputy president of the African National Congress, in 1990.

1852: LYING IN STATE The Rotunda of the Capitol, completed in 1824, has been used to pay final tribute to very eminent citizens. The first person laid in state in the Rotunda was Henry Clay on July 1, 1852; a former secretary of state and frequent presidential contender, Clay also served as a senator and U.S. representative, and was elected three times as speaker of the House.

Civil rights activist Rosa Parks was the first woman to lie in honor on Oct. 30-31, 2005.

The first president to lie in state in the Rotunda was Abraham Lincoln, April 19-21, 1865. Nine other presidents have lain there in state: James Garfield (1881), William McKinley Jr. (1901), Warren G. Harding (1923), William Howard Taft (1930), John F. Kennedy (1963), Herbert Hoover (1964), Dwight D. Eisenhower (1969), Lyndon B. Johnson (1973), and Ronald Reagan (2004).

1870: AFRICAN-AMERICAN REPRESENTATIVE The first African-American to serve in the House was Joseph Rainey, elected as a Republican from South Carolina on Dec. 12, 1870, during the Reconstruction Era. The son of a barber who bought his family's freedom, he was reelected four times.

1899: MAJORITY, MINORITY LEADERS The House of Representatives established the positions of majority and minority leaders in 1899. They are elected every two years in secret balloting by the party caucus or conference. The first House majority leader was Sereno E. Payne (R, NY); the first minority leader was James D. Richardson (D, TN).

1916: WOMEN The first woman to serve in Congress was Jeannette Rankin (R, MT). She was elected to the House in 1916. Instead of seeking reelection, she ran an unsuccessful campaign for the U.S. Senate.

THE LAST TIME...

The last time a former member of the House was elected president was in 1988, when George H.W. Bush defeated Gov. Michael Dukakis. Bush served in the House from Jan. 3, 1967, to Jan. 3, 1971.

But nearly a quarter century after making political history, Rankin won election to the House again, in 1940.

Margaret Chase Smith (R, ME) became the first woman elected to both houses of Congress. She was first elected to the House on June 3, 1940, to replace her deceased husband, and was reelected four times. In 1948 she ran successfully for a Senate seat, serving another four terms there.

1933: 20TH AMENDMENT The 20th Amendment to the Constitution, ratified on Feb. 6, 1933, established the third day of January as the opening day for each Congress, unless Congress by law appoints a different day. Prior to passage of the amendment, Congress had generally convened in either December or March.

SOMETHING TO THINK ABOUT

THE AMERICAN PASTIME

The only member of Congress to pitch a perfect game in a major-league baseball game is Jim Bunning (R, KY); he did it for the Philadelphia Phillies in 1964. But Bunning is not the only member of Congress who enjoys the national pastime. At one time in the late 1980s there were over 300 teams playing in three congressional softball leagues in Washington, DC; there are about 150 teams playing now.

A Few Congressional Softball Players, Present and Past

LEGISLATOR	TEAM NAME
Sen. Strom Thurmond	Strom's Right Swingers
Sen. Bill Bradley	Dollar Bills
Sen. David Boren	Boren To Run
Sen. Dale Bumpers	Bumpers Stickers
Sen. Bob Graham	Graham Crackers
Rep. Philip Crane	Whooping Cranes
Rep. Dan Burton	Hoosier Daddies
Rep. Barney Frank	Congressional Franks
Rep. John Dingell	Dingell's Dingbats
Rep. Dennis Hastert	Denny's Grand Slams

SUPERLATIVES

MOST REPRESENTATIVES With 53 representatives, California has almost double the number of second-ranked Texas, which has 32. New York is the only state to have gone through over 1,000 representatives, having elected 1,396 by Nov. 2004.

FEWEST REPRESENTATIVES OF A STATE Alaska, Delaware, Montana, North Dakota, South Dakota, Vermont, and Wyoming all have only one representative.

OLDEST REPRESENTATIVE The oldest person ever to win an election to the House of Representatives was Claude Pepper (D, FL), in 1988; he was then 88 years, 2 months old. A House member for 26 years over 13 terms, he served until his death on May 30, 1989. Pepper had served in the Senate from 1937 to 1951.

YOUNGEST REPRESENTATIVE The Constitution sets the minimum age for House members at 25 years. Contrary to the rules, the youngest person to serve in the House, William Claiborne (D, TN), ran for and won a House seat in 1797 at age 22. Claiborne was already a Tennessee Supreme Court judge and had started as a congressional clerk at the age of 15. He became the first territorial governor of Mississippi in 1801 at age 26.

LONGEST SERVICE The longest-serving member of Congress was Carl Hayden (D, AZ), who served 56 consecutive years from Feb. 19, 1912, to Jan. 3, 1969. He was elected as the first representative of Arizona just five days after its entry to the Union, and won a seat in the Senate in 1927. Hayden served under 10 presidents, from William Howard Taft to Lyndon B. Johnson.

LONGEST-SERVING HOUSE SPEAKER The longest service as speaker of the House was the 17 years that Sam Rayburn (D, TX) held the post, in three separate stretches: 1940-47, 1949-53, and 1955-61.

Rayburn was also the oldest person to win an election to the speaker's chair, when he was reelected on Jan. 3, 1961, at age 78 years, 11 months.

SHORTEST TERM AS SPEAKER The shortest term of any speaker was the one day served by Theodore Pomeroy (R, NY), on March 3, 1869, the last day the 40th Congress was in session.

YOUNGEST SPEAKER The youngest person elected speaker of the House was Robert Hunter (Whig, VA), chosen for the 26th Congress on Dec. 16, 1839, at age 30 years, 7 months.

MOST UNBALANCED HOUSE In the 16th Congress (1819-1821) there were 160 Jeffersonian Republicans—86% of the membership—with only 26 Federalists.

Supreme Court

THE SUPREME COURT OF THE UNITED STATES is the highest federal court. It consists of a chief justice and a number of associate justices as determined by Congress (since 1869, the number has been 9). The president nominates the justices, with confirmation required by the Senate.

The Court's term begins each year on the first Monday in October and ordinarily ends in late June. Justices wear black robes and sit in an order determined by seniority.

MILESTONES

1789: FIRST SESSION The Judiciary Act of 1789 required the Supreme Court to sit in the nation's capital; the first assembly of the Court was set for Feb. 1, 1790, in the Merchants Exchange Building in New York City, then the capital. It had to be postponed for one day because some of the justices were not able to get there in time.

1790: FIRST BENCH The first Supreme Court consisted of a chief justice and five associate justices. All six members of the original Court were appointed by George Washington. John Jay was the first chief justice, and the five original associate justices were: John Rutledge, William Cushing, James Wilson, John Blair, and James Iredell.

1803: JUDICIAL REVIEW The power of judicial review, the Supreme Court's authority to strike down legislation that it finds to conflict with the Constitution, was not specifically granted to the Court in the Constitution. It was not clearly established until it was invoked by Chief Justice John Marshall in the case of *Marbury v. Madison* in 1803.

Marshall said that the Court's power to overturn unconstitutional legislation was a necessary consequence of its sworn duty to uphold the Constitution.

1826: FEDERAL JUDGE ELEVATED Robert Trimble served as judge of the U.S. District Court in Kentucky, and on June 16, 1826, became the first federal judge to be nominated and confirmed as a justice of the Supreme Court, under President John Quincy Adams. He served only two years before he died at 51.

With the appointment of Harry Blackmun by President Richard Nixon on June 9, 1970, the Supreme Court for the first time had a majority of justices with experience on the lower federal courts.

1935: SUPREME COURT BUILDING Unlike the president and Congress, the Supreme Court did not have its own building until 1935, 146 years after the Court was established. Congress agreed to provide the funds after being urged to do so by Chief Justice and former President William H. Taft. Before 1935 the Court had met in at least nine different locations, including the Old Senate Chamber in the Capitol.

1967: AFRICAN-AMERICAN JUSTICE The first African-American to serve on the Supreme Court was Thurgood Marshall. Appointed by President Lyndon B. Johnson, Marshall took the oath of office on Oct. 2, 1967. He served for 23 years until his retirement on June 28, 1991. Of Marshall's historic elevation to the Supreme Court, Johnson said: "It was the right thing to do, the right time to do it, the right man and the right place."

The only other African-American justice is Clarence Thomas. Appointed by President George H. W. Bush, he took the oath of office on Oct. 23, 1991, and still serves on the court.

1981: WOMAN JUSTICE The first woman to serve on the Supreme Court was Sandra Day O'Connor. Appointed by President Ronald Reagan, O'Connor took the oath of office on Sept. 25, 1981, and announced her retirement on July 1, 2005.

The second woman to serve on the Court was Ruth Bader Ginsburg. Appointed to the bench by President Bill Clinton, she took the oath of office on Aug. 10, 1993.

Chief Justice John Roberts (center) and Justices in 2005

THE LAST TIME...

The last time a president did not get to nominate a Supreme Court justice was during the presidency of Jimmy Carter. President Gerald Ford appointed Justice John Paul Stevens to the bench on Dec. 19, 1975; the next appointment was of Justice Sandra Day O'Connor by President Ronald Reagan on Sept. 25, 1981.

SOMETHING TO THINK ABOUT

TRADITION

Like many institutions the Supreme Court scrupulously maintains its traditions, even if they appear outdated. For instance, on each day the Court sits, white quills are placed at the lawyers' tables. This practice dates to the earliest sessions of the Court. A more recent tradition is the "conference handshake," the brainchild of Chief Justice Melville W. Fuller in the late 19th century. Each justice shakes hands with all the other justices when they assemble to go on the bench and before private conferences. Fuller started the practice to remind the Court that differences of opinions did not preclude overall harmony of purpose.

SUPERLATIVES

OLDEST CHIEF JUSTICE The oldest person appointed chief justice was Harlan Fiske Stone. Elevated to the chief justice position from his spot as an associate justice by President Franklin D. Roosevelt, Stone took the oath of office on July 3, 1941, at the age of 68 years, 261 days.

Stone served as chief justice until his death on April 22, 1946. His term as head of the court, four years, nine months, 19 days, was the second-shortest on record.

The oldest chief justice to leave office was Roger Brooke Taney, at 87 years, 194 days. Appointed to head the court by President Andrew Jackson, Taney served from March 28, 1836, until his death on Oct. 12, 1864.

YOUNGEST CHIEF JUSTICE The youngest judge to serve as chief justice was John Jay. The first chief justice, he was appointed to the post by George Washington. Jay took the oath of office at the age of 44 years, 307 days on Oct. 19, 1789; he served until June 29, 1795.

LONGEST-SERVING CHIEF JUSTICE The longest tenure as chief justice was the 34 years, 152 days served by John Marshall. The fourth chief justice, Marshall was appointed to the post by John Adams. He took the oath of office on Feb. 4, 1801, and served until July 6, 1835.

LONGEST-SERVING ASSOCIATE JUSTICE The longest serving associate justice was William O. Douglas, who sat on the Court for 36 years, 209 days. Appointed by Franklin D. Roosevelt, Douglas took the oath of office on April 17, 1939, and served until Nov. 12, 1975.

LONGEST UNCHANGED COURT The longest period when the Court went without a vacancy was a little over 11 years, 1 month, from Feb. 3, 1812, when Joseph Story took his seat, to March 18, 1823, when Justice Henry Brockhurst Livingston died.

The second-longest was the period starting with the installation of Justice Stephen Breyer on Aug. 3, 1994 and ending with the death of Chief Justice William Rehnquist on Sept. 3, 2005.

NARROWEST MARGIN OF CONFIRMATION Clarence Thomas was confirmed as an associate justice in 1991 by the narrowest vote margin in the 20th century, 52-48. Lucius Q.C. Lamar was confirmed with the same margin, passing by a vote of 32-28 in 1888.

The narrowest ever margin recorded occurred during the confirmation of Stanley Matthews, who passed by one vote when he was confirmed by the Senate, 24-23, in 1881.

Alabama to California

THE 13 ORIGINAL COLONIES ALONG THE ATLANTIC COAST joined the Union when they ratified the Constitution, starting with Delaware in Dec. 1787. The last of the 50 states was Hawaii, admitted to the Union in August 1959.

[*Note*: Records exclude time when state was in secession. City populations are Census Bureau estimates for mid-2004.]

ALABAMA

Alabama entered the Union on Dec. 14, 1819, as the 22nd state. The state seceded from the Union in 1861 and was readmitted in 1868. The "Heart of Dixie" ranks 30th in total area (542,419 sq mi) and 23rd in population (4,530,182 in 2004). It has seven seats in the House of Representatives and casts nine electoral votes.

STATE RECORDS		
First Governor	William Bibb	1819-20
First Woman Governor	Lurleen Wallace	1967-68
Highest Point	Cheaha Mountain	2,407 ft
Lowest Point	Gulf of Mexico	sea level
Hottest Temperature	112°F	Centerville, Sept. 5, 1925
Coldest Temperature	-27°F	New Market, Jan. 30, 1966
Tallest Building	RSA Battlehouse Tower, Mobile	750 ft, 41 floors (under construction as of Jan. 2006)
Largest City	Birmingham	pop. 233,149 (2004 est.)
HERE ARE SOME U.S. RECORDS CLAIMED BY ALABAMA:		
Fastest Average Speed, NASCAR race	186.288 mph by Bill Elliott	Talladega Superspeedway, Talladega, May 5, 1985
Most Related Governors	10: 4 father-son: William Wyatt Bibb & Thomas Bibb; James Folsom, Sr. & Jr.; Gabriel Moore & Samuel B. Moore; Edward Asbury O'Neal & Emmet O'Neal. 1 husband-wife: George C. Wallace & Lurleen Wallace	

ALASKA

Alaska was purchased from Russia for $7.2 million in 1867. It became a territory in 1884, and entered the Union as the 49th state Jan. 3, 1959. The "Last Frontier" is ranked 1st in area (663,267 sq mi) and 47th in population (655,435 in 2004), and has the lowest population density (1.1 person per sq mi of land). It has one seat in the U.S. House of Representatives and casts three electoral votes.

STATE RECORDS		
First Governor	William A. Egan	1959-66, 1970-74
Highest Point (also U.S. record)	Mount McKinley (Denali)	20,320 ft
Lowest Point	Pacific Ocean	sea level
Hottest Temperature	100°F	Fort Yukon, June 27, 1915
Coldest Temperature (also U.S. record)	-80°F	Prospect Creek Camp, Jan. 23, 1971
Tallest Building	Conoco Phillips Bldg., Anchorage (1983)	296 ft, 22 floors
Largest City	Anchorage	pop. 272,687 (2004 est.)
HERE ARE SOME U.S. RECORDS CLAIMED BY ALASKA:		
Longest Shoreline	33,904 mi	
Largest National Park	Wrangell-St. Elias	8,323,148 acres
Northernmost City	Barrow, AK	71 ° 17' N
Westernmost City	Atka, AK	174 ° 12' W
Easternmost Settlement[1]	Amchitka Island	179 ° 15' E

(1) Because Alaska's Aleutian Islands extend into the eastern hemisphere, they technically contain the easternmost points in the U.S.

ARIZONA

Arizona became part of the United States in 1848 after the Mexican War. The area below the Gila River was obtained from Mexico in the Gadsden Purchase in 1853. Arizona became a territory in 1863, and entered the Union on Feb. 14, 1912, as the 48th state. The "Grand Canyon State" is ranked 6th in total area (113,998 sq mi) and 18th in population (5,743,834 in 2004). It has eight seats in the U.S. House of Representatives and casts 10 electoral votes.

STATE RECORDS		
First Governor	George W.P. Hunt	1912-19, 1923-29, 1931-33
First Hispanic Governor	Raul Castro	1975-77
First Woman Governor	Rose Mofford	1988-91
Highest Point	Humphreys Peak	12,633 ft
Lowest Point	Colorado River (Yuma)	70 ft
Hottest Temperature	128°F	Lake Havasu City, June 29, 1994
Coldest Temperature	-40°F	Hawley Lake, Jan. 7, 1971
Tallest Building	Bank One Center, Phoenix (1972)	483 ft, 40 floors
Largest City	Phoenix	pop. 1,418,041 (2004 est.)
HERE ARE SOME U.S. RECORDS CLAIMED BY ARIZONA:		
Largest Gorge	Grand Canyon, Colorado River	277 mi long, 600 ft-18 mi wide, 1 mi deep
Tallest Fountain	Fountain, Fountain Hills	spurt reaches 562 ft every 15 minutes

ARKANSAS

Arkansas became part of the United States with the Louisiana Purchase in 1803. It became a territory in 1819 and entered the Union on June 15, 1836. Arkansas seceded in 1861, and was readmitted in 1868. The "Natural State" is ranked 29th in total area (53,179 sq mi) and 32nd in population (2,752,629 in 2004). Based on the 2000 census, it has four seats in the U.S. House of Representatives and casts six electoral votes.

STATE RECORDS		
First Governor	James S. Conway	1836-40
Highest Point	Magazine Mountain	2,753 ft
Lowest Point	Ouachita River (Ashley-Union)	55 ft
Hottest Temperature	120°F	Ozark, Aug. 10, 1936
Coldest Temperature	-29°F	Pond, Feb. 13, 1905
Tallest Building	MetropolitanTower, Little Rock (1986)	546 ft, 40 floors
Largest City	Little Rock	pop. 184,071 (2004 est.)
HERE ARE SOME U.S. RECORDS CLAIMED BY ARKANSAS:		
Largest Retail Firm Headquarters	Wal-Mart, Bentonville; 4,800+ stores	$2.9 billion in revenues, 2004
Recent Sighting of Ivory-Billed Woodpecker	Big Woods region	thought extinct, 1944; rediscovered, 2005

CALIFORNIA

California became part of the United States at the end of the Mexican War in 1848. It entered the Union on Sept. 9, 1850. The "Golden State" ranks 3rd in total area (163,696 sq mi) and 1st in population (35,893,799 in 2004). It has 53 seats in the U.S. House of Representatives and casts 55 electoral votes.

STATE RECORDS		
First Governor	Peter H. Burnett	1850-51
First Hispanic Governor	Romualdo Pacheco	1875
Highest Point	Mount Whitney	14,494 ft
Lowest Point (also U.S. record)	Death Valley	282 ft. below sea level
Hottest Temperature (also U.S. record)	134°F	Greenland Ranch, July 10, 1913
Coldest Temperature	-45°F	Boca, Jan. 20, 1937
Tallest Building	US Bank Tower, Los Angeles (1989)	1,018 ft, 73 floors
Largest City	Los Angeles	pop. 3,845,541 (2004 est.)
HERE ARE SOME U.S. RECORDS CLAIMED BY CALIFORNIA:		
Lowest Settlement	Calipatria	184 ft below sea level
Largest Native American Population	627,562	2000 Census
Largest Living Tree	Giant sequoia "General Sherman," Sequoia National Park	275 ft tall, weighs about 6,167 tons
Highest Waterfall	Yosemite Falls	2,425 ft (total in 3 sections)

COLORADO

Eastern Colorado was acquired with the Louisiana Purchase in 1803. The rest of the state was ceded to the U.S. from Mexico after the Mexican War in 1848. Colorado entered the Union on Aug. 1, 1876. The "Centennial State" is ranked 8th in total area (104,094 sq mi) and 22nd in population (4,601,403 in 2004). It has seven seats in the U.S. House of Representatives and casts nine electoral votes.

STATE RECORDS		
First Governor	John L. Routt	1876-79, 1891-93
Highest Point	Mt. Elbert	14,433 ft
Lowest Point	Arikaree River	3,315 ft
Hottest Temperature	118°F	Bennett, July 11, 1888
Coldest Temperature	-61°F	Maybell, Feb. 1, 1985
Tallest Building	Republic Plaza, Denver (1984)	714 ft, 56 floors
Largest City	Denver	pop. 556,835 (2004 est.)
Here are some U.S. records claimed by COLORADO:		
Highest Settlement	Climax, CO	11,360 ft
Highest Bridge	Royal Gorge, CO	1,053 ft above water
Longest Street	Colfax Avenue, Denver	26 mi

CONNECTICUT

One of the original 13 colonies, Connecticut became the fifth state to ratify the Constitution, on Jan. 9, 1788. The "Constitution State" is ranked 48th in total area (5,543 sq mi) and 29th in population (3,503,604 in 2004). It has five seats in the U.S. House of Representatives and casts seven electoral votes.

STATE RECORDS		
First Governor	Samuel Huntington	1788-96
First Woman Governor	Ella T. Grasso	1975-80
Highest Point	Mt. Frissell	2,380 ft
Lowest Point	Long Island Sound	sea level
Hottest Temperature	106°F	Danbury, July 15, 1995
Coldest Temperature	-32°F	Coventry, Jan. 22, 1961
Tallest Building	City Place, Hartford (1980)	535 ft, 38 floors
Largest City	Bridgeport	pop. 139,910 (2004 est.)
Here are some U.S. records claimed by CONNECTICUT:		
Oldest Existing U.S. Newspaper	The Hartford Courant	Oct. 29, 1764
Worst Circus Fire	Ringling Circus at Hartford, July 6, 1944	168 killed; 700 injured

DELAWARE

One of the original 13 colonies, Delaware became the first state to ratify the Constitution, on Dec. 7, 1787. The "First State" is ranked 49th in total area (2,489 sq mi) and 45th in population (830,364 in 2004). It has one seat in the U.S. House of Representatives and casts three electoral votes.

STATE RECORDS		
First Governor	Joshua Clayton	1789-96
First Woman Governor	Ruth Ann Minner	2001-
Highest Point	Ebright Road, New Castle	448 ft
Lowest Point	Atlantic Ocean	sea level
Hottest Temperature	110°F	Millsboro, July 21, 1930
Coldest Temperature	-17°F	Millsboro, Jan. 17, 1893
Tallest Building	Chase Manhattan Center, Wilmington (1988)	330 ft, 23 floors
Largest City	Wilmington	pop. 72,784 (2004 est.)
Here are some U.S. records claimed by DELAWARE:		
First U.S. State	Dec. 7, 1787	
First Scheduled Steam Railroad	New Castle	1831

FLORIDA

Spain ceded Florida to the U.S. in 1819, and it entered the Union on March 3, 1845. Florida seceded from the Union in 1861 and was readmitted in 1868. The "Sunshine State" is ranked 22nd in total area (65,755 sq mi) and fourth in population (17,397,161 in 2004). It has 25 seats in the U.S. House of Representatives and casts 27 electoral votes.

STATE RECORDS		
First Governor	William D. Moseley	1845-49
Highest Point	Britton Hill	345 ft
Lowest Point	Atlantic Ocean	sea level
Hottest Temperature	109°F	Monticello, June 29, 1931
Coldest Temperature	-2°F	Tallahassee, Feb. 13, 1899
Tallest Building	Four Seasons Hotel and Tower, Miami (2003)	789 ft, 64 floors
Largest City	Jacksonville	pop. 777,704 (2004 est.)
Here are some U.S. records claimed by FLORIDA:		
Most Consecutive Sunny Days	St. Petersburg, Feb. 9, 1967-Mar. 17, 1969	768 days
Largest Amusement Resort	Disney World, Orlando	30,000 acres; opened 1971
First Federal Wildlife Refuge	Pelican Island, Indian River Co.	5,413 acres; opened 1903

GEORGIA

One of the original 13 colonies, Georgia became the fourth state to ratify the Constitution, on Jan. 2, 1788. Georgia seceded from the Union in 1861 and was readmitted in 1870. The "Peach State" is ranked 24th in total area (59,425 sq mi) and ninth in population (8,829,383 in 2004). It has 13 seats in the U.S. House of Representatives and casts 15 electoral votes.

STATE RECORDS		
First Governor	George Handley	1788-89
Highest Point	Brasstown Bald	4,784 ft
Lowest Point	Atlantic Ocean	sea level
Hottest Temperature	112°F	Greenville, Aug. 20,1983
Coldest Temperature	-17°F	CCC Camp F-16, Jan. 27, 1940
Tallest Building	Bank of America Plaza, Atlanta (1993)	1,023 ft, 55 floors
Largest City	Atlanta	pop. 419,122 (2004 est.)
Here are some U.S. records claimed by GEORGIA:		
Busiest Airport	Hartsfield Int'l Airport, Atlanta	83.6 million passengers (2004)
Biggest Peanut Producer	1,511,655,000 lbs (2003)	45% of U.S. peanut crop

HAWAI'I

Hawai'i was annexed by the U.S. in 1898. It became the 50th state of the Union, on Aug. 21, 1959. The "Aloha State" is ranked 43rd in total area (10,931 sq mi) and 42nd in population (1,262,840 in 2004). It has two seats in the U.S. House of Representatives and casts four electoral votes.

STATE RECORDS		
First Governor	William F. Quinn	1959-62
First Asian-American Governor	George R. Ariyoshi	1974-86
First Woman Governor	Linda Lingle	2002-
Highest Point	Mauna Kea	13,796 ft
Lowest Point	Pacific Ocean	sea level
Hottest Temperature	100°F	Pahala, April 27, 1931
Coldest Temperature	12°F	Mauna Kea Obs., May 17, 1979
Tallest Building	First Hawaiian Center, Honolulu (1996)	429 ft, 30 floors
Largest City	Honolulu	pop. 377,260 (2004 est.)
Here are some U.S. records claimed by HAWAI'I:		
Southernmost Point	Ka Lae, Island of Hawai'i	18° 55' N
Southernmost City	Hilo, Island of Hawai'i	19° 44' N
Rainiest Location (also world record)	Mount Waialeale, Kauai	average annual rainfall 460 in

Idaho to Kentucky

IDAHO

Idaho was organized as a territory in 1863 and entered the Union on July 3, 1890. The "Gem State" is ranked 14th in total area (83,570 sq mi) and 39th in population (1,393,262 in 2004). It has two seats in the U.S. House of Representatives and casts four electoral votes.

First Governor	George L. Shoup	1890
Highest Point	Borah Peak	12,662 ft
Lowest Point	Snake River	710 ft
Hottest Temperature	118°F	Orofino, July 28, 1930
Coldest Temperature	-60°F	Island Park Dam, Jan. 18, 1943
Tallest Building	US Bank Plaza, Boise (1978)	267 ft, 20 floors
Largest City	Boise	pop. 190,122 (2004 est.)
Here are some U.S. records claimed by IDAHO:		
Deepest Gorge (w/ Oregon)	Hell's Canyon, Snake River	7,900 ft
Biggest Potato Producer	13.2 billion lbs (2004)	30% of U.S. crop

ILLINOIS

Sections of present-day Illinois became part of the U.S. when Gen. George Rogers Clark took Kaskaskia from the British in 1778. In 1787, the area became part of the Northwest Territory. Illinois entered the Union on Dec. 3, 1818. The "Prairie State" is ranked 25th in total area (57,914 sq mi) and fifth in population (12,713,634 in 2004). It has 19 seats in the U.S. House of Representatives and casts 21 electoral votes.

First Governor	Shadrach Bond	1818-22
Highest Point	Charles Mound	1,235 ft
Lowest Point	Mississippi River	279 ft
Hottest Temperature	117°F	East St. Louis, July 14, 1954
Coldest Temperature	-36°F	Congerville, Jan. 5, 1999
Tallest Building (also U.S. record)	Sears Tower, Chicago (1974)	1,450 ft, 108 floors
Largest City	Chicago	pop. 2,862,244 (2004 est.)
Here are some U.S. records claimed by ILLINOIS:		
First Metal-Frame Skyscraper	Home Insurance Bldg., Chicago (1885)	180 ft, 12 floors

INDIANA

Great Britain ceded Indiana to the U.S. at the end of the Revolutionary War. In 1787, the area became part of the Northwest Territory. Indiana entered the Union on Dec. 11, 1816. The "Hoosier State" is ranked 38th in total area (36,418 sq mi) and 14th in population (6,237,569 in 2004). It has nine seats in the U.S. House of Representatives and casts 11 electoral votes.

First Governor	Jonathan Jennings	1816-22
Highest Point	Hoosier Hill	1,257 ft
Lowest Point	Ohio River	320 ft
Hottest Temperature	116°F	Collegeville, July 14, 1936
Coldest Temperature	-36°F	New Whiteland, Jan. 19, 1994
Tallest Building	Bank One Tower, Indianapolis (1990)	811 ft, 49 floors
Largest City	Indianapolis	pop. 784,242 (2004 est.)
Here are some U.S. records claimed by INDIANA:		
First Long-Distance Auto Track Race	Indianapolis Motor Speedway, May 30, 1911	Ray Harroun won, avg. speed 74.602 mph
First Electrically Lighted City	Wabash	March 31, 1880

IOWA

Iowa became part of the U.S. through the Louisiana Purchase in 1803 and was recognized as a territory in 1838. It entered the Union on Dec. 28, 1846. The "Hawkeye State" is ranked 26th in total area (56,272 sq mi) and 30th in population (2,954,451 in 2004). It has five seats in the U.S. House of Representatives and casts seven electoral votes.

STATE RECORDS		
First Governor	Ansel Briggs	1846-50
Highest Point	Hawkeye Point	1,670 ft
Lowest Point	Mississippi River	480 ft
Hottest Temperature	118°F	Keokuk, July 20, 1934
Coldest Temperature	-47°F	Elkader, Feb. 3, 1996
Tallest Building	801 Grand, Des Moines (1991)	630 ft, 44 floors
Largest City	Des Moines	pop. 194,311 (2004 est.)
Here are some U.S. records claimed by IOWA:		
Shortest and Steepest Railroad	Dubuque (1882)	296 ft long; rises 60°
First Presidential Birthplace West of Mississippi River	West Branch	Herbert Hoover, Aug. 10, 1874

KANSAS

The U.S. took over most of modern-day Kansas with the Louisiana Purchase in 1803. Kansas became a territory in 1854 and entered the Union on Jan. 29, 1861. The "Sunflower State" ranks 15th in total area (82,277 sq mi) and 33rd in population (2,735,502 in 2004). It has four seats in the U.S. House of Representatives and casts six electoral votes.

STATE RECORDS		
First Governor	Charles Robinson	1861-63
First Woman Governor	Joan Finney	1991-95
Highest Point	Mount Sunflower	4,039 ft
Lowest Point	Verdigris River	679 ft
Hottest Temperature	121°F	(near) Alton, July 24, 1936
Coldest Temperature	-40°F	Lebanon, Feb. 13, 1905
Tallest Building	Epic Center, Wichita (1989)	325 ft, 22 floors
Largest City	Wichita	pop. 353,823 (2004 est.)
Here are some U.S. records claimed by KANSAS:		
First Female Elected Mayor	Susanna Medora Salter	Argonia, 1887
Wheat Production	480 mil bushels (2003)	21% of U.S. crop
Largest Circus Audience (Tent)	Ringling Bros., Barnum & Bailey Circus, Concordia	capacity, 16,702 people; erected Sept. 13, 1924
Geographic Center of the U.S.	Barton, 15 mi NE of Great Bend	

KENTUCKY

Kentucky was the first area west of the Alleghenies settled by American pioneers. After Virginia dropped its claims to the region, Kentucky entered the Union on June 1, 1792. The "Bluegrass State" ranks 37th in total area (40,409 sq mi) and 26th in population (4,145,922 in 2004). It has six seats in the U.S. House of Representatives and casts eight electoral votes.

First Governor	Isaac Shelby	1792-96
First Woman Governor	Martha Layne Collins	1983-87
Highest Point	Black Mountain	4,145 ft
Lowest Point	Mississippi River	257 ft
Hottest Temperature	114°F	Greensburg, July 28, 1930
Coldest Temperature	-37°F	Shelbyville, Jan. 19, 1994
Tallest Building	Aegon Center, Louisville (1993)	549 ft, 35 floors
Largest City	Lexington	pop. 266,358 (2004 est.)
Here are some U.S. records claimed by KENTUCKY:		
Largest Gold Bullion Holdings	Fort Knox	147.3 million oz (worth c. $65.7 billion), 2005
Longest Cave	Mammoth Cave System	360 mi of mapped passages

Louisiana to Michigan

LOUISIANA

The U.S. bought Louisiana from France as part of the Louisiana Purchase in 1803, and it became a state on April 30, 1812. The "Pelican State" ranks 31st in total area (51,840 sq mi) and 24th in population (4,515,770 in 2004). It has seven seats in the U.S. House of Representatives and casts nine electoral votes.

STATE RECORDS		
First Governor	William C.C. Claiborne	1812-16
First African-American Governor	P.B.S. Pinchback	1872-73
First Woman Governor	Kathleen Blanco	2004-
Highest Point	Driskill Mountain	535 ft
Lowest Point	New Orleans	8 ft below sea level
Hottest Temperature	114°F	Plain Dealing, Aug. 10, 1936
Coldest Temperature	-16°F	Minden, Feb. 13, 1899
Tallest Building	One Shell Square, New Orleans (1972)	697 ft, 51 floors
Largest City	New Orleans	pop. 462,269 (2004 est.)
Here are some U.S. records claimed by LOUISIANA:		
Longest Causeway	Second Lake Pontchartrain Causeway (1969)	23 mi, 1,538 yd

MAINE

Originally part of Massachusetts, Maine broke off and became a separate state on March 15, 1820. The "Pine Tree State" ranks 39th in total area (35,385 sq mi) and 40th in population (1,317,253 in 2004). It has two seats in the U.S. House of Representatives and casts four electoral votes.

STATE RECORDS		
First Governor	William King	1820-21
Highest Point	Mount Katahdin	5,268 ft
Lowest Point	Atlantic Ocean	sea level
Hottest Temperature	105°F	North Bridgton, July 10, 1911
Coldest Temperature	-48°F	Van Buren, Jan. 19, 1925
Largest City	Portland	pop. 63,905 (2004 est.)
Here are some U.S. records claimed by MAINE:		
Easternmost City	Eastport	66°58'49 W
Easternmost Settlement in Lower 48 States	Lubec	66°59'05 W
Largest Lobster Producer	63.2 million lbs; worth $253.5 million (2004)	57% of U.S. lobster catch

MARYLAND

One of the original 13 colonies, Maryland became the seventh state to ratify the Constitution, on April 28, 1788. The "Old Line State" ranks 42nd in total area (12,407 sq mi) and 19th in population (5,558,058 in 2004). It has eight seats in the U.S. House of Representatives and casts 10 electoral votes.

STATE RECORDS		
First Governor	William Smallwood	1788
Highest Point	Hoye-Crest	3,360 ft
Lowest Point	Atlantic Ocean	sea level
Hottest Temperature	109°F	Cumberland & Frederick, July 10, 1936
Coldest Temperature	-40°F	Oakland, Jan. 13, 1912
Tallest Building	Legg Mason Bldg., Baltimore (1973)	529 ft, 40 floors
Largest City	Baltimore	pop. 636,251 (2004 est.)
Here are some U.S. records claimed by MARYLAND:		
Oldest Continually Operated Airport	College Park Airport	established in 1909
First Telegraph Line	Baltimore to Washington, DC	May 24, 1844

MASSACHUSETTS

One of the original 13 colonies, Massachusetts became the sixth state to ratify the Constitution on Feb. 6, 1788. The "Bay State" ranks 44th in total area (10,555 sq mi) and 13th in population (6,416,505 in 2004). It has 10 seats in the U.S. House of Representatives and casts 12 electoral votes.

STATE RECORDS		
First Governor	John Hancock	1788-93
First Woman Governor	Jane Swift	2001-03
Highest Point	Mount Greylock	3,491 ft
Lowest Point	Atlantic Ocean	sea level
Hottest Temperature	107°F	Chester, New Bedford, July 10, 1936
Coldest Temperature	-35°F	Chester, Jan. 12, 1981
Tallest Building	John Hancock Tower, Boston (1976)	790 ft, 60 floors
Largest City	Boston	pop. 569,165 (2004 est.)
Here are some U.S. records claimed by MASSACHUSETTS:		
First Institution of Higher Learning	Harvard, 1636	Began with 9 students, 1 instructor
First Revolutionary War Battle	Lexington, April 19, 1775	8 Minutemen killed

MICHIGAN

Britain ceded the area of modern-day Michigan to the U.S. after the Revolutionary War, though it did not withdraw immediately. In 1787, the area became part of the Northwest Territory, and Michigan entered the Union on Jan. 26, 1837. The "Great Lakes State" ranks 11th in total area (96,716 sq mi) and 8th in population (10,112,620 in 2004). It has 15 seats in the U.S. House of Representatives and casts 17 electoral votes.

STATE RECORDS		
First Governor	Stevens T. Mason	1837-40
First Woman Governor	Jennifer M. Granholm	2003-
Highest Point	Mount Arvon	1,979 ft
Lowest Point	Lake Erie	571 ft
Hottest Temperature	112°F	Mio, July 13, 1936
Coldest Temperature	-51°F	Vanderbilt, Feb. 9, 1934
Tallest Building	Marriot Renaissance Center, Detroit (1977)	726 ft, 73 floors
Largest City	Detroit	pop. 900,198 (2004 est.)
Here are some U.S. records claimed by MICHIGAN:		
First State Fair	Michigan State Fair	Detroit, Sept. 25-27, 1849
First Land-Grant University	Michigan State University (1855)	East Lansing
First Moving Assembly Line	Ford Motor Company	Highland Park, 1913

Minnesota to Nebraska

MINNESOTA

The U.S. gained the eastern section of modern-day Minnesota from Britain after the Revolutionary War. Most of western Minnesota became part of the U.S. with the Louisiana Purchase in 1803. In 1849, the territory of Minnesota was created, and the state entered the Union on May 11, 1858. The "North Star State" ranks 21st in population (5,100,958 in 2004). It has eight seats in the U.S. House of Representatives and casts 10 electoral votes.

First Governor	Henry S. Sibley	1858-60
Highest Point	Eagle Mountain	2,301 ft
Lowest Point	Lake Superior	602 ft
Hottest Temperature	114°F	Moorhead, July 6, 1936
Coldest Temperature	-60°F	Tower, Feb. 2, 1996
Tallest Building	IDS Tower, Minneapolis (1973)	792 ft, 55 floors
Largest City	Minneapolis	pop. 373,943 (2004 est.)
Here are some U.S. records claimed by MINNESOTA:		
Largest Shopping Mall	Mall of America, Bloomington (1992)	4.2 million sq ft, 520+ stores
Northernmost settlement in contiguous 48 states	Angle Inlet	49° 21'N
Northernmost point in contiguous 48 states	Northwest Angle	49° 23 'N

MISSISSIPPI

The U.S. acquired Mississippi's territory from Britain at the end of the Revolutionary War, though Spain had seized part of the land during the war and maintained its interests there until 1798. Mississippi became a territory in 1798 and entered the Union on Dec. 10, 1817. The state seceded in 1861 and was readmitted in 1870. The "Magnolia State" ranks 32nd in total area (48,430 sq mi) and 31st in population (2,902,966 in 2004). It has four seats in the U.S. House of Representatives and casts six electoral votes.

First Governor	David Holmes	1817-20, 1826
Highest Point	Woodall Mountain	806 ft
Lowest Point	Gulf of Mexico	sea level
Hottest Temperature	115°F	Holly Springs, July 29, 1930
Coldest Temperature	-19°F	Corinth, Jan. 30, 1966
Tallest Building	Beau Rivage Casino Hotel, Biloxi (1999)	346 ft, 32 floors
Largest City	Jackson	pop. 179,298 (2004 est.)
Here are some U.S. records claimed by MISSISSIPPI:		
Largest Cactus Plantation	The Cactus Plantation, Edwards	3,000 varieties of cacti
Longest Artificial Beach	Mississippi Gulf Coast, Biloxi to Henderson Point	26 mi
First Public College for Women	Mississippi University for Women, Columbus	created by state legislature, March 12, 1884; 250 women began Oct. 22, 1885

MISSOURI

Missouri was acquired by the U.S. as part of the Louisiana Purchase in 1803 and entered the Union on Aug. 10, 1821, in accordance with the terms of the Missouri Compromise (1820). The "Show Me State" ranks 21st in total area (69,704 sq mi) and 17th in population (5,754,618 in 2004). It has nine seats in the U.S. House of Representatives and casts 11 electoral votes.

STATE RECORDS		
First Governor	Alexander McNair	1821-24
Highest Point	Taum Sauk Mountain	1,772 ft
Lowest Point	St. Francis River	230 ft
Hottest Temperature	118°F	Warsaw, Union, July 14, 1954
Coldest Temperature	-40°F	Warsaw, Feb. 13, 1905
Tallest Building	One Kansas City Place, Kansas City (1988)	632 ft, 42 floors
Largest City	Kansas City	pop. 444,387 (2004 est.)
Here are some U.S. records claimed by MISSOURI:		
Tallest Monument	Gateway to the West Arch, St. Louis	630 ft
Most Neighboring States (tied with Tennessee)	8	Iowa, Illinois, Kentucky, Tennessee, Arkansas, Oklahoma, Kansas, and Nebraska

MONTANA

The U.S. acquired parts of Montana in the Louisiana Purchase of 1803. Additional sections were gained by the exploration of Lewis and Clark (1805-06). The Montana territory was established in 1864. Montana entered the Union on Nov. 8, 1889. The "Treasure State" ranks 4th in total area (147,042 sq mi) and 44th in population (926,865 in 2004). It has one seat in the U.S. House of Representatives and casts three electoral votes.

STATE RECORDS		
First Governor	Joseph K. Toole	1889-93, 1901-08
First Woman Governor	Judy Martz	2001-05
Highest Point	Granite Peak	12,799 ft
Lowest Point	Kootenai River	1,800 ft
Hottest Temperature	117°F	Medicine Lake, July 5, 1937
Coldest Temperature	-70°F	Rogers Pass, Jan. 20, 1954
Tallest Building	First Interstate Center, Billings (1985)	272 ft, 20 floors
Largest City	Billings	pop. 96,977 (2004 est.)
Here are some U.S. records claimed by MONTANA:		
First Elected Congresswoman	Jeanette Rankin (R)	65th Congress, 1917-19
Greatest Temperature Change in a Day	103 degrees, Loma	Jan. 14-15, 1972, from -56°F to 49°F

NEBRASKA

Nebraska was acquired by the U.S. with the Louisiana Purchase of 1803 and entered the Union on March 1, 1867. The "Cornhusker State" ranks 16th in total area (77,354 sq mi) and 38th in population (1,747,214 in 2004). It has three seats in the U.S. House of Representatives and casts five electoral votes.

STATE RECORDS		
First Governor	David Butler	1867-71
First Woman Governor	Kay A. Orr	1987-91
Highest Point	Panorama Point	5,424 ft
Lowest Point	Missouri River	840 ft
Hottest Temperature	118°F	Minden, July 24, 1936
Coldest Temperature	-47°F	Oshkosh, Dec. 22, 1989
Tallest Building	One First National Center (2002)	634 ft, 45 floors
Largest City	Omaha	pop. 409,416 (2004 est.)
Here are some U.S. records claimed by NEBRASKA:		
Only Unicameral State Legislature	By constitutional amendment approved by referendum	1937
Only Non-Partisan State Legislature	49 senators elected to 4-year terms	no party affiliation on ballot

Nevada to New York

NEVADA

Nevada was acquired by the U.S. at the end of the Mexican War in 1848. Nevada entered the Union on Oct. 31, 1864. The "Silver State" ranks 7th in total area (110,561 sq mi) and 35th in population (2,334,771 in 2004). It has three seats in the U.S. House of Representatives and casts five electoral votes.

STATE RECORDS		
First Governor	Henry G. Blasdel	1864-71
Highest Point	Boundary Peak	13,143 ft
Lowest Point	Colorado River	479 ft
Hottest Temperature	125°F	Laughlin, June 29, 1994
Coldest Temperature	-50°F	San Jacinto, Jan. 8, 1937
Tallest Building	Wynn Las Vegas hotel (2005)	614 ft, 50 floors
Largest City	Las Vegas	pop. 534,847 (2004 est.)
Here are some U.S. records claimed by NEVADA:		
Largest Stage	Hilton Theatre, Reno (1959)	42,175 sq ft
Fastest-Growing Metropolitan Area	Las Vegas-Paradise (1990-2000)	85.5% growth

NEW HAMPSHIRE

One of the original 13 colonies, New Hampshire became the ninth state to ratify the Constitution, on June 21, 1788. The "Granite State" ranks 46th in total area (93,350 sq mi) and 41st in population (1,299,500 in 2004). It has two seats in the U.S. House of Representatives and casts four electoral votes.

STATE RECORDS		
First Governor	John Langdon	1788-89
First Woman Governor[1]	Jeanne Shaheen	1997-2001
Highest Point	Mt. Washington	6,288 ft
Lowest Point	Atlantic Ocean	sea level
Hottest Temperature	106°F	Nashua, July 4, 1911
Coldest Temperature	-47°F	Mt. Washington, Jan. 29, 1934
Tallest Building	Hampshire Plaza, Manchester (1972)	259 ft, 20 floors
Largest City	Manchester	pop. 109,310 (2004 est.)
Here are some U.S. records claimed by NEW HAMPSHIRE:		
Oldest and Largest Artists' Colony	MacDowell Colony, Peterborough	founded 1907 by Marian Nevins MacDowell
Longest Covered Bridge	Cornish-Windsor Bridge (1866)	460 ft double-span

(1) Not counting New Hampshire Senate Pres. Vesta Roy, who became governor after the death of Gov. Hugh Gallen in 1982 and served for only one week.

NEW JERSEY

One of the original 13 colonies, New Jersey became the third state to ratify the U.S. Constitution, on Dec. 18, 1787. The "Garden State" ranks 47th in total area (8,712 sq mi) and 10th in population (8,698,879 in 2004), but is the most densely populated (1,173 people per sq mil of land area). It has 13 seats in the U.S. House of Representatives and casts 15 electoral votes.

STATE RECORDS		
First Governor	William Livingston	1787-1790
First Woman Governor	Christine Todd Whitman	1994-2001
Highest Point	High Point, Sussex	1,803 ft
Lowest Point	Atlantic Ocean	sea level
Hottest Temperature	110°F	Runyon, July 10, 1936
Coldest Temperature	-34°F	River Vale, Jan. 5, 1904
Tallest Building	30 Hudson St., Jersey City (2004)	781 ft, 42 floors
Largest City	Newark	pop. 280,451 (2004 est.)
Here are some U.S. records claimed by NEW JERSEY:		
First College Football Game	New Brunswick, Nov. 6, 1869	Rutgers beat Princeton, 6-4
First Boardwalk	Atlantic City	built in 1870

NEW MEXICO

Gen. Stephen Kearny took Santa Fe on Aug. 18, 1846, and declared New Mexico part of the U.S. The 1848 treaty ending the Mexican War made New Mexico officially part of the U.S. It became a territory in 1850 and entered the Union on Jan. 6, 1912. The "Land of Enchantment" ranks 5th in total area (121,589 sq mi) and 36th in population (1,903,289 in 2004). It has three seats in the U.S. House of Representatives and casts five electoral votes.

STATE RECORDS		
First Governor	William C. McDonald	1912-17
First Hispanic Governor	Ezequiel Cabeza de Baca	1917
Highest Point	Wheeler Peak	13,161 ft
Lowest Point	Red Bluff Reservation	2,862 ft
Hottest Temperature	122°F	Waste Isolat. Pilot Plant, June 27, 1994
Coldest Temperature	-50°F	Gavilan, Feb. 1, 1951
Tallest Building	Albuquerque Plaza, Albuquerque (1990)	351 ft, 22 floors
Largest City	Albuquerque	pop. 484,246 (2004 est.)
Here are some U.S. records claimed by NEW MEXICO:		
Highest Capital City	Santa Fe	6,989 ft
First Atomic Bomb Detonation	Trinity Site, White Sands Testing Range, near Alamogordo	19 kiloton explosion, July 16, 1945

NEW YORK

One of the original 13 colonies, New York became the 11th state to ratify the U.S. Constitution, on July 26, 1788. The "Empire State" ranks 27th in total area (54,556 sq mi) and 3rd in population (19,227,088 in 2004). It has 29 seats in the U.S. House of Representatives and casts 31 electoral votes.

STATE RECORDS		
First Governor	George Clinton	1788-95, 1801-04
Highest Point	Mount Marcy	5,344 ft
Lowest Point	Atlantic Ocean	sea level
Hottest Temperature	108°F	Troy, July 22, 1926
Coldest Temperature	-52°F	Old Forge, Feb. 18, 1979
Tallest Building	Empire State Bldg., New York City (1931)	1,250 ft, 102 floors
Largest City (also U.S. record)	New York City	pop. 8,104,079 (2004 est.)
Here are some U.S. records claimed by NEW YORK:		
Longest Bridge Span	Verrazano-Narrows	4,260 ft
Most Extensive Subway System	2,058 mi of track, 468 stations	NYC; first opened Oct. 27, 1904
Largest Department Store	Macy's, NYC	over 1 million sq ft of retail space

North Carolina to Oregon

NORTH CAROLINA

One of the original 13 colonies, North Carolina became the 12th state to ratify the U.S. Constitution, on Nov. 21, 1789. North Carolina seceded from the Union in 1861 and was readmitted in 1868. The "Tar Heel State" ranks 28th in total area (53,819 sq mi) and 11th in population (8,541,221 in 2004). It has 13 seats in the U.S. House of Representatives and casts 15 electoral votes.

STATE RECORDS		
First Governor	Samuel Johnston	1787-89
Highest Point	Mount Mitchell	6,684 ft
Lowest Point	Atlantic Ocean	sea level
Hottest Temperature	110°F	Fayetteville, Aug. 21, 1983
Coldest Temperature	-34°F	Mt Mitchell, Jan. 21, 1985
Tallest Building	Bank of America Corporate Center, Charlotte (1992)	871 ft, 60 floors
Largest City	Charlotte	pop. 594,359 (2004 est.)
Here are some U.S. records claimed by NORTH CAROLINA:		
Largest Freshwater Sound	Albemarle Sound	50 mi long, 5-14 mi wide
First Successful Heavier-than-Air Flight	Orville Wright, Wilbur Wright	near Kitty Hawk, Dec. 17, 1903
Most Visited National Park System Site	Blue Ridge Parkway (NC-VA)	17,999,116 visits (2004)

NORTH DAKOTA

The U.S. acquired half of North Dakota with the Louisiana Purchase in 1803, and gained ownership of the other half by an agreement with Britain in 1818. North Dakota entered the Union on Nov. 2, 1889. The "Peace Garden State" ranks 19th in total area (70,700 sq mi) and 48th in population (634,366 in 2004). It has one seat in the U.S. House of Representatives and casts three electoral votes.

STATE RECORDS		
First Governor	John Miller	1889-90
Highest Point	White Butte	3,506 ft
Lowest Point	Red River of the North	750 ft
Hottest Temperature	121°F	Steele, July 6, 1936
Coldest Temperature	-60°F	Parshall, Feb. 15, 1936
Tallest Building	Capitol Building, Bismarck (1934)	242 ft, 19 floors
Largest City	Fargo	pop. 91,048 (2004 est.)
Here are some U.S. records claimed by NORTH DAKOTA:		
Tallest Structure	KVLY-TV tower, near Fargo	2,063 ft
Biggest Scrap Metal Sculpture	"Geese in Flight" by Gary Greff (2001)	110 ft tall, 154 ft wide; 157,659 lbs

OHIO

Britain gave up its claim to Ohio in the terms of the 1783 Treaty of Paris, and in 1787, the area became part of the Northwest Territory. Ohio entered the Union on March 1, 1803. The "Buckeye State" ranks 34th in total area (44,825 sq mi) and 7th in population (11,459,011 in 2004). It has 18 seats in the U.S. House of Representatives and casts 20 electoral votes.

STATE RECORDS		
First Governor	Edward Tiffin	1803-07
First Woman Governor	Nancy Hollister	1998-99
Highest Point	Campbell Hill	1,550 ft
Lowest Point	Ohio River	455 ft
Hottest Temperature	113°F	near Gallipolis, July 21, 1934
Coldest Temperature	-39°F	Milligan, Feb. 10, 1899
Tallest Building	Key Tower, Cleveland (1991)	947 ft, 57 floors
Largest City	Columbus	pop. 730,008 (2004 est.)
Here are some U.S. records claimed by OHIO:		
First State with Official Rock Song	"Hang on Sloopy" (1985)	by House Resolution, 1985
First Coeducational College	Oberlin College	1833

OKLAHOMA

Acquired by the U.S. as part of the Louisiana Purchase in 1803, Oklahoma was established as "Indian Territory." From 1828 to 1846, it was home to the "Five Civilized Tribes" after the forced removal of Native Americans from the eastern U.S. Oklahoma entered the Union on Nov. 16, 1907. The "Sooner State" ranks 20th in total area (69,898 sq mi) and 28th in population (3,523,553 in 2004). It has five seats in the U.S. House of Representatives and casts seven electoral votes.

STATE RECORDS		
First Governor	Charles N. Haskell	1907-11
Highest Point	Black Mesa	4,973 ft
Lowest Point	Little River	289 ft
Hottest Temperature	120°F	Tipton, June 27, 1994
Coldest Temperature	-27°F	Watts, Jan. 18, 1930
Tallest Building	Williams Center, Tulsa (1975)	667 ft, 52 floors
Largest City	Oklahoma City	pop. 528,042 (2004 est.)
Here are some U.S. records claimed by OKLAHOMA:		
Largest Measured Tornado	near Mulhall, May 2, 1999	5,250 ft diameter
Deepest Well	Washita County	31,441 ft

OREGON

Settlers first arrived in the Willamette Valley in 1834. Oregon entered the Union on Feb. 14, 1859. The "Beaver State" ranks 9th in total area (98,381 sq mi) and 27th in population (3,594,586 in 2004). It has five seats in the U.S. House of Representatives and casts seven electoral votes.

STATE RECORDS		
First Governor	John Whiteaker	1859-62
First Woman Governor	Barbara Roberts	1991-95
Highest Point	Mount Hood	11,239 ft
Lowest Point	Pacific Ocean	sea level
Hottest Temperature	119°F	Pendleton, Aug. 10, 1898
Coldest Temperature	-54°F	Seneca, Feb. 10, 1933
Tallest Building	Wells Fargo Center, Portland (1973)	546 ft, 40 floors
Largest City	Portland	pop. 533,492 (2004 est.)
Here are some U.S. records claimed by OREGON:		
Deepest Lake	Crater Lake	1,932 ft
Deepest Gorge (w/Idaho)	Hells Canyon, Snake River	7,900 ft
Largest Fungus	Honey Mushroom (*Armillaria ostoyae*), 2,200 acres	Malheur National Forest, Blue Mountains

STATE BY STATE

Pennsylvania to Tennessee

PENNSYLVANIA

One of the original 13 colonies, Pennsylvania became the second state to ratify the U.S. Constitution, on Dec. 12, 1787. The "Keystone State" ranks 33rd in total area (44,817 sq mi) and 6th in population (12,406,292 in 2004). It has 19 seats in the U.S. House of Representatives and casts 21 electoral votes.

STATE RECORDS		
First Governor	Thomas Mifflin	1790-99
Highest Point	Mount Davis	3,213 ft
Lowest Point	Delaware River	sea level
Hottest Temperature	111°F	Phoenixville, July 10, 1936
Coldest Temperature	-42°F	Smethport, Jan. 5, 1904
Tallest Building	One Liberty Place, Philadelphia (1987)	945 ft, 61 floors
Largest City	Philadelphia	pop. 1,470,151 (2004 est.)
Here are some U.S. records claimed by PENNSYLVANIA:		
Oldest Bridge in Continuous Use	Philadelphia	Frankford Ave. Bridge (1697)
Oldest Zoo	Philadelphia Zoo	chartered 1859; opened July 1, 1874

RHODE ISLAND

One of the original 13 colonies, Rhode Island became the 13th state to ratify the U.S. Constitution, on May 29, 1790. "Little Rhody" ranks 50th in total area (1,545 sq mi) and 43rd in population (1,080,632 in 2004). It has two seats in the U.S. House of Representatives and casts four electoral votes.

STATE RECORDS		
First Governor	Arthur Fenner	1790-1805
Highest Point	Jerimoth Hill	812 ft
Lowest Point	Atlantic Ocean	sea level
Hottest Temperature	104°F	Providence, Aug. 2, 1975
Coldest Temperature	-25°F	Greene, Feb. 5, 1996
Tallest Building	Fleet Bank Bldg., Providence (1927)	428 ft, 26 floors
Largest City	Providence	pop. 178,126 (2004 est.)
Here are some U.S. records claimed by RHODE ISLAND:		
Smallest State	1,545 sq mi	about 429 Rhode Islands could fit inside Alaska
First Town Founded by a Woman	Portsmouth (1638)	Anne Hutchinson
First and Oldest U.S. Synagogue	Touro Synagogue, 1763	Newport

SOUTH CAROLINA

One of the original 13 colonies, South Carolina became the eighth state to ratify the U.S. Constitution, on May 23, 1788. South Carolina was the first state to secede from the Union in 1860. It was readmitted in 1868. The "Palmetto State" ranks 40th in total area (32,020 sq mi) and 25th in population (4,198,068 in 2004). It has six seats in the U.S. House of Representatives and casts eight electoral votes.

STATE RECORDS		
First Governor	Thomas Pinckney	1788-89
Highest Point	Sassafras Mountain	3,560 ft
Lowest Point	Atlantic Ocean	sea level
Hottest Temperature	111°F	Camden, June 28, 1954
Coldest Temperature	-19°F	Caesar's Head, Jan. 21, 1985
Tallest Building	Capitol Center, Columbia (1987)	349 ft, 25 floors
Largest City	Columbia	pop. 116,331 (2004 est.)
Here are some U.S. records claimed by SOUTH CAROLINA:		
Longest-serving U.S. Senator	Strom Thurmond	Dec. 1954 - Jan. 2003
First Civil War Battle	Fort Sumter, Charleston Harbor	April 12-14, 1861

SOUTH DAKOTA

South Dakota was acquired by the U.S. in the Louisiana Purchase of 1803, and gold was discovered in 1874. South Dakota entered the Union on Nov. 2, 1889. The "Coyote State" ranks 17th in total area (77,116 sq mi) and 46th in population (770,883 in 2004). It has one seat in the U.S. House of Representatives and casts three electoral votes.

STATE RECORDS		
First Governor	Arthur C. Mellette	1889-93
Highest Point	Harney Peak	7,242 ft
Lowest Point	Big Stone Lake	966 ft
Hottest Temperature	120°F	Gannvalley, July 5, 1936
Coldest Temperature	-58°F	McIntosh, Feb. 17, 1936
Largest City	Sioux Falls	pop. 136,695 (2004 est.)
Here are some U.S. records claimed by SOUTH DAKOTA:		
Geographic Center of U.S. (incl. AK & HI)	West of Castle Rock, Butte County	44° 58′ N, 103° 46′ W
Largest/Most Complete T-Rex Skeleton	"Sue"; found in Hell Creek Formation, near Faith, Aug. 1990	13 ft tall, 41 ft long; approx. 90% complete
Largest Presidential Portraits	Mount Rushmore	4 portraits 50 to 70 ft high

TENNESSEE

Virginians established the first permanent settlement in the region in 1769. Tennessee entered the Union on June 1, 1796. It seceded from the Union in 1861 and was readmitted in 1866. The "Volunteer State" ranks 36th in total area (42,143 sq mi) and 16th in population (5,900,962 in 2004). It has nine seats in the U.S. House of Representatives and casts 11 electoral votes.

First Governor	John Sevier	1796-1801, 1803-09
Highest Point	Clingmans Dome	6,643 ft
Lowest Point	Mississippi River	178 ft
Hottest Temperature	113°F	Perryville, Aug. 9, 1930
Coldest Temperature	-32°F	Mountain City, Dec. 30, 1917
Tallest Building	Bell South Tower, Nashville (1994)	490 ft (incl. spire), 33 floors
Largest City	Memphis	pop. 671,929 (2004 est.)
Here are some U.S. records claimed by TENNESSEE:		
Longest-Running Live Radio Program	Grand Ole Opry	weekly on WSM, Nashville, since Nov. 28, 1925
Most Visited National Park	Great Smoky Mountains Nat. Park (NC-TN)	9,167,049 visitors (2004)
Most Neighboring States (tied with Missouri)	8	Arkansas, Missouri, Kentucky, Virginia, North Carolina, Georgia, Alabama, Mississippi

Texas to Washington

TEXAS

Texas won its independence from Mexico in 1836, and the Republic of Texas functioned as an independent nation until it entered the Union on Dec. 29, 1845. The "Lone Star State" ranks 2nd in total area (268,581 sq mi) and second in population (22,490,022 in 2004). It has 32 seats in the U.S. House of Representatives and casts 34 electoral votes.

STATE RECORDS		
First Governor	James P. Henderson	1846-47
First Woman Governor	Miriam A. "Ma" Ferguson	1925-27, 1933-35
Highest Point	Guadalupe Peak	8,749 ft
Lowest Point	Gulf of Mexico	sea level
Hottest Temperature	120°F	Monahans, July 28, 1994
Coldest Temperature	-23°F	Seminole, Feb, 8, 1933
Tallest Building	JP Morgan Chase Tower, Houston (1982)	1,002 ft, 75 floors
Largest City	Houston	pop. 2,012,626 (2004 est.)
Here are some U.S. records claimed by TEXAS:		
Petroleum	1,073,000 barrels per day	2004
Cotton Production	4.25 mil bushels (2003)	24% of U.S. crop
Largest Bat Colony	Bracken Cave, San Antonio	up to 20 million Mexican free-tailed bats
Most Interstate Highway Mileage	3,233.45 miles in 17 routes	

UTAH

The permanent settlement of Utah began with the arrival of Mormons in 1847. In 1850, the territory of Utah was established, and Utah entered the Union on Jan. 4, 1896. The "Beehive State" ranks 13th in total area (84,889 sq mi) and 34th in population (2,389,039 in 2004). It has three seats in the U.S. House of Representatives and casts five electoral votes.

STATE RECORDS		
First Governor	Heber M. Wells	1896-1905
First Woman Governor	Olene Walker	2003-04
Highest Point	Kings Peak	13,528 ft
Lowest Point	Beaver Dam Wash	2,000 ft
Hottest Temperature	117°F	St. George, July 5, 1985
Coldest Temperature	-69°F	Peter's Sink, Feb. 1, 1985
Tallest Building	Wells Fargo Center, Salt Lake City (1998)	422 ft, 24 floors
Largest City	Salt Lake City	pop. 178,605 (2004 est.)
Here are some U.S. records claimed by UTAH:		
Most Jell-O Consumed (per capita)	Estimated at twice the national average	Declared official state snack, Jan. 2001
Biggest Mormon Temple	Salt Lake LDS Temple, Salt Lake City (1893)	253,000 sq ft floor area

VERMONT

Vermont entered the Union on March 4, 1791, the first state not formerly one of the 13 original colonies. The "Green Mountain State" ranks 45th in total area (9,614 sq mi) and 49th in population (621,394 in 2004). It has one seat in the U.S. House of Representatives and casts three electoral votes.

STATE RECORDS		
First Governor	Thomas Chittenden	1791-97
First Woman Governor	Madeleine Kunin	1985-91
Highest Point	Mount Mansfield	4,393 ft
Lowest Point	Lake Champlain	95 ft
Hottest Temperature	105°F	Vernon, July 4, 1911
Coldest Temperature	-50°F	Bloomfield, Dec. 30, 1933
Largest City	Burlington	pop. 38,934 (2004 est.)
Here are some U.S. records claimed by VERMONT:		
Smallest State Capital (pop.)	Montpelier	pop. 8,013 (2004 est.)
First Social Security Beneficiary	Ida Mae Fuller, Ludlow	received first check for $22.50, Feb. 1940

VIRGINIA

One of the original 13 colonies, Virginia became the tenth state to ratify the U.S. Constitution on June 25, 1788. Virginia seceded from the Union in 1861 and was readmitted in 1870. The "Old Dominion" state ranks 35th in total area (42,774 sq mi) and 12th in population (7,459,827 in 2004). It has 11 seats in the U.S. House of Representatives and casts 13 electoral votes.

STATE RECORDS		
First Governor	Beverley Randolph	1788-91
First African-American Governor	L. Douglas Wilder	1990-94
Highest Point	Mount Rogers	5,729 ft
Lowest Point	Atlantic Ocean	sea level
Hottest Temperature	110°F	Balcony Falls, July 15, 1954
Coldest Temperature	-30°F	Mountain Lake Bio. Station, Jan. 22, 1985
Tallest Building	James Monroe Bldg., Richmond (1981)	449 ft, 29 floors
Largest City	Virginia Beach	pop. 440,098 (2004 est.)
Here are some U.S. records claimed by VIRGINIA:		
Largest Skatepark	Vans Skatepark, Potomac Mills Mall, Prince William	61,640 sq ft
Largest Office Building	The Pentagon , Arlington	77,025,000 cu ft; 29 acres

WASHINGTON

The final agreement with Britain on the Washington-Canada border was made in 1846. Washington became part of the Oregon Territory in 1848, and entered the Union as a state on Nov. 11, 1889. The "Evergreen State" ranks 18th in total area (71,300 sq mi) and 15th in population (6,203,788 in 2004). It has nine seats in the U.S. House of Representatives and casts 11 electoral votes.

STATE RECORDS		
First Governor	Elisha P. Ferry	1889-93
First Woman Governor	Dixy Lee Ray	1977-81
First Asian-American Governor	Gary Locke	1997-2005
Highest Point	Mt. Rainier	14,411 ft
Lowest Point	Pacific Ocean	sea level
Hottest Temperature	118°F	Ice Harbor Dam, Aug. 5, 1961
Coldest Temperature	-48°F	Mazama & Winthrop, Dec. 30, 1968
Tallest Building	Bank of America Center, Seattle (1985)	933 ft, 76 floors
Largest City	Seattle	pop. 571,480 (2004 est.)
Here are some U.S. records claimed by WASHINGTON:		
Largest Building	Boeing Manufacturing Plant, Everett	472 million cu ft; 98 acres
Most Snowfall (12-month period)	Paradise, Mount Rainier	1,224.5 in, Feb. 19, 1971-Feb. 18, 1972

STATE BY STATE

West Virginia to Wyoming

WEST VIRGINIA

The anti-secession western counties of Virginia declared themselves the state of Kanawha when Virginia seceded from the Union in 1861. Renamed West Virginia, the state entered the Union on June 20, 1863. The "Mountain State" ranks 41st in total area (24,230 sq mi) and 37th in population (1,815,354 in 2004). It has three seats in the U.S. House of Representatives and casts five electoral votes.

STATE RECORDS		
First Governor	Arthur I. Boreman	1863-69
Highest Point	Spruce Knob	4,863 ft
Lowest Point	Potomac River	240 ft
Hottest Temperature	112°F	Martinsburg, July 10, 1936
Coldest Temperature	-37°F	Lewisburg, Dec. 30, 1917
Largest City	Charleston	pop. 51,685 (2004 est.)
Here are some U.S. records claimed by WEST VIRGINIA:		
Longest Single-Span Steel Arch Bridge	New River Gorge, Fayetteville (1977)	1,700 ft
First World War I Memorial Bldg.	Welch	dedicated May 30, 1923

WISCONSIN

The U.S. acquired Wisconsin after the Revolutionary War, and in 1787, the area became part of the Northwest Territory, though the British maintained a presence there until after the War of 1812. Wisconsin entered the Union on May 29, 1848. The "Badger State" ranks 23rd in total area (65,498 sq mi) and 20th in population (5,509,026 in 2004). It has eight seats in the U.S. House of Representatives and casts 10 electoral votes.

STATE RECORDS		
First Governor	Nelson Dewey	1848-52
Highest Point	Timms Hill	1,951 ft
Lowest Point	Lake Michigan	579 ft
Hottest Temperature	114°F	Wisconsin Dells, July 13, 1936
Coldest Temperature	-55°F	Couderay, Feb. 4, 1996
Tallest Building	U.S. Bank Center, Milwaukee (1973)	601 ft, 42 floors
Largest City	Milwaukee	pop. 583,624 (2004 est.)
Here are some U.S. records claimed by WISCONSIN:		
Deadliest Fire	Peshtigo, WI, forest fire	1,000+ killed, Oct. 8, 1871
First Kindergarten	Established by Karl and Margarethe Meyer Schurz	Watertown, 1858

WYOMING

Wyoming became a territory in 1868, and granted women the right to vote a year later. Wyoming entered the Union on July 10, 1890. The "Cowboy State" ranks 10th in total area (97,814 sq mi) and 50th in population (506,529 in 2004). It has one seat in the U.S. House of Representatives and casts three electoral votes.

STATE RECORDS		
First Governor	Francis E. Warren	1890
First Woman Governor	Nellie Tayloe Ross (also U.S. record)[1]	1925-27
Highest Point	Gannett Peak	13,804 ft
Lowest Point	Belle Fourche River	3,099 ft
Hottest Temperature	115°F	Basin, Aug. 8, 1983
Coldest Temperature	-66°F	Riverside R.S., Feb. 9, 1933
Tallest Building	White Hall Dormitory, Laramie (1967)	12 floors
Largest City	Cheyenne	pop. 55,362 (2004 est.)
Here are some U.S. records claimed by WYOMING:		
First National Monument	Devil's Tower, Sept. 24, 1906	Proclaimed by Pres. Theodore Roosevelt
Biggest Coal Producer	376,878,000 short tons (2003)	About 35% of national total

(1) Term began 15 days before that of Miriam Ferguson (TX)

District of Columbia, Puerto Rico

DISTRICT OF COLUMBIA

The District of Columbia was chosen as the site of the nation's capital by Pres. George Washington in Oct. 1790, and covers 68 square miles of territory ceded by Virginia and Maryland. Extensively planned by Pierre Charles L'Enfant, Andrew Elicott, and Benjamin Banneker, it became the capital on June 10, 1800. The District, coextensive with the city of Washington, DC, is smaller in area (68 sq mi) than any state. It is also smaller in population (553,523 in 2004) than any state except Wyoming. Its citizens were not represented in the Electoral College until 1964 (under the 23rd Amendment). The District has one delegate in the U.S. House of Representatives—who may vote in committee but not on the floor—and three electoral votes.

STATE RECORDS		
First (elected) Mayor	Walter Washington	1975-79
First Woman Mayor	Sharon Pratt Kelly (neé Dixon)	1991-95
Highest Point	Tenleytown	410 ft
Lowest Point	Potomac River	1 ft
Here are some U.S. records claimed by the DISTRICT OF COLUMBIA:		
Biggest Museum (world record)	Smithsonian Institution	18 museums (14 in DC), 144 million objects
Biggest Library (world record)	Library of Congress	130 million items, 530 mi of shelves

COMMONWEALTH OF PUERTO RICO

Puerto Rico was ceded to the U.S. under the treaty ending the Spanish-American War in 1898 and voted in favor of commonwealth status in 1952. The commonwealth (area, 3,515 sq mi; pop. 3,894,855 in 2004) does not vote in presidential elections; it is represented in Congress by an elected resident commissioner who may vote in committee, but not on the floor.

STATE RECORDS		
First (elected) Governor	Luis Muñoz Marín	1949-65
First Woman Governor	Sila M. Calderón	2001-05
Highest Point	Cerro de Punta	4,390 ft
Lowest Point	Atlantic Ocean	sea level
Largest City	San Juan	pop. 433,319 (2004 est.)
Here are some U.S. records claimed by PUERTO RICO:		
Biggest Radio Telescope	Arecibo Radio Telescope	1,000 ft diameter, 167 ft deep

Photo Credits

This product/publication includes images from Artville, Comstock, Corbis Royalty-Free, Corel Stock Photo Library, Digital Stock, Digital Vision, EyeWire Images, Ingram Publishing, One Mile Up Inc., PhotoDisc, Rubberball Productions, which are protected by the copyright laws of the U.S., Canada, and elsewhere. Used under license.

COVER: Background, digitalvision. Hot dog eating contest, NASCAR, Peyton Manning, and Beyoncé, AP/Wide World Photos. Harry Potter, Warner Bros./Photofest. The Simpsons, Fox/Photofest. Franklin, Library of Congress Prints and Photographs Division, Reproduction #LC-USZC2-2004. **BACK COVER:** Shark, © James D. Watt/SeaPics.com. Hank Aaron, Louis Requena/MLB Photos via Getty Images. **INSIDE COVER:** LeBron James, Aaron Josefczyk/Reuters/Landov. Eng & Cheng, Courtesy, Mütter Museum, College of Physicians of Philadelphia. Halle Berry, AP/Wide World Photos. **TABLE OF CONTENTS:** SR-71, NASA. King Kong, Weta Digital Ltd./Universal Studios. Venus Williams, AP/Wide World Photos. Bush, Bush & Clinton, White House photo by Tina Hager. **7:** Janek Mela and Danny Way, AP/Wide World Photos. Earthship, Steve Northup/Time Life Pictures/Getty Images. **10-11:** Cook, LOC P&P, Rep. #LC-USZ62-119526. **11:** Norge, AP/Wide World Photos. **12:** NOAA Corps Collection. **13:** Treasures of the NOAA Library Collection/Archival Photograph by Mr. Steve Nicklas, NOS, NGS. **16:** AP/Wide World Photos. **18:** U.S. Air Force photo by Tech. Sgt. Michael Haggerty. **19:** LOC P&P, Rep. #LC-DIG-ppprs-00626. **25:** Courtesy of Troy Waters. **30:** ©James D. Watt/SeaPics.com. **39:** LOC P&P, Rep. #LC-USZ62-29499. **42, 44-45:** AP/Wide World Photos. **46:** World Almanac 1868, World Almanac Books. **46:** Harry Potter, Arthur A. Levin Books/Scholastic, Inc. **51:** Courtesy of Microsoft Archives. **52-53:** U.S. Army Photo. **55:** Courtesy of GUIdebook. **56:** World Almanac Books. **58:** Courtesy of Sony Electronics Inc. **60:** LOC P&P, Rep. #LC-USZC4-5001. **61:** ©Edward A. Thomas. **62:** LOC P&P, Rep. #LC-USZ62-104276. **66-67:** Kingda Ka, Six Flags Theme Parks Inc. Pentagon, DoD photo by Master Sgt. Ken Hammond, U.S. Air Force. **70-71:** AP/Wide World Photos. **72-73:** Courtesy of the Bureau of Reclamation. **74-75:** COURTESY OF LUCASFILM LTD. *Star Wars: Episode III - Revenge of the Sith* ©2005 Lucasfilm ltd. & TM. All rights reserved. Used under authorization. Unauthorized duplication is a violation of applicable law. **76:** AP/Wide World Photos. **77-78:** Photofest. **80:** New Line Cinema/Photofest. **81:** King Kong, left, Weta Digital Ltd./Universal Studios. right, Pierre Vinet. **82-83:** CBS/Photofest. **85:** AP/Wide World Photos. **86:** Photo courtesy of Jeopardy! Productions, Inc. **87-89:** CBS/Landov. **90:** RCA photo courtesy of Thomson, Inc. **92:** Mike Blake/Reuters/Landov. **94-95:** AP/Wide World Photos. **97:** Wright Bros., LOC P&P, Rep. #LC-USZ62-00626. **97:** Earhart, Hillary and Norgay, AP/Wide World Photos. Everest, Barry C. Bishop National Geographic/Getty Images. Nimrod, NOAA Corps Collection. **98:** Walkingstick, Ernest Janes/BRUCE COLEMAN INC. Snake, Bianca LaviesNational Geographic/Getty Images. Bats, Kenneth Gunnar/BRUCE COLEMAN INC. **99:** Eggs, LIOR RUBIN/Peter Arnold, Inc. Fish, Jane Burton/BRUCE COLEMAN INC. Termites, JORGEN SCHYTTE/Peter Arnold, Inc. Cheetah, Photos.com. Cheeta, NEEMA FREDERIC/GAMMA. **100:** Painting, AP/Wide World Photos. ENIAC, U.S. Army Photo. Chess, Stan Honda/AFP/Getty Images. **101:** Empire State Bldg., Lewis W. Hine/George Eastman House/Getty Images. **102:** Dylan, Photofest. Edison, LOC P&P, Brady-Handy Photo. Coll., Rep. #LC-DIG-cwpbh-04044. *Star Wars*, Lucasfilm Ltd./Twentieth Century Fox Film Corp./Photofest. **103:** Beatles, Central Press/Getty Images. Cheers and Lion King, AP/Wide World Photos. *Trip to the Moon*, Star Film/Edison Manufacturing Company/Photofest. *Jaws*, Universal Pictures/Photofest. **104-105:** Tsunami, John Russell/AFP/Getty Images. Buddha, Liu Jin/AFP/Getty Images. Others, AP/Wide World Photos. **106-107:** Laface/Zomba. **108-109:** LOC P&P, Rep. #LC-USZ62-111094. **111:** RSO Records/Photofest. **112:** Library of Congress. **114:** JVC Company of America. **115:** Shannon Stapleton/Reuters /Landov. **120:** AP/Wide World Photos. **122:** Winchester Mystery House, San Jose, CA. **124:** LOC P&P, Rep. #LC-USZ62-67635. **126:** Top, Mary Bloom/Westminster Kennel Club. Bottom, Lisa Croft Elliott/Westminster KC. **128:** Courtesy of Mall of America. **129:** Photo courtesy of Bob Cole. **134:** LOC P&P, Rep. #LC-USZ62-63968. **137:** LOC P&P, Rep. #LC-DIG-ggbain-00160. **150:** National Archives. **151:** DoD photo by Airman Danielle Sosa, U.S. Navy. **154, 158-161:** AP/Wide World Photos. **162:** Promosedia, organizers of the International Chair Exhibition (30th edition to be held in Udine-Italy 9th-12th September 2005). **165:** Seppo Sirkka/EPA/Landov. **183:** www.goldenpalace.com. **184:** Robert A. Siegel Auction Galleries Inc. **185:** ©Edward A. Thomas. **188-189:** Las Vegas News Bureau. **210:** FEMA/Liz Roll. **211:** FEMA/Mark Wolfe. **214-215:** Courtesy of "Toyota Motor Corporation". **216:** Special Collections, University of Vermont. **218:** Courtesy: Airbus. **220:** LOC P&P, Rep. #LC-USZ62-117340. **221:** Cunard Line. **222-223:** COURTESY OF THE OAKLAND MUSEUM OF CALIFORNIA. **224:** LOC P&P, Rep. #LC-USZ62-105442. **225:** Photograph courtesy of the Harley-Davidson Motor Company Archives. **231:** AP/Wide World Photos. **232:** Published in *Collier's Weekly*, August 13, 1910. **233:** AP/Wide World Photos. **235:** Fox/Photofest. **236:** Lionel image courtesy of Lionel LLC. **239:** Image by Gil Potts courtesy of the Liberace Museum. **241:** LOC P&P, Rep. #LC-USZC4-1599. *Wizard of Oz* movie, MGM/Photofest. **254:** Image copyright History of Science Collections, University of Oklahoma Libraries. **255:** LOC P&P, Rep. #LC-USZC4-4940 . **260:** National Archives. **264:** NASA-JPL. **265:** Wallendas, Pascal Guyot/AFP/Getty Images. Marathon, Pierre Verdy/AFP/Getty Images. Chair, Promosedia, organizers of the International Chair Exhibition (30th edition to be held in Udine-Italy 9th-12th September 2005). **266:** Kingda Ka, Andrew Gombert/EPA/Landov. MacArthur, Stephen Hird/Reuters/Landov. **266-267:** Petit, dinner party, Monopoly, fish, Pac-Man, AP/Wide World Photos. **267:** Stamps, Robert A. Siegel Auction Galleries Inc. **268:** Flower and iceberg, AP/Wide World Photos. Tree, Peter Essick/Aurora/Getty Images. Hurricane, NOAA Photo Library, NOAA Central Library. OAR/ERL/National Severe Storms Laboratory (NSSL). Tornado, NASA/Jeff Schmaltz, MODIS Land Rapid Response Team. **269:** Steve Marcus/Reuters/Landov. Usher, Simpsons, Fox/Photofest. Bikini, Keystone/Getty Images. Jackson 2005, Justin Sullivan/EPA/Landov. Jackson 1975, Anwar Hussein/Getty Images. **270:** Soldiers and blackout, AP/Wide World Photos. Newton, History of Science Collections, University of Oklahoma Libraries. Franklin, LOC P&P, Rep. #LC-DIG-ppmsca-09853. Curie, LOC P&P, Rep. #LC-DIG-ggbain-06354. **271:** SpaceShipOne, Armando Arorizo/EPA /Landov. Space Walk and man on moon, NASA. **272:** Nebula, NASA, ESA, STScI, Jeff Hester and Paul Scowen (Arizona State University). Saturn, NASA Goddard Space Flight Center. Olympus Mons, NASA Jet Propulsion Laboratory. **275:** NASA. **276-277:** The Hubble Heritage Team (AURA/STScI/NASA). **282:** NASA. **283:** NASA-JPL-Caltech/UMD. **289:** NOAA Corps Collection. **295:** ©Edward A. Thomas. **296, 326:** AP/Wide World Photos. **329:** George Bush Presidential Library. **337:** AP/Wide World Photos. **348:** LOC P&P, Rep. #LC-USZ62-77759. **354:** Courtesy of www.vicepresidentdanquayle.com. **358, 362-363, 366, 373, 374, 377, 379-381:** AP/Wide World Photos. **382-383:** Christine Chew /UPI Photo/Landov. **384, 388, 390:** AP/Wide World Photos. **392-393:** Major League Soccer. **395, 396, 399, 400:** AP/Wide World Photos. **401, 402-403:** Kilamanjaro, Lutz Bongarts/Bongarts/Getty Images. Iceberg, Josh Landis, National Science Foundation. Bollywood, Monopole-Pathé/Photofest. Others, AP/Wide World Photos. **404-405, 406-407:** Patrick, Mike Segar/Reuters/Landov. Woods and Nicklaus, Mike Nelson/AFP/Getty Images. Robinson, LOC P&P, Rep. #LC-USZC4-6144 DLC. Earnhardts, Mark Wallheiser/Reuters/Landov. **405:** Donovan, Major League Soccer. Jordan, Mike Blake/Reuters/Landov. Others, AP/Wide World Photos. **408:** Rushmore and woodpecker, AP/Wide World Photos. River, NASA/JPL-Caltech. Las Vegas, Las Vegas News Bureau. **410, 414-415, 419:** AP/Wide World Photos. **420:** LOC P&P, Rep. #LC-DIG-ggbain-10782. **421, 424, 427, 430:** AP/Wide World Photos. **431:** LOC P&P, Rep. #LC-USZ62-29331. **433:** Courtesy of Wabash College. **434:** PBA LLC. **438:** LOC P&P, Rep. #LC-USZC4-5122. **439:** LOC P&P, Rep. #LC-USZ61-1285. **440:** Courtesy of U.S. Speedskating. **442, 444:** AP/Wide World Photos. **445:** LOC P&P, Rep. #LC-USZ62-27663. **447:** Jason Lee /Reuters/Landov. **448-449:** Rick Wilking /Reuters/Landov. **457:** © 1967 Dover Publications. Library of Congress. **458:** George Bush Presidential Library. **460-461:** LOC P&P, Rep. #LC-USZ62-67895. **465:** AP/Wide World Photos. **504:** Lincoln, LOC P&P, Rep. #LC-USZ62-13016. Wie & Blackout, AP/Wide World Photos.

Subject Index

Index entries for chapters appear in **BOLDFACE CAPITALS**. The titles of page spreads appear in **boldface**. Page numbers for photos in insert sections are in *italics*. Following this Subject Index there is a separate index of Superlatives.

SUPERLATIVES

Abraham Lincoln ▲

Michelle Wie ►

New York City, 2003 Blackout ►